HOLT
ELEMENTS OF
LITERATURE

Fifth Course

**ESSENTIALS OF
AMERICAN LITERATURE**

HOLT, RINEHART AND WINSTON

A Harcourt Education Company

Orlando • **Austin** • New York • San Diego • Toronto • London

EDITORIAL
Editorial Vice President: Laura Wood
Project Directors: Kathleen Daniel, Mescal Evler
Executive Editors: Kristine E. Marshall, Laura Mongello
Senior Editors: John Haffner Layden, Susan K. Lynch, Kathryn Rogers, Jennifer Tench, Hester Weeden
Managing Editor: Marie Price
Senior Product Manager: Don Wulbrecht
Editorial Staff: Abraham Chang, Steven Fechter, Michael Fleming, Christine Han, Crystal Wirth, Michael Zakhar
Copyediting Manager: Michael Neibergall
Copyediting Supervisor: Mary Malone
Copyeditors: Christine Altgelt, Elizabeth Dickson, Emily Force, Leora Harris, Anne Heausler, Kathleen Scheiner, Nancy Shore
Associate Managing Editors: Lori De La Garza, Elizabeth LaManna
Editorial Support: Danielle Greer, Erik Netcher
Editorial Permissions: Carrie Jones, Susan Lowrance, Erik Netcher

ART, DESIGN, AND PRODUCTION
Director: Athena Blackorby
Senior Design Director: Betty Mintz
Design and Composition: Preface, Inc.
Prepress: Lehigh Digital
Production Manager: Carol Trammel

COVER
Photo Credits: (Inset) *From Brooklyn Heights* (1925) by George Copland Ault. Oil on canvas. Collection of The Newark Museum, 28.1802/Art Resource, NY.

	Collection 1 Encounters and Foundations to 1800	Collection 2 American Romanticism 1800–1860	Collection 3 American Masters: Whitman and Dickinson
Literary Response	Evaluate the historical and social influences of the foundations and colonial period in America. Analyze archetypes drawn from myth and tradition. Analyze an author's style. Analyze characteristics of subgenres of poetry and prose. Analyze the use of figures of speech. Analyze political points of view on a topic. Compare and contrast works from different literary periods.	Evaluate the historical and social influences of the Romantic period in America. Analyze an author's style. Analyze theme. Analyze the use of poetic and literary devices. Analyze characteristics of subgenres of poetry and short stories. Analyze political points of view on a topic. Analyze an author's style. Analyze archetypes drawn from myth and tradition. Compare and contrast works from different literary periods.	Analyze genres and traditions in American literature. Analyze characteristics of subgenres in poetry. Analyze the use of poetic and literary devices. Analyze an author's tone. Compare and contrast works from different literary periods.
Reading Public Documents and Informational Text	Analyze features of public documents. Recognize and analyze modes of persuasion.	Analyze implicit and explicit philosophical assumptions. Critique arguments in public documents. Recognize and analyze modes of persuasion.	
Vocabulary	Understand and identify synonyms. Understand prefixes and suffixes. Create semantic maps. Understand and use context clues. Understand etymologies of words used in political science and history.	Understand and use context clues. Analyze word analogies. Create semantic maps. Use Latin, Greek, and Anglo-Saxon affixes to infer meaning of terms used in math and science.	Understand multiple-meaning words.
Writing, Listening, and Speaking	Write an editorial. Present and evaluate speeches.	Write a short story.	Write a reflective essay. Present a reflection.

	Collection 4 The Rise of Realism: The Civil War to 1914	Collection 5 The Moderns 1914–1939	Collection 6 Contemporary Literature 1939–Present
Literary Response	Evaluate the historical and social influences of the Realist period, from the Civil War to 1914. Analyze political points of view on a topic. Analyze the use of literary devices. Analyze point of view. Analyze literary elements. Analyze American Indian Oratory. Analyze an author's style. Analyze characteristics of satire. Analyze philosophical assumptions in literary works. Analyze connotations. Compare literary works of different literary periods.	Evaluate the historical and social influences of the Modernist period in America, from 1914–1939. Analyze the use of poetic devices. Analyze characteristics of drama, short stories, poetry, and prose. Analyze the protagonist. Analyze archetypes drawn from myth and tradition. Analyze theme. Analyze an author's style. Compare and contrast works from different literary periods.	Evaluate the historical and social influences of contemporary America, from 1939 to the present. Analyze political points of view on a topic. Analyze the use of poetic and literary devices. Analyze objective and subjective writing. Analyze theme. Analyze characteristics of subgenres of short stories, nonfiction, and poetry. Analyze an author's tone and style. Analyze archetypes drawn from myth and tradition. Analyze a poem's speaker. Compare literary works of different literary periods.
Reading Public Documents and Informational Text	Analyze features of public documents.	Analyze implicit and explicit philosophical assumptions.	Evaluate the credibility of an author's argument. Analyze a writer's message. Analyze features of public documents. Identify historical context.
Vocabulary	Understand and use context clues. Analyze synonyms and antonyms. Understand noun-forming suffixes. Analyze Greek and Latin roots in terms used in math and science. Understand word origins. Analyze word analogies.	Understand synonyms and antonyms. Understand and use context clues. Analyze Greek and Latin roots in terms used in math and science. Analyze connotations. Analyze word analogies. Create semantic maps.	Understand connotations and denotations. Identify synonyms. Use context clues. Analyze word analogies. Understand etymologies of words used in political science and history. Analyze word analogies.
Writing, Listening, and Speaking	Report historical research. Present historical research.	Write a descriptive essay. Analyze literature. Write a biographical narrative. Analyze a novel. Present a literary analysis.	Write an autobiographical narrative. Analyze nonfiction. Analyze and use media. Recite literature.

LITERARY SKILLS	Grade 6	Grade 7	Grade 8	Grade 9	Grade 10	Grade 11	Grade 12
Alexandrine							■
Allegory				■	■	■	■
Alliteration	■	■	■	■	■	■	■
Allusion	■	■	■	■	■	■	■
Ambiguity				■	■	■	
American Indian oratory						■	
Analogy		■	■	■	■	■	■
Anecdote	■	■	■			■	■
Antagonist			■	■	■	■	■
Anticlimax							■
Antithesis							■
Aphorism						■	■
Apostrophe							■
Approximate rhyme			■	■	■	■	
Archetype						■	■
Argument					■	■	
Arthurian legend		■			■		■
Aside				■	■		
Assonance			■	■		■	■
Atmosphere		■	■	■	■	■	■
Autobiography	■	■	■	■	■	■	■
Ballad			■	■	■	■	■
Biography	■	■	■	■	■	■	■
Blank verse				■	■	■	■
Cadence						■	
Caesura							■
Catalog poem				■		■	■
Carpe Diem							■
Character	■	■	■	■	■	■	■
Character interactions		■		■	■		
Character traits	■	■	■	■	■		

LITERARY SKILLS	Grade 6	Grade 7	Grade 8	Grade 9	Grade 10	Grade 11	Grade 12
Characterization	■	■	■	■	■	■	■
Chronological order	■	■	■	■	■	■	
Classicism							■
Climax	■	■	■	■	■	■	■
Comedy			■	■	■	■	■
Comic devices			■			■	
Comparing texts	■	■	■	■	■	■	■
Conceit							■
Conflict	■	■	■	■	■	■	■
Connotation	■	■	■	■	■	■	■
Contradiction				■	■		
Couplet		■	■	■	■	■	■
Deism						■	■
Denotation	■	■	■	■	■		
Denouement				■	■	■	■
Description	■	■	■	■	■	■	■
Dialect	■	■	■	■	■	■	■
Dialogue	■	■	■	■	■	■	■
Diction			■	■	■	■	■
Didactic literature	■	■	■				■
Direct characterization	■	■	■	■	■		
Drama	■	■	■	■	■		■
Dramatic monologue				■	■	■	■
Dramatic irony			■	■	■	■	■
Elegy		■	■			■	■
End rhyme	■	■	■	■	■		
Epic			■	■			■
Epic conventions							■
Epic hero			■	■			■
Epic simile							■
Epigram							■

CONTENTS IN BRIEF

Collection 1

Encounters and Foundations to 1800

Collection 2

American Romanticism 1800–1860

Collection 3

American Masters

Whitman and Dickinson

Collection 4

The Rise of REALISM

The Civil War to 1914

Collection 5

THE MODERNS

1914–1939

MODERN AMERICAN FICTION

THE HARLEM RENAISSANCE

COLLECTION 5: SKILLS REVIEW

Collection 6

Contemporary Literature

1939 to Present

CONTEMPORARY FICTION

CONTEMPORARY NONFICTION

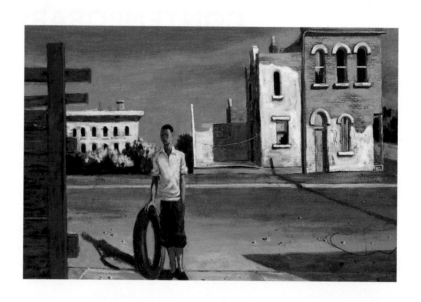

CONTEMPORARY POETRY

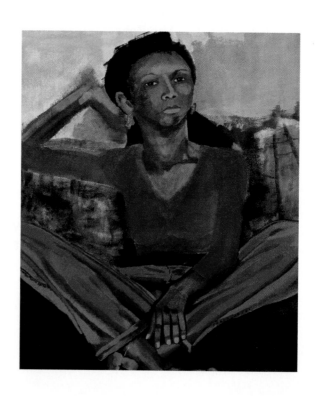

Resource Center

SKILLS, WORKSHOPS, AND FEATURES

SKILLS

LITERARY SKILLS

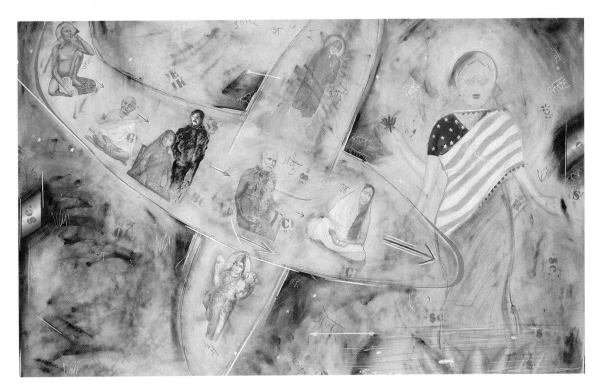

READING SKILLS

WORKSHOPS

FEATURES

PRIMARY SOURCES

GRAMMAR LINK

LANGUAGE HANDBOOK

SKILLS REVIEW

THE WORLD OF WORK

WRITER'S HANDBOOK

TEST SMARTS

SELECTIONS BY GENRE

FICTION

POETRY

NONFICTION AND INFORMATIONAL TEXT

APHORISMS

ARTICLE

AUTOBIOGRAPHIES

OP-ED ARTICLE

PERSONAL NARRATIVE

REPORTAGE

TRIBUTE

PUBLIC DOCUMENTS

EULOGY

INTERVIEWS

OPEN LETTER

POLITICAL ESSAY

POLICY STATEMENTS

SERMON

SPEECHES

Elements of Literature on the Internet

TO THE STUDENT

At the *Elements of Literature* Internet site, you can analyze the work of professional writers and learn the inside stories behind your favorite authors. You can also build your word power and analyze messages in the media. As you move through *Elements of Literature,* you will find the best online resources at **go.hrw.com.**

Here's how to log on:

1. Start your Web browser, and enter **go.hrw.com** in the Address or Location field.

Back   Forward   Reload   Home   Search

Location: http://go.hrw.com

2. Note the keyword in your textbook.

INTERNET

Speeches

Keyword: LE5 11-1

3. Enter the keyword and click "go."

http://go.hrw.com

LE5 11-1   go!

Enter keyword

FEATURES OF THE SITE

More About the Writer

Author biographies provide the inside stories behind the lives and works of great writers.

More Writer's Models

Interactive Writer's Models present annotations and reading tips to help you with your own writing. Printable Professional Models and Student Models provide you with quality writing by real writers and students across the country.

Interactive Reading Model

Interactive Reading Workshops guide you through high-interest informational articles and allow you to share your opinions through pop-up questions and polls.

Vocabulary Practice

Interactive vocabulary-building activities help you build your word power.

Cross-Curricular Connection

Short informational readings relate the literature you read in your textbook to your other studies and to real life.

Projects and Activities

Projects and activities help you extend your study of literature through writing, research, art, and public speaking.

Speeches

Video clips from historical speeches provide you with the tools you need to analyze elements of great speechmaking.

Media Tutorials

Media tutorials help you dissect messages in the media and learn to create your own multimedia presentations.

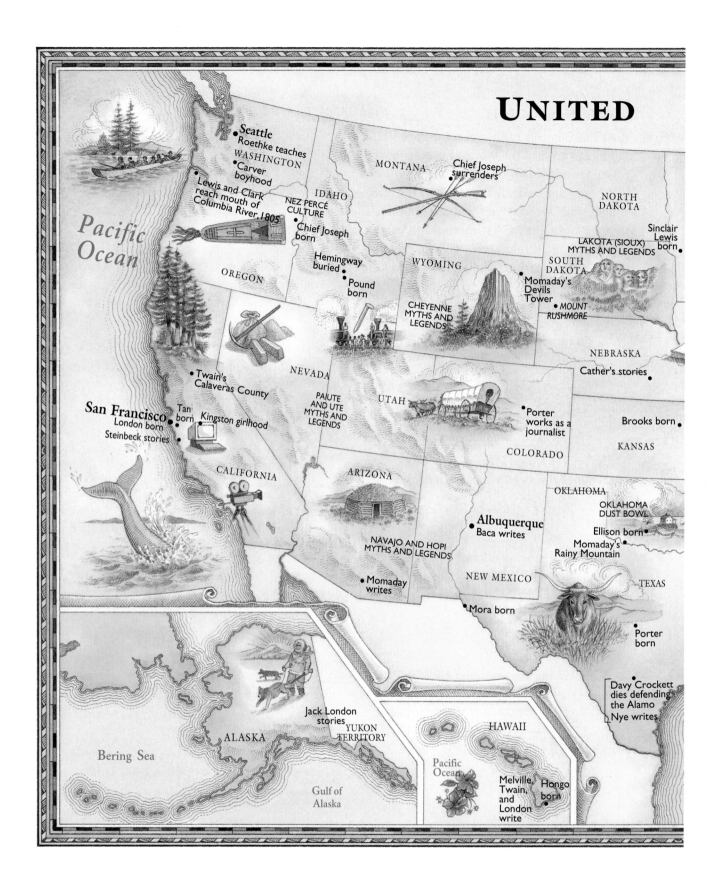

UNITED

Pacific Ocean

Seattle
Roethke teaches
WASHINGTON
Carver boyhood
Lewis and Clark reach mouth of Columbia River, 1805

MONTANA
Chief Joseph surrenders

IDAHO
NEZ PERCÉ CULTURE
Chief Joseph born
Hemingway buried
Pound born

OREGON

WYOMING
CHEYENNE MYTHS AND LEGENDS

NORTH DAKOTA

SOUTH DAKOTA
LAKOTA (SIOUX) MYTHS AND LEGENDS
Sinclair Lewis born
Momaday's Devils Tower
MOUNT RUSHMORE

NEBRASKA
Cather's stories

NEVADA
Twain's Calaveras County
San Francisco
Tan born
London born
Kingston girlhood
Steinbeck stories

PAIUTE AND UTE MYTHS AND LEGENDS

UTAH

COLORADO
Porter works as a journalist

KANSAS
Brooks born

CALIFORNIA

ARIZONA
NAVAJO AND HOPI MYTHS AND LEGENDS
Momaday writes

OKLAHOMA
OKLAHOMA DUST BOWL
Ellison born
Momaday's Rainy Mountain

Albuquerque
Baca writes

NEW MEXICO
Mora born

TEXAS
Porter born

Davy Crockett dies defending the Alamo
Nye writes

ALASKA
Bering Sea
Gulf of Alaska

Jack London stories
YUKON TERRITORY

HAWAII
Pacific Ocean
Melville, Twain, and London write
Hongo born

STATES

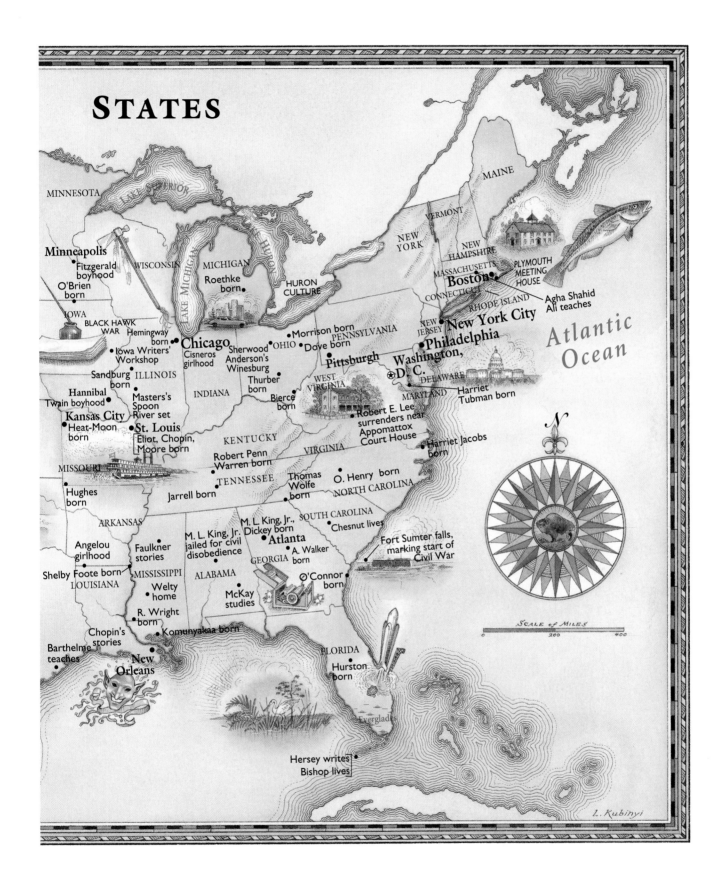

MINNESOTA

LAKE SUPERIOR

Minneapolis
- Fitzgerald boyhood
- O'Brien born

WISCONSIN

IOWA

BLACK HAWK WAR

LAKE MICHIGAN

MICHIGAN
- Roethke born

LAKE HURON

HURON CULTURE

Hemingway born
- Iowa Writers' Workshop
- Sandburg born

Chicago

ILLINOIS

Cisneros girlhood

Sherwood Anderson's Winesburg

OHIO
- Morrison born
- Dove born

PENNSYLVANIA

Pittsburgh

Philadelphia

Washington, D.C.

DELAWARE

MARYLAND

Harriet Tubman born

NEW YORK

VERMONT

NEW HAMPSHIRE

MAINE

MASSACHUSETTS

Boston

CONNECTICUT

RHODE ISLAND

NEW JERSEY

New York City

PLYMOUTH MEETING HOUSE

Agha Shahid Ali teaches

Atlantic Ocean

Hannibal
Twain boyhood

INDIANA

Thurber born

Bierce born

Masters's Spoon River set

WEST VIRGINIA

Kansas City
- Heat-Moon born

St. Louis
Eliot, Chopin, Moore born

KENTUCKY

Robert Penn Warren born

VIRGINIA

Robert E. Lee surrenders near Appomattox Court House

Harriet Jacobs born

MISSOURI

TENNESSEE

Jarrell born

Thomas Wolfe born

O. Henry born

NORTH CAROLINA

- Hughes born

ARKANSAS

- Angelou girlhood

- Shelby Foote born

LOUISIANA

Faulkner stories

M. L. King, Jr. jailed for civil disobedience

MISSISSIPPI

Welty home

R. Wright born

M. L. King, Jr., Dickey born

Atlanta

A. Walker born

GEORGIA

O'Connor born

SOUTH CAROLINA

Chesnut lives

Fort Sumter falls, marking start of Civil War

ALABAMA

McKay studies

Chopin's stories

Barthelme teaches

New Orleans

Komunyakaa born

FLORIDA

Hurston born

Everglades

Hersey writes
Bishop lives

N

Scale of Miles

0   200   400

L. Kubinyi

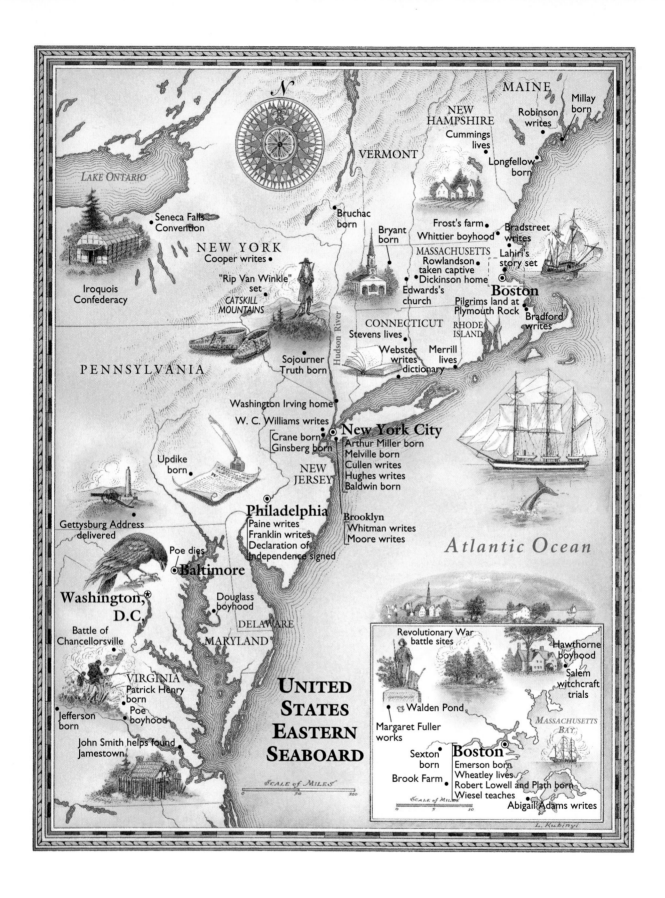

United States Eastern Seaboard

MAINE
Millay born
Robinson writes

NEW HAMPSHIRE
Cummings lives
Longfellow born

VERMONT
Bruchac born

Frost's farm
Whittier boyhood
Bradstreet writes

MASSACHUSETTS
Rowlandson taken captive
Dickinson home
Lahiri's story set

Bryant born

Edwards's church

Boston

LAKE ONTARIO
Seneca Falls Convention

NEW YORK
Cooper writes

Iroquois Confederacy

"Rip Van Winkle" set
CATSKILL MOUNTAINS

Pilgrims land at Plymouth Rock
Bradford writes

CONNECTICUT
Stevens lives

RHODE ISLAND

Webster writes dictionary
Merrill lives

PENNSYLVANIA

Sojourner Truth born

Washington Irving home
W. C. Williams writes
Crane born
Ginsberg born

New York City
Arthur Miller born
Melville born
Cullen writes
Hughes writes
Baldwin born

Updike born

NEW JERSEY

Philadelphia
Paine writes
Franklin writes
Declaration of Independence signed

Brooklyn
Whitman writes
Moore writes

Atlantic Ocean

Gettysburg Address delivered

Poe dies

Baltimore

Washington, D.C.

Battle of Chancellorsville

DELAWARE

Douglass boyhood

MARYLAND

VIRGINIA
Patrick Henry born
Poe boyhood

Jefferson born

John Smith helps found Jamestown

UNITED STATES EASTERN SEABOARD

Scale of Miles
0   50   100

Revolutionary War battle sites

Hawthorne boyhood

Salem witchcraft trials

Walden Pond

MASSACHUSETTS BAY

Margaret Fuller works

Sexton born

Brook Farm

Boston
Emerson born
Wheatley lives
Robert Lowell and Plath born
Wiesel teaches

Abigail Adams writes

Scale of Miles
0   5   10

L. Kubinyi

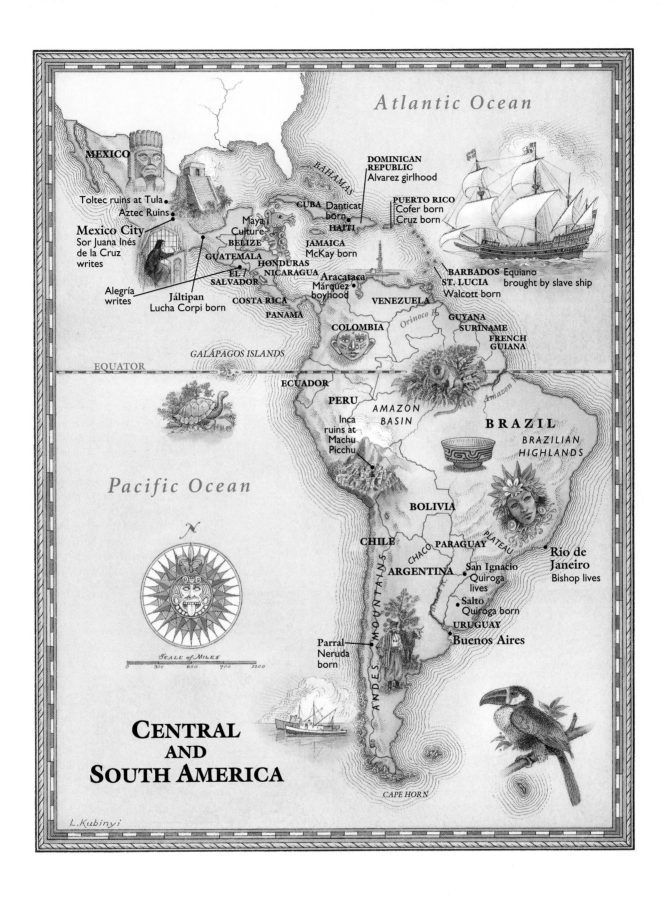

Atlantic Ocean

MEXICO

Toltec ruins at Tula
Aztec Ruins

Mexico City
Sor Juana Inés
de la Cruz
writes

Alegría
writes

Jáltipan
Lucha Corpi born

BAHAMAS

DOMINICAN
REPUBLIC
Alvarez girlhood

CUBA Danticat
born
HAITI

PUERTO RICO
Cofer born
Cruz born

Maya
Culture
BELIZE

GUATEMALA
HONDURAS
EL NICARAGUA
SALVADOR

COSTA RICA

PANAMA

JAMAICA
McKay born

Aracataca
Márquez
boyhood

VENEZUELA

COLOMBIA

Orinoco R.

BARBADOS Equiano
ST. LUCIA brought by slave ship
Walcott born

GUYANA
SURINAME
FRENCH
GUIANA

GALÁPAGOS ISLANDS

EQUATOR

ECUADOR

PERU
Inca
ruins at
Machu
Picchu

AMAZON
BASIN

Amazon

BRAZIL

BRAZILIAN
HIGHLANDS

Pacific Ocean

N

SCALE of MILES
0   300   600   900   1200

BOLIVIA

CHILE

ANDES MOUNTAINS

CHACO

PARAGUAY

PLATEAU

ARGENTINA

San Ignacio
Quiroga
lives

Salto
Quiroga born

URUGUAY

Buenos Aires

Río de
Janeiro
Bishop lives

Parral
Neruda
born

CENTRAL
AND
SOUTH AMERICA

CAPE HORN

L. Kubinyi

A Walk Through
Elements of Literature

The ***Elements of Literature*** *Student Edition* is the primary tool for building knowledge and understanding of literature and language skills. Opportunities for practice and remediation, reteaching, and assessing are offered throughout the program.

Collections

The collections in ***Elements of Literature*** are organized chronologically to cover each literary period's historical, political, and social contexts. Informational texts include introductions to literary periods, public documents, and features such as Political and Social Milestones, Political Points of View, and A Closer Look. Opportunities are provided for students to compare pieces of literature. Students will also examine the literature of other cultures with Literature of the Americas in the Fifth Course. Each collection offers multiple opportunities for students to master each skill, as well as a review section.

Introduction to the Literary Period

Introduction to the Literary Period gives students an understanding of the literary period and the historical forces that shaped it. It includes a Political and Social Milestones section as well as a detailed Time Line.

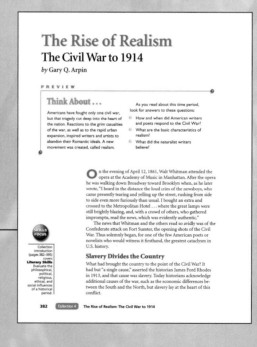

Author Biography

An **author biography** appears before each literature selection, providing students with comprehensive background on the author.

Mark Twain
(1835–1910)

Mark Twain is the most celebrated humorist in American history. His ability to make us laugh has contributed to the singular popularity of his books, not just in Twain's own time but in following generations. It is even more surprising to find that Twain's appeal has traveled throughout the world.

The great humorist is also, ironically, our great realist. Behind the backwoods humor—especially in his novel *Adventures of Huckleberry Finn*—is a revelation of the illusions that exist in American life. Huck's journey on a raft with the escaped slave Jim is not a "hymn to boyhood." It is a dramatization of the grim realities of a slaveholding society.

Although Twain became remarkably successful, his later life was shadowed by disappointment and tragedy, and as he grew older, he turned into a bitter man. He once told his friend William Dean Howells, the influential novelist and editor of *The Atlantic Monthly*, "Everyone is a moon and has a dark side which he never shows to anybody."

"Mark Twain!"

Twain was born Samuel Langhorne Clemens in the backwoods of Missouri. His father, John Clemens, a bright, ambitious, but impractical Virginian, had married Jane Lampton, a witty, dynamic woman who was also a great beauty. When John's store failed in 1839, he moved his hopes and his family to Hannibal, Missouri—the Mississippi River town that Sam, writing as Mark Twain, would later fashion into the setting of the most renowned boyhood in American literature, that of Tom Sawyer.

Sam's own carefree boyhood ended at twelve when his father died. To help support his mother and sister, he went to work setting type and editing copy for the newspaper started by his older brother Orion. At eighteen, Sam set out on his own. Over the next fifteen years, he worked as a printer in various towns from Missouri to the East Coast. Smitten by a love for the magical steamboats that plied the Mississippi, he apprenticed himself to the great steamboat pilot Horace Bixby. From Bixby, Sam Clemens learned the bends and shallows of the great river. It was the leadsman's cry of "Mark twain!"—announcing a water depth of two fathoms (twelve feet)—that provided Clemens with his celebrated pen name.

A Gold Mine of Humor

For a short time during the Civil War, Twain was a soldier with a company of Confederate irregulars, but he soon abandoned the military life for that of a gold prospector in Nevada. While he found little gold there, he did discover the rich mine of storytelling within himself. With his Missouri drawl and relaxed manner, Twain captivated audiences. In pretending not to recognize the coarseness or absurdity of his material, Twain maintained a deadpan attitude that added to his material's hilarity.

Mark Twain (1935) by Frank Edwin Larson. Oil on canvas (48" × 36").

Mark Twain   457

Before You Read

The Lowest Animal

Make the Connection
Quickwrite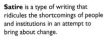

Americans have always had a high regard for progress and self-improvement. Mark Twain couples this admirable national trait with a blistering vision of how far, in his opinion, the human race falls short of its ideals. Think about what you would like to change about human nature, and freewrite your ideas.

Literary Focus
Satire: The Weapon of Laughter

Mark Twain wrote that we have only "one really effective weapon—laughter. Power, money, persuasion, supplication—these can lift a colossal humbug—push it a little—weaken it a little, century by century; but only laughter can blow it to rags and atoms at a blast."

Satire uses humor to critique people or institutions with the intention of improving them. One of the favorite techniques of the satirist is **exaggeration**—overstating something to make it look ridiculous. Another technique is **irony**—stating the opposite of what's really meant.

Like many other great satires, this famous essay is clearly outrageous. Twain doesn't really mean much of what he says, but sometimes the most exaggerated and maddening pieces of writing force us to think critically.

> **Satire** is a type of writing that ridicules the shortcomings of people and institutions in an attempt to bring about change.
>
> For more on Satire, see the Handbook of Literary and Historical Terms.

Reading Skills 🖰
Recognizing a Writer's Purpose

In general, a writer's **purpose** can be to describe, to inform, to narrate, to entertain, to analyze, or to persuade. Satires are usually exaggerated and humorous, but the true satirist intends to do more than simply make you laugh. Real-world change; reform; honest reexamination of values; the development of new goals, attitudes, and perspectives—these are the satirist's deeper purposes. To get to the deeper meaning of a satire, consider the following questions:

- What is the writer's philosophical position?
- What are the writer's religious, political, and social beliefs?
- Whom or what is the writer aiming to improve? What is his or her target?
- What does the writer want me to believe and—most important—to *do*?

Vocabulary Development

dispositions (dis′pə·zish′ənz) *n. pl.:* natures; characters.

allegiance (ə·lē′jəns) *n.:* loyalty.

caliber (kal′ə·bər) *n.:* quality or ability.

wantonly (wänt′'n·lē) *adv.:* carelessly, often with ill will.

transition (tran·zish′ən) *n.:* passage from one condition, form, or stage to another.

scrupled (skro͞o′pəld) *v.:* hesitated because of feelings of guilt.

appease (ə·pēz′) *v.:* satisfy; pacify.

avaricious (av′ə·rish′əs) *adj.:* greedy.

atrocious (ə·trō′shəs) *adj.:* evil; very bad.

sordid (sôr′did) *adj.:* dirty; cheap; shameful.

INTERNET
Vocabulary Practice
•
More About Mark Twain
•
Keyword: LE5 11-4

SKILLS FOCUS

Literary Skills
Understand the characteristics of satire.

Reading Skills
Analyze a writer's purpose.

Before You Read

Before You Read precedes every selection, giving students adequate prereading information, motivation, and a purpose for reading. The skills focus is listed on the page so students know what skills they will be learning.

Make the Connection asks students to think or write about issues they will encounter in the literature they are about to read.

Literary Focus enables students to learn about or review a key literary element in the selection.

Reading Skills introduces a skill that will help students' reading comprehension, such as making inferences, summarizing, or making predictions.

Background provides students with necessary information that will help them understand the context of the literature.

Vocabulary Development lists the key vocabulary words from the selection and their definitions.

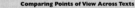

Introducing **Political Points** *of* **View**
Slavery

You will be reading the five selections listed above in this Political Points of View feature on slavery. In the top corner of each page of this feature, you'll find three stars. Smaller versions of the stars appear next to the questions on pages 404 and 411 that focus on this political issue. At the end of the feature (page 421), you'll compare the various points of view on slavery expressed in the selections.

Examining the Issue: Slavery

The fact that slavery could flourish in a nation so fervently dedicated to the ideals of equality and freedom is perhaps the greatest paradox, or seeming contradiction, in our nation's history. It would take the upheaval of civil war to confront this American paradox and force a change.

Slavery is an issue that makes clear the close relationship between the personal and the political. The laws governing the slave system were not mere technicalities. They defined people, determined the course of their lives, and controlled all their relationships. As you read the selections in this section, note how, for the writers, the political is personal.

Reading Skills
Comparing Points of View Across Texts

The readings in this section describe several ways by which human beings opposed the horrors of slavery. In order to compare these points of view, make a chart like the one below. For each reading, note how slavery is opposed, and then describe the writer's point of view.

SKILLS FOCUS

Pages 396–421
cover
Literary Skills
Analyze political points of view on a topic.

Reading Skills
Compare points of view across texts.

Selection	Opposition to Slavery	Point of View
Narrative of the Life of Frederick Douglass	Endures beating; complains to "master"; fights Covey	Defiant resistance revives dignity and hope for freedom.

396 Collection 4 The Rise of Realism: The Civil War to 1914

Political Points of View

Political Points of View features throughout the book provide opportunities for students to examine different political points of view on issues pertinent to the historical period. The selections included in these features span a variety of genres, including public documents, informational text, poetry, and prose.

Public Documents

Public Documents give students an opportunity to examine and critique the arguments on an issue of public concern. These documents include speeches, essays, policy statements, interviews, and newspaper articles.

Political Points *of* **View**
Before You Read

The blood bath of Gettysburg, fought on July 1–3, 1863, was the greatest single battle of the Civil War and its turning point. The battle left 5,660 dead, 27,000 wounded, and 10,500 missing. A few days after the battle, President Abraham Lincoln commented that he was "not prepared to make [a speech] worthy of the occasion." Several months later, at the dedication of a Gettysburg memorial cemetery on November 19, Lincoln did in fact deliver this "worthy" speech, probably the most memorable of his career.

SPEECH

The Gettysburg Address
Abraham Lincoln

Fourscore and seven[1] years ago our fathers brought forth on this continent a new nation, conceived[2] in Liberty, and dedicated to the proposition that all men are created equal.

Now we are engaged in a great civil war, testing whether that nation, or any nation so conceived and so dedicated, can long endure. We are met on a great battlefield of that war. We have come to dedicate a portion of that field as a final resting place for those who here gave their lives that that nation might live. It is altogether fitting and proper that we should do this.

But, in a larger sense, we cannot dedicate—we cannot consecrate[3]—we cannot hallow[4]—this ground. The brave men, living and dead, who struggled here, have consecrated it far above our poor power to add or detract. The world will little note nor long remember what we say here, but it can never forget what they did here. It is for us the living, rather, to be dedicated here to the unfinished work which they who fought here have thus far so nobly advanced. It is rather for us to be here dedicated to the great task remaining before us—that from these honored dead we take increased devotion to that cause for which they gave the last full measure of devotion—that we here highly resolve that these dead shall not have died in vain—that this nation, under God, shall have a new birth of freedom—and that government of the people, by the people, for the people, shall not perish from the earth.

---
1. **fourscore and seven:** eighty-seven. A score is a set of twenty.
2. **conceived** *v.* used as *adj.*: developed; imagined.
3. **consecrate** *v.*: set apart as sacred or holy.
4. **hallow** *v.*: make holy.

448 Collection 4 The Rise of Realism: The Civil War to 1914

Connection

A number of selections are followed by a **Connection** feature: an additional work, often in a different genre, that makes a pertinent literary connection to the main selection. Newspaper articles, poems, and essays appear as **Connection** features, enabling students to compare and contrast different treatments of a theme and make relevant personal connections.

CONNECTION / OP-ED ARTICLE **INFORMATIONAL TEXT**

This article was written shortly after the terrorist attack that brought down the World Trade Center towers in New York City on September 11, 2001.

A Time of Gifts
Stephen Jay Gould

The patterns of human history mix decency and depravity in equal measure. We often assume, therefore, that such a fine balance of results must emerge from societies made of decent and depraved people in equal numbers. But we need to expose and celebrate the fallacy of this conclusion so that, in this moment of crisis, we may reaffirm an essential truth too easily forgotten and regain some crucial comfort too readily forgone. Good and kind people outnumber all others by thousands to one. The tragedy of human history lies in the enormous potential for destruction in rare acts of evil, not in the high frequency of evil people. Complex systems can only be built step by step, whereas destruction requires but an instant. Thus, in what I like to call the Great Asymmetry, every spectacular

Firefighters leaving rescue area near World Trade Center, September 13, 2001.

incident of evil will be balanced by ten thousand acts of kindness, too often unnoted and invisible as the "ordinary" efforts of a vast majority.

We have a duty, almost a holy responsibility, to record and honor the victorious weight of these innumerable little kindnesses when an unprecedented act of evil so threatens to distort our perception of ordinary human behavior. I have stood at ground zero, stunned by the twisted ruins of the largest human structure ever destroyed in a catastrophic moment. (I will discount the claims of a few biblical literalists for the Tower of Babel.) And I have contemplated a single day of carnage that our nation has not suffered since battles that still evoke passions and tears, nearly 150 years later: Antietam, Gettysburg, Cold Harbor. The scene is insufferably sad, but not at all depress-

474 Collection 4 The Rise of Realism: The Civil War to 1914

READ ON: FOR INDEPENDENT READING

FICTION
A Family Saga
When Alex Haley was a child, his grandmother told him tales of an ancestor known only as the African—a man torn from his Mandingo people and forced into slavery in America. When Haley grew up, he discovered that the African had a real name—Kunta Kinte—and a story that had the power to reach people everywhere. *Roots* is a fictionalized chronicle spanning the period between Kunta's birth in 1750 and the death of Haley's father, a college professor, in the twentieth century.

FICTION
The Great American Novel
Ernest Hemingway wrote, "All modern American literature comes from one book by Mark Twain called *Huckleberry Finn*." Widely regarded as Twain's masterpiece, *Adventures of Huckleberry Finn* is a wise and funny novel about a young boy coming of age on the Mississippi River.

This title is available in the HRW Library.

NONFICTION
The War Between the States
For an inside look at the most dramatic war waged on U.S. soil, consider *The Civil War: An Illustrated History* by Geoffrey C. Ward and others. This companion volume to the PBS series, produced by Ric and Ken Burns, features essays; interviews; and an arresting series of photographs depicting generals, soldiers, and everyday citizens from the North and the South. The historical narrative and stunning images trace the war from the first shots at Fort Sumter through the bloody battlefields and finally to General Lee's surrender at Appomattox.

FICTION
The Wild Frontier
The late nineteenth century was a time in which the United States became a nation of immigrants—a time when people from many lands were drawn to the promise of the western frontier. Willa Cather's classic novel *My Ántonia* is the story of one such immigrant family—the Shimerdas of Bohemia—and their new life in Nebraska. At the center of the story is the Shimerdas's daughter Ántonia, who captures the heart and imagination of a lonely neighbor boy.

Read On   **527**

Read On
At the end of each collection, **Read On** provides students with suggestions for independent reading of fiction and nonfiction. The recommended books have themes or subjects similar to those in the collection.

Writing Workshops

Writing Workshops at the end of each collection guide students through the writing process. Each workshop covers a different mode of writing, such as narration, persuasion, description, or exposition, and is a logical extension of the literary and informational selections covered in the collection.

Prewriting provides step-by-step instruction to help students get started and think about the audience they want to reach.

Writer's Framework shows students how to structure their papers.

Writer's Model demonstrates the workshop assignment with annotations to help students understand the structure and development of an essay.

Editor in Charge offers a three-step process with specific actions for students to take to locate and correct weaknesses in their papers.

Style Guidelines encourage students to revise their papers a second time for precise and effective language.

Writing Workshop

Reporting Historical Research

Writing Assignment
Write a paper investigating a historical event that intrigues you.

Paralleling the rise of realism in American literature was a rise in realism for historians, who began to take a more scientific and objective approach to gathering and interpreting evidence about historical events. Instead of writing to glorify or justify conquerors, historians would analyze and evaluate all the available evidence about an event before drawing any conclusions. Now you will have the opportunity to **investigate a historical event** by analyzing several different historical records about it, explaining the similarities and differences among the records, and drawing conclusions about the event.

Prewriting

Choose and Narrow a Topic

Travel to the Past You investigate a historical event so you can draw your own conclusions about the event and its significance. When you read a single record of a historical event—the attack on Pearl Harbor or the assassination of President John F. Kennedy, the fall of the Berlin Wall—you are likely to be reading information that represents only one **perspective**, or point of view, on that event. To understand a historical event fully, you need to examine a wide variety of sources representing all relevant perspectives on the event.

As you consider a topic for your paper, look for a controversial event that interests you and for which you will be able to find a variety of sources. You should also make sure that the topic is narrow enough to be covered well in a paper of 1,500 words. To choose an appropriate topic, follow the example in the student model below.

What historical event am I interested in?	I'm interested in the Civil War.
How can I narrow this topic, if necessary?	I can focus on one important event: General Sherman's march from Atlanta to Savannah.
Can I find a variety of sources on this topic?	Yes—records and newspaper accounts written during the war, memoirs and books written after the war are available.
Can I find sources representing all relevant perspectives on this topic?	Yes, there should be plenty of information representing various points of view, such as those of Northerners, Southerners, soldiers, and civilians.

Listening & Speaking Workshop

Presenting and Evaluating Speeches

Speaking Assignment
Adapt your written editorial for a persuasive speech and deliver it to an audience. Then, listen to and evaluate the persuasive speeches of others.

Effective **persuasive speeches** incorporate the same techniques that are used to write editorials. A speech, though, allows you to use your voice and body as well as words to make your point. In this workshop you will learn how to use the techniques of persuasion in a speech and how to listen to and evaluate the persuasive speeches of others.

Adapt Your Editorial

Part by Part A persuasive speech consists of the same introduction, body, and conclusion arrangement your written editorial had. However, you might need to make alterations to each of these parts of your editorial so they will be better suited for a speech.

- The **introduction** to an effective persuasive speech is dramatic. Consider using a thought-provoking literary quotation, a touching anecdote that illustrates an aspect of the issue you're dealing with, or a reference to an authority on the subject of your speech. Then, state your **distinct perspective** on the issue in a strong but simple opinion statement, perhaps even repeating it for dramatic effect and impact.

 TIP Keep in mind that your reasoning will be evaluated as you present your speech. Therefore, you should avoid faulty logic and the use of propaganda. For more on **logical fallacies and propaganda**, see page 125.

- The **body** of a persuasive speech supports the opinion statement and must consist of **solid reasoning**. To fit within your time limits, choose only the most effective reasons from your written editorial based on the makeup of your audience. For example, an audience composed exclusively of classmates might respond favorably to reasons that appeal to their emotions. An audience of city council members might respond best to reasons that appeal to logic or ethics.

- The **conclusion** to an effective speech should be memorable. First, summarize the main points and restate your opinion directly. Finally, call the audience to action, using specific language.

Take the Right Approach There are two basic ways to organize the body of a persuasive speech—deductively or inductively. You can use either to make sure that your speech is coherent and focused.

 SKILLS FOCUS

Listening and Speaking Skills
Present and evaluate a persuasive speech.

- **The Deductive Approach** Deductive reasoning moves from general to specific. State your opinion in the introduction, and give specific reasons and evidence in the body of the speech.

- **The Inductive Approach** Inductive reasoning m_____ to general. You present the reasons and evidence _____ your opinion at the beginning and build to your _____ (the general) in the conclusion.

Listening and Speaking Workshop

Some collections feature a **Listening and Speaking Workshop** that guides students in delivering focused, coherent presentations and in evaluating a variety of oral and media communications.

Each **Listening and Speaking Workshop** is tied to a **Writing Workshop** and focuses on a different kind of presentation, such as narration, exposition, persuasion, research, and response to literature.

Practice and Apply encourages students to follow easy steps to help them construct, deliver, and evaluate a presentation.

Skills Review

A **Skills Review** at the end of each collection provides standardized-test practice for the vocabulary and writing skills taught in the collection. Students also compare and contrast two literary works from different time periods, completing both **multiple-choice** questions and an **essay**.

Collection 4: Skills Review
Comparing Literature

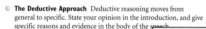 **Test Practice** The following two pieces of literature were written almost a hundred years apart. Both deal with the horrors of war.

Stephen Crane (1871–1900) was born after the Civil War, but his best-known work is *The Red Badge of Courage*, a short novel that supposedly takes place at the battle of Chancellorsville in Virginia. This classic work of fiction is told through the eyes of young Henry Fleming, a Union soldier.

The poet Yusef Komunyakaa (1947–   ) won the Pulitzer Prize in 1994 for his poetry collection *Neon Vernacular*. Much of Komunyakaa's work, including "Camouflaging the Chimera," is based on his experiences in the Vietnam War, where he served as an information specialist.

DIRECTIONS: Read the following novel excerpt and poem. Then, read each multiple-choice question that follows, and write the letter of the best response.

This excerpt from The Red Badge of Courage *describes a column of soldiers headed into battle. The "youth" is Henry Fleming, Crane's protagonist in the novel.*

from The Red Badge of Courage

Stephen Crane

Presently the calm head of a forward-going column of infantry[1] appeared in the road. It came swiftly on. Avoiding the obstructions gave it the sinuous movement of a serpent. The men at the head butted mules with their musket stocks. They prodded teamsters[2] indifferent to all howls. The men forced their way through parts of the dense mass by strength. The blunt head of the column pushed. The raving teamsters swore many strange oaths.

The commands to make way had the ring of a great importance in them. The men were going forward to the heart of the din. They were

 SKILLS FOCUS

Pages 550–553 cover
Literary Skills
Compare and contrast works from different literary periods.

1. **infantry** *n.:* foot soldiers.
2. **teamsters** *n. pl.:* drivers of teams of horses used for hauling.

Reading Matters

Reading Matters is a handbook that offers students strategies designed to improve their reading skills. It focuses on issues such as reading comprehension and reading rate.

Reading Matters

When the Text Is Tough

Remember the reading you did back in first, second, and third grades? Big print. Short texts. Easy words. In high school, however, the texts you read are often filled with small print, long chapters, and complicated plots or topics. Also, you now find yourself reading a variety of material—from your driver's-ed handbook to college applications, from job applications to income-tax forms, from e-mail to e-zines, from classics to comics, from textbooks to checkbooks.

Doing something every day that you find difficult and tedious isn't much fun—and that includes reading. So this section of this book is designed to show you what to do when the text gets tough. Let's begin to look at some reading matters.

READING UP CLOSE: HOW TO USE THIS SECTION

- **This section is for you.** Turn to it whenever you need to remind yourself about what to do when the text gets tough. Don't wait for your teacher to assign this section for you to read. It's your handbook. Use it.

- **Read the sections that you need.** You don't have to read every word. Skim the headings, and find the information you need.

- **Use this information to help you with reading for other classes,** not just for the reading you do in this book.

- **Don't be afraid to re-read the information** you find in Reading Matters. The best readers constantly re-read information.

- **If you need more help, then check the index.** The index will direct you to other pages in this book with information on reading skills and strategies.

The World of Work

You will use reading and writing skills almost every day of your life. For example, a police officer must write coherent reports. A parent must understand school policies. A car buyer must understand the contract. A dissatisfied employee must document unfair treatment in an effective memo. In your life and in the world of work, you will use reading and writing skills to learn new information, to communicate effectively, and to get the results you want.

Reading

Reading is an important decision-making tool that helps you analyze information, weigh arguments, and make informed choices. Much of the real-life reading you will do will come from **informative documents** and **persuasive documents**.

Informative Documents Informative documents focus on providing facts and information, and they can be good places to check when you want to verify or clarify information from other sources. For example, suppose a co-worker sends you an e-mail complaining about a new vacation policy. Before responding, you can read the memo that explains the policy to see if your co-worker has understood the information correctly. Informative documents include **consumer documents** and **workplace documents**.

Consumer Documents As a consumer, you will face thousands of buying decisions. Maybe you've heard the warning: "Let the buyer beware!" That warning means that buyers are responsible for reading and understanding information about products and services. This information can be found in consumer documents, which spell out details about products and the legal rights and responsibilities of the buyer and the companies that produce and sell the product. Consumer documents you're likely to see include **warranties, contracts, product information,** and **instruction manuals.**

- **Warranties** describe what happens if the product breaks down or doesn't work properly. Warranties such as the one below note how long the product is covered for repair or replacement, which repairs the warranty does and does not cover, and how to receive repair service.

The MovieBuff DVD player is guaranteed to be free of defects in material or workmanship under normal use for a period of one (1) year from the date of purchase. Equipment covered by the warranty will be repaired by MovieBuff merchants WITHOUT CHARGE, except for insurance, transportation, and handling charges. A copy of this warranty card and proof of purchase must be enclosed when returning equipment for warranty service. The warranty does not apply in the following cases:

- if loss or damage to the equipment is due to abuse
- if the equipment is defective due to leaking batteries or liquid damage
- if the equipment has been serviced by unauthorized repair technicians

The World of Work **1135**

World of Work

World of Work includes information about and examples of **consumer documents** (such as warranties), **workplace documents** (such as memos), and **public documents** (such as policy statements). It also includes guidelines for writing resumes and completing job applications.

Test Smarts

by Flo Ota De Lange and Sheri Henderson

Strategies for Taking Multiple-Choice Tests

You have now reached your junior year and are almost at the end of your high school career. To graduate, however, you still need to pass a lot of tests. You'll have plenty of quizzes, midterm exams, and finals to get through. You'll take the state's standardized tests, and if you plan to go on to college, you'll need to tackle the *Scholastic Assessment Test* (SAT) or the *American College Testing Program* (ACT).

The following pages can help you prepare for all your standardized tests. They are designed to help you meet three goals:

- to become familiar with the different types of questions you will be asked
- to learn some strategies for approaching the questions
- to discover the kinds of questions that give you trouble

Once you have met those goals, you will want to practice answering the kinds of questions that give you trouble until you feel comfortable with them. Here are some basic strategies that will help you approach your multiple-choice tests with confidence:

Stay Calm

You have studied the material, and you know your stuff, but you're still nervous. That's OK. A little nervousness helps you focus, but so does a calm body. **Take a few deep breaths** before you begin.

Track Your Time

First, take a few minutes to estimate how much time you have for each question. Then, set checkpoints for yourself—how many questions should be completed at a quarter of the time, half the time, and so on. That way you can **pace yourself** as you work through the test. If you're behind, you can speed up. If you're ahead, you can—and should—slow down.

Master the Directions

Read the directions carefully to be sure you know exactly what to do and how to do it. If you are supposed to fill in a bubble, fill it in cleanly and carefully. Be careful to match each question's number to the number on the answer sheet.

Study the Questions

Read each question once, twice, three times—until you are absolutely certain you know what the question is asking you. Watch out for words like *not* and *except:* They tell you to look for choices that are false, different, or opposite.

Anticipate Answers

Once you are sure you understand the question, **anticipate the answer** before you read the choices. If the answer you guessed is there, it is probably correct. To be sure, though, check out each choice. If you understand the question but don't know the answer, eliminate any choices you think are wrong. Then, make an educated—not a wild—guess. Take care to **avoid distracters,** choices that are true but don't fit the question.

Don't Give Up

If you are having a hard time with a test, take a deep breath, and **keep on going.** On most tests the questions do not get more difficult as you go, and an easier question is probably coming up soon. The last question on a test is worth just as many points as the first, so give your all—all the way to the end.

Types of Test Questions

You will feel more confident if you are familiar with the kinds of questions given on a test. Following are examples of and tips for taking the different types of questions on many standardized tests.

Test Smarts **1153**

Test Smarts

Test Smarts is a handbook that gives students strategies for taking multiple-choice tests and writing tests. It includes questions for reading comprehension, vocabulary, and analogies.

Language Handbook

1 THE PARTS OF SPEECH

PART OF SPEECH	DEFINITION	EXAMPLES
NOUN	Names person, place, thing, or idea	poet, Sylvia Plath, city, Chicago, awards, Nobel Prize, *Of Mice and Men*, books, crew, herd, Harlem Renaissance, realism
PRONOUN	Takes place of one or more nouns or pronouns	
Personal	Refers to one(s) speaking (first person), spoken to (second person), spoken about (third person)	I, me, my, mine, we, us, our, ours you, your, yours he, him, his, she, her, hers, it, its, they, them, their, theirs
Reflexive	Refers to subject and directs action of verb back to subject	myself, ourselves, yourself, yourselves, himself, herself, itself, themselves
Intensive	Refers to and emphasizes noun or another pronoun	(same as examples for Reflexive)
Demonstrative	Refers to specific one(s) of group	this, that, these, those
Interrogative	Introduces question	what, which, who, whom, whose
Relative	Introduces subordinate clause	that, which, who, whom, whose
Indefinite	Refers to one(s) not specifically named	all, any, anyone, both, each, either, everybody, many, none, nothing, someone
ADJECTIVE	Modifies noun or pronoun by telling *what kind, which one, how many,* or *how much*	**a large black** box, **an able-bodied** worker, **that** one, **the five Iroquois** nations, **enough** time, **less** money, **many** choices
VERB	Shows action or state of being	
Action	Expresses physical or mental activity	write, receive, run, think, imagine, understand
Linking	Connects subject with word identifying or describing it	appear, be, seem, become, feel, look, smell, sound, taste
Helping	Assists another verb to express time, voice, or mood	be, have, may, can, shall, will, would
	Modifies verb, adjective, or adverb by telling *how, when, where,* or *to what extent*	speaks **clearly, quite** interesting, **rather** calmly, arrived **there** late
	Relates noun or pronoun to another word	about, at, by, for, of, in, on, through, according to, in front of, out of

(continued)

Language Handbook

Language Handbook

The **Language Handbook** is a quick reference guide that gives students an overview of important issues in grammar, usage, and mechanics.

Handbook of Literary and Historical Terms

You will find more information about the terms in this Handbook on the pages given at the ends of the entries. To learn more about **Ambiguity**, for example, turn to pages 696, 724, and 1039 in this book.

Cross-references at the ends of some entries refer to other entries in the Handbook containing related information. For instance, at the end of **Antagonist,** you are referred to **Protagonist.**

ABSTRACT LANGUAGE A term used to describe language that deals with generalities and intangible concepts. Words such as *happiness, despair, hope, beauty,* and *evil* are examples of the abstract. Abstract language is useful in dealing with philosophical ideas.

See page 1078.
See also *Concrete Language.*

ALLEGORY A story or poem in which characters, settings, and events stand for other people or events or for abstract ideas or qualities. An allegory can be read on one level for its literal meaning and on a second level for its symbolic, or allegorical, meaning. The most famous allegory in the English language is *The Pilgrim's Progress* (1678) by the English Puritan writer John Bunyan, in which Christian, on his journey to the Celestial City, meets such personages as Mr. Worldly Wiseman, Hopeful, and Giant Despair and travels to such places as the Slough of Despond, the Valley of Humiliation, and Doubting Castle. Puritans were trained to see their own lives as allegories of biblical experiences. Nathaniel Hawthorne's and Edgar Allan Poe's fictions are often called allegorical.

See page 227.

ALLITERATION The repetition of the same or similar consonant sounds in words that are close together. Alliteration is used to create musical effects and to establish mood. In the following line from "The Tide Rises, the Tide Falls" (Collection 2) by

Henry Wadsworth Longfellow, the repetition of the *s* sound is an example of alliteration:

> But the sea, the sea in darkness calls

See pages 171, 279, 313, 1082.
See also *Assonance, Onomatopoeia, Rhyme.*

ALLUSION A reference to someone or something that is known from history, literature, religion, politics, sports, science, or some other branch of culture. T. S. Eliot drew on his knowledge of the Bible when he alluded to the raising of Lazarus from the dead in "The Love Song of J. Alfred Prufrock" (Collection 5). The title of Sandra Cisneros's essay "Straw into Gold" (Collection 6) is an allusion to the folk tale about Rumpelstiltskin.

You won't understand the cartoon below unless you recognize the fairy tale it alludes to.

See pages 36, 583, 721, 1024, 1075.

"They're offering a deal—you can pay court costs and damages, they drop charges of breaking and entering."

Drawing by Maslin. © 1988 The New Yorker Magazine, Inc.

AMBIGUITY A technique by which a writer deliberately suggests two or more different, and sometimes conflicting, meanings in a work.

Handbook of Literary and Historical Terms **1169**

Handbook of Literary and Historical Terms

The **Handbook of Literary and Historical Terms** serves as a reference guide to the important literary terms and concepts students will encounter throughout the text.

Program Resources

HOLT
ELEMENTS OF LITERATURE
ESSENTIALS OF AMERICAN LITERATURE
Fifth Course

Holt Assessment
Writing, Listening, and Speaking

Includes Tests and Answer Key

HOLT
ELEMENTS OF LITERATURE
ESSENTIALS OF AMERICAN LITERATURE
Fifth Course

Holt Assessment
Literature, Reading, and Vocabulary

HOLT
ELEMENTS OF LITERATURE
ESSENTIALS OF AMERICAN LITERATURE
Fifth Course

The Holt Reader

- Historical Essays and Literary Selections from *Elements of Literature*
- Additional Literary and Informational Texts

HOLT
ELEMENTS OF LITERATURE
ESSENTIALS OF AMERICAN LITERATURE
Fifth Course

Holt Reading Solutions

Kylene Beers

Solutions for
- Intervention
- English Language Learners
- Special Education

HOLT
ELEMENTS OF LITERATURE
ESSENTIALS OF AMERICAN LITERATURE
Fifth Course

Holt Adapted Reader

Instruction in Reading Literature and Informational Materials

Planning

Annotated Teacher's Edition

This planning and teaching tool offers

- Specific questions to help reinforce and evaluate reading and literary skills for each selection

- Special approaches for learners having difficulty, English-language learners, and advanced learners

- Planning charts in the interleaf pages for each collection that provide information about the collection's scope and sequence of skills, core content, and resources

- Specific sequencing suggestions to ensure coverage of grade-level skills, effective testing, and remediation and reteaching opportunities

One-Stop Planner CD-ROM with ExamView Test Generator

This time-saving planning software contains print-based teaching resources, clips from the video program, and valuable assessment tools. The *One-Stop Planner* also

- Simplifies lesson planning and management

- Includes all the teaching resources for *Elements of Literature*

- Includes printable program resources and an easy-to-use test generator

- Offers previews of all teaching resources, including assessments and worksheets linked to the **Student Edition**

- Launches directly to the **go.hrw.com** Web site

PowerNotes for Literature and Reading

- Contains fully editable instructional PowerPoint® presentations that teach literary elements and reading skills and that introduce literary periods

- Includes teacher's notes with discussion questions and student note-taking worksheets with graphic organizers for each presentation

Professional Development

Web-Based Professional Development

Teaching Literacy to All Students, Grades 6–12, is a 9-module online professional development program that is ideal for all subject areas. *Teaching Reading to All Students, Grades 6–8,* is a 16-module online professional development program designed for middle school language arts teachers. Each module provides video demonstrations of best teaching practices tied to web-based content that includes explanations and examples, interactive applications to the teacher's own classroom, graphic organizers and lesson-planning templates, printable classroom handouts, and assessment instruments. The modules cover topics such as

- Planning schoolwide literacy programs
- Using assessment data to drive instruction
- Modifying instruction for English language learners
- Helping struggling readers with comprehension and fluency
- Integrating standards-based instruction

Face-to-Face Professional Development

Holt, Rinehart and Winston provides customized, comprehensive teacher training to assist school districts and individual teachers in the effective implementation of *Elements of Literature*.

- The training is facilitated by highly qualified professional development providers with language arts and reading expertise.

- Training institute and workshop topics include effective teaching practices, evidence-based research, and standards-based instruction.

Differentiating Instruction

The Holt Reader

This worktext includes alternative direct instruction and additional practice for the skills taught in each collection of *Elements of Literature*. The consumable format offers students' an interactive, hands-on approach to building reading, vocabulary, and literary analysis skills. Students circle, underline, and write responses in the margins of the selections.

- **Part I** contains key literary selections from *Elements of Literature* and additional literary selections that extend student's practice. Instruction is focused on vocabulary, literary elements, and reading skills.

- **Part 2** contains informational texts such as magazine and newspaper articles, editorials, and essays. Also offered are vocabulary exercises and standardized-test practice.

Holt Adapted Reader

This consumable worktext contains the literary and informational adaptations found in *Holt Reading Solutions*. With scaffolded instruction that provides guided support, the *Holt Adapted Reader* can be used with struggling readers while other students in the class read the same selection in *The Holt Reader* or the **Student Edition**.

- Adaptations are within the reading range of English-language learners, special education students, and reluctant readers

- "Here's How" annotations model vocabulary, literary analysis, and reading comprehension skills; "Your Turn" annotations ask students to answer a question using the skill just modeled

- Graphic organizers help students review and consolidate what they've learned

Holt Reading Solutions

This book pulls together all of the reading resources in the *Elements of Literature* program to create a powerful tool for intervention and whole-class instruction. It includes

- Diagnostic assessment tools
- Lesson plans for English-language learners and special education students
- Adaptations of selected reading selections
- Vocabulary and comprehension worksheets
- Information on phonics and decoding
- Additional instruction and practice in remedial reading skills and strategies

Supporting Instruction in Spanish

Provides the following Spanish-language materials as extra support for students who are making the transition from Spanish to English:

- Summaries of selections in *Elements of Literature*
- Criteria for major writing modes
- Definitions and examples of key grammar terms and concepts
- Introductions and summaries of Visual Connections segments

Audio CD Library

- Includes dramatic readings by professional actors that bring to life nearly every reading selection in *Elements of Literature*

Audio CD Library, Selections and Summaries in Spanish

- Includes Spanish translations of key selections in *Elements of Literature* that assist students in reading and developing their own sense of a selection
- Includes recordings of summaries in Spanish of virtually every selection in *Elements of Literature* that serve as a valuable tool for English-language learners

Workshop Resources: Writing, Listening, and Speaking

Supports instruction and assignments in the **Student Edition**

- Includes worksheets for each Writing Workshop and each Listening and Speaking Workshop
- Includes exercises and lesson plans with alternative teaching strategies for English-language learners and special education students

Family Involvement Activities in English and Spanish

- Offers a selection of letters written for the parents or guardians of students using *Elements of Literature*
- Suggests activities that can be completed at home to extend the material in the **Student Editions**
- Allows parents or guardians to participate in students' education and helps foster an atmosphere in the home that encourages academic success

Reading/Literature/Vocabulary

The Holt Reader

This worktext includes alternative direct instruction and additional practice for the skills taught in each collection of *Elements of Literature*. The consumable format offers students' an interactive, hands-on approach to building reading, vocabulary, and literary analysis skills. Students circle, underline, and write responses in the margins of the selections.

- **Part 1** contains key literary selections from *Elements of Literature* and additional literary selections that extend student's practice. Instruction is focused on vocabulary, literary elements, and reading skills.
- **Part 2** contains informational texts such as magazine and newspaper articles, editorials, and essays. Also offered are vocabulary exercises and standardized-test practice.

Holt Adapted Reader

This consumable worktext contains the literary and informational adaptations found in *Holt Reading Solutions*. With scaffolded instruction that provides guided support, the *Holt Adapted Reader* can be used with struggling readers while other students in the class read the same selection in *The Holt Reader* or the **Student Edition**.

- Adaptations are within the reading range of English-language learners, special education students, and reluctant readers
- "Here's How" annotations model vocabulary, literary analysis, and reading comprehension skills; "Your Turn" annotations ask students to answer a question using the skill just modeled
- Graphic organizers help students review and consolidate what they've learned

Holt Reading Solutions

This book pulls together all of the reading resources in the *Elements of Literature* program to create a powerful tool for intervention and whole-class instruction. It includes

- Diagnostic assessment tools
- Lesson plans for English-language learners and special education students
- Adaptations of selected reading selections
- Vocabulary and comprehension worksheets
- Information on phonics and decoding
- Additional instruction and practice in remedial reading skills and strategies

Vocabulary Development

- Includes copying master worksheets that expand on students' ability to define and use the Vocabulary words identified in the **Student Edition**
- Includes cumulative reviews that reinforce students' mastery of the Vocabulary words

HRW Library

- Offers a comprehensive selection of the best novels, works of nonfiction, anthologies, and connected readings, with selections drawn from a variety of cultures
- Includes Study Guides that help motivate students and enhance their appreciation and understanding of classic and contemporary literature

Writing/Grammar and Language/Listening and Speaking

Workshop Resources: Writing, Listening, and Speaking

Supports instruction and assignments in the **Student Edition**

- Includes worksheets for each Writing Workshop and each Listening and Speaking Workshop
- Includes exercises and lesson plans with alternative teaching strategies for English-language learners and special education students

Language Handbook Worksheets

- Includes practice and reinforcement worksheets that cover the material presented in the Language Handbook section of *Elements of Literature*
- Includes tests at the end of each section of the booklet that can be used either for assessment or as end-of-section reviews

Daily Language Activities

A notebook of transparencies that reinforce skills in reading, writing, grammar, usage, and mechanics that are covered in *Elements of Literature*. Transparencies are grouped into the following categories:

- Proofreading Warm-ups
- Vocabulary
- Analogies
- Sentence Combining
- Critical Reading

Assessment

Holt Assessment: Literature, Reading, and Vocabulary

Contains diagnostic, progress, and summative assessment tests, as follows:

- An Entry-Level Test and diagnostic tests for each collection assess students' level of preparation
- Tests for every reading selection provide ongoing evaluation of students' skill development
- Summative tests for each collection and an End-of-Year Test then offer cumulative assessment opportunities

Holt Assessment: Writing, Listening, and Speaking

- Includes assessment of writing, listening, and speaking skills in a variety of test formats, including standardized tests
- Provides scales and rubrics for each workshop assignment

Holt Online Assessment

- Includes entry-level and summative assessments
- Provides tools to monitor student progress through tracking student mastery and recording and analyzing scores

One-Stop Planner CD-ROM with ExamView Test Generator

Time-saving planning software that includes a printable version of all the tests from *Holt Assessment: Reading, Literature, and Vocabulary* and *Holt Assessment: Writing, Listening, and Speaking* as well as an easy-to-use test generator.

Holt Online Essay Scoring

- Provides writing prompts for the types of writing most common in state assessments
- Instantly scores and gives holistic and analytic feedback on student essays
- Provides writing tips, activities, and model essays geared to students' results

Technology

Internet

Elements of Literature Basic Online Edition

A Web-based version of the print edition of *Elements of Literature*, this "digital textbook"

- Delivers the content of the textbook in an online format that lightens the load students carry in their backpacks
- Enables students to complete homework online
- Includes access to an online notebook for storing student work, taking notes, and responding to the same questions and activities that appear in the student book

Elements of Literature Enhanced Online Edition

In addition to all the features of the Basic Online Edition described above, the Enhanced Online Edition includes a number of selections from the student text that are enhanced with various interactive features. The Enhanced Online Edition

- Provides point-of-use interactive critical thinking and literary response questions that pop up in the Notebook, where students can type responses, edit, save, and print their work
- Includes audio excerpts from the selection in both English and Spanish
- Features vocabulary links in English and Spanish, with accompanying audio
- Delivers links to high-interest video clips that enhance students' understanding of selections and build their prior knowledge

- Provides Spanish summaries of selections, in audio
- Includes highlighting and annotation tools for use by both students and teachers
- Features an Image Gallery where students can click to see art and graphics from their textbook

AuthorSpace

A Web environment available on *Elements of Literature Enhanced Online Edition* that provides students opportunities to dig deeper into the lives and works of various authors

- Uses a variety of interactive features such as timelines, maps, and illustrated "webs of influence" to help students gain a more detailed understanding of an author's life and his or her place in literary history
- Gives students a chance to read additional literary works, as well as primary source documents, by featured authors

go.hrw.com

At **go.hrw.com** students put their reading, writing, listening, and speaking skills into action in real-world situations. The GO Site

- Reinforces the study of literature through additional biographical information about authors, a variety of cross-curricular projects connected to the literature in the student textbook, and literary elements activities
- Includes interactive reading workshops that guide students through informational texts
- Includes interactive writers' models that illustrate various types of writing
- Includes vocabulary-building activities, through which students explore synonyms, antonyms, etymologies, and multiple meanings

Holt Online Assessment

- Includes entry-level and summative assessments
- Provides tools to monitor student progress through tracking student mastery and recording and analyzing scores

Holt Online Essay Scoring

- Provides writing prompts for the types of writing most common in state assessments
- Instantly scores and gives holistic and analytic feedback on student essays
- Provides writing tips, activities, and model essays geared to students' results

Teaching Literacy to All Students, Grades 6–12

This online professional development program provides video demonstrations of best teaching practices combined with interactive exercises, graphic organizers, and lesson-planning templates; printable classroom handouts; and assessment instruments. The program contains 9 lesson-segments covering literacy topics such as

- Schoolwide literacy programs
- Assessment driving instruction
- English language learners and intensive learners
- Comprehension and fluency
- Strategies in language arts

Media

Visual Connections Videocassette Program

- Consists of author biographies, interviews, historical summaries, and cross-curricular connections that motivate students and enrich and extend learning

Fine Art Transparencies

- Features stunning examples of classic and contemporary art to complement the literature selections in *Elements of Literature*
- Helps students explore literary characters and ideas through visual representations
- Encourages students to make cross-curricular connections

One-Stop Planner CD-ROM with ExamView Test Generator

- Time-saving planning software that contains print-based teaching resources, clips from the video program, and valuable assessment tools

PowerNotes for Literature and Reading

- Fully editable instructional PowerPoint presentations that teach literary elements and reading skills and that introduce literary periods

Audio CD Library

- Includes dramatic readings by professional actors that bring to life nearly every reading selection in *Elements of Literature*

Audio CD Library, Selections and Summaries in Spanish

- Includes Spanish translations of key selections in *Elements of Literature*
- Includes recordings of summaries in Spanish of virtually every selection in *Elements of Literature*

Diagnosis and Prescription: Tracking Student Mastery

The Entry-Level and End-of-Year tests can be used to inform instructional planning, chart student progress, and provide individual and group snapshots of core language arts skills proficiency.

CORE SKILLS	Entry-Level Test	End-of-Year Test	Collection Diagnostic Test	Collection Summative Test	Reteaching	Remediation
Collection 1						
Archetypes			Item 1		*The Holt Reader,* Collection 1	*Holt Reading Solutions:* • ELL Lesson Plans • Special Ed Lesson Plans
Style	Item 7		Item 5		*The Holt Reader,* Collection 1	*Holt Reading Solutions:* • Adapted Readings *Holt Adapted Reader*
Persuasion		Item 19	Items 6–8	Item 14	*The Holt Reader,* Collection 1	*Holt Reading Solutions:* • ELL Lesson Plans • Special Ed Lesson Plans • Adapted Readings *Holt Adapted Reader*
Figures of speech	Items 3, 9, 24, 30	Item 22			*The Holt Reader,* Collection 1	*Holt Reading Solutions:* • ELL Lesson Plans • Special Ed Lesson Plans • Adapted Readings • MiniReads *Holt Adapted Reader*
Autobiography		Item 1	Item 4		*The Holt Reader,* Collection 1	*Holt Reading Solutions:* • ELL Lesson Plans • Special Ed Lesson Plans
Making inferences about an author's beliefs		Items 1, 5–11, 26–29		Items 6–12	*The Holt Reader,* Collection 1	*Holt Reading Solutions:* • ELL Lesson Plans • Special Ed Lesson Plans • Adapted Readings • MiniReads *Holt Adapted Reader*
Context clues			Item 9		*The Holt Reader,* Collection 1	
Etymology			Item 10		*The Holt Reader,* Collection 1	
Collection 2						
Meter			Item 2		*The Holt Reader,* Collection 2	*Holt Reading Solutions:* • ELL Lesson Plans • Special Ed Lesson Plans
Symbol			Item 5		*The Holt Reader,* Collection 2	*Holt Reading Solutions* • Adapted Readings *Holt Adapted Reader*
Sound effects			Item 6		*The Holt Reader,* Collection 2	*Holt Reading Solutions:* • ELL Lesson Plans • Special Ed Lesson Plans • Adapted Reader *Holt Adapted Reader*
Analyzing political assumptions		Items 20, 23, 25			*The Holt Reader,* Collection 2	*Holt Reading Solutions:* • ELL Lesson Plans • Special Ed Lesson Plans

CORE SKILLS	Entry-Level Test	End-of-Year Test	Collection Diagnostic Test	Collection Summative Test	Reteaching	Remediation
Drawing inferences		Items 1, 5–11, 26–29		Items 7, 9–10, 13	*The Holt Reader,* Collection 2	Holt Reading Solutions: • ELL Lesson Plans • Special Ed Lesson Plans • Adapted Reader • MiniReads *Holt Adapted Reader*
Analogies			Item 9		*The Holt Reader,* Collection 2	

Collection 3

Free verse			Item 1		*The Holt Reader,* Collection 3	Holt Reading Solutions: • ELL Lesson Plans • Special Ed Lesson Plans • Adapted Reader • MiniReads *Holt Adapted Reader*
Theme	Items 8, 28, 29		Item 6		*The Holt Reader,* Collection 3	Holt Reading Solutions: • ELL Lesson Plans • Special Ed Lesson Plans • Adapted Reader • MiniReads *Holt Adapted Reader*
Slant rhyme			Item 3		*The Holt Reader,* Collection 3	Holt Reading Solutions: • ELL Lesson Plans • Special Ed Lesson Plans
Irony	Item 17		Item 5		*The Holt Reader,* Collection 3	Holt Reading Solutions: • ELL Lesson Plans • Special Ed Lesson Plans • MiniReads *Holt Adapted Reader*
Comparing themes across texts					*The Holt Reader,* Collection 3	Holt Reading Solutions: • ELL Lesson Plans • Special Ed Lesson Plans • Adapted Reader • MiniReads *Holt Adapted Reader*

Collection 4

Metaphor	Items 24–25			Item 15	*The Holt Reader,* Collection 4	Holt Reading Solutions: • ELL Lesson Plans • Special Ed Lesson Plans • Adapted Reader • MiniRead *Holt Adapted Reader*
Situational irony			Item 3		*The Holt Reader,* Collection 4	Holt Reading Solutions: • ELL Lesson Plans • Special Ed Lesson Plans • Adapted Reader *Holt Adapted Reader*

CORE SKILLS	Entry-Level Test	End-of-Year Test	Collection Diagnostic Test	Collection Summative Test	Reteaching	Remediation
Motivation			Item 5		*The Holt Reader,* Collection 4	*Holt Reading Solutions:* • ELL Lesson Plans • Special Ed Lesson Plans • Adapted Reader *Holt Adapted Reader*
Analyzing a writer's purpose	Items 7, 13–14, 20	Items 24, 28	Item 4		*The Holt Reader,* Collection 4	*Holt Reading Solutions:* • ELL Lesson Plans • Special Ed Lesson Plans • Adapted Reader *Holt Adapted Reader*
Analyzing historical context		Items 14, 20, 25, 30	Item 6		*The Holt Reader,* Collection 4	*Holt Reading Solutions:* • ELL Lesson Plans • Special Ed Lesson Plans • Adapted Reader *Holt Adapted Reader*
Affixes			Item 10			

Collection 5

CORE SKILLS	Entry-Level Test	End-of-Year Test	Collection Diagnostic Test	Collection Summative Test	Reteaching	Remediation
Imagery	Item 26		Item 1	Item 12	*The Holt Reader,* Collection 5	*Holt Reading Solutions:* • ELL Lesson Plans • Special Ed Lesson Plans
Dramatic monologue			Item 2		*The Holt Reader,* Collection 5	*Holt Reading Solutions:* • ELL Lesson Plans • Special Ed Lesson Plans
Setting			Item 3		*The Holt Reader,* Collection 5	*Holt Reading Solutions:* • ELL Lesson Plans • Special Ed Lesson Plans • Adapted Reader *Holt Adapted Reader*
Stream of consciousness					*The Holt Reader,* Collection 5	*Holt Reading Solutions:* • ELL Lesson Plans • Special Ed Lesson Plans • Adapted Reader *Holt Adapted Reader*
Narrative poetry			Item 7		*The Holt Reader,* Collection 5	*Holt Reading Solutions:* • ELL Lesson Plans • Special Ed Lesson Plans
Mood	Item 4			Item 15	*The Holt Reader,* Collection 5	*Holt Reading Solutions:* • ELL Lesson Plans • Special Ed Lesson Plans
Identifying main ideas	Items 11, 14, 16, 18	Items 10, 23–24		Item 11	*The Holt Reader,* Collection 5	*Holt Reading Solutions:* • ELL Lesson Plans • Special Ed Lesson Plans • MiniReads

CORE SKILLS	Entry-Level Test	End-of-Year Test	Collection Diagnostic Test	Collection Summative Test	Reteaching	Remediation
Making inferences about character	Item 6	Items 4, 8–10, 17			*The Holt Reader,* Collection 5	*Holt Reading Solutions:* • ELL Lesson Plans • Special Ed Lesson Plans • Adapted Reader • MiniReads *Holt Adapted Reader*
Word roots			Item 9		*The Holt Reader,* Collection 5	
Analogies			Item 10		*The Holt Reader,* Collection 5	

Collection 6

CORE SKILLS	Entry-Level Test	End-of-Year Test	Collection Diagnostic Test	Collection Summative Test	Reteaching	Remediation
Implied metaphor			Item 1		*The Holt Reader,* Collection 6	*Holt Reading Solutions:* • ELL Lesson Plans • Special Ed Lesson Plans
Magic realism					*The Holt Reader,* Collection 6	*Holt Reading Solutions:* • ELL Lesson Plans • Special Ed Lesson Plans
Personal essay		Item 1			*The Holt Reader,* Collection 6	*Holt Reading Solutions:* • ELL Lesson Plans • Special Ed Lesson Plans
Allusion					*The Holt Reader,* Collection 6	*Holt Reading Solutions:* • ELL Lesson Plans • Special Ed Lesson Plans
Concrete and abstract language	Items 24–26				*The Holt Reader,* Collection 6	*Holt Reading Solutions:* • ELL Lesson Plans • Special Ed Lesson Plans

Harvey A. Daniels
Professor of Education
National-Louis University
Evanston, IL

RESEARCH

Atwell, N. 2002.
In the Middle: New Understandings About Writing, Reading, and Learning.
Portsmouth: Heinemann Educational Books.

Graves, D. 1983.
Writing: Teachers and Children at Work.
Portsmouth: Heinemann Educational Books.

Newman, F. 1996.
Authentic Achievement: Restructuring Schools for Intellectual Quality.
San Francisco: Jossey-Bass.

National Council of Teachers of English/International Reading Association. 1999.
Standards for the English Language Arts.
Newark: NCTE/IRA.

Zemelman, S., H. Daniels, and A. Hyde. 1998.
Best Practice: New Standards for Teaching and Learning in America's Schools, 2nd ed.
Portsmouth: Heinemann Educational Books.

Best Practices in Writing

"There is a process to follow. There is a process to learn. That's the way it is with a craft, whether it be teaching or writing. There is a road, a journey to travel, and there is someone to travel with us, someone who has already made the trip." —**Donald Graves**

The Process of Writing

Over the past twenty-five years, the "process" model of writing has been strongly validated by educational research. A generation ago, many viewed writing as a somewhat magical act in which flawless texts flowed from the pens of a few muse-blessed artists. Today, we understand that writing is not so much a rare talent but a definable series of cognitive operations that can be learned by anyone who can read. For even the most skilled writer, composing is a sequential process of constructing meaning: gathering information, organizing material, trying out ideas in draft, revising and restructuring text, proofreading and editing, and sharing text with readers and using their feedback for further refinement. No, these stages aren't linear and lockstep; indeed, recursive and even idiosyncratic approaches are normal and useful. But the underlying cognitive reality remains: Just like reading, writing is a staged cognitive process of building up meaning.

New Teacher Roles

Once we understand that writing is more craft than magic, we can recast the teacher as a master craftsperson, helping apprentices to learn a trade. Process-writing teachers model, mentor, and coach; they create a classroom workshop where students build a repertoire of strategies for starting, developing, and polishing written products over a wide range of genres. The teacher's first job is to show how writing gets made, by serving as a live example of an adult writer at work. This doesn't mean teachers must be paragons or professionals, just journeyman composers eager to share their own writings and explain their own strategies. Then they can add rich literary models, bathing the workshop in fine literature, so students have great writers to learn from. That's why the *Elements of Literature* series includes collections of great and varied literature, followed by activities that help students draw directly upon these models to create their own original pieces.

Instructional Implications

Young writers need plenty of writing practice. In the workshop approach, students start many pieces, save all materials in a portfolio, and gradually develop selected drafts to a highly polished and public form. At the core of this work is deep revision: Students are constantly helped to re-see ideas and rethink organization, as well as to follow carefully the conventions of written language. Where possible, writing is not just graded, but shared with real audiences. This makes the work more rhetorically genuine and provides authentic feedback that can help writers grow. All these features of writing-process instruction remind us that—when the trade secrets are revealed, explained, and practiced—writing is not a mysterious practice reserved for the gifted, but a trade that's open to all.

Effective Vocabulary Instruction

Kylene Beers, Ph.D.
Clinical Associate Professor
University of Houston
Houston, TX

RESEARCH

Beers, K.   2002.
When Kids Can't Read—What Teachers Can Do.
Portsmouth: Heinemann.

Blachowicz, C. L. Z., and Fisher, P.   2000.
"Vocabulary Instruction." *Handbook of Reading Research.* Eds. P. D. Pearson, R. Barr, M. Kamil, and P. Mosenthal.
White Plains: Longman. 503–524.

Tierney, R., and Cunningham, J.   1984.
"Research on Teaching Reading Comprehension." *Handbook of Reading Research.* Eds. P. D. Pearson, R. Barr, M. Kamil, and P. Mosenthal.
White Plains: Longman. 609–656.

"Preteaching vocabulary . . . requires that the words to be taught must be key words, . . . be taught in semantically and topically related sets, . . . and that only a few words be taught per lesson."   **—Tierney and Cunningham**

Preteaching Vocabulary

When students don't know the meaning of words that are used in a text, their ability to understand that text is diminished. They can use the context as a clue to get the gist of the meaning, but sometimes the context doesn't provide enough information and other times the gist isn't helpful enough. In those cases, we must preteach the vocabulary. To do so effectively, focus on which words you teach, the number that you teach, and how you teach them.

The Right Words and the Right Number

Deciding which words to teach is linked to deciding how many to teach. Twenty new words per week are probably too many for struggling readers, especially when you consider that the list of twenty is just for English class. The more vocabulary words we give students to learn weekly, the less chance they have of learning a word to the level needed to move it from short term to long term memory. Keeping the number between five and ten means students have a better chance of retaining that word beyond the end of the week (Beers, 2002).

Consequently, choose wisely the words to be taught. Avid readers benefit by studying rare words—those highly unusual ones—because they already have a solid vocabulary of the more common ones. Struggling readers, however, benefit by focusing on high-utility words—those more common words that they are likely to see in other contexts. So, in this sentence, "The boys banked the canoe to the lee side of the rock," the inclination might be to teach the word *lee*, a rare word. However, if students don't know what *banked* means in this context or don't know the word *canoe*, it matters little what *lee* means. For struggling readers, a focus on high-utility words is more beneficial than a focus on rare words.

The Right Instructional Approach

Tierney and Cunningham (1984) explain that offering students a list of vocabulary words with their definitions is not as effective as placing each word within a semantic context. Students learn how to use words as they read or hear them used correctly. *Elements of Literature* provides a short list of words on the "Before You Read" page of each selection that are defined and then used in a sentence. It is this semantic placement that most helps students learn words. Choosing the right number of the right words and presenting words in a semantic context helps students build their vocabulary and, as a consequence, improve their comprehension.

Kylene Beers, Ph.D.
Clinical Associate Professor
University of Houston
Houston, TX

RESEARCH

Baumann, J. 1984.
"Effectiveness of a Direct Instruction Paradigm for Teaching Main Idea Comprehension."
Reading Research Quarterly, 20: 93–108.

Beers, K. 2002.
When Kids Can't Read—What Teachers Can Do.
Portsmouth: Heinemann.

Dole, J., Brown, K., and Trathen, W. 1996.
"The Effects of Strategy Instruction on the Comprehension Performance of At-risk Students."
Reading Research Quarterly, 31: 62–89.

Duffy, G. 2002.
"The Case for Direct Explanation of Strategies."
Comprehension Instruction: Research-Based Best Practices. Eds. C. Block and M. Pressley.
New York: Guilford Press. 28–41.

Pearson, P. D. 1984.
"Direct Explicit Teaching of Reading Comprehension." *Comprehension Instruction: Perspectives and Suggestions*. Eds. G. Duffy, L. Roehler, and J. Mason.
New York: Longman. 222–233.

Teaching Comprehension

"Comprehension is both a product and a process, something that requires purposeful, strategic effort on the reader's part as he or she predicts, visualizes, clarifies, questions, connects, summarizes, and infers."
—Kylene Beers

When the Text Is Tough

"Comprehension is only tough when you can't do it," explained the eleventh-grader. I almost dismissed his words until I realized what truth they offered. We aren't aware of all the thinking we do to comprehend a text until faced with a difficult text. Then, all too clearly, we're aware of what words we don't understand, what syntax seems convoluted, what ideas are beyond our immediate grasp. As skilled readers, we know what to do: We slow our pace, re-read, ask questions, connect whatever we do understand to what we don't understand, summarize what we've read thus far, make inferences about what the author is saying. In short, we make that invisible act of comprehension visible as we consciously push our way through the difficult text. At those times, we realize that, indeed, comprehension is tough.

Reading Strategies for Struggling Readers

It's even tougher if you lack strategies that would help you through the difficult text. Many struggling readers believe they aren't successful readers because that's just the way things are (Beers, 2002); they believe successful readers know some secret that they haven't been told (Duffy, 2002). While we don't mean to keep comprehension a secret, at times we do. For instance, though we tell students to "re-read," we haven't shown them how to alter their reading. We tell them to "make inferences" or "make predictions," but we haven't taught them how to do such things. In other words, we tell them what to do, but don't show them how to do it, in spite of several decades of research showing the benefit of direct instruction in reading strategies to struggling readers. (Baumann, 1984; Pearson, P. D., 1984; Dole, et al., 1996; Beers, 2002).

Direct Instruction

Direct instruction means telling students what you are going to teach them, modeling it for them, providing assistance as they practice it, then letting them practice it on their own. It's not saying, "Visualize while you read," but instead explaining, "Today, I'm going to read this part aloud to you. I'm going to focus on seeing some of the action in my mind as I read. I'm going to stop occasionally and tell you what I'm seeing and what in the text helped me see that." When we directly teach comprehension strategies to students via modeling and repeated practice, we show students that good readers don't *just* get it. They work hard to get it. *Elements of Literature* takes the secret out of comprehension as it provides teachers the support they need to reach struggling readers.

The Technology Connection

Nancy Patterson, Ph.D.
Assistant Professor, School of Education
Grand Valley State University
Grand Rapids, MI

RESEARCH

Bolter, Jay David. 1991.
Writing Space: The Computer, Hypertext, and the History of Writing.
Mahwah: Lawrence Erhlbaum Associates.

Henderson, Kathryn. 1995.
"The Visual Culture of Engineers."
The Cultures of Computing. Ed. Susan Leigh Star.
Cambridge: Blackwell Publishers. 196–218.

Joyce, Michael. 1995.
Of Two Minds: Hypertext Pedagogy and Poetics.
Ann Arbor: University of Michigan Press.

Snyder, Ilana. 1997.
Hypertext: The Electronic Labyrinth.
New York: New York University Press.

Weaver, Constance. 1994.
Reading Process and Practice: From Socio-Psycholinguistics to Whole Language, 2nd ed.
Portsmouth: Heinemann.

"Reading comprehension is a process that involves the orchestration of the reader's prior experience and knowledge about the world and about language." —**Bartoli and Botel**

Technology Promotes Thinking Skills

Without technology, there would be no reading. It takes technology to create text. Whether that technology has been the invention of the scroll, the moveable printing press, or e-books, each new innovation in text-creation technology brings new challenges for readers and writers. Computer technology is no exception, especially when it comes to helping readers access, and even create, the necessary prior knowledge needed for efficient reading.

Michael Joyce (1995) believes that Internet technology offers the possibility for students to use the same thinking skills "that experts routinely, subtly, and self-consciously apply in accomplishing intellectual tasks"—as it "promises to unlock these skills for novice learners and to empower and enfranchise their learning." The Internet offers this promise because it allows readers to act physically on the associations or mental connections they make when reading. Hyperlinks effectively placed in a piece of online text can help students make connections between what they are reading and what they already know. Hyperlinks support students' thinking by prompting them through the wording of the links, and when they activate a link, allowing them to immediately learn more information about a given topic.

Webbed Text and Thinking

Constance Weaver (1994) explains that prior knowledge develops through our experience with the world. Readers create some of those experiences through active participation with webbed texts. So, when the appropriate prior knowledge does not exist, students can gain knowledge via hyperlinks associated with a selection.

Jay Bolter (1991) believes that webbed texts bring the usually unconscious transaction between reader and writer to the forefront. The writer invites the reader to choose paths—or click on links. The reader considers the author's invitations and follows various paths through the links-as-invitation. Students experience the satisfaction of physically clicking on a link that addresses the same topic they may have been thinking about as they read. Those connections to more information increase their prior knowledge.

But webbed text can provide more than just information. We cannot ignore the importance of visual literacy in our culture today. In a world where images convey so much meaning, students must understand how images affect meaning. The more they are able to construct meaning with images, the better they will become at that mode of meaning construction (Henderson, 196). The effective combination of text and visually rich images on many Web pages, coupled with reflections on those elements, can help students build the literacies they need in this complex world.

Dale Allender
Associate Executive Director
National Council of Teachers of English
Urbana, IL

RESEARCH

Allender, D.   2002
"The Myth Ritual Theory and the
Teaching of Multicultural Literature."
English Journal 5: 52–55.

Barthes, R.   1981
"Theory of the Text." *Untying the Text: A
Poststructuralist Reader.* Ed. R Young.
London: Routledge.

Bloome, D. and Egan-Robertson, A.   1993
"The Social Construction of Intertextuality in
Classroom Reading and Writing Lessons."
Reading Research Quarterly 28: 304–333.

Callahan, Meg   2002
"Intertextual Composition: The Power of the
Digital Pen." *English Education* 35: 46–64.

Spears-Bunton, L.   1999
"Calypso, Jazz, Reggae, and Salsa: Literature
Response and the African Diaspora." *Reader
Response in Secondary and College Classrooms.*
Ed. N. Karolides. Mahway, New Jersey:
Lawrence Erlbaum Associates.

Multicultural Literacy

"Inherent in the theory of text is the notion of intertextuality."
—Meg Callahan

Finding a Way In

Multicultural literature affirms and celebrates the rich diversity of our classrooms. That very same literature, however, can be a source of confusion and frustration for some readers, as it often contains unfamiliar references and unfamiliar words or phrases. We can overcome these surface problems by using intertextual readings.

Intertextual Reading

At first glance, intertextual reading looks like paired reading via novel sets or themed reading. However, it is far more. It is an activity for before, during, and after reading; and it can be led by the teacher or students. When reading intertextually, teachers and students read widely within and across genres, canons and eras as a way of exploring one novel, short story or poem (Barthes 1981; Bloome and Egan-Robinson, 1993). This is a particularly helpful strategy when the core selection represents a nonwhite cultural group. Students begin to build an understanding of the core selection by reading various other selections. Some students will read primary-source documents from the era of the literary work; others will look at contemporary media with related content. Still others will look at student-produced research papers, Web sites, CDs, or poetry. Everything is fair game, as long as it has some relationship to the literature the whole class is reading. It is helpful if the additional material is short—a newspaper article, letter, poem, video clip, song, or excerpt from a reference book. Short pieces allow students to read and re-read quickly and not get bogged down in something intended to help with the primary reading task.

From Text to Talk

All of the additional reading can then be discussed in relation to the primary work as a way of illuminating, challenging, or affirming it through various reading, writing, and speaking activities. For example, students might use a Venn diagram to compare information in a newspaper account of a historic event to the representation of that event in the literature. Or they can interview each other about the literature in light of the related reading. They might ask a partner who read an article or studied a photograph how the literature shapes or expresses the event in a different way from the image or article. They might ask if the literature adds colorful language or if it changes facts and information. Such intertextual reading will help students understand multicultural literature. In fact, such reading extends the meaning of reading multiculturally so that now it includes reading multiple sources about a diversity of experiences and communities. *Elements of Literature,* with its thematic grouping of literature and its wide variety of genres, offers readers repeated opportunities for intertextual reading.

Literary Analysis: Beyond Response

Carol Jago
English Teacher
Santa Monica High School
Santa Monica, CA
and
Director
California Reading and Literature Project
University of California,
Los Angeles, CA

RESEARCH

Emig, J.   1990.
"Our Missing Theory." *Conversations: Contemporary Critical Theory and the Teaching of Literature.* Eds. C. Moran and E.F. Penfield. Urbana: National Council of Teachers of English. 87–96.

Greene, M.   1988.
The Dialectic of Freedom.
New York: Teachers College Press.

Rosenblatt, L.   1968.
Literature as Exploration. 2nd ed.
New York: Noble & Noble.

Scholes, R.   1985.
Textual Power: Literary Theory and the Teaching of English.
New Haven: Yale University Press.

"When there is active participation in literature—the reader living through, reflecting on, and criticizing his own responses to the text—there will be many kinds of benefits."   **—Louise Rosenblatt**

Literary Analysis

Literary analysis is hard work that begins with readers' initial response to a literary work and deepens as readers measure that response against the richness of the text. That richness includes ideas presented in the text, symbols embedded in the text, and persuasive devices the author offers throughout the text. As readers do as Rosenblatt suggested and live through, reflect on, and criticize their own responses to the text, there are indeed many benefits. Those benefits become most evident when analysis follows response. As Robert Scholes explains in *Textual Power*, reading "requires both interpretation and criticism for completion."

Reading Stances

During the process of reading, readers take a series of stances toward the text. A reader's initial stance is a first impression including surface features of a text such as genre, content, and language. Moving through the text, the reader becomes caught up in the story or is carried along by a persuasive argument. Upon completion, readers step back and reflect on their own experience and prior knowledge. The text may cause them to rethink what they know. Finally, readers step back from their reading and reflect upon the context within which this piece of literature was created. Sometimes this stance includes thinking about the reading experience itself. These stances are not a hierarchy of skills, nor are they ever really independent of one another. Each adds a different dimension to the reader's understanding.

Critical Literary Stances

A stance can also refer to the point of view a reader adopts towards a text. Formal approaches to teaching literary analysis include psychological theories: psychoanalytic criticism drawing on the theories of Sigmund Freud, biographical approaches exploring the influence of the author's life upon the text, reader response approaches focusing upon what the reader brings to the text, and archetypal approaches examining universal responses to text. Other critical stances that readers may adopt include Marxist readings, new historicist readings, cultural readings, postcolonial readings, feminist readings, gender readings, and deconstructionist readings.

Maxine Greene argues that, "Learning to look through multiple perspectives, young people may be helped to build bridges among themselves; attending to a range of human stories, they may be provoked to heal and to transform." Throughout *Elements of Literature*, students are given the tools to build those bridges as they read texts and form initial responses and deepen them as they consider texts from multiple perspectives, examine literary techniques, and recognize the author's biases and purposes.

Collection 1
Encounters and Foundations to 1800

About Collection 1

In Collection 1, students will master the following skills:

- **Literary Skills:** Evaluate the philosophical, political, religious, ethical, and social influences of a historical period; analyze archetypes, plain style, allusions, the sonnet, aphorisms, figures of speech, persuasion, parallelism; analyze and compare political points of view on a topic.
- **Reading Skills:** Analyze cultural characteristics, the use of inversion, chronological order, inferences about a writer's beliefs, modes of persuasion; compare main ideas across texts.
- **Vocabulary Skills:** Understand synonyms, prefixes and suffixes, the etymology of words used in political science and history; use context clues.
- **Writing Skills:** Develop, write, and revise an editorial.
- **Listening and Speaking Skills:** Present and evaluate a persuasive speech.

Minimum Course of Study

Most skills can be taught with a minimum number of selections and features. In the chart to the right, lessons highlighted in green constitute the minimum course of study that provides coverage of the skills taught in Collection 1.

Scope and Sequence

Selection ▪ Feature	Literary Skills
Encounters and Foundations to 1800 *by* Gary Q. Arpin	• Evaluate the philosophical, political, religious, ethical, and social influences of a historical period
Native American Oral Traditions: • The Sun Still Rises in the Same Sky: Native American Literature *by* Joseph Bruchac ↔ *at grade level* • The Sky Tree *retold by* Joseph Bruchac ↓ *below grade level* • The Earth Only *composed by* Used-as-a-Shield ↓ *below grade level* • Coyote Finishes His Work *retold by* Barry Lopez ↓ *below grade level*	• Analyze archetypes
Here Follow Some Verses upon the Burning of Our House, July 10, 1666 *by* Anne Bradstreet ↔ *at grade level*	• Analyze the use of plain style
Literature of the Americas: Mexico World, in hounding me . . . /En perseguirme, mundo . . . *by* Sor Juana Inés de la Cruz ↑ *above grade level*	• Analyze a Petrarchan sonnet
from A Narrative of the Captivity . . . *by* Mary Rowlandson ↔ *at grade level*	• Analyze allusions
from Sinners in the Hands of an Angry God *by* Jonathan Edwards ↑ *above grade level*	• Analyze figures of speech
from The Interesting Life of Olaudah Equiano *by* Olaudah Equiano ↔ *at grade level*	• Analyze the characteristics of an autobiography

Resource Manager

(see pp. 1E–1H)
Lesson and workshop resources are referenced in the Resource Manager on the pages that follow. These resources can be used to reinforce the skills taught in Collection 1, remediate students who are having difficulty, and provide supporting activities for English-language learners.

Reading Skills	Vocabulary Skills	Writing ■ Grammar and Language ■ Listening and Speaking Skills
• Analyze cultural characteristics		• Write an essay analyzing myths
• Analyze the use of inversion		• Write an essay analyzing the writer's attitude • Present an oral performance of a poem
		• Write an essay comparing poems from different cultures
• Analyze chronological order	• Understand synonyms	• Write an essay analyzing a narrative
	• Understand prefixes and suffixes	• Write an essay analyzing tone
• Analyze inferences about an author's beliefs	• Create semantic charts • Use context clues to determine the meaning of words	• Write a book for children about African American heritage

(continued)

Scope and Sequence

Selection ■ Feature	Literary Skills	Reading Skills
from The Autobiography ↔ *at grade level* *from* Poor Richard's Almanack *by* Benjamin Franklin ↓ *below grade level*	• Analyze aphorisms	• Make inferences about a writer's beliefs
Speech to the Virginia Convention *by* Patrick Henry ↑ *above grade level*	• Analyze the use of persuasion	• Analyze modes of persuasion, including appeals to reason and appeals to emotion
from The Crisis, No. 1 *by* Thomas Paine ↑ *above grade level*	• Analyze the characteristics of style	• Analyze modes of persuasion, including appeals to logic, appeals to emotion, and analogy
Introducing Political Points of View: Freedom and Equality **Main Reading:** *from* The Autobiography: The Declaration of Independence *by* Thomas Jefferson ↔ *at grade level*	• Analyze and compare political points of view on a topic • Analyze the use of parallelism	• Compare main ideas across texts
Connected Readings: • *from* The Iroquois Constitution *by* Dekanawida ↓ *below grade level* • Letter to John Adams *by* Abigail Adams ↓ *below grade level* • *from* Declaration of Sentiments of the Seneca Falls Woman's Rights Convention *by* Elizabeth Cady Stanton ↔ *at grade level*		
Writing Workshop: *Writing an Editorial*		
Listening and Speaking Workshop: *Presenting and Evaluating Speeches*		
Skills Review: *Literary Skills* *Vocabulary Skills* *Writing Skills*	• Compare works from different literary periods	

Vocabulary Skills	Writing ■ Grammar and Language ■ Listening and Speaking Skills
• Demonstrate word knowledge	• Write an essay comparing two writers • Use coordinating conjunctions • Write a handbook with aphorisms
• Understand synonyms	• Write an essay comparing a speech and a sermon
• Analyze synonyms	• Write an essay analyzing a persuasive essay
	• Write an essay evaluating documents • Write an editorial
• Demonstrate word knowledge • Understand the etymology of terms used in political science and history	• Write an essay analyzing a political point of view
	• Write an editorial
	• Present and evaluate a persuasive speech
• Use context clues to determine the meaning of words	• Write an editorial

Resource Manager

Selection ▪ Feature	Planning	Differentiating Instruction ▪ Lesson Plans with ELL Strategies and Practice	Reading ▪ Vocabulary
Encounters and Foundations to 1800 *by* Gary Q. Arpin	• PowerNotes: The Puritan Legacy	• Holt Adapted Reader	• Holt Adapted Reader
Native American Oral Traditions: • The Sun Still Rises in the Same Sky: Native American Literature *by* Joseph Bruchac • The Sky Tree *retold by* Joseph Bruchac The Earth Only *composed by* Used-as-a-Shield • Coyote Finishes His Work *retold by* Barry Lopez	• One-Stop Planner with ExamView Test Generator	• The Holt Reader • Holt Reading Solutions: Lesson Plans • Supporting Instruction in Spanish NOTE: All selections appear on • Audio CD Library, discs 1 and 2 • Audio CD Library, Selections and Summaries in Spanish	• The Holt Reader • Holt Reading Solutions
Here Follow Some Verses upon the Burning of Our House, July 10, 1666 *by* Anne Bradstreet	• One-Stop Planner with ExamView Test Generator	• The Holt Reader • Holt Adapted Reader • Holt Reading Solutions: Lesson Plans • Supporting Instruction in Spanish	• The Holt Reader • Holt Adapted Reader • Holt Reading Solutions
Literature of the Americas: Mexico World, in hounding me . . . / En perseguirme, mundo . . . *by* Sor Juana Inés de la Cruz	• One-Stop Planner with ExamView Test Generator	• The Holt Reader • Holt Reading Solutions: Lesson Plans • Supporting Instruction in Spanish	• The Holt Reader • Holt Reading Solutions
from A Narrative of the Captivity . . . *by* Mary Rowlandson	• One-Stop Planner with ExamView Test Generator	• The Holt Reader • Supporting Instruction in Spanish	• The Holt Reader • Holt Reading Solutions • Vocabulary Development, p. 1
from Sinners in the Hands of an Angry God *by* Jonathan Edwards	• One-Stop Planner with ExamView Test Generator	• The Holt Reader • Holt Adapted Reader • Holt Reading Solutions: Lesson Plans • Supporting Instruction in Spanish	• The Holt Reader • Holt Adapted Reader • Holt Reading Solutions • Vocabulary Development, p. 2
from The Interesting Narrative of the Life of Olaudah Equiano *by* Olaudah Equiano	• One-Stop Planner with ExamView Test Generator	• The Holt Reader • Holt Reading Solutions: Lesson Plans • Supporting Instruction in Spanish	• The Holt Reader • Holt Reading Solutions • Vocabulary Development, p. 3

The Holt Reader

The Holt Reader is a consumable paperback book which can be used alone or to accompany *Elements of Literature*. It offers guided support throughout the reading process and encourages students to become active readers by circling, underlining, questioning, and jotting down responses as they read. *The Holt Reader* works well for homework, students who have missed class, additional instructional time, reteaching, and remediation.

Holt Reading Solutions (HRS)

Holt Reading Solutions pulls together reading resources in the *Elements of Literature* program to create a powerful tool for intervention and whole-class instruction. *HRS* includes diagnostic assessment tools, lesson plans for English-language learners and special education students, adaptations of selected reading selections, vocabulary and comprehension worksheets, information on phonics and decoding, and additional instruction and practice in remedial reading skills.

Writing ▪ Grammar and Language ▪ Listening and Speaking	Assessment
• Daily Language Activities	• Holt Assessment: Literature, Reading, and Vocabulary • Holt Online Assessment • One-Stop Planner with ExamView Test Generator
• Daily Language Activities	• See "Native American Oral Traditions" above
• Daily Language Activities	• See "Native American Oral Traditions" above
• Daily Language Activities	• See "Native American Oral Traditions" above
• Daily Language Activities	• See "Native American Oral Traditions" above
• Daily Language Activities	• See "Native American Oral Traditions" above

Technology

INTERNET

- go.hrw.com
- Holt Online Assessment
- Holt Online Essay Scoring
- Elements of Literature Online

MEDIA

 • One-Stop Planner with ExamView Test Generator

 • PowerNotes

 • Audio CD Library, discs 1 and 2

• Audio CD Library, Selections and Summaries in Spanish

 • Visual Connections Videocassette Program, Segments 1 and 2

 • Fine Art Transparencies, 1, 2, and 3

 Transparency   Video

 CD-ROM   Audio CD

One-Stop Planner with ExamView Test Generator

The *One-Stop Planner* CD-ROM contains electronic versions of print-based teaching resources, clips from the video program, and valuable assessment tools. The *One-Stop Planner* resources are presented in easy-to-follow, point-and-click menu formats. To preview resources or print out worksheets and tests, you simply make a selection and click.

■ **1493**
Askia Muhammad

Askia Muhammad ascends the throne of the Songhai Empire of West Africa. This statesman, scholar, and strategist brings the empire to its height and reestablishes its capital, Tombouctou, as a cultural center.

■ **1517**
Martin Luther

To protest policies of the Roman Catholic Church, the German priest posts a list of criticisms on the door of the cathedral in Wittenberg. The Ninety-five Theses, as the list comes to be known, paves the way for the Reformation and the spread of Protestantism.

■ **1635**
Church and State

Roger Williams is banished from the Massachusetts Bay Colony after criticizing the colony's Puritan doctrine. The next year he establishes a colony in Providence, Rhode Island. The colony becomes known for its religious freedom and the separation of church and state.

■ **1748**
Checks and Balances

French philosopher and jurist Montesquieu, in *The Spirit of Laws,* proposes the system of checks and balances that has come to characterize the United States government: three branches curbing one another's powers.

Encounters and Foundations to 1800

LITERARY EVENTS

1490		1700	
1605, 1615 Spain's Miguel de Cervantes publishes his novel *Don Quixote* in two parts	**1620–1647** William Bradford writes *Of Plymouth Plantation*	**1719** England's Daniel Defoe publishes *Robinson Crusoe,* considered one of the first English novels	**1741** Jonathan Edwards delivers his vivid sermon "Sinners in the Hands of an Angry God"
1605–1606 England's William Shakespeare writes *King Lear* and *Macbeth*	**1650** Anne Bradstreet's *The Tenth Muse Lately Sprung Up in America* is published in England	**1726** England's Jonathan Swift publishes the satiric novel *Gulliver's Travels*	**1749** England's Henry Fielding publishes the novel *The History of Tom Jones*
	1682 Mary Rowlandson's captivity narrative is published	**1728** William Byrd writes *The History of the Dividing Line*	**1754, 1763** John Woolman publishes antislavery essays

POLITICAL AND SOCIAL EVENTS

1490		1700	
1492 Christopher Columbus lands on an island in the Caribbean	**1620** *Mayflower* Pilgrims land at Plymouth	**1700** About 251,000 European settlers live in what is now the United States	**1740–1745** The Great Awakening is touched off by a traveling English preacher
c. 1500 Mohawk leader Dekanawida establishes the Iroquois Confederacy	**c. 1630** Great Migration of Puritans to New England begins	**1721** Smallpox epidemic hits Boston	**1742** George Frideric Handel's *Messiah* is first performed, in Dublin, Ireland
1517 Protestant Reformation starts in Germany	**1632–1638** Mughal emperor Shah Jahan builds Taj Mahal in northern India	**1729** German composer Johann Sebastian Bach completes the oratorio *St. Matthew Passion*	**1748** France's Montesquieu publishes *The Spirit of Laws,* a study of government later reflected in the U.S. Constitution
1521 Aztec Empire falls to Spanish army	**1675** Metacomet's war on Massachusetts colonies begins		
1528–1536 Spanish explorer Álvar Núñez Cabeza de Vaca lands in Florida and spends eight years walking through modern-day Texas, New Mexico, and Arizona	**1687** England's Isaac Newton explains laws of motion and gravity in *Principia Mathematica*		
	1690 Slavery exists in all English colonies in North America		
1607 Settlement founded at Jamestown, Virginia	**1692** Twenty people are executed in witch trials in Salem, Massachusetts		

Arresting a witch in the streets of Salem.
The Granger Collection, New York.

Using the Time Line

Activity. Pair students, and assign each pair two events from the lower part of the time line. Give the pairs several minutes to write down what they know about the events or to make inferences about Colonial life in America by examining the rest of the time line and scanning the introductory essay on pp. 6–19. For example, a pair assigned the Boston smallpox epidemic of 1721 could examine the time line further and note that Edward Jenner developed a smallpox vaccine in 1796; the students might infer that smallpox remained a health menace in the Colonies until that time. They will find more information on p. 8 and pp. 15–17. Ask students to read their notes to the class. You might have other students verify and supplement information by using an encyclopedia or

COMMON SENSE:
ADDRESSED TO THE INHABITANTS
OF A...

1755 England's Samuel Johnson publishes his monumental *Dictionary of the English Language*

1762 Benjamin Franklin's sister-in-law Anne Franklin becomes first woman printer in New England

1771 Benjamin Franklin begins to write his *Autobiography*

1773 Phillis Wheatley publishes *Poems on Various Subjects, Religious and Moral*

1775 Patrick Henry demands liberty from British rule, at the Virginia Convention

1776 Thomas Paine publishes *Common Sense*

1785 Thomas Jefferson publishes *Notes on the State of Virginia*

1787–1788 *The Federalist*, a series of essays by Alexander Hamilton, James Madison, and John Jay, urges voters to approve the U.S. Constitution

1789 Olaudah Equiano publishes *The Interesting Narrative of the Life of Olaudah Equiano*

1798 England's Samuel Taylor Coleridge publishes *The Rime of the Ancient Mariner*, a long Romantic poem

1752 Benjamin Franklin's experiments with a kite and a key prove that lightning is a manifestation of electricity

1763 French and Indian War officially ends as British gain control of most French North American territory

1765 American colonists hold Stamp Act Congress to protest a direct British tax (British repeal tax in 1766)

Stamp from Stamp Act, 1765.

Negative number 41127. © Collection of The New-York Historical Society.

1773 Boston Tea Party occurs in Boston Harbor

April 19, 1775 First shots of American Revolution are fired at Lexington and Concord, Massachusetts

George Washington.

July 4, 1776 Second Continental Congress adopts Declaration of Independence

October 1781 American Revolutionary War ends as British surrender at Yorktown, Virginia (peace treaty signed in 1783)

1781–1788 America is governed under Articles of Confederation

1787 Austrian composer Wolfgang Amadeus Mozart finishes the opera *Don Giovanni*

1789 George Washington is inaugurated as first president under U.S. Constitution

1789 French Revolution begins

1790 First census in America sets population at about 3.9 million

1792 New York Stock Exchange is organized

1793 Invention of cotton gin leads to increase in slave labor

1796 English physician Edward Jenner develops smallpox vaccine

1799 Napoleon Bonaparte becomes dictator of France

1800 Library of Congress is established

1800 Washington, D.C., is named capital of the United States

Encounters and Foundations to 1800   **3**

■ 1771
Ben Franklin

Franklin's autobiography is the first American rags-to-riches story.

■ 1775–1781
Revolutionary War

During the war, twenty-two-year-old Deborah Sampson, a school-teacher, becomes the first American woman to serve as a combat soldier. She disguises herself as a man, and using the name Robert Shurtleff, she enlists in a regiment. She fights in a number of battles and is wounded at least twice. To protect her identity, she conceals a serious leg wound; but when she is hospitalized for a high fever, her disguise is discovered. General Washington grants her an honorable discharge.

■ 1787–1788
The Federalist Papers

The eighty-five essays collectively known as *The Federalist Papers* or *The Federalist* appeared in New York newspapers between October 1787 and August 1788. Alexander Hamilton writes fifty-one of the essays; James Madison, twenty-nine; and John Jay, five.

As delegates to the Constitutional Convention, the three writers are involved in its strife over the issue of central government. In *The Federalist*, No. 10, the most famous of the essays, Madison argues that a unified federal government can work, even in a country as large as the United States, because a large population will inevitably break into many factions, ensuring that no one faction can grow powerful enough to control the government.

---

an electronic database. The ability to work with graphic organizers that reflect the structure and content of texts is a critical comprehension skill.

Activity. Ask students to examine the introductory essay on pp. 6–19. Have students indicate each of the following events correctly on the time line:

- The Pilgrims sign the Mayflower Compact. [1620]
- The first printing press in America is set up. [1639]
- The *Bay Psalm Book* is first published. [1640]

Next, have students research the following events and indicate where they would be placed on the time line.

- After one failure, the English establish a colony on Roanoke Island. [1587]
- The war between colonists and the Pequots of Connecticut ends in a massacre. [1637]
- Cotton Mather explains his support for the Salem witch trials in *Wonders of the Invisible World*. [1693]

■ Clash of Cultures

Many scholars classify American Indian populations at the time of early European contact into nine major cultural and geographic groups:

- **Eastern Woodlands** (Minnesota east to Atlantic, south to North Carolina)—Hunters, farmers, and fishers; mined copper; descended from the Hopewell and Mississippian mound cultures that had cities and vast trade networks; some peoples formed federations.

- **Southeast** (southern Atlantic coast, west to Central Texas)—Hunters managed wildlife in pine forests; developed farming; had built a large town with central temple plaza two thousand years before Mississippians; some peoples formed federations.

- **Plains** (Midwest to Rockies, southern Canada to Mexico)—Nomadic hunters and traders of the grasslands; most groups lived in tepees and followed bison herds; a few groups farmed river valleys.

- **Southwest** (Arizona, New Mexico, southern Colorado)—Hunter-gatherers, farmers, and herders; descendants of Hohokam and Anasazi cultures, with cliff towns and pueblos of stone and adobe; engineered complex irrigation networks.

- **California Intermountain** (Utah, Nevada, California)—Hunters, fishers, and gatherers; maintained seasonal villages; crafted artifacts ranging from baskets to seagoing plank boats; established broad trade networks.

- **Plateau** (Idaho, eastern Oregon and Washington, western Montana)— Hunter-gatherers and salmon fishers; maintained a permanent market town as a trade hub between the Pacific Coast and the Plains.

Political and Social

Clash of Cultures

During the 1490s, when the great wave of European exploration of the Americas started, numerous groups of American Indians were living all over North America. These societies were diverse, and each had its own long history. Most were made up of a few thousand people. (The Aztec Empire, in what is now Mexico, was the largest Native American civilization in the fifteenth century, with millions of people living within its borders.)

What's important to remember is that there were people on this continent when the Europeans arrived; descendants of those original people are still here, and their traditions remain. In 1994, for example, the Pequots—whom the English met when they arrived in what is now Connecticut, Rhode Island, and Massachusetts—donated ten million dollars to the new National Museum of the American Indian in Washington, D.C., to promote and save native cultures.

Native Americans and a Puritan in a village (19th century).

Puritan Dominance

In many respects the American character has been shaped by the moral, ethical, and religious convictions of the Puritans. In 1620, just before Christmas, the first and most famous group of these English Puritans landed on the tip of Cape Cod. They were followed ten years later by about seven hundred more Puritan settlers. By 1640, as many as twenty thousand English Puritans had sailed to what they called New England.

Although the real commerce of the Puritans was with heaven, they were competent in the business of the world as well. It is important to remember that the founding of a new society in North America was a business venture as well as a spiritual one. For the Puritans the everyday world and the spiritual world were closely intertwined.

- **Northwest Pacific Coast** (southern Alaska to northern California)—Fishers and forest dwellers; carved totem poles; built large wooden houses; traded as far as northern Asia for iron.

- **Subarctic** (Canada)—Nomadic trappers and fishers; hunted moose and followed caribou herds.

- **Arctic** (coastal Alaska and Arctic)—Fishers and hunters of caribou, seal, and whale; traveled in hide boats and dog sleds; lived in houses of sod or hides; built igloos as temporary shelters.

Milestones to 1800

The First Thanksgiving by Jennie Augusta Brownscombe.

Reverend Jonathan Edwards (detail) by Joseph Badger.

Rise of Rationalism and Independence

Beginning in Europe near the end of the seventeenth century, a group of philosophers and scientists began calling themselves rationalists. This marked the start of the Age of Reason, which soon had a growing influence in America. These rationalists believed that people can discover truth by using their own reason rather than relying on only religious faith or intuition. Along with a homegrown American sense of practicality, the ideas of these European thinkers inspired many of the triumphs of eighteenth-century American life. The great by-product of rationalism in America was the mind-set that resulted in the Declaration of Independence and the American Revolution.

The Declaration of Independence, July, 1776 by John Trumbull. Oil on canvas.

Yale University Art Gallery, Trumbull Collection.

■ Puritan Dominance

Many historians feel that the Puritan ethic of thrift, hard work, and self-sufficiency contributed to the success of capitalism in the New World. Because the Puritans believed that wealth was a sign of God's favor, they strove to attain it.

■ Rise of Rationalism and Independence

Philosophical rationalism arose in conjunction with developments in the sciences. The father of rationalism, René Descartes (1596–1650) of France, devised the proposition "I think, therefore I am" as a basis for philosophical reasoning. He also made significant contributions in analytic geometry, algebra, and physics. Other influential rationalists include German mathematician Gottfried Wilhelm von Leibniz (1646–1716), who discovered the laws of calculus, and English scientist Sir Isaac Newton (1642–1727), who pioneered revolutionary advances in astronomy, physics, mathematics, and optics.

Grade-Level Skills

■ **Literary Skills**

Evaluate the philosophical, political, religious, ethical, and social influences of the historical period.

Preview

Think About . . .

Encourage students to preview the historical essay by examining its verbal and graphic elements: headings, subheadings, illustrations, and captions. You might ask students which topics catch their interest.

DIRECT TEACHING

Ⓐ Exploring the Historical Period
EUROPEAN EXPLORATION

The first Europeans known to land in North America were Norse colonists from Iceland and Greenland, who attempted to settle Newfoundland in A.D. 1000. Medieval Icelandic sagas describe North America as a "kind" land, abounding in game, wild rice, and wild grapes. The sagas also describe encounters with American Indians. The Norse settlements failed, and almost five hundred years passed before Christopher Columbus's 1492 landfall in the West Indies.

Encounters and Foundations to 1800

by Gary Q. Arpin

PREVIEW

Think About . . .

The United States is a land of immigrants. The first people began entering North America on foot many thousands of years ago. Then people came in wooden sailing ships. Later millions were brought against their will in the stifling holds of slave ships. Millions of others, lacking money for better accommodations, endured weeks of discomfort in the cramped, uncomfortable steerage sections of passenger or merchant ships.

As you read about this period, look for answers to these questions:

● What effect did European settlement have on American Indians—the people who already lived on this vast continent?

● Who were the Puritans, and what were their beliefs about human nature?

● How did rationalism differ from Puritanism, and what effect did rationalism have on the new American political system?

Collection introduction (pages 6–19) covers **Literary Skills** Evaluate the philosophical, political, religious, ethical, and social influences of a historical period.

About five hundred years ago European explorers first set foot on land in our hemisphere. In some ways their voyages must have seemed as daring and ultimately triumphant as Neil Armstrong's first steps on the moon in 1969. However, European feet were not the first to tread on American soil. American Indians lived here for thousands of years before the first Europeans stumbled across what they called the New World. As J. H. Parry states in his book *The Spanish Seaborne Empire,* "Columbus did not discover a new world; he established contact between two worlds, both already old."

Forming New Relationships

The first interactions between Europeans and American Indians largely involved trading near various harbors and rivers of North America. As the English began to establish colonies on these new shores, a mutual curiosity and increasing interdependence grew between the cultures. The Europeans relied on the American Indians to teach them survival skills, such as how to make canoes and

DIFFERENTIATING INSTRUCTION

Learners Having Difficulty
Students might use the condensed version of this essay in *The Holt Reader,* either as a practice for reading or as an alternate assignment.

English-Language Learners
To build background, you might begin by showing the videocassette segment titled "The Puritan Experience," available in

Spanish and English, which brings the Puritan era to life with vivid visual images and auditory effects.

Advanced Learners
Acceleration. Show the videocassette segment "The Puritan Experience" before students read the essay. Encourage students to list names of literary figures mentioned in the video, the essay, and the essay's sidebars. For

each name, have students record the genre(s) in which the person worked. Students might use their lists to develop an overview of the genres common in various historical periods.

Jacques Cartier's Discovery of the St. Lawrence River (1957) by Thomas H. Benton.
Tempera on canvas (7′ × 6′).

VIEWING THE ART

Thomas H. Benton
(1889–1975) was a regionalist known for murals depicting America at the birth of the modern era. He painted workers and other ordinary Americans, as well as the houses, tenements, nightclubs, cornfields, shacks, and skyscrapers they lived in; in short, he sought to capture the modern American experience. His stylized, muscular figures celebrate the vigor and energy of the American people. In *Jacques Cartier's Discovery of the St. Lawrence River,* Benton depicts an earlier time period but characteristically highlights the strength of the men and women who already lived on the North American continent and of those who came to explore it.

Activity. Ask students to imagine the impact created by the sheer size of this seven-foot-by-six-foot painting. Then, ask how Benton portrays the way Native Americans received the explorers. [Possible response: The Native American figures in the foreground may be welcoming or may be wary.] **How does Benton call attention to Cartier and his group?** [He places them and a symbolic flag center-top.]

Powhatan, 1609
Powhatan (1550?–1618) led a confederacy of tribes who aided John Smith and other English colonists in the early 1600s in what is now Virginia. Smith reported the following 1609 speech by Powhatan:

"Why will you take by force what you may obtain by love? Why will you destroy us who supply you with food? What can you get by war? . . . We are unarmed, and willing to give you what you ask, if you come in a friendly manner. . . .

"I am not so simple as not to know it is better to eat good meat, sleep comfortably, live quietly with my women and children, laugh and be merry with the English, and being their friend, trade for their copper and hatchets, than to run away from them. . . .

"Take away your guns and swords . . . or you may die in the same manner."

VIEWING THE ART

American artist **George Catlin** (1796–1872) dedicated himself to capturing the vanishing culture of native peoples of the American West and Central America.

Activity. Have students discuss what impression Black Coat might have made on European settlers and why. [Possible responses: They might have thought him violent and confrontational because of the arrow in his hair, or they might have been reassured by his amiable expression and the pipe in his hand.]

A **Content-Area Connections**

Science: Smallpox
The World Health Organization officially declared this lethal viral disease eradicated from the world in 1979, after a thirteen-year global vaccination campaign. No new cases of smallpox have been reported since 1977. Smallpox, which was highly contagious, was spread by airborne droplets. Victims suffered a rash of pustules and a high fever. Many victims died when the virus infected internal organs; others died of secondary bacterial infections. Survivors usually gained lifelong immunity, though some were left blind or infertile.

Black Coat, a Cherokee Chief (1836) by George Catlin. Oil on canvas.

The Granger Collection, New York.

Columbus did not discover a new world; he established contact between two worlds, both already old.

—J.H. Parry,
The Spanish Seaborne Empire (1966)

shelters, how to fashion clothing from buckskin, and how to plant their crops. At the same time and in exchange, the American Indians were eager to acquire European firearms, textiles, and steel tools.

In the early years of European settlement, American Indians vastly outnumbered the colonists. Historians estimate that in 1600, the total American Indian population of New England alone was from 70,000 to 100,000 people—more than the English population of New England would be two centuries later.

Battling New Diseases

The arrival of the European settlers had a deadly impact on Native Americans. Because the ancestors of American Indians probably crossed the ancient land bridge from Asia to North America during the Ice Age, their descendants weren't exposed to the diseases that had wracked Europe over the centuries. When European settlers made contact with Native Americans, the settlers unwittingly exposed them to diseases to which they had no immunity. These diseases, especially smallpox, sometimes killed off a village's entire population.

Here is how William Bradford (1590–1657), who was elected governor of Plymouth Colony thirty times, described the horrors of smallpox visited upon the American Indians:

A

    66 For want of bedding and linen and other helps . . . they fall into a lamentable condition as they lie on their hard mats, the pox breaking and mattering and running one into another, their skin cleaving by reason thereof to the mats they lie on. When they turn them, a whole side will flay off at once as it were, and they will be all of a gore blood, most fearful to behold. And then being very sore, what with cold and other distempers, they die like rotten sheep. 99

—*Of Plymouth Plantation 1620–1647*

Against enormous odds some Native Americans managed to survive the epidemics. Many of these survivors, however, were eventually forced to vacate their land and homes by settlers, who, now able to survive on their own, no longer needed the American Indians' friendship and guidance. Historian Francis Jennings writes bitterly of the effects of the European settlements:

    66 Europeans did not find a wilderness here; rather, however involuntarily, they made one. Jamestown, Plymouth, Salem, Boston, Providence, New Amsterdam, Philadelphia—all grew upon sites previously occupied by Indian communities. So did Quebec and Montreal and Detroit and Chicago. The so-called

Canassatego, 1744
A leader of the Iroquois Confederation, Canassatego replied to an offer by the Colonial Virginia Legislature to educate Native American youths at the College of William and Mary: "[Y]ou who are so wise must know that different Nations have different Conceptions of things; and you will not therefore take it amiss, if our Ideas of this kind of Education happens not to be the same with yours. We have had some experience of it. Several of our young People were formerly brought up in the Colleges of the Northern Provinces; they were instructed in all your Sciences; but, when they came back to us, they were bad Runners, ignorant of every means of living in the Woods, unable to bear either Cold or Hunger, knew neither how to build a Cabin, take a deer, nor kill an enemy, spoke our language imperfectly, were therefore neither fit for Hunters, Warriors, nor Counsellors; they were totally good for nothing. We are however not the less obliged for your kind Offer . . . and to show our grateful Sense of it, if the Gentlemen of Virginia shall send us a Dozen of their Sons, we will take great care of their Education, instruct them in all we know, and make Men of them."

settlement of America was a resettlement, a reoccupation of a land made waste by the diseases and demoralization introduced by the newcomers. **"**

—*The Invasion of America* (1975)

Explorers' Writings

The first detailed European observations of life on this vast continent were recorded in Spanish and French by explorers of the fifteenth and sixteenth centuries. These writings open a window onto a time when the so-called New World was the focus of the dreams and desires of an entire era. Christopher Columbus (c. 1451–1506), Francisco Vásquez de Coronado (c. 1510–1554), and many other explorers described the Americas in a flurry of eagerly read letters, journals, and books. Hoping to receive funding for further expeditions, the explorers emphasized the Americas' abundant resources, the peacefulness and hospitality of the inhabitants, and the promise of unlimited wealth to be gained from fantastic treasuries of gold.

■ Cabeza de Vaca's Expedition

In 1528, only thirty-six years after Columbus first sighted a flickering fire on the beach of San Salvador, a Spaniard named Álvar Núñez Cabeza de Vaca (c. 1490–1557) landed with an expedition (he was its treasurer) on the west coast of what is now Florida. Cabeza de Vaca and others left the ship and marched inland. They did not return. Their fleet waited an entire year for them, then departed for Mexico, giving up the explorers for dead. Lost in the Texas Gulf area, Cabeza de Vaca and his companions wandered for the next eight years in search of other Europeans who would help them to get home. Cabeza de Vaca's narrative of his journeys through what is now Texas is a gripping adventure story. It is also a firsthand account of the habits of some of the American Indians in what is now the southwestern United States: what they ate (very little), how they housed themselves, and what their religious beliefs were. Cabeza de Vaca also provides the first account of some animals and plants that the Europeans had never known existed.

Cabeza de Vaca and his shipmates were alternately captives and companions of the various

Cabeza de Vaca in the Desert (1906) by Frederic Remington. Oil on canvas.
Courtesy Frederic Remington Art Museum, Ogdensburg, New York.

DIRECT TEACHING

B Exploring the Historical Period
ENCOMIENDA

The Spanish *conquistadores* ("conquerors") introduced the *encomienda* system to the Americas. This system virtually enslaved the Native Americans of the West Indies and brought decades of suffering, malnutrition, and death. It officially ended in 1542.

C Background
Cabeza de Vaca

Cabeza de Vaca's eight-year journey through the New World was a remarkable feat of endurance. However, his account is more than a chronicle of his travels. In his work he also undertakes an inward journey; he transforms himself from a competent conquistador and Spanish gentleman into a new American who sympathizes with and appreciates the native peoples he encounters. He spent much of the rest of his time in America fighting for justice for them.

VIEWING THE ART

Although he spent most of his life in New York, **Frederic Remington** (1861–1909) produced paintings, illustrations, and sculptures depicting the American West.

Activity. How does Remington show the starkness of the desert landscape? [The landscape is barren; the land is rendered in one ocher color, suggesting the land's dry condition.]

Primary Source

Bartolomé de Las Casas
One critic of *encomienda* was Bartolomé de Las Casas (1474–1566), a Spanish lawyer who settled on Hispaniola in 1502. He later became a priest, gave up his *encomienda,* and condemned the system in his 1542 *Very Brief Account of the Destruction of the Indies,* as shown in the following quotation: "The reason why the [Europeans] have killed and destroyed such infinite numbers of souls is

solely because they have made gold their ultimate aim, seeking to load themselves with riches in the shortest time. . . . These lands, being so happy and so rich, and the people so humble, so patient, and so easily subjugated, they have . . . taken no more account of them . . . than—I will not say of animals, for would to God that they had considered and treated them as animals—but as even less than the dung in the streets."

In his 1566 *Apologetic History of the Indies,* Las Casas championed the native peoples: "Not only have the Indians shown themselves to be very wise peoples and possessed of lively and marked understanding . . . governing and providing for their nations . . . but they have equaled many diverse nations of the . . . past and present . . . and exceed by no small measure the wisest of these."

In the winter of 1692, two girls in Salem, Massachusetts, dramatically accused three local people of witchcraft, touching off a yearlong wave of further accusations, biased trials, and hasty executions; causes of the bizarre episode remain unclear.

DIRECT TEACHING

A Reading Skills

❓ **Speculating.** What do you think might explain the girls' symptoms? [Possible responses: The girls were playacting (while suffering from skin rashes). The girls really believed themselves possessed, and their convulsions and hallucinations stemmed from fear and hysteria.]

B Background
The Youngest Witch

Dorcas Good was four years old when she was accused and convicted of being a witch. Her mother and baby sister died in prison; she survived but suffered emotional difficulties for the rest of her life.

Native American peoples they encountered on their long trek. Here is part of his report of the expedition's experiences with a people in the Gulf Coast area, who are struggling to survive a famine:

> 66 Their support is principally roots, of two or three kinds, and they look for them over the face of all the country. The food is poor and gripes the persons who eat it. The roots require roasting two days: Many are very bitter, and withal difficult to be dug. They are sought the distance of two or three leagues, and so great is the want these people experience, that they cannot get through the year without them. Occasionally they kill deer, and at times take fish; but the quantity is so small and the famine so great, that they eat spiders and the eggs of ants, worms, lizards, salamanders, snakes, and vipers that kill whom they strike; and they eat earth and wood, and all that there is, the dung of deer, and other things that I omit to mention; and I honestly believe that were there stones in that land they would eat them. 99

—*La relación* (*The Report*)

A CLOSER LOOK: SOCIAL INFLUENCES

The Salem Witchcraft Trials

INFORMATIONAL TEXT

During the cold, dreary winter of 1691–1692, the daughter and the niece of Samuel Parris, a minister in Salem, Massachusetts, began to dabble in magic. By February the two girls started having seizures. Lesions appeared on their skin, and it seemed as if they were being choked by invisible hands. A doctor diagnosed the girls as victims of malicious witchcraft.

Urged to name those responsible for bewitching them, the girls accused Sarah Good and Sarah Osborne, two unpopular women from the village, and Tituba, a slave whom Samuel Parris had brought back from Barbados. During the subsequent trial the girls writhed and moaned and behaved as if they were being choked. Based on this "evidence," Sarah Good was condemned to death. In an attempt to save her own life, Tituba confessed to being a witch. She claimed that there was a coven of witches in Massachu-

setts and testified that she had seen several names written in blood in the Devil's book. The witch hunt had begun.

Zealous ministers like Cotton Mather argued that the epidemic of witchcraft proved beyond a doubt that New England was a holy place, since the Devil was so interested in it. Mather and others demanded that all witches be rooted out and severely punished. Hundreds of people from Salem and other eastern Massachusetts towns came forward to testify that they were victims of witchcraft.

Before long the prisons were overcrowded, and a special court was established in Salem. Within the next ten months about 150 people in this small community were accused of witchcraft. Neighbors, especially those with long-standing quarrels, turned on one another. Between June and September nineteen people were hanged, and one man, Giles Corey, who had refused to plead either innocent or guilty, was crushed to death under a pile of stones.

Literary Criticism

Critic's Commentary: Cabeza de Vaca

In *Empires Lost and Won: The Spanish Heritage in the Southwest*, historian Albert Marrin finishes the account of Álvar Núñez Cabeza de Vaca's life after his eight-year trek: "Cabeza de Vaca returned to Spain in 1537. We do not know whether he rejoined his wife, or, for that matter, if she was still alive. What is certain is that his fame preceded him and that His Majesty promised him high office as

a reward for his achievements. After three years of waiting, he was named governor of the province of Rio de la Plata in South America. From 1540 to 1543 he explored the jungles south of the Equator. His humane treatment of the Indians, however, made enemies among the colonists. They had him arrested on false charges and sent back to Spain in chains. For six years he lay

in a dungeon with scarcely enough light to see his hand in front of his face. Upon his release, he vanished from history. It is believed that Álvar Núñez Cabeza de Vaca spent his last years in loneliness and poverty. The date of his death is unknown. He never knew that his travels had opened a new chapter in American history."

The Puritan Legacy

Central to the development of the American literary tradition have been the writings of the Puritans of New England. *Puritan* is a broad term, referring to a number of Protestant groups that, beginning about 1560, sought to "purify" the Church of England, which since the time of Henry VIII (who reigned from 1509 to 1547) had been virtually inseparable from the country's government. Like other Protestant reformers on the European continent, English Puritans wished to return to the simpler forms of worship and church organization that are described in the Christian Scriptures. For them religion was first of all a personal, inner experience. They did not believe that the clergy or the government should or could act as an intermediary between the individual and God.

The examination of Sarah Good at the Salem witchcraft trials.

What really happened at Salem? Many historians believe that Salem experienced a mass hysteria, a sort of shared delusion. Still others have suggested that a more restrictive form of government recently imposed on the Massachusetts Bay Colony, in addition to new economic pressures in the colony's towns, may have led to bitterness, aggression, and outright paranoia. Perhaps the strict society of Puritan New England finally erupted under the strain of its repression. A recent theory proposes that fear of unusual or powerful nonconformists—particularly women—may have led to an attempt to constrain their behavior. Statistics show that the majority of the "witches" were unmarried women between the ages of forty and sixty, eccentric and independent loners with abrasive personalities. Some of them may have been "cunning folk," that is, midwives or people with unusual healing abilities and knowledge of herbal remedies. Some of these were women who could potentially come into their fathers' inheritances and therefore may have been seen as threats to male power.

The Salem trials fascinate to this day. They are the subject of one of the great American plays, Arthur Miller's *The Crucible* (1953). Set in 1692 Salem, *The Crucible* draws parallels between the Salem witch trials and the 1950s hunt for Communists in the U.S. government conducted by Senator Joseph McCarthy.

C Exploring the Culture
PROTESTANT DENOMINATIONS

The Puritans protested against the Anglican Church (called Episcopalians in the United States) for retaining aspects of the organization and ritual of the Roman Catholic Church. Other groups, such as the Lutherans and the Calvinists formed established churches, also maintaining that the Protestants did not go far enough to establish a more austere form of Christianity.

D Exploring the Historical Period
SALEM SOCIOLOGY

Some historians examining the Salem hysteria theorize that it expressed hostilities between the wealthy residents of the Salem seaport, who had made money in trade, and the poorer farmers, who lived outside town in Salem Village. These historians contend that many of the accusers were villagers and the accused were largely townsfolk.

E Exploring the Historical Period
SALEM'S AFTERMATH

In 1696, after the wave of hysteria had passed, one Salem judge repented; then, twelve jurors repented. Eventually Ann Putnam, one of the chief accusers, apologized. In 1711, the state reimbursed heirs of most of the victims with up to 150 pounds sterling.

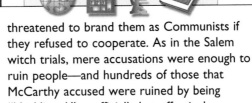

CONTENT-AREA CONNECTIONS

Political Science: McCarthyism
In 1950, Senator Joseph McCarthy of Wisconsin seized the political spotlight by charging that Communists had infiltrated the State Department. He produced almost no hard evidence, but his accusations fueled people's fears at the height of the cold war. McCarthy launched an investigation, summoned hundreds of Americans to testify, and threatened to brand them as Communists if they refused to cooperate. As in the Salem witch trials, mere accusations were enough to ruin people—and hundreds of those that McCarthy accused were ruined by being "blacklisted," unofficially but effectively prohibited from working in their chosen professions. In 1954, the U.S. Senate condemned McCarthy's misconduct and abuse of power.

VIEWING THE ART

Painting was not common in the early days of the American Colonies, as the economy required to support such activity took some time to develop. Because people wanted images of themselves, however, it is not surprising that almost all of the earliest paintings in the Colonies were portraits. The painter of this portrait is unknown, but one of the subjects, Mrs. Freake, was a rich Bostonian. Her wealth is evident in her choice of clothing and the well-crafted chair she sits in. It is thought that the artist updated the portrait shortly after first painting it, changing her clothing to a more fashionable style and adding the baby that is sitting on her lap.

Activity. Ask students what the painting tells them about childhood in this era. [Mrs. Freake appears proud and protective of her daughter, suggesting the importance of children to the Puritans.]

Ⓐ Reading Skills

❓ Summarizing. In your own words, what are three to five tenets that taken together sum up the Puritan credo? [Possible response: Humans are sinful by nature; most are damned for eternity; salvation belongs to the elect, who can be identified by their virtue; hard work and worldly success are signs of God's grace; people should live in a thrifty, self-reliant, and simple way.]

Mrs. Freake and Baby Mary (1674).

The Granger Collection, New York.

Many Puritans suffered persecution in England. Some were put in jail and whipped, their noses slit and their ears chopped off. Some fled England for Holland. A small group in Holland, fearing that they would lose their identity as English Protestants, set sail in 1620 for what was advertised as the New World. There they hoped to build a new society patterned after God's word.

Puritan Beliefs: Sinners All?

For a people who were so convinced that they were right, the Puritans had to grapple with complex uncertainties. At the center of Puritan theology was an uneasy mixture of certainty and doubt. The certainty was that because of Adam and Eve's sin of disobedience, most of humanity would be damned for all eternity. However, the Puritans were also certain that God in his mercy had sent his son Jesus Christ to earth to save particular people.

The doubt centered on whether a particular individual was one of the saved (the "elect") or one of the damned (the "unregenerate").

How did you know if you were saved or damned? As it turns out, you did not know. A theology that was so clear-cut in its division of the world between saints and sinners was fuzzy when it came to determining which were which. There were two principal indications of the state of your soul, neither of them completely certain. You were saved by the grace of God, and you could *feel* this grace arriving in an intensely emotional fashion. The inner arrival of God's grace was demonstrated by your outward behavior. After receiving grace, you were "reborn" as a member of the community of saints, and you behaved like a saint. People hoping to be among the saved examined their inner lives closely for signs of grace and tried to live exemplary lives. Thus, American Puritans came to value self-reliance, industriousness, temperance, and simplicity. These were, coincidentally, the ideal qualities needed to carve out a new society in a strange land.

Warrant for the arrest of Ann Pudeator, accused of witchcraft (1692).

Courtesy Peabody Essex Museum, Salem, Massachusetts.

The Puritan Deacon Samuel Chapin (1899) by Augustus Saint-Gaudens. Bronze model.

James Graham & Sons, Inc. New York.

Page from *The Day of Doom* by Michael Wigglesworth.

Puritan Politics: Government by Contract

In the Puritan view a covenant, or contract, existed between God and humanity. This spiritual covenant was a useful model for worldly social organization as well: Puritans believed that people should enter freely into agreements concerning their government. On the *Mayflower*, for example, in 1620, the Puritans composed and signed the Mayflower Compact, outlining how they would be governed once they landed. In this use of a contractual agreement, they prepared the ground for American constitutional democracy.

On the other hand, because the Puritans believed the saintly elect should exert great influence on government, their political views tended to be undemocratic. There was little room for compromise. In 1692, the witchcraft hysteria in Salem, Massachusetts, resulted in part from fear that the community's moral foundation was threatened and therefore its political unity was also in danger.

VIEWING THE ART

Augustus Saint-Gaudens (1848–1907) was born in Dublin, Ireland, but raised in New York City. His most highly regarded works include the expressive figure of Abraham Lincoln in Chicago's Lincoln Park; the shrouded, seated woman of the Adams Memorial in Rock Creek Cemetery, Washington, D.C.; and the equestrian statue of General William Tecumseh Sherman in New York City's Central Park.

Activity. Have students generate a list of adjectives that capture the Puritan spirit by examining the stance and bearing of Deacon Chapin. [Possible responses: sternness; dignity; pride; steadfastness; faith; religious fervor.]

B **Exploring the Culture**
THE PURITAN COVENANT
The Puritans believed that their covenant with God enjoined them to create a society governed by the Bible, in which everyone worked together for the common good. They demanded strict conformity: Dissenters were often flogged, banished, or on occasion put to death.

Primary Source

The Mayflower Compact
Here is the first voluntary compact of government written in the New World:
"We, whose names are here underwritten . . . Having undertaken for the Glory of God, and Advancement of the Christian Faith, and the Honour of our King and Country, a Voyage to plant the first colony in the northern Parts of Virginia; Do by these Presents [this document], solemnly and mutually in the Presence of God and one another, covenant and combine ourselves together into a civil Body Politick, for our better Ordering and Preservation, and Furtherance of the Ends aforesaid; And by Virtue hereof do enact, constitute, and frame, such just and equal Laws, Ordinances, Acts, Constitutions, and Offices, from time to time, as shall be thought most meet and convenient for the general Good of the Colony; unto which we promise all due Submission and Obedience."

A Exploring the Culture
HIGHER EDUCATION

Harvard was followed by the College of William and Mary (1693), Yale College (1701), Princeton College (1746). Although these were the first colleges in North America, it was not until the mid-twentieth century that they began to offer female students the same privileges and opportunities as male students. By contrast, Oberlin College in northeastern Ohio opened its doors to female students as soon as it was founded in 1833.

B Exploring the Culture
DEISM

The view that God created a well-ordered universe, controlled by immutable laws and operating without divine intervention, is the central belief of deism. Deists generally accepted naturalistic explanations for miracles in the Bible and allegorical interpretations of biblical prophecies. Adherents saw deism as a philosophy that could reconcile religion and science. Deists' beliefs, however, clashed with the Puritan emphasis on revelation, divine providence, and the final judgment.

Characteristics of Puritan Writing

- The Bible provided a model for Puritan writing. The Puritans viewed each individual life as a journey to salvation. Puritans looked for direct connections between biblical events and events in their own lives.
- Diaries and histories were the most common forms of literary expression in Puritan society; in them writers described the workings of God.
- Puritans favored a plain style of writing. They admired clarity of expression and avoided complicated figures of speech.

The Bible in America

The Puritans read the Bible as the story of the creation, fall, wanderings, and rescue of the human race. Within this long and complex narrative, each Puritan could see connections to events in his or her own life or to events in the life of the community. Each Puritan was trained to see life as a pilgrimage, or journey, to salvation. Each Puritan learned to read his or her life the way a literary critic reads a book.

The Puritans believed that the Bible was the literal word of God. Reading the Bible was a necessity for all Puritans, as was the ability to understand theological debates. For these reasons the Puritans placed great emphasis on education. Thus, Harvard College, originally intended to train Puritan ministers for the rapidly expanding colony, was founded in 1636, only sixteen years after the first Pilgrims had landed. Just three years later the first printing press in the American Colonies was set up.

Their beliefs required the Puritans to keep a close watch on both their spiritual and their public lives. This focus of the Puritan mind greatly affected their writings. Diaries and histories were important forms of Puritan literature because they were used to record the workings of God.

The Age of Reason: Tinkerers and Experimenters

By the end of the seventeenth century, new ideas that had been fermenting in Europe began to present a challenge to the unshakable faith of the Puritans.

The Age of Reason, or the Enlightenment, began in Europe with the philosophers and scientists of the seventeenth and eighteenth centuries who called themselves rationalists. **Rationalism** is the belief that human beings can arrive at truth by using reason, rather than by relying on the authority of the past, on religious faith, or on intuition.

The Puritans saw God as actively and mysteriously involved in the workings of the universe; the rationalists saw God differently. The great English rationalist Sir Isaac Newton (1642–1727), who formulated the laws of gravity and motion, compared God to a clockmaker. Having created the perfect mechanism of this universe, God then left his creation to run on its own, like a clock. The rationalists believed that God's special gift to humanity is reason—the ability to think in an ordered, logical manner. This gift of reason enables people to discover both scientific and spiritual truth. According to the rationalists, then, everyone has the capacity to regulate and improve his or her own life.

While the theoretical background for the Age of Reason took shape in Europe, a homegrown practicality and interest in scientific tinkering or experimenting was already thriving in the American Colonies. From the earliest Colonial days, Americans had to be generalists and tinkerers; they had to make do with what was on hand, and they had to achieve results.

The Smallpox Plague

The unlikely hero of America's first foray into scientific exploration was the strict Puritan minister Cotton Mather (1663–1728), who was interested in natural science and medicine.

In April 1721, a ship from the West Indies docked in Boston Harbor. This was not unusual, for trade with the West Indies was one of the foundations of New England economic life. This ship was different, though. For in addition to its cargo of sugar and molasses, this ship carried smallpox.

The Rationalist Worldview

- People arrive at truth by using reason rather than by relying on the authority of the past, on religion, or on nonrational mental processes, such as intuition.
- God created the universe but does not interfere in its workings.
- The world operates according to God's rules, and through the use of reason, people can discover those rules.
- People are basically good and perfectible.
- Since God wants people to be happy, they worship God best by helping other people.
- Human history is marked by progress toward a more perfect existence.

Title page of the *Bay Psalm Book* (1640).

The Granger Collection, New York.

Hornbook used to teach the alphabet to children.

Rare Book Department, Free Library of Philadelphia.

C **Background**
Cotton Mather
A child prodigy who went to Harvard at age twelve, Cotton Mather came from a prominent New England family of theologians and thinkers. His grandfather Richard and his father, Increase, were both well-known ministers, writers, and orators. Beginning in the 1680s, Mather and his father both preached at Boston's Second Church. There (in spite of a serious stutter), Mather became famous for his rousing sermons and his interest in science, witchcraft, and prophecies about the end of the world. Mather is now praised for his attempts to prevent smallpox through inoculations. Nevertheless, some historians have criticized Mather for his support of the Salem witch trials, which he wrote about in *The Wonders of the Invisible World.*

CONTENT-AREA CONNECTIONS

Humanities: Education
A hornbook was a type of children's primer used from the fifteenth to eighteenth centuries. A lesson was printed on a sheet of parchment or paper and covered for protection with a thin, transparent sheet of animal horn. Both sheets were then fastened to a board, which usually had a perforated handle that could be attached to a child's belt or to

a cord worn around the neck. Lessons included the alphabet in capitals and lowercase and a variety of other material, such as Roman numerals or the Lord's Prayer. The contents of hornbooks and early primers reflect the fact that the curricula of the earliest schools in the North American Colonies centered on religion.

Whole-class activity. Ask students to contrast the way Colonial children learned the alphabet and "three R's" and the way children learn these things today. [Children today learn from parents, teachers, and television shows such as *Sesame Street.* Commercial television and public schools avoid religious content.]

A ## Background
The Iroquois Confederacy

The confederacy's complex and egalitarian constitution, preserved for centuries in the oral tradition, united the Seneca, Oneida, Mohawk, Onondaga, and Cayuga tribes of the Northeast. A sixth tribe, the Tuscarora, joined in 1722.

B ## Background
The Turkish Connection

From the fourteenth through the early twentieth century, Turkey anchored the vast Ottoman Empire. In 1716, when Britain appointed Edward Montagu ambassador to Turkey, his strong-willed wife shocked London society by joining him. Lady Mary Wortley Montagu spent the next two years diligently observing Turkish customs; one of these customs was inoculation against smallpox. Returning home in 1718, she worked to introduce inoculation to England.

FAST FACTS
Political Highlights

A • The Mohawk leader Dekanawida establishes the Iroquois Confederacy around 1500, uniting Native American peoples who used to be rivals.

• The *Mayflower* Pilgrims adopt the Mayflower Compact and land at Plymouth, Massachusetts, in 1620.

• Mounting tension between the colonists and the British Empire results in the Revolutionary War (1775–1783).

• The Second Continental Congress adopts the Declaration of Independence on July 4, 1776.

In the seventeenth and eighteenth centuries, smallpox was one of the scourges of life, just as AIDS and the Ebola virus are today. The disease spread rapidly, disfigured its victims, and was often fatal. The outbreak in Boston in 1721 was a major public-health problem. What was to be done?

■ An Unlikely Cure

At the time of the smallpox epidemic, Cotton Mather was working on what would be the first scholarly essay on medicine written in America. In his opening sentences he reveals his Puritan perspective: "Let us look upon sin as the cause of sickness." Mather's religious point of view did not, however, prevent him from seeking **B** cures for specific diseases. He had heard of a method, devised by a Turkish physician, for dealing with smallpox. The method seemed illogical, but it apparently worked. It was called inoculation. In June 1721, as the smallpox epidemic spread throughout Boston, Mather began a public campaign for inoculation.

Boston's medical community was violently opposed to such an experiment, especially one invented by a Muslim. The debate was vigorous, raging all summer and into the fall. Controversy developed into violence: In November, Mather's house was bombed.

Despite such fierce opposition, Mather succeeded in inoculating

16

Primary Source

Benjamin Franklin

Smallpox epidemics continued throughout the eighteenth century. In his *Autobiography,* Benjamin Franklin provides a poignant personal perspective: "In 1736 I lost one of my sons, a fine boy of four years old, by the smallpox, taken in the common way. I long regretted bitterly, and still regret that I had not given it to him by inoculation. This I mention for the sake of parents who omit that operation, on the supposition that they should never forgive themselves if a child died under it, my example showing that the regret may be the same either way, and that, therefore, the safer should be chosen."

nearly 300 people. By the time the epidemic was over, in March of the following year, only 6 of these people had died. Of the almost 6,000 other people who contracted the disease (nearly half of Boston's population), about 850 had died. The evidence, according to Mather's figures, was clear: Whether or not inoculation made much sense to scientists, it worked.

■ A Practical Approach to Change

The smallpox controversy illustrates two interesting points about American life in the early eighteenth century. First, it shows that contradictory qualities of the American character often existed side by side. Puritan thinking was not limited to a rigid and narrow interpretation of the Bible; a devout Puritan like Mather could also be a practical scientist.

Mather's experiment also reveals that a practical approach to social change and scientific research was necessary in America. The frontier farmer with little access to tools shared a problem with the scientist who had few books and a whole new world of plants and animals to catalog. American thought had to be thought in action: Improving the public welfare required a willingness to experiment, to try things out, no matter what the authorities might say.

FAST FACTS

Philosophical Views

- Native American worldviews, passed down through oral tradition, stress not progress but the cyclical nature of existence.

- The Puritans regard life as a journey toward salvation and look for signs of self-improvement and for the workings of God in their daily lives.

- The rationalists regard reason and logic as God-given gifts and try to find order in the universe.

Social Influences

- Slavery is legal and common in all New England colonies in 1620.

- Hysteria and paranoia build as more than one hundred people are accused of witchcraft in Salem, Massachusetts.

- An epidemic of smallpox strikes Boston in 1721, affecting nearly half the city's population.

DIRECT TEACHING

C Exploring the Historical Period
THE BATTLE AGAINST SMALLPOX

Inoculation, the method Cotton Mather advocated in 1721, involved deliberate infection with smallpox. A doctor would inject a healthy person with matter from the sores of a person who had a light case of the disease. In most instances the inoculated person would get only a light case, survive, and gain lifelong immunity. Since the concept of *viruses* was still unknown, scientists as well as laypeople were mystified that the procedure worked. Despite Mather's success, many people shied away from inoculation, for even a light case of smallpox could be dangerous. Not until the end of the century did Edward Jenner of England devise the safer technique called vaccination. This procedure involved injection of a far milder disease, cowpox, which also conferred immunity from smallpox.

D Exploring the Culture
SLAVERY IN THE COLONIES

Serious opposition to slavery did not arise in the Colonies until the Revolutionary War era, a time when greater attention was given to the issues of equality and human rights. Leaders of the new government introduced measures aimed at gradually ending slavery in the northern states. The first measure, passed in Pennsylvania in 1780, provided that all children born to slaves in the future would be freed when they reached the age of twenty-eight.

? Evaluating. More than two centuries ago, a French man made this bold prediction about America's future. In your judgment, has his prediction come true? [Possible responses: Yes, America's Constitution, economy, and foreign policy have had a huge impact on world affairs; No, America is still not truly free from "ancient prejudices."]

B Background
Michel-Guillaume Jean de Crèvecoeur

Born and educated in France, Crèvecoeur (1735–1813) traveled throughout the Colonies before buying a New York farm. His volume of essays, *Letters from an American Farmer,* overflows with details and insights about American life during the Revolutionary War era.

C Background
Deists

American deists included prominent revolutionaries such as Benjamin Franklin, Thomas Jefferson, George Washington, and Thomas Paine.

VIEWING THE ART

Activity. Compare this portrait of Thomas Jefferson by Rembrandt Peale to Charles Willson Peale's portrait on p. 95. Which might Jefferson have preferred? Why? [Possible responses: Charles Willson's, because Jefferson seems younger and more cheerful; or Rembrandt's, because Jefferson seems wiser and more philosophical.]

What then is . . . this new man? . . . He is an American, who, leaving behind him all his ancient prejudices and manners, receives new ones from the new mode of life he has embraced, the new government he obeys, and the new rank he holds. . . .

[In America] individuals of all nations are melted into a new race of men, whose labors . . . will one day cause great changes in the world.

—Michel-Guillaume Jean de Crèvecoeur, *Letters from an American Farmer* (1782)

Deism: Are People Basically Good?

Like the Puritans, the rationalists discovered God through the medium of the natural world, but in a different way. Rationalists thought it unlikely that God would choose to reveal himself only at particular times to particular people. It seemed much more reasonable to believe that God had made it possible for *all* people at *all* times to discover natural laws through their God-given power of reason.

This outlook, called **deism** (dē′iz′əm), was shared by many eighteenth-century thinkers, including many founders of the American nation. American deists came from different religious backgrounds, but they avoided supporting specific religious groups. They sought instead the principles that united all religions.

Deists believed that the universe was orderly and good. In contrast to the Puritans, deists stressed humanity's goodness. They believed in the perfectibility of every individual through the use of reason. God's objective, in the deist view, was the happiness of his creatures. Therefore, the best form of worship was to do good for others. There already existed in America an impulse to improve people's lives, as Cotton Mather's struggle to save Boston from smallpox illustrates. Deism elevated this impulse to one of the nation's highest goals. To this day social welfare is still a political priority and still the subject of fierce debate.

The American struggle for independence was justified largely by appeals to rationalist principles. The arguments presented in the Declaration of Independence are based on rationalist assumptions about the relations between people, God, and natural law.

Self-made Americans

Most of the literature written in the American Colonies during the Age of Reason was, understandably, rooted in reality. This

*Thomas Jefferson (1805)
by Rembrandt Peale. Oil on canvas.
© Collection of the New-York Historical Society (1867.306).*

Advanced Learners
Enrichment. Point out that the eighteenth century saw enormous social and cultural changes sweep over the American Colonies.
Activity. Invite students to deepen their understanding of American life during the eighteenth century by searching the Internet for primary sources from the period. Using *U.S. history sources* as keywords in a search engine, they may examine sources such as the journals of John Woolman, William Byrd, or Sarah Kemble Knight; the essays and articles of Michel-Guillaume Jean de Crèvecoeur; or the correspondence of John and Abigail Adams. Have students choose excerpts from any of these sources to present in a class seminar exploring aspects of daily life in eighteenth-century America.

was an age of pamphlets, since most literature was intended to serve practical or political ends. Following the Revolutionary War (1775–1783), the problems of organizing and governing the new nation were of the highest importance.

The unquestioned masterpiece of the American Age of Reason is *The Autobiography* by Benjamin Franklin (page 67). Franklin used the autobiographical narrative, a form common in Puritan writing, and omitted its religious justification. Written in clear, witty prose, this account of the development of the self-made American provided the model for a story that would be told again and again. In the twentieth century it appeared in F. Scott Fitzgerald's novel *The Great Gatsby* (1925). It is still found in the countless biographies and autobiographies of self-made men and women that appear on the bestseller lists today.

Benjamin Franklin.
Drawing by David Levine.

Reprinted with permission from *The New York Review of Books.* Copyright © 1967 NYREV, Inc.

REVIEW

Talk About . . .

Turn back to the Think About questions at the start of the introduction to this period (page 6), and discuss your views.

Write About . . .

Contrasting Literary Periods

Who are we? Answers then and now. Consider what you've learned about the dominant philosophical and religious beliefs in early America. The **Puritans** believed that the world was fallen and that people were sinners who could be redeemed only through the grace of God. The **rationalists** believed that the universe was basically good and that doing good for others was the best way to worship God. How do people today regard the universe and human nature itself? Write a brief essay explaining whether you find evidence of Puritanism and rationalism in American society today.

Review

Talk About . . .

- **Modeling.** You might model answering the first bulleted question on p. 6 by saying, "European settlement ravaged American Indian populations and cultures; we read about disease and horrific treatment during *encomienda,* for example. Yet some parts of these rich, resilient cultures endured and, belatedly, gained respect."

- Possible response: The Puritans were Protestants who wanted to create a government that followed biblical rules; they believed that most humans were damned through original sin but could be saved through God's grace.

- Possible response: Unlike Puritanism, rationalism was the belief that people were basically good and that truth could be arrived at through human reasoning alone; rationalist ideals inspired the Declaration of Independence.

Write About . . .

Who are we? Answers then and now. To start students off, you might suggest that they examine views of current social and political critics and reformers. Which ones assume that the world is going downhill ("fallen") or that people are basically untrustworthy? Which ones assume that life is getting better or that social welfare programs ("doing good for others") are keys to progress?

Check Test: Short Answer

Guide the class in answering these comprehension questions. Have students support their responses with passages from the text.

1. Puritans believed they could be saved by _____. [God's grace]

2. Four qualities that the Puritans valued were _____. [self-reliance, industriousness, temperance, and simplicity]

3. Cotton Mather proposed combating the smallpox epidemic by _____. [inoculating the uninfected]

4. Deists believed the universe was _____. [orderly and good]

5. Most literature written in America during the Age of Reason consisted of _____. [political tracts]

Grade-Level Skills

■ **Literary Skills**

Analyze archetypes drawn from myth and tradition.

■ **Reading Skills**

Analyze cultural characteristics in literary traditions.

More About the Writers

Background. Ironically, Joseph Bruchac's grandfather never told Native American stories to his grandson; it was not until his college days that Bruchac began to gather stories from Native American elders. Bruchac says, "The central themes in my work are simple ones—that we have to listen to each other and to the earth, that we have to respect each other and the earth, that we never know anyone until we know what they have in their heart."

Barry Lopez, from whose critically acclaimed collection of coyote tales "Coyote Finishes His Work" is taken, has a special interest in the culture of the Northwest Indians. He may be better known as a travel and natural history writer, but even in those books he explores spiritual connections between humanity and the natural world. Lopez claims that he writes out of a deep desire to "contribute to a literature of hope."

Native American Oral Traditions

Shield cover, once the property of Pretty Bear, a Crow chief.
Museum of the American Indian (20/7130).

Joseph Bruchac (1942–   ) was born in Saratoga Springs, New York, and was raised there by his grandfather, a member of the Abenaki people. Bruchac has edited several anthologies of poetry and has written short stories, poems, and novels, many of which incorporate myths from the Abenaki heritage.

"The Sky Tree" is a creation myth of the **Huron,** a Native American people of the eastern woodlands, the region around the Great Lakes and toward the Atlantic Ocean. The Huron lived in villages along the St. Lawrence River, where they competed in the fur trade with the peoples of the Iroquois League. Rivalry with the Iroquois League and European settlers gradually forced the Huron west into the north central United States and Canada and then into Kansas and Oklahoma.

"The Earth Only" comes from the oral tradition of the **Teton Sioux,** a North American Plains Indian people who are sometimes called the Dakota. The Sioux led a nomadic life, following the buffalo and traveling in established cycles across the rolling plains of what is now Minnesota, North Dakota, and South Dakota. The Sioux offered intense resistance to the westward expansion of the United States.

"Coyote Finishes His Work" has been handed down through the tradition of the **Nez Perce,** a Native American people of the Plateau culture who lived in what is now Idaho, Oregon, and Washington. The French coined the name *nez percé*, meaning "pierced nose," because some of the people wore nose pendants. Following the establishment of the Oregon Trail and aggravated by the mania of the nineteenth-century gold rush, fierce conflicts erupted over the Nez Perce land. In 1877, the Nez Perce leader, Chief Joseph, surrendered to federal troops with the now famous words "I will fight no more forever."

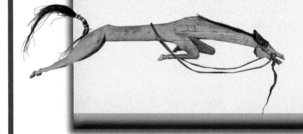

Teton Sioux horse sculpture.
Robinson Museum, Pierre, South Dakota.

20   Collection 1   Encounters and Foundations to 1800

RESOURCES: READING

Planning
■ *One-Stop Planner* CD-ROM with ExamView Test Generator

Differentiating Instruction
■ *Holt Reading Solutions*
■ *The Holt Reader*
■ *Supporting Instruction in Spanish*
■ *Audio CD Library, Selections and Summaries in Spanish*

Grammar and Language
■ *Daily Language Activities*

Assessment
■ *Holt Assessment: Literature, Reading, and Vocabulary*
■ *One-Stop Planner* CD-ROM with ExamView Test Generator
■ *Holt Online Assessment*

Internet
■ go.hrw.com (Keyword: LE5 11-1)
■ *Elements of Literature Online*

Media
■ *Audio CD Library*
■ *Audio CD Library, Selections and Summaries in Spanish*

Before You Read

The Sun Still Rises... • The Sky Tree • The Earth Only • Coyote Finishes His Work

Make the Connection
Quickwrite ✏

People have always asked questions about the origins of the world and about their place in the natural order of things. To answer their questions, people have told themselves stories. The stories, which are almost always connected with religious rituals, explain the world the people live in and their traditions. These stories, called **myths,** also comfort people when they are afraid and give them a sense of cultural identity. Take some notes on myths you are familiar with. What do they explain to people? What comfort might they offer?

Literary Focus
Archetypes

Most myths contain archetypes. An **archetype** (är′kə·tīp′) is an old imaginative pattern that has appeared in literature throughout the ages. The tree in the Huron myth here is an archetype—that of the life-giving tree. Coyote in the Nez Perce myth is an archetype—that of the trickster hero. Archetypes cross cultural and national boundaries.

Archetypes can be plots (the death of the hero, boy wins girl, the quest), characters (the trickster, the savior, the rescued maiden), or images (a place where people never die, a golden cup, hoarded treasure). The life-giving tree is an archetypal image found in Native American myths as well as in Norse and Middle Eastern myths. The trickster hero is a character archetype found in African and Scandinavian myths and in modern fiction (and comics).

> An **archetype** is an old imaginative pattern that appears across cultures and is repeated through the ages. An archetype can be a character, a plot, or an image.
>
> *For more on Archetype, see the Handbook of Literary and Historical Terms.*

Reading Skills 📖
Understanding Cultural Characteristics

In reading works by members of different cultures, it is important to recognize differences in literary traditions. Since American Indian literature was handed down orally by storytellers, these pieces lose some of their power in written form. As you read, try to imagine each piece being spoken by a skilled storyteller to an eager audience—or, better yet, read each piece aloud.

SKILLS FOCUS

Quapaw ceramic turtle-effigy vessel (late Mississippian period, A.D. 1300–1500).
The University Museum, University of Arkansas, Fayetteville.

Literary Skills
Understand archetypes.

Reading Skills
Understand cultural characteristics.

Native American Oral Traditions   **21**

PRETEACHING

Summary ⟷ *at grade level*

In this essay, Joseph Bruchac gives an overview of Native American literature. He points out the difficulty that Western scholars have had in coming to terms with the existence and analysis of this literature. Bruchac offers several generalizations about Native American literature and concludes by stressing its importance as a means of preserving historical continuity.

Skills Starter

Build review skills. Begin to tell a story to the class: "Once upon a time, a poor but kindly couple had a son. Although he owned little of this world's wealth, the child was cheerful and clever. . . ." Discuss the adventures such a character might have. Explain that such a character—a person who has few possessions but whose optimism and cleverness see him or her through most situations—appears in stories from around the world. Such a character is an archetype. You also might point out that this archetype usually takes the role of the hero, or central character. Invite students to consider what these four selections suggest about archetypal figures.

A Literary Focus

? Cross-cultural relationships.
According to Bruchac, what is one important thing that Native American literature has in common with ancient European classics? [Both bodies of literature are rooted in oral tradition.]

B Content-Area Connections

Social Science: Native American Languages
Researchers estimate that when Columbus arrived in the Americas, approximately 2,000 independent people speaking at least 350 languages in about 60 language groups were spread across the North American continent. Since writing did not exist among the group, it is not surprising that many treasures in the oral tradition went undiscovered for years.

C Reading Skills

? Understanding cultural characteristics. Consider what Bruchac says about the authors whom he names. What have these writers done for Native American literature? [Possible response: They have brought it to life—for Native and non-Native readers alike—by combining its ancient culture and traditions with a modern English sensibility.]

The Sun Still Rises in the Same Sky: Native American Literature

Joseph Bruchac

22

Learners Having Difficulty
Invite learners having difficulty to read "Coyote Finishes His Work" in interactive format in *The Holt Reader* and to use the sidenotes as aids to understanding the selection. The interactive version provides additional instruction, practice, and assessment of the literary skill standard taught in the Student Edition. Monitor students' responses

to the selection, and correct any misconceptions that arise.

Special Education Students
For lessons designed for English-language learners and special education students, see *Holt Reading Solutions*.

Advanced Learners
Enrichment. Ask an advanced learner to read "The Sun Still Rises . . . " and give classmates prereading help by telling what he or she thinks the title means.

Few peoples have been as appreciated and, at the same time, as misrepresented as the many different cultures today called American Indian or Native American. Images of Indians are central to mainstream America, from Longfellow's misnamed epic poem *The Song of Hiawatha* (which actually tells the story of the Chippewa hero Manabozho, not the Iroquois Hiawatha) to the "cowboys and Indians" tradition of movies about the Old West. Yet it's only recently that the authentic literary voices of Native Americans have received serious attention. Native American literature has been a living oral tradition, but it was never treated with the same respect as European, or Western, literature. But Western literature itself has its roots firmly planted in the oral tradition—such ancient classics as the *Odyssey*[1] and *Beowulf*,[2] long before they were written down, were stories kept alive by word of mouth. The vast body of American Indian oral literature, encompassing dozens of epic narratives and countless thousands of stories, poems, songs, oratory, and chants, was not even recognized by Western scholars until the late 1800s. Until then, it was assumed that Native Americans had no literature.

Part of the problem scholars had in recognizing the rich traditions of American Indian literature was translating the texts from hundreds of different languages—a task often best done by Native Americans themselves. Over the decades, various American Indian writers—N. Scott Momaday, Louise Erdrich, Simon J. Ortiz, and Leslie Marmon Silko, among others—have revitalized Native American literature by combining their fluency in English with a deep understanding of their own languages and traditions.

We can make some important generalizations about American Indian oral traditions. First of all, Native American cultures use stories to teach moral lessons and convey practical information about the natural world. A story from the Abenaki people of Maine, for example, tells how Gluskabe catches all of the game animals. He is then told by his grandmother to return the animals to the woods. They will die if they are kept in his bag, she tells him, and if they do die, there will be no game left for the people to come. In this one brief tale, important, life-sustaining lessons about greed, the wisdom of elders, and game management are conveyed in an entertaining and engaging way.

American Indian literature also reflects a view of the natural world that is more inclusive than the one typically seen in Western literature. The Native American universe is not dominated by human beings. Animals and humans are often interchangeable in myths and folk tales. Origin myths may even feature animals as the instruments of creation.

All American Indian cultures also show a keen awareness of the power of metaphor. Words are as powerful and alive as the human breath that carries them. Songs and chants can make things happen—call game animals, bring rain, cure the sick, or destroy an enemy. For Native Americans, speech, or oratory—often relying on striking similes drawn from nature—is a highly developed and respected literary form.

Passed on from generation to generation, oral traditions preserve historical continuity. But these traditions are also, like the Native American peoples themselves, tenacious, dynamic, and responsive to change. The American Indian worldview is not that of a progressive straight line, but of an endless circle. This cyclical nature of existence is reflected both in the natural world itself, with its changing seasons and cycles of birth, death, and rebirth, and in Native American ceremonies repeated year after year. Each summer, for example, the Lakota people have their Sun Dance. In pre-Columbian times, they went to the Sun Dance on foot; after the coming of the Spanish, they rode horses to the annual event. Today, the Lakota arrive by automobile. While a European eye might see the technology of transport as the important point of this anecdote, to a Lakota the issue of changing transportation is unimportant. It is, after all, only a different way of getting to the same place. The sun still rises in the same sky.

1. *Odyssey:* ancient Greek epic poem, attributed to Homer.
2. *Beowulf:* epic poem composed in Old English between A.D. 700 and 750.

Literary Criticism

Critic's Commentary: Native American Voices

According to critic Margaret Atrov, "Until recently . . . the popular concept of Indian literature was shaped not by the Indian and not even by his translator but by the white American writer or moviemaker. . . . There is no better way to correct the misrepresentations that have ingrained themselves in our folklore than to listen to the genuine voices of the Indian peoples. Since their poems are really songs meant to be chanted or sung as part of various rituals, it is indeed the voices of the Indians, ancient and authentic, despite the drawbacks of translation, that we hear when we read them." Call on volunteers to explain what they think Atrov means by *authentic voices* and how these selections help support what she says about those voices.

DIRECT TEACHING

D Content-Area Connections

Literature: Gluskabe
Explain that Gluskabe, according to Abenaki legend, was a giant who came from across the sea in a stone canoe. He established the human race, it is said, by splitting open an ash tree and allowing the human beings to come out.

E Literary Focus

? Characteristics of subgenres of prose. Ask students to think of (or do research into) some well-known, highly effective pieces of oratory. [Examples might include Lincoln's Gettysburg Address and King's "I Have a Dream" speech.] Compare students' comments about those speeches with Bruchac's comments about Native American oratory, especially with respect to their use of figurative language.

F Content-Area Connections

Culture: The Sun Dance
The Sun Dance is a yearly ceremony of the Plains Indians. For three to four days, dancers gather around a central pole topped with a buffalo skull. This pole represents the east/west axis of the world. The ceremony celebrates the concept of sacrifice by having dancers endure a ritual ordeal. In the 1800s, this ordeal required putting skewers tied to the central pole through the chest muscles of the dancers, who then danced until the skewers pulled loose. Today the ceremonial sacrifice is fasting. Despite the change of ordeal, the principles of the sacrificial rite are timeless and are the highest expression of the Plains Indians' religion.

Summary ⬇ *below grade level*

In "The Sky Tree," a creation myth, Aataentsic cuts down the Sky Tree because her ailing husband, the chief of Sky Land, asks for the tree's healing fruit. When the Sky Tree falls through a hole in the sky, she throws herself after it. Animals on the water-covered earth hurry to build an island upon Turtle's back, where Aataentsic and the Sky Tree can come to rest. Eventually, the Sky Tree takes root in the new earth.

"The Earth Only" is a poem that celebrates the permanence of the natural world—and the wisdom of those who recognize that truth.

Ⓐ Content-Area Connections

Literature: The Earth Diver Myth
In the earth diver myth, common among Northeast Native American cultures, the earth is covered by water, and some creature (usually an otter, loon, or beaver) dives down to bring up a piece of it. That clump is placed on the back of a great turtle—which is why some Native American groups call North America "Turtle Island."

Ⓑ Literary Focus

❓ **Symbolism.** What does the rooting of the tree represent? [Possible response: It symbolizes rebirth in that the tree will grow again, and life will not end.]

The Sky Tree

In the beginning, Earth was covered with water. In Sky Land, there were people living as they do now on Earth. In the middle of that land was the great Sky Tree. All of the food which the people in that Sky Land ate came from the great tree.

The old chief of that land lived with his wife, whose name was Aataentsic,° meaning "Ancient Woman," in their longhouse near the great tree. It came to be that the old chief became sick, and nothing could cure him. He grew weaker and weaker until it seemed he would die. Then a dream came to him, and he called Aataentsic to him.

"I have dreamed," he said, "and in my dream I saw how I can be healed. I must be given the fruit which grows at the very top of Sky Tree. You must cut it down and bring that fruit to me."

Aataentsic took her husband's stone ax and went to the great tree. As soon as she struck it, it split in half and toppled over. As it fell, a hole opened in Sky Land, and the tree fell through the hole. Aataentsic returned to the place where the old chief waited.

"My husband," she said, "when I cut the tree, it split in half and then fell through a great hole. Without the tree, there can be no life. I must follow it."

Then, leaving her husband, she went back to the hole in Sky Land and threw herself after the great tree.

───────
°**Aataentsic** (ä′tä·ent′sik).

Coyote-effigy platform pipe (Middle Woodland period, 200 B.C.–A.D. 100). Ohio Hopewell culture.

Photograph © The Detroit Institute of Arts, 1995. Collection of Ohio Historical Society, Columbus. Photo courtesy © The Detroit Institute of Arts, Dirk Bakker, photographer (WL-117).

As Aataentsic fell, Turtle looked up and saw her. Immediately Turtle called together all the water animals and told them what she had seen.

"What should be done?" Turtle said.

Beaver answered her. "You are the one who saw this happen. Tell us what to do."

Navajo sand painter at Hubbell Trading Post, Ganado, Arizona.

"All of you must dive down," Turtle said. "Bring up soil from the bottom, and place it on my back."

Immediately all of the water animals began to dive down and bring up soil. Beaver, Mink, Muskrat, and Otter each brought up pawfuls of wet soil and placed the soil on Turtle's back until they had made an island of great size. When they were through, Aataentsic settled down gently on the new Earth, and the pieces of the great tree fell beside her and took root.

—from the Huron tradition,
retold by Joseph Bruchac

The Earth Only

Wica'hcala kin	The old men
heya'pelo'	say
maka' kin	the earth
lece'la	only
tehan yunke'lo	endures
eha' pelo'	You spoke
ehan'kecon	truly
wica' yaka pelo'	You are right.

—composed by Used-as-a-Shield (Teton Sioux), translated in 1918

24

Delivering narrative presentations. Ask students to imagine themselves as storytellers in a Huron long house or a Nez Perce tepee. They must tell in their own words either "The Sky Tree" or "Coyote Finishes His Work."

Activity. Have students form small groups; each group should select one of the stories for a group oral interpretation. Ask groups to consider how best to represent the theme of the tale. They can discuss vocal techniques— pitch, volume, and tone—and nonverbal techniques—the use of gestures, facial expressions, and movements—to achieve desired effects. Ask them to think about the best way to express sensory details and to adjust the pacing of the narrative's action to accommodate changes in setting or mood. Allow time in class for each group to present one of the stories.

Coyote Finishes His Work

From the very beginning, Coyote was traveling around all over the earth. He did many wonderful things when he went along. He killed the monsters and the evil spirits that preyed on the people. He made the Indians, and put them out in tribes all over the world because Old Man Above wanted the earth to be inhabited all over, not just in one or two places.

He gave all the people different names and taught them different languages. This is why Indians live all over the country now and speak in different ways.

He taught the people how to eat and how to hunt the buffalo and catch eagles. He taught them what roots to eat and how to make a good lodge and what to wear. He taught them how to dance. Sometimes he made mistakes, and even though he was wise and powerful, he did many foolish things. But that was his way.

Coyote liked to play tricks. He thought about himself all the time, and told everyone he was a great warrior, but he was not. Sometimes he would go too far with some trick and get someone killed. Other times, he would have a trick played on himself by someone else. He got killed this way so many times that Fox and the birds got tired of bringing him back to life. Another way he got in trouble was trying to do what someone else did. This is how he came to be called Imitator.

Coyote was ugly too. The girls did not like him. But he was smart. He could change himself around and trick the women. Coyote got the girls when he wanted.

One time, Coyote had done everything he could think of and was traveling from one place to another place, looking for other things that needed to be done. Old Man saw him going along and said to himself, "Coyote has now done almost everything he is capable of doing. His work is almost done. It is time to bring him back to the place where he started."

So Great Spirit came down and traveled in the shape of an old man. He met Coyote. Coyote said, "I am Coyote. Who are you?"

Old Man said, "I am Chief of the earth. It was I who sent you to set the world right."

"No," Coyote said, "you never sent me. I don't know you. If you are the Chief, take that lake over there and move it to the side of that mountain."

"No. If you are Coyote, let me see you do it."

Coyote did it.

"Now, move it back."

Coyote tried, but he could not do it. He thought this was strange. He tried again, but he could not do it.

Chief moved the lake back.

Coyote said, "Now I know you are the Chief."

Old Man said, "Your work is finished, Coyote. You have traveled far and done much good. Now you will go to where I have prepared a home for you."

Then Coyote disappeared. Now no one knows where he is anymore.

Old Man got ready to leave, too. He said to the Indians, "I will send messages to the earth by the spirits of the people who reach me but whose time to die has not yet come. They will carry messages to you from time to time. When their spirits come back into their bodies, they will revive and tell you their experiences.

"Coyote and myself, we will not be seen again until Earth-woman is very old. Then we shall return to earth, for it will require a change by that time. Coyote will come along first, and when you see him, you will know I am coming. When I come along, all the spirits of the dead will be with me. There will be no more Other Side Camp. All the people will live together. Earthmother will go back to her first shape and live as a mother among her children. Then things will be made right."

Now they are waiting for Coyote.

—from the Nez Perce tradition,
retold by Barry Lopez

Coyote Crooner by Rosemary "Apple Blossom" Lonewolf. Pottery ($3^1/2'' \times 4^1/2''$). Santa Clara Pueblo, New Mexico.

DIRECT TEACHING

Summary ⬇ *below grade level*

This Nez Perce myth relates how trickster Coyote created the Indians, and taught them how to live but also plays tricks on them. When the Great Spirit decides that Coyote's work on earth is completed, he sends Coyote to a resting place but tells the people that one day he and Coyote will return.

C Literary Focus

❷ Archetypes. The trickster often takes the form of an animal. What traits of Coyote help him to be a trickster? [Possible responses: Coyote is creative, imaginative, and mischievous; he is wise but fallible, self-centered but also generous.]

GUIDED PRACTICE

Monitoring students' progress. Guide the class in answering the following comprehension questions.

Short Answer

1. When did Western scholars begin to realize that Native Americans had an oral literature? [the late 1800s]

2. In "The Sky Tree," which animals make a place where Aataentsic can land? [Turtle, Beaver, Mink, Muskrat, and Otter]

3. According to "The Earth Only," which people speak the truth? [the old men]

4. Where does Old Man Above send Coyote? [to a place that Old Man Above (the Great Spirit) has prepared for him]

FAMILY/COMMUNITY ACTIVITY

Invite students to research the Native American cultures of their area. If there are no Native Americans in your class, you might have students begin at local cultural organizations and museums or the archives department of the local government or library. To complement the oral tradition represented in the text, you might ask students to present their findings orally, using photographs or other graphics as visual aids. If one or more students are Native American, they may want to invite a parent or other adult relative to present information about the community's Native past in class.

Response and Analysis

The Sun Still Rises . . .

Reading Check

1. It was a living oral tradition.
2. They teach lessons; their view is more inclusive of the natural world; they contain powerful metaphors.
3. Students should identify comparisons from paragraphs 3–5.

Thinking Critically

4. To Native Americans the nature of existence is cyclical.
5. Possible answer: They value communication between generations.

The Sky Tree

Reading Check

1. It was covered with water.
2. It falls through a great hole.
3. Animals heap soil onto Turtle's back, which becomes the new earth.

Thinking Critically

4. Supportive—they exist only because the earth does.
5. The tree; students may compare it with the tree of knowledge in the Bible.

The Earth Only

Thinking Critically

1. They are respected.
2. Humans will not endure.

Coyote Finishes His Work

Reading Check

1. The myth explains the origin of people and their customs.
2. Coyote and Great Spirit change; the earth is to change.
3. Everything "will be made right."

Thinking Critically

4. Possible answer: Great Spirit will restore earth according to his original plan.

Response and Analysis

The Sun Still Rises . . .

Reading Check

1. Why did scholars have problems recognizing the traditions of Native American literature?
2. What three generalizations does Bruchac make about American Indian oral traditions?
3. Identify three comparisons Bruchac makes between American Indian and Western views of the world.

Thinking Critically

4. What does Bruchac's **title** suggest?
5. What does the emphasis on oral literature tell you about Native American cultures?

The Sky Tree

Reading Check

1. According to this myth, what was the world like in the beginning?
2. What happens when Aataentsic cuts the tree?
3. How does this myth explain the origin of the earth as we know it today?

Thinking Critically

4. Would the people who told this myth feel hostile or supportive toward the natural world? Why?
5. What aspects of the settings in this **myth** are **archetypes**? What other stories have used the same archetypes?

The Earth Only

Thinking Critically

1. What does the idea repeated in the last three lines of this chant signify about the position of old men in this culture?

SKILLS FOCUS

Literary Skills Analyze archetypes.

Reading Skills Analyze cultural characteristics.

Writing Skills Write an essay analyzing myths.

2. What profound philosophical comment does "The Earth Only" make by what it leaves out? In other words, what does *not* endure?

Coyote Finishes His Work

Reading Check

1. What aspects of life on earth are explained in this myth?
2. **Metamorphoses,** or shape changes, are common in myths of all cultures. What metamorphoses take place in this myth?
3. What does this myth promise for the future?

Thinking Critically

4. Old Man says that when he returns, earth "will require a change." What do you think he means?
5. What does the **archetype** of the Earth-mother in this story reveal about the Nez Perce vision of nature?

Sand painting representing storm, lightning, and the four seasons, by Michael Tsosie.

WRITING

Learning Lessons

Each of these selections offers insights into an aspect of human experience. In an **essay,** analyze the myths. First, discuss these topics: what "The Sky Tree" reveals about the origins of the earth and our relationship to nature; what "The Earth Only" reminds us about our life on earth; and what "Coyote Finishes His Work" promises for the future. Then, explain how these myths relate to what Bruchac says about Native American myths in his essay. Finally, present your own thoughts on the universal, cross-cultural appeal of myths like these.

---

5. Possible answer: It shows faith in nature.

ASSESSING

Assessment

■ *Holt Assessment: Literature, Reading, and Vocabulary*

RETEACHING

For a lesson reteaching archetypes, see **Reteaching,** p. 1117A.

Anne Bradstreet
(1612–1672)

Who could have guessed that the writer who would begin the history of American poetry would be an immigrant teenage bride? This fact seems less far-fetched when we know something about the life of the young woman who came from England to America when the Colonies were no more than a few villages precariously perched between the ocean and the wilderness.

Shakespeare was still alive when Anne Bradstreet was born, and like many budding poets, she found in Shakespeare, and in other great English poets, sources of inspiration and technique that would one day run like threads of gold through the fabric of her own work. However, what most determined the course of Anne Bradstreet's life was not a poetic influence but a religious one.

Anne Bradstreet was born into a family of Puritans. She accepted their reformist views as naturally as most children accept the religious teachings of a parent. When she was about sixteen, she married a well-educated and zealous young Puritan by the name of Simon Bradstreet. Two years later, in 1630, Simon, Anne, and Anne's father journeyed across the Atlantic to the part of New England around Salem that would become known as the Massachusetts Bay Colony. There her father and then her husband rose to prominence, each serving as governor of the colony, while Anne kept house first in Cambridge, then Ipswich, and finally in Andover. She raised four boys and four girls and, without seeking an audience or publication, found time to write poems.

Bradstreet's poems might never have come to light had it not been for John Woodbridge, her brother-in-law and a minister in Andover. In 1648, he went to England and, in 1650, without consulting the author herself, published Bradstreet's poems in London under the title

The Tenth Muse Lately Sprung Up in America.

In one stroke an obscure wife and mother from the meadows of New England was placed among the nine Muses of art and learning sacred to the ancient Greeks. In itself this was embarrassing enough, but in the middle of the seventeenth century, the real arrogance was that a woman would aspire to a place among the august company of established male poets. *The Tenth Muse* fared better with critics and the public than Anne expected (later even the learned Puritan minister Cotton Mather praised her work), and she felt encouraged to write for the rest of her life.

Today Anne Bradstreet is remembered not for her elaborate earlier poems, which focus on public events, but for a few simple, personal lyrics on such topics as the birth of children, the death of grandchildren, her love for her husband, her son's departure for England, and her own illnesses and adversities. In a letter to her children just before she died, she wrote, "Among all my experiences of God's gracious dealings with me I have constantly observed this, that He hath never suffered me long to sit loose from Him, but by one affliction or other hath made me look home, and search what was amiss."

Anne Bradstreet (detail) (1948) by Harry Grylls. Stained glass.

Reproduced by kind permission of the vicar and church wardens of St. Botolph's Church, Boston, England.

SKILLS FOCUS, pp. 27–30

Grade-Level Skills

■ **Literary Skills**
Analyze the way an author's use of plain style achieves specific rhetorical or aesthetic purposes.

■ **Reading Skills**
Analyze the use of inversion.

More About the Writer
Background. The Puritans believed that woman was created as man's "helpmate" and subordinate; a good wife thus was expected to be compliant and self-effacing. Given this atmosphere, it is not surprising that Anne Bradstreet never attempted to publish her poetry herself. In fact, when her first book was published without her permission, she maintained that she was embarrassed by the "rambling brat."

RESOURCES: READING

Planning
■ *One-Stop Planner* CD-ROM with ExamView Test Generator

Differentiating Instruction
■ *Holt Reading Solutions*
■ *The Holt Reader*
■ *Holt Adapted Reader*
■ *Supporting Instruction in Spanish*

■ *Audio CD Library, Selections and Summaries in Spanish*

Grammar and Language
■ *Daily Language Activities*

Assessment
■ *Holt Assessment: Literature, Reading, and Vocabulary*
■ *One-Stop Planner* CD-ROM with ExamView Test Generator

■ *Holt Online Assessment*

Internet
■ go.hrw.com (Keyword: LE5 11-1)
■ *Elements of Literature Online*

Media
■ *Audio CD Library*
■ *Audio CD Library, Selections and Summaries in Spanish*

Summary *at grade level*

Awakened by shouts of "Fire!" the speaker escapes from her burning house and then watches as the flames consume it. Later, passing the ruins, she scolds herself for mourning the loss of her worldly goods. She reminds herself that God gave her those goods and was not unjust in taking them away. She concludes by affirming that her true riches lie in her relationship with God and her hope of Heaven.

Selection Starter

Motivate. Invite students to freewrite about how it would feel to suddenly lose all of one's possessions. Then, have them turn to Bradstreet's poem to analyze how a woman who lived four centuries ago responded to that very situation.

Build background. Although the Puritans were industrious and often acquired material goods, they considered it sinful to place too much pride on personal possessions. Bradstreet's emotional conflict between the loss of a comfortable, memory-filled home and her Puritan belief that such a loss should not overwhelm her is what gives this poem its emotional and spiritual power.

Before You Read

Here Follow Some Verses upon the Burning of Our House, July 10, 1666

Make the Connection
Quickwrite

This poem is a response to a terrible personal loss. The event that is the focus of the poem took place hundreds of years ago, but it could be a story in today's newspapers. In trying to work through her loss, this poet portrays an internal debate, a dialogue between herself and her soul. As you read, notice the points at which Bradstreet questions her own thoughts and emotions. Note also your own responses: How would you deal with the destruction of a home? Before you read, take some notes on what your response might be if all the material things you hold dear went up in flames.

Literary Focus
The Plain Style

In their style of writing, as well as in their manner of worship, the Puritans favored the plain and unornamented. Though the style used by Puritan writers now seems hard to read, in the 1600s it was considered simple and direct. This **plain style** emphasized uncomplicated sentences and the use of everyday words from common speech.

The Puritan plain style differed greatly from the ornate "high style" that was in fashion in England at the time—a style that used classical allusions, Latin quotations, and elaborate figures of speech, as in this example from the poet and Anglican clergyman John Donne:

> First, for the incomprehensibleness of God, the understanding of man hath a limited, a determined latitude; it is an intelligence able to move that sphere which it is fixed to, but could not move a greater:

I can comprehend *naturam naturatam*, created nature, but for that *natura naturans*, God himself, the understanding of man cannot comprehend.

Although Bradstreet uses figurative language in her poetry, her writing is still influenced by strong, simple Puritan style and diction. Rather than narrating a straightforward account of the burning of her house, Bradstreet records her journey from grief to spiritual solace. Present too in the poem is Bradstreet's realization that her love of material things is in danger of eclipsing her love of things divine.

> The **plain style** is a way of writing that stresses simplicity and clarity of expression.
>
> *For more on Plain Style, see the Handbook of Literary and Historical Terms.*

Reading Skills
Analyzing Text Structures: Inversion

In order to accommodate the demands of **meter** and **rhyme**, poets through the centuries have used **inversion**. In an inversion the words of a sentence or phrase are wrenched out of normal English syntax, or word order: for example, "In silent night when rest I took" instead of "In silent night when I took rest." As you read Bradstreet's poem, pay close attention to her use of inversion. Then, go through the poem line by line, and rewrite it so that these words appear in normal order.

SKILLS FOCUS

Literary Skills
Understand the characteristics of plain style.

Reading Skills
Understand the use of inversion. Rewrite inverted text in normal order.

DIFFERENTIATING INSTRUCTION

Learners Having Difficulty
Modeling. To help students read the poem, model the reading skill of analyzing inverted text. Say, "Look at the title of this poem. Bradstreet has inverted—switched around—the word order to put the emphasis on *here*. In everyday English, the title would be 'Some Verses . . . Follow Here.'" Have students rephrase other examples of inversion as they read.

Invite learners having difficulty to read "Here Follow Some Verses upon the Burning of Our House, July 10, 1666," in interactive format in *The Holt Reader* and to use the sidenotes as aids to understanding the selection.

English-Language Learners
Help students determine the meaning of such archaic English words as *oft* (often), *e'er* (ever), and *'gin* (begin).

Here Follow Some Verses upon the Burning of Our House, July 10, 1666

Anne Bradstreet

In silent night when rest I took
For sorrow near I did not look
I wakened was with thund'ring noise
And piteous shrieks of dreadful voice.
5   That fearful sound of "Fire!" and "Fire!"
Let no man know is my desire.
I, starting up, the light did spy,
And to my God my heart did cry
To strengthen me in my distress
10 And not to leave me succorless.°
Then, coming out, beheld a space
The flame consume my dwelling place.
And when I could no longer look,
I blest His name that gave and took,°
15 That laid my goods now in the dust.
Yea, so it was, and so 'twas just.
It was His own, it was not mine,
Far be it that I should repine;
He might of all justly bereft
20 But yet sufficient for us left.
When by the ruins oft I past
My sorrowing eyes aside did cast,
And here and there the places spy
Where oft I sat and long did lie:
25 Here stood that trunk, and there that chest,
There lay that store I counted best.
My pleasant things in ashes lie,
And them behold no more shall I.
Under thy roof no guest shall sit,
30 Nor at thy table eat a bit.
No pleasant tale shall e'er be told,
Nor things recounted done of old.
No candle e'er shall shine in thee,
Nor bridegroom's voice e'er heard shall be.

35 In silence ever shall thou lie,
Adieu, Adieu, all's vanity.
Then straight I 'gin my heart to chide,
And did thy wealth on earth abide?
Didst fix thy hope on mold'ring dust?
40 The arm of flesh didst make thy trust?
Raise up thy thoughts above the sky
That dunghill mists away may fly.
Thou hast an house on high erect,
Framed by that mighty Architect,
45 With glory richly furnished,
Stands permanent though this be fled.
It's purchased and paid for too
By Him who hath enough to do.
A price so vast as is unknown
50 Yet by His gift is made thine own;
There's wealth enough, I need no more,
Farewell, my pelf,° farewell my store.
The world no longer let me love,
My hope and treasure lies above.

---

52. pelf *n.:* wealth or worldly goods (sometimes used as a term of contempt).

---

10. succorless (suk′ər·lis) *adj.:* without aid or assistance; helpless.

14. that gave and took: allusion to Job 1:21, "The Lord gave, and the Lord hath taken away; blessed be the name of the Lord."

Embroidered chair-seat cover (1725–1750) owned by the Bradstreet family. Colored wool embroidered on cotton and linen twill (44 cm × 54 cm).

Museum of Fine Arts, Boston, Gift of Samuel Bradstreet (19.602).

Anne Bradstreet   **29**

INDEPENDENT PRACTICE

Response and Analysis

Thinking Critically

1. In l. 37 the speaker begins putting her material losses into spiritual perspective.

2. Her inner strength comes from her faith that her true treasure lies in Heaven. Students might suggest that many people today would be far more angry.

3. The house is Heaven, whose architect is God (l. 44). It is better than the poet's earthly home because it is richly furnished with spiritual glory.

4. She may feel that her earthly treasures have caused her to minimize the treasure of eternal life.

5. Answers should cover this progression: "When I heard the flames and 'Fire!' I cried out to God and ran from my house. I stared at the fire and blessed God. Now, when I pass the ruins, I think about my lost goods, my memories, and the events that will never take place in my house. Then I chide myself, for I have a better 'house' in Heaven."

Extending and Evaluating

6. Her faith does seem to help her overcome the human impulse to lament her misfortune.

Literary Criticism

7. Among the beliefs expressed are that God takes an interest in the individual; that all belongs to God; that earthly things have only temporary value; that there is a sanctuary in Heaven for the believer, thanks to God.

Thinking Critically

1. In this poem, Bradstreet first narrates an incident and then moves on to draw conclusions from it. What do you think is the turning point of the poem?

2. Where does Bradstreet get her inner strength to face the loss of her house? How do you think someone today might deal with the same situation? Look back at your Quickwrite notes for ideas.

3. Bradstreet speaks of another "house" in an **extended metaphor** at the end of the poem. What is this house, who is its architect, and how is it better than the house she has lost?

4. *Pelf*—a word designating riches or worldly goods—is usually used only when the riches or goods are considered to be slightly tainted, ill-gotten, or stolen. Why do you suppose Bradstreet uses such a bitter word in line 52 to describe her own cherished treasures?

5. Using your "noninverted" version of the poem as a starting point, write a paraphrase of the entire poem. (A **paraphrase** is a restatement of a text in your own words.)

Extending and Evaluating

6. Some readers have felt that by so lovingly enumerating her losses, Bradstreet is crying out to heaven in a way that unconsciously reveals more attachment to her earthly possessions than she would admit to. On the other hand, what Bradstreet does not reveal in this poem is significant: Hundreds of books, as well as her papers and all her unpublished poems, were also lost in the fire. Using specific examples from the text, explain why you are, or are not, convinced that the speaker means what she says.

go.hrw.com

INTERNET
Projects and Activities
Keyword: LE5 11-1

SKILLS FOCUS

Literary Skills
Analyze the use of plain style.

Writing Skills
Write an essay analyzing a writer's attitude.

Listening and Speaking Skills
Present an oral performance of a poem.

Literary Criticism

7. Think about the major Puritan beliefs as you re-read this poem. What philosophical beliefs about God and the purpose of human life are reflected in Bradstreet's poem?

WRITING

Trials and Tribulations

In the Book of Job from the Bible, Job endures great misery, yet he is still able to say, "The Lord gave, and the Lord hath taken away; blessed be the name of the Lord" (Job 1:21). Bradstreet expresses a similar attitude in her poem; twice she checks herself from mourning over the loss of her beloved possessions. The first instance is in lines 14–20; the second begins with line 37. In a brief **essay,** discuss Bradstreet's attitude toward earthly suffering and the providence of God. Cite details from the poem to support your analysis.

LISTENING AND SPEAKING

Oral Performance

Get together with a partner, and practice reading Bradstreet's poem aloud. Pay close attention to the meter, the inexact rhymes, and the pronunciation of unfamiliar words. Then, present an oral performance of the poem. Decide who will speak at what point, which words to emphasize, and how to use body language to enhance the reading.

ASSESSING

Assessment

■ *Holt Assessment: Literature, Reading, and Vocabulary*

RETEACHING

For a lesson reteaching irony, tone, and author's style see **Reteaching,** p. 1117A.

Literature of the Americas

Mexico

Sor Juana Inés de la Cruz
(1651–1695)

Even as a child growing up in a Mexican village, Juana Ramirez de Asbaje displayed an extraordinary love of learning. At six, she begged her mother to dress her as a boy and send her to the university in Mexico City. Her request was denied, so the child threw herself into reading in her grandfather's library—a world of books that in the seventeenth century was generally available only to men. Young Juana was hard on herself; she cut off her hair if she failed to learn Latin grammar according to her own schedule.

At sixteen, Juana was presented at the court of the Spanish viceroy in Mexico City, where she charmed everyone, according to reports. She served as a lady-in-waiting for four years, then abruptly entered a convent, taking the name Sor (Sister) Juana Inés de la Cruz. Her career is summed up by Octavio Paz (1914–1998), the Nobel Prize–winning poet from Mexico who wrote a critical study of Sor Juana's life and work:

❝There was nothing ordinary about her person or her life. She was exceptionally beautiful, and poor. She was the favorite of a Vicereine [wife of a viceroy] and lived at court, courted by many; she was loved and perchance she loved. Abruptly she gives up worldly life and enters a convent—yet far from re-nouncing the world entirely, she converts her cell into a study filled with books, works of art, and scientific instruments and transforms the convent locutory [room for conversation] into a literary and intellectual salon. She writes love poems, verses for songs and dance tunes, profane comedies, sacred poems, an essay in theology, and an autobiographical defense of the right of women to study and cultivate their minds. She becomes famous, sees her plays performed, her poems published, and her genius applauded in all the Spanish dominions, half the Western world. Then suddenly she gives up everything; surrenders her library and collections; renounces literature; and finally, during an epidemic, after ministering to stricken sisters in the convent, dies at the age of forty-six.❞

Sister Juana Inés de la Cruz (1750) by Miguel Cabrera (1695–1768). Oil on canvas.

SKILLS FOCUS, pp. 31–34

Grade-Level Skills

■ **Literary Skills**

Analyze characteristics of subgenres of poetry, including Petrarchan sonnets.

Review Skills

■ **Literary Skills**

Analyze various literary devices, including figurative language, imagery, allegory, and symbolism.

VIEWING THE ART

Miguel Cabrera (1695–1768) of Mexico City specialized in portraits and religious paintings. The two types of art are combined in this idealized portrait, created several decades after Sor Juana's death.

Activity. Ask students what they can infer about Sor Juana's personality from the portrait. [Possible response: She is quiet, intense, and serious.] After students read selections from Sor Juana's biography, ask them if they think the portrait depicts her accurately. [Possible responses: Yes, it shows her engaged in the scholarship for which she is famous. No, for it shows only one side of her personality.]

SOR JVANA INES DE LA CRVZ

RESOURCES: READING

Planning

■ *One-Stop Planner* CD-ROM with ExamView Test Generator

Differentiating Instruction

■ *Holt Reading Solutions*

■ *The Holt Reader*

■ *Supporting Instruction in Spanish*

■ *Audio CD Library, Selections and Summaries in Spanish*

Grammar and Language

■ *Daily Language Activities*

Assessment

■ *Holt Assessment: Literature, Reading, and Vocabulary*

■ *One-Stop Planner* CD-ROM with ExamView Test Generator

■ *Holt Online Assessment*

Internet

■ go.hrw.com (Keyword: LE5 11-1)

■ *Elements of Literature Online*

Media

■ *Audio CD Library*

■ *Audio CD Library, Selections and Summaries in Spanish*

Summary ⬆ *above grade level*

> Instead of setting her mind on achieving wealth and comeliness, the speaker chooses to focus on things of beauty—a treasure that will outlast all earthly vanities.

Skills Starter

Motivate. Explain that song lyrics are poetry; they usually have a structure, rhythm, and rhyme scheme.

More About the Writer

Background. Sor (Sister) Juana critiqued a sermon given years before by Antonio de Vieyra. In response, the bishop of Puebla published the comments, and wrote a letter under the pen name "Sor Philotea de la Cruz," in which he criticized her scholarly pursuits. In 1691, Sor Juana published her *Reply to Sor Philotea*. She wrote of the importance of studying "all the things that God created." Not long afterward, Sor Juana sold books, scientific equipment, and musical instruments and donated the money to the poor; shortly after that, Sor Juana signed a confession and dedicated her life solely to religious duties.

Before You Read

World, in hounding me . . .

Make the Connection
Quickwrite ✏

To *hound* means to "chase or follow; nag." Consider the title of this poem. What does it mean when the world hounds you? Write down your first thoughts on the significance of the poem's title.

Literary Focus
Sonnet

The **sonnet** is a fourteen-line lyric poem that is built around a strict structure. Sor Juana's sonnet is a **Petrarchan sonnet,** a form popularized in the fourteenth century by the Italian poet Petrarch. The Petrarchan sonnet is divided into two parts: an eight-line octave (from the Latin *octo,* meaning "eight"), with the rhyme scheme *abba abba,* and a six-line sestet (from the Latin *sex,* meaning "six"), with the rhyme scheme *cde cde* or *cdc dcd.* (The letters simply indicate a rhyming sound: Each line that ends with one rhyming sound is marked "a," each line that ends with another rhyming sound is marked "b," and so on.) In a strict Petrarchan sonnet the octave poses a question or states an idea, and the sestet then answers the question or restates the poet's point more forcefully.

You might ask why some poets choose to follow such tough rules. Perhaps these poets enjoy the challenge of expressing their ideas within strict forms. Robert Frost, a great American poet, said that writing poetry without paying attention to structure is like playing tennis without the net.

SKILLS FOCUS

Literary Skills
Understand the characteristics of a Petrarchan sonnet.

> A **sonnet** is a rhymed fourteen-line poem, usually written in iambic pentameter.
>
> *For more on Sonnet, see the Handbook of Literary and Historical Terms.*

Background

In her time, Sor Juana was called "the tenth muse from Mexico," just as Anne Bradstreet was called "the tenth muse lately sprung up in America." Although both poets possessed a strong creative force, the personal lives of Bradstreet and Sor Juana were vastly different. Bradstreet was fundamentally a private person, a Puritan wife and mother, who wrote poems but did not seek publication. Sor Juana, although a devout Catholic nun, had served at court, acquired the education of a scholar, written plays and song lyrics, and presided over a salon—a regular gathering of distinguished literary and intellectual guests.

Octavio Paz considered Sor Juana's poems to be among "the most elegant and refined in Spanish. Few poets in our language equal her, and those who surpass her can be counted on the fingers of one hand." Her style is an example of Spanish baroque writing in the Americas, with its intricate verse forms, its interplay of the intellectual and the sensual, and its verbal dexterity and wit. In 1974, at a ceremony in Mexico, Sor Juana was awarded the title First Feminist of the Americas.

In the following poem by Sor Juana, the word *vanity* plays an important role. It means an empty pursuit that is characterized by conceit and is ultimately worthless. For Sor Juana the word would also have carried echoes of the powerful exclamation of the preacher at the beginning of Ecclesiastes in the Bible: "Vanity of vanities; all is vanity."

DIFFERENTIATING INSTRUCTION

Learners Having Difficulty
Line breaks. As students approach Sor Juana's poem, point out that line breaks do not necessarily mean breaks in thought. Point out, for example, how l. 2 needs l. 3 to complete its thought. Have students try reading the sonnet sentence by sentence instead of line by line.

Invite learners having difficulty to read

"World, in hounding me . . ." in interactive format in *The Holt Reader* and to use the side-notes as aids to understanding the selection.

English-Language Learners
You might have students whose first language is Spanish focus on the Spanish text of the sonnet. Other English-language learners might master the poem by listing the things that the speaker says could occupy one's mind and

World, in hounding me…

Sor Juana Inés de la Cruz

translated by **Alan S. Trueblood**

World, in hounding me, what do you gain?
How can it harm you if I choose, astutely,
rather to stock my mind with things of beauty,
than waste its stock on every beauty's claim?

5　　Costliness and wealth bring me no pleasure;
the only happiness I care to find
derives from setting treasure in my mind,
and not from mind that's set on winning treasure.
　　I prize no comeliness.° All fair things pay
10　to time, the victor, their appointed fee
and treasure cheats even the practiced eye.
　　Mine is the better and the truer way:
to leave the vanities of life aside,
not throw my life away on vanity.

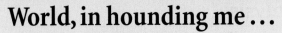

°**comeliness** *n.:* beauty.

En perseguirme, mundo…

Sor Juana Inés de la Cruz

En perseguirme, mundo, ¿qué interesas?
¿En qué te ofendo, cuando sólo intento
poner bellezas en mi entendimiento
y no mi entendimiento en las bellezas?

5　　Yo no estimo tesoros ni riquezas;
y así, siempre me causa más contento
poner riquezas en mi pensamiento
que no mi pensamiento en las riquezas.
　　Y no estimo hermosura que, vencida,
10　es despojo civil de las edades,
ni riqueza me agrada fementida,
　　teniendo por mejor, en mis verdades,
consumir vanidades de la vida
que consumir la vida en vanidades.

SOR JVANA INES DE LA CRVZ

33

Response and Analysis

Thinking Critically

1. Possible answer: World, what good does it do you to hunt me down? How am I hurting you if I wisely choose to fill my mind with true spiritual beauty instead of false earthly beauty?

2. In l. 8, she is referring to the worldly wealth that she disdains; in l. 7, the "treasure" is spiritual beauty or knowledge.

3. Possible answer: The "fair things" are personified as someone who is "paying" time, which is personified as "the victor"; treasure is personified as a "cheat." Possible restatement: "All physical beauty is eventually conquered by time, and treasure escapes even those who were the most skillful at accumulating it."

4. Possible answer: "The things of this physical life that people care about the most—wealth and physical beauty—ultimately fade, so I will fill my mind with the kinds of beauty and treasure that last." The speaker says this in ll. 3–4, ll. 6–8, and ll. 12–14.

5. Students may point out that the Spanish-language rhyme scheme is on target (although the rhyme in the English translation is approximate) but that the sonnet does not follow the Petrarchan standard of devoting the octave to a question and the sestet to its answer; instead, the main idea is developed throughout.

Extending and Evaluating

6. Students may feel that the title is ineffective because its thought or attitude clearly is incomplete. Comparisons will vary and need not be shared; some students may decide that their Quickwrite thoughts are not as "spiritual" as the speaker's.

Response and Analysis

Thinking Critically

1. The first four lines of "World, in hounding me . . ." consist of two **rhetorical questions**—questions that are asked for effect. Rhetorical questions don't need to be answered because the answers are obvious. Restate Sor Juana's opening questions in your own words.

2. The word *treasure* is used in different ways in lines 7 and 8. What kind of treasure is Sor Juana referring to in each of these lines?

3. In lines 9–11, Sor Juana uses **personification** in talking about "fair things," "time," and "treasure." How does she personify these three nonhuman things? Restate these lines in your own words.

4. How would you state the **theme** of the poem? Which words or lines convey the theme most clearly for you?

5. How closely has Sor Juana followed the structure of the **Petrarchan sonnet**? (See the Literary Focus on page 32.) To answer this question, focus first on the original Spanish. Then, analyze the English translation.

Extending and Evaluating

6. How effective is the poem's title in conveying the speaker's attitude toward the world? How does it compare with your own point of view? (Check your Quickwrite notes.) ✎

SKILLS FOCUS

Literary Skills
Analyze a Petrarchan sonnet.

Writing Skills
Write an essay comparing and contrasting poems from different cultures.

WRITING

Comparing Literature

Religion strongly influenced Sor Juana's and Anne Bradstreet's writings. Sor Juana, however, was from Latin America and had a Catholic background, while Bradstreet was from New England and had a Puritan background. Re-read Bradstreet's poem "Here Follow Some Verses upon the Burning of Our House, July 10, 1666" (page 29). In a brief essay, **compare and contrast** the two poems, including the use of the word *vanity* in each. Before you write, gather your details in a chart like the one that follows. Remember to use specific quotations from the poems to support your ideas.

	Sor Juana	Bradstreet
Topic		
Theme		
Use of metaphor		
Use of rhyme		
Key words in poem		

ASSESSING

Assessment

■ *Holt Assessment: Literature, Reading, and Vocabulary*

Mary Rowlandson
(c. 1636–c. 1711)

From June 1675 to August 1676, the Wampanoag chief, Metacomet, called King Philip by the colonists, carried out a series of bloody raids on Colonial settlements in what is now called King Philip's War. This conflict was the natural result of growing encroachments by the settlers on American Indian land. The native people of New England had been forced into ever more restricted areas, and although they had sold the land, they rejected conditions stipulating that they could no longer hunt on it. To them "selling" meant selling the right to share the land with the buyers, not selling its exclusive ownership.

Matters came to a head when Metacomet's former assistant, who had given information to the colonists, was killed by his own people. His killers were tried and hanged by the Puritans. This was too much for Metacomet to bear, and two weeks later the most severe war in the history of New England began. Its tragic result was the virtual extinction of the indigenous way of life in the region. Among the war's victims was Mary Rowlandson, the wife of the Congregational minister of Lancaster, a frontier town that was located thirty miles west of Boston. In February 1676, she and her three children were carried away by a Wampanoag raiding party that wanted to trade hostages for money. After eleven weeks and five days of captivity, Rowlandson's ransom was paid.

Not long after the family's reunion, which included the return of their two surviving children, the Rowlandsons resettled in Wethersfield, Connecticut. In 1678, Mary's husband, Joseph, died, and the following year she married Capt. Samuel Talcott, a wealthy landowner. Mary Rowlandson lived in Wethersfield until her death, around 1711.

Rowlandson's story was horrific, but it is important to realize that her captors were only slightly better off than their prisoners. Virtually without food, the Wampanoag were chased from camp to camp by Colonial soldiers. Their captives, they thought, were the only currency with which to buy supplies and food. In a graphic passage, Rowlandson describes the lengths to which the Wampanoag were driven by their hunger, eating horses, dogs, frogs, skunks, rattlesnakes, and even tree bark. "They would pick up old bones," she wrote, "and cut them to pieces at the joints, and if they were full of worms and maggots, they would scald them over the fire to make the vermin come out, and then boil them, and drink up the liquor. . . . They would eat horse's guts, and ears, and all sorts of wild birds which they could catch. . . . I can but stand in admiration," she concluded, "to see the wonderful power of God in providing for such a vast number of our enemies in the wilderness, where there was nothing to be seen."

Rowlandson's narrative not only presents a terrifying and moving tale of frontier life but also provides insight into how the Puritans viewed their lives—with a characteristic double vision. For Rowlandson, as for other Puritans, events had both a physical and a spiritual significance. She did not want merely to record her horrifying experience; she wished to demonstrate how it revealed God's purpose. The full title of her narrative (as published in 1682) illustrates this intention: *The Soveraignty and Goodness of God, Together with the Faithfulness of His Promises Displayed: Being a Narrative of the Captivity and Restauration of Mrs. Mary Rowlandson.*

Courtesy of American Antiquarian Society.

SKILLS FOCUS, pp. 35–43

Grade-Level Skills

■ **Literary Skills**
Analyze the way an author's style, including the use of allusions, affects the meaning of the text.

■ **Reading Skills**
Analyze the way patterns of organization, including chronological order, affect the meaning of a text.

More About the Writer

Background. Mary Rowlandson was born in England as Mary White, one of John and Joan White's ten children. The family left England for Salem, Massachusetts, in 1639. They moved in 1653 to the new village of Lancaster, where Mary later became a wife and mother. When the raid on Lancaster came, John Rowlandson was in Boston, seeking help from the Massachusetts General Assembly in regard to the problems with the Wampanoag. The townspeople who were killed in the raid included Mary's sister and her sister's family. Mary and her children were among the townspeople taken captive.

RESOURCES: READING

Planning
■ *One-Stop Planner* CD-ROM with ExamView Test Generator

Differentiating Instruction
■ *Supporting Instruction in Spanish*
■ *Audio CD Library, Selections and Summaries in Spanish*

Vocabulary
■ *Vocabulary Development*

Grammar and Language
■ *Daily Language Activities*

Assessment
■ *Holt Assessment: Literature, Reading, and Vocabulary*
■ *One-Stop Planner* CD-ROM with ExamView Test Generator

■ *Holt Online Assessment*

Internet
■ *go.hrw.com (Keyword: LE5 11-1)*
■ *Elements of Literature Online*

Media
■ *Audio CD Library*
■ *Audio CD Library, Selections and Summaries in Spanish*

Summary ⬌ at grade level

Mary Rowlandson chronicles her experience as a captive of the Wampanoag during King Philip's War. After being kidnapped by the retreating tribe, she tries to take care of her daughter Sarah, who has been wounded in the raid. The weather, however, is cold; they have no food and little water; and Sarah soon dies. Rowlandson visits briefly with her son and her other daughter, also captives, and she accepts the gift of a Bible from a Native American warrior. Throughout her captivity, the Wampanoag are on the run from the English. Although food is scarce, Rowlandson earns money and tidbits of meat by sewing. Many of her captors treat her kindly, but what ultimately sustains her is reading the Bible and trusting in God.

Skills Starter

Build review skills. Explain to students that chronological order often is signaled by a variety of words and expressions. In Rowlandson's narrative, the subheads provide some sense of sequence, but time signals also appear throughout the text. Offer these examples: "this day in the afternoon"; "when I came"; "till they came"; "then"; "during my abode"; "afterward."

Point out that time signals may indicate events that happened before, after, or during other events.

Before You Read

from A Narrative of the Captivity . . .

Make the Connection
Quickwrite ✏️

Who hasn't listened with rapt attention to stories of people enduring life-threatening circumstances—a flood, a plane crash on a snowy mountain, an earthquake, or captivity as a hostage? Perhaps our fascination with such stories comes from wondering how we would survive if we were put to the same test. In your notebook, write your thoughts on what might help a person survive a life-threatening situation.

Literary Focus
Allusions

The Puritans regarded biblical captivity narratives, such as that of the enslavement of the Israelites by the ancient Egyptians, as allegories representing the Christians' liberation from sin through the intervention of God's grace. Rowlandson views her experiences as a repetition of the biblical pattern and uses **allusions** to reflect her own situation. Through apt quotations from the Bible, Rowlandson places her experiences in the context of the ancient biblical captivities.

INTERNET

Vocabulary Practice
•
Cross-Curricular Connection

Keyword: LE5 11-1

> An **allusion** is a reference to someone or something well known from history, literature, religion, politics, sports, science, or some other branch of culture.
>
> *For more on Allusion, see the Handbook of Literary and Historical Terms.*

SKILLS FOCUS

Literary Skills
Understand allusions.

Reading Skills
Understand chronological order.

Reading Skills 📖
Analyzing Text Structures: Chronological Order

As you read, keep track of events and their impact on Rowlandson by taking notes in a three-column chart. Use the first column to list events in **chronological order** (also called time or sequential order). Use the second column to note where Rowlandson links her sufferings with those of people in the Bible. Use the third column to record her comments about her captors in relation to some of the events. In those comments, be sure to note Rowlandson's **word choice,** especially her use of emotional language. You will have more entries in the first column than in either of the other two.

Events in chrono- logical order	References to Bible	Comments about captors

Vocabulary Development

tedious (tē′dē·əs) *adj.*: tiring; dreary.

lamentable (lam′ən·tə·bəl) *adj.*: regrettable; distressing.

entreated (en·trēt′id) *v.*: asked sincerely; begged.

afflictions (ə·flik′shənz) *n. pl.*: pains; hardships.

plunder (plun′dər) *n.*: goods seized, especially during wartime.

melancholy (mel′ən·käl′ē) *adj.*: sad; sorrowful.

savory (sā′vər·ē) *adj.*: appetizing; tasty.

bewitching (bē·wich′iŋ) *v.* used as *adj.*: enticing; irresistible.

Previewing Vocabulary

Have students read the definitions of the Vocabulary words on p. 36 and express each definition in their own words. Then, have students complete the following sentences with the correct Vocabulary words.

1. The sad story of captivity makes the reader feel _____. [melancholy]

2. The _____ song of the whales lured them to the water's edge. [bewitching]

3. The Puritans stole corn from the Indians and shared this _____. [plunder]

4. Rowlandson _____ King Philip to free her and her children. [entreated]

5. She was blind and lame, but these _____ did not prevent her from succeeding. [afflictions]

6. Were those first Thanksgiving turkeys as _____ as ours? [savory]

7. How you will regret those _____ words! [lamentable]

8. That _____ task both bored and fatigued us. [tedious]

In the opening part of her narrative, Mary Rowlandson describes the attack on Lancaster, in which twelve people were killed and twenty-four taken captive, and the assault on her own house. During the raid, Mary and her six-year-old child Sarah, whom she refers to as her "babe," were wounded. The first part of this selection recounts Mary's move from Princeton to Braintree, Massachusetts, two days after the raid in Lancaster.

from A Narrative of the Captivity . . .

Mary Rowlandson

The Move to an Indian Village on the Ware River, Near Braintree (February 12–27)

The morning being come, they prepared to go on their way. One of the Indians got up upon a horse, and they set me up behind him, with my poor sick babe in my lap. A very wearisome and tedious day I had of it; what with my own wound, and my child's being so exceeding sick, and in a lamentable condition with her wound. It may be easily judged what a poor feeble condition we were in, there being not the least crumb of refreshing that came within either of our mouths from Wednesday night to Saturday night, except only a little cold water. This day in the afternoon, about an hour by sun, we came to the place where they intended, *viz.*[1] an Indian town, called Wenimesset, norward of Quabaug. . . . I sat much alone with a poor wounded child in my lap, which moaned night and day, having nothing to revive the body, or cheer the spirits of her, but instead of that, sometimes one Indian would come and tell me one hour, that your master will knock your

A

B

child in the head, and then a second, and then a third, your master will quickly knock your child in the head.

This was the comfort I had from them, miserable comforters are ye all, as he said.[2] Thus

C

___

2. **he said:** The biblical allusion is to Job 16:2. In the passage cited, Job addresses those who try to console him. God had severely tested Job's faith by causing Job to lose his children and his money and to break out in boils all over his body.

___

Vocabulary
tedious (tē′dē·əs) *adj.:* tiring; dreary.
lamentable (lam′ən·tə·bəl) *adj.:* regrettable; distressing.

___

1. ***viz.:*** abbreviation for the Latin word *videlicet,* for "namely."

Mary Rowlandson **37**

A Reading Skills

? Analyzing text structures: Chronological order. How do you think the chronological order of the narrative relates to Rowlandson's emotional state? [Possible response: Her precision in structuring the account suggests that she is trying to recall every detail of a profound experience.]

B Literary Focus

? Characterization. Consider what Rowlandson says about herself. What does her reaction to her daughter's death and burial suggest about her character? [Possible response: She is both sad about and resigned to her situation. She also is clearheaded and full of faith.]

C Advanced Learners

Enrichment. Ask students to provide more information about this allusion to Genesis 42:36. [Direct students to Genesis 37–48 for more information. Jacob's favorite son, Joseph, is sold into slavery by his ten older brothers, who are jealous of him. Years later, during a famine, Jacob sends the ten to Egypt to procure food. Now the Pharaoh's administrator, Joseph helps them without revealing his true identity; but he tells them to bring their youngest brother, Benjamin, to Egypt. Simeon remains behind in Egypt to ensure that the brothers comply. Although Rowlandson may be dwelling on Jacob's grief upon hearing this news, she also may be remembering that the story ends with a joyful family reunion—much as she hopes to have with her surviving family members.]

nine days I sat upon my knees, with my babe in my lap, till my flesh was raw again; my child being even ready to depart this sorrowful world, they bade me carry it out to another wigwam (I suppose because they would not be troubled with such spectacles) whither I went with a very heavy heart, and down I sat with the picture of death in my lap. About two hours in the night, my sweet babe like a lamb departed this life, on February 18, 1675. It being about six years and five months old. It was nine days from the first wounding, in this miserable condition, without any refreshing of one nature or another, except a little cold water. I cannot but take notice, how at another time I could not bear to be in the room where any dead person was, but now the case is changed; I must and could lie down by my dead babe, side by side all the night after. I have thought since of the wonderful goodness of God to me, in preserving me in the use of my reason and senses, in that distressed time, that I did not use wicked and violent means to end my own miserable life. In the morning, when they understood that my child was dead they sent for me home to my master's wigwam: (by my master in this writing, must be understood Quanopin, who was a Sagamore,[3] and married King Philip's wife's sister; not that he first took me, but I was sold to him by another Narragansett Indian, who took me when first I came out of the garrison). I went to take up my dead child in my arms to carry it with me, but they bid me let it alone: There was no resisting, but go I must and leave it. When I had been at my master's wigwam, I took the first opportunity I could get, to go look after my dead child: When I came I asked them what they had done with it. Then they told me it was upon the hill: Then they went and showed me where it was, where I saw the ground was newly digged, and there they told me they had buried it: There I left that child in the wilderness, and must commit it, and myself also in this wilderness condition, to him who is above all. God having taken away

this dear child, I went to see my daughter Mary, who was at this same Indian town, at a wigwam not very far off, though we had little liberty or opportunity to see one another. She was about ten years old, and taken from the door at first by a Praying Ind.[4] and afterward sold for a gun. When I came in sight, she would fall aweeping; at which they were provoked, and would not let me come near her, but bade me be gone; which was a heart-cutting word to me. I had one child dead, another in the wilderness, I knew not where, the third they would not let me come near to: "Me (as he said) have ye bereaved of my Children, Joseph is not, and Simeon is not, and ye will take Benjamin also, all these things are against me."[5] I could not sit still in this condition, but kept walking from one place to another. And as I was going along, my heart was even overwhelmed with the thoughts of my condition, and that I should have children, and a nation which I knew not ruled over them. Whereupon I earnestly entreated the Lord, that He would consider my low estate, and show me a token for good, and if it were His blessed will, some sign and hope of some relief. And indeed quickly the Lord answered, in some measure, my poor prayers: For as I was going up and down mourning and lamenting my condition, my son came to me, and asked me how I did; I had not seen him before, since the destruction of the town, and I knew not where he was, till I was informed by himself, that he was amongst a smaller parcel of Indians, whose place was about six miles off; with tears in his eyes, he asked me whether his sister Sarah was dead; and told me he had seen his sister Mary; and prayed me, that I would not be troubled in reference to

---

4. **Praying Ind.:** American Indians who converted to Christianity were known as praying Indians. The Colonial assemblies allowed these converts to live in self-governing towns.
5. **Me . . . against me:** Rowlandson quotes Jacob's lament in Genesis 42:36. Jacob had only his youngest son, Benjamin, at home.

Vocabulary
entreated (en·trēt′id) v.: asked sincerely; begged.

---

3. **Sagamore** (sag′ə·môr′) n.: secondary chief in the hierarchy of several American Indian peoples.

Secondary Source

Women and Power

In an essay about King Philip's War, David Rickert of Georgetown University writes of the conflict between Rowlandson and Wetamo: "Wetamo was a 'squaw sachem'— a woman who led the Wampanoag village of Pocasset. Wetamo had allied herself with King Philip (Metacom) early in the war, and despite the tradition of wifely obedience to one's hus- band was, on her own initiative, one of the key leaders during the conflict. Mary Rowlandson, however, never recognized Wetamo's independent authority, which caused conflict between the two throughout her captivity. . . . As part of a more patriar- chal society, Mrs. Rowlandson found it difficult to understand Wetamo's behavior as other

himself. . . . I cannot but take notice of the wonderful mercy of God to me in those afflictions, in sending me a Bible. One of the Indians that came from Medfield fight, had brought some plunder, came to me, and asked me, if I would have a Bible, he had got one in his basket. I was glad of it, and asked him, whether he thought the Indians would let me read. He answered, yes: So I took the Bible, and in that melancholy time, it came into my mind to read first the 28th chapter of Deuteronomy,[6] which I did, and when I had read it, my dark heart wrought on this manner, that there was no mercy for me, that the blessings were gone, and the curses come in their room, and that I had lost my opportunity. But the Lord helped me still to go on reading till I came to Chapter 30 the seven first verses, where I found, there was mercy promised again, if we would return to Him by repentance; and though we were scattered from one end of the earth to the other, yet the Lord would gather us together, and turn all those curses upon our enemies. I do not desire to live to forget this Scripture, and what comfort it was to me. . . .

The Fifth Remove **F**

The occasion (as I thought) of their moving at this time, was, the English Army, it being near and following them: For they went, as if they had gone for their lives, for some considerable way, and then they made a stop, and chose some of their stoutest men, and sent them back to hold the English Army in play while the rest escaped: And then, like Jehu,[7] they marched on furiously, with their old, and with their young: Some carried their old decrepit[8] mothers, some carried one, and some another. Four of them

---

6. **28th chapter of Deuteronomy:** In Deuteronomy 28, Moses warns that God will bless those who obey Him and curse those who do not.
7. **Jehu** (jē′hōō′): Israelite king of the ninth century B.C. Jehu was said to be a "furious driver" (2 Kings 9:20), and Rowlandson's allusion here is to the speed and fury with which her captors moved away from the English army.
8. **decrepit** *adj.:* run-down; worn out by age or use.

carried a great Indian upon a bier; but going through a thick wood with him, they were hindered, and could make no haste; whereupon they took him upon their backs, and carried him, one at a time, till they came to Bacquaug River. Upon a Friday, a little after noon we came to this river. When all the company was come up, and were gathered together, I thought to count the number of them, but they were so many, and being somewhat in motion, it was beyond my skill. In this travel, because of my wound, I was somewhat favored in my load; I carried only my knitting work and two quarts of parched meal: Being very faint I asked my mistress to give me one spoonful of the meal, **G** but she would not give me a taste. They quickly fell to cutting dry trees, to make rafts to carry them over the river: and soon my turn came to go over: By the advantage of some brush which they had laid upon the raft to sit upon, I did not wet my foot (which many of themselves at the other end were midleg deep) which cannot but be acknowledged as a favor of God to my weakened body, it being a very cold time. I was not before acquainted with such kind of doings or dangers. "When thou passeth through the waters I will be with thee, and through the Rivers they shall not overflow thee," Isaiah, 43:2. A certain number of us got over the river that night, but it was the night after the Sabbath before all the company was got over. On the Saturday they boiled an old horse's leg which they had got, and so we drank of the broth, as soon as they thought it was ready, and when it was almost gone, they filled it up again.

The first week of my being among them, I hardly ate anything; the second week, I found my stomach grow very faint for want of something; and yet it was very hard to get down their filthy trash: but the third week, though I could think how formerly my stomach would turn

Vocabulary

afflictions (ə·flik′shənz) *n. pl.:* pains; hardships.
plunder (plun′dər) *n.:* goods seized, especially during wartime.
melancholy (mel′ən·käl′ē) *adj.:* sad; sorrowful.

than just a woman being excessively assertive. Wetamo, however, was acting out a role which was acceptable in her own culture. It is also of interest to note that, as a minister's wife, Mary Rowlandson was a high-status individual in her own Puritan society. Yet she would have no chance to have the kind of power which Wetamo possessed."

DIRECT TEACHING

D **Content-Area Connections**

Culture: Puritans and the Bible
❓ Think of what you know about the Puritans. Why would acquiring a Bible be so important to Rowlandson? [Possible responses: As a Puritan, she regards the Bible as a holy book; the Bible contains many stories and other writings that comfort her; it is a familiar object.]

E **Reading Skills**
❓ **Identifying cause and effect.** Why does this biblical passage comfort Rowlandson? [Possible response: It gives her hope that she will be reunited with her family—either by the Puritans in this life or by God in heaven.]

F **Correcting Misconceptions**

Students may be confused about Rowlandson's title for this new section. Explain that *remove* here is a noun, not a verb, and that it means "occasion of moving from one location to another." Students will read that the reason for this "remove" is pursuit by the English army.

G **Vocabulary Development**
❓ **Words in context.** In this setting, the term *mistress* means "a woman who employs servants." Given what you know of Rowlandson's situation, what other word or words might she have used? [Since Rowlandson was sold by the Indian who took her captive (p. 38), she might use words such as *owner* or *slaveholder*.]

A Vocabulary Development

? Synonyms. In general use, what is another word for *pagans*? [Possible responses: *nonbelievers; infidels; heathens.*] What is another word that you think Rowlandson would have used? [Possible responses: *Indians; Wampanoag.*]

B Reading Skills

? Speculating. When Rowlandson wants to comfort herself, she turns to the Bible. The Wampanoag try to comfort her by giving her food. Why do you think they do this? [Possible responses: Since food is life-sustaining, it would show her that they do not mean to harm her; it is tangible proof of their good will—and food is the only thing they have that Rowlandson wants.]

A Closer Look: Social Influences

To help students understand the captivity experience, ask them in groups of three to research various Native American groups—such as the Iroquois, Abenaki, Mohawk, Huron, Penobscot, Cherokee, Shawnee, and Comanche—who took captives or were in contact with captives. Students should explore why these groups took such actions. Have each group elect one student to sit on a panel that relates the groups' findings to the rest of the class.

against this or that, and I could starve and die before I could eat such things, yet they were sweet and savory to my taste. . . .

The Sixth Remove

We traveled on till night; and in the morning, we must go over the river to Philip's crew. When I was in the canoe, I could not but be amazed at the numerous crew of pagans that were on the bank on the other side. When I came ashore, they gathered all about me, I sitting alone in the midst: I observed they asked one another questions, and laughed, and rejoiced over their gains and victories. Then my heart began to fail: And I fell aweeping which was the first time to my remembrance, that I wept before them. Although I had met with so much affliction, and my heart was many times ready to break, yet could I not shed one tear in their sight: but rather had been all this while in a maze, and like one astonished: But now I may say as, Psalm 137:1, "By the rivers of Babylon, there we sat down: yea, we wept when we remembered Zion." There one of them asked me, why I wept, I could hardly tell what to say: Yet I answered, they would kill me: "No," said he, "none will

Vocabulary

savory (sā′vər·ē) *adj.:* appetizing; tasty.

A CLOSER LOOK: SOCIAL INFLUENCES

Captivity Narratives

INFORMATIONAL TEXT

A Narrative of the Captivity, Sufferings, and Removes of Mrs. Mary Rowlandson was one of the most widely read prose works of the seventeenth century. It was especially popular in England, where people were eager for lurid tales of native inhabitants of the Americas. Rowlandson's story went through at least thirty editions, and it inspired a mass of imitations that were often partially or purely fictional. These "captivity" stories became one of the most widely produced forms of entertainment in America, but they had a tragic side effect: They contributed to the further deterioration of relations between American Indians and colonists.

Between the seventeenth and nineteenth centuries, as settlers moved westward and occupied American Indian lands, tensions between the two groups increased. American Indians, in retaliation for various injustices, raided settlements and took captives to ransom, enslave, or sell to the French or to other native peoples. These captives didn't necessarily suffer grim fates: Some captives actually chose to remain with their captors and were adopted by them; a few married American Indi-

ans and never expressed any desire to return to their original homes. Many of those who escaped or were ransomed recorded their experiences when they returned home. Eventually thousands of captivity tales—of varying quality and accuracy—sprouted up all over the country. Scarcely any first editions of these books remain, as they were literally read and re-read to shreds by an eager public.

From Providence to propaganda. Because early captivity narratives were almost all told from the limited first-person point of view, they often failed to mention settlers' actions that may have provoked American Indian aggression. Typically seventeenth-century captivity narratives begin with a brief description of a raid and the rounding up of hostages; they then focus on the gritty details of the day-to-day struggle for survival. The captives in these early narratives generally accept their condition as a punishment sent by God to test their faith, and any relief from their suffering is always evidence of divine Providence, not sympathy from their captors. By the eighteenth century, continuing animosity between settlers and American Indians, aggravated by the French and Indian War, led to a different kind of captivity narrative, one that was an undisguised ex-

Analyzing genre. Explain to students that because Mary Rowlandson writes from the heart, her narrative reveals inconsistencies, which commonly mark personal writing. **Activity.** Have small groups of students use these questions to discuss the concept. (Possible responses are given.)

• In the first paragraph on p. 37, why do you think that Rowlandson isn't more clear about what made the day "wearisome and tedious"? [Perhaps she was so concerned with her daughter's care that she didn't remember the specifics of other aspects of the day; perhaps it just saddened her too much to remember more details.]

• In what subtle ways does Rowlandson change over the course of the narrative? **Explain.** [She grows emotionally stronger. For example, she resolves to spend the night with the body of her daughter and, later, to eat food that formerly would have revolted her.]

hurt you." Then came one of them and gave me two spoonfuls of meal to comfort me, and another gave me half a pint of peas; which was more worth than many bushels at another time. Then I went to see King Philip, he bade me come in and sit down, and asked me whether I would smoke it (a usual compliment nowadays amongst saints and sinners) but this no way suited me. For though I had formerly used tobacco, yet I had left it ever since I was first taken. It seems to be a bait, the devil lays to make men lose their precious time: I remember with shame, how formerly, when I had taken two or three pipes, I was presently ready for another, such a bewitching thing it is: But I thank **C**

God, He has now given me power over it; surely there are many who may be better employed than to lie sucking a stinking tobacco pipe.

Now the Indians gather their forces to go against North Hampton: Overnight one went about yelling and hooting to give notice of the design. Where upon they fell to boiling of groundnuts, and parching of corn (as many as had it) for their provision: And in the morning away they went. During my abode[9] in this place, **D**

---

9. abode (ə·bōd′) *n.*: stay.

Vocabulary
bewitching (bē·wich′iŋ) *v.* used as *adj.*: enticing; irresistible.

pression of hatred toward American Indians. No longer were captivity narratives instructive tales of physical and spiritual survival in the wilderness; now they were inflammatory propaganda, assertions of European superiority.

Sensationalism and stereotypes.
By the early nineteenth century, propaganda had turned into pure sensationalism. Journalists and authors of lurid fiction, gifted at manipulating the fantasies and prejudices of the reading public, revised the original narratives. They pulled out all the stops, using melodramatic plot devices and long passages of grisly detail. The public eagerly read these penny dreadfuls (the popular term for cheap magazines with tales of horror and crime), shuddering with mixed fascination and horror at fictional tales of American Indian atrocities and the suffering of innocent captives. The tawdriness of these publications didn't go unnoticed by more educated readers. Many actual nineteenth-century captives were reluctant to publish their stories, afraid that by association with sleazy popular magazines, their experiences would not be taken seriously.

Some historians have argued that captivity narratives, by advancing the stereotype of the "savage Indian," made it easier for settlers to justify occupation of American Indian lands. By

Museum of Art, Rhode Island School of Design. Gift of Mr. Robert Winthrop (48.246).

Portrait of Ninigret II, Chief of the Niantic Indians (detail) (c. 1681). Oil on canvas (33 1/8″ × 30 1/8″).

the late nineteenth century, with the "Indian threat" a thing of the past, captivity narratives gradually became less popular. Unfortunately, though, stereotypes of the "bad" Indian and the "virtuous" European settler remained in the popular imagination well into the twentieth century, appearing in countless western novels, Hollywood movies, and television programs.

Mary Rowlandson **41**

C **Content-Area Connections**
Culture: Tobacco
The Wampanoag believe that tobacco is a sacred substance that comes from the bones of the First Mother. To them, smoking signifies commitment and a request for support. Discuss why Rowlandson refuses King Philip's offer of a smoke and how Philip might have reacted. [Possible response: She viewed tobacco as a temptation of the devil; to Philip, it was a way to make contact with the spiritual world, and he may have been insulted by her refusal.]

D **Reading Skills**
? **Analyzing text structures: Chronological order.** At what point in this group of events do the Wampanoag prepare provisions of groundnuts and corn? [after word is received about the plan for attack and before the warriors leave the encampment]

VIEWING THE ART

Portrait of Ninigret II shows a chief who was a contemporary of Rowlandson. Colonial portrait painters found Native Americans fascinating subjects because of their colorful costumes and (to the European eye) exotic features.

Activity. Ask students what kind of character Ninigret seems to have, based on the portrait. [Possible response: He seems strong and decisive but does not look cruel; on the other hand, the presence of the club and knife suggests that he can be intimidating when necessary.]

Advanced Learners
Enrichment. Explain to students that King Philip was angry that some settlers had used alcohol to entice the Wampanoag to sell their land. He said that "only a small part of the land of my ancestors remains and I am determined not to live until I have no country." Tell students that King Philip did not live to see this catastrophe, for he was defeated and killed within a year. His head was displayed on

a pike in Plymouth for at least twenty years after his death. Given this background information, have students choose partners and role-play the conversation between Rowlandson and King Philip. Partners should discuss why Rowlandson wanted to see the chief, why he agreed to see her, and what they might have discussed. Students can enact the conversation for the class.

❓ Analyzing text structures: Chronological order. How would you characterize the way in which, over time, Rowlandson's relationship with her captors changes? [Possible response: As the weeks pass, Rowlandson grows more courageous, and the relationship becomes one of economic interdependence. She becomes less like a prisoner and more like a paid servant, although occasionally she is treated like a guest or acts like a host.]

GUIDED PRACTICE

Monitoring students' progress. Guide the class in answering these comprehension questions. Direct students to locate passages in the text that support their responses.

True-False

1. After her capture by the Wampanoag, Rowlandson is not allowed to see her children. [F]

2. One of Rowlandson's captors gives her a stolen Bible. [T]

3. Despite the constant travel and cold, the Native Americans have plenty of food. [F]

4. Rowlandson smokes a pipe with King Philip to avoid offending him. [F]

5. Rowlandson interprets her captivity as God's test of her faith. [T]

Philip spoke to me to make a shirt for his boy, which I did, for which he gave me a shilling: I offered the money to my master, but he bade me keep it: And with it I bought a piece of horseflesh. Afterward he asked me to make a cap for his boy, for which he invited me to dinner. I went, and he gave me a pancake, about as big as two fingers; it was made of parched wheat, beaten, and fried in bear's grease, but I thought I never tasted pleasanter meat in my life. There was a squaw who spoke to me to make a shirt for her *sannup*,[10] for which she gave me a piece of bear. Another asked me to knit a pair of stockings, for which she gave me a quart of peas: I boiled my peas and bear together, and invited my master and mistress to dinner, but the proud gossip, because I served them both in one dish, would eat nothing, except one bit that he gave her upon the point of his knife. . . .

A

The Move to the Ashuelot Valley, New Hampshire

But instead of going either to Albany or homeward, we must go five miles up the river, and then go over it. Here we abode awhile. Here lived a sorry Indian, who spoke to me to make him a shirt. When I had done it, he would pay me nothing. But he living by the riverside, where I often went to fetch water, I would often be putting of him in mind, and calling for my pay: At last he told me if I would make another shirt, for a papoose not yet born, he would give me a knife, which he did when I had done it. I carried the knife in, and my master asked me to give it him, and I was not a little glad that I had anything that they would accept of, and be pleased with. When we were at this place, my master's maid came home, she had been gone three weeks into the Narragansett country, to fetch corn, where they had stored up some in the ground: She brought home about a peck and half of corn. This was about the time that

their great captain, Naananto, was killed in the Narragansett country. My son being now about a mile from me, I asked liberty to go and see him, they bade me go, and away I went: but quickly lost myself, traveling over hills and through swamps, and could not find the way to him. And I cannot but admire at the wonderful power and goodness of God to me, in that, though I was gone from home, and met with all sorts of Indians, and those I had no knowledge of, and there being no Christian soul near me; yet not one of them offered the least imaginable miscarriage to me. I turned homeward again, and met with my master, he showed me the way to my son. . . .

But I was fain[11] to go and look after something to satisfy my hunger, and going among the wigwams, I went into one, and there found a squaw who showed herself very kind to me, and gave me a piece of bear. I put it into my pocket, and came home, but could not find an opportunity to broil it, for fear they would get it from me, and there it lay all that day and night in my stinking pocket. In the morning I went to the same squaw, who had a kettle of groundnuts boiling; I asked her to let me boil my piece of bear in her kettle, which she did, and gave me some groundnuts to eat with it: And I cannot but think how pleasant it was to me. I have sometime seen bear baked very handsomely among the English, and some like it, but the thoughts that it was bear, made me tremble: But now that was savory to me that one would think was enough to turn the stomach of a brute creature.

One bitter cold day, I could find no room to sit down before the fire: I went out, and could not tell what to do, but I went in to another wigwam, where they were also sitting round the fire, but the squaw laid a skin for me, and bid me sit down, and gave me some groundnuts, and bade me come again: and told me they would buy me, if they were able, and yet these were strangers to me that I never saw before. . . . ■

---

10. *sannup* (san′up′) *n.:* husband.

11. **fain** *adj.:* archaic word meaning "glad; ready."

FAMILY/COMMUNITY ACTIVITY

One of the thoughts that sustains Mary Rowlandson in her captivity is the hope that she will see her husband and children again. Thus, the importance of family is a thread that runs throughout the narrative. Urge students to tell their families about Rowlandson's ordeal. In addition, invite students to work with one or more family members to create a piece of artwork (such as a collage or a quilt) that expresses their unity as a family. Allow interested students to share the results of this activity.

Response and Analysis

Reading Check

1. List in **chronological order** the main events of Rowlandson's narrative.

2. How is Rowlandson treated by her captors?

3. Find details that reveal that Rowlandson's captors are themselves desperate to find food.

Thinking Critically

4. What conflicting attitudes, if any, does Rowlandson reveal toward her captors? Do you think her attitude changes as the narrative progresses? Explain.

5. The Puritans' habit of seeing spiritual meanings in their experiences helped them find significance in even minor events. Describe at least two **allusions** to biblical stories that Rowlandson makes during her captivity. In what specific ways does each of these biblical stories resemble Rowlandson's experiences?

6. Rowlandson's narrative was enormously popular in England. What reasons can you propose for its popularity? What aspects of Rowlandson's narrative might have promoted stereotyped and hostile views toward American Indians?

Extending and Evaluating

7. Despite her efforts to be accurate, Rowlandson's narrative is full of **subjective reporting.** Instead of using neutral language, she relies on emotionally loaded words—words with strong positive or negative **connotations.** Select any extract from Rowlandson's narrative, and find the emotionally loaded words or phrases that reveal her attitude toward her captors. What words or phrases does Rowlandson use that a detached, objective historian would *not* use?

WRITING

Survival Skills

In his classic work of psychology, *Man's Search for Meaning,* Viktor Frankl, a survivor of the Nazi concentration camps of World War II, claims that survival in the camps depended less on physical endurance and general health than on an internal sense that the experience, no matter how horrifying, had some ultimate meaning for the prisoner. Those who had strong religious faith, committed political views, or even just a strong love of family were far more likely to survive, both physically and mentally. In a brief **essay,** identify and discuss Mary Rowlandson's ultimate source of strength. How does her story compare with other captivity stories you've read or seen dramatized on TV? Be sure to provide details from Rowlandson's account in your response. ✏️

Vocabulary Development

Synonyms

Match each Vocabulary word from the list below with the word that is closest in meaning. When you have finished matching, find the place in the text where the Vocabulary word is underlined. Can its synonym be substituted for Mary Rowlandson's original word, or are there subtle distinctions between the meanings of the two words?

1. tedious	asked
2. lamentable	delicious
3. entreated	enchanting
4. afflictions	hardships
5. plunder	loot
6. melancholy	sad
7. savory	tiresome
8. bewitching	unfortunate

INTERNET

Projects and Activities

Keyword: LE5 11-1

SKILLS FOCUS

Literary Skills
Analyze allusions.

Reading Skills
Analyze chronological order.

Writing Skills
Write an essay analyzing a narrative.

Vocabulary Skills
Understand synonyms.

Mary Rowlandson 43

Response and Analysis

5. Possible answers: Like Job, she endures hardships; she compares herself to Jacob, who laments for his children; she feels that they are being driven like the Israelites.

6. Students' answers will vary. Possible answers: The account does not relate the colonists' mistreatment of Native Americans, and it makes her captors appear overly cruel.

Extending and Evaluating

7. Possible answers: She calls her captors "miserable comforters" (p. 37); she calls the food "filthy trash" (p. 39).

Vocabulary Development

Answers

1. tiresome	5. loot
2. unfortunate	6. sad
3. asked	7. delicious
4. hardships	8. enchanting

ASSESSING

Assessment

■ *Holt Assessment: Literature, Reading, and Vocabulary*

RETEACHING

For a lesson reteaching patterns of organization, see **Reteaching,** p. 1117A.

Reading Check

1. See Summary on p. 36 for a chronology of the narrative's main events.

2. Rowlandson's captors treat her with some cruelty but also give her a Bible and food and pay her fairly for her sewing.

3. boiling the horse's leg; rationing meat

Thinking Critically

4. At first, Rowlandson dislikes her captors for not being troubled by events such as her daughter's death. However, she eventually sees them as being capable of kindness and generosity.

Grade-Level Skills

■ **Literary Skills**

Analyze ways poets use figures of speech.

Review Skills

■ **Literary Skills**

Identify the literary devices that define a writer's style.

More About the Writer

Background. Edwards was also the loving, affectionate, and thoughtful father of eleven children. When his daughter Esther was nine years old, she wrote movingly about a ride in the woods that they took together: "Though father is usually taciturn or preoccupied . . . today he discoursed to me of the awful sweetness of walking with God in nature. He seems to feel God in the woods, the sky, and the grand sweep of the river. . . ."

VIEWING THE ART

Jonathan Edwards's portrait is one of about 150 that **Joseph Badger** (1708–1765), at one time the chief portrait artist of Boston, painted between about 1740 and 1765. Some art historians consider Badger something of an amateur and call his style stiff and repetitive; it should be remembered, however, that Badger succeeded in his own time even though he did not have access to formal (specifically, European) artistic training.

Activity. Have students think about this portrait as they read the excerpt from "Sinners in the Hands of an Angry God." What in the portrait makes them believe or not believe that the person it depicts preached the fiery sermon?

Jonathan Edwards
(1703–1758)

Yale University Art Gallery. Bequest of Eugene Phelps Edwards (1938.74).

Despite his fire-and-brimstone imagery, Jonathan Edwards was not merely a stern, zealous preacher. He was a brilliant, thoughtful, and complicated man. Science, reason, and observation of the physical world confirmed Edwards's deeply spiritual vision of a universe filled with the presence of God.

Edwards's abilities were recognized early. Groomed to succeed his grandfather as pastor of the Congregational Church in Northampton, Massachusetts, Edwards entered Yale when he was only thirteen. When his grandfather died in 1729, Edwards mounted the pulpit and quickly established himself as a strong-willed and charismatic pastor.

Edwards's formidable presence and vivid sermons helped to bring about the religious revival known as the Great Awakening. This revival began in Northampton in the 1730s and, during the next fifteen years, spread throughout the Eastern Seaboard. The Great Awakening was marked by waves of conversions that were so intensely emotional as to amount at times to mass hysteria.

The Great Awakening began at a time when enthusiasm for the old Puritan religion was declining. To offset the losses in their congregations, churches had been accepting growing numbers of "unregenerate" Christians—people who accepted church doctrine and lived upright lives but who had not confessed to being born again in God's grace, and so were not considered to be saved.

Edwards became known for his extremism as a pastor. In his sermons he didn't hesitate to accuse prominent church members by name of relapsing into sin. Edwards's strictness eventually proved to be too much for his congregation, and in 1750, he was dismissed from

Reverend Jonathan Edwards (1750–1755) by Joseph Badger. Oil on canvas (28½″ × 22″).

his prestigious position as pastor of Northampton. After rejecting a number of pastorships offered to him, Edwards relocated to the raw and remote Mohican community of Stockbridge, Massachusetts. After eight years of missionary work in virtual exile, shared with his wife, Sarah, Edwards was named president of the College of New Jersey (later called Princeton University). Three months after assuming this position, he died of a smallpox inoculation—a modern medical procedure that, ironically, had been promoted by the fierce Puritan minister Cotton Mather.

Intellectually, Edwards straddled two ages: the modern, secular world exemplified by such men as Benjamin Franklin (page 67) and the religious world of his zealous Puritan ancestors. He believed (like Franklin) in reason and learning, the value of independent intellect, and the power of the human will. On the other hand, he believed (like Mather) in the lowliness of human beings in relation to God's majesty and in the ultimate futility of merely human efforts to achieve salvation. Edwards, as "the last Puritan," stood between Puritan America and modern America. Tragically, he fit into neither world.

Before You Read

from Sinners in the Hands of an Angry God

Make the Connection
Quickwrite ✏️

Many people would agree that fear is one of the most powerful motivators of human behavior. Fear of injury makes us buckle our seat belts. Fear of failure makes us study or work harder. Edwards and other pastors used harsh warnings in their sermons to make "sinners" understand the precariousness of their situation by actually *feeling* the fear and horror of their sinful state. Do you think fear is a great motivator? Take a few moments to write about what motivates you and whether you would use fear to motivate someone else.

Literary Focus
Figures of Speech

Figures of speech describe one thing in terms of another, very different thing. Although Edwards's belief in eternal damnation is literal, he uses figures of speech to compare God's wrath to ordinary, everyday things that his listeners could relate to and understand.

> **Figures of speech** are words or phrases that compare one thing to another, unlike thing.
>
> *For more on Figures of Speech, see the Handbook of Literary and Historical Terms.*

Background

This is Edwards's most famous sermon, which he delivered on a visit to the congregation at Enfield, Connecticut, in 1741. The "natural men" he was trying to awaken were those in the congregation who had not been "born again," meaning they had not accepted Jesus as their savior. Edwards was influenced by the work of the English philosopher John Locke (1632–1704). Locke believed that everything we know comes from experience, and he emphasized that understanding and feeling were two distinct kinds of knowledge. (To Edwards the difference between these two kinds of knowledge was like the difference between reading the word *fire* and actually being burned.) Edwards's sermon had a powerful effect; several times he had to ask his shrieking and swooning audience for quiet.

Vocabulary Development

provoked (prə·vōkt′) *v.* used as *adj.:* angered.

appease (ə·pēz′) *v.:* calm; satisfy.

constitution (kän′stə·tōō′shən) *n.:* physical condition.

contrivance (kən·trī′vəns) *n.:* scheme; plan.

inconceivable (in′kən·sēv′ə·bəl) *adj.:* unimaginable; beyond understanding.

omnipotent (äm·nip′ə·tənt) *adj.:* all-powerful.

abhors (ab·hôrz′) *v.:* scorns; hates.

abominable (ə·bäm′ə·nə·bəl) *adj.:* disgusting; loathsome.

ascribed (ə·skrībd′) *v.:* regarded as coming from a certain cause.

induce (in·dōōs′) *v.:* persuade; force; cause.

INTERNET
Vocabulary Practice
Keyword: LE5 11-1

SKILLS FOCUS

Literary Skills
Understand figures of speech.

Jonathan Edwards   45

PRETEACHING

Summary ⬆️ *above grade level*

In this fire-and-brimstone sermon, Edwards uses extended metaphors to argue that those who have not accepted Christ as their Savior live on the brink of damnation and the torments of Hell. Edwards believes that these people's only chance for salvation is a transforming religious experience. He warns those who are not "born again" to realize that God could drop them into the gaping pit of Hell at any moment. By stressing the tenuousness of their everyday lives, Edwards hopes that these "natural men" will abandon their wickedness, throw themselves upon God's mercy, and ask to be saved.

Selection Starter

Build background. Students do not need theological training to understand Edwards, but they may appreciate his sermon more if you explain its evangelistic intent. Note that *evangelism* literally means "the bringing of good news"—specifically, the good news of salvation through faith in Jesus Christ. If students find it hard to reconcile the sharing of "good news" with the fiery tone of Edwards's sermon, point out that he was trying to awaken people who already knew about the Gospel (the biblical accounts of Jesus' ministry, death, and resurrection) but who, he felt, had never made a personal commitment to its message and who were complacent in their religious tradition.

Previewing Vocabulary

Have students work in pairs to study the Vocabulary words on p. 45 and test one another's mastery by playing a game. One partner generates synonyms for each word; the other tries to guess the word from the synonyms. Have partners change roles and play another round. To review, students can match the following synonyms (left-hand column) with the Vocabulary words (right-hand column).

1. enraged [e]
2. unimaginable [h]
3. attributed [j]
4. satisfy [d]
5. all-powerful [i]
6. persuade [b]
7. plan [f]
8. disgusting [c]
9. hates [a]
10. physical condition [g]

a. abhors
b. induce
c. abominable
d. appease
e. provoked
f. contrivance
g. constitution
h. inconceivable
i. omnipotent
j. ascribed

from

Sinners in the Hands of an Angry God

Jonathan Edwards

A **Literary Focus**

? **Figures of speech.** In personification, a writer speaks of nonhuman things as if they were people. In this passage, how does Edwards personify Hell and its fires? [He says that Hell is "gaping," as if it has a mouth, and that its flames want to "lay hold on" and "swallow" natural men.] What detail does he use to personify God? [He speaks of God as having hands.]

Response to Boxed Question

1. It drives home the concept that sinners live on the brink of Hell and enumerates some of the torments that await them there.

S o that, thus it is that natural men[1] are held in the hand of God, over the pit of hell; they have deserved the fiery pit, and are already sentenced to it; and God is dreadfully <u>provoked</u>, His anger is as great toward them as to those that are actually suffering the executions of the fierceness of His wrath in hell, and they have done nothing in the least to <u>appease</u> or abate[2] that anger, neither is God in the least bound by any promise to hold them up one moment: The devil is waiting for them, hell is gaping for them, the flames gather and flash about them, **①** and would fain[3] lay hold on them, and swallow them up; the fire pent up in

①

Note how Edwards uses **parallelism** in these lines: "The devil is waiting for them, hell is gaping for them, the flames gather and flash about them."

? *How does the parallel structure build a sense of horror?*

---

1. **natural men:** people who have not been "reborn."
2. **abate** *v.:* reduce in amount or intensity.
3. **fain** *adv.:* archaic word meaning "happily" or "gladly."

Vocabulary

provoked (prə·vōkt′) *v.* used as *adj.:* angered.
appease (ə·pēz′) *v.:* calm; satisfy.

The Progress of Sin (detail) (1744) by Benjamin Keach.
Sinclair Hamilton Collection no. 21. Graphic Arts Division. Department of Rare Books and Special Collections. Princeton University Library.

Learners Having Difficulty
Planning a reading strategy. To help students keep on track as they read this excerpt from "Sinners in the Hands of an Angry God," urge them to create a KWL chart. In the first column, have them note some things that they know about the Puritans and their religion. In the second column, students should list a few questions that they hope the selection will answer. As students read, they can use the third column to note information that they have learned from the selection.

Invite learners having difficulty to read "Sinners in the Hands of an Angry God" in interactive format in *The Holt Reader* and to use the sidenotes as aids to understanding the selection.

English-Language Learners
For lessons designed for English-language learners and special education students, see *Holt Reading Solutions*.

their own hearts is struggling to break out: And they have no interest in any Mediator,[4] there are no means within reach that can be any security to them.

In short, they have no refuge, nothing to take hold of; all that preserves them every moment is the mere arbitrary will, and uncovenanted, unobliged forbearance[5] of an incensed[6] God.

The use of this awful subject may be for awakening unconverted persons in this congregation. This that you have heard is the case of every one of you that are out of Christ. ❷ That world of misery, that lake of burning brimstone, is extended abroad under you. There is the dreadful pit of the glowing flames of the wrath of God; there is hell's wide gaping mouth open; and you have nothing to stand upon, nor anything to take hold of; there is nothing between you and hell but the air; it is only the power and mere pleasure of God that holds you up.

You probably are not sensible of this; you find you are kept out of hell, but do not see the hand of God in it; but look at other things, as the good state of your bodily <u>constitution</u>, your care of your own life, and the <u>means</u> you use for your own preservation. But indeed these things are nothing; if God should withdraw His hand, they would avail no more to keep you from falling, than the thin air to hold up a person that is suspended in it.

Your wickedness makes you as it were heavy as lead, and to tend downward with great weight and pressure toward hell; and if God should let you go, you would immediately sink and swiftly descend and plunge into the bottomless gulf, and your healthy constitution, and your own care and prudence, and best <u>contrivance</u>, and all your righteousness, would

? *Whom does Edwards address in his sermon, and what does he hope it will accomplish?*

have no more influence to uphold you and keep you out of hell, than a spider's web would have to stop a fallen rock. . . . ❸

The wrath of God is like great waters that are dammed for the present; they increase more and more, and rise higher and higher, till an outlet is given; and the longer the stream is stopped, the more rapid and mighty is its course, when once it is let loose. It is true, that judgment against your evil works has not been executed hitherto; the floods of God's vengeance have been withheld; but your guilt in the meantime is constantly increasing, and you are every day treasuring up more wrath; the waters are constantly rising, and waxing more and more mighty; and there is nothing but the mere pleasure of God that holds the waters back, that are unwilling to be stopped, and press hard to go forward. If God should only withdraw His hand from the floodgate, it would immediately fly open, and the fiery floods of the fierceness and wrath of God, would rush forth with inconceivable fury, and would come upon you with <u>omnipotent</u> power; and if your strength were ten thousand times greater than it is, yea, ten thousand times greater than the strength of the stoutest, sturdiest devil in hell, it would be nothing to withstand or endure it.

The bow of God's wrath is bent, and the arrow made ready on the string, and justice bends the arrow at your heart, and strains the bow, and it is nothing but the mere pleasure of God, and that of an angry God, without any promise or obligation at all, that keeps the arrow one moment from being made drunk

❸ Edwards uses a **metaphor** here to dramatize human powerlessness: People who think they can escape Hell on their own have as little chance of doing so as a spider's web has of stopping a falling rock.

Vocabulary

constitution (kän′stə·tōō′shən) *n.*: physical condition.
contrivance (kən·trī′vəns) *n.*: scheme; plan.
inconceivable (in′kən·sēv′ə·bəl) *adj.*: unimaginable; beyond understanding.
omnipotent (äm·nip′ə·tənt) *adj.*: all-powerful.

---

4. **Mediator:** Jesus Christ. In general, one who intervenes between two parties in conflict.
5. **forbearance** *n.*: tolerance or restraint.
6. **incensed** *v.* used as *adj.*: angered; enraged.

Jonathan Edwards **47**

READING MINI-LESSON

Developing Word-Attack Skills

Use the word *omnipotence* to illustrate that a word's pronunciation is not always the sum of its parts. Point out that the word is made up of the combining form *omni–,* which means "all," and *potence,* which is a variation of *potency,* meaning "strength." However, if you pronounce the word by just combining the two parts—/äm′ni/ and /pōt′əns/—you would pronounce it incorrectly. The word is

correctly pronounced /äm·nip′ə·təns/. Cite *extraordinary* as another example. Instead of /eks′trə·ôrd′′n·er′ē/, the word is pronounced /ek·strôrd′′n·er′ē/.

Point out that not all words with the combining forms *omni–* and *extra–* have this shift in stress. In fact, only a limited number do. To illustrate this, have students compare *omnipotence* with *omnipresence* and *extraordinary* with *extrasensory.*

Activity. Display these sets of prefixes or combining forms and words. Have volunteers combine the parts, say the word, and indicate if the stress shifts (as it does in *omnipotence*) or stays the same (as it does in *omnipresence*).

1. omni– science [äm·nish′əns—shift]
2. extra– mural [eks′trə·myoor′əl—no shift]
3. para– meter [pə·ram′ ət·ər—shift]
4. para– graph [par′ ə·graf′—no shift]

Jonathan Edwards **47**

A **Reading Skills**

? **Recognizing persuasive technique.** What do you think makes this final paragraph especially persuasive? [Possible responses: the heart-rending "O sinner!"; the passion with which he speaks; the distillation of his argument into a few sentences that dramatically build, detail upon detail.]

Responses to Boxed Questions

4. Possible response: Like an archer ready to loose an arrow, God is ready to send justice upon the nonbeliever.

5. Possible response: The listeners may be good people, but unless they have experienced a profound spiritual transformation, they are doomed. The Spirit of God will convince them.

6. The two creatures are a spider and a poisonous snake.

7. Call on volunteers to identify previous statements of this idea in the sermon.

8. Repeating the word *nothing* emphasizes his statement that people cannot be saved by anything but their acceptance of God's grace. The repetition suggests the urgency of the call to repentance.

Monitoring students' progress. Direct students to locate three statements that when taken together provide an accurate summary of Edwards's sermon. [Possible response: "That world of misery, that lake of burning brimstone, is extended abroad under you"; "Thus all you that never passed under a great change of heart . . . are in the hands of an angry God"; "Consider the fearful danger you are in. . . . "]

---

with your blood. **4** Thus all you that never passed under a great change of heart, by the mighty power of the Spirit of God upon your souls; all you that were never born again, and made new creatures, and raised from being dead in sin, to a state of new, and before altogether unexperienced light and life, are in the hands of an angry God. However you may have reformed your life in many things, and may have had religious affections,[7] and may keep up a form of religion in your families and closets,[8] and in the house of God, it is nothing but His mere pleasure that keeps you from being this moment swallowed up in everlasting destruction. However unconvinced you may now be of the truth of what you hear, by and by you will be fully convinced of it. **5** Those that are gone from being in the like circumstances with you, see that it was so with them; for destruction came suddenly upon most of them; when they expected nothing of it, and while they were saying, peace and safety: Now they see, that those things on which they depended for peace and safety, were nothing but thin air and empty shadows.

The God that holds you over the pit of hell, much as one holds a spider, or some loathsome insect over the fire, abhors you, and is dreadfully provoked: His wrath toward you burns like fire; He looks upon you as worthy of nothing else but to be cast into the fire; He is of purer eyes than to bear to have you in His sight; you are ten thousand times more abominable in His eyes than the most hateful venomous serpent is in ours. **6** You have offended Him infinitely more than

4 Edwards uses a **metaphor** to describe God's wrath. Explain this metaphor in your own words.

? **5** What main point does Edwards want his listeners to understand? Who or what does he say will convince them?

? **6** What two creatures does Edwards compare sinners to in this passage?

7. **affections** *n. pl.:* feelings.
8. **closets** *n. pl.:* rooms for prayer and meditation.

---

ever a stubborn rebel did his prince; and yet it is nothing but His hand that holds you from falling into the fire every moment. It is to be ascribed to nothing else, that you did not go to hell the last night; that you was suffered to awake again in this world, after you closed your eyes to sleep. And there is no other reason to be given, why you have not dropped into hell since you arose in the morning, but that God's hand has held you up. There is no other reason to be given why you have not gone to hell, since you have sat here in the house of God, provoking His pure eyes by your sinful wicked manner of attending His solemn worship. Yea, there is nothing else that is to be given as a reason why you do not this very moment drop down into hell. **7**

O sinner! Consider the fearful danger you are in: It is a great furnace of wrath, a wide and bottomless pit, full of the fire of wrath, that you are held over in the hand of that God, whose wrath is provoked and incensed as much against you, as against many of the damned in hell. You hang by a slender thread, with the flames of divine wrath flashing about it, and ready every moment to singe it, and burn it asunder;[9] and you have no interest in any Mediator, and nothing to lay hold of to save yourself, nothing to keep off the flames of wrath, nothing of your own, nothing that you ever have done, nothing that you can do, to induce God to spare you one moment. . . . **8**

7 Here Edwards repeats one of his **main ideas:** that the only reason his listeners have not fallen into the fires of Hell is that God has held them up.

? **8** How does Edwards use **repetition** to increase the emotional effect of his sermon?

9. **asunder** *adv.:* into pieces.

Vocabulary

abhors (ab·hôrz′) *v.:* scorns; hates.
abominable (ə·bäm′ə·nə·bəl) *adj.:* disgusting; loathsome.
ascribed (ə·skrībd′) *v.:* regarded as coming from a certain cause.
induce (in·doos′) *v.:* persuade; force; cause.

Whether or not students agree with Edwards's doctrine, they might be prompted by his sermon to discuss spiritual matters with family members. Alternatively, students and families might find out which churches in the community acknowledge themselves as spiritual descendants of Jonathan Edwards.

Response and Analysis

Reading Check

1. Find the direct statement in which Edwards sets forth the **purpose** of his sermon.

2. According to the sermon, what keeps sinners out of the fiery "pit of hell"?

3. Identify the three famous **figures of speech** that Edwards develops in the fourth through seventh paragraphs. What things is he comparing in each one?

Thinking Critically

4. What references in the sermon reveal Edwards's implicit philosophical beliefs about divine mercy?

5. Edwards was directing his sermon to what he calls "natural men," those members of his congregation who had not been "reborn." What **images** and **figures of speech** might have helped Edwards's listeners to *feel* the peril of their sinful condition?

6. Edwards struck fear into the hearts of his listeners in order to persuade them to act to avoid everlasting torment. Which specific **metaphors** and **similes** in the sermon were probably the most persuasive?

Extending and Evaluating

7. If you had a chance to respond to Edwards, what would you say?

8. Edwards believed that fear was a great motivator, yet many philosophers and politicians have disagreed. For example, President Franklin Delano Roosevelt, in his first inaugural address, made this famous comment about fear: "The only thing we have to fear is fear itself." What do you think of the use of fear as a motivator? Before you answer, look back at your Quickwrite notes. What motivation might work better than fear?

WRITING

The Tone of the Time

Edwards's fiery words were delivered to the congregation of a church he was visiting. What is Edwards's **tone,** or attitude toward his audience, and what effect does this attitude have on his listeners? Consider how Edwards's sermon would differ if he had chosen a different style or diction. Write a brief **essay** in which you analyze Edwards's tone and then consider what would happen if that tone were different. Would the sermon be as effective?

Vocabulary Development
Prefixes and Suffixes

provoked	contrivance	abominable
appease	omnipotent	ascribed
constitution	abhors	induce

Just a few letters tacked onto the beginning of a word (a **prefix**) or the end of a word (a **suffix**) can change its meaning and often its part of speech. When you find an unfamiliar word, look for prefixes and suffixes that provide clues to how the base form of the word changes. Keep in mind that –s, –ed, and –ing are inflectional suffixes (suffixes that indicate the tense or case of a word rather than changing its meaning). Fill out a chart like the one below for each remaining Vocabulary word. Consult a dictionary to find the origins of words and the meanings of prefixes and suffixes.

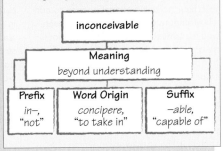

INTERNET

Projects and Activities

Keyword: LE5 11-1

SKILLS FOCUS

Literary Skills
Analyze figures of speech.

Writing Skills
Write an essay analyzing tone.

Vocabulary Skills
Understand prefixes and suffixes.

Jonathan Edwards   **49**

Response and Analysis

5. Edwards's sensory images—such as flames, "thin air," and the description of singeing and burning—make listeners feel the danger.

6. Students may cite any of the images cited above or the simile of God looking at sinners in the way in which one looks at a spider or a serpent.

Extending and Evaluating

7. Answers will vary. Some students may say they hope that God is more merciful than Edwards thinks.

8. Some students may feel that if fear is the only way to motivate someone to necessary action, its use of fear might be justified. Other students may suggest that people can be motivated by compassion, patriotism, or other noble feelings.

ASSESSING

Assessment

■ *Holt Assessment: Literature, Reading, and Vocabulary*

RETEACHING

For lessons reteaching irony, tone, and authors style, see **Reteaching,** p. 1117A.

Reading Check

1. Edwards's statement of purpose appears in the third paragraph: "The use of this awful subject may be for awakening unconverted persons in this congregation."

2. Only God's authority keeps sinners from falling into Hell.

3. The wrath of God is compared to dammed waters, with God holding back the "fiery floods"; a bent bow, whose tension is increasing as justice prepares to loose the arrow of God's vengeance upon those "out of Christ." Sinners are compared to "loathsome" spiders held over the fire and threatened with being dropped into the flames.

Thinking Critically

4. Possible answers: Edwards's ideas about mercy are couched in figurative language—for example, his reference to Christ as the "Mediator" and to God's hand holding his listeners out of Hell.

Grade-Level Skills

■ **Literary Skills**
Understand the characteristics of subgenres of prose, including autobiographies.

■ **Reading Skills**
Make inferences about an author's beliefs.

More About the Writer

Background. In 1762, four years before Equiano finally bought his freedom, he thought he was about to become a free man. The British naval officer he had served with during the Seven Years' War had promised to free Equiano after the war. Instead, he tricked him and sold him to a ship captain, who brought Equiano to the West Indies: "Thus, at the moment I expected all my toils to end, was I plunged . . . in a new slavery: in comparison of which all my service hitherto had been perfect freedom. . . ."

The name *Olaudah* means "one favored," especially with the ability to speak well. Equiano spoke out through his autobiography, which is one of the classic slave narratives of all times.

Olaudah Equiano
(c. 1745–1797)

Olaudah Equiano (ō·lōō′dä ek′wē·än′ō) was the first African writer to reach a sizable audience of American readers. A member of the Ibo people, Equiano was born in a part of West Africa that is now Nigeria. When he was only eleven years old, Equiano, along with his sister, was kidnapped from his home by African raiders involved in the slave trade. Over a period of six or seven months, during which he and his sister were separated, the slave traders took Equiano to a series of way stations. When he reached the coast, Equiano was put aboard one of the infamous slave ships bound for Barbados, an island in the West Indies, in the Caribbean. There was a great demand for slaves to work on the sugar plantations in the Caribbean. In his narrative, Equiano vividly describes this cruel and horrifying part of the slave route, which was known as the Middle Passage.

After a short stay in Barbados, Equiano was sold to a British military officer, who gave him the name Gustavus Vassa, after a Swedish king. Equiano served with this officer during the Seven Years' War between England and France and gained great skill as a seaman. In time a Quaker merchant from Philadelphia purchased Equiano. From his own profitable business ventures while managing his master's business, Equiano saved enough money to purchase his freedom in 1766, after having been enslaved for almost ten years. He was about twenty-one years old.

After buying his freedom, Equiano worked as a sailor and led an exciting and adventurous life, sailing on exploratory expeditions to the Arctic and Central America. He finally settled in England, where he made his living as a free servant, a musician, and a barber. He also became active in the antislavery movement. In 1781, the captain of the *Zong*, which was transporting more than four hundred Africans to Jamaica, threw a third of the shackled captives overboard in order to collect the insurance. In 1783, Equiano was instrumental in bringing this atrocity to the attention of the public and the British naval authorities. When the abolition of the slave trade became a hotly debated issue in the English Parliament, Equiano actively campaigned against slavery, writing letters to officials and newspapers and visiting abolitionist leaders.

Equiano's autobiography, published in England in 1789, was titled *The Interesting Narrative of the Life of Olaudah Equiano, or Gustavus Vassa, the African*. Reprinted in New York in 1791, the book—considered the first great black autobiography—proved popular with readers in the United States as well as abroad. The author's account of the horrors he suffered struck a responsive chord with northern abolitionists. In 1792, Equiano married an Englishwoman, Susanna Cullen.

Though Equiano traveled widely, he never returned to the United States. Nor did he ever again see his native Africa, to which he dreamed of returning. He defined himself, to the end of his life, simply as "the African."

Portrait of a Negro Man, Olaudah Equiano in 1780s. English School (eighteenth century), previously attributed to Joshua Reynolds. Oil on canvas.

Royal Albert Memorial Museum, Exeter, Devon, UK/Bridgeman Art Library.

RESOURCES: READING

Planning
■ *One-Stop Planner* CD-ROM with ExamView Test Generator

Differentiating Instruction
■ *Holt Reading Solutions*
■ *The Holt Reader*
■ *Supporting Instruction in Spanish*
■ *Audio CD Library, Selections and Summaries in Spanish*

Vocabulary
■ *Vocabulary Development*

Grammar and Language
■ *Daily Language Activities*

Assessment
■ *Holt Assessment: Literature, Reading, and Vocabulary*
■ *One-Stop Planner* CD-ROM with ExamView Test Generator

■ *Holt Online Assessment*

Internet
■ go.hrw.com (Keyword: LE5 11-1)
■ *Elements of Literature Online*

Media
■ *Audio CD Library*
■ *Audio CD Library, Selections and Summaries in Spanish*

Before You Read

from The Interesting Narrative of the Life of Olaudah Equiano

Make the Connection
Quickwrite ✏️

The first Africans in the Americas were unwilling immigrants who arrived on slave ships before 1600. Between the seventeenth and nineteenth centuries, about ten million people were captured in Africa and shipped to North and South America and the islands of the West Indies, where they were sold as slaves.

Before you read Equiano's account, make a KWL chart like the one below. Fill out the first two columns—what you already know about slavery and the slave trade in the eighteenth century and what you'd like to learn about it. Leave the third column blank.

K What I Know	W What I Want to Know	L What I Learned

Literary Focus
Autobiography

Equiano's **autobiography** was one of the first of a number of slave narratives, so called because they were firsthand accounts written by ex-slaves. The publication of these narratives was encouraged by abolitionists in the nineteenth century to fuel the crusade against slavery.

> An **autobiography** is a firsthand account of the writer's own life.
>
> *For more on Autobiography, see the Handbook of Literary and Historical Terms.*

Reading Skills 📖
Making Inferences About an Author's Beliefs

An **inference** is an educated guess based on what you already know and what you learn from reading a text. To make an inference, you look beyond what's being stated directly in a text and think about what is implicit, or hinted at. As you read, be alert for phrases or passages that give you insight into an author's beliefs about a subject. What do you think are Equiano's philosophical or fundamental beliefs about human cruelty?

Vocabulary Development

assailant (ə·sāl′ənt) *n.:* attacker.

distraction (di·strak′shən) *n.:* mental disturbance or distress.

apprehensions (ap′rē·hen′shənz) *n. pl.:* feelings of anxiety or dread.

alleviate (ə·lē′vē·āt′) *v.:* relieve; reduce.

interspersed (in′tər·spʉrst′) *v.* used as *adj.:* placed at intervals.

commodious (kə·mō′dē·əs) *adj.:* spacious.

consternation (kän′stər·nā′shən) *n.:* confusion resulting from fear or shock.

improvident (im·präv′ə·dənt) *adj.:* careless; not providing for the future.

avarice (av′ə·ris) *n.:* greed.

INTERNET
Vocabulary Practice
Keyword: LE5 11-1

SKILLS FOCUS

Literary Skills
Understand the characteristics of autobiography.

Reading Skills
Make inferences about an author's beliefs.

Olaudah Equiano **51**

PRETEACHING

Summary ⬄ *at grade level*

Equiano begins by briefly describing his life as the beloved youngest son in a large Ibo family. When he is eleven, he and his sister are kidnapped by other Africans. Soon separated from his sister, Equiano is sold to a series of African slave owners, who treat him kindly. He eventually ends up on a slave ship bound for the West Indies. Terrified of the white crew, he is put in the ship's hold. The miserable overcrowding and terrible stench cause many of his fellow captives to die and a few to attempt suicide by jumping into the ocean. When the ship arrives in Barbados, Equiano and the other captives are sold to eager merchants and planters. The excerpt ends with Equiano's passionate denouncement of the hypocrisy of so-called Christians who, by tearing apart families and friends, go beyond avarice to add "fresh horrors even to the wretchedness of slavery."

Selection Starter

Build background. The first slaves in the North American Colonies arrived in 1619 to work in the tobacco fields of Virginia. Eventually, about ten million slaves were shipped to the Americas. On the voyage from Africa—known as the Middle Passage—approximately 1.5 million captives died at sea because of inhuman conditions, abuse, disease, and suicide.

Previewing Vocabulary

Have students read the Vocabulary words and definitions listed on this page. Then, have them complete the following sentences with the correct Vocabulary word.

1. Peter came home in a state of _____; he was highly agitated and distraught. [distraction]

2. Jan said she had witnessed the assault but had trouble describing the _____. [assailant]

3. This house is hardly _____ enough for our large family. [commodious]

4. It was _____ of you to spend your whole month's salary on a pair of shoes. [improvident]

5. His _____ led him to charge his clients for work he hadn't performed. [avarice]

6. A hot shower will do a lot to _____ your back pain. [alleviate]

7. An occasional birch tree was _____ among the pines. [interspersed]

8. My _____ were confirmed when my favorite team lost the game. [apprehensions]

9. Ethan's _____ made him turn bright red and knock over his water glass. [consternation]

VIEWING THE ART

This painting of a slave ship reflects conditions at the height of the African slave trade during the eighteenth century.

Activity. When students have reached the section of the narrative that describes the conditions of the captives in the hold (pp. 56–58), ask them to look back at this watercolor. How does it compare with Equiano's description? [Possible response: The painting shows inhumanely crowded conditions, but the slaves are apparently able to move around. Equiano describes an even more horrifying situation of people crammed together like cargo, "so crowded that each had scarcely room to turn himself." Students may also point out that the painting is not as horrifying as Equiano's verbal depiction because it cannot evoke the "loathsome" stench or the pitiful shrieks that he describes.]

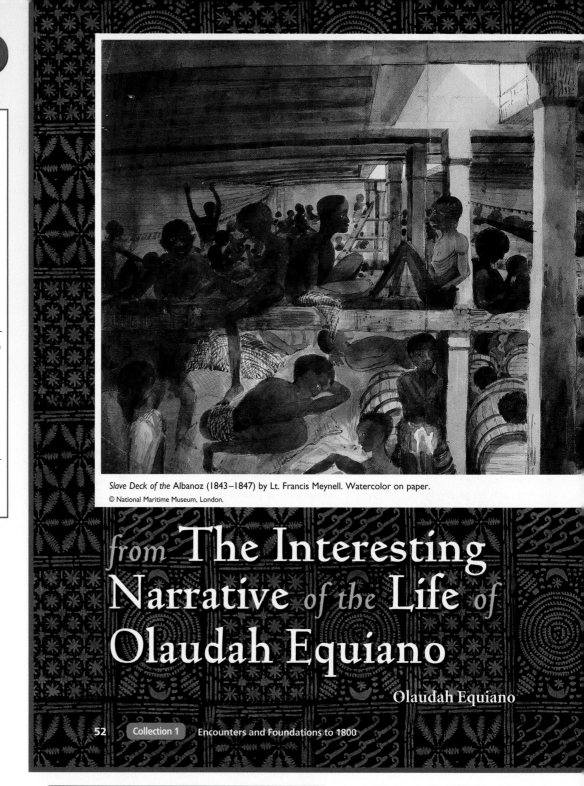

Slave Deck of the Albanoz *(1843–1847) by Lt. Francis Meynell. Watercolor on paper.*
© National Maritime Museum, London.

from The Interesting Narrative of the Life of Olaudah Equiano

Olaudah Equiano

DIFFERENTIATING INSTRUCTION

Learners Having Difficulty
Modeling. To help students read the excerpt from *The Interesting Narrative of the Life of Olaudah Equiano,* model the skill of making inferences about an author's beliefs. You might say: "As I read, I notice that Equiano is sometimes quite matter-of-fact about events or situations that I would find upsetting. At other points, however, he expresses his feelings strongly or provides clues about his attitude." Encourage students to think about how Equiano expresses or implies his beliefs— particularly, about slavery and human cruelty.

Invite learners having difficulty to read *The Interesting Narrative of the Life of Olaudah Equiano* in interactive format in *The Holt Reader* and to use the sidenotes as aids to understanding the selection.

Kidnapped

My father, besides many slaves, had a numerous family of which seven lived to grow up, including myself and a sister who was the only daughter. As I was the youngest of the sons I became, of course, the greatest favorite with my mother and was always with her; and she used to take particular pains to form my mind. I was trained up from my earliest years in the art of war, my daily exercise was shooting and throwing javelins, and my mother adorned me with emblems after the manner of our greatest warriors. In this way I grew up till I was turned the age of 11, when an end was put to my happiness in the following manner. Generally when the grown people in the neighborhood were gone far in the fields to labor, the children assembled together in some of the neighbors' premises to play, and commonly some of us used to get up a tree to look for any assailant or kidnapper that might come upon us, for they sometimes took those opportunities of our parents' absence to attack and carry off as many as they could seize. One day, as I was watching at the top of a tree in our yard, I saw one of those people come into the yard of our next neighbor but one to kidnap, there being many stout young people in it. Immediately on this I gave the alarm of the rogue[1] and he was surrounded by the stoutest of them, who entangled him with cords so that he could not escape till some of the grown people came and secured him.

But alas! ere long it was my fate to be thus attacked and to be carried off when none of the grown people were nigh. One day, when all our people were gone out to their works as usual and only I and my dear sister were left to mind the house, two men and a woman got over our walls, and in a moment seized us both, and without giving us time to cry out or make resistance they stopped our mouths and ran off with us into the nearest wood. Here they tied our hands and continued to carry us as far as they could till night came on, when we reached a small house where the robbers halted for refreshment and spent the night. We were then unbound but were unable to take any food, and being quite overpowered by fatigue and grief, our only relief was some sleep, which allayed our misfortune for a short time. The next morning we left the house and continued traveling all the day. For a long time we had kept to the woods, but at last we came into a road which I believed I knew. I had now some hopes of being delivered, for we had advanced but a little way before I discovered some people at a distance, on which I began to cry out for

---

1. **rogue** *n.*: rascal; scoundrel.

Vocabulary
assailant (ə·sāl′ənt) *n.*: attacker.

Olaudah Equiano   **53**

DIRECT TEACHING

A **Content-Area Connections**
History: Slavery in Africa
Students may be surprised and distressed to learn that Africans enslaved one another. According to historian Herbert S. Klein, slavery existed in Africa from recorded times, but it was a relatively minor institution before the emergence of the Atlantic slave trade in the early sixteenth century.

B **Content-Area Connections**
History: The Slave Trade
Again, students may be shocked to learn that the slave catchers, or kidnappers, were other Africans. According to Herbert S. Klein, "All African slaves were purchased from local African owners. . . . European buyers were totally dependent on African sellers for the delivery of slaves."

C **Learners Having Difficulty**
Finding the sequence of events.
Point out time sequence phrases such as "the next morning." Ask students to use these sequencing clues to create a time line of the events in the autobiography. This exersise will help them track Equiano's movements west. (Students may want to work on time lines with partners.)

English-Language Learners
Point out that English was not Equiano's first language. He heard it for the first time when he was eleven or twelve, yet his autobiography is written in a fluent and effective English prose style.

Special Education Students
For lessons designed for special education students, see *Holt Reading Solutions*.

Advanced Learners
Enrichment. Some students may be interested in reading more of Equiano's autobiography. Web sites offer excerpts from the work.

A Reading Skills

❓ Making inferences. Why do you think Equiano and his sister refused the food? [Possible responses: They were too upset to eat. They didn't trust their kidnappers or their food.]

B Reading Skills

Making inferences about an author's beliefs. Equiano suggests his belief that one of the cruelest aspects of slavery is the way it often tears apart families.

C Reading Skills

❓ Making inferences about an author's beliefs. Today most people are horrified by the idea of slavery, so students may be surprised by Equiano's matter-of-fact attitude. Although he is grief-stricken at being separated from his sister, he seems to accept being a slave. Why might he react this way? [Possible responses: Slavery was the custom of his culture. He didn't know societies could be different.]

D Reading Skills

❓ Interpreting. Why do you think the slavers carried Equiano? [Possible responses: They may have felt sorry for him or wanted to keep him healthy so that they would receive a higher price at auction.]

E Reading Skills

❓ Making inferences about an author's beliefs. What can we infer about Equiano's beliefs from his use of the phrase "sable destroyers of human rights"? [His word choice implies that he strongly condemns these African slave traders, despite their kindness.]

---

assistance: But my cries had no other effect than to make them tie me faster and stop my mouth, and then they put me into a large sack. They also stopped my sister's mouth and tied her hands, and in this manner we proceeded till we were out of the sight of these people.

When we went to rest the following night they offered us some victuals, but we refused it, and the only comfort we had was in being in one another's arms all that night and bathing each other with our tears. But alas! we were soon deprived of even the small comfort of weeping together. The next day proved a day of greater sorrow than I had yet experienced, for my sister and I were then separated while we lay clasped in each other's arms. It was in vain that we besought them not to part us; she was torn from me and immediately carried away, while I was left in a state of distraction not to be described. I cried and grieved continually, and for several days I did not eat anything but what they forced into my mouth. At length, after many days' traveling, during which I had often changed masters, I got into the hands of a chieftain in a very pleasant country. This man had two wives and some children, and they all used me extremely well and did all they could to comfort me, particularly the first wife, who was something like my mother. Although I was a great many days' journey from my father's house, yet these people spoke exactly the same language with us. This first master of mine, as I may call him, was a smith, and my principal employment was working his bellows,[2] which were the same kind as I had seen in my vicinity. They were in some respects not unlike the stoves here in gentlemen's kitchens, and were covered over with leather; and in the middle of that leather a stick was fixed, and a person stood up and worked it in the same manner as is done to pump water out of a cask with a hand pump. I believe it was gold he worked, for it was of a lovely bright yellow color and was worn by the women on their wrists and ankles. . . .

---

2. **bellows** *n.:* device that produces a strong air current, used for blowing fires.

Soon after this my master's only daughter and child by his first wife sickened and died, which affected him so much that for some time he was almost frantic, and really would have killed himself had he not been watched and prevented. However, in a small time afterward he recovered and I was again sold. I was now carried to the left of the sun's rising, through many different countries and a number of large woods. The people I was sold to used to carry me very often when I was tired either on their shoulders or on their backs. I saw many convenient well-built sheds along the roads at proper distances, to accommodate the merchants and travelers who lay in those buildings along with their wives, who often accompany them; and they always go well armed.

From the time I left my own nation I always found somebody that understood me till I came to the seacoast. The languages of different nations did not totally differ, nor were they so copious[3] as those of the Europeans, particularly the English. They were therefore easily learned, and while I was journeying thus through Africa I acquired two or three different tongues. In this manner I had been traveling for a considerable time, when one evening, to my great surprise, whom should I see brought to the house where I was but my dear sister! As soon as she saw me she gave a loud shriek and ran into my arms—I was quite overpowered: Neither of us could speak, but for a considerable time clung to each other in mutual embraces, unable to do anything but weep. Our meeting affected all who saw us, and indeed I must acknowledge, in honor of those sable destroyers of human rights, that I never met with any ill-treatment or saw any offered to their slaves except tying them, when necessary, to keep them from running away.

When these people knew we were brother and sister they indulged us to be together, and

---

3. **copious** *adj.:* here, wordy.

Vocabulary
distraction (di·strak′shən) *n.:* mental disturbance or distress.

DIFFERENTIATING INSTRUCTION

English-Language Learners
Point out that Equiano picks up new languages easily when they are similar to his own. Ask students who are learning English if they listen for words that sound similar to ones in their native language. What English words have they learned in this way? How similar is their first language to English?

Have students conduct a poll to find out how many different languages or dialects are spoken by class members (or students throughout the school). What is the most number of languages that one student speaks or understands? Students can present their poll results as graphs or other illustrations.

---

the man to whom I supposed we belonged lay with us, he in the middle while she and I held one another by the hands across his breast all night; and thus for a while we forgot our misfortunes in the joy of being together: But even this small comfort was soon to have an end, for scarcely had the fatal morning appeared when she was again torn from me forever! I was now more miserable, if possible, than before. The small relief which her presence gave me from pain was gone, and the wretchedness of my situation was redoubled by my anxiety after her fate and my apprehensions lest her sufferings should be greater than mine, when I could not be with her to alleviate them. . . .

I did not long remain after my sister. I was again sold and carried through a number of places till, after traveling a considerable time, I came to a town called Tinmah in the most beautiful country I had yet seen in Africa. It was extremely rich, and there were many rivulets which flowed through it and supplied a large pond in the center of town, where the people washed. Here I first saw and tasted coconuts, which I thought superior to any nuts I had ever tasted before; and the trees, which were loaded, were also interspersed amongst the houses, which had commodious shades adjoining and were in the same manner as ours, the insides being neatly plastered and whitewashed. Here I also saw and tasted for the first time sugar cane. Their money consisted of little white shells the size of the fingernail. I was sold here for 172 of them by a merchant who lived and brought me there. I had been about two or three days at his house when a wealthy widow, a neighbor of his, came there one evening, and brought with her an only son, a young gentleman about my own age and size. Here they saw me; and, having taken a fancy to me, I was bought of the merchant, and went home with them. Her house and premises were situated close to one of those rivulets I have mentioned, and were the finest I ever saw in Africa: They were very extensive, and she had a number of slaves to attend her. The next day I was washed and perfumed, and when mealtime came I was led into the presence of my mistress, and ate and drank before her with her son. This filled me with astonishment; and I could scarce help expressing my surprise that the young gentleman should suffer me, who was bound, to eat with him who was free; and not only so, but that he would not at any time either eat or drink till I had taken first, because I was the eldest, which was agreeable to our custom. Indeed everything here, and all their treatment of me, made me forget that I was a slave. The language of these people resembled ours so nearly that we understood each other perfectly. They had also the very same customs as we. There were likewise slaves daily to attend us, while my young master and I with other boys sported with our darts and bows and arrows, as I had been used to do at home. In this resemblance to my former happy state I passed about two months; and I now began to think I was to be adopted into the family, and was beginning to be reconciled to my situation, and to forget by degrees my misfortunes, when all at once the delusion vanished; for without the least previous knowledge, one morning early, while my dear master and companion was still asleep, I was wakened out of my reverie to fresh sorrow, and hurried away even amongst the uncircumcised.

Thus at the very moment I dreamed of the greatest happiness, I found myself most miserable; and it seemed as if fortune wished to give me this taste of joy only to render the reverse more poignant. The change I now experienced was as painful as it was sudden and unexpected. It was a change indeed from a state of bliss to a scene which is inexpressible by me, as it discovered to me an element I had never before beheld and till then had no idea of, and wherein such instances of hardship and cruelty continually occurred as I can never reflect on but with horror. . . .

Vocabulary

apprehensions (ap′rē·hen′shənz) n. pl.: feelings of anxiety or dread.
alleviate (ə·lē′vē·āt′) v.: relieve; reduce.
interspersed (in′tər·spʉrst′) v. used as adj.: placed at intervals.
commodious (kə·mō′dē·əs) adj.: spacious.

F Content-Area Connections

History: Slavery in Africa Students may be surprised at the physical closeness between slaves and owner.

G Literary Focus

Autobiography. Equiano's autobiography is not simply an account of the hardship he endured. He also includes descriptions of the people, places, and customs he experiences.

H Reading Skills

❓ Speculating. Why do you think the widow and her son treated Equiano so well? [Possible response: The son may have been lonely for a friend. The widow may have wished she had another child.]

I Literary Focus

Autobiography. According to Vincent Carretta, an editor of an edition of the *Narrative*, Equiano's book falls within the genre of the "spiritual autobiography," recounting the hero's journey toward salvation. To that end, Equiano places his tale within a Judeo-Christian context, often drawing analogies between Africans and Jews. According to Carretta, he uses the "contemptuous label" *uncircumcised* "to distinguish other races from his own" and to "remind his readers of the Jewish-African relationship he sees."

Secondary Source

Critical Comment: The Institution of Slavery

In the introduction to his edition of *The Interesting Narrative,* Vincent Carretta provides this analysis: "Equiano appears to offer the transformation of his own attitude toward the varieties of eighteenth-century slavery as a model for the moral progress of his readers as individuals and of the society he now shares with them. Through personal experience and observation, Equiano becomes an expert on the institution of slavery as well as on the effects of the African slave trade. Many twentieth-century readers are surprised to discover that eighteenth-century slavery was not a monolithic institution, simply divided into White owners and Black chattel. Equiano's initial encounter with slavery is in Africa, where, in its native African form, it is domestic, where the slaves are treated almost like members of their owners' families because of close personal contact. Thus it seems benign, and not obviously dehumanizing. Slavery is neither racially based nor hereditary. . . . But, like an infectious disease, the European slave trade with Africa has gradually spread further inland until it destroys even the tranquility of Equiano's homeland."

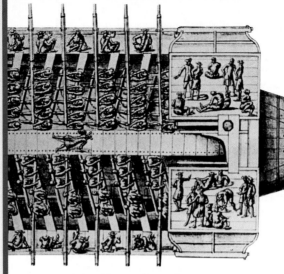

A slave ship manned by captives.

The Slave Ship

The first object which saluted[4] my eyes when I arrived on the coast was the sea, and a slave ship which was then riding at anchor and waiting for its cargo. These filled me with astonishment, which was soon converted into terror when I was carried on board. I was immediately handled and tossed up to see if I were sound by some of the crew, and I was now persuaded that I had gotten into a world of bad spirits and that they were going to kill me. Their complexions too differing so much from ours, their long hair and the language they spoke (which was very different from any I had ever heard) united to confirm me in this belief. Indeed such were the horrors of my views and fears at the moment that, if ten thousand worlds had been my own, I would have freely parted with them all to have exchanged my condition with that of the meanest[5] slave in my own country. When I looked round the ship too and saw a large furnace or copper boiling and a multitude of black people of every description chained together, every one

———————
4. **saluted** v.: met.
5. **meanest** adj.: lowest.

of their countenances[6] expressing dejection and sorrow, I no longer doubted of my fate; and quite overpowered with horror and anguish, I fell motionless on the deck and fainted. When I recovered a little I found some black people about me, who I believed were some of those who had brought me on board and had been receiving their pay; they talked to me in order to cheer me, but all in vain. I asked them if we were not to be eaten by those white men with horrible looks, red faces, and loose hair. They told me I was not, and one of the crew brought me a small portion of spirituous liquor in a wineglass, but being afraid of him I would not take it out of his hand. One of the blacks therefore took it from him and gave it to me, and I took a little down my palate, which instead of reviving me, as they thought it would, threw me into the greatest consternation at the strange feeling it produced, having never tasted such any liquor before. Soon after this the blacks who brought me on board went off, and left me abandoned to despair.

I now saw myself deprived of all chance of returning to my native country or even the least glimpse of hope of gaining the shore, which I now considered as friendly; and I even wished for my former slavery in preference to my present situation, which was filled with horrors of every kind, still heightened by my ignorance of what I was to undergo. I was not long suffered to indulge my grief; I was soon put down under the decks, and there I received such a salutation in my nostrils as I had never experienced in my life: So that with the loathsomeness of the stench and crying together, I became so sick and low that I was not able to eat, nor had I the least desire to taste anything. I now wished for the last friend, death, to relieve me; but soon, to my grief, two of the white men offered me eatables,

———————
6. **countenances** n. pl.: faces.

Vocabulary
consternation (kän′stər·nā′shən) n.: confusion resulting from fear or shock.

CONTENT-AREA CONNECTIONS

History: The Slave Trade
Not all whites remained insensitive to the human misery on slave ships. The English clergyman John Newton (1725–1807), writer of the hymn "Amazing Grace," was for a time the manager of a slave "factory" and captain of a slave ship. He later regretted his work in the slave trade and wrote the pamphlet *Thoughts upon the African Slave Trade* to promote the abolition of slavery.

Small-group activity. Ask a group of students to research Newton's work and report to the class.

and on my refusing to eat, one of them held me fast by the hands and laid me across, I think, the windlass,[7] and tied my feet while the other flogged[8] me severely. I had never experienced anything of this kind before, and although, not being used to the water, I naturally feared that element the first time I saw it, yet nevertheless could I have got over the nettings I would have jumped over the side, but I could not; and besides, the crew used to watch us very closely who were not chained down to the decks, lest we should leap into the water: And I have seen some of these poor African prisoners most severely cut for attempting to do so, and hourly whipped for not eating. This indeed was often the case with myself. In a little time after, amongst the poor chained men I found some of my own nation, which in a small degree gave ease to my mind. I inquired of these what was to be done with us; they gave me to understand we were to be carried to these white people's country to work for them. I then was a little revived, and thought if it were no worse than working, my situation was not so desperate: But still I feared I should be put to death, the white people looked and acted, as I thought, in so savage a manner; for I had never seen among my people such instances of brutal cruelty, and this not only shown toward us blacks but also to some of the whites themselves. One white man in particular I saw, when we were permitted to be on deck, flogged so unmercifully with a large rope near the foremast[9] that he died in consequence of it; and they tossed him over the side as they would have done a brute. This made me fear these people the more, and I expected nothing less than to be treated in the same manner. I could not help expressing my fears and apprehensions to some of my countrymen: I asked them if these people had no country but lived in this hollow place (the ship): They told me they did not, but came from a distant one. "Then,"

said I, "how comes it in all our country we never heard of them?" They told me because they lived so very far off. I then asked where were their women? Had they any like themselves? I was told they had: "And why," said I, "do we not see them?" They answered, because they were left behind. I asked how the vessel could go? They told me they could not tell, but that there were cloths put upon the masts by the help of the ropes I saw, and then the vessel went on; and the white men had some spell or magic they put in the water when they liked in order to stop the vessel. I was exceedingly amazed at this account and really thought they were spirits. I therefore wished much to be from amongst them for I expected they would sacrifice me: But my wishes were vain, for we were so quartered that it was impossible for any of us to make our escape.

While we stayed on the coast I was mostly on deck, and one day, to my great astonishment, I saw one of these vessels coming in with the sails up. As soon as the whites saw it they gave a great shout, at which we were amazed; and the more so as the vessel appeared larger by approaching nearer. At last she came to an anchor in my sight, and when the anchor was let go I and my countrymen who saw it were lost in astonishment to observe the vessel stop, and were now convinced it was done by magic. Soon after this the other ship got her boats out, and they came on board of us, and the people of both ships seemed very glad to see each other. Several of the strangers also shook hands with us black people, and made motions with their hands, signifying I suppose we were to go to their country; but we did not understand them. At last, when the ship we were in had got in all her cargo, they made ready with many fearful noises, and we were all put under deck so that we could not see how they managed the vessel.

But this disappointment was the least of my sorrow. The stench of the hold[10] while we were on the coast was so intolerably loathsome that it was dangerous to remain there for any time, and

---

7. **windlass** (wind′ləs) *n.:* device used to raise and lower heavy objects, like a ship's anchor.
8. **flogged** *v.:* beat with a rod or whip.
9. **foremast** *n.:* mast closest to the bow, or front, of a ship.

---

10. **hold** *n.:* enclosed area below a ship's deck, where cargo is usually stored.

Olaudah Equiano   **57**

DIRECT TEACHING

D **Reading Skills**

❓ **Making inferences.** Why were Equiano and the other prisoners whipped for refusing to eat? [They were considered property. If a captive died of starvation, the slavers lost money because they couldn't sell him or her.] You might point out to students that the nettings Equiano refers to were placed along the sides of the boat specifically to prevent the slaves from jumping overboard.

E **Content-Area Connections**

History: The Crew
In fact, slave-ship captains were so brutal toward their crews that abolitionists (hoping to convince white people of the evils of slavery) often argued that the slave trade was deadlier for the crew than for the slaves.

F **Learners Having Difficulty**

❓ **Monitoring comprehension.** What is this "spell or magic"? [the anchor]

G **Reading Skills**

❓ **Speculating.** Why didn't the crew want the slaves to see how they managed the ship? [Possible response: It was in their interest to keep the slaves ignorant, so that they were scared of the sailors and thought they used magic, and therefore were afraid to attempt a mutiny.]

CONTENT-AREA CONNECTIONS

Literature: Slave Narratives
The first example of a slave narrative—an autobiographical account of the life of a slave—was published in 1760 under the title *A Narrative of the Uncommon Sufferings and Surprising Deliverance of Briton Hammon, a Negro Man.* Others, like Equiano's work in 1789, soon followed. The historian Marion Wilson Starling reports that of the estimated sixty thousand slaves who escaped to freedom, more than six thousand wrote down or told their stories to interviewers. Slave narratives were filled with accounts of inhuman cruelty, horrendous suffering, the intense desire for freedom, successful and unsuccessful escape attempts, and religious meditations (or in Equiano's narrative, actual conversion to Christianity). Many slave narratives were written specifically to support the cause of abolishing slavery, or at least the slave trade.

Individual activity. Have students compare and contrast Equiano's narrative with another slave narrative: either the excerpt from the *Narrative of the Life of Frederick Douglass* (p. 398) or the excerpt from *Incidents in the Life of a Slave Girl,* by Harriet Jacobs (p. 406).

A **Content-Area Connections**

History: The Middle Passage
Each captive on a slave ship had about six feet by sixteen inches of space. Captives were wedged together horizontally and were unable to stand up or even turn over. The men were shackled to one another or to the deck to prevent mutiny or suicide (by jumping overboard). The main causes of death were gastrointestinal disorders and fevers, with dysentery probably the most common disease. Mortality rates during the Middle Passage have been estimated at 15 to 30 percent.

B **Reading Skills**

? **Interpreting.** What does Equiano mean when he refers to the slavers' "improvident avarice"? [If the slavers had been less greedy, they would have put fewer slaves on a ship and created better conditions, thereby resulting in fewer deaths, more slaves to sell, and therefore greater profits.]

C **Reading Skills**

? **Recognizing the author's purpose.** Why does Equiano include this anecdote about the sailors and the fish? [Possible response: He wants to emphasize the spiteful cruelty of the slavers.]

D **Literary Focus**

Autobiography. Once again, Equiano includes details about the new things he sees and learns. His autobiography often reads like a travel or adventure book.

---

some of us had been permitted to stay on the deck for the fresh air; but now that the whole ship's cargo were confined together it became absolutely pestilential.[11] The closeness of the place and the heat of the climate, added to the number in the ship, which was so crowded that each had scarcely room to turn himself, almost suffocated us. This produced copious perspirations, so that the air soon became unfit for respiration from a variety of loathsome smells, and brought on a sickness among the slaves, of which many died, thus falling victims to the improvident avarice, as I may call it, of their purchasers. This wretched situation was again aggravated by the galling of the chains, now become insupportable, and the filth of the necessary tubs,[12] into which the children often fell and were almost suffocated. The shrieks of the women and the groans of the dying rendered the whole a scene of horror almost inconceivable. Happily perhaps for myself I was soon reduced so low here that it was thought necessary to keep me almost always on deck, and from my extreme youth I was not put in fetters.[13] In this situation I expected every hour to share the fate of my companions, some of whom were almost daily brought upon deck at the point of death, which I began to hope would soon put an end to my miseries. Often did I think many of the inhabitants of the deep much more happy than myself. I envied them the freedom they enjoyed, and as often wished I could change my condition for theirs. Every circumstance I met with served only to render my state more painful, and heighten my apprehensions and my opinion of the cruelty of the whites. One day they had taken a number of fishes, and when they had killed and satisfied themselves with as many as they thought fit, to our astonishment who were on the deck, rather than give any of them to us to eat as we expected, they tossed the remaining fish into the sea again, although we begged and prayed for some as well as we could, but in vain;

and some of my countrymen, being pressed by hunger, took an opportunity when they thought no one saw them of trying to get a little privately; but they were discovered, and the attempt procured them some very severe floggings.

One day, when we had a smooth sea and moderate wind, two of my wearied countrymen who were chained together (I was near them at the time), preferring death to such a life of misery, somehow made through the nettings and jumped into the sea: Immediately another quite dejected fellow, who on account of his illness was suffered to be out of irons, also followed their example; and I believe many more would very soon have done the same if they had not been prevented by the ship's crew, who were instantly alarmed. Those of us that were the most active were in a moment put down under the deck, and there was such a noise and confusion amongst the people of the ship as I never heard before, to stop her and get the boat out to go after the slaves. However two of the wretches were drowned, but they got the other and afterward flogged him unmercifully for thus attempting to prefer death to slavery. In this manner we continued to undergo more hardships than I can now relate, hardships which are inseparable from this accursed trade. Many a time we were near suffocation from the want of fresh air, which we were often without for whole days together. This and the stench of the necessary tubs carried off many.

During our passage I first saw flying fishes, which surprised me very much: They used frequently to fly across the ship and many of them fell on the deck. I also now first saw the use of the quadrant; I had often with astonishment seen the mariners make observations with it, and I could not think what it meant. They at last took notice of my surprise, and one of them, willing to increase it as well as to gratify my curiosity, made me one day look through it.

---

11. **pestilential** *adj.:* deadly; harmful.
12. **necessary tubs:** toilets.
13. **fetters** *n. pl.:* shackles or chains for the feet.

Vocabulary
improvident (im·präv′ə·dənt) *adj.:* careless; not providing for the future.
avarice (av′ə·ris) *n.:* greed.

SKILLS REVIEW

Analyzing persuasive techniques. Review the different techniques that writers (and speakers) use to try to persuade their readers (or audience) to think or act in a certain way. They can appeal to our logic by presenting well-reasoned arguments that are supported by facts and examples. They can also appeal to our emotions by using loaded words, a passionate style, and even compelling personal anecdotes (like the one about the sailors with the fish).

Activity. Here are two questions for discussion:
• What is Equiano trying to persuade his readers to think or do? [He is trying to persuade them that slavery and the slave trade are cruel and un-Christian and should be abolished.]

The clouds appeared to me to be land, which disappeared as they passed along. This heightened my wonder, and I was now more persuaded than ever that I was in another world and that everything about me was magic. At last we came in sight of the island of Barbados, at which the whites on board gave a great shout and made many signs of joy to us. We did not know what to think of this, but as the vessel drew nearer we plainly saw the harbor and other ships of different kinds and sizes, and we soon anchored amongst them off Bridgetown. Many merchants and planters now came on board, though it was in the evening. They put us in separate parcels and examined us attentively. They also made us jump, and pointed to the land, signifying we were to go there. We thought by this we should be eaten by these ugly men, as they appeared to us; and when soon after we were all put down under the deck again, there was much dread and trembling among us, and nothing but bitter cries to be heard all the night from these apprehensions, insomuch that at last the white people got some old slaves from the land to pacify us. They told us we were not to be eaten but to work, and were soon to go on land where we should see many of our countrypeople. This report eased us much; and sure enough soon after we were landed there came to us Africans of all languages.

We were conducted immediately to the merchant's yard, where we were all pent up together like so many sheep in a fold without regard to sex or age. As every object was new to me everything I saw filled me with surprise. What struck me first was that the houses were built with stories, and in every other respect different from those in Africa: But I was still more astonished on seeing people on horseback. I did not know what this could mean, and indeed I thought these people were full of nothing but magical arts. While I was in this astonishment one of my fellow prisoners spoke to a countryman of his about the horses, who said they were the same kind they had in their country. I understood them though they were from a distant part of Africa, and I thought it odd I had not seen any horses there; but afterward when I came to converse with different Africans I found they had many horses amongst them, and much larger than those I then saw.

We were not many days in the merchant's custody before we were sold after their usual manner, which is this: On a signal given (as the beat of a drum) the buyers rush at once into the yard where the slaves are confined, and make choice of that parcel they like best. The noise and clamor with which this is attended and the eagerness visible in the countenances of the buyers serve not a little to increase the apprehensions of the terrified Africans, who may well be supposed to consider them as the ministers of that destruction to which they think themselves devoted. In this manner, without scruple,[14] are relations and friends separated, most of them never to see each other again. I remember in the vessel in which I was brought over, in the men's apartment there were several brothers who, in the sale, were sold in different lots; and it was very moving on this occasion to see and hear their cries at parting. O, ye nominal Christians! might not an African ask you, Learned you this from your God who says unto you, Do unto all men as you would men should do unto you? Is it not enough that we are torn from our country and friends to toil for your luxury and lust of gain? Must every tender feeling be likewise sacrificed to your avarice? Are the dearest friends and relations, now rendered more dear by their separation from their kindred, still to be parted from each other and thus prevented from cheering the gloom of slavery with the small comfort of being together and mingling their sufferings and sorrows? Why are parents to lose their children, brothers their sisters, or husbands their wives? Surely this is a new refinement in cruelty which, while it has no advantage to atone for it, thus aggravates distress and adds fresh horrors even to the wretchedness of slavery. ■

---

14. **scruple** *n.:* unease or doubt arising from difficulty in determining what is right.

Olaudah Equiano 59

DIRECT TEACHING

E Reading Skills

? Recognizing persuasive techniques. In this passage, what is Equiano trying to persuade his readers to think or do? [He wants to persuade his readers, who are primarily white Christians, that slavery and the slave trade are unnecessarily cruel and contrary to the teachings of their religion.] Point out that Equiano here is presenting an ethical appeal directed toward the audience's moral beliefs.

F Learners Having Difficulty

Breaking down difficult text. Have students paraphrase this complicated sentence, breaking it down into several simpler sentences and replacing the pronoun *this* with the noun phrase *it* refers to. [Possible response: This tearing apart of families takes cruelty to a new level. It offers no advantage to justify itself. Instead, it worsens the already horrible suffering of slavery.]

GUIDED PRACTICE

Monitoring students' progress. Guide the class in answering these comprehension questions.

True-False

1. Equiano and his sister are kidnapped when he is eleven. [T]
2. Equiano is treated brutally by African slave owners. [F]
3. Equiano is frightened by the white crew of the slave ship. [T]
4. The crew members make no attempt to prevent the captives from committing suicide. [F]

- What persuasive techniques does he use, and how effectively? [Possible response: He effectively uses both logical and emotional appeals. Facts about conditions on the ship are horrifying; anecdotes add emotional weight.]

FAMILY/COMMUNITY ACTIVITY

Encourage students to re-read Equiano's narrative with family members and then discuss one of its powerful themes: slavery's cruelty in tearing families apart. What passage or images from Equiano's account does each family member find the most memorable or moving or horrifying? Why?

Connection

Summary ⬌ *at grade level*

In this stanza, addressed to a British government official, the speaker explains the origin of her love of freedom. Because she was stolen from her home and enslaved as a child, she understands the misery that the loss of freedom creates. Therefore, she prays that others will be spared similar tyranny—by which she means not slavery but rather the tyranny of British rule over the American Colonies.

DIRECT TEACHING

Ⓐ Background
George Washington
Washington had read Wheatley's lofty poem "To His Excellency, General Washington," which praised his military prowess and virtue. Washington invited Wheatley to meet him, and she did so in Cambridge, Massachusetts, in 1776.

Ⓑ Background
Birthplace
Wheatley was born in what is now Senegal.

Ⓒ Background
Learning English
Wheatley learned English in just sixteen months. She soon went on to master the highly rhetorical English poetic forms and conventions of her time.

Ⓓ Literary Focus
Style. Like the English poets John Dryden and Alexander Pope, Wheatley also uses a poetic style rich in classical allusions.

Phillis Wheatley: A Revolutionary Woman

Ⓐ   **A**ll the odds were stacked against her— she was an African held in slavery, she was young, and she was female. But Phillis Wheatley (c. 1753–1784) published her first poem when she was barely thirteen, and by the time she was twenty years old she had developed a reputation as a poet whose work was praised by George Washington and Thomas Jefferson (page 95).

Ⓑ   When Phillis Wheatley was about seven or eight years old, she, like Olaudah Equiano, was stolen from her home in West Africa. She arrived in America onboard a slave ship in 1761. At first, of course, she spoke no English. But she was purchased by the Wheatley family of Boston to assist Mrs. Susanna Wheatley and was treated Ⓒ kindly. Pleased to find this young woman intelligent and eager to learn, the Wheatleys provided her with an excellent education, equal to that of any free person in Boston at the time.

Susanna Wheatley arranged the London publication of a volume of Phillis's poems in 1773; the book received generally encouraging reviews, and it was read widely in England, France, and the American Colonies. Around this time, Phillis was given her freedom, though she chose to remain with the Wheatleys. When they died, she married John Peters, a freeman, in 1778.

Ⓓ   Wheatley's poems imitate the style popular in the poetry of her time: She uses a Latinate vocabulary, inversions, and elevated diction. The stanza on page 61 is from her poem to the earl of Dartmouth, who had just been appointed secretary of state in charge of the American Colonies (1772). Dartmouth, she hopes, will be open to the colonists' grievances.

Phillis Wheatley (1773). Frontispiece of *Poems* by Phillis Wheatley. Engraving.
The Granger Collection, New York.

Wheatley's life ended on a tragic note. Her married life was filled with personal, financial, and familial hardships. Wheatley bore three children, but none of them survived. When she herself was sick and poor, the same society that had lavished attention on her as a kind of "sideshow attraction"—an enslaved woman who could write lofty poetry—abandoned her to a position of powerlessness and anonymity. She died in her early thirties, destitute and grieving, without having published another book of poems. Since her death, however, her poems have been reprinted and, in the twentieth century, have again attracted lavish attention. Today Phillis Wheatley is praised as a true pioneer—the first African American poet.

from To the Right Honorable William, Earl of Dartmouth, His Majesty's Principal Secretary of State for North America, etc.

Phillis Wheatley

Should you, my lord, while you peruse my song,
Wonder from whence my love of *Freedom* sprung,
Whence flow these wishes for the common good,
By feeling hearts alone best understood,
5   I, young in life, by seeming cruel fate
Was snatch'd from *Afric's* fancy'd happy seat:
What pangs excruciating must molest,
What sorrows labor in my parent's breast?
Steel'd was that soul and by no misery mov'd
10 That from a father seiz'd his babe belov'd:
Such, such my case. And can I then but pray
Others may never feel tyrannic sway?

Connection

Summary ⬇ *below grade level*

This 1997 newspaper article tells about an annual ceremony called the Tribute to the Ancestors of the Middle Passage. Gathering in Coney Island, Brooklyn, participants pay tribute to the millions of Africans who were captured and transported across the Atlantic Ocean to be slaves in the Americas. The ceremony honors those who died during the voyage, known as the Middle Passage, as well as those who survived. It also provides a ritual for participants to honor their African heritage.

DIRECT TEACHING

Ⓐ Content-Area Connections

History: The Middle Passage
The mortality rate during the Middle Passage—the actual ship voyage across the Atlantic—is a controversial statistic. Estimates vary. Historian Howard Zinn, in *A People's History of the United States, 1492–Present,* uses the one-third figure cited in this article. However, Vincent Carretta, in an edition of *The Interesting Narrative . . . ,* says that modern estimates of the mortality rate are 15 percent.

Ⓑ Content-Area Connections

Culture: Honoring the Dead
Ask students to think about some of the ways different groups and cultures honor their dead—particularly large numbers of people who died in wars, atrocities, and accidents. [Possible responses: Students might mention the Vietnam Veterans Memorial, the Holocaust Memorial Museum, the AIDS quilt, and newspaper features devoted to telling about the lives of the thousands of people who died in the terrorist attacks on September 11, 2001.]

Honoring African Heritage

Halimah Abdullah

Ignoring the creaking of rusting amusement rides behind him, Ahsana Adae kept his gaze focused ahead, toward the horizon, where the gray expanse of overcast sky met the brackish waves.

"When I look out across those waters," Mr. Adae said, "I feel like walking across them back home."

For Mr. Adae and others who gathered in Coney Island on June 14 for a ceremony known as the Tribute to the Ancestors of the Middle Passage celebration, the ocean view represented a symbolic connection to their African ancestors' voyages here.

Ⓐ For four hundred years, millions of Africans were enslaved and transported across the Atlantic. Experts estimate that one third died on their journeys.

"The Atlantic Ocean is the largest single graveyard in the world, with over thirty million people buried in that ocean," said Zala Chandler, a professor of English and black and women's studies at Medgar Evers College and an organizer of the event.

"We're paying tribute to both those who died during that African holocaust and the survivors," she said of the celebration, now in its eighth year. "We ask that those present receive the blessings of those lost spirits."

Mr. Adae said he hoped that by setting adrift a photo of his great-grandparents, the children of slave mothers, they would symbolically return to their mothers' homelands.

"It's important for us to do these things to regain a sense of pride," he said. "Every other race that I know of is proud of who they are.

Spectators at the Middle Passage Monument, Riverbank State Park, New York City.

So it's about us learning to like ourselves. We have to learn that our African heritage is nothing to be ashamed of."

The gathering, swathed in colorful African prints, paid tribute through song, dance, and prayers. Some participants sat quietly in beach chairs facing the waves, reflecting.

"We as a people need to really take some time out and look at what happened during the Middle Passage," one participant, Tony Akeem, said. "We need to think about what they must have gone through."

Ⓑ As a solemn drumbeat sounded, the group proceeded to the water's edge and cast flowers, fruit, and pictures of dead relatives along the waves, offering whispered prayers. A scratched sepia° photo bobbed wildly as the current carried it toward open waters.

"The real story there," Mr. Akeem said, "is in the bottom of that briny deep."

—*The New York Times,* June 22, 1997

°**sepia** *adj.:* dark reddish brown.

Comparing and Contrasting Texts

As a springboard to discussion, you might ask a student to read the tenth paragraph aloud (the quotation by Tony Akeem, beginning "We as a people . . ."). Then, ask the class to consider how slave narratives like Equiano's might help accomplish Akeem's purpose: to get people to think about "what happened during the Middle Passage" and what the captives "must have gone through." [Possible response: Such narratives provide readers with concrete details about what the captives experienced.] **Are books as important as rituals for coming to terms with horrific events such as the Middle Passage?** [Possible response: Both are necessary—factual information plus cathartic ritual.]

Response and Analysis

Reading Check

1. How was Equiano treated by his captors and owners while he was held in slavery in West Africa?

2. Under what circumstances was Equiano twice parted from his sister?

3. How did some Africans onboard the ship try to escape life in bondage?

4. Why did the ship's crew keep Equiano on deck most of the time?

Thinking Critically

5. Fill in the third column of the KWL chart that you made in your Quickwrite. Has your understanding of slavery and the slave trade changed? Did the article "Honoring African Heritage" add to your understanding? (See the **Connection** on page 62.) Explain your responses.

6. Equiano was "handled and tossed up" by some of the crew as soon as he was taken onboard. Why? What would have happened to him if the crew had found him unsatisfactory?

7. Look back at the notes you took while reading. What **inferences** did you make about Equiano's beliefs? Why do you think Equiano described the flogging of a crew member?

8. What is the basic contradiction between the crew's main goal and their treatment of the captives?

Extending and Evaluating

9. What characteristics of Equiano's **autobiography** distinguish it from the poem by Phillis Wheatley (see the **Connection** on page 60)? How does the message in his autobiography differ from that in Wheatley's poem?

10. How do you account for the depth of human cruelty described in parts of this autobiography? What current events reveal a similar capacity for cruelty in human nature?

WRITING

Teach Your Children Well

Create a **book** for children that will teach them about some aspect of the African American heritage—perhaps something that you've just learned from Equiano's account. Research your topic, and report your findings in clear, easy-to-read language for children. You might even want to write in poetic form. (You may illustrate your book if you wish.)

Vocabulary Development

Getting Information

assailant	commodious
distraction	consternation
apprehensions	improvident
interspersed	avarice

This chart organizes some basic information about the word *alleviate*. With a partner or small group, use a dictionary to make similar charts for the other Vocabulary words.

alleviate
Meaning   *make more bearable; lighten*
Origin   *ad–,* "to" + *levis,* "light"
Synonyms   *relieve; lessen; reduce*
Sample Sentence   *This painkiller will alleviate the patient's suffering.*

SKILLS FOCUS

Literary Skills
Analyze the characteristics of an autobiography.

Reading Skills
Analyze inferences about an author's beliefs.

Writing Skills
Write a book for children about African American heritage.

Vocabulary Skills
Create semantic charts.

Olaudah Equiano   63

INDEPENDENT PRACTICE

Response and Analysis

Thinking Critically

5. Students may say that they hadn't known Africans participated in the slave trade. Students may say that the article taught them that those who died during the Middle Passage have not been forgotten.

6. They wanted to see if he was healthy enough to travel and fetch a good price. If not, they might have killed or sold him.

7. Possible answer: Equiano believed that slavery was immoral and contrary to the teachings of Christianity. He included the description to show that the slavers acted brutally to one another.

8. When harsh treatment causes slaves to die, then the slavers have gone against their own financial interests.

Extending and Evaluating

9. Possible answer: Equiano's autobiography is a personal, first-hand account of the horrors of slavery. His purpose is to convey the message that slavery and the slave trade are immoral. Wheatley's purpose is to convey the message that England is acting tyrannically toward the colonists.

10. Possible answer: Greed and racism are the main causes. Genocidal wars, terrorist attacks, and hate crimes reveal a similar cruelty.

Vocabulary Development

Sample word chart

- *distraction.* Meaning—mental disturbance or distress. *Origin—dis–,* "apart" + *trahere,* "draw." *Synonym*—agitation. *Sentence*—Reading about the disaster can cause distraction for most readers.

Reading Check

1. His African captors and owners treated him humanely.

2. They were first separated a few days after their kidnapping. Later, they met again but were separated the next morning.

3. They attempted suicide by refusing food or leaping overboard.

4. They kept him on deck because the stench of the hold made him so sick that he might have died.

Vocabulary Development

Practice

In the following sample sentences, Vocabulary words are underlined, context clues are in italics, and the type of context clue is in brackets.

- Separated from his sister, Equiano was left in a state of <u>distraction</u>, too *grief-stricken* and *upset to eat.* [definition/restatement]

- Equiano was filled with <u>apprehensions</u> when he was carried aboard the slave ship, and his *fears* increased when he saw a large furnace. [synonym]

- A crew member offered him some liquor, thinking it would <u>alleviate</u> his terror, but instead it only *made him feel worse.* [contrast]

- Descriptions of the new things he sees are <u>interspersed</u> within the narrative, *rather than collected* into a single chapter. [contrast]

- In Africa the wealthy widow's house was <u>commodious</u>, the most *spacious* dwelling Equiano had ever seen. [synonym]

- Three captives jumped overboard, much to the <u>consternation</u> of the crew, who were *alarmed* that others might follow. [synonym]

- *Careless about their future* profits, the slavers were <u>improvident</u> to let captives die from horrid conditions. [definition]

- Equiano denounces the <u>avarice</u> of the slavers, whose *greed* goes against their supposed Christian values. [synonym]

Vocabulary Development

Context Clues

A word's **context**—the words and sentences that surround it—often gives clues to the word's meaning. Look at this example from *The Interesting Narrative of the Life of Olaudah Equiano.*

> "Some of us used to get up a tree to look for any <u>assailant</u> or kidnapper that might come upon us, for they sometimes took those opportunities of our parents' absence to attack and carry off as many as they could seize." (page 53)

You can infer from the context that an assailant is a "kidnapper" or someone who would "attack" and "carry off" someone. The context has given you an **example** of an assailant.

You will find many different types of context clues in your reading. An example is one type of clue. Here are three other common types to look for:

1. **Definition or restatement.** Look for an actual definition or a rephrasing of the word in more familiar terms.

   As a child, Equiano was trained to shoot and throw <u>javelins</u>, or light spears.

   "Light spears" is the definition of *javelins.*

2. **Synonyms.** Look for clues indicating that an unfamiliar word is similar in meaning to a familiar word or phrase.

   The closest relations were deprived of the comfort of companionship and separated from their <u>kindred</u>.

   Kindred is a synonym for "closest relations."

3. **Contrast.** An unfamiliar word may sometimes be contrasted with a more familiar word or concept.

   Sleep was Equiano's only relief from his overpowering <u>fatigue</u>.

   Fatigue is contrasted with the word *sleep.* Since sleep was Equiano's "only relief," you can infer that *fatigue* means "exhaustion" or "weariness."

PRACTICE

For each of the other Vocabulary words, construct a sentence that gives the meaning of the word in a context clue. Model your sentences after the sentences above. Include a definition or rephrasing of the word in more familiar terms.

distraction	interspersed	improvident
apprehensions	commodious	avarice
alleviate	consternation	

SKILLS FOCUS

Vocabulary Skills
Use context clues to determine the meaning of words.

ASSESSING

Assessment

- *Holt Assessment: Literature, Reading, and Vocabulary*

Benjamin Franklin
(1706–1790)

Benjamin Franklin (1777) after Jean Baptiste Greuze. Oil on canvas (28⅝″ × 22⅝″).

Few people have been so energetically devoted to improvement as Benjamin Franklin. Born in Boston, one of seventeen children, he rose from poverty to eminence even though he had to leave school early in order to work. By the time he was twenty-four, Franklin was a prosperous merchant, owner of a successful print shop, and publisher of *The Pennsylvania Gazette*. He helped found the Academy of Philadelphia (which became the University of Pennsylvania), the American Philosophical Society, and the first public library in America. Franklin was a scientist and an important inventor: His research, especially on electricity, resulted in his election to England's Royal Society. In addition, he invented an open heating stove (called a Franklin stove), bifocal eyeglasses, a type of harmonica, and a rocking chair that could swat flies.

Franklin also possessed uncommon talents as a diplomat and negotiator, and he used these skills in the service of his state and his country. Franklin lived in London in the 1750s and '60s, representing the interests of Pennsylvania as an agent of the Pennsylvania Assembly. A decade later he was back in London lobbying for the Colonies in their dispute with Britain, hoping to bring about a reconciliation that would prevent war. Franklin's wit and charm made him enormously popular in London for many years; he once said that he was invited out to dinner there six nights a week. But by 1774, when he was sixty-eight, the stress between Britain and the Colonies had become too great. The king's Privy Council publicly attacked Franklin for his policies, and the British press called him an "old snake." Franklin finally relinquished his hopes for peace and sailed for America in 1775.

When Franklin arrived home, he was greeted with news that the first battles of the Revolutionary War had been fought at Lexington and Concord, Massachusetts. "The shot heard round the world" had been fired. After helping to draft the Declaration of Independence in 1776, Franklin left for Paris to negotiate the treaty that brought the French into the war on America's side.

In Paris, Franklin was even more popular than he had once been in England. He played the role of the sophisticated but homespun American to the hilt. When the Revolution was over, he helped negotiate the peace. In 1787, Franklin served as a member of the Constitutional Convention. His death three years later was cause for international mourning.

Franklin's practicality, like the success story of his life, is typically American, but it has not been universally admired throughout the nation's history. The American novelist Herman Melville deplored Franklin's lack of imagination: "Jack-of-all-trades, master of each and mastered by none—the type and genius of his land. Franklin was everything but a poet."

Summary  *at grade level*

In "Arrival in Philadelphia," Franklin describes his first day in the city. Hungry, tired, dirty, and poor, he buys three rolls, then ends up giving two of them to a woman and child. He then follows a group of people into a Quaker meeting house, where he falls asleep. In "Arriving at Moral Perfection," Franklin describes his plan for achieving a perfectly virtuous life— that is, to "live without committing any fault at any time." To arrive at this state of moral perfection, Franklin devises a list of thirteen virtues and an ambitious plan for mastering each one, in order, one at a time.

Selection Starter

Motivate. Ask students if they have ever made a New Year's resolution to accomplish something or change a bad habit. How successful were they at achieving their goals? What obstacles did they face?

Before You Read

from The Autobiography

Make the Connection
Quickwrite 🖉

From founding a nation to flying to the moon, Americans have always believed in the possibility of progress. Progress, however, can be measured in many ways— technological, financial, educational, social, and even spiritual. Just as Benjamin Franklin invented devices to improve the quality of life in America, he also tried to invent a moral "machine" to improve the quality of his own character. Today a walk through a bookstore or a glance at TV commercials quickly reveals that self-improvement is still a hot topic. Jot down the titles of any self-help books you know of or of TV self-help programs that you have seen. Why do you think so many of these books and programs are popular?

Reading Skills
Making Inferences

One of the pleasures of reading an autobiography is getting to know the writer's personality, as well as his or her philosophical beliefs and attitudes—in other words, what makes the writer "tick." In many cases, though, writers don't directly reveal this information. Readers need to look beneath the surface of the text to **infer,** or use clues to guess, the writer's implicit, or suggested but unstated, beliefs.

As you read this excerpt from *The Autobiography,* jot down any words or phrases that help you infer Franklin's attitudes and beliefs. For example, how do you think Franklin felt about being self-reliant and practical?

go. hrw .com

INTERNET

Vocabulary Practice
•
More About Benjamin Franklin
•
Keyword: LE5 11-1

SKILLS FOCUS

Reading Skills
Make inferences about a writer's beliefs.

Background

Franklin began *The Autobiography* when he was sixty-five and continued working on it intermittently for years, although he never finished it and it was not published during his lifetime. When Franklin was a teenager, he was apprenticed to his older brother James, who printed a Boston newspaper. Disputes arose between the brothers, and the younger Franklin fled Boston for Philadelphia to escape from a second, secret indenture, or contract of service, that his brother had forced him to sign. This selection begins with Franklin's arrival in Philadelphia.

Vocabulary Development

arduous (är′jōō·əs) *adj.:* difficult.

rectitude (rek′tə·tōōd′) *n.:* correctness.

facilitate (fə·sil′ə·tāt′) *v.:* make easier.

subsequent (sub′si·kwənt) *adj.:* following.

eradicate (ē·rad′i·kāt′) *v.:* eliminate.

Odometer used by Benjamin Franklin to measure postal routes.

Previewing Vocabulary

To reinforce students' understanding of the Vocabulary words on p. 66, have them complete the following sentences with the correct word.

1. He used his uncle's influence to _____ his promotion. [facilitate]

2. Good deeds can't _____ past mistakes. [eradicate]

3. Her moral _____ prevented her from lying. [rectitude]

4. Writing the book was a long, _____ task. [arduous]

5. Her _____ actions showed how much she had learned on the job. [subsequent]

Benjamin Franklin Drawing Electricity from the Sky (c. 1805) by Benjamin West. Oil on paper on canvas (13¼″ × 10″).

from The Autobiography

Benjamin Franklin

VIEWING THE ART

The American painter **Benjamin West** (1738–1820) achieved meteoric fame during his lifetime. A Quaker, he was born in Pennsylvania and began painting portraits professionally at the age of eighteen. In 1763, after spending three years in Italy, West moved to London, where he was soon celebrated as a prodigy from the American wilderness. Establishing himself as a painter of prominent subjects, West originated the style of placing these figures in contemporary dress (freeing the genre from the convention of painting modern subjects wearing Roman togas). In 1769, West gained the patronage and friendship of King George III, and in 1792, he became president of the prestigious Royal Academy of Arts. Because of his Quaker beliefs, however, West turned down the British knighthood.

Activity. This painting exhibits the Romantic style that West adopted later in his life—a style marked by emotional intensity, concern with the mysterious aspects of nature, and a focus on awe-inspiring subjects. Ask students to cite elements in the painting that demonstrate each of these characteristics. [Students might mention such Romantic elements as Franklin's intent gaze and swirling cape; the fact that Franklin and the cherubs are performing a scientific experiment with a mysterious force of nature; and the dramatic lightning-streaked sky.]

Primary Source

Franklin's Epitaph
Franklin wrote the following epitaph for himself when he was in his early twenties: "The body of Benjamin Franklin, Printer (like the cover of an old book, its contents torn out and stripped of its lettering and gilding), lies here food for worms; but the work shall not be wholly lost, for it will . . . appear once more in a new and more elegant edition, revised and corrected by the Author."

Comparing and contrasting authors' beliefs. Point out that although Franklin's thirteen virtues were deeply rooted in Puritanism, he offers them as a practical formula for improving himself and his society —not as a way to win or demonstrate God's approval. Ask students to compare Franklin's beliefs about virtues, faults, and human perfectibility with Jonathan Edwards's ideas about salvation, sin, and predestination (p. 46).

Ⓑ Literary Focus

❷ Irony. Elsewhere in *The Autobiography*, Franklin says that he tacked on the thirteenth virtue after a friend told him that he was considered proud. What irony or discrepancy can you find in this addition? [It is hardly humble of Franklin to think that he can imitate Jesus and Socrates.]

---

names of virtues all that at that time occurred to me as necessary or desirable, and annexed to each a short precept,[4] which fully expressed the extent I gave to its meaning.

These names of virtues, with their precepts, were:

1. Temperance. *Eat not to dullness; drink not to elevation.*

2. Silence. *Speak not but what may benefit others or yourself; avoid trifling[5] conversation.*

3. Order. *Let all your things have their places; let each part of your business have its time.*

4. Resolution. *Resolve to perform what you ought; perform without fail what you resolve.*

5. Frugality. *Make no expense but to do good to others or yourself; i.e., waste nothing.*

6. Industry. *Lose no time; be always employed in something useful; cut off all unnecessary actions.*

7. Sincerity. *Use no hurtful deceit; think innocently and justly, and, if you speak, speak accordingly.*

8. Justice. *Wrong none by doing injuries, or omitting the benefits that are your duty.*

9. Moderation. *Avoid extremes; forbear resenting injuries so much as you think they deserve.*

10. Cleanliness. *Tolerate no uncleanliness in body, clothes, or habitation.*

11. Tranquility. *Be not disturbed at trifles, or at accidents common or unavoidable.*

---

4. **precept** *n.:* rule of moral conduct; principle.
5. **trifling** *adj.:* unimportant; shallow.

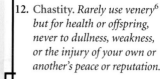

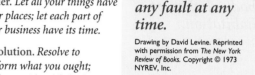

I wished to live without committing any fault at any time.

Drawing by David Levine. Reprinted with permission from *The New York Review of Books.* Copyright © 1973 NYREV, Inc.

12. Chastity. *Rarely use venery[6] but for health or offspring, never to dullness, weakness, or the injury of your own or another's peace or reputation.*

13. Humility. *Imitate Jesus and Socrates.[7]*

My intention being to acquire the habitude of all these virtues, I judged it would be well not to distract my attention by attempting the whole at once, but to fix it on one of them at a time; and, when I should be master of that, then to proceed to another, and so on, till I should have gone through the thirteen; and, as the previous acquisition of some might facilitate the acquisition of certain others, I arranged them with that view, as they stand above. *Temperance* first, as it tends to procure that coolness and clearness of head, which is so necessary where constant vigilance was to be kept up, and guard maintained against the unremitting[8] attraction of ancient habits, and the force of perpetual temptations. This being acquired and established, *silence* would be more easy; and my desire being to gain knowledge at the same time that I improved in virtue, and considering that in conversation it was obtained rather by the use of the ears than of the tongue, and therefore wishing to break a habit I was getting into of prattling, punning, and joking, which only made me acceptable to trifling com-

---

6. **venery** (ven'ər·ē) *n.:* sex.
7. **Socrates** (säk'rə·tēz') (470?–399 B.C.): Greek philosopher who is said to have lived a simple, virtuous life.
8. **unremitting** *adj.:* not stopping; persistent.

Vocabulary
facilitate (fə·sil'ə·tāt') *v.:* make easier.

Analyzing connotations. Remind students that while the denotations, or dictionary definitions, of two words may be similar, their connotations, or emotional overtones, may be quite different. For example, the word *slim* usually has positive connotations, while *skinny* does not. *Dining* is an elegant experience; *chowing down* is just the opposite.
Activity. To demonstrate the power of connotation, discuss with students the

differences between the following word pairs. Then, have them write pairs of sentences that demonstrate the two different shades of meaning.

1. temperance, self-denial
2. silence, reticence
3. order, fussiness
4. resolution, stubbornness
5. frugality, stinginess

6. industry, workaholism
7. sincerity, bluntness
8. justice, righteousness
9. moderation, halfheartedness
10. cleanliness, sterility
11. tranquility, lethargy
12. humility, nonassertiveness

pany, I gave *silence* the second place. This and the next, *order,* I expected would allow me more time for attending to my project and my studies. *Resolution,* once become habitual, would keep me firm in my endeavors to obtain all the <u>subsequent</u> virtues; *frugality* and *industry* freeing me from my remaining debt, and producing affluence and independence, would make more easy the practice of *sincerity* and *justice,* etc., etc. Conceiving then, that, agreeably to the advice of Pythagoras[9] in his Golden Verses, daily examination would be necessary, I contrived the following method for conducting that examination.

I made a little book, in which I allotted a page for each of the virtues. I ruled each page with red ink, so as to have seven columns, one for each day of the week, marking each column with a letter for the day. I crossed these columns with thirteen red lines, marking the beginning of each line with the first letter of one of the virtues, on which line, and in its proper column, I might mark, by a little black spot, every fault I found upon examination to have been committed respecting that virtue upon that day.

I determined to give a week's strict attention to each of the virtues successively. Thus, in the first week, my great guard was to avoid every[10] the least offense against *temperance,* leaving the other virtues to their ordinary chance, only marking every evening the faults of the day. Thus, if in the first week I could keep my first line, marked T, clear of spots, I supposed the habit of that virtue so much strengthened, and its opposite weakened, that I might venture extending my attention to include the next, and for the following week keep both lines clear of spots. Proceeding thus to the last, I could go through a course complete in thirteen weeks, and four courses in a year. And like him who, having a garden to weed, does not attempt to <u>eradicate</u> all the bad herbs at once, which would exceed his reach and his strength, but works on one of the beds at a time, and, having accom-

Form of the Pages

Temperance							
Eat not to dullness. Drink not to elevation.							
	S	M	T	W	T	F	S
T							
S							
O							
R							
F							
I							
S							
J							
M							
Cl							
T							
Ch							
H							

plished the first, proceeds to a second, so I should have, I hoped, the encouraging pleasure of seeing on my pages the progress I made in virtue, by clearing successively my lines of their spots, till in the end, by a number of courses, I should be happy in viewing a clean book, after a thirteen weeks' daily examination. . . . ■

---

9. **Pythagoras** (pi·thag′ə·rəs): Greek philosopher and mathematician of the sixth century B.C.
10. **every:** archaic for "even."

Vocabulary
subsequent (sub′si·kwənt) *adj.:* following.
eradicate (ē·rad′i·kāt′) *v.:* eliminate.

Benjamin Franklin   71

DIRECT TEACHING

C **Reading Skills**

❓ **Making inferences.** What does Franklin's plan reveal about his character? [Possible responses: It reveals that he is diligent, orderly, organized, methodical, and logical. It shows that he attempts to control emotional behavior with reason. Some students might say that his plan shows that he is unrealistic, naive, or arrogant.]

D **Vocabulary Development**

❓ **Analogy.** What analogy does Franklin use to explain why he doesn't try to tackle all the virtues at once? [He compares eliminating faults with pulling weeds from a garden.] **What point is he making?** [If you try to get rid of all your faults at once, you'll get frustrated and tired. It's better to attack them one at a time.]

GUIDED PRACTICE

Monitoring students' progress. Guide the class in answering these comprehension questions.

True-False

1. When Franklin arrived in Philadelphia, he was poor. [T]
2. Franklin refused to pay for his passage to Philadelphia. [F]
3. Franklin felt that temperance was the first virtue to master. [T]
4. Franklin gave up his plan after thirteen weeks. [F]

READING MINI-LESSON

Developing Word-Attack Skills
Remind students that a final *e* usually signals that the preceding vowel sound is long. This is almost always true for one-syllable words. Display these examples:

fate   pride   drove   rude

Explain that the vowel–consonant–final *e* pattern at the end of a multisyllable word doesn't always indicate a long vowel sound. Write

these words on the chalkboard:

passage   imagine   rectitude

Then, have volunteers read them aloud and tell which word has a long vowel sound in the final syllable.

Activity. Have students read each pair of words and decide in which word or words the vowel–consonant–final *e* pattern signals a long vowel sound.

1. aggravate [long]   immediate
2. suffice [long]   office
3. favorite   parasite [long]
4. infantile [long]   fragile
5. magnitude [long]   interlude [long]

Connection

Summary ⬇ *below grade level*

In this excerpt, Fulghum states that we learn the basic values of life when we are in kindergarten. He then lists sixteen precepts—beginning with "Share everything" and ending with "LOOK"—that he believes we should follow as adults.

DIRECT TEACHING

A Vocabulary Development

? **Using context clues.** What context clue provides the definition of *credo*? ["personal statement of belief"]

B Reading Skills

? **Expressing an opinion.** Do you agree with all of Fulghum's precepts? Can you think of anything you learned in kindergarten (or at any other point in your childhood) that you could add to his list? [Possible responses: Take turns. Everyone gets to play. No cutting in line. Look both ways before crossing. Put the cap back on the glue. Take what you want, but eat or use what you take.]

C Literary Focus

? **Diction.** Why do you think Fulghum uses the word *blankies* here? [Possible response: The childhood term humorously suggests that the comforts of childhood are still valid in adulthood.]

CONNECTION / ESSAY

Behind Benjamin Franklin's project for achieving moral perfection lies what seems to be a common human impulse—the need to simplify life, to get at the root of what's fundamental to us. In 1986, Robert Fulghum published some thoughts of his own about how to live a full and happy life. The book became a bestseller.

from All I Really Need to Know I Learned in Kindergarten

Robert Fulghum

Each spring, for many years, I have set myself the task of writing a personal statement of belief: a Credo. When I was younger, the statement ran for many pages, trying to cover every base, with no loose ends. It sounded like a Supreme Court brief, as if words could resolve all conflicts about the meaning of existence.

The Credo has grown shorter in recent years—sometimes cynical, sometimes comical, sometimes bland—but I keep working at it. Recently I set out to get the statement of personal belief down to one page in simple terms, fully understanding the naive idealism that implied. . . .

I realized then that I already know most of what's necessary to live a meaningful life—that it isn't all that complicated. *I know it.* And I have known it for a long, long time. Living it—well, that's another matter, yes? Here's my Credo:

All I really need to know about how to live and what to do and how to be I learned in kindergarten. Wisdom was not at the top of the graduate-school mountain, but there in the sandpile at Sunday school. These are the things I learned:

Share everything.
Play fair.
Don't hit people.
Put things back where you found them.
Clean up your own mess.
Don't take things that aren't yours.
Say you're sorry when you hurt somebody.
Wash your hands before you eat.
Flush.
Warm cookies and cold milk are good for you.
Live a balanced life—learn some and think some and draw and paint and sing and dance and play and work every day some.
Take a nap every afternoon.
When you go out into the world, watch out for traffic, hold hands, and stick together.
Be aware of wonder. Remember the little seed in the Styrofoam cup: The roots go down and the plant goes up and nobody really knows how or why, but we are all like that.
Goldfish and hamsters and white mice and even the little seed in the Styrofoam cup—they all die. So do we.
And then remember the Dick-and-Jane books and the first word you learned—the biggest word of all—LOOK.

. . . Think what a better world it would be if we all—the whole world—had cookies and milk about three o'clock every afternoon and then lay down with our blankies for a nap. Or if all governments had as a basic policy to always put things back where they found them and to clean up their own mess.

And it is still true, no matter how old you are—when you go out into the world, it is best to hold hands and stick together.

Comparing and Contrasting Texts

Ask students to think about how Franklin might respond to Fulghum's sixteen precepts and how Fulghum might respond to Franklin's thirteen virtues. Introduce a scenario in which each writer has been transported into the other's time period to serve as his editor. What specific revisions might each editor suggest? What positive feedback might he offer? [Students might imagine that Franklin would advise Fulghum to reword his precepts to be less metaphorical and more direct or to combine related ideas (such as "Put things back where you found them," "Clean up your own mess," and "Flush"). Students might imagine that Fulghum would object to Franklin's ornate diction and would suggest more down-to-earth language. He might also encourage Franklin to consider the virtues of wonder and observation.]

Before You Read

from Poor Richard's Almanack

Make the Connection
Quickwrite ✏️

TV talk shows, radio call-in programs, newspaper columns, how-to books, inspirational speakers—sometimes today's world seems to overflow with people who want to give advice. Dispensing wisdom—or at least reflections on one's own experience—has become an American industry. Why do you think so many readers and listeners flock to advice givers? Make a list of three pieces of advice you would give to an incoming freshman at your school.

Literary Focus
Aphorisms

An **aphorism** is a brief, cleverly worded statement that makes a wise observation about life. Aphorisms grow out of speeches, sermons, religious texts such as the Bible ("Love your neighbor"), poems and stories, advertisements, and most commonly, the expressions of ordinary people in ordinary situations.

Aphorisms can serve many purposes. They entertain, especially through their humor, wit, and wordplay; they instruct, suggesting ways to overcome obstacles, solve problems, and achieve success; and they inspire, often providing a kind of moral uplift. Aphorisms can also **satirize,** using humor to mock and criticize the way things are. They can address any subject—from war and peace to the fleas on a dog.

> An **aphorism** is a brief, cleverly worded statement that makes a wise observation about life.
>
> *For more on Aphorisms, see the Handbook of Literary and Historical Terms.*

Background

With the publication of *Poor Richard's Almanack* in 1732, Franklin found his biggest publishing success, and he continued to publish his almanac for twenty-five years. Almost every house had an almanac. Almanacs calculated the tides and the phases of the moon, forecast the weather for the next year, and even provided astrological advice. Many almanacs also supplied recipes, jokes, and aphorisms. Poor Richard was an imaginary astrologer with a critical wife named Bridget. One year Bridget wrote the aphorisms to answer those her husband had written the year before on female idleness. Another time Bridget included "better" weather forecasts so that people would know the good days for drying their clothes.

Franklin's practicality shows itself not only in the content of his almanacs but also in the way he put them together: He took his wit and wisdom wherever he found it. He printed old sayings translated from other languages, lifted some aphorisms from other writers, and adapted others from popular and local sources. An American to the core, Franklin never hesitated to rework what he found to suit his own purposes. For example, for the 1758 almanac, Franklin skimmed all his previous editions to compose a single speech on economy. This speech, called "The Way to Wealth," has become one of the best known of Franklin's works. It has been mistakenly believed to be representative of Poor Richard's wisdom. Poor Richard often called for prudence and thrift, but he just as often favored extravagance.

INTERNET
More About Benjamin Franklin
Keyword: LE5 11-1

Literary Skills
Understand aphorisms.

PRETEACHING

Summary ⬌ *at grade level*

These nineteen aphorisms from *Poor Richard's Almanack* give students a glimpse of Franklin's legendary humor, insight into human nature, and philosophy of life.

Skills Starter

Motivate. You might begin by telling students that contemporary aphorisms are the kinds of witty statements you might see on bumper stickers, T-shirts, and advertising displays. Ask students to recall some examples they've seen and to create an original aphorism they would like to see on a bumper sticker. [Here are some examples of contemporary bumper sticker wisdom: "Don't judge a book by its movie"; "Cleanliness is next to impossible"; "Aliens smart enough to visit Earth would be smart enough not to."]

Benjamin Franklin   **73**

Primary Source

Poor Richard's Persona

To give students an idea of the persona and voice Franklin created for Poor Richard, read aloud the following section from the preface to the first *Poor Richard's Almanack* of 1733: "COURTEOUS READER, . . . The plain Truth of the Matter is, I am excessive poor, and my Wife, good Woman, is, I tell her, excessive proud; she cannot bear, she says, to sit spinning in her Shift of Tow [chemise], while I do nothing but gaze at the Stars; and has threatened more than once to burn all my Books and Rattling-Traps (as she calls my Instruments) if I do not make some profitable Use of them for the good of my Family."

A **Reading Skills**

? **Synthesizing.** Would Poor Richard agree or disagree with the following statements? Support your answers with references to specific aphorisms. (1) Even close friends need some privacy from each other. [agree; 1] (2) Live for tomorrow. [disagree; 8] (3) May all your wishes come true. [disagree; 14] (4) There is dignity in hard work. [agree; 17] (5) A mind is a terrible thing to waste. [agree; 2]

GUIDED PRACTICE

Monitoring students' progress. For each of the following statements, guide the class in identifying one of Poor Richard's aphorisms that essentially says the same thing.

Matching Item

1. Be careful what you wish for. [14]

2. Good fences make good neighbors. [1]

3. Seize the day. [8]

4. Give a man a fish, and he'll eat for a day. Teach him how to fish, and he'll eat forever. [2]

5. A rumor goes in one ear and out many mouths. [3]

---

from Poor Richard's Almanack

Benjamin Franklin

Panel from an engraving for Benjamin Franklin's *Poor Richard Illustrated* (c. 1800).
The Granger Collection, New York.

1. Love your neighbor; yet don't pull down your hedge.

2. If a man empties his purse into his head, no man can take it away from him. An investment in knowledge always pays the best interest.

3. Three may keep a secret if two of them are dead.

4. Tart words make no friends; a spoonful of honey will catch more flies than a gallon of vinegar.

5. Glass, china, and reputation are easily cracked and never well mended.

6. Fish and visitors smell in three days.

7. He that lieth down with dogs shall rise up with fleas.

8. One today is worth two tomorrows.

A 9. A truly great man will neither trample on a worm nor sneak to an emperor.

10. A little neglect may breed mischief; for want of a nail the shoe was lost; for want of a shoe the horse was lost; for want of a horse the rider was lost; for want of the rider the battle was lost.

11. If you would know the value of money, go and try to borrow some; he that goes a-borrowing goes a-sorrowing.

12. He that composes himself is wiser than he that composes books.

13. He that is of the opinion that money will do everything may well be suspected of doing everything for money.

14. If a man could have half his wishes, he would double his troubles.

15. 'Tis hard for an empty bag to stand upright.

16. A small leak will sink a great ship.

17. A plowman on his legs is higher than a gentleman on his knees.

18. Keep your eyes wide open before marriage, half shut afterward.

19. Nothing brings more pain than too much pleasure; nothing more bondage than too much liberty.

DIFFERENTIATING INSTRUCTION

Learners Having Difficulty
Students may need help understanding the implied metaphors in some of the aphorisms, such as 2, 4, 7, 9, 15, and 16. You might ask, "What does it mean to empty one's purse into one's head?" Then, ask for a volunteer to paraphrase the expression, using more literal language. [Possible response: Spend money on education.]

English-Language Learners
Students may need help understanding the puns in some of the aphorisms. You might explain that aphorism 12 relies on the two meanings of the word *compose*: "to write" and "to make oneself calm."

Response and Analysis

from The Autobiography

Reading Check

1. What was Franklin's condition in life when he arrived in Philadelphia?
2. What does Franklin say must happen before people can depend on correct moral behavior?
3. Why does Franklin place temperance first on his list?
4. How many "courses" of his list of virtues does Franklin plan to go through in one year?

Thinking Critically

5. What **inferences** can you make about Franklin's attitudes and beliefs, based on his plan to achieve moral perfection? If Franklin were alive today, what modern causes might he support? Explain.
6. Franklin writes about "arriving at moral perfection" just as he had earlier written about his arrival in the city of Philadelphia. What does this similarity in his language reveal about Franklin's philosophical assumptions?

✓ Extending and Evaluating

7. Compare Robert Fulghum's list of things learned in kindergarten (see the **Connection** on page 72) to Franklin's list of virtues. Which list do you think would be more useful to people today? In general, how does Franklin's scheme for moral perfection compare with the self-help books available today? Be sure to refer to your Quickwrite notes. 🖉

Literary Criticism

8. Reactions to *The Autobiography* have sometimes been negative. Read the following comment by satirist Mark Twain. What is Twain's **tone** in this paragraph—that is, his attitude toward Ben Franklin?

> [Franklin had] a malevolence which is without parallel in history; he would work all day and then sit up nights and let on to be studying algebra by the light of a smoldering fire, so that all the boys might have to do that also, or else have Benjamin Franklin thrown upon them. Not satisfied with these proceedings, he had a fashion of living wholly on bread and water, and studying astronomy at mealtime—a thing which has brought affliction to millions of boys since, whose fathers had read Franklin's pernicious biography.
>
> —Mark Twain

The word *pernicious* (pər·nish′əs), in the last sentence, means "deadly." What elements of Franklin's autobiography is Twain attacking? How do you feel about Twain's grumblings?

from Poor Richard's Almanack

Thinking Critically

1. Poor Richard's aphorisms often succeed because of their **implied metaphors,** or metaphors that do not state explicitly the two things being compared. Re-read aphorisms 4, 7, 15, and 16. Then, identify what each of the following images might mean: a spoonful of honey, lying down with dogs, an empty bag, a small leak.
2. Many of Poor Richard's aphorisms convey moral lessons. Choose one of the aphorisms, and restate it in your own words, explaining its moral lesson.
3. Which of the aphorisms reveals a healthy skepticism and humor about human nature?

INTERNET
Projects and Activities
Keyword: LE5 11-1

SKILLS FOCUS

Literary Skills
Analyze aphorisms.

Reading Skills
Make inferences about a writer's beliefs.

Writing Skills
Write a handbook with aphorisms. Write an essay comparing and contrasting two writers.

Vocabulary Skills
Demonstrate word knowledge.

Benjamin Franklin   **75**

Response and Analysis

Extending and Evaluating

7. Possible answer: Franklin's list is applicable in any age. Fulghum's list reflects today's emphasis on social relationships. Both share a concern for justice and order. Franklin's list emphasizes the goals of virtue, self-control, and responsibility, while most self-help books emphasize goals like personal fulfillment and high self-esteem.

Literary Criticism

8. Twain's tone is ironic, showing that despite his resentment toward Franklin's diligence, he doesn't really view Franklin as malevolent. Twain is attacking the elements of Franklin's autobiography that present Franklin as a role model that no one else can live up to. Students may say Twain makes a good point.

from Poor Richard's Almanack

Thinking Critically

1. *Spoonful of honey*—a small amount of praise, love, sweetness. *Lying down with dogs*—associating with lowly people, riffraff. *An empty bag*—a person who doesn't have much intelligence or character. *A small leak*—a minor flaw.
2. Possible answer: "Protect your reputation, because once it's damaged, it's hard to fix" (aphorism 5).
3. Possible answers: 1, 3, 6, 15, 18, and 19.

---

from The Autobiography

Reading Check

1. He was tired, dirty, hungry, and poor.
2. They must first break bad habits and acquire good ones.
3. Temperance helps guard against other bad habits and temptations.
4. four

Thinking Critically

5. Possible answers: Franklin believes in the virtues of practicality, discipline, and self-reliance. If he were alive today, he might support antidrug and stay-in-school programs.
6. Possible answer: He assumes that one can plot a course to achieve moral perfection.

Vocabulary Development

Completed sentences should read as follows:

In order to <u>facilitate</u> his task, Franklin tried to <u>eradicate</u> everything that stood in the way of moral <u>rectitude</u>. It was an <u>arduous</u> program, but his <u>subsequent</u> career proved it was worth the effort.

WRITING

Becoming Virtuous

Using your Quickwrite notes, write a short handbook titled *Surviving Freshman Year*. Create **aphorisms** to make your advice short and memorable.

Comparing Texts

In an **essay,** compare and contrast Franklin with Jonathan Edwards (page 44). Be sure to consider each man's goals in life and the philosophy behind those goals. Are these Americans alike in any ways?

Vocabulary Development

Fill in the blanks with the appropriate word from the list below:

⁴ arduous   ¹ facilitate   ² eradicate
³ rectitude   ⁵ subsequent

In order to _____ his task, Franklin tried to _____ everything that stood in the way of moral _____. It was an _____ program, but his _____ career proved it was worth the effort.

Grammar Link

Linking It Up: Coordinating Conjunctions

Here's one way to describe one of Benjamin Franklin's projects for self-improvement:

> Benjamin Franklin knew that arriving at moral perfection would be difficult. He was willing to give it a try.

Here's a better way to express the same information:

> Benjamin Franklin knew that arriving at moral perfection would be difficult, yet he was willing to give it a try.

In the second example, the writer combined two related thoughts into a single sentence with a connective word—in this case, the coordinating conjunction *yet*. A **coordinating conjunction** joins words or word groups that are used in the same way. Separating two thoughts into two sentences is not incorrect; there are times when short, simple sentences sound best. However, using coordinating conjunctions to combine two thoughts into one sentence can result in more graceful syntax, or sentence structure.

Some Connective Words and What They Indicate	
Conjunction	**Indicates**
and	similarity, addition
but	opposition, contrast
yet	opposition, contrast
or	choice
nor	negation
so	cause and effect, result
for	explanation

SKILLS FOCUS

Grammar Skills
Use coordinating conjunctions.

All the words in the chart above function as coordinating conjunctions, but some can also function as other parts of speech.

For example, *for* is a preposition in the sentence *We went to the store for apples.* However, the word *for* is a coordinating conjunction in the sentence *We went to a store downtown, for the store on our block was closed.* To combine two related sentences into a single sentence, you will need to select an appropriate coordinating conjunction.

PRACTICE

Combine each pair of sentences into one sentence by using the most appropriate coordinating conjunction from the chart. Make necessary revisions so that the resulting sentence reads smoothly.

1. Benjamin Franklin was practically penniless when he arrived in Philadelphia. He was able to buy some rolls.
2. Franklin wished to achieve moral perfection. He devised a book in which he could record his transgressions and his progress.
3. Franklin wanted to avoid wrongdoing. He thought self-improvement was important.

Apply to Your Writing

Take out a writing assignment you are working on now or have already completed. Use coordinating conjunctions to combine any short, choppy sentences that have a clear relationship to one another.

▶ **For more help, see Combining by Coordinating Ideas, 10c, in the Language Handbook.**

The American Spelling Book by Noah Webster.

Grammar Link

Practice

1. Benjamin Franklin was practically penniless when he arrived in Philadelphia, *but* he was able to buy some rolls.
2. Franklin wished to achieve moral perfection, *so* he devised a book in which he could record his transgressions and his progress. [Also accept *and.*]
3. Franklin wanted to avoid wrongdoing, *for* he thought self-improvement was important.

ASSESSING

Assessment

■ *Holt Assessment: Literature, Reading, and Vocabulary*

RETEACHING

For a lesson reteaching philosophical assumptions and beliefs, see **Reteaching**, p. 1117A.

DIFFERENTIATING INSTRUCTION

Learners Having Difficulty

To provide students with additional practice, write the following pairs of sentences on the chalkboard. Have students use a coordinating conjunction to combine each pair into one sentence.

1. Benjamin Franklin was born in Boston. He moved to Philadelphia when he was a teenager. [but]

2. Franklin was a successful, self-made man. Not everyone admired him. [yet, but]

3. Tensions between Britain and the Colonies increased. Franklin decided to return home to America. [so]

4. Franklin was an accomplished scientist. He wrote several books, including his autobiography. [and]

Grade-Level Skills

■ **Literary Skills**

Analyze characteristics of persuasion.

■ **Reading Skills**

Critique the validity, appeals, and truthfulness of public documents, including appeals to reason and appeals to emotion.

More About the Writer

Background. The historian Garry Wills described Patrick Henry this way: "He had the actor's trick, in his oratory, of lifting his whole body up toward climaxes, along with his voice, as if he could add cubits by wanting to. . . . No one who beheld him incandescent with a Cause ever forgot the experience."

Patrick Henry

(1736–1799)

Patrick Henry (1820–1830), attributed to Asahel L. Powers. Oil on canvas.

Photograph by Ken Burns. © Shelburne Museum, Shelburne, Vermont.

One fiery act can catapult someone from obscurity to fame. That is what happened to Patrick Henry, a young representative who stood up in the Virginia House of Burgesses one day in 1765. He delivered a dynamic, thundering speech against the hated Stamp Act, with which the British Parliament instituted taxes on all newspapers and public documents. For the ten years following his declaration of resistance, Henry—a tall, lank, somber-looking man who favored the kind of clothing a preacher might wear—was recognized as one of the most persuasive figures in Virginia politics.

Henry had not always been so successful. Born in a frontier region of Virginia, he was raised in a cultured but modest environment. During his youth the country was undergoing the religious revival known as the Great Awakening, and young Patrick often accompanied his mother to hear the sermons of the traveling preachers. Later, as a young man, he made several unsuccessful stabs at farming and merchant life before discovering his love of oratory and his true calling: the law.

In 1765, the twenty-nine-year-old lawyer was chosen to represent his region in the Virginia House of Burgesses. Henry's speech against the Stamp Act was the first of the two most famous speeches in American Colonial history. The second, his famous "liberty or death" speech, came ten years later in 1775 as the Colonies were nearing the breaking point with England. Following the Boston Tea Party in December 1773, the British had closed the port of Boston and instituted other harsh measures referred to by the colonists as the Intolerable Acts. When the First Continental Congress protested these acts, the British Crown relieved the Colonies of taxation on a number of conditions. One condition was that the colonists fully support British rule and contribute toward the maintenance of British troops in America, whose numbers were increasing greatly. On March 20, 1775, the Virginia House of Burgesses held a convention in St. John's Episcopal Church in Richmond to decide how to respond to the growing British military threat. George Washington and Thomas Jefferson (page 95) were both present.

On March 23, after several speeches in favor of compromise with the British, Patrick Henry rose to defend his resolution to take up arms. Later, a clergyman who was present recalled that during Henry's speech he felt "sick with excitement." As the speech reached its climax, Henry is said to have grabbed an ivory letter opener and plunged it toward his chest at the final word *death*.

Henry persuaded the delegation. The Virginia Convention voted to arm its people against England. On April 19, 1775, the Battle of Lexington, Massachusetts, ignited the Revolutionary War.

RESOURCES: READING

Planning
■ *One-Stop Planner* CD-ROM

Differentiating Instruction
■ *Holt Reading Solutions*
■ *The Holt Reader*
■ *Holt Adapted Reader*
■ *Supporting Instruction in Spanish*
■ *Audio CD Library, Selections and Summaries in Spanish*

Vocabulary
■ *Vocabulary Development*

Grammar and Language
■ *Daily Language Activities*

Assessment
■ *Holt Assessment: Literature, Reading, and Vocabulary*
■ *One-Stop Planner* CD-ROM with ExamView Test Generator

■ *Holt Online Assessment*

Internet
■ go.hrw.com (Keyword: LE5 11-1)
■ *Elements of Literature Online*

Media
■ *Audio CD Library*
■ *Fine Art Transparencies*
■ *Audio CD Library, Selections and Summaries in Spanish*

Before You Read

Speech to the Virginia Convention

Make the Connection
Quickwrite ✏

Words shape us; they make us who we are. The American dream, as we loosely call our aspirations toward freedom, self-reliance, and self-creation, is defined in large part by the words of the men and women who helped shape America in its early years. Blood and suffering resulted from Henry's famous impassioned cry "give me liberty, or give me death!" yet his words generate pride to this day. Write a few sentences about what liberty means to you.

Literary Focus
Persuasion

Persuasion is a form of speaking or writing that aims to convince an audience to take a specific action. A good persuasive speaker or writer appeals to both head and heart—or **logic** and **emotion**—to win over an audience. To be persuasive, a writer or speaker must provide reasons to support a particular opinion or course of action. In the final analysis, audiences are often won over by the speaker's ability to address their concerns as much as by forceful arguments and a powerful personality.

> **Persuasion** is a form of discourse that uses logical and emotional appeals to convince another person to think or act in a certain way.
>
> *For more on Persuasion, see the Handbook of Literary and Historical Terms.*

Reading Skills 📖
Recognizing Modes of Persuasion

Patrick Henry uses two modes of **persuasion**: appeals to **reason** and appeals to **emotions** or values. As you read, track

these types of appeals in a two-column chart. In the left column, list Henry's logical appeals for wanting war. In the right column, write down his emotional appeals. As you take notes, mark a star next to those appeals that you find most effective. Mark an X next to appeals that strike you as deceptive or faulty.

Background

Although Henry's 1775 speech is one of the most famous in all American oratory, no manuscript of it exists. William Wirt, a biographer of Henry, pieced together the traditionally accepted text forty years after it was delivered, using notes of people who were present at the speech. As you read Henry's speech, try to envision the physical surroundings where it was delivered: a church in eighteenth-century Richmond, Virginia, on an early spring day. Try also to imagine the manner in which Henry delivered his speech.

INTERNET
Vocabulary Practice
Keyword: LE5 11-1

Vocabulary Development

solace (säl′is) *v.:* comfort.

insidious (in·sid′ē·əs) *adj.:* sly; sneaky.

martial (mär′shəl) *adj.:* warlike.

supplication (sup′lə·kā′shən) *n.:* plea; prayer.

avert (ə·vurt′) *v.:* prevent; turn away.

spurned (spurnd) *v.:* rejected.

inviolate (in·vī′ə·lit) *adj.:* uncorrupted.

adversary (ad′vər·ser′ē) *n.:* opponent.

vigilant (vij′ə·lənt) *adj.* used as *n.:* those who are watchful.

inevitable (in·ev′i·tə·bəl) *adj.:* not avoidable.

SKILLS FOCUS

Literary Skills
Understand the characteristics of persuasion.

Reading Skills
Recognize modes of persuasion, including appeals to reason and appeals to emotion.

Previewing Vocabulary

Have volunteers pronounce each vocabulary word on p. 79 with a tone or look that corresponds to its meaning. For example, one might add a villainous sneer when saying "insidious." Then, ask students to choose the Vocabulary word that fits best in each of the following statements:

1. A letter from home can ――― a soldier. [solace]

2. Patrick Henry knew that war was ―――. [inevitable]

3. Britain ――― the offers for peace. [spurned]

4. Americans struggle to keep the principles of democracy ―――. [inviolate]

5. The soldiers took on a ――― air before the battle. [martial]

6. His heartfelt ――― was denied by his captors. [supplication]

7. Spies must use ――― tactics. [insidious]

8. England was the Colonies' ―――. [adversary]

9. Guards must remain ―――. [vigilant]

10. Could negotiation ――― war? [avert]

VIEWING THE ART

Patrick Henry Arguing the Parson's Cause is attributed to **George Cooke** (1793–1849), an American artist who painted portraits, landscapes, and historical subjects. Cooke is remembered primarily for his depictions of Native American dignitaries.

Activity. Ask students how this image of Patrick Henry (the central figure with the upraised arm), which depicts him in a scene from his early legal career, compares with the portrait on p. 78. [Possible responses: The faces are similar, especially the noses; the portrait depicts Henry as older, with gray sideburns. In Cooke's work he is shown in action; in the portrait, Henry is transformed into an icon of liberty.]

A **Content-Area Connections**

History: Motion Before the House Henry was speaking before the Virginia assembly in support of his motion to form a Colonial militia, which previous speakers had argued would only provoke England. Even though Thomas Jefferson supported Henry's motion, the resolution passed by only five votes.

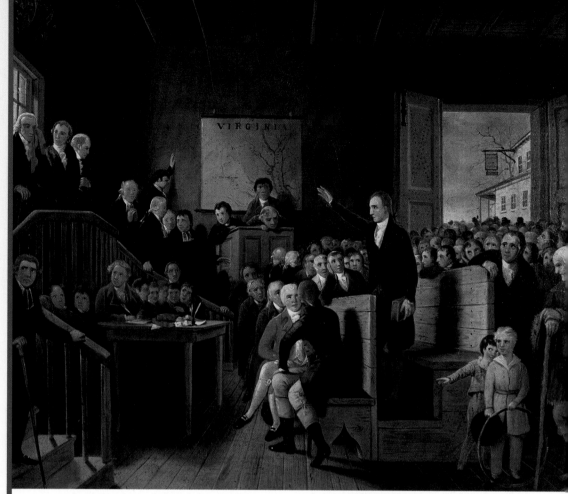

Patrick Henry Arguing the Parson's Cause (c. 1830), attributed to George Cooke. Oil on canvas.

Speech to the Virginia Convention

PUBLIC DOCUMENT

Patrick Henry

A   r. President:[1] No man thinks more highly than I do of the patriotism, as well as abilities, of the very worthy gentlemen who have just addressed the House. But different men often see the same subject in different lights; and, therefore, I hope that it will not be

---

1. **Mr. President:** Peyton Randolph (1721–1775), president of the Virginia Convention.

Learners Having Difficulty
Modeling. To help students read "Speech to the Virginia Convention," model the reading skill of recognizing modes of persuasion. Say: "When I know someone is trying to persuade me, I watch to see how he or she goes about it. I know the person is trying to move me emotionally when he or she uses charged language about things I care a lot about, such as home, family, security, and freedom. I know

the person is appealing to my intelligence and common sense when he or she makes cause-and-effect and other logical arguments." As they read, encourage students to ask themselves questions such as "What does the speaker want me to think or feel?"

Invite learners having difficulty to read "Speech to the Virginia Convention" in interactive format in *The Holt Reader* and to use the sidenotes as aids to understanding the selection.

thought disrespectful to those gentlemen, if, entertaining[2] as I do, opinions of a character very opposite to theirs, I shall speak forth my sentiments freely and without reserve. This is no time for ceremony. ❶ The question before the House is one of awful moment[3] to this country. For my own part I consider it as nothing less than a question of freedom or slavery; and in proportion to the magnitude of the subject ought to be the freedom of the debate. It is only in this way that we can hope to arrive at truth, and fulfill the great responsibility which we hold to God and our country. Should I keep back my opinions at such a time, through fear of giving offense, I should consider myself as guilty of treason toward my country, and of an act of disloyalty toward the majesty of heaven, which I revere above all earthly kings. ❷

Mr. President, it is natural to man to indulge in the illusions of hope. We are apt to shut our eyes against a painful truth, and listen to the song of that siren, till she transforms us into beasts.[4] Is this the part of wise men, engaged in a great and arduous struggle for liberty? Are we disposed to be of the number of those who, having eyes, see not, and having ears, hear not, the things which so nearly concern their temporal salvation? For my part, whatever anguish of spirit it may cost, I am willing to know the whole truth; to know the worst and to provide for it.

❶
In his opening remarks, Henry makes a respectful appeal to his audience. He anticipates their objections to what he is about to say.
? *What effect might his appeal have on his audience?*

❷
? *Simply put, how does Henry describe the question or debate that is before the Convention?*

---

2. **entertaining** *v.:* having in mind; considering.
3. **awful moment:** great importance.
4. **listen . . . beasts:** In Greek mythology, the sirens are sea maidens whose seductive singing lures men to wreck their boats on coastal rocks. In the *Odyssey*, Circe, an enchanter, transforms Odysseus's men into swine after they arrive at her island home. Henry's allusion combines these two stories.

I have but one lamp by which my feet are guided; and that is the lamp of experience. I know of no way of judging of the future but by the past. And judging by the past, I wish to know what there has been in the conduct of the British ministry for the last ten years, to justify those hopes with which gentlemen have been pleased to solace themselves and the House? Is it that insidious smile with which our petition[5] has been lately received? Trust it not, sir; it will prove a snare to your feet. Suffer not yourselves to be betrayed with a kiss. Ask yourselves how this gracious reception of our petition comports[6] with these warlike preparations which cover our waters and darken our land. Are fleets and armies necessary to a work of love and reconciliation? Have we shown ourselves so unwilling to be reconciled, that force must be called in to win back our love? Let us not deceive ourselves, sir. These are the implements of war and subjugation;[7] the last arguments to which kings resort. ❸

I ask gentlemen, sir, what means this martial array, if its purpose be not to force us to submission? Can gentlemen assign any other possible motives for it? Has Great Britain any enemy, in this quarter of the world, to call for all this accumulation

❸
Henry asks his listeners to look back on past experiences. He lists the recent actions of King George III and the English army to support his **main idea**—that the colonists are mistaken in thinking that the British are ready to compromise.

---

5. **our petition:** The First Continental Congress had recently protested against new tax laws. King George III had withdrawn the laws conditionally, but the colonists were unwilling to accept his conditions.
6. **comports** *v.:* agrees.
7. **subjugation** *n.:* conquest; domination.

Vocabulary
solace (säl′is) *v.:* comfort.
insidious (in·sid′ē·əs) *adj.:* sly; sneaky.
martial (mär′shəl) *adj.:* warlike.

Patrick Henry   **81**

DIRECT TEACHING

B Literary Focus
? Persuasion. What might be seen as a logical fallacy in Henry's declaration? [Possible response: He oversimplifies the issue by presenting only two extreme choices. This is often called the either-or fallacy.]

C Reading Skills
? Recognizing modes of persuasion. Figurative language is often used to support an emotional appeal. What metaphor does Henry use here, and how does it illustrate his argument? [He calls the past experience of British oppression the only "lamp" that the colonists have to illuminate the future with and implies that those who hope for an improvement in British conduct are walking blindly in the dark.]

D English-Language Learners
Simplifying syntax. Point out that in contemporary English, we would add the words *they are* after the semicolon.

Responses to Boxed Questions

1. Possible response: Henry's respectful tone and air of gravity will appeal to his audience's sense of themselves as fair and responsible leaders and will dispose them to listen carefully to him.

2. He sees the question as a matter of patriotic, even religious, duty versus disloyalty to God and country.

English-Language Learners
To help students follow Henry's arguments, have them first listen to the speech read aloud, and then have them read it silently.

Special Education Students
For lessons designed for special education students, see *Holt Reading Solutions*.

Advanced Learners
Enrichment. Ask students to develop logical arguments and emotional appeals that counter Henry's points. Have them draft a rebuttal that one of Henry's opponents might have made.

A Literary Focus

? **Persuasion.** What emotions does Henry appeal to with his imagery of binding chains? [He is appealing to his listeners' love of liberty and fear of coercion.]

B Literary Focus

? **Persuasion.** A periodic sentence is one in which the main clause is postponed until the end. What is the effect of such a sentence? [The sentence builds to a conclusion, to a dramatic climax.] Ask students to recast the sentence, putting the main clause ("we must fight") first and to compare the effect.

C Literary Focus

? **Persuasion.** What technique is Henry using here? [repetition] Why? [Henry uses repetition to stress his main idea, "we must fight!" He even announces this intention—"I repeat it, sir"—to pound the point home.] Where does Henry use the same technique in the next paragraph? [in the final two sentences]

Responses to Boxed Questions

4. By raising questions before his opponents do, he gives the impression that he has thought through all their objections and can answer all of them.

5. Henry argues that the colonists have already used all possible peaceful means to persuade England to rethink its policies and that fighting is the only course left to them.

---

of navies and armies? No, sir, she has none. They are meant for us; they can be meant for no other. They are sent over to bind and rivet upon us those chains which the British ministry have been so long forging. And what have we to oppose to them? Shall we try argument? Sir, we have been trying that for the last ten years. Have we anything new to offer on the subject? Nothing. We have held the subject up in every light of which it is capable; but it has been all in vain. Shall we resort to entreaty and humble supplication? What terms shall we find which have not been already exhausted? Let us not, I beseech you, sir, deceive ourselves longer. **4** Sir, we have done everything that could be done, to avert the storm which is now coming on. We have petitioned; we have remonstrated;[8] we have supplicated; we have prostrated ourselves before the throne, and have implored its interposition[9] to arrest the tyrannical hands of the ministry and Parliament. Our petitions have been slighted; our remonstrances have produced additional violence and insult; our supplications have been disregarded; and we have been spurned, with contempt, from the foot of the throne. In vain, after these things, may we indulge the fond[10] hope of peace and reconciliation. There is no longer any room for hope. If we wish to be free—if we mean to preserve inviolate those inestimable privileges for which we have been so long contending—if we mean not basely to abandon the noble struggle in which we have been so long engaged, and which we have pledged ourselves never to abandon until the glorious object of our contest shall be obtained, we must fight! I repeat it, sir, we must fight! An appeal to arms and to the

God of Hosts is all that is left us! **5**

They tell us, sir, that we are weak; unable to cope with so formidable[11] an adversary. But when shall we be stronger? Will it be the next week, or the next year? Will it be when we are totally disarmed, and when a British guard shall be stationed in every house? Shall we gather strength by irresolution and inaction? Shall we acquire the means of effectual resistance, by lying supinely on our backs, and hugging the delusive[12] phantom of hope, until our enemies shall have bound us hand and foot? Sir, we are not weak, if we make a proper use of the means which the God of nature hath placed in our power. Three millions of people, armed in the holy cause of liberty, and in such a country as that which we possess, are invincible by any force which our enemy can send against us. Besides, sir, we shall not fight our battles alone. There is a just God who presides over the destinies of nations; and who will raise up friends to fight our battles for us. The battle, sir, is not to the strong alone; it is to the vigilant, the active, the brave. Besides, sir, we have no election.[13] If we were base[14] enough to desire it, it is now too late to retire from the contest. There is no retreat, but in submission and slavery! Our chains are forged! Their clanking may be heard on the plains of Boston! The war is inevitable—

---

4 Note Henry's use of **rhetorical questions,** or questions asked for effect with no answer anticipated.

? *How do these questions help anticipate the arguments of his opponents?*

5 **?** *What appeals to reason does Henry make in this paragraph? What does he want the colonists to understand?*

---

8. **remonstrated** *v.:* objected; complained.
9. **interposition** *n.:* intervention; stepping in to try to solve the problem.
10. **fond** *adj.:* foolishly optimistic.

11. **formidable** *adj.:* powerful; difficult to defeat.
12. **delusive** *adj.:* deceptive; misleading.
13. **election** *n.:* choice.
14. **base** *adj.:* showing little courage, honor, or decency.

Vocabulary
supplication (sup′lə·kā′shən) *n.:* plea; prayer.
avert (ə·vʉrt′) *v.:* prevent; turn away.
spurned (spʉrnd) *v.:* rejected.
inviolate (in·vī′ə·lit) *adj.:* uncorrupted.
adversary (ad′vər·ser′ē) *n.:* opponent.
vigilant (vij′ə·lənt) *adj.* used as *n.:* those who are watchful.
inevitable (in·ev′i·tə·bəl) *adj.:* not avoidable.

CONTENT-AREA CONNECTIONS

Mathematics: Economics of War
Remind students that Henry was asking the Virginia delegates not only to declare their willingness to fight Britain, but also to allocate funds to raise a militia.
Mixed-ability group activity. Have students do research and create a bar graph showing (1) how much money the Virginia

Convention allotted to arming its people, (2) what this amount equals in today's dollars, (3) how much money Virginia contributed to the maintenance of British troops in the Colonies. In light of their findings, ask students to discuss the monetary cost of the war.

and let it come! I repeat it, sir, let it come! ⑤

It is in vain, sir, to extenuate[15] the matter. Gentlemen may cry peace, peace—but there is no peace. The war is actually begun! The next gale that sweeps from the north will bring to our ears the

 ⑥ What fiery language and **loaded words** does Henry use in this paragraph? What effect do you think his words would have had on the audience?

---
15. **extenuate** *v.:* weaken.

clash of resounding arms! Our brethren are already in the field! Why stand we here idle? What is it that gentlemen wish? What would they have? Is life so dear, or peace so sweet, as to be purchased at the price of chains and slavery? Forbid it, Almighty God! I know not what course others may take; but as for me, give me liberty, or give me death! ⑦

⑦ To wrap up his speech, Henry uses a final strong **appeal to emotion.** What makes his conclusions so powerful?

Response and Analysis

Reading Check

1. According to the first two paragraphs of this speech, why is Henry speaking out?

2. In the third paragraph, what facts does Henry offer to convince his listeners that Great Britain will not respond to peaceful petitions?

3. In the fourth paragraph, what facts does Henry offer to prove that the colonists have tried everything and that war is now the only solution?

4. According to the fifth paragraph, what answers does Henry give to those who say that the colonists cannot win the war?

5. In the sixth paragraph, how does Henry wrap up his argument?

Thinking Critically

6. Review your two-column chart, noting especially the appeals you starred and those you marked with an *X.* What made these appeals powerful or weak? Explain whether you are more convinced by Henry's appeals to **reason** or his appeals to **emotion.**

7. In the fourth paragraph, what **metaphors** does Henry use to describe the coming war?

8. Henry makes use of the **rhetorical question**—a question that is asked for effect. Rhetorical questions, which are often used in **persuasion,** presume that the audience agrees with the speaker on the answers and so no answer is expected or required. Find the series of rhetorical questions in the fifth paragraph of this speech. How does this technique make Henry's speech more persuasive?

9. Because his audience knew the Bible, as well as classical mythology, Henry knew he could count on certain **allusions** to produce emotional effects. Look up the classical or biblical passages that Henry alludes to in each of the following statements from his speech. How would each allusion relate to the conflict in Virginia in 1775? Could any of them relate to life today? Explain.

   • "We are apt to . . . listen to the song of that siren, till she transforms us into beasts." (*Odyssey,* Books 10 and 12)

   • "Are we disposed to be of the number of those who, having eyes, see not, and having ears, hear not, the things which so nearly concern their temporal salvation?" (Ezekiel 12:2)

INTERNET
Projects and Activities
Keyword: LE5 11-1

SKILLS FOCUS

Literary Skills
Analyze the use of persuasion.

Reading Skills
Analyze modes of persuasion, including appeals to reason and appeals to emotion.

Writing Skills
Write an essay comparing and contrasting a speech with a sermon.

Vocabulary Skills
Understand synonyms.

Patrick Henry **83**

Reading Check

1. Henry feels the colonists are in danger of losing their liberty if they do not face up to the reality of their situation.

2. He points to British war preparations and the movements of Great Britain's armies and navies in the direction of the Colonies.

3. He states that the colonists have been trying to reason with the British for ten years to no avail.

4. He says that three million people fighting for their liberty with God on their side cannot lose.

5. He says that death is better than peace without liberty and that he is willing to die for liberty.

Responses to Boxed Questions

6. Examples include "lying supinely on our backs"; "hugging the delusive phantom of hope"; "bound us hand and foot"; "armed in the holy cause of liberty"; and "Our chains are forged! Their clanking may be heard on the plains of Boston!" The language would have stirred up the audience's fighting spirit and love of liberty.

7. Henry declares himself willing to die for liberty and by extension offers his listeners the same stark and powerful choice.

INDEPENDENT PRACTICE

Response and Analysis

Thinking Critically

6. Students are likely to admire the reasoning in the speech but be more viscerally affected by the rhythm, imagery, and rhetoric. They may conclude that an effective persuasive speech appeals to both logic and emotion.

7. Henry uses metaphors of confinement in chains and of an approaching storm.

8. Henry's rhetorical questions allow him to attack his opponents' arguments indirectly by reframing them in a negative light and then asking his audience if they still agree with the arguments.

9. Possible answers:
   • The allusion reminds listeners not to surrender to a seductive offer.
   • The allusion reminds listeners not to be heedless of signs from England.
   • The allusion warns listeners not to be deceived by the apparently mild British reaction to the colonists' petitions against the tax laws.

10. Possible answer: Henry's arguments are sound because they are based on facts as well as on valid appeals to the colonists' values, especially their love of liberty. Research of the period can back up this assertion.

Extending and Evaluating

11. Students' answers will vary, but many may feel that there are some fundamental human rights and freedoms worth fighting for, and perhaps dying for.

Vocabulary Development

1. supplication
2. martial; inevitable
3. solace
4. vigilant; adversary
5. insidious
6. avert
7. spurned
8. inviolate

Assessment

■ *Holt Assessment: Literature, Reading, and Vocabulary*

For a lesson reteaching critiquing public documents, see **Reteaching,** p. 1117A.

- "Suffer not yourselves to be betrayed with a kiss." (Luke 22:47–48)
10. An **assertion** is a statement that declares a position on some issue or topic. What assertions would you make about Patrick Henry's arguments that the Colonies should arm for war? How will you back up your assertions? Be sure to discuss your assertions in class.

Extending and Evaluating

11. Look back at your Quickwrite notes on your feelings about liberty. Do you think liberty is more important than life itself? Explain your answers. 🖉

WRITING

Politician Versus Preacher

In a brief essay, **compare and contrast** Patrick Henry's speech with Jonathan Edwards's sermon "Sinners in the Hands of an Angry God" (page 46). Consider the specific ways in which the speech and sermon are alike and the ways they are different. Use the following chart to help organize your material:

Elements of the Oration	Edwards	Henry
Speaker's purpose and audience		
Main idea		
Appeals to reason and emotion		
Use of metaphors		
Use of rhetorical questions		
Overall effectiveness		

Vocabulary Development

In Other Words

solace	spurned
insidious	inviolate
martial	adversary
supplication	vigilant
avert	inevitable

Replace the underlined word or words below with a word from the list above.

1. The British failed to respond to the plea of the Colonies.
2. Henry thought a warlike confrontation was impossible to avoid.
3. Some colonists found comfort in ignoring the danger signs.
4. The watchful will outwit their opponent.
5. Henry believed that the true plans of the British were underhanded.
6. We must try to turn away the approaching troops.
7. The British rejected with contempt the colonists' attempts to compromise.
8. Henry would fight to keep his rights sacred and protected.

Learners Having Difficulty

You may want to concentrate on the Reading Check questions and on questions 6 and 10, which rely more heavily on students' own experiences. In addition, help students to think of situations in which political leaders might have to ask citizens to make sacrifices or even risk their lives for the public good.

Advanced Learners

When answering question 10, students should be urged to evaluate the logical validity of Henry's arguments as well as their effectiveness in persuading his audience to take the action he is proposing. You might also ask students to make assertions about the relative effectiveness of Henry's logical and emotional appeals.

Thomas Paine
(1737–1809)

The most persuasive writer of the American Revolution came from an unlikely background. Thomas Paine, the poorly educated son of a corset maker, was born in England and spent his first thirty-seven years drifting through occupations—corset maker, grocer, tobacconist, schoolteacher, tax collector. In 1774, Paine was dismissed from his job as a tax collector for attempting to organize the employees in a demand for higher wages (an unusual activity in those days). Like many others at that time and since, he came to America to make a new start.

With a letter of introduction from Benjamin Franklin (page 65), whom he had met in London, Paine went to Philadelphia, where he worked as a journalist. In the conflict between England and the Colonies, he quickly identified with the underdog. In January 1776, he published the most important written work in support of American independence: *Common Sense*, a forty-seven-page pamphlet that denounced King George III as a "royal brute" and asserted that a continent should not remain tied to an island. The pamphlet sold a half-million copies—in a country whose total population was roughly two and a quarter million.

After the Revolution, Paine lived peacefully in New York and New Jersey until 1787, when he returned to Europe. There he became involved once more in radical revolutionary politics, supporting the French Revolution. In 1791, he began to compose *The Rights of Man*, a reply to the English statesman Edmund Burke's condemnation of the French revolt. *The Rights of Man* was an impassioned defense of republican government and a call to the English people to overthrow their king. Although he was living in France at the time, Paine was tried for treason in England and

banned from the country. Safe in France from English law, he was briefly celebrated as a hero of the French Revolution, but Paine was soon imprisoned for being a citizen of an enemy nation (England). James Monroe, the American minister to France at the time, gained his release in 1794 by insisting that Paine was an American citizen.

Paine's final notable work, *The Age of Reason*, was published in two parts, the first in 1794 and the second in 1796. Expounding the principles of deism (page 18), the book was controversial in America. Americans did not fully understand Paine's ideas and thought he was an atheist—that he did not believe in God. When Paine returned to America in 1802, he was a virtual outcast, scorned as a dangerous radical and nonbeliever. He was stripped of his right to vote, had no money, and was continually harassed. When he died in New York in 1809, he was denied burial in consecrated ground. His body was buried on his farm in New Rochelle.

Even in death, though, Thomas Paine was not allowed to rest. In 1819, an English sympathizer named William Cobbett dug up Paine's body and removed it and the coffin to England, intending to erect a memorial to the author of *The Rights of Man*. No monument was ever built. The last record of Paine's remains shows that the coffin and the bones were acquired by a furniture dealer in England in 1844.

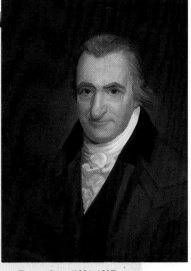

Thomas Paine (1806–1807) by John Wesley Jarvis. Oil on canvas.

©1998 Board of Trustees, National Gallery of Art, Washington, D.C. Gift of Marion B. Maurice.

Thomas Paine   85

More About the Writer
Background. The excerpt below from *The Crisis, No. 13*, written after the war, offers a reflective contrast to the fiery rhetoric of *No. 1*.

"'The times that tried men's souls,' are over—and the greatest and completest Revolution the world ever knew, gloriously and happily accomplished. . . .

"To see it in our power to make a world happy—to teach mankind the art of being so—to exhibit on the theatre of the universe a character hitherto unknown—and to have, as it were, a new creation entrusted in our hands, are honors that command reflection, and can neither be too highly estimated, nor too gratefully received.

"In this pause then of reflection—while the storm is ceasing, and the long agitated mind vibrating to a rest, let us look back on the scenes we have passed, and learn from experience what is yet to be done."

VIEWING THE ART

John Wesley Jarvis (1780–1840) was known for producing competent, precise portraits of famous figures. Later on his style relaxed, and his work became more expressive and romantic. Primarily a painter of faces, he often collaborated with others who painted the backgrounds and costumes.
Activity. Contrast Paine's clothing and hairstyle with that of Jonathan Edwards (p. 44) and Washington Irving (p. 150).

Summary ⬆ *above grade level*

In this persuasive essay, Paine urges the colonists to renew their struggle against the British. He argues that no prize worth fighting for is easily won and that the British objective is nothing less than the enslavement of the Colonies. War for independence is inevitable, he insists, and only a selfish Tory father would leave it for his children to fight. In a provocative analogy, Paine compares King George's actions to those of a common burglar and insists that the colonists refuse to accept any reconciliation with him. To do so, Paine asserts, would invite the destruction of Colonial society at the hands of the Native American tribes, the British army, and German mercenaries. Thus, the colonists must act now to ensure a "glorious issue" to the conflict.

Selection Starter

Motivate. Tell students that this essay is one of the most powerful calls to battle in American history and that it begins with a line that became famous: "These are the times that try men's souls." Using this line as an example, point out that the effectiveness of Paine's essay resides equally in his message and in the language in which he expresses his call to arms.

Before You Read

from The Crisis, No. 1

Make the Connection
Quickwrite ✏

At various times in life, we have to make personal sacrifices for a common cause. The early American colonists were urged to do just that by Thomas Paine in *The Crisis, No. 1*. Record your thoughts on the crucial decision facing the colonists: Should they kneel as British subjects or stand together as Americans? Try to identify the conflicts this posed for the colonists.

Literary Focus
Style

A writer's **style** is the distinctive way in which he or she uses language. Style is largely determined by **sentence structure, word choice,** and use of **figurative language** and **imagery.** Paine uses a combination of styles: Direct, common speech is mixed with heightened expressions that are sharpened by dramatic rhetorical techniques. Paine says that he speaks "in language as plain as A, B, C," yet he also includes such lofty declarations as "What we obtain too cheap, we esteem too lightly."

INTERNET
Vocabulary Practice
Keyword: LE5 11-1

SKILLS FOCUS

Literary Skills
Understand the characteristics of style.

Reading Skills
Recognize modes of persuasion, including appeals to logic, appeals to emotion, and analogy.

Style is the distinctive way in which a writer uses language.

For more on Style, see the Handbook of Literary and Historical Terms.

Reading Skills 📖
Recognizing Modes of Persuasion

A good writer of **persuasion** advances his or her argument by using a variety of appeals. By citing evidence, facts, and statistics, a writer can appeal to **logic,** or the reason of the audience. By using loaded words, figurative language, and personal experiences, the writer can arouse the **emotions** of the audience.

In *The Crisis,* watch especially for these two literary techniques—an **analogy** that compares the king with a thief and an **anecdote** about a tavern keeper and his child. As you read, write down the extent to which each technique appeals to both reason and emotion.

Background

In 1776, Paine joined the Continental army as it retreated across New Jersey to Philadelphia. The exhausted and demoralized army was heavily outnumbered by the enemy. As he traveled with the army, Paine began writing a series of sixteen pamphlets called *The American Crisis,* commenting on the war and urging Americans not to give up the fight. The first of these pamphlets was read to General George Washington's troops in December 1776, a few days before the army recrossed the Delaware River to attack the British-held city of Trenton, New Jersey.

Vocabulary Development

tyranny (tir′ə·nē) *n.:* cruel use of power.

consolation (kän′sə·lā′shən) *n.:* comfort.

celestial (sə·les′chəl) *adj.:* divine; perfect.

impious (im′pē·əs) *adj.:* irreverent.

ravage (rav′ij) *n.:* violent destruction.

relinquished (ri·liŋ′kwishd) *v.:* given up.

pretense (prē·tens′) *n.:* false claim.

dominion (də·min′yən) *n.:* rule.

eloquence (el′ə·kwəns) *n.:* forceful, fluent, and graceful speech.

perseverance (pʉr′sə·vir′əns) *n.:* persistence.

86 Collection 1   Encounters and Foundations to 1800

Previewing Vocabulary

Have students choose the antonym of each of the following Vocabulary words from p. 86.

1. discontinuation [perseverance]
2. construction [ravage]
3. genuineness [pretense]
4. democracy [tyranny]
5. incoherence [eloquence]
6. retained [relinquished]
7. aggravation [consolation]
8. servitude [dominion]
9. reverent [impious]
10. earthly [celestial]

Colonial campfire reenactment, Valley Forge, Pennsylvania.

(Swords) The Granger Collection, New York.

from The Crisis, No. 1

Thomas Paine

PUBLIC DOCUMENT

These are the times that try men's souls. The summer soldier and the sunshine patriot will, in this crisis, shrink from the service of his country; but he that stands it NOW, deserves the love and thanks of man and woman. Tyranny, like hell, is not easily conquered; yet we have this consolation with us, that the harder the conflict, the more glorious the triumph. What we obtain too cheap, we esteem[1] too lightly; 'tis dearness only that gives everything its value. Heaven knows how to put a proper price upon its goods; and it would be strange indeed, if so celestial an article as FREEDOM should not be highly rated. Britain, with an army to enforce her tyranny, has declared that she has a right (*not only to* TAX) but "to BIND *us in* ALL CASES

---

1. **esteem** *v.:* value; hold in high regard.

Vocabulary

tyranny (tir′ə·nē) *n.:* cruel use of power.
consolation (kän′sə·lā′shən) *n.:* comfort.
celestial (sə·les′chəl) *adj.:* divine; perfect.

DIFFERENTIATING INSTRUCTION

Learners Having Difficulty
Modeling. Model recognizing modes of persuasion. Say: "As I read, I will look for examples of concrete evidence, facts, and statistics that are intended to appeal to my ability to reason and think logically. I will also look for examples of charged language, figures of speech, and accounts of personal experiences that are intended to appeal to my emotions." Encourage students as they read to ask themselves, "Is this a spot where Paine is moderately, highly, or least persuasive?"

English-Language Learners
Point out some of Paine's sentences that sound like aphorisms. Paine often connects two such clauses with a semicolon to create a compound sentence. An example is in the first paragraph, the sentence beginning "Tyranny, like hell . . ." Ask students to find three more examples of Paine's aphoristic compound sentences and then to create one of their own.

Analyzing Political Points of View

Freedom and Equality

The questions on this page ask you to analyze the views on freedom and equality in the preceding four selections.

Thomas Jefferson . . . . *from* **The Autobiography: The Declaration of Independence**

Dekanawida . . . . *from* **The Iroquois Constitution**

Abigail Adams . . . . **Letter to John Adams**

Elizabeth Cady Stanton . . . . . *from* **Declaration of Sentiments**

Comparing Political Assumptions

1. Review the chart you made analyzing each document's **main ideas** (see page 94). Now consider the historical period and context in which each document was written, and add another column to the chart identifying the **purpose** behind each of the documents.

2. These powerful documents were not written to spare feelings. Discuss the effectiveness of each document. Do you see any flaws in their reasoning? Explain your responses.

3. Has the passage of time made any of the writers' points of view irrelevant or questionable, or are their ideas timeless? How do their ideas compare with your own? (Look back at your Quickwrite notes from page 94.)

WRITING

Evaluating the Documents

Review the selections about freedom and equality that you've just read. First, examine each piece separately, and evaluate the clarity and strength of the author's argument. Next, consider the texts as a group, and think about the various points of view represented. Note especially those points of view that are in agreement or disagreement. Then, write a brief **essay** evaluating the documents. Do you consider the pieces powerful documents? Taken together, are they an effective grouping? Be sure to use examples from the texts to support your points.

How Equal?

"All men are created equal" are perhaps the most famous words of the Declaration of Independence or of any document in American history. What do you think the statement really meant to Jefferson and the men who revised his draft—considering that they went on to form a government in which slavery was legal, women could not vote, and Native Americans were called merciless savages? Write an **editorial** in which you analyze your ideas about freedom and equality. Do you feel that some people in America, in fact, are not yet equal?

➤ Use "Writing an Editorial," pages 114–121, for help with this assignment.

SKILLS FOCUS

Pages 94–112 cover
Literary Skills Analyze and compare political points of view on a topic.

Reading Skills Compare main ideas across texts.

Writing Skills Write an essay evaluating documents. Write an editorial.

Analyzing Political Points of View

Comparing Political Assumptions

1. Possible answers: *Purpose of Declaration of Independence—to justify the colonists' desire to end a political relationship with Great Britain. Purpose of Iroquois Constitution—to forge a peaceful and voluntary union among Native American nations. Purpose of Letter to John Adams—to request that women's rights be addressed in the founding documents of the new American nation. Purpose of Declaration of Sentiments—to demand that the rights for men be immediately extended to women, including the right to vote*

2. The Declaration of Independence proved its effectiveness in 1776 as a document that Americans rallied around. Its tone and omissions probably contributed to its effectiveness. The Iroquois Constitution, although impressive in its appeal to the highest human motives, may rely too heavily on the virtue of leaders and not enough on laws and systems. Abigail Adams's appeal is argued more on the basis of what is good for men than what is owed to women. The Declaration of Sentiments was a strong statement for its time and has spurred the realization of at least some of its ideals.

3. Possible answer: Abigail Adams's view that men (but not women) are naturally tyrannical might be controversial today.

Conducting a Historical Investigation

In order to help students in their research activities, make sure that they understand the difference between primary and secondary sources. For most assignments, they should seek sources of both kinds, being especially careful to check the credentials of their secondary sources, especially when they get information from the Internet. Legitimate sources include professional historians with university connections and journalists who write for established newspapers and periodicals.

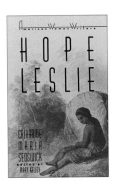

FICTION
Hope in a New World

Set in seventeenth-century New England, *Hope Leslie* by Catharine Maria Sedgwick tells the story of an independent, freethinking young woman living in a repressive Puritan society. Determined to follow her own principles, she battles the injustices suffered by the Native Americans and champions the independence of women. The novel centers around Hope's friendship with Magawisca, the passionate and articulate daughter of a Pequot chief. Through their friendship, Hope and Magawisca transcend the restrictive boundaries of their cultures.

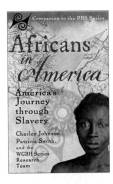

FICTION / NONFICTION
A New Perspective

Africans in America by Charles Johnson and Patricia Smith chronicles the history of slavery in America. Smith's vivid narrative—which uses diaries, letter excerpts, and historical documents—is coupled with Johnson's fictional histories to bring a new perspective to the slave experience, one told from the African point of view.

For another fictional perspective on Africans in America, read Johnson's **Middle Passage.** A National Book Award winner, this novel tells the story of a newly freed slave who stows away on a ship without realizing it is a slave ship bound for Africa.

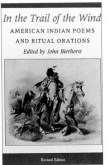

POETRY
Guiding Voices

In the Trail of the Wind: American Indian Poems and Ritual Orations, edited by John Bierhorst, tells the history of the original inhabitants of our land through their own rich oral tradition. These songs, dreams, and prayers from Indian cultures of North and South America paint a vivid picture of peoples both ancient and living.

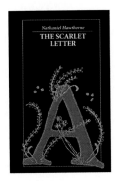

FICTION
Puritan Principles

A famous fictional account of the Puritan era is Nathaniel Hawthorne's powerful novel *The Scarlet Letter,* which examines the consequences of private sin and public penance. It touches on many familiar conflicts in literature—emotion versus reason, love versus hate, and the individual versus society.

This title is available in the HRW Library.

Read On

For Independent Reading

If students enjoyed the themes and topics explored in this collection, you might recommend the following titles for independent reading.

Assessment Options

The following projects can help you evaluate and assess your students' outside reading.

- **Review on a card.** Have students write a brief book review on an index card. The card should include the title, author, subject, brief plot synopsis, and a rating based on a system all students agree to follow. Students should turn in and file their review cards, according to topic, in an index card box to which all students have access. Students who are looking for books to read about a particular topic may then find suggestions in the index card box.

- **Research a related topic.** Have students research a specific topic that the book addresses. For *The Scarlet Letter,* students could research the consequences of breaking a law—civil or church—in Puritan times. Students can report their findings to the class with an oral presentation or illustrated poster.

- **Storytelling circle.** Have students work in storytelling groups of five or six. Have each group sit in a circle, and have each student portray a character from the book he or she has read, telling the story from that character's point of view. Storytelling circles may include students who have read different books or students who have all read the same book but are depicting different characters.

Differentiating Instruction

Estimated Word Counts and Reading Levels of Read On Books:

Fiction			Nonfiction		
Hope Leslie	↔	145,600	Africans in America	↔	151,700
			Poetry		
The Scarlet Letter	↑	67,400	In the Trail of the Wind	↓	80,000

KEY: ↑ *above grade level*   ↔ *at grade level*   ↓ *below grade level*

PRETEACHING

Skills Starter

Motivate. Ask students to answer these questions about commercials they have seen on TV:

- What visual techniques do the commercials use to get the viewer's attention?

- What do the commercials say to convince the viewer to buy their products?

Lead students to recognize that the persuasive techniques used in commercials often appear in more serious messages, such as political advertisements, debates, and editorials. Point out that these techniques may be of use as students complete this workshop.

DIFFERENTIATING INSTRUCTION

Learners Having Difficulty

If students have trouble visualizing their audience, suggest that they imagine a person who takes the position opposite theirs on the issue about which they are writing. Throughout the writing process, students should keep that specific person in mind as their audience.

DIRECT TEACHING

Analyze Your Audience

Tell students that, as the speakers in their editorials, they will want to adopt the correct tone. Explain that tone is the attitude writers express toward a subject and an audience through their language. Remind students to take a polite, respectful, and rational tone when writing their editorials.

Writing an Editorial

Writing Assignment
Write an editorial that conveys a well-defined perspective and a tightly reasoned argument.

When you read Patrick Henry's famous speech to the Virginia Convention, you probably noted the strength and eloquence of the arguments he used to try to persuade his peers to take up arms against Great Britain. In this workshop you'll get to try your hand at using language to persuade others to take a particular action on an issue by writing an **editorial** for your school newspaper.

Prewriting

Choose a Specific Issue

Add Incite to Insight Inciting people to riot is a crime. Inciting them to think is not—at least not in free societies. Editorial writers incite people to think about controversial **issues**—topics about which people disagree—for the **purpose** of convincing readers that a particular stand on the issue is the correct one. As a "guest editor" for your school newspaper, encourage your readers to think about and agree with the position you support on an issue that concerns them. To find an issue, try these strategies.

- Talk to friends and classmates about issues that concern them.

- Read editorials or letters to the editor in local, state, and national newspapers or magazines or online.

- Attend meetings of your school's student council, your school district's board of education, or your local city council.

   Make a list of several issues that you're interested in and that you believe would interest readers of your school newspaper. Then, create a ratings chart and rate each issue from one to five on the following criteria: 1) it is narrow enough to be argued in a short editorial, 2) each side can make a strong case for its position, 3) people have strong feelings about the issue. Choose the issue with the highest total of points to defend or attack in an editorial.

Analyze Your Audience

The Object of Your Persuasion To write effective editorials, first become familiar with your **audience**—the readers of your school newspaper. Here are some questions you can use.

- **How much do my readers know?** If your issue is unfamiliar, fill readers in on its basic points. If the issue is front-page news, assume your readers know about it.

SKILLS FOCUS

Writing Skills
Write an editorial.
Choose a topic.
Analyze the
audience.

RESOURCES: WRITING

Planning
- *One-Stop Planner* CD-ROM with ExamView Test Generator

Differentiating Instruction
- *Workshop Resources: Writing, Listening, and Speaking*
- *Family Involvement Activities in English and Spanish*

- *Supporting Instruction in Spanish*

Writing and Language
- *Workshop Resources: Writing, Listening, and Speaking*
- *Daily Language Activities*
- *Language Handbook Worksheets*

- **What are the concerns of readers who disagree with my position?**
Anticipate that some readers will disagree with your views. What will their counterarguments be and how can you address them?

Plan Your Thesis

Make Your Point The **thesis** of an editorial is a statement of the writer's basic opinion on the issue. Plan your thesis by jotting down an **opinion statement,** one or two sentences that identify the issue and state your perspective on it. Here is an example of an opinion statement one student wrote for an editorial opposing a curfew law for teenagers.

 DO THIS

[issue]   [opinion]
The city's new curfew law for teenagers should be repealed.

TIP If your opinion statement suggests that a certain action should be taken, you might issue a **call to action** in the conclusion of your editorial. For example, the student opposed to the curfew law calls upon readers to contact their city council members and ask that the law be repealed.

Gather and Shape Support

Convince Me! In order to persuade your audience, you must explain to them why your opinion is valid. Back up your opinion statement with the **reasons** for your opinion. Each of these reasons should appeal to readers' sense of logic, to their emotions, or to their ethical beliefs. Support your reasons with relevant **evidence**—precise and pertinent facts, statistics, examples, anecdotes, and expert opinions. If the connection between a reason and its supporting evidence is not self-evident, elaborate upon the evidence, showing how it connects to the reason. When you support the reasons for your opinion with evidence and elaboration of that evidence, you form **sustained arguments.** Take a look at the chart below to see one student's support of his opinion statement and an analysis of that support.

Opinion Statement: The city's new curfew law for teenagers should be repealed.

Reason	Evidence	Analysis
The law will have no effect on crime.	Teenage crime makes up only 11 percent of the city's total; Dr. Chang says statistics show most teen crime occurs between 4 and 9 p.m.	Evidence consists of facts, some cited by expert. Appeal is to logic.
The law further burdens an already overburdened police force.	Police chief says, "The curfew won't do a thing, except to make officers waste their time enforcing it." Only 5 percent of officers support the law. A poll of officers shows that 93 percent think more officers and equipment are needed, not a new law.	Evidence consists of expert opinions and facts. Appeal is mostly to logic, but also to emotions and ethics.

(continued)

MODELING AND DEMONSTRATION

Gather and Shape Support
To help students become familiar with ethical appeals—appeals to an audience's sense of right and wrong—you may want to model these examples:

- Conceding a point: "True, many young people would benefit from more structured after-school activities."
- A demonstration of fairness: "Is arbitrarily placing restrictions on one group in keeping with our country's concept of equal protection under the law?"

Ask volunteers to demonstrate examples of ethical appeals that they plan to use in their own editorials.

DIFFERENTIATING INSTRUCTION

English-Language Learners
Ask students to read their opinion statements aloud to you, and offer responses that begin in these ways: "I agree because . . ." or "I disagree because . . ." Guide students to recognize when they give irrelevant facts or phrase their opinions as facts. Then, have students suggest ways in which a troublesome opinion statement could be rewritten. You may want to suggest using marker words for an opinion, such as *should* or *would*.

Assessment
- *Holt Assessment: Writing, Listening, and Speaking*
- *One-Stop Planner* CD-ROM with ExamView Test Generator
- *Holt Online Assessment*
- *Holt Online Essay Scoring*

Internet
- go.hrw.com (Keyword: LE5 11-1)
- Elements of Literature Online

School activities often require later hours than curfew allows.

Sports teams and school-sponsored clubs often get back late from competitions and conventions. Activities like Bowl-a-Thon, which has raised $17,000 for charity, require late hours.

Evidence consists of examples. Appeal is to logic, emotions, and ethics.

RETEACHING

Organize Your Support

If students have difficulty organizing their support, have them use a visual organizer such as the one below. This organizer can also help them shape their body paragraphs.

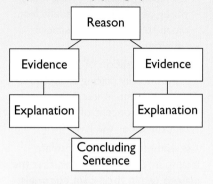

DIRECT TEACHING

Integrating with Grammar, Usage, and Mechanics

As students start their editorials, they may have trouble correctly recognizing and using parts of speech and the parts of a sentence. You may want to review sections 1 and 8 in the Language Handbook.

PRACTICE & APPLY 1

Guided and Independent Practice

Guide students by reviewing with them the steps they will follow to choose an issue, analyze their audience, write an opinion statement, and develop and organize their support. Then, have students complete **Practice and Apply 1** as independent practice.

The Art of Persuasion Shape your support in a persuasive and sophisticated way by using **rhetorical devices,** techniques writers use to enhance their arguments and make their writing effective. Here are some rhetorical devices you can use in your editorial.

RHETORICAL DEVICES AND EXAMPLES	
Repetition is the repeated use of a word, phrase, or clause more than once for emphasis.	The curfew law should be **repealed—repealed** immediately in fairness to the community, the police, and the students.
Parallelism is the repetition of the same grammatical form to express equal, or parallel, ideas. A noun is paired with a noun, a phrase with a phrase, a clause with a clause, and so on.	This week, the Riverdale High School student council had to cancel its annual charity Bowl-a-Thon—**not because of a lack of interest, not because of a shortage of funds, and not because of a failure to sign up enough enthusiastic volunteers.**
Rhetorical questions are questions that are not meant to be answered but are asked for effect.	Should students who are out late because of such events be jailed or fined? Should such school activities be dropped?
Argument by analogy draws a parallel between basically dissimilar events or situations.	If the curfew law aims to reduce youth crime, it mistakenly targets the wrong hours. **It's much like shutting the corral gate after the horses have escaped.**

Organize Your Support

Right This Way The body paragraphs of your editorial should develop each of the reasons in your argument by presenting and elaborating on evidence. Most writers arrange their reasons from strongest to weakest when they want to grab the attention of the audience and from weakest to strongest when they want to leave readers with the strongest possible impression. Some writers use a combination such as beginning with the second strongest reason, going next to the third strongest, and ending with the strongest. Use the pattern you think will have the greatest impact on your audience.

SKILLS FOCUS

Writing Skills
Organize your support. Use rhetorical devices.

PRACTICE & APPLY 1

Use the instruction in this section to develop an editorial for your school newspaper. Choose an issue that is important to you and others.

Writing

Writing an Editorial

A Writer's Framework

Introduction

- Grab readers' attention, perhaps by explaining how the issue affects them.
- Give background information on the issue.
- Include a clear opinion statement.

Body

- Support your position with reasons and evidence.
- Use rhetorical devices to shape your support.
- Organize reasons and evidence on the basis of relative strength.

Conclusion

- Restate your opinion.
- Consider providing a summary of your reasons.
- Call readers to action by telling them what they can do to change the situation.

A Writer's Model

Cancel the Curfew

This week, the Riverdale High School student council had to cancel its annual charity Bowl-a-Thon—not because of a lack of interest, not because of a shortage of funds, and not because of an inadequate number of enthusiastic volunteers. The student council had to cancel the popular charity event because the Bowl-a-Thon would cause participants to violate the law.

The Riverdale city council's new curfew law is an attempt to crack down on a perceived rise in teenage crime. Under the new law, anyone under the age of eighteen found in a public area after 10:00 P.M. on weekdays or 11:00 P.M. on weekends will be fined or jailed. While something should be done about teenage crime, the measure is a reckless overreaction on the city council's part to the complaints of a few influential business owners and groups. Because the new curfew law is unfair and unnecessary, it should be repealed.

The curfew law will have absolutely no effect on the city's crime rate. Most crimes are not committed by teenagers. According to the Riverdale Police Department's recent report on city crime, teenage crime is a mere 11 percent of the total. Of those offenses that are committed by teenagers, according to Dr. Theodore Chang in his study "Child Criminals," almost all occur between 4:00 P.M. and 9:00 P.M., which is before the curfew. The curfew law, then, is akin to shutting the corral gate after the horses have escaped.

(continued)

INTRODUCTION
Attention-grabber
Parallelism

Background information

Opinion statement

BODY
Second strongest reason

Statistic
Expert opinion

Analogy

A Writer's Model
Point out to students that one of the best ways to capture their audience's attention is to surprise them. Encourage students to begin their editorials with a fact, quotation, or anecdote that will surprise their audience. Students who have trouble thinking of such an item on their issues may need to extend their research or simply ask themselves this question: "What do I find most surprising about my issue?"

(continued)

Third strongest reason Expert opinion Statistics	Creating a new, unnecessary law only further burdens an already overburdened police department. Diane McCasland, the Riverdale police chief, says, "The curfew won't do a thing, except to make officers waste their time enforcing it." According to a recent poll, only 5 percent of police officers support the new law. When asked what would help stop city crime, 93 percent of the officers polled said more officers and equipment, not new laws, are needed to reduce crime.
Counterargument addressed Facts Rhetorical question	Some people will correctly point out that many cities in the region have instituted curfew laws in the past twelve months. The fact is, however, that they have had very little success. According to the *Riverdale Gazette,* neighboring Hillview's eight-month-old curfew law has had no effect on the city's crime rate, while Springdale's and Morgan's laws have been followed by an increase in overall crime. Is there any reason to think Riverdale's results will be any different?
Strongest reason Examples Rhetorical questions Repetition	While it is true that Riverdale's teens have no business being out late without a good reason, the strongest argument against the curfew law is that school activities often require late hours. Sports teams and school-sponsored clubs, for example, often get back late from competitions and conventions. Events such as the Riverdale High School student council's annual Bowl-a-Thon, which has raised a total of seventeen thousand dollars for local charities over the past three years, also require students to be out after curfew. Should students who are out late because of such events be jailed or fined? Should such school activities be dropped? No. Instead, the curfew law should be repealed—repealed immediately in fairness to the community, the police, and the students.
CONCLUSION Restatement of opinion Call to action	Even if the city council's new curfew law were to withstand legal challenges, clearly the measure is unnecessary and misguided. It is also a complete waste of the police department's time and energy. A law that restricts the rights of an entire group for the transgressions of a small minority is neither fair nor effective. If you value fair play, if you believe that the many should not be punished for the transgressions of the few, I urge you to contact your city council members and ask that the law be repealed.

go.
hrw
.com

INTERNET
More Writer's
Models
Keyword: LE5 11-1

PRACTICE & APPLY 2 Refer to the framework and Writer's Model as you write the first draft of your editorial. If necessary, return to the instructions in the Prewriting section to refresh your understanding of the basics of persuasion.

PRACTICE & APPLY 2

Guided and Independent Practice

Guide students through the writing process by giving them these tips:

• Do not worry about the length of the editorial in the drafting stage; material can be added or taken out during the revision stages.

• Keep your notes of evidence close by. Even though you might have made a detailed outline, you may decide while writing to include a piece of evidence you had not planned to use.

Then, have students complete **Practice and Apply 2** as independent practice.

Revising

Evaluate and Revise Your Editorial

The Editorial Touch An editorial is a serious piece of writing. When you write one, you want people to pay attention to what you have to say. Therefore, because you want everything about your editorial to contribute to its persuasive effect, you need to evaluate and revise it carefully. The guidelines in the chart below and in the chart on the next page will help you.

PEER REVIEW

Give your editorial to a peer to read. He or she may be able to offer hints on how to elaborate on your evidence.

➤ **First Reading: Content and Organization** An editorial succeeds or fails first on the basis of its content. How the editorial is organized affects readers' understanding of that content. Evaluating and revising the content and organization of your editorial is an integral part of the process of producing an effective editorial. Use the tips in the chart below to evaluate and revise the content and organization of your editorial.

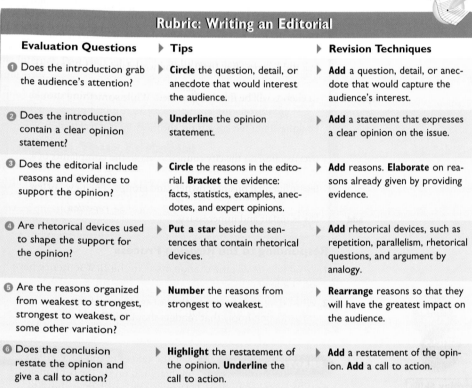

Rubric: Writing an Editorial

Evaluation Questions	▶ Tips	▶ Revision Techniques
❶ Does the introduction grab the audience's attention?	▶ **Circle** the question, detail, or anecdote that would interest the audience.	▶ **Add** a question, detail, or anecdote that would capture the audience's interest.
❷ Does the introduction contain a clear opinion statement?	▶ **Underline** the opinion statement.	▶ **Add** a statement that expresses a clear opinion on the issue.
❸ Does the editorial include reasons and evidence to support the opinion?	▶ **Circle** the reasons in the editorial. **Bracket** the evidence: facts, statistics, examples, anecdotes, and expert opinions.	▶ **Add** reasons. **Elaborate** on reasons already given by providing evidence.
❹ Are rhetorical devices used to shape the support for the opinion?	▶ **Put a star** beside the sentences that contain rhetorical devices.	▶ **Add** rhetorical devices, such as repetition, parallelism, rhetorical questions, and argument by analogy.
❺ Are the reasons organized from weakest to strongest, strongest to weakest, or some other variation?	▶ **Number** the reasons from strongest to weakest.	▶ **Rearrange** reasons so that they will have the greatest impact on the audience.
❻ Does the conclusion restate the opinion and give a call to action?	▶ **Highlight** the restatement of the opinion. **Underline** the call to action.	▶ **Add** a restatement of the opinion. **Add** a call to action.

First Reading: Content and Organization

Explain to students that using think sheets when reading models or drafts can help them to organize their thoughts on the reading and to remember ideas for their own writing and revision. Students might consider using the questions from the **Guidelines: Writing an Editorial** chart as a think sheet. A sample think sheet might look something like the following:

Text	Responses

CRITICAL THINKING

To help students strengthen the arguments in their editorials, draw attention to the brief anecdote used to introduce **A Writer's Model** on p. 117. Ask students to analyze and discuss how they think the anecdote helps make the situation real and important to readers. Ask students to consider how including an anecdote might make their editorials more effective.

DIFFERENTIATING INSTRUCTION

Advanced Learners

Enrichment. Since persuasive writing requires finding common ground with the reader, writers may find it difficult to avoid using clichés. Challenge students to be on the lookout for such tired expressions by asking this question:

What are other ways in which a writer may make a reader feel comfortable while at the same time challenging his or her assumptions?

Have students discuss the question and use the resulting suggestions in their own editorials.

Collection 2

In Collection 2, students will encounter the fiction of famous early American writers such as Washington Irving and Nathaniel Hawthorne. They will also read non-fiction works by the Transcendentalist writers Henry David Thoreau and Ralph Waldo Emerson. Students will analyze political points of view of civil disobedience by reading works by Martin Luther King, Jr., and Mohandas Gandhi. Other skills taught in this collection include analyzing figures of speech and symbolic meaning, and making predictions. Finally, in the writing workshop, students will be asked to write and publish a short story of their own.

VIEWING THE ART

Americans looked to untamed nature as inspiration for a uniquely American art. **Thomas Cole** (1801–1848) was a leader of this new American landscape painting. In this painting of the Adirondack Mountains, Cole erases all signs of white settlement, and depicts a Native American as the lone inhabitant.

Activity. Ask students what attitudes toward nature are suggested by Cole's painting. [Possible response: The painting suggests reverence toward and inspiration from nature.]

Indian Pass (1847) by Thomas Cole. Oil on canvas (40¹/₁₆″ × 29³/₄″).

COLLECTION 2 RESOURCES: READING

Planning
- *One-Stop Planner* CD-ROM with ExamView Test Generator

Differentiating Instruction
- *Holt Reading Solutions*
- *The Holt Reader*
- *Holt Adapted Reader*
- *Family Involvement Activities in English and Spanish*

- *Supporting Instruction in Spanish*
- *Audio CD Library, Selections and Summaries in Spanish*

Vocabulary
- *Vocabulary Development*

Grammar and Language
- *Language Handbook Worksheets*
- *Daily Language Activities*

Assessment
- *Holt Assessment: Literature, Reading, and Vocabulary*
- *One-Stop Planner* CD-ROM with ExamView Test Generator
- *Holt Online Assessment*

Internet
- go.hrw.com (Keyword: LE5 11-2)
- *Elements of Literature Online*

practical sen
human perfe

■ Emerson

Though Em
ideas and pr
member of t
developed b
rope and Asi
Its American
eighteenth-c
and the Ron
(page 165).

The Purit
through the
Jonathan Ed
experience i
woods for n
of the glory
what I know
lated; to lie i
mysticism—
thought. "Ev
spiritual fac

■ Emersor

Emerson's n
from intuiti
neously and
through our
son believed
like Benjam
presence of
thing to be c

An intens
belief that v
God works
natural ever
be explained
of life. Acco
separated fr
simply trust
know God c
of the Divir
Emerson'
who lived ir

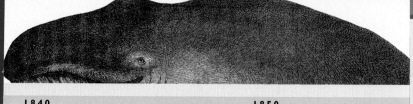

1840

1841 Ralph Waldo Emerson publishes his first collection, *Essays*, including "Self-Reliance" and "The Over-Soul"

1845 Margaret Fuller publishes *Woman in the Nineteenth Century*, the first full-length study of women's position in American society

1845 Edgar Allan Poe publishes *The Raven and Other Poems*

1848 James Russell Lowell publishes *The Biglow Papers*, satirical poems opposing the Mexican War and written in a Yankee dialect

1850

1850 Nathaniel Hawthorne publishes *The Scarlet Letter*

1851 Herman Melville publishes *The Whale, or Moby-Dick*

1854 Henry David Thoreau publishes *Walden*

1855 Walt Whitman publishes the first edition of his book of poems, *Leaves of Grass*

1858
gins
into

1858
Wad
Long
publi
Court
Miles

1840

1840 U.S. population is 17.1 million

1841 Brook Farm undertakes experiment in cooperative living

1842 By Treaty of Nanking, China cedes Hong Kong to Great Britain and opens five ports to foreign trade

1845 Alexander Cartwright formulates rules to regulate modern game of baseball

1845 United States annexes Texas (leads to war with Mexico, 1846–1848)

1846 Famine in Ireland due to potato-crop failure causes increased emigration from Ireland to United States

1848 Lucretia Mott and Elizabeth Cady Stanton organize first women's-rights convention in the United States in Seneca Falls, New York

1849 California gold rush begins as thousands of gold miners travel to Sacramento area

1850

1851 *The New York Times* is founded

1854 Modern Republican party is organized to oppose the extension of slavery

1854 Commodore Matthew Perry opens two Japanese ports to U.S. trade

1857 U.S. Supreme Court's *Dred Scott* decision antagonizes antislavery forces

1858 After Indian revolt against British East India Company rule, British government takes over administration of India

1858 A
and S
stage
seven
dates
in the

Title page from a
gold-mining manual
(detail) (1849).

Lincoln
debate

American Romanticism: 180

Collection 2

American Romanticism 1800–1860

We will walk on our own feet;
we will work with our own hands;
we will speak our own minds.

—Ralph Waldo Emerson

INTERNET
Collection
Resources
Keyword: LE5 11-2

133

THE QUOTATION
Ralph Waldo Emerson was a leading figure in the American Romantic movement. An essayist, poet, orator, and critic, Emerson based his philosophy on the ideals of optimism, individualism, and self-reliance. Ask students to discuss whether the quotation describes an American ideal that is alive and well today. [Possible response: Most students will agree that independence is still highly valued in America.]

all groups t
they record

Advanced
Enrichme

books of p
Holmes, ar
interests th
aspects of

Activity. Have students use a reference source to place these events on the time line.

- Elizabeth Blackwell becomes the first female physician in the United States. [1849]
- Sequoyah, a Cherokee, creates the first system for writing Native American languages and publishes parts of the Bible and a newspaper, *The Cherokee Phoenix*. [1820s]

- William Lloyd Garriso
of *The Liberator*, an infl
newspaper. [1831]
- American Samuel Mor
Code. [1838]
- Sojourner Truth delive
defense of the rights c
Woman?" [1851]

Media
■ *Audio CD Library*
■ *Audio CD Library, Selections and Summaries in Spanish*
■ *Fine Art Transparencies*
■ *Visual Connections Videocassette Program*
■ *PowerNotes*

Time Line

- **1798**
English Romantics

The publication of *Lyrical Ballads* is generally considered the beginning of Romantic poetry in Britain. Wordsworth's preface to the second edition (1800) emphasizes the role of emotion in poetry and urges poets to draw inspiration from the everyday life and speech of ordinary people.

- **1814**
The National Anthem

Francis Scott Key wrote "The Star-Spangled Banner" as a poem. It was later set to the music of "To Anacreon in Heaven," composed by John Stafford Smith, an Englishman. The song officially became the national anthem by an act of Congress in 1931.

- **1828**
Noah Webster

In addition to his dictionaries, Noah Webster published a grammar book and a speller that sold sixty million copies and distinguished American spelling from British spelling. Webster also edited political journals and campaigned for a strong federal government.

- **1835**
Alexis de Tocqueville

Alexis de Tocqueville was sent to the United States by the French government in 1831 to study the penitentiary system, but he ultimately wrote the earliest and most enduringly influential analysis of American democracy. In addition to studying government and administration, he evaluated social conditions and American literature, which he found lacking.

Ameri

1800–18

LITERARY

1790

1792 England's Mary Wollstonecraft publi *A Vindication of the R of Woman*

1798 William Wordsworth and Samuel Taylor Coleridge publish *Lyrical Ballads,* a landmark of English Romanticism

POLITICAL

1790

1791 First ten amendments, or Bill of Rights, is added to U.S. Constitution

1794 Eli Whitney's improved cotton gin increases U.S. cotton cultivation and expan demand for slave labo

1800 U.S. population is 5.3 million

1800 Washington, D.C becomes U.S. capital

1803 President Thoma Jefferson negotiates Louisiana Purchase from France, more th doubling U.S. territory

---

Using the Time Li

Activity. Assign two ever half of the time line to pair give them three minutes to much information as they events. In some cases, stud much about the events the they may make inferences learn from examining the For example, in 1803, Thor

---

A Exp
AM

Even tho the Rom English America social co a kind o America foundati such as Dickinso poetry i

B Ba
Walt V

In 1855, of Walt collectio (See pp. readers and rad gave the agemen into the Emerso blind to gift of *L* most ex and wis tributed things s As Eme works as som poems— express

C Ba
Plato's

Plato's interes relate t ple, he human of diffe using a cluded in com the *for*

SKILLS FOCUS, pp. 150–164

Grade-Level Skills

- **Literary Skills**
Analyze the way an author's style, including the use of mood, achieves specific rhetorical or aesthetic purposes.

- **Reading Skills**
Make predictions.

Review Skills

- **Literary Skills**
Evaluate the aesthetic qualities of style, including the effect of diction and mood.

More About the Writer

Background. Just as he Americanized European folk tales, Washington Irving helped popularize various Dutch, German, and British yuletide traditions in America—the most famous being the gift-bearing Saint Nicholas (familiarly known as Sinter Klaas by the Dutch, and later as Santa Claus), whom Irving introduced to American readers in one of his Knickerbocker writings. The sociable and popular Irving hobnobbed with the rich and famous in both the United States and Europe. He declined an invitation to run for mayor of New York City, although he did agree to serve as the first president of the Astor Library, which eventually became the New York Public Library. Irving's delightful residence on the banks of the Hudson River, reflecting the old Dutch style and aptly named Sunnyside, remains a favorite tourist spot in upstate New York.

Washington Irving
(1783–1859)

Washington Irving (1809) by John Wesley Jarvis. Oil on wood panel (33″ × 26″).
Historic Hudson Valley, Tarrytown, New York.

Many people in Europe and England felt that America would never develop a literary voice of its own. But then came Washington Irving, the youngest and not too well educated son of a pious hardware importer and his amiable wife. Irving, who was from New York City, had a genius for inventing comic fictional narrators. (In fact, he did not sign his real name to his work until he was over fifty.) The first of these narrators Irving called Jonathan Old style, Gent.—a caricature of those British writers who could not accept the simple values of the new nation.

Irving's second invented narrator was called Diedrich Knickerbocker. Irving pretended that Knickerbocker was the author of a book called *A History of New York, from the Beginning of the World to the End of the Dutch Dynasty.* The mysterious Knickerbocker is supposed to have left the manuscript to his landlord in payment of back rent. This fake and comical history, in which the entire American past is ridiculed, established Washington Irving as the foremost New York satirist.

All this time Irving was enjoying the literary societies that were popular then in New York. His interest in law, which he practiced half-heartedly, was lukewarm. In 1815, he was sent off by his father to Liverpool, England, to look after the failing overseas branch of the family business. Irving found the business beyond repair, but he loved the British literary scene and stayed abroad for seventeen years. He was particularly attracted to the works of the Romantic novelist Sir Walter Scott (1771–1832), who gave Irving advice that was to make his reputation. Scott told the younger writer to read the German Romantics and find inspiration in folklore and legends.

Now Irving decided against putting further energy into business and its "sordid, dusty, soul-killing way of life." He would give himself entirely to writing. In 1817, Irving began to write the first drafts of stories based on German folk tales. These were narrated by yet another of Irving's comic voices, Geoffrey Crayon, and the stories were collected under the title *The Sketch Book* (1819–1820). This book carried Irving to the summit of international success.

Even though Irving borrowed openly from a European past, he brought to his material a droll new voice, as inflated as a preacher's or a politician's at one moment and self-mocking the next. It was a voice the new nation recognized as its own.

Irving gave his country its first international literary celebrity. This was a role Irving enjoyed exploiting to the fullest. He had always loved parties and people and praise. Now he had access to the literary circles of the world. It was a remarkable achievement for the unpromising child of a middle-class American family.

His next book, *Tales of a Traveller* (1824), which included "The Devil and Tom Walker," met with such unfavorable reviews that Irving stopped writing fiction altogether. He never again wrote anything that matched the success of the two great comic tales in *The Sketch Book.* Today we remember Irving for Rip Van Winkle, who slept through the American Revolution, and the Headless Horseman, who plagued the lovelorn Yankee schoolteacher Ichabod Crane in the dreamy glen of Sleepy Hollow, in New York's lush Hudson Valley.

RESOURCES: READING

Planning
- *One-Stop Planner* CD-ROM with ExamView Test Generator

Differentiating Instruction
- Supporting Instruction in Spanish
- Audio CD Library, Selections and Summaries in Spanish

Vocabulary
- *Vocabulary Development*

Grammar and Language
- *Daily Language Activities*

Before You Read

The Devil and Tom Walker

Make the Connection

Many cultures tell tales of characters bargaining with the devil in order to get what they think they want. You might know some of these stories, most of which offer a moral lesson about pride, greed, or just plain stupidity. Washington Irving's Tom Walker demonstrates all three of these characteristics in his dealings with the devil, or Old Scratch. The devil's unusual name comes from the Old German word *scraz*, which means "goblin."

Literary Focus
Mood

Mood—the overall feeling or atmosphere of a story, play, or poem—may be the most difficult literary element to define. After all, mood is intangible; you can't point to mood in a text.

In order to identify a story's mood, start with the **setting**. Pay close attention to the details of time and place, and ask yourself how the setting makes you feel. Look carefully at the writer's **word choice**. For example, is a tree *budding* or *rotting*? Then, consider the **plot**. Does it end happily, or does it present a bitter or tragic outlook on life?

The mood of most stories can be identified with one or two adjectives: *gloomy, romantic, threatening,* and so on. Remember that even though you may sense several moods in some stories one dominant feeling (humor in the midst of horror, for example) will usually prevail.

> The **mood** of a story, play, or poem is its overall feeling or atmosphere.
>
> *For more on Mood, see the Handbook of Literary and Historical Terms.*

Reading Skills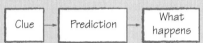
Making Predictions

When you make an inference about a text, you make an educated guess based on clues in the text and on your own knowledge and experience. A **prediction** is a special type of inference—an educated guess about what will happen later. Not all predictions turn out to be accurate, and adjusting them is an essential part of active reading. As you read "The Devil and Tom Walker," take notes in chart form. Identify a clue that suggests or foreshadows what may happen further along in the story. Then, make a prediction based on the clue. Later, note what actually happens. How often did the writer surprise you?

Clue	→	Prediction	→	What happens

Background

"The Devil and Tom Walker" is an American version of the archetypal story of Faust, the sixteenth-century German philosopher who sells his soul to the devil for knowledge and power. An **archetype** (är′kə·tīp′) is an original or fundamental imaginative pattern that is repeated through the ages. An archetype can be a plot, an event, a character, a setting, or an object. The story of a person who sells his or her soul to the devil for worldly gain is an archetypal plot. The most famous and influential version of the tale is *Faust*, a play by Johann Wolfgang von Goethe (1749–1832). Each retelling of the Faustian legend puts a different spin on the story, and the ending may change: The Faust character, for example, may face eternal flames, find forgiveness and love, or somehow cleverly beat the devil.

INTERNET

Vocabulary Practice

Keyword: LE5 11-2

SKILLS FOCUS

Literary Skills
Understand mood.

Reading Skills
Make predictions.

Washington Irving **151**

PRETEACHING

Summary ↔ *at grade level*

In 1727, the miserly New Englander Tom Walker meets a mysterious "black man" near a swamp. This personage, who may be the devil, offers Tom hidden pirate gold on certain conditions that Tom never reveals. Later, Tom tells his shrewish wife about the encounter, swearing that he refused the bargain. She decides to deal for herself, but never returns from her second meeting with the black man. It becomes rumored that Tom found her apron in a tree, holding a heart and liver.

With his wife gone, Tom makes his own bargain with the mysterious man. He gets the pirate gold and, as requested by the devil, becomes a moneylender notorious for his hard terms. He prospers, but as he grows old, Tom becomes a zealous and harshly dogmatic churchgoer, perhaps fearing for his soul. Nonetheless, the black man finally summons Tom, who is last seen howling on the back of a horse, galloping into an old Indian fort that is immediately destroyed by lightning. His name becomes linked with the devil's in the familiar New England saying "the devil and Tom Walker."

Selection Starter

Build background. Tell students that this story is set outside Boston, thirty-five years after the Salem witch trials and almost fifty years before the American Revolution.

Assessment
- *Holt Assessment: Literature, Reading, and Vocabulary*
- *One-Stop Planner* CD-ROM with ExamView Test Generator
- *Holt Online Assessment*

Internet
- go.hrw.com (Keyword: LE5 11-2)
- *Elements of Literature Online*

Media
- *Audio CD Library*
- *Audio CD Library, Selections and Summaries in Spanish*

Vocabulary Development

prevalent (prev′·ə·lənt) *adj.*: widely existing; frequent.

stagnant (stag′nənt) *adj.*: not flowing or moving.

precarious (pri·ker′ē·əs) *adj.*: uncertain; insecure; risky.

impregnable (im·preg′nə·bəl) *adj.*: impossible to capture or enter by force.

melancholy (mel′ən·käl′ē) *adj.*: sad; gloomy.

obliterate (ə·blit′ər·āt′) *v.*: erase or destroy.

avarice (av′ə·ris) *n.*: greed.

resolute (rez′ə·lo͞ot′) *adj.*: determined; resolved; unwavering.

parsimony (pär′sə·mō′nē) *n.*: stinginess.

superfluous (sə·pʉr′flo͞o·əs) *adj.*: more than is needed or wanted; useless.

Previewing Vocabulary

Have students complete each of the following sentences with the correct Vocabulary word from p. 152.

1. The safe was nearly _____ because it was hidden in a wall. [impregnable]

2. Because of his _____, the miser seldom replaced his worn-out clothes. [parsimony]

3. The miser regarded all non-food purchases as _____. [superfluous]

4. Stories about money often focus on the sin of _____. [avarice]

5. It is a _____ belief that money can't buy happiness. [prevalent]

6. The heat made the pond _____. [stagnant]

7. The cemetery entrance was a _____ place. [melancholy]

8. The hiker was _____ in his effort to walk ten miles each day. [resolute]

9. Incomes based on risky investments are usually _____. [precarious]

10. He wanted to _____ his unhappy memories. [obliterate]

The DEVIL and TOM WALKER

Washington Irving

A few miles from Boston in Massachusetts, there is a deep inlet, winding several miles into the interior of the country from Charles Bay, and terminating in a thickly wooded swamp or morass. On one side of this inlet is a beautiful dark grove; on the opposite side the land rises abruptly from the water's edge into a high ridge, on which grow a few scattered oaks of great age and immense size. Under one of these gigantic trees, according to old stories, there was a great amount of treasure buried by Kidd the pirate.[1] The inlet allowed a facility to bring the money in a boat secretly and at night to the very foot of the hill; the elevation of the place permitted a good lookout to be kept that no one was at hand; while the remarkable trees formed good landmarks by which the place might easily be found again. The old stories add, moreover, that the devil presided at the hiding of the money, and took it under his guardianship; but this, it is well known, he always does with buried treasure, particularly when it has been ill-gotten. Be that as it may, Kidd never returned to recover his wealth; being shortly after seized at Boston, sent out to England, and there hanged for a pirate.

1. **Kidd the pirate:** William Kidd (1645?–1701), known as Captain Kidd, a famous pirate in the late 1690s.

Washington Irving 153

DIRECT TEACHING

A Reading Skills

? Making predictions. Point out that this detail about the pirate's buried gold does more than spice up the story's setting. What possible plot developments does the mention of buried gold allow? [Possible responses: The mention of buried gold could lead readers to expect a story about a hunt for the gold, or about people fighting over it. The fact that it is pirate's gold, and therefore stolen, hints that the story may deal with wrongdoing, as does the next reference to Kidd's hanging.]

B Literary Focus

? Archetype. What do the phrases "well known" and "he always does" suggest about the old stories? [Possible responses: They suggest that these stories about the devil are widely known and are based on predictable patterns of the devil's behavior; the references also connect the gold with evil and suggest that the stories teach lessons about greed.]

DIFFERENTIATING INSTRUCTION

English-Language Learners
These students may find Irving's highly descriptive style somewhat challenging. Help them to break down Irving's longer sentences and to paraphrase them.

Advanced Learners
Enrichment. Invite students to think about the connections among the story's pre-Revolutionary, post-Puritanical Boston; Washington Irving's America a century later; and our own world, almost three centuries later. What lessons about morality and money-grubbing materialism may Irving have intended for nineteenth-century merchants who participated in such dubious enterprises as the slave trade? In what ways does this folkloric story still speak to Americans of the twenty-first century?

? **Mood.** How does the description of Tom's house affect the mood of the story? What words are significant? [The description adds a sense of hardship and misery; significant words include *forlorn, alone, straggling, sterility.*]

B **Literary Focus**

? **Stereotyped characters.** What female stereotype is Irving drawing on here? How might this stereotype contribute to the feeling that the story is based on a folk tale? [Possible responses: Irving is using the stereotype of the shrewish, nagging wife in characterizing Mrs. Walker. The use of this stereotype makes the story more like a folk tale.]

C **Literary Focus**

? **Mood.** What mood does this description create, and what words in particular heighten this mood? What might be Irving's purpose in creating this mood? [Possible responses: The description creates a mood of danger, foreboding, or oppression. The words that create this impression include *ill-chosen, swamp, gloomy, dark, quagmires, betrayed, smothering, stagnant, half drowned, half rotting,* as well as the references to reptiles. Irving's purpose may be to make the reader expect something evil to happen in this setting.]

About the year 1727, just at the time that earthquakes were <u>prevalent</u> in New England, and shook many tall sinners down upon their knees, there lived near this place a meager,[2] miserly fellow, of the name of Tom Walker. He had a wife as miserly as himself: They were so miserly that they even conspired to cheat each other. Whatever the woman could lay hands on, she hid away; a hen could not cackle but she was on the alert to secure the new-laid egg. Her husband was continually prying about to detect her secret hoards, and many and fierce were the conflicts that took place about what ought to have been common property. They lived in a forlorn-looking house that stood alone, and had an air of starvation. A few straggling savin trees,[3] emblems of sterility, grew near it; no smoke ever curled from its chimney; no traveler stopped at its door. A miserable horse, whose ribs were as articulate as the bars of a gridiron, stalked about a field, where a thin carpet of moss, scarcely covering the ragged beds of puddingstone,[4] tantalized and balked his hunger; and sometimes he would lean his head over the fence, look piteously at the passerby, and seem to petition deliverance from this land of famine.

The house and its inmates had altogether a bad name. Tom's wife was a tall termagant,[5] fierce of temper, loud of tongue, and strong of arm. Her voice was often heard in wordy warfare with her husband; and his face sometimes showed signs that their conflicts were not confined to words. No one ventured, however, to interfere between them. The lonely wayfarer shrunk within himself at the horrid clamor and clapperclawing;[6] eyed the den of discord askance;[7] and hurried on his way, rejoicing, if a bachelor, in his celibacy.

One day that Tom Walker had been to a distant part of the neighborhood, he took what he considered a shortcut homeward, through the swamp. Like most shortcuts, it was an ill-chosen route. The swamp was thickly grown with great gloomy pines and hemlocks, some of them ninety feet high, which made it dark at noonday, and a retreat for all the owls of the neighborhood. It was full of pits and quagmires,[8] partly covered with weeds and mosses, where the green surface often betrayed the traveler into a gulf of black, smothering mud: There were also dark and <u>stagnant</u> pools, the abodes of the tadpole, the bullfrog, and the watersnake, where the trunks of pines and hemlocks lay half drowned, half rotting, looking like alligators sleeping in the mire.

Tom had long been picking his way cautiously through this treacherous forest; stepping from tuft to tuft of rushes and roots, which afforded <u>precarious</u> footholds among deep sloughs;[9] or pacing carefully, like a cat, along the prostrate trunks of trees; startled now and then by the sudden screaming of the bittern, or the quacking of wild duck rising on the wing from some solitary pool. At length he arrived at a firm piece of ground, which ran out like a peninsula into the deep bosom of the swamp. It had been one of the strongholds of the Indians during their wars with the first colonists. Here they had thrown up a kind of fort, which they had looked upon as almost <u>impregnable</u> and had used as a place of refuge for their squaws and children. Nothing remained of the old Indian fort but a few embankments, gradually sinking to the level of the surrounding earth, and already

---

2. **meager** *adj.:* thin.
3. **savin trees:** juniper trees.
4. **puddingstone** *n.:* rock consisting of pebbles embedded in cement.
5. **termagant** *n.:* quarrelsome, scolding woman.
6. **clapperclawing** *v.* used as *n.:* scratching or clawing with the fingernails.
7. **askance** *adv.:* with a sideways glance.

8. **quagmires** *n. pl.:* areas of land with soft, muddy surfaces; bogs.
9. **sloughs** (slōōz) *n. pl.:* swamps or marshes, usually parts of inlets.

Vocabulary

prevalent (prev′ə·lənt) *adj.:* widely existing; frequent.
stagnant (stag′nənt) *adj.:* not flowing or moving.
precarious (pri·ker′ē·əs) *adj.:* uncertain; insecure; risky.
impregnable (im·preg′nə·bəl) *adj.:* impossible to capture or enter by force.

CONTENT-AREA CONNECTIONS

History: Warfare with American Indians

At the time of the story, almost all the white inhabitants of the Boston area had emigrated from England and were Protestants. Before these settlers came to the area in 1620, the Native Americans of the region had suffered greatly from diseases brought to America by European explorers, and native populations had been greatly reduced during epidemics from 1616–1618. During the late 1600s, the English settlers fought a series of wars with the French, who were allied with Native Americans of the area. At the time of the story, the area was enjoying a long break from these conflicts, but the wars erupted again in the 1750s, finally ending in 1763 with a British victory. The old fort that Irving uses as the setting may be a relic of the wars of the previous generation.

overgrown in part by oaks and other forest trees, the foliage of which formed a contrast to the dark pines and hemlocks of the swamp.

It was late in the dusk of evening when Tom Walker reached the old fort, and he paused there awhile to rest himself. Anyone but he would have felt unwilling to linger in this lonely, melancholy place, for the common people had a bad opinion of it, from the stories handed down from the time of the Indian wars, when it was asserted that the savages held incantations here, and made sacrifices to the evil spirit.

Tom Walker, however, was not a man to be troubled with any fears of the kind. He reposed himself for some time on the trunk of a fallen hemlock, listening to the boding cry of the tree-toad, and delving with his walking staff into a mound of black mold at his feet. As he turned up the soil unconsciously, his staff struck against something hard. He raked it out of the vegetable mold, and lo! a cloven[10] skull, with an Indian tomahawk buried deep in it, lay before him. The rust on the weapon showed the time that had elapsed since this deathblow had been given. It was a dreary memento of the fierce struggle that had taken place in this last foothold of the Indian warriors.

"Humph!" said Tom Walker, as he gave it a kick to shake the dirt from it.

"Let that skull alone!" said a gruff voice. Tom lifted up his eyes, and beheld a great black man seated directly opposite him, on the stump of a tree. He was exceedingly surprised, having neither heard nor seen anyone approach; and he was still more perplexed on observing, as well as the gathering gloom would permit, that the stranger was neither Negro nor Indian. It is true he was dressed in a rude half-Indian garb, and had a red belt or sash swathed round his body; but his face was neither black nor copper color, but swarthy and dingy, and begrimed with soot, as if he had been accustomed to toil among fires and forges. He had a shock of coarse black hair, that stood out from his head in all directions, and bore an ax on his shoulder.

_____
10. **cloven** _adj._: split.

He scowled for a moment at Tom with a pair of great red eyes.

"What are you doing on my grounds?" said the black man, with a hoarse, growling voice.

"Your grounds!" said Tom, with a sneer, "no more your grounds than mine; they belong to Deacon Peabody."

"Deacon Peabody be d—d," said the stranger, "as I flatter myself he will be, if he does not look more to his own sins and less to those of his neighbors. Look yonder, and see how Deacon Peabody is faring."

Tom looked in the direction that the stranger pointed, and beheld one of the great trees, fair and flourishing without, but rotten at the core, and saw that it had been nearly hewn through, so that the first high wind was likely to blow it down. On the bark of the tree was scored the name of Deacon Peabody, an eminent man, who had waxed[11] wealthy by driving shrewd bargains with the Indians. He now looked around, and found most of the tall trees marked with the name of some great man of the colony, and all more or less scored by the ax. The one on which he had been seated, and which had evidently just been hewn down, bore the name of Crowninshield; and he recollected a mighty rich man of that name, who made a vulgar display of wealth, which it was whispered he had acquired by buccaneering.[12]

"He's just ready for burning!" said the black man, with a growl of triumph. "You see I am likely to have a good stock of firewood for winter."

"But what right have you," said Tom, "to cut down Deacon Peabody's timber?"

"The right of a prior claim," said the other. "This woodland belonged to me long before one of your white-faced race put foot upon the soil."

"And pray, who are you, if I may be so bold?" said Tom.

_____
11. **waxed** _v._: become or grown.
12. **buccaneering** _v._ used as _n._: robbery at sea; piracy.

Vocabulary
melancholy (mel′ən·käl′ē) _adj._: sad; gloomy.

155

DIRECT TEACHING

D Literary Focus

❓ Archetype. Why is it appropriate that this place is associated with an "evil spirit"? [Possible response: The gloom and foreboding of the setting seem to go beyond mere unpleasantness to something supernatural.]

E Literary Focus

Influences of the historical period. Discuss Irving's use of the word _savages_ here. Explain that at the time of the story's publication in 1824, this would have been a common way of referring to Native Americans. Today such usage is considered culturally offensive.

F Literary Focus

❓ Archetype. How do the details describing the dark man make him special and strange? [Possible responses: He appears without making a sound; he is dark but not of a recognizable race; he wears some Native American garb but is not a Native American; his face is covered with soot as if he works around fire, even though there is no forge at the swamp; he carries an ax.]

G Literary Focus

❓ Symbol. What might the great tree, rotten at the core, symbolize? [Possible response: It might symbolize a man who outwardly appears to be great, but who is rotten inside.]

H Reading Skills

❓ Drawing conclusions. What conclusion can you draw from the fact that these men's names have been hacked into the trees and the fact that the black man carries an ax? [Possible response: The man has hacked the names into the trees, as if claiming the men's souls for himself.]

CONTENT-AREA CONNECTIONS

History: Puritan Failings

In the devil's introduction, Irving makes a satiric point by allying the devil with the religious but intolerant Puritans. The Puritans were notorious for their lack of tolerance of other religions, and several early settlements in New England were established by colonists who had come to Massachusetts and then fled the colony in search of religious freedom.

In the 1692 Salem witch trials near Boston, also referred to in this passage, several young girls accused nineteen people of consorting with the devil. A Puritan judge officially tried and convicted the accused, then executed them.

The devil also refers to slave dealers. Traffic in slaves had begun with the first American colony in Virginia. At the time of the story, slavery was legal throughout the colonies, including Massachusetts.

A Literary Focus

? Archetype. What range of evil activity does this paragraph attribute to the devil? [Possible response: It attributes to him grisly human sacrifices, religious intolerance, the slave trade, and the witch trials.] **In what way might Irving be commenting on his own society?** [Religious intolerance and slavery would be applicable to Irving's day, so he is making his position on those issues clear.]

B Reading Skills

? Making predictions. What do you predict Tom will do, now that he is face to face with the devil? [Possible responses: Tom may try to strike a bargain with the devil, perhaps to get rid of Tom's wife; he may try to trick the devil in some way.]

A "Oh, I go by various names. I am the wild huntsman in some countries; the black miner in others. In this neighborhood I am known by the name of the black woodsman. I am he to whom the red men consecrated this spot, and in honor of whom they now and then roasted a white man, by way of sweet-smelling sacrifice. Since the red men have been exterminated by you white savages, I amuse myself by presiding at the persecutions of Quakers and Anabaptists;[13] I am the great patron and prompter of slave dealers, and the grand master of the Salem witches."

13. **Quakers and Anabaptists:** In Puritan New England, where this story is set, Quakers were known primarily for their pacifism and refusal to take oaths, and Anabaptists were known for their opposition to infant baptism.

"The upshot of all which is, that, if I mistake not," said Tom, sturdily, "you are he commonly called Old Scratch."

"The same, at your service!" replied the black man, with a half-civil nod.

Such was the opening of this interview, according to the old story; though it has almost too familiar an air to be credited. One would think that to meet with such a singular personage, in this wild, lonely place, would have **B** shaken any man's nerves; but Tom was a hard-minded fellow, not easily daunted, and he had lived so long with a termagant wife, that he did not even fear the devil.

It is said that after this commencement they had a long and earnest conversation together, as Tom returned homeward. The black man told him of great sums of money buried by Kidd the

Comparing and Contrasting Texts

Invite students to compare this story with Jonathan Edwards's famous sermon, "Sinners in the Hands of an Angry God" (pp. 46–48). Edwards delivered his sermon in Connecticut in 1741, so it is almost contemporary with the story's setting (Massachusetts in 1727). Ask students to find what the story and the sermon have in common and where they differ in their characterizations of the relationship between human beings and supernatural justice. Edwards's sermon focuses on divine power and the precariousness of human life, and so is meant to strike fear into his audience. Ask if Irving's story shares any of that perspective and objective, and whether human beings are as helpless in the story as in the sermon. Ask students which work is more effective in persuading humans to behave morally.

pirate, under the oak trees on the high ridge, not far from the morass. All these were under his command, and protected by his power, so that none could find them but such as propitiated[14] his favor. These he offered to place within Tom Walker's reach, having conceived an especial kindness for him; but they were to be had only on certain conditions. What these conditions were may be easily surmised, though Tom never disclosed them publicly. They must have been very hard, for he required time to think of them, and he was not a man to stick at trifles when money was in view. When they had reached the edge of the swamp, the stranger paused. "What proof have I that all you have been telling me is true?" said Tom. "There's my signature," said the black man, pressing his finger on Tom's forehead. So saying, he turned off among the thickest of the swamp, and seemed, as Tom said, to go down, down, down, into the earth, until nothing but his head and shoulders could be seen, and so on, until he totally disappeared.

When Tom reached home, he found the black print of a finger burnt, as it were, into his forehead, which nothing could obliterate.

The first news his wife had to tell him was the sudden death of Absalom Crowninshield, the rich buccaneer. It was announced in the papers with the usual flourish, that "A great man had fallen in Israel."[15]

Tom recollected the tree which his black friend had just hewn down, and which was ready for burning. "Let the freebooter[16] roast," said Tom. "Who cares!" He now felt convinced that all he had heard and seen was no illusion.

He was not prone to let his wife into his confidence; but as this was an uneasy secret, he willingly shared it with her. All her avarice was awakened at the mention of hidden gold, and she urged her husband to comply with the black man's terms, and secure what would make them wealthy for life. However, Tom might have felt disposed to sell himself to the devil, he was determined not to do so to oblige his wife; so he flatly refused, out of the mere spirit of contradiction. Many and bitter were the quarrels they had on the subject; but the more she talked, the more resolute was Tom not to be damned to please her.

At length she determined to drive the bargain on her own account, and if she succeeded, to keep all the gain to herself. Being of the same fearless temper as her husband, she set off for the old Indian fort toward the close of a summer's day. She was many hours absent. When she came back, she was reserved and sullen in her replies. She spoke something of a black man, whom she met about twilight hewing at the root of a tall tree. He was sulky, however, and would not come to terms: She was to go again with a propitiatory offering, but what it was she forbore to say.

The next evening she set off again for the swamp, with her apron heavily laden. Tom waited and waited for her, but in vain; midnight came, but she did not make her appearance: Morning, noon, night returned, but still she did not come. Tom now grew uneasy for her safety, especially as he found she had carried off in her apron the silver teapot and spoons, and every portable article of value. Another night elapsed, another morning came; but no wife. In a word, she was never heard of more.

What was her real fate nobody knows, in consequence of so many pretending to know. It is one of those facts which have become confounded by a variety of historians. Some asserted that she lost her way among the tangled mazes of the swamp, and sank into some pit or slough; others, more uncharitable, hinted that she had eloped with the household booty, and

---

14. **propitiated** (prō·pish′ē·āt′id) v.: gained the goodwill of.
15. **A great man had fallen in Israel:** popular expression, drawn from the Bible (2 Samuel 3:38), to refer to the death of a prominent member of the community.
16. **freebooter** n.: pirate.

Vocabulary
obliterate (ə·blit′ər·āt′) v.: erase or destroy.
avarice (av′ə·ris) n.: greed.
resolute (rez′ə·lōot′) adj.: determined; resolved; unwavering.

C Reading Skills

? Making inferences. What do you think the conditions of the bargain are? [Possible responses: The man may have asked Tom to exchange his soul for the pirate gold; he may have asked Tom to commit some terrible crime.]

D Literary Focus

? Archetype. What is the meaning of the black fingerprint branded into Tom's forehead, and what does it imply about Tom's future? [Possible response: The fingerprint is probably an indication that the man is the devil. Even though Tom has not yet accepted the devil's terms, the fingerprint suggests that Tom will belong to the devil.]

E Learners Having Difficulty

Paraphrasing. Have students paraphrase this passage. [Possible response: Tom's wife set out to bargain for herself. She went to the old fort late one day and was gone for a long time. When she returned, she was unusually quiet. She did say that she had met the black man, but that they couldn't reach an agreement. She was supposed to return later with some kind of gift for him, but she wouldn't say what.]

F Reading Skills

? Making predictions. What do you think has happened to Tom's wife? [Possible responses: She may have run off with the goods she took; she may have been taken by the devil.]

DEVELOPING FLUENCY

Paired activity. This story contains a number of colorful descriptions. Have pairs of students choose a favorite passage from the story to divide and read aloud to each other. Ask students to practice individually at first, determining where they will raise or lower their voices, speed up or slow down for emphasis, or pause for suspense. As partners read to each other, have the listener note several specific places where the reader was particularly effective, and explain why.

A Reading Skills

❓ Determining author's purpose. What is the purpose of reporting the diverse opinions—both prosaic and supernatural—about the fate of Tom's wife? [Possible responses: The reports add to the mystery of the story; they indicate that it was told far and wide; they cover a wide range of human reactions, both common-sensical and superstitious. The storyteller thus gives the reader the option of choosing a prosaic, everyday explanation, as opposed to a thrilling, supernatural one.]

B Literary Focus

❓ Mood. What is the mood of this passage, and what words create this mood? How does this passage heighten the suspense about the fate of Tom's wife? [Possible responses: The mood is eerie and somewhat melancholy. Particularly effective words include *gloomy, repeatedly, nowhere, screaming, croaked dolefully, bats, clamor, carrion crows, vulture.* Tom's wife has not been a sympathetic character, but the passage makes readers suspect that she has met an awful fate.]

C Literary Focus

❓ Archetype. What "generally understood" terms does the narrator refer to here? Why do you think he doesn't state the terms explicitly? [Possible responses: The usual terms of a bargain with the devil involve exchanging one's soul for some large material advantage. The narrator says that these terms do not need to be stated because everyone knows them, but his real reason may be to preserve some mystery, or perhaps to make the bargain seem darker by not being specific about it.]

made off to some other province; while others surmised that the tempter had decoyed her into a dismal quagmire, on the top of which her hat was found lying. In confirmation of this, it was said a great black man, with an ax on his shoulder, was seen late that very evening coming out of the swamp, carrying a bundle tied in a check apron, with an air of surly triumph.

The most current and probable story, however, observes, that Tom Walker grew so anxious about the fate of his wife and his property, that he set out at length to seek them both at the Indian fort. During a long summer's afternoon he searched about the gloomy place, but no wife was to be seen. He called her name repeatedly, but she was nowhere to be heard. The bittern alone responded to his voice, as he flew screaming by; or the bullfrog croaked dolefully from a neighboring pool. At length, it is said, just in the brown hour of twilight, when the owls began to hoot, and the bats to flit about, his attention was attracted by the clamor of carrion crows[17] hovering about a cypress tree. He looked up, and beheld a bundle tied in a check apron, and hanging in the branches of the tree, with a great vulture perched hard by, as if keeping watch upon it. He leaped with joy; for he recognized his wife's apron, and supposed it to contain the household valuables.

"Let us get hold of the property," said he, consolingly to himself, "and we will endeavor to do without the woman."

As he scrambled up the tree, the vulture spread its wide wings, and sailed off, screaming, into the deep shadows of the forest. Tom seized the checked apron, but, woeful sight! found nothing but a heart and liver tied up in it!

Such, according to this most authentic old story, was all that was to be found of Tom's wife. She had probably attempted to deal with the black man as she had been accustomed to deal with her husband; but though a female scold is generally considered a match for the devil, yet in this instance she appears to have had the worst

of it. She must have died game, however; for it is said Tom noticed many prints of cloven feet stamped upon the tree, and found handfuls of hair, that looked as if they had been plucked from the coarse black shock of the woodman. Tom knew his wife's prowess by experience. He shrugged his shoulders, as he looked at the signs of a fierce clapperclawing. "Egad," said he to himself, "Old Scratch must have had a tough time of it!"

☛ Tom consoled himself for the loss of his property, with the loss of his wife, for he was a man of fortitude. He even felt something like gratitude toward the black woodman, who, he considered, had done him a kindness. He sought, therefore, to cultivate a further acquaintance with him, but for some time without success; the old black legs played shy, for whatever people may think, he is not always to be had for calling for: He knows how to play his cards when pretty sure of his game.

At length, it is said, when delay had whetted Tom's eagerness to the quick, and prepared him to agree to anything rather than not gain the promised treasure, he met the black man one evening in his usual woodman's dress, with his ax on his shoulder, sauntering along the swamp, and humming a tune. He affected to receive Tom's advances with great indifference, made brief replies, and went on humming his tune.

By degrees, however, Tom brought him to business, and they began to haggle about the terms on which the former was to have the pirate's treasure. There was one condition which need not be mentioned, being generally understood in all cases where the devil grants favors; but there were others about which, though of less importance, he was inflexibly obstinate. He insisted that the money found through his means should be employed in his service. He proposed, therefore, that Tom should employ it in the black traffic; that is to say, that he should fit out a slave ship. This, however, Tom resolutely refused: He was bad enough in all conscience; but the devil himself could not tempt him to turn slave trader.

Finding Tom so squeamish on this point, he did not insist upon it, but proposed, instead,

---

17. **carrion crows** *n. pl.:* crows that feed on decaying flesh.

SKILLS REVIEW

Analyzing setting. Review the definition of *setting* as the place and time in which a work of literature unfolds. Invite students to discuss the way setting influences other elements of the story by asking them to imagine stories in various hypothetical settings (for instance, in an abandoned old house, on a Civil War battlefield, or in a distant galaxy) and the kinds of plots, characters, and moods that would be appropriate to such settings.

Activity. Have half the class focus on the purely physical details of the setting, as described by Irving. Ask students, "How do these details affect the story's mood and meaning?"

that he should turn usurer;[18] the devil being extremely anxious for the increase of usurers, looking upon them as his peculiar[19] people.

To this no objections were made, for it was just to Tom's taste.

"You shall open a broker's shop in Boston next month," said the black man.

"I'll do it tomorrow, if you wish," said Tom Walker.

"You shall lend money at two percent a month."

"Egad, I'll charge four!" replied Tom Walker.

"You shall extort bonds, foreclose mortgages, drive the merchants to bankruptcy—"

"I'll drive them to the d—l," cried Tom Walker.

"You are the usurer for my money!" said black legs with delight. "When will you want the rhino?"[20]

"This very night."

"Done!" said the devil.

"Done!" said Tom Walker. So they shook hands and struck a bargain.

A few days' time saw Tom Walker seated behind his desk in a countinghouse in Boston.

His reputation for a ready-moneyed man, who would lend money out for a good consideration, soon spread abroad. Everybody remembers the time of Governor Belcher,[21] when money was particularly scarce. It was a time of paper credit. The country had been deluged with government bills; the famous Land Bank[22] had been established; there had been a rage for speculating; the people had run mad with schemes for new settlements, for building cities in the wilderness; land jobbers[23] went about

with maps of grants, and townships, and Eldorados,[24] lying nobody knew where, but which everybody was ready to purchase. In a word, the great speculating fever which breaks out every now and then in the country, had raged to an alarming degree, and everybody was dreaming of making sudden fortunes from nothing. As usual the fever had subsided; the dream had gone off, and the imaginary fortunes with it; the patients were left in doleful plight, and the whole country resounded with the consequent cry of "hard times."

At this propitious time of public distress did Tom Walker set up as usurer in Boston. His door was soon thronged by customers. The needy and adventurous, the gambling speculator, the dreaming land jobber, the thriftless tradesman, the merchant with cracked credit; in short, everyone driven to raise money by desperate means and desperate sacrifices hurried to Tom Walker.

Thus Tom was the universal friend of the needy, and acted like a "friend in need"; that is to say, he always exacted good pay and good security. In proportion to the distress of the applicant was the hardness of his terms. He accumulated bonds and mortgages; gradually squeezed his customers closer and closer; and sent them at length, dry as a sponge, from his door.

In this way he made money hand over hand, became a rich and mighty man, and exalted his cocked hat upon 'Change.[25] He built himself, as usual, a vast house, out of ostentation;[26] but left the greater part of it unfinished and unfurnished, out of parsimony. He even set up a carriage in the fullness of his vainglory, though he nearly starved the horses which drew it; and as

---

18. **usurer** *n.*: one who lends money at excessive rates of interest.
19. **peculiar** *adj.*: here, special or particular.
20. **rhino** *n.*: slang for "money."
21. **Governor Belcher:** Jonathan Belcher (1681?–1757) was governor of the Massachusetts Bay Colony from 1730 to 1741.
22. **Land Bank:** loan system by which the province advanced money in exchange for mortgages on land. When the bank was outlawed, many people faced financial ruin.
23. **land jobbers** *n. pl.*: people who buy and sell land for profit.

24. **Eldorados:** Spanish word meaning "the gilded"; places of fabulous wealth.
25. **cocked hat upon 'Change:** Tom's cocked hat was a three-corner hat worn at the time. *'Change* is short for "the Exchange," a place where merchants and stockbrokers meet to do business.
26. **ostentation** *n.*: showy display.

Vocabulary
parsimony (pär′sə·mō′nē) *n.*: stinginess.

159

DIRECT TEACHING

D Literary Focus

? Mood. How does this plot development and change of setting affect the mood? [Possible responses: The story has left the gloomy marsh for the practical, everyday world of business, and Tom has gone from being a poor miser to being a moneylender. The mood shifts from the haunted feeling of a ghost story to a factual, almost news-like account of social and economic developments. Perhaps Irving is showing the everyday face of evil here.]

E Advanced Learners
Enrichment. Encourage students to unearth more information about the specific boom and bust cycle during the 1730s that Irving describes here. Invite them to draw comparisons between that get-rich-quick economic cycle and the dot-com phenomenon of the late 1990s.

F Literary Focus

? Verbal irony. What is Irving saying here, actually? [Irving is sarcastically saying that Tom is making money from the misfortunes of others. He lends them money when they need it (hence, he acts like a friend), but his terms are so harsh that the borrowers are worse off than before.]

Have the other half focus on the social and historical setting, as presented in the story and in any other information you would like to provide. Ask students, "How do these details shape mood and meaning?"

Have the class as a whole put the pieces together: the eerie marsh, trees carved with the names of supposedly upstanding men; the

abandoned fort; the widespread materialism; the slave trade; the persecution of religious minorities. Then, ask students the following questions:

• What kind of world does Tom Walker live in?

• How has it made him the sort of man he is?

• Does it resemble our own world in any way?

A Reading Skills

❓ Making predictions. What do you think is going to happen to Tom? [Possible responses: He will have to go with the devil when he dies; he may figure out a way to cheat the devil.]

B Literary Focus

❓ Satire. What aspect of society is Irving satirizing in showing Tom's change? [Possible response: He is making fun of insincere piety that serves as a cover for sin.]

C Literary Focus

❓ Mood. How does the mood shift here, and what is the effect of this anecdote about Tom's horse? [Possible response: The mood shifts to the darkly comic and superstitious. The narrator leaves off satirizing Puritan life and returns to the realm of the folk tale. The narrator also sets up a contrast between this story and the "authentic old legend" about Tom's disappearance, which is to follow.]

D English-Language Learners

Archaic idiom. Explain that the expression *brought upon the parish* is an old-fashioned way of saying "have to accept charity." The parish is the social organization of a church, and in the days before government assistance, such organizations would take care of those who needed help.

E Literary Focus

❓ Irony. How do Tom's words ironically bring about his own fate here? [He says, "The devil take me . . . if I have made a farthing," asserting that he has not made money. But Tom has made much more than a farthing, and his own hypocrisy, appropriately, seems to summon the devil to collect him.]

---

the ungreased wheels groaned and screeched on the axletrees, you would have thought you heard the souls of the poor debtors he was squeezing.

As Tom waxed old, however, he grew thoughtful. Having secured the good things of this world, he began to feel anxious about those of the next. He thought with regret on the bargain he had made with his black friend, and set his wits to work to cheat him out of the conditions. He became, therefore, all of a sudden, a violent churchgoer. He prayed loudly and strenuously, as if heaven were to be taken by force of lungs. Indeed, one might always tell when he had sinned most during the week, by the clamor of his Sunday devotion. The quiet Christians who had been modestly and steadfastly traveling Zionward,[27] were struck with self-reproach at seeing themselves so suddenly outstripped in their career by this new-made convert. Tom was as rigid in religious as in money matters; he was a stern supervisor and censurer of his neighbors, and seemed to think every sin entered up to their account became a credit on his own side of the page. He even talked of the expediency of reviving the persecution of Quakers and Anabaptists. In a word, Tom's zeal became as notorious as his riches.

Still, in spite of all this strenuous attention to forms, Tom had a lurking dread that the devil, after all, would have his due. That he might not be taken unawares, therefore, it is said he always carried a small Bible in his coat pocket. He had also a great folio Bible on his countinghouse desk, and would frequently be found reading it when people called on business; on such occasions he would lay his green spectacles in the book, to mark the place, while he turned round to drive some usurious bargain.

Some say that Tom grew a little crackbrained in his old days, and that, fancying his end approaching, he had his horse new shod, saddled and bridled, and buried with his feet uppermost; because he supposed that at the last day the world would be turned upside down; in

which case he should find his horse standing ready for mounting, and he was determined at the worst to give his old friend a run for it. This, however, is probably a mere old wives' fable. If he really did take such a precaution, it was totally *superfluous*; at least so says the authentic old legend, which closes his story in the following manner:

One hot summer afternoon in the dog days, just as a terrible black thunder gust was coming up, Tom sat in his countinghouse, in his white linen cap and India silk morning gown. He was on the point of foreclosing a mortgage, by which he would complete the ruin of an unlucky land speculator for whom he had professed the greatest friendship. The poor land jobber begged him to grant a few months' indulgence. Tom had grown testy and irritated, and refused another day.

"My family will be ruined and brought upon the parish," said the land jobber. "Charity begins at home," replied Tom. "I must take care of myself in these hard times."

"You have made so much money out of me," said the speculator.

Tom lost his patience and his piety. "The devil take me," said he, "if I have made a farthing!"

Just then there were three loud knocks at the street door. He stepped out to see who was there. A black man was holding a black horse, which neighed and stamped with impatience.

"Tom, you're come for," said the black fellow, gruffly. Tom shrank back, but too late. He had left his little Bible at the bottom of his coat pocket, and his big Bible on the desk buried under the mortgage he was about to foreclose: Never was sinner taken more unawares. The black man whisked him like a child into the saddle, gave the horse the lash, and away he galloped, with Tom on his back, in the midst of the thunderstorm. The clerks stuck their pens behind their ears, and stared after him from the windows. Away went Tom Walker, dashing

---

27. **Zionward:** toward Zion, or Heaven.

Vocabulary
superfluous (sə·pʉr′flo̅o̅·əs) *adj.*: more than is needed or wanted; useless.

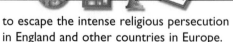

CONTENT-AREA CONNECTIONS

History: Quakers and Anabaptists
The Quakers (known more formally as the Society of Friends) and Anabaptists were regarded as fringe groups within European Protestantism. Both groups were pacifist and believed strongly in the separation of church and state. (By contrast, church and state had been intertwined in the Massachusetts colony, and those who didn't conform had to relocate.) Both groups came to the New World to escape the intense religious persecution in England and other countries in Europe.

The Quakers believed that religion was an inward experience and that each individual must wait patiently for the "inner light," or private apprehension of God. The Anabaptists believed that adult baptism was the only valid form of the sacrament, requiring that the decision to become a Christian be a conscious choice.

down the streets, his white cap bobbing up and down, his morning gown fluttering in the wind, and his steed striking fire out of the pavement at every bound. When the clerks turned to look for the black man, he had disappeared.

Tom Walker never returned to foreclose the mortgage. A countryman, who lived on the border of the swamp, reported that in the height of the thunder gust he had heard a great clattering of hoofs and a howling along the road, and running to the window caught sight of a figure, such as I have described, on a horse that galloped like mad across the fields, over the hills, and down into the black hemlock swamp toward the old Indian fort; and that shortly after a thunderbolt falling in that direction seemed to set the whole forest in a blaze.

The good people of Boston shook their heads and shrugged their shoulders, but had been so much accustomed to witches and goblins, and tricks of the devil, in all kinds of shapes, from the first settlement of the colony, that they were not so much horror-struck as might have been expected. Trustees were appointed to take charge of Tom's effects. There was nothing, however, to administer upon. On searching his coffers,[28] all his bonds and mortgages were found reduced to cinders. In place of gold and silver, his iron chest was filled with chips and shavings; two skeletons lay in his stable instead of his half-starved horses, and the very next day his great house took fire and burnt to the ground.

Such was the end of Tom Walker and his ill-gotten wealth. Let all griping money brokers lay this story to heart. The truth of it is not to be doubted. The very hole under the oak trees whence he dug Kidd's money is to be seen to this day; and the neighboring swamp and old Indian fort are often haunted in stormy nights by a figure on horseback, in morning gown and white cap, which is doubtless the troubled spirit of the usurer. In fact the story has resolved itself into a proverb, and is the origin of that popular saying, so prevalent throughout New England, of "The Devil and Tom Walker." ■

---

28. **coffers** *n. pl.:* containers for money and valuables.

Washington Irving 161

Literary Criticism

Critic's Commentary: Moralist or Artist?

Scholar Norman Foerster characterizes Irving's writing in the following way: "He commanded an admirable prose style, long considered a model for youth in the schools. It is easy, natural . . . not without romantic richness. Through it he conveyed an attitude toward life which is genial—warmly good-natured with a twinkle in the eye—and sometimes sentimental. . . . In writing, he conceived it his business to please as an artist rather than instruct as a moralist."
Individual activity. To what extent is this description applicable to Irving's writing in "The Devil and Tom Walker"? Would you say that Irving's purpose is to "please as an artist" or to "instruct as a moralist"?

[Possible response: This story reflects Irving's talent for writing description, and there is some humor in it. However, there also seems to be a strong message, or moral, to the story.]

Response and Analysis

Reading Check

1. Possible Answer

   Conflict—devil offers wealth for Tom's soul. *Events*—Tom meets the devil; Tom's wife tries to bargain with the devil; she disappears; Tom encounters the devil again; Tom acquires wealth; Tom tries to be religious. *Climax*—the devil carries Tom off. *Resolution*—Tom's goods disappear; people react to Tom's fate.

Thinking Critically

2. Students may have predicted that Tom would give up his soul or bargain with the devil. Surprises may include the wife's fate and Tom's religious fervor.

3. Possible answers: Tom is greedy and brave at first but crueler later. Mrs. Walker meets her end because she fights with the devil.

4. Possible details: "begrimed with soot," red eyes, his stock of firewood. Specific references to America: the extermination of Native Americans, Salem witch trials, persecuting Quakers and Anabaptists, and a request that Tom take up slave trade.

5. Possible details: reference to the devil's presence (p. 153); the swamp, "dark at noonday"; "sacrifices to the evil spirit" (p. 155); the devil's statement that "the woodland belonged to me" (p. 155); the reported haunting (p. 161).

6. The dark setting reflects the moral decay of the characters.

7. Irving mocks greed, stinginess, religious intolerance, spiritual hypocrisy, and the inhumane treatment of others. He criticizes the Puritans for their persecution of Quakers and Anabaptists, the Salem witch trials, and their practice of usury.

Response and Analysis

Reading Check

1. Fill out a graph like the following one to show the elements that make up the **plot** of this story. Add as many key events as you think are necessary.

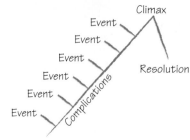

Event — Climax
Event
Event
Event — Resolution
Event
Event
Complications

Basic situation (conflict)

Thinking Critically

SKILLS FOCUS

Literary Skills
Analyze mood.

Reading Skills
Review predictions.

Writing Skills
Write an essay analyzing how a work is representative of Romanticism.

Vocabulary Skills
Use context clues to determine the meanings of words.

2. Usually we look for surprises in stories; we would be disappointed if a story turned out just the way we predicted. What did you predict would happen to Tom and his wife? Did any particular detail or event in the story surprise or shock you?

3. Irving's **characters** in this story are one-dimensional people who represent one or two character traits. In fact, Mrs. Tom Walker is a stereotype of the nagging wife, still a source of comedy today. What character traits are represented by Tom Walker? Why do you think Mrs. Walker met with such a nasty end?

4. In stories about the devil, this character takes on many forms. Look back at the first description of the devil, on page 155. What details suggest at once that he comes from a region of hellfire? What details refer to the devil's special dealings in America?

5. This story opens in Puritan New England in 1727. The Salem witch trials had taken place in 1692, only thirty-five years earlier. Identify five details describing the **setting** that suggest something sinister and supernatural.

6. How does the physical **setting** of the story reflect the moral decay of the characters and, indeed, of the whole society presented in this story?

7. A **tragedy** is a story about the fall of a great person. A **satire** is a story that mocks some human folly. Plots built on bargains with the devil are often tragic, as in the story told by Christopher Marlowe about Dr. Faustus. If Irving's story is a satire, what human follies is Irving mocking? What details in the story reveal that Irving was specifically critical of the values held by the Puritans of Boston?

8. How would you describe the **mood,** or atmosphere, created in the story? What details help to create that mood?

9. As the narrator tells the story—which certainly has its gruesome and fearful aspects—what **tone** prevails? Is it comic, frightening, bitter, romantic, or something else? Find details from the story that support your response.

10. Irving's story opens in 1727 in Boston, Massachusetts. What if the story were set in another time and place? Consider the following questions:
    • Would the theme remain the same?
    • Who would the characters be?
    • What bargain would they drive with the devil?
    • What would the devil look like, and where would he hang out?

8. Possible answer: At first the story's mood is dark, but it lightens when Tom makes the bargain; the mood is darkly comic as Tom is carried off to Hell. The physical details of the swamp create the story's dark mood. The details of Tom's business dealings lighten the mood later, and the image of him on horseback creates the final mood.

9. Possible answer: Irving's tone is that of a detached, witty observer telling a good yarn with a moral lesson. The tone has comic and frightening moments along with strongly satiric ones.

10. Students may feel that the theme of greed is still relevant, but that the setting and characters for a contemporary version might be more sophisticated.

Extending and Evaluating

11. This story was first published in 1824, long before people's consciousness had been raised about the cruelty of viewing other people as stereotypes. It was a time, for example, when women characters were housewives, when African Americans were looked down on, and when American Indians were feared as "savages." These views are reflected in Irving's story. How do you feel about reading literature like this today?

WRITING

Literary Criticism

Review the characteristics of American Romanticism on page 143. In a brief **essay,** describe the characteristics of this story that make it an example of American Romanticism. At the end of your essay, respond to these questions: How would a contemporary American writer be likely to handle the same plot—say, Stephen King? Would the story's tone change?

Vocabulary Development
Context Clues

Respond to each numbered item below. Then, indicate the context clues that give you hints to the meaning of the underlined words in each sentence.

1. If a swampy terrain is filled with stagnant pools, are mosquitoes likely to be prevalent there?

2. Why would it be superfluous for an inexperienced soldier to storm an impregnable fortress?

3. Is someone whose heart is filled with avarice more likely to show parsimony or to make a charitable donation?

4. Name three pleasant things that might help you obliterate a melancholy feeling.

5. If you faced a long and precarious climb up a mountain, why would you want a partner who was especially resolute?

Vocabulary Development

Analogies

A kind of comparison called an **analogy** often appears as a logic problem on standardized tests. An analogy begins with a related pair of words or phrases. The goal is to identify a second pair of words with a similar relationship.

LARGE : GIGANTIC ::

a. depressed : happy   c. round : square

b. noisy : excited   d. tired : weary

The colon (:) stands for the phrase "is related to." The double colon (::) can be read as "in the same way that." Thus, you'd read the above analogy question like this: "*Large* is related to *gigantic* in the same way that . . ."

Finding the connection. Now you have to do two things: Identify the relationship of the first word pair as precisely as possible, and choose a second pair whose relationship is most similar to that of the first pair. In the example above, you could say, "*Large* is similar in meaning to *gigantic.*" *Is similar in meaning to* is the relationship. Next, check to see which answer choices include a pair of words whose meanings are

SKILLS FOCUS

Vocabulary Skills
Analyze word analogies.

Extending and Evaluating

11. Answers will vary. Some students may feel it is instructive to learn the mind-set of an earlier time, if only to see how casually such attitudes were accepted.

Vocabulary Development

1. Yes, mosquitoes lay eggs in stagnant water. *Context clues— swampy* and *pools.*

2. An impregnable fortress could not be taken, even by an accomplished soldier. *Context clues—inexperienced* and *fortress.*

3. A greedy person is more likely to show parsimony, which means "stinginess." *Chief context clue— opposition between show parsimony* and *make a charitable contribution.*

4. Singing, reading something funny, or taking a brisk walk might make one feel better. *Context clues—pleasant, help,* and *feeling.*

5. One would want a resolute partner because the journey would be very challenging and dangerous. *Context clues—long, climb, mountain, want.*

Vocabulary Development

Practice 1

1. synonym
2. antonym
3. characteristic
4. characteristic
5. antonym
6. synonym

Practice 2

1. c
2. c
3. d
4. a

ASSESSING

Assessment

■ *Holt Assessment: Literature, Reading, and Vocabulary*

RETEACHING

For a lesson reteaching irony, tone, and author's style, see **Reteaching,** p. 1117A.

---

similar. The only choice that contains words with similar meanings is d. The word *tired* is similar in meaning to *weary*.

Classifying analogies. Most analogies can be classified into one of about ten relationships. Here are three types of analogy relationships. (For other types of analogies, see pages 714 and 950.)

Type	Relationship	Example
Synonym	is similar in meaning to	SMART : CLEVER
Antonym	is opposite in meaning of	GREED : GENEROSITY
Characteristic	is characteristic of	LOYAL : PATRIOT

Test-taking strategies. Keep the following guidelines in mind when doing analogies in which you have to choose a second pair of words with the same relationship as the first pair:

1. Look for a second pair with a clear, precise relationship.
2. Compare the relationship, not the words.
3. Know the precise denotation, or dictionary definition, of words. Consult a dictionary frequently when dealing with unfamiliar words.

PRACTICE 1

Using the information given in the chart above, identify the type of relationship that exists in each of the following word pairs:

1. NOISE : SOUND
2. TRIVIAL : IMPORTANT
3. FREEZING : ICE
4. CARNIVOROUS : TIGER
5. COURAGE : TIMIDITY
6. WONDER : AWE

PRACTICE 2

Select the lettered word pair that best expresses a relationship similar to that of the capitalized word pair. (In each capitalized pair, the first word is from "The Devil and Tom Walker.")

1. INTERIOR : EXTERIOR ::
   a. beautiful : gorgeous
   b. tired : sleepy
   c. immense : small
   d. smoke : chimney

2. GLOOMY : DISMAL ::
   a. soothing : irritating
   b. cautious : careless
   c. meek : humble
   d. quiet : noisy

3. CONFIDENCE : TRUST ::
   a. illusion : reality
   b. contradiction : agreement
   c. determination : unease
   d. authenticity : truth

4. DESPERATE : HOPELESS ::
   a. strict : stern
   b. rich : poor
   c. unlucky : fortunate
   d. miserable : joyous

William Cullen Bryant
(1794–1878)

William Cullen Bryant (1833)
by James Frothingham. Oil
on canvas (21″ × 17½″).

Courtesy Museum of Fine Arts,
Boston. Gift of Maxim Karolik for
the M. and M. Karolik Collection
of American Paintings, 1815–1865
(62.271).

Poetry is a lonely occupation but not a solitary one. Poets of any consequence rarely write in isolation from the influence of their predecessors or from the influence of other poets of their own time. When William Cullen Bryant was still an adolescent, he read a book of poems that would change his life: *Lyrical Ballads,* published in 1798 by his great English contemporaries William Wordsworth and Samuel Taylor Coleridge. This volume of poetry and theory focused the expression and much of the philosophy of the Romantic era. The book was a powerful source of inspiration for poets who wanted to replace conventional poetic diction with the common speech of their own time. Bryant was one of these poets—the first mature American Romantic, the country boy who translated the messages of English Romanticism into his native tongue.

Two other important factors supported the influence of English Romanticism on Bryant's poetry. One factor was Bryant's own growing attraction to the philosophy of deism (page 18), which held that divinity could be found in nature. The other factor was the geography of his surroundings, which placed Bryant in immediate contact with everything that supported this philosophy.

By the time of Bryant's birth, western Massachusetts was no longer a Colonial frontier but a widely settled countryside. Over the next hundred years and more, its farms, steepled towns, and mountain forests would be the homes of many poets. These writers would find in their surroundings metaphors to express their sense of correspondence between human life and the life of nature. After Bryant, the same New England seasons would turn for Herman Melville and Emily Dickinson and later for Robert Frost and Richard Wilbur. All these poets were intimate with the shadows and whispers of the Berkshires and the adjacent Green Mountains. All would make their own small plot of ground part of the permanent landscape of American poetry.

Bryant was born in Cummington, Massachusetts. His father was a physician, and his mother came from a family of clergy. Bryant's literary gifts were evident from an early age: By the age of nine, he was already writing poetry and had earned a reputation as a prodigy.

Bryant was tutored for a career as a lawyer, but with the publication of "Thanatopsis," his literary future was assured. In his late twenties he moved to New York City and for many years played the triple role of editor, critic, and poet.

Bryant became not only a famous literary figure but also an influential voice in religion and politics. An outspoken liberal, Bryant supported social reform, free speech, and the growing movement for the abolition of slavery. He was also one of the founders of the Republican party, which, in his lifetime, would produce one of America's greatest presidents, Abraham Lincoln. When Bryant died, at the age of eighty-three, he was a millionaire and so widely honored at home and abroad that he had become a kind of national monument, the widely acknowledged father of American poetry.

SKILLS FOCUS,
pp. 165–169

Grade-Level Skills

■ **Literary Skills**
Analyze the way the theme of a selection represents a comment on life.

■ **Reading Skills**
Recognize inverted sentences.

More About the Writer

Background. During his long and illustrious career as a professional writer, Bryant worked for several periodicals, serving as editor for the *New York Review* and *Athaeneum Magazine* and then as editor and co-owner of the New York *Evening Post.* In spite of his involvement in city life, Bryant retained his love for nature, particularly the Berkshire Mountains of western Massachusetts and the mountains of the Hudson Valley. In "Kindred Spirits," one of the most famous paintings of the Hudson River School, Bryant appears with his friend, the artist Thomas Cole.

Summary at grade level

> The speaker celebrates and reflects upon Nature as a mirror that matches his happy moods and offers comfort and balm for his darker thoughts—especially those of death. In death, our individual beings intermingle with Nature's elements, and we join the company of all who have gone before. The speaker advises us to live in such a way that when our time to die comes, we can go to the grave sustained by trust, like a sleeper expecting pleasant dreams.

Selection Starter

Build background. Bryant wrote this poem while walking through the woods on a day off. At Williams College, he had been reading eighteenth-century British poems such as Robert Blair's "The Grave," which might have inspired him to write this Romantic meditation on death. The poem was published anonymously a few years later when his father sent it to an important literary magazine in Boston. The editors could not believe that such a young man had written such a profound, accomplished poem, and assumed that his father had written it. When first published, the poem lacked ll. 1–17 and the conclusion, ll. 66–81; Bryant added these two sections later.

Before You Read

Thanatopsis

Make the Connection

Romantic poets looked to nature for lessons—lessons that we too can learn by looking around us. One of the ever-present lessons of nature is the organic cycle of birth, growth, death, and rebirth. Think of some of the ways that nature reminds us of this recurring cycle. Do you find this aspect of nature disturbing or comforting?

Literary Focus
Theme

Bryant composed the first version of "Thanatopsis" when he was only sixteen years old, during solitary walks in the woods. Despite his youth, though, or perhaps because of it, he tackled the most serious questions a poet can explore: What happens to us after we die, and how should we think or feel about death? Bryant's answers to these questions represent the **theme** of this poem—its central insight into human experience. As you read "Thanatopsis," pay special attention to lines 17–72, where the "still voice" of Nature speaks. What spiritual "teachings" does Nature offer?

> The **theme** of a literary work is the insight it offers into human experience.
>
> *For more on Theme, see the Handbook of Literary and Historical Terms.*

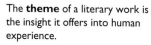

SKILLS FOCUS

Literary Skills
Understand theme.

Reading Skills
Understand inverted sentences.

Reading Skills
Reading Inverted Sentences

In order to maintain his **meter** and create certain sound effects, Bryant makes use of **inversion**—a reversal or rearranging of the usual word order in sentences. The usual word order in English sentences is subject, then verb, and then object or complement. In lines 17–19, Bryant reverses this order: "Yet a few days, and thee / The all-beholding sun shall see no more / In all his course." The normal word order would be "Yet a few days, and thee shall see no more the all-beholding sun in all his course." *Thee* is the subject, *see* is the verb, and *sun* is the object. If you're having trouble understanding a line or passage, look for the subject and the verb, and then restate the sentence in normal English word order.

Background

Thanatopsis is a word Bryant coined by joining two Greek words, *thanatos*, "death," and *opsis*, "sight." The new word is defined by the poem: a way of looking at and thinking about death.

Learners Having Difficulty

Explain that the human speaker is present in the poem's beginning (ll. 1–17) and ending (ll. 73–81), but that a personified Nature speaks the rest of the poem. Remind students that personification gives human qualities to inhuman things such as time, nature, and countries. Ask students to think about the sort of person Nature is represented as being in this poem.

English-Language Learners

This poem contains poetic vocabulary, inverted word order, and omitted words—sometimes all in one sentence. Read, for example, ll. 32–33: "nor couldst thou wish / Couch more magnificent." Translated, this reads "You could not wish [to have a] more magnificent couch." Have students work in mixed-ability groups to decode the poem, following this model.

Advanced Learners

Enrichment. On first reading, encourage students to notice the poet's use of nature imagery. On later readings, focus students'

Thanatopsis

William Cullen Bryant

To him who in the love of Nature holds
Communion with her visible forms, she speaks
A various language; for his gayer hours
She has a voice of gladness, and a smile

5 And eloquence of beauty, and she glides
Into his darker musings, with a mild
And healing sympathy, that steals away
Their sharpness, ere he is aware. When thoughts
Of the last bitter hour come like a blight

10 Over thy spirit, and sad images
Of the stern agony, and shroud, and pall,°
And breathless darkness, and the narrow house,°
Make thee to shudder, and grow sick at heart;—
Go forth, under the open sky, and list°

15 To Nature's teachings, while from all around—
Earth and her waters, and the depths of air—
Comes a still voice.—
                            Yet a few days, and thee
The all-beholding sun shall see no more
In all his course; nor yet in the cold ground,

20 Where thy pale form was laid, with many tears,
Nor in the embrace of ocean, shall exist
Thy image. Earth, that nourished thee, shall claim
Thy growth, to be resolved to earth again,
And, lost each human trace, surrendering up

25 Thine individual being, shalt thou go
To mix forever with the elements,
To be a brother to the insensible rock
And to the sluggish clod, which the rude swain°
Turns with his share,° and treads upon. The oak

30 Shall send his roots abroad, and pierce thy mold.

    Yet not to thine eternal resting place
Shalt thou retire alone, nor couldst thou wish
Couch more magnificent. Thou shalt lie down
With patriarchs of the infant world—with kings,

35 The powerful of the earth—the wise, the good,
Fair forms, and hoary seers° of ages past,
All in one mighty sepulcher. The hills
Rock-ribbed and ancient as the sun,—the vales
Stretching in pensive quietness between;

8. Ere *means "before."* What does Nature do for those who communicate with her?

11. pall (pôl) *n.:* coffin cover.
12. narrow house: grave.

14. list *v.:* archaic for "listen."

17. *Here the voice of Nature begins to speak. When you get to line 30, sum up Nature's advice to those who think sad thoughts of death.*

28. rude swain: uneducated country youth.
29. share *n.:* short for "plowshare."

36. hoary seers°: white-haired prophets.
37. *A sepulcher is a burial place.* What does Nature say to those who fear the solitude of death?

attention on the speaker's philosophical views, which can be labeled Stoic in the classic tradition of Zeno, Seneca, and Marcus Aurelius. Invite students to discuss the kind of afterlife, if any, the speaker imagines and how consoling this view of death may or may not be.

A Reading Skills
Reading inverted sentences. Show students how to rephrase the opening clauses as follows: "Nature speaks in various ways to those who love and commune with her." Encourage students to use this technique as they read on their own.

B Literary Focus
Imagery. In l. 10, the speaker refers to "sad images" that make us "grow sick at heart." What are these images, and to what do they refer? [The images include the "stern agony" of the mortally ill, the "shroud" and "pall" in which a dead person and coffin are wrapped, the "breathless darkness" and "narrow house." These images all refer to death—from the pain of a fatal illness to enclosure and burial in a coffin.]

C Literary Focus
Personification. What quality of Nature does the "still voice" suggest? [Possible responses: Nature is soothing, easing our fears; Nature is subtle, and one must listen carefully to hear her.]

D Learners Having Difficulty
Breaking down difficult text. Explain that Nature begins to speak to the reader in l. 17. What is the main idea expressed in ll. 22–23 and ll. 25–26? [Possible response: In death the earth reclaims us and we mix with the elements.]

Responses to Margin Questions
Line 8. Nature comforts those who communicate with her, sometimes even before they know they are sad.
Line 17. Soon they will have no individual being, but merge with Earth.
Line 37. They will not be alone, because they will join all the people who have died before them.

Ⓐ Literary Focus

❓ Metaphor and theme. How does the metaphor here support the poem's theme? [The speaker calls the earth a "tomb" for all humanity; this metaphor emphasizes that death is natural and universal.]

Ⓑ Content-Area Connections

History: The Living and the Dead Explain that in Bryant's day the number of people living was smaller than the number who had previously lived and died. The population explosion of the twentieth century reversed that relationship.

Ⓒ Literary Focus

❓ Sound and tone. What is the tone of these lines, and what sounds help create the tone? [Possible responses: The tone is soothing and somewhat melancholy; the repetition of o's and u's—as in *continuous, lose, woods, rolls, Oregon, no, sound*—contribute to this quality, as do the *n*'s in some of these words.]

Ⓓ Literary Focus

❓ Metaphor and theme. What does the phrase "chase / his favorite phantom" imply about the living? [Possible response: It implies that they pursue illusory or trivial things.]

Ⓔ Reading Skills

❓ Evaluating. The original version of this poem did not contain ll. 1–17 and ll. 66–81; these were added later. Which version seems better? [Possible response: The longer version is better because it provides a human point of reference.]

---

40 The venerable woods—rivers that move
In majesty, and the complaining brooks
That make the meadows green; and, poured round all,
Old Ocean's gray and melancholy waste,—
Ⓐ Are but the solemn decorations all
45 Of the great tomb of man. The golden sun,
The planets, all the infinite host of heaven,
Are shining on the sad abodes of death,
Through the still lapse of ages. All that tread
Ⓑ The globe are but a handful to the tribes
50 That slumber in its bosom.—Take the wings
Of morning,° pierce the Barcan wilderness,°
Or lose thyself in the continuous woods
Ⓒ Where rolls the Oregon,° and hears no sound,
Save his own dashings—yet the dead are there:
55 And millions in those solitudes, since first
The flight of years began, have laid them down
In their last sleep—the dead reign there alone.
So shalt thou rest, and what if thou withdraw
In silence from the living, and no friend
60 Take note of thy departure? All that breathe
Will share thy destiny. The gay will laugh
When thou art gone, the solemn brood of care
Plod on, and each one as before will chase
Ⓓ His favorite phantom; yet all these shall leave
65 Their mirth and their employments, and shall come
And make their bed with thee. As the long train
Of ages glides away, the sons of men,
The youth in life's fresh spring, and he who goes
In the full strength of years, matron and maid,
70 The speechless babe, and the gray-headed man—
Shall one by one be gathered to thy side,
By those, who in their turn shall follow them.

So live, that when thy summons comes to join
The innumerable caravan, which moves
75 To that mysterious realm, where each shall take
His chamber in the silent halls of death,
Ⓔ Thou go not, like the quarry slave at night,
Scourged to his dungeon, but, sustained and soothed
By an unfaltering trust, approach thy grave,
80 Like one who wraps the drapery of his couch
About him, and lies down to pleasant dreams.

45. *What decorates the "tomb of man"?*

51. Take . . . morning: allusion to Psalm 139:9: "If I take the wings of the morning . . ." **Barcan wilderness:** desert near Barca (now al-Marj), in Libya, North Africa. **53. Oregon:** early name for the Columbia River, which flows between Washington and Oregon.

57. *What examples does the speaker use to explain that the dead are everywhere?*

72. *What comfort does Nature offer in lines 58–72?*

73. *The speaker's voice resumes here. When you get to the end of the poem, sum up the speaker's message in lines 73–81.*

Responses to Margin Questions

Line 45. Everything we see on the earth—seas, rivers, hills, rocks—decorates the "tomb of man."

Line 57. If you go to the desert of North Africa, or to the Oregon woods, or other solitary places, you will stand where people are buried.

Line 72. Those who survive us will join us in death one day.

Line 73. Live in such a way that death will not seem a punishment, but a needed rest.

Response and Analysis

Thinking Critically

1. As the poem opens, Nature is **personified** as someone who speaks "a various language." How does Nature speak to us in our "gayer hours"? How does Nature respond to our "darker musings"?

2. Lines 17–30 have a sad, tragic **tone.** Describe the shift in tone that occurs in line 31. What **metaphors** and **images** in this section of the poem reinforce the change in tone?

3. After Nature's speech (lines 17–72), the human speaker's voice resumes for the concluding section, or summing up. In your own words, summarize the speaker's advice in lines 73–81. What **images** does the poet make you see in these lines?

4. Do you find this speaker's attitude toward death comforting or disturbing, or do you have some other reaction? Explain.

5. How does "Thanatopsis" reveal the Romantic conviction that the universe, far from operating like a machine, is really a living organism that undergoes constant cyclical changes? How does the human speaker feel about this view of the universe?

Extending and Evaluating

6. Today many readers view a poem like "Thanatopsis" as simply a period piece with only historical interest, yet Bryant's intent was to offer serious spiritual counsel. Does Bryant's poem still speak to us today? Or are his musings no longer meaningful? Give reasons for your opinion.

Literary Criticism

7. Some readers think this poem expresses a traditional notion of an afterlife in heaven. Others find in it a very untraditional view of an afterlife, in which people rejoin the great chain of Nature instead of ascending to a heavenly realm. Which interpretation strikes you as a more valid reading of the poem's **theme**?

WRITING

A Puritan Writes to a Romantic

How might Anne Bradstreet (page 27) or Jonathan Edwards (page 44) have reacted to Bryant's meditation on death? Write a **letter** from Bradstreet or Edwards to Bryant, conveying a Puritan reaction to "Thanatopsis." In your letter, be sure to cite specific lines from the poem.

LISTENING AND SPEAKING

Performing a Poem

Working with a partner, present an oral reading of "Thanatopsis." One reader can take the part of the human speaker (lines 1–17 and 73–81), and the other can be the voice of Nature (lines 17–72). As you rehearse, pay attention to where sentences begin and end, since the poem has many run-on lines and sentences that end in the middle of a line. To avoid a singsong rhythm, stop only at punctuation marks (pause briefly at commas, and stop at periods). Before you perform, be sure you have identified lines in the poem that use **inverted syntax.**

SKILLS FOCUS

Literary Skills
Analyze theme.

Reading Skills
Recognize inverted sentences.

Writing Skills
Write a letter reacting to a poem.

Listening and Speaking Skills
Present an oral reading of a poem.

William Cullen Bryant   **169**

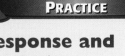

Response and Analysis

Thinking Critically

1. In our "gayer hours" Nature mirrors our happiness with her own beauty and harmony; in our "darker musings," she consoles and heals us.

2. The tone shifts from stern finality to consolation. *Metaphor*—the earth as man's tomb with its natural wonders as the tomb's decorations. *Images*—various landscapes—deserts and woods—where people have lived and died; diverse multitudes lying down together in death.

3. Possible answer: The speaker tells us to regard death with trust, not fear, and to approach it as we do sleep each night, hoping for peaceful dreams. Images include joining a caravan of the dead not as a suffering slave but as a willing guest; the final image is that of the serene sleeper, wrapped in comfort, settling down to dream.

4. Possible answer: The speaker's view is comforting because we must all die, and it is better not to be afraid.

5. The poem reveals the Romantic view that the universe is a living organism by showing how the dead become part of Nature's rebirth. This thought comforts the speaker because it emphasizes the unity of the living and the dead.

Extending and Evaluating

6. Possible answer: The question of how to understand and face death is just as relevant today as it was in Bryant's time.

Literary Criticism

7. Possible answer: It is more valid to say that the poem expresses a less traditional vision of the afterlife by focusing on becoming one with Nature.

William Cullen Bryant   **169**

ASSESSING

Assessment

■ *Holt Assessment: Literature, Reading, and Vocabulary*

RETEACHING

For a lesson reteaching theme and meaning, see **Reteaching,** p. 1117A.

Grade-Level Skills

- **Literary Skills**

Analyze the way a poet uses meter and sounds.

- **Literary Skills**

Analyze characteristics of subgenres of poetry, including sonnets.

More About the Writer

Background. Longfellow's facility with language extended beyond his masterfully crafted poems. As a student at Bowdoin College, he displayed such fluency in translating that he was offered a professorship in modern languages upon graduation. Longfellow's translation of Dante's *Divine Comedy* from the Italian, initiated after the tragic death of his second wife, is one of the best translations of that time.

Henry Wadsworth Longfellow
(1807–1882)

Longfellow was and still is the most popular poet America has ever produced. With the possible exception of Robert Frost (page 716), no twentieth-century poet has ever become a household name, let alone achieved the kind of recognition suggested by the word *popular*.

Longfellow's immense popularity was based largely on his appeal to an audience hungry for sermons and lessons. That audience wanted assurances that their cherished values would prevail over the new forces of history

Henry Wadsworth Longfellow. Photograph by Julia Margaret Cameron.
Courtesy of George Eastman House.

—such as industrialization—that were threatening to destroy them. The values Longfellow endorsed were positive forces in the making of the American character, but his tendency to leave these values unexamined led to poetry that often offered easy comfort at the expense of illumination.

Born in Portland, Maine, Longfellow was never far from the rocks and splashing waves of the Atlantic Coast or from the cultural and religious influences of the well-to-do families who lived north of Boston. Longfellow's early interest in foreign languages and literature led him naturally to an academic career. He attended Bowdoin College (where Nathaniel Hawthorne was one of his classmates) and then pursued three additional years of study in France, Spain, Italy, and Germany. When Longfellow returned, he joined the Bowdoin faculty, married, and began to write a series

of sketches about his experiences abroad.

During a second European trip in 1835, Longfellow's young wife died of a miscarriage. When he returned to America, the young widower became a professor of French and Spanish at Harvard; seven years later he married Frances (Fanny) Appleton, whom he had met in Europe after his first wife's death. He settled into eighteen years of happily married life, fathering six children and producing some of his most celebrated poetry, much of it based on American legends, such as *Evangeline* (1847) and *The Song of Hiawatha* (1855).

By 1854, Longfellow had devoted himself to writing full time. Seven years later, though, a second tragedy struck: His wife, Frances, died in a fiery accident at home, when a lighted match or hot sealing wax ignited her summer dress. Longfellow tried to save her, smothering the flames with a rug, and was badly burned himself.

Longfellow now devoted himself to his work with a religious and literary zeal. By the end of his long and productive life, he had become for Americans the symbolic figure of the Poet: wise, graybearded, haloed with goodness, and living in a world of undiminished romance. Two years after his death, Longfellow's marble image was unveiled in the Poets' Corner in London's Westminster Abbey. He was the first American to be so honored.

RESOURCES: READING

Planning

- *One-Stop Planner* CD-ROM with ExamView Test Generator

Differentiating Instruction

- *Holt Reading Solutions*
- *The Holt Reader*
- *Supporting Instruction in Spanish*
- *Audio CD Library, Selections and Summaries in Spanish*

Grammar and Language

- *Daily Language Activities*

Assessment

- *Holt Assessment: Literature, Reading, and Vocabulary*
- *One-Stop Planner* CD-ROM with ExamView Test Generator
- *Holt Online Assessment*

Before You Read

The Tide Rises, the Tide Falls

Make the Connection

Think of how nature repeats its cycles over and over again: Summer turns to winter and returns again; day follows night and returns again; the tide rises and falls and rises again. Then, think of individual human lives. Are our lives like these endlessly repeated cycles of the natural world, or is a human life different?

Literary Focus

Meter: A Pattern of Sounds

Meter is a pattern of stressed and unstressed syllables in poetry. **Scanning** a poem means marking the stressed syllables with one symbol (') and the unstressed syllables with another (˘).

A metrical unit of poetry is called a **foot**. A foot always contains at least one stressed syllable and usually one or more unstressed syllables. A common type of foot is the **iamb** (ī'amb')—an unstressed syllable followed by a stressed syllable. The meter of

"The Tide Rises, the Tide Falls" is essentially iambic. Read this line aloud, stressing the syllables marked with the stress symbol.

˘ / ˘ / ˘ / ˘ /
Along / the sea- / sands damp / and brown

Poets often vary their metrical patterns to avoid a mechanical, singsong effect. In this poem's first line, notice how Longfellow avoids a purely iambic meter by pairing two stressed syllables. This kind of metrical foot is called a **spondee**.

Read the entire poem aloud to hear how the rise and fall of its rhythm mimics the rise and fall of the tide.

> **Meter** is a pattern of stressed and unstressed syllables in poetry.
>
> *For more on Meter, see the Handbook of Literary and Historical Terms.*

Portion of the original manuscript of "The Cross of Snow" by Henry Wadsworth Longfellow.

Summary ↔ *at grade level*

At twilight a traveler hurries along the shore to the town. In the night, waves efface the footprints left in the sand. At daybreak, normal activities in the town resume, but the traveler does not return to the shore. Through it all, the tide rises and the tide falls.

Selection Starter

Building background. Literary critic Cecil Williams says of this poem: "In 1879, when he was seventy-two and only three years from death, Longfellow wrote the lovely 'The Tide Rises, the Tide Falls.' . . . He returns again to his boyhood in Portland, where he had loved to listen to the sound of the waves and to the gentle rush of the tide coming in. As he visualized in old age the phenomena of water behavior, it became symbolic of life."

SKILLS FOCUS

Literary Skills
Understand meter.

Henry Wadsworth Longfellow **171**

Internet
- go.hrw.com (Keyword: LE5 11-2)
- *Elements of Literature Online*

Media
- *Audio CD Library*
- *Fine Art Transparencies*
- *Audio CD Library, Selections and Summaries in Spanish*

The Cross of Snow

Thinking Critically

1. The phrase means that the speaker lies awake at night thinking of his dead wife.

2. He suggests that she was religious, virtuous, and courageous in the face of death. Other images are the halo, the description of her soul as "white," or pure, and the comparison of her life to those of the saints.

3. Deep ravines might shade a cross of snow from sunlight. Similarly, the poet's grief is too deep to be melted by any ray of happiness.

4. Possible answer: In Christianity, the cross is a potent symbol of grief; it serves as a constant reminder of the martyrdom of Jesus Christ, just as Longfellow's cross reminds him of his wife's terrible death. Longfellow also emphasizes the saintliness of his wife, so a religious symbol is an apt reminder of her life and death.

Literary Criticism

5. Longfellow expresses sadness at the transience of life and deep grief for the death of a loved one, both universal sentiments.

Literary Focus

• The rhyme scheme is *abba, abba, cde, cde.* The octave describes the saintliness of the poet's dead wife. The sestet describes the cross of snow on the mountain as an analogy to the poet's grief.

• In l. 1, Longfellow begins the poem with two unstressed syllables followed by two stressed syllables. Lines 5, 6, and 12 open with a stressed syllable followed by two unstressed syllables.

The Cross of Snow

Thinking Critically

1. The phrase "watches of the night" usually refers to the rounds made by a guard. What does the phrase mean in line 1?

2. The image "martyrdom of fire" in line 6 might confuse readers who do not know that Longfellow's wife died in a fire. (A martyr is a person who dies for his or her faith. Many early Christian martyrs were burned to death.) What is Longfellow suggesting about his wife's character by using this powerful **image**? What other image reinforces this characterization of his wife as saintly?

3. Explain how *sun-defying* (line 10) suggests conditions of weather and geology that might actually produce a permanent cross of snow on the side of a mountain. How does the poet relate this idea to his own feelings of grief?

4. Why might Longfellow have chosen to use a cross as the **symbol** of his grief?

Literary Criticism

5. In his article on Longfellow (see the **Connection** on page 175), J. D. McClatchy says that Queen Victoria was surprised that her servants read Longfellow. What universal human experiences do you think Longfellow has expressed in these two poems that might account for his popularity?

WRITING

Comparing Poems

In a brief **essay,** compare and contrast the attitudes toward death in "The Tide Rises, the Tide Falls" and "The Cross of Snow." How important is it that one poem is about an unnamed traveler—probably standing for everyone—while the other is about a specific person?

List of characters from
Tales of a Wayside Inn.

An Image of Grief

Refer to your Quickwrite notes, and write a brief **poem** in which you use an image from nature to stand for an experience of grief.

Literary Focus

What Is a Sonnet?

☑ A sonnet has fourteen lines arranged in a specific pattern. It uses a set rhyme scheme.

☑ The typical rhyme scheme in a Petrarchan, or Italian, sonnet is *abba, abba, cde, cde.*

☑ The usual rhyme scheme in a Shakespearean sonnet is *abab, cdcd, efef, gg.*

☑ The first part of a sonnet usually introduces a subject. The last group of lines makes a comment on the subject. When you read a sonnet, look for the subject and the comment on the subject.

• Longfellow chose to write "The Cross of Snow" in the form of a **Petrarchan sonnet.** Identify the **rhyme scheme** of the sonnet. What question or idea does the **octave** (lines 1–8) present? What answer or response does the **sestet** (lines 9–14) offer?

• This sonnet is written in **iambic pentameter.** This is the most common meter used in English poetry because it sounds the most like ordinary speech. Where does Longfellow vary his iambic pentameter?

Assessment

■ *Holt Assessment: Literature, Reading, and Vocabulary*

For lessons reteaching poetic devices, see **Reteaching,** p. 1117A.

Ralph Waldo Emerson
(1803–1882)

Shortly before the poet Walt Whitman died, he honored a man whose ideas had influenced him profoundly throughout his own long and controversial career. "America in the future," he wrote, "in her long train of poets and writers, while knowing more vehement and luxurious ones, will, I think, acknowledge nothing nearer [than] this man, the actual beginner of the whole procession."

"This man" was Ralph Waldo Emerson. Emerson expressed, better than anyone before him, the advantages of a young land—its freedom from the old, corrupt, and dying thought and the customs of Europe; its access to higher laws directly through nature rather than indirectly, through books and the teachings of the past; its energy; and its opportunity to reform the world.

Emerson was one of those rare writers who appealed both to intellectuals and to the general public. His influence on the popular mind—thanks to the thousands of lectures he gave throughout the United States—was strong. Although Emerson had something of a reputation for being hard to understand, his lectures were usually quite accessible. "I had heard of him as full of transcendentalisms, myths, and oracular gibberish," Herman Melville wrote a friend after hearing Emerson lecture. "To my surprise, I found him quite intelligible." Melville added wryly, "To say truth, they told me that that night he was unusually plain."

Despite Emerson's great influence, it is difficult even to classify what kind of writer he was. *Essayist* is too limited a term, and *philosopher* is too broad. The best term, perhaps, is *poet*—a poet whose best work was not always in verse.

"I am born a poet," Emerson wrote to his fiancée, Lydia Jackson, in 1835, "of a low class without doubt, yet a poet. That is my nature

Ralph Waldo Emerson (c. 1867) by William Henry Furness, Jr. Oil on canvas (45³/₄″ × 36⁵/₁₆″).

The Pennsylvania Academy of the Fine Arts, Philadelphia. Gift of Horace Howard Furness (1899.8).

and vocation. My singing, be sure, is very 'husky,' and is for the most part in prose. Still am I a poet in the sense of a perceiver and dear lover of the harmonies that are in the soul and in matter. . . ."

The Burden of Expectation

Emerson was born in Boston in 1803 to a family that was cultured but poor. When he was not quite eight years old, his father, a Unitarian minister, died of tuberculosis. His mother, left with six growing children to care for, opened a boardinghouse.

In the lives of the Emerson children, their father's place was taken by an aunt, Mary Moody Emerson. She was a strict Calvinist who emphasized self-sacrifice and whose enormous energy drove the Emerson boys to achievement. "She had the misfortune," Emerson later wrote, "of spinning with a greater velocity than any of the other tops."

Every step of Emerson's life had been laid out for him from an early age. He was to go to Harvard and become a minister, like the eight generations of Emersons before him. Emerson uncomfortably obeyed. His life was a series of attempts to establish his own identity against this background of expectation.

Young Rebel

Emerson entered Harvard at fourteen. He was an indifferent student, although he read widely in philosophy and theology. Upon graduation,

SKILLS FOCUS,
pp. 179–188

Grade-Level Skills

■ **Literary Skills**
Analyze ways writers use imagery and figures of speech.

■ **Literary Skills**
Analyze an author's philosophical assumptions and beliefs about a subject.

■ **Reading Skills**
Monitor your reading.

More About the Writer

Background. At age twenty-one, Emerson took stock of himself in the following terms: "My bearing in the world is the direct opposite of that good humoured independence & self esteem which should mark the gentleman. . . . I am unfortunate also . . . in a propensity to laugh & snicker. I am ill at ease therefore among men. I criticize with hardness; I lavishly applaud. I weakly argue; and I wonder with a foolish face of praise. . . . What is called a warm heart, I have not."

RESOURCES: READING

Planning
■ *One-Stop Planner* CD-ROM with ExamView Test Generator

Differentiating Instruction
■ *Holt Reading Solutions*
■ *The Holt Reader*
■ *Holt Adapted Reader*
■ *Supporting Instruction in Spanish*

Vocabulary
■ *Vocabulary Development*

Grammar and Language
■ *Daily Language Activities*

Assessment
■ *Holt Assessment: Literature, Reading, and Vocabulary*
■ *One-Stop Planner* CD-ROM with ExamView Test Generator

■ *Holt Online Assessment*

Internet
■ go.hrw.com (Keyword: LE5 11-2)
■ *Elements of Literature Online*

Media
■ *Audio CD Library*
■ *Audio CD Library, Selections and Summaries in Spanish*

More About the Writer

Emerson on writing. "No man can write well who thinks there is any choice of words for him," Emerson wrote in 1831. "The laws of composition are as strict as those of sculpture & architecture. There is always one line that ought to be drawn or one proportion that should be kept & every other line or proportion is wrong. . . . So in writing, there is always a right word, & every other than that is wrong. There is no beauty in words except in their collocation. The effect of a fanciful word misplaced, is like that of a horn . . . growing on a human head."

Emerson on the sacred. Emerson believed that the true path to spiritual reality was found in the faculties of the human mind. Emerson rejected the easy authority of religious texts and mocked the fatuous movements of Spiritualism and Mesmerism that were popular in Boston society at the time. He wrote, "Shun them as you would shun the secrets of the undertaker, of the butcher, the secrets of the jakes and the dead-cart. [Remember that] nothing is sacred but the integrity of your own mind."

Emerson took a job at a school run by his brother and prepared himself, with many doubts, for the Unitarian ministry. In 1829, at the age of twenty-five, he accepted a post at Boston's Second Church; that same year he married Ellen Tucker, a beautiful but fragile seventeen-year-old already in the early stages of tuberculosis. Seventeen months later Ellen died.

Emerson's grief coincided with a growing disbelief in some of the central doctrines of his religion. In June 1832, he shocked his congregation by resigning from the ministry and setting off on an extended tour of Europe. There he met and conversed with the Romantic poets William Wordsworth and Samuel Taylor Coleridge, as well as other influential writers.

Emerson's "New Pulpit"

Returning to the United States in late 1833, Emerson settled in Concord, Massachusetts, and soon married Lydia Jackson. He began to supplement his meager income by giving lectures and found in that occupation "a new pulpit," as he once wrote. Emerson's view was distinctively American in that he denied the importance of the past: "Let us unfetter ourselves of our historical associations and find a pure standard in the idea of man."

The last phrase points to Emerson's focus on humanity. Individual men and women were part of this "idea of man" in the same way that individual souls were part of a larger entity, which Emerson later called the Over-Soul. The idea of nature also corresponded to the "idea of man"—both were part of a universal whole in which people could see their souls reflected.

Over the years, Emerson's influence grew. In 1837, he excited students at Harvard with the lecture now known as "The American Scholar." In the speech, Emerson demanded that American scholars free themselves from the shackles of the past. "Our day of dependence," he declared, "our long apprenticeship to the learning of other lands, draws to a close."

A year later Emerson was invited back to Harvard to speak to a group of divinity students. His speech, "Divinity-School Address," called for a rejection of institutional religion in favor of a personal relation with God. Religious truth, Emerson said, is "an intuition. It cannot be received at secondhand." The lecture so outraged Harvard authorities (who heard in it a denial of the divinity of Jesus) that three decades passed before Emerson was allowed to speak there again.

Twilight of an Idol

With the author's growing fame, Concord increasingly became a destination for truth-seeking young people who looked to Emerson as their guru. The young responded to Emerson's predictions that they were on the verge of a new age; intellectuals responded to his philosophical ideas about the relations among humanity, nature, and God; and society as a whole responded to his optimism.

That optimism was dealt a severe blow in 1842, when Emerson's son Waldo died of scarlet fever at the age of five. By nature a rather reserved man, Emerson had found in Waldo someone to whom he could show his love spontaneously. At the child's death he shrank into an emotional shell from which he never emerged. "How can I hope for a friend," he wrote in his journal, "who have never been one?"

In later years, Emerson suffered from a severe loss of memory and had difficulty recalling the most ordinary words. This affliction resulted in his increasing public silence, and when he did appear in public, he read from notes.

In the autumn of 1881, Walt Whitman paid Emerson a visit of respect and was asked to dinner. Whitman wrote that Emerson, "though a listener and apparently an alert one, remained silent through the whole talk and discussion. A lady friend [Louisa May Alcott] quietly took a seat next to him, to give special attention. A good color in his face, eyes clear, with the well-known expression of sweetness, and the old clear-peering aspect quite the same." Six months later Emerson was dead.

Secondary Source

Emerson's Politics

Literary scholar Brooks Atkinson explains that in spite of being actively involved in local affairs in Concord regarding national politics, Emerson was a reluctant participant: "From the first he had believed that the slaves should be freed. But he avoided as long as possible the radical societies that were promoting abolition. . . . But as the slavery clamor increased Emerson began to join in it. When the Fugitive Slave Law was passed, and Emerson believed his hero, Daniel Webster, had betrayed public trust, Emerson appeared at public meetings in Concord, Boston, and New York and spoke with a bitterness strange in so serene a person. In spite of the fact that all his instincts were against taking part in political action and in spite of his distrust of his own knowledge of practical affairs, he actively associated himself with the abolitionist cause after the passage of the Fugitive Slave Law. Once he observed to one of his children who had to write a school essay on building a house that no house should be

Before You Read

from Nature

Make the Connection
Quickwrite ✏

Emerson was exhilarated by nature's beauty and grandeur. In the presence of nature, Emerson felt he was in tune with his better self and in harmony with eternal things. How do you feel about nature? Jot down your thoughts on anything that nature has taught or revealed to you.

Literary Focus
Imagery

In this essay, Emerson the poet helps Emerson the philosopher. Here Emerson *shows* us scenes of nature that have moved him; he doesn't just *tell* us how he feels. As you read, look for **imagery**, or descriptive language that appeals to your senses. How do the images help you share the writer's experiences?

> **Imagery** is the use of language to evoke a picture or a concrete sensation of a person, a thing, a place, or an experience.
>
> *For more on Imagery, see the Handbook of Literary and Historical Terms.*

Reading Skills 📖
Monitoring Your Reading

As you read these essays, look for key passages that state or suggest a **main idea.** If a statement puzzles you, try to **paraphrase** it, or restate it in your own words. Check the footnotes, and use a dictionary to look up the definitions of difficult words. Above all, read the essay more than once, and be sure to ask questions of the text.

Background

In his introduction to the book *Nature*, from which the following chapter is taken, Emerson offers a clue to his underlying purpose when he encourages his contemporaries to look directly at nature:

> Our age is retrospective. It builds the sepulchers [tombs] of the fathers. It writes biographies, histories, and criticism. The foregoing generations beheld God and nature face to face; we, through their eyes. Why should we not also enjoy an original relation to the universe? Why should we not have a poetry and philosophy of insight and not of tradition, and a religion by revelation to us, and not the history of theirs?

In his quest for original religious insight and a uniquely American literary expression, Emerson inspired the American renaissance. In *Nature* he made it clear to those who wished to see that the magnificent American landscape itself could be the basis for spiritual rebirth.

Vocabulary Development

admonishing (ad·män′ish·iŋ) *v.* used as *adj.*: gently warning.

integrate (in′tə·grāt′) *v.*: unify.

perennial (pə·ren′ē·əl) *adj.*: persistent; constant.

blithe (blīth) *adj.*: carefree.

occult (ə·kult′) *adj.*: hidden.

go.hrw.com

INTERNET

Vocabulary Practice
•
More About Ralph Waldo Emerson
•

Keyword: LE5 11-2

SKILLS FOCUS

Literary Skills
Understand the use of imagery. Analyze an author's philosophical beliefs.

Reading Skills
Monitor reading by identifying main ideas and paraphrasing.

PRETEACHING

Summary ⬆ *above grade level*

> In this excerpt from *Nature*, Emerson uses vivid imagery to describe the exaltation human beings can experience when they really see the natural world around them. Most people, Emerson believes, lose that sense of wonder and delight in nature as they grow older, but those adults who retain that sense remain youthful in spirit all their lives. Emerson explains that humans and plants are both part of the same natural world and that our delight in nature comes from our perception of this relationship. Beauty and grandeur are not only to be found in nature but also in our perception of and response to it.

Skills Starter

Motivate. Write the following sentences on the chalkboard: "The sun shone. I walked beneath the trees. The wind blew in the branches." Remind students that imagery helps to paint a scene. Ask volunteers to improve upon the three simple sentences by adding colorful images and sensory details to flesh out the scene.

---

built without having in it a space to hide a runaway slave. He entertained John Brown in his house, contributed to the cause of abolition beyond his means and spoke in defense of John Brown after Harpers Ferry."

Previewing Vocabulary

Have students find the Vocabulary word on p. 181 that corresponds to each of the following synonyms.

1. recurring [perennial]
2. merry [blithe]
3. combine [integrate]
4. secret [occult]
5. scolding [admonishing]

Ⓐ Literary Focus

❓ Imagery. Which of the five senses does Emerson appeal to here? [sight] How does he feel when he looks at the stars? [awed; thrilled; reverent; admiring]

Ⓑ Reading Skills

❓ Tracing recurring themes. Elsewhere in *Nature* Emerson says that "[t]he invariable mark of wisdom is to see the miraculous in the common." How might you apply this remark to Emerson's observation about people taking the stars for granted? [Possible response: The stars seem common because they are always there, but wise people perceive that they are truly miraculous.]

Ⓒ Reading Skills

Monitoring reading. Ask students to paraphrase this paragraph. [Possible response: The poet looks at nature as an organic whole rather than a group of distinct objects or features. People own particular plots of land, but no one "owns the landscape."]

Responses to Boxed Questions

1. People would be filled with faith in and love for God, and they would remember the experience of the sublime for many generations.

2. It can integrate the parts of nature into a landscape.

3. The lover of nature is a person whose inner and outer senses are still aligned, who remains young at heart, and who feels the necessity of communing with nature on a daily basis.

---

from Nature
Ralph Waldo Emerson

To go into solitude, a man needs to retire as much from his chamber[1] as from society. I am not solitary while I read and write, though nobody is with me. But if a man would be alone, let him look at the stars. The rays that come from those heavenly worlds, will separate between him and vulgar things. One might think the atmosphere was made transparent with this design, to give man, in the heavenly bodies, the perpetual presence of the sublime.[2] Seen in the streets of cities, how great they are! If the stars should appear one night in a thousand years, how would men believe and adore; and preserve for many generations the remembrance of the city of God which had been shown! But every night come out these envoys[3] of beauty, and light the universe with their admonishing smile. ❶

The stars awaken a certain reverence, because though always present, they are always inaccessible; but all natural objects make a kindred impression, when the mind is open to their influence. Nature never wears a mean appearance. Neither does the wisest man extort all her secrets, and lose his curiosity by finding out all her perfection. Nature never became a toy to a wise spirit. The flowers, the animals, the mountains, reflected all the wisdom of his best hour, as much as they had delighted the simplicity of his childhood.

When we speak of nature in this manner, we have a distinct but most poetical sense in the mind. We mean the integrity of impression made by manifold[4] natural objects. It is this which distinguishes the stick of timber of the woodcutter, from the tree of the poet. The charming landscape which I saw this morning, is indubitably[5] made up of some twenty or thirty farms. Miller owns this field, Locke that, and Manning the woodland beyond. But none of them owns the landscape. There is a property in the horizon which no man has but he whose eye can integrate all the parts, that is, the poet. This is the best part of these men's farms, yet to this their warranty deeds[6] give no title. ❷

To speak truly, few adult persons can see nature. Most persons do not see the sun. At least they have a very superficial seeing. The sun illuminates only the eye of the man, but shines into the eye and the heart of the child. The lover of nature is he whose inward and outward senses are still truly adjusted to each other; who has retained the spirit of infancy even into the era of manhood. His intercourse with heaven and earth, becomes part of his daily food. In the presence of nature, a wild delight runs through the man, in spite of real sorrows. ❸ Nature says—he is my creature, and

❓ ❶ According to this first paragraph, how would people respond if the stars came out only one night every thousand years?

❓ ❷ What can the poet's eye do when he or she looks at nature?

❓ ❸ How does Emerson define the "lover of nature"?

---

1. **chamber** *n.:* room.
2. **sublime** *adj.* used as *n.:* something that inspires awe. Here, Emerson refers to the divine.
3. **envoys** *n. pl.:* messengers.

4. **manifold** *adj.:* many and varied.
5. **indubitably** *adv.:* without a doubt.
6. **warranty deeds** *n. pl.:* legal documents showing ownership of property.

Vocabulary
admonishing (ad·män′ish·iŋ) *v.* used as *adj.:* gently warning.
integrate (in′tə·grāt′) *v.:* unify.

English-Language Learners
Even proficient English-speakers may have some difficulty with the complexity of Emerson's concepts and language. Guide the class in paraphrasing passages that prove troublesome. For difficult sentences and words (such as *maugre*), paraphrases or definitions could be written on the chalkboard. Divide the essay into smaller passages, each of which can be analyzed by a group of students.

Special Education Students
For lessons designed for special education students, see *Holt Reading Solutions*.

maugre[7] all his impertinent griefs, he shall be glad with me. Not the sun or the summer alone, but every hour and season yields its tribute of delight; for every hour and change corresponds to and authorizes a different state of the mind, from breathless noon to grimmest midnight. Nature is a setting that fits equally well a comic or a mourning piece. In good health, the air is a cordial[8] of incredible virtue. Crossing a bare common, in snow puddles, at twilight, under a clouded sky, without having in my thoughts any occurrence of special good fortune, I have enjoyed a perfect exhilaration. Almost I fear to think how glad I am. In the woods too, a man casts off his years, as the snake his slough,[9] and at what period soever of life, is always a child. In the woods, is perpetual youth. Within these plantations of God, a decorum[10] and sanctity reign, a perennial festival is dressed, and the guest sees not how he should tire of them in a thousand years. In the woods, we return to reason and faith. There I feel that nothing can befall me in life—no disgrace, no calamity (leaving me my eyes), which nature cannot repair. Standing on the bare ground—my head bathed by the blithe air, and uplifted into infinite space—all mean egotism vanishes. I become a transparent eyeball. I am nothing. I see all. The currents of the Universal Being circulate through me; I am part or particle of God. The name of the nearest friend sounds then foreign and accidental. To be brothers, to be acquaintances—master or servant, is then a trifle and a disturbance. I am the lover of uncontained and immortal beauty. In the wilderness, I find something more dear and connate[11] than in streets or villages. In the tranquil landscape, and especially in the distant line of the horizon, man beholds somewhat[12] as beautiful as his own nature. ●4

The greatest delight which the fields and woods minister, is the suggestion of an occult relation between man and the vegetable. I am not alone and unacknowledged. They nod to me and I to them. The waving of the boughs in the storm, is new to me and old. It takes me by surprise, and yet is not unknown. Its effect is like that of a higher thought or a better emotion coming over me, when I deemed I was thinking justly or doing right. ●5

Yet it is certain that the power to produce this delight, does not reside in nature, but in man, or in a harmony of both. It is necessary to use these pleasures with great temperance. For, nature is not always tricked[13] in holiday attire, but the same scene which yesterday breathed perfume and glittered as for the frolic of the nymphs, is overspread with melancholy today. Nature always wears the colors of the spirit. To a man laboring under calamity, the heat of his own fire hath sadness in it. Then, there is a kind of contempt of the landscape felt by him who has just lost by death a dear friend. The sky is less grand as it shuts down over less worth in the population. ●6 ■

---

7. **maugre** (mô′gər) *prep.*: archaic for "in spite of; despite."
8. **cordial** (kôr′jəl) *n.*: medicine, food, or drink that stimulates the heart.
9. **slough** (sluf) *n.*: outer layer of a snake's skin, which is shed periodically.
10. **decorum** *n.*: orderliness.
11. **connate** *adj.*: having the same nature.

12. **somewhat** *pron.*: something.
13. **tricked** *v.*: dressed up.

Vocabulary
perennial (pə·ren′ē·əl) *adj.*: persistent; constant.
blithe (blīth) *adj.*: carefree.
occult (ə·kult′) *adj.*: hidden.

Ralph Waldo Emerson   **183**

? ●4 What does Emerson think and feel when he stands in the woods?

? ●5 What is the greatest delight the fields and woods give us, according to Emerson?

? ●6 What does Emerson say about how our own moods can affect the way we look at nature?

DIRECT TEACHING

●D Reading Skills
Monitoring reading. Pause at this point, and have students re-read this long and complex paragraph. Then, have them make a list of Emerson's main ideas and the supporting details that he provides. [Possible responses should include the following ideas: The lover of nature remains young through an emotional and aesthetic appreciation of nature that most adults lose; nature assuages our troubles by taking us outside ourselves and reconnecting us to the grandeur of divine creation.]

●E Literary Focus
? Imagery. What are the images in this line? [bare common, snow puddles, twilight, clouded sky] **What effect does this description have on the reader?** [Possible response: Emerson's direct language evokes the brisk exhilaration of the scene and causes the reader to see the treeless patch of ground and to feel the slush and cold.]

●F Literary Focus
? Imagery. What image does Emerson conjure up here? [the "vegetable" world nodding and waving to him] **What effect does that image have on him?** [It carries him to a higher level of thought and emotion.]

Responses to Boxed Questions

4. He feels peaceful, young, and at one with God and all creation.

5. They give us the feeling that we are part of nature, "not alone and unacknowledged."

6. An unhappy or unworthy person will see the landscape as melancholy or less grand.

Advanced Learners
Enrichment. Have students read Emerson's famous Harvard lectures "The American Scholar" and "The Divinity School Address." Students can then form small groups to discuss the main idea of each of the lectures and how those ideas relate to the main idea of the excerpt from *Nature*. They might also consider whether the three selections form a coherent or inconsistent philosophical system and whether they agree with Emerson's ideas.

Summary *at grade level*

In this essay, Emerson makes a persuasive argument for nonconformity and self-sufficiency, finds sanctity in the individual mind, and calls upon us to express ourselves strongly rather than meekly. He insists that only as individuals do we know the best course of action and that imitation of others is ignorance.

Skills Starter

Build review skills. Write the following sentence on the chalkboard: "Society is a joint-stock company." Point out to students that Emerson does not mean that society is in fact a business with shareholders, but that he is comparing the two in order to say something about society. Ask students to think about their own experience of society as they read the excerpt. Do they agree with Emerson?

Before You Read

from Self-Reliance

Make the Connection

As citizens of a bold, young nation, Americans have always taken tremendous pride in their personal liberty. Emerson nourished this individualistic creed with his essay "Self-Reliance." What associations do you make with the word *self-reliance*? How does *self-reliance* differ from *selfishness* and *self-centeredness*?

Literary Focus
Figures of Speech

Emerson said he was "born a poet" who sang "for the most part in prose." One sign of his poetic nature is the way he uses figures of speech in his philosophical arguments. **Figures of speech** are imaginative comparisons of things that are basically unalike. Emerson often compares abstract ideas to ordinary things or events—such as when he says, "Society is a joint-stock company." Here Emerson compares society to a business where the shareholders or owners are held personally liable.

INTERNET

Vocabulary
Practice

More About
Ralph Waldo
Emerson

Keyword: LE5 11-2

SKILLS
FOCUS

Literary Skills
Understand
figures of
speech.

Reading Skills
Interpret
difficult figures
of speech.

A **figure of speech** is a word or phrase that describes one thing in terms of another, very different thing. Figures of speech are not meant to be taken literally. The most common figures of speech are **simile, metaphor, personification,** and **symbol.**

For more on Figure of Speech, see the Handbook of Literary and Historical Terms.

Reading Skills
Understanding Figures of Speech

In a good figure of speech, a characteristic of one thing helps us see the other, unlike thing in a new, imaginative way. Some of Emerson's figures of speech are difficult and require re-reading and analysis. When you come across a figure of speech—especially a complex one—ask yourself, "What do these two things have in common?" and "Why has the writer chosen this particular comparison?"

Vocabulary Development

conviction (kən·vik′shən) *n.:* fixed or strong belief.

imparted (im·pärt′id) *v.:* revealed.

manifest (man′ə·fəst′) *adj.:* plain; clear.

transcendent (tran·sen′dənt) *adj.:* excelling; surpassing.

integrity (in·teg′rə·tē) *n.:* sound moral principles; honesty.

Previewing Vocabulary

Have students complete each of the following sentences with the correct Vocabulary word from p. 184.

1. Emerson_____ wisdom to his audiences. [imparted]

2. He spoke with_____; he meant what he said. [conviction]

3. His honesty and _____ were rarely questioned. [integrity]

4. Emerson viewed a winter stroll as a _____ experience, transporting him beyond petty egotism and worry. [transcendent]

5. The ripening corn stalks make _____ the arrival of summer. [manifest]

Long Island Farmer Husking Corn (1833–1834) by William Sidney Mount. Oil on canvas mounted on panel (20⅞″ × 16⅞″).

The Long Island Museum of American Art, History and Carriages. Gift of Mr. and Mrs. Ward Melville, 1975.

from Self-Reliance

Ralph Waldo Emerson

There is a time in every man's education when he arrives at the <u>conviction</u> that envy is ignorance; that imitation is suicide; that he must take himself for better, for worse, as his portion; that though the wide universe is full of good, no kernel of nourishing corn can come to him but through his toil bestowed on that plot of ground which is given to him to till. The power which resides in him is new in nature, and none but he knows what that is which he can do, nor does he know until he has tried. Not for nothing one face, one character, one fact makes much impression on him, and another none. This sculpture in the memory is not without preestablished harmony. ❶ The eye was placed where one ray should fall, that it might testify of that particular ray. We but half express ourselves, and are

❶
Emerson believes that each person has unique talents and passions that can be discovered only on one's own.

? *What does he mean by "this sculpture in the memory"?*

Vocabulary
conviction (kən·vik′shən) *n.:* fixed or strong belief.

Ralph Waldo Emerson **185**

Ralph Waldo Emerson **185**

Ⓐ Literary Focus

❓ Making and supporting assertions. Does Emerson see society as a positive or a negative force? [Emerson sees society as being harmful to individuals.] **What elements in the text support your interpretation?** [Possible response: Emerson characterizes society as a "conspiracy" against the self-reliance of individuals.]

Responses to Boxed Questions

2. A person is relieved and happy having done his or her best.

3. One should trust oneself.

4. society

5. a nonconformist

6. Emerson says that "foolish consistency" can prevent people from growing, changing, and fulfilling their potential.

---

ashamed of that divine idea which each of us represents. It may be safely trusted as proportionate[1] and of good issues, so it be faithfully imparted, but God will not have his work made manifest by cowards. A man is relieved and gay when he has put his heart into his work and done his best; but what he has said or done otherwise, shall give him no peace. It is a deliverance which does not deliver. In the attempt his genius deserts him; no muse befriends; no invention, no hope. ❷

Trust thyself: Every heart vibrates to that iron string. Accept the place the divine Providence has found for you; the society of your contemporaries, the connection of events. Great men have always done so and confided themselves childlike to the genius of their age, betraying their perception that the absolutely trustworthy was seated at their heart, working through their hands, predominating[2] in all their being. And we are now men, and must accept in the highest mind the same transcendent destiny; and not minors and invalids in a protected corner, not cowards fleeing before a revolution, but guides, redeemers, and benefactors, obeying the Almighty effort, and advancing on Chaos and the Dark. . . . ❸

Ⓐ These are the voices which we hear in solitude, but they grow faint and inaudible as we enter into the world. Society everywhere is in conspiracy against the manhood of every one of its members. Society is a joint-stock company in which the members agree for the better securing of his bread to each shareholder, to surrender the liberty and culture of the eater. The virtue in most request is conformity. Self-reliance is its aversion.[3] It loves not realities

> **❷ ❓** According to Emerson, when is a person relieved and happy?

> **❸ ❓** Who or what should every person trust?

---

1. **proportionate** *adj.:* having a correct relationship between parts; balanced.
2. **predominating** *v.* used as *adj.:* having influence or power.
3. **aversion** *n.:* object of intense dislike or opposition.

---

and creators, but names and customs. ❹

Whoso would be a man must be a non-conformist. He who would gather immortal palms[4] must not be hindered by the name of goodness, but must explore if it be goodness. Nothing is at last sacred but the integrity of your own mind. Absolve[5] you to yourself, and you shall have the suffrage of the world. . . . ❺

A foolish consistency is the hobgoblin of little minds, adored by little statesmen and philosophers and divines. With consistency a great soul has simply nothing to do. He may as well concern himself with his shadow on the wall. Speak what you think now in hard words, and tomorrow speak what tomorrow thinks in hard words again, though it contradict everything you said today—"Ah, so you shall be sure to be misunderstood"—Is it so bad then to be misunderstood? Pythagoras was misunderstood, and Socrates, and Jesus, and Luther, and Copernicus, and Galileo, and Newton,[6] and every pure and wise spirit that ever took flesh. To be great is to be misunderstood. . . . ❻ ■

> **❹ ❓** What is the opposite, or "aversion," of self-reliance?

> **❺ ❓** According to Emerson, what must a person be?

> **❻ ❓** What does Emerson say about "foolish consistency"?

---

4. **he who . . . immortal palms:** he who would win fame. In ancient times, palm leaves were carried as a symbol of victory or triumph.
5. **absolve** *v.:* pronounce free from guilt or blame.
6. **Pythagoras . . . Newton:** people whose contributions to scientific, philosophical, and religious thought were ignored or suppressed during their lifetimes.

Vocabulary
imparted (im·pärt′id) *v.:* revealed.
manifest (man′ə·fəst) *adj.:* plain; clear.
transcendent (tran·sen′dənt) *adj.:* excelling; surpassing.
integrity (in·teg′rə·tē) *n.:* sound moral principles; honesty.

Learners Having Difficulty

Invite learners having difficulty to read "Self-Reliance" in interactive format in *The Holt Reader* and to use the sidenotes as aids to understanding the selection. The interactive version provides additional instruction, practice, and assessment of the literary skill taught in the Student Edition. Monitor students' responses to the selection, and correct any misconceptions that arise.

Advanced Learners

Enrichment. To elaborate on Emerson's point in the final paragraph of this excerpt, ask students to research one of the great men listed to discover what he accomplished, what new ideas he introduced, and how the world responded to him during his lifetime. Students can present their research to the class. Afterward, ask students if they agree that "to be great is to be misunderstood."

Response and Analysis

from Nature

Reading Check

1. Review each paragraph of the essay. Then, write down one statement from each paragraph that you think sums up the **main idea** of that paragraph. You should have six main ideas.

Thinking Critically

2. In the first paragraph, Emerson says that our attitude toward the stars would change if they appeared only once every thousand years. What point is Emerson making about nature with this striking example?

3. What do you think Emerson means in the third paragraph by a "poetical sense" of looking at nature?

4. Emerson's **image** of a "transparent eyeball" in the fourth paragraph is one of the most famous passages in all of his works. (See the caricature on this page.) In your own words, tell how you interpret Emerson's image. What effect does this unusual image have on you?

5. "Nature always wears the colors of the spirit," Emerson says in the sixth paragraph. What does Emerson mean by this statement? How does the statement demonstrate Emerson's Romantic beliefs?

Extending and Evaluating

6. "To speak truly," Emerson says, "few adult persons can see nature." Emerson sees children as having the advantage over adults when it comes to experiencing nature directly. Do you agree with Emerson? What do people seem to lose as they grow older?

7. Emerson's expectations of nature were immense, and they formed the basis of his philosophy. How would his views of nature be received today? Be sure to check your Quickwrite notes for your own thoughts about nature. ✏

8. Implicit in the fourth paragraph is the assumption that city life can't help us feel the "currents of the Universal Being." How do you feel about this assumption?

Caricature of Emerson by Christopher Pearce Cranch from *Illustrations of the New Philosophy*.

from Self-Reliance

Thinking Critically

1. In the first paragraph, what do you think Emerson means by "that divine idea which each of us represents"? How does this philosophical assumption influence the entire essay?

2. Describe what Emerson compares to these things and events: planting corn, an iron string, a joint-stock company, a shadow on the wall.

go.
hrw
.com

INTERNET
Projects and Activities
Keyword: LE5 11-2

SKILLS FOCUS

Literary Skills
Analyze imagery and figures of speech.

Reading Skills
Monitor reading by identifying main ideas. Analyze figures of speech.

Writing Skills
Write a reflective essay about aphorisms. Write an essay analyzing an author's philosophical beliefs.

Vocabulary Skills
Demonstrate word knowledge.

Ralph Waldo Emerson   **187**

Response and Analysis

Thinking Critically

2. Possible answer: Emerson is saying that people take the beauty of nature for granted.

3. Possible answer: This phrase means looking at nature as a sublime and integrated whole.

4. Interpretations should include the idea that Emerson loses all sense of self in order to feel like he is a part of the nature that is around him. Students may say that the image lends strength to Emerson's ideas, or they may feel that the image is distracting.

5. Emerson means that we see our emotions reflected in nature. This highlights the belief that nature and the human mind act upon one another.

Extending and Evaluating

6. Answers will vary. Students may say that adults lose a sense of wonder at the world.

7. Students may say that today people have even less of a connection with nature. They may find Emerson's ideas naive and optimistic, or they may say that today people need to connect with the natural world.

8. Students may agree, or they may say that because nature is rare in a city, it is more appreciated.

from Self-Reliance

Thinking Critically

1. Possible answer: Emerson means the individuality of each person. He believes that relying on and expressing ourselves is an act of prayer and praise to God.

2. *Planting corn*—doing good deeds and working hard. *Iron string*—trusting oneself. *Joint-stock company*—society. *Shadow on the wall*—consistency.

---

from Nature

Reading Check

1. Possible Answers

"But if a man would be alone, let him look at the stars."

"All natural objects make a kindred impression, when the mind is open to their influence."

"There is a property in the horizon which no man has but he whose eye can integrate all the parts, that is, the poet."

"The lover of nature is he whose inward and outward senses are still truly adjusted to each other."

"The greatest delight which the fields and woods minister, is the suggestion of an occult relation between man and the vegetable."

"Nature always wears the colors of the spirit."

Response and Analysis

from **Self-Reliance**

Extending and Evaluating

3. Students' opinions will vary. Their theories about Emerson's opinion will vary according to their feelings about the first question.

4. Students' opinions will vary. Students may feel that the success of mass marketing and the mass media shows the high value Americans place on conformity. Students may cite examples of times when conformity is a positive thing.

Vocabulary Development

Students' justifications will vary.

1. no	6. yes
2. yes	7. no
3. no	8. no
4. no	9. no
5. yes	10. yes

Dover Plains, Dutchess County, New York (1848) by Asher Brown Durand. Oil on canvas (42½" × 60½").

National Museum of American Art/Smithsonian Institution/Art Resource, NY: Gift of Thomas M. Evans and Museum Purchase through the Smithsonian Collections Acquisition Program.

Extending and Evaluating

3. Do you think that there is too little or too much emphasis on self-reliance and individualism in America today? What might Emerson think of today's focus on the individual?

4. "The virtue in most request is conformity," Emerson says. A paraphrase of this sentence might read: "The virtue that is most often demanded of us is that we conform to what someone else thinks." What is your opinion of this belief? Do you think this belief holds true today? Is conformity always a negative? Explain your responses.

WRITING

Sage Sayings

Emerson's work is filled with memorable sayings, called **aphorisms** (af'ə·riz'əmz). These are short statements that express wise or clever observations about life, such as "Trust thyself: Every heart vibrates to that iron string." Pick an aphorism from one of Emerson's writings, and write a **reflective essay** on what that saying means to you. In your essay, consider whether the statement needs updating to apply to today's

world. Be sure to quote the aphorism in your essay and to tell which work of Emerson's it comes from.

▶ Use "Writing a Reflective Essay," pages 360–367, for help with this assignment.

Analyze Emerson's Philosophy

In an **essay**, analyze one of Emerson's philosophical beliefs, about either nature or self-reliance. Be sure to use passages from the essays to support your analysis. Follow this structure:

• Tell in your own words what the philosophical belief is.

• Quote passages to support your summary.

• Make an assertion or statement of your own about the belief, and provide details to explain or support your assertion.

Vocabulary Development
Yes or No?

Answer yes or no to the following questions, and justify your answers:

1. If you wanted to integrate a classroom, would you divide it into parts?

2. Is someone with perennial happiness often happy?

3. Would a jury that arrives at the conviction that a man is innocent pronounce him guilty?

4. Is an admonishing remark comforting?

5. Would you trust a person with integrity?

6. If a song gives you a transcendent feeling, does it make you joyful?

7. When you're feeling blithe, are you weighed down with worry?

8. Would a secret be imparted by you to someone you don't trust?

9. Is occult information common knowledge?

10. If you have a manifest intention, can people recognize it easily?

ASSESSING

<u>Assessment</u>

■ *Holt Assessment: Literature, Reading, and Vocabulary*

RETEACHING

For a lesson reteaching philosophical assumptions and beliefs, see **Reteaching,** p. 1117A.

Henry David Thoreau
(1817–1862)

Henry David Thoreau (1856).
Photograph by Benjamin D. Maxham.

On July 4, 1845 (the date was apparently accidental), a young man ended a three-year stay at the house of a friend and moved to a cabin on the shores of Walden Pond in Massachusetts. He was almost twenty-eight years old and, to all appearances, a failure. He had lasted only two weeks as a schoolteacher (he refused to whip a child, then a mandatory form of punishment); his public lectures had been uninspiring; the woman to whom he had proposed marriage had turned him down; and he had little interest in the family business. Despite his impressive Harvard education, he had not realized his literary ambitions.

If ever a person looked like a self-*unmade* man, a man who had squandered the advantages of intelligence, education, and the friendship of brilliant and successful people, it was Henry David Thoreau. On top of all his other problems, Thoreau was difficult to get along with. Three days before Thoreau went to Walden, Nathaniel Hawthorne (page 225) wrote to a New York publisher that Thoreau was "tedious, tiresome, and intolerable." Hawthorne added, "And yet he has great qualities of intellect and character."

Even his closest friends had doubts about Thoreau. "He seemed born for great enterprise and for command," Ralph Waldo Emerson said years later at Thoreau's funeral, "and I so much regret the loss of his rare powers of action, that I cannot help counting it a fault in him that he had no ambition. Wanting this, instead of engineering for all America, he was the captain of a huckleberry party."

What Emerson failed to see, and what Thoreau knew (or hoped) all along, was that by leading a berry-picking party on a jaunt in the woods he could "engineer for all America" in the most profound way. This paradox is at the center of Thoreau's life and work.

The Student Who Wouldn't Wear Black

Thoreau was born in Concord, Massachusetts, in 1817. His father was a moderately successful manufacturer of pencils. His mother took in boarders, among them the sister of Emerson's wife, thus establishing the relationship between the two families. As a boy, Thoreau tramped the woods and fields around Concord, often with a fishing rod and seldom with a gun.

Thoreau entered Harvard in 1833 and graduated four years later. Independent and eccentric even then, he attended chapel in a green coat, "because," he wrote, "the rules required black." Thoreau never ranked higher than the middle of his class, but he was extremely well read. He became thoroughly familiar with English literature and with the German philosophers who provided many of the underpinnings of Transcendentalism.

After returning to Concord and teaching school, Thoreau went to New York in 1843, but he pined for his hometown. After six months of struggling, he gave up and returned to Concord. A friend proposed that Thoreau and he sail to Europe and work their way across the Continent, but Thoreau turned him down. He appeared to be floundering, but in

SKILLS FOCUS, pp. 189–207

Grade-Level Skills

■ **Literary Skills**
Analyze ways authors use figures of speech, including metaphors.

■ **Reading Skills**
Make generalizations about a writer's beliefs.

VIEWING THE ART

Benjamin D. Maxham took this daguerreotype of Thoreau on June 18, 1856, in his portrait studio in Worcester, Massachusetts, known as the "Daguerrean Palace." The daguerreotype process, named after its French inventor, Louis Daguerre, employed light-sensitive, silver-plated copper sheets to capture images. Maxham and others championed this new technology as a cheap, practical, and realistic alternative to traditional portraiture.

Activity. Ask students to describe what impression of Thoreau this daguerreotype conveys. [Possible responses: He seems thoughtful, good-humored, quiet, and calm.]

More About the Writer

Background. Thoreau and his brother John opened a private school in 1839 that lasted only two years. The brothers, however, instituted a new educational practice—field trips for nature study. Thoreau's love of nature was also interwoven with his love for writing. He once wrote, "A writer . . . is the scribe of all nature; he is the corn and the grass and the atmosphere writing. It is always essential that we love to do what we are doing, do it with a heart."

fact he knew what he was doing: Thoreau's voyage would be inward, and it would depart from Walden Pond, where Emerson had offered him the use of some land.

Walden: Life in Its Essence

The experiment at Walden Pond was an attempt to rediscover the grandeur of a simple life led close to nature. Though only two miles from town, Walden offered a focus for Thoreau's contemplative urge. "I wish to meet the facts of life," he wrote in his journal, "the vital facts, which are the phenomena or actuality the gods meant to show us . . . and so I came down here."

This private confrontation was to Thoreau's mind the truly heroic enterprise of his time. "I am glad to remember tonight as I sit by my door," he wrote on the evening of July 7, "that I too am at least a remote descendant of that heroic race of men of whom there is a tradition. I too sit here on the shore of my Ithaca, a fellow wanderer and survivor of Ulysses."

When he looked toward town, Thoreau saw his fellow citizens so caught up in making a living that they had become one-dimensional. "The mass of men," as one of the most famous sentences in *Walden* puts it, "lead lives of quiet desperation." He hoped to wake them up and show them that the heroic enterprise of confronting the "vital facts of life" lay literally in their own backyards.

Walden—one of the most well-known works ever produced in America—owes much of its artistic success to Thoreau's blending of style and content. He looked to nature, rather than to the stylists of the past, for a model. To Thoreau a style that imitated nature would speak fundamental spiritual truths. Thoreau wished to build sentences "which lie like boulders on the page, up and down or across; which contain the seed of other sentences, not mere repetition, but creation; which a man might sell his grounds and castles to build."

Thoreau the Protester

It was while he was at Walden that Thoreau's other famous act took place. As a protest against the Mexican War, which he and many

others saw as an attempt to extend American slaveholding territory, Thoreau refused to pay his poll tax and spent a night in jail as a result. While at Walden and again in 1851 (after the Fugitive Slave Act had been passed), Thoreau helped fugitives escaping slavery make their way to Canada. In 1859, he was one of the first defenders of John Brown, the radical abolitionist who staged a famous raid on the federal arsenal at Harpers Ferry in Virginia.

Thoreau remained at Walden for a little more than two years. In 1847, he left the cabin and moved back into the Emersons' house in exchange for a few hours a day of odd jobs and gardening. During the next few years he worked on *Walden* (which was published in 1854) and essays such as "Resistance to Civil Government" (page 211). The latter, delivered as a lecture in 1848 and published as an essay in 1849, had little immediate influence, but few essays have had such an overwhelming long-term effect on human history. It was especially important in helping to inspire the passive resistance used by Mohandas K. Gandhi in India and later by Martin Luther King, Jr., in the United States.

Thoreau moved back into his parents' house in 1848 and lived there the rest of his life. He supported himself by making pencils, taking odd jobs (he was an excellent carpenter, mason, and gardener), and doing survey work on the land around Concord. Thoreau became a kind of local record keeper, a fount of knowledge about the amount of rainfall and snowfall and the first days of frost. He could predict to the day when each wildflower in the area would bloom.

In 1860, Thoreau caught a cold, and it soon became clear that beneath the cold lay incurable tuberculosis. He faced his coming death with great calm. The town constable, Sam Staples (who had jailed Thoreau for refusing to pay his poll tax), told Emerson that he "never saw a man dying with so much pleasure and peace."

"Henry, have you made your peace with God?" his aunt is said to have asked him toward the end. "Why, Aunt," he replied, "I didn't know we had ever quarreled."

Literary Criticism

Critic's Commentary: Thoreau on Rhetorical Style

"When I hear the hypercritical quarreling about grammar and style, the position of the particles, etc., etc., stretching or contracting every speaker to certain rules . . . I see that they forget that the first requisite and rule is that expression shall be vital and natural," wrote Thoreau around 1859. "Essentially,

your truest poetic sentence is as free and lawless as a lamb's bleat. The grammarian is often one who can neither cry nor laugh, yet thinks that he can express human emotions.

"When I read some of the rules for speaking and writing the English language correctly,—as that a sentence must never end with a particle,—and perceive how implicitly even the learned obey it, I think—

Any fool can make a rule
And every fool will mind it."

Whole-class activity. Ask students whether they agree with Thoreau that writers should be allowed to bend the rules of grammar to achieve their rhetorical and aesthetic purposes. Have students support their answers with examples from other readings and from their own writing.

Before You Read

from Walden, or Life in the Woods

Make the Connection

A temporary move to a site on a large pond in Concord, Massachusetts, resulted in a work of literature that has become an American classic. Thoreau moved to Walden because he wanted to find out what life is. That is a question people still ask; it is something people the world over have always asked, when they have the leisure to think about it. As you read, imagine yourself in the woods near this pond. How would you have responded to a life that offered little more in excitement than a battle between ants, no company other than the visit of a bird?

Literary Focus
Metaphor

A **metaphor** is a figure of speech that makes an imaginative comparison between two unlike things. A metaphor is direct; unlike a simile it does not use a specific word of comparison, such as *like, as, than,* or *resembles*. Thoreau's metaphors are highly visual. They are drawn from nature and from simple, everyday things that he and his audience are familiar with. To be sure you understand the points that Thoreau is making with his metaphors, try to **paraphrase** each metaphor you encounter—that is, try to explain what is being compared to what.

> A **metaphor** is a figure of speech that makes a comparison between two unlike things without using a specific word of comparison, such as *like, as, than,* or *resembles*.
>
> *For more on Metaphor, see the Handbook of Literary and Historical Terms.*

Reading Skills
Making Generalizations About a Writer's Beliefs

Active readers can often make generalizations about a writer's beliefs, based on specific information they get from a text. A **generalization** is a type of **inference** in which a conclusion is drawn from explicit examples in the text. For example, after reading Thoreau, you might make this generalization: Thoreau believed people should eliminate unnecessary complexity and lead lives focused on what matters most to them.

As you read *Walden,* take notes in the form of a double-entry journal. In the left column, list Thoreau's explicit ideas. In the right column, make generalizations about Thoreau's beliefs that you think logically follow from his views.

Vocabulary Development

pertinent (p∙rt′'n∙ənt) *adj.:* to the point; applying to the situation.

encumbrance (en∙kum′brəns) *n.:* burden; hindrance.

impervious (im∙pur′vē∙əs) *adj.:* resistant; incapable of being penetrated.

temporal (tem′pə∙rəl) *adj.:* temporary.

superficial (soo′pər∙fish′əl) *adj.:* not profound; shallow.

effete (e∙fēt′) *adj.:* sterile; unproductive.

incessantly (in∙ses′ənt∙lē) *adv.:* without stopping.

derision (di∙rizh′ən) *n.:* ridicule; contempt.

tumultuous (too∙mul′choo∙əs) *adj.:* noisy and disorderly; stormy.

ethereal (ē∙thir′ē∙əl) *adj.:* not earthly; spiritual.

go.
hrw
.com

INTERNET

Vocabulary Practice
•
More About Henry David Thoreau
•

Keyword: LE5 11-2

SKILLS FOCUS

Literary Skills
Understand metaphor.

Reading Skills
Make generalizations about a writer's beliefs.

Henry David Thoreau **191**

from

Walden, or Life in the Woods

Henry David Thoreau

Learners Having Difficulty
Modeling. To help students read *Walden,* model the reading skill of making generalizations. Say, "Suppose you read these facts in the selection: Thoreau builds a cabin near a pond in the woods, where he lives for two years; Thoreau wants to learn about the true meaning of life. You could use these facts to make the following generalization: *Thoreau* *believes that we can learn much from solitude and nature.*" Encourage students to use similar facts and examples in the selection to form generalizations.

English-Language Learners
Have students make a list of unfamiliar words as they read. Student pairs can then compare word lists and work together to learn new words.

Advanced Learners
Enrichment. Have students read the entire text of one section of *Walden.* Ask them to discuss their reading in small groups and to make a cluster diagram with the main idea in the center and the supporting arguments and evidence radiating from it. Have students determine what kind of appeal (logical, emotional, or ethical) each argument makes.

I went to the woods because I wished to live deliberately,
to front only the essential facts of life,
and see if I could not learn what it had to teach, and not,
when I came to die, discover that I had not lived.

from Economy

When I wrote the following pages, or rather the bulk of them, I lived alone, in the woods, a mile from any neighbor, in a house which I had built myself, on the shore of Walden Pond, in Concord, Massachusetts, and earned my living by the labor of my hands only. I lived there two years and two months. At present I am a sojourner in civilized life again.

I should not obtrude my affairs so much on the notice of my readers if very particular inquiries had not been made by my townsmen concerning my mode of life, which some would call impertinent, though they do not appear to me at all impertinent, but, considering the circumstances, very natural and pertinent. Some have asked what I got to eat; if I did not feel lonesome; if I was not afraid; and the like. Others have been curious to learn what portion of my income I devoted to charitable purposes; and some, who have large families, how many poor children I maintained. I will therefore ask those of my readers who feel no particular interest in me to pardon me if I undertake to answer some of these questions in this book. In most books, the I, or first person, is omitted; in this it will be retained; that, in respect to egotism, is the main difference. We commonly do not remember that it is, after all, always the first person that is speaking. I should not talk so much about myself if there were anybody else whom I knew as well. Unfortunately, I am confined to this theme by the narrowness of my experience. Moreover, I, on my side, require of every writer, first or last, a simple and sincere account of his own life, and not merely what he has heard of other men's lives; some such account as he would send to his kindred from a distant land; for if he has lived sincerely, it must

have been in a distant land to me. Perhaps these pages are more particularly addressed to poor students. As for the rest of my readers, they will accept such portions as apply to them. I trust that none will stretch the seams in putting on the coat, for it may do good service to him whom it fits. . . .

By the middle of April, for I made no haste in my work, but rather made the most of it, my house was framed and ready for the raising. I had already bought the shanty of James Collins, an Irishman who worked on the Fitchburg Railroad, for boards. James Collins's shanty was considered an uncommonly fine one. When I called to see it he was not at home. I walked about the outside, at first unobserved from within, the window was so deep and high. It was of small dimensions, with a peaked cottage roof, and not much else to be seen, the dirt being raised five feet all around as if it were a compost heap. The roof was the soundest part, though a good deal warped and made brittle by the sun. Doorsill there was none, but a perennial passage for the hens under the door board. Mrs. C. came to the door and asked me to view it from the inside. The hens were driven in by my approach. It was dark, and had a dirt floor for the most part, dank, clammy, and aguish,[1] only here a board and there a board which would not bear removal. She lighted a lamp to show me the inside of the roof and the walls, and also that the board floor extended under the bed, warning

---

1. **aguish** (ā′gyo͞o·ish) *adj.:* likely to cause ague, or fever and chills.

Vocabulary
pertinent (pʉrt′'n·ənt) *adj.:* to the point; applying to the situation.

Ⓐ Vocabulary Development

❓ Multiple-meaning words. Direct students' attention to the definition of *pertinent* at the bottom of the page. Explain that *impertinent* has two meanings: "rude" and "not relevant." What play on words is Thoreau making using these meanings? [He is saying that his neighbors' queries about his lifestyle were perhaps rude but nevertheless relevant to his beliefs.]

Ⓑ Reading Skills

❓ Recognizing persuasive techniques. Why does Thoreau include these objections and questions concerning his lifestyle? Why is this an effective persuasive technique? [By introducing his work as a simple response to his neighbors' questions, Thoreau anticipates potential criticism.]

Ⓒ Literary Focus

❓ Metaphor. To what does Thoreau compare his writing? [a coat] What does he mean when he expresses a hope that some of his readers will not "stretch the seams" of the coat? [Possible response: He hopes that his readers will not alter or stretch his philosophy if it does not fit their own beliefs.]

CONTENT-AREA CONNECTIONS

Music: Charles Ives's *Concord, Mass.*
Widely praised for his innovative approach to music, composer Charles Ives (1847–1954) drew on many aspects of American culture. The second of his two piano sonatas, subtitled *Concord, Mass., 1840–60,* celebrates the New England literary renaissance of those decades. The sonata's four movements are subtitled with the names of writers of that renaissance:

"Emerson," "Hawthorne," "The Alcotts," and "Thoreau."
Whole-class activity. Play the first and last movements, "Emerson" and "Thoreau," from *Sonata for Piano No. 2.* Have students try to guess which movements Ives subtitled "Emerson" and which "Thoreau." Afterward, have students explain their guesses in a group discussion in which they cite details from the writings of both authors.

A Reading Skills

❓ Making generalizations.
Based on this passage, what generalization can you make about Thoreau's abilities as a house builder? [Thoreau's use of recycled materials and his appropriation of the woodchuck's burrow show his thrift and resourcefulness.] What generalization can you draw from this passage about Thoreau's personal philosophy? [Possible response: He believes that human beings and animals share the same survival strategies, such as digging "burrows" for warmth.]

B Content-Area Connections

History: Root Cellars
Before refrigeration, people often dug root cellars, or pits in the ground, where they stored fresh root vegetables (such as carrots or potatoes) covered with dirt. The cool ground preserved the vegetables during the winter, and the walls kept animals away from the food.

C Advanced Learners
Enrichment. Direct students' attention to footnote 3. Have students speculate about what the "raisers" discussed as they worked.

me not to step into the cellar, a sort of dust hole two feet deep. In her own words, they were "good boards overhead, good boards all around, and a good window"—of two whole squares originally, only the cat had passed out that way lately. There was a stove, a bed, and a place to sit, an infant in the house where it was born, a silk parasol, gilt-framed looking glass, and a patent new coffee mill nailed to an oak sapling, all told. The bargain was soon concluded, for James had in the meanwhile returned. I to pay four dollars and twenty-five cents tonight, he to vacate at five tomorrow morning, selling to nobody else meanwhile: I to take possession at six. It were well, he said, to be there early, and anticipate certain indistinct but wholly unjust claims on the score of ground rent and fuel. This he assured me was the only <u>encumbrance</u>. At six I passed him and his family on the road. One large bundle held their all—bed, coffee mill, looking glass, hens—all but the cat; she took to the woods and became a wild cat, and, as I learned afterward, trod in a trap set for woodchucks, and so became a dead cat at last.

I took down this dwelling the same morning, drawing the nails, and removed it to the pond side by small cartloads, spreading the boards on the grass there to bleach and warp back again in the sun. One early thrush gave me a note or two as I drove along the woodland path. I was informed treacherously by a young Patrick that neighbor Seeley, an Irishman, in the intervals of the carting, transferred the still tolerable, straight, and drivable nails, staples, and spikes to his pocket, and then stood when I came back to pass the time of day, and look freshly up, unconcerned, with spring thoughts, at the devastation; there being a dearth of work, as he said. He was there to represent spectatordom, and help make this seemingly insignificant event one with the removal of the gods of Troy.[2]

---

2. **the gods of Troy:** Thoreau loved classical allusions. Here he humorously compares taking down a little cabin to the destruction of the great ancient city of Troy. In the *Aeneid* by Virgil, the conquering Greeks carry off the images of the Trojan gods after the fall of Troy.

I dug my cellar in the side of a hill sloping to the south, where a woodchuck had formerly dug his burrow, down through sumac and blackberry roots, and the lowest stain of vegetation, six feet square by seven deep, to a fine sand where potatoes would not freeze in any winter. The sides were left shelving, and not stoned; but the sun having never shone on them, the sand still keeps its place. It was but two hours' work. I took particular pleasure in this breaking of ground, for in almost all latitudes men dig into the earth for an equable temperature. Under the most splendid house in the city is still to be found the cellar where they store their roots as of old, and long after the superstructure has disappeared posterity remark its dent in the earth. The house is still but a sort of porch at the entrance of a burrow.

At length, in the beginning of May, with the help of some of my acquaintances, rather to improve so good an occasion for neighborliness than from any necessity, I set up the frame of my house. No man was ever more honored in the character of his raisers[3] than I. They are destined, I trust, to assist at the raising of loftier structures one day. I began to occupy my house on the 4th of July, as soon as it was boarded and roofed, for the boards were carefully feather-edged and lapped,[4] so that it was perfectly impervious to rain, but before boarding I laid the foundation of a chimney at one end, bringing two cartloads of stones up the hill from the pond in my arms. I built the chimney after my hoeing in the fall, before a fire became necessary for warmth, doing my cooking in the mean-

---

3. **raisers** *n.:* Thoreau's helpers included the Transcendentalist writers Ralph Waldo Emerson (page 179), Bronson Alcott, and William Ellery Channing; hence the reference in the next sentence to raising loftier structures one day.
4. **featheredged and lapped:** The edges were cut at an angle and overlapped.

Vocabulary
encumbrance (en·kum′brəns) *n.:* burden; hindrance.
impervious (im·pur′vē·əs) *adj.:* resistant; incapable of being penetrated.

Understanding allusions. Remind students that an allusion is a reference a writer makes to an event, another text, a historical or fictional character, or any other significant cultural item. Point out that Thoreau's *Walden* contains numerous allusions to the history and culture of ancient Greece.
Activity. As they read, have students note references and allusions to the *Iliad,* the Trojan War, and other aspects of the classical age. Then, have students discuss why Thoreau might have alluded to the ancient Greeks so often. What thematic implications do these references have for Thoreau's account? How might Thoreau have considered his experiment as a journey or as a return to the classical themes of simplicity, beauty, and harmony?

while out of doors on the ground, early in the morning: which mode I still think is in some respects more convenient and agreeable than the usual one. When it stormed before my bread was baked, I fixed a few boards over the fire, and sat under them to watch my loaf, and passed some pleasant hours in that way. In those days, when my hands were much employed, I read but little, but the least scraps of paper which lay on the ground, my holder, or tablecloth, afforded me as much entertainment, in fact answered the same purpose as the *Iliad*.[5]

It would be worth the while to build still more deliberately than I did, considering, for instance, what foundation a door, a window, a cellar, a garret, have in the nature of man, and perchance never raising any superstructure until we found a better reason for it than our temporal necessities even. There is some of the same fitness in a man's building his own house that there is in a bird's building its own nest. Who knows but if men constructed their dwellings with their own hands, and provided food for themselves and families simply and honestly enough, the poetic faculty would be universally developed, as birds universally sing when they are so engaged? But alas! we do like cowbirds and cuckoos, which lay their eggs in nests which other birds have built, and cheer no traveler with their chattering and unmusical notes. Shall we forever resign the pleasure of construction to the carpenter? What does architecture amount to in the experience of the mass of men? I never in all my walks came across a man engaged in so simple and natural an occupation as building his house. . . .

Before winter I built a chimney, and shingled the sides of my house, which were already impervious to rain, with imperfect and sappy shingles made of the first slice of the log, whose edges I was obliged to straighten with a plane.

I have thus a tight shingled and plastered house, ten feet wide by fifteen long, and eight-foot posts, with a garret and a closet, a large window on each side, two trapdoors, one door at the end, and a brick fireplace opposite. The exact cost of my house, paying the usual price for such materials as I used, but not counting the work, all of which was done by myself, was as follows; and I give the details because very few are able to tell exactly what their houses cost, and fewer still, if any, the separate cost of the various materials which compose them—

Boards,	$ 8 03 ½	Mostly shanty boards
Refuse shingles for roof and sides,	4 00	
Laths,	1 25	
Two secondhand windows with glass,	2 43	
One thousand old brick,	4 00	
Two casks of lime,	2 40	That was high
Hair,	0 31	More than I needed
Mantle-tree iron,	0 15	
Nails,	3 90	
Hinges and screws,	0 14	
Latch,	0 10	
Chalk,	0 01	
Transportation,	1 40	I carried a good part on my back
In all,	$28 12 ½	

. . . Before I finished my house, wishing to earn ten or twelve dollars by some honest and agreeable method, in order to meet my unusual expenses, I planted about two acres and a half of light and sandy soil near it chiefly with beans, but also a small part with potatoes, corn, peas, and turnips. The whole lot contains eleven acres, mostly growing up to pines and hickories, and was sold the preceding season for eight dollars and eight cents an acre. One farmer said that it was "good for nothing but to raise cheeping squirrels on." I put no manure whatever on this land, not being the owner, but merely a

---

5. **the *Iliad*:** Homer's epic about the Greek siege of Troy.

Vocabulary
temporal (tem'pə·rəl) *adj.:* temporary.

D ▶ **Reading Skills**

❷ Recognizing rhetorical devices. What rhetorical device does Thoreau use in this passage? Why do you think he does this? [Possible response: By asking a question, Thoreau causes readers to think about the similarities between humans' homes and birds' nests and humans' poems and birds' songs. He also reinforces his argument that building fosters creativity.]

E ▶ **Reading Skills**

❓ Extending the text. Compare the size of Thoreau's house with your own. Could you live contentedly in a house this size? Why or why not? [Possible responses: Yes, small houses are cozy; no, there is no room to have friends come and stay or to store possessions.]

F ▶ **Reading Skills**

❓ Interpreting graphic aids. What can you learn about Thoreau by examining this statement of his account? [Possible response: Thoreau is thrifty, independent, environmentally conscious, and meticulous.]

SKILLS REVIEW

Using text organizers. Review the categories and purposes of text organizers. Headings break a text into sections and indicate the contents of those sections. Graphic features, such as tables, present information in a way that stands out from the text. Illustrations provide visual supplements for a written text.

Activity. Have students locate examples of these three types of text organizers in *Walden*. [Each section has a heading. Page 195 includes a numerical table. Several selection pages have illustrations.] Then, tell students that the tables on p. 195 exist in every edition of *Walden*. Ask why Thoreau decided to set off this information from the text.

[Possible responses: because it is easier to understand numbers in a table than mixed in with text; to stress how cheaply one can live if one wants to.] Finally, have students discuss pages that have no organizers or illustrations (for example, pp. 194 and 201). Is a full page of text without text organizers more or less confusing for readers? more interesting? more difficult? Have students provide reasons.

A Reading Skills

? Making generalizations. Why does Thoreau believe that he did better with his small profit than any other farmer in Concord? [Although the actual amount Thoreau earns is small, his percentage of profit is probably higher than that of the average farmer.] What generalization about earning a living can be made from this? [Possible response: If your needs are simple, you can meet them, still be independent, and enjoy life.]

B Reading Skills

? Understanding implicit assumptions. What does Thoreau value more than a good profit? [He values the state of his soul and time to ponder the essential facts of life.]

C Reading Skills

? Interpreting. Based on this paragraph, what do you think Thoreau hopes to discover by spending time in solitude surrounded by nature? [Possible response: Through solitude, he hopes to understand the rudimentary forces of life and thus to understand himself and society more clearly.] Note that Thoreau is also following the precepts set down by Emerson, who wrote, "To go down into solitude, a man needs to retire as much from his chamber as from society" (p. 182).

D Reading Skills

? Recognizing implicit assumptions. Thoreau makes a generalization that most people are uncertain about the meaning of life and hastily conclude that it is to glorify God. What implicit assumption is Thoreau making by questioning this generalization? [People should not accept the received wisdom about the purpose of life but discover it themselves through experience. Thoreau wants to "live deep and suck out all the marrow of life," and "to know [life] by experience."]

---

squatter, and not expecting to cultivate so much again, and I did not quite hoe it all once. I got out several cords of stumps in plowing, which supplied me with fuel for a long time, and left small circles of virgin mold, easily distinguishable through the summer by the greater luxuriance of the beans there. The dead and for the most part unmerchantable wood behind my house, and the driftwood from the pond, have supplied the remainder of my fuel. I was obliged to hire a team and a man for the plowing, though I held the plow myself. My farm outgoes for the first season were, for implements, seed, work, etc., \$14.72½. The seed corn was given me. This never costs anything to speak of, unless you plant more than enough. I got twelve bushels of beans, and eighteen bushels of potatoes, beside some peas and sweet corn. The yellow corn and turnips were too late to come to anything. My whole income from the farm was

A

	\$23 44,
Deducting the outgoes,	14 72 ½
There are left,	\$ 8 71 ½

beside produce consumed and on hand at the time this estimate was made of the value of \$4.50—the amount on hand much more than balancing a little grass which I did not raise. All things considered, that is, considering the importance of a man's soul and of today, notwithstanding the short time occupied by my experiment, nay, partly even because of its transient character, I believe that that was doing better than any farmer in Concord did that year. . . .

from **Where I Lived, and What I Lived For**

B . . . I went to the woods because I wished to live deliberately, to front only the essential facts of life, and see if I could not learn what it had to teach, and not, when I came to die, discover that I had not lived. I did not wish to live what was

not life, living is so dear; nor did I wish to practice resignation, unless it was quite necessary. I wanted to live deep and suck out all the marrow of life, to live so sturdily and Spartan-like[6] as to put to rout all that was not life, to cut a broad **C** swath and shave close, to drive life into a corner, and reduce it to its lowest terms, and, if it proved to be mean, why then to get the whole and genuine meanness of it, and publish its **D** meanness to the world; or if it were sublime, to know it by experience, and be able to give a true account of it in my next excursion. For most men, it appears to me, are in a strange uncertainty about it, whether it is of the devil or of God, and have *somewhat hastily* concluded that it is the chief end of man here to "glorify God and enjoy him forever."[7]

Still we live meanly, like ants; though the fable tells us that we were long ago changed into men; like pygmies we fight with cranes;[8] it is error upon error, and clout upon clout, and our best virtue has for its occasion a superfluous and evitable[9] wretchedness. Our life is frittered away by detail. An honest man has hardly need to count more than his ten fingers, or in extreme cases he may add his ten toes, and lump the rest. Simplicity, simplicity, simplicity! I say, let your affairs be as two or three, and not a hundred or a thousand; instead of a million count half a dozen, and keep your accounts on your thumbnail. In the midst of this chopping sea of civilized life, such are the clouds and storms and quicksands and thousand-and-one items to be allowed for, that a man has to live, if he would not founder and go to the bottom and not make his port at all, by dead reckoning, and

---

6. **Spartan-like:** like the Spartans, the hardy, frugal, and highly disciplined citizens of the ancient Greek city-state Sparta.
7. **glorify . . . forever:** answer to catechism question "What is the chief end of man?"
8. **the fable . . . cranes:** In a Greek fable, Zeus changes ants into men. In the *Iliad,* Homer compares the Trojans to cranes fighting with pygmies.
9. **superfluous and evitable:** unnecessary and avoidable.

Secondary Source

Spartan Simplicity

To help students evaluate Thoreau's allusions to Spartan culture, have them consider the following analysis by historian Dr. John Buckler: "Suppression of the individual together with emphasis on military prowess led to a barracks state. . . . Once Spartan boys reached the age of twelve, they were enrolled in separate companies. . . . They slept outside on reed mats and underwent rugged physical and military training until age twenty-four, when they became frontline soldiers. . . . The older men were expected to be models of endurance, frugality, and sturdiness. . . . Spartan men were expected to train vigorously, disdain luxury and wealth, do with little, and like it." Ask students which aspects of Spartan culture Thoreau would embrace or reject.

he must be a great calculator indeed who succeeds. Simplify, simplify. Instead of three meals a day, if it be necessary eat but one; instead of a hundred dishes, five; and reduce other things in proportion. Our life is like a German Confederacy,[10] made up of petty states with its boundary forever fluctuating, so that even a German cannot tell you how it is bounded at any moment. The nation itself, with all its so-called internal improvements, which, by the way are all external and superficial, is just such an unwieldy and overgrown establishment, cluttered with furniture and tripped up by its own traps, ruined by luxury and heedless expense, by want of calculation and a worthy aim, as the million households in the land; and the only cure for it, as for them, is in a rigid economy, a stern and more than Spartan simplicity of life and elevation of purpose. It lives too fast. Men think that it is essential that the *Nation* have commerce, and export ice, and talk through a telegraph, and ride thirty miles an hour, without a doubt, whether *they* do or not; but whether we should live like baboons or like men, is a little uncertain. If we do not get out sleepers,[11] and forge rails, and devote days and nights to the work, but go to tinkering upon our *lives* to improve *them,* who will build railroads? And if railroads are not built, how shall we get to heaven in season? But if we stay at home and mind our business, who will want railroads? We do not ride on the railroad; it rides upon us. Did you ever think what those sleepers are that underlie the railroad? Each one is a man, an Irishman, or a Yankee man. The rails are laid on them, and they are covered with sand, and the cars run smoothly over them. They are sound sleepers, I assure you. And every few years a new lot is laid down and run over; so that, if some have the pleasure of riding on a rail, others have the misfortune to be ridden upon. And when they run over a man that is walking in his sleep, a supernumerary[12] sleeper in the wrong position, and wake him up, they suddenly stop the cars, and make a hue and cry about it, as if this were an exception. I am glad to know that it takes a gang of men for every five miles to keep the sleepers down and level in their beds as it is, for this is a sign that they may sometime get up again. . . .

from Solitude

. . . Some of my pleasantest hours were during the long rainstorms in the spring or fall, which confined me to the house for the afternoon as well as the forenoon, soothed by their ceaseless roar and pelting; when an early twilight ushered in a long evening in which many thoughts had time to take root and unfold themselves. In those driving northeast rains which tried the village houses so, when the maids stood ready with mop and pail in front entries to keep the deluge out, I sat behind my door in my little house, which was all entry, and thoroughly enjoyed its protection. In one heavy thundershower the lightning struck a large pitch pine across the pond, making a very conspicuous and perfectly regular spiral groove from top to bottom, an inch or more deep, and four or five inches wide, as you would groove a walking stick. I passed it again the other day, and was struck with awe on looking up and beholding that mark, now more distinct than ever, where a terrific and resistless bolt came down out of the harmless sky eight years ago. Men frequently say to me, "I should think you would feel lonesome down there, and want to be nearer to folks, rainy and snowy days and nights especially." I am tempted to reply to such—This whole earth which we inhabit is but a point in space. How far apart, think you, dwell the two most distant inhabitants of yonder star, the breadth of whose disk cannot be appreciated by our instruments?

---

10. **German Confederacy:** At the time Thoreau was writing, Germany was not yet a unified nation.
11. **sleepers** *n. pl.:* British usage for "railroad ties," so called because they lie flat.

---

12. **supernumerary** (soo′pər·noo′mə·rer′ē) *adj.:* additional; unnecessary.

Vocabulary
superficial (soo′pər·fish′əl) *adj.:* not profound; shallow.

Henry David Thoreau   **197**

VIEWING THE ART

Andrew Wyeth (1917–), son of N. C. Wyeth, belongs to a distinguished family of American painters. Best known for land-scapes of the Brandywine River Valley and of rural Maine, Wyeth has been successful and popular, although critical opinion of his works is divided.

Activity. Ask students to com-pare Wyeth's attitude toward nature with Thoreau's. [Possible response: Both seem to believe that human beings can learn much about themselves and their environment by studying nature's smallest details.]

A Reading Skills

❷ Extending philosophical arguments. Thoreau argues that solitude is not created by physical distance between people but by dis-tance between their points of view. He also maintains that solitude in nature brings us close to the source of all life—and thus to other people. In light of these beliefs, do you think the hours people spend in front of televisions and computers today serve to bring people together or to isolate them? [Responses will vary, but students should note that Thoreau would probably not approve of tech-nological solitude.]

B Content-Area Connections

History: Beacon Hill and the Five Points
Beacon Hill has traditionally been the home of wealthy people in Boston, while the Five Points was a slum in New York during the 1800s.

C Reading Skills

❷ Making generalizations. According to Thoreau, what advan-tages does solitude offer? [the opportunity to connect to the "perennial source of our life"]

Quaker Ladies (1956) by Andrew Wyeth. Watercolor and drypoint.

Why should I feel lonely? Is not our planet in the Milky Way? This which you put seems to me not to be the most important question. What sort of space is that which separates a man from his fellows and makes him solitary? I have found that no exertion of the legs can bring two minds much nearer to one another. What do we want most to dwell near to? Not to many men surely, the depot, the post office, the barroom, the meetinghouse, the schoolhouse, the grocery, Beacon Hill, or the Five Points, where men most congregate, but to the perennial source of our life, whence in all our experience we have found that to issue, as the willow stands near the water and sends out its roots in that direction. This will vary with different natures, but this is the place where a wise man will dig his cellar. . . .

from **The Bean Field**

Meanwhile my beans, the length of whose rows, added together, was seven miles already planted, were impatient to be hoed, for the earliest had

CONTENT-AREA CONNECTIONS

Botany: Native Plants
Quaker Ladies, the title of the Andrew Wyeth painting above, is another name for bluets (*Houstonia*), an American wildflower.
Paired activity. Have students determine the genus of other native plants Thoreau mentions—such as cinquefoil, johnswort, and pigweed—and present sketches, verbal descriptions, or both of each. Students can also choose an object from nature and explain how it teaches a lesson about life, using Thoreau's work as a model.

Courtesy Winterthur Museum, Winterthur, Delaware.

Heaven knows. This was my curious labor all summer—to make this portion of the earth's surface, which had yielded only cinquefoil, blackberries, johnswort, and the like, before, sweet wild fruits and pleasant flowers, produce instead this pulse.[14] What shall I learn of beans or beans of me? I cherish them, I hoe them, early and late I have an eye to them; and this is my day's work. It is a fine broad leaf to look on. My auxiliaries are the dews and rains which water this dry soil, and what fertility is in the soil itself, which for the most part is lean and effete. My enemies are worms, cool days, and most of all woodchucks. The last have nibbled for me a quarter of an acre clean. But what right had I to oust johnswort and the rest, and break up their ancient herb garden? Soon, however, the remaining beans will be too tough for them, and go forward to meet new foes. . . .

It was a singular experience that long acquaintance which I cultivated with beans, what with planting, and hoeing, and harvesting, and threshing, and picking over and selling them—the last was the hardest of all—I might add eating, for I did taste. I was determined to know beans. When they were growing, I used to hoe from five o'clock in the morning till noon, and commonly spent the rest of the day about other affairs. Consider the intimate and curious acquaintance one makes with various kinds of weeds—it will bear some iteration in the account, for there was no little iteration in the labor—disturbing their delicate organizations so ruthlessly, and making such invidious distinctions with his hoe, leveling whole ranks of one species, and sedulously cultivating another. That's Roman wormwood—that's pigweed—that's sorrel—that's pipergrass—have at him, chop him up, turn his roots upward to the sun, don't let him have a fiber in the shade, if you do

 **D**

grown considerably before the latest were in the ground; indeed they were not easily to be put off. What was the meaning of this so steady and self-respecting, this small Herculean labor, I knew not. I came to love my rows, my beans, though so many more than I wanted. They attached me to the earth, and so I got strength like Antaeus.[13] But why should I raise them? Only

---

13. **Antaeus** (an·tē′əs): in Greek mythology the giant who draws strength from the earth, his mother.

---

14. **pulse** *n.*: beans, peas, and other edible seeds of plants having pods.

Vocabulary
effete (e·fēt′) *adj.*: sterile; unproductive.

Henry David Thoreau **199**

DIRECT TEACHING

A Literary Focus

? Metaphor. What two things are being compared in this paragraph? [Weeding a bean field is compared to fighting a war.] **What is the effect of the military language?** [By comparing himself to a warrior fighting the Trojan weeds, Thoreau adds self-mocking humor to the essay; most weeds are tough, and readers will identify with the comparison to a battle. Thoreau, however, also uses the comparison to point out the heroic qualities of daily labor.]

B Vocabulary Development

Context clues. Ask students to use the context of the passage to figure out the meanings of and distinction between *duellum* and *bellum*. [The context shows that both mean "combat." Thoreau explains *bellum* as "a war between two races of ants" rather than one between just two individual ants.]

C Literary Focus

? Personification. How does Thoreau personify the newly arrived ant? [He compares it to a fresh recruit, to a young and ignorant soldier eager for the excitement of the fight.]

D Advanced Learners

Enrichment. Remind students that before the Civil War, most battles involved hand-to-hand combat, as opposed to battles with mechanized weapons and weapons of mass destruction that are used today. Interested students may want to conduct research to learn more about the battles to which Thoreau alludes: the battles between Greeks and Trojans in the *Iliad*, the Napoleonic War battles of Austerlitz and Dresden, and the Battle of Concord.

he'll turn himself t'other side up and be as green as a leek in two days. A long war, not with cranes, but with weeds, those Trojans who had sun and rain and dews on their side. Daily the beans saw me come to their rescue armed with a hoe, and thin the ranks of their enemies, filling up the trenches with weedy dead. Many a lusty crest-waving Hector,[15] that towered a whole foot above his crowding comrades, fell before my weapon and rolled in the dust. . . .

from Brute Neighbors

. . . One day when I went out to my woodpile, or rather my pile of stumps, I observed two large ants, the one red, the other much larger, nearly half an inch long, and black, fiercely contending with one another. Having once got hold they never let go, but struggled and wrestled and rolled on the chips incessantly. Looking farther, I was surprised to find that the chips were covered with such combatants, that it was not a *duellum*, but a *bellum*,[16] a war between two races of ants, the red always pitted against the black, and frequently two red ones to one black. The legions of these Myrmidons[17] covered all the hills and vales in my wood yard, and the ground was already strewn with the dead and dying, both red and black. It was the only battle which I have ever witnessed, the only battlefield I ever trod while the battle was raging; internecine[18] war; the red republicans on the one hand, and the black imperialists on the other. On every side they were engaged in deadly combat, yet without any noise that I could hear, and human soldiers never fought so resolutely. I watched a couple that were fast locked in each other's embraces, in a little sunny valley amid the chips, now at noonday prepared to fight till the sun went down, or life went out. The smaller red champion had fastened himself

like a vise to his adversary's front, and through all the tumblings on that field never for an instant ceased to gnaw at one of his feelers near the root, having already caused the other to go by the board; while the stronger black one dashed him from side to side, and, as I saw on looking nearer, had already divested him of several of his members. They fought with more pertinacity than bulldogs. Neither manifested the least disposition to retreat. It was evident that their battle cry was "Conquer or die." In the meanwhile there came along a single red ant on the hillside of this valley, evidently full of excitement, who either had dispatched his foe, or had not yet taken part in the battle; probably the latter, for he had lost none of his limbs; whose mother had charged him to return with his shield or upon it.[19] Or perchance he was some Achilles, who had nourished his wrath apart, and had now come to avenge or rescue his Patroclus.[20] He saw this unequal combat from afar—for the blacks were nearly twice the size of the red—he drew near with rapid pace till he stood on his guard within half an inch of the combatants; then, watching his opportunity, he sprang upon the black warrior, and commenced his operations near the root of his right foreleg, leaving the foe to select among his own members; and so there were three united for life, as if a new kind of attraction had been invented which put all other locks and cements to shame. I should not have wondered by this time to find that they had their respective musical bands stationed on some eminent chip, and playing their national airs the while, to excite the slow and cheer the dying combatants. I was myself excited somewhat even as if they had been men.

---

15. **Hector:** In the *Iliad*, Hector is the Trojan prince killed by the Greek hero Achilles.
16. **not a *duellum*, but a *bellum*:** not a duel, but a war.
17. **Myrmidons:** Achilles' soldiers in the *Iliad*. *Myrmex* is Greek for "ant."
18. **internecine** (in′tər·nē′sin) *adj.*: harmful to both sides of the group.

19. **return . . . upon it:** echo of the traditional charge of Spartan mothers to their warrior sons: in other words, return victorious or dead.
20. **Achilles . . . Patroclus** (pə·trō′kləs): In the *Iliad*, Achilles withdraws from the battle at Troy but rejoins the fight after his friend Patroclus is killed.

Vocabulary
incessantly (in·ses′ənt·lē) *adv.*: without stopping.

CONTENT-AREA CONNECTIONS

Architecture: Design
Individual activity. Have students design a simple cabin that would provide sufficient shelter for living in a wilderness area located in their state or region. Remind them to consider the demands of the climate, the characteristics of the site, and the materials native to the natural ecosystem. Students should create a blueprint and describe how the cabin is to be constructed to meet the unique conditions of its location. Display the blueprints in the classroom.

The more you think of it, the less the difference. And certainly there is not the fight recorded in Concord history, at least, if in the history of America, that will bear a moment's comparison with this, whether for the numbers engaged in it, or for the patriotism and heroism displayed. For numbers and for carnage it was an Austerlitz or Dresden.[21] Concord Fight! Two killed on the patriots' side, and Luther Blanchard wounded! Why here every ant was a Buttrick— "Fire! for God's sake fire!"—and thousands shared the fate of Davis and Hosmer.[22] There was not one hireling there. I have no doubt that it was a principle they fought for, as much as our ancestors, and not to avoid a three-penny tax on their tea; and the results of this battle will be as important and memorable to those whom it concerns as those of the Battle of Bunker Hill, at least.

I took up the chip on which the three I have particularly described were struggling, carried it into my house, and placed it under a tumbler on my windowsill, in order to see the issue. Holding a microscope to the first-mentioned red ant, I saw that, though he was assiduously gnawing at the near foreleg of his enemy, having severed his remaining feeler, his own breast was all torn away, exposing what vitals he had there to the jaws of the black warrior, whose breastplate was apparently too thick for him to pierce; and the dark carbuncles of the sufferer's eyes shone with ferocity such as war only could excite. They struggled half an hour longer under the tumbler, and when I looked again the black soldier had severed the heads of his foes from their bodies, and the still living heads were hanging on either side of him like ghastly trophies at his saddlebow, still apparently as firmly fastened as ever, and he was endeavoring with feeble struggles, being without feelers and with

only the remnant of a leg, and I know not how many other wounds, to divest himself of them; which at length, after half an hour more, he accomplished. I raised the glass, and he went off over the windowsill in that crippled state. Whether he finally survived that combat, and spent the remainder of his days in some Hôtel des Invalides,[23] I do not know; but I thought that his industry would not be worth much thereafter. I never learned which party was victorious, nor the cause of the war; but I felt for the rest of that day as if I had had my feelings excited and harrowed by witnessing the struggle, the ferocity and carnage, of a human battle before my door. . . .

In the fall the loon (*Colymbus glacialis*) came, as usual, to molt and bathe in the pond, making the woods ring with his wild laughter before I had risen. At rumor of his arrival all the Milldam sportsmen are on the alert, in gigs and on foot, two by two and three by three, with patent rifles and conical balls and spyglasses. They come rustling through the woods like autumn leaves, at least ten men to one loon. Some station themselves on this side of the pond, some on that, for the poor bird cannot be omnipresent; if he dive here he must come up there. But now the kind October wind rises, rustling the leaves and rippling the surface of the water, so that no loon can be heard or seen, though his foes sweep the pond with spyglasses, and make the woods resound with their discharges. The waves generously rise and dash angrily, taking sides with all waterfowl, and our sportsmen must beat a retreat to town and shop and unfinished jobs. But they were too often successful. When I went to get a pail of water early in the morning I frequently saw this stately bird sailing out of my cove within a few rods.[24] If I endeavored to overtake him in a boat, in

21. **Austerlitz or Dresden:** major battles of the Napoleonic Wars.

22. **Luther . . . Hosmer:** All these men fought at the Battle of Concord, the first battle of the Revolutionary War. Maj. John Buttrick led the minutemen who defeated the British. Isaac Davis and David Hosmer were the two colonists killed.

23. **Hôtel des Invalides** (ō·tel′ dez a*n*′vä·lēd′): Home for Disabled Soldiers, a veterans' hospital in Paris, France. The body of Napoleon I (1769–1821) is buried there.

24. **rods** *n. pl.:* one rod measures 16½ feet.

E Reading Skills

❓ Determining author's purpose. What effect does Thoreau hope to achieve with the suggestion that the ants were fighting for a principle? [Possible response: He wishes to add humor (since ants would probably fight only over food or territory), but he also wants to suggest that humans should fight only for a lofty principle, not because of a petty three-penny tax on tea.]

F Literary Focus

❓ Tone. What tone does Thoreau take toward his subject in this passage? [He maintains a compassionate yet satirical tone.]

G Literary Focus

❓ Point of view. Look back over this section. What point of view does Thoreau use to describe the battle? [His point of view is a mix of first person and objective. He witnesses the battle but is not involved in it; nevertheless, he interprets the battle as more than just insect behavior.] What is the effect of this point of view? [The section reads like a war correspondent's report; Thoreau does not take sides yet is still caught up in the excitement of the battle.]

CONTENT-AREA CONNECTIONS

Science: Laughing Loons

Loons live in fresh and salt waters in northern climates. Clumsy on land, they fly and swim exceptionally well, and they can dive deeper than any other bird except penguins, reaching depths of up to two hundred feet in pursuit of fish. During mating season, the only time they are on land, loons develop striking black and white dorsal plumage, which offsets their usually dull gray and white coat. Both male and female loons take care of the hatchlings, which often ride on their parents' backs for the first few weeks of life. Loons are famous for their distinctive call, often likened to wailing or insane shrieking.

Whole-class activity. Have the class listen to and comment on a recording of a loon laughing from a collection such as *Stokes Field Guide to Bird Songs: Eastern Region* by Donald and Lillian Stokes and Lang Elliot.

VIEWING THE ART

John James Audubon
(1785–1851) was born in Haiti and lived in France as a boy. He came to the United States in 1803. Audubon spent his life on the ambitious project of producing life-sized, accurate watercolor paintings of every bird in America. His two massive works, *The Birds of America* (1827–1838) and *Ornithological Biography* (1831–1839), are valuable scientific resources, as well as works of art, because his renderings of the birds and their environments are meticulously accurate as well as aesthetically beautiful.

Activity. Ask students to write a paragraph describing how the painting helps readers appreciate Thoreau's long description of loons. Students should compare Audubon's impressions of the loon's "personality" with Thoreau's.

Ⓐ Reading Skills

❷ Determining author's purpose. This section, which contains Thoreau's description of the loon, is a digressive piece of nature writing. What might be the purpose of the section? [Possible answer: It is a philosophical metaphor about the relationship between people and nature, or between people and the elusive meaning of their own existence.]

Ⓑ Literary Focus

❷ Metaphor. To what does Thoreau compare the loon in the "game" they are playing. What does this comparison convey? [Thoreau compares the loon to a checker that disappears beneath a playing board and then pops up again. His comparison conveys Thoreau's surprise each time the loon reappears on the surface.]

Common Loon (1833) by John James Audubon. Watercolor, graphite, gouache, pastel.
© Collection of the New-York Historical Society.

order to see how he would maneuver, he would dive and be completely lost, so that I did not discover him again, sometimes, till the latter part of the day. But I was more than a match for him on the surface. He commonly went off in a rain.

Ⓐ   As I was paddling along the north shore one very calm October afternoon, for such days especially they settle onto the lakes, like the milkweed down, having looked in vain over the pond for a loon, suddenly one, sailing out from the shore toward the middle a few rods in front of me, set up his wild laugh and betrayed himself. I pursued with a paddle and he dived, but when he came up I was nearer than before. He dived again, but I miscalculated the direction he would take, and we were fifty rods apart when he came to the surface this time, for I had helped to widen the interval; and again he

laughed long and loud, and with more reason than before. He maneuvered so cunningly that I could not get within half a dozen rods of him. Each time, when he came to the surface, turning his head this way and that, he coolly surveyed the water and the land, and apparently chose his course so that he might come up where there was the widest expanse of water and at the greatest distance from the boat. It was surprising how quickly he made up his mind and put his resolve into execution. He led me at once to the widest part of the pond, and could not be driven from it. While he was thinking one thing in his brain, I was endeavoring to divine his Ⓑ thought in mine. It was a pretty game, played on the smooth surface of the pond, a man against a loon. Suddenly your adversary's checker disappears beneath the board, and the problem is to place yours nearest to where his will appear

CONTENT-AREA CONNECTIONS

Visual Art: Bird Images
Whole-class activity. Have students look at a copy of Audubon's *Birds of America* and compare his paintings to photographs in modern nature guides. Which do students prefer? Which show more detail? Which do they find more visually appealing? Which might better serve the interests of the average bird watcher?

Economics: Budget
Individual activity. Have students discuss Thoreau's use of the word *Economy* on p. 193. Point out that it comes from the Greek root *oikos,* or "house." Next, have students summarize the steps Thoreau took to economize and then write a journal entry on how they could economize in their own finances. What possessions or activities could they eliminate?

again. Sometimes he would come up unexpectedly on the opposite side of me, having apparently passed directly under the boat. So long-winded was he and so unwearieable, that when he had swum farthest he would immediately plunge again, nevertheless; and then no wit could divine where in the deep pond, beneath the smooth surface, he might be speeding his way like a fish, for he had time and ability to visit the bottom of the pond in its deepest part. It is said that loons have been caught in the New York lakes eighty feet beneath the surface, with hooks set for trout—though Walden is deeper than that. How surprised must the fishes be to see this ungainly visitor from another sphere speeding his way amid their schools! Yet he appeared to know his course as surely underwater as on the surface, and swam much faster there. Once or twice I saw a ripple where he approached the surface, just put his head out to reconnoiter, and instantly dived again. I found that it was as well for me to rest on my oars and wait his reappearing as to endeavor to calculate where he would rise; for again and again, when I was straining my eyes over the surface one way, I would suddenly be startled by his unearthly laugh behind me. But why, after displaying so much cunning, did he invariably betray himself the moment he came up by that loud laugh? Did not his white breast enough betray him? He was indeed a silly loon, I thought. I could commonly hear the plash of the water when he came up, and so also detected him. But after an hour he seemed as fresh as ever, dived as willingly, and swam yet farther than at first. It was surprising to see how serenely he sailed off with unruffled breast when he came to the surface, doing all the work with his webbed feet beneath. His usual note was this demoniac laughter, yet somewhat like that of a waterfowl; but occasionally, when he had balked me most successfully and come up a long way off, he uttered a long-drawn unearthly howl, probably more like that of a wolf than any bird; as when a beast puts his muzzle to the ground and deliberately howls. This was his looning—perhaps the wildest sound that is ever heard here, making the woods ring far and wide. I concluded that he laughed in derision of my efforts confident of his own resources. Though the sky was by this time overcast, the pond was so smooth that I could see where he broke the surface when I did not hear him. His white breast, the stillness of the air, and the smoothness of the water were all against him. At length, having come up fifty rods off, he uttered one of those prolonged howls, as if calling on the god of loons to aid him, and immediately there came a wind from the east and rippled the surface, and filled the whole air with misty rain, and I was impressed as if it were the prayer of the loon answered, and his god was angry with me; and so I left him disappearing far away on the tumultuous surface. . . .

from Conclusion

. . . I left the woods for as good a reason as I went there. Perhaps it seemed to me that I had several more lives to live, and could not spare any more time for that one. It is remarkable how easily and insensibly we fall into a particular route, and make a beaten track for ourselves. I had not lived there a week before my feet wore a path from my door to the pond side; and though it is five or six years since I trod it, it is still quite distinct. It is true, I fear, that others may have fallen into it, and so helped to keep it open. The surface of the earth is soft and impressible by the feet of men; and so with the paths which the mind travels. How worn and dusty, then, must be the highways of the world, how deep the ruts of tradition and conformity! I did not wish to take a cabin passage, but rather to go before the mast and on the deck of the world, for there I could best see the moonlight amid the mountains. I do not wish to go below now.

I learned this, at least, by my experiment:

Vocabulary
derision (di·rizh′ən) *n.:* ridicule; contempt.
tumultuous (to͞o·mul′cho͞o·əs) *adj.:* noisy and disorderly; stormy.

C **English-Language Learners**
Interpreting idioms. Explain that the phrase *no wit could divine* means "no one could figure out."

D **Reading Skills**
❓ **Making judgments.** Go over Thoreau's description of his encounter with the loon. How does Thoreau personify the bird? [He suggests that the loon is deliberately challenging and playing with him; he attributes to it such characteristics as coolness, resolution, cunning, and a sense of humor.] Does this view of the loon seem realistic or fanciful? [Possible responses: realistic—animals often demonstrate a sense of play; fanciful—birds usually avoid human beings.]

E **Reading Skills**
❓ **Making generalizations.** What is Thoreau suggesting? What generalizations would he like readers to draw? [Possible responses: People should always strive for growth and change in their lives; people need different things at different stages of their lives; even a nonconformist can get into a rut and should avoid leading others into it.]

F **English-Language Learners**
Interpreting archaisms. Explain that *to go before the mast* means "working on a ship to pay for one's passage." This expression suggests adventure, as if life were a sea voyage. "Going below," in this context, means taking the passive role of a passenger rather than the active role of a sailor.

CONTENT-AREA CONNECTIONS

Science: Nature Observation
Individual activity. Discuss with students the fact that Thoreau learned many lessons from careful observations of nature. Take or assign students to visit a park or nature preserve. Tell them to sit quietly apart from one another and to record their sensory impressions. The following day, have students read over their material and develop a preliminary thesis for an essay about their experience.

Allow their essays to follow any direction that arises from their reflections on the natural surroundings. Students may want to read selected chapters of *Pilgrim at Tinker Creek* by Annie Dillard as models for their essay.

A **Reading Skills**

? **Assessing the author's argument.** Do you agree with Thoreau that people will meet with success by following their dreams? [Possible responses: Yes, people can achieve anything they really set their minds to; no, life is full of limitations.]

B **Reading Skills**

? **Making generalizations.** What generalization is Thoreau making in this passage? [Anyone can discover a unique path in life, but this discovery comes at different times for different people.]

C **Literary Focus**

? **Metaphor.** What does Thoreau imply about society through the comparison in this passage? [The idea of human life buried inside dead-wood is a strong indictment of the way society oppresses many people.]

D **Reading Skills**

? **Recognizing persuasive techniques.** Thoreau closes with a ringing call to action. What does he want people to do? [Possible response: not merely to allow time to pass but to reflect on the significance of their lives and to explore and learn.]

GUIDED PRACTICE

Monitoring students' progress. Guide the class in answering these true-false statements.

True-False

1. Thoreau observes nature. [T]
2. Thoreau plays a game of hide-and-seek with a loon. [T]
3. Thoreau leaves Walden Pond because he feels ready to move on. [T]
4. Thoreau values nonconformity. [T]

A That if one advances confidently in the direction of his dreams, and endeavors to live the life which he has imagined, he will meet with a success unexpected in common hours. He will put some things behind, will pass an invisible boundary; new, universal, and more liberal laws will begin to establish themselves around and within him; or the old laws be expanded, and interpreted in his favor in a more liberal sense, and he will live with the license of a higher order of beings. In proportion as he simplifies his life, the laws of the universe will appear less complex, and solitude will not be solitude, nor poverty poverty, nor weakness weakness. If you have built castles in the air, your work need not be lost; that is where they should be. Now put the foundations under them. . . .

Some are dinning in our ears that we Americans, and moderns generally, are intellectual dwarfs compared with the ancients, or even the Elizabethan men. But what is that to the purpose? A living dog is better than a dead lion.[25] Shall a man go and hang himself because he belongs to the race of pygmies, and not be the biggest pygmy that he can? Let everyone mind his own business, and endeavor to be what he was made.

B Why should we be in such desperate haste to succeed and in such desperate enterprises? If a man does not keep pace with his companions, perhaps it is because he hears a different drummer. Let him step to the music which he hears, however measured or far away. It is not important that he should mature as soon as an apple tree or an oak. Shall he turn his spring into summer? If the condition of things which we were made for is not yet, what were any reality which we can substitute? We will not be shipwrecked on a vain reality. Shall we with pains erect a heaven of blue glass over ourselves, though when it is done we shall be sure to gaze still at the true ethereal heaven far above, as if the former were not? . . .

The life in us is like the water in the river. It may rise this year higher than man has ever

---

known it, and flood the parched uplands; even this may be the eventful year, which will drown out all our muskrats. It was not always dry land where we dwell. I see far inland the banks which the stream anciently washed, before science began to record its freshets. Everyone has heard the story which has gone the rounds of New England, of a strong and beautiful bug which came out of the dry leaf of an old table of apple-tree wood, which had stood in a farmer's kitchen for sixty years, first in Connecticut, and afterward in Massachusetts—from an egg deposited in the living tree many years earlier still, as appeared by counting the annual layers be- **C** yond it; which was heard gnawing out for several weeks, hatched perchance by the heat of an urn. Who does not feel his faith in a resurrection and immortality strengthened by hearing of this? Who knows what beautiful and winged life, whose egg has been buried for ages under many concentric layers of woodenness in the dead dry life of society, deposited at first in the alburnum[26] of the green and living tree, which has been gradually converted into the semblance of its well-seasoned tomb—heard perchance gnawing out now for years by the astonished family of man, as they sat round the festive board—may unexpectedly come forth from amidst society's most trivial and hand-selled[27] furniture, to enjoy its perfect summer life at last!

D I do not say that John or Jonathan[28] will realize all this; but such is the character of that morrow which mere lapse of time can never make to dawn. The light which puts out our eyes is darkness to us. Only that day dawns to which we are awake. There is more day to dawn. The sun is but a morning star. ■

---

26. **alburnum** *n.*: sapwood, soft wood between the inner bark and the hard core of a tree.
27. **handselled** *v.* used as *adj.*: given as a mere token of good wishes; therefore, of no great value in itself.
28. **John or Jonathan:** John Bull and Brother Jonathan were traditional personifications of England and the United States, respectively.

Vocabulary
ethereal (ē·thir′ē·əl) *adj.*: not earthly; spiritual.

---

25. **A living dog ... lion:** Ecclesiastes 9:4.

READING MINI-LESSON

Developing Word-Attack Skills
Remind students that compound words are two words written together as one. Reading an unfamiliar compound word requires that you identify the smaller words that make it up.

Write *pipergrass* on the chalkboard. Have students identify the words that make up the compound (*piper* and *grass*). Have students use context and other clues to draw conclusions about the word's meaning.

Activity. Have students identify the two words that make up each compound word. The first word in each compound word is indicated with boldface letters.

1. **savin**trees
2. **pudding**stone
3. **grid**iron
4. **worm**wood
5. **clapper**clawing
6. **way**farer
7. **fore**noon
8. **saddle**bow

Don Henley (of the rock group the Eagles) founded the Walden Woods Project to protect a part of Walden Woods under threat of real estate development. Here Henley talks about how Thoreau and Emerson contributed to his "spiritual awakening" and his commitment to the preservation of Walden Woods.

from Heaven Is Under Our Feet

Don Henley

I honestly don't remember when I was first introduced to the works of Henry David Thoreau or by whom. It may have been my venerable high school English teacher, Margaret Lovelace, or it may have been one of my university professors. I was lucky enough to have a few exceptional ones and that is sometimes all a kid needs—just one or two really good teachers can make all the difference in the world. It can inspire and change a life. . . .

Thoreau's writing struck me like a thunderbolt. Like all great literature, it articulated something that I knew intuitively, but could not quite bring into focus for myself. I loved Emerson, too, and his essay "Self-Reliance" was instrumental in giving me the courage to become a songwriter. The works of both men were part of a spiritual awakening in which I rediscovered my hometown and the beauty of the surrounding landscape, and, through that, some evidence of a "Higher Power," or God, if you like. This epiphany brought great comfort and relief. . . .

. . . [T]here has been a great deal of curiosity, speculation, and, in some quarters, skepticism bordering on cynicism, as to how and why I came to be involved in the movement to preserve the stomping grounds of Henry David Thoreau and his friend and mentor, Ralph Waldo Emerson. What, in other words, is California rock and roll trash doing meddling around in something as seemingly esoteric and high-minded as literature (pronounced "LIT-tra-chure"), philosophy, and history—the American Transcendentalist Movement and all its ascetic practitioners. Seems perfectly natural to me. American Literature, like the air we breathe, belongs—or should belong—to everybody. . . . The great halls of learning may keep Thoreau's literature and principles alive, but they will be of little help in fortifying the well from whence they sprang.

. . . Unfortunately, the focus of preservation efforts has come to rest on the pond and its immediate surroundings. That is all well and good, except that there remain approximately two thousand six hundred acres that are inside the historic boundaries of Walden Woods and deserve protection as well. Thoreau did not live *in* Walden Pond; he lived beside it. The man did not walk on water, he walked several miles a day through the woods, and his musings and writings therein figure at least as prominently in his literature as Walden Pond does. In other words, the width and breadth of his inspiration, the scope of his legacy is not limited to one sixty-two-acre pond, and it is absurd to think so. Walden Woods is not a pristine, grand tract of wilderness, but it is still, for the most part, exceedingly beautiful and inspiring. It is, for all intents and purposes, the cradle of the American environmental movement and should be preserved for its intrinsic, symbolic value or, as Ed Schofield, Thoreau Society president, so succinctly put it, "When Walden goes, all the issues radiating out from Walden go, too. If the prime place can be disposed of, how much easier to dispose of the issues it represents." Otherwise, we might just as well turn all our national parks, our monuments to freedom and independence, into theme parks and shopping malls.

Comparing and Contrasting Texts

Connecting Henley to Thoreau and Emerson. Ask students to consider how Don Henley is living up to Thoreau's and Emerson's ideals. [Possible response: Henley has learned from Emerson to rely on himself, to listen to his own conscience, and to broaden his thinking. These abilities help him to speak out against the commercial development of Walden Woods. Henley has also learned from Thoreau. He has come to appreciate not only the beauty of Walden Woods but also the beauty of his own hometown. He has acquired the self-confidence to ignore those who criticize him for meddling in this issue. In fact, in his professional and personal life, he marches to the beat of his own drummer.]

Connection

Summary ⬇ *below grade level*

In this essay, Eagles's drummer Don Henley recalls how the writings of Emerson and Thoreau gave him the courage to become a musician and inspired a spiritual awakening in him. He goes on to explain that because of its symbolic value to American literature and to the American environmental movement, Walden Pond, as well as the entire 2,680-acre tract of Walden Woods, where Thoreau roamed and wrote, should be preserved.

DIRECT TEACHING

E **Reading Informational Text**

❓ **Finding the main idea.** Henley says that reading Thoreau's writing was like being struck by lightning. He makes this comparison to draw attention to his main idea that follows. What is that idea? [The ideas expressed by Thoreau and Emerson changed his life by inspiring him both professionally and spiritually.]

F **Reading Informational Text**

❓ **Making assertions about the argument.** Henley argues that Walden Pond and Walden Woods should be preserved because they are the "cradle of the American environmental movement." What do you think of this argument? [Possible response: Henley offers no evidence to prove that Thoreau was the first American environmentalist or that Walden Woods is the first and most important symbol of American environmentalism. His argument does gain some persuasiveness by citing an authority on Thoreau, Ed Schofield.]

Response and Analysis

Reading Check

1. He wants to give "a simple and sincere account" of himself; he knows himself best.

2. He lived in a cabin in the woods; he lived as fully and deliberately as possible.

3. He is a part of the Milky Way; he is surrounded by countless living creatures; he feels close to the natural sources of life.

4. He learns all about them. They make him feel as if he is rooted to the earth.

Thinking Critically

5. **a.** I hope my readers will take only what suits them personally in my work and not distort my philosophy.

   b. I wanted to participate in and enjoy every experience that life has to offer.

   c. If someone lives in his or her own way, it may be because of beliefs and a destiny that differ from everyone else's. Let that person live according to his or her own convictions.

6. People and nations carry the potential for dramatic and beautiful change inside them—even after years of thoughtless conformity.

7. The full possibilities of life will open up to us only when we are committed to living fully.

Extending and Evaluating

8. Possible generalizations: A person can achieve anything he or she truly wants. A person must believe in himself or herself and avoid the course charted by others. A busy life is not necessarily a satisfying life.

Response and Analysis

Reading Check

1. According to the second paragraph in "Economy," why has Thoreau decided to write about his life?

2. How does Thoreau answer the questions implied in the title "Where I Lived, and What I Lived For"?

3. What arguments does Thoreau present in "Solitude" to demonstrate that he is not lonely in his isolated cabin?

4. What satisfactions does Thoreau find in the labor of raising beans in "The Bean Field"?

Thinking Critically

5. Thoreau's **metaphors** are highly visual. Though they're clever and original, they aren't far-fetched. Thoreau takes his comparisons from nature and from other things he and his audience are familiar with, such as clothes and sailing. To be sure you understand Thoreau's figures of speech, **paraphrase** the following metaphors:

   a. "As for the rest of my readers, they will accept such portions as apply to them. I trust that none will stretch the seams in putting on the coat, for it may do good service to him whom it fits." (page 193)

   b. "I wanted to live deep and suck out all the marrow of life." (page 196)

   c. "If a man does not keep pace with his companions, perhaps it is because he hears a different drummer. Let him step to the music which he hears, however measured or far away." (page 204)

6. A **parable** is a very brief story that teaches a moral or ethical lesson. What do you think is the lesson of the parable involving the bug in the wood table at the conclusion of *Walden*?

7. What do you think Thoreau means in his final paragraphs by these words: "Only that day dawns to which we are awake"?

Extending and Evaluating

8. Review the double-entry journal you kept as you read *Walden*. What **generalizations** can you make about Thoreau's beliefs? For example, you might make a generalization about Thoreau's beliefs on technological progress, based on what he says about railroads and other inventions.

INTERNET
Projects and Activities
Keyword: LE5 11-2

SKILLS FOCUS

Literary Skills
Analyze metaphor.

Reading Skills
Make generalizations about a writer's beliefs.

Writing Skills
Write an essay analyzing a work.

Vocabulary Skills
Complete word analogies.

Thoreau's journals and a writing box.

DIFFERENTIATING INSTRUCTION

Learners Having Difficulty
You may simplify this assignment by discussing only the Reading Check questions. Point out that these questions focus on the main ideas of Thoreau's writing. Help students find details from the selection that support these main ideas.

Advanced Learners
After students have paraphrased the metaphors in the Interpretations questions, lead a discussion in which they evaluate the effectiveness of the metaphors. Do the metaphors help readers better understand Thoreau's arguments, or do they distract from his ideas? Do his comparisons "fit" his ideas, or would other comparisons work better?

WRITING

How Romantic?

In a brief **essay,** evaluate evidence of the Romantic point of view in *Walden*—for instance, the emphasis on intuition, the power of nature, and individual autonomy. In your opinion, is Thoreau a Romantic, or can you identify strong non-Romantic strains in his thinking? (Review the characteristics of Romanticism on page 143.) Be sure to quote from *Walden* to support your evaluation.

A journal page (1845)
by Henry David Thoreau.

Vocabulary Development
Analogies

In an analogy two pairs of words have the same relationship. For example, in each pair the words could be synonyms or antonyms, or one word could describe a characteristic or be an example of the other word. Fill in each blank below with the Vocabulary word that completes the analogy. (For more help with analogies, see pages 163, 714, and 950.)

pertinent	effete
encumbrance	incessantly
impervious	derision
temporal	tumultuous
superficial	ethereal

1. VIOLENT : PEACEFUL :: _____ : tranquil
2. SOLID : ROCK :: _____ : heaven
3. FREQUENTLY : OFTEN :: _____ : continuously
4. RESPECT : ADMIRATION :: _____ : ridicule
5. ESSENTIAL : NECESSARY :: _____ : relevant
6. HOSTILE : AGGRESSIVE :: _____ : shallow
7. BOLD : MEEK :: _____ : eternal
8. HEALTHY : ROBUST :: _____ : unproductive
9. PRAISE : COMPLIMENT :: _____ : obstacle
10. ABSORBENT : SPONGE :: _____ : fortress

Vocabulary Development

1. tumultuous
2. ethereal
3. incessantly
4. derision
5. pertinent
6. superficial
7. temporal
8. effete
9. encumbrance
10. impervious

Assessment

■ *Holt Assessment: Literature, Reading, and Vocabulary*

For lessons reteaching poetic devices and philosophical assumptions and beliefs, see **Reteaching,** p. 1117A.

Political Points of View

Grade-Level Skills

■ **Literary Skills**

Analyze political points of view in a selection of literary works on a topic.

■ **Literary Skills**

Analyze the way an author's style, including the use of paradox, achieves specific rhetorical or aesthetic effects.

■ **Reading Skills**

Critique the validity, appeals, and truthfulness of arguments in public documents.

■ **Reading Skills**

Recognize persuasive techniques.

Political Issue: Civil Disobedience

The selections in this feature address a central American political issue—to what extent does a citizen have a right, or even a responsibility, to break the country's laws? This question had, and continues to have, special relevance to a nation established through revolution and founded on the principle of the consent of the governed. Thoreau's seminal essay articulates this vital aspect of the relationship between government and the individual, and influenced civil rights movements and passive resistance movements around the world.

Skills Starter

Build review skills. Be sure students understand the meaning of *civil*, as in "civil government" and "civil disobedience." Define the term as "relating to citizens, citizenship, and the interrelationship of people with their government." You might point out that the word derives from the Latin word *civis*, meaning "citizen," and that it has the same root as *civics*—the branch of political science that deals with the rights and responsibilities of citizens.

Introducing *Political Points of View*

Civil Disobedience

Main Reading

You will be reading the three selections listed above in this Political Points of View feature on civil disobedience. In the top corner of the pages in this feature, you'll find three stars. Smaller versions of the stars appear next to the questions on page 217 that focus on civil disobedience. At the end of the feature (pages 223–224), you'll compare the various points of view expressed in the selections.

Examining the Issue: Civil Disobedience

The phrase *civil disobedience* was coined by Henry David Thoreau when he chose to disobey a law he considered unjust. Think about people who hold rallies, boycotts, or hunger strikes today to protest a perceived injustice. Do you think they are abusing the role of citizens or fulfilling that role in a responsible way? When protesters accept beatings, imprisonment, or even death as a consequence for disobeying laws they view as unjust, are they criminals or patriots? Henry David Thoreau, Mohandas K. Gandhi, and Martin Luther King, Jr., viewed civil disobedience as an important expression of citizenship. In the writings that follow, each man attempts to explain to his fellow citizens the reasons he chose the path of civil disobedience.

Make the Connection

Quickwrite ✏

Sometimes a government enforces a law that is intended to protect or benefit people but actually infringes on their rights, such as the right to free speech. Reflect for a few minutes on the policies or laws already existing or proposed in your school or community (for example, curfews, dress codes, or smoking regulations). Freewrite for a few minutes on what you think are the strongest arguments for and against one of these policies or laws.

Reading Skills 📖

Recognizing Persuasive Techniques

Speakers and writers who want to move an audience to think, feel, or act in a certain way make use of several persuasive techniques:

SKILLS FOCUS

Pages 208–224 cover
Literary Skills
Analyze political points of view on a topic.
Reading Skills
Recognize persuasive techniques (logical, ethical, and emotional appeals).

208 Collection 2 American Romanticism: 1800–1860

- **Logical appeals** consist of facts, examples, and well-reasoned arguments.

  Because 85 percent of the taxpayers are senior citizens and do not have school-age children, they should not be expected to pay for academic expenses. The school budget should be cut.

- **Ethical appeals** are arguments based on widely accepted values or moral standards.

  America has a long-standing tradition in which every taxpayer is obliged to support the education of our young people. If it were not for the help of all taxpayers, our young people would not get the future they deserve.

- **Emotional appeals** consist of language and anecdotes that arouse strong feelings.

  Senior taxpayers are sick and tired of seeing their taxes used to support expensive nonacademic programs like wrestling.

As you read the selections that follow, note examples of each of these persuasive techniques.

Political Points of View: Civil Disobedience   209

Summary at grade level

Thoreau argues that government should serve individuals, who are the real agents of change and progress. He criticizes people for passively accepting governmental actions with which they disagree; he says that if people defied the government in such a case, it would have to show more accountability to its citizens. He tests his theory of civil disobedience by serving a jail sentence rather than paying a tax he believes will help finance war with Mexico and the expansion of slavery. During his time in jail, Thoreau recognizes that few of his neighbors will have the courage to follow his example. He concludes with the hope that one day the state will be truly "free and enlightened."

Before You Read

from Resistance to Civil Government

Political Points *of* View

In July 1846, Thoreau's stay at Walden Pond was interrupted by a night in jail. Thoreau was arrested because he refused on principle to pay a tax to the state. He refused to pay the tax because he was opposed to the U.S. war with Mexico, which he believed was an excuse to expand America's slave-holding territory. The police in Concord offered to pay the tax for Thoreau, but he refused that also. He was forced, therefore, to spend the night in jail. Thoreau might have spent more time there, except that someone, probably his aunt, paid the tax for him. This night in jail was the inspiration for the essay known as "Resistance to Civil Government" or "Civil Disobedience." Some people have suggested that the essay shows that Thoreau merely wanted to withdraw from life and all its hard questions. Others see Thoreau's action as the logical outcome of his beliefs. You will have to decide for yourself if Thoreau's position is admirable or not.

INTERNET

Vocabulary
Practice
•
More About
Henry David
Thoreau
•
Keyword: LE5 11-2

SKILLS FOCUS

Literary Skills
Analyze political
points of view
on a topic.
Understand
paradox.

Literary Focus

Paradox

A **paradox** is a statement that expresses the complexity of life by showing how opposing ideas can be both contradictory and true at the same time. When the poet Emily Dickinson wrote the line "Much Madness is divinest Sense" (page 350), she was expressing a paradox. William Shakespeare is expressing another paradox when he has one of his young lovers say, "Parting is such sweet sorrow." Paradox was one of Thoreau's favorite literary devices; look for it as you read his essay.

A **paradox** is a statement that appears to be self-contradictory but that actually reveals a kind of truth.

For more on Paradox, see the Handbook of Literary and Historical Terms.

Vocabulary Development

expedient (ek·spē′dē·ənt) *n.:* convenience; means to an end.

perverted (pər·vurt′id) *v.:* misdirected; corrupted.

posterity (päs·ter′ə·tē) *n.:* generations to come.

alacrity (ə·lak′rə·tē) *n.:* promptness in responding; eagerness.

inherent (in·hir′ənt) *adj.:* inborn; built-in.

eradication (ē·rad′i·kā′shən) *n.:* utter destruction; obliteration.

insurrection (in′sə·rek′shən) *n.:* rebellion; revolt.

penitent (pen′i·tənt) *adj.:* sorry for doing wrong.

effectual (e·fek′chōō·əl) *adj.:* productive; efficient.

impetuous (im·pech′ōō·əs) *adj.:* impulsive.

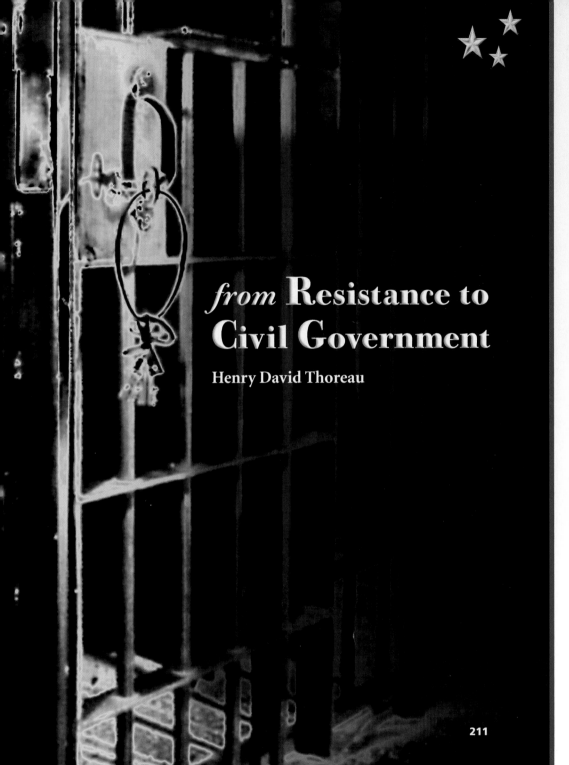

from Resistance to Civil Government

Henry David Thoreau

211

PRETEACHING

Selection Starter

Motivate. Numerous popular sayings give voice to the idea that you must be willing to stand up for what you believe in, from "Put your money where your mouth is," to "Put up or shut up." Ask students under what circumstances they would be willing to risk a fine, punishment, or even jail for a moral or political principle. Have them discuss examples of people who have endured physical suffering in order to demonstrate their commitment to an idea.

Previewing Vocabulary

Working with a partner, each student should look up five Vocabulary words in a dictionary and note their prefixes, suffixes, and roots (all the Vocabulary words in this selection are derived from Latin roots). Partners can then quiz each other on the Latin roots they have learned and create lists of other words with those roots that might prove useful.

Next, have students match each of the following words from p. 210 with its synonym.

1. insurrection [c]
2. expedient [h]
3. penitent [f]
4. inherent [a]
5. alacrity [d]

a. inborn
b. impulsive
c. rebellion
d. eagerness
e. corrupted

6. effectual [i]
7. impetuous [b]
8. eradication [g]
9. perverted [e]
10. posterity [j]

f. sorry
g. obliteration
h. means
i. productive
j. descendants

A Reading Skills

Recognizing persuasive techniques. Logical reasoning is Thoreau's first persuasive weapon. He begins with a paradox that challenges the reader to think logically: Can there be, simultaneously, government and no government? He then makes what appears to be a logical analogy: Because a standing government is like a standing army, it should be disbanded as soon as it is no longer needed. He ends the paragraph with another logical point: A government is subject to being manipulated by a few, contrary to the will of the many.

B Political Issue

Civil disobedience. Explain that many Americans, including Thoreau, believed that the United States had provoked the Mexican War in order to expand its slaveholding territory. Mexico had never recognized the independence of Texas and was clearly ready to go to war in order to prevent the loss of this enormous area.

C Reading Skills

? Recognizing persuasive techniques. What is Thoreau's logical argument here? [He argues that the government is not as forceful as one individual and accomplishes nothing on its own.] How does Thoreau add to the emotional appeal of his argument? [He increases its force by using parallelism and repetition ("It does not"), as if he were a speaker pointing his finger and raising his voice.]

Responses to Boxed Questions

1. He may mean that governments should trust their citizens to make their own decisions or that, in an ideal world, people would not need governments at all.

I heartily accept the motto—"That government is best which governs least";[1] and I should like to see it acted up to more rapidly and systematically. Carried out, it finally amounts to this, which also I believe—"That government is best which governs not at all"; and when men are prepared for it, that will be the kind of government which they will have. ❶ Government is at best but an expedient; but most governments are usually, and all governments are sometimes, inexpedient. The objections which have been brought against a standing army, and they are many and weighty, and deserve to prevail, may also at last be brought against a standing government. The standing army is only an arm of the standing government. The government itself, which is only the mode which the people have chosen to execute their will, is equally liable to be abused and perverted before the people can act through it. Witness the present Mexican war, the work of comparatively a few individuals using the standing government as their tool; for, in the outset, the people would not have consented to this measure.[2] ❷

This American government—what is it but a tradition, though a recent one,

> ❶ Thoreau opens his essay with a radical **paradox:** "That government is best which governs not at all."
>
> **?** *What does Thoreau mean?*

> ❷ Thoreau uses **logic** in providing an example of the problems with government.
>
> **?** *What is the example?*

endeavoring to transmit itself unimpaired to posterity, but each instant losing some of its integrity? It has not the vitality and force of a single living man; for a single man can bend it to his will. It is a sort of wooden gun to the people themselves; and, if ever they should use it in earnest as a real one against each other, it will surely split. But it is not the less necessary for this; for the people must have some complicated machinery or other, and hear its din, to satisfy that idea of government which they have. Governments show thus how successfully men can be imposed on, even impose on themselves, for their own advantage. It is excellent, we must all allow; yet this government never of itself furthered any enterprise, but by the alacrity with which it got out of its way. *It does not keep the country free. It does not settle the West. It does not educate.* ❸ The character inherent in the American people has done all that has been accomplished; and it would have done somewhat more, if the government had not sometimes got in its way. For government is an expedient by which men would fain[3] succeed in letting one another alone; and, as has been said, when it is most expedient, the governed are most let alone by it. Trade and commerce, if they were not made of India rubber, would never manage to bounce over the obstacles which legislators are continually putting in their way; and, if one

> ❸ Thoreau uses an **emotional appeal** in citing what the government does *not* do.
>
> **?** *What does government not do?*

---

1. **That ... least:** This statement, attributed to Thomas Jefferson, was the motto of the New York *Democratic Review,* which had published two of Thoreau's essays.
2. **this measure:** On May 9, 1846, President James K. Polk received word that Mexico had attacked U.S. troops. He then asked Congress to declare war, which it did on May 13. Some Americans, including Thoreau, thought the war was unjustified. Because Thoreau would not pay taxes to support the war, he went to jail.

3. **fain** *adv.:* archaic for "gladly; willingly."

Vocabulary

expedient (ek·spē′dē·ənt) *n.:* convenience; means to an end.
perverted (pər·vʉrt′id) *v.:* misdirected; corrupted.
posterity (päs·ter′ə·tē) *n.:* generations to come.
alacrity (ə·lak′rə·tē) *n.:* promptness in responding; eagerness.
inherent (in·hir′ənt) *adj.:* inborn; built-in.

---

2. His example is that the government has declared war on Mexico although the vast majority of Americans do not want war.

3. Government does not keep the country free, settle the West, or educate—all these actions are accomplished by individuals.

Learners Having Difficulty

Explain that this essay is a persuasive argument for civil disobedience—responsible refusal to obey laws that violate personal conscience. Encourage students to note the logical, ethical, and emotional arguments that Thoreau offers. As they read, students should decide whether they agree or disagree with each supporting argument.

were to judge these men wholly by the effects of their actions, and not partly by their intentions, they would deserve to be classed and punished with those mischievous persons who put obstructions on the railroads.

But, to speak practically and as a citizen, unlike those who call themselves no-government men, I ask for, not at once no government, but *at once* a better government. Let every man make known what kind of government would command his respect, and that will be one step toward obtaining it.

After all, the practical reason why, when the power is once in the hands of the people, a majority are permitted, and for a long period continue, to rule, is not because they are most likely to be in the right, nor because this seems fairest to the minority, but because they are physically the strongest. But a government in which the majority rule in all cases cannot be based on justice, even as far as men understand it. Can there not be a government in which majorities do not virtually decide right and wrong, but conscience?—in which majorities decide only those questions to which the rule of expediency is applicable? Must the citizen ever for a moment, or in the least degree, resign his conscience to the legislator? Why has every man a conscience, then? I think that we should be men first, and subjects afterward. It is not desirable to cultivate a respect for the law, so much as for the right. The only obligation which I have a right to assume, is to do at any time what I think right. . . . ❹

It is not a man's duty, as a matter of course, to devote himself to the eradication of any, even the most enormous wrong; he may still properly have other concerns to engage him; but it is his duty, at least, to wash his hands of it, and, if he gives it no thought longer, not to give it practically his support. If I devote myself to other pursuits and contemplations, I must first see, at least, that I

> **❓ ❹** What conflict does Thoreau see between majority rule and individual conscience?

do not pursue them sitting upon another man's shoulders. I must get off him first, that he may pursue his contemplations too. See what gross inconsistency is tolerated. I have heard some of my townsmen say, "I should like to have them order me out to help put down an insurrection of the slaves, or to march to Mexico—see if I would go"; and yet these very men have each, directly by their allegiance, and so indirectly, at least, by their money, furnished a substitute. The soldier is applauded who refuses to serve in an unjust war by those who do not refuse to sustain the unjust government which makes the war; is applauded by those whose own act and authority he disregards and sets at nought; as if the State were penitent to that degree that it hired one to scourge it while it sinned, but not to that degree that it left off sinning for a moment. Thus, under the name of order and civil government, we are all made at last to pay homage to and support our own meanness. After the first blush of sin, comes its indifference and from immoral it becomes, as it were, *un*moral, and not quite unnecessary to that life which we have made. . . . ❺

I meet this American government, or its representative the State government, directly, and face to face, once a year, no more, in the person of its tax gatherer; this is the only mode in which a man situated as I am necessarily meets it; and it then says distinctly, Recognize me; and the simplest, the most effectual, and, in the present posture of affairs, the indispensablest mode of treating with it on this head, of expressing your

> **❓ ❺** What ethical appeals does Thoreau make in this paragraph?

Vocabulary

eradication (ē·rad′i·kā′shən) *n.:* utter destruction; obliteration.

insurrection (in′sə·rek′shən) *n.:* rebellion; revolt.

penitent (pen′i·tənt) *adj.:* sorry for doing wrong.

effectual (e·fek′chōō·əl) *adj.:* productive; efficient.

Henry David Thoreau **213**

DIRECT TEACHING

ⓓ Political Issue

❓ Civil disobedience. What political assumption lies behind Thoreau's statement? [Thoreau assumes that all citizens bear the responsibility of communicating their ideas about the kind of government they want.]

ⓔ Literary Focus

❓ Paradox. What paradoxical behavior is Thoreau criticizing? [People in Concord disapprove of slavery and of America's war with Mexico; but when they purchase cotton or tobacco products, they add to the slavers' profits, and when they pay taxes, they support the war effort.]

Responses to Boxed Questions

4. Thoreau sees that majority rule runs the risk of usurping the role of individual conscience.

5. Thoreau asserts that each person has a moral duty to not support wrongdoing, even obliquely. The individual has an obligation to be consistent, not publicly saying one thing while silently allowing contrary things to happen.

Invite learners having difficulty to read "Resistance to Civil Government" in interactive format in *The Holt Reader* and to use the side-notes as aids to understanding the selection.

English-Language Learners
Help students summarize the major points that Thoreau makes: Government is a means to an end; people have a duty to not support what they feel is wrong; the "enlightened" state recognizes "the individual as a higher power."

A Reading Skills

Recognizing persuasive techniques. Point out to students that writers do not necessarily create an emotional appeal merely by using direct address and exclamation points. An emotional appeal can be generated by invoking a common experience. In this case, Thoreau uses the common experience of paying taxes (to a local official) to try to persuade readers that government forces people to consider one another in sometimes adversarial roles.

B Political Issue

? Civil disobedience. What is the political assumption behind Thoreau's belief in "one HONEST man"? [Thoreau believes fervently that one honest man can inspire others.]

C Literary Focus

? Paradox. Why does Thoreau not feel confined in prison? [His body is in prison, but his thoughts and convictions are free.]

Responses to Boxed Questions

6. Thoreau humanizes his argument by placing it in the context of his personal relationship with the tax gatherer and appealing for mutual respect. Students are likely to agree that one person can instigate change.

7. The comment about the abusive boys emphasizes the immaturity and mean-spiritedness of the State. The comparison to the woman with silver spoons suggests that the State is fearful of imaginary crimes, as a lonely, wealthy person is afraid of imaginary thieves.

---

little satisfaction with and love for it, is to deny it then. My civil neighbor, the tax gatherer, is the very man I have to deal with—for it is, after all, with men and not with parchment that I quarrel—and he has voluntarily chosen to be an agent of the government. How shall he ever know well what he is and does as an officer of the government, or as a man, until he is obliged to consider whether he shall treat me, his neighbor, for whom he has respect, as a neighbor and well-disposed man, or as a maniac and disturber of the peace, and see if he can get over this obstruction to his neighborliness without a ruder and more impetuous thought or speech corresponding with his action? I know this well, that if one thousand, if one hundred, if ten men whom I could name—if ten *honest* men only—aye, if *one* HONEST man, in this State of Massachusetts, *ceasing to hold slaves,* were actually to withdraw from this copartnership, and be locked up in the county jail therefor, it would be the abolition of slavery in America. For it matters not how small the beginning may seem to be: What is once well done is done forever.... ❻

I have paid no poll tax[4] for six years. I was put into a jail once on this account, for one night; and, as I stood considering the walls of solid stone, two or three feet thick, the door of wood and iron, a foot thick, and the iron grating which strained the light, I could not help being struck with the foolishness of that institution which treated me as if I were mere flesh and blood and bones, to be locked up. I wondered that it should have concluded at length that this was the best use it could put me to, and had never thought to avail itself of my

> ❻
> **? What emotional appeal** does Thoreau make in this paragraph? Do you think he is correct about one person being able to change the system?

---
4. **poll tax:** fee some states and localities required from each citizen as a qualification for voting. It is now considered unconstitutional in the United States to charge such a tax.

---

services in some way. I saw that, if there was a wall of stone between me and my townsmen, there was a still more difficult one to climb or break through, before they could get to be as free as I was. I did not for a moment feel confined, and the walls seemed a great waste of stone and mortar. I felt as if I alone of all my townsmen had paid my tax. They plainly did not know how to treat me, but behaved like persons who are underbred. In every threat and in every compliment there was a blunder; for they thought that my chief desire was to stand the other side of that stone wall. I could not but smile to see how industriously they locked the door on my meditations, which followed them out again without let or hindrance, and *they* were really all that was dangerous. As they could not reach me, they had resolved to punish my body; just as boys, if they cannot come at some person against whom they have a spite, will abuse his dog. I saw that the State was half-witted, that it was timid as a lone woman with her silver spoons, and that it did not know its friends from its foes, and I lost all my remaining respect for it, and pitied it.... ❼

The night in prison was novel and interesting enough. The prisoners in their shirt sleeves were enjoying a chat and the evening air in the doorway, when I entered. But the jailer said, "Come, boys, it is time to lock up"; and so they dispersed, and I heard the sound of their steps returning into the hollow apartments. My roommate was introduced to me by the jailer, as "a first-rate fellow and a clever man." When the door was locked, he showed me where to hang my hat, and how he managed matters there. The rooms were white-

> ❼
> **? Why might** Thoreau include this **anecdote** about the boys and the dog? What is the purpose of the comparison of the state to a woman with her silver spoons?

Vocabulary
impetuous (im·pech′o͞o·əs) adj.: impulsive.

Primary Source

Emerson on Thoreau

"If I knew only Thoreau, I should think cooperation of good men impossible," Emerson wrote. Yet he admired Thoreau's writing. In 1863, Emerson wrote: "In reading Henry Thoreau's journal, I am very sensible of the vigour of his constitution. That oaken strength which I noted whenever he walked, or worked, or surveyed woodlots, the same unhesitating hand with which a field-labourer accosts a piece of work, which I should shun as a waste of strength, Henry shows in his literary task. He has muscle, and ventures on and performs feats which I am forced to decline. In reading him, I find the same thought, the same spirit that is in me, but he takes a step beyond, and illustrates by excellent images that which I should have conveyed in a sleepy generality." Ask students whether they think Emerson's assessment of Thoreau is accurate.

washed once a month; and this one, at least, was the whitest, most simply furnished, and probably the neatest apartment in the town. He naturally wanted to know where I came from, and what brought me there; and, when I had told him, I asked him in my turn how he came there, presuming him to be an honest man, of course; and, as the world goes, I believe he was. "Why," said he, "they accuse me of burning a barn; but I never did it." As near as I could discover, he had probably gone to bed in a barn when drunk, and smoked his pipe there; and so a barn was burnt. He had the reputation of being a clever man, had been there some three months waiting for his trial to come on, and would have to wait as much longer; but he was quite domesticated and contented, since he got his board for nothing, and thought that he was well treated.

He occupied one window, and I the other; and I saw, that, if one stayed there long, his principal business would be to look out the window. I had soon read all the tracts that were left there, and examined where former prisoners had broken out, and where a grate had been sawed off, and heard the history of the various occupants of that room; for I found that even here there was a history and a gossip which never circulated beyond the walls of the jail. Probably this is the only house in the town where verses are composed, which are afterward printed in a circular form, but not published. I was shown quite a long list of verses which were composed by some young men who had been detected in an attempt to escape, who avenged themselves by singing them.

I pumped my fellow prisoner as dry as I could, for fear I should never see him again; but at length he showed me which was my bed, and left me to blow out the lamp.

It was like traveling into a far country, such as I had never expected to behold, to lie there for one night. It seemed to me that I never had heard the town clock strike before, nor the evening sounds of the village; for we slept with the windows open, which were inside the grat-

ing. It was to see my native village in the light of the middle ages, and our Concord was turned into a Rhine stream, and visions of knights and castles passed before me. They were the voices of old burghers that I heard in the streets. I was an involuntary spectator and auditor of whatever was done and said in the kitchen of the adjacent village inn—a wholly new and rare experience to me. It was a closer view of my native town. I was fairly inside of it. I never had seen its institutions before. This is one of its peculiar institutions; for it is a shire town.[5] I began to comprehend what its inhabitants were about. ❽

In the morning, our breakfasts were put through the hole in the door, in small oblong square tin pans, made to fit, and holding a pint of chocolate, with brown bread, and an iron spoon. When they called for the vessels again, I was green enough to return what bread I had left; but my comrade seized it, and said that I should lay that up for lunch or dinner. Soon after, he was let out to work at haying in a neighboring field, whither he went every day, and would not be back till noon; so he bade me good day, saying that he doubted if he should see me again.

When I came out of prison—for someone interfered, and paid the tax—I did not perceive that great changes had taken place on the common, such as he observed who went in a youth, and emerged a tottering and gray-headed man; and yet a change had to my eyes come over the scene—the town, and State, and country—greater than any that mere time could effect. I saw yet more distinctly the State in which I lived. I saw to what extent the people among whom I lived could be trusted as good neighbors and friends; that their friendship was for summer

> ❓ To what does Thoreau compare his night in jail? How does he explain his unusual comparison?

---

5. **shire town:** town where a court sits, like a county seat.

A **Political Issue**

? **Civil disobedience.** How does this passage summarize the political assumption that justifies civil disobedience? [Thoreau admits that he is willing to be governed only by laws that he has agreed to. In any other circumstances, he is free to disobey.]

B **Reading Skills**

Recognizing persuasive techniques. Ask students to explain Thoreau's final ethical appeal to his reader. [Thoreau's argument appeals to the widely accepted value of progress—that government has evolved from absolute monarchy to democracy and can improve further by recognizing the final authority of the individual.]

C **Literary Focus**

? **Paradox.** How could citizens live "aloof" from government and still fulfill the duties of "neighbors and fellow men"? [People could refuse to pay certain taxes, for example, and thus not receive certain governmental benefits—but still be honest and patriotic citizens.]

Responses to Boxed Questions

9. He criticizes his neighbors harshly for running no risks to stand up for what they profess to believe, and walking "straight and useless" paths to "save their souls."

10. He envisions a government that has the consent of the governed, that respects the individual as "a higher and independent power," and that is just to all people.

---

weather only; that they did not greatly purpose to do right; that they were a distinct race from me by their prejudices and superstitions, as the Chinamen and Malays are; that, in their sacrifices to humanity, they ran no risks, not even to their property; that, after all, they were not so noble but they treated the thief as he had treated them, and hoped, by a certain outward observance and a few prayers, and by walking in a particular straight though useless path from time to time, to save their souls. This may be to judge my neighbors harshly; for I believe that most of them are not aware that they have such an institution as the jail in their village. **⑨**

⑨
? Why does Thoreau criticize his neighbors so harshly?

It was formerly the custom in our village, when a poor debtor came out of jail, for his acquaintances to salute him, looking through their fingers, which were crossed to represent the grating of a jail window, "How do ye do?" My neighbors did not thus salute me, but first looked at me, and then at one another, as if I had returned from a long journey. I was put into jail as I was going to the shoemaker's to get a shoe which was mended. When I was let out the next morning, I proceeded to finish my errand, and, having put on my mended shoe, joined a huckleberry party, who were impatient to put themselves under my conduct; and in half an hour—for the horse was soon tackled[6]—was in the midst of a huckleberry field, on one of our highest hills, two miles off; and then the State was nowhere to be seen.

---
6. **tackled** v.: harnessed.

This is the whole history of "My Prisons." . . . The authority of government, even such as I am willing to submit to—for I will cheerfully obey those who know and can do better than I, and in many things even those who neither **A** know nor can do so well—is still an impure one: To be strictly just, it must have the sanction and consent of the governed. It can have no pure right over my person and property but what I concede to it. The progress from an absolute to a limited monarchy, from a limited monarchy to a democracy, is a progress toward a true respect for the individual. Is a democracy, such as we know it, the last improvement possible in government? Is it not possible to take a step further toward recognizing and organizing the rights of man? There will never be a really **B** free and enlightened State, until the State comes to recognize the individual as a higher and independent power, from which all its own power and authority are derived, and treats him accordingly. I please myself with imagining a State at last which can afford to be just to all men, and to treat the individual with respect as a neighbor; which even would not think it inconsistent with its own repose, if a few were to live **C** aloof from it, not meddling with it, nor embraced by it, who fulfilled all the duties of neighbors and fellow men. A State which bore this kind of fruit, and suffered it to drop off as fast as it ripened, would prepare the way for a still more perfect and glorious State, which also I have imagined, but not yet anywhere seen. **⑩** ■

⑩
Thoreau sums up his political ideas about ideal government.
? What does he envision as a truly just government?

DEVELOPING FLUENCY

Paired activity. Students can practice fluency by reading passages of the essay as if they were responses to questions in an interview. Have students work in pairs to write down three questions that can be answered by specific passages in the essay. Then, have them take turns asking the questions and reading aloud the answering passages.

FAMILY/COMMUNITY ACTIVITY

Ask students to use the library or the archives of their local newspapers to find stories of civil disobedience that have occurred in their town, city, county, or state. Then, have them present an oral report on the controversy, how the act of civil disobedience was carried out, how the community and law enforcement authorities responded, and to what extent the act achieved its goals. If possible, have them interview someone who participated.

Response and Analysis

Reading Check

1. Explain what Thoreau finds wrong with majority rule. What does he say is the only obligation he has the right to assume?

2. What does Thoreau predict about slavery in America?

3. Why was Thoreau put in jail? What were his feelings about the government while he was in jail?

4. At the end of the essay, what qualities does Thoreau envision in an ideal "perfect and glorious State"?

Thinking Critically

5. Identify the opposing ideas, and then explain the truth contained in each of these **paradoxes:**

   a. "I saw that, if there was a wall of stone between me and my towns-men, there was a still more difficult one to climb or break through, before they could get to be as free as I was." (page 214)

   b. "I felt as if I alone of all my town-men had paid my tax." (page 214)

6. How are Thoreau's perceptions of his fellow citizens changed by his night in jail?

7. What point is Thoreau making by telling us that he got his shoe fixed and led the huckleberry party on the day he was released?

Extending and Evaluating

8. Which of Thoreau's arguments did you find convincing, and which did you disagree with? What would be the effect on civil order if each person always followed his or her own conscience? Explain.

9. When Thoreau accepted release from jail (because someone else paid his tax), did he become just like the people he criticized—those who opposed the Mexican War and the expansion of slavery but supported it indirectly with their tax money? If he wanted to make a truly courageous and effective protest, should he have insisted on staying in jail? Explain your response.

Literary Criticism

10. From what you know about American Romanticism (pages 138–149), would you say that the assumptions and values that Thoreau reveals in this essay are fundamentally Romantic? Explain.

11. What influences of Emerson can you find in Thoreau's "Resistance to Civil Government"?

WRITING

Taking a Stand ✏️

What issue is important in your community today? Select an issue you feel strongly about, and write an **essay** using "Resistance to Civil Government" as your model. Argue for or against a particular solution to the issue. (Be sure to check your Quickwrite notes.) Be aware of the kinds of appeals you are using: Emotional appeals can be powerful, but logical ones will provide stronger support. Use a chart like the one below to organize your essay:

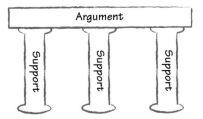

Argument / Support / Support / Support

Henry David Thoreau   217

go.hrw.com

INTERNET
Projects and Activities
Keyword: LE5 11-2

SKILLS FOCUS

Literary Skills
Analyze political points of view on a topic. Analyze paradox.

Writing Skills
Write a persuasive essay.

Vocabulary Skills
Create semantic maps. Clarify word meanings.

Response and Analysis

Thinking Critically

5. **a.** Although Thoreau is physically in prison, he is more free, intellectually and spiritually, than those who are imprisoned by conformity.

   b. By following his conscience and trying to improve the moral condition of his society, Thoreau feels he has figuratively paid his tax.

6. He thinks that they are hypocrites.

7. His point is that being jailed for one's conscience can be a normal part of life's duties and pleasures.

Extending and Evaluating

8. Some students may be impressed with the ethical argument that every individual has a responsibility to act according to conscience. Some students may feel that civil order would break down if each person followed his or her conscience without respect for the law.

9. Possible answers: No, staying in jail would have accomplished nothing. Yes, acceptance of that "interference" was a compromise.

Literary Criticism

10. Possible answer: Thoreau asserts the importance of being true to oneself and being wary of government's potentially corrupting power. He also shares the preference for nature over "civilization" and freedom of the imagination over conformity.

11. Thoreau puts into practice and radicalizes Emerson's ideas of self-reliance, integrity, and shaping one's own destiny.

Reading Check

1. Majority rule does not represent everyone's conscience, and it does not necessarily make just decisions. His only obligation is to do what he thinks is right.

2. Slavery will begin to break down when people are arrested for protesting it.

3. He refused to pay his poll tax. In jail, he lost respect for the State.

4. He envisions a State that recognizes the individual's ultimate authority and accepts the principled protests of nonconformists.

INDEPENDENT PRACTICE

Response and Analysis

Vocabulary Development

Sample Word Map Answer

Word—posterity. *Etymology*—from Latin *posterus*, "after." *Meaning*—descendants; future generations. *Related Words*—posterior, posthumous.

Language and Style

1. **a.** *Neutrality* denotes a refusal to take sides. *Apathy* denotes a lack of interest. Here, *indifference* means "moral apathy."

   b. *Unmoral* means that morality does not apply. *Immoral* means "corrupt."

2. **a.** It is a tax on each voter.

   b. A *pollster* takes people's "votes" in a non-electoral survey (a *poll*). Each word denotes a form of "counting heads," or gauging opinions.

ASSESSING

Assessment

- *Holt Assessment: Literature, Reading, and Vocabulary*

RETEACHING

For a lesson reteaching making assertions, see **Reteaching,** p. 1117A.

Vocabulary Development
Etymology

expedient	eradication
perverted	insurrection
posterity	penitent
alacrity	effectual
inherent	impetuous

You can learn the history of a word, or its **etymology,** by checking a good dictionary. Information about a word's etymology is usually found in brackets or parentheses before the word's definition(s). Make an etymology map like the one below for the remaining Vocabulary words in the list. In the "Related Words" box, list as many words as you can with the same origin.

> **Word**
> insurrection
>
> **Etymology**
> from L *insurgere*
> *in–,* = "in; upon" + *surgere,*
> "to rise"
>
> **Meaning**
> rising up against authority; rebellion
>
> **Related Words**
> insurgent, surge, resurgent, resurrect

Language and Style
Determining the Precise Meanings of Words

1. "After the first blush of sin," writes Thoreau on page 213, "comes its indifference and from immoral it becomes, as it were, *unmoral....*"

   a. The word *indifference* can mean "neutrality" or "apathy." What is the difference between the two meanings? Which meaning does the word *indifference* have in Thoreau's sentence?

   b. How is *unmoral* different from *immoral*?

2. Thoreau was arrested because he did not pay a "poll tax."

   a. The word *poll* comes from a Middle English word for "top of the head." Usage has added other meanings, including the sense of "individual" ("one head"). What do you think a poll tax is?

   b. What do the words *poll* and *pollster* mean today? How are they related to the sense of "head"?

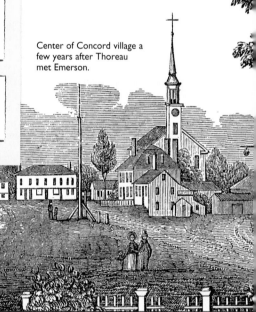

Center of Concord village a few years after Thoreau met Emerson.

DIFFERENTIATING INSTRUCTION

Learners Having Difficulty

In the writing assignment on p. 217, some students may have difficulty using Thoreau's "Resistance to Civil Government" as a model for a persuasive essay. The following questions may help them structure their essays:

- What is the problem or issue?
- What solution are you in favor of (or against)?

- How will the solution solve (or not solve) the problem?
- What is the logical reason for your position?
- What facts, examples, or personal experiences support your position?
- Why do you feel strongly about your position?
- Why should the reader agree with you?

Connected Readings

Civil Disobedience

Mohandas K. Gandhi ...... *from* **On Nonviolent Resistance**

Martin Luther King, Jr. ..... *from* **Letter from Birmingham City Jail**

You have just read Thoreau's "Resistance to Civil Government" and considered the views it expresses about civil disobedience. The next two selections—by Mohandas K. Gandhi and Martin Luther King, Jr.—present other points of view on civil disobedience. After you read these two selections, you'll find questions on pages 223–224 asking you to compare all three selections.

Political Points *of* View

Before You Read

Mohandas K. Gandhi (1869–1948), leader of India's fight for independence from British rule, is considered the father of his country. As a young lawyer, Gandhi worked for the rights of Indians living under the racist and repressive government of South Africa. From the 1920s to the mid-1940s, he led a prolonged *satyagraha* (noncooperation) campaign for Indian independence from the rule of Great Britain. Though Gandhi was often arrested and imprisoned for his actions, he urged his followers to hold to the principles of nonviolent resistance even in the face of violent tactics by those in power. After independence was granted by the British crown, Gandhi, himself a Hindu, fought desperately, and in the end ineffectively, to ease the religious tension between India's Muslims and Hindus. In 1948, Gandhi was assassinated by a Hindu fanatic.

Today Mohandas K. Gandhi (also called Mahatma, meaning "Great Soul") has assumed mythic stature as the embodiment of the principle of civil disobedience, or noncooperation with unjust laws.

The following is an excerpt from a 1916 speech on the principle of *satyagraha* and its use in the fight against the South African government. The speech was made to Gandhi's Hindu supporters after a prayer meeting at Kochrab Ashram in India, the retreat that served as Gandhi's first headquarters.

Mahatma Gandhi (August 1942).

Mohandas K. Gandhi　　**219**

Connected Reading

Summary ⬌ *at grade level*

In this speech, Mohandas K. Gandhi explains that *satyagraha*, or noncooperation, is a better means of combating injustice than violence and war, in which both sides ultimately suffer defeat. He bases his position on the firm belief that government depends upon the consent of the governed.

Selection Starter

Build background. When Gandhi was working for Indian rights in South Africa, he edited and published a newspaper, *Indian Opinion*. He had read "Civil Disobedience," which made a "deep impression" on him, and, as he wrote years later, "translated a portion for the readers of *Indian Opinion* [and] made copious extracts for the English part of the paper." Gandhi included a short biography of Thoreau and five columns of excerpts from "Civil Disobedience" that contained the essence of Thoreau's argument. Gandhi emphasized that Thoreau's "incisive logic is unanswerable" and that he "taught nothing he was not prepared to practice in himself."

CONTENT-AREA CONNECTIONS

Film and Music: Works on Gandhi

Two recent works have presented Gandhi's life and beliefs to a wide audience. In 1982, Richard Attenborough's film *Gandhi* dramatized the major events in his life. In 1980, American composer Philip Glass (born 1937) presented his opera *Satyagraha*, based on incidents in Gandhi's life. Each act of the opera focuses on an encounter with a historical figure renowned for nonviolence.

SPEECH

from On Nonviolent Resistance
Mohandas K. Gandhi

There are two ways of countering injustice. One way is to smash the head of the man who perpetrates injustice and to get your own head smashed in the process. All strong people in the world adopt this course. Everywhere wars are fought and millions of people are killed. The consequence is not the progress of a nation but its decline. . . . Pride makes a victorious nation bad-tempered. It falls into luxurious ways of living. Then for a time, it may be conceded, peace prevails. But after a short while, it comes more and more to be realized that the seeds of war have not been destroyed but have become a thousand times more nourished and mighty. No country has ever become, or will ever become, happy through victory in war. A nation does not rise that way; it only falls further. In fact, what comes to it is defeat, not victory. And if, perchance, either our act or our purpose was ill-conceived, it brings disaster to both belligerents.

But through the other method of combating injustice, we alone suffer the consequences of our mistakes, and the other side is wholly spared. This other method is *satyagraha*. One who resorts to it does not have to break another's head; he may merely have his own head broken. He has to be prepared to die himself suffering all the pain. In opposing the atrocious laws of the Government of South Africa, it was this method that we adopted. We made it clear to the said Government that we would never bow to its outrageous laws. No clapping is possible without two hands to do it, and no quarrel without two persons to make it. Similarly, no State is possible without two entities, the rulers and the ruled. You are our sovereign, our Government, only so long as we consider ourselves your subjects. When we are not subjects, you are not the sovereign either. So long as it is your endeavor to control us with justice and love, we will let you to do so. But if you wish to strike at us from behind, we cannot permit it. Whatever you do in other matters, you will have to ask our opinion about the laws that concern us. If you make laws to keep us suppressed in a wrongful manner and without taking us into confidence, these laws will merely adorn the statute books. We will never obey them. Award us for it what punishment you like; we will put up with it. Send us to prison and we will live there as in a paradise. Ask us to mount the scaffold and we will do so laughing. Shower what sufferings you like upon us; we will calmly endure all and not hurt a hair of your body. We will gladly die and will not so much as touch you. But so long as there is yet life in these our bones, we will never comply with your arbitrary laws.

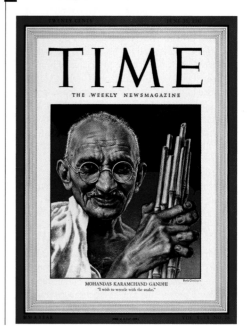

MOHANDAS KARAMCHAND GANDHI
"I wish to wrestle with the snake."

Literature and History: Thoreau's Influence

Thoreau scholar George Hendrick puts the influence of "Civil Disobedience" in perspective: "Gandhi found in Thoreau a practical man willing to practice his beliefs. It is a mistake, however, to overestimate Thoreau's influence upon Gandhi and the *Satyagraha* movement—to maintain that Gandhi did nothing original and merely applied Thoreauvian teachings. Gandhi himself protested to P. Kodanda Rao in 1935, 'The statement that I derived my idea of Civil Disobedience from the writings of Thoreau is wrong. The resistance to authority . . . was well advanced before I got the essay. . . .' The Passive Resistance movement, however, had not been tested when Gandhi first read 'Civil Disobedience,' and the essay offered confirmation of the effectiveness of deliberate resistance to unjust laws."

Martin Luther King, Jr., being booked for loitering as his stunned wife, Coretta, looks on (1958).

Political Points of View

Before You Read

Martin Luther King, Jr., the brilliant and eloquent leader of the U.S. civil rights movement in the 1960s, was inspired by the ideas of both Thoreau and Gandhi. King's courageous commitment to nonviolence and passive resistance captured the attention and respect of the nation. In April 1963, he led a campaign in Birmingham, Alabama, to end racial segregation at lunch counters and discrimination in hiring. While King and his supporters were on a peaceful march toward city hall, the police turned fire hoses on them and then arrested them. On April 16, 1963, while serving his sentence for marching without a permit, King wrote this open letter explaining his philosophy of nonviolent resistance.

OPEN LETTER

from Letter from Birmingham City Jail
Martin Luther King, Jr.

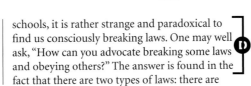

You express a great deal of anxiety over our willingness to break laws. This is certainly a legitimate concern. Since we so diligently urge people to obey the Supreme Court's decision of 1954 outlawing segregation in the public schools, it is rather strange and paradoxical to find us consciously breaking laws. One may well ask, "How can you advocate breaking some laws and obeying others?" The answer is found in the fact that there are two types of laws: there are

Connected Reading

Summary ⬌ *at grade level*

In this famous open letter, Martin Luther King, Jr. articulates the ethical and religious foundations of his theory of civil disobedience. He draws a distinction between just laws, which uphold the moral law of God, and those that violate it—such as the segregationist policies of the Alabama legislature. Such laws should not be defied or evaded for selfish reasons, but broken openly, with a willingness to pay the penalty for one's conscience. This, King concludes, is a moral act that upholds the highest principle of law itself.

Selection Starter

Build background. King was in Birmingham to lead a boycott against discriminatory stores. The goals of the boycott were to desegregate store facilities and establish fair hiring practices. On April 12, 1963, King defied an injunction against marching and led about fifty protesters in a peaceful march toward City Hall. Four blocks into the march, he was arrested.

DIRECT TEACHING

D Literary Focus

❓ Paradox. What is the paradox King admits? [He urges both obedience to and the deliberate breaking of the law.] **How does he explain the paradox?** [There are two types of laws—just and unjust.]

A Reading Skills

❓ Recognizing persuasive techniques. What persuasive technique does King use here? [He cites an authority—the brilliant theologian and moral philosopher Saint Augustine of Hippo (354–430).]

B Reading Skills

❓ Recognizing persuasive techniques. What persuasive techniques does King use here? [He uses logic, in analyzing Alabama's election process. He uses fact, in citing that there are counties without African Americans registered to vote. He uses a rhetorical question, with the sentence that begins "Can any law...." He uses personal experience when he refers to his own arrest.]

C Political Issue

❓ Civil disobedience. What political assumptions lie behind King's advocacy of civil disobedience? [He emphasizes that defiance of the law must be done with forethought, love of the principles involved, openness, and willingness to bear the penalty.]

D Reading Skills

❓ Recognizing persuasive techniques. Does King's final sentence appeal to the reader's reason, emotions, or morals? [Such an appeal to conscience is an ethical or moral argument.]

A just and there are unjust laws. I would agree with Saint Augustine that "An unjust law is no law at all."

Now what is the difference between the two? How does one determine when a law is just or unjust? A just law is a man-made code that squares with the moral law or the law of God. An unjust law is a code that is out of harmony with the moral law. . . .

B An unjust law is a code inflicted upon a minority which that minority had no part in enacting or creating because they did not have the unhampered right to vote. Who can say that the legislature of Alabama which set up the segregation laws was democratically elected? Throughout the state of Alabama all types of conniving methods are used to prevent Negroes from becoming registered voters and there are some counties without a single Negro registered to vote despite the fact that the Negro constitutes a majority of the population. Can any law set up in such a state be considered democratically structured?

These are just a few examples of unjust and just laws. There are some instances when a law is just on its face and unjust in its application. For instance, I was arrested Friday on a charge of parading without a permit. Now there is nothing wrong with an ordinance which requires a permit for a parade, but when the ordinance is used to preserve segregation and to deny citizens the First Amendment privilege of peaceful assembly and peaceful protest, then it becomes unjust.

I hope you can see the distinction I am trying to point out. In no sense do I advocate evading or defying the law as the rabid segregationist

C would do. This would lead to anarchy. One who breaks an unjust law must do it *openly, lovingly* (not hatefully as the white mothers did in New Orleans when they were seen on television screaming, "nigger, nigger, nigger"), and with a willingness to accept the penalty. I submit that an individual who breaks a law that conscience tells him is unjust, and willingly accepts the

D penalty by staying in jail to arouse the conscience of the community over its injustice, is in reality expressing the very highest respect for law.

Martin Luther King, Jr., in Birmingham City Jail, November 3, 1963.

CONTENT-AREA CONNECTIONS

Social Studies: Impetus for King's Letter

King wrote his famous letter in response to criticism of the Birmingham demonstration by clergymen whom King had believed to be at least passive supporters of his nonviolent protest. The clergymen's denunciation appeared in a newspaper article that King saw after being jailed. In *Parting the Waters,* Taylor Branch writes, "To King, these preachers never had risked themselves for true morality through all the years when [Birmingham civil rights leader Fred] Shuttlesworth was being bombed, stabbed, and arrested, and even now could not make themselves state forthrightly what was just. Instead, they stood behind the injunction and the jailers to dismiss his spirit along with his body. King could not let it go. He sat down and began scribbling around the margins of the newspaper. 'Seldom, if ever, do I pause to answer criticism of my work and ideas,' he began."

Analyzing **Political Points** *of* **View**

Civil Disobedience

The questions on this page ask you to analyze the views on civil disobedience that were expressed in the preceding three selections.

Henry David Thoreau . . . . . *from* **Resistance to Civil Government**
Mohandas K. Gandhi . . . . . . *from* **On Nonviolent Resistance**
Martin Luther King, Jr. . . . . . *from* **Letter from Birmingham City Jail**

Comparing Political Assumptions

1. In "Resistance to Civil Government," what does Thoreau mean by saying that he must not pursue his own interests while "sitting upon another man's shoulders. . . . I must get off him first" (page 213)? What details from the speech and letter show that Gandhi and King held this same idea?

2. Look back over the three texts, and list in chart form the **logical, ethical,** and **emotional appeals** you find in each one. Which of these arguments do you think is the most effective? Which is weakest? 📖

Kind of Appeal	Thoreau	Gandhi	King
Logical			
Ethical			
Emotional			

3. King and Gandhi drew their inspiration from Thoreau, who argues that if one honest man truly protested slavery and went willingly to jail for his belief, "it would be the abolition of slavery" (page 214). Explain how that single night in jail serves as the "small beginning" that expanded the campaigns of King and Gandhi?

4. Each writer you have read had specific ideas about the consequence of disobeying laws. Consider the following statements:

   a. "I did not for a moment feel confined, and the walls seemed a great waste. . . ." (Thoreau)

   b. "Send us to prison and we will live there as in a paradise." (Gandhi)

   c. "[Stay] in jail to arouse the conscience of the community. . . ." (King)

   What do these statements assume about the power of ideas and moral action versus the power of walls and physical punishment?

5. Consider the consistency of the political assumptions underlying Thoreau's essay, King's letter, and Gandhi's speech. What do all three writers believe about these questions:

SKILLS FOCUS

Pages 208–224 cover
Literary Skills
Analyze and compare political points of view on a topic.

Reading Skills
Analyze persuasive techniques (logical, ethical, and emotional appeals).

Writing Skills
Write a research report about civil disobedience.

Listening and Speaking Skills
Conduct a debate on the topic of civil disobedience.

Comparing and Contrasting Texts

Recognizing archetypes. Have students consider the different meanings of civil disobedience as expressed by Thoreau, Gandhi, and King. How do the men think and act alike? How do the men think and act differently? Have students share outside knowledge they have of each of the three men. Finally, have students articulate qualities that these men have in common that have led people to consider them heroes—qualities such as moral integrity, deep concern for other people, a vision of an ideal community, and commitment to putting ideals into practice.

Analyzing Political Points of View

Comparing Political Assumptions

1. Thoreau means that he must not support government actions that hurt others. Ghandi supports a method of protest in which "one who resorts to it does not have to break another's head," and King advocates breaking unjust laws "*lovingly.*"

2. Possible Answers

   Thoreau. Logical—because government rules by consent of the governed, he has a right to resist it; *Ethical*—action or inaction must not harm others; *Emotional*—experience of jail.

   Gandhi. Logical—violence leads only to defeat; *Ethical*—he will endure pain but will not hurt others; *Emotional*—assertion that "we will never obey."

   King. Logical—just laws should be obeyed, unjust laws resisted; *Ethical*—unjust laws are inflicted on a minority; *Emotional*—jail experience and African Americans denied the right to vote.

   Students may feel that logical and ethical arguments are stronger than emotional ones.

3. In Thoreau's example, Gandhi and King saw how civil disobedience worked in the real world. Thoreau's night in jail validated the principle of nonviolence and inspired the two leaders.

4. They assume that ideas and moral actions are more powerful than physical punishment.

5. They believe that the individual is the source of government's power; that consent of the governed determines whether a law is just; that only nonviolent protest succeeds; and that people must accept the consequences of their actions.

A Reading Skills

❓ Identifying details. Upon feeling the effects of the water, Colonel Killigrew begins to ogle and praise the widow. How is this in keeping with his behavior as a young man? [The colonel had "wasted his best years" in the pursuit of "sinful pleasures."]

the deep and sad inscriptions which Father Time had been so long engraving on their brows. The Widow Wycherly adjusted her cap, for she felt almost like a woman again.

"Give us more of this wondrous water!" cried they, eagerly. "We are younger—but we are still too old! Quick!—give us more!"

"Patience, patience!" quoth Dr. Heidegger, who sat watching the experiment, with philosophic coolness. "You have been a long time growing old. Surely, you might be content to grow young in half an hour! But the water is at your service."

Again he filled their glasses with the liquor of youth, enough of which still remained in the vase to turn half the old people in the city to the age of their own grandchildren. While the bubbles were yet sparkling on the brim, the doctor's four guests snatched their glasses from the table, and swallowed the contents at a single gulp. Was it <u>delusion</u>? Even while the draft[20] was passing down their throats, it seemed to have wrought a

change on their whole systems. Their eyes grew clear and bright; a dark shade deepened among their silvery locks; they sat around the table, three gentlemen of middle age and a woman, hardly beyond her buxom prime.

"My dear widow, you are charming!" cried Colonel Killigrew, whose eyes had been fixed ⒜ upon her face, while the shadows of age were flitting from it like darkness from the crimson daybreak.

The fair widow knew, of old, that Colonel Killigrew's compliments were not always measured by sober truth; so she started up and ran to the mirror, still dreading that the ugly visage of an old woman would meet her gaze. Meanwhile, the three gentlemen behaved in such a manner, as proved that the water of the Fountain of Youth possessed some intoxicating qualities; unless, indeed, their exhilaration of spirits were merely a lightsome dizziness, caused by the

---

20. **draft** *n.:* serving of a drink; large swallow.

Vocabulary
delusion (di·lōō′zhən) *n.:* false belief or opinion.

Developing Word-Attack Skills
Write these words from the selection on the chalkboard:

peculiar   riot   folio   marriage
patience   cordial   politician   illusion

Ask students what these eight words have in common. Help them recognize that in each word the letter *i* precedes another vowel, but the letter *i* stands for different sounds in

different words. Have volunteers read the words aloud and discuss the sound represented by *i* or the effect of *i* on the sound of the preceding consonant letter.

In *peculiar, i* stands for /y/.
In *riot, i* stands for a long *i.*
In *folio, i* stands for a long *e.*
In *marriage, i* is silent.
In *patience, i* after *t* stands for /sh/.

B **Advanced Learners**

❓ **Analyzing satire.** What might you infer about Hawthorne's view of politicians based on his description of Mr. Gascoigne? [Possible response: Hawthorne seems to be saying that politicians tend to utter the same empty phrases about patriotism and people's rights decade after decade while secretly making underhanded deals and promises.]

C **Literary Focus**

❓ **Subgenre: Allegory.** Think about the actions of the guests once they feel young again. What moral point does Hawthorne seem to make? [Possible response: People often seem unable to overcome certain character flaws; given the chance, they will indulge in the same destructive behavior that has proved disastrous in the past.]

Response to Boxed Question

6. Colonel Killigrew begins to flirt with the Widow Wycherly and sings a drinking song. Mr. Gascoigne utters a well-worn political speech. Mr. Medbourne dreams up a speculative scheme to harness whales to icebergs. Widow Wycherly primps coquettishly in the mirror.

sudden removal of the weight of years. Mr. Gascoigne's mind seemed to run on political topics, but whether relating to the past, present, or future, could not easily be determined, since the same ideas and phrases have been in vogue these fifty years. Now he rattled forth full-throated sentences about patriotism, national glory, and the people's right; now he muttered some perilous stuff or other, in a sly and doubtful whisper, so cautiously that even his own conscience could scarcely catch the secret; and now, again, he spoke in measured accents, and a deeply deferential tone, as if a royal ear were listening to his well-turned periods. Colonel Killigrew all this time had been trolling forth a jolly bottle song and ringing his glass in symphony with the chorus, while his eyes wandered toward the buxom figure of the Widow Wycherly. On the other side of the table, Mr. Medbourne was involved in a calculation of dollars and cents, with which was strangely intermingled a project for supplying the East Indies with ice, by harnessing a team of whales to the polar icebergs.

As for the Widow Wycherly, she stood before the mirror, curtsying and simpering[21] to her own image, and greeting it as the friend whom she loved better than all the world beside. She thrust her face close to the glass, to see whether some long-remembered wrinkle or crow's-foot had indeed vanished. She examined whether the snow had so entirely melted from her hair, that the venerable cap could be safely thrown aside. At last, turning briskly away, she came with a sort of dancing step to the table. ❻

"My dear old doctor," cried she, "pray favor me with another glass!"

> ❻ **How does each elderly subject in the experiment behave after his or her metamorphosis, or change in form?**

21. **simpering** *v.* used as *adv.*: smiling in a silly, self-conscious manner.

Vocabulary
deferential (def′ər·en′shəl) *adj.*: showing respect or courteous regard.

Nathaniel Hawthorne   **233**

Haw
As th
"Dr.
sugge
of the
lives.
journ:
time,
alway
ities

In *cordial*, *i* after *d* stands for /j/.
In *politician*, *i* with *c* stands for /sh/.
In *illusion*, *i* after *s* stands for /zh/.
Activity. Display the sets of words that follow. Have volunteers read the words and tell in which two words the letter *i* stands for the same sound. Encourage students to check pronunciations in a dictionary. Answers are underlined.

1. veracious	curious	precious
2. prandial	cordial	meridian
3. mysterious	delirium	audacious
4. foliage	carriage	foliated
5. deferential	magnolias	brilliant
6. delusion	mansion	intrusion

26. cc

VIEWING THE ART

Julius Gari Melchers (1860–1932) settled in Holland, where a sermon in a Dutch Reformed Church inspired this painting.

Activity. Have students identify which figures best illustrate the attitude of Mr. Hooper's parishioners the first time he preaches in his veil. [All of the parishioners, except for the one shown sleeping and the one who is observing her, would be fascinated by the minister's strange appearance.]

Ⓐ Reading Skills

❓ Drawing inferences. How would you explain the supposed movement of the corpse in this scene? [Possible response: The superstitious old woman imagines the shuddering based on her own response to Mr. Hooper.]

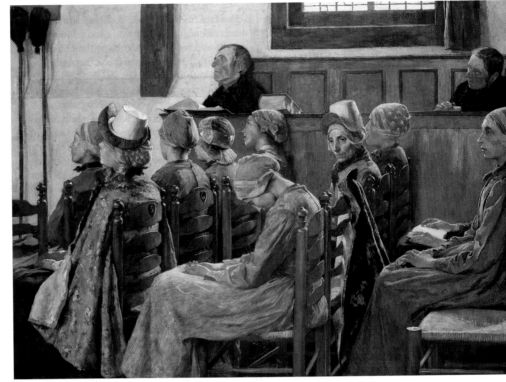

The Sermon (1886) by Julius Gari Melchers. Oil on canvas.

The afternoon service was attended with similar circumstances. At its conclusion, the bell tolled for the funeral of a young lady. The relatives and friends were assembled in the house, and the more distant acquaintances stood about the door, speaking of the good qualities of the deceased, when their talk was interrupted by the appearance of Mr. Hooper, still covered with his black veil. It was now an appropriate emblem. The clergyman stepped into the room where the corpse was laid, and bent over the coffin, to take a last farewell of his deceased parishioner. As he stooped, the veil hung straight down from his forehead, so that, if her eyelids had not been closed forever, the dead maiden might have seen his face. Could Mr. Hooper be fearful of her glance, that he so hastily caught back the black veil? A person, who watched the interview be-

Ⓐ tween the dead and living, scrupled[19] not to affirm, that, at the instant when the clergyman's features were disclosed, the corpse had slightly shuddered, rustling the shroud[20] and muslin cap, though the countenance retained the composure of death. A superstitious old woman was the only witness of this prodigy.[21] From the coffin, Mr. Hooper passed into the chamber of the mourners, and thence to the head of the staircase, to make the funeral prayer. It was a tender and heart-dissolving prayer, full of sorrow, yet so imbued with celestial[22] hopes, that the music

---

19. **scrupled** *v.*: hesitated.
20. **shroud** *n.*: cloth used to wrap a body for burial.
21. **prodigy** *n.*: something extraordinary or inexplicable.
22. **celestial** *adj.*: heavenly.

242 Collection 2 American Romanticism: 1800–1860

READING SKILLS REVIEW

Analyzing sentence structure. Review the process of breaking down long sentences by first finding the main subject and verb and then adding subsidiary clauses one by one. For example, point out that the sentence beginning on the last line of the first column on this page begins with the subject—*A person*. Instruct students to omit the clause within the commas and look for the main verb *scrupled*. With the base sentence in place, encourage students to add the other clauses one by one. This process would proceed as follows: (1) "The person who watched Mr. Hooper and the corpse did not hesitate to state that the corpse had shuddered." (2) "The person, who watched Mr. Hooper and the corpse, did not hesitate to affirm that, at the moment when the veil fell forward, the corpse had shuddered." (3) Build sentence until it is complete.

Activity. Have students repeat this process with a different sentence.

of a heavenly harp, swept by the fingers of the dead, seemed faintly to be heard among the saddest accents of the minister. The people trembled, though they but darkly understood him, when he prayed that they, and himself, and all of mortal race, might be ready, as he trusted this young maiden had been, for the dreadful hour that should snatch the veil from their faces. The bearers went heavily forth, and the mourners followed, saddening all the street, with the dead before them, and Mr. Hooper in his black veil behind.

"Why do you look back?" said one in the procession to his partner.

"I had a fancy," replied she, "that the minister and the maiden's spirit were walking hand in hand."

"And so had I, at the same moment," said the other. ❸

❸ What might this vision of the minister and the maiden's spirit symbolize?

That night, the handsomest couple in Milford village were to be joined in wedlock. Though reckoned a melancholy man, Mr. Hooper had a placid cheerfulness for such occasions, which often excited a sympathetic smile, where livelier merriment would have been thrown away. There was no quality of his disposition which made him more beloved than this. The company at the wedding awaited his arrival with impatience, trusting that the strange awe, which had gathered over him throughout the day, would now be dispelled. But such was not the result. When Mr. Hooper came, the first thing that their eyes rested on was the same horrible black veil, which had added deeper gloom to the funeral, and could portend nothing but evil to the wedding. Such was its immediate effect on the guests, that a cloud seemed to have rolled duskily from beneath the black crape, and dimmed the light of the candles. The bridal pair stood up before the minister. But the bride's cold fingers quivered in the tremulous[23] hand of the bridegroom, and her deathlike paleness caused a whisper, that the maiden who had been buried a few hours before, was come from

23. **tremulous** *adj.:* trembling.

her grave to be married. If ever another wedding were so dismal, it was that famous one, where they tolled the wedding knell.[24] After performing the ceremony, Mr. Hooper raised a glass of wine to his lips, wishing happiness to the new-married couple, in a strain of mild pleasantry that ought to have brightened the features of the guests, like a cheerful gleam from the hearth. At that instant, catching a glimpse of his figure in the looking glass, the black veil involved his own spirit in the horror with which it overwhelmed all others. His frame shuddered—his lips grew white—he spilt the untasted wine upon the carpet—and rushed forth into the darkness. For the Earth, too, had on her Black Veil. ❹

❹ How does the black veil affect the wedding?

The next day, the whole village of Milford talked of little else than Parson Hooper's black veil. That, and the mystery concealed behind it, supplied a topic for discussion between acquaintances meeting in the street, and good women gossiping at their open windows. It was the first item of news that the tavern keeper told to his guests. The children babbled of it on their way to school. One imitative little imp covered his face with an old black handkerchief, thereby so affrighting his playmates, that the panic seized himself, and he well nigh lost his wits by his own waggery.[25]

It was remarkable, that, of all the busybodies and impertinent people in the parish, not one ventured to put the plain question to Mr. Hooper, wherefore he did this thing. Hitherto, whenever there appeared the slightest call for such interference, he had never lacked advisers, nor shown himself averse to be guided by their judgment. If he erred at all, it was by so painful a degree of self-distrust, that even the mildest

24. **If . . . wedding knell:** reference to Hawthorne's story "The Wedding Knell." A knell is the ringing of a bell.
25. **waggery** *n.:* joke.

Vocabulary
portend (pôr·tend′) *v.:* signify.

Nathaniel Hawthorne   243

Literary Criticism

Critic's Commentary: James on Hawthorne
The great novelist Henry James (1843–1916) offered this assessment of Hawthorne: "The fine thing in Hawthorne is that he cared for the deeper psychology. . . . This natural, yet fanciful familiarity with it, . . . constitutes the originality of his tales. And then they have the further merit of seeming, for what they are, to

spring up so freely and lightly. The author has all the ease, indeed, of a regular dweller in the moral, psychological realm; he goes to and fro in it, as a man who knows his way. His tread is a light and modest one, but he keeps the key in his pocket."

Whole-class activity. Have students discuss whether James's opinion holds true for this story.

B Literary Focus
Allusion. Explain that the phrase *darkly understood* is a reference to I Corinthians 13:12 in the Bible: "For now we see through a glass, darkly, but then face to face: now I know in part; but then shall I know even as also I am known."

C Literary Focus
❓ **Symbolism.** What does the snatching away of the veil symbolize in this context? [It symbolizes the moment of death, when, according to Puritan beliefs, the external trappings of this life are cast aside, and one stands exposed before God's judgment.]

D Reading Skills
❓ **Drawing inferences.** What does the narrator mean when he says, "For the Earth, too, had on her Black Veil"? [Possible responses: Literally, he means it was night. Figuratively, he means that the material world and all its inhabitants have sins to veil.]

E Reading Skills
❓ **Drawing inferences.** Why doesn't anyone ask Mr. Hooper directly why he wears the veil? [Possible response: People are intimidated by the sight of it and don't really want to learn the answer. Deep down they suspect it has to do with their own sins.]

Responses to Boxed Questions

3. The vision might symbolize that the minister had some secret relationship with the maiden or that the minister can communicate with spirits.

4. The veil casts a dark cloud over the wedding, even frightening Mr. Hooper himself.

A Reading Skills

? Drawing inferences. The deputation defers the matter of the veil to the synod not because it is "too weighty" but because they see Hooper's veil as "a symbol of a fearful secret between him and them." What do you think this secret might really be, based on the story so far? [Possible response: The deputies' secret awareness that they themselves, like the minister, are less pious and more sinful than they appear in public.]

B Reading Skills

Speculating. Have students note that Mr. Hooper chooses to set himself off from the world—and even from his fiancée. Ask students to speculate about his motives. [Some students will feel that he has chosen to separate himself as a sacrifice to God and as an example for his congregation; others will feel that he does so as penance for some misdeed or out of pride.]

Responses to Boxed Questions

5. The members of the delegation become so frightened by the veil and what it might mean that they decide not to broach the subject.

6. The passage shows that the minister will never remove the veil and suggests that he sees it as a symbol of the world's separation from God.

---

censure[26] would lead him to consider an indifferent action as a crime. Yet, though so well acquainted with this amiable[27] weakness, no individual among his parishioners chose to make the black veil a subject of friendly remonstrance.[28] There was a feeling of dread, neither plainly confessed nor carefully concealed, which caused each to shift the responsibility upon another, till at length it was found expedient to send a deputation[29] of the church, in order to deal with Mr. Hooper about the mystery, before it should grow into a scandal. Never did an embassy so ill discharge its duties. The minister received them with friendly courtesy, but became silent, after they were seated, leaving to his visitors the whole burden of introducing their important business. The topic, it might be supposed, was obvious enough. There was the black veil, swathed round Mr. Hooper's forehead, and concealing every feature above his placid mouth, on which, at times, they could perceive the glimmering of a melancholy smile. But that piece of crape, to their imagination, seemed to hang down before his heart, the symbol of a fearful secret between him and them. Were the veil but cast aside, they might speak freely of it, but not till then. Thus they sat a considerable time, speechless, confused, and shrinking uneasily from Mr. Hooper's eye, which they felt to be fixed upon them with an invisible glance. Finally, the deputies returned abashed to their constituents, pronouncing the matter too weighty to be handled, except by a council of the churches, if, indeed, it might not require a general synod.[30]

5

? What happens when the church sends a delegation to talk to Mr. Hooper?

But there was one person in the village, unappalled by the awe with which the black veil had impressed all beside herself. When the

---

26. **censure** *n.:* expression of strong disapproval or criticism.
27. **amiable** *adj.:* friendly; likable.
28. **remonstrance** *n.:* protest; complaint.
29. **deputation** *n.:* group of representatives.
30. **synod** (sin′əd) *n.:* governing body of a group of churches.

---

deputies returned without an explanation, or even venturing to demand one, she, with the calm energy of her character, determined to chase away the strange cloud that appeared to be settling round Mr. Hooper, every moment more darkly than before. As his plighted[31] wife, it should be her privilege to know what the black veil concealed. At the minister's first visit, therefore, she entered upon the subject, with a direct simplicity, which made the task easier both for him and her. After he had seated himself, she fixed her eyes steadfastly upon the veil, but could discern nothing of the dreadful gloom that had so overawed the multitude: It was but a double fold of crape, hanging down from his forehead to his mouth, and slightly stirring with his breath.

"No," said she aloud, and smiling, "there is nothing terrible in this piece of crape, except that it hides a face which I am always glad to look upon. Come, good sir, let the sun shine from behind the cloud. First lay aside your black veil: Then tell me why you put it on."

Mr. Hooper's smile glimmered faintly.

"There is an hour to come," said he, "when all of us shall cast aside our veils. Take it not amiss, beloved friend, if I wear this piece of crape till then."

"Your words are a mystery too," returned the young lady. "Take away the veil from them, at least."

"Elizabeth, I will," said he, "so far as my vow may suffer me. Know, then, this veil is a type and a symbol, and I am bound to wear it ever, both in light and darkness, in solitude and before the gaze of multitudes, and as with strangers, so with my familiar friends. No mortal eye will see it withdrawn. This dismal shade must separate me from the world: Even you, Elizabeth, can never come behind it!"

6

? Why is this a key passage in the story?

"What grievous affliction hath befallen you," she earnestly inquired, "that you should thus darken your eyes forever?"

---

31. **plighted** *v.* used as *adj.:* promised.

CONTENT-AREA CONNECTIONS

Social Studies: Puritanism in New England

In Puritan New England, sin was a constant topic of conversation and a frequent sermon subject. To the Puritans, sin most often meant "original sin," the belief that humans are born in a state of sin, an innate alienation from God resulting from the first, or original, sin of Adam and Eve. Calvinists of the Puritan era believed that people were predestined by God either to be saved from sin or to be damned. Puritans were anxious to determine whether they were saved and tended to view a moral lifestyle and material success as evidence of such salvation.

In addition to original sin, sin could mean any violation of the Ten Commandments or a minor offense such as speaking harshly to a neighbor.

> Her eyes were fixed insensibly on the black veil,
> when, like a sudden twilight in the air, its terrors fell around her.

"If it be a sign of mourning," replied Mr. Hooper, "I, perhaps, like most other mortals, have sorrows dark enough to be typified by a black veil."

"But what if the world will not believe that it is the type of an innocent sorrow?" urged Elizabeth. "Beloved and respected as you are, there may be whispers, that you hide your face under the consciousness of secret sin. For the sake of your holy office, do away this scandal!"

The color rose into her cheeks, as she intimated the nature of the rumors that were already abroad in the village. But Mr. Hooper's mildness did not forsake him. He even smiled again—that same sad smile, which always appeared like a faint glimmering of light, proceeding from the obscurity beneath the veil.

"If I hide my face for sorrow, there is cause enough," he merely replied; "and if I cover it for secret sin, what mortal might not do the same?"

And with this gentle, but unconquerable obstinacy,[32] did he resist all her entreaties. At length Elizabeth sat silent. For a few moments she appeared lost in thought, considering, probably, what new methods might be tried, to withdraw her lover from so dark a fantasy, which, if it had no other meaning, was perhaps a symptom of mental disease. Though of a firmer character than his own, the tears rolled down her cheeks. But, in an instant, as it were, a new feeling took the place of sorrow: Her eyes were

---

32. **obstinacy** *n.:* stubbornness; willfulness.

fixed insensibly on the black veil, when, like a sudden twilight in the air, its terrors fell around her. She arose, and stood trembling before him.

"And do you feel it then at last?" said he mournfully.

She made no reply, but covered her eyes with her hand, and turned to leave the room. He rushed forward and caught her arm.

"Have patience with me, Elizabeth!" cried he passionately. "Do not desert me, though this veil must be between us here on earth. Be mine, and hereafter there shall be no veil over my face, no darkness between our souls! It is but a mortal veil—it is not for eternity! Oh! you know not how lonely I am, and how frightened to be alone behind my black veil. Do not leave me in this miserable obscurity forever!"

"Lift the veil but once, and look me in the face," said she.

"Never! It cannot be!" replied Mr. Hooper.

"Then, farewell!" said Elizabeth.

She withdrew her arm from his grasp, and slowly departed, pausing at the door, to give one long, shuddering gaze, that seemed almost to penetrate the mystery of the black veil. But, even amid his grief, Mr. Hooper smiled to think that only a material emblem had separated him from happiness, though the horrors which it shadowed forth, must be drawn darkly between the fondest of lovers. ❼

From that time no attempts were made to

> ❼ What is the result of the encounter between Elizabeth and Mr. Hooper?

Nathaniel Hawthorne   245

Nathaniel Hawthorne   245

A Literary Focus

? Symbolism. How does the black veil affect Mr. Hooper's relationship with the villagers? [Possible responses: Some people say he is eccentric, and most avoid him whenever possible; some say he is responsible for a great crime; he is cut off from love and sympathy.]

B Reading Skills

? Drawing inferences. Why do people come to deeply respect Mr. Hooper as a clergyman? [Possible responses: In personally taking on this mysterious emblem of sin and sorrow, Hooper makes people feel the moral and spiritual stakes of their own lives. Much more than a personal symbol of guilt, Hooper's veil comes to symbolize sin itself and makes sinners feel that he, above all, understands their struggles and can lead them to goodness.]

Response to Boxed Question

8. Many villagers whisper that Mr. Hooper must have committed some great crime; others suspect he can see the spirits of the dead and uses the veil to hide them from his sight.

A remove Mr. Hooper's black veil, or, by a direct appeal, to discover the secret which it was supposed to hide. By persons who claimed a superiority to popular prejudice, it was reckoned merely an eccentric whim, such as often mingles with the sober actions of men otherwise rational, and tinges them all with its own semblance of insanity. But with the multitude, good Mr. Hooper was irreparably a bugbear.[33] He could not walk the streets with any peace of mind, so conscious was he that the gentle and timid would turn aside to avoid him, and that others would make it a point of hardihood to throw themselves in his way. The impertinence of the latter class compelled him to give up his customary walk, at sunset, to the burial ground; for when he leaned pensively over the gate, there would always be faces behind the gravestones, peeping at his black veil. A fable went the rounds, that the stare of the dead people drove him thence. It grieved him, to the very depth of his kind heart, to observe how the children fled from his approach, breaking up their merriest sports, while his melancholy figure was yet afar off. Their instinctive dread caused him to feel, more strongly than aught else, that a preternatural[34] horror was interwoven with the threads of the black crape. In truth, his own antipathy to the veil was known to be so great, that he never willingly passed before a mirror, nor stooped to drink at a still fountain, lest, in its peaceful bosom, he should be affrighted by himself. This was what gave plausibility to the whispers, that Mr. Hooper's conscience tortured him for some great crime, too horrible to be entirely concealed, or otherwise than so obscurely intimated. Thus, from beneath the black veil, there rolled a cloud into the sunshine, an ambiguity of sin or sorrow, which enveloped the poor minister, so that love or sympathy could never reach him. It was said, that ghost and fiend consorted with him there. With self-shudderings and outward terrors, he walked continually in its shadow, groping darkly within his own soul,

---

33. **bugbear** *n.*: source of irrational fears.
34. **preternatural** *adj.*: abnormal; supernatural.

---

or gazing through a medium that saddened the whole world. Even the lawless wind, it was believed, respected his dreadful secret, and never blew aside the veil. But still good Mr. Hooper sadly smiled, at the pale visages of the worldly throng as he passed by. **8**

B Among all its bad influences, the black veil had the one desirable effect, of making its wearer a very efficient clergyman. By the aid of his mysterious emblem—for there was no other apparent cause—he became a man of awful power, over souls that were in agony for sin. His converts always regarded him with a dread peculiar to themselves, affirming, though but figuratively, that, before he brought them to celestial light, they had been with him behind the black veil. Its gloom, indeed, enabled him to sympathize with all dark affections. Dying sinners cried aloud for Mr. Hooper, and would not yield their breath till he appeared; though ever, as he stooped to whisper consolation, they shuddered at the veiled face so near their own. Such were the terrors of the black veil, even when Death had bared his visage! Strangers came long distances to attend service at his church, with the mere idle purpose of gazing at his figure, because it was forbidden them to behold his face. But many were made to quake ere they departed! Once, during Governor Belcher's[35] administration, Mr. Hooper was appointed to preach the election sermon. Covered with his black veil, he stood before the chief magistrate, the council, and the representatives, and wrought so deep an impression, that the legislative measures of that year, were characterized by

8 *What do the villagers think is the reason their pastor wears the veil?*

---

35. **Governor Belcher's:** Jonathan Belcher (1681?–1757) was governor of the Massachusetts Bay Colony from 1730 to 1741.

Vocabulary

pensively (pen′siv·lē) *adv.*: thinking deeply or seriously.
antipathy (an·tip′ə·thē) *n.*: strong dislike.
plausibility (plô′zə·bil′ə·tē) *n.*: believability.

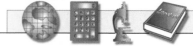

CONTENT-AREA CONNECTIONS

Social Studies: Veils

Individual activity. Have students report on the wearing of veils in different cultures around the world. Ask students to investigate the historical, religious, and political origins of these customs as well as their present-day purposes. Ask students to address the following questions:

- Who wears veils?
- Why and when do they wear veils?
- What countries have laws governing the wearing of veils?
- How do various women's and human rights groups respond to these laws?
- How are veil-wearing customs around the world similar? How are they different?

all the gloom and piety of our earliest ancestral sway. **9**

In this manner Mr. Hooper spent a long life, irreproachable[36] in outward act, yet shrouded in dismal suspicions; kind and loving, though unloved, and dimly feared; a man apart from men, shunned in their health and joy, but ever summoned to their aid in mortal anguish. As years wore on, shedding their snows above his sable veil, he acquired a name throughout the New England churches, and they called him Father Hooper. Nearly all his parishioners, who were of mature age when he was settled, had been borne away by many a funeral: He had one congregation in the church, and a more crowded one in the churchyard; and having wrought so late into the evening, and done his work so well, it was now good Father Hooper's turn to rest.

Several persons were visible by the shaded candlelight, in the death chamber of the old clergyman. Natural connections he had none. But there was the decorously grave, though un-moved physician, seeking only to mitigate[37] the last pangs of the patient whom he could not save. There were the deacons, and other emi-nently pious members of his church. There, also, was the Reverend Mr. Clark, of Westbury, a young and zealous divine, who had ridden in haste to pray by the bedside of the expiring minister. There was the nurse, no hired hand-maiden of death, but one whose calm affection had endured thus long, in secrecy, in solitude, amid the chill of age, and would not perish, even at the dying hour. Who, but Elizabeth! And there lay the hoary head of good Father Hooper upon the death-pillow, with the black veil still swathed about his brow and reaching down over his face, so that each more difficult gasp of his faint breath caused it to stir. All through life that piece of crape had hung between him and the world: It had separated him from cheerful

9 ? How does the veil affect Mr. Hooper?

brotherhood and woman's love, and kept him in that saddest of all prisons, his own heart; and still it lay upon his face, as if to deepen the gloom of his darksome chamber, and shade him from the sun-shine of eternity. **10**

10 ? What do we learn about Elizabeth, whom Hooper has loved?

For some time previous, his mind had been confused, wavering doubt-fully between the past and the present, and hov-ering forward, as it were, at intervals, into the indistinctness of the world to come. There had been feverish turns, which tossed him from side to side, and wore away what little strength he had. But in his most convulsive struggles, and in the wildest vagaries of his intellect, when no other thought retained its sober influence, he still showed an awful solicitude lest the black veil should slip aside. Even if his bewildered soul could have forgotten, there was a faithful woman at his pillow, who, with averted eyes, would have covered that aged face, which she had last beheld in the comeliness of manhood. At length the death-stricken old man lay quietly in the torpor[38] of mental and bodily exhaus-tion, with an imperceptible pulse, and breath that grew fainter and fainter, except when a long, deep, and irregular inspiration[39] seemed to prelude the flight of his spirit.

The minister of Westbury approached the bedside.

"Venerable Father Hooper," said he, "the mo-ment of your release is at hand. Are you ready for the lifting of the veil, that shuts in time from eternity?"

Father Hooper at first replied merely by a feeble motion of his head; then, apprehensive, perhaps, that his meaning might be doubtful, he exerted himself to speak.

"Yea," said he, in faint accents, "my soul hath a patient weariness until that veil be lifted."

"And is it fitting," resumed the Reverend Mr. Clark, "that a man so given to prayer, of such a

---

36. **irreproachable** *adj.*: blameless.
37. **mitigate** *v.*: make less painful.

38. **torpor** *n.*: dull or sluggish state.
39. **inspiration** *n.*: inhaling.

Nathaniel Hawthorne **247**

DIRECT TEACHING

C **Learners Having Difficulty**

? **Paraphrasing.** How might this text be paraphrased? [He had served the church for so long that his deceased parishioners outnumbered his living ones; having worked so hard for so long, he deserved the peace of death.]

D **Literary Focus**

? **Symbolism.** In what sense can the human heart be a prison? [Possible responses: For someone who harbors a sense of guilt, the heart (or soul or psyche) is a prison. A sense of sin can make people suffer.]

Responses to Boxed Questions

9. The veil leaves him sad and unloved but makes him a better clergyman because sinners see in him a kindred spirit.

10. Elizabeth has continued to love Hooper over the years and serves as his nurse in his dying hours.

Literary Criticism

Critic's Commentary: Canaday and Poe on "The Minister's Black Veil"

Critic Nicholas Canaday argues that the black veil stands not for secret sin but pride. "At the end of his life, Mr. Hooper pridefully reveals his so-called motive for donning the black veil, that it typifies the veiling deceptions of all men. In his famous comment on this story, Poe rightly calls this speech,

'The moral put into the mouth of the dying minister' and correctly sees that this overt moral is not 'the true import of the narrative.' Yet the true import escapes Poe. Hawthorne is not stressing secret sin in this tale, especially sexual sin as Poe suggests. [See p. 249, ques-tion 13.] Rather he is exploring the sin of pride with its demoniac pretensions and inhuman results. The misguided minister,

aware of the finiteness of the human condition, yet daring to resent it, seeks to compensate for it and thus to overcome it. With satanic irony Mr. Hooper dons the veil in order to gain an absolute perspective on life. The final irony is Hawthorne's, for whom the veil must symbolize the imperfect human vision, which, because of the finiteness of the human condition, sees only darkly."

Nathaniel Hawthorne **247**

> There he sat, shivering with the arms of death around him, while the black veil hung down...

❓ Symbolism. Why does Mr. Hooper claim to see a black veil on every human face? What is he saying in this final argument? [Hooper points out that he has not been shunned and isolated for any "horrible crime" of his own, but because the mystery of his symbolic gesture reminded people of their own secret sins, their own "black veils." He insists that he is no monster, and that his only goal was to be honest before God and humanity about a truth that everyone else hides.]

Ⓑ Reading Skills

❓ Evaluating. Is Mr. Hooper a sympathetic or unsympathetic character, and how does Elizabeth's character help to define his? [Most students will say that they feel sorry for Hooper and that Elizabeth's character illuminates both Hooper's strengths and failures.] Discuss Hawthorne's purpose. Is he examining the destructive effect of guilt for some dark deed? the destructive effect of public hypocrisy (or the need for such hypocrisy)? the "veils" people hide behind? all of these? something else? Does Hawthorne succeed in his purpose? Explain your response.

Responses to Boxed Questions

11. Reverend Clark suggests that leaving the veil on will leave a shadow on Hooper's name, which suggests that he had not led a triumphant Christian life.

12. Hooper suggests that people's own sins cause them to react with fear and horror to the veil, making the symbol all the more awful.

---

blameless example, holy in deed and thought, so far as mortal judgment may pronounce; is it fitting that a father in the church should leave a shadow on his memory, that may seem to blacken a life so pure? I pray you, my venerable brother, let not this thing be! Suffer us to be gladdened by your triumphant aspect, as you go to your reward. Before the veil of eternity be lifted, let me cast aside this black veil from your face!" ⑪

> ⑪
> ❓ What reasons does Reverend Clark give for lifting the black veil?

And thus speaking, the Reverend Mr. Clark bent forward to reveal the mystery of so many years. But, exerting a sudden energy, that made all the beholders stand aghast, Father Hooper snatched both his hands from beneath the bedclothes, and pressed them strongly on the black veil, <u>resolute</u> to struggle, if the minister of Westbury would contend with a dying man.

"Never!" cried the veiled clergyman. "On earth, never!"

"Dark old man!" exclaimed the affrighted minister, "with what horrible crime upon your soul are you now passing to the judgment?"

Father Hooper's breath heaved; it rattled in his throat; but, with a mighty effort, grasping forward with his hands, he caught hold of life, and held it back till he should speak. He even raised himself in bed; and there he sat, shivering with the arms of death around him, while the black veil hung down, awful, at that last moment, in the gathered terrors of a lifetime. And yet the faint, sad smile, so often there, now

seemed to glimmer from its obscurity, and linger on Father Hooper's lips.

"Why do you tremble at me alone?" cried he, turning his veiled face round the circle of pale spectators. "Tremble also at each other! Have men avoided me, and women shown no pity, and children screamed and fled, only for my black veil? What, but the mystery which it obscurely typifies, has made this piece of crape so awful? When the friend shows his inmost heart to his friend; the lover to his best beloved; when man does not vainly shrink from the eye of his Creator, loathsomely treasuring up the secret of his sin; then deem me a monster, for the symbol beneath which I have lived, and die! I look around me, and, lo! on every visage a Black Veil!" ⑫

> ⑫
> This is the **climax** of the story.
> ❓ What does Hooper say has made the veil so awful?

While his auditors shrank from one another, in mutual affright, Father Hooper fell back upon his pillow, a veiled corpse, with a faint smile lingering on the lips. Still veiled, they laid him in his coffin, and a veiled corpse they bore him to the grave. The grass of many years has sprung up and withered on that grave, the burial stone is moss-grown, and good Mr. Hooper's face is dust; but awful is still the thought, that it moldered beneath the Black Veil! ∎

Vocabulary
resolute (rez′ə·loot′) *adj.:* determined.

Monitoring students' progress. Ask students to respond to these statements.

True-False

1. The veil makes Hooper an effective minister. [T]

2. Hooper himself is horrified to see what he looks like with the veil on. [T]

3. No one besides his fiancée ever asks Hooper why he wears the veil. [T]

4. Hooper draws back his veil before dying. [F]

Response and Analysis

Reading Check

1. How does the congregation respond at first to Mr. Hooper's black veil? Why?

2. In a single afternoon, Hooper presides at both a funeral and a wedding. How do people react to the presence of the veil at each event?

3. What explanation does Hooper give to Elizabeth, his fiancée, for wearing the veil? What arguments against wearing the veil does she make?

Thinking Critically

4. Briefly describe Hooper's **character** as revealed in the story's opening paragraphs. What does the congregation's attitude toward him seem to have been before the appearance of the veil?

5. Explain the narrator's remark on page 247 about the human heart being the "saddest of all prisons." Do you agree or disagree? Do you think this observation refers only to Hooper, or is it true of everyone in the story? Explain your response.

6. **Tone** is the attitude a writer takes toward a subject. Would you describe this narrator's tone as neutral or emotional? (Think particularly of the words the narrator uses in referring to the veil.) Write down words and phrases that contribute to the story's tone.

7. Trace the progression of Elizabeth's responses to the veil. How do you explain her changing attitudes?

8. On his deathbed, Hooper says, "I look around me, and, lo! on every visage a Black Veil!" What does Hooper mean? In what ways is Hooper's veil a **symbol**?

9. Look for evidence in the story that suggests more than one **symbolic meaning** for the black veil. What are some of these meanings?

10. Does Hooper's veil have any positive effects during his long life? Use details from the story to support your answer.

11. Why do you think the villagers bury Hooper without removing the veil?

12. What would you say is the moral lesson of this **parable**—the **theme,** or insight it provides about our human existence?

Extending and Evaluating

12. Edgar Allan Poe said that Hooper wore the veil because "a crime of dark dye (having reference to the 'young lady') has been committed." What do you think Poe is referring to? Do you think the story would be more effective if Hawthorne had revealed precisely why Hooper wears the veil? Explain.

INTERNET
Projects and Activities
Keyword: LE5 11-2

WRITING

Behind the Veil: Analyzing the Story

In a brief **essay,** analyze the way that the black veil functions in this story. Trace Hooper's use of the veil and its effects on him and people in the community. Using the inferences you made while reading, follow the effects of the veil right through to its shocking appearance on Hooper's face on his deathbed. Conclude with your interpretation of what the black veil **symbolizes.**

Comparing Literature

In a brief **essay,** compare and contrast the attitudes revealed in Hawthorne's story to attitudes held by Puritans such as Jonathan Edwards (see "Sinners in the Hands of an Angry God," page 46). Consider especially attitudes toward sin, guilt, and the conditions necessary for salvation. How do you think Hawthorne felt about the tenets of Puritanism?

SKILLS FOCUS

Literary Skills
Analyze symbolism.

Reading Skills
Make inferences.

Writing Skills
Write an essay analyzing a symbol. Write an essay comparing and contrasting authors' attitudes.

Vocabulary Skills
Create semantic charts. Use context clues to understand archaic words.

Nathaniel Hawthorne **249**

Response and Analysis

Thinking Critically

4. Hooper is neat, gentle, and kind, and his congregation seems to have been fond of him.

5. Anyone who cannot share emotions regarding shame and sin is in a personal prison.

6. The narrator presents unusual events in a detached way, but he also adds to the tragic tone with connotative language such as "darkened aspect" and "gloomy shade."

7. At first, Elizabeth is loving, but when Hooper resists her pleas to remove his veil, she becomes sad and then terrified. She may fear that he has committed a crime; she may fear his preoccupation with universal sin; she may fear for her own soul.

8. He may mean that everyone is a sinner; the veil represents something in addition to itself.

9. Symbolic meanings include Hooper's own secret sin; the sins of his parishioners; Hooper's (and everyone's) isolation from God.

10. It makes Mr. Hooper a more effective minister, especially with people who have sinned.

11. They do so out of respect or fear.

12. Possible themes: We should all admit we are secret sinners; we should not be too quick to judge others; we must learn to acknowledge our sins but also welcome God's forgiveness and people's love.

Extending and Evaluating

13. Poe suggests an illicit sexual relationship between Hooper and the woman whose funeral he conducted. Students might suggest that by leaving the symbolism ambiguous, Hawthorne forces us to think more deeply about the story.

Nathaniel Hawthorne **249**

Reading Check

1. The congregation is threatened by this sign of personal and universal sin.

2. At the funeral, the people find the veil appropriate. At the wedding, the guests regard the veil as an ominous portent.

3. He says that the veil is a symbol of universal secret sin and that he is bound to wear it forever. Elizabeth says that the world may not believe that the veil is the sign of an innocent sorrow. She warns Hooper that people will gossip about him and will say that he has been involved in some scandal, and that his ministry may be compromised. She appeals to their love and asks him to cast the veil aside once for her sake.

1. *Archaic words*—sensible; unwonted. *Modern English passage*—The audience could sense something unusual in their minister. *New meanings*—Today *sensible* means "reasonable," and *unwonted,* which is seldom used, means "not common" or "rare."

2. *Archaic word*—prodigy. *Modern English passage*—A superstitious woman was the only witness of this marvel. *New meaning*—Today *prodigy* refers to "a child genius."

3. *Archaic words*—well nigh; waggery. *Modern English passage*—He almost lost his wits by joking. *New meanings*—Both have the same meaning today but are not commonly used.

4. *Archaic word*—wrought. *Modern English passage*—having worked so late. *New meaning*—Today *wrought* means "formed" or "made."

Vocabulary Development

Possible Answers

- *semblance. Definition*—outward appearance. *Origin*—L *similis,* "like." *Related word*—resemblance. *Sample sentence*—There was no <u>semblance</u> of justice in the kangaroo court.

- *iniquity. Definition*—wickedness. *Origin*—L *iniquus,* "unequal." *Related word*—iniquitous. *Sample sentence*—The <u>iniquity</u> of the terrorists on September 11, 2001, will go down in history.

- *ostentatious. Definition*—deliberately attracting notice. *Origin*—L *ob–* + *ostendere,* "to stretch before, expose." *Related words*—ostentation; ostensible. *Sample sentence*—The gold fixtures made an <u>ostentatious</u> display of wealth.

- *portend. Definition*—signify. *Origin*—L *portendere,* "to stretch forth, foretell." *Related words*—portentous; portent. *Sample sentence*—The black funnel in the distance may <u>portend</u> a twister.

- *obscurity. Definition*—the state of being hidden or concealed.

Illustration by Elenore Plaisted Abbott for "The Minister's Black Veil," from the 1900 edition of *Twice-Told Tales.*

Language and Style
Understanding Archaic Language

If modern readers have trouble with Hawthorne, it is usually because of his **archaic,** or old-fashioned, language. **Context clues** (page 64) can often help you figure out unfamiliar vocabulary. Which word or words in each of the following passages from the story are rarely used today? Rephrase each passage in Modern English. Are any of these words still in use today but with different meanings?

- "So sensible were the audience of some unwonted attribute in their minister . . ." (page 241)

- "A superstitious old woman was the only witness of this prodigy." (page 242)

- ". . . He well nigh lost his wits by his own waggery." (page 243)

- ". . . having wrought so late into the evening . . ." (page 247)

Vocabulary Development
Word Charts

Fill out a chart like the one below for each of the Vocabulary words. Use a dictionary to find basic information about each word.

semblance	portend
obscurity	pensively
iniquity	antipathy
ostentatious	plausibility
sagacious	resolute

Word	sagacious
Definition	wise; keenly perceptive
Origin	L *sagax,* "wise, forseeing"; akin to *sagire,* "to perceive acutely"
Related words	sagacity, sage
Sample sentence	Mrs. Keller was a shrewd and <u>sagacious</u> businesswoman.

Origin—L *obscurus,* "covered over." *Related word*—obscurantism. *Sample sentence*—The former movie star was forgotten and lived in <u>obscurity</u>.

- *pensively. Definition*—thoughtfully. *Origin*—L *pensare,* "to weigh or consider." *Related words*—pensive; pensiveness. *Sample sentence*—The homesick students thought <u>pensively</u> of their families.

- *antipathy. Definition*—strong dislike. *origin*—Gr *anti–,* "against" + *patheia,* "feeling."

Related words—pathos; pathetic. *Sample sentence*—I have a strong <u>antipathy</u> to bullies.

- *plausibility. Definition*—believability. *Origin*—L *plaudere, plausibilis,* "deserving applause." *Related word*—plausible. *Sample sentence*—Because he was caught in the act, the <u>plausibility</u> of his alibi was nil.

- *resolute. Definition*—determined. *Origin*—L *resolutus,* "loosened, released, freed." *Related word*—resolution. *Sample sentence*—We are <u>resolute</u> in our faith.

Grammar Link

Avoiding Sentence Fragments and Run-on Sentences: Respecting Boundaries

Just because a group of words looks like a sentence does not mean it is one. It may be a sentence fragment or a run-on sentence.

Sentence Fragments

A **sentence** is a group of words that has a **subject** and a **verb** and expresses a complete thought. A **sentence fragment** lacks one of these elements. It may be missing a subject or a verb or both, or the fragment may depend on a nearby sentence to make sense. The following items are examples of fragments:

> Roused the fears of the congregation. [no subject]
> Even on his deathbed. [not a complete thought]

Although sentence fragments are acceptable in informal writing and dialogue, you should avoid using them in formal writing. There are two ways to correct a fragment.

1. Add the missing subject or verb.

   The black veil roused the fears of the congregation. [subject added]

2. Rewrite the fragment to make it a complete sentence. (Sometimes this involves connecting the fragment to a neighboring sentence.)

   Reverend Hooper wore the veil even on his deathbed. [subject and predicate added]

Run-on Sentences

While a fragment is not a complete thought, a **run-on sentence** contains two or more complete thoughts running into one another, without respect for boundaries. There are two common types of run-on sentences: A **fused sentence** has no punctuation at all between its complete thoughts. A **comma splice** has only a comma between the two complete thoughts.

> The sexton rang the bell the people walked toward the church. [fused sentence]
> The sexton rang the bell, the people walked toward the church. [comma splice]

There are several ways to fix a run-on sentence.

1. Turn the run-on sentence into two or more separate sentences.

   The sexton rang the bell. The people walked toward the church.

SKILLS FOCUS

Grammar Skills
Revise run-on sentences and sentence fragments.

Nathaniel Hawthorne   **251**

Grammar Link

Practice

Possible Answers

1. CS.   At the beginning of Hawthorne's story, readers probably suspect that Mr. Hooper wears the veil because he has committed a sin. By the end, they may not be so sure.

2. SF.   Hooper refuses to remove the veil, although Elizabeth, his fiancée, begs him to lift it and let her see his face.

3. SF.   On his deathbed, Hooper insists that he sees a black veil covering every human face.

4. FS.   Some readers may view Hooper as morally courageous; others may view him as arrogant and obsessive.

ASSESSING

Assessment

■ *Holt Assessment: Literature, Reading, and Vocabulary*

2. Add a **coordinating conjunction** (*and, but, or, nor, for, so, yet*), and if the run-on sentence is a fused sentence, add a comma before the conjunction.

   The sexton rang the bell**,** <u>and</u> the people walked toward the church.

3. Separate the complete thoughts with a semicolon.

   The sexton rang the bell**;** the people walked toward the church.

4. Add a **subordinating conjunction** (such as *because, although, until,* or *when*) and, if necessary, a comma before the conjunction.

   The sexton rang the bell <u>while</u> the people walked toward the church.

5. Use a semicolon and a conjunctive adverb.

   The sexton rang the bell**;** <u>consequently,</u> the people walked toward the church.

PRACTICE

In the following items, indicate whether each example is a **sentence fragment** (SF), a **fused sentence** (FS), or a **comma splice** (CS). Then, correct each sentence fragment or run-on sentence, using whichever method you think works best.

1. At the beginning of Hawthorne's story, readers probably suspect that Mr. Hooper wears the veil because he has committed a sin, by the end they may not be so sure.

2. Hooper refuses to remove the veil. Although Elizabeth, his fiancée, begs him to lift it and let her see his face.

3. On his deathbed, Hooper insists that he sees a black veil. Covering every human face.

4. Some readers may view Hooper as morally courageous others may view him as arrogant and obsessive.

Apply to Your Writing

Re-read a current writing assignment or a piece of writing that you've already completed. Can you find any sentence fragments or run-on sentences? If so, revise each of them according to what you have learned.

For more help, see Obstacles to Clarity, 9d–e, in the Language Handbook.

Edgar Allan Poe
(1809–1849)

"The want of parental affection," wrote Poe, "has been the heaviest of my trials." Edgar Allan Poe was, indeed, most unfortunate in his parents. His father, David Poe, was a mediocre traveling actor who drank heavily. His mother, Elizabeth Arnold, was a talented actress who was deserted by her husband when Edgar was still a baby. She died on tour in Richmond, Virginia, leaving Edgar virtually an orphan before his third birthday.

The boy was taken in by John and Frances Allan, a charitable and childless couple in Richmond. John Allan, an ambitious and self-righteous merchant, became Edgar's guardian (and the source of the writer's middle name). He provided generously for Edgar's early education, but he never formally adopted the boy.

Although Frances Allan was kind to Edgar, the boy grew up feeling both the lack of a natural father and the disapproval of his foster father. John Allan made no secret of his disappointment in Edgar—in his idleness, in his indifference to business life, and in his literary ambitions. Surely Allan's criticism added to Edgar's growing moodiness.

Breaking Away

At seventeen, Edgar entered the University of Virginia. He did well in his studies but was resentful of the meager allowance Allan gave him. When he tried to earn extra money by gambling, he went deep into debt. On discovering this, Allan refused to help his foster son and instead withdrew him from college.

After an especially bitter quarrel with Allan, Poe ran off to Boston to make his own way in the world. There, in 1827, he published a small volume of poems, *Tamerlane.* The book did not attract much attention, and Poe could find no other work. In despair he joined the army. He was promoted to the rank of sergeant major, but he disliked the enlisted man's life and appealed to Allan for help. At the request of his wife, who was dying, Allan interceded for Poe (for the last time) and agreed to help him enter the U.S. Military Academy at West Point. Poe's motive in going to the academy was probably to please his foster father.

While waiting to get into the academy, Poe published a second book of poems, *Al Aaraaf,* in 1829 and received his first real recognition as a writer. The next year, while at West Point, Poe learned that Allan (now a widower) had remarried and that the woman was young enough to have children. Since this appeared to end all hope of becoming Allan's heir, Poe had himself dismissed from West Point.

Exploring the Darkness and the Depths

Poe moved in with an aunt, Maria Poe Clemm, in Baltimore, Maryland. In 1835, he married her thirteen-year-old daughter, Virginia. The difference in their ages and Virginia's poor health resulted in a very odd marriage, but need and a strong sense of family drew the three housemates together.

Poe supported his family by working as an editor at various magazines. He wrote when he could find the time, completing his only full-length novel, *The Narrative of Arthur Gordon Pym,* several years after his marriage. It was his short stories, however, that had the greatest effect on other writers.

In "The Gold Bug" and in the tales built around the intuitive sleuth C. Auguste Dupin, "The Purloined Letter" and "The Murders in the Rue Morgue," Poe laid the foundations for the modern detective story. In fact, he inspired Sir Arthur Conan Doyle to create Sherlock Holmes. In tales such as "The Tell-Tale Heart" and "The Cask of Amontillado," Poe inspired the Russian novelist Fyodor Dostoyevsky

SKILLS FOCUS, pp. 253–272

Grade-Level Skills

■ **Literary Skills**
Analyze various literary devices, including symbolism.

■ **Reading Skills**
Retell the story.

More About the Writer

Background. Mrs. Gove Nichols, a contemporary of Poe, recalls an incident that occurred during a visit she made to his cottage in New York: "So neat, so poor, so unfurnished, and yet so charming a dwelling I never saw." Although Poe was depressed by his wife's tuberculosis, his inability to write as much as he needed to, and his poverty, he took a stroll in the woods with his visitors and challenged them to a broad-jumping contest. He won, but broke his old gaiters, which he could not afford to replace. At the cottage, Poe's aunt pleaded with Nichols to talk to a certain magazine editor regarding Poe's latest poem. Nichols could not understand the poem, and even considered it "a hoax," but she generously spoke to the editor, who bought it, enabling Poe to buy new gaiters.

RESOURCES: READING

Planning
■ *One-Stop Planner* CD-ROM with ExamView Test Generator

Differentiating Instruction
■ *Holt Adapted Reader*
■ *Supporting Instruction in Spanish*
■ *Audio CD Library, Selections and Summaries in Spanish*

Vocabulary
■ *Vocabulary Development*

Grammar and Language
■ *Daily Language Activities*

Assessment
■ *Holt Assessment: Literature, Reading, and Vocabulary*
■ *One-Stop Planner* CD-ROM with ExamView Test Generator

■ *Holt Online Assessment*

Internet
■ go.hrw.com (Keyword: LE5 11-2)
■ *Elements of Literature Online*

Media
■ *Audio CD Library*
■ *Audio CD Library, Selections and Summaries in Spanish*

For Independent Reading

■ Tell students reading "The Fall of the House of Usher" that Poe's classic tale has had a profound influence on American composer Philip Glass (1937–   ), who wrote an opera based on Poe's work. Encourage students to research Glass's work and play segments of his opera to the class.

A CLOSER LOOK

This feature provides five bulleted facts that prove Edgar Allan Poe is a legend of popular culture.

DIRECT TEACHING

A **Reading Informational Text**

? **Critiquing the argument.** How convincing are these facts in proving that Poe is a legendary figure? [Most students will say that they are convincing because Poe plays a role in several different areas. The first three facts relate to literature, and the last two concern popular arts and film, respectively.]

B **Reading Skills**

? **Speculating.** Poe might be surprised to learn that he is a legendary figure. In a class discussion, invite students to speculate about how he might have handled fame and financial success in his lifetime. Would it have made him happy? How might it have changed him and his work?

(1821–1881) to explore the criminal mind.

Poe was a master of the psychological thriller. His tales of the ghastly and the grotesque are peopled with distraught narrators, deranged heroes, and doomed heroines, yet his purpose in creating such characters was not to present readers with convincing likenesses of human beings—nor merely to shock and frighten. Instead, Poe wanted to take us behind the curtain that separates the everyday from the incredible. He wanted to leave behind the sunlit, tangible, rational world and discover the unsettling truth that lies in the dark, irrational depths of the human mind.

Small Triumphs and Great Tragedy

Poe produced a considerable body of work in spite of humiliating poverty and a serious drinking problem. The slightest amount of alcohol made him senseless, yet he drank to escape a reality he found agonizing. Publication of his poem "The Raven" in 1845 brought Poe some fame at last, but financial security still eluded him.

When Virginia died of tuberculosis in 1847, Poe and "Muddy" (Virginia's mother) were left alone. Poe grew more unstable. He pursued romance relentlessly, always looking for someone to "adopt" him. In 1849, on his way home after a visit to Virginia to see a woman he hoped to marry, Poe disappeared. A week later, he was found in a Baltimore tavern—delirious and in cheap clothing that was not his, wet through from a raging storm. Four days later, having passed in and out of delirium, Poe died, leaving critics to argue endlessly about this final mystery. What happened during those last days in Baltimore?

For Independent Reading

For more of Poe's horror stories, read these titles:

• "The Fall of the House of Usher"
• "The Oval Portrait"

A CLOSER LOOK: SOCIAL INFLUENCES

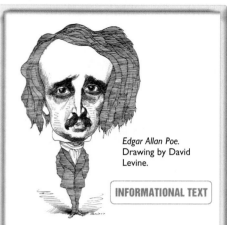

Edgar Allan Poe. Drawing by David Levine.

INFORMATIONAL TEXT

Poe the Pop Icon

Can you guess what Edgar Allan Poe has in common with Elvis Presley, Marilyn Monroe, the Beatles, and Michael Jordan? Like all of the above, Poe is a legend of popular culture. Consider these facts:

• Poe's works have been translated into virtually every language.

• Such popular writers as Stephen King and Ray Bradbury point to Poe as their literary forefather.

A • The Mystery Writers of America annually honors great achievements in mystery writing with the Edgar—the equivalent of an Oscar or an Emmy.

• Poe has been immortalized in the popular arts, on everything from posters, buttons, and coffee mugs to bumper stickers and T-shirts.

• Poe has been "ushered" into pop culture through dozens of film adaptations, including *The Masque of the Red Death, The Black Cat, The Tomb of Ligeia,* and *The Pit and the Pendulum.*

Keep your eye out for Poe. He may be **B** closer than you think.

Before You Read

The Pit and the Pendulum

Make the Connection
Quickwrite ✎

Here is Edgar Allan Poe's famous story of confinement in an extraordinary prison cell in Toledo, Spain, during the brutal Spanish Inquisition. Poe's story is powerful for many reasons, one being its point of view. It is the prisoner himself who tells this story. Given this fact, do you already know at the outset that he will survive the torture—or could he possibly die?

The other powerful device in the story is the form of torture itself, which gradually takes on symbolic meaning. Before you read the story, freewrite for a few minutes about one of your fears and the images you associate with it.

Literary Focus
Symbolic Meaning

When we read, we often sense that a story means more than what simply happens on the surface level. For instance, if a young girl in a story is in conflict with her parents over wearing certain earrings, we suspect that those earrings represent something important to her—perhaps her self-expression or independence. A **symbol** is a concrete object, a person, a place, or an action that works on at least two levels: It functions as itself, and it also suggests a deeper meaning. As you read "The Pit and the Pendulum," consider what elements may have broader symbolic significance.

> The **symbolic meaning** of a story emerges from an overall interpretation of the story's individual symbols.
>
> *For more on Symbol, see the Handbook of Literary and Historical Terms.*

Reading Skills 📖
Retelling

Good readers sometimes stop at key points in a story in order to retell what has happened so far. Try this retelling strategy with Poe's story. You'll find boxed questions at certain points in the story. Stop at these points, and retell the key events that have taken place so far. Focus also on causes and their effects. Ask yourself, "What has *caused* this event to happen?" and "What is the *effect* of this action?"

Background

The Spanish Inquisition was a kind of religious court set up by the Catholic Church and the monarchy in Spain during the fifteenth century to accuse and punish those who

INTERNET

Vocabulary Practice
•
Cross-Curricular Connection
•
More About Edgar Allan Poe
•
Keyword: LE5 11-2

SKILLS FOCUS

Literary Skills
Understand symbolic meaning.

Reading Skills
Retell key events.

Edgar Allan Poe   **255**

PRETEACHING

Summary ⬆ *above grade level*

This classic horror tale, rich in symbolic overtones, opens in Toledo, Spain, in the final days of the Spanish Inquisition. After an agonizing trial, the first-person narrator hears judges condemn him to death. He faints and awakens in a pitch-dark dungeon, where he narrowly escapes a fatal fall into a pit. He sleeps, awakens to find food and water nearby, drinks, and loses consciousness. Reviving from a drugged stupor, he finds himself bound to a frame. He sees a glow from beneath the walls, realizes that they are solid metal, then looks up to see a scythe-like pendulum descending toward him. One of his arms is free, and a bowl of meat is nearby. He rubs meat scraps on his bindings so that rats eat through them. As he rolls free, the dungeon walls, now glowing hot, move inward, forcing him toward the pit. At the last second, he hears a confused din. The walls rush back. Fainting, he topples into the pit. A strong arm catches him; it is General Lasalle of France, whose army has just taken Toledo.

Selection Starter

Build background. To prepare students for Poe's images of the Spanish Inquisition (1478–1834), you might point out that torture of prisoners still occurs today. Have students share what they know of organizations working to end torture, such as the United Nations Human Rights Commission, the Red Cross, and Amnesty International.

A Reading Skills

❓ Speculating. What events might you expect in a horror story that involves a pit and a pendulum? [Have students write their responses, which can be discussed after reading this tale.]

B English-Language Learners

Build background knowledge. Be sure students know that a pendulum is a swinging weight, often used in clocks. Ask a volunteer to draw a clock with a pendulum. Explain that the image of a swinging pendulum suggests the gradual but irreversible passage of time.

failed to comply with the church or royal authority. Poe may have gotten the idea for this story from a book by Juan Antonio Llorente. Poe read a review of this book, which contains the following passage:

> 66 The Inquisition was thrown open, in 1820, by the orders of the Cortes of Madrid. Twenty-one prisoners were found in it. . . . Some had been confined three years, some a longer period, and not one knew perfectly the nature of the crime of which he was accused. One of these prisoners had been condemned and was to have suffered on the following day. His punishment was to be death by the Pendulum. The method of thus destroying the victim is as follows: The condemned is fastened in a groove, upon a table, on his back; suspended above him is a Pendulum, the edge of which is sharp, and it is so constructed as to become longer with every movement. The wretch sees this implement of destruction swinging to and fro above him, and every moment the keen edge approaching nearer and nearer. 99

Vocabulary Development

imperceptible (im′pər·sep′tə·bəl) *adj.*: not clear or obvious to the senses or mind.

ponders (pän′dərz) *v.*: thinks deeply.

lucid (lōō′sid) *adj.*: clearheaded; not confused.

tumultuous (tōō·mul′chōō·əs) *adj.*: violent; greatly agitated or disturbed.

insuperable (in·sōō′pər·ə·bəl) *adj.*: incapable of being overcome.

prostrate (präs′trāt′) *adj.*: lying flat.

potent (pōt′'nt) *adj.*: powerful or effective.

lethargy (leth′ər·jē) *n.*: abnormal drowsiness.

proximity (präk·sim′ə·tē) *n.*: nearness.

averted (ə·vurt′id) *v.*: turned away; prevented.

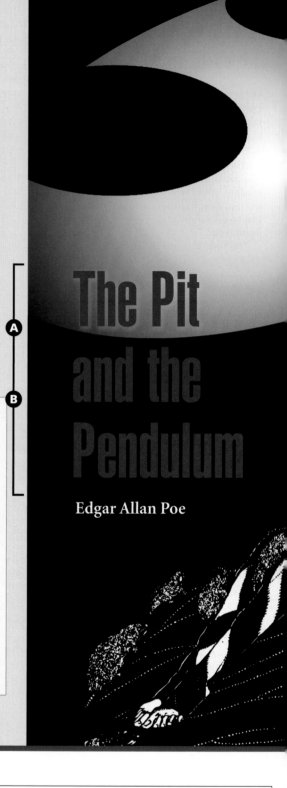

The Pit and the Pendulum

Edgar Allan Poe

Previewing Vocabulary

After students review the definitions in the Student Edition, have them use the Vocabulary words on p. 256 to complete the following analogies.

1. _____ : UNBEATABLE :: brilliant : bright [INSUPERABLE]

2. _____ : CONSIDERS :: wanders : meanders [PONDERS]

3. _____ : UNCLEAR :: accept : reject [LUCID]

4. PEACEFUL : _____ :: calm : nervous [TUMULTUOUS]

5. INVISIBLE : _____ :: weep : cry [IMPERCEPTIBLE]

6. WEAK : _____ :: love : hate [POTENT]

7. _____ : UPRIGHT :: ordinary : unique [PROSTRATE]

8. DEEP : PROFOUND :: deflected : _____ [averted]

9. LIGHT : DARK :: distance : _____ [proximity]

10. _____ : VIGOR :: horror : delight [LETHARGY]

Any horror but this!

I was sick—sick unto death with that long agony; and when they at length unbound me, and I was permitted to sit, I felt that my senses were leaving me. The sentence—the dread sentence of death—was the last of distinct accentuation which reached my ears. After that, the sound of the Inquisitorial voices seemed merged in one dreamy, indeterminate hum. It conveyed to my soul the idea of *revolution*[1]—perhaps from its association in fancy[2] with the burr of a mill wheel. This only for a brief period, for presently I heard no more. Yet for a while, I saw—but with how terrible an exaggeration! I saw the lips of the black-robed judges. They appeared to me white—whiter than the sheet upon which I trace these words—and thin even to grotesqueness; thin with the intensity of their expression of firmness—of immovable resolution—of stern contempt of human torture. I saw that the decrees of what to me was Fate were still issuing from those lips. I saw them writhe with a deadly locution.[3] I saw them fashion the syllables of my name; and I shuddered because no sound succeeded.[4] I saw, too, for a few moments of delirious horror, the soft and nearly imperceptible waving of the sable draperies which enwrapped the walls of the apartment. And then my vision fell upon the seven tall candles upon the table. At first they wore the aspect of charity and seemed white, slender angels who would save me; but then, all at once, there came a most deadly nausea over my spirit, and I felt every fiber in my frame thrill as if I had touched the wire of a galvanic battery, while the angel forms became meaningless specters, with heads of flame, and I saw that from them there would be no help. And then there stole into my fancy, like a rich musical note, the thought of what sweet rest there must

---

1. **revolution** *n.:* rotation; turning motion.
2. **fancy** *n.:* imagination.
3. **locution** (lō·kyōō′shən) *n.:* utterance; statement.
4. **succeeded** *v.:* followed.

Vocabulary

imperceptible (im′pər·sep′tə·bəl) *adj.:* not clear or obvious to the senses or the mind.

Edgar Allan Poe 257

DIRECT TEACHING

C Reading Skills

? Retelling. What happened to the narrator before the story opened? [He endured a trial that was a "long agony," during which he was tied up and forced to remain standing.] **What does he hear now?** [He hears his death sentence.]

D Vocabulary Development

? Greek, Latin, and Anglo-Saxon affixes. The Latin suffix *–al* means "related to." An Inquisitor (from Latin *in–,* "into" + *quaerere,* "to seek") is an official of the Inquisition. What do you think *Inquisitorial* means? ["related to members of the Inquisition"]

E Literary Focus

? Symbolic meaning. The narrator sees the candles literally and then symbolically. What two different things does he say the candles symbolize for him? [At first they seem to be angels who might save him; then they become "meaningless specters."]

DIFFERENTIATING INSTRUCTION

Learners Having Difficulty
Modeling. To help students read "The Pit and the Pendulum," model the reading skill of retelling. Say, "Suppose you read a long, complicated passage with detailed descriptions of a character's thoughts, feelings, and actions. You could retell it by listing the main actions and mentioning the thoughts that caused them." Encourage students, as they read, to ask themselves, "What is the action? What are its causes?"

A Learners Having Difficulty

? Varying your reading rate.
As the narrator meditates on consciousness and dreams, Poe builds suspense by making readers wait to learn what happens next. How might you read the paragraph to find out what happens next quickly? [Skim it, or scan for action sequences.]

Response to Boxed Question

1. The narrator has been tried by the Inquisition. He hears his own death sentence, slips into a hallucinatory stupor, and faints.

A CLOSER LOOK

This feature provides historical background on the Inquisition in Spain from 1478 to 1834.

B Background

The Inquisition Worldwide
Point out that the Inquisition took place in France, Germany, Portugal, Italy, and Latin America, as well as in Spain. England had its own version, the Tribunal, which attempted to control the Protestant Reformation. (In colonial America, the Inquisitorial mind-set flared briefly but horribly in the Salem witch trials.) The Inquisition was established in Italy in the 1200s as an attempt to curb heresy and dissent in the Roman Catholic Church. Its most common method of execution was burning, because the Church was not allowed to shed blood.

---

be in the grave. The thought came gently and stealthily, and it seemed long before it attained full appreciation; but just as my spirit came at length properly to feel and entertain it, the figures of the judges vanished, as if magically, from before me; the tall candles sank into nothingness! Their flames went out utterly; the blackness of darkness supervened; all sensations appeared swallowed up in a mad rushing descent, as of the soul into Hades. Then silence, and stillness, and night were the universe. ◑

I had swooned;[5] but still will not say that all of consciousness was lost. What of it there remained I will not attempt to define, or even to describe; yet all was not lost. In the deepest

___
5. **swooned** *v.:* fainted.

> ◐ The narrator has just explained what has happened to him.
>
> **?** In your own words, **retell** what has happened so far.

slumber—no! In delirium—no! In a swoon—no! In death—no! Even in the grave all *is not* lost. Else there is no immortality for man. Arousing from the most profound of slumbers, we break the gossamer web of *some* dream. Yet in a second afterward (so frail may that web have been), we remember not that we have dreamed. In the return to life from the swoon, there are two stages: first, that of the sense of mental or spiritual; second, that of the sense of physical existence. It seems probable that if, upon reaching the second stage, we could recall the impressions of the first, we should find these impressions eloquent in memories of the gulf beyond. And that gulf is—what? How at least shall we distinguish its shadows from those of the tomb? But if the impressions of what I have termed the first stage are not, at will, recalled, yet, after long interval, do they not come unbidden, while we marvel whence they come? He who has never swooned is not he who finds

A CLOSER LOOK: POLITICAL INFLUENCES

The Inquisition: Power, Greed, and Suffering

INFORMATIONAL TEXT

B King Ferdinand and Queen Isabella of Spain had political as well as religious motives for establishing the Spanish Inquisition in 1478. The Catholic monarchs wished to regain control over a fragmented country that had been ruled for centuries by the Moors (Muslims from North Africa) and that had a large population of influential Jews, many of whom had converted to Christianity. By finding Spanish Jews and Muslims guilty of converting to Christianity not out of true religious conviction but from a desire to keep their lands and property, the monarchy used the Inquisition to seize the converts' wealth and destroy their influence. The methods of the Inquisition included imprisonment, torture, confiscation of property, and public execution. At its height, from 1483 to 1498, a Dominican priest, Tomás de Torquemada, presided over thousands of trials and about

two thousand burnings at the stake. These burnings were preceded by a public religious ceremony, called an auto-da-fé (Portuguese for "act of faith"), in which the accused was marched in procession into a church, a Mass was held, and the death sentence was read. Then the convicted person was handed over to the state authorities for execution.

The Inquisition was temporarily halted in 1808, when Napoleon's army invaded and defeated Spain. General Lasalle commanded the French troops who seized the city of Toledo. Napoleon proclaimed his older brother king of Spain, but in 1813, he was ousted by the Spanish with British aid. The Spanish monarchy was restored and with it the Inquisition, which persisted in a limited form in Spain and Latin America until 1834.

DIFFERENTIATING INSTRUCTION

English-Language Learners
Be sure students understand that "The Pit and the Pendulum" is a horror story, a tale intended to frighten. To help students with Poe's complex, archaic style and intricate imagery, you might provide a basic scenario: the story is set in Toledo, Spain, in the mid-1800s; the narrator is near collapse after being tried by the Inquisition for a crime that is

never made clear; at the beginning of the story, he is sentenced to death and taken to a mysterious dungeon. For more background on the Inquisition, have students read A Closer Look on p. 258.

Advanced Learners
Enrichment. Move students toward advanced genre study by discussing the subgenres of horror stories (short stories

designed to frighten) and Gothic novels (usually set in eerie castles, ruins, dungeons, or tombs).
Activity. Ask students what makes works in these subgenres effective. [Possible response: The frightening parts must be believable; this requires credible characters, settings, causes, and effects.]

strange palaces and wildly familiar faces in coals that glow; is not he who beholds floating in midair the sad visions that the many may not view; is not he who ponders over the perfume of some novel flower; is not he whose brain grows bewildered with the meaning of some musical cadence which has never before arrested his attention.

Amid frequent and thoughtful endeavors to remember, amid earnest struggles to regather some token of the state of seeming nothingness into which my soul had lapsed, there have been moments when I have dreamed of success; there have been brief, very brief, periods when I have conjured up remembrances which the lucid reason of a later epoch assures me could have had reference only to that condition of seeming unconsciousness. These shadows of memory tell, indistinctly, of tall figures that lifted and bore me in silence down—down—still down—till a hideous dizziness oppressed me at the mere idea of the interminableness of the descent. They tell also of a vague horror at my heart, on account of that heart's unnatural stillness. Then comes a sense of sudden motionlessness throughout all things; as if those who bore me (a ghastly train!) had outrun, in their descent, the limits of the limitless, and paused from the wearisomeness of their toil. After this I call to mind flatness and dampness; and then all is *madness*—the madness of a memory which busies itself among forbidden things. ❷

❷ What has the narrator dreamed, and what does he realize at this moment?

Very suddenly there came back to my soul motion and sound—the tumultuous motion of the heart and, in my ears, the sound of its beating. Then a pause in which all is blank. Then again sound, and motion, and touch—a tingling sensation pervading my frame. Then the mere consciousness of existence, without thought—a condition which lasted long. Then, very suddenly, *thought,* and shuddering terror, and earnest endeavor to comprehend my true state. Then a strong desire to lapse into insensibility. Then a rushing revival of soul and a suc-

cessful effort to move. And now a full memory of the trial, of the judges, of the sable draperies, of the sentence, of the sickness, of the swoon. Then entire forgetfulness of all that followed; of all that a later day and much earnestness of endeavor have enabled me vaguely to recall.

So far, I had not opened my eyes. I felt that I lay upon my back, unbound. I reached out my hand, and it fell heavily upon something damp and hard. There I suffered[6] it to remain for many minutes, while I strove to imagine where and *what* I could be. I longed, yet dared not, to employ my vision. I dreaded the first glance at objects around me. It was not that I feared to look upon things horrible, but that I grew aghast lest there should be *nothing* to see. At length, with a wild desperation at heart, I quickly unclosed my eyes. My worst thoughts, then, were confirmed. The blackness of eternal night encompassed me. I struggled for breath. The intensity of the darkness seemed to oppress and stifle me. The atmosphere was intolerably close. I still lay quietly, and made effort to exercise my reason. I brought to mind the Inquisitorial proceedings and attempted from that point to deduce my real condition. The sentence had passed; and it appeared to me that a very long interval of time had since elapsed. Yet not for a moment did I suppose myself actually dead. Such a supposition, notwithstanding what we read in fiction, is altogether inconsistent with real existence—but where and in what state was I? The condemned to death, I knew, perished usually at the autos-da-fé, and one of these had been held on the very night of the day of my trial. Had I been remanded to my dungeon, to await the next sacrifice, which would not take place for many months? This I at once saw could not be. Victims had been in immediate

_____

6. **suffered** *v.:* allowed; tolerated.

_____

Vocabulary

ponders (pän′dərz) *v.:* thinks deeply.
lucid (lōō′sid) *adj.:* clearheaded; not confused.
tumultuous (tōō·mul′chōō·əs) *adj.:* violent; greatly

Edgar Allan Poe **259**

El Greco (1541–1614) was one of the most original painters of his era. Born in Greece, he spent his last decades in Toledo, Spain, where "The Pit and the Pendulum" is set. He is known for portraits revealing his fascination with effects of movement and light. During his long career, he painted at least two landscapes of Toledo. In *View of Toledo,* intense colors and slightly distorted shapes suggest a thunderstorm's strong winds and shifting light.

Activity. Invite students to describe the mood of the painting. [ominous, nightmarish] Then, ask students what symbolic meanings the storm gathering over Toledo might carry for them. [Possible responses: The storm might suggest war, civil unrest, or fear.]

The Metropolitan Museum of Art, H. O. Havemeyer Collection, Bequest of Mrs. H. O. Havemeyer, 1929 (29.100.6). Photograph ©1992 The Metropolitan Museum of Art.

View of Toledo (1608) by El Greco. Oil on canvas.

demand. Moreover, my dungeon, as well as all the condemned cells at Toledo, had stone floors, and light was not altogether excluded.

A fearful idea now suddenly drove the blood in torrents upon my heart, and for a brief period I once more relapsed into insensibility. Upon recovering, I at once started to my feet, trembling convulsively in every fiber. I thrust my arms wildly above and around me in all di-rections. I felt nothing; yet dreaded to move a step, lest I should be impeded by the walls of a *tomb*. Perspiration burst from every pore and stood in cold, big beads upon my forehead. The agony of suspense grew at length intolerable, and I cautiously moved forward, with my arms extended and my eyes straining from their sockets in the hope of catching some faint ray of light. I proceeded for many paces; but still all

My confusion of
serving that I be;
left and ended it

I had been de
shape of the enc
found many ang
great irregularity
darkness upon o
sleep! The angle;
slight depression
The general shap
What I had taken
be iron, or some
whose sutures or
sion. The entire
sure was rudely
repulsive devices
stition of the m
of fiends in aspe
forms, and othe
overspread and
that the outlines
sufficiently disti
faded and blurre
from the effects
atmosphere. I n
the floor, too, w
stone. In the cen
the circular pit f
jaws I had escap
was the only on
dungeon. ❸

All this I saw
for my personal
changed during
back, and at full
framework of w
bound by a long
It passed in man
and body, leavin
my left arm to s

10. **daubed** *v.*: pai
11. **charnel** *adj.*: s
   is a tomb or pl
   deposited.
12. **surcingle** (sur
   or a pack to a l

was blackness and vacancy.
I breathed more freely. It
seemed evident that mine
was not, at least, the most
hideous of fates. ❸

And now, as I still con-
tinued to step cautiously
onward, there came
thronging upon my recol-
lection a thousand vague
rumors of the horrors of
Toledo. Of the dungeons there had been strange
things narrated—fables I had always deemed
them—but yet strange, and too ghastly to repeat, save in a whisper. Was I left to perish of
starvation in the subterranean world of darkness; or what fate, perhaps even more fearful,
awaited me? That the result would be death, and
a death of more than customary bitterness, I
knew too well the character of my judges to
doubt. The mode and the hour were all that occupied or distracted me.

My outstretched hands at length encountered
some solid obstruction. It was a wall, seemingly
of stone masonry—very smooth, slimy, and
cold. I followed it up, stepping with all the careful distrust with which certain antique narratives had inspired me. This process, however,
afforded me no means of ascertaining the dimensions of my dungeon, as I might make its
circuit and return to the point whence I set out
without being aware of the fact, so perfectly
uniform seemed the wall. I therefore sought the
knife which had been in my pocket when led
into the Inquisitorial chamber, but it was gone;
my clothes had been exchanged for a wrapper of
coarse serge. I had thought of forcing the blade
in some minute crevice of the masonry, so as to
identify my point of departure. The difficulty,
nevertheless, was but trivial; although, in
the disorder of my fancy, it seemed at first
insuperable. I tore a part of the hem from the
robe and placed the fragment at full length and
at right angles to the wall. In groping my way
around the prison, I could not fail to encounter
this rag upon completing the circuit. So, at least,
I thought; but I had not counted upon the ex-

> The narrator now
> is relieved that "the
> most hideous of
> fates" is not for him.
> ❓ **What is this
> fate? How
> does the narrator
> come to realize
> that this punishment
> is not his?**

tent of the dungeon, or upon my own weakness.
The ground was moist and slippery. I staggered
onward for some time, when I stumbled and
fell. My excessive fatigue induced me to remain
prostrate; and sleep soon overtook me as I lay.

Upon awaking and stretching forth an arm, I
found beside me a loaf and a pitcher with water.
I was too much exhausted to reflect upon this
circumstance, but ate and drank with avidity.[7]
Shortly afterward, I resumed my tour around
the prison and, with much toil, came at last
upon the fragment of the serge. Up to the period when I fell, I had counted fifty-two paces,
and upon resuming my walk, I had counted
forty-eight more—when I arrived at the rag.
There were in all, then, a hundred paces; and,
admitting two paces to the yard, I presumed the
dungeon to be fifty yards in circuit. I had met,
however, with many angles in the wall, and thus
I could form no guess at the shape of the vault,
for vault I could not help supposing it to be.

I had little object—certainly no hope—in
these researches; but a vague curiosity prompted
me to continue them. Quitting the wall, I resolved to cross the area of the enclosure. At first,
I proceeded with extreme caution, for the floor,
although seemingly of solid material, was
treacherous with slime. At length, however, I
took courage and did not hesitate to step
firmly—endeavoring to cross in as direct a line
as possible. I had advanced some ten or twelve
paces in this manner when the remnant of the
torn hem of my robe became entangled between my legs. I stepped on it and fell violently
on my face.

In the confusion attending my fall, I did not
immediately apprehend a somewhat startling
circumstance, which yet, in a few seconds afterward and while I still lay prostrate, arrested my
attention. It was this—my chin rested upon the

---

7. **avidity** (ə·vid′ə·tē) *n.*: great eagerness.

agitated or disturbed.

Vocabulary

insuperable (in·soo′pər·ə·bəl) *adj.*: incapable of being
overcome.

Edgar Allan Poe   **261**

Ⓐ Literary Focus

❓ Symbolic meaning. The narrator repeatedly refers to the total
darkness and earlier expresses his
terror of it. What do you think the
darkness might symbolize for him?
[Possible responses: death; perdition;
ignorance (he does not know where
he is or what will happen to him); the
"dark" malice of his torturers; the
"dark" dementia he struggles against.]

Ⓑ Advanced Learners

❓ Enrichment. How would you
characterize Poe's writing style in
this story? [He uses formal diction
and long sentences with complicated
structures.] What purpose do you
think the style achieves? [Possible
response: It makes the narrator seem
educated, intelligent, and credible.]

Ⓒ Reading Skills

❓ Retelling. How would you
retell what has happened since the
narrator found the wall? [He set off
around the cell's perimeter, tearing a
strip from his clothes to mark his
starting point. He fell and slept,
awoke to find food and water nearby,
ate and drank, and went on till he
reached the cloth strip again. He then
tried to cross the cell but tripped and
fell facedown.]

**Response to Boxed
Question**

3. The "most hideous of fates" is
   being entombed alive; he knows
   it is not his punishment when he
   tries walking in his prison and
   finds that it is too big to be a
   tomb.

CONTENT-

Science: Fou
A Foucault pen
French physicis
(1819–1868), H
motion in a sir
of upright bloc
Small-group
ested students
the Foucault pe
diagrams and r

CONTENT-AREA CONNECTIONS

Health: Definition of Death

The narrator's great fear after first awakening
is that he has been placed alive in a tomb. Poe
himself was preoccupied with the possibility of
being buried alive. At one time, people were,
in fact, sometimes buried alive. Scientifically
accurate methods for determining death had
not been devised, and on rare occasions a
person who was merely unconscious was mistaken for dead. One practical purpose of the
funeral wake was to provide an opportunity
for friends and family to watch for signs of life.
Individual activity. Invite interested students to investigate and report on the medical
definition of death. Students might also report
on the implications of the definition for the
patient, the patient's family, and the public—
for example, in regard to organ donations.

DIRECT TEACHING

A Literar

? Symboli

symbolic cor
tor make be
masonry and
happens to tl
have happene
had not tripp

B Literar

? Theme.

Inquisition de
after discove
response: The
as the wildest
claimed.]

C Readin

? Retelling

retell what h
narrator deci
his cell? [He
and water ne
which was dr
sciousness. W
was lit by an

D Readin

? Analyzin

motive might
preoccupatio
details of his
He is busying
hopes to find

Response
Boxed Qu

4. In total da
was in a tc
not. He gr
the cell's p
tried to cr
tripped, la
over a pit.
masonry v
below. He
narrow es
stop explo

A Content-Area Connections

Science: Physics
A pendulum has a regular *period* (the time it takes to swing once in each direction) that relates directly to its *arc* (the distance of the swing).

B Literary Focus

? Symbolic meaning. Here the narrator uses the word *typical* to mean "archetypal" or "symbolic." What does this passage reveal about the symbolism of the pit? [Possible response: To the narrator, it symbolizes hell.]

C English-Language Learners

? Archaic language. The phrase *what boots it* means "of what use is it?" and the word *ere* means "until." How does a dictionary label these meanings for *boot* and *ere*? [Possible responses: archaic or obsolete.]

D Literary Focus

? Symbolic meaning. How does this sentence reinforce the idea that the dungeon symbolizes Hell for the narrator? [Possible response: He refers to his torturers as "demons."]

E Reading Skills

? Retelling. How would you retell what goes on in the narrator's mind when he takes a bite of food? [Possible response: He gets a half-formed idea that gives him hope, but his mind is too far gone to focus on the idea or remember it.]

In the center yawned the circular pit from whose jaws I had escaped . . .

A imperfect note of time), before I again cast my eyes upward. What I then saw confounded and amazed me. The sweep of the pendulum had increased in extent by nearly a yard. As a natural consequence its velocity was also much greater. But what mainly disturbed me was the idea that it had perceptibly *descended*. I now observed—with what horror it is needless to say—that its nether extremity[15] was formed of a crescent of glittering steel, about a foot in length from horn to horn; the horns upward, and the under edge evidently as keen as that of a razor. Like a razor also, it seemed massy and heavy, tapering from the edge into a solid and broad structure above. It was appended to a weighty rod of brass, and the whole *hissed* as it swung through the air.

B I could no longer doubt the doom prepared for me by monkish ingenuity in torture. My cognizance[16] of the pit had become known to the Inquisitorial agents—*the pit*, whose horrors had been destined for so bold a recusant[17] as myself—*the pit*, typical of hell and regarded by rumor as the ultima Thule[18] of all their punishments. The plunge into this pit I had avoided by the merest of accidents, and I knew that surprise, or entrapment into torment, formed an important portion of all the grotesquerie of these dungeon deaths. Having failed to fall, it was no part of the demon plan to hurl me into the abyss, and thus (there being no alternative) a different and a milder destruction awaited me.

---

15. **nether extremity:** lower end.
16. **cognizance** (käg′nə·zəns) *n.:* awareness.
17. **recusant** (rek′yoo·zənt) *n.:* person who stands out stubbornly against an established authority.
18. **ultima Thule** (ul′ti·mə thōō′lē) most extreme. The term is Latin for "northernmost region of the world."

Milder! I half smiled in my agony as I thought of such application of such a term.

C What boots it[19] to tell of the long, long hours of horror more than mortal, during which I counted the rushing vibrations of the steel! Inch by inch—line by line—with a descent only appreciable at intervals that seemed ages—down and still down it came! Days passed—it might have been that many days passed—ere it swept so closely over me as to fan me with its acrid breath. The odor of the sharp steel forced itself into my nostrils. I prayed—I wearied heaven with my prayer for its more speedy descent. I grew frantically mad and struggled to force myself upward against the sweep of the fearful scimitar.[20] And then I fell suddenly calm and lay smiling at the glittering death, as a child at some rare bauble.

There was another interval of utter insensibility; it was brief; for, upon again lapsing into life, there had been no perceptible descent in the pendulum. But it might have been long—for I **D** knew there were demons who took note of my swoon and who could have arrested the vibration at pleasure. Upon my recovery, too, I felt very—oh! inexpressibly—sick and weak, as if through long inanition.[21] Even amid the agonies of that period, the human nature craved food. With painful effort I outstretched my left arm as far as my bonds permitted and took possession of the small remnant which had been spared me by the rats. As I put a portion of it within my lips, there rushed to my mind a half-formed thought of joy—of hope. Yet what business had *I* with hope? It was, as I say, a half-formed thought—man has many such, **E** which are never completed. I felt that it was of joy—of hope; but I felt also that it had perished in its formation. In vain I struggled to perfect—to regain it. Long suffering had nearly annihilated all my ordinary powers of mind. I was an imbecile—an idiot.

---

19. **what boots it:** of what use is it.
20. **scimitar** (sim′ə·tər) *n.:* sword with a curved blade, used mainly by Arabs and Turks.
21. **inanition** (in′ə·nish′ən) *n.:* weakness from lack of food.

DEVELOPING FLUENCY

Mixed-ability group activity. Encourage purposeful re-reading by assigning small, mixed-ability groups to prepare news feature stories about the narrator's imprisonment. Direct students to divide the story among themselves—for example, beginning, middle, and end—and to re-read their story section and to list its key events and pertinent details.

Students should then assume individual roles, such as illustrator, writer, editor, and announcer. Tell each group to prepare a tantalizing "teaser" for its feature story ("News from the pit! Details at eleven.") and then to present the story to the class.

The vibration of the pendulum was at right angles to my length. I saw that the crescent was designed to cross the region of the heart. It would fray the serge of my robe—it would return and repeat its operations—again—and again. Notwithstanding its terrifically wide sweep (some thirty feet or more) and the hissing vigor of its descent, sufficient to sunder these very walls of iron, still the fraying of my robe would be all that, for several minutes, it would accomplish. And at this thought I paused. I dared not go further than this reflection. I dwelt upon it with a pertinacity[22] of attention—as if, in so dwelling, I could arrest[23] *here* the descent of the steel. I forced myself to ponder upon the sound of the crescent as it should pass across the garment—upon the peculiar thrilling sensation which the friction of cloth produces on the nerves. I pondered upon all this frivolity until my teeth were on edge.

Down—steadily down it crept. I took a frenzied pleasure in contrasting its downward with its lateral velocity. To the right—to the left—far and wide—with the shriek of a damned spirit! to my heart, with the stealthy pace of the tiger! I alternately laughed and howled, as the one or the other idea grew predominant.

Down—certainly, relentlessly down! It vibrated within three inches of my bosom! I struggled violently—furiously—to free my left arm. This was free only from the elbow to the hand. I could reach the latter, from the platter beside me, to my mouth, with great effort, but no farther. Could I have broken the fastenings above the elbow, I would have seized and attempted to arrest the pendulum. I might as well have attempted to arrest an avalanche!

Down—still unceasingly—still inevitably down! I gasped and struggled at each vibration. I shrunk convulsively at its every sweep. My eyes followed its outward or upward whorls with the eagerness of the most unmeaning despair; they closed themselves spasmodically at the descent, although death would have been a relief, oh,

how unspeakable! Still I quivered in every nerve to think how slight a sinking of the machinery would precipitate that keen, glistening ax upon my bosom. It was *hope* that prompted the nerve to quiver—the frame to shrink. It was *hope*— the hope that triumphs on the rack—that whispers to the death-condemned even in the dungeons of the Inquisition.

I saw that some ten or twelve vibrations would bring the steel in actual contact with my robe, and with this observation there suddenly came over my spirit all the keen, collected calmness of despair. For the first time during many hours—or perhaps days—I *thought*. It now occurred to me that the bandage, or surcingle, which enveloped me, was *unique*. I was tied by no separate cord. The first stroke of the razorlike crescent athwart any portion of the band would so detach it that it might be unwound from my person by means of my left hand. But how fearful, in that case, the proximity of the steel! The result of the slightest struggle, how deadly! Was it likely, moreover, that the minions[24] of the torturer had not foreseen and provided for this possibility? Was it probable that the bandage crossed my bosom in the track of the pendulum? Dreading to find my faint and, as it seemed, my last hope frustrated, I so far elevated my head as to obtain a distinct view of my breast. The surcingle enveloped my limbs and body close in all directions—*save in the path of the destroying crescent.* ❼

Scarcely had I dropped my head back into its original position when there flashed upon my mind what I cannot better describe than as the unformed half of that idea of deliverance to which I had previously alluded, and of which a moiety[25] only floated indeterminately through my brain when I raised food to my burning lips.

> ❼ **Retell** what has happened to the narrator since he first saw the rats coming out of the pit.

---

24. **minions** *n. pl.*: servants; followers.
25. **moiety** (moi′ə·tē) *n.*: part.

Vocabulary
proximity (präk·sim′ə·tē) *n.*: nearness.

---

22. **pertinacity** (purt′′n·as′ə·tē) *n.*: stubborn persistence.
23. **arrest** *v.*: stop.

F **Literary Focus**

❓ **Symbolic meaning.** How does the phrase "damned spirit" reinforce the symbolic meaning of the dungeon? [Possible response: "Damned spirit" can refer to a soul condemned to Hell.]

G **Reading Skills**

❓ **Making inferences.** What had the narrator been doing when he *wasn't* thinking? [Possible responses: His mind was fixated on the motion of the pendulum; he was overcome with a series of extreme emotions; he was in shock.]

H **Reading Skills**

❓ **Making predictions.** What do you predict the narrator's idea will be? [Possible responses: to use the food dish somehow; to use the food; to use the rats.]

Response to Boxed Question

7. As the rats nibble his food, he sees that the pendulum is sharp and slowly descending toward his heart. He eats a bit, then drifts in and out of consciousness, his attention focused on the pendulum, which his torturers always halt until he revives. Much time passes. When the blade is very near, he thinks that it may cut his bonds but then sees that it will not.

Literary Criticism

Critic's Commentary:
D. H. Lawrence on Poe

D. H. Lawrence remarked, "Poe is rather a scientist than an artist. He is reducing his own self as a scientist reduces a salt in a crucible. It is an almost chemical analysis of the soul and consciousness. Whereas in true art there is always the double rhythm of creating and destroying. This is why Poe calls his things 'tales.' They are a concatenation of cause and effect. His best pieces, however, are not tales. They are more. They are ghastly stories of the human soul in its disruptive throes."

Whole-class activity. Ask students if they feel that "The Pit and the Pendulum" is a "ghastly" story "of the human soul in its disruptive throes." Why or why not?

A **Reading Skills**

? **Recognizing rhetorical devices.** The narrator knows the answer to his question, and so do you. What is it? [The rats have eaten other prisoners who fell into the pit.]

B **Reading Skills**

? **Retelling.** How would you retell what the narrator has just done? [He has taken what is left of the food and smeared it on the strap that ties him to the frame.]

C **Literary Focus**

? **Symbolic meaning.** Which details suggest that, to the narrator, the rats symbolize death and decay? [Possible response: The rats' "cold lips" touch his like a kiss of death; they "chill" his heart "with a heavy clamminess"; they fill him with a "disgust" beyond words.]

D **Reading Skills**

? **Retelling.** What does the narrator notice and do after he rolls free? [He stands up and sees the pendulum stop and retract into the ceiling. He then sees that the cell walls are separate from the floor, with light coming from beneath them. He tries to look through the crack.]

Response to Boxed Question

8. He wants to get the rats to gnaw through his bonds. They increase his horror by swarming over him and licking at his lips, but they do eventually eat through the straps, freeing him.

The whole thought was now present—feeble, scarcely sane, scarcely definite—but still entire. I proceeded at once, with the nervous energy of despair, to attempt its execution.

For many hours the immediate vicinity of the low framework upon which I lay had been literally swarming with rats. They were wild, bold, ravenous—their red eyes glaring upon me as if they waited but for motionlessness on my part to **A** make me their prey. "To what food," I thought, "have they been accustomed in the well?"

B They had devoured, in spite of all my efforts to prevent them, all but a small remnant of the contents of the dish. I had fallen into a habitual seesaw or wave of the hand about the platter; and, at length, the unconscious uniformity of the movement deprived it of effect. In their voracity, the vermin frequently fastened their sharp fangs in my fingers. With the particles of the oily and spicy viand which now remained, I thoroughly rubbed the bandage wherever I could reach it; then, raising my hand from the floor, I lay breathlessly still.

At first, the ravenous animals were startled and terrified at the change—at the cessation of movement. They shrank alarmedly back; many sought the well. But this was only for a moment. I had not counted in vain upon their voracity. Observing that I remained without motion, one or two of the boldest leaped upon the framework and smelled at the surcingle. This seemed the signal for a general rush. Forth from the well they hurried in fresh troops. They clung to the wood—they overran it and leaped in hundreds upon my person. The measured movement of the pendulum disturbed them not at all. Avoiding its strokes, they busied themselves with the anointed bandage. They pressed—they swarmed upon me in ever accumulating heaps. They **C** writhed upon my throat; their cold lips sought my own; I was half stifled by their thronging pressure; disgust for which the world has no name swelled my bosom and chilled, with a heavy clamminess, my heart. Yet one minute, and I felt that the struggle would be over. Plainly I perceived the loosening of the bandage. I knew that in more than one place it must be already severed. With a more than human resolution I lay *still.*

Nor had I erred in my calculations—nor had I endured in vain. I at length felt that I was *free.* The surcingle hung in ribbons from my body. But the stroke of the pendulum already pressed upon my bosom. It had divided the serge of the robe. It had cut through the linen beneath. Twice again it swung, and a sharp sense of pain shot through every nerve. But the moment of escape had arrived. At a wave of my hand my deliverers hurried tumultuously away. With a steady movement—cautious, sidelong, shrinking, and slow—I slid from the embrace of the bandage and beyond the reach of the scimitar. For the moment, at least, *I was free.* **8**

8 **?** Why does the narrator rub the binding with the meat? What effect does this have on his situation?

Free!—and in the grasp of the Inquisition! I had scarcely stepped from my wooden bed of horror upon the stone floor of the prison when the motion of the hellish machine ceased, and I beheld it drawn up, by some invisible force, through the ceiling. This was a lesson which I took desperately to heart. My every motion was undoubtedly watched. **D** Free!—I had but escaped death in one form of agony to be delivered unto worse than death in some other. With that thought I rolled my eyes nervously around on the barriers of iron that hemmed me in. Something unusual—some change which at first I could not appreciate distinctly—it was obvious, had taken place in the apartment. For many minutes of a dreamy and trembling abstraction, I busied myself in vain, unconnected conjecture. During this period, I became aware, for the first time, of the origin of the sulfurous light which illumined the cell. It proceeded from a fissure, about half an inch in width, extending entirely around the prison at the base of the walls, which thus appeared, and were, completely separated from the floor. I endeavored, but of course in vain, to look through the aperture.

As I arose from the attempt, the mystery of the alteration in the chamber broke at once

Analyzing cause and effect. Review cause and effect with students, reminding them that in fiction, each event that advances the plot has its own causes and effects. Point out that many plot events involve multiple causes and effects. For example, on p. 262, the narrator is thirsty (cause), so he drinks water (effect). The Inquisitors have drugged the water (cause) so he falls asleep (effect), enabling them to bind him beneath the pendulum (second effect). Remind students that personality traits of characters can also affect a story's plot.

Activity. Assign students one page from "The Pit and the Pendulum," and direct them to list key events, specific causes, and corresponding effects. Then, ask students to consider how cause-and-effect relationships advance the plot of "The Pit and the Pendulum" as a whole. What major causes and effects govern the narrator's situation and actions?

A scene from "The Pit and the Pendulum," illustrated by John Byam Shaw.

VIEWING THE ART

John Byam Shaw (1872–1919) illustrated numerous books with watercolors and drawings. Influenced by the composition and intense use of color of the Pre-Raphaelites, Shaw was known for his romantic flair. In his later work, he enjoyed painting allegories that combined realistic details with fantasy images.

Activity. Invite students to compare the composition of this illustration and the one on pp. 256–257, which shows nearly the same scene. [In Shaw's illustration, diagonal lines, real and implied, draw the eye toward two points of convergence: the prisoner and the pit. At the upper right, the pendulum seems poised to fall, and the white-hot glow beneath the walls bisects the painting. On pp. 256–257, the pit is not shown. The stylized pendulum blade, conveyed by negative space, takes up almost half the drawing, glowing gold-white and crowding the figure of the prisoner.]

A **Literary Focus**

Subgenre: The horror story.
Challenge students to list characteristics of the horror story (a subgenre pioneered by Poe) and to explain how this story demonstrates those characteristics. [Possible response: The story creates mounting fear and anxiety and makes the incredible credible by developing the character of the narrator in a realistic way and by building the increasingly bizarre setting (the dungeon) with realistic details taken from a real-life situation (the Inquisition).]

B **Literary Focus**

❓ Symbolic meaning. On a symbolic level, who is the "King of Terrors"? [the Devil; Satan]

C **Reading Skills**

❓ Evaluating credibility. How believable do you find the setting? [Possible responses: It is credible because it is based on a historical situation and includes realistic details and logical explanations; it isn't credible because the complexity of the dungeon's machinery strains belief.]

D **Literary Focus**

❓ Symbolic meaning. What symbolic meaning might Lasalle's arrival have? [Possible response: God's pardoning of the damned.]

Response to Boxed Question

9. The metal walls and ceiling of the dungeon glow red-hot and close in on him, forcing him toward the pit.

---

upon my understanding. I had observed that, although the outlines of the figures upon the walls were sufficiently distinct, yet the colors seemed blurred and indefinite. These colors had now assumed and were momentarily assuming, a startling and most intense brilliance that gave to the spectral and fiendish portraitures an aspect that might have thrilled even firmer nerves than my own. Demon eyes, of a wild and ghastly vivacity, glared upon me in a thousand directions where none had been visible before, and gleamed with the lurid luster of a fire that I could not force my imagination to regard as unreal.

Unreal!—even while I breathed, there came to my nostrils the breath of the vapor of heated iron! A suffocating odor pervaded the prison! A deeper glow settled each moment in the eyes that glared at my agonies! A richer tint of crimson diffused itself over the pictured horrors of blood. I panted! I gasped for breath! There could be no doubt of the design of my tormenters—oh! most unrelenting! oh! most demoniac of men! I shrank from the glowing metal to the center of the cell. Amid the thought of the fiery destruction that impended, the idea of the coolness of the well came over my soul like balm. I rushed to its deadly brink. I threw my straining vision below. The glare from the enkindled roof illumined its inmost recesses. Yet for a wild moment did my spirit refuse to comprehend the meaning of what I saw. At length it forced—it wrestled its way into my soul—it burned itself in upon my shuddering reason.—Oh! for a voice to speak!—oh! horror! —oh! any horror but this! With a shriek, I rushed from the margin and buried my face in my hands—weeping bitterly.

The heat rapidly increased, and once again I looked up, shuddering as with a fit of the ague.[26] There had been a second change in the cell—and now the change was obviously in the *form.* As before, it was in vain that I at first endeavored to appreciate or understand what was taking place. But not long was I left in doubt. The Inquisitorial vengeance had been hurried by my

---

26. **ague** (ā′gyōō′) *n.:* chills.

---

twofold escape, and there was to be no more dallying with the King of Terrors. The room had been square. I saw that two of its iron angles were now acute[27]—two, consequently, obtuse.[28] The fearful difference quickly increased with a low rumbling or moaning sound. In an instant the apartment had shifted its form into that of a lozenge.[29] But the alteration stopped not here—I neither hoped nor desired it to stop. I could have clasped the red walls to my bosom as a garment of eternal peace. "Death," I said, "any death but that of the pit!" Fool! Might I not have known that *into the pit* it was the object of the burning iron to urge me? Could I resist its glow? Or if even that, could I withstand its pressure? And now, flatter and flatter grew the lozenge, with a rapidity that left me no time for contemplation. Its center, and of course its greatest width, came just over the yawning gulf. I shrank back—but the closing walls pressed me resistlessly onward. At length, for my seared and writhing body, there was no longer an inch of foothold on the firm floor of the prison. I struggled no more, but the agony of my soul found vent in one loud, long, and final scream of despair. I felt that I tottered upon the brink—I averted my eyes— ❾

There was a discordant hum of human voices! There was a loud blast as of many trumpets! There was a harsh grating as of a thousand thunders! The fiery walls rushed back! An outstretched arm caught my own as I fell, fainting, into the abyss. It was that of General Lasalle. The French army had entered Toledo. The Inquisition was in the hands of its enemies. ■

> **❓** What third crisis does the narrator face after he escapes from his "bed of horror"?

---

27. **acute** *adj.:* of less than 90 degrees.
28. **obtuse** *adj.:* of more than 90 degrees and less than 180 degrees.
29. **lozenge** *n.:* diamond shape.

Vocabulary
averted (ə·vurt′id) *v.:* turned away; prevented.

Analyzing point of view. Review with students the three possible points of view that a story may have: first-person, third-person limited, and third-person omniscient. Ask students to recall key characteristics for each point of view. Then, ask students to recall the differences between a subjective and an objective point of view.

Activity. Have students identify specific sentences in "The Pit and the Pendulum" that reveal the point of view. Then, have students analyze in a brief discussion how the point of view and choice of narrator affect the story's tone and credibility. Finally, have students list what they would like to learn from a narrator with a different point of view. For example, they may want to know what the Inquisitors are thinking, what the prisoner's name is, what he looks like, and what he is accused of.

Response and Analysis

Reading Check

1. The retellings you did while reading the story should help you fill out a story map like the one below. Add as many events as you think are necessary.

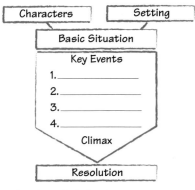

```
Characters        Setting
    Basic Situation
      Key Events
  1._____
  2._____
  3._____
  4._____
        Climax
      Resolution
```

Thinking Critically

2. The **setting** of this story may be its most unforgettable element. List at least six of its horrible details. Did any of these horrors tap into the fear you described in your Quickwrite notes?

3. Some critics read Poe's text **symbolically,** as the story of a man who dies and almost loses his soul in the pit of hell but is saved at the end by God. See if the story works with this symbolic interpretation. Consider the following items:

   • The man, above all, fears falling into the pit. What could the pit symbolize?

   • What does a pendulum suggest to you, and what does an old man with a scythe represent? What connection might there be between these two symbols and the scythe on the pendulum in Poe's story?

   • Rats are often used as symbols of death and decay. How does the prisoner's response to these rats—especially when they crawl over him—suggest that he might see them in this way?

• What sounds are usually associated with Judgment Day, at the end of the world? Do you hear these sounds at the story's end?

   Do you think this symbolic reading makes sense, or is it stretching the meaning of a simple horror story too far? Explain.

4. Stories of imprisonment and torture often explore **themes** of power and its abuse. What comment do you think Poe may be making about the political, religious, and social situation in the historical period in which this story takes place?

Extending and Evaluating

5. Did General Lasalle's arrival seem an exceptionally lucky coincidence to you? If so, did the last-minute rescue lessen the story's credibility or your enjoyment of the story? Explain your opinion.

WRITING

The Story as Springboard

On page 258, you read a brief feature about the political situation in Spain during the fifteenth century. These details shed some interesting light on Poe's brutal story. Select a topic that is featured in the story or in *A Closer Look,* and write a **research report.** You might focus on one of these topics:

• the Spanish Inquisition

• the Moors in Spain during the Middle Ages

• the Jewish presence in Spain in the Middle Ages

• El Greco (see the art on page 260)

Before you begin, formulate a series of questions about the topic you choose. As you find the answers to those broad questions, make decisions that will narrow the focus of your research.

▶ Use "Reporting Historical Research," pages 528–547, for help with this assignment.

SKILLS FOCUS

Literary Skills
Analyze symbolic meaning.

Reading Skills
Retell key events.

Writing Skills
Write a historical research report. Write an updated horror story.

Vocabulary Skills
Use context clues to determine the meanings of words.

Edgar Allan Poe **269**

Reading Check

1. *Characters*—narrator, judges, unseen torturers, Gen. Lasalle. *Setting*—courtroom and dungeon in Toledo, Spain during the Inquisition. *Situation*—narrator is condemned to death by torture. *Key Events*—*1.* Narrator is put in dungeon, trips, and discovers pit. *2.* Narrator is bound to frame under pendulum. *3.* Narrator gets rats to chew his bindings and rolls free at last minute. *4.* Walls heat up and close in, forcing narrator toward the pit where rats wait. *Climax*—Narrator teeters at brink of pit; strange noises erupt, and walls recede. *Resolution*—Narrator faints, falls, and is rescued.

INDEPENDENT PRACTICE

Response and Analysis

Thinking Critically

2. Sample answers: total darkness, silence, tomb-like enclosure, deep pit, smell of decay, rats, pendulum with a razor-sharp edge, walls closing in; fire; falling. Students may connect any of these with their own fears.

3. Some students may feel that a symbolic interpretation is plausible but prefer simply to enjoy the story as a masterful tale of horror. Most students will agree that a symbolic interpretation is valid because it recognizes the depth in a story that includes the following symbols:

   • pit—death or Hell

   • pendulum—time; old man with scythe—Grim Reaper (death); the scythe on the pendulum suggests time running out for the prisoner and death coming to claim him.

   • The rats horrify and disgust the prisoner. His responses connect them with death and decay.

   • sounds—human wails and trumpet blasts herald Judgment Day. At the story's end, we hear discordant voices, trumpet blasts, and thunder, suggestive of Judgment Day.

4. By exploring the internal torment as well as the external torture that the narrator suffers, and by characterizing the torturers as two-dimensional, faceless, and thoroughly sadistic, Poe shows that he considers the Spanish Inquisition's abuse of power grotesque and inhuman.

Extending and Evaluating

5. Some students may find the ending contrived, improbable, or disappointing; others may feel that since the entire story is a series of surprising, dramatic turns, one more at the end does not seem out of place.

Edgar Allan Poe **269**

Vocabulary Development

1. Clear instructions would help someone thinking about how to operate a complex device. *Context clues*—"simple"; "how to operate." *Poe's clues*—"lucid reason" contrasted with confused, vague memories; "he who ponders over the perfume . . . he whose brain. . . ."

2. Quiet breathing followed by sounds of battle. *Context clues*—"faintly"; "shocking." *Poe's clues*—"soft and nearly imperceptible"; "tumultuous motion of the heart . . . beating."

3. She turned her eyes away because she was so close that the flash would hurt them. *Context clues*—"standing in proximity to"; "blinding flash." *Poe's clues*—"how fearful . . . the proximity of the [sharp] steel!" "I averted my eyes [from the feared pit]."

4. They might lie flat in fear or submission if the enemy were impossible to beat. *Context clues*—"desperate"; "lie . . . on the ground." *Poe's clues*—"The difficulty . . . was but trivial, although . . . it seemed at first insuperable"; "fatigue induced me to remain prostrate . . . as I lay."

5. Skunk, smoke, and gas are three powerful smells that would rouse someone from drowsiness. *Context clues*—"smells . . . rouse"; "rouse . . . summer afternoon's." *Poe's clues*—"I had been deceived . . . so potent is the effect of total darkness"; "lethargy or sleep."

WRITING

Terror Today

"The Pit and the Pendulum" is a classic psychological horror story. Do you think the events in the story—or something like them—could take place today? Fill out a chart like the following one for help organizing your thoughts:

	Poe's Story	Updated Story
Setting (when and where?)		
Protagonist (What is his or her crime?)		
Punishment		
Opponents or jailers		
Rescuers		

Then, write your own modern retelling.

▶ Use "Writing a Short Story," pages 284–291, for help with this assignment.

Illustration by Wilfred Satty for "The Fall of the House of Usher" by Edgar Allan Poe.

Vocabulary Development

Using Context Clues

Justify your responses to each numbered item below. Then, indicate the context clues in each sentence that gave you hints to the meaning of each underlined word. When you've identified the context clues in the sentences, go back to Poe's story, and write down any context clues he gives for the underlined Vocabulary words.

1. Why would simple, lucid instructions help someone who ponders the operation of a videocassette recorder?

2. A mystery movie's soundtrack begins faintly, with an almost imperceptible noise, quickly followed by shocking, tumultuous sounds. Suggest examples of each type of sound.

3. Explain why a woman standing in proximity to a blinding flash of light would have averted her eyes.

4. Why might desperate people facing an insuperable enemy lie prostrate on the ground?

5. Name three potent smells that would rouse you from a summer afternoon's lethargy.

Vocabulary Development

Greek, Latin, and Anglo-Saxon Affixes in Math and Science

Prefixes and suffixes are examples of **affixes,** word parts that are attached to the beginning or end of a base word or root to make a new word. Knowing some frequently used affixes can help you quickly unlock the meanings of some difficult words.

Prefixes are added to the beginning of a base word and always change its meaning. The following chart shows prefixes commonly used in mathematical and scientific terms:

Latin Prefixes	Meanings	Examples
co–, col–, com–	with; together	coefficient, collide, compute
circum–	around	circumvent, circumnavigate
di–, dis–	away; lack of	disinfect, dilute
re–	again; back	research, reproduce
Greek Prefixes	**Meanings**	**Examples**
ant–, anti–	against; opposing	antibiotic, antidote
hypo–	under; below	hypothesis, hypodermic
micro–	enlarging; small	microscope, microorganism
Anglo-Saxon Prefixes	**Meanings**	**Examples**
mis–	badly or wrongly; not	misdiagnose, miscalculate
over–	too much	overdose, overestimate
un–	not	unconscious, unknown

(continued)

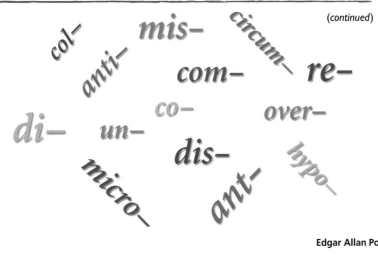

SKILLS FOCUS

Vocabulary Skills
Use Latin, Greek, and Anglo-Saxon affixes to infer meanings of scientific and mathematical terms.

Vocabulary Development

Practice

1. *Word*—cognizance. *Base*—cognoscere, "to learn of; to become aware of." *Suffix*—–ance, "state or quality of being." *Meaning*—"state of awareness."

2. *Word*—intensity. *Base*—intense, "extreme in degree." *Suffix*—–ity, "state of." *Meaning*—"state of being intense."

3. *Word*—alteration. *Base*—alter, "to change." *Suffix*— –tion, "action of." *Meaning*—"action of changing."

4. *Word*—sulfurous. *Base*—sulfur, a chemical element. *Suffix*— –ous, "full of." *Meaning*—"full of sulfur."

5. *Word*—circumstance. *Prefix*—circum–, "around." *Base*—stare, "to stand." *Suffix*— –ance, "state or quality of being." *Meaning*—"condition surrounding."

6. *Word*—insensibility. *Prefix*— in–, "not." *Base*—sense, "feeling." *Suffixes*— –ible, "able to," + –ity, "state of." *Meaning*—"state of being unable to feel."

7. *Word*—relapsed. *Prefix*—re–, "back." *Base*—lapse, "fall." *Meaning*—"fell back."

8. *Word*—disorder. *Prefix*—dis–, "lack of." *Base*—order, "proper arrangement." *Meaning*—"lack of proper arrangement."

9. *Word*—evidently. *Base*—evident, "clear, obvious." *Suffix*— –ly, "characteristic of." *Meaning*—"characteristic of what is obvious."

10. *Word*—limitless. *Base*—limit, "end." *Suffix*— –less, "without." *Meaning*—"without end."

Suffixes are added to the end of a base word or root. **Inflectional suffixes,** like –ed and –ing, usually just change the tense, the person, or the number of a word (generally a verb). **Derivational suffixes,** like the ones listed below, change the meaning of a root or base word. This chart shows suffixes commonly used in math and science:

Greek and Latin Suffixes	Meanings	Examples
–ance, –ence	state or quality of being	buoyance, turbulence
–able, –ible	able to; likely to	malleable, combustible
–tion	action of; condition of	respiration, condensation
–ous	full of	igneous, deciduous
–cy	condition of; state of	accuracy, currency
–ity	state of; condition of	possibility, regularity
Anglo-Saxon Suffixes	**Meanings**	**Examples**
–ness	quality or state of being	consciousness, sickness
–dom	state of being; rank of or domain of	kingdom, wisdom
–ly	like; characteristic of	internally, regressively
–less	lacking; without	motionless, bloodless

This chart shows one way in which you can do an affix analysis to get at the meaning of a difficult word:

Word	Prefix + Its Meaning	Base/Root Word + Its Meaning	Suffix + Its Meaning	Meaning of Word
unconsciousness	un–, "not"	conscious, "knowing; feeling"	–ness, "quality or state of being"	the state of not knowing or feeling

PRACTICE

Make your own affix-analysis chart for these words from "The Pit and the Pendulum." Use a dictionary for help.

1. cognizance
2. intensity
3. alteration
4. sulfurous
5. circumstance
6. insensibility
7. relapsed
8. disorder
9. evidently
10. limitless

–ness –ous –ly –tion –able –dom –ance

ASSESSING

Assessment

■ *Holt Assessment: Literature, Reading, and Vocabulary*

Before You Read

The Raven

Make the Connection

"The Raven"—one of the most famous poems ever written—is a narrative poem with a story line that leads the reader from curiosity to horror. The poem explores one aspect of the dark side of human nature—what Poe himself called "that species of despair which delights in self-torture." In the jargon of psychology, the narrator projects or puts onto the bird whatever his own wild imagination dredges up.

Literary Focus
Sound Effects

One of the reasons "The Raven" electrified the public is that it's catchy in the way a song can be. Like many songs, the poem has evocative rhythms, clever rhymes, alliteration, and other pleasing sound effects. These devices make you want to read the poem aloud or listen to it being read aloud. You want to hear not only the story but also the *sound* of the story.

As you read or listen, bear in mind that literary sound effects—just like movie sound effects—have a purpose. What is Poe trying to accomplish with the sound effects he creates in "The Raven"?

Background

When "The Raven" was first published, in 1845 in a New York newspaper, it was a hit—an enormous popular success with the same kind of impact that a new CD might have today. Back then it seemed as if everyone was reading "The Raven," reciting it, and talking about it. As a result of the poem's success, Poe's name became a household word—yet he received only about ten dollars for his work.

INTERNET

More About Edgar Allan Poe

Keyword: LE5 11–2

SKILLS FOCUS

Literary Skills
Understand sound effects in poetry.

Edgar Allan Poe   273

Grade-Level Skills

■ **Literary Skills**
Analyze ways poets use sound effects.

PRETEACHING

Summary ⬌ *at grade level*

The speaker in this narrative poem, a weary student, is studying at midnight and mourning his dead love, Lenore. He hears a faint knock, and opening the shutter, he finds a mysterious raven. The talking bird amuses the speaker at first, but its refrain of "Nevermore," in answer to the speaker's pleading questions about meeting Lenore after death, drives him to despair and madness. As the poem closes, the bird settles in to stay, a brooding symbol and symptom of the speaker's desperate state of mind.

Selection Starter

Build background. You might share with students Poe's explanation of his choice of subject matter: "I asked myself 'Of all melancholy topics, what, according to the universal understanding of mankind, is the most melancholy?' Death—was the obvious reply. 'And when,' I said, 'is this most melancholy of topics most poetical?' . . . the answer, here also, is obvious—'When it most closely allies itself to *Beauty*: The death then, of a beautiful woman is, unquestionably, the most poetical topic in the world. . . .'"

RESOURCES: READING

Planning
■ *One-Stop Planner* CD-ROM with ExamView Test Generator

Differentiating Instruction
■ *Holt Reading Solutions*
■ *The Holt Reader*
■ *Holt Adapted Reader*
■ *Supporting Instruction in Spanish*

Grammar and Language
■ *Daily Language Activities*

Assessment
■ *Holt Assessment: Literature, Reading, and Vocabulary*
■ *One-Stop Planner* CD-ROM with ExamView Test Generator
■ *Holt Online Assessment*

Internet
■ go.hrw.com (Keyword: LE5 11-2)
■ *Elements of Literature Online*

Media
■ *Audio CD Library*
■ *Audio CD Library, Selections and Summaries in Spanish*

A Literary Focus

? Sound effects. What is the poem's rhyme scheme? [*abcbbb*] The entire poem uses the same *b* end rhyme. What difficulties does this pose for the writer? [Possible response: The writer must come up with many rhyming words for the /ôr/ sound.]

The Raven

Edgar Allan Poe

Once upon a midnight dreary, while I pondered, weak and weary,
Over many a quaint and curious volume of forgotten lore—
While I nodded, nearly napping, suddenly there came a tapping,
As of someone gently rapping, rapping at my chamber door—
5   " 'Tis some visitor," I muttered, "tapping at my chamber door—
    Only this and nothing more."

274   Collection 2   American Romanticism: 1800–1860

DIFFERENTIATING INSTRUCTION

Learners Having Difficulty
Build background knowledge by pointing out that in Western cultures, ravens have long been considered portentous and wise. In Greek and Roman epics, they function as omens. In Norse mythology, two ravens, Thought and Memory, keep watch on the world and advise the high god Odin. In

Christian lore, the raven occurs as a symbol of sin, the devil, or death.

Instruct learners having difficulty to read "The Raven" in interactive format in *The Holt Reader* and to use the sidenotes as aids to understanding the selection.

English-Language Learners
The insistent rhyme and rhythm of "The Raven" may distract students from the narrative. Suggest that they read the poem at least twice: first for the sound and then for the story.

Ah, distinctly I remember it was in the bleak December;
And each separate dying ember wrought its ghost upon the floor.
Eagerly I wished the morrow;—vainly I had sought to borrow
10   From my books surcease° of sorrow—sorrow for the lost Lenore—
For the rare and radiant maiden whom the angels name Lenore—
      Nameless *here* for evermore.

And the silken, sad, uncertain rustling of each purple curtain
Thrilled me—filled me with fantastic terrors never felt before;
15   So that now, to still the beating of my heart, I stood repeating
" 'Tis some visitor entreating° entrance at my chamber door—
Some late visitor entreating entrance at my chamber door;—
      This it is and nothing more."

Presently my soul grew stronger; hesitating then no longer,
20   "Sir," said I, "or Madam, truly your forgiveness I implore;°
But the fact is I was napping, and so gently you came rapping,
And so faintly you came tapping, tapping at my chamber door,
That I scarce was sure I heard you"—here I opened wide the door;—
      Darkness there and nothing more.

25   Deep into that darkness peering, long I stood there wondering, fearing,
Doubting, dreaming dreams no mortal ever dared to dream before;
But the silence was unbroken, and the stillness gave no token,
And the only word there spoken was the whispered word, "Lenore?"
This I whispered, and an echo murmured back the word, "Lenore!"
30   Merely this and nothing more.

Back into the chamber turning, all my soul within me burning,
Soon again I heard a tapping somewhat louder than before.
"Surely," said I, "surely that is something at my window lattice;°
Let me see, then, what thereat is, and this mystery explore—
35   Let my heart be still a moment and this mystery explore;—
      'Tis the wind and nothing more!"

10. surcease *n.:* end.

16. entreating *v.:* begging; asking.

20. implore *v.:* plead; ask.

33. lattice *n.:* shutter or screen formed by strips or bars overlaid in a crisscross pattern.

Edgar Allan Poe   **275**

DIRECT TEACHING

B **Reading Skills**

❓ **Interpreting.** What do you think *here* means, and which parts of this stanza show its meaning? [Possible response: It means "in this life" or "on earth"; Lenore is "Nameless *here* for evermore" because to the speaker's "sorrow," she is "lost"—she has died. She is now with "the angels."]

C **Reading Skills**

❓ **Tracing a recurring theme.** What idea about Lenore's death does the word *evermore* suggest? [Possible responses: It reinforces the finality of Lenore's death. It suggests she is gone from earth for good.]

D **Literary Focus**

❓ **Sound effects.** What refrains close the first four stanzas? [*and nothing more* and *for evermore*] With which name do these refrains rhyme? [Lenore] What effect is achieved by these sound effects? [The disappearance of Lenore is made to seem absolute and eternal.]

Special Education Students
For lessons designed for special education students, see *Holt Reading Solutions*.

Advanced Learners
Acceleration. To lead students toward more advanced study of sound effects, discuss the term *feminine rhyme,* defining it as "a rhyme of two or more syllables, with the final syllable unstressed" (for example, *gratitude* and *latitude*), and the term *slant rhyme,* defining it as "a rhyming sound that is not exact" (for example, *upper* and *dapper*). Encourage students to notice Poe's uses of feminine rhyme and slant rhyme in "The Raven."

❓ Symbol. In Greek mythology, ravens symbolize wisdom and prophecy. What does the raven's perching on the bust of Athena imply? [Possible responses: that the raven will offer wisdom; that the raven has the powers of an oracle.]

B **Learners Having Difficulty**

❓ Interpreting. Why does the speaker think at first that Nevermore is the bird's name? [The bird says that word in answer to "Tell me what thy lordly name is" (l. 47).] Now *Nevermore* becomes the poem's new refrain. At the end of each stanza, ask yourself what specific comment or question the word *Nevermore* relates to.

C **English-Language Learners**

❓ Reading inverted text. In these two lines, Poe inverts standard English word order. How would you paraphrase the first line? [I was surprised to hear the clumsy bird talk so clearly.]

D **Literary Focus**

❓ Tone. How do the speaker's expectations reveal an increasingly despairing attitude? [The speaker expects that the raven will soon abandon him, just as "Other friends have flown before."]

E **Literary Focus**

❓ Sound effects. What sound effects does Poe employ in these three lines? [repetition ("fancy," "ominous"); alliteration ("grim, ungainly, ghastly, gaunt"); and onomatopoeia ("croaking")] What do they reveal about the speaker's state of mind? [Possible response: They show that he now sees the bird as a symbol of his unending sorrow.]

Open here I flung the shutter, when, with many a flirt and flutter,
In there stepped a stately Raven of the saintly days of yore;°
Not the least obeisance° made he; not a minute stopped or stayed he;
40 But, with mien° of lord or lady, perched above my chamber door—
Perched upon a bust of Pallas° just above my chamber door—
            Perched, and sat, and nothing more.

Then this ebony bird beguiling° my sad fancy into smiling,
By the grave and stern decorum of the countenance it wore,
45 "Though thy crest be shorn and shaven, thou," I said, "art sure no craven,
Ghastly grim and ancient Raven wandering from the Nightly shore—
Tell me what thy lordly name is on the Night's Plutonian shore!"°
            Quoth the Raven "Nevermore."

Much I marveled this ungainly° fowl to hear discourse so plainly,
50 Though its answer little meaning—little relevancy bore;
For we cannot help agreeing that no living human being
Ever yet was blessed with seeing bird above his chamber door—
Bird or beast upon the sculptured bust above his chamber door,
            With such name as "Nevermore."

55 But the Raven, sitting lonely on the placid bust, spoke only
That one word, as if his soul in that one word he did outpour.
Nothing farther then he uttered—not a feather then he fluttered—
Till I scarcely more than muttered "Other friends have flown before—
On the morrow *he* will leave me, as my Hopes have flown before."
60   Then the bird said "Nevermore."

Startled at the stillness broken by reply so aptly spoken,
"Doubtless," said I, "what it utters is its only stock and store
Caught from some unhappy master whom unmerciful Disaster
Followed fast and followed faster till his songs one burden bore—
65 Till the dirges of his Hope that melancholy burden bore
            Of 'Never—nevermore.'"

But the Raven still beguiling my sad fancy into smiling,
Straight I wheeled a cushioned seat in front of bird, and bust and door;
Then, upon the velvet sinking, I betook myself to linking
70 Fancy unto fancy, thinking what this ominous bird of yore—
What this grim, ungainly, ghastly, gaunt, and ominous bird of yore
            Meant in croaking "Nevermore."

38. Raven . . . of yore: *Of yore* is an obsolete way of saying "of time long past." Poe's allusion is to 1 Kings 17:1–6, which tells of the prophet Elijah being fed by ravens in the wilderness.
39. obeisance (ō · bā′səns) *n.*: gesture of respect.
40. mien (mēn) *n.*: manner.
41. Pallas: Pallas Athena, the Greek goddess of wisdom.
43. beguiling *v.* used as *adj.*: deceiving.
47. Plutonian shore: Pluto is the Greek god of the underworld—the land of darkness—called Hades (hā′dēz′). Hades is separated from the world of the living by several rivers; hence, the mention of a shore.
49. ungainly *adj.*: unattractive.

CONTENT-AREA CONNECTIONS

Music: Tone Poems
During the mid-1800s and early 1900s, composers began creating tone poems, which are works in which a literary or descriptive idea serves as the basis of a musical composition. One famous, dark symphonic poem is *Danse Macabre* (*Macabre Dance*) by French composer Camille Saint-Saëns (1835–1921). This piece "tells" of a wintry midnight when Death plays a tune on his violin, setting skeletons dancing until a rooster's crow ushers in the dawn.
Mixed-ability group activity. Play a recording of *Danse Macabre*. Ask students to identify the sounds that signal the stroke of midnight, the eerie violin tune, the wild dancing of the skeletons, and the rooster's crow. Then, group students of mixed abilities, and invite them to present a reading of "The Raven," using *Danse Macabre* as background music.

This I sat engaged in guessing, but no syllable expressing
To the fowl whose fiery eyes now burned into my bosom's core;
75 This and more I sat divining,° with my head at ease reclining
On the cushion's velvet lining that the lamplight gloated o'er,
But whose velvet-violet lining with the lamplight gloating o'er,
　　　　She shall press, ah, nevermore!

Then, methought, the air grew denser, perfumed from an unseen censer
80 Swung by seraphim° whose footfalls tinkled on the tufted floor.
"Wretch," I cried, "thy God hath lent thee—by these angels he hath sent thee
Respite—respite and nepenthe° from thy memories of Lenore;
Quaff,° oh quaff this kind nepenthe and forget this lost Lenore!"
　　　　Quoth the Raven "Nevermore."

85 "Prophet!" said I, "thing of evil!—prophet still, if bird or devil!—
Whether Tempter sent, or whether tempest tossed thee here ashore,
Desolate yet all undaunted,° on this desert land enchanted—
On this home by Horror haunted—tell me truly, I implore—
Is there—*is* there balm in Gilead?°—tell me—tell me, I implore!"
90 　　　　Quoth the Raven "Nevermore."

"Prophet!" said I, "thing of evil!—prophet still, if bird or devil!
By that Heaven that bends above us—by that God we both adore—
Tell this soul with sorrow laden if, within the distant Aidenn,°
It shall clasp a sainted maiden whom the angels name Lenore—
95 Clasp a rare and radiant maiden whom the angels name Lenore."
　　　　Quoth the Raven "Nevermore."

"Be that word our sign of parting, bird or fiend!" I shrieked, upstarting—
"Get thee back into the tempest and the Night's Plutonian shore!
Leave no black plume as a token of that lie thy soul hath spoken!
100 Leave my loneliness unbroken!—quit the bust above my door!
Take thy beak from out my heart, and take thy form from off my door!"
　　　　Quoth the Raven "Nevermore."

And the Raven, never flitting, still is sitting, *still* is sitting
On the pallid° bust of Pallas just above my chamber door;
105 And his eyes have all the seeming of a demon's that is dreaming,
And the lamplight o'er him streaming throws his shadow on the floor;
And my soul from out that shadow that lies floating on the floor
　　　　Shall be lifted—nevermore!

Side glossary:

75. divining *v.* used as *adj.*: guessing; supposing.

80. seraphim *n. pl.*: highest of the nine ranks of angels.

82. nepenthe (nē·pen′thē) *n.*: sleeping potion that people once believed would relieve pain and sorrow.

83. quaff *v.*: drink heartily.

87. undaunted *adj.*: unafraid.

89. Is . . . Gilead: literally, Is there any relief from my sorrow? Poe paraphrases a line from Jeremiah 8:22: "Is there no balm in Gilead?" Gilead was a region in ancient Palestine known for its healing herbs, such as balm, a healing ointment.

93. Aidenn: Arabic for "Eden; Heaven."

104. pallid *adj.*: pale.

DIRECT TEACHING

F Literary Focus

❓ Sound effects. In the fourth and fifth lines of every stanza, Poe uses repetition as well as internal rhymes and end rhymes. What do these sound effects usually emphasize? [Possible response: They emphasize the depressing idea in each stanza.]

G Literary Focus

❓ Sound effects. Line 91 repeats l. 85. What does the repetition suggest about the speaker's state of mind? [He is becoming obsessed; the same phrases keep running through his mind.]

H Advanced Learners

❓ Acceleration. What internal slant rhyme does Poe use in this line? [evil/devil] Is this a masculine or a feminine rhyme? [feminine] What key idea receives added emphasis from these sound effects? [Possible response: the idea that the speaker now sees the bird as a devil or an evil omen.]

I Literary Focus

❓ Sound effects. Why is the meaning of "Nevermore" in this stanza especially painful for the narrator? [Possible response: The raven's "Nevermore" seems to dash the speaker's last hope of meeting Lenore in an afterlife.]

Edgar Allan Poe　**277**

DEVELOPING FLUENCY

Individual activity. Invite students to write humorous parodies of "The Raven" and to read them aloud for the class. To get students started, you might tell them that Poe barely scratched the surface with his rhyming /ôr/ words. He left out such gems as *bore, snore, sore, galore, albacore, kitchen floor, carnivore, semaphore, convenience store,* and *two-by-four.*

Direct students to use rhyming dictionaries if they wish and to make their parodies at least two stanzas in length.

This feature is based on excerpts from Poe's essay on writing "The Raven." Poe says that he first established his goal: to create a melancholy effect on his audience. He chose the refrain and then the bird to help produce that effect. Only then did he choose the topic: the death of a beloved, beautiful woman. The first lines he wrote were ll. 85–90, a dramatic confrontation between the speaker and the raven. After that, he composed the rest of the poem to reflect "the human thirst for self-torture" as the speaker aggravates his own sorrow by pursuing the "conversation" with the raven.

DIRECT TEACHING

A **Reading Informational Text**

? **Making generalizations.** Do you think most writers begin with a desire to evoke a single emotion, as Poe claims he did, or is it more common to begin with a desire to tell a story or explore a theme? **Explain your reasoning.** [Possible responses: the latter, because storytelling is a universal human impulse; the former, because it's more challenging artistically.]

B **Reading Informational Text**

? **Finding details in the text to support the argument.** In your view, which details about the raven reinforce Poe's statement that it is "emblematical [symbolic] . . . of *Mournful and never ending Remembrance*"? [Possible responses: the raven's somber looks and demeanor; its repetition of "Nevermore," which sounds like a long moan; the fact that it will not leave; its effect on the soul of the speaker, pushing him into despair.]

PRIMARY SOURCE / ESSAY

Poe's Process: Writing "The Raven"

INFORMATIONAL TEXT

Several years after the hugely successful publication of "The Raven," Poe wrote an essay describing how he composed it. He described the writing of the poem as though he were solving a mathematical puzzle. Here are the first stages of Poe's writing process:

1. He decided he wanted to write a poem with a melancholy effect.
2. Then he decided that the melancholy would be reinforced by the refrain "Nevermore" (he liked its sound) and that a raven would utter the refrain. (Before he settled on a raven, though, he considered an owl and even a parrot.)
3. Finally, he decided his subject would be what he thought was the most melancholy subject in the world: a lover mourning for a beautiful woman who has died.

Now Poe was ready to write. The first stanza he wrote, he claimed, was the climactic one, lines 85–90. From there he set about choosing his details: the interior space in which the lover, who is a student, and the raven are brought together; the tapping that introduces the raven; the fact that the night is stormy rather than calm; and the action of the raven alighting on the bust of Pallas.

Then Poe goes on to describe his writing process:

> 66 The raven addressed, answers with its customary word, 'Nevermore'—a word which finds immediate echo in the melancholy heart of the student, who, giving utterance aloud to certain thoughts suggested by the occasion, is again startled by the fowl's repetition of 'Nevermore.'

Drawing by Chas. Addams. Courtesy of Tee and Charles Addams Foundation.

"One more time."

The student now guesses the state of the case, but is impelled, as I have before explained, by the human thirst for self-torture, and in part by superstition, to propound such queries to the bird as will bring him, the lover, the most of the luxury of sorrow, through the anticipated answer 'Nevermore.' . . .

It will be observed that the words 'from out my heart' involve the first metaphorical expression in the poem. They, with the answer 'Nevermore,' dispose the mind to seek a moral in all that has been previously narrated. The reader begins now to regard the raven as emblematical [symbolic]— but it is not until the very last line of the very last stanza, that the intention of making him emblematical of *Mournful and never ending Remembrance* is permitted distinctly to be seen. . . . 99

Literary Criticism

Critic's Commentary: Pure Fiction?
Critic Daniel Hoffman believes that Poe's explanation of how he wrote "The Raven" is pure fiction. Hoffman thinks Poe's essay is more a defense of theories of poetry than an actual account of writing "The Raven." Read Hoffman's comments to students, and ask them to explain whom they find more credible—Hoffman or Poe.

"Poe . . . does warn us, at the very end of his essay, to look more deeply than his autopsy of 'The Raven' delved: look, he says, for 'some undercurrent, however indefinite, of meaning.' Even as he revels in having so dexterously performed a complete anatomy of his poem, he cannot stop his mouth from whispering 'This wonderful dissection has merely skinned my Raven, it hasn't exposed the vital organs of the soul.'"

Response and Analysis

Reading Check

1. What is the **setting**—the time and place—of the poem?

2. Trace the main events of the story, starting with the rap on the door (stanza 1) and ending with the raven's sitting on the sculpture above the chamber door (stanza 18). Include the questions the narrator asks the raven.

Thinking Critically

3. How does the significance of the word *nevermore* change each time it is spoken? Though the speaker says his beloved will be nameless, he uses her name in lines 28–29, 82–83, and 94–95. How does the raven's answer to the speaker's queries keep reminding you of her?

4. How would you describe the **mood,** or feeling, created by the **setting**? Which **images** in the beginning of the poem help create this mood?

5. In line 101, what do you think the speaker means when he begs the bird, "Take thy beak from out my heart"?

6. The speaker's **tone,** or attitude toward his visitor, changes as the raven gradually turns from a slightly comic figure into a demonic one. Trace these changes in tone. Is there any evidence suggesting that the speaker is going mad? Explain.

7. What, in your opinion, does the raven **symbolize**? Why do you suppose Poe chose a raven to carry this meaning, rather than a chicken, an owl, a parrot, or any other bird? (For Poe's thoughts on "The Raven," see the *Primary Source* on page 278.)

Extending and Evaluating

8. Look back at the *Primary Source* where the first three steps of Poe's writing process for "The Raven" are outlined. How do you evaluate the results of Poe's intention to write "a poem with a melancholy effect"?

Literary Focus

Interpreting Sound Effects

In writing "The Raven," Poe deliberately set out to produce an original verse form and to create novel effects using rhyme and alliteration.

The poem is a virtuoso performance in the use of **internal rhyme**—rhyme that occurs within the lines or repetition of an end rhyme within a line. "Dreary" and "weary" in line 1 prepare us for a pattern of internal rhyming sounds. "Napping," "tapping," and "rapping" in lines 3–4 make us expect more. Some of the rhymes are ingenious. Not many writers, for example, would think of rhyming "window lattice" with "what threat is" (lines 33–34).

The technique of **alliteration** (the repetition of a consonant sound) is sometimes used to create **onomatopoeia**—the use of words with sounds that actually echo their sense. Often alliteration is used merely to create a striking sound effect; at times it becomes so exaggerated that we might even wonder if Poe is mocking himself. A good example of the excessive use of alliteration is in line 71, where the hard *g* is repeated four times, almost resulting in a tongue twister: "this grim, ungainly, ghastly, gaunt, and ominous bird of yore."

- What other examples of internal rhyme can you find?
- Where in lines 13–18 and 37–42 is alliteration used to create onomatopoeia?

INTERNET
Projects and Activities
Keyword: LE5 11-2

SKILLS FOCUS

Literary Skills
Analyze sound effects in poetry.

Edgar Allan Poe **279**

Reading Check

1. The setting is the speaker's room at midnight in "bleak December."

2. The speaker hears a tapping, opens the door, and finds no one. He opens the window, and a raven enters to perch on a bust of Athena. The speaker asks the raven's name; it says, "Nevermore." It repeats this when he murmurs that it will probably abandon him soon, as others have done; when he says that it has been sent for his benefit; when he asks if there is any relief from his sorrow; and when he asks if he will meet Lenore in heaven. Finally he shrieks for the raven to leave, but it croaks "Nevermore." It's still there when the poem closes.

3. "Nevermore" first means that the raven will not forsake the speaker; then that there is no relief, and he will not see Lenore again; and finally that the raven will give him no peace. "Nevermore" rhymes with Lenore.

4. *Mood*—ominous. *Images*—"bleak December," "dying ember," and "ghost upon the floor."

5. The bird's "prophecies" pierce the speaker's heart.

6. The speaker is first amused (ll. 37–54) and then reflective (ll. 57–78). In ll. 87–102, his tone grows desperate. By ll. 103–108, his wild despair suggests insanity.

7. Possible answers: The raven symbolizes death, loss, or despair. The raven suits the speaker's mournful tone and tormented projections.

Extending and Evaluating

8. Most students will agree that the poem is melancholy, powerfully evoking despair. Some may say Poe defeats his purpose by overwriting.

Literary Focus

- Internal rhymes occur in the first, third, and fourth lines of each stanza.
- *Line 13*—"silken, sad, uncertain rustling of each purple curtain." *Line 37*—"flung the shutter, when with many a flirt and flutter."

ASSESSING

Assessment

■ *Holt Assessment: Literature, Reading, and Vocabulary*

RETEACHING

For lessons reteaching poetic devices, see **Reteaching,** p. 1117A.

SKILLS FOCUS, pp. 280–282

Grade-Level Skills

■ **Literary Skills**
Analyze archetypes drawn from myth and tradition.

PRETEACHING

Summary ⇔ *at grade level*

A brightly-clad knight sets off on an archetypal quest in search of Eldorado. As his journey continues, he grows old and discouraged, and his strength begins to fail. Meeting a traveling pilgrim—a shadow—he asks the way to Eldorado. The pilgrim replies that if the knight wants to find it, he must carry on "boldly" beyond the "Mountains of the Moon" and through the "Valley of the Shadow."

Skills Starter

Motivate. Tell students that the quest for a land of great riches springs from an even more basic archetype, the quest itself. You might define *quest* as "any long and challenging journey in search of a reward that may be tangible, intangible, or both." The archetypal quest pattern recurs from the earliest literature known—the Sumerian *Epic of Gilgamesh*—through the most modern stories in popular culture. Invite students to list books, films, and computer games based on the quest archetype. For each quest, have students name the reward sought.

Make the Connection

Quickwrite

The poem you are about to read is about a quest for Eldorado, a mythical land of great wealth. What quests do people take today to find great wealth? What are the results of some of those quests? Take notes on your responses to these questions.

Literary Focus

Archetype

The quest for a place of fabulous wealth is an archetype. Throughout history and literature this search for a golden land has been repeated, with different characters and varying endings. America itself once took on the aura of a paradise on earth. Europeans who were fleeing starvation or persecution imagined America as a place where the streets were paved with gold. From *Paradise Lost* to *The Wizard of Oz*, the message of this enduring archetype seems to be that as long as people can imagine a land where money practically grows on trees, they will continue to search for it.

go.hrw.com

INTERNET

More About Edgar Allan Poe

Keyword: LE5 11-2

> An **archetype** is an original, imaginative pattern that appears across cultures and is repeated through the ages. An archetype can be a character, a plot, a setting, or an object.
>
> *For more on Archetype, see the Handbook of Literary and Historical Terms.*

SKILLS FOCUS

Literary Skills
Understand the use of archetype.

Background

El Dorado is Spanish for "the gilded one." The term is associated with the conquistadors, who had heard repeatedly about a ruler who lived in what is now Colombia. Every year the ruler would be covered in gold dust, which would then be rinsed from his body in Lake Guatavita. During the ceremony, emeralds and other precious stones would be thrown into the depths of the lake. The conquistadors became convinced that if only they could find it, a country of vast riches would be theirs. Eldorado was never found.

In 1849, the year in which this poem was written, Eldorado took on a new meaning. The discovery of gold in California convinced thousands of Americans that a land of golden opportunity was at hand. Thus began the great rush that would take the gold seekers to the vicinity of Sutter's Mill and the muddy streets of San Francisco.

Behind this poem, then, lie both the legend passed on by the frustrated conquistadors and the reality reported in the daily newspapers. For Poe, though, Eldorado was predominantly an idea, as it remains for us today. "Eldorado" speaks to a universal human hope that somewhere lies a great, good place, the land of our hearts' desires.

RESOURCES: READING

Planning
■ *One-Stop Planner* CD-ROM with ExamView Test Generator

Differentiating Instruction
■ *Supporting Instruction in Spanish*
■ *Audio CD Library, Selections and Summaries in Spanish*

Grammar and Language
■ *Daily Language Activities*

Assessment
■ *Holt Assessment: Literature, Reading, and Vocabulary*
■ *One-Stop Planner* CD-ROM with ExamView Test Generator
■ *Holt Online Assessment*

Internet
■ *go.hrw.com* (Keyword: LE5 11-2)
■ *Elements of Literature Online*

Media
■ *Audio CD Library*
■ *Audio CD Library, Selections and Summaries in Spanish*

Eldorado

Edgar Allan Poe

Gaily bedight,°
  A gallant knight,
In sunshine and in shadow,
  Had journeyed long,
5   Singing a song,
In search of Eldorado.

  But he grew old—
  This knight so bold—
And o'er his heart a shadow
10   Fell as he found
  No spot of ground
That looked like Eldorado.

  And, as his strength
  Failed him at length,
15 He met a pilgrim shadow—
  "Shadow," said he,
  "Where can it be—
This land of Eldorado?"

  "Over the Mountains
20   Of the Moon,°
Down the Valley of the Shadow°
  Ride, boldly ride,"
  The shade replied,
"If you seek for Eldorado!"

---

 1. **bedight** *adj.:* archaic for bedecked; dressed.
20. **Mountains of the Moon:** legendary source of the Nile River.
21. **Valley of the Shadow:** The "valley of the shadow of death" is mentioned in Psalm 23.

(Opposite and right), Gold sculpture showing the ceremony in Lake Guatavita that started the search for Eldorado.

A Literary Focus

? Archetype. A young person setting off on a quest is a familiar archetypal figure. What does the opening stanza suggest about the character of the knight when he starts? [Possible response: He is optimistic, cheerful, determined, bold, and hopeful.]

B Reading Skills

? Interpreting. How is the connotation of *shadow* in stanza 2 different from its connotation in stanza 1? [In stanza 1, *shadow* has a literal connotation. In stanza 2, *shadow* has the figurative connotation of "darkness of the heart."]

C Literary Focus

? Archetype. The archetypal figure of the *pilgrim,* someone journeying for religious reasons, recurs throughout world literature. How would you contrast the characters of the pilgrim and the knight in this poem? [Possible responses: The pilgrim seems wiser and more experienced, but less optimistic and less substantial; the pilgrim is a shade, or spirit, whereas the knight is human.]

Advanced Learners
Enrichment. Lead students to consider broader implications of the archetypal quest for a land of plenty. In many Native American myths, for example, the earth itself is created when people in proto-worlds seek a better place to live. Archeological evidence suggests that the Americas were peopled by early explorers—trekkers on the Bering land bridge, before seafarers from Europe explored the continents, seeking a fabled land.
Activity. Encourage students to discuss the human yearning for "a great, good place" as they see it manifested in the history and literature of the Americas. Which historical events and literary works reflect the archetypal quest for a land of plenty?

Response and Analysis

Reading Check

1. He grows old and discouraged as he fails to find Eldorado.

2. It tells him to ride boldly "over the Mountains of the Moon" and "down the Valley of the Shadow."

Thinking Critically

3. Answers will vary. Some students may say the shadow is saying that Eldorado exists only in dreams or after death.

4. In stanza 1, *shadow* literally means "shade." In stanza 2, it carries a figurative meaning of sorrow or discouragement. In stanza 3, it refers to the mysterious pilgrim figure. In stanza 4, it alludes to death. These changes in meaning reflect the darkening of the poem's tone in successive stanzas.

5. Possible answers: The knight may represent innocence, optimism, or boldness; the pilgrim shadow may represent experience, pessimism, or endurance.

6. According to the pilgrim, this quest will carry the knight beyond the farthest reaches of the known world ("Over the Mountains of the Moon") and perhaps into death ("Down the Valley of the Shadow").

7. Possible answers: People today seek wealth, pleasure, thrills, cures for diseases, world peace, social justice, wisdom, and love. Compared to the knight's quest, most of these goals are clearer; some more practical, some more philanthropic; some are shallower.

Extending and Evaluating

8. Possible answers: Poe might have struggled with a sense of failure as a poet or saw his writing as a quest to push beyond known boundaries, with the hope of success after death.

Response and Analysis

Reading Check

1. Paraphrase what happens to the knight in the first two stanzas of the poem.

2. What directions does the shadow give the knight?

Thinking Critically

3. The response the shadow makes to the knight is **ambiguous,** or open to interpretation. Explain what you think the shadow's answer really means.

4. How do the meanings of the word *shadow* change from stanza to stanza? How do these changes reflect a shift in the poem's **tone**—the attitude the speaker reveals about the quest?

5. The characters of the knight and the shadow have a **symbolic** meaning. What types of persons, attitudes, or values might these two characters represent?

6. This poem is based on an **archetypal** story pattern: the quest or perilous journey taken to find something of great value. According to the pilgrim shadow, what will be the result of this quest for the land of Eldorado?

7. Refer to the notes about quests that you wrote for the Quickwrite. What contemporary Eldorados are people searching for? How do their quests compare with the quest in "Eldorado"?

SKILLS FOCUS

Literary Skills
Analyze archetypes.

Writing Skills
Write an essay comparing two poems.

Extending and Evaluating

8. Suppose this questing knight is a symbol of the poet himself. What then would the fate of this knight and his quest mean, in terms of Poe's feelings about his poetry?

WRITING

Comparing Poems

In a brief **essay,** compare "Eldorado" with "The Raven." Before you write, gather your details in a chart like the following one. Be sure to quote lines from the poems to support your comparison.

	The Raven	Eldorado
What raven symbolizes		
What Eldorado symbolizes		
Fate of main character		
Theme of poem		
Mood created by poem		

Gold mask from the pre-Columbian period (predating Columbus's arrival in the Western Hemisphere).

Assessment

■ *Holt Assessment: Literature, Reading, and Vocabulary*

For a lesson reteaching archetypes, see **Reteaching,** p. 1117A.

READ ON: FOR INDEPENDENT READING

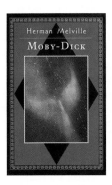

FICTION
Death to Moby-Dick!

A literary masterpiece of the Romantic era, Herman Melville's *Moby-Dick* is the epic tale of a man's obsession that is both dark and tragic. Captain Ahab, the strange captain of the whaling ship *Pequod,* has one goal in life: to destroy the white whale that cost him his right leg. *Billy Budd,* another masterwork written by Melville, is the story of an innocent, young sailor aboard the H.M.S. *Indomitable* who inadvertently kills John Claggart, the ship's master-at-arms, who is envious of Billy.

FICTION
The Face of One Long Dead

Longfellow's "The Cross of Snow" is a poem of mourning for a lost love whose absence still haunts the speaker. For another treatment of this theme, read Emily Brontë's classic novel *Wuthering Heights.* Inspired by many of the same Romantic poets that influenced Longfellow, Brontë's novel chronicles a tragic love of such intensity that it transcends even death.

This title is available in the HRW Library.

NONFICTION
On America's Highways

Thoreau went to Walden Pond to experience the simplicity of nature in his own corner of America. In *Blue Highways: A Journey into America,* William Least Heat-Moon does the exact opposite—he hits the asphalt and travels the back roads of America. In the faces of people, in the beauty of the landscape, and in the small towns with names like Bear Wallow, Mud Lick, and Love Joy, Heat-Moon celebrates the human spirit and the American way of life.

NONFICTION
Nature Revisited

Emerson deeply loved the natural world. He believed that in the presence of nature "a wild delight" would fill a person "in spite of real sorrows." What can renew us when we find sorrow in nature? Rachel Carson's *Silent Spring,* written in 1962, chronicles the dire effects of pesticides on songbird populations across America. This meticulously researched book helped launch environmental campaigns and ecological movements that are still active today.

DIFFERENTIATING INSTRUCTION

Estimated Word Counts and Reading Levels of Read On Books:

Fiction			Nonfiction		
Moby-Dick	↔	255,300	*Blue Highways: A Journey into America*	↓	165,600
Wuthering Heights	↔	147,600	*Silent Spring*	↑	90,900

KEY: ↑ *above grade level*   ↔ *at grade level*   ↓ *below grade level*

Read On

For Independent Reading

If students enjoyed the themes and topics explored in this collection, you might recommend the following titles for independent reading.

Assessment Options

The following projects can help you evaluate and assess your students' outside reading.

- **Plan a movie.** Students can work on a proposal for a movie version of *Moby-Dick.* Students who have seen the 1956 Hollywood film with Gregory Peck or the 1998 television remake with Patrick Stewart may work together, pooling ideas for a new version. The proposal can be presented as a notebook with photographs, set designs, character and costume sketches, an outline. and a list of preferred actors for the parts.

- **Design a book jacket.** Have students design a book jacket for a new edition of *Wuthering Heights.* The front cover should include the title, the author's name, and a graphic that conveys the book's theme. On the back cover, have students include biographical information about Emily Brontë and critical comments chosen to present the heart of the book.

- **Videotape an interview.** Students who read *Blue Highways: A Journey into America* might stage an interview between Heat-Moon and someone he meets on his journey. The student portraying Heat-Moon can prepare a list of questions, and the interviewee can try to capture the spirit of his or her American place.

- **Create an editorial comic strip.** Students can create an editorial comic strip based on Rachel Carson's *Silent Spring.* Suggest that students come up with a one- or two-sentence summary of Carson's main idea and then think of an effective way to illustrate this concept in a short series of panels.

PRETEACHING

Skills Starter

Motivate. Using a literature book or art history book, find a piece of artwork that depicts a scene from a story. Show the artwork to the class, and ask a student volunteer to describe what is happening in the picture. Then, ask another volunteer to speculate about what might have happened before the action shown in the picture, and ask yet another student to tell what might have happened afterward. Point out to students that these descriptions and speculations could be used to create a short story.

DIRECT TEACHING

Consider Audience, Purpose, and Tone

You may want to remind students that there is more than one form in which to present a story. Some forms may be more appropriate, depending on students' purpose and audience. For example, a dramatic presentation might be an appropriate form to present a story to an audience of young children. If the audience is a teacher, a written document is probably the most appropriate form for presenting a story.

Integrating with Grammar, Usage, and Mechanics

As students start their short stories, they may have trouble with phrases and clauses. You may want to review sections 6 and 7 in the Language Handbook.

Writing a Short Story

Writing Assignment
Write a short story of at least 1,500 words with an interesting plot and well-developed characters.

If a minister begins wearing an unexplained black veil, how will his congregation respond? If a man makes a bargain with the devil about the fate of his soul, can he escape the consequences? As you've seen in this chapter, Nathaniel Hawthorne and Washington Irving answer these questions in **short stories**—short, fictional narratives that create imaginative worlds in very few pages. In this workshop you will learn how to develop a story idea into an interesting short story—to make readers cry, laugh, or shriek in terror.

Prewriting

Consider Audience, Purpose, and Tone

Have You Heard the One About . . . ? The kind of story you will write will be short enough for your readers—or **audience**—to complete in one sitting. When you write a short story, your **purpose** is a literary one—that is, you use language creatively to express an idea. The attitude you have toward your readers and your subject establishes your **tone,** which may be serious, comic, or ironic.

Explore Story Ideas

"What if . . . ?" Situations Many authors say that their best ideas for short stories come from real life—from a news story, an interesting-looking person, or an everyday situation. To find a story idea, try looking around and making note of your observations. Next, brainstorm a "What if?" question about each news event, person, or situation you have recorded. Then, choose the most interesting idea for your short story.

Imagine Characters and Setting

Who? Once you have a story idea, imagine the people who will appear in the story—the **characters,** or the fictional individuals that have human traits (even if the characters are animals). Your short story will usually have one or more main characters and perhaps one or two secondary characters. Because believable characters act and behave in stories the way people do in real life, use **concrete sensory details** in making the characters come to life. To help you create complex characters, write responses to the following analysis questions for each character.

SKILLS FOCUS

Writing Skills
Write a short story. Create characters, setting, and plot.

● **What is the character's appearance?** How does he or she speak and move? Does this character have distinctive actions and gestures?

COLLECTION 2 RESOURCES: WRITING

Planning
- *One-Stop Planner* CD-ROM with ExamView Test Generator

Differentiating Instruction
- *Workshop Resources: Writing, Listening, and Speaking*
- *Family Involvement Activities in English and Spanish*
- *Supporting Instruction in Spanish*

Writing and Language
- *Workshop Resources: Writing, Listening, and Speaking*
- *Daily Language Activities*
- *Language Handbook Worksheets*

- **How does the character behave?** What actions or reactions could help develop and reveal information about the character?

- **What motivates the character?** What is important to this person? What does he or she want?

Where? As you develop your characters, also develop the times and places—or the **settings**—for their actions and speech. Locate the scenes in your short story in specific places with unique sights, sounds, and smells, which you will describe, again using concrete sensory details. Limit the number of settings in your story to one or two places to avoid confusing your reader. Here is how one writer used sensory language to make one of the settings of her short story immediately recognizable for the reader.

> They walked into the permanent sausage-and-potato-salad smell of the restaurant.

Plot Your Story

Make Trouble To keep your readers interested in the situation, characters, and setting you've chosen, something has to happen. The sequence of events in a short story is called the **plot.** To develop a plot for your story, answer the questions in the chart below. One writer's responses to the questions appear in the right-hand column.

QUESTIONS FOR DEVELOPING PLOT

Questions	Examples
1. **What's the conflict—the problem in the story?** The conflict can be **external,** in which a character struggles against an outside force such as another character or the environment; or it can be **internal,** in which a character struggles against his or her own feelings.	Leticia and her best friend Jennifer have a misunderstanding. Jennifer has decided she won't go to college after all, and Leticia doesn't understand her reasons.
2. **What happens next?** The characters' actions or decisions complicate the plot. They make up the **rising action** that advances the plot toward the climax.	Leticia begins to change; she has a new friend and a new hairstyle. She tells Jennifer she wants everything to be new. Jennifer thinks Leticia wants a new best friend, too.
3. **Will things like this go on forever?** The **climax,** or crisis point, is usually the moment when the outcome of the conflict is imminent.	Leticia apologizes for saying she wanted everything to be new, but Jennifer tells her she doesn't need her sympathy.
4. **What happens to the characters at the end?** The resolution of the conflict is the **denouement,** the results or significance of the story's events for the characters.	Jennifer explains that she wants to help her dad with the restaurant. It's a choice she has made. Leticia realizes that things change, even friendships.

Assessment

- *Holt Assessment: Writing, Listening, and Speaking*
- *One-Stop Planner* CD-ROM with ExamView Test Generator
- *Holt Online Assessment*
- *Holt Online Essay Scoring*

Internet

- go.hrw.com (Keyword: LE5 11-2)
- *Elements of Literature Online*

MODELING AND DEMONSTRATION

Make Trouble

Model how to plot a short story in a brainstorming session. Invite students to volunteer story ideas. Write the ideas on the chalkboard, and have students choose one idea to develop as a class. Then, ask students to think of a conflict that might work well with the story idea and have them explain why. List several conflicts next to the story idea, and have the class choose one. Continue by asking students to offer possible resolutions to the conflict, and list these next to the conflict. Then, have a volunteer come to the chalkboard and demonstrate the process of producing his or her own story idea, conflict, and resolution.

CRITICAL THINKING

Studying resolutions can help students avoid dull or trite endings and be aware of the wide variety of possible resolutions. Have students list endings of familiar stories and categorize the different resolutions. Students can use the list as a reference when planning the resolution to their stories.

Collection 3

INTRODUCING THE COLLECTION

In Collection 3, students will read the works of Walt Whitman and Emily Dickinson and learn how their writing influenced American literature. Students will also compare and contrast Whitman's style with the modern Chilean poet Pablo Neruda. In this collection, students will analyze an author's use of free verse, symbolism, slant rhyme, and paradox and summarize text. The collection concludes with a writing workshop and a listening and speaking workshop that gives students the opportunity to write and present a reflective essay.

VIEWING THE ART

The photograph shows a solitary man in a baseball cap crossing an old planked bridge with his head down and his hands in his pockets.

Activity. Ask students to speculate about what the solitary figure in this photograph might suggest about the writers in the collection that follows. [Possible responses: The writers may have worked in isolation from others; the writers may have dealt with subjects close to the heart of the average American; the writers may have cherished nature and the opportunity to reflect on its lessons in solitude.]

COLLECTION 3 RESOURCES: READING

Planning
- *One-Stop Planner* CD-ROM with Exam View Test Generator

Differentiating Instruction
- *Holt Reading Solutions*
- *The Holt Reader*
- *Holt Adapted Reader*

- *Family Involvement Activities in English and Spanish*
- *Supporting Instruction in Spanish*
- *Audio CD Library, Selections and Summaries in Spanish*

Grammar and Language
- *Language Handbook Worksheets*
- *Daily Language Activities*

Assessment
- *Holt Assessment: Literature, Reading, and Vocabulary*
- *One-Stop Planner* CD-ROM with ExamView Test Generator
- *Holt Online Assessment*

Internet
- go.hrw.com (Keyword: LE5 11-3)
- *Elements of Literature Online*

x

American Masters

Whitman and Dickinson

If you want me again look for me
under your boot-soles.

—Walt Whitman

This is my letter to the World
That never wrote to Me—

—Emily Dickinson

go.hrw.com

INTERNET

Collection
Resources

Keyword: LE5 11-3

299

Media
- *Audio CD Library*
- *Audio CD Library, Selections and Summaries in Spanish*
- *Fine Art Transparencies*
- *Visual Connections Videocassette Program*
- *PowerNotes*

Time Line

■ **1831**

Edgar Allan Poe

This volume of poetry was published soon after Poe purposely got himself expelled from West Point. As a gesture of support, Poe's friends at the academy made up a subscription for his book, which included revisions of earlier poems as well as new poems such as "Israfel."

■ **1850–1855**

Hawthorne, Melville, Stowe, Thoreau, Whitman

Remarkably, one six-year period produced five of the most important books in American literary history.

■ **1852**

Harriet Beecher Stowe

The antislavery novel *Uncle Tom's Cabin* was first serialized in 1851–1852 in the abolitionist newspaper *The National Era*. When it was published in book form in 1852, it became an overnight sensation, selling 350,000 copies in its first year and becoming the second biggest bestseller of the nineteenth century. Written in protest against the Fugitive Slave Act of 1850, *Uncle Tom's Cabin* was so influential in arousing abolitionist sentiments that it is often cited as one of the causes of the Civil War. Despite its antislavery message, however, critics later objected to the book's stereotypical depiction of the docile slave Uncle Tom; the expression "Uncle Tom" became a term of contempt for an African American whose behavior toward whites is considered fawning or servile.

American Masters
Whitman and Dickinson

1810		1850	
1819 Walt Whitman is born in Long Island, New York (his home, as it looks today, is pictured at far right, page 301)	**1836** Ralph Waldo Emerson publishes *Nature*	**1850** Nathaniel Hawthorne publishes *The Scarlet Letter*, which sells four thousand copies in ten days	**1854** Henry David Thoreau publishes *Walden*
1830 Emily Dickinson is born in Amherst, Massachusetts	**1848** In New Orleans, Whitman first encounters the vast American landscape		**1855** Walt Whitman publishes first edition of *Leaves of Grass;* Emily Dickinson visits Philadelphia and Washington, perhaps meeting a married clergyman whom she has fallen in love with
1831 Edgar Allan Poe publishes third volume of *Poems*, including "To Helen"	**1848** Dickinson spends a year at Mount Holyoke Female Seminary	**1851** Herman Melville publishes *Moby-Dick; or The Whale*	
		1852 Harriet Beecher Stowe publishes *Uncle Tom's Cabin*	**1861** Civil War begins

Harriet Beecher Stowe.

Portrait of Private George A. Stryker, New York Regiment.

Using the Time Line

Activity. Have students use reference sources to place the following literary, cultural, and historical events on the time line:

- Charles Dickens publishes *David Copperfield.* [1850]
- Karl Marx and Friedrich Engels publish *The Communist Manifesto.* [1848]
- Charlotte Brontë publishes *Jane Eyre.* [1847]
- In a migration that has come to be known as the Trail of Tears, the Cherokee are evicted from their land in Georgia and forced to march to Oklahoma—a grueling journey during which four thousand Cherokee die. [1838–1839]
- Horatio Alger publishes *Ragged Dick,* a popular rags-to-riches novel. [1868]

■ **1876–1879**

Alexander Graham Bell and Thomas Alva Edison

Perhaps the two greatest American inventors of all time, Alexander Graham Bell (1847–1922) and Thomas Alva Edison (1847–1931), had a lot in common. They were born the same year (1847), Bell in Scotland and Edison in Ohio. Both lacked formal education: Bell attended school for a few years but was largely home-schooled and self-taught, while Edison dropped out of school when he was about twelve years old. Each man worked closely with an assistant who compensated for the inventor's shortcomings— Bell with Thomas Watson, who provided skill in making models, and Edison with Francis Upton, who provided mathematical and scientific expertise. Both inventors were motivated by an interest in deafness and the challenge of transmitting sound: Bell pioneered techniques for teaching speech to the deaf and married one of his deaf students; Edison was partially deaf himself. Though Bell was the first to patent the telephone, Edison experimented with methods to improve the audibility of sounds transmitted by telephone, and in 1877, he invented the carbon-button transmitter, which is still used in telephone speakers and microphones today. In 1877, Edison also invented the phonograph, or record player—a device that reproduces sound.

1862 Dickinson begins correspondence with Thomas Wentworth Higginson; Whitman travels to Virginia and begins caring for Civil War wounded; Abraham Lincoln issues Emancipation Proclamation

1863 Louisa May Alcott publishes *Hospital Sketches*, about her experiences as Civil War nurse

1864 Dickinson is treated for eye disease in Boston

1865 Civil War ends; Lincoln is assassinated; Whitman publishes *Drum-Taps*, including elegy for Lincoln, "When Lilacs Last in the Dooryard Bloom'd"

1869 Dickinson is no longer leaving her house in Amherst (the house is pictured above, as it looks today)

First printing of some of Dickinson's poems.

1870 Higginson is one of the few visitors to Amherst whom Dickinson meets in person

1873 Whitman moves to Camden, New Jersey

1876 Alexander Graham Bell patents the telephone

1879 Thomas Alva Edison invents the incandescent lamp

1882 Ralph Waldo Emerson dies

1884 Mark Twain publishes *Adventures of Huckleberry Finn*

1886 Emily Dickinson dies of a kidney disease

1890 Dickinson's *Poems* published by Higginson and Mabel Loomis Todd

1891 Whitman publishes *Leaves of Grass,* Deathbed Edition

1892 Whitman dies of a stroke

301

- Frederick Douglass publishes his autobiography, *Narrative of the Life of Frederick Douglass.* [1845]
- The U.S. Congress passes the Chinese Exclusion Act, which prohibits the immigration of Chinese laborers into the United States for a period of ten years. [1882]

Activity. To help the class understand how Whitman and Dickinson fit into the period called American Romanticism, have students mentally superimpose the events covered in this time line onto the Chapter 2 time line (pp. 134–135). Remind students that they will have to divide the events in the Chapter 3 time line into the two categories used in the Chapter 2 time line: "Literary Events" and "Political and Social Events."

Background. "Be simple and clear" were the first words that Whitman wrote in one of his notebooks. He felt that a poet had to express himself frankly, fully, and intelligibly. His poetry was addressed to all people, regardless of their status; he invited everyone to share his emotions, his philosophy, and his bodily experience.

and stingy Nature, as if too much handi-work, or too much lymph in the temperament, were making our Western wits fat and mean.

I give you joy of your free and brave thought. I have great joy in it. I find incomparable things said incomparably well, as they must be. I find the courage of treatment which so delights us, and which large perception only can inspire.

I greet you at the beginning of a great career, which yet must have had a long foreground somewhere, for such a start. I rubbed my eyes a little, to see if this sunbeam were no illusion; but the solid sense of the book is a sober certainty. It has the best merits, namely, of fortifying and encouraging.

I did not know until I last night saw the book advertised in a newspaper that I could trust the name as real and available for a post-office. I wish to see my benefactor, and have felt much like striking my tasks and visiting New York to pay you my respects.

R. W. Emerson

The "long foreground" of which Emerson wrote had not been the careful, confident period of preparation to which many poets devote themselves before they are ready to publish. Instead, it had been a precarious existence. Journalism had kept Whitman going financially, but not even the editorials he wrote for the *Brooklyn Eagle* had brought him distinction. On the surface at least, his "long foreground" of preparation had been a mixture of hack work and jack-of-all-trades ingenuity.

By the time he was ready to declare himself a poet and to publish the first version of his book, Walt Whitman was unique. *Leaves of Grass* is a masterpiece that Whitman was to expand and revise through many editions. Its process of growth did not end until the ninth, "deathbed" edition was published in 1891,

thirty-six years after its first appearance. It is a spiritual autobiography that tells the story of an enchanted observer who says who he is at every opportunity and claims what he loves by naming it. "Camerado," he wrote, "this is no book / Who touches this touches a man."

In the Crowd, but Not of It

The figure we know today as Walt Whitman was conceived and created by the poet himself. Whitman endorsed his image and sold it to the public with a promoter's skill worthy of P. T. Barnum, the great show manager of the nineteenth century. At first glance that figure is a bundle of contradictions. Whitman seems to have had the theatrical flair of a con artist and the selfless dignity of a saint; the sensibility of an artist and the carefree spirit of a hobo; the blustery egotism of a braggart and the demure shyness of a shrinking violet. On second glance these contradictions disappear: Walt Whitman was everything he seemed to be. The figure he so carefully crafted and put on display was not a surrogate but the man himself.

"One would see him afar off," wrote the great naturalist John Burroughs, "in the crowd but not of it—a large, slow-moving figure, clad in gray, with broad-brimmed hat and gray beard—or, quite as frequently, on the front platform of the street horse-cars with the driver. . . . Whitman was of large mold in every way, and of bold, far-reaching schemes, and is very sure to fare better at the hands of large men than of small. The first and last impression which his personal presence always made upon one was of a nature wonderfully gentle, tender, and benignant. . . . I was impressed by the fine grain and clean, fresh quality of the man. . . . He always had the look of a man who had just taken a bath."

If there is a side of Whitman that today we would associate with image building, or self-promotion, there is nothing in his poetry to suggest that it was anything but the product of

Literary Criticism

Critic's Commentary: The Common Man as Hero

According to literary critic Roger Asselineau, Whitman always maintained faith in the average American and in the strength of American democracy. Asselineau explains, "The Civil War revealed to him the heroism and the spirit of sacrifice of the average American and confirmed his faith in man 'en-masse.' . . . When he

happened to sing of Lincoln . . . he showed him . . . not as a great leader of men, but . . . as a magnificent example of the virtues of the average man whom power does not corrupt."

Activity. Have students apply Asselineau's comment to the poems in this chapter. Ask them to look for ways in which Whitman places the mighty and the average on a level field of honor.

The Walt Whitman House in Camden, New Jersey. Whitman lived here from 1884 until his death.

the kind of genius that permanently changes the history of art. He modified standard, king's-English diction and abandoned traditional rhyme schemes and formal meters in favor of the rhythms and speech patterns of free verse.

Everything Under the Sun

The result was poetry that could sing and speak of everything under the sun. Its sweep was easy, and its range was broad. Suddenly poetry was no longer a matter of organized word structures that neatly clicked shut at the last line; instead, it was a series of open-ended units of rhythm that flowed one into the other and demanded to be read in their totality.

"Whitman throws his chunky language at the reader," writes the critic Paul Zweig. "He cajoles and thunders; he chants, celebrates, chuckles, and caresses. He spills from his capacious American soul every dreg of un-Englishness, every street sound thumbing its nose at traditional subject matter and tone. Here is Samson pulling the house of literature down around his ears, yet singing in the ruins."

Walt Whitman had invented a way of writing poetry that perfectly accommodated his way of seeing. His form is loose enough to allow for long lists and catalogs abundant in detail; it is also flexible enough to include delicate moments of lyricism as well as stretches of blustering oratory. This form served Whitman as observer and prophet—as a private man tending the wounded in the hospital wards of the Civil War and as the public man who gave voice to the grief of a nation in his great elegy for the slain Abraham Lincoln, "When Lilacs Last in the Dooryard Bloom'd."

An American Epic

When Whitman died, in 1892, he had met a great personal goal. He had enlarged the possibilities of American poetry to include the lyricism of simple speech and the grand design of the epic.

How is *Leaves of Grass* like an epic? Who is its hero? What is its action? The hero is the poet, and he is a hero not of the ancient past but of the future. As in all epics the action takes the form of a journey. In *Leaves of Grass,* the journey is the one the speaker takes as he becomes a poet:

> I am the poet of the Body and I am the
>   poet of the Soul . . .
> I am the poet of the woman the same as
>   the man . . .
> I am not the poet of goodness only, I do
>   not decline to be the poet of wickedness
>   also. . . .

By the end of his epic journey, which even takes him down into a kind of hell, the poet has also been transformed. The "I" has become identified with every element in the universe and has been reborn as something divine. The poet has become the saving force that Whitman believed was the true role of the American poet.

Nothing quite like it had ever been done in America before.

Short Answer

Monitoring students' progress. Guide students in answering the following comprehension questions.

1. Whitman was a native of what state? [New York]

2. What were three jobs that Whitman held before he was twenty? [office clerk, printer's assistant, school teacher]

3. As an adult, Whitman spent many years in what profession? [journalism]

4. Why was *Leaves of Grass* largely ignored when it was published? [People found it too bold and strange.]

5. How did Whitman make people aware of the publication of *Leaves of Grass*? [He sent copies to reviewers and other readers.]

6. Which writer said to Whitman, "I greet you at the beginning of a great career"? [Emerson]

7. In appearance, how did Whitman strike people? [large, kind, gentle, aloof, unusual]

8. What was Whitman's influence on poetry? [He changed the traditional way that poetry was written.]

Critic's Commentary: Whitman's Readers

American literature scholar Sculley Bradley suggests that Whitman was the only poet who was "persistently overrated and steadily underrated at the same time and for so long. . . . even Tennyson, who lived in a totally different world, saw in Whitman 'a great big something,' which he could not quite identify as a poet."

Activity. Once students have finished reading Whitman's work, ask them to elaborate on Tennyson's comment about Whitman by asking themselves, "What is that 'great big something' that the English poet saw in the American?"

Summary at grade level

In this lyric poem, Whitman's first-person, all-embracing "I" catalogs the unique "songs" expressed by the labors of mechanics, carpenters, masons, shoemakers, young wives, seamstresses, and other ordinary workers. The poem celebrates the spirit of candor and joy that infuses these Americans who work for themselves and their country.

Selection Starter

Motivate. Have students read employment ads in a newspaper or on a Web site and share the jobs that they think they would like with the class. Ask students what conclusions they can draw about the variety of everyday work that people do in a nation.

Before You Read

I Hear America Singing

Make the Connection
Quickwrite

This famous poem appears near the beginning of *Leaves of Grass* and introduces one of the poet's major themes—the tremendous variety and individuality in American life. Whitman celebrates the American enterprise, in all its forms, through the varied carols, or songs, of men and women who take pride in their occupations. Why do you think a poet who celebrates America would focus on *work* songs? List a few of the jobs you would expect to be celebrated in an American epic written today.

Literary Focus
Catalog

One of the most obvious characteristics of Whitman's poetry is his frequent use of **catalogs**—long lists of related things, people, or events. By selecting and naming items in this way, Whitman expresses his unbounded love for everything and everyone in the world. He also, by means of the catalog, creates a kind of rhythm built on the repetition of certain sentence patterns. To hear the effect of cataloging, read aloud this poem and others in this Whitman collection.

go.hrw.com

INTERNET

More About Walt Whitman

Keyword: LE5 11-3

> A **catalog** is a list of things, people, or events.
>
> *For more on Catalog, see the Handbook of Literary and Historical Terms.*

SKILLS FOCUS

Literary Skills
Understand the use of catalogs in poetry.

310 Collection 3

Construction of the Dam (1937) by William Gropper. Mural study, Department of the Interior, National Park Service.

© Smithsonian American Art Museum, Washington, D.C./Art Resource, NY.

Learners Having Difficulty

Invite learners having difficulty to read "I Hear America Singing" in interactive format in *The Holt Reader* and to use the sidenotes as aids to understanding the selection. The interactive version provides additional instruction, practice, and assessment of the literary skills taught in the Student Edition. Monitor students' responses to the selection, and correct any misconceptions that arise.

English-Language Learners

Here and in other Whitman poems, have students list unfamiliar nouns and verbs. Provide definitions. Ask students to re-read the poem and develop a summary statement.

I Hear America Singing

Walt Whitman

I hear America singing, the varied carols I hear,
Those of mechanics, each one singing his as it should be blithe and strong,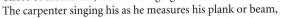
The carpenter singing his as he measures his plank or beam,
The mason singing his as he makes ready for work, or leaves off work,
5   The boatman singing what belongs to him in his boat, the deckhand singing on the
       steamboat deck,
The shoemaker singing as he sits on his bench, the hatter singing as he stands,
The wood-cutter's song, the plowboy's on his way in the morning, or at noon
       intermission or at sundown,
The delicious singing of the mother, or of the young wife at work, or of the girl sewing
       or washing,
Each singing what belongs to him or her and to none else,
10   The day what belongs to the day—at night the party of young fellows, robust, friendly,
Singing with open mouths their strong melodious songs.

Walt Whitman   **311**

DIRECT TEACHING

VIEWING THE ART

William Gropper (1897–1977) was a social-protest painter who was dismissed from the *New York Tribune*, where he worked as a political cartoonist, for his radical political views.

Activity. Discuss how the mural relates to the poem. [Possible response: Both idealize the beauty and heroism of ordinary workers.]

A Reading Skills

❓ Hypothesizing. Why does the speaker say that each person's singing "should be blithe and strong"? [Possible response: Like Emerson and Thoreau, he believes that each person should express his or her individuality without fear.]

B Learners Having Difficulty

Reading elliptical constructions. Explain to students that elliptical constructions are sentences with words left out and that their meaning can be inferred from nearby sentences with a similar structure. Then, have students explain the meaning of "The day what belongs to the day." [The day is singing what belongs to the day.]

C Literary Focus

❓ Characteristics of subgenres of poetry. This whole poem can be viewed as a catalog. What is Whitman using the catalog to celebrate? [Possible response: the optimistic, energetic spirit of working Americans—all with a common pride in their labors.]

Special Education Students
For lessons designed for special education students, see *Holt Reading Solutions*.

Advanced Learners
Enrichment. Ask students to classify the kinds of workers named in the poem. Ask them who Whitman seems to feel is building America. [working-class people—people who work with their hands] At this point you might challenge students to expand on their Quickwrite list.

Response and Analysis

Thinking Critically

1. He names mechanics, the carpenter, the mason, the boatman, the deckhand, the shoemaker, the hatter, the woodcutter, the plowboy, the mother, the young wife, and a girl who sews or washes. Each sings a song that is unique to himself or herself.

2. Possible answers: The diversity of American people should be celebrated; Each person should celebrate one's self-expression in work and culture.

3. Possible answers: It seems to be a romanticized view. Perhaps in Whitman's day, people were happier in their work. The variety of singers and songs and the implied sense of pride in their work are realistic aspects of American life.

4. Possible answer: Whitman would hear songs that have more to do with feelings and interpersonal relationships than with work.

5. The most frequent parallelism is "[worker] singing as [activity]." Other examples include "makes ready for work, or leaves off work" (l. 4) and "in the morning, or at noon intermission or at sundown" (l. 7).

ASSESSING

Assessment

- *Holt Assessment: Literature, Reading, and Vocabulary*

Response and Analysis

Thinking Critically

1. Name the people the speaker hears in lines 2–8. According to line 9, what does each person sing?

2. What Whitman has in mind here are not the actual work songs associated with various trades and kinds of physical labor but something more subtle. What would you say is the real **theme** of this poem—what is the speaker saying about the American people?

3. A feeling of acceptance, even contentment, runs through many of these voices. Considering the long hours and low pay of laborers in the nineteenth century, would you say Whitman is romanticizing or idealizing the lot of workers? Instead, do the songs express a positive and realistic aspect of American life? Explain your response, and support it with specific references to the poem.

4. Imagine the kinds of singing Whitman would hear if he were alive today. In what ways might these work songs be different from those he heard in his own time? In what ways would they be the same? Before you answer, review your Quickwrite notes.

5. The **catalog** in this poem uses **parallel structures** to create a kind of rhythm. What parallel structures can you find repeated in the poem? Read them aloud to hear the rhythm they create.

SKILLS FOCUS

Literary Skills
Analyze the use of catalogs in poetry.

Walt Whitman.
Courtesy of Ohio Wesleyan University, Bayley-Whitman Collection, Delaware, Ohio.

312   Collection 3

DIFFERENTIATING INSTRUCTION

Learners Having Difficulty
To help students respond to question 3, ask them to recall what they have heard from the adults they know (or in some cases, their peers) about their jobs. How do those comments compare to Whitman's?

English-Language Learners
Students with strong ties to other cultures might enjoy "translating" Whitman's poem.

Urge them to focus on jobs from their native countries. If you wish, give them the option of creating a bilingual poem.

Advanced Learners
Have students expand upon question 1 by writing a "strong melodious song" for a worker of their choice. Students may use the melody of a familiar song or create an original tune. Allow volunteers to perform their songs in class.

Before You Read

from Song of Myself, Numbers 10 and 33

Make the Connection

Whitman tries to feel what other people feel, to step into their lives, even to become the person or thing he is talking about. Perhaps you have experienced this blend of imagination and empathy—the ability to share in another's thoughts or feelings—which is at the heart of *Song of Myself.* The poem juxtaposes a wide variety of scenes and emotions in movielike glimpses into the broad American scene. Each experience—whether real or fictional, or a bit of both—provides Whitman with an opportunity for empathy, a chance to feel joy (as in number 10) or to share in heroic suffering (as in number 33).

As you read, look for words and phrases that reveal Whitman's ability to feel empathy with people quite different from himself.

Literary Focus
Free Verse

Today we are so used to poetry written in free verse that we take it for granted. In Whitman's time, however, Americans preferred poetry that was like that being written in England: They expected a poem to show strict concern for **meter** and **rhyme.** Thus, Whitman's sprawling lines were revolutionary, as was his daring use of American slang, foreign words, and words he occasionally made up to suit his purpose. Whitman's free verse is said to have been inspired by the roll and sweep of passages from the King James Bible and even by the measured cadence of Emerson's essays.

Free verse is poetry that is written without regular rhyme schemes and meter. It is not really free at all. Whitman abandoned meter and regular rhyme schemes, but he made full use of these other traditional elements of poetry:

- **alliteration**—the repetition of similar consonant sounds
- **assonance**—the repetition of similar vowel sounds
- **imagery**—the use of language to evoke visual pictures, as well as sensations of smell, hearing, taste, and touch
- **onomatopoeia**—the use of words whose sounds echo their meaning (such as *buzz*)
- **parallel structure**—the repetition of phrases, clauses, or sentences that have the same grammatical structure

Most important, when you read Whitman's lines aloud, you hear **cadence,** the musical run of words that rises and falls as the poet sings the song. As you can hear in Whitman's poems, cadence does not depend on a strict count of stressed and unstressed syllables.

Poets who, like Whitman, choose to write in cadence have nothing but their own sense of balance and proportion to tell them when a line should end and when it should continue. They must rely completely on their own sense of spacing and timing and on their own feeling about what sounds right. In Whitman's poems, lines can be any length at all—three syllables or thirty syllables.

> **Free verse** is poetry that does not conform to a regular meter or rhyme scheme.
>
> *For more on Free Verse, see the Handbook of Literary and Historical Terms.*

INTERNET

More About Walt Whitman

Keyword: LE5 11-3

SKILLS FOCUS

Literary Skills
Understand the characteristics of free verse.

Walt Whitman **313**

Summary ⬌ *at grade level*

In number 10 of *Song of Myself,* the speaker describes hunting in the wilderness, sharing chowder with clam-diggers, witnessing a trapper's marriage into a Native American family, and sheltering a runaway slave. These vignettes convey Whitman's vision of a self who embraces nature, others, and the cosmos.

In number 33, the speaker takes on the voices of unsung heroes: a skipper in a storm, a mother burnt as a witch in front of her children, a hunted slave, a firefighter crushed by a falling building, and a dying general under fire. The speaker proclaims, "All these I feel or am" (l. 16).

PRETEACHING

Skills Starter

Motivate. Write the following sentences on strips of paper:

- Whitman the poet praised the power and potential of the people.
- Whitman insisted that manual work was rich with significance.
- The clatter and clank of engines inspired Whitman.

Call on volunteers to read these sentences aloud. Without using the literary terms, ask students to discuss the use of words beginning with the same consonant sound in the first sentence, words with the same internal vowel sounds in the second sentence, and words that imitate the sound that they describe in the third sentence. Discuss how the sounds and the structures are not only pleasant to say and hear, but also contribute to the coherence of each thought.

DIFFERENTIATING INSTRUCTION

Learners Having Difficulty

Whitman's style is so detailed and rich in imagery that students may need to pause, reread, and ponder as they go along. Urge students to stop briefly after each stanza of *Song of Myself,* number 10, and summarize what they have just read.

Invite learners having difficulty to read *Song of Myself,* number 33, in interactive format in *The Holt Reader* and to use the sidenotes as aids to understanding the selection.

English-Language Learners

Whitman uses apostrophe and the letter *d* instead of *-ed* several times, as in "Gather'd," "reach'd," and "thinn'd." Whitman also uses "stopt" and "drest" instead of their more familiar past-tense forms. Alert students to these spellings.

Ⓐ Learners Having Difficulty

❓ Rearranging syntax. Have students re-read the first sentence. What is the simple subject? [*I*] What is the simple predicate? [*hunt*] Explain that in traditional syntax the first line would be, "I hunt alone, far in the wilds and mountains." Also, explain that the participial phrases in the first stanza ("Wandering . . ., Kindling . . . broiling . . ., Falling asleep . . .") all describe the simple subject.

Ⓑ Literary Focus

Elements of free verse. Read this stanza aloud or play the recording in the *Audio CD Library*. Ask students what makes the stanza free verse. [lack of rhyme and meter] Emphasize that the poem does not sound like ordinary prose: Cadenced lines add rhythm and melody.

Ⓒ Content-Area Connections

Culture: Nineteenth-Century Americana
Explain the following references:

- Yankee clippers (l. 6) were some of the fastest and most popular sailing vessels of Whitman's time.

- The "red girl" (l. 11) is a Native American. The term *red* was commonly used by whites to describe Native Americans at that time. Today the term is considered offensive.

Ⓓ Literary Focus

❓ Imagery. What emotions do you think Whitman wants the readers to feel in this scene? [Possible response: He wants readers to feel affection, pride, and respect for the married couple.]

---

from **Song of Myself**

Walt Whitman

10

Ⓐ Alone far in the wilds and mountains I hunt,
     Wandering amazed at my own lightness and glee,
     In the late afternoon choosing a safe spot to pass the night,
Ⓑ Kindling a fire and broiling the fresh-kill'd game,
5   Falling asleep on the gather'd leaves with my dog and gun by my side.

     The Yankee clipper is under her sky-sails,° she cuts the sparkle and scud,°
     My eyes settle the land, I bend at her prow or shout joyously from the deck.

Ⓒ The boatmen and clam-diggers arose early and stopt for me,
     I tuck'd my trowser-ends in my boots and went and had a good time;
10   You should have been with us that day round the chowder-kettle.

     I saw the marriage of the trapper in the open air in the far west, the bride was a red girl,
     Her father and his friends sat near cross-legged and dumbly smoking, they had moccasins to
           their feet and large thick blankets hanging from their shoulders,
     On a bank lounged the trapper, he was drest mostly in skins, his luxuriant beard and curls
Ⓓ   protected his neck, he held his bride by the hand,
     She had long eyelashes, her head was bare, her coarse straight locks descended upon her
           voluptuous limbs and reach'd to her feet.

15   The runaway slave came to my house and stopt outside,
     I heard his motions crackling the twigs of the woodpile,
     Through the swung half-door of the kitchen I saw him limpsy° and weak,
     And went where he sat on a log and led him in and assured him,
Ⓔ And brought water and fill'd a tub for his sweated body and bruis'd feet,
20   And gave him a room that enter'd from my own, and gave him some coarse clean clothes,
Ⓕ And remember perfectly well his revolving eyes and his awkwardness,
     And remember putting plasters on the galls° of his neck and ankles;
     He stayed with me a week before he was recuperated and pass'd north,
     I had him sit next me at table, my fire-lock lean'd in the corner.

---

6. **sky-sails** *n.:* small sails atop a square-rigged mast.   **scud** *n.:* windblown sea spray or foam.
17. **limpsy** *adj.:* limp; exhausted.
22. **galls** *n. pl.:* sores.

314 Collection 3 **American Masters: Whitman and Dickinson**

SKILLS REVIEW

Analyzing the effect of using a persona. Remind students that a persona is the voice a writer assumes when telling a story. By using a first-person narrator, the writer takes on the persona of one character. In the omniscient point of view, an all-knowing narrator tells the story, using third-person pronouns such as *he, she,* and *they.* In narrating the vignettes in *Song of Myself,* however, Whitman uses an omniscient first-person narrator—a speaker who can enter any consciousness and yet remain *I.*

Activity. Ask students to find and list examples of the omniscient first-person point of view in the poems.

Activity. Have the class write Whitman-esque catalogs using this point of view. Ask each student to contribute a line describing a different type of person who might be seen in the United States today.

Lost on the Prairie (1837) by Alfred Jacob Miller. Watercolor on paper (9¼″ × 13½″).
Stark Museum of Art, Orange, Texas.

Walt Whitman   **315**

E **Content-Area Connections**

History: Whitman as Free-Soiler
Whitman was a member of the Free-Soil Party (1848–1854), a coalition political party opposed to the extension of slavery into the new U.S. territories. In 1848—thirteen years before the outbreak of the Civil War—Whitman signaled his strong antislavery sentiments by serving as a delegate at the party's New York convention.

F **Literary Focus**

Theme. Have students recall the title of the poem and discuss how one person (Whitman) could represent such varied images of America.

VIEWING THE ART

Alfred Jacob Miller
(1810–1874) might not have become the first important painter of the American West had he not met a Scottish adventurer who wanted to decorate his family castle with paintings of Native Americans. Previously a Baltimore portrait painter, Miller joined William Drummond Stewart's wagon train from Missouri to the Rockies in 1837, his only duty being to sketch what he liked.

Activity. Ask students what phrases from *Song of Myself,* number 10, could serve as titles for this painting. [Possible responses: "Alone far in the wilds" (l. 1); "choosing a safe spot to pass the night" (l. 3); "the trapper" (l. 11).]

A Ride for Liberty—The Fugitive Slaves (c. 1862) by Eastman Johnson. Oil on board (22″ × 26¼″).
The Brooklyn Museum of Art, Gift of Miss Gwendolyn O. L. Conkling (40.59.A).

from Song of Myself

Walt Whitman

from 33

I understand the large hearts of heroes,
The courage of present times and all times,
How the skipper saw the crowded and rudderless wreck of the
    steam-ship, and Death chasing it up and down the storm,
How he knuckled tight and gave not back an inch, and was faithful
    of days and faithful of nights,

And chalk'd in large letters on a board, *Be of good cheer, we will not*
5   *desert you;*
How he follow'd with them and tack'd with them three days and
    would not give it up,
How he saved the drifting company at last,
How the lank loose-gown'd women look'd when boated from the
    side of their prepared graves,
How the silent old-faced infants and the lifted sick, and the sharp-
    lipp'd unshaved men;
10 All this I swallow, it tastes good, I like it well, it becomes mine,
I am the man, I suffer'd, I was there.°

The disdain and calmness of martyrs,
The mother of old, condemn'd for a witch, burnt with dry wood,
    her children gazing on,
The hounded slave that flags in the race, leans by the fence,
    blowing, cover'd with sweat,
The twinges that sting like needles his legs and neck, the
15   murderous buckshot and the bullets,
All these I feel or am.

I am the hounded slave, I wince at the bite of the dogs,
Hell and despair are upon me, crack and again crack the
    marksmen,

1–11. I understand . . . I was there: This stanza was inspired by an incident that occurred in 1853. According to reports in the New York *Weekly Tribune* of January 21, 1854, the ship *San Francisco* sailed from New York City on December 22, 1853, destined for South America. A violent storm hit the ship several hundred miles out of port, washing many passengers overboard. The captain of another ship helped rescue the survivors. A copy of the newspaper story was found among Whitman's papers after his death.

SKILLS REVIEW

Analyzing the significance of literary devices: Anecdotes. Explain to students that sharing an anecdote, or a brief story, can be an effective way for a writer to emphasize his or her ideas. Anecdotes engage the audience's emotions as well as intellect and allow the author to explore ethics and values without overtly preaching.

Activity. Ask small groups of students to identify the anecdotes in *Song of Myself,* number 33. Some are as short as one line (l. 13); others are longer (ll. 3–9). Have students discuss what values are implicit in each anecdote.

I clutch the rails of the fence, my gore dribs,° thinn'd with the ooze
  of my skin,
20 I fall on the weeds and stones,
The riders spur their unwilling horses, haul close,
Taunt my dizzy ears and beat me violently over the head with
  whip-stocks.

Agonies are one of my changes of garments,
I do not ask the wounded person how he feels, I myself become the
  wounded person,
25 My hurts turn livid upon me as I lean on a cane and observe.

I am the mash'd fireman with breast-bone broken,
Tumbling walls buried me in their debris,
Heat and smoke I inspired,° I heard the yelling shouts of my
  comrades,
I heard the distant click of their picks and shovels,
30 They have clear'd the beams away, they tenderly lift me forth.

I lie in the night air in my red shirt, the pervading hush is for
  my sake,
Painless after all I lie exhausted but not so unhappy,
White and beautiful are the faces around me, the heads are bared
  of their fire-caps,
The kneeling crowd fades with the light of the torches.

35 Distant and dead resuscitate,
They show as the dial or move as the hands of me, I am the clock
  myself.

I am an old artillerist, I tell of my fort's bombardment,
I am there again.

Again the long roll of the drummers,
40 Again the attacking cannon, mortars,
Again to my listening ears the cannon responsive.

I take part, I see and hear the whole,
The cries, curses, roar, the plaudits for well-aim'd shots,
The ambulanza° slowly passing trailing its red drip,
45 Workmen searching after damages, making indispensable repairs,
The fall of grenades through the rent roof, the fan-shaped
  explosion,
The whizz of limbs, heads, stone, wood, iron, high in the air.

Again gurgles the mouth of my dying general, he furiously waves
  with his hand,
He gasps through the clot *Mind not me—mind—the entrenchments.*

19. **dribs** *n. pl.*: dribbles.

28. **inspired** *v.*: breathed in.

44. **ambulanza** (äm·bo͞o·länt′sə):
Italian for "ambulance."

Walt Whitman   317

Walt Whitman   317

Response and Analysis

Song of Myself, Number 10
Thinking Critically

1. *Scene*—hunting in the wilderness. *Emotion*—contentment. *Scene*—sailing a clipper. *Emotion*—joy. *Scene*—digging for clams. *Emotion*—humor. *Scene*—a wedding. *Emotion*—admiration. *Scene*—aiding a runaway. *Emotion*—sorrow.

2. Students might mention any image but should note why it is vivid.

3. In the first three scenes, the speaker is joyous. In the fourth and fifth, he is more reverent. The change creates a poignant contrast with the optimism of ll. 1–10.

4. The cadence is created by a sequence of present participles in ll. 2–5 and the repetition of verbs connected by *and* in ll. 18–22. The cadence might underscore the sense of passing time.

5. The speaker treats the slave as an equal.

from **Song of Myself, Number 33**
Thinking Critically

1. *Scene*—a skipper rescuing survivors of a shipwreck. *Emotion*—sympathy. *Scene*—a woman burned in front of her children. *Emotion*—outrage. *Scene*—a runaway slave found and beaten. *Emotion*—compassion. *Scene*—a fallen firefighter. *Emotions*—grief, respect. *Scene*—a dying general. *Emotion*—admiration.

2. He makes restatements in ll. 16, 17, 26, 36, 37, 38, and 42. They stress the scenes' immediacy and the speaker's compassion.

3. Possible answers: *Alliteration*—"lank loose-gown'd women look'd" (l. 8). *Assonance*—"thinn'd with the ooze of my skin" (l. 19). *Imagery*—"fan-shaped explosion" (l. 46). *Onomatopoeia*—"Again gurgles the mouth" (l. 48). *Parallel structure*—"How he follow'd with them and tack'd with them three days" (l. 6).

Response and Analysis

Song of Myself, Number 10
Thinking Critically

1. In the five stanzas of this poem, the **speaker** observes and participates in five American scenes. Describe the scene in each stanza. What emotion does each scene evoke?

2. Identify at least three **images** of sight, sound, or touch in the poem that are most vivid to you.

3. **Tone** is the attitude a writer takes toward a subject. A writer can change tone by manipulating language. Whitman changes the **tone** of this poem in the fourth and fifth scenes. Identify the tone of the first three scenes. Then, tell how the tones of the fourth and fifth scenes are different. What effect do you think the poet hoped to create by changing tones?

4. Read this **free-verse** poem aloud. What repetitions of sentence patterns help to create a **cadence**—a rhythmic rise and fall of your voice as the lines are spoken aloud? How does the sound of the poem contribute to its meaning?

5. In the last scene the "runaway slave" is one of thousands who entrusted their lives to those who would help them escape. What do you think this stanza shows about the speaker's relationship with his guest?

from **Song of Myself, Number 33**
Thinking Critically

1. As in number 10, the **speaker** in number 33 observes and participates in several American scenes. Identify the scenes, and describe the emotions they evoke in the speaker.

SKILLS FOCUS

Literary Skills
Analyze the characteristics of free verse.

2. One of Whitman's most famous lines is found in number 33. At what moments does the speaker restate the point that "I am the man, I suffer'd, I was there"? What is the effect of these restatements?

3. To see how Whitman uses various poetic devices in his poems, fill out a chart like the following one. Quote lines from the poem that illustrate his use of these devices.

Poetic Device	Quotations
Alliteration	
Assonance	
Imagery	
Onomatopoeia	
Parallel structure	

4. How would you describe the speaker's **tone** in this song? In other words, how does he feel about the heroes he describes?

5. Find examples of very long lines and very short lines. Read the poem aloud to feel the effects of these long and short lines. How do they force you to vary your rate of reading and your emphasis?

6. Based on the scenes in this section of *Song of Myself*, how do you think Whitman defines heroism?

7. If you were to add a contemporary hero (or heroes) to this poem, whom would you choose? Why?

---

4. The tone is empathetic. He takes pride in the heroes' courage and mourns their losses.

5. Short lines usually are the most emphatic; see ll. 11, 16, 38, and 42. They might be spoken slowly and forcefully.

6. He might define *heroism* as the willingness to suffer or sacrifice oneself in the pursuit of freedom, justice, honor, or compassion.

7. Answers will vary.

ASSESSING

Assessment
- *Holt Assessment: Literature, Reading, and Vocabulary*

Before You Read

from Song of Myself, Number 52

Make the Connection

In this final section, Whitman restates some of the themes that run through *Song of Myself*. The poet weaves these themes in and out of this final verse, like a composer filling a song with familiar refrains. Since the most insistently present element throughout *Song of Myself* is the mind and spirit of the speaker himself, this passage is highly personal. True to his nature, Whitman mocks his own egotism. True to his confidence in himself, he also proclaims his importance—and his inescapability.

Reading Skills
Comparing Themes Across Texts

The final section of *Song of Myself* is not only the poet's farewell to the reader but also a **coda**—a summing up and restatement of the themes of the entire poem. As you read this concluding section a second time, write down your observations of how particular lines and phrases echo themes you've already encountered in the Whitman poems you've read.

INTERNET

More About
Walt Whitman

Keyword: LE5 11-3

SKILLS FOCUS

Reading Skills
Compare themes across texts.

---

from Song of Myself

Walt Whitman

52

The spotted hawk swoops by and accuses me, he complains
　　of my gab and my loitering.

I too am not a bit tamed, I too am untranslatable,
I sound my barbaric yawp over the roofs of the world.

The last scud° of day holds back for me,
5　It flings my likeness after the rest and true as any on the shadow'd wilds,
It coaxes me to the vapor and the dusk.

I depart as air, I shake my white locks at the runaway sun,
I effuse° my flesh in eddies, and drift it in lacy jags.

I bequeath myself to the dirt to grow from the grass I love,
10　If you want me again look for me under your boot-soles.

---

4. **scud** *n.:* windblown mist and low clouds.
8. **effuse** *v.:* spread out.

Walt Whitman   **319**

Summary *at grade level*

Whitman's epic *I* declares his union with the soil and nature and claims his involvement in the readers' lives, whom he addresses directly.

PRETEACHING

Selection Starter

Motivate. Invite students to freewrite about a time when they looked upon a scene and felt that they truly were a part of it. Ask students to refer to their notes as they read Whitman's lines.

DIRECT TEACHING

Ⓐ Literary Focus

❓ Figures of speech. In l. 1, the cry of a hawk is compared to a human complaint. In l. 2, the speaker compares himself to the hawk. What is the point of these metaphors? [Possible response: The speaker claims a poetic voice that has the power of a hawk's cry because it is not tame and because it cannot be translated or understood by conventional standards of beauty.]

Ⓑ Reading Skills

❓ Comparing themes across texts. What passages from number 52 link to lines elsewhere in *Song of Myself?* [Lines 7–10 express Whitman's identification with nature, as does ll. 6 and 13 in number 10; the themes of good health and loafing also appear in both; the theme of empathy appears in l. 16 of number 52 and throughout numbers 10 and 33.]

DEVELOPING FLUENCY

Paired activity. Have students look up the meanings of words they do not understand. Each partner should practice re-reading aloud the lines that contain the unfamiliar words and then paraphrase those lines. Finally, partners should read the lines aloud together, focusing on correct pronunciation and phrasing.

Response and Analysis

Thinking Critically

1. Possible answer: He says in ll. 2–3 that he is not tamed and that his voice, like the hawk's cry, is untranslatable.

2. Possible answer: He might mean that his poetry is everywhere.

3. Possible answer: He dissipates into nature. He offers his body to nourish the soil.

4. Possible answer: The ideas in his poetry will spiritually enrich and ennoble the reader.

5. Present tense (except for ll. 11–12, which are in the future tense). The poem might have lost its immediacy and intensity if Whitman had used the past tense.

6. These lines show Whitman's preoccupation with the self as a universal poetic current that communes with nature and with other people. The last line reminds the readers that this *I*, this voice, is always accessible to them.

7. Possible answer: The pact is unified with nature, empathizes with other humans, and finds courage in being oneself.

8. Possible answer: Whitman wrote in a freer style; he abandoned the conventions of earlier poetry. Also, his self-celebration was not what one would expect to see in earlier poets' work.

Assessment

■ *Holt Assessment: Literature, Reading, and Vocabulary*

For a lesson reteaching theme and meaning, see **Reteaching**, p. 1117A.

You will hardly know who I am or what I mean,
But I shall be good health to you nevertheless,
And filter and fiber your blood.

Failing to fetch me at first keep encouraged,
15 Missing me one place search another,
I stop somewhere waiting for you.

Response and Analysis

Thinking Critically

1. How does Whitman show his connection to the natural world in this section of *Song of Myself*? For example, what qualities does he say he shares with the spotted hawk?

2. What might Whitman mean by line 10: "If you want me again look for me under your boot-soles"?

3. As Whitman departs (lines 7–8), what happens to him, and what does he become? Explain in your own words his final bequest (line 9).

4. How can Whitman be "good health" to the reader (line 12)?

5. What verb tense does Whitman use in this poem and in other parts of *Song of Myself*? How would the effect of the poem have been different if the speaker had used a different verb tense?

6. The first line of *Song of Myself* is "I celebrate myself, and sing myself" (see page 370), and the last line is "I stop somewhere waiting for you." Taking into account all that you have learned of the poet's character and the range of his poetry, tell what you think the last words of number 52 reveal about Whitman's purpose in writing *Song of Myself*.

Reading Skills
Compare themes across texts.

7. Re-read the Whitman poems, and review your reading notes. Then, sum up the **themes** restated in number 52, the coda to *Song of Myself*.

8. You've already studied some of the American poets who preceded Whitman—Longfellow (page 170), Bryant (page 165), Poe (page 253)—as well as other Romantics. Based on what you know about the work of these earlier poets, what do you think Whitman means when he describes his own poetry as his "barbaric yawp" (line 3)?

From Williamsburg Bridge (1928) by Edward Hopper.

Literary Criticism

Critic's Commentary: Coming Full Circle
Robert C. Sickels refers to number 52 as "Whitman's denouement." He explains, "The spotted hawk swoops and complains, but the narrator has come full circle. No longer is the narrator merely an observer of the hawk, . . . [he] joyously joins with the hawk, . . . symbolizing the reconciliation of the seemingly opposite natural and man-made worlds. . . .

Although 'Song of Myself' has been interpreted in innumerable ways, the poem cumulatively chronicles humanity's inextricable place in the regenerative natural world. By the time the poet has returned to the earth, his readers have been reborn to play our part in the cosmic drama." Ask students to be alert to similar critical responses to contemporary poets.

Union hospital at Fair Oaks, Virginia (1862). Photograph by James F. Gibson.

Before You Read

A Sight in Camp in the Daybreak Gray and Dim

Make the Connection
A common emotional focus in Whitman's poetry is empathy—an understanding so intimate that the feelings and thoughts of other people are actually experienced by someone else. In the following poem, Whitman's empathy extends to the wounded of the Civil War. If you have ever felt that you actually *shared* the pain or sorrow of another person, you have felt empathy.

Literary Focus
Symbol
In literature a **symbol** is a person, a thing, or an event that functions as itself and as something broader than itself as well. A writer rarely makes a symbol obvious by directly stating what it means. Most symbols are more subtle; you as the reader must make inferences about their wider meanings.

In this poem, Whitman sees three faces. After you read the poem the first time, go back and re-read it. What could each of these faces symbolize?

> A **symbol** is a person, a place, a thing, or an event that functions as itself as well as something broader.
> *For more on Symbol, see the Handbook of Literary and Historical Terms.*

Background
In December 1862, Whitman traveled to Virginia to care for his brother George, who had been wounded at the First Battle of Fredericksburg. Though George's injuries were minor, Whitman stayed on to assist the staffs of hospitals who were caring for the wounded. Whitman comforted and fed the injured and dying men, cleaned and bandaged their wounds, read to them, and wrote letters home to their families. By the end of the war, Whitman had probably met thousands of soldiers.

go.
hrw
.com

INTERNET

Vocabulary
Practice
•
More About
Walt Whitman
•
Keyword: LE5 11-3

SKILLS
FOCUS

Literary Skills
Understand
symbolism.

Walt Whitman   321

Summary ⬄ *at grade level*

Early one morning in an army camp, the speaker peers at the faces of three dead soldiers: an old man, a youth, and a man whose face seems like the face of Jesus Christ. These anonymous soldiers thus come to represent not only the range of human tragedy in war, but perhaps also the possibility of redemption.

PRETEACHING

Skills Starter
Build review skills. Ask students to recall what they know about the Civil War. You may wish to use a cluster diagram or concept web to record students' facts, images, and opinions relating to the conflict. You may also wish to add to the graphic organizer the fact that about 620,000 soldiers were casualties of the war. Ask students, as they read the poem, to consider how it connects to descriptions of more recent wars.

VIEWING THE ART

James F. Gibson (b. 1828) took many photographs during the Civil War. The Civil War was the first fully modern war involving the United States, and it was the first American war to be documented by photography.

Activity. What can you tell about conditions of life in this hospital from the photograph? [Possible response: Tents imply the temporary and overcrowded nature of the hospital.]

DIFFERENTIATING INSTRUCTION

Learners Having Difficulty
To help students read this poem, ask them to write the following four headings down the side of a sheet of paper, with writing space between each heading: Introduction, First Soldier, Second Soldier, Third Soldier. Under each heading, have students note what they consider to be the most important details from that part of the poem. Students can refer to their notes when participating in class discussion or when answering Response and Analysis questions.

English-Language Learners
Depending on their background, students may vary in their familiarity with Christian symbolism and may need an outline of the story of Jesus Christ. After students have read the poem, elicit comments about the meaning of the final line.

A Reading Skills

❓ Analyzing imagery. What details shape the overall image of Whitman's setting? [the time of day—very early in the morning; the light—gray and dim; the quality of the air—fresh but cool]

B Learners Having Difficulty

Rearranging syntax. Ask students to rearrange the syntax in clauses, such as "Curious I halt and silent stand" (l. 7), by first reading aloud Whitman's phrasing and then experimenting with the effect of an alternative word order.

C Literary Focus

❓ Symbol. In what sense is the dead soldier like Christ? [Possible responses: Both suffered and gave their lives for the good of others; both have a beatific air in death; both are viewed as representing humanity as a whole.]

GUIDED PRACTICE

Monitoring students' progress. Direct students to locate passages in the text that support their responses to these questions.

True-False

1. The speaker wanders through the encampment shortly after dark. [F]

2. He looks at the faces of three dead soldiers. [T]

3. The first two corpses are those of an elderly soldier and a very young soldier. [T]

4. The speaker wishes that he could learn the identity of each man. [F]

Wounded Drummer Boy (c. 1862–1865) by William Morris Hunt. Oil on canvas (14″ × 19¼″).

Museum of Fine Arts, Boston/Gift from the Isaac Fenno Collection (18.393).

A Sight in Camp in the Daybreak Gray and Dim

Walt Whitman

A sight in camp in the daybreak gray and dim,
As from my tent I emerge so early sleepless,
As slow I walk in the cool fresh air the path near by the hospital tent,
Three forms I see on stretchers lying, brought out there untended lying,
5   Over each the blanket spread, ample brownish woolen blanket,
Gray and heavy blanket, folding, covering all.

Curious I halt and silent stand,
Then with light fingers I from the face of the nearest the first just lift the blanket;
Who are you elderly man so gaunt and grim, with well-gray'd hair, and flesh all sunken
        about the eyes?
10   Who are you my dear comrade?

Then to the second I step—and who are you my child and darling?
Who are you sweet boy with cheeks yet blooming?

Then to the third—a face nor child nor old, very calm, as of beautiful yellow-white ivory;
Young man I think I know you—I think this face is the face of the Christ himself,
15   Dead and divine and brother of all, and here again he lies.

322 Collection 3   American Masters: Whitman and Dickinson

CONTENT-AREA CONNECTIONS

Humanities: Mixed Media
Whole-class activity. Ask students to review the Whitman poems that they have read and to consider the poems in relation to the idea of heroism. Then, invite the class to collaborate on one or more artistic interpretations of heroism as Whitman presents it. The results should incorporate some text from the poems.

The following extracts are from Whitman's "memoranda book," which he called Specimen Days.

from Specimen Days

The Inauguration

March 4, 1865—The President[1] very quietly rode down to the Capitol in his own carriage, by himself, on a sharp trot, about noon, either because he wished to be on hand to sign bills, or to get rid of marching in line with the absurd procession, the muslin temple of liberty, and pasteboard monitor. I saw him on his return, at three o'clock, after the performance was over. He was in his plain two-horse barouche,[2] and looked very much worn and tired; the lines, indeed, of vast responsibilities, intricate questions, and demands of life and death, cut deeper than ever upon his dark brown face; yet all the old goodness, tenderness, sadness, and canny shrewdness, underneath the furrows. (I never see that man without feeling that he is one to become personally attached to, for his combination of purest, heartiest tenderness, and native western form of manliness.) By his side sat his little boy, of ten years. There were no soldiers, only a lot of civilians on horseback, with huge yellow scarves over their shoulders, riding around the carriage. (At the inauguration four years ago, he rode down and back again surrounded by a dense mass of armed cavalrymen eight deep, with drawn sabers; and there were sharpshooters stationed at every corner on the route.) I ought to make mention of the closing levee[3] of

1. **The President:** Abraham Lincoln. He would be assassinated in April, just a month after Whitman wrote this.
2. **barouche** (bə·rōōsh′) *n.:* four-wheeled, horse-drawn carriage.
3. **levee** *n.:* reception.

Saturday night last. Never before was such a compact jam in front of the White House—all the grounds filled, and away out to the spacious sidewalks. I was there, as I took a notion to go—was in the rush inside with the crowd—surged along the passageways, the Blue and other rooms, and through the great East Room. Crowds of country people, some very funny. Fine music from the Marine band, off in a side place. I saw Mr. Lincoln, dressed all in black, with white kid gloves and a claw-hammer coat, receiving, as in duty bound, shaking hands, looking very disconsolate, and as if he would give anything to be somewhere else.

The Real War Will Never Get in the Books

And so goodbye to the war. I know not how it may have been, or may be, to others—to me the main interest I found (and still, on recollection, find) in the rank and file of the armies, both sides, and in those specimens amid the hospitals, and even the dead on the

Walt Whitman 323

Primary Source

Whitman first published *Specimen Days* in 1882, but he made his notes for the Civil War sections of the book at the time of the events themselves—while he was working as a government clerk and war correspondent in Washington, D.C.

Whitman called his book *Specimen Days* because these journal entries offered "specimens" of his life. In the first excerpt, Whitman sketches an admiring portrait of Abraham Lincoln at his second inauguration. The second excerpt explores the human tragedy of the war—in the fields, among ordinary soldiers, and in the makeshift hospitals where Whitman worked—the part of the story of the war that was not told to the public.

DIRECT TEACHING

Ⓐ Reading Informational Text

❓ Analyzing implicit assumptions. From his comments here, what does Whitman assume about Lincoln's view of the presidency? Where does Whitman himself stand on this question? [Possible response: In using the adjective *absurd* to describe the procession and by drawing attention to the flimsy appearance of emblems in the procession (the "muslin temple," and "pasteboard monitor"), Whitman seems to think that Lincoln had little use for the ceremonial aspects of his office. The reference to signing bills implies that Lincoln was more interested in serving the American people. In choosing to describe these particular details, Whitman seems to support Lincoln's views.]

CONTENT-AREA CONNECTIONS

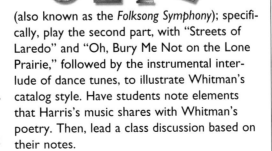

Music: Sound Catalogs
Like Whitman, composer Roy Harris "heard America singing" and often incorporated American popular and folk tunes and themes into his music. Among Harris's compositions for choral performance is the *Whitman Triptych,* based on some of Walt Whitman's poems.
Whole-class activity. Locate and play for the class a recording of Harris's *Symphony No. 4*

(also known as the *Folksong Symphony*); specifically, play the second part, with "Streets of Laredo" and "Oh, Bury Me Not on the Lone Prairie," followed by the instrumental interlude of dance tunes, to illustrate Whitman's catalog style. Have students note elements that Harris's music shares with Whitman's poetry. Then, lead a class discussion based on their notes.

Writing

1. Reading Nature

Ask students to organize their thoughts by using a three-column chart. Have students list at least three examples of how each writer "reads" nature.

Whitman	Emerson	Thoreau
	[The Universal Being circulates through people who are close to nature.]	[Farming enables one to become strengthened by the earth.]

2. My Walt Whitman

Encourage students to brainstorm topics as a group and then individually to list nouns to include in their poems. After the poems are written, let students pairs read them to each other; the listener should give specific feedback (especially regarding imagery and sound effects) and point out similarities to and differences from Whitman's poems.

3. A Close Look

Remind students that every point they make in their essays needs a quotation from or reference to the text and an explanation of how the example supports the point.

4. You Hear America Singing

Encourage students to review a family scrapbook or interview family members as they compile lists of experiences, people, and places. Suggest that a statement such as "In my eyes, America looks . . . " might be a good way both to begin and to conclude the essay—an essay that students may want to keep private and reflect upon in the future.

Listening and Speaking

Ask students to decide which audience they want to invite to the reading—for example, family members or another class. Urge students to keep the audience in mind as they try a variety of approaches to the reading and to then choose the one that they like best. If possible, tape the performances for review and enjoyment.

WRITING

1. Reading Nature

Nature is a major element in Whitman's writing, as it is in the writings of the Transcendentalists. In a brief essay, **compare and contrast** Whitman's "reading" of nature with Emerson's *Self-Reliance* (page 185) or Thoreau's *Walden* (page 192). You may want to create a chart to organize your ideas and reveal your points of comparison more clearly. Focus your comparison by asking and answering a specific question about the selections, such as

- What does nature *teach* the author?

- Is nature a source of *comfort* or *anxiety* to the author?

- What aspects of *self* does nature enable the author to understand?

- What aspects of the *divine* or the *sublime* does nature enable the author to understand?

2. My Walt Whitman

Write a free-verse **poem** in the tradition of Walt Whitman, using one of the poems you have read as a model. Consider beginning with one of Whitman's openers, such as "I hear America singing" or "I understand the large hearts of heroes." When you write in free verse (see page 313), you are not restricted to the use of rhymes and regular meters. However, you will want to use **imagery** and **sound effects** (alliteration, repetition, parallel structure), as well as one or more of Whitman's techniques: catalogs, rolling cadences, and changes of voice that result in a specific tone.

3. A Close Look

In a **critical essay,** analyze the Whitman poems you have read. Focus on analyzing one aspect of Whitman's poems that inter-

ests you: perhaps his **themes,** his everyday **diction,** his use of **catalogs,** his use of **free verse,** his **commonplace subject matter,** or his celebration of the **ordinary person** as hero. Open your essay with a thesis statement that clearly states your main idea. Be sure to use evidence from the poems to support your main points. When you quote directly from a poem, be sure to use quotation marks and to indicate the poem you are citing.

4. You Hear America Singing

How does Whitman's America differ from the America you know? How have social, historical, religious, and ethical influences changed from his time to yours? Reflect upon your own life, and then create a catalog of items that describe America as you see it today. Using that catalog as a starting point, write a **reflective essay** on the experiences you have had and the people and places that have influenced your life. How does America look in your eyes?

▶ **Use "Writing a Reflective Essay," pages 360–367, for help with this assignment.**

LISTENING AND SPEAKING

Performance

Prepare a public reading of Whitman's poems. You will have to decide when you will use solo readers and when you will use a chorus. For some poems you might want to use musical accompaniment. Be sure to ask your audience to evaluate your performance.

SKILLS FOCUS

Writing Skills
Write an essay comparing and contrasting literary works. Write a free-verse poem. Write a critical essay analyzing poems. Write a reflective essay about a personal experience.

Listening and Speaking Skills
Prepare and present a public reading of a poem.

DIFFERENTIATING INSTRUCTION

Learners Having Difficulty

You might allow students to respond to some of these activities in a form other than writing. For example, they might turn the free-verse poem or the reflective essay into a mural or collage. Alternatively, you might have students work in groups on some of the activities, such as "A Close Look."

Advanced Learners

Students might expand upon the "Reading Nature" essay by adding a fourth column to their charts, labeled with their own last name. They should then compare and contrast their own reading of nature with those of Emerson, Thoreau, and Whitman, giving examples and anecdotes both from their writing and from their lives.

Vocabulary Development

Multiple-Meaning Words

Many English words that are spelled the same have multiple meanings and sometimes different pronunciations. For example, the noun *desert*, with stress on the first syllable, means "dry, barren, sandy region." The verb *desert*, with stress on the second syllable, means "abandon," as in this line from Whitman's *Song of Myself*, number 33.

> "*Be of good cheer, we will not desert you*"

Often, however, words carry multiple meanings even when pronunciation and the part of speech don't change. Suppose, for example, that someone asks for a *roll*. Depending on the situation, the person might be requesting a class list, a cylinder of cloth, a piece of bread, a flight maneuver, or a rapid drumbeat. To understand which meaning is intended, you must pay attention to the word's **context**—the surrounding words and sentences. Which meaning of *roll* does Whitman intend in this line from *Song of Myself*, number 33?

> "Again the long roll of the drummers"

Using a dictionary. When you look up a word like *desert* or *roll*, you will find separate entries (or parts of an entry) for the word's use as a verb and as a noun. Some dictionaries start with the word's oldest meaning and end with its most recent meaning. Other dictionaries start with the modern meanings and then list old, rare, or obsolete meanings.

Studying origins. Word origins usually appear in brackets at the beginning of a dictionary entry. Some words have the same origin for all of their meanings. Other words, such as *desert* (dez′ərt) and *desert* (di·zurt′) have different origins—it is an accident of language history that the words ended up with the same spelling. Read the lines below by Louisa May Alcott, and note her use of the word *pale*. Then, study the chart. Which meaning of the word *pale* did Alcott intend?

> "Round the great stove was gathered the dreariest group I ever saw—ragged, gaunt and pale, mud to the knees, with bloody bandages untouched since put on days before . . ."

Word	Origin	Present Meaning
1. pale	Latin *pallidus*, "pale"	of a colorless complexion; wan
2. pale	Latin *palus*, "stake"	narrow, pointed stake; picket

PRACTICE

1. Use a dictionary to look up the origin and different meanings of all five words listed below. Then, choose two of the words. Use each of them in two different contexts to show its different meanings.

   a. sound   **d.** form
   b. bank   **e.** room
   c. limbs

2. Read the line below from Whitman's *Song of Myself*, number 33. Then, choose the lettered sentence that uses *hand* in the same sense as Whitman uses the word.

   > "Again gurgles the mouth of my dying general, he furiously waves with his hand. . . ."

   a. Please give me a hand with this shoveling.
   b. The hired hand was plowing the field.
   c. Let's play another hand of bridge.
   d. He asked her for her hand in marriage.
   e. My hand aches from writing.

Vocabulary Skills
Understand multiple-meaning words.

Vocabulary Development

Practice

1. Sentences will vary, but contexts should support the following meanings:

   a. *sound*—"auditory impression" or "in good health"
   b. *bank*—"a rise of ground next to a river or stream" or "an establishment for transactions with money"
   c. *limbs*—"large tree branches" or "arms or legs"
   d. *form*—"shape or external appearance" or "a printed document with blank spaces to be filled in"
   e. *room*—"a partitioned part of a building" or "an area of space"

2. The sentence for answer e is the only choice in which *hand* means literally a part of the anatomy, as it does in the quotation.

ASSESSING

Assessment

■ *Holt Assessment: Literature, Reading, and Vocabulary*

RETEACHING

For a lesson reteaching poetic devices, see **Reteaching**, p. 1117A.

Grade-Level Skills

■ **Reading Skills**
Compare and contrast poems.

More About the Writer

Background. Neftalí Ricardo Reyes Basoalto, the son of a railway worker and a schoolteacher, took the pen name Pablo Neruda in 1920 in honor of Jan Neruda, a nineteenth-century Czech poet.

During his years as a diplomat, Neruda continued to write poetry. His works from that period include *Residencia en la tierra* (*Residence on Earth*), a collection of surrealistic poems about the harmful effects of civilization, and *Canto general* (*General Song*), an epic poem about South American history.

For Independent Reading

Students may think that good poets and poetry address only grand topics. Neruda's poems, however, often focus on everyday or commonplace life. Two of the three recommended odes exemplify this characteristic.

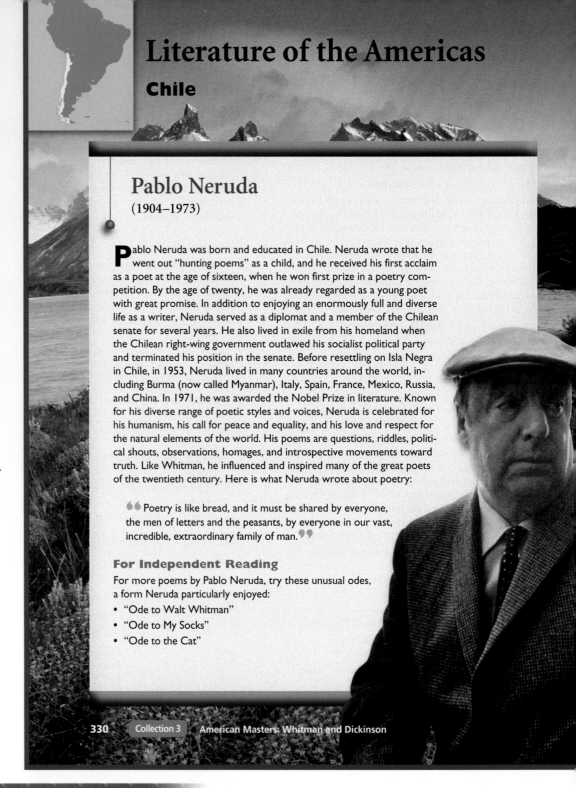

Literature of the Americas
Chile

Pablo Neruda
(1904–1973)

Pablo Neruda was born and educated in Chile. Neruda wrote that he went out "hunting poems" as a child, and he received his first acclaim as a poet at the age of sixteen, when he won first prize in a poetry competition. By the age of twenty, he was already regarded as a young poet with great promise. In addition to enjoying an enormously full and diverse life as a writer, Neruda served as a diplomat and a member of the Chilean senate for several years. He also lived in exile from his homeland when the Chilean right-wing government outlawed his socialist political party and terminated his position in the senate. Before resettling on Isla Negra in Chile, in 1953, Neruda lived in many countries around the world, including Burma (now called Myanmar), Italy, Spain, France, Mexico, Russia, and China. In 1971, he was awarded the Nobel Prize in literature. Known for his diverse range of poetic styles and voices, Neruda is celebrated for his humanism, his call for peace and equality, and his love and respect for the natural elements of the world. His poems are questions, riddles, political shouts, observations, homages, and introspective movements toward truth. Like Whitman, he influenced and inspired many of the great poets of the twentieth century. Here is what Neruda wrote about poetry:

❝ Poetry is like bread, and it must be shared by everyone, the men of letters and the peasants, by everyone in our vast, incredible, extraordinary family of man. ❞

For Independent Reading

For more poems by Pablo Neruda, try these unusual odes, a form Neruda particularly enjoyed:
• "Ode to Walt Whitman"
• "Ode to My Socks"
• "Ode to the Cat"

330 Collection 3 American Masters: Whitman and Dickinson

RESOURCES: READING

Planning
■ *One-Stop Planner* CD-ROM with ExamView Test Generator

Differentiating Instruction
■ *Holt Reading Solutions*
■ *The Holt Reader*
■ *Supporting Instruction in Spanish*
■ *Audio CD Library, Selections and Summaries in Spanish*

Grammar and Language
■ *Daily Language Activities*

Assessment
■ *Holt Assessment: Literature, Reading, and Vocabulary*
■ *One-Stop Planner* CD-ROM with ExamView Test Generator
■ *Holt Online Assessment*

Internet
■ go.hrw.com (Keyword: LE5 11-3)
■ *Elements of Literature Online*

Media
■ *Audio CD Library*
■ *Audio CD Library, Selections and Summaries in Spanish*

Full Powers

Make the Connection

Like many great writers, Pablo Neruda was deeply inspired by Walt Whitman's *Leaves of Grass*. A year before his death, Neruda made the following remarks:

> ❝ I was barely fifteen when I discovered Walt Whitman, my primary creditor. I stand here among you today still owing this marvelous debt that has helped me to live.
>
> To renegotiate this debt is to begin by making it public, by proclaiming myself the humble servant of the poet who measured the earth with long, slow strides, pausing everywhere to love and to examine, to learn, to teach, and to admire.... Clearly, he feared neither mortality nor immortality, nor did he attempt to define the boundaries between pure and impure poetry. He is the first absolute poet, and it was his intention not only to sing but to impart his vast vision of the relationships of men and of nations. In this sense, his obvious nationalism is part of an organic universality. He considers himself indebted to happiness and sorrow, to advanced cultures and primitive societies.... In Whitman's poetry the ignorant are never humbled, and the human condition is never derided.
>
> We are still living in a Whitmanesque epoch.... The bard complained of the all-powerful European influence that continued to dominate the literature of his time. In fact, it was he, Walt Whitman, in the persona of a specific geography, who for the first time in history brought honor to an American name. ❞

Reading Skills
Comparing and Contrasting Poems

In many ways, Whitman and Neruda are cut from the same cloth, even though they emerged from different cultures years apart. Read Neruda's poem twice. After the second reading, jot down **images** or phrases that remind you of lines from any of the poems in *Song of Myself*.

SKILLS FOCUS

Reading Skills
Compare and contrast poems.

Pablo Neruda 331

Summary ⬆ *above grade level*

The speaker of this poem says that he writes in the sun, in the street, by the sea. He is inhibited by night, yet in darkness he forges keys, perhaps keys that lead to understanding. The poem suggests that it is the ambiguity between "being" and "non-being," between silent death and defiant song, that makes both living and writing possible. Death is not an object of fear; rather, it evokes speculation about "origins" and a commitment to keep on singing. Several lines in the poem can be read as allusions to Whitman's *Song of Myself*.

PRETEACHING

Selection Starter

Build background. In *Song of Myself,* number 52, Whitman bequeaths himself to the dirt in order to filter or nourish the blood of others. Neruda expresses a related sentiment in the closing line of his long poem *The Heights of Macchu Picchu*. The two poets share an elemental love of the earth and humanity. In different ways, both poets' lives also reflect a continuing devotion to civic life: Whitman as a journalist and hospital volunteer and Neruda as a professional diplomat.

DIFFERENTIATING INSTRUCTION

Learners Having Difficulty

After students have read "Full Powers" once, focus their attention on ll. 1, 17, and 19–20. Then, have them re-read "I Hear America Singing" (p. 311). Once students see the parallels between Whitman and Neruda, they will have an easier time interpreting the poem.

Invite learners having difficulty to read "Full Powers" in interactive format in *The Holt Reader* and to use the sidenotes as aids to understanding the selection.

English-Language Learners

For lessons designed for intermediate and advanced English-language learners, see *Holt Reading Solutions*.

Special Education Students

For lessons designed for special education students, see *Holt Reading Solutions*.

Advanced Learners

Enrichment. Encourage students who know Spanish to attempt a new English translation of "Full Powers." They can use a Spanish-English dictionary, an English dictionary, and an English thesaurus. English- and Spanish-speaking classmates can then discuss the challenges of capturing the connotations and feelings of one language in another.

A **English-Language Learners**

Reading aloud. If any students are fluent in Spanish, invite them to read these lines aloud. Ask students to listen to the assonance and alliteration in Neruda's original. Then, have students look for sound devices in the same lines of the English translation (the *m* sounds in l. 7, for example, and the various *o* sounds in ll. 9–11).

Plenos poderes

Pablo Neruda

A puro sol escribo, a plena calle,
a pleno mar, en donde puedo canto,
sólo la noche errante me detiene
pero en su interrupción recojo espacio,
5 recojo sombra para mucho tiempo.

A
El trigo negro de la noche crece
mientras mis ojos miden la pradera
y así de sol a sol hago las llaves:
busco en la oscuridad las cerraduras
10 y voy abriendo al mar las puertas rotas
hasta llenar armarios con espuma.

Y no me canso de ir y de volver,
no me para la muerte con su piedra,
no me canso de ser y de no ser.

15 A veces me pregunto si de donde
si de padre o de madre o cordillera
heredé los deberes minerales,

los hilos de un océano encendido
y sé que sigo y sigo porque sigo
20 y canto porque canto y porque canto.

No tiene explicación lo que acontece
cuando cierro los ojos y circulo
como entre dos canales submarinos,
uno a morir me lleva en su ramaje
25 y el otro canta para que yo cante.

Así pues de no ser estoy compuesto
y como el mar asalta el arrecife
con cápsulas saladas de blancura
y retrata le piedra con la ola,
30 así lo que en la muerte me rodea
abre en mí la ventana de la vida
y en pleno paroxismo estoy durmiendo.
A plena luz camino por la sombra.

332

Tracing recurring themes. Neruda seems to be saying in "Full Powers" that some of his inspiration comes from an awareness of death. How is the same theme seen in Whitman's writing? [Possible response: In the concluding image of *Song of Myself,* Whitman describes the earth's absorption of his own dead body to evoke the reader's absorption of Whitman's poetry. He is inspired by the threat of death when he praises various heroes in the same poem, also touching upon the theme when recounting his hospital experiences in *Specimen Days.*]

Activity. Both Neruda and Whitman wrote during troubled times in their homelands. Have students use library or Internet resources to identify another poet who wrote during a time of national conflict and compare his or her writing to that of Neruda and Whitman.

Full Powers

Pablo Neruda

translated by **Ben Belitt** *and* **Alastair Reid**

I write in the clear sun, in the teeming street,
at full sea-tide, in a place where I can sing;
only the wayward night inhibits me,
but, interrupted by it, I recover space,
5 I gather shadows to last me a long time.

The black crop of the night is growing
while my eyes meanwhile take measure of the
    meadows.
So, from one sun to the next, I forge the keys.
In the darkness, I look for the locks
10 and keep on opening broken doors to the sea,
for it to fill the wardrobes with its foam.

And I do not weary of going and returning.
Death, in its stone aspect, does not halt me.
I am weary neither of being nor of non-being.

15 Sometimes I puzzle over origins—
was it from my father, my mother, or the
    mountains

that I inherited debts to minerality,
the fine threads spreading from a sea on fire?
And I know that I keep on going for the going's
    sake,
20 and I sing because I sing and because I sing.

There is no way of explaining what does happen
when I close my eyes and waver
as between two lost channels under water.
One lifts me in its branches toward my dying,
25 and the other sings in order that I may sing.

And so I am made up of a non-being,
and, as the sea goes battering at a reef
in wave on wave of salty white-tops
and drags back stones in its retreating wash,
30 so what there is in death surrounding me
opens in me a window out to living,
and, in the spasm of being, I go on sleeping.
In the full light of day, I walk in the shade.

Response and Analysis

Thinking Critically

1. In the first stanza, why might the night inhibit the speaker from writing?

2. What could the "keys" in line 8 unlock for the speaker? What do you think he means by "night" and "darkness" in the second stanza?

3. In line 14, what does the speaker mean by "I am weary neither of being nor of non-being"? Explain.

4. What could the speaker mean by his "debts to minerality" (line 17)?

5. Why does the speaker "keep on going," according to lines 19–20?

6. Why might the poem be titled "Full Powers"? What is the source of the speaker's creative powers?

WRITING

Comparing and Contrasting Poems

Look back at the notes you took on your second reading of "Full Powers." Based on these notes, write a brief **essay** comparing and contrasting "Full Powers" with the songs in *Song of Myself*. Here are some general points to focus on: the poets' use of **imagery**, their attitudes toward death, and their views of themselves in relation to others. In your essay, cite lines or passages from the poems to support your comparisons.

SKILLS FOCUS

Reading Skills
Compare and contrast poems.

Writing Skills
Write an essay comparing and contrasting two poems.

Pablo Neruda **333**

For a lesson reteaching poetic devices, see **Reteaching,** p. 1117A.

Pablo Neruda 333

DIRECT TEACHING

B **Literary Focus**
Analyzing the sound of language.
Have students describe and comment on the cadence in these lines (for example, the inclusion of a question in ll. 16–17 and the repetition of "I sing" in l. 20). Also, discuss the role of the translator in trying to be faithful to the sound effects in the original poem

INDEPENDENT PRACTICE

Response and Analysis

4. He may be referring to his origins in the land or earth; he may be expressing his dependence upon his own physical existence.

5. He feels compelled to write about the things that he experiences and feels; he is driven by eagerness to share things that he has not yet experienced or experiences that he thus far has kept to himself.

6. Neruda is exploring multiple aspects of life and living, of existence and death, of emotion and physicality; he may be saying that the source of his full creative powers lies in this interplay of death and life.

ASSESSING

Assessment
■ *Holt Assessment: Literature, Reading, and Vocabulary*

RETEACHING

Thinking Critically

1. Possible answer: The night alters or makes it hard for the speaker to see the things that inspire him ("teeming street," "full sea-tide"); night might remind the speaker of death or stasis.

2. Possible answer: The "keys" might unlock realms of the unconscious or the ability to

create again. The "night" and "darkness" may be as yet unexplored areas for the speaker's consideration.

3. Possible answer: The speaker may mean that he enjoys the creative exploration and recording of experiences related not only to the physical world ("being") but also to the realm of the mind and the spirit or soul ("non-being").

The speaker longs for the return of an absent loved one and imagines that any amount of time would go by quickly if only the date of their reunion were known. It is the uncertainty of the length of separation that seems difficult for the speaker to bear.

DIRECT TEACHING

Ⓐ Literary Focus

❓ **Imagery.** How do the words *brush by* and *spurn* reveal the speaker's feelings? [Possible responses: *Brush by* reveals the speaker's determination to pay only fleeting attention to present experiences in order to see her beloved more quickly; *spurn* reveals that the speaker scorns the present, seeing it only as a time of waiting.]

Ⓑ Reading Skills

❓ **Analyzing style.** How does the speaker use understatement to make a point in the second stanza? [She speaks of "only Centuries" as though one hundred years are a brief amount of time. Her love is so strong that she is willing to wait for a very long time.]

Ⓒ Literary Focus

❓ **Figures of speech.** What do ll. 13–16 say about the speaker's feelings for the absent "you"? [Possible responses: She cares more for this person than for her own life; she would discard this life if she knew she would be with her lover eternally.]

Before You Read

If you were coming in the Fall

Make the Connection
Poetry is called metaphysical when the simplest thoughts and emotions are described using fantastic and often highly intellectual **imagery** and **figures of speech.** In metaphysical poetry, private emotions, such as unfulfilled love, take on the importance of great and profound events. See if you think this poem qualifies as metaphysical.

INTERNET

More About Emily Dickinson

Keyword: LE5 11-3

If you were coming in the Fall

Emily Dickinson

Ⓐ
> If you were coming in the Fall,
> I'd brush the Summer by
> With half a smile, and half a spurn,
> As Housewives do, a Fly.

5 If I could see you in a year,
I'd wind the months in balls—
And put them each in separate Drawers,
For fear the numbers fuse—

Ⓑ
> If only Centuries, delayed,
> 10 I'd count them on my Hand,
> Subtracting, till my fingers dropped
> Into Van Dieman's Land.°

Ⓒ
> If certain, when this life was out—
> That your's and mine, should be
> 15 I'd toss it yonder, like a Rind,
> And take Eternity—

But, now, uncertain of the length
Of this, that is between,
It goads me, like the Goblin Bee—
20 That will not state—it's sting.

12. Van Dieman's (dē′mənz) **Land:** former name of Tasmania, an island that is a state of Australia.

Literary Criticism

Critic's Commentary: Rhyme and Reason
Scholar Joel Conarroe writes that Dickinson "employed off rhymes, or near rhymes, to ensure that the quatrains, couched in the language of surprise, were neither conventional nor predictable. . . . Rarely containing so much as an unnecessary syllable, the poems are almost all characterized by epigrammatic precision. . . . A reader soon learns the pleasures of collaboration, filling in the missing keys she has deliberately left out."

George Inness (1825–1894) painted with poetic impressionism, depicting the soft effects of early spring and the glowing hues of autumn.

Activity. Have students speculate about how the speaker of the poem might respond to *Pastoral Scene*. [Possible response: The fall might look as idyllic as this scene to the speaker if the absent person addressed were to arrive.]

Pastoral Scene by George Inness. Oil on canvas (51 cm × 76 cm).
Courtesy Davis Art Slides.

Emily Dickinson   **339**

Literary Criticism

Critic's Commentary:
An Original Voice

Essayist and editor Thomas Wentworth Higginson was among the first outside of Dickinson's family and friends to read her poetry. Later, he wrote of the experience: "The impression of a wholly new and original poetic genius was as distinct on my mind at the first reading of these four poems as it is now, after half a century of further knowledge; and with it came the problem never yet solved, what place ought to be assigned in literature to what is so remarkable, yet so elusive of criticism. The bee himself did not evade the schoolboy more than she evaded me; and even at this day I still stand somewhat bewildered, like the boy."

Activity. After students have read the poems in this group, have them return to this statement by Higginson. Then, invite students to share their responses to his comments about Dickinson's originality and elusiveness.

Primary Source

This feature includes Dickinson's poem with the corrections by her earliest editors. Students can contrast Dickinson's phrasing and punctuation with the conventional style imposed by her first editors.

DIRECT TEACHING

Ⓐ Content-Area Connections

Literature: Textual Scholarship
Because Dickinson's early editors mistook originality for error, they freely changed her texts. Her poems did not appear in print as she wrote them until the 1950s. Dickinson's frequent dashes, capitalization, and elliptical phrasing were unconventional in her time and they still remain so.

Ⓑ Learners Having Difficulty

Proofreading marks. Make sure students understand the marks used. You might draw each on the chalkboard and explain, for instance, that a slash through a letter means "change to lowercase," a slash with a loop at the top means "delete," and a caret means "insert."

Ⓒ Content-Area Connections

Literature: The Editor's Role
Ask students to discuss the role of an editor. [Possible responses: fixing errors; helping writers to better express their ideas.] Encourage students to take sides and debate the question of whether it is acceptable for an editor to change a writer's work without the writer's permission.

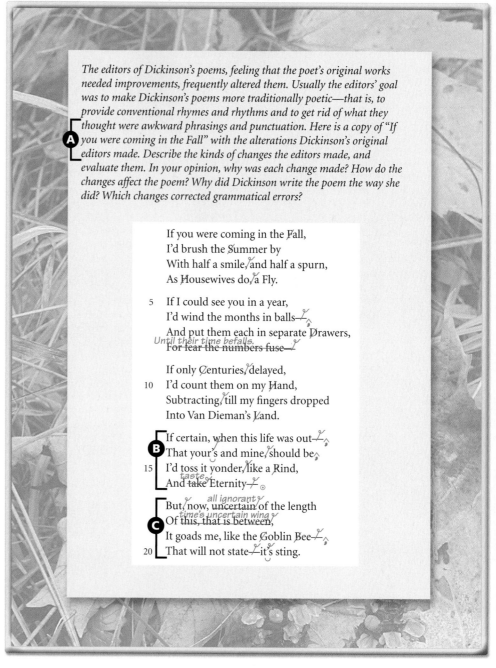

Ⓐ *The editors of Dickinson's poems, feeling that the poet's original works needed improvements, frequently altered them. Usually the editors' goal was to make Dickinson's poems more traditionally poetic—that is, to provide conventional rhymes and rhythms and to get rid of what they thought were awkward phrasings and punctuation. Here is a copy of "If you were coming in the Fall" with the alterations Dickinson's original editors made. Describe the kinds of changes the editors made, and evaluate them. In your opinion, why was each change made? How do the changes affect the poem? Why did Dickinson write the poem the way she did? Which changes corrected grammatical errors?*

If you were coming in the Fall,
I'd brush the Summer by
With half a smile, and half a spurn,
As Housewives do, a Fly.

5　If I could see you in a year,
I'd wind the months in balls—
And put them each in separate Drawers,
Until their time befalls.
For fear the numbers fuse—

If only Centuries, delayed,
10　I'd count them on my Hand,
Subtracting, till my fingers dropped
Into Van Dieman's Land.

Ⓑ If certain, when this life was out—
That your's and mine, should be
15　I'd toss it yonder, like a Rind,
taste.
And take Eternity—

all ignorant
But, now, uncertain of the length
time's uncertain wing
Ⓒ Of this, that is between,
It goads me, like the Goblin Bee—
20　That will not state—it's sting.

Literary Criticism

Critic's Commentary: Dickinson's Diction

According to Thomas H. Johnson, who compiled and edited the complete 1955 edition of Emily Dickinson's poems, "Emily Dickinson loved words ardently. Her feeling about them amounted to veneration and her selection of them was ritualistic. . . . 'A word that breathes distinctly / Has not the power to die' [she wrote]. . . . Near the end of her life she wrote to a close friend, 'I hesitate which word to take, as I can take but few and each must be the chiefest. . . .'" Another critic, Joel Conarroe, also focuses on Dickinson's love of words. "What mainly held her attention, year after year," Conarroe says, "was the mysterious power of words."

Response and Analysis

The Soul selects her own Society

Thinking Critically

1. Dickinson uses **personification**, attributing human feelings, thoughts, or attitudes to a soul. What does the soul do in the last stanza of the poem?

2. *Majority* has at least two meanings: "the greater part of something" and "having reached full legal age." An older, obsolete meaning of *majority* is "superiority." What do you think *majority* means in this poem? What kind of person does the adjective *divine* suggest?

3. Do you think the phrase "Valves of her attention" is derived from organic things (valves of the heart) or mechanical ones (valves of a faucet)? What do you picture happening here?

4. Dickinson's early editors changed the word *Valves* to *lids* in line 11. How does this change the **metaphor**? How does it change what you see?

5. Look at the **meter** of lines 10 and 12. How does their rhythmical pattern differ from the corresponding lines in the first and second stanzas? What is the effect of this difference?

6. Dickinson gave very few of her poems titles. (The titles in this text are the first lines of the poems.) Her early editors called this poem "Exclusion." In what ways does this title apply? In what ways is it a limiting title?

7. An example of **slant rhyme** in this poem occurs in the third stanza, where Dickinson rhymes *stone* with *one*. Why is it important that the word *stone* be emphasized? To hear the difference, imagine that Dickinson had ended her poem with the words "And be done."

Find another example of slant rhyme in this poem.

8. Do you think the "soul selects her own society" in the strict way that is described in the poem? Do you think that most people make choices the way the speaker in this poem does? Explain your response.

If you were coming in the Fall

Thinking Critically

1. How would you describe the speaker's situation? How does she feel about it?

2. What two things are being compared in the **simile** in the first stanza?

3. In the second stanza, what domestic articles are the months compared to? Why does the speaker put them in separate drawers?

4. Van Dieman's Land, besides being the old name of Tasmania, also refers to those places on the globe farthest away from the United States. Given this information, how would you **paraphrase** the third stanza?

5. How would you describe the speaker's **tone** in the first four stanzas? How does the tone change in the fifth stanza, where her exaggerations disappear? What goads, or pushes, her against her will?

6. In folklore a goblin is a tormenting creature. What might Dickinson be suggesting when she says that the bee is a goblin and will not "state" its sting?

7. Do you think the hopes expressed in this poem are fairly common, or are they rare or odd? Explain your responses.

SKILLS FOCUS

Literary Skills
Analyze exact rhyme and slant rhyme.

Emily Dickinson   **341**

The Soul selects her own Society

Thinking Critically

1. The soul chooses one and closes the valves of her attention.

2. Possible answers: "the greater part," since the person the soul selects outweighs all others; "maturity," since the soul controls her life; "superiority," since the soul finds only one who meets her standards. "Divine" suggests one who is godlike.

3. Possible answer: In shutting out people, she seems to be closing the valves of her heart (love).

4. Lids suggest eyelids. The edited metaphor suggests shutting out unwanted sights. It creates a more human image than Dickinson's original.

5. Unlike the four syllable words in the first and second stanzas, the two syllable lines in ll. 10 and 12 slow the rhythm and add emphasis.

Response and Analysis

6. It applies to the soul's excluding many people, but fails to convey the passion with which the soul selects a soulmate.

7. As the last word *Stone* affects the overall impression the poem makes on the reader and the word *stone* emphasizes the power of the soul's exclusion. Other slant rhymes include *society/majority, Gate/Mat, nation/attention.*

8. Possible answer: No, most people remain open to forming friendships, even close ones, with more than one person.

If you were coming in the Fall

Thinking Critically

1. She is tortured by the uncertainty of when her lover will return.

2. Making the summer pass quickly is compared to brushing away a fly.

3. The months are compared to balls of yarn. She separates them so she won't lose count.

4. If mere centuries delayed you, I could tick them off indefinitely.

5. The tone changes from hopeful to frustrated. Continual uncertainty has become a torture.

6. Possible answer: She would prefer knowledge—the bee's sting—no matter how painful.

7. Possible answer: Many people find prolonged uncertainty harder to bear than definite bad news.

Assessment

■ *Holt Assessment: Literature, Reading, and Vocabulary*

For a lesson reteaching poetic devices, see **Reteaching,** p. 1117A.

Emily Dickinson   **341**

The poet compares truth to a blinding light and suggests that truth can be fully comprehended only if it is revealed obliquely.

A Reading Skills

? Interpreting. What is a major difference between the two expressions "slant the truth" and "tell all the truth slant"? [To "slant the truth" means to deliberately mislead, but to "tell all the truth slant" means to tell the truth partially, gradually, or indirectly.]

B Learners Having Difficulty

Breaking down difficult text. Of all the poems in this group, "Tell all the Truth . . ." may be the most fragmented in terms of normal sentence structure. Have students choose partners and go over the poem in pairs, breaking it down into a series of paraphrased thoughts and images.

C Reading Skills

? Expressing an opinion. In your opinion, what kinds of truths might need to be revealed "slant" (indirectly), or gradually? [Possible responses: truths that challenge people's established beliefs or core values; personal truths that can damage someone's self-image.]

Before You Read

Tell all the Truth but tell it slant

Make the Connection
Quickwrite 🖉

Dickinson's famous line "Tell all the Truth but tell it slant" may reveal her method of survival as well as the essence of her own poetry. What do you think it would mean to tell the truth "slant"? Is truth told slant the same as a lie? Jot down your thoughts.

Tell all the Truth but tell it slant

Emily Dickinson

A Tell all the Truth but tell it slant—
Success in Circuit° lies
B Too bright for our infirm Delight
The Truth's superb surprise
As Lightning to the Children eased
With explanation kind
C The Truth must dazzle gradually
Or every man be blind—

2. **circuit** *n.*: indirect path.

INTERNET
More About Emily Dickinson
Keyword: LE5 11-3

DIFFERENTIATING INSTRUCTION

Advanced Learners
Enrichment. This poem, unlike many of Dickinson's others, contains no slant rhymes. Ask students whether Dickinson might have been making an ironic comment on the word *slant*. [Possible response: The lack of slant rhymes is ironic since it contradicts what the word *slant* leads readers to expect. The word *slant* has different meanings in the phrases "tell all the truth but tell it slant" and "slant rhymes."] Have students suggest what the rhymes in the poem contribute to the meaning. [Possible response: The rhymes add emphasis to key words: *Lies* puts stress on *surprise; kind,* on *blind.*]

Rooms by the Sea (1951) by Edward Hopper. Oil on canvas.
Yale University Art Gallery, Bequest of Stephen Clark, B.A., 1903.

American realist painter **Edward Hopper** (1882–1967) studied and spent most of his life in Manhattan. His work often presents archetypally empty scenes and isolated, often melancholy figures. Large geometric shapes, sharp angles, and an austere play of light and shadow are recurrent compositional elements in his paintings. For many people, his work has come to symbolize modern alienation.

Activity. Ask students what surrealistic element is featured in Hopper's *Rooms by the Sea.* [The door opens directly onto the water.] Ask how the title is a "slant" on the usual meaning of the phrase "by the sea." ["By the sea" usually means on a beach, not directly on the water.] Ask in what other way the painting connects with Dickinson's poem. [Possible responses: Light and surprise are elements of both; the slanting line of light in the painting provides a visual analogy for the verbal image of truth as light in the poem.]

Emily Dickinson   **343**

CONTENT-AREA CONNECTIONS

Humanities: Modernism
Tell students that there are many connections between modern painting and modern poetry. Tell them also that in many ways Dickinson's work prefigures the poetry of the twentieth century, with its emphasis on concision and imagery.

Paired activity. Have student pairs explore further how "telling the truth slant" applies to modern painting as well as to poetry. Have them identify artists who present their subjects straightforwardly and artists who present them "slant." Students should explain which elements of modern painting are analogous to modern poetry and what both modern art and modern poetry require of the audience. Ask students to share their observations; they should use art reproductions to illustrate their points.

Summary ↔ *at grade level*

At the height of its beauty, a flower is indifferently killed by the frost. Nevertheless, God approves, as the sun rises and sets, following the beautiful yet merciless progress of the seasons.

DIRECT TEACHING

A Literary Focus

❓ Word choice. What does Dickinson mean by "accidental"? [Possible responses: The frost cannot control its own power; it has no conscious intention to hurt or harm.]

B English-Language Learners

Interpreting capitalization. Explain to students that Dickinson capitalizes many common nouns that do not ordinarily take capitals. Often, but not always, she capitalizes words that she personifies. Examples of this practice include *Flower, Frost, Sun.* However, be sure students understand that not every unusual capitalization by Dickinson is an example of personification.

C Literary Focus

❓ Tone. What is the speaker saying about God's attitude toward nature? [Possible response: The cycles of light and dark and even of death and life are part of God's plan and therefore good and acceptable.]

Before You Read

Apparently with no surprise

INTERNET
More About
Emily Dickinson
Keyword: LE5 11–3

Literary Skills
Understand tone.

Make the Connection
Quickwrite ✏

Dickinson had only to look out her window to see the powers of nature at work. In her poetry she uses deceptively innocent observations about birds, flies, and flowers to reveal deep and sometimes disturbing ideas about life and death. Think about nature for a few minutes: Do you think nature is nurturing and helpful, or is it threatening and hostile? Create a double-column chart in which you write evidence of nature's benevolence in one column and evidence of nature's destructiveness in the other.

Literary Focus
Tone

A writer's attitude toward a subject, or even toward an audience, is called **tone.** Tone is most often revealed by word choice. Tone can be described in a single word: *optimistic, pessimistic, sarcastic, playful, loving, awed,* and so on. We cannot say we have understood any piece of literature until we have understood, or heard, its tone.

> **Tone** is the attitude a writer takes toward the subject of a work, the characters in it, or the audience.
>
> *For more on Tone, see the Handbook of Literary and Historical Terms.*

Apparently with no surprise

Emily Dickinson

Apparently with no surprise
To any happy Flower
The Frost beheads it at its play—
In accidental power—
The blonde Assassin passes on—
The Sun proceeds unmoved
To measure off another Day
For an Approving God.

CONTENT-AREA CONNECTIONS

Art: Lessons from Nature
Though self-confined to a very narrow world for much of her life, Dickinson keenly observed the people and things around her, and from these particulars, she expressed themes and feelings about life, love, nature, and immortality. Suggest that students reread the poems in this group and focus on

how the poet evokes images of nature and subtly personifies them.
Individual activity. Ask students to observe a natural object carefully and to think deeply about how the object makes them feel. Suggest that they imagine the object as a human being or as having a human experience. Then, have them draw

the natural object in a way that conveys its human characteristics. A simple example of this would be a flower drawn with a smiling face.

Before You Read

Success is counted sweetest

Make the Connection
Quickwrite 🖉

In 1862, Dickinson sent this poem along with three others to Thomas Wentworth Higginson, a literary critic and editor for *The Atlantic Monthly,* to ask his advice about her poems. It is one of several poems that shows Dickinson's feelings about success and her struggles with the values of the world. Write down some of your own thoughts about success. How do you think people who always encounter failure feel?

Background

Literary scholars debate Dickinson's lack of interest in publishing and in public recognition. This poem, included in *A Masque of Poets,* is one of the poems that Dickinson did publish during her lifetime. Ironically many readers thought it was written by Ralph Waldo Emerson (page 179).

Success is counted sweetest

Emily Dickinson

Success is counted sweetest
By those who ne'er succeed.
To comprehend a nectar°
Requires sorest° need. **D**

5　Not one of all the purple Host°
Who took the Flag today
Can tell the definition
So clear of Victory

As he defeated—dying—
10　On whose forbidden ear
The distant strains of triumph
Burst agonized and clear!

---

3. **nectar** *n.:* name for the drink of the Greek and Roman gods; also, a term applied to any delicious beverage.
4. **sorest** *adv.:* deepest; most extreme.
5. **purple host:** royal army.

Taps (detail) (c. 1907–1909) by Gilbert Gaul.
Oil on canvas (32¾″ × 43″).
Collection of the Birmingham Museum of Art, Birmingham, Alabama. Gift of John Meyer.

INTERNET
More About Emily Dickinson
Keyword: LE5 11-3

Emily Dickinson　345

Literary Criticism

Critic's Commentary: Bittersweet Success

In an introduction to a volume of Dickinson's poems, Robert N. Linscott writes: "She lived a life, outwardly uneventful, inwardly dedicated to a secret and self-imposed assignment—the mission of writing a 'letter to the world' that would express, in poems of absolute truth and of the utmost economy, her concepts of life and death, of love and nature, and of what Henry James called 'the landscape of the soul.' Unpublished in her lifetime, unknown at her death in 1886, her poems, by chance and good fortune, reached, at last, the world to which they had been addressed. 'If fame belonged to me,' she had written in 1861, 'I could not escape her; if she did not, the longest day would pass me on the chase, and the approbation of my dog would forsake me.' The long day passed and fame was finally hers."

Response and Analysis

Tell all the Truth . . .

Thinking Critically

1. "Slant" is an indirect revelation; "lying" is a distortion of the truth.

2. *Circuit* means "going around the truth." "Truth's superb surprise" is too bright.

3. Fears of lightning are eased when children are gently given an explanation of what it is.

4. The surprise of direct truth is too shocking. *Dazzle* may mean "enlighten." *Blind* may mean "uncomprehending."

5. an intense light

Extending and Evaluating

6. Poetry tells the truth "slant"— with implication, metaphor, allusion, and symbols.

Apparently with no . . .

Thinking Critically

1. It is the frost—something beautiful in its own right but deadly.

2. The flower—a happy child; the frost—an accidental killer; the sun—an indifferent passerby.

3. *Unmoved* means either "unfeeling" or "stationary;" and since *proceeds* means "moves ahead," the sun "moves unmoved."

4. God approves. The speaker feels disturbed by, yet resigned to, this reality.

5. Possible answer: *awed,* as suggested by God's and nature's power to take life.

6. Emerson focuses on nature's majesty; the speaker here focuses on the indifferent constancy of nature's laws. Charts will vary.

Extending and Evaluating

7. Possible answer: God calmly allows death and destruction as well as life. Opinions will vary.

Response and Analysis

Tell all the Truth but tell it slant

Thinking Critically

1. Look back at your Quickwrite notes. How would you define the word *slant* as it is used in the poem? How is telling something "slant" different from lying?

2. Explain the meaning of *circuit* (line 2) in the context of the poem. What is "Too bright for our infirm Delight" (line 3)?

3. Lines 5 and 6 provide an example to illustrate the poet's point about truth. As is typical of Dickinson's **style,** she omits several words in these lines. How would you rephrase the lines to make a full sentence?

4. According to the last two lines, why must the truth be told "slant"? How would you define *dazzle* and *blind* here?

5. What **metaphor** is implied in line 7? What is "Truth" being compared to?

Extending and Evaluating

6. Do you agree with the poet's message? In what way can this lyric be seen as a reference to the way poetry works?

Apparently with no surprise

Thinking Critically

1. What is the "blonde Assassin"?

2. How are the flower, the frost, and the sun **personified** in this poem? What kind of person does each seem to be compared to?

3. A **pun** is a play on words, based on the multiple meanings of a single word or on words that sound alike but mean different things. What pun do you find in line 6? How would you explain it?

4. According to the speaker, how does God feel about the flower's beheading? How do you think the speaker feels?

SKILLS FOCUS

Literary Skills
Analyze tone.

5. What word would you use to describe the **tone** of this poem: *optimistic, pessimistic, awed, defiant?* Be sure to find details in the poem to support your response.

6. How does this speaker's attitude toward nature differ from Emerson's attitude in the excerpt from his essay *Nature* (page 182)? Is either point of view supported by the chart you made before reading the poem? Explain.

Extending and Evaluating

7. What do you think is the **theme** of this poem? Do you find the theme shocking, reassuring, or something else? Explain.

Success is counted sweetest

Thinking Critically

1. According to the speaker, who is likely to count success as sweetest? Do you think the poet is accurate in describing the feelings of people who fail? Be sure to review your Quickwrite notes.

2. Purple is a color associated with blood shed in battle (the Purple Heart medal is given to soldiers wounded or killed in action). It is also a color associated with royalty and nobility. What do you think is the "purple Host" in line 5?

3. Whose ear is mentioned in line 10? Why is the ear "forbidden"?

4. Describe the **image** you see in the last stanza. How could this image be extended to refer to other situations in life? Explain.

5. Have you ever been like the soldier in the last stanza—in agony because someone else is proclaimed winner? What other circumstances in life (other than a wartime battle) could this situation be applied to? (Could it describe the feelings of a poet who could not publish her work?)

Success is counted sweetest
Thinking Critically

1. The defeated. Possible answers: Yes, what is out of reach is most desirable; no, after a great effort, winners count success sweetest.

2. The victorious army; its wounded soldiers.

3. The dying soldier's ear is forbidden to hear of victory for *his* side.

4. Possible answer: The image of a soldier dying on a battlefield could be extended to refer to any unsuccessful person.

5. Possible answer: A political candidate who loses a race; yes, an unpublished writer.

ASSESSING

Assessment

■ *Holt Assessment: Literature, Reading, and Vocabulary*

RETEACHING

For a lesson reteaching poetic devices, see **Reteaching,** p. 1117A.

Before You Read

Because I could not stop for Death

Make the Connection

Like many other metaphors in Dickinson's poetry, the one in this poem "tames" or "domesticates" the most awesome and inevitable of human experiences—death. The literal elements of the metaphor are simple: Dying is compared to an unexpected ride in a horse-drawn carriage.

Literary Focus
Irony

The success of this poem depends on **irony**, on gradual comprehension, and on a light-hearted, witty tone that contrasts with the subject of the story being told. In this poem what seems to be a pleasant carriage ride turns into a trip of eternal significance. As you read, pay careful attention to details which give the poem an ironic twist.

In general, **irony** is a discrepancy between appearances and reality, between what seems suitable or appropriate and what actually happens.

For more on Irony, see the Handbook of Literary and Historical Terms.

Reading Skills
Summarizing a Text

Dickinson uses time in an unusual way in this poem. It will help, as you read, to pause at the end of each stanza and note *when* the events are occurring.

INTERNET
More About
Emily Dickinson
Keyword: LE5 11-3

SKILLS FOCUS

Pages 347–349
cover
Literary Skills
Understand irony.
Reading Skills
Summarize a text.

Because I could not stop for Death

Emily Dickinson

Because I could not stop for Death—
He kindly stopped for me—
The Carriage held but just Ourselves—
And Immortality.

5   We slowly drove—He knew no haste
And I had put away
My labor and my leisure too,
For His Civility—

We passed the School, where Children strove
10 At Recess—in the Ring—
We passed the Fields of Gazing Grain—
We passed the Setting Sun—

Or rather—He passed Us—
The Dews drew quivering and chill—
15 For only Gossamer,° my Gown—
My Tippet—only Tulle°—

We paused before a House that seemed
A Swelling of the Ground—
The Roof was scarcely visible—
20 The Cornice°—in the Ground—

Since then—'tis Centuries—and yet
Feels shorter than the Day
I first surmised the Horses' Heads
Were toward Eternity—

---

15. **gossamer** *n.*: thin, soft material.
16. **tippet . . . tulle:** shawl made of fine netting.
20. **cornice** *n.*: molding at the top of a building.

Emily Dickinson   **347**

CONTENT-AREA CONNECTIONS

Music: American Geniuses
Brooklyn native **Aaron Copland** (1900–1990) is recognized as one of the greatest composers of the twentieth-century. Sometimes called the "dean of American music," Copland infused his compositions with a distinctly American sound. In his song cycle *Twelve Poems of Emily Dickinson,* Copland respectfully gave a predominant role to the poet's words.

Mixed-ability group activity. After students read "Because I could not stop for Death," have them listen to Copland's version of this poem, which he called "The Chariot" (its title in earlier editions of Dickinson). Then, have students create their own music for this or another of Dickinson's poems. The style doesn't need to be classical or choral—it can be rock, pop, hip-hop, country, folk, or any style students wish.

VIEWING THE ART

Andrew Newell Wyeth
(1917–   ), the son of American illustrator N.C. Wyeth (1882–1945), is known for his austere paintings of rural New England scenes and his spare, uncluttered style. His paintings use egg tempera, which is made of earth and mineral colors combined with egg yolk and water. Wyeth once said that he appreciates the medium for its feeling of "dry lostness." Somewhat conservative in both technique and subject matter, Wyeth is one of the few critically recognized contemporary artists to focus on rural subjects.

Activity. What makes Wyeth's *Wind from the Sea* a suitable work to accompany this poem? [Possible responses: Both have images of light, air, and a window; the rush of air through the window might parallel the extinguishing of the speaker's consciousness.]

Wind from the Sea (1947) by Andrew Wyeth. Tempera on panel (18½″ × 27½″).
Mead Art Museum, Amherst College. Gift of Charles and Janet Morgan (EL1984.51). © Andrew Wyeth.

Before You Read

I heard a Fly buzz—when I died

Make the Connection
Quickwrite ✏️

One of Dickinson's most brilliantly original works, this poem begins with such boldness and continues with such quick shifts of attention that we may not stop to think about what we are hearing—a voice from the dead. Write down what you would expect someone to sense at the time of death—that ultimate moment when we cannot "see to see."

I heard a Fly buzz— when I died

Emily Dickinson

I heard a Fly buzz—when I died—
The Stillness in the Room
Was like the Stillness in the Air—
Between the Heaves of Storm—

5 The Eyes around—had wrung them dry—
And Breaths were gathering firm
For that last Onset—when the King
Be witnessed—in the Room—

I willed my Keepsakes—Signed away
10 What portion of me be
Assignable—and then it was
There interposed a Fly—

With Blue—uncertain stumbling Buzz—
Between the light—and me—
15 And then the Windows failed—and then
I could not see to see—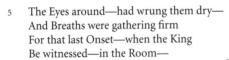

Emily Dickinson 349

Summary *at grade level*

The speaker describes her own death as others wait for death to come to her. She is giving away her last possessions. A buzzing fly positions itself between the speaker and the light as death overtakes her.

DIRECT TEACHING

A Literary Focus

❓ **Mood.** What is the mood created in ll. 2–8? [Possible responses: solemnity, expectation.] **What changes the mood?** [the fly; the introduction of an insignificant everyday event]

B Learners Having Difficulty

Paraphrasing. To help students grasp the two senses in which the speaker uses the word *see*, paraphrase the line as "My vision failed, and I could no longer understand what was happening."

READING MINI-LESSON

Developing Word-Attack Skills
Write and say the word *buzz*, from a Dickinson poem, and the word *yawp*, from one of Whitman's. Help students recognize that both are imitative or echoic words. *Buzz* sounds like the sound made by a flying insect. *Yawp* sounds like a loud, harsh cry.

Activity. Display these sentences. Have students read the sentences aloud and identify the words that are imitative words.

1. The cat stood motionless, <u>purring</u> softly.
2. Birds <u>twittered</u> all around her.
3. Her paw <u>swooshed</u> out at an unsuspecting sparrow.
4. She managed only to <u>whack</u> the air.
5. The air filled with raucous <u>caws</u>.
6. A crow <u>guffawed</u> at the cat's failure.

Summary ⬌ *at grade level*

This poem asserts that those judged mad are often the sane ones and those deemed sensible are truly mad. The poem warns that those who do not conform to society's expectations will be labeled mad and punished.

DIRECT TEACHING

A Literary Focus

❓ Author's style. Why does the poet choose to use the word *divinest* here? [Possible response: to suggest that madness is in reality a gift from God.]

B Reading Skills

❓ Interpreting. What is the speaker saying about creativity and conformity in these lines? [Possible responses: Those who go against the majority are often thought of as being mad and are shunned. To the speaker, such madness is actually divine inspiration.]

C Literary Focus

❓ Imagery. What does the image in the last line suggest? [Possible response: Dissenters will be chained up like wild animals.]

Before You Read

Much Madness is divinest Sense

Make the Connection

Since her death, Dickinson has often been portrayed as an eccentric recluse. In fact, Dickinson lived as many other great poets (and quite a few "ordinary" people) have lived—deliberately choosing solitude for contemplation, reading, and writing.

Literary Focus
Paradox

A **paradox** is a statement that seems to be self-contradictory. For example, when Juliet says "Parting is such sweet sorrow," she uses a paradox: She is sad to be leaving Romeo, but kissing him goodbye (over and over again) is very sweet. The very title of this poem states an interesting paradox.

> A **paradox** is a statement that appears to be self-contradictory but reveals a kind of truth.
>
> *For more on Paradox, see the Handbook of Literary and Historical Terms.*

Much Madness is divinest Sense

Emily Dickinson

Ⓐ Much Madness is divinest Sense—
To a discerning Eye—
Much Sense—the starkest Madness—
'Tis the Majority
Ⓑ In this, as All, prevail—
Assent—and you are sane—
Demur—you're straightway dangerous—
Ⓒ And handled with a Chain—

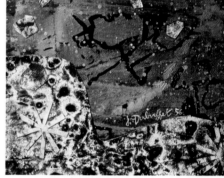

Path with Grass Border (detail) (1956) by Jean Dubuffet. Oil on canvas cutout with sand, earth, and pebbles. Dubuffet was a French artist who coined the term *art brut*, or "outsider art."

SKILLS FOCUS

Literary Skills
Understand paradox.

SKILLS REVIEW

Analyzing the speaker. Remind students that the speaker of a poem is not the poet but a creation of the poet, a distinct voice that the poet consciously manipulates. Tell students that many readers mistakenly assume that the speaker of Dickinson's poems is the poet herself. However, this is not a safe assumption: too little is known of her life, her feelings, or her personality to confirm such an idea.

Activity. Have students read through Dickinson's poems and take brief notes about the speaker of each poem.
- What clues are there to each speaker's age, gender, or position in life?
- How would students describe each speaker's personality and tone?
- How credible or believable is each speaker?

Activity. Ask students to look over their notes and compare speakers. Then, hold a class discussion in which students debate whether all the speakers are the same persona. Encourage students to defend their positions by citing details from the poems.

"I sing . . . because I am afraid"

In 1862, Emily Dickinson sent the editor and critic Thomas Wentworth Higginson a letter and four poems, asking for critical help. Dickinson saw him as a mentor, and they corresponded for several years. Four years after Dickinson's death, Higginson assisted Mabel Loomis Todd (a friend of Austin Dickinson, Emily's brother) in editing Dickinson's poems. The following excerpts are from two of Dickinson's letters. The first was written after Dickinson asked Higginson for some criticism, which she referred to as "surgery."

April 26, 1862

Mr. Higginson,—Your kindness claimed earlier gratitude, but I was ill, and write today from my pillow.

Thank you for the surgery; it was not so painful as I supposed. I bring you others, as you ask. . . .

You asked how old I was? I made no verse, but one or two, until this winter, sir.

I had a terror since September, I could tell to none; and so I sing, as the boy does of the burying ground, because I am afraid.

You inquire my books. For poets, I have Keats, and Mr. and Mrs. Browning. For prose, Mr. Ruskin, Sir Thomas Browne, and the Revelations. I went to school, but in your manner of the phrase had no education. When a little girl, I had a friend who taught me Immortality; but venturing too near, himself, he never returned. Soon after my tutor died, and for several years my lexicon was my only companion. Then I found one more, but he was not contented I be his scholar, so he left the land.

You ask of my companions. Hills, sir, and the sundown, and a dog large as myself, that my father bought me. They are better than beings because they know, but do not tell; and the noise in the pool at noon excels my piano.

I have a brother and sister; my mother does not care for thought, and father, too busy with his briefs to notice what we do. He buys me many books, but begs me not to read them, because he fears they joggle the mind. They are religious, except me. . . .

But I fear my story fatigues you. I would like to learn. Could you tell me how to grow, or is it unconveyed, like melody or witchcraft?

You speak of Mr. Whitman. I never read his book, but was told that it was disgraceful. . .

In the second excerpt, Dickinson responds to Higginson's request for her picture.

July 1862

Could you believe me without? I had no portrait, now, but am small, like the wren; and my hair is bold, like the chestnut bur; and my eyes, like the sherry in the glass, that the guest leaves. Would this do just as well?

It often alarms father. He says death might occur, and he has molds [photographs] of all the rest, but has no mold of me. . . .

E. Dickinson

Emily Dickinson   351

Primary Source

In the first letter, Dickinson evades Higginson's questions regarding her experience as a poet, her education, her friends, and her family—claiming nature as her companion and hinting at a vague "terror" in the past. She asks for Higginson's advice on growing as a poet and demurely deflects his suggestion that she read Whitman. In the second letter, she responds to his request for a picture with a brief, evocative description of her appearance.

DIRECT TEACHING

D Reading Informational Text

? Extending ideas through analysis. In an article Higginson wrote about these letters, he described Dickinson as evading him "with a naive skill such as the most experienced coquette might envy." What are some examples of her evasions? ["You asked me how old I was? I made no verse, but one or two, until this winter, sir"; "I had a terror since September, I could tell to none"; "I went to school, but . . . had no education."] What might have motivated Dickinson to make such evasions? [Possible responses: She was embarrassed about deficiencies; she thought some of Higginson's inquiries were intrusive; she wanted to make herself interesting by engaging in a verbal flirtation.]

Comparing and Contrasting Texts

Poems and letters. After students have finished reading the excerpts from Dickinson's letters, you might ask them to look for any attitudes or feelings in the letters that are echoed in her poetry. Have students point out similarities and differences in a class discussion. [Possible responses: Dickinson's comment about "terror" might echo feelings in "Because I could not stop for Death"; her comment about a friend "who never returned" recalls "If you were coming in the Fall"; her comments about her companions suggest "The Soul selects her own Society."]

Response and Analysis

Because I could not stop for Death

Thinking Critically

1. There are two, the speaker and Immortality.

2. Death is kind, polite, and unhurried.

3. They pass a schoolyard, fields of grain, and a sunset.

4. The sun's passing brings nightfall. It becomes cold, suggesting the body's temperature after death.

5. She surmises that she is heading for Eternity.

6. Possible paraphrase: Because I could not stop my busy life, Death put a stop to it. *Kindly* is ironic.

7. Humans tend to be fearful of death. That both death and the dead speaker are civil is thus an extension of the irony of the first stanza.

8. The house is the speaker's grave.

9. Possible answers: There is a tone of terror—the day of the speaker's realization seems to last longer than centuries; there is a tone of acceptance—the centuries have passed quickly.

Literary Criticism

10. Answers will vary. "Eternity" may mean permanent death or everlasting life, or something in between.

I heard a Fly buzz— when I died

Thinking Critically

1. Possible paraphrase: When I was dying, I heard a fly buzz. The air in the room was still—like the calmness between claps of thunder in a storm.

Response and Analysis

Because I could not stop for Death

Thinking Critically

1. How many passengers are in Death's carriage? Who are they?

2. How is Death **personified**? What are his human characteristics?

3. What three things do the riders pass in the third stanza?

4. What is significant about the sun passing the carriage in the fourth stanza? How does the temperature now change?

5. What has the speaker surmised, or guessed, in the last stanza?

6. How would you paraphrase the first two lines in a way that emphasizes their **irony**? What word in line 2 tells you that the tone is ironic?

7. In the second stanza, *civility* means "politeness; good manners." How does this kind of behavior on the part of both Death and the speaker extend the **irony** of the first stanza?

8. The fifth stanza is a riddle in itself. What is the house that is nearly buried?

9. Do you think the concluding stanza introduces a **tone** of terror, because the speaker has suddenly realized she will ride on forever, conscious of being dead? Or is the poem really an expression of trust and even triumph? Explain your response.

Literary Criticism

10. The critic Alfred Kazin said of the last stanza of this poem: "What that famous Eternity is, we cannot say." Do you agree with Kazin? What do *you* think Dickinson meant by the "Eternity" the horses were going toward?

SKILLS FOCUS

Literary Skills
Analyze irony and paradox.

Reading Skills
Summarize a text.

New England Cemetery—Augusta, Maine (1997) by Fred Danziger (20″ × 23″).

---

2. The mourners cry until their tears dry up, and they catch their breaths in expectation. The speaker gives away her possessions.

3. The contrast between what they expect to appear—God or Christ ("the King")—and what does appear—a fly—creates irony.

4. "Heaves" expresses the spasms of a dying person or a weeping mourner gasping for breath.

4. In line 4, Dickinson uses the word *heaves* to refer to the behavior of storms. Why is *heaves* an appropriate word to describe what is happening in this poem?

5. How does the poet use pauses and specific words in lines 12–13 to make the appearance of the fly dramatic and lively?

6. In the third stanza, what portion of the speaker is "assignable"? What portion, by implication, is *not* assignable?

7. What does the phrase "the Windows failed" (line 15) mean?

8. What **tone** do you hear in this poem? Why might Dickinson insert the fly into this deathbed scene? (Refer to your notes about the expectations most people have about death and dying.)

Much Madness is divinest Sense

Thinking Critically

1. What is the meaning of the two **paradoxes,** or apparent contradictions, in the first three lines?

2. The word *assent* means "agree to." The word *demur* means "hesitate; object." What does the "Majority" say about those who assent and those who demur? In what situations in life might someone be considered dangerous because he or she demurred?

3. What do you think is the poem's **theme**? (Consider what the speaker thinks about the individual's proper relationship to society.)

4. Dickinson liked to use dashes—a mark of punctuation her first editors removed. How do dashes help emphasize certain ideas in this poem?

5. What would you say is Dickinson's **tone** in this poem? What similarities do you notice to other poems in this collection?

I heard a Fly buzz—when I died

Thinking Critically

1. How would you **paraphrase** the first stanza—that is, how would you rephrase it in your own words?

2. According to the second and third stanzas, how have the speaker and those around her prepared for death?

3. Whom are the dying person and those around her expecting to find in the room? What appears instead, and why is this **ironic**?

Emily Dickinson   **353**

Much Madness is divinest Sense

Thinking Critically

1. The paradoxes are that the mad make sense and much that is deemed sane is nonsense. They convey the poem's message that originality is often misunderstood and suppressed.

2. If you assent or agree, you are sane in the eyes of the "Majority." If you demur or disagree, you are dangerous. Possible situations might include a pacifist in time of war or an artist whose work challenges established ideas of beauty or decency.

3. People should follow their own beliefs and convictions. Majority opinion should be questioned.

4. Possible answer: They suggest that the speaker is spontaneous, "mad," and proud of it.

5. Possible tone: defiant, ironic. Other poems also promote nonconformity.

ASSESSING

Assessment
■ *Holt Assessment: Literature, Reading, and Vocabulary*

RETEACHING

For a lesson reteaching irony, tone, and author's style, see **Reteaching,** p. 1117A.

5. The dashes and the formal word "interposed" suggest drama. The pause in l. 13 sets a staccato rhythm that mirrors the flight of the fly.

6. Material possessions are assignable, while her spirit is not.

7. The phrase may refer to the speaker's eyes failing or to a lack of spiritual revelation.

8. Possible answer: The tone is first solemn, then sad or ironic. The poet is disappointed that a commonplace fly blocked a spiritual revelation. The poet is puncturing the supposed portentousness of death. Most people expect the deathbed scene to be horrifying or revelatory, not ordinary or uneventful.

Connection

Summary ⟷ *at grade level*

In this free-verse poem, the Hispanic American speaker explores her actual as well as her imagined relationship to Emily Dickinson. She feels that she and Emily Dickinson are kindred spirits despite cultural, religious, and temporal divides.

DIRECT TEACHING

A Reading Skills

❓ Interpreting details. What item does the speaker imagine that she and Emily Dickinson would each own? [a treasure chest filled with doilies] What does this item suggest about the speaker's values? [Possible response: She values tradition, domestic life, and the legacies passed down by female forebears.]

B Learners Having Difficulty

Changing reading strategies. Advise students that when they encounter a foreign or unfamiliar word, they should slow their reading rate and try to infer the word's meaning by using context clues and footnotes.

C Literary Focus

❓ Theme. What theme is supported by the combination of English and Spanish words? [Possible response: Although the speaker and Dickinson come from different cultures, they can communicate.]

CONNECTION / POEM

In the season of change

Teresa Palomo Acosta

A If E. Dickinson and I had been friends,
we would have each owned a treasure chest
filled with doilies for laying under our silverware,
for showing off atop our china cabinets.
5 For softening the scars in the 300-year-old dining room tables
we would have inherited
from our great-grandmothers.

B But our bisabuelas° never met,
exchanged glances or
10 sat next to each other in church.
And I only discovered E. Dickinson
in the few pages she was allowed
to enter in my high school literature texts.

Only years later did
15 I finally pore over her words,
believing that
her songs held
my name inscribed within.
And that they might fill the air
20 with the ancient signs of kinship
that women can choose to pass along.

And thus left on our own,
E. Dickinson and I
sat down at the same table,
25 **C** savoring her rhubarb pie and my cafecito°
chatting and chismeando°
and trading secrets
despite decrees demanding silence between us:

women from separate corners of the room.

Two Girls Talking
by Pierre-Auguste Renoir
(15.3″ × 20.1″).

---

8. **bisabuelas** (bēs·ä·bwä′läs) *n. pl.:* great-grandmothers.
25. **cafecito** (kä′fä·sē′tô) *n.:* little cup of coffee.
26. **chismeando** (chēs·mä·än′dô) *adj.:* gossiping.

Comparing and Contrasting Texts

Activity. Have student pairs make a double-column chart in which they list similarities and differences between the speaker and Dickinson. Suggest that students also use information they have learned about Dickinson in this chapter. Urge them to look at the concrete details and the choice of words in Acosta's poem as they make their lists. Then, have all pairs discuss as a group whether each difference could actually be overcome and, if so, how.

Activity. Have students make a chart comparing and contrasting a poem by Emily Dickinson with "In the season of change." Ask them to consider categories such as verse form, diction, compression of language, imagery, and theme.

Emily Dickinson

Linda Pastan

We think of her hidden in a white dress
among the folded linens and sachets
of well-kept cupboards, or just out of sight
sending jellies and notes with no address

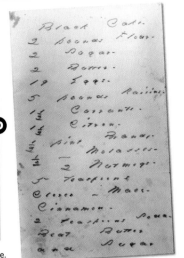

Dickinson's handwritten recipe for black cake.

5   to all the wondering Amherst neighbors.
Eccentric as New England weather
the stiff wind of her mind, stinging or gentle,
blew two half-imagined lovers off.
Yet legend won't explain the sheer sanity
10 of vision, the serious mischief
of language, the economy of pain.

Emily Dickinson

Gary Smith

I've defended you against the many
who have made a madcap of you—
citing the middle years, how feverishly
you paced the house in bridal whites,
5   the longing of every poem you wrote—
how easily they spill into nothing.
We like to own the poets we keep—
to mother each word like obsessions.
Your company is not easily kept—
10 too soon, too soon you retire to bed.
A peevish old maid worrying Puritans.
If heaven had been given to you in gold,
before singing your hymns of praise,
you would have discovered copper within.

Emily Dickinson's bedroom window.

Emily Dickinson   **355**

Connection

Summary ⬌ *at grade level*

Pastan's poem asserts that the legend of Dickinson as a reclusive New England eccentric does not explain the brilliance and breadth of her poetry. Addressing Emily Dickinson directly, the speaker in Smith's poem tells her that he has defended her. But he also suggests that she is difficult to know and "own."

DIRECT TEACHING

D Reading Skills

? Synthesizing. What picture of Dickinson do ll. 1–5 create? [Possible responses: a serious, quiet, shy woman; a person who feels vulnerable outside her domestic environment.] **What picture do ll. 9–11 create?** [Possible responses: an intelligent but odd person who views the world with a vivid imagination; a poet who compresses language to express difficult and complex feelings]

E Advanced Learners

Enrichment. Ask students to research Dickinson's "two half-imagined lovers" to find out what happened between her and them.

F Literary Focus

? Style. How does Gary Smith use language in ways similar to Dickinson's? [Possible response: His language is spare, elusive, and compressed, requiring the reader to fill in what has been left out.]

Comparing and Contrasting Texts

The speaker in Pastan's poem describes the poetry of Emily Dickinson as having the following qualities: "sheer sanity of vision," "serious mischief of language," and "economy of pain."
Activity. Ask students to evaluate the speaker's judgment by reexamining Dickinson's poetry in search of examples of the qualities cited. Students can organize their findings in a chart, adding and subtracting categories if they think the speaker of "Emily Dickinson" has overlooked or overemphasized any aspects of Dickinson's poetry.
Activity. Have student pairs or small groups compare and contrast the portraits of Emily Dickinson in the poems by Acosta, Pastan, and Smith. Get students started by raising the following questions: How does each poet evaluate Dickinson as a poet? What are the views of each on the relationship of audience and artist? To what extent does each Connection poet imitate Dickinson in his or her own work? Which of the three views of Dickinson comes closest to your own? After the discussion, direct students to write brief essays comparing and contrasting the Connections poets.

Writing

1. Analyzing Dickinson

Suggest to students that they begin by re-reading the poems in this chapter and listing the ones that have death and the ones that have immortality as a central theme. Students may also want to read additional Dickinson poems to see if Frye's generalization is supported. Encourage them to cite specific poems and to use quotations from those poems to support their thesis.

2. Echoes of Dickinson

Students may choose to echo Dickinson's themes or address her directly without imitating her style. They may instead want to use other forms of poetry such as a sonnet or haiku. Encourage students to use their imagination and to write in a style that best expresses their ideas.

3. Comparing Poems

Students may also find a comparison of Dickinson and Whitman interesting. If students prefer to compare prose and poetry, they may want to examine ways in which themes concerning nature and religion are addressed in Dickinson's poetry and in the excerpts from Emerson's *Nature* (p. 182) and Thoreau's *Walden* (p. 192).

Listening and Speaking

4. Dickinson Onstage

Suggest that students obtain a videotape of William Luce's 1976 play about Emily Dickinson, *The Belle of Amherst,* in which Julie Harris plays the poet in an award-winning performance. Alternatively, students can read a biography of Dickinson to get further insight into her life and views. Suggest that group members all work together in shaping the script and performance, but each member should take on a primary role, such as writer, director, or performer.

WRITING

SKILLS FOCUS

Writing Skills
Write an essay analyzing a critical comment. Write a poem. Write an essay comparing and contrasting poems by two poets.

Listening and Speaking Skills
Present a performance using a prepared script.

Grammar Skills
Understand and use subordinating conjunctions.

1. Analyzing Dickinson

The critic Northrop Frye had this to say about Dickinson's poetry:

> The most cursory glance at Emily Dickinson will reveal that she is a deeply religious poet, preoccupied, to the verge of obsession, with the themes of death and immortality.

In a brief **essay,** discuss this comment, and tell whether or not you agree with it and why. At the end of your essay, explain how you feel about Dickinson's themes and the tone she reveals in talking about them.

2. Echoes of Dickinson

On pages 354–355, you read three poems inspired by Emily Dickinson. Write a **poem** of your own—either one addressed to Dickinson or one that treats one of the subjects that engaged Emily Dickinson: love and loss, the life of the spirit, death and immortality, the nature of nature, or the power of imagination. You might even use one of Dickinson's lines as your opener and try out Dickinson's style of punctuation and capitalization.

3. Comparing Poems

In a brief **essay,** compare and contrast one of Dickinson's poems with a poem by another poet. You might choose a work by an earlier poet, such as "Upon the Burning of Our House" by Anne Bradstreet (page 29), or "Thanatopsis" by William Cullen Bryant (page 167), or "The Cross of Snow" by Henry Wadsworth Longfellow (page 174). Look for poems that have something in common—a similar subject or theme. Before you write, collect your points of comparison and contrast in a chart like the one below:

	Dickinson Poem	Other Poem
Subject matter		
Theme		
Tone		
Figures of speech		

LISTENING AND SPEAKING

Dickinson Onstage

With a partner or a small group, prepare a script for a performance called *An Evening with Emily Dickinson.* Let Dickinson tell about her life, her views of poetry and language, and her feelings about nature, faith, and eternity. Include readings of selected poems. You might want to include Teresa Palomo Acosta's poem "In the season of change" (see the **Connection** on page 354), Linda Pastan's poem "Emily Dickinson" (see the **Connection** on page 355), or Gary Smith's poem "Emily Dickinson" (see the **Connection** on page 355). Present your performance for the class.

Grammar Link

Using Subordinating Conjunctions: Showing Relationships

When you write, part of your job is to clarify the relationships between ideas. In the following example sentence the two clauses are joined with the coordinating conjunction *and*. As you will see, this conjunction fails to indicate the relationship between the two parts of the sentence.

> Emily Dickinson published only a handful of poems during her lifetime, <u>and</u> she is now considered one of the most important American poets.

By using a **subordinating conjunction** instead of a co-ordinating conjunction, you can join the same clauses in a way that clearly conveys the relationship between ideas.

> <u>Although</u> Emily Dickinson published only a handful of poems during her lifetime, she is now considered one of the most important American poets.

A subordinating conjunction is a linking word (or group of words) that connects two complete ideas by making one of the ideas subordinate, or less important than the other. A subordinate clause is sometimes called a **dependent clause** because it can't stand on its own as a sentence—it depends on an independent clause to express a complete thought. A subordinating conjunction may come between two clauses, or it may appear at the beginning of a sentence.

When you're writing sentences with subordinate clauses, choose a subordinating conjunction that pinpoints the precise relationship you want to convey between the two ideas (cause, purpose, time, contrast, comparison, and so on). Here are some possibilities:

Some Common Subordinating Conjunctions		
although	in order to	that
as	rather than	unless
because	since	until
before	so that	when
even if	than	while

Some subordinate clauses begin with a **relative pronoun** (*that, which, who, whom, whose*) rather than a subordinating conjunction.

Basket at Emily Dickinson's window.

Learners Having Difficulty

Write the following sets of sentences and subordinating conjunctions on the chalkboard. Have students write a single sentence containing a subordinating clause for each set.

1. Dickinson's poems are short. They require careful reading. Although [Although Dickinson's poems are short, they require careful reading.]

2. Charles Wadsworth moved from Philadelphia to San Francisco. Dickinson was devastated. When [When Charles Wadsworth moved from Philadelphia to San Francisco, Dickinson was devastated.]

3. Thomas Higginson was impressed by Dickinson's poems. He encouraged her. Because [Because Thomas Higginson was impressed by Dickinson's poems, he encouraged her.]

4. Whitman died in 1892. He had revised *Leaves of Grass* many times. Before [Before Whitman died in 1892, he had revised *Leaves of Grass* many times.]

Grammar Link

Practice

Possible Answers

1. Dickinson's early editors altered her poems *because* they wanted to make her work more conventionally poetic.

2. Readers did not get a chance to read what Dickinson actually wrote *until* Thomas H. Johnson published a new edition of her poetry in 1955.

3. *Although* Dickinson's punctuation, rhymes, syntax, and diction were often baffling, Johnson restored her poems to their original form.

Rewrite these sentences, replacing *and* with a subordinating conjunction that more precisely explains the relationship between the two clauses.

1. Dickinson's early editors altered her poems, and they wanted to make her work more conventionally poetic.

2. Readers did not get a chance to read what Dickinson actually wrote, and Thomas H. Johnson published a new edition of her poetry in 1955.

3. Dickinson's punctuation, rhymes, syntax, and diction were often baffling, and Johnson restored her poems to their original form.

Apply to Your Writing

Look through a current writing assignment or a work that you've already completed. Can you find any sentences in which the relationship between the clauses is vague? If so, try replacing coordinating conjunctions with subordinating conjunctions that express your meaning more clearly.

▶ **For more help, see Combining by Subordinating Ideas, 10d, in the Language Handbook.**

Center of Amherst, Massachusetts (c. 1875), Dickinson's hometown, by George A. Thomas.

Courtesy of the Amherst History Museum.

READ ON: FOR INDEPENDENT READING

POETRY

Legacy in Latin America

Who's the most popular U.S. poet in Latin America? The answer is probably Walt Whitman. One of his greatest admirers was the Cuban poet José Martí, who introduced Whitman's work to Spanish-speaking audiences at the turn of the century. Whitman's influence on Martí's own verse is evident in *José Martí: Major Poems,* a bilingual edition with English translations by Elinor Randall, edited by Philip Foner.

FICTION

Meet the Marches

Meg, Jo, Beth, and Amy—to those who grew up with Louisa May Alcott's classic *Little Women,* these names conjure images of four spirited New England girls bound together through comedy and tragedy. This enduring story, whose events closely resemble those of Alcott's own life, offers up an unforgettable portrait of the four March sisters, who must grow up in a hurry after their father is sent to fight in the Civil War.

NONFICTION

Beholder of Mysteries

"I am no scientist," Annie Dillard says of herself. "I am a wanderer with a background in theology and a penchant for quirky facts." In *Pilgrim at Tinker Creek,* Dillard draws on her experiences in an isolated Virginia valley to create a memorable reflection on life, death, and the mysteries of nature.

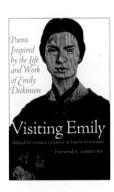

POETRY

A Tribute to Emily

Something about Emily Dickinson—her shadowy reclusiveness, her fierce, driven poems—has captured people's imaginations in a way few other writers have. *Visiting Emily,* edited by Sheila Coghill and Thom Tammaro, is a collection of poems inspired by the life and work of Emily Dickinson, featuring such poets as Richard Wilbur, Robert Bly, and Adrienne Rich. Some are in imitation of Dickinson's style; others are tributes to the woman herself.

Differentiating Instruction

Estimated Word Counts and Reading Levels of Read On Books:

Poetry			Fiction		
Simple Verses	⬌	11,100	*Little Women*	⬇	235,200
Nonfiction			**Poetry**		
Pilgrim at Tinker Creek	⬌	100,600	*Visiting Emily*	⬇	20,600

KEY: ⬆ *above grade level*   ⬌ *at grade level*   ⬇ *below grade level*

Read On

For Independent Reading

If students enjoyed the themes and topics explored in this collection, you might recommend the following titles for independent reading.

Assessment Options

The following projects can help you evaluate and assess your students' outside reading.

- **Record a radio ad.** Radio advertisements rely on the power of words and the voice of the announcer or actors, music, and sound effects to create a commercial that captures the audience's attention. Have students work alone or with a partner to create a radio commercial for a book they have read. Remind students that their commercial should include specific details from the book.

- **Prepare a catalog entry.** Have students imagine that they are the marketing director for a publishing company. Their job is to write copy and select (or make) illustrations that will promote the book they've just read. Their copy and illustrations should be designed to attract and serve the needs of several audiences: the company's sales force, book stores, online book sellers, libraries, and readers.

- **Hold a literary reading.** Have students choose a poem or prose excerpt that they particularly like and then present a literary reading to the class. Students should prepare by practicing in front of a partner or family member in order to read with appropriate expression. At the reading, students should begin by introducing the work they are about to read, explaining why they chose it and what it means to them. After students read, they should invite questions from the audience about the selection they have presented.

Writing a Reflective Essay

Writing Assignment
Write a reflective essay in which you explore an experience from your life and share its significance with readers.

Some discoveries that you read about, such as the detection of a distant solar system, make headlines around the globe. Other discoveries are smaller and more personal, such as Emily Dickinson's discovery that "The Soul selects her own Society—." Writing a **reflective essay** leads to discoveries, too. When you write about an experience from your life—the white-water rafting trip you took this summer or your first driving lesson—you explore the meaning of the experience and your beliefs about life in general.

Prewriting

Consider Your Purpose

Sense of Purpose Before you start thinking of your life experiences, think about why you are writing so that you can pick the best experience. Your **purpose** in writing a reflective essay is to express and explore your thoughts and feelings. You'll not only discover and share the **significance** of the experience you describe, but you'll also go beyond the specifics to show how it compares and connects to the beliefs you hold important and to the ideas you have about life.

Choose an Experience

Sifting Through Memories Think back on the experiences that have been important in your life. The experience you write about might be something as simple as feeding a pet or overhearing a conversation; however, it must be an experience that has taught you something about yourself or the world. For example, feeding a pet may have taught you responsibility and compassion for all living things. Journals, diaries, and photo albums are good places to look for significant experiences. You might also try reading published reflective essays, such as memoirs or biographies, for ideas. Think of your **audience** when selecting an experience to explore—be sure you'll feel comfortable sharing the experience with the people who will be reading your essay.

Reflect on Meaning

The Heart of the Matter Once you've chosen an experience to explore, spend some time reflecting not only on what the experience meant to you at the time it occurred, but also on what it means to you now. As a springboard for reflection, ask yourself the questions in the left-hand column of the chart on the next page. Look also at one

SKILLS FOCUS

Writing Skills
Write a reflective essay. Choose an experience and reflect on its meaning. Gather details.

360 Collection 3 American Masters: Whitman and Dickinson

student's answers in the right-hand column. These answers are based on her experience doing community service at a retirement center.

REFLECTION QUESTIONS

Questions	Answers
What did I feel during this experience? What did I feel when I thought about it shortly afterwards? How do I feel about it now?	At first I felt dread and disappointment at having to spend my spring break doing community service. Later, I felt pleasantly surprised. When I think about it now, I feel grateful.
What did I learn about others and myself from this experience?	I learned that you can find friends in unexpected places and that you might find that you have things in common with people who seem very different from you.
How did this experience influence what I believe about people or life in general? How have my beliefs changed or developed since then?	I came to believe that life is unpredictable—something you don't want to do may end up being something you enjoy. Since then, I try to keep an open mind about new situations.

Sum It All Up Answer the questions in the chart above. Then, write a sentence that sums up the significance of your experience. This sentence will appear at the end of your essay, but writing down your ideas now will remind you of the larger meaning you want to convey to readers. Every detail you include in your essay should help communicate the importance of the experience. The following example shows what the student writer learned while working in a retirement center.

> I've gained a new belief: Life is unpredictable, and sometimes an experience brings you a surprise—a new perspective.

Recall and Record Details

A Detailed Account Now, gather the details that will bring the experience to life and will convince your readers that it is significant. First, list the individual events that made up the experience. Here are some suggestions to help you recall as many events as you can.

- Close your eyes and visualize the experience.
- Discuss your experience with a friend or family member. Talking about it may help to bring it all back.
- Allow yourself to daydream by looking through photos or souvenirs of the experience.

Next, add details to your list that provide a more complete picture of each event that made up the experience. Use **narrative and descriptive**

DO THIS

TIP Try to **balance** how much time you spend relating each event, and try to connect each event to **general** or **abstract ideas** about life.

- *One-Stop Planner* CD-ROM with ExamView Test Generator
- *Holt Online Assessment*
- *Holt Online Essay Scoring*

Internet
- go.hrw.com (Keyword: LE5 11-3)
- *Elements of Literature Online*

Sum It All Up
Students may have difficulty drawing some larger meaning from their personal experiences and may benefit from your modeling the process. You can use the questions in the **Reflection Questions** chart to walk students orally through an experience of your own, such as going off to a summer camp, learning how to drive, or leaving home for college. Then, have volunteers take turns using the chart to answer selected questions for the experiences about which they intend to write.

RETEACHING

Recall and Record Details
To help students recall details, suggest that they audiotape themselves speaking about their experiences or set themselves a time limit in which they freewrite as quickly as possible about their experiences. Students can then review the tape or their notes and pick out details that surprise them or that they thought they had forgotten. Direct students to concentrate especially on remembering details that relate to the five senses. Discuss with students how sensory details bring an experience to life for a reader.

Additionally, students may find that looking through photos of the time period during which the experience happened can help refresh their memories.

DIRECT TEACHING

Integrating with Grammar, Usage, and Mechanics
As students start their reflective essays, they may have trouble with agreement and using pronouns correctly. You may want to review sections 2 and 4 in the Language Handbook.

Learners Having Difficulty

Tell students having difficulty evaluating and arranging their details that they should only include a detail in their accounts if it meets at least one of the following criteria:

- makes the experience clear
- adds necessary background information
- makes the experience seem more real
- clarifies the experience's overall meaning
- adds insight to the experience

Special Education Students

If a student needs additional help recalling and recording details, ask a helper to assist him or her in composing a brief e-mail or note to a friend about the experience. This informal beginning may provide ideas to develop in students' essays.

PRACTICE & APPLY 1

Guided and Independent Practice

Guide students to collect ideas about the significance of their experiences by having them fill in the blanks in the following sentence: Before [the experience], I _____, but now I _____. For example, "Before working at the retirement center, I thought my spring break experience would be a waste of time, but now I can see how fortunate I was to make a new friend." Students should complete **Practice and Apply 1** for independent practice.

---

details that flesh out the sequence of events by describing the people involved and the places where the events took place. The following chart gives explanations and examples of these types of details.

ADDING NARRATIVE AND DESCRIPTIVE DETAILS

Types of Details	Examples
Narrative details • tell the actions, thoughts, and feelings of the people involved • include **dialogue,** words spoken by people involved in the experience, and **interior monologue,** your internal flow of thoughts	"Are you in there, Mrs. Anderson?" I called, after knocking on her open door at the Summerdale Retirement Center. All I could think was, "This is going to be a long week."
Descriptive details • describe **appearances** of people involved • describe the **setting** • use **sensory language** that appeals to the five senses (sight, hearing, smell, taste, and touch)	Mrs. Anderson had curly hair, smooth skin, and eyes crinkled with age. The staff at the center had decorated the hallways for the Fourth of July. On the door hung a huge, white straw hat with shiny red and blue strings of stars and red, white, and blue streamers.

Arrange the Details

Truth and Consequences Once you've recalled the events and details of your experience, decide how you'll organize them. Often, reflective essays use **chronological order**—the order in which events occurred. Within that order, though, writers may arrange details **spatially** or in **order of importance** to describe a person or a place.

Look at the following example to see how one writer organized her essay to give an early hint at the significance of her experience and to create a sense of how her reflections have deepened over time. Notice that she plans to start her essay in the present and then use a **flashback** to skip backward in time. She'll use chronological order within the flashback to recount the experience. Finally, she'll conclude her essay with further reflection and some thoughts on life in general.

| Begin with most recent visit to the center. | → | Flashback to first day I went to the center. | → | Event 1: Secretary asks me to get Pierre, the parrot. | → | Event 2: Meet Mrs. Anderson. We share stories. | → | Relate the significance of the experience. |

PRACTICE & APPLY 1 Choose an experience to write about, think about its significance, and write a sentence that expresses that significance. Then, recall, record, and arrange details that will make the experience come alive for readers.

Writing

Writing a Reflective Essay

A Writer's Framework

Introduction	Body	Conclusion
• Engage readers' attention with an anecdote, question, or interesting statement.	• Narrate the events that make up the experience.	• State the significance of the experience to you.
• Provide background information to establish a context for the experience.	• Provide narrative and descriptive details about each event.	• Make a final connection between the experience and life in general.
• Hint at the significance of your experience.	• Make the order of the events clear for the reader.	

A Writer's Model

A Spring Break Surprise

"Are you in there, Mrs. Anderson?" I called, after knocking on her open door at the Summerdale Retirement Center. The staff at the center had decorated the hallways for the Fourth of July. On Mrs. Anderson's door hung an enormous white straw hat, its brim wrapped with shiny red and blue strings of stars, its crown trailing red, white, and blue streamers. I let the streamers run through my fingers as I remembered how much I'd learned from the person inside the room.

"Why, Amy!" she laughed. "Is that you coming back to see me?"

Even though it was midsummer, Mrs. Anderson still remembered me. A week at the retirement center had not been my first choice of recreation for my spring break. Unfortunately, however, the fall before I'd gotten a ticket for failure to yield right of way. In my court appearance, the judge had assigned me, instead of a hefty fine, twelve hours of community service to be completed within a four-month period. Of course my schoolwork had kept me so busy that my only time to fulfill this requirement was during my spring break. I was not at all happy with the prospects for the week's entertainment.

The day I first arrived at the center, the secretary said, "Sign our volunteer register first. Then, get Pierre out of his cage."

Pierre, I found out, was the pet parrot kept in a cage by the front office. He had beautiful blue and green feathers on his back, yellow breast feathers with streaks of orange, golden feet, and a wicked-looking

(continued)

INTRODUCTION
Attention-grabbing anecdote

Descriptive details

Hint at significance

Dialogue

Background information

Narrative details

BODY
Event one of flashback

Descriptive details

A Writer's Framework
Point out to students that **A Writer's Model** begins with a line of dialogue. Encourage students to be creative in writing introductions that capture their audience's interest. You may also want to tell students that making the order of events clear for their readers does not necessarily mean they should relate every event in strict chronological order. If they find one or two flashbacks useful in relating their accounts, they should not hesitate to use the device.

DIFFERENTIATING INSTRUCTION

Advanced Learners
Enrichment. Explain to students that college applications often require brief reflective essays or "statements of purpose." Ask students to imagine they are applying to a college or for a job and to list specific details or experiences that show how they have been working toward this purpose. Then, have students look at the details they listed and think of one or two sentences that explain the meaning of the details and how they support each student's purpose.

CORRECTING MISCONCEPTIONS

Students who are unsure or uncomfortable drawing meaning from their experiences might mistakenly tack on to the ends of their narratives a reflection upon meaning. Remind students that their reflections on meaning should be an essential, integrated part of their essays and should be used to help shape their essays.

Students may have an easier time drawing out meaning if they ask themselves the following additional questions:

• What feelings does remembering the experience raise in me?

• What are the reasons for those feelings?

CRITICAL THINKING

Help students consider how a writer might include too much elaboration. Give students a sentence, such as "One rainy morning, I noticed cars driving around a sharp curve too fast for the road conditions." Have students experiment with adding descriptive details to the sentence. For instance, someone might offer, "One *early* rainy morning, I noticed *both big and small* cars driving *crazily* around a sharp curve too fast for the *wet, slippery* road conditions." Encourage students to determine which details are helpful and which seem excessive. Have students explain the criteria they use in making their evaluations.

DIFFERENTIATING INSTRUCTION

English-Language Learners

Students' cultural perspectives might become particularly apparent in the writing of reflective essays. Individual student conferences could serve two purposes: You could be alerted to any potentially sensitive topics, and you could help students see the value of their cultural points of view. In addition, an awareness of students' topics could be helpful in grouping students for peer revision.

PRACTICE & APPLY 2

Guided and Independent Practice

To help students include sufficient narrative and descriptive details, ask them the following questions:

- How does your introduction engage the reader?

- Which details help the reader sense what you are describing? Which details make the experience real and interesting?

- How do the details relate to the meaning of the experience?

Have students then complete **Practice and Apply 2** as independent practice.

Narrative details

Interior monologue

Event two of flashback

Descriptive details

Narrative details

black eye. He talked. He also nipped my ear, cracked sunflower seeds into my shirt pocket, and dug his claws into my shoulder. The residents, however, loved him. My volunteer job, the secretary told me, was to carry this cranky, unpleasant bird on my shoulder around the halls, stopping to talk to residents who were outside their rooms or in the recreation areas. All I could think was, "This is going to be a long week."

On that first day, however, I also met Mrs. Amelia Anderson. She had curly hair, smooth skin, and eyes crinkled with age. Even though she sat in a wheelchair most of the time because of her chronic back trouble, she had a cheerful personality and sweet smile. She reminded me of my grandmother, who had died the preceding year. When I told her why I was at the center, she clucked her tongue in sympathy. "I know just how you feel," she said.

It seems that Mrs. Anderson had had an experience similar to mine when she was in her twenties. She'd also failed to yield the right of way, but in her case, her carelessness had caused a wreck in rush-hour traffic at a busy intersection. The police officer had given her a ticket, despite her protests.

We began to laugh over our similar experiences, especially since she told me that, as an adult, she had been given no choice but to pay the fine. I should feel lucky, she said, because all I had to do was dodge Pierre's flapping feathers. From that moment on, we became friends. We really didn't even need Pierre to start our conversations. Every day we shared stories about our families. She was interested in my friends and schoolwork, and I in turn became interested in her life as a former high school teacher.

CONCLUSION

Significance of experience

Statement about life

Now when I think of my time with Mrs. Anderson and the friendship we developed, I realize I've gained a new belief: Life is unpredictable and sometimes an experience brings you a surprise—a new perspective. I now try to keep an open mind about meeting unfamiliar people and facing new situations. Where I had once been uninterested in, maybe even dismissive of, older people, I now know that they can make interesting, valuable friends.

INTERNET

More Writer's Models

Keyword: LE5 11-3

PRACTICE & APPLY 2

Using the framework on page 363 as a guide, write the first draft of your reflective essay. Refer to the Writer's Model beginning on that same page to give you ideas for writing your own work.

Revising

Evaluate and Revise Your Draft

Did I Say That? Not even professional writers get everything right the first time. The revision process gives you the chance to make your writing as clear and as interesting as you can make it. To polish your writing, read through your paper at least twice. Using the guidelines below, read first for content and organization. Then, use the guidelines on page 366 to read your essay for style, concentrating on letting your personality show through your writing.

> **PEER REVIEW**
>
> Ask a peer to review your essay by using the guidelines in this section for content, organization, and style. He or she may have ideas about where you should include additional narrative or descriptive details. Carefully consider his or her suggestions.

▶ **First Reading: Content and Organization** Use the chart below to look for ways to improve the content and organization of your reflective essay. Ask yourself the questions in the left-hand column. Then, use the middle column for practical tips. To revise your paper, use the suggestions in the right-hand column.

Rubric: Writing a Reflective Essay

Evaluation Questions	▶ Tips	▶ Revision Techniques
❶ Does the introduction capture readers' attention?	▶ **Bracket** any attention-getting anecdote, question, or interesting statement.	▶ **Add** an anecdote, a question, or an interesting statement.
❷ Does the introduction give a hint about the significance of the experience?	▶ **Underline** the sentence or sentences in the introduction that hint at the significance of the experience.	▶ **Add** a sentence or two that hints at the significance of the experience.
❸ Are the specific events of the experience presented clearly and in an order that makes sense?	▶ **Number** each event. If the events are not presented clearly or in a logical order, revise.	▶ **Add** missing events, or **delete** events that do not relate to the experience. **Rearrange** events to make the chronology clear to the reader.
❹ Do narrative and descriptive details describe the people, places, and events?	▶ **Circle** the sentences that help readers imagine the events, people, and places.	▶ **Add** details that clarify the experience, including details about what people do, say, or think, and **add** sensory details.
❺ Does the conclusion make the significance of the experience clear? Does it include a final statement that connects the experience to life in general?	▶ **Star** the sentence that relates the meaning of the experience. **Double star** the statement that relates ideas about life in general.	▶ **Add** a sentence that states the importance of the experience, or **revise** sentences so that they clearly convey the importance. **Add** a sentence that makes a generalization about life.

Rubric: Writing a Reflective Essay

Advise students to use the **Rubric** chart on this page as a think sheet by having them answer the questions in their notebooks. Explain that using think sheets to summarize their notes allows students to place their thoughts, observations, and questions on paper, which, in turn, helps improve the content and organization of their reflections.

Elaboration

Draw students' attention to the precise sensory language used in **A Writer's Model,** particularly in the description of the parrot. Point out to students that the description is important because the bird serves as the writer's own introduction to her memorable experience. Ask students to pick out an important element in their own essays and to revise the section to make their descriptive language more precise and vivid.

Selection ▪ Feature	Planning	Differentiating Instruction ▪ Lesson Plans with ELL Strategies and Practice	Reading ▪ Vocabulary
• *from* A Diary from Dixie *by* Mary Chesnut • *from* Men at War: An Interview with Shelby Foote *by* Ken Burns			
"I Will Fight No More Forever" *by* Chief Joseph	• One-Stop Planner with ExamView Test Generator	• The Holt Reader • Supporting Instruction in Spanish • Audio CD Library, disc 10	• The Holt Reader • Holt Reading Solutions
The Celebrated Jumping Frog of Calaveras County The Lowest Animal *by* Mark Twain	• One-Stop Planner with ExamView Test Generator	• The Holt Reader • Supporting Instruction in Spanish • Audio CD Library, disc 11	• The Holt Reader • Holt Reading Solutions • Vocabulary Development, pp. 25, 26–27
To Build a Fire *by* Jack London	• One-Stop Planner with ExamView Test Generator	• The Holt Reader • Holt Adapted Reader • Supporting Instruction in Spanish • Audio CD Library, disc 12	• The Holt Reader • Holt Adapted Reader • Holt Reading Solutions • Vocabulary Development, p. 28
Literature of the Americas: Chile What Do You Feel Underground? *by* Gabriela Mistral	• One-Stop Planner with ExamView Test Generator	• The Holt Reader • Supporting Instruction in Spanish • Audio CD Library, disc 12	• The Holt Reader • Holt Reading Solutions
A Pair of Silk Stockings *by* Kate Chopin	• One-Stop Planner with ExamView Test Generator	• The Holt Reader • Holt Adapted Reader • Holt Reading Solutions: Lesson Plans • Supporting Instruction in Spanish • Audio CD Library, disc 12 and 13	• The Holt Reader • Holt Adapted Reader • Holt Reading Solutions • Vocabulary Development, p. 29
A Wagner Matinée *by* Willa Cather	• One-Stop Planner with ExamView Test Generator	• The Holt Reader • Supporting Instruction in Spanish • Audio CD Library, disc 13	• The Holt Reader • Holt Reading Solutions • Vocabulary Development, p. 30
Richard Cory Miniver Cheevy *by* Edwin Arlington Robinson	• One-Stop Planner with ExamView Test Generator	• The Holt Reader • Supporting Instruction in Spanish • Audio CD Library, disc 13	• The Holt Reader • Holt Reading Solutions
Writing Workshop: *Reporting Historical Research*	• One-Stop Planner with ExamView Test Generator	• Workshop Resources: Writing, Listening, and Speaking • Family Involvement Activities in English and Spanish • Supporting Instruction in Spanish	
Listening and Speaking Workshop: *Presenting Historical Research*	• One-Stop Planner with ExamView Test Generator	• Workshop Resources: Writing, Listening, and Speaking • Supporting Instruction in Spanish	
Skills Review: *Literary Skills* *Vocabulary Skills* *Writing Skills*			

Writing ▪ Grammar and Language ▪ Listening and Speaking	Assessment
• Daily Language Activities	• Holt Assessment: Literature, Reading, and Vocabulary • Holt Online Assessment • One-Stop Planner with ExamView Test Generator
• Daily Language Activities	• See "I Will Fight No More Forever" above
• Daily Language Activities • Language Handbook Worksheets, pp. 64, 67, 69	• See "I Will Fight No More Forever" above
• Daily Language Activities	• See "I Will Fight No More Forever" above
• Daily Language Activities	• See "I Will Fight No More Forever" above
• Daily Language Activities	• See "I Will Fight No More Forever" above
• Daily Language Activities	• See "I Will Fight No More Forever" above
• Daily Language Activities • Workshop Resources: Writing, Listening, and Speaking	• See "I Will Fight No More Forever" above
• Daily Language Activities • Workshop Resources: Writing, Listening, and Speaking	• Holt Assessment: Writing, Listening, and Speaking • One-Stop Planner with ExamView Test Generator
	• Holt Assessment: Writing, Listening, and Speaking • One-Stop Planner with ExamView Test Generator

Internet
- go.hrw.com
- *Elements of*

Media
- *Audio CD Li*
- *Audio CD Li* in Spanish

Technology

INTERNET
- go.hrw.com
- Holt Online Assessment
- Holt Online Essay Scoring
- Elements of Literature Online

MEDIA
 • One-Stop Planner with ExamView Test Generator

 • PowerNotes

 • Audio CD Library, discs 9, 10, 11, 12, and 13

 • Audio CD Library, Selections and Summaries in Spanish

 • Visual Connections Videocassette Program, Segment 7

• Fine Art Transparencies, 8, 9, and 10

 Transparency　 Video

CD-ROM　Audio CD

Coll

INTR...
COLL...

The Ame...
transforr...
the histo...
Collectic...
political ...
such as F...
Harriet J...
ery. They ...
ing views ...
works by ...
inal news ...
Tubman. ...
authors ii ...
are Mark ...
Stephen C ...
cludes wi ...
a listening ...
that give ...
to write a ...
report.

THE Q

Before the ...
States wa: ...
confident, ...
Ask stude ...
Stephen C ...
gests happ ...
as a result ...
response: ...
their purpc ...
verse was

COLL

Planning
- *One-Stc*
  ExamV
Differen
- *The Ho*
- Holt Ad
- Holt Re

DIRECT TEACHING

A Background
A Clash of Ideals

Both the North and the South were motivated by a combination of ideology and economics. Northerners fought to end slavery and to preserve the constitutional Union of the nation's founders. Southerners fought to uphold states' rights and to defend the Southern way of life from what they saw as the crass materialism of the industrial North. Both sides fought to protect their economic interests.

VIEWING THE ART

Mathew Brady (c. 1823?–1896) pioneered wartime photography during the Civil War. He and his staff traveled with the Union armies and took more than 3,500 photographs.

Activity. Have students discuss what the photograph reveals about the state of the Union soldiers. [Students may point to the primitive, unsanitary-looking conditions or the despair and exhaustion of the wounded man.]

> War is at best barbarism.... Its glory is all moonshine.... War is hell.
>
> —Union Gen. William Tecumseh Sherman

From the personal accounts of people held in slavery—such as Frederick Douglass and Harriet A. Jacobs—we learn firsthand about the horrors and injustices of slavery. Increasing numbers of Northerners viewed slaveholding as a monstrous violation of the basic American principle of equality, but Southerners wanted to preserve the institution of slavery. The conflict reached a fever pitch and erupted at Fort Sumter. As soldiers went off to battle, emotions ran high through a divided country.

A Response to the War: Idealism

In Concord, Massachusetts, home of Ralph Waldo Emerson, Henry David Thoreau, Nathaniel Hawthorne, and many other intellectual leaders of the nation, army volunteers met in 1861 at the bridge that Emerson had immortalized in "Concord Hymn," his famous poem about the beginning of the American Revolution. Emerson had for decades warned that this day would come if slavery were not abolished. Now that the day had arrived, he was filled with patriotic fervor. He watched the Concord volunteers march to Boston, and he visited a navy yard, declaring that "sometimes gunpowder smells good."

Photograph by Mathew Brady.

Secondary Source

Civil War Casualties

Bruce Catton, a leading Civil War historian, offers this explanation for the war's shockingly high casualties: "Neither side in the Civil War was prepared to stop anywhere short of complete victory. In the old days, wars had been formalized; two nations fought until it seemed to one side or the other that it would not be worthwhile to fight any longer, and some sort of accommodation would be reached—and, in the last analysis, nothing would have been changed very much. But in the Civil War it was all or nothing. The Southern States wanted absolute independence, and the Northern States wanted absolute union; once a little blood had been shed, there was no halfway point at which the two sides could get together and make a compromise. So the stakes were immeasurably increased, and this too affected the way in which men fought."

Wounded Soldier Being Given a Drink from a Canteen (1864) by Winslow Homer. Charcoal and white chalk on green paper (36.5 cm × 50 cm).

Emerson had great respect for the Southern will to fight, however, and he suspected, quite rightly, that the war would not be over in a few months, as some people had predicted. When the Concord volunteers returned a few months later from the First Battle of Bull Run (July 1861), defeated and disillusioned, many of them unwilling to reenlist, Emerson maintained his conviction that the war must be pursued.

A Reality of the War: Appalling Suffering

Late in 1862, Walt Whitman traveled to Virginia to find his brother George, who had been wounded in battle. After George was nursed back to health, Whitman remained in Washington off and on, working part time and serving as a volunteer hospital visitor, comforting the wounded and writing to their loved ones. The condition of the wounded was appalling. Many of the injured had to remain on the battlefield for two or three days until the camp hospitals had room for them. Antiseptics were primitive, as were operating-room techniques. A major wound meant amputation or even death.

Whitman estimated that in three years as a camp hospital volunteer, he visited tens of thousands of wounded men. "I am the man," he had written in "Song of Myself," "I suffer'd, I was there," and now he *was* there, in the real heart of America. In his poems he had presented a panoramic vision of America; now America passed

> *Future years will never know the seething hell and the black infernal background of the countless minor scenes and interiors . . . and it is best they should not— the real war will never get in the books.*
>
> —Walt Whitman

Primary Source

Walt Whitman on Bull Run

Walt Whitman recorded this gloomy description of Union troops returning to Washington after the first battle of Bull Run: "The defeated troops commenced pouring into Washington over the Long Bridge at daylight on Monday, 22nd . . . all the men with this coating of murk and sweat and rain, now recoiling back, pouring over the Long Bridge—a horrible march of twenty miles, returning to Washington baffled, humiliated, panic-struck. Where are the vaunts, and the proud boasts with which you went forth? Where are your banners, and your bands of music, and your ropes to bring back your prisoners? Well, there isn't a band playing—and there isn't a flag but clings ashamed and lank to its staff."

DIRECT TEACHING

VIEWING THE ART

Although **Winslow Homer** (1836–1910) painted a number of typical American scenes of farm life and children at play, it was his pictures of the Civil War that made him one of the best-known American artists of the nineteenth century.

Activity. Have students compare and contrast this painting with the photograph of actual soldiers on p. 384.

B **Exploring the Historical Period**
FIRST BATTLE OF BULL RUN

Some historians think the war could have ended with this battle, given the disorganization and lack of training on both sides. At the beginning of the battle, the Union nearly broke the left flank of the Confederate line. Had it done so, the Confederates would likely have lost the battle and the war. Late in the battle, the Union retreated, and if the Confederates had pursued them, they might have captured Washington, D.C.

C **Reading Skills**
Expressing an opinion. Ask students whether they agree with Whitman that citizens are better off not seeing "the real war" or whether they believe citizens have a duty to learn about the wars waged by their government.

D **Background**
Appalling Suffering
Rifle balls often shattered soldiers' bones, forcing doctors to amputate arms and legs. The limbs were often piled up on a cart outside the surgeon's tent. Ignorant of the importance of sterile conditions for surgery, surgeons frequently honed their scalpels on the soles of their boots, so infections ran rampant in the field hospitals. There were no antibiotics so even minor wounds could prove deadly.

VIEWING THE ART

This painting of a boy at war is a study for a work by **Winslow Homer** (1836–1910). Homer captures the soldier's youth through his stance, physical characteristics, and ill-fitting uniform.

Activity. Have students read selections from "Political Points of View: The Civil War" (p. 432) and then write a letter home that the young soldier may have composed.

A Reading Skills

❷ **Making inferences.** What do you think Whitman saw in the soldiers that gave him cause for such optimism? [Possible responses: The men were loyal to their cause; the men on each side developed strong bonds; the men showed great courage in the face of death.]

B Reading Skills

❷ **Interpreting.** Compare this proverb with a statement made by Herbert Hoover in 1944, while World War II raged: "Older men declare war. But it is youth that must fight and die." In what ways do both "graybeards" and youth grieve after a war? [Possible response: Older people mourn the loss of their children. Younger people mourn their lost comrades and their lost youth. Both mourn the physical and spiritual destruction of their country.]

C Reading Skills

❷ **Drawing conclusions.** How do Whitman's and Melville's attitudes toward the soldiers differ? [Possible response: Whitman saw the courage and patriotism of the soldiers he encountered, while Melville saw their naiveté and recklessness.]

Young Soldier: Separate Study of a Soldier Giving Water to a Wounded Companion (1861) by Winslow Homer. Oil, gouache, and black crayon on canvas (36 cm × 17.5 cm).

Cooper-Hewitt, National Design Museum, Smithsonian Institution; Gift of Charles Savage Homer, Jr./Courtesy Art Resource, New York.

A through the hospital tents in the form of wounded men from every state in the Union and the Confederacy. Nevertheless, out of the horror that he viewed, Whitman was able to derive an optimistic vision of the American character, of "the actual soldier of 1862–65 . . . with all his ways, his incredible dauntlessness, habits, practices, tastes, language, his fierce friendship, his appetite, rankness, his superb strength—and a hundred unnamed lights and shades."

A Result of the War: Disillusionment

The war that strengthened Whitman's optimism served at the same time to justify Herman Melville's pessimism. Melville's poems about the war, collected in *Battle-Pieces and Aspects of the War* (1866), were often dark and foreboding. Of the elation following the firing on Fort Sumter, Melville wrote:

> O, the rising of the People
>   Came with the springing of the grass,
> They rebounded from dejection
>   After Easter came to pass.
> And the young were all elation
>   Hearing Sumter's cannon roar. . . .
> But the elders with foreboding
>   Mourned the days forever o'er,
> And recalled the forest proverb,
>   The Iroquois' old saw:
> **B** *Grief to every graybeard*
>   *When young Indians lead the war.*

Melville was fascinated by the war, but he never wrote a novel about it. The poems in *Battle-Pieces,* based on newspaper accounts of the battles as well as visits to battlefields, record the heroism and futility of the fighting on both sides and demonstrate respect for **C** Southern soldiers as well as Northern troops. In some of Melville's best poems, though, there is a sense of human nature being stripped bare, revealing not the heroism and strength that Whitman found, but rather humanity's basic evil.

Civil War ambulance.

Literary Criticism

Critic's Commentary: Melville's War Writing

Richard Chase contends that Herman Melville's *Battle-Pieces and Aspects of the War* is "the only volume of verse in the meager body of distinguished writing about the war that may be favorably compared with Whitman's *Drum Taps.*" He says, "Melville does not write as a partisan. The war as he sees it is a catastrophe that has happened not so much because of a Southern insurrection but because of innate imperfections in man's very nature, because of historical forces no man or group could fully control, and because of certain weaknesses in American democracy that the war itself has made ominously apparent."

How do Melville's views about the war confirm that Melville is one of the Dark Romantics? (See pp. 148–149.)

Eyes of an Era

INFORMATIONAL TEXT

Television's close-up coverage of modern warfare has made the thick of battle a common sight on the nightly news, but during the American Civil War, photographs were the closest thing to newscasts. By the latter part of the 1800s, technical advances began to allow for truly mobile photographers. As a result, the Civil War **D** became the first war to be fully documented in pictures. Cameras went on the march, up in observation balloons, and to sea on battleships.

Cameras of the time could not capture motion; charging troops and thrusting bayonets came out as hazy blurs. However, cameras richly recorded the preparations and the aftermath of war. After battles, photographers roamed the killing fields, shooting pictures while wearing handkerchiefs across their faces to block the stench of death. They captured the war's still lifes—fields and forests filled with dead soldiers; blasted cities and landscapes; and scenes inside prisons, hospitals, and camps.

The most famous of these war photographers was Mathew Brady (1823?–1896). Brady was among the first photographers to bring portable darkrooms to combat zones. Though Brady helped to inspire Civil War photography, he often employed courageous photographers, such as Alexander Gardner and Timothy O'Sullivan, to take their cameras onto the battlefields.

Gardner came closer than anyone else to capturing an actual battle scene when he set his camera on a ridge overlooking the Battle of Antietam in Maryland in 1862. He recognized that "verbal representations" of the war "may or may not have the merit of accuracy; but photographic presentments of them will be accepted by posterity with an undoubting faith."

Alexander Gardner (seated) and his portable darkroom.

O'Sullivan was one of the most fearless and brilliant of Brady's assistants. When bridge builders whom O'Sullivan was photographing were targeted by enemy sharpshooters, he calmly continued taking pictures while men screamed and fell.

Photographers struggled with heavy equipment, stray bullets, rain, mud, insects, foliage, wandering livestock, and frozen hands. Processing photographs in the field was complicated and messy: Many pictures were ruined when they were washed in streams, where debris could stick to the gummy image.

Sadly, most Civil War photographers and their work fell into obscurity after the war. **E** Hundreds of glass negatives were sold for use as greenhouse windows, and decades later many of the glass plates ended up in gas masks worn by soldiers in World War I. **F**

The Rise of Realism: The Civil War to 1914   **387**

A CLOSER LOOK

This feature describes the efforts of Mathew Brady and others to create a photographic record of the war.

DIRECT TEACHING

D **Exploring the Culture**
EARLY PHOTOGRAPHY
The first image to be captured and photochemically fixed was made in 1826 by a French military officer and inventor, Joseph-Nicéphore Niepce. Niepce's process took hours, and was therefore impractical. In 1851, the British photographer Frederick Scott Archer created a process that reduced the time it took to produce a picture to just a few seconds, but the picture had to be developed at once. This was the process Brady and his staff used during the Civil War—hence the need for mobile darkrooms.

E **Reading Informational Text**
❓ Hypothesizing. Why do you think the pictures taken by Brady and others were neglected after the war? [Possible responses: People did not want to remember a war that had caused them so much pain; people did not realize that the plates were an irreplaceable part of history.]

F **Reading Informational Text**
❓ Understanding author's purpose. What is the author's main purpose in writing this essay? [to provide a brief description of early photography, to convey the difficulties faced by its practitioners, and to show how they revolutionized war reporting by capturing images of battle on film]

DIFFERENTIATING INSTRUCTION

Learners Having Difficulty
Encourage students to create a glossary of the terms they encounter while reading this essay.

English-Language Learners
Have students do research on the role their state played during the Civil War. Possible topics for students to investigate include the number of troops the state provided and the number lost; important historical figures; and local Civil War memorials.

Advanced Learners
Enrichment. Ask students to prepare charts or graphs showing the human and financial costs of the Civil War.

VIEWING THE ART

Jacob Lawrence (1917–2000) painted subjects from African American history. He painted a thirty-one-panel series on Harriet Tubman, the famous guide, or conductor, on the Underground Railroad. "I was the conductor of the Underground Railroad for eight years," Tubman once remarked, "and I can say what most conductors can't say—I never ran my train off the track and I never lost a passenger."

Activity. Ask students to examine the use of color and line in this painting. How does Lawrence use these elements to emphasize the constraints of slavery? [Possible response: He uses heavy, dark chains and "prison stripes" to suggest bondage.]

A Reading Skills

Analyzing. After the Civil War, Walt Whitman predicted that "a great literature will . . . arise out of the era of those four years." As the text states, there was little literary output during the war. Since then, however, the conflict has inspired more than sixty thousand scholarly books and articles, a figure matched by few other wars. Discuss with students whether such works fulfill Whitman's prediction.

B Literary Connections

Where Were The Literary Giants?

A number of important American writers of the time were silent on the war. Henry Wadsworth Longfellow was busy raising his children after his wife's death; Oliver Wendell Holmes was working as a professor at Harvard; William Cullen Bryant was working as editor of the *New York Evening Post*.

The Harriet Tubman Series (1939–1940), No. 9, by Jacob Lawrence. Hardboard (12″ × 17⅛″).

Harriet Tubman dreamt of freedom ("Arise! Flee for your life!") and in the visions of the night she saw the horsemen coming. Beckoning hands were ever motioning her to come, and she seemed to see a line from the land of slavery to the land of freedom.

The War in Literature

A Although many works of historical interest—soldiers' letters and diaries, as well as journalistic writings—came out of the war, works of literary significance were rare, prompting the question, Why did an event of such magnitude result in such a scanty literary output?

Modern readers think that one byproduct of a war is literary accounts, largely in the form of novels and poems by participants in the war. Modern writers like Ernest Hemingway went to war intending to return with the material for novels. This was not the case with the Civil War. Few major American writers saw the Civil War first-hand. Emerson was in Concord during most of the war, "knitting socks and mittens for soldiers," as he wrote to his son, and "writing patriotic lectures." Thoreau, who had been a fervent abolitionist, **B** died in 1862, and Hawthorne died two years later. Emily Dickinson remained in Amherst, Massachusetts, and the country's grief over the war seems not to have informed her poetry. Of the younger generation of writers, William Dean Howells, Henry James, and Henry Adams were abroad.

388   Collection 4   The Rise of Realism: The Civil War to 1914

DIFFERENTIATING INSTRUCTION

Learners Having Difficulty
Have students plan a ceremony to confer awards on civilian heroes of the Civil War, such as Walt Whitman, writer and nurse; Clara Barton, army nurse; and Mathew Brady, photographer. Have students work in small groups researching these or other honorees and devising appropriate awards. Tell students to decide who will serve as master of ceremonies and who will play the heroes.

Advanced Learners
Enrichment. Invite students to write a diary entry from the point of view of someone experiencing the Civil War firsthand, such as a Southern slave, a Northern freeman or free-woman, a Union or Confederate soldier, a battlefield nurse, or President Lincoln. Encourage students to use their character's perspective to tell how the war is affecting his or her everyday life.

Perhaps most important, the traditional literary forms of the time were inadequate to express the horrifying details of the Civil War. The literary form most appropriate for handling such strong material—the **realistic novel**—had not yet been fully developed in the United States. Thus, the great novel of the war, *The Red Badge of Courage*, had to wait to be written by a man who was not born until six years after the war had ended: Stephen Crane.

The Rise of Realism

One of the most enduring subjects of prose fiction has been the exploits of larger-than-life heroes. Born of the chivalric romance, the **Romantic novel** presents readers with lives lived idealistically—beyond the level of everyday life. The heroes and heroines of the novels of James Fenimore Cooper, for example, engage in romantic adventures filled with courageous acts, daring chases, and exciting escapes.

In America the great fiction writers of the mid–nineteenth century, Edgar Allan Poe, Nathaniel Hawthorne, and Herman Melville, shared an aversion to simple realism. These writers used romance

> *With malice toward none; with charity for all; with firmness in the right, as God gives us to see the right, let us strive on to finish the work we are in; to bind up the nation's wounds; to care for him who shall have borne the battle, and for his widow, and his orphan—to do all which may achieve and cherish a just and lasting peace, among ourselves, and with all nations.*
>
> —President Abraham Lincoln, Second Inaugural Address, March 4, 1865

Woman freed from slavery, learning to read.
Leib Image Archives, York, Pennsylvania.

389

DIRECT TEACHING

C Background

Stephen Crane

Tell students that Stephen Crane based his writings about the Civil War on stories told by veterans and on war photographs.

D Literary Connections

James Fenimore Cooper

Cooper (1789–1851) described the exploits of his uniquely American hero, Natty Bumppo, in a series of novels called the Leatherstocking Tales. The most famous of these books, *The Last of the Mohicans*, was made into a movie starring Daniel Day-Lewis.

Literary Criticism

Critic's Commentary: Mark Twain on Cooper

Although Cooper's books won a wide readership, not everyone was enamored of his writing. Mark Twain skewered Cooper for his "literary offenses," such as his dependence on hackneyed literary devices. According to Twain, Cooper "prized his broken twig above all the rest of his effects, and worked it the hardest. It is a restful chapter in any book of his when somebody doesn't step on a dry twig and alarm all the reds and whites for two hundred yards about. Every time a Cooper person is in peril, and absolute silence is worth four dollars a minute, he is sure to step on a dry twig. There may be a hundred handier things to step on, but that wouldn't satisfy Cooper. Cooper requires him to turn out and find a dry twig; and if he can't do it, go and borrow one. In fact, the Leather Stocking Series ought to have been called the Broken Twig Series."

VIEWING THE ART

Frederic Remington
(1861–1909) is famous for his bronzes and his paintings of the American West. Remington was born in Canton, New York, and was educated at New York City's Art Students League. He served as a war correspondent and artist during the Spanish-American War, but the American West was always his favorite subject. In more than 2,700 paintings and drawings, numerous sculptures, and several books, he explored the myth of the rugged American West.

Activity. Remington's paintings often have a strong narrative element that captures the flavor of life on the vanishing frontier. Ask students to describe the story this painting tells. [As the title suggests, it shows how mail was delivered by the pony express; it conveys the tension and excitement of the mail carriers' work.]

Ⓐ Literary Connections
Huckleberry Finn
The book *Adventures of Huckleberry Finn*—and, by extension, its author Mark Twain—did not always occupy a place of honor in American literature. When *Huckleberry Finn* was first published in 1884, it offended many readers. It was called "vulgar," "trashy," "semiobscene," and "vicious." Although today the novel is generally regarded as a masterpiece, some people are offended by the novel's portrayal of Jim, which they consider racially stereotyped.

Coming and Going of the Pony Express (1900) by Frederic Remington. Oil on canvas (26″ × 39″).

> *All modern American literature comes from one book by Mark Twain called* Huckleberry Finn.
> —Ernest Hemingway

at the expense of the realities of a social world that relied on slavery. Realism as a literary movement in the United States went far beyond regionalism in its concern for accuracy in portraying social conditions and human motivation.

Mark Twain is the best-known example of a regional writer whose realism far surpassed local bounds. Although he first established his reputation as a regional humorist, Twain evolved into a writer whose comic view of society became increasingly satiric. His best novel, *Adventures of Huckleberry Finn* (1884), describes the moral growth of a comic character in an environment that is at the same time physically beautiful and morally repugnant. *Huckleberry Finn* combines a biting picture of some of the injustices inherent in pre–Civil War life with a lyrical portrait of the American landscape.

Literary Criticism

Critic's Commentary: The National Epic

The literary critic Clifton Fadiman described the significance of Mark Twain's novel this way: "This is the book with which we as a literary people begin. Two thousand years from now American professors of literature—if such still exist—will speak of *Huckleberry Finn* as English professors of literature now speak of Chaucer. For *Huckleberry Finn* is our Chaucer, our Homer, our Dante, our Virgil. It is the source of the stream, the seedbed, the book which, read or unread, has influenced a thousand American writers, the first great mold within which the form and pattern of our speech were caught. . . .

"It is the nearest thing we have to a national epic."

Realism and Naturalism:
A Lens on Everyday Life

■ "Smiling Realism"

The most active proponent of realism in American fiction was William Dean Howells, editor of the influential magazine *The Atlantic Monthly*. In both his fiction and his critical writings, Howells insisted that realism should deal with the lives of ordinary people, be faithful to the development of character even at the expense of action, and discuss the social questions perplexing Americans. Howells's "smiling realism" portrayed an America where people may act foolishly but where their good qualities eventually win out.

Other realistic novelists viewed life as a much rougher clash of contrary forces. The Californian Frank Norris, for example, agreed with Howells that the proper subject for fiction was the ordinary person, but he found Howells's fiction too strait-laced and narrow. It was, Norris said, "as respectable as a church and proper as a deacon." Norris was an earthier writer, interested in the impact of large social forces on individuals. His best-known novel, *The Octopus* (1901), is about the struggles between wheat farmers and the railroad monopoly in California. Norris was not the first to use the novel to examine social institutions with the aim of reforming them; Harriet Beecher Stowe's novel *Uncle Tom's Cabin* (1852) had been published

Elements of Naturalism
• Attempt to analyze human behavior objectively, as a scientist would • Belief that human behavior is determined by heredity and environment • Sense that human beings cannot control their own destinies • Sense of life as a losing battle against an uncaring universe

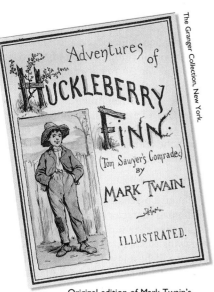

The Granger Collection, New York.

Original edition of Mark Twain's *Adventures of Huckleberry Finn* (1885).

Advertisement for Harriet Beecher Stowe's antislavery novel *Uncle Tom's Cabin* (1852).

B **Literary Connections**
Howells's Support of Realism
Before 1900, Howells spearheaded the battle for realism in America. He used his position as the editor-in-chief of *The Atlantic Monthly* to proclaim his sympathies and to encourage young American writers who wanted to break with convention and write what they saw and knew.

C **Exploring the Culture**
NORRIS ON NATURALISM
Benjamin Franklin (Frank) Norris scorned the pale and bloodless romances of his time—the "literature of chambermaids," he called them. Along with Theodore Dreiser and Jack London, he combined realism with Darwinism to create naturalism. By the end of his life, however, Norris came to reject the brutally individualistic vision of naturalism and to feel that people are basically interdependent. As the rancher Annixter says in Norris's novel *The Octopus,* "I began to see that a fellow can't live *for* himself any more than he can live *by* himself. He's got to think of others."

Literary Criticism

Critic's Commentary:
Uncle Tom's Cabin
Undoubtedly the most influential novel of the era, *Uncle Tom's Cabin* is the story of the hard life and cruel death of an enslaved man called Uncle Tom. Among the most famous scenes are the death of Little Eva, the daughter of the plantation owner; the escape of an enslaved woman named Eliza and her baby across the ice floes of the Ohio River; and the escape of Eliza's husband, George, by way of the Underground Railroad. Although some people view Uncle Tom negatively (his name is sometimes used as a pejorative term), others see him as a character of great nobility and dignity. More polemical than literary, the novel strengthened the abolitionists' arguments against slavery. The first edition of five thousand copies sold out in forty-eight hours, and in the following two years, the presses never caught up with the demand. Total book sales were in the millions, and soon after its publication the novel was adapted into a play that ran continuously from 1853 to 1930. Upon meeting the diminutive Stowe for the first time, President Lincoln is reported to have said, "So this is the little lady who started this big war."

A Literary Connections
Zola's Vision
Emile Zola wrote a series of twenty novels called *Les Rougon-Macquart: The Natural and Social History of a Family Under the Second Empire.* These books reflect Zola's belief that heredity determines human nature and that people with weak or evil ancestors are condemned to a bleak fate. In Zola's view, undesirable qualities could be eliminated only through education and medicine.

B Reading Skills
❓ Identifying the main idea.
What is the main focus of Jamesian realism? [psychological motivation]

C Exploring the Historical Period
FAST FACTS
Ask students to discuss how the reformers and muckrakers of the period both reflected and challenged the philosophies of realism and naturalism. [Possible response: Reflecting the rise of realism, these reformers looked at such topics as prostitution and described them as they were. Because their aim was to bring about change, they opposed the dark fatalism of the naturalists.]

D Literary Connections
Crane as Ironist
Although Stephen Crane's ironic naturalism has been more closely studied in his novels and short stories, it is also evident in his poems, as this excerpt from *War Is Kind* shows:

The wayfarer
Perceiving the pathway to truth
Was struck with astonishment.
It was thickly grown with weeds.
"Ha," he said.
"I see that none has passed here
In a long time."
Later he saw that each weed
Was a singular knife.
"Well," he mumbled at last.
"Doubtless there are other roads."

FAST FACTS

Political Highlights
- Civil War (1861–1865) results in the loss of more than 600,000 men and a reunited but bitter republic.
- Slavery, a leading cause of the Civil War, is abolished in 1865.
- Abraham Lincoln is assassinated in Ford's Theatre, Washington, D.C., on April 14, 1865.

Philosophical Views
- Romanticism is overtaken by more realistic attitudes toward art and life.
- Advances in sociology and psychology lead to growing interest in analyzing everyday life and the behavior of society as a whole.

Social Influences
- Reformers and muck-raking journalists expose abuses in industries such as mining and meatpacking.
- Large numbers of immigrants from Europe settle in American cities.
- In 1908, Henry Ford introduces the Model T, an invention that will drastically change the landscape and re-shape the American way of life.

---

before the Civil War and, according to Lincoln (and many historians), played a part in bringing about the war. But *Uncle Tom's Cabin* was more melodrama than realistic fiction.

■ Grim Naturalism

Norris is generally considered a **naturalist.** Following the lead of the French novelist Émile Zola, naturalists relied heavily on the emerging scientific disciplines of psychology and sociology. In their fiction, the naturalists attempted to dissect human behavior with as much objectivity as a scientist would use. For naturalists, human behavior was determined by forces beyond the individual's power, especially by biology and environment. The naturalists tended to look at human life as a grim losing battle. Their characters usually have few choices. In the eyes of some naturalist writers, human beings are totally subject to the natural laws of the universe; like animals, they live crudely, by instinct, unable to control their own destinies.

Psychological Realism: Inside the Human Mind

■ Exploring Motivation

On the other hand, the New York–born Henry James, considered America's greatest writer of the psychological novel, concentrated principally on fine distinctions in character motivation. James was a realist, but no realist could be further from the blunt, naturalistic view that people were driven by animal-like instincts. In his finely tuned studies of human motivation, James was mainly interested in complex social and psychological situations. Many of his novels, including *Daisy Miller* (1879) and *The Portrait of a Lady* (1881), take place in Europe, because James considered European society to be both more complex and more sinister than American society. He frequently contrasts innocent, eager Americans with sophisticated, more manipulative Europeans. In a typical James novel a straightforward American confronts the complexities of European society and either defeats or is defeated by them.

■ Examining Characters in Crisis

Stephen Crane was as profound a psychologist as James, but his principal interest was the human character at moments of stress. For James the proper setting for an examination of human behavior under pressure was the drawing room; for Crane it was the battlefield, the streets of a slum, or a lifeboat lost at sea. Although Crane is sometimes referred to as a naturalist, he is probably best thought of as an **ironist;** he was the first of many modern American writers—later including Ernest Hemingway and Kurt Vonnegut, Jr.—to juxtapose human illusions with the indifference of the universe. Of all the nineteenth-century realists, only Crane could describe a stabbing death (in his story "The Blue Hotel") in this coolly cynical manner: "[The blade] shot forward, and a human body, this citadel of virtue, wisdom, power, was pierced as easily as if it had been a melon." It would take this sensibility to get the "real war" in the books at last.

Endings and Beginnings

The period from around the turn of the century up to 1914 saw the continuation of many nineteenth-century trends and, at the same time, the early flowerings of modernism. Some writers worked to sustain earlier visions of America, such as Edwin Arlington Robinson, with his classic New England characters. Others, like Willa Cather, reminded readers of the heroic struggle to settle the vanishing frontier. Still, the currents of realism and naturalism evoked by the Civil War continued to dominate American literature.

In the period between the end of the Civil War and the outbreak of World War I in 1914, the American nation was transformed from an isolated, rural nation to an industrialized world power. Even these changes would soon be dwarfed, however. World War I would rock the world and shake people's faith in humanity. Idealism would turn to cynicism, and thinkers and writers called modernists would seek new literary forms for exploring the social and spiritual upheavals wrought once again by war.

> [Crane's] importance lies not only in those few works of his which completely come off, like "The Open Boat," but in his constantly seeking the primitive facts, the forbidden places, the dangerous people.
>
> —Alfred Kazin

E **F**

R E V I E W

Talk About ...

Turn back to the Think About questions at the start of this introduction to the period (page 382), and discuss your views.

Write About ...

Contrasting Literary Periods

The Romantics and the realists. The shift from Romanticism to realism brought about new literary forms, new styles, and, most important, new attitudes in writers and readers. Write a brief essay in which you compare and contrast the basic atti-

tudes and beliefs of the Romantic writers with those of the realist writers. Consider, for example, the writers' subjects, characters, and attitudes toward human nature and their views on the purpose of literature.

The Rise of Realism: The Civil War to 1914   **395**

E **Literary Connections**
Robinson's Traditional Vision
Edwin Arlington Robinson (1869–1935) was the most prominent American poet between 1890 and 1910 and has enjoyed lasting popularity. Robinson used traditional poetic forms to express his wise and ironic views on human nature.

F **Literary Connections**
Willa Cather's Pioneers
Willa Cather (1873–1947) grew up among immigrant pioneers on the Nebraska prairie. In her novels *O Pioneers!* (1913) and *My Ántonia* (1918), she describes the difficult lives of pioneers struggling to cultivate a wild new land.

Review

Talk About ...

- **Modeling.** You might model answering the first bulleted question on p. 382 by saying, "I noted that the first great novel about the war, *The Red Badge of Courage*, wasn't published until 1895. Maybe the shock of the war was so great that writers needed some distance from it before they could deal with it."

- Characteristics of realist writing include rejection of the Romantic hero, a focus on the lives of ordinary people and on urban life, the use of slang and dialect to reveal class distinctions, and concern about social issues and ethics.

- Naturalist writers were fatalistic; they believed that human behavior and destiny were predetermined and that people were at the mercy of an uncaring universe.

Write About ...

The Romantics and the realists.
To help students get started, have them review the boxed features on Romanticism and realism.

Check Test: Short Answer
Monitoring students' progress. Guide the class in answering these questions.

1. What type of novel idealizes people and their lives? [Romantic]

2. What type of novel is meant to mirror daily life and deal with social issues? [realistic]

3. Which writer exemplifies idealism about the Civil War? Which writer exemplifies

disillusionment with the war?
[Walt Whitman; Herman Melville]

4. Which humorous regional writer expanded his vision to become a perceptive realist and social satirist? [Mark Twain]

5. What type of novel shows the effects of environment and heredity on people trapped in a cold, indifferent universe? [naturalistic]

Political Points of View

SKILLS FOCUS, pp. 396–421

Grade-Level Skills

■ **Literary Skills**
Analyze political points of view in a selection of literary works on a topic.

■ **Reading Skills**
Compare and contrast points of view across texts.

Political Issue: Slavery

Open a discussion of slavery by asking students to write down their own definitions of the word. Then, have students share their definitions. Have the class create a master definition, and write it on the chalkboard.

Skills Starter

Build prerequisite skills. To help students understand political assumptions, pose these questions:

• If you recommend a mystery novel to a friend, what assumption have you made about how your friend spends his or her free time? [the assumption that he or she reads for fun]

• What assumption or belief would allow a person to buy another human being? [the belief that some people are less human or have fewer rights than others]

Help students see that a *political assumption* is an unsubstantiated belief about how a government, a society, or a member of a society should act or think.

SKILLS FOCUS

Pages 396–421
cover
Literary Skills
Analyze political points of view on a topic.

Reading Skills
Compare points of view across texts.

Introducing *Political Points of View*

Slavery

Main Readings
Frederick Douglass . . . *from* **Narrative of the Life of Frederick Douglass** . . 399
Harriet A. Jacobs . . . . . *from* **Incidents in the Life of a Slave Girl** 407

You will be reading the five selections listed above in this Political Points of View feature on slavery. In the top corner of each page of this feature, you'll find three stars. Smaller versions of the stars appear next to the questions on pages 404 and 411 that focus on this political issue. At the end of the feature (page 421), you'll compare the various points of view on slavery expressed in the selections.

Examining the Issue: Slavery

The fact that slavery could flourish in a nation so fervently dedicated to the ideals of equality and freedom is perhaps the greatest paradox, or seeming contradiction, in our nation's history. It would take the upheaval of civil war to confront this American paradox and force a change.

Slavery is an issue that makes clear the close relationship between the personal and the political. The laws governing the slave system were not mere technicalities. They defined people, determined the course of their lives, and controlled all their relationships. As you read the selections in this section, note how, for the writers, the political is personal.

Reading Skills

Comparing Points of View Across Texts

The readings in this section describe several ways by which human beings opposed the horrors of slavery. In order to compare these points of view, make a chart like the one below. For each reading, note how slavery is opposed, and then describe the writer's point of view.

Selection	Opposition to Slavery	Point of View
Narrative of the Life of Frederick Douglass	Endures beating; complains to "master"; fights Covey	Defiant resistance revives dignity and hope for freedom.

Frederick Douglass
(1817?–1895)

Chester County Historical Society, West Chester, Pennsylvania.

Frederick Douglass was born into slavery in Talbot County, on the Eastern Shore of Maryland, and was separated from his mother soon after his birth. "The practice of separating children from their mothers," wrote Douglass years later, "and hiring the latter out at distances too great to admit of their meeting, except at long intervals, is a marked feature of the cruelty and barbarity of the slave system. But it is in harmony with the grand aim of slavery, which, always and everywhere, is to reduce man to a level with the brute. It is a successful method of obliterating from the mind and heart of the slave all just ideas of the sacredness of *the family.*"

Since birth records were not kept for children born into slavery, Douglass was never sure of his exact age. "Genealogical trees do not flourish among slaves," he was to remark ironically later. Although Douglass received no formal education, he did teach himself to read with the help, at first, of members of the household he served. Later these same people became furious when they saw Douglass reading a book or a newspaper; education, they decided, was incompatible with being enslaved.

When Douglass was about twenty-one, he satisfied his hunger for freedom by escaping to Massachusetts, where he married and soon started to make public speeches in support of the abolitionist cause. He changed his last name from Bailey to Douglass, after the hero of the Romantic novel *The Lady of the Lake* by Sir Walter Scott.

In 1845, Douglass went to England, largely because of the danger he faced as a fugitive, especially after the publication that same year of his autobiography *Narrative of the Life of Frederick Douglass, an American Slave.* In England he mobilized antislavery sentiment and became independent when British friends collected around seven hundred dollars to purchase his freedom.

When he returned to the United States, in 1847, Douglass founded a newspaper, the *North Star.* (The name was chosen because escapees used this star as a guide north.) In his newspaper, Douglass championed the abolition of slavery. In 1855, he published a revised version of his life story, titled *My Bondage and My Freedom.* Escape narratives, like earlier captivity stories (page 37), were enormously popular, and Douglass's were widely read and very influential in the abolitionist cause.

When the Civil War began, Douglass worked ardently for the Underground Railroad, the secret network of abolitionists that helped many people held in slavery escape to the North. He also energetically helped to recruit black soldiers for the Union armies.

Continuing to write and lecture after the war, Douglass argued that the surest way to rehabilitate his tragically scarred people was through education. In 1881, he published yet another version of his autobiography, titled *The Life and Times of Frederick Douglass.* Today Douglass is revered for the courage with which he insistently proclaimed his profoundly humane values, and he is admired for the quiet eloquence of his writing style.

Frederick Douglass **397**

SKILLS FOCUS,
pp. 397–404

Grade-Level Skills

■ **Literary Skills**
Analyze ways authors use figures of speech, including metaphors.

■ **Literary Skills**
Analyze political points of view on a topic.

■ **Reading Skills**
Analyze a writer's purpose.

More About the Writer

Background. As a boy living in Baltimore, Frederick Douglass considered himself lucky to learn to read and write at a time when it was an "unpardonable offense to teach slaves to read." Douglass would carry a book with him on errands, finish his work early, and find a poor white boy to give him a lesson in exchange for bread. After he learned to write a few letters of the alphabet through his work at a shipyard, Douglass would boast to other boys that he could write as well as they. When the boys took the bait, Douglass would use the opportunity to learn more letters.

RESOURCES: READING

Planning
■ *One-Stop Planner* CD-ROM with ExamView Test Generator

Differentiating Instruction
■ *The Holt Reader*
■ *Holt Reading Solutions*
■ *Holt Adapted Reader*
■ *Supporting Instruction in Spanish*

Vocabulary
■ *Vocabulary Development*

Grammar and Language
■ *Daily Language Activities*

Assessment
■ *Holt Assessment: Literature, Reading, and Vocabulary*
■ *One-Stop Planner* CD-ROM with ExamView Test Generator

■ *Holt Online Assessment*

Internet
■ go.hrw.com (Keyword: LE5 11-4)
■ *Elements of Literature Online*

Media
■ *Audio CD Library*
■ *Audio CD Library, Selections and Summaries in Spanish*
■ *Fine Art Transparencies*

Summary at grade level

In this excerpt from his autobiography, Frederick Douglass recalls an incident during his enslavement. At the time a man named Covey had rented his services from his "owner," Thomas, for one year. One day, Douglass collapsed while working and was beaten by Covey. Douglass sustained a head wound, and fearing that he would be injured further, he struggled through the woods to Thomas's farm. Despite Douglass's pleas, Thomas refused Douglass sanctuary and ordered him to return to Covey. Douglass managed to elude Covey for a day, during which a slave named Sandy Jenkins offered Douglass a root to protect him from beatings. The next day, Covey treated Douglass decently, but only because it was Sunday. On Monday, Covey and a hired hand tried to tie up Douglass and beat him. Douglass fought back and managed to get the better of them, thus regaining a measure of dignity. For the remainder of the year, Covey treated Douglass with cautious respect.

Skills Starter

Build review skills. Remind students that a metaphor compares different things by implying that one thing *is* the other: *He is a snake.* Writers often use metaphors to help readers understand unfamiliar concepts. For example, Douglass uses metaphors that help readers who have never experienced slavery understand how it feels to live under—and overcome—bondage.

Before You Read

from Narrative of the Life of Frederick Douglass

Political Points *of* View

Quickwrite

While he was still enslaved, Frederick Douglass fought to assert his human rights and defend his dignity against a brutal social institution. His courageous action became a turning point in his life. Think of other heroic men and women who have fought against slavery, and jot down the qualities or attitudes you admire in them.

Literary Focus
Metaphor

Writers and poets use **metaphors** to make creative comparisons. Near the end of the selection, Douglass uses a metaphor that compares his triumph over Mr. Covey to resurrection from the dead: "It was a glorious resurrection, from the tomb of slavery, to the heaven of freedom." The metaphor adds a spiritual dimension to the story by connecting a physical victory to a victory of the soul.

> A **metaphor** is a figure of speech that makes a comparison between two unlike things without the use of a specific word of comparison, such as *like, as, than,* or *resembles.*
>
> *For more on Metaphor, see the Handbook of Literary and Historical Terms.*

go.hrw.com

INTERNET

Vocabulary Practice
•
More About Frederick Douglass
•
Keyword: LE5 11-4

SKILLS FOCUS

Literary Skills
Analyze political points of view on a topic. Understand metaphor.

Reading Skills
Analyze a writer's purpose.

Reading Skills
Analyzing a Writer's Purpose

In many cases, writers combine several modes of expression—such as description, narration, exposition, and persuasion—in order to accomplish their purpose. Douglass's writing provides a good example. He does not rely on *persuasion* to prove that slavery is dehumanizing. Instead, he *describes* the life of a slave and *narrates* his experiences in order to persuade readers to take action against slavery.

Background

In the following selection, Douglass provides a graphic account of a critical incident that occurred when he was sixteen years old. Earlier in his narrative he explains to his readers "how a man was made a slave"; now he sets out to explain "how a slave was made a man." At the time, Douglass was "owned" by a man named Thomas, who had rented Douglass's services out for a year to a man named Covey.

Vocabulary Development

intimated (in'tə·māt'id) *v.*: stated indirectly; hinted.

comply (kəm·plī') *v.*: obey; agree to a request.

interpose (in'tər·pōz') *v.*: put forth in order to interfere.

afforded (ə·fôrd'id) *v.*: gave; provided.

solemnity (sə·lem'nə·tē) *n.*: seriousness.

render (ren'dər) *v.*: make.

singular (siŋ'gyə·lər) *adj.*: remarkable.

attributed (ə·trib'yōo̅t·id) *v.*: thought of as resulting from.

expiring (ek·spīr'iŋ) *v.* used as *adj.*: dying.

Previewing Vocabulary

Have students work in pairs, with one partner reading aloud each word and its definition from p. 398 and the other creating a sentence with the word. Have students switch roles and repeat the activity. When students have demonstrated an understanding of the words, have them test their knowledge by writing the Vocabulary word that is opposite in meaning to each word or phrase on the following list.

1. proclaimed [intimated]
2. resist [comply]
3. gaiety [solemnity]
4. ordinary [singular]
5. living [expiring]
6. withdraw [interpose]
7. dissociated [attributed]
8. fail to make [render]
9. withheld [afforded]

from Narrative of the Life of Frederick Douglass

Frederick Douglass

The Battle with Mr. Covey

I have already intimated that my condition was much worse, during the first six months of my stay at Mr. Covey's, than in the last six. The circumstances leading to the change in Mr. Covey's course toward me form an epoch[1] in my humble history. You have seen how a man was made a slave; you shall see how a slave was made a man. On one of the hottest days of the month of August, 1833, Bill Smith, William Hughes, a slave named Eli, and myself, were engaged in fanning wheat.[2] Hughes was clearing the fanned wheat from before the fan, Eli was turning, Smith was feeding, and I was carrying wheat to the fan. The work was simple, requiring strength rather than intellect; yet, to one entirely unused to such work, it came very hard.

About three o'clock of that day, I broke down; my strength failed me; I was seized with a violent aching of the head, attended with extreme dizziness; I trembled in every limb. Finding what was coming, I nerved myself up, feeling it would never do to stop work. I stood as long as I could stagger to the hopper with grain. When I could stand no longer, I fell, and felt as if held down by an immense weight. The fan of course stopped; everyone had his own work to do; and no one could do the work of the other, and have his own go on at the same time.

Mr. Covey was at the house, about one hundred yards from the treading yard where we were fanning. On hearing the fan stop, he left immediately, and came to the spot where we were. He hastily inquired what the matter was. Bill answered that I was sick, and there was no one to bring wheat to the fan. I had by this time crawled away under the side of the post-and-rail fence by which the yard was enclosed, hoping to find relief by getting out of the sun. He then asked where I was. He was told by one of the hands.

He came to the spot, and, after looking at me awhile, asked me what was the matter. I told him as well as I could, for I scarce had strength to speak. He then gave me a savage kick in the side, and told me to get up. I tried to do so, but fell back in the attempt. He gave me another kick, and again told me to rise. I again tried, and succeeded in gaining my feet; but, stooping to get the tub with which I was feeding the fan, I again staggered and fell. While down in this situation, Mr. Covey took up the hickory slat with which Hughes had been striking off the half-bushel measure, and with it gave me a heavy blow upon the head, making a large wound, and the blood ran freely; and with this again told me to get up. I made no effort to comply, having now made up my mind to let him do his worst. In a short time after receiving this blow, my head grew better. Mr. Covey had now left me to my fate.

At this moment I resolved, for the first time, to go to my master, enter a complaint, and ask his protection. In order to [do] this, I must that afternoon walk seven miles; and this, under the circumstances, was truly a severe undertaking. I was exceedingly feeble; made so as much by the kicks and blows which I received, as by the severe fit of sickness to which I had been subjected. I, however, watched my chance, while Covey was looking in an opposite direction, and started for St. Michael's. I succeeded in

---

1. **epoch** (ep′ək) *n*.: noteworthy period of time.
2. **fanning wheat:** separating out usable grain.

Vocabulary
intimated (in′tə·māt′id) *v*.: stated indirectly; hinted.
comply (kəm·plī′) *v*.: obey; agree to a request.

Frederick Douglass **399**

VIEWING THE ART

Jacob Lawrence (1917–2000) was an African American painter who depicted scenes from black history in a spare, expressionistic style. His use of simplified forms and blocks of color makes his paintings look like posters. The paintings on this page and p. 403 come from his series on Frederick Douglass. He also painted a thirty-one-panel series on Harriet Tubman (see p. 388) and a sixty-panel series on the mass migration of African Americans to the North during the early decades of the twentieth century (see p. 741).

Activity. After they read the selection, ask students which painting—*Frederick Douglass Series No. 10,* shown here, or *No. 9,* on p. 403—illustrates the excerpt from Douglass's autobiography. [*No. 10* shows Douglass's fight with Covey.] What do you find most striking about this painting? [Students may mention the red and yellow of Covey's shirt, suggesting anger, blood, or cowardice.]

Hampton University Museum, Hampton, Virginia. © Gwendolyn Knight Lawrence, courtesy of the Jacob and Gwendolyn Lawrence Foundation.

The Life of Frederick Douglass (1938–1939), No. 10, by Jacob Lawrence. "The master of Douglass, seeing he was of a rebellious nature, sent him to a Mr. Covey, a man who had built up a reputation as a 'slave breaker.' A second attempt by Covey to flog Douglass was unsuccessful. This was one of the most important incidents in the life of Frederick Douglass: He was never again attacked by Covey. His philosophy: A slave easily flogged is flogged oftener; a slave who resists flogging is flogged less." (17⅛" × 12").

Learners Having Difficulty
Following the sequence of events. As students read, have them sketch a map of the route Douglass took from Covey's farm to Thomas's store and back and to label the places at which he stopped along the way. Remind them to include Sandy Jenkins's cabin and Covey's barn. Then, ask students to add a short description of what happened at each spot and to number the descriptions and

place them in chronological order along the route.

Special Education Students
For lessons designed for special education students, see *Holt Reading Solutions.*

Advanced Learners
Enrichment. Explain that Douglass was famous for his oratory as well as his writing. In fact, many opponents were so impressed

with his speaking that they refused to believe he had ever been enslaved. Invite students to find passages that show Douglass's skill with rhythm, alliteration, and other sound effects, such as pauses. For example, students might point out the pause in "You have seen how a man was made a slave; you shall see how a slave was made a man."

getting a considerable distance on my way to the woods, when Covey discovered me, and called after me to come back, threatening what he would do if I did not come. I disregarded both his calls and his threats, and made my way to the woods as fast as my feeble state would allow; and thinking I might be overhauled by him if I kept the road, I walked through the woods, keeping far enough from the road to avoid detection, and near enough to prevent losing my way.

I had not gone far before my little strength again failed me. I could go no farther. I fell down, and lay for a considerable time. The blood was yet oozing from the wound on my head. For a time I thought I should bleed to death; and think now that I should have done so, but that the blood so matted my hair as to stop the wound. After lying there about three quarters of an hour, I nerved myself up again, and started on my way, through bogs and briers, barefooted and bareheaded, tearing my feet sometimes at nearly every step; and after a journey of about seven miles, occupying some five hours to perform it, I arrived at master's store. I then presented an appearance enough to affect any but a heart of iron. From the crown of my head to my feet, I was covered with blood. My hair was all clotted with dust and blood; my shirt was stiff with blood. My legs and feet were torn in sundry places with briers and thorns, and were also covered with blood. I suppose I looked like a man who had escaped a den of wild beasts, and barely escaped them.

In this state I appeared before my master, humbly entreating him to interpose his authority for my protection. I told him all the circumstances as well as I could, and it seemed, as I spoke, at times to affect him. He would then walk the floor, and seek to justify Covey by saying he expected I deserved it. He asked me what I wanted. I told him, to let me get a new home; that as sure as I lived with Mr. Covey again, I should live with but to die with him; that Covey would surely kill me; he was in a fair way for it.

Master Thomas ridiculed the idea that there was any danger of Mr. Covey's killing me, and said that he knew Mr. Covey; that he was a good man, and that he could not think of taking me from him; that, should he do so, he would lose the whole year's wages; that I belonged to Mr. Covey for one year, and that I must go back to him, come what might; and that I must not trouble him with any more stories, or that he would himself *get hold of me.* After threatening me thus, he gave me a very large dose of salts, telling me that I might remain in St. Michael's that night (it being quite late), but that I must be off back to Mr. Covey's early in the morning; and that if I did not, he would *get hold of me,* which meant that he would whip me.

I remained all night, and, according to his orders, I started off to Covey's in the morning (Saturday morning), wearied in body and broken in spirit. I got no supper that night, or breakfast that morning. I reached Covey's about nine o'clock; and just as I was getting over the fence that divided Mrs. Kemp's fields from ours, out ran Covey with his cowskin, to give me another whipping. Before he could reach me, I succeeded in getting to the cornfield; and as the corn was very high, it afforded me the means of hiding. He seemed very angry, and searched for me a long time. My behavior was altogether unaccountable. He finally gave up the chase, thinking, I suppose, that I must come home for something to eat; he would give himself no further trouble in looking for me. I spent that day mostly in the woods, having the alternative before me—to go home and be whipped to death, or stay in the woods and be starved to death.

That night, I fell in with Sandy Jenkins, a slave with whom I was somewhat acquainted. Sandy had a free wife who lived about four miles from Mr. Covey's; and it being Saturday,

---

Vocabulary

interpose (in′tər·pōz′) v.: put forth in order to interfere.
afforded (ə·fôrd′id) v.: gave; provided.

A **English-Language Learners**

Archaic language. Douglass's statement that he thought he "should bleed" to death may be confusing. Explain that Douglass did not feel an obligation to bleed to death but rather was amazed that he didn't actually do so.

B **Reading Skills**

Analyzing a writer's purpose. Why do you think Douglass describes his physical condition in so much detail? [Possible responses: He wants to emphasize the extent to which he had been degraded and to suggest that he would be justified in fighting back; he hopes to evoke sympathy in the reader.]

C **Literary Focus**

Figures of speech. Why does Douglass compare himself to someone who has just "escaped a den of wild beasts"? How is this simile ironic? [Possible response: Covey did act like a beast. The irony arises from the fact that slaveholders regarded people held in slavery as less than human.]

D **Reading Skills**

Making inferences. Describe Thomas's behavior. Why do you think he reacted this way? [Possible responses: Thomas acted uneasy and seemed ambivalent. He may have been motivated by financial worries, a desire to uphold white authority, or fear of Covey.]

E **Reading Skills**

Hypothesizing. What other options might Douglass have pursued? [Possible responses: He could have returned to Covey and acted contrite; he could have returned to Covey and tried to defend himself.]

Architecture: Plantation Design
Individual activity. Ask students to research historic plantations, such as Thomas Jefferson's Monticello. Invite them to give a presentation on plantation housing, using graphic aids. Tell them to address the following questions:

- How did the homes of plantation owners and slaves differ?
- How many slaves shared a single dwelling?
- Where were the slaves' quarters located in relation to the plantation owner's house?

A Reading Skills

❓ Evaluating religious influences. Why did Covey treat Douglass kindly during this encounter? Would you call Covey's behavior gentlemanly or hypocritical? Why? [Possible response: Covey treated Douglass kindly because it was Sunday. This behavior is hypocritical because Covey treated Douglass like a brute on other days.]

B Reading Skills

❓ Making assertions about a writer's arguments. Before saying that he had resolved to fight back, Douglass admits that "from whence came the spirit I don't know." How does this description of his state of mind add to the persuasiveness of his argument? [Possible response: Douglass is suggesting that even in the face of grave danger, the human spirit is a powerful force that acts almost of its own accord; in this way he suggests that people will almost instinctively strike back when they are treated unjustly.]

he was on his way to see her. I told him my circumstances, and he very kindly invited me to go home with him. I went home with him, and talked this whole matter over, and got his advice as to what course it was best for me to pursue. I found Sandy an old advisor.[3] He told me, with great solemnity, I must go back to Covey; but that before I went, I must go with him into another part of the woods, where there was a certain *root*, which, if I would take some of it with me, carrying it *always on my right side,* would render it impossible for Mr. Covey, or any other white man, to whip me. He said he had carried it for years; and since he had done so, he had never received a blow, and never expected to while he carried it. I at first rejected the idea, that the simple carrying of a root in my pocket would have any such effect as he had said, and was not disposed to take it; but Sandy impressed the necessity with much earnestness, telling me it could do no harm, if it did no good. To please him, I at length took the root, and, according to his direction, carried it upon my right side. This was Sunday morning.

I immediately started for home; and upon entering the yard gate, out came Mr. Covey on his way to meeting. He spoke to me very kindly, made me drive the pigs from a lot nearby, and passed on toward the church. Now, this singular conduct of Mr. Covey really made me begin to think that there was something in the *root* which Sandy had given me; and had it been on any other day than Sunday, I could have attributed the conduct to no other cause than the influence of that root; and as it was, I was half inclined to think the *root* to be something more than I at first had taken it to be. All went well till Monday morning. On this morning, the virtue of the *root* was fully tested.

Long before daylight, I was called to go and rub, curry, and feed the horses. I obeyed, and was glad to obey. But while thus engaged, while in the act of throwing down some blades from

---

3. **an old advisor:** someone who can offer good advice.

the loft, Mr. Covey entered the stable with a long rope; and just as I was half out of the loft, he caught hold of my legs, and was about tying me. As soon as I found what he was up to, I gave a sudden spring, and as I did so, he holding to my legs, I was brought sprawling on the stable floor. Mr. Covey seemed now to think he had me, and could do what he pleased; but at this moment—from whence came the spirit I don't know—I resolved to fight; and, suiting my action to the resolution, I seized Covey hard by the throat; and as I did so, I rose. He held on to me, and I to him. My resistance was so entirely unexpected, that Covey seemed taken all aback. He trembled like a leaf. This gave me assurance, and I held him uneasy, causing the blood to run where I touched him with the ends of my fingers. Mr. Covey soon called out to Hughes for help. Hughes came, and, while Covey held me, attempted to tie my right hand. While he was in the act of doing so, I watched my chance, and gave him a heavy kick close under the ribs. This kick fairly sickened Hughes, so that he left me in the hands of Mr. Covey.

This kick had the effect of not only weakening Hughes, but Covey also. When he saw Hughes bending over with pain, his courage quailed.[4] He asked me if I meant to persist in my resistance. I told him I did, come what might; that he had used me like a brute for six months, and that I was determined to be used so no longer. With that, he strove to drag me to a stick that was lying just out of the stable door. He meant to knock me down. But just as he was leaning over to get the stick, I seized him with both hands by his collar, and brought him by a

---

4. **quailed** *v.:* faltered.

Vocabulary
solemnity (sə·lem′nə·tē) *n.:* seriousness.
render (ren′dər) *v.:* make.
singular (sin′gyə·lər) *adj.:* remarkable.
attributed (ə·trib′yōot·id) *v.:* thought of as resulting from.

READING MINI-LESSON

Developing Word-Attack Skills
Write the words *aching* and *arching* on the chalkboard, and ask students to compare the sounds of *ch* in the two words. Tell students that in English the combination *ch* typically stands for the sound /ch/ but that there are some words in which *ch* stands for /k/. Many of these words, such as *chord* and *chronic*,

derive from Greek. Have students scan the first paragraph of the selection to find a word in which *ch* stands for the sound /k/. [epoch]

Activity. Write the following word pairs on the chalkboard. Have students read each pair and identify the word in which *ch* stands for /k/. Tell them to consult a dictionary, if

necessary, to check pronunciation. Answers are underlined.

<u>chores</u>   <u>chorus</u>
<u>lichen</u>   lichee
<u>anchor</u>   archery
<u>archetype</u>   eschew
orchard   <u>orchid</u>
<u>dichotomy</u>   discharge

The Life of Frederick Douglass (1938–1939), No. 9, by Jacob Lawrence. "Transferred back to the eastern shore of Maryland, being one of the few Negroes who could read or write, Douglass was approached by James Mitchell, a free Negro, and asked to help teach a Sabbath School. However, their work was stopped by a mob who threatened them with death if they continued their class—1833." (12″ × 17⅞″).

Hampton University Museum, Hampton, Virginia. © Gwendolyn Knight Lawrence, courtesy of the Jacob and Gwendolyn Lawrence Foundation.

sudden snatch to the ground. By this time, Bill came. Covey called upon him for assistance. Bill wanted to know what he could do. Covey said, "Take hold of him, take hold of him!" Bill said his master hired him out to work, and not to help to whip me; so he left Covey and myself to fight our own battle out. We were at it for nearly two hours. Covey at length let me go, puffing and blowing at a great rate, saying that if I had not resisted, he would not have whipped me half so much. The truth was, that he had not whipped me at all. I considered him as getting entirely the worst end of the bargain; for he had drawn no blood from me, but I had from him. The whole six months afterward, that I spent with Mr. Covey, he never laid the weight of his finger upon me in anger. He would occasionally say, he didn't want to get hold of me again. "No," thought I, "you need not; for you will come off worse than you did before."

This battle with Mr. Covey was the turning point in my career as a slave. It rekindled the

few expiring embers of freedom, and revived within me a sense of my own manhood. It recalled the departed self-confidence, and inspired me again with a determination to be free. The gratification afforded by the triumph was a full compensation for whatever else might follow, even death itself. He only can understand the deep satisfaction which I experienced, who has himself repelled by force the bloody arm of slavery. I felt as I never felt before. It was a glorious resurrection,[5] from the tomb of slavery, to the heaven of freedom. My long-crushed spirit rose, cowardice departed, bold defiance took its place; and I now resolved that, however long I might remain a slave in form, the day had passed forever when I could be a slave in fact. ■

---

5. **resurrection** *n.:* coming back to life.

Vocabulary
expiring (ek·spīr′iŋ) *v.* used as *adj.:* dying.

Frederick Douglass   **403**

Response and Analysis

Reading Check

1. Douglass fled to Thomas and asked for protection. Thomas ordered Douglass to return to Covey.

2. Sandy Jenkins gave Douglass shelter and a root to protect Douglass from harm.

Thinking Critically

3. Douglass thought the root might have protected him when he returned to Covey's and Covey spoke kindly to him. Douglass discovered that his inner strength was more powerful than the root.

4. Students may characterize Douglass as levelheaded, determined, courageous, and strong.

5. The metaphor compares the battle to a fire that reignited Douglass's desire to seek freedom. This metaphor is related to rebirth because, like reignited embers, Douglass's spirit was born anew.

6. To Douglass a "slave in form" is someone who is enslaved but acts to maintain his or her inner freedom. A "slave in fact" is someone who submits to his or her enslavement without resisting. This distinction illustrates Douglass's theme: the importance of affirming one's dignity by acting against injustice.

7. Douglass describes events in a sober, restrained manner. This style convinces Douglass's audience that he is reliable and intelligent.

Literary Criticism

8. Because of slavery, Douglass was separated as an infant from his mother, denied an education, and treated cruelly. These wrongs strengthened his resolve to seek freedom and to help other oppressed people.

Response and Analysis

Reading Check

1. What action did Douglass take after Covey struck him? What did Thomas order Douglass to do?

2. Explain how Sandy Jenkins helped Douglass.

Thinking Critically

3. The root Douglass carried was thought to have supernatural powers. What made him think the root was magical? What did he discover was more powerful than the root?

4. Based on this account, how would you **characterize** the young Frederick Douglass? Did he possess any of the qualities or attributes you noted in the Quickwrite? Explain.

5. Explain the **metaphor** implied in this line: "It [the battle with Covey] rekindled the few expiring embers of freedom." How is the metaphor related to the idea of rebirth?

6. At the end of the selection, Douglass distinguishes between being "a slave in form" and "a slave in fact." How does this distinction support the **theme** of this selection?

7. Think about Douglass's **purpose** in writing this narrative. Consider Douglass's **style,** including his objectivity and restraint in describing painful incidents. How does Douglass win over an audience that might be uneasy at the idea of a black man's fighting a white man?

Literary Criticism

8. **Political approach.** In every period of history, certain conditions and events shape the character of people who live during that time. How was Douglass influenced by slavery, and in what ways does his story influence the institution of slavery?

WRITING

Douglass Writes Back

American literature abounds with writers who have championed principles of freedom—such as Jefferson, Paine, Emerson, and Thoreau. Write a **letter** in which Douglass responds to one of these writers. Have Douglass express his views on slavery and then comment on the author's writings and beliefs.

Vocabulary Development
Context Clues

intimated	afforded	singular
comply	solemnity	attributed
interpose	render	expiring

Look back at the selection now, and see if there are any clues in the **context** (the surrounding sentences) that would help you figure out the meaning of each underlined Vocabulary word. Record your findings in a chart like this one:

curry
↓
Meaning: comb and groom
↓
Clues: "I was called to go and rub, curry, and feed the horses." Curry must be something done to a horse.
↓
Possible meaning from context: He is rubbing and feeding the horses; perhaps he is washing and combing them as well.

go. hrw .com

INTERNET
Projects and Activities
Keyword: LE5 11-4

SKILLS FOCUS

Literary Skills
Analyze political points of view on a topic. Analyze metaphor.

Reading Skills
Analyze a writer's purpose.

Writing Skills
Write a letter expressing political views.

Vocabulary Skills
Use context clues to determine the meanings of words.

Vocabulary Development

Sample Answer

intimated. Meaning—hinted. *Clues*—"I have already intimated" suggests that the narrator has already mentioned something. *Possible meaning from context*—"said" or "hinted."

Harriet A. Jacobs
(1813?–1897)

Slave, fugitive, abolitionist, author, and mother—Harriet A. Jacobs led an extraordinary life. Born into slavery in Edenton, North Carolina, Jacobs was orphaned when she was only six years old. She was then taken into the home of her first mistress and trained as a house servant. There Jacobs learned how to read and write—vital skills usually forbidden to slaves. When her mistress died, Jacobs was "willed" to her mistress's young niece and sent to live at the home of Dr. James Norcom.

As a teenager, Jacobs was subjected to repeated harassment by her second owner, Dr. Norcom. Furious at her refusals of his advances, he sent her away to do hard labor as a plantation slave and then threatened to do the same to her two young children. Luckily Jacobs escaped from the plantation and found shelter with sympathetic relatives and friends, both black and white.

In her grandmother's house in Edenton, she found the safest place of all, a tiny crawl space above a storeroom. Jacobs hid there for seven years—reading (mainly the Bible), writing, sewing, and catching treasured glimpses of her children. All she ever wanted, she said, was freedom and a home for her children and herself. In 1842, Jacobs escaped to New York City, where she found work as a nursemaid and was eventually reunited with her children. She spent the next ten years as a fugitive, but in 1852, she finally gained her freedom.

Jacobs began writing the story of her life in 1853 and published it herself in 1861, using the pen name Linda Brent. *Incidents in the Life of a Slave Girl, Written by Herself* is an emotionally charged personal account and a fierce indictment of the slave system. Jacobs wrote on the title page:

> 66 Northerners know nothing at all about Slavery. They think it is perpetual bondage only. They have no conception of the depth of *degradation* involved in that word, *Slavery;* if they had, they would never cease their efforts until so horrible a system was overthrown. 99

After the publication of her book, Jacobs became active in the abolitionist movement. During the Civil War she worked tirelessly to relieve the poverty and suffering of other former slaves. Jacobs distributed clothes and supplies, raised money, and helped to establish schools and orphanages in Philadelphia, New York, Washington, D.C., Alexandria, and Savannah.

Although Jacobs's writing at times resembles the popular melodramas of her day, her story nevertheless retains an authentic power. *Incidents in the Life of a Slave Girl*—its raw facts of experience told with skill and honesty—provides modern readers with a chilling first-hand look at the particular plight of someone who was both a woman and a slave.

Harriet A. Jacobs   **405**

Grade-Level Skills
■ **Literary Skills**
Analyze political points of view on a topic.

Review Skills
■ **Literary Skills**
Analyze influences on characters (such as internal and external conflict) and the way those influences affect the plot.

■ **Literary Skills**
Analyze the way a work of literature relates to the themes and issues of its historical period. (Historical approach)

More About the Writer
Background. Harriet Jacobs's actions were motivated in large part by her love for her children. During her early years in hiding, Jacobs wrote many letters to Norcom claiming that she had escaped to the North. She hoped that this news would prompt Norcom to sell her children. Eventually Norcom unwittingly sold the children to their father and they were brought to Jacobs's grandmother's house, where Jacobs was able to watch them through a peephole she had drilled. Many years later, in a letter to a fellow abolitionist, Jacobs wrote, "thank God the bitter cup is drained of its last dreg. there is no more need of hiding places to conceal slave Mothers. yet it was little to . . . save my Children from the misery and degradation of Slavery."

RESOURCES: READING

Planning
■ *One-Stop Planner* CD-ROM with ExamView Test Generator

Differentiating Instruction
■ *Supporting Instruction in Spanish*
■ *Audio CD Library, Selections and Summaries in Spanish*

Vocabulary
■ *Vocabulary Development*

Assessment
■ *Holt Assessment: Literature, Reading, and Vocabulary*
■ *One-Stop Planner* CD-ROM with ExamView Test Generator
■ *Holt Online Assessment*

Internet
■ go.hrw.com (Keyword: LE5 11-4)
■ *Elements of Literature Online*

Media
■ *Audio CD Library*
■ *Audio CD Library, Selections and Summaries in Spanish*

Summary ⟷ *at grade level*

In "The Flight" and "Months of Peril," Harriet Jacobs (who calls herself Linda Brent in her narrative) describes her escape from the home of her "owner," Dr. Norcom (called Dr. or Mr. Flint in the narrative). Late one night, Jacobs crawled through a window of Norcom's house and ran to her grandmother's home. After telling a friend her plan and checking on her sleeping children, she departed for the home of another friend. She stayed there for a week, after which she was given refuge by the wife of another slaveholder. When Jacobs's small children were put in jail, she yearned to go to them, but stayed put on the advice of friends and family.

Skills Starter

Motivate. Ask students what forces or influences have helped shape them. [Possible responses: family, religion, friends, school, the times in which we live.] **Point out that similar influences shape the characters of literary works. Invite students to think about the political and social influences that shaped the people they will read about in this excerpt.

Selection Starter

Build background. Clarify these facts before students read:

• Harriet Jacobs's grandmother was a free black woman who owned her own house. Although no Southern slave had the legal right to earn freedom or own property, slaveholders sometimes used such privileges to motivate or reward people they held as slaves.

• "Mr. Sands" is actually Samuel Sawyer, a white attorney, an ally of Jacobs and the father of her children.

Before You Read

from Incidents in the Life of a Slave Girl

Political Points *of* View

The most obvious influence in Harriet Jacobs's life was slavery. It established her identity, ruled her daily existence, controlled her family life, and dominated her ideas and emotions. Jacobs was not only a slave, though; she was also a woman and a mother. Her autobiography brings us this additional perspective on the dehumanizing effects of slavery.

Literary Focus
Internal and External Conflict

Conflict is central to Jacobs's narrative. She experienced **external conflicts** when she escaped from her furious owner and tried to avoid recapture. In a larger context her life can be seen as one long struggle against the slave system.

Jacobs's **internal conflicts** were just as intense (for example, she pondered whether she dared abandon her children or involve her friends). These internal conflicts also had a direct influence on how her external conflicts were resolved.

INTERNET

Vocabulary Practice

Keyword: LE5 11-4

SKILLS FOCUS

Literary Skills
Analyze political points of view on a topic. Understand internal and external conflict.

> **Conflict** is the struggle between opposing forces or characters in a story. Conflict can be **internal** (a character struggles with conscience, for example) or **external** (a character struggles with another person or with society).
>
> *For more on Conflict, see the Handbook of Literary and Historical Terms.*

Background

Harriet Jacobs's autobiography is an authentic historical narrative. She used language and dialect that were typical of her time but would be considered offensive by today's readers. Although *Incidents in the Life of a Slave Girl* is nonfiction, Jacobs used made-up names for the characters. The narrator, who says she is writing her autobiography, is called Linda Brent. Dr. James Norcom, the slaveholder who pursued Jacobs for years, is called Dr. or Mr. Flint.

Vocabulary Development

malice (mal′is) *n.*: ill will; desire to harm.

fervently (fur′vənt·lē) *adv.*: with intense feeling.

unnerve (un·nurv′) *v.*: cause to lose one's courage.

provocation (präv′ə·kā′shən) *n.*: something that stirs up action or feeling.

distressed (di·strest′) *adj.*: suffering; troubled.

cunning (kun′iŋ) *adj.*: sly or crafty.

compelled (kəm·peld′) *v.*: driven; forced.

impulse (im′puls′) *n.*: sudden desire or urge.

Previewing Vocabulary

Have students work in pairs to read the definitions of the Vocabulary words on p. 406. Then, have them use the words to create an add-a-sentence story. One student begins the story by making up a sentence containing the first word on the Vocabulary list; the other student adds a sentence containing the second word, and so on. When students are finished, have them create another story, switching the order in which they give sentences. Afterward, reinforce students' knowledge of the Vocabulary words by having students compose a story on their own, using the Vocabulary words in any order they choose.

from Incidents in the Life of a Slave Girl

Harriet A. Jacobs

The Flight

Mr. Flint was hard pushed for house servants, and rather than lose me he had restrained his malice. I did my work faithfully, though not, of course, with a willing mind. They were evidently afraid I should leave them. Mr. Flint wished that I should sleep in the great house instead of the servants' quarters. His wife agreed to the proposition, but said I mustn't bring my bed into the house, because it would scatter feathers on her carpet. I knew when I went there that they would never think of such a thing as furnishing a bed of any kind for me and my little one. I therefore carried my own bed, and now I was forbidden to use it. I did as I was ordered. But now that I was certain my children were to be put in their power, in order to give them a stronger hold on me, I resolved to leave them that night. I remembered the grief this step would bring upon my dear old grandmother; and nothing less than the freedom of my children would have induced me to disregard her advice. I went about my evening work with trembling steps. Mr. Flint twice called from his chamber door to inquire why the house was not locked up. I replied that I had not done my work. "You have had time enough to do it," said he. "Take care how you answer me!"

I shut all the windows, locked all the doors, and went up to the third story, to wait till midnight. How long those hours seemed, and how fervently I prayed that God would not forsake[1] me in this hour of utmost need! I was about to risk everything on the throw of a die; and if I failed, Oh what would become of me and my poor children? They would be made to suffer for my fault.

At half past twelve, I stole softly downstairs. I stopped on the second floor, thinking I heard a noise. I felt my way down into the parlor, and

---

1. **forsake** *v.*: abandon; give up.

looked out of the window. The night was so intensely dark that I could see nothing. I raised the window very softly and jumped out. Large drops of rain were falling, and the darkness bewildered me. I dropped on my knees, and breathed a short prayer to God for guidance and protection. I groped my way to the road, and rushed toward the town with almost lightning speed. I arrived at my grandmother's house, but dared not see her. She would say, "Linda,[2] you are killing me," and I knew that would unnerve me. I tapped softly at the window of a room occupied by a woman who had lived in the house several years. I knew she was a faithful friend, and could be trusted with my secret. I tapped several times before she heard me. At last she raised the window, and I whispered, "Sally, I have run away. Let me in, quick." She opened the door softly, and said in low tones, "For God's sake, don't. Your grandmother is trying to buy you and de chillern. Mr. Sands was here last week. He tole her he was going away on business, but he wanted her to go ahead about buying you and de chillern, and he would help her all he could. Don't run away, Linda. Your grandmother is all bowed down wid trouble now."

I replied, "Sally, they are going to carry my children to the plantation tomorrow; and they will never sell them to anybody so long as they have me in their power. Now, would you advise me to go back?"

"No, chile, no," answered she. "When dey finds you is gone, dey won't want de plague ob de chillern; but where is you going to hide? Dey knows ebery inch ob dis house."

---

2. **Linda:** Jacobs's made-up name for herself (see Background, page 406).

Vocabulary
malice (mal′is) *n.*: ill will; desire to harm.
fervently (fur′vənt·lē) *adv.*: with intense feeling.
unnerve (un·nurv′) *v.*: cause to lose one's courage.

Harriet A. Jacobs **407**

African American schoolchildren, New Bern, North Carolina (c. 1862). (Inset) Advertisement for the capture of an escaped slave (1835).

$100 REWARD!

RANAWAY

From the undersigned, living on Current River, about twelve miles above Doniphan, in Ripley County, Mo., on 2nd of March, 1860, A MU-LATTO, about 30 years old, weighs about 160 pounds; high forehead, with a scar on it; had on brown pants and coat very much worn, and an old black wool hat; shoes size No. 11.

The above reward will be given to any person who may apprehend this said fugitive out of the State, and fifty dollars if apprehended in the State within six miles of Ripley county, or $25 if taken in Ripley county.

APOS TUCKER.

DIFFERENTIATING INSTRUCTION

Advanced Learners

Enrichment. Explain that the conflicts described in this narrative reflect broad social struggles. Have students analyze Jacobs's narrative in relation to these struggles. First, have students work in groups to identify and examine Jacobs's external conflicts. Then ask, "What larger social conflict lay at the heart of her experience?" Encourage students to look beyond the institution of slavery and identify a fundamental belief or assumption that Jacobs and other enslaved people struggled against. [Possible response: They struggled against the idea that certain groups of people have no rights.] When students reach a consensus, have them discuss the internal conflicts that resulted from this external struggle.

I told her I had a hiding place, and that was all it was best for her to know. I asked her to go into my room as soon as it was light, and take all my clothes out of my trunk, and pack them in hers; for I knew Mr. Flint and the constable[3] would be there early to search my room. I feared the sight of my children would be too much for my full heart; but I could not go out into the uncertain future without one last look. I bent over the bed where lay my little Benny and baby Ellen. Poor little ones! Fatherless and motherless! Memories of their father came over me. He wanted to be kind to them; but they were not all to him, as they were to my womanly heart. I knelt and prayed for the innocent little sleepers. I kissed them lightly, and turned away.

As I was about to open the street door, Sally laid her hand on my shoulder, and said, "Linda, is you gwine all alone? Let me call your uncle."

"No, Sally," I replied, "I want no one to be brought into trouble on my account."

I went forth into the darkness and rain. I ran on till I came to the house of the friend who was to conceal me.

Early the next morning Mr. Flint was at my grandmother's inquiring for me. She told him she had not seen me, and supposed I was at the plantation. He watched her face narrowly, and said, "Don't you know anything about her running off?" She assured him that she did not. He went on to say, "Last night she ran off without the least provocation. We had treated her very kindly. My wife liked her. She will soon be found and brought back. Are her children with you?" When told that they were, he said, "I am very glad to hear that. If they are here, she cannot be far off. If I find out that any of my niggers have had anything to do with this damned business, I'll give 'em five hundred lashes." As he started to go to his father's, he turned round and added, persuasively, "Let her be brought back, and she shall have her children to live with her."

---
3. **constable** *n.:* officer of the law, ranking just below sheriff.

The tidings[4] made the old doctor rave and storm at a furious rate. It was a busy day for them. My grandmother's house was searched from top to bottom. As my trunk was empty, they concluded I had taken my clothes with me. Before ten o'clock every vessel northward bound was thoroughly examined, and the law against harboring[5] fugitives was read to all on-board. At night a watch was set over the town. Knowing how distressed my grandmother would be, I wanted to send her a message; but it could not be done. Everyone who went in or out of her house was closely watched. The doctor said he would take my children, unless she became responsible for them; which of course she willingly did. The next day was spent in searching. Before night, the following advertisement was posted at every corner, and in every public place for miles round:

$300 REWARD! Ran away from the subscriber,[6] an intelligent, bright mulatto[7] girl, named Linda, 21 years of age. Five feet four inches high. Dark eyes, and black hair inclined to curl; but it can be made straight. Has a decayed spot on a front tooth. She can read and write, and in all probability will try to get to the Free States. All persons are forbidden, under penalty of the law, to harbor or employ said slave. $150 will be given to whoever takes her in the state, and $300 if taken out of the state and delivered to me, or lodged in jail.

Dr. Flint

---
4. **tidings** *n. pl.:* news.
5. **harboring** *v.* used as *n.:* providing protection or shelter.
6. **subscriber** *n.:* literally, the person whose name is "written below"; that is, Dr. Flint.
7. **mulatto** *adj.:* of mixed black and white ancestry.

Vocabulary

provocation (präv'ə·kā'shən) *n.:* something that stirs up action or feeling.

distressed (di·strest') *adj.:* suffering; troubled.

Harriet A. Jacobs **409**

Harriet A. Jacobs **409**

A Content-Area Connections

History: Patrick Henry
The sentence "Give me liberty or give me death" was originally spoken by the American statesman Patrick Henry. Henry was urging the Virginia militia to mobilize and fight the English forces shortly before the Revolutionary War.

B Reading Skills

❓ **Comparing points of view across texts.** What main idea does Jacobs express in these sentences? State it in your own words. [Possible response: Enslaved people are forced to use cunning because it is the only weapon they have with which to defend themselves against slaveholders.] Would Douglass agree? Why or why not? [Possible response: No; he believes that physical resistance can be used as a weapon as well.]

C Literary Focus

❓ **Conflict.** Describe Jacobs's internal conflict. [She yearned to go to her children but knew that their eventual freedom depended upon her escape.]

D English-Language Learners

Dialect. Be sure students understand these last few lines of dialect, which contain one of the narrative's main themes—that freedom is worth great sacrifices.

Jacobs (Linda) passed a terrifying week in hiding. Then one night she heard her pursuers nearby. Afraid of capture, she rushed out of her friend's house and concealed herself in a thicket, where she was bitten by a poisonous reptile. Determined not to give up, Jacobs adopted the motto "Give me liberty, or give me death." With the aid of her friend Betty, she found shelter with the sympathetic wife of a local slaveholder. The woman urged Jacobs never to reveal who had helped her, and she hid the fugitive in a small upstairs storeroom.

Months of Peril

I went to sleep that night with the feeling that I was for the present the most fortunate slave in town. Morning came and filled my little cell with light. I thanked the heavenly Father for this safe retreat. Opposite my window was a pile of feather beds. On the top of these I could lie perfectly concealed, and command a view of the street through which Dr. Flint passed to his office. Anxious as I was, I felt a gleam of satisfaction when I saw him. Thus far I had outwitted him, and I triumphed over it. Who can blame slaves for being cunning? They are constantly compelled to resort to it. It is the only weapon of the weak and oppressed against the strength of their tyrants.

I was daily hoping to hear that my master had sold my children; for I knew who was on the watch to buy them. But Dr. Flint cared even more for revenge than he did for money. My brother William, and the good aunt who had served in his family twenty years, and my little Benny, and Ellen, who was a little over two years old, were thrust into jail, as a means of compelling my relatives to give some information about me. He swore my grandmother should never see one of them again till I was brought back. They kept these facts from me for several days. When I heard that my little ones were in a loathsome jail, my first impulse was to go to them. I was encountering dangers for the sake of freeing them, and must I be the cause of their death? The thought was agonizing. My benefac-

tress[8] tried to soothe me by telling me that my aunt would take good care of the children while they remained in jail. But it added to my pain to think that the good old aunt, who had always been so kind to her sister's orphan children, should be shut up in prison for no other crime than loving them. I suppose my friends feared a reckless movement on my part, knowing, as they did, that my life was bound up in my children. I received a note from my brother William. It was scarcely legible, and ran thus: "Wherever you are, dear sister, I beg of you not to come here. We are all much better off than you are. If you come, you will ruin us all. They would force you to tell where you had been, or they would kill you. Take the advice of your friends; if not for the sake of me and your children, at least for the sake of those you would ruin."

Poor William! He also must suffer for being my brother. I took his advice and kept quiet. My aunt was taken out of jail at the end of a month, because Mrs. Flint could not spare her any longer. She was tired of being her own housekeeper. It was quite too fatiguing to order her dinner and eat it too. My children remained in jail, where brother William did all he could for their comfort. Betty went to see them sometimes, and brought me tidings. She was not permitted to enter the jail; but William would hold them up to the grated window while she chatted with them. When she repeated their prattle,[9] and told me how they wanted to see their ma, my tears would flow. Old Betty would exclaim, "Lors, chile! what's you crying 'bout? Dem young uns vil kill you dead. Don't be so chick'n-hearted! If you does, you vil nebber git thro' dis world." ∎

---

8. **benefactress** *n.:* woman who gives aid.
9. **prattle** *n.:* chatter; babble.

Vocabulary
cunning (kun'iŋ) *adj.:* sly or crafty.
compelled (kəm·peld') *v.:* driven; forced.
impulse (im'puls') *n.:* sudden desire or urge.

Conducting a Historical Investigation

Have students use library or Internet resources to find another slave narrative. Tell them to read a portion of it and write a short essay comparing and contrasting it with Jacobs's.

Response and Analysis

Reading Check

1. Why did Jacobs finally decide to escape?

2. What did Jacobs ask Sally to do for her at dawn?

3. What did Jacobs's grandmother tell Dr. Flint about the escape?

4. What did Dr. Flint assume Jacobs would try to do?

5. What advice did Jacobs receive from her brother William?

Thinking Critically

6. How would you describe Jacobs's **character**? Find details in the text that reveal her character traits.

7. Describe how Jacobs resolved one of her **internal conflicts.** How did her decision affect the **external conflict** she faced?

8. Cite specific passages in Jacobs's narrative that illustrate the religious influences that affected Jacobs and her decisions.

Extending and Evaluating

9. Explain Jacobs's **purpose** in writing and publishing her story. Judging from this excerpt, do you think she achieved her purpose? Why or why not?

10. Jacobs's writing has been criticized as resembling too much the melodramatic novels popular in her time. Do you think her story rings true, or do you find parts of it sentimental? How might you change the language or alter her word choice to update the selection?

Literary Criticism

11. **Political approach.** Frederick Douglass (page 397) and Harriet Jacobs narrate two different episodes of slave life. Compare and contrast their situations, their actions, their emotions, and their opinions. How do their attitudes and views contribute to their credibility? In other words, what do they believe, and do you believe them?

WRITING

Across the Lines

Imagine that Jacobs escaped to the North and sent a written message back to one of the characters in the excerpt—Sally, Betty, her grandmother, the woman who hid her in the storeroom, or Dr. Flint. Write the **message,** explaining Jacobs's motivations, expressing her feelings, and describing her plans and hopes for the future.

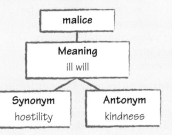

Vocabulary Development
Mapping Meanings

Create a word map like the one below for each of the remaining Vocabulary words. (Not all words will have an antonym.)

malice   provocation   compelled
fervently   distressed   impulse
unnerve   cunning

SKILLS FOCUS

Literary Skills
Analyze political points of view on a topic. Analyze internal and external conflict.

Writing Skills
Write a message or letter from the point of view of a character.

Vocabulary Skills
Create semantic maps with synonyms and antonyms.

Harriet A. Jacobs   411

Response and Analysis

7. Internal conflicts include Jacobs's competing desires to free her children and to avoid causing them pain and her desire to go to her imprisoned children and her awareness that she must remain in hiding. In both cases, Jacobs resolved the conflict by choosing what she saw as the greater good—freedom. Her choices exacerbated her external conflict with Flint.

8. Passages include "I prayed that God would not forsake me in this hour of utmost need!" and "I . . . breathed a short prayer to God for guidance and protection".

Extending and Evaluating

9. Jacobs's purpose was to reveal the trials enslaved females suffered. Students' opinions about her success will vary.

10. Some students may find certain passages sentimental. Students should discuss what changes in language would update the selection.

Literary Criticism

11. Students should observe that both felt justified in taking action against slaveholders. Jacobs relied on her cunning to escape, while Douglass relied on his physical strength. Most students will feel that both writers' narratives are heartfelt and believable.

Vocabulary Development

Use a thesaurus or a dictionary of synonyms and antonyms to check students' word maps.

Assessment

■ *Holt Assessment: Literature, Reading, and Vocabulary*

Reading Check

1. She decided to escape because her children were about to be given over to the Flints.

2. Jacobs asked Sally to move her clothes into Sally's trunk.

3. She told Dr. Flint that she knew nothing about the escape.

4. He assumed that she would try to escape to the North.

5. William advised Jacobs to remain in hiding rather than come out to see her children.

Thinking Critically

6. Possible answer: Jacobs is generous, loving, determined, and courageous. The details students choose should illustrate the traits they have named.

Connected Reading

Summary ⬌ *at grade level*

In this portion of *My Bondage and My Freedom*, Douglass reflects on the songs sung by people held in slavery. The songs fill him with sadness for the slaves' suffering and hatred for the dehumanizing institution of slavery.

Selection Starter

Build background. Tell students that *My Bondage and My Freedom* was the second of three autobiographies Frederick Douglass published during his lifetime. In *My Bondage and My Freedom,* Douglass expanded on his first autobiography, *Narrative of the Life of Frederick Douglass* (1845). By the time the book appeared, in 1855, Douglass had moved to the forefront of the abolitionist movement in the United States and had become deeply involved in the Underground Railroad.

Connected Readings

Slavery

Frederick Douglass . . . . *from* **My Bondage and My Freedom**
Spirituals . . . . **Go Down, Moses/Follow the Drinking Gourd/ Swing Low, Sweet Chariot**
Commonwealth and
Freeman's Record . . . . **The Most Remarkable Woman of This Age**

You have just read selections from the autobiographies of Frederick Douglass and Harriet A. Jacobs describing their experiences of slavery. The next three selections you will be reading—another piece by Douglass, some spirituals, and an article about Harriet Tubman—present other views on slavery. As you read, ask yourself how the experiences and views expressed in the selections are alike and how they are different. At the end, on page 421, you'll find questions asking you to compare all five selections in this Political Points of View feature on slavery.

Political Points *of* View
Before You Read

In this excerpt from *My Bondage and My Freedom,* Frederick Douglass writes eloquently about the songs of slavery—compositions later called sorrow songs by the African American writer W.E.B. DuBois. In his 1903 book *The Souls of Black Folk,* DuBois made the following comments about sorrow songs:

> 66 Through all the sorrow of the Sorrow Songs there breathes a hope—a faith in the ultimate justice of things. The minor cadences of despair change often to triumph and calm confidence. Sometimes it is faith in life, sometimes a faith in death, sometimes assurance of boundless justice in some fair world beyond. But whichever it is, the meaning is always clear: that sometime, somewhere, men will judge men by their souls and not by their skins. 99

In the same way, when Frederick Douglass describes his intense responses to those "wild notes" in *My Bondage and My Freedom,* he demonstrates how a literary composition, born out of hard real-world experience, can ultimately have a political impact.

African American girl picking cotton on a Georgia plantation (1895).

412 Collection 4 The Rise of Realism: The Civil War to 1914

Literary Criticism

Critic's Commentary: Slave Songs
W.E.B. DuBois once described "sorrow songs" as "not simply . . . the sole American music, but as the most beautiful expression of human experience born on this side of the seas . . . the singular spiritual heritage of the nation and the greatest gift of the Negro people." Tell students that DuBois was born after the Civil War, was the first African

American to receive a doctorate from Harvard, and later taught history and economics at Atlanta University. **Individual activity.** Have students write a short essay comparing and contrasting Douglass's and DuBois's perspectives on the songs of the slaves. Encourage students to speculate on the historical and political forces that influenced each writer's thinking.

from My Bondage and My Freedom

Frederick Douglass

Slaves are generally expected to sing as well as to work. A silent slave is not liked by masters or overseers. *"Make a noise, make a noise,"* and *"bear a hand"* are the words usually addressed to the slaves when there is silence amongst them. This may account for the almost constant singing heard in the southern states. . . . On allowance day, those who visited the great house farm were peculiarly excited and noisy. While on their way, they would make the dense old woods, for miles around, reverberate with their wild notes. These were not always merry because they were wild. On the contrary, they were mostly of a plaintive[1] cast, and told a tale of grief and sorrow. In the most boisterous out-bursts of rapturous sentiment, there was ever a tinge of deep melancholy.[2] I have never heard any songs like those anywhere since I left slav-ery, except when in Ireland. There I heard the same *wailing notes,* and was much affected by them. It was during the famine of 1845–1846. In all the songs of the slaves, there was ever some expression in praise of the great house farm; something which would flatter the pride of the owner, and, possibly, draw a favorable glance from him.

. . . I cannot better express my sense of them now, than ten years ago, when, in sketching my life, I thus spoke of this feature of my plantation experience:

". . . The hearing of those wild notes always depressed my spirits, and filled my heart with ineffable[3] sadness. The mere recurrence, even now, afflicts my spirit, and while I am writing

Frederick Douglass (detail) (c. 1844), attributed to Elisha Hammond. Oil on canvas (27½" × 22½").

National Portrait Gallery, Smithsonian Institution. Courtesy Art Resource, New York.

these lines, my tears are falling. To those songs I trace my first glimmering conceptions of the dehumanizing character of slavery. I can never get rid of that conception. Those songs still fol-low me, to deepen my hatred of slavery, and quicken my sympathies for my brethren in bonds. If anyone wishes to be impressed with a sense of the soul-killing power of slavery, let him go to Colonel Lloyd's plantation, and, on allowance day, place himself in the deep, pine woods, and there let him, in silence, thought-fully analyze the sounds that shall pass through the chambers of his soul, and if he is not thus impressed, it will only be because 'there is no flesh in his obdurate[4] heart.'"

---

1. **plaintive** *adj.:* mournful; sad.
2. **melancholy** *n.:* sadness; gloom.
3. **ineffable** *adj.:* too great to be expressed; indescribable.

---

4. **obdurate** *adj.:* without sympathy; pitiless.

Frederick Douglass **413**

Comparing and Contrasting Texts

Analyzing Douglass's texts. Remind students that Douglass wrote this text about ten years after he wrote *Narrative of the Life of Frederick Douglass.* After students review both texts, have them work with a partner to com-pare and contrast the selections. In addition to identifying the similarities and differences between the texts, students should discuss the tone, theme, style, and purpose of each piece. Have students record their conclusions and report them to the class. Then, have the class discuss the question, "Which text makes a stronger case against slavery?"

DIRECT TEACHING

A **Political Issue**
? Slavery. Why do you think a "silent slave" made masters and overseers uncomfortable? [Possible responses: A noisy slave could be found easily; a silent slave might be lost in his or her own thoughts and possibly plotting an escape; silence sometimes signals antagonism.]

B **Content-Area Connections**
History: The Irish Potato Famine Under British rule, Irish farmers were forced to export their grain to England and eat potatoes instead. In 1845–1846, a blight wiped out the potato crop, and close to one mil-lion people died of starvation or famine-related diseases.

C **Political Issue**
? Slavery. Why might Douglass have first felt the "dehumanizing" character of slavery through these songs? [Possible responses: The songs reflected the deep sorrow of enslaved people; they often flattered the slaveholder; they were "wild" and "wailing."]

D **Advanced Learners**
? Acceleration. In the discipline of rhetoric, an emotional appeal like this one is known as pathos. (The word *pathos* means "suffering" in Greek.) Writers use pathos to appeal to readers' emotions and their imaginations. Why do you think Douglass uses such an appeal here? [Possible response: He wants to evoke in his readers the deep emotions he feels; he wants his readers to imagine the scenario he has described; he wants to end the passage on an emotional note.]

Summary ⟷ *at grade level*

In the midst of a heated Civil War battle, Private Fred Collins decides to risk death to get some water. Egged on by his comrades, he sets out across a meadow under bombardment, fills an old bucket at a well, and, with shells landing all about, heads back to his company's position. On the way back, he passes a dying officer, who asks him for a drink. Collins initially refuses but then turns back to give the officer some water. Upon his return, two lieutenants playfully grab the bucket and accidentally overturn it, spilling the water on the ground.

Selection Starter

Motivate. One reason Crane's war stories were popular was that they were told from a common soldier's point of view. Earlier fiction dealing with war had focused largely on the exploits of officers, who tended to be well educated, wealthy, and aristocratic. Ask students who they would rather hear narrate a war story—a general, an officer in the field, a common soldier, or a war correspondent. Discuss with them the differences in point of view you would expect from these narrators.

Before You Read

A Mystery of Heroism

Political Points *of* View

Quickwrite ✏️

Imagine this scene: In the midst of the frightful noise and bloody destruction of a Civil War battlefield, a soldier suddenly decides to jump up and run straight into the enemy line to get something. To his fellow soldiers it is an impulse that seems simply crazy, but could he be a hero?

The above scene is the one Crane describes in this story. Although he never experienced the war himself, Crane had read firsthand accounts of the mayhem of Civil War battlefields, where often one soldier would escape death and another would die by the merest chance. Dazed by battle, soldiers often struggled later to explain their actions.

Before you read, jot down your thoughts about what makes someone a hero during war. Then, as you read, think about Crane's view of heroism.

Literary Focus

Situational Irony

Situational irony occurs when what actually happens differs from what one expects will happen. For example, suppose a heroic soldier is wounded as he battles through war-torn terrain to rescue a fallen comrade—only to find out that the comrade is quite safe and never needed help. The irony of the situation shocks—or at least surprises—both the hero and the reader.

INTERNET

Vocabulary Practice
•
More About Stephen Crane

Keyword: LE5 11-4

SKILLS FOCUS

Literary Skills
Analyze political points of view on a topic. Understand situational irony.

> **Situational irony** takes place when there is a discrepancy between what is expected to happen and what actually happens.
>
> *For more on Irony, see the Handbook of Literary and Historical Terms.*

Background

In war the military chain of command makes it possible for an army to function. When reading stories about war, you can better understand not only the military action but also the relationships between soldiers by knowing the different military ranks. Here are the ranks mentioned in "A Mystery of Heroism," from highest to lowest:

Colonel
Lieutenant Colonel
Major
Captain
Lieutenant
Sergeant
Private

> **Vocabulary Development**
>
> **conflagration** (kän′flə·grā′shən) *n.*: huge fire.
>
> **stolidity** (stə·lid′ə·tē) *n.*: absence of emotional reactions.
>
> **ominous** (äm′ə·nəs) *adj.*: threatening; menacing.
>
> **gesticulating** (jes·tik′yoo·lāt′iŋ) *v.* used as *adj.*: gesturing, especially with the hands and arms.
>
> **provisional** (prə·vizh′ə·nəl) *adj.*: temporary; serving for the time being.
>
> **retraction** (ri·trak′shən) *n.*: withdrawal.
>
> **indolent** (in′də·lənt) *adj.*: lazy.
>
> **blanched** (blancht) *v.* used as *adj.*: drained of color.

Previewing Vocabulary

Have students read the words listed under Vocabulary Development on p. 434, along with their definitions. Next, have students work in pairs making flashcards, using all the Vocabulary words. Encourage students to use the cards to help one another learn the words and their meanings. Then, hold a class vocabulary bee: Read the words aloud, and have teams take turns giving definitions. Afterward, have students complete the following matching exercise.

1. blanched [d]
2. conflagration [c]
3. stolidity [h]
4. provisional [e]
5. retraction [b]
6. ominous [f]
7. gesticulating [a]
8. indolent [g]

a. gesturing
b. withdrawal
c. huge fire
d. drained of color
e. temporary
f. foreboding
g. lazy
h. lack of emotion

from My Bondage and My Freedom

Frederick Douglass

Slaves are generally expected to sing as well as to work. A silent slave is not liked by masters or overseers. *"Make a noise, make a noise,"* and *"bear a hand"* are the words usually addressed to the slaves when there is silence amongst them. This may account for the almost constant singing heard in the southern states. . . . On allowance day, those who visited the great house farm were peculiarly excited and noisy. While on their way, they would make the dense old woods, for miles around, reverberate with their wild notes. These were not always merry because they were wild. On the contrary, they were mostly of a plaintive[1] cast, and told a tale of grief and sorrow. In the most boisterous outbursts of rapturous sentiment, there was ever a tinge of deep melancholy.[2] I have never heard any songs like those anywhere since I left slavery, except when in Ireland. There I heard the same *wailing notes,* and was much affected by them. It was during the famine of 1845–1846. In all the songs of the slaves, there was ever some expression in praise of the great house farm; something which would flatter the pride of the owner, and, possibly, draw a favorable glance from him.

. . . I cannot better express my sense of them now, than ten years ago, when, in sketching my life, I thus spoke of this feature of my plantation experience:

". . . The hearing of those wild notes always depressed my spirits, and filled my heart with ineffable[3] sadness. The mere recurrence, even now, afflicts my spirit, and while I am writing

Frederick Douglass (detail) (c. 1844), attributed to Elisha Hammond. Oil on canvas (27½″ × 22½″).

National Portrait Gallery, Smithsonian Institution. Courtesy Art Resource, New York.

these lines, my tears are falling. To those songs I trace my first glimmering conceptions of the dehumanizing character of slavery. I can never get rid of that conception. Those songs still follow me, to deepen my hatred of slavery, and quicken my sympathies for my brethren in bonds. If anyone wishes to be impressed with a sense of the soul-killing power of slavery, let him go to Colonel Lloyd's plantation, and, on allowance day, place himself in the deep, pine woods, and there let him, in silence, thoughtfully analyze the sounds that shall pass through the chambers of his soul, and if he is not thus impressed, it will only be because 'there is no flesh in his obdurate[4] heart.'"

---

1. **plaintive** *adj.:* mournful; sad.
2. **melancholy** *n.:* sadness; gloom.
3. **ineffable** *adj.:* too great to be expressed; indescribable.

---

4. **obdurate** *adj.:* without sympathy; pitiless.

Frederick Douglass   **413**

Comparing and Contrasting Texts

Analyzing Douglass's texts. Remind students that Douglass wrote this text about ten years after he wrote *Narrative of the Life of Frederick Douglass.* After students review both texts, have them work with a partner to compare and contrast the selections. In addition to identifying the similarities and differences between the texts, students should discuss the tone, theme, style, and purpose of each piece. Have students record their conclusions and report them to the class. Then, have the class discuss the question, "Which text makes a stronger case against slavery?"

Connected Reading

Summary ⬇ *below grade level*

> These three spirituals use different images to express a single longing—for liberation.

Selection Starter

Build background. Remind students that many Africans encountered Christianity for the first time when they were brought to America as slaves. Some enslaved Africans viewed the religion as hypocritical: Although it espoused brotherly love, it was practiced by slaveholders who asserted ownership over, and frequently mistreated, fellow human beings. Still, many slaves were drawn to biblical stories about oppressed people like them. Spirituals often allude to biblical figures, places, and events, such as Moses and the Promised Land.

VIEWING THE ART

One important influence on **Winslow Homer** (1836–1910) was a trip he made to France, which exposed him to European art of his time. In the mid-1870s, Homer made a number of trips to Virginia, where he painted several pictures of African American workers. Although the subject of *The Cotton Pickers* is uniquely American, the painting resembles the work of the French artist Jean-François Millet in its sympathetic depiction of working people.

Activity. Ask students to explain how Homer uses the painting's composition to convey his sympathy with the workers. [Possible responses: The viewer looks up at the girls; the girls are at the front of the painting, with their heads above the horizon.]

The Cotton Pickers (1876) by Winslow Homer. Oil on canvas (61.0 cm x 97.1 cm).

Political Points *of* View

Before You Read

The moving and intensely emotional songs known as spirituals developed largely from the oral traditions of Africans held in slavery in the South before the Civil War. Spirituals, like other kinds of folk literature and music, were composed by anonymous artists and passed on orally. They often combine African melodies and rhythms with elements of white southern religious music.

Even though individuals probably composed the spirituals, the ideas and the language came from a common group of images and idioms. As the songs were passed from generation to generation by word of mouth, lines were changed and new stanzas were added, so that numerous versions of a particular spiritual might exist.

Spirituals were concerned above all with issues of freedom: spiritual freedom in the form of salvation and literal freedom from the shackles of slavery. The biblical Moses delivered the ancient Israelites from slavery in Egypt. Many people during the time of slavery were therefore called Moses by those longing for deliverance. Harriet Tubman, for example, used Moses as her code name with the Underground Railroad. A Methodist minister named Francis Asbury was also known as Moses, and according to some scholars, the spiritual "Go Down, Moses" is really a plea for Asbury's help.

Some of the songs were code songs, or signal songs—that is, songs with details that provided runaways with directions, times, and meeting places for their escapes. For example, in "Follow the Drinking Gourd," the drinking gourd refers literally to the shell of a vegetable related to the squash or melon, dried and hollowed out for drinking. Slaves, however, knew that the drinking gourd was also the Big Dipper, a group of stars. Two stars in the bowl of the Big Dipper point to the North Star—and the direction of freedom.

Go Down, Moses

Go down, Moses,
Way down in Egypt land
Tell old Pharaoh
To let my people go.

5   When Israel was in Egypt land
Let my people go
Oppressed so hard they could not stand
Let my people go.

Go down, Moses,
10   Way down in Egypt land
Tell old Pharaoh,
"Let my people go."

"Thus saith the Lord," bold Moses said,
"Let my people go;
15   If not I'll smite your firstborn dead
Let my people go."

Go down, Moses,
Way down in Egypt land,
Tell old Pharaoh,
20   "Let my people go!"

Follow the Drinking Gourd

When the sun comes back and the first
   quail calls,
   Follow the drinking gourd,
For the old man is a-waiting for to carry
   you to freedom
   If you follow the drinking gourd.

[Refrain]

5   Follow the drinking gourd,
   Follow the drinking gourd,
For the old man is a-waiting for to carry
   you to freedom
   If you follow the drinking gourd.

The river bank will make a very good road,
10   The dead trees show you the way,
Left foot, peg foot traveling on
   Follow the drinking gourd.

[Refrain]

The river ends between two hills,
   Follow the drinking gourd.
15   There's another river on the other side,
   Following the drinking gourd.

[Refrain]

Where the little river meets the great big
   river,
   Follow the drinking gourd.
The old man is a-waiting for to carry you
   to freedom,
20   If you follow the drinking gourd.

[Refrain]

Spirituals   **415**

CONTENT-AREA CONNECTIONS

Humanities: The Story of Moses

The events described in "Go Down, Moses" come from Exodus 3–12. Moses asks the pharaoh (probably Ramses II) to allow the Israelites to leave Egypt. The pharaoh refuses, whereupon Moses's staff turns into a serpent, the waters of the Nile River flow blood-red, and Egypt is afflicted with plagues of frogs, gnats, and flies. Next, an epidemic decimates the Egyptians' flocks, and people and animals become festered with boils. Fierce lightning and hail, locusts, and daytime darkness follow. Finally, after the firstborn sons of the Egyptians, including his own, are struck dead, the pharaoh agrees to free the Israelites.

Music: Spirituals

Paired activity. Play several recordings of spirituals to acquaint students with their tones and cadences. Then, pair students who enjoy music with those who enjoy creative writing, and have them compose their own spiritual. Invite pairs to perform their song, to record it and play it for the class, or to display their lyrics and musical arrangements in the classroom.

A Literary Focus

❓ **Symbolism.** What might the chariot represent in religious terms? [Possible responses: death; a hearse; God; Jesus.] **What might "home" be?** [heaven] **As a symbol of a transport toward freedom, what might the chariot signify?** [Possible responses: the Underground Railroad; any means of escape; a leader such as Harriet Tubman.] **What might "home" signify?** [Possible responses: the North; freedom.]

B English-Language Learners

Interpreting idioms. Explain that "coming after me" means "coming to get me," not "behind me."

C Literary Focus

❓ **Refrain.** What is the refrain of this song? ["Coming for to carry me home"] **How might this refrain have affected slaves who sang the song?** [Possible response: They may have found it comforting or inspiring.]

Swing Low, Sweet Chariot

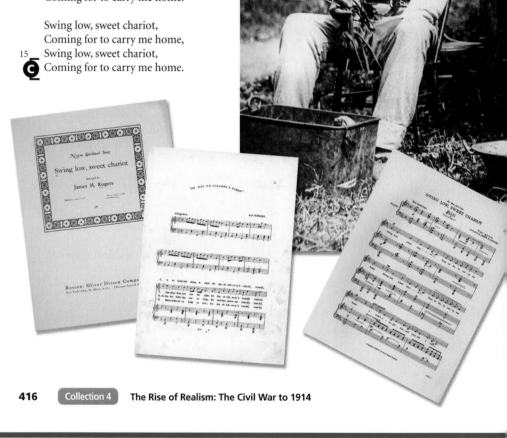

A Swing low, sweet chariot,
Coming for to carry me home,
Swing low, sweet chariot,
Coming for to carry me home.

5 I looked over Jordan and what did I see
Coming for to carry me home,
B A band of angels, coming after me,
Coming for to carry me home.

If you get there before I do,
10 Coming for to carry me home,
Tell all my friends I'm coming too,
Coming for to carry me home.

Swing low, sweet chariot,
Coming for to carry me home,
15 Swing low, sweet chariot,
C Coming for to carry me home.

416 Collection 4 The Rise of Realism: The Civil War to 1914

CONTENT-AREA CONNECTIONS

History: Coded Quilts

Because it was illegal to teach enslaved people to read and write, many were illiterate. Enslaved people and abolitionists used songs, stories, and even quilts to send signals to one another along the Underground Railroad. Often fugitives traveling on the railroad would look for quilts displayed outside the homes of railroad supporters. The patterns on the quilts told the fugitives whether they had reached a safe stopping point. Common patterns included stars (signifying the North Star), arrows (pointing along the direction of the route), and zigzag lines, which mimicked the staggered arrangement of safehouses.

Music: Lyrics

Whole-class activity. Have students listen to the spirituals included in the *Audio CD Library,* or play other recordings of these spirituals. Ask students to think about the effect the songs might have had on the people who heard them. Have them note any differences between the lyrics in the recordings they hear and the lyrics in their textbooks. Then, have students discuss whether the attitude conveyed by the spirituals is one of hope or despair.

These people were formerly held in slavery.

Harriet Tubman (c. 1860s).

Political Points *of* View

Before You Read

The most famous "conductor" on the Underground Railroad, a secret system organized to help fugitive slaves escape to free states, was Harriet Tubman, herself an escaped slave. Tubman, who went by the code name Moses, made nineteen dangerous journeys back into slave territory, rescuing more than three hundred people from bondage in the 1850s. When the Civil War broke out, she not only tended to wounded soldiers but also served as a scout and a spy, once leading more than 750 people to safety. She was never captured.

The following selection, which is based on interviews with Tubman, appeared in regional newspapers in 1863 and 1865.

Harriet Tubman   417

Connected Reading

Summary ⬌ *at grade level*

In this selection from interviews in two regional newspapers, we learn about the years when Harriet Tubman was held in slavery and her later years as a courageous leader.

Selection Starter

Build background. The Underground Railroad was neither underground nor a railroad, but it did resemble a railroad in certain ways: It moved its passengers rapidly and anonymously from point to point; stopping points were called stations; the people who brought the passengers from one station to the next were called conductors. Although the Underground Railroad was an informal operation, it helped thousands of people escape from the South to the North between 1830 and 1860. After 1850, when Congress passed the Fugitive Slave Act, the Underground Railroad led thousands of fugitives across the border into Canada.

DIRECT TEACHING

Ⓐ Content-Area Connections

Math: Reward Sum
The $40,000 reward posted for the capture of Harriet Tubman would be worth almost $864,800 today.

Ⓑ Content-Area Connections

History: The New England Freedmen's Aid Society
The New England Freedmen's Aid Society was one of many associations formed in the 1860s to assist people fleeing slavery and freedmen seeking refuge in the North. The general aim of the Freedmen's Aid movement was first to supply basic necessities, such as clothing and shelter, and later to educate people who had been enslaved and help them find work.

Ⓒ Content-Area Connections

Humanities: Moses
Remind students that according to the Bible, Moses led the enslaved Israelites out of Egypt and to the Promised Land of Canaan (later called Palestine).

NEWSPAPER ARTICLE

INFORMATIONAL TEXT

The Most Remarkable Woman of This Age

from *Commonwealth*, July 17, 1863, and *Freeman's Record*, March 1865

Magee house (c. 1855) in Canesto, New York, a safe house on the Underground Railroad.

Ⓐ Harriet Tubman, the famous fugitive slave from Maryland, risks her life sneaking into slave territory to free slaves. Slaveholders posted a forty thousand dollar reward for the capture of the "Black Moses."

Ⓑ One of the teachers lately commissioned by the New England Freedmen's Aid Society is probably the most remarkable woman of this age. That is to say, she has performed more wonderful deeds by the native power of her own spirit against adverse circumstances than any other. She is well known to many by the various names which her eventful life has given her, Harriet Garrison, Gen. Tubman, and so on, but among the slaves Ⓒ she is universally known by her well-earned title of Moses— Moses the deliverer. She is a rare instance, in the midst of high civilization and intellectual culture, of a being of great native powers, working powerfully, and to beneficent[1] ends, entirely untaught by schools or books.

Her maiden name was Araminta Ross.[2] She is the granddaughter of a native African, and has not a drop of white blood in her veins. She

1. **beneficent** (bə·nef'ə·sənt) *adj.*: showing kindness or charity.
2. **Araminta Ross** (1820?–1913): Tubman was also known as Araminta Greene; she was the daughter of Benjamin Ross and Harriet Greene.

DIFFERENTIATING INSTRUCTION

Learners Having Difficulty
Have students work in groups of four to analyze the description of the young Harriet Tubman in paragraphs 3–6. Tell students that each group member should read one paragraph aloud. Group members should then generate a list of adjectives that describe Tubman's words or actions in that paragraph.

Afterward, ask students to decide on the three or four most important characteristics for a conductor on the Underground Railroad to have. Then, challenge them to explain why these characteristics would be so important.

was born in 1820 or 1821, on the Eastern Shore of Maryland. Her parents were slaves, but married and faithful to each other, and the family affection is very strong. . . .

She seldom lived with her owner, but was usually "hired out" to different persons. She once "hired her time," and employed it in the rudest farming labors, ploughing, carting, driving the oxen, and so on, to so good advantage that she was able in one year to buy a pair of steers worth forty dollars.

When quite young, she lived with a very pious mistress; but the slaveholder's religion did not prevent her from whipping the young girl for every slight or fancied fault. Araminta found that this was usually a morning exercise; so she prepared for it by putting on all the thick clothes she could procure to protect her skin. She made sufficient outcry, however, to convince her mistress that her blows had full effect; and in the afternoon she would take off her wrappings, and dress as well as she could. When invited into family prayers, she preferred to stay on the landing, and pray for herself. "And I prayed to God," she says, "to make me strong and able to fight and that's what I've allers prayed for ever since."

In her youth she received a severe blow on her head from a heavy weight thrown by her master at another slave, but which accidentally hit her. The blow produced a disease of the brain which was severe for a long time, and still makes her very lethargic.[3] . . . She was married about 1844 to a free colored man named John Tubman, but never had any children. Owing to changes in her owner's family, it was determined to sell her and some other slaves; but her health was so much injured that a purchaser was not easily found. At length she became convinced that she would soon be carried away, and she decided to escape. Her brothers did not agree with her plans, and she walked off alone, following the guidance of the brooks, which she had observed to run North. . . .

She remained two years in Philadelphia working hard and carefully hoarding her money. Then she hired a room, furnished it as well as she could, bought a nice suit of men's clothes, and went back to Maryland for her husband. But the faithless man had taken to himself another wife. Harriet did not dare venture into her presence, but sent word to her husband where she was. He declined joining her. At first her grief and anger were excessive. . . . But finally she thought . . . "if he could do without her, she could without him," and so "he dropped out of her heart," and she determined to give her life to brave deeds. Thus all personal aims died out of her heart; and with her simple brave motto, "I can't die but once," she began the work which has made her Moses—the deliverer of her people. Seven or eight times she has returned to the neighborhood of her former home, always at the risk of death in the most terrible forms, and each time has brought away a company of fugitive slaves, and led them safely to the free States, or to Canada. Every time she went, the dangers increased. In 1857, she brought away her old parents, and, as they were too feeble to walk, she was obliged to hire a wagon, which added greatly to the perils of the journey. In 1860, she went for the last time, and among her troop was an infant whom they were obliged to keep stupefied with laudanum[4] to prevent its outcries. This was at the period of great excitement, and Moses was not safe even in New York State; but her anxious friends insisted upon her

---

3. **lethargic** *adj.*: abnormally drowsy; sluggish.

4. **laudanum** *n.*: solution of opium in alcohol.

Harriet Tubman   **419**

DIRECT TEACHING

D Reading Skills

? Analyzing tone. How would you describe the tone of this comment about the slaveholder's religion? [Possible responses: ironic; sarcastic; wry; critical.]

E Reading Skills

? Analyzing motives. Is Tubman's motive rooted in hope or in despair? [Possible responses: Tubman's motive is rooted in despair— she seems to no longer value her own life; Tubman's motive is rooted in hope—she has transcended her personal desires to devote herself to a larger cause.]

Primary Source

Tubman on Freedom
When Tubman crossed the Pennsylvania border at the end of her own ninety-mile journey to freedom, she later said, "I looked at my hands to see if I was the same person now I was free. There was such a glory over everything, the sun came like gold through the trees, and over the fields, and I felt like I was in heaven."

A Content-Area Connections

Philosophy: Utilitarianism
Tubman's thinking reflects a theory of morality that developed during the late 1700s and early 1800s. The theory, known as utilitarianism, held that an act is moral if it yields the greatest good for the greatest number of people. Utilitarianism stands in opposition to absolute codes of behavior, such as the Ten Commandments, which, for example, state that killing a person is always wrong.

B Content-Area Connections

Philosophy: Transcendentalism
The authors of this article may have wanted to link Tubman to a philosophical movement known as Transcendentalism, which flourished in the United States during the mid-1800s. Transcendentalist thinkers, such as Thoreau and Emerson, believed that truth resides in all human beings and that people can find this truth by looking within rather than to external authorities, such as church and state. They also believed that each individual could achieve transcendence—a mystical state of connection with the universe—through meditation or immersion in nature, work, or art.

---

taking refuge in Canada. So various and interesting are the incidents of the journeys, that we know not how to select from them. She has shown in them all the characteristics of a great leader: courage, foresight, prudence, self-control, ingenuity, subtle perception, command over others' minds. . . .

She always came in the winter when the nights are long and dark, and people who have homes stay in them. She was never seen on the plantation herself, but appointed a rendezvous[5] for her company eight or ten miles distant, so that if they were discovered at the first start she was not compromised.[6] She started on Saturday night; the slaves at that time being allowed to go away from home to visit their friends—so that they would not be missed until Monday morning. Even then they were supposed to have loitered on the way, and it would often be late on Monday afternoon before the flight would be certainly known. If by any further delay the advertisement was not sent out before Tuesday morning, she felt secure of keeping ahead of it; but if it were, it required all her ingenu-

5. **rendezvous** (rän′dā·vōo′) *n.:* meeting place.
6. **compromised** *v.:* laid open to danger.

ity to escape. She resorted to various devices; she had confidential friends all along the road. She would hire a man to follow the one who put up the notices, and take them down as soon as his back was turned. She crossed creeks on railroad bridges by night; she hid her company in the woods while she herself, not being advertised, went into the towns in search of information. . . .

The expedition was governed by the strictest rules. If any man gave out, he must be shot. "Would you really do that?" she was asked. "Yes," she replied, "if he was weak enough to give out, he'd be weak enough to betray us all, and all who had helped us; and do you think I'd let so many die just for one coward man." "Did you ever have to shoot anyone?" she was asked. "One time," she said, "a man gave out the second night. His feet were sore and swollen; he couldn't go any further. He'd rather go back and die, if he must." They tried all arguments in vain, bathed his feet, tried to strengthen him; but it was of no use, he would go back. Then she said, "I told the boys to get their guns ready, and shoot him. They'd have done it in a minute; but when he heard that, he jumped right up and went on as well as anybody."

When going on these jour-

Graue Mill in Oak Brook, Illinois, a stop on the Underground Railroad.

neys, she often lay alone in the forests all night. Her whole soul was filled with awe of the mysterious Unseen Presence, which thrilled her with such depths of emotion that all other care and fear vanished. Then she seemed to speak with her Maker "as a man talketh with his friend"; her childlike petitions had direct answers, and beautiful visions lifted her up above all doubt and anxiety into serene trust and faith. No man can be a hero without this faith in some form; the sense that he walks not in his own strength, but leaning on an almighty arm. Call it fate, destiny, what you will, Moses of old, Moses of today, believed it to be Almighty God.

DIFFERENTIATING INSTRUCTION

Advanced Learners
Enrichment. Have students analyze the newspaper article to identify the authors' biases. First, pose the following questions:

• What do the authors believe about Tubman? about slavery? about God?

• What evidence in the article supports your conclusions?

Then, have students write a hypothetical profile of the authors of the article. Where did they live? To what groups might they have belonged? What political and philosophical assumptions did they hold? Invite students to read their profiles aloud.

Analyzing **Political Points** *of* **View**

Slavery

The questions on this page ask you to analyze the views on slavery reflected in the following five selections:

Frederick Douglass .... *from* **Narrative of the Life of Frederick Douglass**

Harriet A. Jacobs ...... *from* **Incidents in the Life of a Slave Girl**

Frederick Douglass .... *from* **My Bondage and My Freedom**

Spirituals .... **Go Down, Moses / Follow the Drinking Gourd / Swing Low, Sweet Chariot**

Commonwealth and
Freeman's Record ...... **The Most Remarkable Woman of This Age**

Comparing Political Assumptions

1. What assumptions about slavery did you infer from the narratives of Frederick Douglass and Harriet Jacobs?

2. Compare the forms of resistance to slavery that each of these readings describes. Which form of resistance do you think was the most effective? Explain your opinion.

3. Consider the readings in this Political Points of View feature and the genre in which each is written. What qualities do the autobiographies have that make them different from the newspaper article and the spirituals? In which readings do you find the political message the most clear and powerful? Explain.

4. Do you think that reading and discussing these historical narratives and spirituals can have an effect on a contemporary understanding of slavery? Why or why not?

WRITING

Historical Research

Write a one- or two-page **research report** about one aspect of slavery exposed in these readings. You might consider, for example, the treatment of slave children, fugitive slave laws, or the Underground Railroad. A vast amount of material has been written about slavery, so remember that it is essential to limit your topic.

▶ **Use "Reporting Historical Research," pages 528–547, for help with this assignment.**

CAUTION!!
COLORED PEOPLE
OF BOSTON, ONE & ALL,
You are hereby respectfully **CAUTIONED** and advised, to avoid conversing with the
Watchmen and Police Officers of Boston,
For since the recent **ORDER OF THE MAYOR & ALDERMEN,** they are empowered to act as
KIDNAPPERS
AND
Slave Catchers,
And they have already been actually employed in **KIDNAPPING, CATCHING, AND KEEPING SLAVES.** Therefore, if you value your **LIBERTY,** and the *Welfare of the Fugitives* among you, **Shun** them in every possible manner, as so many *HOUNDS* on the track of the most unfortunate of your race.
Keep a **Sharp Look Out** for **KIDNAPPERS,** and have **TOP EYE** open.
APRIL 24, 1851.

SKILLS FOCUS

Placard issued by the Vigilance Committee of Boston in 1851.

Pages 396–421 cover
Literary Skills
Analyze and compare political points of view on a topic.

Reading Skills
Compare points of view across texts.

Writing Skills
Write a historical research report.

Political Points of View: Slavery　　**421**

Grade-Level Skills

■ **Reading Skills**
Analyze a sequence of events.

Review Skills

■ **Literary Skills**
Analyze the way voice, tone, and choice of narrator affect characterization and the plot.

More About the Writer

Background. Bierce was fascinated with the psychology of war. His obsession grew out of his own traumatic Civil War experiences. Once a Confederate sentinel shot at him unexpectedly in the dark of night. He later recalled being "cut off from my comrades, groping about an unknown country, surrounded by invisible perils . . . the flash and shock of that firearm were unspeakably dreadful!" A similar sense of terror and disorientation is evident in "An Occurrence at Owl Creek Bridge."

VIEWING THE ART

In this portrait of Ambrose Bierce, the artist **J.H.E. Partington** (1843–1899) captures Bierce's fascination with death and with human anatomy.

Activity. Before students read "An Occurrence at Owl Creek Bridge," ask them what they can infer about Bierce's character from his posture and facial expression and from the prop depicted in this portrait. [Possible response: Bierce's expression and posture suggest a man who is casual in manner but intellectually serious. The skull suggests a fear of or fascination with death.]

Ambrose Bierce
(1842–1914?)

Ambrose Bierce by J.H.E. Partington (1843–1899). Oil on canvas.

The Huntington Library, Art Collections, and Botanical Gardens, San Marino, California/SuperStock.

Ambrose Bierce infused his writing with an attitude of scorn for all the sentimental illusions human beings cling to. His dark vision of life centers on warfare and the cruel joke it plays on humanity. This bleak vision assures Bierce's place in our literary history.

Bierce was born in 1842, the tenth of thirteen children in the family of an eccentric and unsuccessful farmer named Marcus Aurelius Bierce. The Bierces lived in a log cabin in Meigs County, Ohio. Bierce was educated primarily through exploring his father's small library.

At nineteen, Bierce joined the Ninth Indiana Volunteers and saw action at the bloody Civil War battles of Shiloh and Chickamauga. He was also part of General Sherman's march to the sea in 1864. Bierce was once severely wounded and was cited for bravery no fewer than fifteen times.

At the war's end, Bierce reenlisted, but several years in the peacetime army left him discouraged about his prospects. He left the army and joined his brother Albert to work at the United States Mint in San Francisco.

He began to contribute caustically witty short pieces to the city's weeklies.

A growing reputation as a muckraking reporter brought Bierce the editorship of the San Francisco *News Letter* and the acquaintance of the literary community, including Mark Twain (page 457). When the financier Collis P. Huntington, head of the Southern Pacific Railroad, asked Bierce's price for silence on the railroad's tax fraud case, Bierce is said to have replied, "My price is about seventy-five million dollars, to be handed to the treasurer of the United States." Bierce's disillusionment with the deceit and greed of his times continued to spur his pen and earned him the nickname "Bitter Bierce."

Bierce married in 1871 and moved to England, where he spent the next four years editing and contributing to humor magazines and making his first attempts at fiction. On his return to San Francisco in 1876, he wrote a regular column. This was the most active and fruitful time of Bierce's life. He became the witty scholar and literary dictator of the West Coast, but he never achieved wide recognition for his stories.

The Devil's Dictionary, first published in 1906 as *The Cynic's Word Book,* was more successful. In his dictionary, Bierce offered a collection of definitions filled with irony and sardonic humor. He defined war as a "byproduct of the arts of peace," and peace as "a period of cheating between two periods of fighting." A cynic was a person who "sees things as they are, not as they ought to be. Hence the custom among the Scythians of plucking out a cynic's eyes to improve his vision."

In 1913, when Bierce was lonely and weary of his life, he asked his few friends to "forgive him in not perishing where he was." He set off for Mexico to report on or join in its revolution. "Goodbye," he wrote. "If you hear of my being stood up against a Mexican stone wall and shot to rags please know that I think it a pretty good way to depart this life. It beats old age, disease, or falling down the cellar stairs." No further word was ever heard from him.

RESOURCES: READING

Planning

■ *One-Stop Planner* CD-ROM with ExamView Test Generator

Differentiating Instruction

■ *Supporting Instruction in Spanish*

■ *Audio CD Library, Selections and Summaries in Spanish*

Vocabulary

■ *Vocabulary Development*

Assessment

■ *Holt Assessment: Literature, Reading, and Vocabulary*

■ *One-Stop Planner* CD-ROM with ExamView Test Generator

■ *Holt Online Assessment*

Before You Read

An Occurrence at Owl Creek Bridge

Make the Connection

Can we ever really understand the complexities of the human mind? What's real? What's imaginary? When someone we love is late or missing, we can conjure up the details of disaster in a few seconds and make ourselves sick with worry. Imagine, then, the extremes to which the human imagination might go if a person were threatened with imminent death. What thoughts might pass through his or her mind?

Literary Focus
Point of View

In the different sections of Bierce's story, watch for these variations in **point of view:** (1) **omniscient,** in which the narrator seems to know everything about all the characters or events; (2) **objective,** in which the narrator reports without comment, much as a camera would record a scene; and (3) **third-person-limited,** in which the narrator zooms in on the thoughts and feelings of a single character.

> **Point of view** is the vantage point from which a writer tells a story.
>
> *For more on Point of View, see the Handbook of Literary and Historical Terms.*

Reading Skills
Analyzing Sequence of Events

As you read Bierce's story, make a list of the major events in the order in which they're presented in the story. After you've finished reading, put the events in chronological order on a time line, showing the order in which they actually happened. Think about why Bierce chose to relate the events of the story out of sequence.

Background

The belief that life will prove gratifying and will reward our virtues is so strong that it has become a main current in storytelling. This romantic notion, however, has its inevitable counterpart in realism and naturalism—fiction that conforms to the truth as it is experienced rather than as we would like it to be.

Bierce's no-punches-pulled story is set in the Deep South during the Civil War (1861–1865). The horrors of war serve as only an external setting for the landscape that *really* interests the writer. That landscape is the inside of the mind of a man condemned to death.

Vocabulary Development

sentinel (sent'n·əl) *n.:* guard; sentry.

deference (def'ər·əns) *n.:* respect.

perilous (per'ə·ləs) *adj.:* dangerous.

encompassed (en·kum'pəst) *v.* used as *adj.:* surrounded; enclosed.

oscillation (äs'ə·lā'shən) *n.:* regular back-and-forth movement.

pivotal (piv'ət·'l) *adj.:* central; acting as a point around which other things turn.

appalling (ə·pôl'iŋ) *adj.:* frightful.

gyration (jī·rā'shən) *n.:* circular movement; whirling.

abrasion (ə·brā'zhən) *n.:* scrape.

malign (mə·līn') *adj.:* harmful; evil.

INTERNET

Vocabulary Practice

Keyword: LE5 11-4

SKILLS FOCUS

Literary Skills
Understand point of view.

Reading Skills
Analyze a sequence of events.

Ambrose Bierce **423**

PRETEACHING

Summary *at grade level*

Bierce's psychological drama is set during the Civil War. The protagonist, Peyton Farquhar, is a wealthy Confederate planter who has been lured by a Union spy into attempting to sabotage a bridge in Union-held territory. As the story opens, he has been captured by Union forces and is about to be hanged from the bridge. Instead of immediately witnessing his death, however, we first step into Farquhar's perspective and accompany him on an incredible escape: The rope snaps; he falls into the river and, dodging bullets fired by the Union soldiers, runs into the woods and back to his plantation. At the end of this extended narrative, we learn that the escape was merely a fantasy that passes through Farquhar's mind during the last few moments of his life.

Selection Starter

Motivate. Ask students whether they have ever experienced the bending of time—that is, moments that seemed extraordinarily long or drawn out. Such moments are usually induced by feelings of anxiety. Ask students to tell about these experiences if they wish.

Previewing Vocabulary

Internet
- go.hrw.com (Keyword: LE5 11-4)
- *Elements of Literature Online*

Media
- *Audio CD Library*
- *Audio CD Library, Selections and Summaries in Spanish*

To reinforce students' understanding of the Vocabulary words on p. 423, have them work with partners on the following activities.

1. Use your hands to demonstrate the difference between <u>oscillation</u> and <u>gyration</u>.

2. Use <u>malign</u> and <u>sentinel</u> to describe the threat of an approaching army.

3. Explain how someone might receive an <u>abrasion</u>.

4. Draw a compass, and label its <u>pivotal</u> point.

5. Use <u>appalling</u> and <u>deference</u> to describe the behavior of people at a funeral.

6. Describe a <u>perilous</u> journey.

7. Draw a picture of land <u>encompassed</u> by water.

A **Reading Skills**

? **Making predictions.** After reading the title, what predictions can you make about this story? What does the word *occurrence* suggest? [Possible response: The title suggests that something will happen at the Owl Creek bridge—and nowhere else. The vague word *occurrence* suggests that what happens at the bridge is too mysterious or ambiguous to be described more concretely.]

B **Literary Focus**

? **Point of view.** From what point of view is the beginning of the story told? [objective] How does this point of view resemble the perspective of a camera recording the opening scene of a movie? [Possible responses: Both set the scene and introduce the main character from without; both are highly visual.]

C **Reading Skills**

? **Determining the author's slant.** Is Bierce trying to elicit sympathy for the condemned man, or is he as neutral as the sentinels are? [Possible response: Bierce indirectly elicits sympathy through his description of the cold detachment of the sentinels.]

An Occurrence at Owl Creek Bridge

Ambrose Bierce

I

A man stood upon a railroad bridge in northern Alabama, looking down into the swift water twenty feet below. The man's hands were behind his back, the wrists bound with a cord. A rope closely encircled his neck. It was attached to a stout cross-timber above his head, and the slack fell to the level of his knees. Some loose boards laid upon the sleepers[1] supporting the metals of the railway supplied a footing for him and his executioners— two private soldiers of the Federal army, directed by a sergeant who in civil life may have been a deputy sheriff. At a short remove[2] upon the same temporary platform was an officer in the uniform of his rank, armed. He was a captain. A sentinel at each end of the bridge stood with his rifle in the position known as "support," that is to say, vertical in front of the left shoulder, the hammer resting on the forearm thrown straight across the chest—a formal and unnatural position, enforcing an erect carriage of the body. It did not appear to be the duty of these two men to know what was occurring at the center of the bridge; they merely blockaded the two ends of the foot planking that traversed it.

Beyond one of the sentinels nobody was in sight; the railroad ran straight away into a forest for a hundred yards, then, curving, was lost to view. Doubtless there was an outpost farther along. The other bank of the stream was open ground—a gentle acclivity[3] topped with a stockade of vertical tree trunks, loopholed for rifles, with a single embrasure through which protruded the muzzle of a brass cannon

3. **acclivity** *n.:* uphill slope.

Vocabulary
sentinel (sent′n • əl) *n.:* guard; sentry.

1. **sleepers** *n. pl.:* railroad ties.
2. **remove** *n.:* distance.

Learners Having Difficulty
Modeling. To help students read the story, model the reading skill of analyzing sequence of events. Say, "At the beginning of this story, no real action has occurred. The narrator is simply describing the scene at a single point in time. This scene does tell me that a certain event—a hanging—will probably happen very soon." Encourage students to ask themselves whether each event in the story takes place before or after the opening moment.

English-Language Learners
Before students read, point out that the story is divided into three parts. Explain that even though the same verb tense—the past tense—is used in each part, the order in which events are described differs from the order in which they occur. The events of Part II happen first, the events of Part I happen second, and the events of Part III happen last. Read the story aloud with students, stopping to point out each shift in the time frame as it occurs.

Advanced Learners
Enrichment. Bierce's work is often categorized as Gothic, a word that refers to

commanding the bridge. Midway of the slope between bridge and fort were the spectators—a single company of infantry in line, at "parade rest," the butts of the rifles on the ground, the barrels inclining slightly backward against the right shoulder, the hands crossed upon the stock. A lieutenant stood at the right of the line, the point of his sword upon the ground, his left hand resting upon his right. Excepting the group of four at the center of the bridge, not a man moved. The company faced the bridge, staring stonily, motionless. The sentinels, facing the banks of the stream, might have been statues to adorn the bridge. The captain stood with folded arms, silent, observing the work of his subordinates, but making no sign. Death is a dignitary who when he comes announced is to be received with formal manifestations of respect, even by those most familiar with him. In the code of military etiquette, silence and fixity[4] are forms of deference.

The man who was engaged in being hanged was apparently about thirty-five years of age. He was a civilian, if one might judge from his habit, which was that of a planter. His features were good—a straight nose, firm mouth, broad forehead, from which his long, dark hair was combed straight back, falling behind his ears to the collar of his well-fitting frock coat. He wore a moustache and pointed beard, but no whiskers; his eyes were large and dark gray, and had a kindly expression which one would hardly have expected in one whose neck was in the hemp. Evidently this was no vulgar assassin. The liberal military code makes provision for hanging many kinds of persons, and gentlemen are not excluded.

The preparations being complete, the two private soldiers stepped aside and each drew away the plank upon which he had been standing. The sergeant turned to the captain, saluted, and placed himself immediately behind that officer, who in turn moved apart one pace. These movements left the condemned man and the sergeant standing on the two ends of the same plank, which spanned three of the crossties of

---

4. **fixity** *n.:* steadiness; motionlessness.

the bridge. The end upon which the civilian stood almost, but not quite, reached a fourth. This plank had been held in place by the weight of the captain; it was now held by that of the sergeant. At a signal from the former, the latter would step aside, the plank would tilt and the condemned man go down between two ties. The arrangement commended itself to his judgment as simple and effective. His face had not been covered nor his eyes bandaged. He looked a moment at his "unsteadfast footing," then let his gaze wander to the swirling water of the stream racing madly beneath his feet. A piece of dancing driftwood caught his attention, and his eyes followed it down the current. How slowly it appeared to move! What a sluggish stream!

He closed his eyes in order to fix his last thoughts upon his wife and children. The water, touched to gold by the early sun, the brooding mists under the banks at some distance down the stream, the fort, the soldiers, the piece of drift—all had distracted him. And now he became conscious of a new disturbance. Striking through the thought of his dear ones was a sound which he could neither ignore nor understand, a sharp, distinct, metallic percussion like the stroke of a blacksmith's hammer upon the anvil; it had the same ringing quality. He wondered what it was, and whether immeasurably distant or nearby—it seemed both. Its recurrence was regular, but as slow as the tolling of a death knell.[5] He awaited each stroke with impatience and—he knew not why—apprehension. The intervals of silence grew progressively longer; the delays became maddening. With their greater infrequency the sounds increased in strength and sharpness. They hurt his ear like the thrust of a knife; he feared he would shriek. What he heard was the ticking of his watch.

He unclosed his eyes and saw again the water below him. "If I could free my hands," he thought, "I might throw off the noose and

---

5. **knell** *n.:* sound of a bell ringing slowly.

Vocabulary
deference (def′ər·əns) *n.:* respect.

D Literary Focus

Analyzing the author's style. How does the formality of the author's style reflect his purpose in this passage? [Possible response: Bierce's formal diction and his personification of death as a dignitary evoke a solemn mood that befits a hanging.]

E Literary Focus

Analyzing the author's style. Why does Bierce use the phrase "engaged in being hanged" rather than "was being hanged" or "was about to be hanged"? [Possible response: The contrast between the matter-of-fact phrase *engaged in* and the violence and brutality of the act creates a powerful sense of irony.]

F English-Language Learners

Archaic language. Explain that in the past, the word *habit* referred to a person's style of dress.

G Literary Focus

Point of view. How does the point of view change? What effect does this shift have on the reader? [The narration shifts from the objective or omniscient point of view to the third-person limited. This shift personalizes Farquhar and prompts the reader to identify with him.]

H Reading Skills

Determining the author's purpose. How do time and sound change in this passage? What effect do the changes create? [Time slows down and sound is amplified. These changes move the narrative wholly into Farquhar's third-person-limited point of view.]

---

literature dealing with death, psychological disturbance, and the macabre. Have students investigate the Gothic genre. What are some characteristics of Gothic fiction? When did it first appear? How has it changed over time? Then, have students write an essay stating whether "An Occurrence at Owl Creek Bridge" should be considered a Gothic work and explaining why or why not.

A **Reading Skills**

❓ **Making predictions.** Take a look at the number of pages left in the story. What do you predict the rest of the story will be about? [Possible responses: the prisoner's past; an escape attempt; the aftermath of the hanging.]

B **Literary Focus**

❓ **Point of view.** What point of view does Bierce use in Part II? [objective third person] How is Peyton Farquhar portrayed in the opening paragraph of this section? [Possible response: Farquhar is portrayed as eager to serve the Southern cause but naive about the realities of war.]

C **Reading Skills**

❓ **Analyzing sequence of events.** When does this encounter between Farquhar, his wife, and the "gray-clad soldier" occur? [It occurs one evening sometime before the events at the bridge.]

D **Content-Area Connections**

History: Treason
Treason is the betrayal of one's government. In 1790, the U.S. Congress fixed the punishment for treason as death by hanging. During the Civil War, no Confederates were ever officially tried for treason. Jefferson Davis, the president of the Confederacy, was indicted for treason but was never tried.

E **Learners Having Difficulty**

❓ **Finding details.** Remind students that Confederate soldiers wore gray. In this flashback, however, the gray-clad soldier is not what he seems. What is his real identity? [He is a Federal scout.]

---

spring into the stream. By diving I could evade the bullets and, swimming vigorously, reach the bank, take to the woods, and get away home. My home, thank God, is as yet outside their lines; my wife and little ones are still beyond the invader's farthest advance."

As these thoughts, which have here to be set down in words, were flashed into the doomed man's brain rather than evolved from it, the captain nodded to the sergeant. The sergeant stepped aside.

II

Peyton Farquhar was a well-to-do planter, of an old and highly respected Alabama family. Being a slave owner and, like other slave owners, a politician, he was naturally an original secessionist[6] and ardently devoted to the Southern cause. Circumstances of an imperious[7] nature, which it is unnecessary to relate here, had prevented him from taking service with the gallant army that had fought the disastrous campaigns ending with the fall of Corinth,[8] and he chafed[9] under the inglorious restraint, longing for the release of his energies, the larger life of the soldier, the opportunity for distinction. That opportunity, he felt, would come, as it comes to all in wartime. Meanwhile he did what he could. No service was too humble for him to perform in aid of the South, no adventure too perilous for him to undertake if consistent with the character of a civilian who was at heart a soldier, and who in good faith and without too much qualification assented to at least a part of the frankly villainous dictum[10] that all is fair in love and war.

One evening while Farquhar and his wife were sitting on a rustic bench near the entrance to his grounds, a gray-clad soldier rode up to the gate and asked for a drink of water. Mrs. Farquhar was only too happy to serve him with her own white hands. While she was fetching the water, her husband approached the dusty horseman and inquired eagerly for news from the front.

"The Yanks are repairing the railroads," said the man, "and are getting ready for another advance. They have reached the Owl Creek bridge, put it in order, and built a stockade on the north bank. The commandant has issued an order, which is posted everywhere, declaring that any civilian caught interfering with the railroad, its bridges, tunnels, or trains will be summarily[11] hanged. I saw the order."

"How far is it to the Owl Creek bridge?" Farquhar asked.

"About thirty miles."

"Is there no force on this side the creek?"

"Only a picket post half a mile out, on the railroad, and a single sentinel at this end of the bridge."

"Suppose a man—a civilian and student of hanging—should elude the picket post and perhaps get the better of the sentinel," said Farquhar, smiling, "what could he accomplish?"

The soldier reflected. "I was there a month ago," he replied. "I observed that the flood of last winter had lodged a great quantity of driftwood against the wooden pier at this end of the bridge. It is now dry and would burn like tow."

The lady had now brought the water, which the soldier drank. He thanked her ceremoniously, bowed to her husband, and rode away. An hour later, after nightfall, he repassed the plantation, going northward in the direction from which he had come. He was a Federal scout.

III

As Peyton Farquhar fell straight downward through the bridge, he lost consciousness and was as one already dead. From this state he was awakened—ages later, it seemed to him—by the pain of a sharp pressure upon his throat,

---

6. **secessionist** *n.*: one who favored the separation of Southern states from the Union.
7. **imperious** *adj.*: urgent.
8. **Corinth:** Union forces under Gen. William S. Rosecrans (1819–1898) took Corinth, Mississippi, on October 4, 1862.
9. **chafed** *v.*: became impatient.
10. **dictum** *n.*: statement; saying.

11. **summarily** *adv.*: without delay.

Vocabulary
perilous (per′ə·ləs) *adj.*: dangerous.

CONTENT-AREA CONNECTIONS

History: Civil War Scouts
Both the Confederate and the Union armies used scouts to gather information on their opponents' positions and strategies. Scouts served as the invisible eyes and ears of their commanders, often donning the enemy's uniform in order to infiltrate enemy territory. Scouting was dangerous work; captured scouts were usually put to death.

Individual activity. Ask students to do research on Civil War scouts and spies. Tell them to use the information they find to evaluate the accuracy of Bierce's story. Did many wealthy Southern planters engage in sabotage? Is the conversation between the scout and Farquhar credible?

followed by a sense of suffocation. Keen, poignant agonies seemed to shoot from his neck downward through every fiber of his body and limbs. These pains appeared to flash along well-defined lines of ramification[12] and to beat with an inconceivably rapid periodicity. They seemed like streams of pulsating fire heating him to an intolerable temperature. As to his head, he was conscious of nothing but a feeling of fullness—of congestion. These sensations were unaccompanied by thought. The intellectual part of his nature was already effaced; he had power only to feel, and feeling was torment. He was conscious of motion. Encompassed in a luminous cloud, of which he was now merely the fiery heart, without material substance, he swung through unthinkable arcs of oscillation, like a vast pendulum. Then all at once, with terrible suddenness, the light about him shot upward with the noise of a loud plash; a frightful roaring was in his ears, and all was cold and dark. The power of thought was restored; he knew that the rope had broken and he had fallen into the stream. There was no additional strangulation; the noose about his neck was already suffocating him and kept the water from his lungs. To die of hanging at the bottom of a river!—the idea seemed to him ludicrous. He opened his eyes in the darkness and saw above him a gleam of light, but how distant, how inaccessible! He was still sinking, for the light became fainter and fainter until it was a mere glimmer. Then it began to grow and brighten, and he knew that he was rising toward the surface—knew it with reluctance, for he was now very comfortable. "To be hanged and

drowned," he thought, "that is not so bad; but I do not wish to be shot. No; I will not be shot; that is not fair."

He was not conscious of an effort, but a sharp pain in his wrist apprised[13] him that he was trying to free his hands. He gave the struggle his attention, as an idler might observe the feat of a juggler, without interest in the outcome. What splendid effort!—what magnificent, what superhuman strength! Ah, that was a fine endeavor! Bravo! The cord fell away; his arms parted and floated upward, the hands dimly

---

13. **apprised** *v.*: informed.

Vocabulary

encompassed (en·kum′pəst) *v.* used as *adj.*: surrounded; enclosed.

oscillation (äs′ə·lā′shən) *n.*: regular back-and-forth movement.

Ambrose Bierce   427

DIRECT TEACHING

F Reading Skills

? Interpreting. In what way is this description ambiguous? Which two events does it suggest? Identify phrases that support your interpretation. [Possible responses: It might describe the moment of death, as suggested by the phrases "luminous cloud," "without material substance," "all was cold and dark," and "a gleam of light, but how distant." The passage might also describe the sensation of being hanged ("he swung through unthinkable arcs"), falling into water ("a loud plash"), and rising to the surface (the glimmer "began to grow").]

G Reading Skills

Analyzing sequence of events. Ask students to describe the sequence of events in this passage. [Possible response: Farquhar feels the sensation of swinging through the air. He then feels a downward rush and believes he has fallen into the stream. He sees a glimmer of light above him and begins to rise toward it.]

H Literary Focus

? Point of view. What two points of view does Bierce use here? How do these perspectives convey Farquhar's altered state? [Possible response: Bierce alternates between a first-person and a third-person-limited perspective here—a technique that conveys Farquhar's dreamlike disassociation from his own body.]

READING SKILLS REVIEW

Analyzing chronological order. Remind students that when stories are related in chronological order, the events proceed in sequence from first to last. At first the events of "An Occurrence at Owl Creek Bridge" are related in chronological order. The story then moves into a flashback, a scene that breaks into a narrative to show events that took place earlier.

Activity. Have students list the main events of the story in the order in which they appear. Then, divide the class into groups, and have them put the events in chronological order.

Activity. Have students construct a time line showing the order of events in the story.

Activity. Challenge students to explain why Bierce relates the story the way he does.

[Possible responses: He wishes to focus on Farquhar's mental state; he wants to create a surprise ending.]

---

12. **flash ... ramification:** spread out rapidly along branches from one point.

A **Advanced Learners**

Enrichment. Critics have pointed out that Farquhar's struggle to emerge from the water is like a baby's struggle to emerge from the womb. Note the parallels in taking a first breath and emitting a cry. Bierce himself defines birth as "the first and direst of all disasters."

B **Reading Skills**

❓ Determining the author's purpose. How has Farquhar's vision changed? What purpose might this serve in the narrative? [Possible response: His senses have sharpened, and he now experiences the most minute details with an unnatural intensity. Students might recall that a sharpening of senses is sometimes said to occur at the moment of death, so this passage may offer a clue to Farquhar's real fate.]

C **Reading Skills**

❓ Analyzing sequence of events. How much time do you think has passed since the sergeant stepped off the plank? What details support your speculation? [Possible response: Only a few seconds have passed; the captain and other soldiers are still in position on the bridge.]

seen on each side in the growing light. He watched them with a new interest as first one and then the other pounced upon the noose at his neck. They tore it away and thrust it fiercely aside, its undulations resembling those of a water snake. "Put it back, put it back!" He thought he shouted these words to his hands, for the undoing of the noose had been succeeded by the direst pang that he had yet experienced. His neck ached horribly; his brain was on fire; his heart, which had been fluttering faintly, gave a great leap, trying to force itself out at his mouth. His whole body was racked and wrenched with an insupportable anguish! But his disobedient hands gave no heed to the command. They beat the water vigorously with quick, downward strokes, forcing him to the surface. He felt his head emerge; his eyes were blinded by the sunlight; his chest expanded convulsively, and with a supreme and crowning agony his lungs engulfed a great draft of air, which instantly he expelled in a shriek!

He was now in full possession of his physical senses. They were, indeed, preternaturally[14] keen and alert. Something in the awful disturbance of his organic system had so exalted and refined them that they made record of things never before perceived. He felt the ripples upon his face and heard their separate sounds as they struck. He looked at the forest on the bank of the stream, saw the individual trees, the leaves, and the veining of each leaf—saw the very insects upon them: the locusts, the brilliant-bodied flies, the gray spiders stretching their webs from twig to twig. He noted the prismatic colors in all the dewdrops upon a million blades of grass. The humming of the gnats that danced above the eddies of the stream, the beating of the dragonflies' wings, the strokes of the water spiders' legs, like oars which had lifted their boat—all these made audible music. A fish slid along beneath his eyes, and he heard the rush of its body parting the water.

He had come to the surface facing down the stream; in a moment the visible world seemed to wheel slowly round, himself the <u>pivotal</u> point, and he saw the bridge, the fort, the soldiers upon the bridge, the captain, the sergeant, the two privates, his executioners. They were in silhouette against the blue sky. They shouted and gesticulated, pointing at him. The captain had drawn his pistol, but did not fire; the others were unarmed. Their movements were grotesque and horrible, their forms gigantic.

---

14. **preternaturally** *adv.:* extraordinarily; abnormally.

Vocabulary

pivotal (piv′ət·'l) *adj.:* central; acting as a point around which other things turn.

READING MINI-LESSON

Developing Word-Attack Skills

Write the following words from the selection on the chalkboard:

ignore malign poignant

Read the words aloud, and ask students to identify the sound or sounds represented by *gn* in each word. Help them make the following generalizations:

- In *ignore*, *g* ends one syllable and *n* begins another. The letter *g* stands for /g/, and the letter *n* stands for /n/.

- In *malign*, the letters *g* and *n* appear together at the end of the word. The *g* is silent, and the two letters stands for /n/. The *g* is also silent when *gn* appears at the beginning of a word, as in *gnat* and *gnaw*.

Suddenly he heard a sharp report[15] and something struck the water smartly within a few inches of his head, spattering his face with spray. He heard a second report, and saw one of the sentinels with his rifle at his shoulder, a light cloud of blue smoke rising from the muzzle. The man in the water saw the eye of the man on the bridge gazing into his own through the sights of the rifle. He observed that it was a gray eye and remembered having read that gray eyes were keenest, and that all famous marksmen had them. Nevertheless, this one had missed.

A counterswirl had caught Farquhar and turned him half round; he was again looking into the forest on the bank opposite the fort. The sound of a clear, high voice in monotonous singsong now rang out behind him and came across the water with a distinctness that pierced and subdued all other sounds, even the beating of the ripples in his ears. Although no soldier, he had frequented camps enough to know the dread significance of that deliberate, drawling, aspirated chant; the lieutenant on shore was taking a part in the morning's work. How coldly and pitilessly—with what an even, calm intonation, presaging,[16] and enforcing tranquility in the men—with what accurately measured intervals fell those cruel words:

"Attention, company! . . . Shoulder arms! . . . Ready! . . . Aim! . . . Fire!"

Farquhar dived—dived as deeply as he could. The water roared in his ears like the voice of Niagara, yet he heard the dulled thunder of the volley and, rising again toward the surface, met shining bits of metal, singularly flattened, oscillating slowly downward. Some of them touched him on the face and hands, then fell away, continuing their descent. One lodged between his collar and neck; it was uncomfortably warm and he snatched it out.

As he rose to the surface, gasping for breath, he saw that he had been a long time underwater; he was perceptibly farther downstream—nearer to safety. The soldiers had almost

finished reloading; the metal ramrods flashed all at once in the sunshine as they were drawn from the barrels, turned in the air, and thrust into their sockets. The two sentinels fired again, independently and ineffectually.

The hunted man saw all this over his shoulder; he was now swimming vigorously with the current. His brain was as energetic as his arms and legs; he thought with the rapidity of lightning.

"The officer," he reasoned, "will not make that martinet's[17] error a second time. It is as easy to dodge a volley as a single shot. He has probably already given the command to fire at will. God help me, I cannot dodge them all!"

An appalling plash within two yards of him was followed by a loud, rushing sound, *diminuendo*,[18] which seemed to travel back through the air to the fort and died in an explosion which stirred the very river to its deeps! A rising sheet of water curved over him, fell down upon him, blinded him, strangled him! The cannon had taken a hand in the game. As he shook his head free from the commotion of the smitten water, he heard the deflected shot humming through the air ahead, and in an instant it was cracking and smashing the branches in the forest beyond.

"They will not do that again," he thought; "the next time they will use a charge of grape.[19] I must keep my eye upon the gun; the smoke will apprise me—the report arrives too late; it lags behind the missile. That is a good gun."

Suddenly he felt himself whirled round and round—spinning like a top. The water, the banks, the forests, the now distant bridge, fort, and men—all were commingled and blurred. Objects were represented by their colors only;

---

15. **report** *n.*: explosive noise.
16. **presaging** *v.* used as *adj.*: forewarning; predicting.

17. **martinet's:** A martinet is a disciplinarian of military rigidity.
18. ***diminuendo*** (də·min′yōō·en′dō) *adj.*: decreasing in loudness.
19. **charge of grape:** cannon charge of small iron balls, called grapeshot.

Vocabulary
appalling (ə·pôl′iŋ) *adj.*: frightful.

Ambrose Bierce **429**

DIRECT TEACHING

D Literary Focus

Point of view. Find three verbs that tell what Farquhar did. [*heard, saw,* and *observed*] How do these verbs indicate the point of view being used? [They indicate that the third-person-limited point of view is being used because the narrator sees what Farquhar sees, hears what he hears, and knows what he thinks.]

E Literary Focus

Point of view. How does this description of the military formality of a firing squad differ from the one on p. 425? [Possible response: The earlier passage describes a military ritual performed with "respect," in accordance with "etiquette"; here, the ritual is performed "coldly and pitilessly," and the lieutenant's commands are "cruel."] How do these differences reflect the change in point of view? [Possible response: The earlier passage was told from the point of view of a detached, cynical observer. This passage is told from the point of view of the panicking Farquhar.]

F Literary Focus

Point of view. What is strange about the thoughts going through Farquhar's mind? [Possible response: A person in such a dire situation does not usually think so coherently.] Why might Bierce have put such thoughts in his character's mind? [Possible responses: He wants to show how distorted Farquhar's perceptions are; he wants to hint at the unreality of these events.]

- In *poignant, gn* appears at the end of a syllable. The *g* is silent, but the letters *gn* introduce the sound /y/ at the beginning of the second syllable: pȯin′yənt.

Activity. Display the following list of words. Ask students whether the pronunciation of *gn* matches that in *ignore,* in *malign,* or in *poignant.*

design
malignant
lasagna
gnome
vignette
insignia

alignment
cognitive
cognac
magnetic
feign

pugnacious
gnash
mignon
magnitude
campaign

[*Ignore*—malignant, insignia, cognitive, magnetic, pugnacious, magnitude. *Malign*—design, gnome, alignment, campaign, feign, gnash. *Poignant*—lasagna, vignette, cognac, mignon.]

A Literary Focus

❓ Point of view. How does the point of view add to the strangeness of this scene? [Possible response: Because we see events through Farquhar's eyes, we would expect the landscape to be familiar, since he is not far from his home. Instead, the scene has a surreal, nightmarish quality.]

B Literary Focus

❓ Point of view. Why does Bierce return to the objective point of view in his final sentence? [He wants to show that Farquhar's escape was pure fantasy.]

C Literary Focus

❓ Analyzing the author's rhetorical purpose. How does this story reflect Bierce's scorn for sentimental illusions? [Possible response: Farquhar's romantic illusions about the war end with his capture and execution. The reader's illusion of Farquhar's escape ends with the brutally matter-of-fact final sentence.]

GUIDED PRACTICE

Monitoring students' progress. Guide the class in answering these questions.

True-False

1. Farquhar is a Confederate captain who has been captured during a sabotage attempt. [F]

2. Farquhar was lured by a Union scout into sabotaging a Union-held bridge. [T]

3. Bierce uses a flashback to explain why Farquhar is being executed. [T]

4. At the end of the story, Farquhar is reunited with his wife. [F]

---

circular horizontal streaks of color—that was all he saw. He had been caught in a vortex and was being whirled on with a velocity of advance and gyration that made him giddy and sick. In a few moments he was flung upon the gravel at the foot of the left bank of the stream—the southern bank—and behind a projecting point which concealed him from his enemies. The sudden arrest of his motion, the abrasion of one of his hands on the gravel, restored him, and he wept with delight. He dug his fingers into the sand, threw it over himself in handfuls, and audibly blessed it. It looked like diamonds, rubies, emeralds; he could think of nothing beautiful which it did not resemble. The trees upon the bank were giant garden plants; he noted a definite order in their arrangement, inhaled the fragrance of their blooms. A strange, roseate light shone through the spaces among their trunks, and the wind made in their branches the music of aeolian harps.[20] He had no wish to perfect his escape—was content to remain in that enchanting spot until retaken.

A whiz and rattle of grapeshot among the branches high above his head roused him from his dream. The baffled cannoneer had fired him a random farewell. He sprang to his feet, rushed up the sloping bank, and plunged into the forest.

All that day he traveled, laying his course by the rounding sun. The forest seemed interminable; nowhere did he discover a break in it, not even a woodsman's road. He had not known that he lived in so wild a region. There was something uncanny[21] in the revelation.

By nightfall he was fatigued, footsore, famishing. The thought of his wife and children urged him on. At last he found a road which led him in what he knew to be the right direction. It was as wide and straight as a city street, yet it seemed untraveled. No fields bordered it, no dwelling anywhere. Not so much as the barking of a dog suggested human habitation. The black bodies of the trees formed a straight wall on both sides,

terminating on the horizon in a point, like a diagram in a lesson in perspective. Overhead, as he looked up through this rift in the wood, shone great golden stars looking unfamiliar and grouped in strange constellations. He was sure they were arranged in some order which had a secret and malign significance. The wood on either side was full of singular noises, among which—once, twice, and again—he distinctly heard whispers in an unknown tongue.

His neck was in pain and lifting his hand to it he found it horribly swollen. He knew that it had a circle of black where the rope had bruised it. His eyes felt congested; he could no longer close them. His tongue was swollen with thirst; he relieved its fever by thrusting it forward from between his teeth into the cold air. How softly the turf had carpeted the untraveled avenue—he could no longer feel the roadway beneath his feet!

Doubtless, despite his suffering, he had fallen asleep while walking, for now he sees another scene—perhaps he has merely recovered from a delirium. He stands at the gate of his own home. All is as he left it, and all bright and beautiful in the morning sunshine. He must have traveled the entire night. As he pushes open the gate and passes up the wide white walk, he sees a flutter of female garments; his wife, looking fresh and cool and sweet, steps down from the veranda to meet him. At the bottom of the steps she stands waiting, with a smile of ineffable[22] joy, an attitude of matchless grace and dignity. Ah, how beautiful she is! He springs forward with extended arms. As he is about to clasp her, he feels a stunning blow upon the back of the neck; a blinding white light blazes all about him with a sound like the shock of a cannon—then all is darkness and silence!

Peyton Farquhar was dead; his body, with a broken neck, swung gently from side to side beneath the timbers of the Owl Creek bridge. ■

---

22. **ineffable** *adj.:* indescribable; unspeakable.

Vocabulary
gyration (jī·rā′shən) *n.:* circular movement; whirling.
abrasion (ə·brā′zhən) *n.:* scrape.
malign (mə·līn′) *adj.:* harmful; evil.

---

20. **aeolian** (ē·ō′lē·ən) **harps:** stringed instruments that are played by the wind. Aeolus is the god of the winds in Greek mythology.
21. **uncanny** *adj.:* eerie; weird.

Literary Criticism

Critic's Commentary: Literary Trick or Treat?

The historian and biographer Roy Morris, Jr., writes that "careless readers" misinterpret the story's conclusion as mere sleight of hand. "A more careful reading," he says, "reveals that the ending is no trick—except on the unfortunate and dull-witted Farquhar. Everywhere along the way, Bierce prepares the reader for the story's only possible conclusion. It is, after all, an occurrence—something that occurs—at Owl Creek bridge—on or near the bridge, not downstream, miles away, at Farquhar's home. . . . The story, and Farquhar's story within a story, end with a jolt but not a surprise."

Whole-class activity. Have students revisit the story to look for clues to the story's final "surprise." Then, have them debate the validity of Morris's comments.

Response and Analysis

Reading Check

1. State the situation Peyton Farquhar faces in Part I.

2. Part II of the story is a flashback. List its events in **chronological order.** Be sure to explain who visits Peyton Farquhar and what plan Farquhar conceives as a result of this visit.

3. **Summarize** in one sentence what Farquhar imagines in Part III.

Thinking Critically

4. What **point of view** does the writer use in Part III of the story, which occurs within the few seconds before Farquhar dies? Why is this point of view particularly appropriate?

5. Bierce's **style** is to tell his story out of **chronological order.** How might the impact of the story be different if the events were revealed in order?

6. In this story the Civil War serves as a backdrop; Bierce's main intent is to examine the psychology of someone in a life-or-death situation. What does this story imply about human psychology in the face of death?

Extending and Evaluating

7. Did you think the outcome of this story was credible and powerful, or did you think the surprise ending cheated the reader? Explain.

Literary Criticism

8. **Philosophical approach.** The critics Cleanth Brooks and Robert Penn Warren have said that Bierce's story depends too much on a quirk of human psychology and is thus a mere "case study" that does not reveal anything important about human nature, as good fiction does. Do you agree? Why or why not?

WRITING

Owl Creek Bridge: The Movie

Write a **memorandum** to a film producer outlining your plans for adapting Bierce's story into a movie. Point out scenes where you would use each of the following techniques: (a) close-up shot; (b) moving-camera shot; (c) quick cut to new scene; (d) fast motion; (e) slow motion; (f) fuzzy image; and (g) sound effects. (The story was made into an award-winning film in 1962 in France.)

Vocabulary Development

Synonyms and Antonyms

sentinel	oscillation	abrasion
deference	pivotal	malign
perilous	appalling	
encompassed	gyration	

A **synonym** is a word that has the same, or almost the same, meaning as another word. An **antonym** has the opposite, or nearly the opposite, meaning of another word. Find the Vocabulary word from the list above that answers each of the following questions:

1. What word is a synonym for *rotation?*
2. What word is an antonym for *safe?*
3. What word is a synonym for *crucial?*
4. What word is a synonym for *lookout?*
5. What word is an antonym for *disrespect?*
6. What word is a synonym for *scratch?*
7. What word is a synonym for *shocking?*
8. What word is a synonym for *encircled?*
9. What word is an antonym for *harmless?*
10. What word is a synonym for *vibration?*

go. hrw .com

INTERNET
Projects and Activities
Keyword: LE5 11-4

SKILLS FOCUS

Literary Skills
Analyze point of view.

Reading Skills
Analyze a sequence of events.

Writing Skills
Write a memorandum outlining plans for adapting a story into a movie.

Vocabulary Skills
Identify synonyms and antonyms.

Response and Analysis

5. Possible answer: If the events were related in order, the reader might feel more sympathy for Farquhar before his hanging, diminishing the dramatic contrast between Parts I and III.

6. It implies that the terror of death heightens the senses, distorts perceptions of time, and creates fantasies of escape.

Extending and Evaluating

7. Those who feel cheated may express doubts that someone could imagine such an elaborate, well-ordered sequence of events.

Literary Criticism

8. Students who agree might argue that the escape fantasy described in Part III offers insight only into Farquhar's character. Others might argue that the story explores the human capacity for self-delusion under stress.

Vocabulary Development

1. gyration	6. abrasion
2. perilous	7. appalling
3. pivotal	8. encompassed
4. sentinel	9. malign
5. deference	10. oscillation

ASSESSING

Assessment

■ *Holt Assessment: Literature, Reading, and Vocabulary*

Reading Check

1. He is about to be hanged.

2. A soldier comes to Farquhar's house and tells him that Union soldiers working on the Owl Creek bridge will hang any interfering civilian. At Farquhar's request the soldier tells how someone could burn the bridge. The soldier leaves but returns later, this time traveling north; he is a Union spy.

3. He imagines that the rope breaks, that he escapes, and that he makes it home.

Thinking Critically

4. Bierce uses the third-person-limited point of view to describe Farquhar's desperate flight of imagination. This allows Bierce's narrator to maintain a realist stance—even as his mind flees reality.

Political Points of View

SKILLS FOCUS, pp. 432–453

Grade-Level Skills

■ **Literary Skills**
Analyze the political points of view in a selection of literary works on a topic.

■ **Reading Skills**
Use prior knowledge.

Political Issue: The Civil War

Although the Northern and the Southern states disagreed on slavery and states' rights, the Civil War itself was universally regarded as a hellish, terrifying time of pain and sacrifice. The literature about this period reveals the human cost of the war, as well as the devotion to family and country of both sides.

Skills Starter

Build review skills. Help students define the term *political assumptions.* Remind them that governments are shaped by the fundamental beliefs and values of those who found and maintain them. Sometimes basic assumptions about human rights and civic responsibility are stated explicitly in government documents. Sometimes basic assumptions are unstated, taken for granted, glossed over, or even ignored. Sometimes people in the society make different political assumptions, and conflict may eventually result.

Introducing **Political Points** *of* **View**

The Civil War

You will be reading the seven selections listed above in this Political Points of View feature on the Civil War. In the top corner of each page in this feature, you'll find three stars. Smaller versions of the stars appear next to the questions on page 444 that focus on the Civil War. At the end of the feature (pages 452–453), you'll compare the various points of view expressed in the selections.

Examining the Issue: The Civil War

During the American Civil War many families, especially in the border states, had friends and relatives in both the North and the South. For such families the Civil War was a profoundly personal conflict. What drove supporters of both sides to carry on, despite devastation to themselves and their families? In the readings that follow, you will find surprising similarities in the ways Northerners and Southerners viewed this terrible conflict in American history.

Make the Connection

Quickwrite ✏

The United States was not even one hundred years old when the Civil War began. Neither the North nor the South anticipated how long the war would last and how many lives would be lost before it ended. How would you feel if the United States found itself in a similar controversy today? How would your ideas about what unites the states change? Write a few sentences about your thoughts.

Reading Skills

Using Prior Knowledge

Make a KWL chart in which you write down what you already know about the Civil War and what you want to know. Fill out what you have learned after you've read the selections that follow.

K What I Know	W What I Want to Know	L What I Learned

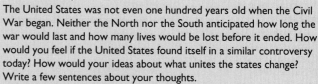

SKILLS FOCUS

Pages 432–453 cover
Literary Skills
Analyze political points of view on a topic.

Reading Skills
Use prior knowledge.

Stephen Crane
(1871–1900)

Stephen Crane was the youngest of the fourteen children of a Methodist minister and his devout wife. Although frail as a child, Stephen grew up—in upstate New York— yearning to become a baseball star. He attended Lafayette College and Syracuse University before deciding to try earning a living as a writer.

When Crane was about sixteen, he took a job at his brother's news agency in New Jersey. Later, working as a reporter in New York City, Crane was drawn to the city's underside. What he called his "artistic education" on the Bowery (Skid Row) left him hungry and often ill.

Crane's first significant fiction, *Maggie: A Girl of the Streets* (1893), was a somber, shocking novel based on his explorations of the city's slums and saloons. This novel revealed Crane as a pioneer of **naturalism**—a literary movement that dissected human instincts and behavior and examined the society that "conditioned" people to turn out as they did. Crane borrowed seven hundred dollars to have it printed. Subsequently the unsold copies lay piled in his room—it was an impossibly grim novel for readers at the time.

Crane's apparent failure with *Maggie* was followed by a triumph—a short novel titled *The Red Badge of Courage* (1895). Using an impressionistic technique, Crane filtered the events of the novel through the eyes of Henry Fleming, a young soldier in the Civil War. (In fiction, **impressionism** is a technique whereby the writer gives us not objective reality but one character's impression of that reality.) Though Crane had never been in battle, he equated war with football. He wrote, "The psychology is the same. The opposing team is the enemy tribe."

The Red Badge of Courage made Crane a celebrity and a national expert on war. He was seen as epitomizing the adventurous war correspondent, living a sensational life, writing about it, and delighting in shocking conservative readers.

Crane had a knack for interweaving his fiction with his real-life experiences. When he sailed from Florida in 1896 to cover a gun-running operation in Cuba, he was shipwrecked and endured a thirty-hour struggle with the sea. The result was his superb story "The Open Boat" (1898).

Before this ill-fated journey, Crane had taken up with a hotel hostess, Cora Taylor. The oddly matched couple later went off to Greece as war correspondents and eventually settled in England. All these adventures were taking their toll on Crane's ever-delicate health. Still he continued to travel and write. In 1899, he produced his second volume of poems, *War Is Kind*. Tuberculosis was sapping his strength, though, and he died in June 1900, at the age of twenty-eight.

For Independent Reading

For more adventures by Crane, try
- "The Open Boat" (short story)
- *The Red Badge of Courage* (novel)

SKILLS FOCUS, pp. 433–444

Grade-Level Skills

- **Literary Skills**
Analyze the political points of view on a topic.

- **Literary Skills**
Analyze the way situational irony achieves specific rhetorical or aesthetic purposes.

More About the Writer

Background. Stephen Crane created the code of manly conduct later associated with Ernest Hemingway. According to the literary critic Joseph Katz, for Crane "it evolved into a tough literary creed which proclaimed, 'A man is born into the world with his own pair of eyes, and he is not responsible for his vision—he is merely responsible for his quality of personal honesty.' "

RESOURCES: READING

Planning
- *One-Stop Planner* CD-ROM with ExamView Test Generator

Differentiating Instruction
- *The Holt Reader*
- *Holt Adapted Reader*
- *Holt Reading Solutions*
- *Supporting Instruction in Spanish*

- *Audio CD Library, Selections and Summaries in Spanish*

Vocabulary
- *Vocabulary Development*

Assessment
- *Holt Assessment: Literature, Reading, and Vocabulary*
- *One-Stop Planner* CD-ROM with ExamView Test Generator

- *Holt Online Assessment*

Internet
- go.hrw.com (Keyword: LE5 11-4)
- *Elements of Literature Online*

Media
- *Audio CD Library*
- *Audio CD Library, Selections and Summaries in Spanish*
- *Fine Art Transparencies*

Summary *at grade level*

In the midst of a heated Civil War battle, Private Fred Collins decides to risk death to get some water. Egged on by his comrades, he sets out across a meadow under bombardment, fills an old bucket at a well, and, with shells landing all about, heads back to his company's position. On the way back, he passes a dying officer, who asks him for a drink. Collins initially refuses but then turns back to give the officer some water. Upon his return, two lieutenants playfully grab the bucket and accidentally overturn it, spilling the water on the ground.

Selection Starter

Motivate. One reason Crane's war stories were popular was that they were told from a common soldier's point of view. Earlier fiction dealing with war had focused largely on the exploits of officers, who tended to be well educated, wealthy, and aristocratic. Ask students who they would rather hear narrate a war story—a general, an officer in the field, a common soldier, or a war correspondent. Discuss with them the differences in point of view you would expect from these narrators.

Before You Read

A Mystery of Heroism

Political Points *of* View

Quickwrite ✏️

Imagine this scene: In the midst of the frightful noise and bloody destruction of a Civil War battlefield, a soldier suddenly decides to jump up and run straight into the enemy line to get something. To his fellow soldiers it is an impulse that seems simply crazy, but could he be a hero?

The above scene is the one Crane describes in this story. Although he never experienced the war himself, Crane had read firsthand accounts of the mayhem of Civil War battlefields, where often one soldier would escape death and another would die by the merest chance. Dazed by battle, soldiers often struggled later to explain their actions.

Before you read, jot down your thoughts about what makes someone a hero during war. Then, as you read, think about Crane's view of heroism.

Literary Focus

Situational Irony

Situational irony occurs when what actually happens differs from what one expects will happen. For example, suppose a heroic soldier is wounded as he battles through war-torn terrain to rescue a fallen comrade—only to find out that the comrade is quite safe and never needed help. The irony of the situation shocks—or at least surprises—both the hero and the reader.

go.hrw.com

INTERNET

Vocabulary Practice
•
More About Stephen Crane
•
Keyword: LE5 11-4

SKILLS FOCUS

Literary Skills
Analyze political points of view on a topic. Understand situational irony.

> **Situational irony** takes place when there is a discrepancy between what is expected to happen and what actually happens.
>
> *For more on Irony, see the Handbook of Literary and Historical Terms.*

Background

In war the military chain of command makes it possible for an army to function. When reading stories about war, you can better understand not only the military action but also the relationships between soldiers by knowing the different military ranks. Here are the ranks mentioned in "A Mystery of Heroism," from highest to lowest:

> Colonel
> Lieutenant Colonel
> Major
> Captain
> Lieutenant
> Sergeant
> Private

Vocabulary Development

conflagration (kän′flə·grā′shən) *n*.: huge fire.

stolidity (stə·lid′ə·tē) *n*.: absence of emotional reactions.

ominous (äm′ə·nəs) *adj*.: threatening; menacing.

gesticulating (jes·tik′yo͞o·lāt′in) *v*. used as *adj*.: gesturing, especially with the hands and arms.

provisional (prə·vizh′ə·nəl) *adj*.: temporary; serving for the time being.

retraction (ri·trak′shən) *n*.: withdrawal.

indolent (in′də·lənt) *adj*.: lazy.

blanched (blancht) *v*. used as *adj*.: drained of color.

434　Collection 4　The Rise of Realism: The Civil War to 1914

Previewing Vocabulary

Have students read the words listed under Vocabulary Development on p. 434, along with their definitions. Next, have students work in pairs making flashcards, using all the Vocabulary words. Encourage students to use the cards to help one another learn the words and their meanings. Then, hold a class vocabulary bee: Read the words aloud, and have teams take turns giving definitions. Afterward, have students complete the following matching exercise.

1. blanched [d]	**a.** gesturing
2. conflagration [c]	**b.** withdrawal
3. stolidity [h]	**c.** huge fire
4. provisional [e]	**d.** drained of color
5. retraction [b]	**e.** temporary
6. ominous [f]	**f.** foreboding
7. gesticulating [a]	**g.** lazy
8. indolent [g]	**h.** lack of emotion

Union soldier.

A Mystery of Heroism

Stephen Crane

The dark uniforms of the men were so coated with dust from the incessant wrestling of the two armies that the regiment almost seemed a part of the clay bank which shielded them from the shells. On the top of the hill a battery[1] was arguing in tremendous roars with some other guns, and to the eye of the infantry, the artillerymen, the guns, the caissons,[2] the horses, were distinctly outlined upon the blue sky. When a piece was fired, a red streak as round as a log flashed low in the heavens, like a monstrous bolt of lightning. The men of the battery wore white duck trousers, which some-

how emphasized their legs, and when they ran and crowded in little groups at the bidding of the shouting officers, it was more impressive than usual to the infantry.

Fred Collins of A Company was saying: "Thunder, I wisht I had a drink. Ain't there any water round here?" Then somebody yelled: "There goes th' bugler!"

As the eyes of half of the regiment swept in one machinelike movement, there was an instant's picture of a horse in a great convulsive leap of a death wound and a rider leaning back with a crooked arm and spread fingers before his face. On the ground was the crimson terror of an exploding shell, with fibers of flame that seemed like lances. A glittering bugle swung

---

1. **battery** *n.*: set of heavy guns.
2. **caissons** (kā'sənz) *n. pl.*: ammunition wagons.

(Background) *Red Badge of Courage* manuscript, Stephen Crane Collection (5505).
Clifton Waller Barrett Library of American Literature, The Albert H. Small Special Collections Library, University of Virginia.

Stephen Crane   **435**

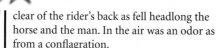

DIRECT TEACHING

A Learners Having Difficulty

❓ Summarizing. List what has been damaged so far. What has remained unharmed? [The house, fence, well house, and barn are all severely damaged. The "fair little meadow" is apparently untouched.]

B Literary Focus

❓ Situational irony. What is ironic about this passage? [Possible responses: The chaos and brutality of the battle scene provide an ironic contrast to the philosophical discussion taking place between Smith and Ferguson.]

C Political Issue

The Civil War. Crane knew that many soldiers did not participate in the Civil War solely to defend lofty political principles such as "national existence." As in any war, Union and Confederate soldiers fought for a variety of reasons—psychological, financial, and religious, as well as political.

D Content-Area Connections

History: Swing Team
A swing team is the middle group of a team of six harnessed horses. The team may be used to move guns from one direction to another in this story. What do the actions of the men and the animals suggest? [Possible response: Both are terrified by the shelling.]

---

clear of the rider's back as fell headlong the horse and the man. In the air was an odor as from a conflagration.

A Sometimes they of the infantry looked down at a fair little meadow which spread at their feet. Its long, green grass was rippling gently in a breeze. Beyond it was the gray form of a house half torn to pieces by shells and by the busy axes of soldiers who had pursued firewood. The line of an old fence was now dimly marked by long weeds and by an occasional post. A shell had blown the well house to fragments. Little lines of gray smoke ribboning upward from some embers indicated the place where had stood the barn.

B From beyond a curtain of green woods there came the sound of some stupendous scuffle as if two animals of the size of islands were fighting. At a distance there were occasional appearances of swift-moving men, horses, batteries, flags, and, with the crashing of infantry, volleys were heard, often, wild and frenzied cheers. In the midst of it all, Smith and Ferguson, two privates of A Company, were engaged in a heated discussion, which involved the greatest questions of

C the national existence.

The battery on the hill presently engaged in a frightful duel. The white legs of the gunners scampered this way and that way and the officers redoubled their shouts. The guns, with their demeanors of stolidity and courage, were typical of something infinitely self-possessed in this clamor of death that swirled around the hill.

D One of a "swing" team was suddenly smitten quivering to the ground and his maddened brethren dragged his torn body in their struggle to escape from this turmoil and danger. A young soldier astride one of the leaders swore and fumed in his saddle and furiously jerked at the bridle. An officer screamed out an order so violently that his voice broke and ended the sentence in a falsetto[3] shriek.

The leading company of the infantry regiment

---

3. **falsetto** *n.* used as *adj.*: artificially high voice.

The Hornet's Nest (1895) by Thomas Corwin Lindsay. Oil on canvas.

was somewhat exposed and the colonel ordered it moved more fully under the shelter of the hill. There was the clank of steel against steel.

A lieutenant of the battery rode down and passed them, holding his right arm carefully in his left hand. And it was as if this arm was not at all a part of him, but belonged to another man. His sober and reflective charger[4] went slowly. The officer's face was grimy and perspiring and his uniform was tousled as if he had been in direct grapple with an enemy. He smiled grimly when the men stared at him. He turned his horse toward the meadow.

---

4. **charger** *n.*: horse trained for battle.

Vocabulary
conflagration (kän′flə·grā′shən) *n.*: huge fire.
stolidity (stə·lid′ə·tē) *n.*: absence of emotional reactions.

DIFFERENTIATING INSTRUCTION

English-Language Learners
For lessons designed for intermediate and advanced English-language learners, see *Holt Reading Solutions*.

Special Education Students
For lessons designed for special education students, see *Holt Reading Solutions*.

Advanced Learners
Enrichment. Explore the differences in people's views on war and the military. Some readers may react negatively to Crane's realistic portrayal of war, while others may believe that it is important to depict war as terrifying and brutal rather than glorious. Remind students that they can debate this issue while respecting one another's views.

Courtesy Cincinnati Historical Society.

Collins of A Company said: "I wisht I had a drink. I bet there's water in that there ol' well yonder!"

"Yes; but how you goin' to git it?"

For the little meadow which intervened was now suffering a terrible onslaught of shells. Its green and beautiful calm had vanished utterly. Brown earth was being flung in monstrous handfuls. And there was a massacre of the young blades of grass. They were being torn, burned, obliterated. Some curious fortune of the battle had made this gentle little meadow the object of the red hate of the shells and each one as it exploded seemed like an imprecation[5] in the face of a maiden.

The wounded officer who was riding across this expanse said to himself: "Why, they couldn't

---

5. **imprecation** *n.:* curse.

---

shoot any harder if the whole army was massed here!"

A shell struck the gray ruins of the house and as, after the roar, the shattered wall fell in fragments, there was a noise which resembled the flapping of shutters during a wild gale of winter. Indeed the infantry paused in the shelter of the bank, appeared as men standing upon a shore contemplating a madness of the sea. The angel of calamity[6] had under its glance the battery upon the hill. Fewer white-legged men labored about the guns. A shell had smitten one of the pieces, and after the flare, the smoke, the dust, the wrath of this blow was gone, it was possible to see white legs stretched horizontally upon the ground. And at that interval to the rear, where it is the business of battery horses to stand with their noses to the fight awaiting the command to drag their guns out of the destruction or into it or wheresoever these incomprehensible humans demanded with whip and spur—in this line of passive and dumb spectators, whose fluttering hearts yet would not let them forget the iron laws of man's control of them—in this rank of brute soldiers there had been relentless and hideous carnage. From the ruck[7] of bleeding and prostrate[8] horses, the men of the infantry could see one animal raising its stricken body with its forelegs and turning its nose with mystic and profound eloquence toward the sky.

Some comrades joked Collins about his thirst. "Well, if yeh want a drink so bad, why don't yeh go git it?"

"Well, I will in a minnet if yeh don't shut up."

A lieutenant of artillery floundered his horse straight down the hill with as great concern as if it were level ground. As he galloped past the colonel of the infantry, he threw up his hand in swift salute. "We've got to get out of that," he roared angrily. He was a black-bearded officer, and his eyes, which resembled beads, sparkled

---

6. **calamity** *n.:* disaster; misfortune.
7. **ruck** *n.:* mass; crowd.
8. **prostrate** *adj.:* lying flat on the ground.

Stephen Crane   **437**

DIRECT TEACHING

A Literary Focus

Situational irony and motive. The plot of this story involves a number of ironies: Collins, an ordinary soldier, is goaded by his comrades into undertaking a task requiring great courage, but the prize for which he is imperiling his life is hardly worth the risk.

B Reading Skills

❓ Making predictions. What do you think will happen? Will the captain grant permission? Will Collins go through with his plan? [Possible responses: Yes—the captain will give permission, because the story presents Collins's thirst as a main conflict. Collins must follow through or risk losing face; perhaps he will change his mind when the time comes to set out.]

C Reading Skills

❓ Making inferences. Why does the colonel call Collins a "lad"? [Possible responses: The colonel feels protective toward Collins, so he uses personal rather than military terms; the colonel is condescending to Collins because of his lower rank.]

D Reading Skills

❓ Analyzing motivation. Why are the officers unsure whether Collins really wants to go? What does this reveal about Collins? [Possible responses: The officers are unsure because Collins is himself unsure. Perhaps battle has dulled his judgment; perhaps he is half aware that he is being driven by his own pride to do something extremely foolish and risky.]

---

like those of an insane man. His jumping horse sped along the column of infantry.

The fat major standing carelessly with his sword held horizontally behind him and with his legs far apart, looked after the receding horseman and laughed. "He wants to get back with orders pretty quick or there'll be no batt'ry left," he observed.

The wise young captain of the second company hazarded[9] to the lieutenant colonel that the enemy's infantry would probably soon attack the hill, and the lieutenant colonel snubbed him.

A private in one of the rear companies looked out over the meadow and then turned to a companion and said: "Look there, Jim." It was the wounded officer from the battery, who some time before had started to ride across the meadow, supporting his right arm carefully with his left hand. This man had encountered a shell apparently at a time when no one perceived him and he could now be seen lying face downward with a stirruped foot stretched across the body of his dead horse. A leg of the charger extended slantingly upward precisely as stiff as a stake. Around this motionless pair the shells still howled.

A There was a quarrel in A Company. Collins was shaking his fist in the faces of some laughing comrades. "Dern yeh! I ain't afraid t' go. If yeh say much, I will go!"

"Of course, yeh will! Yeh'll run through that there medder, won't yeh?"

Collins said, in a terrible voice: "You see, now!" At this ominous threat his comrades broke into renewed jeers.

Collins gave them a dark scowl and went to find his captain. The latter was conversing with the colonel of the regiment.

B "Captain," said Collins, saluting and standing at attention. In those days all trousers bagged at the knees. "Captain, I want t' git permission to go git some water from that there well over yonder!"

---

9. **hazarded** *v.:* risked saying.

The colonel and the captain swung about simultaneously and stared across the meadow. The captain laughed. "You must be pretty thirsty, Collins?"

"Yes, sir; I am."

"Well—ah," said the captain. After a moment he asked: "Can't you wait?"

"No, sir."

C The colonel was watching Collins's face. "Look here, my lad," he said, in a pious[10] sort of a voice. "Look here, my lad." Collins was not a lad. "Don't you think that's taking pretty big risks for a little drink of water?"

"I dunno," said Collins, uncomfortably. Some of the resentment toward his companions, which perhaps had forced him into this affair, was beginning to fade. "I dunno wether 'tis."

The colonel and the captain contemplated him for a time.

"Well," said the captain finally.

"Well," said the colonel, "if you want to go, why go."

Collins saluted. "Much obliged t' yeh."

As he moved away, the colonel called after him. "Take some of the other boys' canteens with you an' hurry back now."

"Yes, sir. I will."

D The colonel and the captain looked at each other then, for it had suddenly occurred that they could not for the life of them tell whether Collins wanted to go or whether he did not.

They turned to regard Collins, and as they perceived him surrounded by gesticulating comrades, the colonel said: "Well, by thunder! I guess he's going."

Collins appeared as a man dreaming. In the midst of the questions, the advice, the warnings, all the excited talk of his company mates, he maintained a curious silence.

---

10. **pious** *adj.:* seemingly virtuous.

Vocabulary

ominous (äm′ə·nəs) *adj.:* threatening; menacing.
gesticulating (jes·tik′yōō·lāt′iŋ) *v.* used as *adj.:* gesturing, especially with the hands and arms.

Literary Criticism

Critic's Commentary: Crane's Irony
The literary scholar R. W. Stallman describes Crane's writing as having the emotional intensity of poetry. He says that Crane's "aim was to immerse the reader in the created experience so that its impact on him would occur simultaneously with the discovery of it by the characters themselves. Instead of panoramic views of a battlefield, Crane paints not the whole scene but disconnected segments of it—all that a participant in an action or a spectator of a scene can possibly take into his view at any one moment." Stallman continues, "Irony is Crane's chief technical instrument. . . . Crane is always dealing with the paradox of man, the paradox of his plight. . . . This . . . conflict, the conflict between ideas and realities, ruled Crane's struggle as artist and gave both his life and his art all their bitter ironies."

He scrambled erect and g...
On the ground near him lay...
with a length of rusty chain...
swiftly into the well. The bu...
water and then turning lazil...
with hand reaching trembli...
hauled it out, it knocked oft...
of the well and spilled some...

In running with a filled b...
adopt but one kind of gait. S...
terrible field over which scr...
angels of death Collins ran i...
a farmer chased out of a dai...

His face went staring whi...
tion—anticipation of a blov...
him around and down. He v...
seen other men fall, the life...
them so suddenly that their...
quick to touch the ground t...
saw the long blue line of the...
comrades were standing loo...
the edge of an impossible st...
some deep wheel ruts and h...
beneath his feet.

The artillery officer who...
meadow had been making g...
of the tempest of sound. Th...
wrenched from him by his a...
only by shells, bullets. Wher...
came running, this officer r...
face contorted and blanche...
about to utter some great b...
suddenly his face straighten...
"Say, young man, give me a...
you?"

Collins had no room am...
for surprise. He was mad fr...
destruction.

"I can't," he screamed, an...
full description of his quaki...
His cap was gone and his h...
clothes made it appear that...
over the ground by the heels...

The officer's head sank d...
crooked. His foot in its bras...

They were very busy in preparing him for his
ordeal. When they inspected him carefully, it
was somewhat like the examination that grooms
give a horse before a race; and they were
amazed, staggered by the whole affair. Their
astonishment found vent in strange repetitions.

"Are yeh sure a-goin'?" they demanded again
and again.

"Certainly I am," cried Collins, at last furiously.

He strode sullenly[11] away from them. He was
swinging five or six canteens by their cords. It
seemed that his cap would not remain firmly
on his head, and often he reached and pulled it
down over his brow.

There was a general movement in the compact column. The long animal-like thing moved
slightly. Its four hundred eyes were turned upon
the figure of Collins.

"Well, sir, if that ain't th' derndest thing.
I never thought Fred Collins had the blood in
him for that kind of business."

"What's he goin' to do, anyhow?"

"He's goin' to that well there after water."

"We ain't dyin' of thirst, are we? That's foolishness."

"Well, somebody put him up to it an' he's
doin' it."

"Say, he must be a desperate cuss."

When Collins faced the meadow and walked
away from the regiment, he was vaguely conscious that a chasm, the deep valley of all prides,
was suddenly between him and his comrades. It
was provisional, but the provision was that he
return as a victor. He had blindly been led by
quaint emotions and laid himself under an
obligation to walk squarely up to the face of
death.

But he was not sure that he wished to make
a retraction even if he could do so without
shame. As a matter of truth he was sure of very
little. He was mainly surprised.

It seemed to him supernaturally strange that
he had allowed his mind to maneuver his body

11. **sullenly** *adv.:* in a resentful manner; sulkily.

into such a situation. He understood that it
might be called dramatically great.

However, he had no full appreciation
of anything excepting that he was actually conscious of being dazed. He could feel his dulled
mind groping after the form and color of this
incident.

Too, he wondered why he did not feel some
keen agony of fear cutting his sense like a knife.
He wondered at this because human expression
had said loudly for centuries that men should
feel afraid of certain things and that all men
who did not feel this fear were phenomena,
heroes.

He was then a hero. He suffered that
disappointment which we would all have if
we discovered that we were ourselves capable
of those deeds which we most admire in history
and legend. This, then, was a hero. After all,
heroes were not much.

No, it could not be true. He was not a hero.
Heroes had no shames in their lives and, as for
him, he remembered borrowing fifteen dollars
from a friend and promising to pay it back the
next day, and then avoiding that friend for ten
months. When at home his mother had aroused
him for the early labor of his life on the farm, it
had often been his fashion to be irritable, childish, diabolical, and his mother had died since he
had come to the war.

He saw that in this matter of the well, the
canteens, the shells, he was an intruder in the
land of fine deeds.

He was now about thirty paces from his
comrades. The regiment had just turned its
many faces toward him.

From the forest of terrific noises there suddenly emerged a little uneven line of men. They
fired fiercely and rapidly at distant foliage on
which appeared little puffs of white smoke. The

Vocabulary

provisional (prə·vizh'ə·nəl) *adj.:* temporary; serving for
the time being.

retraction (ri·trak'shən) *n.:* withdrawal.

DIRECT TEACHING

E **Reading Skills**

? **Drawing conclusions.** What
do you think finally makes Collins
go? [Possible responses: pride;
unwillingness to lose face; thirst; the
colonel's "order" to take canteens
with him; the confusion of battle;
fate.]

F **Literary Focus**

? **Theme.** How does this passage
convey the central theme of the
story? What does it suggest about
the title? [Possible responses: By
showing that Collins is unsure why he
acts as he does, Crane suggests that
uncertainty—or at least a mix of
motives—lies behind much of human
behavior; Crane is suggesting that
heroism is an elusive concept and is
ultimately beyond understanding.]

G **Reading Skills**

? **Analyzing character.** Do
these thoughts seem like ones a
person would be likely to have
under the circumstances? Why or
why not? [Possible responses: Yes,
because Collins suddenly feels that he
is in over his head; yes, because in a
life-or-death situation, people often
feel compelled to be honest with
themselves about their past actions.]

H **Reading Skills**

? **Making judgments.** Is Collins
in fact an "intruder in the land of
fine deeds"? Why or why not?
[Possible responses: No, because he
is about to undertake an action that
requires great courage; yes, because
he is motivated by foolish pride and
pettiness rather than nobility and
heroism.]

CONTENT-AREA CONNECTIONS

Check Test: Short

Monitoring students'
class in answering these

1. What is the setting o...
   takes place during a fu...

2. For what does Collin...
   running across the m...
   get some water.]

Psychology: Battle Fatigue
The anxiety, physical strain, and mortal danger
of war sometimes produce a condition known
as "combat fatigue" or "battle fatigue." The
symptoms of this complex condition include
depression, intense anxiety, irritability,
and grief.

Literature: The Hero
Remind students that literature reflects the
values of a society, including its definition of
heroism. Ancient and medieval heroes—
Odysseus, Beowulf, King Arthur, the Cid—
were judged according to clearly defined
values. In Crane's time, realist and naturalist
writers raised new questions about the concept of heroism.

A Literary Focus

? Diction and atm...
Identify the words in t...
paragraphs that Crane...
vey the hellish atmosph...
[*demon, flying arrows, fla...*
boiling, howled, insane, m...
hootings, yells, howls, fien...

B Content-Area Connections

Literature: Naturalis...
? The naturalist write...
that nature is indiffere...
human struggle for sur...
does this scene reflect...
[Possible response: The...
slowly into the canteen...
Collins's urgency. Collin...
is mocking him.]

VIEWING THE ...

Benjamin West Cli...
red to denote battle,...
Crane does in his nov...
Badge of Courage. The...
uniforms evoke the C...
while the "rockets' re...
the top of the page s...
in general.

Activity. Ask studer...
pare this painting witl...
Lindsay on pp. 436–4...
one conveys the moc...
more effectively? [Pos...
response: This painting...
because the splashes ...
blood, fire, and terror....
Lindsay's painting seen...
almost sedate, in comp...

A Literary Focus

? Comic devices: Hyperbole.
Point out that this is an example of hyperbole. Why is this exaggeration humorous? [Possible response: The idea that someone would follow a bug anywhere, much less all the way to Mexico, is amusingly absurd.]

B Reading Skills

? Understanding vernacular.
How can you figure out the meaning of the word *warn't*? What does it add to the story? [Possible response: The word *warn't*, when spoken aloud, sounds like *weren't*, which makes sense when substituted in the sentence. The use of the vernacular helps the reader hear Wheeler's speech.]

C Literary Focus

? Comic devices: Comic situations. How does Twain add humor to the story about the mare? [Possible response: The words *cavorting, straddling,* and *scattering* help readers picture the ungainly movements of the mare as she blunders across the finish line.]

the spring of '50—I don't recollect exactly, somehow, though what makes me think it was one or the other is because I remember the big flume[4] wasn't finished when he first came to the camp; but anyway, he was the curiousest man about always betting on anything that turned up you ever see, if he could get anybody to bet on the other side; and if he couldn't, he'd change sides. Any way that suited the other man would suit him—any way just so's he got a bet, *he* was satisfied. But still he was lucky, uncommon lucky; he most always come out winner. He was always ready and laying for a chance; there couldn't be no solit'ry thing mentioned but that feller'd offer to bet on it and take any side you please, as I was just telling you. If there was a horse race, you'd find him flush,[5] or you'd find him busted at the end of it; if there was a dog-fight, he'd bet on it; if there was a catfight, he'd bet on it; why if there was a chicken fight, he'd bet on it; why, if there was two birds setting on a fence, he would bet you which one would fly first; or if there was a camp meeting, he would be there reg'lar, to bet on Parson Walker, which he judged to be the best exhorter[6] about here,

A and so he was, too, and a good man. If he even seen a straddlebug start to go anywheres, he would bet you how long it would take him to get wherever he was going to, and if you took him up, he would foller that straddlebug to Mexico but what he would find out where he was bound for and how long he was on the road. Lots of the boys here has seen that Smiley and can tell you about him. Why, it never made no difference to *him*—he would bet on *any-thing*—the dangdest feller. Parson Walker's wife
B laid very sick once, for a good while, and it seemed as if they warn't going to save her; but one morning he come in, and Smiley asked how she was, and he said she was considerable bet-ter—thank the Lord for his inf'nit mercy—and coming on so smart that with the blessing of Prov'dence, she'd get well yet; and Smiley, before he thought, says, "Well, I'll risk twoandahalf that she don't, anyway."

Thish-yer Smiley had a mare—the boys called her the fifteen-minute nag, but that was only in fun, you know, because, of course, she was faster than that—and he used to win money on that horse, for all she was so slow and always had the asthma, or the distemper, or the consumption, or something of that kind. They used to give her two or three hundred yards'
C start and then pass her underway; but always at the end of the race she'd get excited and desper-ate-like, and come cavorting[7] and straddling up, and scattering her legs around limber, some-times in the air, and sometimes out to one side amongst the fences, and kicking up m-o-r-e dust, and raising m-o-r-e racket with her coughing and sneezing and blowing her nose— and always fetch up at the stand just about a neck ahead, as near as you could cipher it down.[8]

And he had a little small bull pup, that to look at him you'd think he wa'n't worth a cent but to set around and look ornery and lay for a chance to steal something. But as soon as money was up on him, he was a different dog; his under-

---

4. **flume** *n.:* man-made waterway.
5. **flush** *adj.:* with a lot of money.
6. **exhorter** (eg·zôrt'ər) *n.:* preacher.

7. **cavorting** *v.* used as *adv.:* running around playfully.
8. **cipher** (sī'fər) **it down:** calculate it.

DIFFERENTIATING INSTRUCTION

Advanced Learners
Have students write a newspaper account in which the "fifteen-minute nag" wins a race at the last minute. The article could be a front-page story, a feature, or a sports story. Tell students to use some of Twain's comic devices.

jaw'd begin to stick out like the fo'castle[9] of a steamboat, and his teeth would uncover and shine savage like the furnaces. And a dog might tackle him, and bullyrag him, and bite him, and throw him over his shoulder two or three times, and Andrew Jackson—which was the name of the pup—Andrew Jackson would never let on but what *he* was satisfied and hadn't expected nothing else—and the bets being doubled and doubled on the other side all the time, till the money was all up; and then all of a sudden he would grab that other dog jest by the j'int of his hind leg and freeze to it—not chaw, you understand, but only jest grip and hang on till they throwed up the sponge,[10] if it was a year. Smiley always come out winner on that pup, till he harnessed a dog once that didn't have no hind legs, because they'd been sawed off by a circular saw, and when the thing had gone along far enough, and the money was all up, and he come to make a snatch for his pet holt,[11] he saw in a minute how he'd been imposed on and how the other dog had him in the door, so to speak, and he 'peared surprised, and then he looked sorter discouraged-like, and didn't try no more to win the fight, and so he got shucked out bad. He give Smiley a look, as much as to say his heart was broke, and it was *his* fault, for putting up a dog that hadn't no hind legs for him to take holt of, which was his main dependence in a fight, and then he limped off a piece and laid down and died. It was a good pup, was that Andrew Jackson, and would have made a name for hisself if he'd lived, for the stuff was in him, and

he had genius—I know it, because he hadn't no opportunities to speak of, and it don't stand to reason that a dog could make such a fight as he could under them circumstances, if he hadn't no talent. It always makes me feel sorry when I think of that last fight of his'n, and the way it turned out.

Well, thish-yer Smiley had rat tarriers, and chicken cocks, and tomcats, and all them kind of things, till you couldn't rest, and you couldn't fetch nothing for him to bet on but he'd match you. He ketched a frog one day, and took him home, and said he cal'klated to edercate him; and so he never done nothing for three months but set in his backyard and learn that frog to jump. And you bet you he *did* learn him, too. He'd give him a little punch behind, and the next minute you'd see that frog whirling in the air like a doughnut—see him turn one summerset, or maybe a couple, if he got a good start, and come down flat-footed and all right, like a cat. He got him up so in the matter of catching flies, and kept him in practice so constant, that he'd nail a fly every time as far as he could see him. Smiley said all a frog wanted was education, and he could do most anything—and I believe him. Why, I've seen him set Dan'l Webster down here on this floor—Dan'l Webster was the name of the frog—and sing out, "Flies, Dan'l, flies!" and quicker'n you could wink, he'd spring straight up, and snake a fly off'n the counter there, and flop down on the floor again as solid as a gob of mud, and fall to scratching the side of his head with his hind foot as indifferent as if he hadn't no idea he'd been doin' any more'n any frog might do. You never see a frog so modest and straightfor'ard as he was, for all he was so gifted. And when it come to fair-and-square jumping on a dead

---

9. **fo'castle** (fōk'səl) *n.:* forecastle, the front part of a ship's upper deck.
10. **throwed up the sponge:** gave up.
11. **pet holt:** favorite grip.

Mark Twain 463

D **Literary Focus**

❓ **Comic devices: Hyperbole and irony.** What comic device does Twain use here? [Twain uses hyperbole when he writes that Andrew Jackson can hold on to another dog's hind leg for a year. He uses irony in describing the fight between Andrew Jackson and the dog with no hind legs.]

E **Reading Skills**
Understanding vernacular. Explain that *a piece* means "a distance."

F **Literary Focus**

❓ **Comic devices: Comic comparisons.** What dissimilar things is Twain comparing here to create humor? [He compares the frog flying through the air to a doughnut and the frog landing on all four feet to a cat.]

G **Literary Focus**

❓ **Personification.** Why is it humorous when Wheeler calls the frog "modest" and "straightfor'ard"? [Modesty and straightforwardness are qualities associated with humans. The notion that a frog might display these qualities is ludicrous.]

History: Angel's Camp
Angel's Camp is located in Calaveras County, west of Yosemite. It was founded in 1848 as a mining camp. Today tourists visit the small town to see its historic buildings—formerly dance halls and saloons—and to take part in frog-jumping contests held in honor of Mark Twain's famous story.

Individual activity. Have students research various aspects of the California Gold Rush: the lives of the miners, the effect on westward expansion, the cultural and environmental legacy, and the literary accounts of writers like Bret Harte and Mark Twain.

A Literary Focus

? Comic devices:
Understatement. What comic
device does Twain use in this sentence? [This is an example of understatement. Smiley speaks slightingly of
his frog to fool the stranger.]

B Literary Focus

? Comic devices: Comic
character. What is humorous
about the stranger? [His sadness
over not having a frog of his own is
faintly ridiculous.]

level, he could get over more ground at one
straddle than any animal of his breed you ever
see. Jumping on a dead level was his strong suit,
you understand; and when it come to that, Smiley would ante up money on him as long as he
had a red.[12] Smiley was monstrous proud of his
frog, and well he might be, for fellers that had
traveled and been everywheres all said he laid
over any frog that ever *they* see.

Well, Smiley kept the beast in a little lattice
box, and he used to fetch him downtown sometimes and lay for a bet. One day a feller—a
stranger in the camp, he was—come across him
with his box, and says:

"What might it be that you've got in the box?"

A And Smiley says, sorter indifferent-like, "It
might be a parrot, or it might be a canary,
maybe, but it ain't—it's only just a frog."

And the feller took it, and looked at it careful,
and turned it round this way and that, and says,
"H'm—so 'tis. Well, what's *he* good for?"

_____
12. **red** *n.*: penny (as in *red cent*).

"Well," Smiley says, easy and careless, "he's
good enough for *one* thing, I should judge—he
can outjump any frog in Calaveras County."

The feller took the box again, and took another long, particular look, and give it back to
Smiley, and says, very deliberate, "Well, I don't
see no p'ints[13] about that frog that's any better'n
any other frog."

"Maybe you don't," Smiley says. "Maybe you
understand frogs, and maybe you don't understand 'em; maybe you've had experience, and
maybe you an't only a amature, as it were.
Anyways, I've got *my* opinion, and I'll risk
forty dollars that he can outjump any frog in
Calaveras County."

B And the feller studied a minute and then
says, kinder sadlike, "Well, I'm only a stranger
here, and I an't got no frog; but if I had a frog,
I'd bet you."

And then Smiley says, "That's all right—

_____
13. **p'ints** *n. pl.*: points, or physical qualities of an
animal, used to judge breeding.

DIFFERENTIATING INSTRUCTION

Learners Having Difficulty
To help students understand vernacular
expressions, model the skill of using context
clues. Direct students' attention to the sentence beginning "Jumping on a dead level,"
near the top of column one on p. 464. Point
out that since you already know that the frog
is an excellent jumper and that Smiley wants
to bet on it, you can guess that *strong suit*

means "area of expertise" and *ante up* means
"bet."

English-Language Learners
It may help students to see the correct
spellings of unfamiliar words in vernacular
expressions. Suggest that they ask a peer
tutor to help them write the correctly spelled
expressions in their reading logs.

that's all right—if you'll hold my box a minute, I'll go and get you a frog." And so the feller took the box, and put up his forty dollars along with Smiley's, and set down to wait.

So he set there a good while thinking and thinking to hisself, and then he got the frog out and prized[14] his mouth open and took a teaspoon and filled him full of quail shot[15]—filled him pretty near up to his chin—and set him on the floor. Smiley he went to the swamp and slopped around in the mud for a long time, and finally he ketched a frog, and fetched him in, and give him to this feller, and says:

"Now, if you're ready, set him alongside of Dan'l, with his forepaws just even with Dan'l, and I'll give the word." Then he says, "One—two—three—jump!" and him and the feller touched up the frogs from behind, and the new frog hopped off, but Dan'l give a heave, and hysted up his shoulders—so—like a Frenchman, but it wan't no use—he couldn't budge; he was planted as solid as an anvil,[16] and he couldn't no more stir than if he was anchored out. Smiley was a good deal surprised, and he was disgusted too, but he didn't have no idea what the matter was, of course.

The feller took the money and started away; and when he was going out at the door, he sorter jerked his thumb over his shoulders—this way—at Dan'l, and says again, very deliberate, "Well, I don't see no p'ints about that frog that's any better'n any other frog."

Smiley he stood scratching his head and looking down at Dan'l a long time, and at last he says, "I do wonder what in the nation that frog throw'd off for—I wonder if there an't something the matter with him—he 'pears to look mighty baggy, somehow." And he ketched Dan'l by the nap of the neck and lifted him up and says, "Why, blame my cats, if he don't weigh five pound!" and turned him upside down, and he belched out a double handful of shot. And

then he see how it was, and he was the maddest man—he set the frog down and took out after that feller, but he never ketched him. And—

[Here Simon Wheeler heard his name called from the front yard and got up to see what was wanted.] And turning to me as he moved away, he said: "Just set where you are, stranger, and rest easy—I an't going to be gone a second."

But, by your leave, I did not think that a continuation of the history of the enterprising vagabond[17] *Jim* Smiley would be likely to afford me much information concerning the Rev. *Leonidas W.* Smiley, and so I started away.

At the door I met the sociable Wheeler returning, and he buttonholed[18] me and recommenced:

"Well, thish-yer Smiley had a yaller one-eyed cow that didn't have no tail, only jest a short stump like a bannanner, and—"

"Oh! hang Smiley and his afflicted cow!" I muttered, good-naturedly, and bidding the old gentleman good day, I departed. ∎

---

14. **prized** *v.:* pried.
15. **shot** *n.:* metal pellets used as ammunition for a shotgun.
16. **anvil** *n.:* iron or steel block on which metal objects are hammered into shape.

17. **vagabond** *n.:* someone who wanders from place to place without a home; drifter.
18. **buttonholed** *v.:* approached aggressively and delayed in conversation.

Mark Twain **465**

Primary Source

This tall tale appeared in the *Saturday Press* on November 18, 1865, creating an instant uproar. Instead of being gratified by his new-found celebrity, Twain, who did not think much of the story, was annoyed that works he regarded more highly had not received a similar amount of attention. In this retranslation, Twain shows not only his skill at manipulating language to achieve an aesthetic purpose but also his ability to create humor out of a disagreeable situation.

DIRECT TEACHING

A Reading Skills

❷ Making inferences. Why do you think Twain said that the French version of his story would bring grief and sickness to anyone who read it? [He was probably commenting on the poor quality of the translation.]

B Literary Focus

❷ Satire. How is this sentence satirical? [Possible response: Twain is using fractured English to poke fun at the peculiarities of the French language.]

C Literary Focus

❷ Comic devices: Comic comparisons. Why do you think Twain retranslates the word *doughnut* as *grease-biscuit*? [Possible response: He is making a humorous reference to the qualities of a doughnut.]

The Frog Jumping of the County of Calaveras

After Twain's story appeared in a New York newspaper in 1865, it became so popular that it was soon reprinted in newspapers across the country. The story, which helped make Twain a national celebrity, was even translated into French. After reading the French version, Twain said it would bring grief and sickness to anyone who read it. He took revenge by retranslating the story into English. Here is an excerpt from "The Frog Jumping of the County of Calaveras":

❝Eh bien! This Smiley nourished some terriers à rats, and some cocks of combat, and some cats, and all sorts of things; and with his rage of betting one no had more of repose. He trapped one day a frog and him imported with him (et l'emporta chez lui), saying that he pretended to make his education. You me believe if you will, but during three months he not has nothing done but to him apprehend to jump (apprendre à sauter) in a court retired of her mansion (de sa maison). And I you respond that he have succeeded. He him gives a small blow by behind, and the instant after you shall see the frog turn in the air like a grease-biscuit, makes one summersault, sometimes two, when she was well started, and re-fall upon his feet like a cat. He him had accomplished in the art of to gobble the flies (gober des mouches), and him there exercised continually—so well that a fly at the most far that she appeared was a fly lost.❞

Mark Twain

Drawing by David Levine. Reprinted with permission from *The New York Review of Books*. Copyright © 1966 NYREV, Inc.

DEVELOPING FLUENCY

Paired activity. Students may find it easier to appreciate the humor of the selection if they hear it read aloud. Provide students with a French-English dictionary, and allow them to translate the French words used in the selection. Then, pair students and have them take turns reading sections aloud to each other.

ASSESSING

Assessment
■ *Holt Assessment: Literature, Reading, and Vocabulary*

RETEACHING

For a lesson reteaching irony, tone, and author's style, see **Reteaching,** p. 1117A.

Response and Analysis

Reading Check

1. What does the narrator hope to learn from Simon Wheeler? What does he learn instead?

2. According to Wheeler, what was Jim Smiley's favorite activity?

3. Which frog wins the jumping contest? Why?

Thinking Critically

4. "The Celebrated Jumping Frog of Calaveras County" is a story within a story—that is, it consists of a **frame story** (at the beginning and the end) and an inner story. What is the basic plot of the frame story?

5. Describe Simon Wheeler's **tone,** or attitude, toward his story. Do you think his tone adds to the humor of Mark Twain's story? Why or why not?

6. Find at least three places in the story where Twain uses the **vernacular.** Explain why the vernacular makes the story more authentic, more vivid, or more comic.

7. Find two or more examples of each of the following **comic devices:** hyperbole, comic comparisons, and comic characters and situations.

8. Compare Twain's retranslated excerpt on page 466 with the original selection, found on page 463. How does this retranslation illustrate Twain's humor and wit?

Extending and Evaluating

9. Do you think "The Celebrated Jumping Frog of Calaveras County" is funny? Why or why not?

Literary Criticism

10. **Tall tales,** like this story by Twain, played a major role in the imaginative life of Americans. Stretchers, whoppers, and embroidered lies became an amazingly popular form of fiction. Do you think Americans today still have this love of exaggeration? Why or why not?

WRITING

Tell the Tale

The narrator leaves when Wheeler starts to tell him about Smiley's "yaller one-eyed cow that didn't have no tail." What amazing story do you think Wheeler might have told about that cow? Write Wheeler's "yaller one-eyed cow" **story.** Include at least two comic devices (such as hyperbole, understatement, comic comparisons, and comic characters and situations). You may also want to try imitating the vernacular that Twain uses or another vernacular that you are familiar with. Read aloud as you write. Remember that much of the humor of this kind of story comes from its *sound.*

▶ **Use "Writing a Short Story," pages 284–291, for help with this assignment.**

Vocabulary Development

Yes or No

Be sure you can justify your answers to these questions.

1. Would a garrulous person be a lively party guest?

2. If the man conjectured that his frog would win the contest, would he bet against it?

3. Would an infamous liar tell the absolute truth in court?

4. Is a dilapidated shack likely to be the home of a millionaire?

5. Is listening to an interminable story enjoyable?

SKILLS FOCUS

Literary Skills
Analyze comic devices.

Reading Skills
Analyze author's style and use of the vernacular.

Writing Skills
Write a story using comic devices.

Vocabulary Skills
Demonstrate word knowledge.

Response and Analysis

6. Possible answer: Examples of vernacular include "sorter discouraged-like," "cal'klated to edercate him," and "ketched." They help the reader imagine the characters and the setting.

7. Possible answers: *Hyperbole*—Smiley's following a straddlebug to Mexico; the frog's catching every fly. *Comic comparisons*—the comparison of the frog to a doughnut; the implied comparison of the frog to a racehorse. *Comic characters and situations*—Smiley teaching the frog to jump; the stranger filling the frog full of shot.

8. Possible answer: Twain is ridiculing the idea of translating his story, which is quintessentially American in its language and humor, into French.

Extending and Evaluating

9. Possible answers: Yes, because the characters and situations are so absurd; no, the story is too far-fetched to be funny.

Literary Criticism

10. Possible answer: Yes, this genre is timeless; it is used in humorous stories, TV shows, and movies.

Vocabulary Development

1. No; other guests probably find him or her boring and tiresome.

2. No; he would expect his frog to win.

3. No; someone known for lying would not be likely to tell the truth.

4. No; a rich person's home is likely to be large and well maintained.

5. No; it would probably make listeners bored and impatient.

Reading Check

1. The narrator asks Wheeler about a man named Leonidas W. Smiley. Wheeler tells him about Jim Smiley instead.

2. Smiley's favorite activity is betting.

3. The stranger's frog wins because the stranger has filled Smiley's frog with shot.

Thinking Critically

4. The narrator asks Wheeler about Leonidas W. Smiley. Wheeler launches into a story about Jim Smiley, someone entirely different. Wheeler is called away, and the narrator escapes.

5. Possible answer: Wheeler's calm, serious tone adds to the humor because it contrasts sharply with the absurdity of the tale.

SKILLS FOCUS,
pp. 468–478

Grade-Level Skills

■ **Literary Skills**
Analyze characteristics of satire.

■ **Reading Skills**
Make reasonable assertions about an author's purpose and arguments by using elements of the text to defend interpretations.

Before You Read

The Lowest Animal

Make the Connection
Quickwrite ✏

Americans have always had a high regard for progress and self-improvement. Mark Twain couples this admirable national trait with a blistering vision of how far, in his opinion, the human race falls short of its ideals. Think about what you would like to change about human nature, and freewrite your ideas.

Literary Focus
Satire: The Weapon of Laughter

Mark Twain wrote that we have only "one really effective weapon—laughter. Power, money, persuasion, supplication—these can lift a colossal humbug—push it a little—weaken it a little, century by century; but only laughter can blow it to rags and atoms at a blast."

Satire uses humor to critique people or institutions with the intention of improving them. One of the favorite techniques of the satirist is **exaggeration**—overstating something to make it look ridiculous. Another technique is **irony**—stating the opposite of what's really meant.

Like many other great satires, this famous essay is clearly outrageous. Twain doesn't really mean much of what he says, but sometimes the most exaggerated and maddening pieces of writing force us to think critically.

INTERNET

Vocabulary Practice
•
More About Mark Twain
•
Keyword: LE5 11-4

SKILLS FOCUS

Literary Skills
Understand the characteristics of satire.

Reading Skills
Analyze a writer's purpose.

> **Satire** is a type of writing that ridicules the shortcomings of people and institutions in an attempt to bring about change.
>
> *For more on Satire, see the Handbook of Literary and Historical Terms.*

Reading Skills 📖
Recognizing a Writer's Purpose

In general, a writer's **purpose** can be to describe, to inform, to narrate, to entertain, to analyze, or to persuade. Satires are usually exaggerated and humorous, but the true satirist intends to do more than simply make you laugh. Real-world change; reform; honest reexamination of values; the development of new goals, attitudes, and perspectives—these are the satirist's deeper purposes. To get to the deeper meaning of a satire, consider the following questions:

• What is the writer's philosophical position?
• What are the writer's religious, political, and social beliefs?
• Whom or what is the writer aiming to improve? What is his or her target?
• What does the writer want me to believe and—most important—to *do*?

Vocabulary Development

dispositions (dis′pə·zish′ənz) *n. pl.:* natures; characters.

allegiance (ə·lē′jəns) *n.:* loyalty.

caliber (kal′ə·bər) *n.:* quality or ability.

wantonly (wänt′'n·lē) *adv.:* carelessly, often with ill will.

transition (tran·zish′ən) *n.:* passage from one condition, form, or stage to another.

scrupled (skr⁻oo′pəld) *v.:* hesitated because of feelings of guilt.

appease (ə·pēz′) *v.:* satisfy; pacify.

avaricious (av′ə·rish′əs) *adj.:* greedy.

atrocious (ə·trō′shəs) *adj.:* evil; very bad.

sordid (sôr′did) *adj.:* dirty; cheap; shameful.

Planning
■ *One-Stop Planner* CD-ROM with ExamView Test Generator

Differentiating Instruction
■ *Supporting Instruction in Spanish*
■ *Audio CD Library, Selections and Summaries in Spanish*

Vocabulary
■ *Vocabulary Development*

Grammar and Language
■ *Daily Language Activities*

Assessment
■ *Holt Assessment: Literature, Reading, and Vocabulary*
■ *One-Stop Planner* CD-ROM with ExamView Test Generator

■ *Holt Online Assessment*

Internet
■ go.hrw.com (Keyword: LE5 11-4)
■ *Elements of Literature Online*

Media
■ *Audio CD Library*
■ *Audio CD Library, Selections and Summaries in Spanish*

The Lowest Animal

Mark Twain

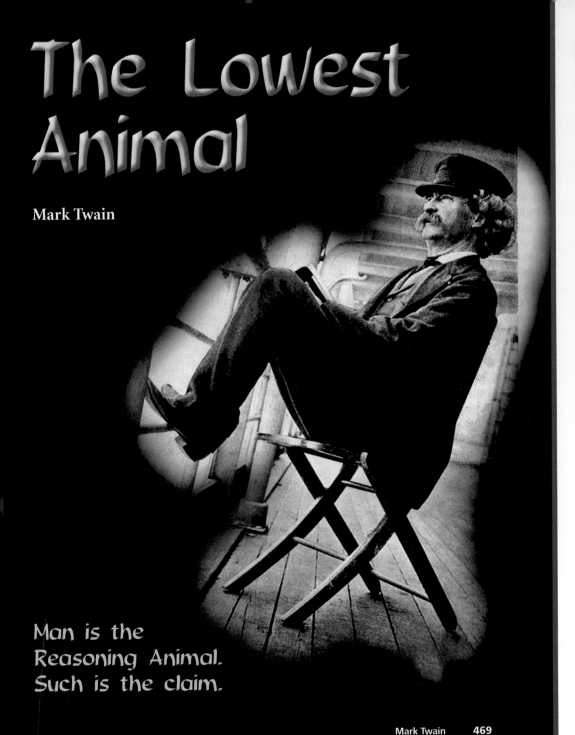

Man is the
Reasoning Animal.
Such is the claim.

PRETEACHING

Summary ⬆ *above grade level*

In "The Lowest Animal," Mark Twain satirizes human nature by describing a series of scientific experiments he purportedly conducted in which he compared humans with the "lower animals." His studies do not shed a favorable light on humans, to put it mildly. Twain points out that humans are the only animals that harm others in the name of religion and patriotism. In fact, Twain asserts that human traits such as cruelty, foolishness, greed, and indecency make humans the lowest—rather than the highest—animals.

Skills Starter

Build review skills. Remind students that to make warranted and reasonable assertions about an author's arguments, they must support their ideas with details and examples from the selection. To identify an author's implicit assumptions about a subject, they should first consider the author's explicit assumptions—those that are clearly stated. They should then use details from the author's arguments to make inferences about the author's implicit message.

Previewing Vocabulary

Have students read the definitions of the Vocabulary words on p. 468 and write their responses to the following questions. (Possible responses are given.)

1. How might you <u>appease</u> children with grumpy <u>dispositions</u>? [by taking them to a park]

2. Name a character whose <u>avaricious</u> nature led him or her to do <u>atrocious</u> things. [the stepmother in "Snow White"]

3. What is one important <u>transition</u> that you will make in the next few years? [I will go to college.]

4. When you pledge <u>allegiance</u> to something, what are you doing? [I am promising to be loyal to it.]

5. If your teacher tells you that your essay is of high <u>caliber</u>, would you expect a good or poor grade on it? [a good grade]

6. If you behave <u>wantonly</u>, how are you acting? [recklessly]

7. What might happen to someone who <u>scrupled</u> to take part in a <u>sordid</u> scheme? [The person might avoid trouble.]

A **Literary Focus**

Satire. What name does Twain suggest for his "new and truer" theory? [the Descent of Man from the Higher Animals] What makes this an example of satire? [Twain pokes fun at commonly held beliefs by turning them upside down. It is this unexpected reversal that makes his suggestion satirical.]

B **Content-Area Connections**

History: Zoological Gardens of London
The Zoological Society of London was founded in 1826. The group's goal was to open a zoo that would be used primarily by scientists. In 1828, the Zoological Gardens opened in Regent's Park; the public was charged an entrance fee to help finance research.

C **Learners Having Difficulty**

Summarizing. In your own words, summarize Twain's three generalizations. [Possible response: Humans form one family. Animals with four legs form another family. All other species, such as insects and birds, belong to the chain of animals in which humans are at the bottom.]

Responses to Boxed Questions

1. Twain's claim is that Darwin's theory of the Ascent of Man from the Lower Animals should be replaced by a new theory called the Descent of Man from the Higher Animals.

2. He says that he has used the scientific method.

I have been studying the traits and dispositions of the "lower animals" (so-called) and contrasting them with the traits and dispositions of man. I find the result humiliating to me. For it obliges me to renounce[1] my allegiance to the Darwinian theory of the Ascent of Man from the Lower Animals, since it now seems plain to me that that theory ought to be vacated[2] in favor of a new and truer one, this new and truer one to be named the *Descent* of Man from the Higher Animals. **❶**

❶ Twain presents his **claim,** explaining his **purpose** in writing this essay. From his tone and statements we can guess that we are reading a **satire.** *What is Twain's claim?*

In proceeding toward this unpleasant conclusion, I have not guessed or speculated or conjectured,[3] but have used what is commonly called the scientific method.[4] That is to say, I have subjected every postulate[5] that presented itself to the crucial test of actual experiment and have adopted it or rejected it according to the result. Thus, I verified and established each step of my course in its turn before advancing to the next. These experiments were made in the London Zoological Gardens and covered many months of painstaking and fatiguing work. **❷**

❷ *What method does Twain use to arrive at his conclusions?*

Before particularizing any of the experiments, I wish to state one or two things which seem to more properly belong in this place than further along. This in the interest of clearness. The massed experiments established to my satisfaction certain generalizations, to wit: **❸**

❸ Here Twain explains that experiments have led him to three main **generalizations,** which he then outlines.

1. **renounce** *v.:* give up; reject.
2. **vacated** *v.:* made void.
3. **conjectured** *v.:* inferred; predicted from incomplete evidence.
4. **scientific method:** research method in which a theory is tested by careful, documented experiments.
5. **postulate** (päs'chə·lit) *n.:* assumption.

1. That the human race is of one distinct species. It exhibits slight variations—in color, stature, mental caliber, and so on—due to climate, environment, and so forth; but it is a species by itself and not to be confounded with any other.

2. That the quadrupeds[6] are a distinct family, also. This family exhibits variations—in color, size, food preferences, and so on; but it is a family by itself.

3. That the other families—the birds, the fishes, the insects, the reptiles, etc.—are more or less distinct, also. They are in the procession. They are links in the chain which stretches down from the higher animals to man at the bottom.

Some of my experiments were quite curious. In the course of my reading, I had come across a case where, many years ago, some hunters on our Great Plains organized a buffalo hunt for the entertainment of an English earl—that, and to provide some fresh meat for his larder.[7] They had charming sport. They killed seventy-two of those great animals and ate part of one of them and left the seventy-one to rot. In order to determine the difference between an anaconda[8] and an earl—if any—I caused seven young calves to be turned into the anaconda's cage. The grateful reptile immediately crushed one of them and swallowed it, then lay back satisfied. It showed no further interest in the calves and no disposition to harm them. I tried this experiment with other anacondas, always with the same result. The fact stood proven that the

6. **quadrupeds** (kwä'drŏŏ·pedz') *n. pl.:* four-footed animals.
7. **larder** *n.:* supply of food or place where food supplies are kept.
8. **anaconda** (an'ə·kän'də) *n.:* long, heavy snake that crushes its prey.

Vocabulary
dispositions (dis'pə·zish'ənz) *n. pl.:* natures; characters.
allegiance (ə·lē'jəns) *n.:* loyalty.
caliber (kal'ə·bər) *n.:* quality or ability.

DIFFERENTIATING INSTRUCTION

Learners Having Difficulty
Modeling. To help students read "The Lowest Animal," model the reading skill of recognizing a writer's purpose. Say, "Writers write to describe, to inform, to entertain, to analyze, and to persuade. I would say that Twain's purpose in writing this essay is to persuade the reader to think about certain issues. I'll look for his main ideas to better understand his position."

English-Language Learners
To highlight the irony of Twain's tone, point out that many of Twain's claims are preposterous and are not meant to be taken at face value.

difference between an earl and an anaconda is that the earl is cruel and the anaconda isn't; and that the earl wantonly destroys what he has no use for, but the anaconda doesn't. This seemed to suggest that the anaconda was not descended from the earl. It also seemed to suggest that the earl was descended from the anaconda, and had lost a good deal in the transition. **4**

? According to Twain, what does the experiment with the earl and the anaconda prove?

I was aware that many men who have accumulated more millions of money than they can ever use have shown a rabid hunger for more, and have not scrupled to cheat the ignorant and the helpless out of their poor servings in order to partially appease that appetite. I furnished a hundred different kinds of wild and tame animals the opportunity to accumulate vast stores of food, but none of them would do it. The squirrels and bees and certain birds made accumulations, but stopped when they had gathered a winter's supply and could not be persuaded to add to it either honestly or by chicane.[9] In order to bolster up a tottering reputation, the ant pretended to store up supplies, but I was not deceived. I know the ant. These experiments convinced me that there is this difference between man and the higher animals: He is avaricious and miserly, they are not. **5**

5

Note Twain's **word choice** in this paragraph, especially his use of words such as *rabid, cheat, helpless, poor,* and *miserly*.

? How do these words increase the effect of Twain's **satire**?

In the course of my experiments, I convinced myself that among the animals man is the only one that harbors[10] insults and injuries, broods over them, waits till a chance offers, then takes revenge. The passion of revenge is unknown to the higher animals.

Roosters keep harems,[11] but it is by consent of their concubines;[12] therefore no wrong is done. Men keep harems, but it is by brute force, privileged by atrocious laws which the other sex was allowed no hand in making. In this matter man occupies a far lower place than the rooster.

Cats are loose in their morals, but not consciously so. Man, in his descent from the cat, has brought the cat's looseness with him but has left the unconsciousness behind—the saving grace which excuses the cat. The cat is innocent, man is not.

Indecency, vulgarity, obscenity—these are strictly confined to man; he invented them. Among the higher animals there is no trace of them. They hide nothing; they are not ashamed. Man, with his soiled mind, covers himself. He will not even enter a drawing room with his breast and back naked, so alive are he and his mates to indecent suggestion. Man is the Animal that Laughs. But so does the monkey, as Mr. Darwin pointed out, and so does the Australian bird that is called the laughing jackass. No—Man is the Animal that Blushes. He is the only one that does it—or has occasion to. **6**

6

Twain repeats his **main idea,** that man is a lower animal.

? What claim does he make here?

At the head of this article[13] we see how "three monks were burnt to death" a few days ago and a prior was "put to death with atrocious cruelty."

___

11. **harems** *n. pl.*: groups of females who mate and live with one male.
12. **concubines** (kän′kyo͞o·bīnz′) *n.*: secondary wives.
13. **at the head of this article:** Twain is referring to 1897 newspaper reports of religious persecution in Crete.

Vocabulary

wantonly (wänt′n·lē) *adv.*: carelessly, often with ill will.

transition (tran·zish′ən) *n.*: passage from one condition, form, or stage to another.

scrupled (skro͞o′pəld) *v.*: hesitated because of feelings of guilt.

appease (ə·pēz′) *v.*: satisfy; pacify.

avaricious (av′ə·rish′əs) *adj.*: greedy.

atrocious (ə·trō′shəs) *adj.*: evil; very bad.

___

9. **chicane** (shi·kān′) *n.*: clever deception; trickery. (*Chicanery* is the more common form.)
10. **harbors** *v.*: clings to; nourishes.

Mark Twain **471**

D **Literary Focus**

Satire. Discuss with students whether Twain actually conducted the experiment with the anacondas. Then, invite them to comment on the point of this claim. [Possible response: Twain's point is that the anaconda kills only what it can eat, whereas the earl kills much more than he can eat. Twain is making the point that the earl's behavior is more abhorrent than that of the anaconda, an animal often viewed with fear and revulsion.]

E **Reading Skills**

? **Recognizing a writer's purpose.** Why does Twain discuss how much food animals store for the winter? [He is making the point that the "higher animals" accumulate only what they need to survive. He contrasts this behavior with that of humans, who accumulate more money than they need and cheat less fortunate people to acquire more.]

F **Literary Focus**

? **Tone.** How would you describe the tone of these sentences? [The tone is bitingly sarcastic.]

Responses to Boxed Questions

4. The experiment proves that humans are more cruel than anacondas and hence are a less-developed life form.

5. The words add weight to Twain's condemnation of human behavior.

6. Humans are the only animals that do shameful things.

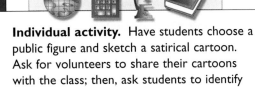

CONTENT-AREA CONNECTIONS

Culture: Satirical Cartoons

Ask students whether they have ever seen satirical cartoons in newspapers or magazines. Point out that these cartoons often ridicule public figures the way Twain ridicules the entire human race.

Individual activity. Have students choose a public figure and sketch a satirical cartoon. Ask for volunteers to share their cartoons with the class; then, ask students to identify the qualities that make a satirical cartoon effective.

A Reading Skills

❼ Recognizing a writer's purpose. What does this example show? Why do you think Twain includes it? [It shows that people sometimes value property more highly than they do other human beings. Twain includes it to suggest that people's values are distorted and corrupt.]

B Reading Skills

❼ Recognizing organizational patterns. What organizational pattern have you begun to notice in Twain's essay? [Twain sums up each section of his argument with sentences such as "Man is the Animal that Blushes" and "Man is the Cruel Animal." These parallel sentences reaffirm Twain's generalizations about human nature.]

C Content-Area Connections

Literature: Twain and Slavery
Explain that Twain's novel *Adventures of Huckleberry Finn* tells the story of a boy named Huck who flees his home with a runaway slave named Jim. One of the book's themes is the inhumanity of slavery.

Responses to Boxed Questions

7. Twain is satirizing people's enjoyment of others' suffering.

8. The words' strong negative connotations help create a powerful emotional appeal for Twain's argument.

Do we inquire into the details? No; or we should find out that the prior was subjected to unprintable mutilations. Man—when he is a North American Indian—gouges out his prisoner's eyes; when he is King John,[14] with a nephew to render untroublesome, he uses a red-hot iron; when he is a religious zealot[15] dealing with heretics[16] in the Middle Ages, he skins his captive alive and scatters salt on his back; in the first Richard's[17] time, he shuts up a multitude of Jewish families in a tower and sets fire to it; in Columbus's time he captures a family of Spanish Jews and—but *that* is not printable; in our day in England, a man is fined ten shillings for beating his mother nearly to death with a chair, and another man is fined forty shillings for having four pheasant eggs in his possession without being able to satisfactorily explain how he got them. Of all the animals, man is the only one that is cruel. He is the only one that inflicts pain for the pleasure of doing it. It is a trait that is not known to the higher animals. The cat plays with the frightened mouse; but she has this excuse, that she does not know that the mouse is suffering. The cat is moderate—unhumanly moderate: She only scares the mouse, she does not hurt it; she doesn't dig out its eyes, or tear off its skin, or drive splinters under its nails—man fashion; when she is done playing with it, she makes a sudden meal of it and puts it out of its trouble. Man is the Cruel Animal. He is alone in that distinction. ❼

The higher animals engage in individual fights, but never in organized

❼
Here Twain uses examples from history and then-current events to support his **main idea.**

❓ *What specific trait of man is Twain **satirizing** in this paragraph?*

masses. Man is the only animal that deals in that atrocity[18] of atrocities, war. He is the only one that gathers his brethren about him and goes forth in cold blood and with calm pulse to exterminate his kind. He is the only animal that for sordid wages will march out, as the Hessians[19] did in our Revolution, and as the boyish Prince Napoleon did in the Zulu war,[20] and help to slaughter strangers of his own species who have done him no harm and with whom he has no quarrel.

Man is the only animal that robs his helpless fellow of his country—takes possession of it and drives him out of it or destroys him. Man has done this in all the ages. There is not an acre of ground on the globe that is in possession of its rightful owner, or that has not been taken away from owner after owner, cycle after cycle, by force and bloodshed.

Man is the only Slave. And he is the only animal who enslaves. He has always been a slave in one form or another, and has always held other slaves in bondage under him in one way or another. In our day he is always some man's slave for wages, and does that man's work; and this slave has other slaves under him for minor wages, and they do *his* work. The higher animals are the only ones who exclusively do their own work and provide their own living. ❽

Man is the only Patriot. He sets himself apart in his

❽
In the previous paragraphs, Twain uses **loaded words,** such as *slaughter, slave,* and *assassins,* to emphasize man's immorality.

❓ *How do these loaded words increase the power of Twain's **satire?***

---

14. **King John:** King of England from 1199 to 1216, known for seizing the throne from his nephew Arthur.
15. **zealot** (zel′ət) *n.:* overly enthusiastic person; fanatic.
16. **heretics** (her′ə·tiks) *n. pl.:* people who hold beliefs opposed to those of the church.
17. **first Richard's:** refers to Richard I (1157–1199), also called Richard the Lion-Hearted, king of England from 1189 to 1199.

18. **atrocity** (ə·träs′ə·tē) *n.:* shockingly cruel and inhuman act.
19. **Hessians** (hesh′ənz): German soldiers who served for pay in the British army during the American Revolution.
20. **Prince Napoleon . . . Zulu war:** In search of adventure, Prince Napoleon, son of Napoleon III, joined the British campaign against Zululand (part of South Africa) in 1879.

Vocabulary
sordid (sôr′did) *adj.:* dirty; cheap; shameful.

READING MINI-LESSON

Developing Word-Attack Skills
Write the word *please* on the chalkboard, and have students read it aloud. Note that the word ends with the letters *se* and the sound /z/. Erase the *p*, and have students read the new word, *lease*. Note that the final sound has changed: In *lease, se* stands for /s/.

Next, write these two sentences on the chalkboard, underlining *excuse* in each one:

The coach won't excuse us from practice.
You don't have a good excuse.

Have volunteers identify the sentence in which *excuse* ends with /z/ (as in *please*) and the sentence in which *excuse* ends with /s/ (as in *lease*). Explain that the verb *excuse* ends with /z/ and the noun *excuse* ends with /s/. Ask students to think of other words in which *se* has a different sound depending on how

---

own country, under his own flag, and sneers at the other nations, and keeps multitudinous uniformed assassins on hand at heavy expense to grab slices of other people's countries and keep *them* from grabbing slices of *his*. And in the intervals between campaigns, he washes the blood off his hands and works for "the universal brotherhood of man"—with his mouth.

Man is the Religious Animal. He is the only Religious Animal. He is the only animal that has the True Religion—several of them. He is the only animal that loves his neighbor as himself, and cuts his throat if his theology isn't straight. He has made a graveyard of the globe in trying his honest best to smooth his brother's path to happiness and heaven. He was at it in the time of the Caesars, he was at it in Mahomet's[21] time, he was at it in the time of the Inquisition, he was at it in France a couple of centuries, he was at it in England in Mary's day,[22] he has been at it ever since he first saw the light, he is at it today in Crete—he will be at it somewhere else tomorrow. The higher animals have no religion. And we are told that they are going to be left out, in the hereafter. I wonder why. It seems questionable taste.

Man is the Reasoning Animal. **❾** Such is the claim. I think it is open to dispute. Indeed, my experiments have proven to me that he is the Unreasoning Animal. Note his history, as sketched above. It seems plain to me that whatever he is, he is *not* a reasoning animal. His record is the fantastic record of a maniac. I consider that the strongest count against his intelligence is the fact that with that record back of him, he blandly sets himself up as the head animal of the lot;

> **❾**
> In this paragraph, Twain begins his final summation. He first presents the theory he is arguing against: that man is a reasoning animal.

whereas by his own standards, he is the bottom one.

In truth, man is incurably foolish. Simple things which the other animals easily learn he is incapable of learning. Among my experiments was this. In an hour I taught a cat and a dog to be friends. I put them in a cage. In another hour I taught them to be friends with a rabbit. In the course of two days I was able to add a fox, a goose, a squirrel, and some doves. Finally a monkey. They lived together in peace, even affectionately.

Next, in another cage I confined an Irish Catholic from Tipperary, and as soon as he seemed tame, I added a Scottish Presbyterian from Aberdeen. Next a Turk from Constantinople, a Greek Christian from Crete, an Armenian, a Methodist from the wilds of Arkansas, a Buddhist from China, a Brahman from Benares. Finally, a Salvation Army colonel from Wapping. Then I stayed away two whole days. When I came back to note results, the cage of Higher Animals was all right, but in the other there was but a chaos of gory odds and ends of turbans and fezzes and plaids and bones and flesh—not a specimen left alive. These Reasoning Animals had disagreed on a theological detail and carried the matter to a higher court. **❿** ■

> **❿**
> To wrap up his argument, Twain presents the disastrous results of the final experiment.
> **?** *Summarize those results.*

Mark Twain   473

---

21. **Mahomet's:** Mohammed (c. A.D. 570–632) was an Arab prophet and founder of Islam.
22. **in Mary's day:** during the reign of Queen Mary (1553–1558), who was given the nickname "Bloody Mary" when she ordered the deaths of many Protestants.

DIRECT TEACHING

❹ Literary Focus

❓ Satire. What do you think Twain wants the reader to think about after reading this passage? [Possible response: Twain wants the reader to examine the role blind patriotism plays in human affairs. He believes that nationalism often divides people and causes them to turn against one another.]

❺ Literary Focus

❓ Satire. What technique is Twain using when he says that man has "made a graveyard of the globe"? [exaggeration]

❻ Reading Skills

❓ Recognizing a writer's purpose. Why do you think Twain ends his essay by describing this "experiment"? [Possible response: Twain wants his readers to reexamine their attitudes toward religious tolerance.]

Response to Boxed Question

10. Twain puts several animals of different kinds in one cage and several people of different nationalities and faiths in another. The animals get along, while the humans annihilate one another.

---

the word is used in a sentence. [Possible responses: *use; abuse; refuse; close.*]

Activity. Display the following sets of words. Ask students to point out the two words in each set that end with the same sound and to identify the sound.

1.	recluse	infuse	amuse [z]
2.	grease	cease	tease [s]
3.	phrase	chase	erase [s]
4.	concise	incise	precise [s]
5.	appraise	abase	appease [z]
6.	whose	chose	dose [z]
7.	disease	increase	malaise [z]
8.	suppose	comatose	lactose [s]

Connection

Summary ⬆ *above grade level*

In this op-ed article, Stephen Jay Gould argues that "good and kind people outnumber all others by thousands to one." He tells about a cook who donated twelve apple brown bettys to the rescue workers toiling in the rubble of the fallen World Trade Center towers. Acts of kindness like this one, Gould argues, outweigh the evil actions of the few.

DIRECT TEACHING

Ⓐ Content-Area Connections

History: World Trade Center Attack

To help students understand this article, remind them that on September 11, 2001, two commercial jets hijacked by terrorists struck the World Trade Center towers, causing their collapse and killing thousands of people. In the days following this event, people from New York City and around the world rushed to help with the recovery, while others sent money, supplies, and good wishes. As a result, a strong sense of unity emerged amid the chaos.

Ⓑ Reading Informational Text

❓ Finding the main idea. What is the main idea behind what Gould calls the Great Asymmetry? [Ten thousand acts of kindness balance every act of evil.]

Ⓒ Reading Informational Text

Understanding terminology.
Explain that the site of the tragedy is referred to as *ground zero*. This term was originally used to refer to an area directly hit by a nuclear bomb.

Ⓐ *This article was written shortly after the terrorist attack that brought down the World Trade Center towers in New York City on September 11, 2001.*

A Time of Gifts

Stephen Jay Gould

Firefighters leaving rescue area near World Trade Center, September 13, 2001.

The patterns of human history mix decency and depravity in equal measure. We often assume, therefore, that such a fine balance of results must emerge from societies made of decent and depraved people in equal numbers. But we need to expose and celebrate the fallacy of this conclusion so that, in this moment of crisis, we may reaffirm an essential truth too easily forgotten and regain some crucial comfort too readily forgone. Good and kind people outnumber all others by thousands to one. The tragedy of human history lies in the enormous potential for destruction in rare acts of evil, not in the high frequency of evil people. Complex systems can only be built step Ⓑ by step, whereas destruction requires but an instant. Thus, in what I like to call the Great Asymmetry, every spectacular incident of evil will be balanced by ten thousand acts of kindness, too often unnoted and invisible as the "ordinary" efforts of a vast majority.

We have a duty, almost a holy responsibility, to record and honor the victorious weight of these innumerable little kindnesses when an unprecedented act of evil so threatens to distort our perception of ordinary human behavior. I have stood at ground zero, Ⓒ stunned by the twisted ruins of the largest human structure ever destroyed in a catastrophic moment. (I will discount the claims of a few biblical literalists for the Tower of Babel.) And I have contemplated a single day of carnage that our nation has not suffered since battles that still evoke passions and tears, nearly 150 years later: Antietam, Gettysburg, Cold Harbor. The scene is insufferably sad, but not at all depress-

---

Comparing and Contrasting Texts

Evaluating assumptions and arguments. In "The Lowest Animal," Mark Twain presents a dark picture of human nature, while in "A Time of Gifts," Stephen Jay Gould affirms his belief in people's basic goodness and decency. Much of Twain's essay deals with institutionalized practices, such as war and slavery, while Gould focuses on individuals' acts of kindness.

Small-group activity. Have small groups of students discuss ways the two writers' essays might counter each other's arguments. Then, ask them to examine each author's underlying philosophical assumptions by citing specific elements of his essay. Suggest that each group share its ideas with the class.

Drawing found taped to a wall on Sixth Avenue and Eleventh Street in New York City, September 25, 2001.

ing. Rather, ground zero can only be described, in the lost meaning of a grand old word, as "sublime," in the sense of awe inspired by solemnity.

In human terms, ground zero is the focal point for a vast web of bustling goodness, channeling unaccountable deeds of kindness from an entire planet—the acts that must be recorded to reaffirm the overwhelming weight of human decency. The rubble of ground zero stands mute, while a beehive of human activity churns within and radiates outward as everyone makes a selfless contribution, big or tiny according to means and skills, but each of equal worth. My wife and stepdaughter established a depot on Spring Street to collect and ferry needed items in short supply, including face masks and shoe inserts, to the workers at ground zero. Word spreads like a fire of goodness, and people stream in, bringing gifts, from a pocketful of batteries to a tenthousand-dollar purchase of hard hats, made on the spot at a local supply house and delivered right to us.

I will cite but one tiny story, among so many, to add to the count that will overwhelm the power of any terrorist's act. And by such tales, multiplied many millionfold, let those few depraved people finally understand why their vision of inspired fear cannot prevail over ordinary decency. As we left a local restaurant to make a delivery to ground zero late one evening, the cook gave us a shopping bag and said: "Here's a dozen apple brown bettys, our best dessert, still warm. Please give them to the rescue workers." How lovely, I thought, but how meaningless, except as an act of solidarity, connecting the cook to the cleanup. Still, we promised that we would make the distribution, and we put the bag of twelve apple brown bettys atop several thousand face masks and shoe pads.

Twelve apple brown bettys into the breach. Twelve apple brown bettys for thousands of workers. And then I learned something important that I should never have forgotten—and the joke turned on me. Those twelve apple brown bettys went like literal hot cakes. These trivial symbols in my initial judgment turned into little drops of gold within a rainstorm of similar offerings for the stomach and soul, from children's postcards to cheers by the roadside. We gave the last one to a firefighter, an older man in a young crowd, sitting alone in utter exhaustion as he inserted one of our shoe pads. And he said, with a twinkle and a smile restored to his face: "Thank you. This is the most lovely thing I've seen in four days—and still warm!"

—*The New York Times*
September 26, 2001

Mark Twain   475

CONTENT-AREA CONNECTIONS

Science: Stephen Jay Gould

Stephen Jay Gould was one of the most widely read scientists of our time. The author of more than twenty popular books on science, he also wrote a monthly column, "This View of Life," for *Natural History* magazine. Gould was born in New York City in 1941 and died there in 2002. He earned a doctorate in paleontology from Columbia University in 1963 and was the Alexander Agassiz Professor of Zoology and Professor of Geology at Harvard University.

Individual activity. Encourage students to read one of Gould's old columns in *Natural History* and summarize his purpose for writing as well as his assumptions and beliefs about his topic.

D **Reading Skills**

❓ Recognizing a writer's purpose. What does Gould hope to achieve by telling this anecdote? [Possible response: Gould believes that telling stories like this one is a way of affirming basic human decency in the face of evil.]

E **Advanced Learners**
Recognizing allusions. Explain that the word *breach* means "opening made in a solid structure or line of defense." Gould is alluding here to a line from Shakespeare's *Henry V*, a play with a patriotic theme: "Once more unto the breach, dear friends, once more. . . ." Tell students that by using this allusion, Gould is likening ground zero to a combat zone. He is also hinting at the scale of the damage done to the nation's psyche and the immensity of what is needed to heal and restore it.

F **Reading Informational Text**

❓ Assessing author's arguments. Do you feel that Gould's story of the apple brown bettys proves his point that most people are good and only a few individuals are responsible for most of the suffering in the world? Why or why not? [Many students will say they are convinced that this act of kindness reaffirms human decency. Others will say that no person is all good or all bad.]

Response and Analysis

Reading Check

1. Twain asserts that humans are one species, that "quadrupeds are a distinct family," and that the other animals, such as birds and insects, also make up distinct families and serve as "links in the chain" extending from the "higher animals" down to humans.

2. Possible answer: They are cruel, greedy, and indecent, and they enslave others of their kind.

3. Twain puts different kinds of animals in one cage and humans of different backgrounds in another. The animals live peacefully together; the humans kill one another.

Thinking Critically

4. Possible answer: Twain's purpose is to urge people to treat one another more humanely. This is a noble but perhaps impractical goal.

5. Twain wants people to stop destroying what they have no use for, accumulating more money than they need, cheating others, taking revenge, treating women unjustly, being hypocritical or cruel, waging war, and committing atrocities in the name of religion and patriotism. Most students will agree that people should strive for these goals.

6. Possible answer: Two examples are "He has made a graveyard of the globe" and "His record is the fantastic record of a maniac." They help readers visualize the devastation humans have brought about.

Extending and Evaluating

7. Possible answer: I agree with Twain that people too often mistreat one another. However, I also feel that humans are capable of kindness, so I believe that Twain's generalizations are only partly valid.

Response and Analysis

Reading Check

1. What are the first three **generalizations** Twain presents as a result of his experiments in the London Zoological Gardens?

2. Name four ways in which human beings are inferior to other animals, according to Twain.

3. Describe Twain's last experiment with the two cages. What are the results of the experiment?

Thinking Critically

4. Summarize Twain's overall **purpose** in this essay. How would you characterize that purpose—as noble, childish, useless, realistic? Give reasons for your opinion.

5. What specific changes in human nature does Twain hope his **satire** will encourage? How do Twain's ideas compare with yours? (Refer to your Quickwrite notes.)

6. Find at least two examples of **exaggeration** in the essay. Do these exaggerations make the satire more effective, or are they just silly? Explain.

Extending and Evaluating

7. Evaluate Twain's philosophical beliefs, as revealed in this essay. In your opinion, are his generalizations about people and their behavior valid, partly valid, or completely invalid? Explain.

WRITING

You're Wrong, Mr. Twain

Write a **rebuttal** of Twain's essay in which you defend the human race as civilized, caring beings. Your rebuttal may be in any form you like: a letter to Twain, a parody of Twain's essay, a serious essay, a poem, an anecdote, an editorial, or something else.

SKILLS FOCUS

Literary Skills
Analyze satire.

Reading Skills
Analyze a writer's purpose.

Writing Skills
Write a rebuttal of an essay.

Vocabulary Skills
Understand noun-forming suffixes.

Support your points with specific examples, just as Twain does. Re-read the **Connection** on page 474 for ideas for your rebuttal.

Vocabulary Development

Suffixes That Form Nouns

dispositions transition atrocious
allegiance scrupled sordid
caliber appease
wantonly avaricious

A **suffix** is a word part added to the end of a word or a **root** (word base) to create a new word. Certain suffixes change words into nouns—for example, the adjective *sordid* and the suffix *–ness* form the noun *sordidness*. Study the following noun-forming suffixes and their meanings.

Suffix	Meaning
–tion	act, result, or state of
–ance	act, process, or quality of
–ment	result or product; means
–ness	quality or state of being

Practice. Write down the words listed above, and indicate whether each one is a noun. If it is a noun and it contains one of the suffixes listed in the chart, circle the suffix. If the word is *not* a noun, turn it into a noun by adding one of the suffixes. (Note: For one of the words, you will have to remove a suffix before you add the noun-forming suffix. For one other word, you need only remove a suffix to form a noun.) Finally, look up the meanings of the new words in a dictionary.

Vocabulary Development

1. noun; dispositions
2. noun; allegiance
3. noun; caliber
4. wantonness—recklessness
5. noun; transition
6. scruple—hesitancy from difficulty of deciding what is right
7. appeasement—act of pacifying
8. avariciousness—greed
9. atrociousness—brutality
10. sordidness—baseness

Vocabulary Development

Greek and Latin Roots in Math and Science

Although the Greek Parthenon and the Roman Colosseum have suffered damage through the centuries, the Greek and Latin languages are alive and well in the English that we speak every day. Thousands of English words have Greek or Latin roots, and recognizing these roots can be a great help to you in improving your vocabulary.

A **root** is a word part that carries the core meaning of a word. In most cases, roots combine with prefixes or suffixes or both to form whole words. Groups of words with the same root are called **word families.**

Many words used in math and science have Greek or Latin roots. This is due in part to the many scientific accomplishments of the Greeks and to the use of Latin as the common language of science for centuries.

In "The Lowest Animal," Mark Twain uses scientific and mathematical terms that have their origins in Greek and Latin roots—for example, *theory, scientific, zoological, verified, species,* and *quadrupeds.* In the following charts, you'll find these words and other common words from math and science that have Greek and Latin roots. (For more about mathematical and scientific terms, see page 271.)

Greek

Word	Root	Meaning of Root	Meaning of Word	Family Words
theory	–theor–	to look at, view	idea or plan that explains how something works	theoretical, theorem
zoological	–log–, –logy–	word, study	having to do with the study of animals	logic, biology
genesis	–gen–	to be born	beginning, origin	genetics, genotype
thermonuclear	–therm–, –thermo–	heat	using heat energy released in nuclear fusion	thermometer, thermal

(continued)

SKILLS FOCUS

Vocabulary Skills
Identify Greek and Latin roots.

Vocabulary Development

Practice

Possible Answers

1. *–theor–*. Family Word—theorize.
   –log–, –logy–. Family Words—
   anthropology, psychology.
   –gen–. Family Words—genealogy,
   generation.
   –therm–, –thermo–. Family Words—
   thermos, thermodynamics.
   –ver–. Family Words—very, aver.
   –scien–. Family Words—omniscient,
   prescient.
   –ped–. Family Word—pedestrian.
   –integ–. Family Word—integrity.
   –ang–. Family Words—angularity,
   quadrangle.

2. *orthodontist*. Meaning of Word—
   dentist who specializes in adjusting and straightening teeth. *Family
   Words*—orthodox, orthopedics.

   epidermis. Meaning of Word—out-
   ermost layer of a vertebrate's
   skin. *Family Word*—dermatitis.

   habitat. Meaning of Word—place
   where an animal or plant normally lives. *Family Words*—inhabit,
   habitual.

   translucent. Meaning of Word—
   permitting light to pass through.
   Family Words—lucid, elucidate.

   symmetry. Meaning of Word—
   correspondence in form, size,
   and position of parts on opposite
   sides of a dividing line or plane.
   Family Words—diameter,
   metronome, geometry.

   equilateral. Meaning of Word—
   having sides of equal length.
   Family Words—bilateral, collateral.

Latin

Word	Root	Meaning of Root	Meaning of Word	Family Words
verified	–ver–	true	proved true	veracity, verdict
scientific	–scien–	to know	systematic and exact	conscience, scientist
quadrupeds	–ped–	foot	animals with four feet	biped, pedal
integer	–integ–	whole	positive or negative whole number or zero	integral, integrate
triangle	–ang–	corner, angle	figure with three angles and three sides	angular, rectangle

PRACTICE

1. For each root listed in the charts, find at least one other word in the same word family. You may use a dictionary for help.

2. For the mathematical and scientific terms below, complete a chart like the one above. The root and the meaning of the root appear in parentheses following each word. Use a dictionary to find the meaning of the word. Then, find at least one family word. (You will note that several words also have common prefixes.)

   orthodontist   (–ortho–, "straight")
   epidermis   (–derm–, "skin")
   habitat   (–hab–, "have; hold")
   translucent   (–luc–, "light")
   symmetry   (–metr–, "measure")
   equilateral   (–lat–, "side")

ASSESSING

Assessment

■ *Holt Assessment: Literature, Reading, and Vocabulary*

RETEACHING

For a lesson reteaching analyzing arguments, see **Reteaching,** p. 1117A.

Jack London
(1876–1916)

In his teens and twenties, Jack London adventured on sea and ice. Then, in the sixteen remaining years of his life, he turned out fifty volumes of essays and fiction. Known during his lifetime as a passionate socialist, London is remembered today not for his political convictions but for his exciting, fast-paced adventure stories.

London was born into a poor family in San Francisco. As a boy he was largely uncared for by his parents. He delivered newspapers, worked on an ice wagon, set up pins in a bowling alley, and worked in a cannery. "Almost the first thing I realized were responsibilities," he said. He graduated from grammar school in Oakland, across the bay from San Francisco.

Meanwhile, London read everything he could find in the public library, especially stories of real-life adventure. In his teens he plunged into danger. "I joined the oyster pirates in the bay; shipped as sailor on a schooner; took a turn at salmon fishing; shipped before the mast and sailed for the Japanese coast on a seal-hunting expedition. After sealing for seven months I came back to California, and took odd jobs. . . ."

London was still in his teens when he settled in Oakland again. He began to write, selling a few pieces to local papers. After attending high school for one year, he passed the entrance exams for the University of California at Berkeley by cramming on his own. The combination of work, school, and writing proved too much, however, and he quit halfway through his freshman year. He submerged himself in writing for the next three months. But he earned practically nothing, so in 1897 he took off to prospect for gold in the Klondike—part of the Yukon Territory in northwestern Canada.

London became sick and had to leave the Klondike in less than a year, but the experience convinced him that life is a struggle in which the strong survive and the weak do not. London's short stories and novels dramatize his belief that "civilized" beings are either destroyed or re-created in savage environments.

London's first major success was a story collection, *The Son of the Wolf* (1900). Readers were thrilled by the shocking brutality of his stories, then hooked by the action and adventure. His most famous novel, *The Call of the Wild* (1903), celebrates the escape to freedom of a sled dog named Buck.

London became a millionaire from his writings, and success greatly altered his life. In 1900, he married and had two daughters, but his wife sued him for divorce in 1905. He remarried and established his home at Glen Ellen in Sonoma County, north of San Francisco. There he intended to create a magnificent ranch estate, but he lost interest when Wolf House, his nearly completed mansion, burned down in 1913. London, for years an alcoholic, suffered in his later years from kidney disease and depression. One evening in November 1916, when the physical pain finally became unendurable, London took a lethal dose of narcotics and lapsed into a coma. He died the next evening; he was forty years old.

For Independent Reading

One of most popular novels in America is London's tale about a sled dog:
- *The Call of the Wild*

SKILLS FOCUS, pp. 479–497

Grade-Level Skills

■ **Literary Skills**
Analyze the philosophical arguments in literary works and their impact on the quality of each work. (Philosophical approach)

■ **Reading Skills**
Analyze cause and effect.

Review Skills

■ **Literary Skills**
Analyze the way a work of literature relates to the themes and issues of its historical period. (Historical approach)

More About the Writer

Background. London saw life as a savage struggle won by those best suited to survival. He regarded people as primitive beasts taking refuge behind a veneer of civilization. London believed that human nature is fierce and cruel, and is tempered only by an equally spontaneous love.

Although he was a socialist, London was heavily influenced by the German philosopher Friedrich Nietzsche's idea of a "superman," who, by force of will, rises above the masses.

For Independent Reading

You might mention that London wrote *The Call of the Wild* from the vantage point of the dog Buck, who, after living with a series of human masters, joins a wolf pack and goes to live in the wild.

RESOURCES: READING

Planning
- *One-Stop Planner* CD-ROM with ExamView Test Generator

Differentiating Instruction
- *Holt Adapted Reader*
- *Supporting Instruction in Spanish*

Vocabulary
- *Vocabulary Development*

Grammar and Language
- *Language Handbook Worksheets*
- *Daily Language Activities*

Assessment
- *Holt Assessment: Literature, Reading, and Vocabulary*
- *One-Stop Planner* CD-ROM with ExamView Test Generator
- *Holt Online Assessment*

Internet
- go.hrw.com (Keyword: LE5 11-4)
- *Elements of Literature Online*

Media
- *Audio CD Library*
- *Audio CD Library, Selections and Summaries in Spanish*
- *Fine Art Transparencies*

Summary ⟷ at grade level

Ignoring the advice of a more experienced man, a rookie prospector in the Yukon attempts a long journey on foot during an intense cold spell, with only his dog as a companion. After proceeding for several hours without incident, the man breaks through the ice of a frozen spring and must stop and build a fire to dry out his footwear. He succeeds at first, but snow falling from a tree suddenly extinguishes the fire. He tries several times to get a new fire going, but he is unable to use his fingers, which have gone numb. Panicking, the man begins to run toward the distant camp where his partners are waiting, but stumbles and falls several times from cold and exhaustion. Finally, realizing that he is too weak to reach the camp, he resigns himself to death and goes to sleep in the snow. The dog remains until it senses that the man is dead; then, seeking warmth and food, it heads toward the camp.

Selection Starter

Build background. The Yukon River valley in Canada remained an uninhabited wilderness until the Klondike gold strike of 1896. The ensuing gold rush, at its peak, swelled the population of the main city, Dawson, to over thirty thousand. One hundred million dollars' worth of gold was mined in the Yukon and transported on the Yukon River between 1896 and 1904. Jack London prospected in the Yukon and was familiar with the kinds of people who sought their fortunes there and the obstacles they faced.

Before You Read

To Build a Fire

Make the Connection

"To Build a Fire" must be the coldest story ever written. London draws on his own experience of prospecting for gold in the Yukon—a bleak region of northwestern Canada—to give authenticity to the story.

This is ultimately far more than a classic "person versus nature" story. It is a grimly realistic tale about a man who is "quick and alert in the things of life, but . . . not in the significances"—an innocent who is not prepared for an unforgiving environment.

Literary Focus
Naturalism

The naturalists were nineteenth-century writers who went beyond realism in an attempt to portray life exactly as it is. Influenced by the scientist Charles Darwin (1809–1882), who put forth the theories of natural selection and survival of the fittest, the naturalist writers believed that human behavior is determined by heredity and environment. Relying on new theories in sociology and psychology, the naturalists dissected human behavior with detachment and objectivity, like scientists dissecting laboratory specimens. Naturalism presents human beings as subject to natural forces beyond their control. This idea is at the center of "To Build a Fire."

INTERNET

Vocabulary Practice
•
More About Jack London
•
Keyword: LE5 11-4

SKILLS FOCUS

Literary Skills
Understand naturalism. Understand philosophical ideas presented in literary works.

Reading Skills
Understand cause and effect.

> **Naturalism** was a nineteenth-century literary movement that claimed to portray life exactly as it is, with detachment and objectivity.
>
> *For more on Naturalism, see the Handbook of Literary and Historical Terms.*

Reading Skills
Analyzing Text Structures: Cause and Effect

Science tells us that for every action there is a reaction. In literature we call this the relationship of **cause** and **effect.** A plot is made up of a string of causes and effects. As you read London's story, keep notes on each action the protagonist takes, and note its effect. You will find that an action as small as a misstep or the lighting of a match can take on critical importance.

Vocabulary Development

intangible (in·tan′jə·bəl) *adj.:* difficult to define; vague.

undulations (un′jə·lā′shənz) *n. pl.:* wave-like motions.

protruding (prō·trōōd′iŋ) *v.* used as *adj.:* sticking out.

apprehension (ap′rē·hen′shən) *n.:* anxious or frightening feeling; dread.

imperative (im·per′ə·tiv) *adj.:* absolutely necessary; urgent.

extremities (ek·strem′ə·tēz) *n. pl.:* limbs of the body, especially hands and feet.

recoiled (ri·koild′) *v.:* shrank away; drew back.

excruciating (eks·krōō′shē·āt′iŋ) *adj.:* intensely painful.

ensued (en·sōōd′) *v.:* resulted.

Previewing Vocabulary

Have students match each of the numbered Vocabulary words from p. 480 with its synonym.

1. intangible [b]
2. undulations [i]
3. protruding [f]

   a. painful
   b. impalpable
   c. dread

4. apprehension [c]
5. imperative [h]
6. extremities [e]
7. recoiled [g]
8. excruciating [a]
9. ensued [d]

   d. followed
   e. hands and feet
   f. bulging
   g. flinched
   h. dire
   i. curves

To Build a Fire

Jack London

D ay had broken cold and gray, exceedingly cold and gray, when the man turned aside from the main Yukon trail and climbed the high earth bank, where a dim and little-traveled trail led eastward through the fat spruce timberland. It was a steep bank, and he paused for breath at the top, excusing the act to himself by looking at his watch. It was nine o'clock. There was no sun or hint of sun, though there was not a cloud in the sky. It was a clear day, and yet there seemed an intangible pall[1] over the face of things, a subtle gloom that made the day dark, and that was due to the absence of sun. This fact did not worry the man. He was used to the lack of sun. It had been days since he had seen the sun, and he knew that a few more days must pass before that cheerful orb, due south, would just peep above the skyline and dip immediately from view.

The man flung a look back along the way he had come. The Yukon lay a mile wide and hidden under three feet of ice. On top of this ice were as many feet of snow. It was all pure white, rolling in gentle undulations where the ice jams of the freeze-up had formed. North and south, as far as his eye could see, it was unbroken

---

1. **pall** *n.:* overspreading atmosphere of gloom and depression.

Vocabulary
intangible (in·tan′jə·bəl) *adj.:* difficult to define; vague.
undulations (un′jə·lā′shənz) *n. pl.:* wavelike motions.

Jack London   481

A Literary Focus

❷ **Naturalism.** How does the protagonist's namelessness reflect London's naturalistic approach? [Possible response: By keeping the protagonist nameless, London suggests that his identity is unimportant in the face of nature's vastness and indifference.]

B Literary Focus

❷ **Foreshadowing.** What does this passage suggest will happen later in the story? [Possible response: It seems to foreshadow doom: The word *pall* can also refer to a cloth draped over a coffin.]

C Reading Skills

❷ **Analyzing cause and effect.** What effects might this attitude produce? [Overconfidence can result in carelessness or unnecessary risk taking.]

DIFFERENTIATING INSTRUCTION

Learners Having Difficulty
Some students may find London's writing difficult to read because of his lengthy sentences, sophisticated vocabulary, and analytical tone. Reassure them that the plot is actually quite simple, marked by several definite points at which the man's fortunes go up or down (usually down). Encourage students to note each time his situation changes, and why.

English-Language Learners
The proper nouns and foreign words in the story may pose challenges for these students. You may wish to help them by pronouncing and defining *Chilkoot* (chil′koot′), and *Chinook* (shə•nook′), the names of two Native American peoples of the Pacific Northwest.

Advanced Learners
Enrichment. Invite students to analyze the way London's description of the environment affects the mood of the story. Help students do a close textual analysis, identifying words and phrases that help create the mood. Then, have students discuss the ways in which the description is naturalistic. What is London saying about the influence of heredity and environment on our survival?

A **Literary Focus**

? **Imagery.** What images do you find in the first stanza? To which senses do they appeal? [The "warmth of this spring" appeals to the sense of touch; the "perfume of honeysuckle" appeals to the sense of smell.]

B **Literary Focus**

? **Imagery.** How do the images in ll. 5–7 contrast with the underground world as the speaker seems to imagine it? [Possible response: The images in these lines—the sky, the mountain water, the "shimmering summit"—suggest vibrancy and brilliance, in sharp contrast to the still, dark world underground.]

C **Reading Skills**

? **Interpreting.** What do you think the poet means by "the sweet liquor of veins"? [Possible responses: the blood flowing in people's veins; the sap that rises in plants; a sense of intoxication; a feeling of vitality and renewal.]

D **Reading Skills**

? **Speculating.** What do these lines suggest about the speaker's relationship with the person being addressed? [Possible responses: The speaker is not sure about the other person's feelings; perhaps the other person has been hurt by the "soft violence" of the speaker's mouth.]

E **Literary Focus**

? **Tone.** What change in tone do you note in the last stanza of the poem? [Possible response: The inquisitive and somewhat hopeful tone changes to one of sorrowful acceptance.]

What Do You Feel Underground?

Gabriela Mistral

translated by **Maria Giachetti**

A
Underground do you feel
the delicate warmth of this spring?
Does the sharp perfume of honeysuckle
reach you through the earth?

5 **B**
Do you remember the sky,
the clear jets of mountain water,
the shimmering summit?
Do you remember the deep-tapestried path,
my still hand in your trembling hand?

10 **C**
This spring perfumes and refines
the sweet liquor of veins.
If only underground your beautiful
closed mouth could savor it!

D
Bordering the river, to this green
15 redolence° you would come.
You might like the ambivalent° warmth
of my mouth, its soft violence.

E
But you are underground—
your tongue silenced by dust;
20 there is no way that you can sing with me
the sweet and fiery songs of this spring.

---

15. **redolence** *n.:* quality of being fragrant; sweetness of scent.
16. **ambivalent** *adj.:* characterized by a mixture of opposite feelings at the same time.

500 Collection 4 The Rise of Realism: The Civil War to 1914

DIFFERENTIATING INSTRUCTION

Learners Having Difficulty
Tell students to follow along in their books as you read the poem aloud. Then, have them make a five-column chart recording images in the poem and their response to each one.

English-Language Learners
Have students list words or phrases in the poem that are unfamiliar or difficult for them. Discuss the meanings of the words with them, helping them see that the words express the poet's feelings about the coming of spring.

Response and Analysis

Thinking Critically

1. Who is the speaker of the poem, and who is being addressed? How would you characterize the relationship between the two people?

2. Find five sensory **images** in the poem, and identify the sense to which each image appeals—sight, hearing, touch, taste, or smell.

3. Describe the **tone** of the speaker's voice (for example, amused, ironic).

4. Mistral uses questions repeatedly throughout the poem. What emotional effect do these repeated questions create?

5. In a sentence, state the **theme** of the poem. What insight into life or love does it reveal? What evidence from the text supports your interpretation?

Extending and Evaluating

6. Is it morbid and unnatural for a poet to address a dead person in a poem, or do poems like Mistral's echo what people think and feel when someone dies? (Consult your Quickwrite notes.) What would you say to someone who thinks such poems are an unnatural way to deal with loss? ✏

Comparing Literature

7. Compare Mistral's use of **sensory images** with Stephen Crane's in "War Is Kind." List the images you find in each poem and the senses to which they appeal. Which poet makes greater use of images evoking touch? sight? Give evidence from the poems to support your conclusions.

8. Mistral's poem was written nearly fifty years after Crane wrote "War Is Kind" (page 443). Crane's poem expresses specific ideas about war, especially about feelings toward war, in the aftermath of the Civil War. Do you think

Crane's readers at that time would have appreciated Mistral's poem and the feelings about death presented in it? Explain your answer.

WRITING

Comparing Poetic Echoes

Develop your comparisons of the poems of Mistral and Crane into an **essay.** Review each poem, and consider the theme, or message, each author is trying to convey. Then, consider the poems' similarities and differences in subject matter, speaker, person addressed, and tone. How successful do you think each poem is in conveying its message?

LISTENING AND SPEAKING

Interpreting Poetry

With one or two classmates, prepare either Crane's "War Is Kind" or Mistral's "What Do You Feel Underground?" for an oral reading. Use textual clues from the poem and insights gained from class discussions to help you orally interpret the meaning of each poem. For example, in Crane's poem, how can you use your voice to convey the speaker's ironic tone? In Mistral's poem, how can you use your voice to suggest the speaker's grief and longing? When you are satisfied that your reading enhances the meaning of the poem, perform it for the class.

Gabriela Mistral receiving the Nobel Prize from King Christian X of Denmark (1945).

SKILLS FOCUS

Literary Skills
Analyze imagery.

Writing Skills
Write an essay comparing and contrasting poems.

Listening and Speaking Skills
Present an oral interpretation of a poem.

Gabriela Mistral   **501**

Response and Analysis

4. The speaker's persistent questioning suggests that he or she has not come to terms with the loss of the lover.

5. Possible answer: We must accept the finality of death; the pleasures of the world are only for the living. This theme is suggested by the speaker's acknowledgment that the lover can no longer join in an appreciation of spring.

Extending and Evaluating

6. Students might suggest that communing with a dead loved one is a normal part of grieving, which helps the bereaved person deal with his or her loss.

Comparing Literature

7. In "War Is Kind," Stephen Crane appeals to the sense of sight, ("threw wild hands toward the sky" and "the yellow trenches") and to the sense of hearing ("Hoarse, booming drums" and "gulped and died"). Mistral appeals to sight and hearing, but includes images that appeal to touch, smell, and taste also ("the delicate warmth of this spring" and "the sweet liquor of veins").

8. Possible answer: Crane's readers who lost a loved one in the war would probably respond sympathetically to Mistral's poem.

Assessment
■ *Holt Assessment: Literature, Reading, and Vocabulary*

For a lesson reteaching poetic devices, see **Reteaching,** p. 1117A.

Thinking Critically

1. The speaker of the poem is a living person, perhaps the poet herself, addressing someone who has died. The speaker may have been the lover of the dead person.

2. Possible answers: "the delicate warmth of this spring" (touch); "the sharp perfume of honeysuckle" (smell); "the shimmering

summit" (sight); "trembling hand" (touch); "the sweet liquor of veins" (taste); "tongue silenced by dust" (hearing); "sweet and fiery songs" (hearing).

3. In the first four stanzas the speaker's tone is quizzical and wistful. In the last stanza the tone changes to one of sorrowful resignation.

Grade-Level Skills

■ **Reading Skills**

Evaluate the philosophical, political, religious, ethical, and social influences of the historical period that shaped the characters, plots, and settings.

Review Skills

■ **Literary Skills**

Analyze influences on characters (including motivation) and the way those influences affect the plot.

More About the Writer

Background. Kate Chopin based her early stories on her experiences in Cloutierville, Louisiana, where her husband owned a plantation store. As the wife of a store owner, she may have known women like Mrs. Sommers. Ironically, Chopin found herself in similarly straitened circumstances when her husband died and she was left alone to raise six children.

For Independent Reading

You might mention to students that *The Awakening* vividly depicts the obstacles faced by American women in the late 1800s.

Kate Chopin
(1851–1904)

The Missouri Historical Society, St. Louis, Missouri.

Kate Chopin's work went unrecognized and was even scorned during her lifetime. Along with many other literary pioneers, Chopin never lived to see her work vindicated.

Kate Chopin was born Katherine O'Flaherty in St. Louis, Missouri, to an Irish immigrant father and a mother descended from French Creole aristocrats. (In the United States, Creoles are people of French or Spanish descent who are born in the states bordering the Gulf of Mexico but who retain their European culture.) Kate's prosperous parents encouraged her early interest in music and reading; her mother invited such a flurry of stimulating visitors to their house that Kate sometimes escaped to the attic to read. She was given lessons in French and piano for a time by her worldly great-grandmother, who stirred the child's imagination with vivid tales of old St. Louis. Kate became a witty and popular young woman with a notably independent turn of mind.

At nineteen, Kate married Oscar Chopin, a French Creole from New Orleans. The Chopins settled in Louisiana and reared a family of six children, but when Kate was thirty-one, Oscar died suddenly from swamp fever. Kate returned to St. Louis, and it was then that she began to write. She published a poem when she was thirty-eight, followed by some short stories. In 1890, she published her first novel.

Chopin's short stories concern the life of French Creoles in Louisiana. Published in national magazines and collected in two volumes called *Bayou Folk* (1894) and *A Night in Acadie* (1897), the stories were praised for their accurate portrayal of the French Creole strand in American culture. Chopin's dominant theme, however, was a much more controversial matter: the repression of women in Victorian America.

This theme was presented most dramatically in her novel *The Awakening* (1899). The novel portrays a dissatisfied New Orleans wife who breaks from the confines of her marriage and, in her quest for freedom, flagrantly defies the Victorian ideals of motherhood and domesticity. The novel was greeted with hostility by American critics, who condemned it as sordid and vulgar. The novel was removed from circulation in St. Louis libraries, some of Chopin's friends shunned her, and the local arts club denied her membership. Chopin was disheartened enough by this rejection to allow her writing to languish, and she produced little more before her death in 1904. After her death, her work fell into obscurity, and often copies of her books couldn't even be obtained.

The Awakening and many of Chopin's other works were rediscovered decades after her death. With the help of discerning critics and the women's movement of the 1960s and 1970s, Kate Chopin is now recognized as a novelist of skill and perception, whose work appeared half a century before its time.

For Independent Reading

Try reading Chopin's most famous novel:

• *The Awakening* (novel)

RESOURCES: READING

Planning

■ *One-Stop Planner* CD-ROM with ExamView Test Generator

Differentiating Instruction

■ *The Holt Reader*
■ *Holt Reading Solutions*
■ *Holt Adapted Reader*
■ *Supporting Instruction in Spanish*

Vocabulary

■ *Vocabulary Development*

Grammar and Language

■ *Daily Language Activities*

Assessment

■ *Holt Assessment: Literature, Reading, and Vocabulary*
■ *One-Stop Planner* CD-ROM with ExamView Test Generator

■ *Holt Online Assessment*

Internet

■ go.hrw.com (Keyword: LE5 11-4)
■ *Elements of Literature Online*

Media

■ *Audio CD Library*
■ *Audio CD Library, Selections and Summaries in Spanish*

Before You Read

A Pair of Silk Stockings

Make the Connection

From time to time, everyone feels trapped by the humdrum duties of daily life. All of us—probably even rock stars and world travelers—fantasize about escape from routines that have come to feel boring or confining. For a nineteenth-century woman of limited means trying to satisfy the needs of her family, even a brief reprieve from the demands of domestic life could be a life-changing bid for freedom and a temporary escape from day-to-day duties.

Literary Focus

Motivation

Motivation is the reasons for a character's actions. As in life the motivations of fictional characters are often complex, so for us to understand why they act the way they do, their motivations must be believable. In Chopin's story, Mrs. Sommers seems swept away in a series of actions that she has not anticipated. As you read, look for her underlying feelings and the reasons behind her unexpected behavior. Are her actions understandable?

> **Motivation** refers to the reasons for a character's behavior.
>
> *For more on Motivation, see the Handbook of Literary and Historical Terms.*

Reading Skills

Analyzing Historical Context

To understand fully a work of literature, you often need to evaluate how the influences from the historical period in which the work was written shape it. In the 1890s, when Chopin wrote "A Pair of Silk Stockings," women in the United States could not vote, were not financially independent, and had few opportunities for education and employment. Although women's rights activists were beginning to seek social justice, progress was slow in coming. As you read Chopin's story, note the differences in the position of women in the 1890s and women today. Consider the ways the story would change if it took place today.

Background

As you read, be aware that nylon had not yet been invented in the 1890s; most women wore long, thick, cotton stockings. Silk stockings ranked as pure luxury. Also, as you'll see in this story, fifteen dollars in the 1890s could buy far more than two meals at a fast-food restaurant.

Vocabulary Development

judicious (jōō·dish′əs) *adj.*: cautious; wise.

appreciable (ə·prē′shə·bəl) *adj.*: measurable.

veritable (ver′i·tə·bəl) *adj.*: genuine; true.

acute (ə·kyōōt′) *adj.*: keen; sharp.

laborious (lə·bôr′ē·əs) *adj.*: difficult; involving much hard work.

reveling (rev′əl·iŋ) *v.*: taking pleasure.

fastidious (fa·stid′ē·əs) *adj.*: difficult to please; critical.

preposterous (prē·päs′tər·əs) *adj.*: ridiculous.

gaudy (gô′dē) *adj.*: showy but lacking in good taste.

poignant (poin′yənt) *adj.*: emotionally moving.

INTERNET

Vocabulary Practice
•
Cross-Curricular Connection
•

Keyword: LE5 11-4

SKILLS FOCUS

Literary Skills
Understand motivation.

Reading Skills
Analyze historical context, especially political and social influences of the time.

Kate Chopin **503**

Summary ⟷ *at grade level*

When Mrs. Sommers unexpectedly finds herself with fifteen dollars (a large sum at the time), she immediately begins thinking about buying clothing for her four children. Inside the department store, she feels faint from hunger and sits down at a counter to rest. As she idly strokes a pair of silk stockings, Mrs. Sommers is seized by an impulse to indulge herself. She treats herself not only to the stockings but also to shoes, gloves, two expensive magazines, a fancy meal, and a theater ticket. As the day draws to a close, Mrs. Sommers boards a cable car and heads home, wishing the journey would never end.

Skills Starter

Build review skills. Remind students that the theme of a work is not the same as its subject but is rather the writer's idea about life conveyed through the subject. Explain that one way to identify a story's theme is to analyze its main character, focusing on the conflicts the character faces and on ways the character changes as a result of the conflicts.

Previewing Vocabulary

To reinforce students' understanding of the Vocabulary words, have them complete the following analogies.

1. MEMORABLE : FORGETTABLE :: facile : _____ [laborious]

2. TEDIOUS : BORING :: moving : _____ [poignant]

3. HEARTLESS : KIND :: reckless : _____ [judicious]

4. RAPID : SLOW :: dull : _____ [acute]

5. PEACOCK : VAIN :: cat : _____ [fastidious]

6. COMMON : RARE :: false : _____ [veritable]

7. SUBDUED : LOUD :: elegant : _____ [gaudy]

8. MOURNING : GRIEVING :: enjoying : _____ [reveling]

9. HILARITY : FUNNY :: incredulity : _____ [preposterous]

10. SEE : VISIBLE :: measure : _____ [appreciable]

A Literary Focus

❓ **Setting.** How do you picture the "little Nebraska village"? [Possible response: as a remote, isolated place.]

B Literary Focus

❓ **Setting.** What does the feeling Clark describes suggest about the city and the farm? [The two settings are totally different; people who live in one environment would not be comfortable in the other.] How do you think Aunt Georgiana will react to the city? [Possible response: She may find it overwhelming or frightening.]

C Literary Focus

❓ **Flashback.** What does the reader learn about Clark from this flashback? [He was once a bashful, awkward farm boy; he practiced on the organ in his aunt's house.]

D Literary Focus

❓ **Characterization.** What impression do you have of Aunt Georgiana? [Possible responses: She seems dazed and bewildered; she seems timid and unassuming.]

E Literary Focus

❓ **Simile.** What do you make of Clark's comparison of his aunt's "misshapen figure" to the battered, weatherbeaten bodies of explorers? [Possible responses: It suggests that Aunt Georgiana's life in Nebraska has been full of hardships and privations; it suggests that she has been living in an alien, uncongenial setting.]

A Wagner Matinée

Willa Cather

I received one morning a letter, written in pale ink on glassy, blue-lined notepaper, and bearing the postmark of a little Nebraska village. This communication, worn and rubbed, looking as though it had been carried for some days in a coat pocket that was none too clean, was from my Uncle Howard and informed me that his wife had been left a small legacy by a bachelor relative who had recently died, and that it would be necessary for her to go to Boston to attend to the settling of the estate. He requested me to meet her at the station and render her whatever services might be necessary. On examining the date indicated as that of her arrival, I found it no later than tomorrow. He had characteristically delayed writing until, had I been away from home for a day, I must have missed the good woman altogether.

The name of Aunt Georgiana called up not alone her own figure, at once pathetic and grotesque, but opened before my feet a gulf of recollection so wide and deep, that, as the letter dropped from my hand, I felt suddenly a stranger to all the present conditions of my existence, wholly ill at ease and out of place amid the familiar surroundings of my study. I became, in short, the gangling farmer boy my aunt had known, scourged[1] with chilblains[2] and bashfulness, my hands cracked and sore from the cornhusking. I felt the knuckles of my thumb tentatively, as though they were raw again. I sat again before her parlor organ, fumbling the scales with my stiff, red hands, while she, beside me, made canvas mittens for the huskers.

The next morning, after preparing my landlady somewhat, I set out for the station. When the train arrived I had some difficulty in finding my aunt. She was the last of the passengers to alight, and it was not until I got her into the carriage that she seemed really to recognize me. She had come all the way in a day coach; her linen duster had become black with soot and her black bonnet gray with dust during the journey. When we arrived at my boardinghouse the landlady put her to bed at once and I did not see her again until the next morning.

Whatever shock Mrs. Springer experienced at my aunt's appearance, she considerably concealed. As for myself, I saw my aunt's misshapen figure with that feeling of awe and respect with which we behold explorers who have left their ears and fingers north of Franz Josef Land,[3] or their health somewhere along the upper Congo.[4] My Aunt Georgiana had been a music teacher at the Boston Conservatory, somewhere back in the latter sixties. One summer, while visiting in the little village among the Green Mountains where her ancestors had dwelt for generations, she had kindled the callow[5] fancy of the most idle and shiftless of all the village lads, and had conceived for this Howard Carpenter one of those extravagant passions which a handsome country boy of twenty-one some-

---

3. **Franz Josef Land:** group of islands in the Arctic Ocean.
4. **upper Congo:** river in West Africa, also called the Zaire.
5. **callow** *adj.*: immature; inexperienced.

Vocabulary
legacy (leg'ə·sē) *n.*: inheritance.
grotesque (grō·tesk') *adj.*: strange; absurd.

---

1. **scourged** *v.*: afflicted; tormented.
2. **chilblains** (chil'blānz') *n. pl.*: inflammation of the hands and feet, caused by exposure to cold.

Learners Having Difficulty
Some students may have difficulty with selection words such as *pathetic, tentatively, extravagant, weakling, ecru,* and *score.* Instruct students to scan the selection for unfamiliar words and to read their definitions in the footnotes or look them up in a dictionary. Suggest that students write down the words and their definitions, creating a glossary to use as they read.

English-Language Learners
Acquaint students with the differences between life on a midwestern farm and life in a northeastern city in the 1800s by displaying and discussing period photographs and a map of the United States.

Advanced Learners
Enrichment. Help students understand the importance of setting in "A Wagner

At the Opera (1879) by Mary Cassatt. Oil on canvas (32" × 26").

Willa Cather **515**

VIEWING THE ART

Mary Cassatt (1844–1926) was one of the most important American artists of the nineteenth century. She left her native Pittsburgh to study art in Paris and remained in France for the rest of her long career. She joined the French Impressionists and won the admiration of such artists as Degas and Manet.

Cassatt painted many portraits of women: mothers with children, sisters, society women. In *At the Opera,* Cassatt carefully modulates detail, color, and line to capture the play of light in the theater box. Point out the man at the upper left who watches the woman in the foreground as intently as she watches the stage.

Activity. Ask students how this painting helps them appreciate Cather's description of the scene in the concert hall. [Possible responses: It conveys the formal, elegant atmosphere of a concert hall; it depicts an audience member absorbed in listening to music.]

Matinée" by asking them to research the theaters, lyceums, and philharmonic groups that flourished in northeastern cities such as Boston during the late 1800s. Have them compare the influence of these institutions on city residents with the influence church socials and other community events may have had on Nebraskans during the same period.

A Content-Area Connections

History: The Homestead Act of 1862

This law, signed by Abraham Lincoln, granted quarter sections (160-acre plots) of public land to people who agreed to occupy and improve the land for five years.

B Literary Focus

❷ Setting. What do these details of Aunt Georgiana's appearance tell you about her Nebraska home?
[Possible responses: Living conditions are harsh; the winds are strong; the water is hard; health care is poor.]

C Literary Focus

❷ Theme. What do you think Aunt Georgiana means when she says, "Pray that whatever your sacrifice may be, it be not that"?
[Possible response: She hopes that Clark will never suffer the pain of losing what he loves most, as she has.]

---

times inspires in an angular, spectacled woman of thirty. When she returned to her duties in Boston, Howard followed her, and the upshot of this inexplicable infatuation was that she eloped with him, eluding the reproaches of her family and the criticisms of her friends by going with **A** him to the Nebraska frontier. Carpenter, who, of course, had no money, had taken a homestead in Red Willow County, fifty miles from the railroad. There they had measured off their quarter section themselves by driving across the prairie in a wagon, to the wheel of which they had tied a red cotton handkerchief, and counting off its revolutions. They built a dugout in the red hillside, one of those cave dwellings whose inmates so often reverted to primitive conditions. Their water they got from the lagoons where the buffalo drank, and their slender stock of provisions was always at the mercy of bands of roving Indians. For thirty years my aunt had not been further than fifty miles from the homestead.

But Mrs. Springer knew nothing of all this, and must have been considerably shocked at what was left of my kinswoman. Beneath the soiled linen duster which, on her arrival, was the most conspicuous feature of her costume, she wore a black stuff[6] dress, whose ornamentation showed that she had surrendered herself unquestioningly into the hands of a country dressmaker. My poor aunt's figure, however, would **B** have presented astonishing difficulties to any dressmaker. Originally stooped, her shoulders were now almost bent together over her sunken chest. She wore no stays,[7] and her gown, which trailed unevenly behind, rose in a sort of peak over her abdomen. She wore ill-fitting false teeth, and her skin was as yellow as a Mongolian's from constant exposure to a pitiless wind and to the alkaline water which hardens the most transparent cuticle into a sort of flexible leather.

I owed to this woman most of the good that ever came my way in my boyhood, and had a reverential affection for her. During the years

---

6. **stuff** *n.:* cloth, usually woolen.
7. **stays** *n. pl.:* corset, or figure-enhancing women's undergarment, stiffened as with whalebone.

---

when I was riding herd for my uncle, my aunt, after cooking the three meals—the first of which was ready at six o'clock in the morning—and putting the six children to bed, would often stand until midnight at her ironing board, with me at the kitchen table beside her, hearing me recite Latin declensions and conjugations,[8] gently shaking me when my drowsy head sank down over a page of irregular verbs. It was to her, at her ironing or mending, that I read my first Shakespeare, and her old textbook on mythology was the first that ever came into my empty hands. She taught me my scales and exercises, too—on the little parlor organ, which her husband had bought her after fifteen years, during which she had not so much as seen any instrument, but an accordion that belonged to one of the Norwegian farmhands. She would sit beside me by the hour, darning and counting while I struggled with the "Joyous Farmer," but she seldom talked to me about music, and I understood why. She was a pious woman; she had the consolations of religion and, to her at least, her martyrdom was not wholly sordid.[9] Once when I had been doggedly[10] beating out some easy passages from an old score of *Euryanthe*[11] I had found among her music books, she came up to me and, putting her hands over my eyes, gently drew my head back upon her shoulder, saying tremulously,[12] "Don't love it so well, **C** Clark, or it may be taken from you. Oh! dear boy, pray that whatever your sacrifice may be, it be not that."

---

8. **Latin declensions and conjugations:** different forms of nouns, pronouns, adjectives, and verbs. Students often memorize these forms when studying Latin or other languages.
9. **sordid** *adj.:* unethical; dishonest.
10. **doggedly** *adv.:* stubbornly; persistently.
11. *Euryanthe:* opera by German composer Carl Maria von Weber.
12. **tremulously** *adv.:* in a trembling or shaking manner.

Vocabulary
eluding (ē·lōōd′iŋ) *v.* used as *adj.:* escaping.
reverential (rev′ə·ren′shəl) *adj.:* deeply respectful.
pious (pī′əs) *adj.:* devoted to one's religion.

READING MINI-LESSON

Developing Word-Attack Skills
Write the selection word *semisomnambulant* on the chalkboard. Tell students that although long words may look intimidating their meaning often becomes clearer when they are divided into parts. Demonstrate this technique with *semisomnambulant*.

- Identify any prefixes: *Semisomnambulant* has the prefix *semi–*.

- Divide the rest of the word into syllables: som-nam-bu-lant.

- Pronounce the prefixes and syllables separately; then, pronounce the whole word.

- Think of words that seem to be related to the unfamiliar word. For *semisomnambulant* these might include *insomnia*, which suggests sleep, and *ambulance*, which suggests movement.

When my aunt appeared on the morning after her arrival, she was still in a semisomnambulant[13] state. She seemed not to realize that she was in the city where she had spent her youth, the place longed for hungrily half a lifetime. She had been so wretchedly trainsick throughout the journey that she had no recollection of anything but her discomfort, and, to all intents and purposes, there were but a few hours of nightmare between the farm in Red Willow County and my study on Newbury Street. I had planned a little pleasure for her that afternoon, to repay her for some of the glorious moments she had given me when we used to milk together in the straw-thatched cowshed and she, because I was more than usually tired, or because her husband had spoken sharply to me, would tell me of the splendid performance of the *Huguenots*[14] she had seen in Paris, in her youth. At two o'clock the Symphony Orchestra was to give a Wagner program, and I intended to take my aunt; though, as I conversed with her, I grew doubtful about her enjoyment of it. Indeed, for her own sake, I could only wish her taste for such things quite dead, and the long struggle mercifully ended at last. I suggested our visiting the Conservatory and the Common before lunch, but she seemed altogether too timid to wish to venture out. She questioned me absently about various changes in the city, but she was chiefly concerned that she had forgotten to leave instructions about feeding half-skimmed milk to a certain weakling calf, "old Maggie's calf, you know, Clark," she explained, evidently having forgotten how long I had been away. She was further troubled because she had neglected to tell her daughter about the freshly opened kit of mackerel in the cellar, which would spoil if it were not used directly.

I asked her whether she had ever heard any of the Wagnerian operas, and found that she had not, though she was perfectly familiar with their respective situations, and had once possessed the piano score of *The Flying Dutchman*. I began to think it would have been best to get her back to Red Willow County without waking her, and regretted having suggested the concert.

From the time we entered the concert hall, however, she was a trifle less passive and inert, and for the first time seemed to perceive her surroundings. I had felt some trepidation lest she might become aware of the absurdities of her attire, or might experience some painful embarrassment at stepping suddenly into the world to which she had been dead for a quarter of a century. But, again, I found how superficially I had judged her. She sat looking about her with eyes as impersonal, almost as stony, as those with which the granite Ramses[15] in a museum watches the froth and fret[16] that ebbs and flows about his pedestal—separated from it by the lonely stretch of centuries. I have seen this same aloofness in old miners who drift into the Brown Hotel at Denver, their pockets full of bullion,[17] their linen soiled, their haggard faces unshaven; standing in the thronged corridors as solitary as though they were still in a frozen camp on the Yukon,[18] conscious that certain experiences have isolated them from their fellows by a gulf no haberdasher[19] could bridge.

We sat at the extreme left of the first balcony, facing the arc of our own and the balcony above us, veritable hanging gardens, brilliant as tulip beds. The matinée audience was made up

---

13. **semisomnambulant** (sem′ē·säm·nam′byo͞o·lənt) *adj.*: confused and unperceiving, as if sleepwalking.
14. ***Huguenots*** (hyo͞o′gə·näts): opera by Giacomo Meyerbeer about the violent struggle between Catholics and Protestants in sixteenth-century France.

---

15. **Ramses** (ram′sēz′): one of the kings of ancient Egypt.
16. **froth and fret:** agitated waters moving around obstacles.
17. **bullion** *n.*: gold.
18. **Yukon:** river in Yukon Territory in northwestern Canada.
19. **haberdasher** (hab′ər·dash′ər) *n.*: one who sells men's clothing. A men's clothing store is sometimes called a haberdashery.

Vocabulary
inert (in·urt′) *adj.*: inactive; dull.
trepidation (trep′ə·dā′shən) *n.*: anxious uncertainty.

Willa Cather **517**

DIRECT TEACHING

D Literary Focus

? Theme. What is Clark referring to when he speaks of Aunt Georgiana's struggle? [Possible response: her struggle to forget her passion for music and to accept her harsh life on the farm.]

E Literary Focus

? Setting and character. What do these worries about the farm reveal about Aunt Georgiana? [They show that her concerns have shifted from high culture to farm and housework.]

F Reading Skills

? Tracing recurring themes. Explore the recurring theme of sleep. On p. 514, Aunt Georgiana is put to bed. On p. 517, she is described as "semisomnambulant." Here Clark regrets "waking her." What do you think the author wants to convey about Aunt Georgiana by using this recurring theme? [Possible response: Sleeping people are unaware of what is happening around them. For Aunt Georgiana, going to Nebraska was like going to sleep. Clark is afraid of reawakening her passion for music.]

G Literary Focus

? Analogy. How is the stone Ramses' relationship to its surroundings like Aunt Georgiana's relationship to hers? [Both seem detached from modern life.]

- Come up with a definition of the word by combining the meaning suggested by the related words with the meanings of the prefixes. Check this definition against the one given in a dictionary or another reference work.

Activity. Write the following words on the chalkboard. Have students study each word and try to find related words that offer clues to its pronunciation and its meaning.

1. superannuated [annual]
2. presupposition [suppose]
3. insurmountable [mount; surmount]
4. interdisciplinary [discipline]
5. unconscionable [conscience]
6. disproportionate [portion; proportion]

? **Context clues.** How can you use context clues to figure out the meaning of *daubs*? [The meaning of *daubs*—"smears; crude strokes"—is suggested by the reference to tube paint and by Cather's earlier description of the audience members' indistinct shapes.]

B **Advanced Learners**

? **Enrichment.** Have a volunteer read this sentence aloud. How does Cather use language to touch the reader in the same way that music first touched Clark? [Possible response: Cather's descriptive phrases and figurative language, such as "forest of fiddle necks," allow the reader to vividly imagine the scene. The steady rhythm of the words suggests the rhythm of music.]

C **Reading Skills**

? **Interpreting.** Why do you think the "frenzy" and "ripping of strings" make Clark recall the Nebraska farm? [Possible response: Clark is struck by the contrast between the richness and passion of the music and the barrenness and squalor of Aunt Georgiana's home.]

D **Learners Having Difficulty**

Breaking down difficult text.
Tell students that breaking down text into shorter segments can help them clarify meaning. Demonstrate by breaking down this long sentence as follows: *I watched her closely through the prelude to* Tristan and Isolde. *I tried vainly to conjecture what that seething turmoil of strings and winds might mean to her. But she sat mutely staring at the violin bows that drove obliquely downward. They were like the pelting streaks of rain in a summer shower.*

---

chiefly of women. One lost the contour of faces and figures, indeed any effect of line whatever, and there was only the color of bodices past counting, the shimmer of fabrics soft and firm, silky and sheer; red, mauve, pink, blue, lilac, purple, ecru, rose, yellow, cream, and white, all the colors that an impressionist[20] finds in a sunlit landscape, with here and there the dead shadow of a frock coat. My Aunt Georgiana regarded them as though they had been so many daubs of tube paint on a palette.

When the musicians came out and took their places, she gave a little stir of anticipation and looked with quickening interest down over the rail at that invariable grouping, perhaps the first wholly familiar thing that had greeted her eye since she had left old Maggie and her weakling calf. I could feel how all those details sank into her soul, for I had not forgotten how they had sunk into mine when I came fresh from plowing forever and forever between green aisles of corn, where, as in a treadmill, one might walk from daybreak to dusk without perceiving a shadow of change. The clean profiles of the musicians, the gloss of their linen, the dull black of their coats, the beloved shapes of the instruments, the patches of yellow light thrown by the green shaded lamps on the smooth, varnished bellies of the cellos and the bass viols in the rear, the restless, wind-tossed forest of fiddle necks and bows—I recalled how, in the first orchestra I had ever heard, those long bow strokes seemed to draw the heart out of me, as a conjurer's[21] stick reels out yards of paper ribbon from a hat.

The first number was the *Tannhäuser*[22] overture. When the horns drew out the first strain of the Pilgrim's chorus, my Aunt Georgiana clutched my coat sleeve. Then it was I first realized that for her this broke a silence of thirty years; the inconceivable silence of the plains. With the battle between the two motives, with

the frenzy of the Venusberg theme and its ripping of strings, there came to me an overwhelming sense of the waste and wear we are so powerless to combat; and I saw again the tall, naked house on the prairie, black and grim as a wooden fortress; the black pond where I had learned to swim, its margin pitted with sundried cattle tracks; the rain-gullied clay banks about the naked house, the four dwarf ash seedlings where the dishcloths were always hung to dry before the kitchen door. The world there was the flat world of the ancients; to the east, a cornfield that stretched to daybreak; to the west, a corral that reached to sunset; between, the conquests of peace, dearer bought than those of war.

The overture closed, my aunt released my coat sleeve, but she said nothing. She sat staring at the orchestra through a dullness of thirty years, through the films made little by little by each of the three hundred and sixty-five days in every one of them. What, I wondered, did she get from it? She had been a good pianist in her day I knew, and her musical education had been broader than that of most music teachers of a quarter of a century ago. She had often told me of Mozart's[23] operas and Meyerbeer's, and I could remember hearing her sing, years ago, certain melodies of Verdi's.[24] When I had fallen ill with a fever in her house she used to sit by my cot in the evening—when the cool, night wind blew in through the faded mosquito netting tacked over the window and I lay watching a certain bright star that burned red above the cornfield—and sing "Home to our mountains, O, let us return!" in a way fit to break the heart of a Vermont boy near dead of homesickness already.

I watched her closely through the prelude to *Tristan and Isolde*, trying vainly to conjecture what that seething turmoil of strings and winds might mean to her, but she sat mutely staring at

---

20. **impressionist** *n.:* one who follows impressionism, a movement in French painting emphasizing the effects of light and color.
21. **conjurer's:** magician's.
22. ***Tannhäuser*** (tän´hoi´zər): Wagner's opera about German minstrels in the thirteenth century.

23. **Mozart's:** Wolfgang Amadeus Mozart (1756–1791), Austrian composer.
24. **Verdi's:** Giuseppe Verdi (1813–1901), Italian composer of opera.

CONTENT-AREA CONNECTIONS

Humanities: Romantic Music
In his "music dramas," Wagner uses the orchestra to express themes and maintain continuity. He pioneered the use of the *leitmotif*, a musical theme assigned to a specific character, event, or idea. The concept of leitmotif has influenced many composers, particularly those who write film scores.

Tannhäuser is based on the story of a legendary German minstrel of the same name. Tannhäuser has been living in Venusberg, the court of Venus. Repenting of his sins, he decides to travel to Rome with a group of pilgrims and ask the pope for forgiveness. The two clashing motives, or motifs, Cather refers to are the Venusberg theme and the Pilgrim's chorus.

the violin bows that drove obliquely downward, like the pelting streaks of rain in a summer shower. Had this music any message for her? Had she enough left to at all comprehend this power which had kindled the world since she had left it? I was in a fever of curiosity, but Aunt Georgiana sat silent upon her peak in Darien.[25] She preserved this utter immobility throughout the number from *The Flying Dutchman*, though her fingers worked mechanically upon her black dress, as though, of themselves, they were recalling the piano score they had once played. Poor old hands! They had been stretched and twisted into mere tentacles to hold and lift and knead with; the palms unduly swollen, the fingers bent and knotted—on one of them a thin, worn band that had once been a wedding ring. As I pressed and gently quieted one of those groping hands, I remembered with quivering eyelids their services for me in other days.

Soon after the tenor began the "Prize Song,"[26] I heard a quick drawn breath and turned to my aunt. Her eyes were closed, but the tears were glistening on her cheeks, and I think, in a moment more, they were in my eyes as well. It never really died, then—the soul that can suffer so excruciatingly and so interminably; it withers to the outward eye only; like that strange moss which can lie on a dusty shelf half a century and yet, if placed in water, grows green again. She wept so throughout the development and elaboration of the melody.

During the intermission before the second half of the concert, I questioned my aunt and found that the "Prize Song" was not new to her. Some years before there had drifted to the farm in Red Willow County a young German, a tramp cowpuncher, who had sung the chorus at Bayreuth,[27] when he was a boy, along with the other peasant boys and girls. Of a Sunday

morning he used to sit on his gingham-sheeted bed in the hands' bedroom which opened off the kitchen, cleaning the leather of his boots and saddle, singing the "Prize Song," while my aunt went about her work in the kitchen. She had hovered about him until she had prevailed upon him to join the country church, though his sole fitness for this step, in so far as I could gather, lay in his boyish face and his possession of this divine melody. Shortly afterward he had gone to town on the Fourth of July, been drunk for several days, lost his money at a faro[28] table, ridden a saddled Texan steer on a bet, and disappeared with a fractured collarbone. All this my aunt told me huskily, wanderingly, as though she were talking in the weak lapses of illness.

"Well, we have come to better things than the old *Trovatore*[29] at any rate, Aunt Georgie?" I queried, with a well-meant effort at jocularity.

Her lip quivered and she hastily put her handkerchief up to her mouth. From behind it she murmured, "And you have been hearing this ever since you left me, Clark?" Her question was the gentlest and saddest of reproaches.

The second half of the program consisted of four numbers from the *Ring*,[30] and closed with Siegfried's funeral march. My aunt wept quietly, but almost continuously, as a shallow vessel overflows in a rainstorm. From time to time her dim eyes looked up at the lights which studded the ceiling, burning softly under their dull glass globes; doubtless they were stars in truth to her. I was still perplexed as to what measure of musical comprehension was left to her, she who had heard nothing but the singing of gospel hymns at Methodist services in the square

---

25. **silent . . . Darien:** allusion to John Keats's "On First Looking into Chapman's Homer," a poem about Keats's awe in the presence of a literary work of art.
26. **"Prize Song":** aria from the third act of Wagner's opera *Die Meistersinger von Nürnberg*.
27. **Bayreuth** (bī·roit′): Bavarian city that hosts an annual festival of Wagnerian music.

28. **faro** (fer′ō) *n.:* gambling game played with cards.
29. *Trovatore* (trô′vä·tô′rä): opera by the Italian composer Giuseppe Verdi.
30. *Ring:* Wagner's *Der Ring des Nibelungen,* a cycle of four operas based on traditional Germanic, Scandinavian, and Icelandic myths and legends.

Vocabulary
obliquely (ō·blēk′lē) *adv.:* at a slant.

Monitoring students' progress.
Ask students whether the following sentences are true or false. Direct students to locate passages in the text that support their responses.

True-False

1. When Clark was young, Aunt Georgiana taught him to play the cello. [F]

2. Although Aunt Georgiana has always loved music, she is not a trained musician. [F]

3. The concert program includes pieces by Verdi and Wagner. [F]

4. Clark invites Aunt Georgiana to stay with him in Boston instead of returning to Nebraska. [F]

INDEPENDENT PRACTICE

Response and Analysis

Reading Check

1. Possible answer: Before her marriage, Aunt Georgiana had a fulfilling career in music, teaching others and attending concerts and operas. After her move, she hears music only in church and must devote her energies to her family and the farm.

2. The narrator is Clark, a young man who lives in Boston. He is grateful to his aunt for introducing him to music and literature.

3. Clark has bought tickets to a concert.

Thinking Critically

4. During the concert, Clark interprets his aunt's thoughts and feelings for the reader. He seems sensitive and kind. Possible answer: Cather is implicitly contrasting the deep sympathy and understanding Clark offers Aunt Georgiana with Howard's apparent callousness and insensitivity.

---

frame schoolhouse on Section Thirteen for so many years. I was wholly unable to gauge how much of it had been dissolved in soapsuds, or worked into bread, or milked into the bottom of a pail.

The deluge of sound poured on and on; I never knew what she found in the shining current of it; I never knew how far it bore her, or past what happy islands. From the trembling of her face I could well believe that before the last numbers she had been carried out where the myriad graves are, into the gray, nameless burying grounds of the sea; or into some world of death vaster yet, where, from the beginning of the world, hope has lain down with hope and dream with dream and, renouncing,[31] slept.

The concert was over; the people filed out of the hall chattering and laughing, glad to relax and find the living level again, but my

---
31. **renouncing** *v.:* giving up.

---

kinswoman made no effort to rise. The harpist slipped its green felt cover over his instrument; the flute players shook the water from their mouthpieces; the men of the orchestra went out one by one, leaving the stage to the chairs and music stands, empty as a winter cornfield.

I spoke to my aunt. She burst into tears and sobbed pleadingly. "I don't want to go, Clark, I don't want to go!"

I understood. For her, just outside the door of the concert hall, lay the black pond with the cattle-tracked bluffs; the tall, unpainted house, with weather-curled boards; naked as a tower, the crookbacked ash seedlings where the dishcloths hung to dry; the gaunt, molting turkeys picking up refuse about the kitchen door. ■

Vocabulary
deluge (del′yo̅o̅j′) *n.:* rush; flood.
myriad (mir′ē·əd) *adj.:* countless.

Response and Analysis

INTERNET
Projects and Activities
Keyword: LE5 11-4

SKILLS FOCUS

Literary Skills
Analyze setting.

Writing Skills
Write an essay comparing and contrasting characters.

Vocabulary Skills
Use context clues.

Reading Check

1. Numerous **flashbacks** in the story provide information about Aunt Georgiana's life before and after she moved to Nebraska. In what ways does her life change as a result of her move?

2. Who is the narrator, and why does he feel he owes a great debt to Aunt Georgiana?

3. What special treat has the narrator planned for Aunt Georgiana in Boston?

Thinking Critically

4. Locate passages in which the first-person **narrator** also functions as an omniscient, or all-knowing, narrator. How would you characterize the narrator? Why do you think Cather chose a male rather than a female narrator to tell this story?

5. The emotional effect of the music and the concert hall on Aunt Georgiana is in direct contrast to the emotional effect on her of the Nebraska frontier—the **setting** we hear about over and over again in the story. How does Cather make you feel about the Nebraska setting? What details from the story create this feeling?

6. Summarize in your own words what you think Clark understands at the end of the story.

7. What series of emotions does Aunt Georgiana experience at the concert? At the end, do you think she finds her pleasure worth the pain of reawakened longings? Why?

8. What seems to be Cather's **theme** in the story? How would you say the central episode of the concert contributes to this theme?

520 Collection 4 The Rise of Realism: The Civil War to 1914

---

5. Using words and phrases such as "silence of the plains," "naked," and "flat," Cather evokes the bleakness of the Nebraska setting.

6. Possible answer: He understands how bleak life without music is for Georgiana.

Extending and Evaluating

9. Aunt Georgiana says to the narrator about music, "Don't love it so well, Clark, or it may be taken from you." Do you agree with this advice, or do you have other ideas on how to cope with losing what you love? Your Quickwrite notes may help you. ✎

Literary Criticism

10. If this story were written by a Romantic rather than a realist, how differently might Aunt Georgiana's visit to Boston have turned out? How do you think a Romantic writer would have described the Nebraska farm setting?

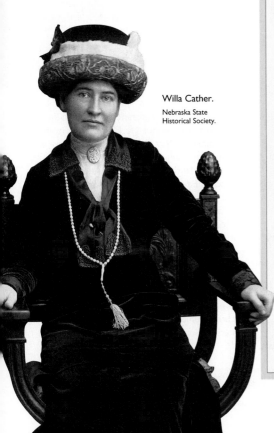

Willa Cather.
Nebraska State
Historical Society.

WRITING

Linked Lives

In what ways is Aunt Georgiana's experience at the concert like the shopping experience of Mrs. Sommers in Kate Chopin's story "A Pair of Silk Stockings" (page 504)? Write a brief essay **comparing and contrasting** the two women and their afternoons of escape. For each character, consider her life at the present and in the past, her emotional needs, and her range of reactions to her "escape" experience.

Vocabulary Development

Diagramming Context

grotesque	pious	obliquely
eluding	inert	deluge
reverential	trepidation	myriad

The diagram below shows how one reader figured out the meaning of the word *legacy* by using **context clues.** After noting this reader's strategies, study the other Vocabulary words where they appear in the story. (You'll find them underlined.) For each word, look for context clues. If you find any, list them and explain how the clues help make the word's meaning clear.

"This communication, worn and rubbed, looking as though it had been carried for some days in a coat pocket that was none too clean, was from my Uncle Howard and informed me that his wife had been left a small legacy by a bachelor relative who had recently died, and that it would be necessary for her to go to Boston to attend to the settling of the estate."

> If she was left something, it might be a gift of some kind.

> Since it was from a relative who died, *legacy* might be some sort of inheritance.

> I've heard this phrase used in reference to a will. *Legacy* is probably related to a will.

Extending and Evaluating

9. Possible answers: Agree; it is better to guard against the pain of loss by not loving too much. Disagree; the joy of loving is worth the risk of suffering. People might cope with losing what they love by developing other interests.

Literary Criticism

10. Possible answer: A Romantic writer might have idealized the rural setting and allowed the concert to bring Aunt Georgiana spiritual solace; a Dark Romantic might have had Aunt Georgiana die of heartbreak.

Vocabulary Development

Possible Answers

- *grotesque:* "pathetic"
- *eluding:* "reproaches"; "criticisms"
- *reverential:* Clues are found in Clark's overall attitude toward Aunt Georgiana.
- *pious:* "religion"; "martyrdom"
- *inert:* "passive"
- *trepidation:* A clue is Clark's protectiveness toward his aunt.
- *obliquely:* "like the pelting streaks of rain"
- *deluge:* "poured"; "current"
- *myriad:* no clues

ASSESSING

Assessment

- *Holt Assessment: Literature, Reading, and Vocabulary*

---

7. At first Aunt Georgiana seems unresponsive, almost apathetic; ultimately she is deeply moved. Possible answers: Yes, the experience has been rewarding; no, it is too painful for her to leave what she loves behind yet again.

8. Possible answers: It is painful to rediscover something one loved and lost, only to lose it once more. The "turmoil of the winds and strings" in the concert suggests the emotional turmoil Aunt Georgiana is experiencing.

Grade-Level Skills

■ **Literary Skills**
Analyze connotations.

■ **Literary Skills**
Analyze the philosophical arguments in literary works and their impact on the quality of each work. (Philosophical approach)

More About the Writer

Background. Edward Arlington Robinson began writing regularly at age eleven; while in high school, he became the youngest member of his town's poetry society. A school-mate described him as "one of those persons whom you cannot influence ever; he went his own way." Robinson had to leave Harvard when a year after his father died, the family's fortune drastically shrank during the economic upheaval known as the panic of 1893. Both of Robinson's older brothers died young, one from alco-holism and the other from mor-phine addiction; these family tragedies may have inspired "Richard Cory" and "Miniver Cheevy." For most of his life, Robinson chose to live in poverty in order to devote himself to poetry.

Edwin Arlington Robinson
(1869–1935)

By the 1890s, the vitality of the nineteenth century seemed exhausted, and the gath-ering forces of modernism were still scattered and obscure. Between 1890 and 1910, many poets were churning out the same old rhymes and meters of Romanticism. In those two decades, one voice spoke out in traditional forms enlivened with an authentic, contempo-rary American accent: the voice of Edwin Arlington Robinson.

The strengths that distinguish Robinson are his native voice and his wise and ironic view of human behavior. Robinson's bedrock realism informs even the most formal of his carefully wrought poems. In some of his poetic por-traits of individuals, he anticipates by a decade the more loosely drawn portraits found in Edgar Lee Masters's *Spoon River Anthology*. In his skill with meter, Robinson foreshadows Robert Frost's gift for bending the strictly counted line to accommodate the ease and flow of vernacular speech.

Robinson was a Yankee from the rocky coast of Maine. Born at Head Tide in 1869, he lived for the next twenty-seven years in the town of Gardiner, except for the two years when he attended Harvard as a special stu-dent. Gardiner became the Tilbury Town of his poems, the home of some of his most famous characters. When he was in his late twenties, Robinson moved to New York City and published his first book. There he sup-ported himself at various jobs, including one as a timekeeper at the construction site of the new subway system.

After a year of such work, Robinson's for-tunes took a surprising turn for the better. Among the young poet's readers was none other than the president of the United States,

Theodore Roosevelt. When Roosevelt learned that the poet he admired was barely scraping by on a laborer's salary, he arranged to have the New York Custom House hire him as a clerk, a position Robinson held for almost five years. One year after Robinson resigned, he pub-lished *The Town Down the River* (1910) and dedi-cated the volume to Roosevelt.

Another form of assistance came in an invi-tation from the famous MacDowell Colony in Peterborough, New Hampshire. The colony is a center for composers, artists, and writers, established by the widow of the American composer Edward MacDowell. There Robinson spent long working summers for the greater part of his life.

Robinson became increasingly popular, and during his career he won the Pulitzer Prize in poetry three times. His traditional poetic forms link him to the nineteenth century, and his sense of irony attach him to the twentieth. At the time of Robinson's death, it was clear that even as modernism flourished, he had secured a unique and permanent place in American literature.

Before You Read

Richard Cory

Make the Connection
Quickwrite

One of the persistent themes of early-twentieth-century American poetry is that the conventions and behaviors common to small-town life are a facade that often obscures unpleasant realities.

Can we accurately determine the inner feelings of a person by observing his or her outward behavior? Write a few sentences stating your opinion, supported by specific reasons.

Literary Focus
Language and Style: Connotations

In Robinson's famous poem an unidentified speaker tells what happened to Richard Cory, a prominent town citizen. Robinson never shows it outright, but he implies that the townspeople see Cory as a king. The poet achieves this effect by using words with connotations of royalty. Words get such **connotations,** or emotional overtones and associations, through shared usage.

It would be hard, for example, for a writer to call a character a lamb without someone familiar with English making an immediate association with innocence and docility. This would be true even for readers who have never seen a lamb; they would only have to be familiar with the Bible or with nursery rhymes to recognize these associations. As you read the poem, be alert for important word connotations.

Literary Skills
Understand connotations.

Richard Cory

Edwin Arlington Robinson

Whenever Richard Cory went downtown,
    We people on the pavement looked at him:
He was a gentleman from sole to crown,
    Clean favored, and imperially slim.

5 And he was always quietly arrayed,
    And he was always human when he talked;
But still he fluttered pulses when he said,
    "Good morning," and he glittered when he walked.

And he was rich—yes, richer than a king—
10   And admirably schooled in every grace:
In fine, we thought that he was everything
    To make us wish that we were in his place.

So on we worked, and waited for the light,
    And went without the meat, and cursed the bread;
15 And Richard Cory, one calm summer night,
    Went home and put a bullet through his head.

Collection of Whitney Museum of American Art (31.128). Photograph ©1998 Whitney Museum of American Art.

Winter Twilight (1930) by Charles Burchfield.
Oil on composition board (27³/₄″ × 39½″).

Edwin Arlington Robinson   **523**

PRETEACHING

Summary   *at grade level*

In this ironic poem a resident of a small town describes Richard Cory—a wealthy, courteous, and refined man who is the envy of his less prosperous neighbors. The poem ends on a shocking note, with the speaker revealing that Cory committed suicide.

DIRECT TEACHING

A Reading Skills

❷ Contrasting. What contrast can you draw between the speaker of the poem and Cory? [The speaker is one of the ordinary townspeople; Cory is regal and distinguished.]

B Literary Focus

❷ Author's style: Connotations. What does the poet imply by using the word *crown* instead of *head* in l.3? [A crown symbolizes kingship; the word connotes royalty.]

C Reading Skills

❷ Making inferences. What assumptions do people make about Cory because he is rich? [Possible responses: They think he is happy; they think he has everything anyone could want.]

D Literary Focus

❷ Irony. Given Richard Cory's fate, why is it ironic that the townspeople envied him? [They had no idea that he was suffering despite his wealth and status; his troubles have turned out to be harder to bear than theirs.]

DIFFERENTIATING INSTRUCTION

Learners Having Difficulty

Ask students to recast this narrative poem as a prose story. Tell them that the story should explain who Richard Cory is and how the other townspeople feel about him. Instruct them to include all the details in the poem.

English-Language Learners

Idioms. You may want to explain several idioms in this poem. When the speaker says that Cory was "always human," he means that Cory never condescended to others. "Fluttered pulses" indicates that Cory's presence excited people, the way a celebrity's appearance might excite people today. "In fine" means "in sum" or "in short."

Response and Analysis

Richard Cory

Thinking Critically

1. Words and phrases include *crown, imperially slim, arrayed, glittered,* and *richer than a king.* Substituting other words softens the contrast between Cory and the townspeople.

2. The word *gentleman* suggests that Cory stands apart from the townspeople; the word *downtown* connotes a workday place far from Cory's exclusive haunts.

3. Since Cory seems so "kingly" his suicide comes as a shock, contrasting with the calm of the night.

4. Yes; readers don't know if problems with Cory's work, friends, or family might have caused him to take his life.

5. He may have felt that the poem expresses Cory's humanity. Brower may have found the tone of the poem unfeeling. Students will probably pity Cory.

6. Cory's fate suggests that material success cannot fulfill our needs.

Extending and Evaluating

7. Possible answers: The poem does not show how Cory's social class affected his fate; Robinson makes it clear that Cory's privileged status caused him unhappiness.

Miniver Cheevy

Thinking Critically

1. Possible answer: No; Cheevy's unhappiness stems from his refusal to take responsibility for his life. He copes by drinking and daydreaming.

2. Possible answers: The phrase connotes bitterness; it suggests that Cheevy sees himself as being above his circumstances.

3. He feels that they are not appreciated.

Response and Analysis

Richard Cory

Thinking Critically

1. Find at least five words or phrases in "Richard Cory" with **connotations** of kingliness or royalty. Replace each of these words or phrases with a neutral one that, in your opinion, has no strong connotations at all. How is the effect of the poem different?

2. Find other words with important **connotations** in the poem. For example, what does the word *gentleman* (line 3) suggest? What does *downtown* (line 1) suggest that *uptown* would not? How do the poet's word choices contribute to the contrast between the townspeople and Richard Cory?

3. Why is it **ironic** that Richard Cory takes his own life? What irony is there in the fact that the night is calm?

4. Does the harsh surprise ending hint that the real story is the one that remains untold? What aspects of Richard Cory's life are not mentioned? How might these hidden or overlooked areas account for his fate?

5. Read Robinson's comments on "Richard Cory" (page 525). What do you think he means when he says there is a lot of "humanity" in the poem? Why do you think the poem made Robinson's correspondent feel "cold"? How does it make you feel?

6. The poem indicates that appearances can be deceiving. Does Cory's tale have a **moral** or message for readers today? (Refer to your Quickwrite notes.) ✏

Extending and Evaluating

7. Is Robinson successful in suggesting how the influences of Cory's social class shaped his personality and fate? Why or why not?

**go.
hrw
.com**

INTERNET
**Projects and
Activities**
Keyword: LE5 11-4

**SKILLS
FOCUS**

Literary Skills
Analyze
connotations.
Analyze
philosophical
ideas presented
in literary works.

Writing Skills
Write an essay
analyzing
character.

Miniver Cheevy

Thinking Critically

1. Do Miniver Cheevy's problems really stem from his having been "born too late"? Explain. How does the disappointed Cheevy cope with his lot in life?

2. What do you think "child of scorn" means? What **connotations** does the expression have? What does it suggest about Cheevy's character?

3. Romance and Art are **personified** in the fourth stanza. What does Cheevy think has happened to romance and art in his own time?

4. How would you describe the overall **tone** of the poem prior to the last stanza? How does the tone shift in the last stanza?

5. Where might Miniver Cheevys be found today? What sorts of worlds do they mourn for? ✏

Literary Criticism

6. **Philosophical approach.** The poet James Dickey wrote that although Robinson has been called a "laureate of failure," he actually chronicled "the delusions necessary to sustain life." How does this statement apply to "Miniver Cheevy"? Do you agree that delusions and illusions can help people get through their lives? Why or why not?

WRITING

Rising Above or Mired Below?

In a brief **essay,** analyze the character of either Richard Cory or Miniver Cheevy to show whether he demonstrates the transcendentalist ideals of self-reliance and individualism championed by Emerson (page 179) and Thoreau (page 189). As the focus of your essay, choose an appropriate quotation from either of these writers.

4. Possible answer: The tone is satirical but not without compassion. In the final stanza the tone becomes darker.

5. Students might compare Cheevy to adults who go to extremes to feel young.

Literary Criticism

6. Cheevy dreams about the past to escape his unhappiness. Possible answer: No—

it is better to face reality without taking refuge in delusions.

ASSESSING

Assessment

■ *Holt Assessment: Literature, Reading, and Vocabulary*

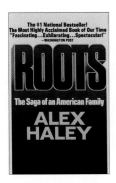

FICTION

A Family Saga

When Alex Haley was a child, his grandmother told him tales of an ancestor known only as the African—a man torn from his Mandingo people and forced into slavery in America. When Haley grew up, he discovered that the African had a real name—Kunta Kinte—and a story that had the power to reach people everywhere. *Roots* is a fictionalized chronicle spanning the period between Kunta's birth in 1750 and the death of Haley's father, a college professor, in the twentieth century.

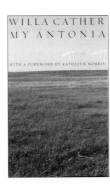

FICTION

The Great American Novel

Ernest Hemingway wrote, "All modern American literature comes from one book by Mark Twain called *Huckleberry Finn*." Widely regarded as Twain's masterpiece, *Adventures of Huckleberry Finn* is a wise and funny novel about a young boy coming of age on the Mississippi River.

This title is available in the HRW Library.

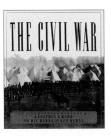

NONFICTION

The War Between the States

For an inside look at the most dramatic war waged on U.S. soil, consider *The Civil War: An Illustrated History* by Geoffrey C. Ward and others. This companion volume to the PBS series, produced by Ric and Ken Burns, features essays; interviews; and an arresting series of photographs depicting generals, soldiers, and everyday citizens from the North and the South. The historical narrative and stunning images trace the war from the first shots at Fort Sumter through the bloody battlefields and finally to General Lee's surrender at Appomattox.

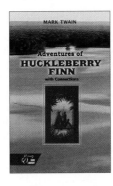

FICTION

The Wild Frontier

The late nineteenth century was a time in which the United States became a nation of immigrants—a time when people from many lands were drawn to the promise of the western frontier. Willa Cather's classic novel *My Ántonia* is the story of one such immigrant family—the Shimerdas of Bohemia—and their new life in Nebraska. At the center of the story is the Shimerdas's daughter Ántonia, who captures the heart and imagination of a lonely neighbor boy.

Read On   527

Read On

For Independent Reading

You might recommend the following titles for independent reading to students who enjoyed the themes and topics explored in this collection.

Assessment Options

Use the following projects to assess your students' understanding of their outside reading.

- **Create a game.** Have groups of three students (all of whom have read the same book) create a game based on the plot and characters of the book. Group members must decide on rules for the game and design the board and game pieces. When other students in the class play the game, they should have a clear understanding of what the book is about.

- **Design a movie poster.** Have students design a poster for a movie based on the book they have read. Tell them to include the title of the book, the author's name, and the names of the main characters, along with the actors who will play the parts. Tell students to choose a scene from the book that will make others want to see the movie.

- **Write a children's book.** Have students write a summary of the book they have read in the form of a children's book. Have them include pictures on each page, an attractive cover, and a new title appropriate for children. Remind students to use simple language that young children will understand.

DIFFERENTIATING INSTRUCTION

Estimated Word Counts and Reading Levels of Read On Books:

Fiction			Nonfiction		
Roots	↔	315,400	The Civil War: An Illustrated History	↔	80,000
Adventures of Huckleberry Finn	↑	95,400			
My Ántonia	↔	79,500			

KEY: ↑ *above grade level*   ↔ *at grade level*   ↓ *below grade level*

Skills Starter

Motivate. Ask students to recall interesting facts about the history of the area in which they live. Write students' comments on the chalkboard, and discuss with the class where such information may be found [books, museums, historical sites, conversations with longtime residents, old photographs]. Students may contribute facts that surprise others or that seem unbelievable. Point out to students that checking and verifying such facts is the job of a historical researcher.

Reporting Historical Research

Writing Assignment
Write a paper investigating a historical event that intrigues you.

Paralleling the rise of realism in American literature was a rise in realism for historians, who began to take a more scientific and objective approach to gathering and interpreting evidence about historical events. Instead of writing to glorify or justify conquerors, historians would analyze and evaluate all the available evidence about an event before drawing any conclusions. Now you will have the opportunity to **investigate a historical event** by analyzing several different historical records about it, explaining the similarities and differences among the records, and drawing conclusions about the event.

Prewriting

Choose and Narrow a Topic

Travel to the Past You investigate a historical event so you can draw your own conclusions about the event and its significance. When you read a single record of a historical event—the attack on Pearl Harbor or the assassination of President John F. Kennedy, the fall of the Berlin Wall—you are likely to be reading information that represents only one **perspective,** or point of view, on that event. To understand a historical event fully, you need to examine a wide variety of sources representing all relevant perspectives on the event.

As you consider a topic for your paper, look for a controversial event that interests you and for which you will be able to find a variety of sources. You should also make sure that the topic is narrow enough to be covered well in a paper of 1,500 words. To choose an appropriate topic, follow the example in the student model below.

What historical event am I interested in?	I'm interested in the Civil War.
How can I narrow this topic, if necessary?	I can focus on one important event: General Sherman's march from Atlanta to Savannah.
Can I find a variety of sources on this topic?	Yes—records and newspaper accounts written during the war, memoirs and books written after the war are available.
Can I find sources representing all relevant perspectives on this topic?	Yes, there should be plenty of information representing various points of view, such as those of Northerners, Southerners, soldiers, and civilians.

COLLECTION 4 RESOURCES: WRITING

Planning
- *One-Stop Planner* CD-ROM with ExamView Test Generator

Differentiating Instruction
- *Workshop Resources: Writing, Listening, and Speaking*
- *Family Involvement Activities in English and Spanish*
- *Supporting Instruction in Spanish*

Writing and Language
- *Workshop Resources: Writing, Listening, and Speaking*
- *Daily Language Activities*
- *Language Handbook Worksheets*

Assessment
- *Holt Assessment: Writing, Listening, and Speaking*

Answering the last two questions in the chart on the previous page might require some preliminary research. If you can't find information representing different perspectives on the event, pick another event that lends itself to hearty investigation.

If you're not sure what historical event you're interested in, thumb through a history book for intriguing topics or ask a history teacher to suggest interesting historical events for you to consider.

Consider Purpose and Audience

Cover the Basics Once you have narrowed your topic, you should consider your **purpose** for writing this investigative paper. Of course you want to inform your **audience**—most likely your classmates and teacher—about your topic. Avoid, however, simply compiling a collection of facts. Instead, focus on creating a historical investigation paper that synthesizes, or combines, information gathered from various sources, and include conclusions you draw about that information based on logical analysis.

TIP Adopt a formal and objective **tone**—your attitude toward your topic and your audience—in your paper. Write from the third-person point of view (avoid the pronoun *I* or *you*), and avoid slang, colloquial expressions, and contractions.

Ask Research Questions

What Do I Want to Know? Clear **research questions** will help you focus your search for sources and will lead you to analyze the different perspectives on the historical event you're investigating. The following chart shows the research questions one writer developed to focus his research on General Sherman's March.

- What are the facts of Sherman's March?
- What perspective is revealed by the written or spoken testimony of each group directly involved in or affected by the march?
- What were the perspectives of Northerners and Southerners not directly involved in or affected by the march?

Find Answers to Research Questions

The Search Begins Begin to track down the answers to your research questions with a general reference work. You'll get an overview of your topic and gain valuable background information. In addition, an article in a general reference work usually mentions other sources you can use in your research. For this initial step, consult a print or CD-ROM encyclopedia, or search the Internet for sites or pages that contain related key words.

Follow the Leads Once you have an overview of your topic, move on to specific sources that can help you answer your research questions. Be creative in developing a research strategy. Avoid restricting yourself to print sources available at your school or community library. Your most valuable information might come from

SKILLS FOCUS

Writing Skills
Write a historical research report. Choose a topic. Consider purpose and audience. Generate research questions, and conduct research.

Consider Purpose and Audience

You may remind students that there is more than one form in which to present historical research. Some forms may be more appropriate depending on students' purpose and audience. For example, an article might be an appropriate form to present information to a magazine audience. If the audience is a teacher, a formal research report is probably the most appropriate form.

MODELING AND DEMONSTRATION

Ask Research Questions

Model for students the kinds of questions they can ask to direct their research by writing on the chalkboard the following questions on the topic of Charlie Parker's contributions to jazz:

- **Who** influenced Charlie Parker's development as a jazz musician?
- **What** major contributions did Parker make to jazz?
- **When** did Parker begin to influence others?
- **Where** did Parker begin his career, and where did it take him?
- **Why** could one argue that Charlie Parker is the most influential musician in the history of jazz?
- **How** did Charlie Parker's influence permanently change jazz?

Then, ask a volunteer to demonstrate the same concept by sharing with the class the questions he or she will use to direct his or her research.

DIRECT TEACHING

The Search Begins

If students research on the Internet, you need to be aware that the World Wide Web often functions as a public forum with unpredictable content.

Point out to students that if they research their topic on the World Wide Web they can make their searches more efficient by using combinations of keywords. For example, if a computer search using the keyword *jazz* yields too much irrelevant information, they might narrow the search by using *jazz + bebop*. Direct students to look for information on advanced searching strategies on the first screen of their search engines.

DIFFERENTIATING INSTRUCTION

English-Language Learners

Locating library resources may be particularly challenging for some students. Talk to a librarian or media specialist about presenting an orientation to show students the areas of the library and to teach useful research tools.

an interview with a historian, a visit to a museum, a letter (or e-mail) requesting additional information, or a visit to an actual historical site. Some sources may lead you to other sources. The chart below lists some information sources in your library and community.

INFORMATION RESOURCES

Library Resources	Sources of Information
Card catalog or online catalog	Books and audiovisuals (separate catalogs in some libraries)
Readers' Guide to Periodical Literature or online periodical indexes	Articles from magazines and journals
Newspaper indexes, specialized reference books, and CD-ROMs	Newspapers (often on microfilm), dictionaries, encyclopedias, and bibliographies
Microfilm or microfiche and online databases	Indexes to major newspapers, back issues of some newspapers and magazines
Community Resources	**Sources of Information**
National, state, and local government offices	Official records
Museums and historical societies	Exhibits, experts
Schools and colleges	Libraries, experts
World Wide Web and online services	Articles, interviews, bibliographies, pictures, videos

The Hard Evidence Your topic may have generated so much interest that you might quickly find yourself buried under information. The following guidelines can help you avoid such a fate.

SKILLS FOCUS

Writing Skills
Use a variety of research sources, including primary and secondary sources.

- **Choose a balance of primary and secondary sources.** A **primary source** is firsthand, original information, such as a letter, an autobiography, a work of literature or art, a historical document, or an interview with a person who participated in the event being researched. A **secondary source** is information derived from, or about, primary sources, or even from other secondary sources. Examples include an encyclopedia or CD-ROM, a documentary film, a biography, a history book, or an interview with a historian. (Sometimes a primary source may be included in a secondary source or another primary source—called an **indirect source.** For example, a book about Sherman's March is the indirect source of a soldier's letter describing the march.)

  For a paper on Sherman's March, primary sources might include General Sherman's memoirs. Secondary sources might include a book about Sherman's March.

- **Choose reliable sources.** Don't assume that all sources are reliable. Memory may be faulty or selective in an autobiography or memoir, and emotions may override facts in a letter or diary. A secondary source may be biased or slanted. Research as much as possible in journals and books published by reputable institutions such as major universities and well-known publishing companies. Factual information from such sources can generally be regarded as reliable and can provide you with a good basis for deciding whether other information you uncover is accurate and objective. The reliability of interpretations of facts can be judged only through logical analysis.

- **Make sure your sources cover all relevant perspectives.** Look for sources that tell the perspectives of all the major groups involved in the event. For instance, plenty of information about Sherman's March is available from the perspectives of Northerners, Sherman and his troops, and Southerners, but less is available from Southern slaves. If information from a certain perspective is scarce, look for hints about what the group thought and felt in information written from other perspectives.

TIP Remember to check any Internet source that you use for its validity and reliability. Usually educational, governmental, or professional Web sites pass muster.

Record and Organize Information

Sources First Using a separate note card or a separate computer file for each source, write complete and accurate information about all the sources you consult, even if you're not sure you will use them in your paper. Include a short note describing the information contained in the source and estimating the value of the source. Such notes will turn your source cards into an **annotated bibliography.** Also, since your *Works Cited* list—the list of sources at the end of your paper—must contain specific publishing information, you will save time if you record that information on sources exactly as it will appear in the *Works Cited* list. Follow the guidelines below to make your source cards.

Reference Note

For sample *Works Cited* entries, see pages 537–539.

GUIDELINES FOR MAKING SOURCE CARDS

1. **Assign each source a number.** Later, when you are taking notes, it will save time to write a number instead of the author and title. (You might also use the author's last name as a source code.)

2. **Record full publishing information.** Consult the Guidelines for Preparing the *Works Cited* List on page 537 and enter publishing information exactly as it appears for each type of entry you have.

3. **Annotate each source.** Write a short note to remind yourself of the content and value of the source.

4. **Note the call number or location.** This information will help you relocate the source quickly.

SKILLS FOCUS

Writing Skills
Record and organize your research.

Integrating with Grammar, Usage, and Mechanics

As students begin their research papers, they might have trouble with clear reference and correct usage of verbs. You may want to review section 3 in the Language Handbook.

Record and Organize Information

Caution students who are using Internet resources to copy Web site addresses very carefully onto source cards, as any errors in spacing, spelling, or punctuation will make the information useless. As an alternative, students may want to cut the address line off the Web page printout and tape it to a source card to avoid any possibility of errors.

As students check Internet sources, you need to be aware that the World Wide Web often functions as a public forum and its content may be unpredictable.

Students conducting interviews should be very careful when noting anything they might want to quote directly. They can read the material to their interview subjects to double-check its accuracy. If they have recorded the interview, they should be sure to transcribe their tapes accurately.

Writing Workshop: Reporting Historical Research **531**

Learners Having Difficulty

To help students keep track of their progress, you might want to encourage them to keep learning logs. Provide a few moments at the end of every class period for students to write entries on what they learned about the process during class. Allow a few volunteers to share their log entries so that students can be exposed to alternative strategies. For example, a sample entry might read:

> Today, I started taking notes on cards. At first, I kept forgetting parts like the source number. Finally, I decided to make a model note card to carry with me to the library. Before I go to the next note, I check the one I have just made against the model to make sure I haven't forgotten anything.

CORRECTING MISCONCEPTIONS

Remind students that informal words or expressions are not acceptable in research papers. If they avoid being informal at the note-taking stage, students will be less likely to incorporate colloquialisms and other informal language into first drafts. It may be helpful to create and distribute a list of unacceptable words and phrases to save time coaching students individually. Examples might include *a lot of, sort of,* and *pretty much.*

Finding the Note Worthy   Now that you have selected, evaluated, and recorded your sources, take notes to answer your research questions. To get started, read each source to be sure that you understand the overall meaning. Then, use the following guidelines for taking notes. See page 533 for sample note cards.

GUIDELINES FOR TAKING NOTES

1. **Use a separate card, half-sheet of paper, or computer file for each source and item of information.** Separate cards or files make rearranging and organizing notes easier when you get ready to write.

2. **Record the source number.** In the upper right-hand corner of each note, write the number (or author's last name) you assigned each source to tell you exactly where you got the information.

3. **Write a label or heading.** In the upper left-hand corner of the card or file, identify the main idea of your note so that you do not have to re-read each note to remind yourself what it is about.

4. **Write the page number(s).** At the end of your note, write the page numbers from which the information comes. Page references, if available, are required for the documentation in your paper.

Reference Note

For more on the use of **ellipsis points,** see Ellipsis Points, 13e, and for more on **brackets** with quotations, see Brackets, 13n, in the Language Handbook.

Decisions, Decisions   As you take notes, decide how to record each piece of information: Will you quote the information directly? summarize it? paraphrase it? Use the following guidelines to decide.

- **Direct quotation**   To capture interesting, well-phrased passages or a passage's technical accuracy, quote an author directly and exactly, including punctuation, capitalization, and spelling. Resist the urge to quote too much. Your task is to synthesize information and draw conclusions from it, not to stitch together a long series of quotations.
  Enclose the passage in quotation marks and remember to use ellipsis points to indicate omissions from quoted text. Use brackets to explain words you have changed for the sense of a sentence.

- **Paraphrase**   If you want to use specific ideas or information from a source without quoting the source, paraphrase the information. Paraphrasing requires completely rewriting the information in your own words and style.

- **Summary**   Summarize information when you want to use the general idea presented in a source. A summary is highly condensed—typically one fourth to one third the length of the original passage.

TIP   To avoid **plagiarizing,** or failing to give credit to an author whose words or ideas you have used, you must completely rewrite paraphrases and summaries. Simply substituting synonyms for some of the words from your source is not enough.

③ — source card number

Sherman's Purpose — label

Major Henry Hitchcock stated, "Evidently it is a — note (quotation)
material element in this campaign to produce among
the people of Georgia a thorough conviction of the
personal misery which attends war . . ."

page 44 — page number

Major Henry Hitchcock observed that making — note (paraphrase)
Georgians completely aware of the terrible consequences that war brings to every individual was
clearly part of Sherman's plan.
page 44

Major Henry Hitchcock observed that Sherman's plan — note (summary)
included convincing Georgians of the miseries of war.
page 44

Analyze Your Information

Accounting for the Records The next step in the historical investigation process is to analyze your information. Begin by separating your note cards by their headings. For example, the student writing about Sherman's March found that he had collected information from the perspectives of Northerners, General Sherman, Southerners, and slaves, and divided his note cards accordingly.

As you analyze the information you have gathered, you will probably find that your sources contain conflicting information or different interpretations of the same facts. How can you account for such differences? Here are a couple of questions you can use to analyze differences in your sources.

1. **What is the background of the author of the information?** Is his or her perspective on the event likely to be biased because of that background? For example, a descendant of a Southerner whose plantation was destroyed by General Sherman's troops might have a biased perspective on the march.

2. **When was the information recorded or the source written?** While material written at the time of an event might have the quality of "eyewitness" news, material written after an event sometimes has the advantage of objectivity. For example, a professional historian writing a century after Sherman's March has had the opportunity to

SKILLS FOCUS

Writing Skills
Analyze your research.

Write a Thesis Statement

Point out to students that there are many possible thesis statements for the same topic, and that thesis statements may change as their research progresses. For example, an alternative to the example on this page is *Northerners and Southerners have different views of Sherman's March, and it seems likely that both of these views are at least partially true, according to historical accounts.*

Learners Having Difficulty

Point out to students that they can write thesis statements from the following formula: topic + your opinion or idea about the topic = thesis statement.

Develop an Outline

As students plan their reports, have them use a visual organizer such as the following to help them shape their body paragraphs.

Subtopic:
#1 Support:
Conclusion:
Conclusion:
#2 Support:
Conclusion:
Conclusion:
Concluding Sentence:

---

examine all the records. What he or she writes is probably more objective than what a victim of Sherman's March might have written.

Here is one student's explanation of an important difference between two historical records.

> **Difference between Sources:** The U.S. Senate and House of Representatives commended Sherman and his men for their "gallantry and good conduct," when Sherman himself was aware that his men had been guilty of "acts of pillage, robbery, and violence."
>
> **Explanation:** Congress commended Sherman's men not only to reward their success but also to spread political propaganda and to increase morale. Sherman, on the other hand, was speaking long after the fact, reflecting honestly on his march through Georgia.

Write a Thesis Statement

So, What's Your Point? How does all your research information fit together? What larger point, or general conclusion, does all the information support? Write a **thesis statement** in which you state your topic and your general conclusion about it. As you support that statement, you will use a combination of rhetorical strategies: **exposition, narration, description.** The following is a sample thesis statement for a historical research paper.

> Northerners, General Sherman, Southerners, and slaves had powerful reasons for their different perspectives on Sherman's March, and the historical record supports them all.

Develop an Outline

Divide and Conquer An outline provides an organizational overview of your paper, and allows you to ensure that your ideas flow in a logical progression, with adequate support for each idea.

First, sort your note cards into groups with similar labels—the information you have written in the left-hand corner of each card. The way you group the labels may immediately suggest the main sections or ideas of your paper. Then, decide how best to order these sections. You'll probably need to use a combination of **chronological order** (the order in which events occur), **logical order** (related ideas grouped together), and **order of importance** (most important idea to least important, or the reverse). Finally, decide how to order the ideas within sections and which supporting details to use.

Now, put your information in a formal outline. A **formal outline** has numerals and letters to identify headings (main ideas), subheadings (supporting ideas and evidence), and details. It provides an overview of your research paper and can serve as a table of contents.

DO THIS

SKILLS FOCUS

Writing Skills
Write a thesis statement.
Develop an outline.

Check with your teacher to see if you should attach a formal outline to the final draft of your paper. Here is part of a student's formal outline for his historical research paper on Sherman's March.

I. Introduction
   A. Overview of research
   B. Thesis: Northerners, General Sherman, Southerners, and slaves had powerful reasons for their different perspectives on Sherman's March, and the historical record supports them all.
II. The view from the North
   A. Military importance
     1. Grant's chief of staff's view
     2. New York Times view
     3. General Grant's view
   B. Conduct of troops
     1. Southerners' view
     2. Public Resolution No. 4

TIP Headings can be used within a research paper to make the paper easier to follow. The headings can be taken from the main ideas in your outline. Notice how the Writer's Model on pages 540–544 uses headings.

Documenting Sources

Give Credit Where Credit Is Due Documenting a paper means identifying the sources of information you use in the paper, as you use them. The rules for *how* to document sources are clearly specified in whatever style guide you follow, for example, the Modern Language Association (MLA) or the American Psychological Association (APA) style guide. The rules about *what* to document are not so clear. Use the following guidelines to decide what to document.

WHAT TO DOCUMENT

Yes	Each direct quotation (unless it's widely known, such as John L. Swigert's famous understatement on Apollo 13: "Okay, Houston, we've had a problem here.")
Yes	Any original theory or opinion that is not your own, even if not directly quoted. Since ideas belong to their authors, you must give the authors credit. Otherwise, you are guilty of plagiarism, a form of cheating.
Yes	Data from surveys, research studies, and interviews
Yes	Unusual, little-known facts or questionable "facts"
No	Information that appears in several sources or in standard reference books, such as the fact that William Tecumseh Sherman was a general in the Union army who led a march through Georgia during the Civil War

Advanced Learners

Enrichment. Encourage students to be creative in using headings from their outlines as subheadings in their finished papers. Students can use direct quotations from various sources as subheads, link their sub-heads together so they follow a discernible pattern (*North, South, East, West,* for example), or link the subheads to photographs or drawings they will use as visuals in their papers. You may want to approve students' subheading ideas before they begin drafting.

Additionally, you may point out to students that their outlines could serve as tables of contents for their final drafts.

DIRECT TEACHING

Documenting Sources

Tell students that for most parenthetical citations, the author's last name and the page number are sufficient. Some exceptions follow:

- A nonprint source such as an interview or videotape will not have a page number.
- A print source of fewer than two pages (such as a one-page letter) will not require a page number.
- For an author named in the sentence, you need give only the page number in parentheses.
- For an author who has more than one work in the Works Cited list, you will also have to give a short form of the title so readers will know which work you are citing.

TECHNOLOGY TIP

Using a computer screen projection system and a word-processing program, demonstrate for students how to insert footnotes or endnotes. You may wish to use one of your student's papers from a past class to demonstrate the footnote/endnote function.

DIFFERENTIATING INSTRUCTION

English-Language Learners

Dealing with the Works Cited format may be especially challenging for some students. Consider setting up a buddy system. Pair English-Language Learners with English-proficient students who can help them work through the finer points of documentation conventions.

Point the Way Sources of information enclosed in parentheses and placed within the body of your paper are called **parenthetical citations.** They point the way to the complete bibliographical information in the *Works Cited* list at the end of your paper. The parenthetical citation should be placed as close as possible to the material it documents without disrupting the flow of the sentence. This means that citations are usually inserted at the ends of sentences. The following example shows two sentences that incorporate material from two sources.

> On November 12, 1864, Sherman set out with an army of 62,000 men on a 250-mile march from Atlanta to Savannah (Inglehart). His army destroyed a strip of land 60 miles wide and inflicted $100 million in damages (Holzer 172).

Parenthetical citations should also be as brief as possible. For most citations, the last name of the author and the page number are sufficient. If the author is named in the sentence, you need give only the page number in parentheses. The following chart shows the form for the most common kinds of sources.

BASIC CONTENT AND FORM FOR PARENTHETICAL CITATIONS

Type of Source	Content of Citation	Example
Sources with one author	Author's last name and a page reference, if any	(Golay 36)
Separate passages in a single source	Author's last name and page references	(Derry 386, 388)
Sources with more than one author	All authors' last names; if over three, use first author's last name and *et al.* (and others)	(Ward, Burns, and Burns 333)
Multivolume source	Author's last name, plus volume and page	(Davis 1: 145–146)
Sources with a title only	Full title (if short) or shortened version	(March of Southern Men 38)
Literary sources published in many editions	Author's last name, title, and division references (act, scene, canto, book, part, or line numbers) in place of page numbers	(Shakespeare, Hamlet. 3.4.107–108)
Indirect sources	Abbreviation *qtd. in* (quoted in) before the source	(qtd. in Miles 175)
More than one source in the same citation	Citations separated with semicolons	(Miles 30; Sherman 64)

SKILLS FOCUS

Writing Skills
Document sources in parenthetical citations and a *Works Cited* list.

TIP Your teacher may want you to use a documentation style different from the parenthetical citation system, such as footnotes or endnotes. A **footnote** is placed at the bottom of the same page where you used the source information, while **endnotes** are listed all together at the end of the paper.

Follow the Forms The *Works Cited* list contains all the sources, print and nonprint, that you credit in your paper. You may have used other sources, but if you do not credit them in your historical research paper you need not include them in a *Works Cited* list. Use the following guidelines to help you prepare your *Works Cited* list.

TIP A bibliography contains only print publications.

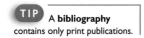

GUIDELINES FOR PREPARING THE WORKS CITED LIST

Center the words *Works Cited*. Ask your teacher whether the list should begin on a new page.

Begin each entry on a separate line. Position the first line of the entry even with the left margin, and indent all other lines five spaces, or one-half inch if you are using a word processor. Double-space all entries.

Alphabetize the sources by the authors' last names. If there is no author, alphabetize by title, ignoring *A, An,* and *The* and using the first letter of the next word.

If you use two or more sources by the same author, include the author's last name only in the first entry. For all other entries, put three hyphens in place of the author's last name (---), followed by a period.

The following sample entries are a reference for preparing your *Works Cited* list. Notice that you include page numbers only for sources that are one part of a whole work, such as one essay in a book of essays.

SAMPLE WORKS CITED ENTRIES

Standard Reference Works If an author is credited in a standard reference work, cite that person's name first in an entry. Otherwise, the title of the book or article appears first. You do not need to cite the editor. Page and volume numbers aren't needed if the work alphabetizes entries. For common reference works, use only the edition (if listed) and the year of publication.

Print Encyclopedia Article
Tebeau, Charlton W. "Sherman, William Tecumseh." The New Encyclopedia Britannica: Micropedia. 15th ed. 1995.
"Civil War." The World Book Encyclopedia. 1998 ed.

Article in a Biographical Reference Book
"Ulysses Simpson Grant." Abridged Encyclopedia of World Biography. 6 vols. Detroit: Gale, 1999.

Books
One Author
Derry, Joseph T. Story of the Confederate States. New York: Arno, 1979.

Two Authors
Catton, William, and Bruce Catton. Two Roads to Sumter. New York: McGraw, 1963.

Three Authors
Ward, Geoffrey C., Ric Burns, and Ken Burns. The Civil War: An Illustrated History. New York: Knopf, 1990.

(continued)

(continued)

Four or More Authors
Beringer, Richard E., et al. <u>Why the South Lost the Civil War</u>. Athens: U of Georgia P, 1986.

No Author Shown
<u>The March of the Southern Men</u>. Richmond: Dunn, 1863.

Editor of a Collection of Writings
Marius, Richard, ed. <u>The Columbia Book of Civil War Poetry</u>. New York: Columbia UP, 1994.

Two or Three Editors
Greenberg, Martin H., and Bill Pronzini, eds. <u>A Treasury of Civil War Stories</u>. New York: Bonanza, 1985.

Bibliography Published as a Book
Moss, William. <u>Confederate Broadside Poems: An Annotated Descriptive Bibliography</u>. Westport: Meckler, 1988.

Translation
Hess, Earl J., ed. <u>A German in the Yankee Fatherland: The Civil War Letters of Henry A. Kircher</u>. Trans. Ernest J. Thode. Kent: The Kent State UP, 1983.

Selections Within Books
From a Book of Works by One Author
Varhola, Michael J. "The Army." <u>Everyday Life During the Civil War</u>. Cincinnati: Writer's Digest, 1999. 129.

From a Book of Works by Several Authors
McMurry, Richard M. "The Atlanta Campaign." <u>The South Besieged: Volume Five of the Image of War, 1861–1865</u>. Ed. William C. Davis. New York: Doubleday, 1983. 240–302.

Introduction, Preface, Foreword, or Afterword
Simpson, Brooks D., and Jean V. Berlin. Introduction. <u>Sherman's Civil War: Selected Correspondence of William T. Sherman, 1860–1865</u>. Chapel Hill: U of North Carolina P, 1999.

Articles from Magazines, Newspapers, and Journals
From a Weekly Magazine
Ebeling, Ashlea. "Battle Cry." <u>Forbes</u>. 5 Oct. 1998: 78–80.

From a Monthly or Quarterly Magazine
Wert, Jeffrey D. "A Month Overrated: April, 1865 in the U.S. Civil War." <u>Civil War Times</u>. May 2001: 20.

Anonymous Author
"South Rises." <u>U.S. News and World Report</u>. 10 May 1999: 8.

From a Scholarly Journal
Brown, William O., and Richard K. Burdekin. "Turning Points in the U.S. Civil War: A British Perspective." <u>Journal of Economic History</u>. 60.1 (216–231).

From a Daily Newspaper, with a Byline
Horwitz, Tony. "Shades of Gray: Did Blacks Fight Freely for the Confederacy?" <u>The Wall Street Journal</u>. 8 May 1997: A1.

From a Daily Newspaper, without a Byline
"The Latest Battle of Gettysburg." <u>New York Times</u>. 4 July 1997: A18.

Unsigned Editorial from a Daily Newspaper, No City in Paper's Title
"Humanity of the War." Editorial. <u>The Christian Recorder</u>. 1 March 1862.

(continued)

DIRECT TEACHING

Sample Works Cited Entries
You may want to explain to students that "U," "P," and "UP" stand for "University," "Press," and "University Press." In the chart at right, these terms are abbreviated according to MLA style.

(continued)

Other Sources

Personal Interview

Norton, Stewart. Personal interview. 14 Aug. 2001.

Telephone Interview

LaRue, Patricia. Telephone interview. 23 May 2001.

Published Interview

Burns, Ken. Interview with Alice Cary. "If Abe Lincoln Were Campaigning for President Today, He
    Wouldn't Win." TV Guide 25 Jan. 1992: 13.

Broadcast or Recorded Interview

Burns, Ken. Interview with Terry Gross. Fresh Air. Natl. Public Radio. WHYY, Philadelphia. 29 Jan. 1997.

Published Letter

Sherman, William T. "To John Sherman." 22 April 1862. Letter in Sherman's Civil War: Selected
    Correspondence of William T. Sherman, 1860–1865. Ed. Brooks D. Simpson and Jean V.
    Berlin. Chapel Hill: U of North Carolina P, 1999.

Unpublished Letter or E-Mail Message

Gumble, Max. Letter to the author. 3 Sept. 2001.

Westmoreland, Margaret. E-mail to the author. 30 Dec. 2001.

Unpublished Thesis or Dissertation

Bass, Patrick Grady. "Fall of Crisis: European Intervention and the American Civil War." Diss.
    Claremont Graduate School, 1986.

Sound Recording

Songs of the Civil War. New World Records, 1976.

Film or Video Recording

The Civil War. Dir. Ken Burns. Videocassette. PBS Video, 1989.

NOTE: Always include the title, director or producer, distributor, and year. For DVD or video recordings,
add a description of the medium (Videodisc or Videocassette) before the distributor's name.

Material Accessed Through the Internet

"American Civil War." Britannica Online. Vers. 1994–2001. Encyclopedia Britannica. 6 June 2001.
    <http://members.eb.com/>.

Article from a CD-ROM Reference Work

Hassler, Jr., Warren W. "Sherman, William Tecumseh." Grolier Multimedia Encyclopedia.
    CD-ROM. Grolier Inc. 2001.

Full-Text Magazine, Newspaper, or Journal Article from a CD-ROM Database

"Here Are the 10 Civil War Battlefields Listed as 'Endangered' by Trust." Knight-Ridder/Tribune News
    Service, 27 Feb. 2001: K2031. Infotrac. CD-ROM. Gale Group, 2001.

PRACTICE & APPLY 1 Following the guidelines in the
Prewriting section, plan your historical
research paper. Remember that accurate records of your research will
make writing and documenting your report easier. Closely follow
the guidelines for making source cards (page 531) and taking notes
(page 532) as you work.

PRACTICE & APPLY 1

Guided and Independent Practice

- As an additional check on topic suitability, ask students to respond to the following prewriting questions: *What are the strengths of your topic? What problems can you foresee?* Challenge students to state how they plan to overcome difficulties they identify.

- Students may meet in small groups to listen to each other's research questions and confirm the suitability of the resources identified. You may circulate among groups to monitor understanding.

- Check that students have recorded notes accurately and legibly so that they will be able to reconstruct the ideas later. Suggest that students keep the resources they are using for the duration of the project, if possible. This will allow them to recheck information if you or they have any questions.

DIRECT TEACHING

A Writer's Framework

Caution students against using phrases such as *I think* or *I believe* throughout their reports. Remind students that research papers should be written in a formal tone, which avoids using the first person or relying on opinion.

RETEACHING

A Writer's Model

Review with students the purpose and role of citations and a Works Cited list by having students use the format of **A Writer's Model** to work backward and identify the exact source of every quotation and original idea or statistic included in it. Do students feel they could find the exact resources cited from each entry? Are quotations and citations inserted into the text in such a way as to maintain the clear, well-organized flow of ideas? Remind students that their readers should feel the same confidence and clarity when reading students' own research.

DIFFERENTIATING INSTRUCTION

Learners Having Difficulty

Students may benefit from studying how the writer uses transitions to make the writing smooth and easy to follow. You may want to select a page of the model and encourage students to identify examples of effective transitions in the section. You can use a graphic organizer drawn on the chalkboard to help students map the relationships expressed by the transitions. Students can use the models to help them include transitions in their own reports.

Reporting Historical Research

A Writer's Framework

Introduction	Body	Conclusion
• Draw readers in with an interesting opener.	• Develop each main idea that supports your thesis.	• Restate your thesis.
• Give readers background information and an overview of your research.	• Include facts and details from a variety of primary and secondary sources.	• Summarize your main points.
• Include your thesis statement.	• Arrange your ideas in a logical order.	• Bring the paper to a close with a concluding thought or a thought-provoking idea.

A Writer's Model

INTRODUCTION
Interesting opener

Background information

Overview of research

Secondary source

Thesis statement

BODY/Heading: First main idea
Point 1: Military importance

Sherman's March: A Civil War Controversy

General William Tecumseh Sherman's army was ready. The sick and wounded and all excess baggage had been sent away. Captain Daniel Oakley of the 2nd Massachusetts wrote, "The army was reduced, one might say, to its fighting weight, no man being retained who was not capable of a long march" (qtd. in Nevin 44). General Sherman sent out last minute dispatches before ordering the telegraph lines be cut, making it impossible for him and his army to communicate further with the Union. His last wire to General Grant reiterated the rationale for the march: "If the North can march an army right through the South, . . . it is proof positive that the North can prevail" (qtd. in Nevin 44). On November 12, 1864, Sherman set out with an army of 62,000 men on a 250-mile march from Atlanta to Savannah (Inglehart). His army destroyed a strip of land 60 miles wide and inflicted $100 million in damages (Holzer 172). While the annals of the American Civil War are filled with controversial actions, Sherman's march across Georgia remains one of the most debated. The U.S. government and many Northerners celebrated Sherman's action as a brilliant military success, but Sherman himself thought it a necessary, if harsh, part of war. Southerners whose homes were destroyed saw it as a lawless act of cruelty. Who was right? Each group had powerful reasons for its perspective, and the historical record supports them all.

The View from the North

Most historical records written from a Northern perspective concentrate on the military importance of Sherman's March. H.W.

Halleck, General Grant's chief of staff, called the march a "splendid success" (qtd. in Sherman, Memoirs 699). A New York Times editorial referred to it as "the most remarkable military achievement of the war" (qtd. in Miles 37). In a letter to Sherman, Grant expressed complete satisfaction with the march: "You have now destroyed the roads of the South" (qtd. in Sherman, Memoirs 682). To read these dry records, one would never know that the action described involved the destruction of citizens' homes. From the distance of Washington or New York, it must have been easy to see the march as a simple movement of troops.

  While Northerners made much of the march's military results, few Northern records focus on how these results were accomplished. Although Southerners complained bitterly of their treatment at the hands of Sherman's troops, the official record of the United States praises their actions. Public Resolution No. 4 states: "[T]he thanks of the people and of the Congress of the United States are due and are hereby tendered to Major-General William T. Sherman, and [his] officers and men, for their gallantry and good conduct . . . " (qtd. in Sherman, Memoirs 706–707). The phrase "gallantry and good conduct" might have been chosen to refute Southerners' claims of abuses.

The View from the Ground: Sherman and His Troops

  While the official records of the U. S. present the march as a military campaign like any other, Sherman was aware that others saw his action as unusual. "[T]he march to the sea," he wrote in his memoirs, "was generally regarded as something extraordinary, something anomalous, something out of the usual order of events . . ." (Sherman, Memoirs 697). However, Sherman remembers the march as a straightforward military tactic: "I considered this march as a means to an end, and not as an essential act of war. . . .[I]n fact, I simply moved from Atlanta to Savannah . . ." (Sherman, Memoirs 697). Sherman's memory, however, is contradicted by his field order of November 9, 1864, ordering commanders to "order and enforce a devastation more or less relentless, according to the measure of such hostility" as his army was shown (Sherman, GeorgiaInfo).

  In fact, it is clear from Sherman's own records and those of his officers that he and his army considered their action more than the movement of troops or the destruction of supplies that Confederates might use. He clearly understood the action's effect on civilians but believed it justified because it would end the war more quickly. "War is cruelty," Sherman stated. "There is no use trying to reform it; the crueler it is, the sooner it will be over" (qtd. in Brother Against Brother 370). Major Henry Hitchcock stated, "Evidently it is a material element in this

(continued)

Margin labels:
- Indirect source
- Direct quotation; Primary source
- Writer's conclusion
- Point 2: Conduct of troops
- Indirect source
- Writer's conclusion
- Second main idea
- Point 1: Military importance
- Direct quotation
- Point 2: Strategy
- Indirect source

Writing Workshop: Reporting Historical Research 541

DIRECT TEACHING

A Writer's Model

Remind students of the proper format for a research paper. **A Writer's Model** has not been double-spaced due to space constraints. Most writing guides, however, recommend double-spacing for both the body and the list of sources in a research paper.

CRITICAL THINKING

Ask students to evaluate the effectiveness of using a logical order to organize this report. Ask students to justify their reasoning. [Some students may feel that chronological order would not have emphasized the enduring differences in opinion held by the different groups affected by the march, and that using order of importance would be difficult because it would be hard to determine which point of view is more important.]

RETEACHING

A Writer's Model

If students have difficulty creating outlines for their reports, you may have them review **A Writer's Model** and create an outline for the report, using the section on outlining on pp. 534–535. Discuss with students their opinions on the success of the writer's organizational plan. An expansion of the sample outline on p. 535 follows.

II. The view from the North (continued)

   C. North's ignorance of details of the march

     1. Official record of the Congress

     2. Southerners' claims

III. The view from the ground

   A. Sherman's view

     1. A simple movement of troops

     2. An order to destroy

   B. Motives for the march

     1. Sherman: end the war quickly

     2. Hitchcock's agreement

   C. Sherman's intentions

     1. Control troops and prevent abuses

     2. Restrictions on troops

     3. Sherman's own admissions of failure

IV. The view from the South

   A. Southerners' view of their nation

     1. Sherman's march as a foreign invasion

     2. Henrietta Lee's sentiments

   B. Southerner's view of Sherman's March

     1. Statement by Confederate Congress

     2. Eyewitness testimony

   C. Efforts by Southern historians to keep memory alive

     1. Account from *Story of the Confederate States*

     2. A more recent account

V. Conclusion

   A. Restatement of thesis

   B. Summary of main ideas

   C. Thought-provoking ending

Writer's conclusion

Point 3: Conduct of troops

Information from two sources

Paraphrase

Third main idea
Point 1: Foreign invasion

Indirect source

Point 2: Conduct of troops
Indirect source
Block quotation
Writer's additions in brackets

---

campaign to produce among the people of Georgia a thorough conviction of the personal misery which attends war" (qtd. in Nevin 44). In today's terms, this is psychological warfare.

    Although Sherman planned to bring war home to Southerners, the record indicates that he intended to control his troops and prevent abuses. The army was walking a fine line. They wanted to break the South's resistance but behave honorably in the process. Sherman directed his army to "forage liberally on the country" (Miles 30; Sherman, <u>GeorgiaInfo</u>). However, he restricted these activities to special foraging parties led by officers and stated that only corps commanders could destroy private buildings. Foragers were to be polite and to leave each family enough to eat (Sherman, <u>GeorgiaInfo</u>). Sherman, however, admitted in his memoirs that these rules were not always followed. "No doubt, many acts of pillage, robbery, and violence were committed by these parties of foragers . . . for I have since heard of jewelry taken from women and the plunder of articles that never reached the commissary"(Sherman, <u>Memoirs</u> 659). Although he sometimes contradicted himself, Sherman saw his march as a harsh but justified action against traitors to the United States who had brought the war upon themselves (Janda 16), an action calculated to bring a quick end to a destructive war. The Southerners saw it differently.

The View from the South

    Southerners saw themselves not as traitors or rebels, but as citizens of a sovereign nation, the Confederate States of America. In their eyes, Sherman's march amounted to a foreign invasion. The manpower of the South had been drained, leaving women, children, and old men undefended at home. For enemy troops to come literally to their doors and take their property—including thousands of slaves who left their masters to follow Sherman's troops ("Sherman and the March to the Sea")—was an outrage. Henrietta Lee voiced the feelings of many Southerners when she wrote to Union General David Hunter: "Your name will stand on history's pages as the Hunter of weak women, and innocent children: the Hunter to destroy defenseless villages and beautiful homes" (qtd. in Clinton 125).

    To Southerners, the conduct of Sherman's troops seemed anything but gallant. The following statement by the Confederate Congress expresses the Southern view of Sherman's March.

       Accompanied by every act of cruelty and pain, the conduct of the enemy has been destitute of [without] that forbearance [restraint] and magnanimity [generosity] which civilization and Christianity have

---

DIFFERENTIATING INSTRUCTION

Advanced Learners

Enrichment. Challenge students to consider how **A Writer's Model** might be enhanced by adding information displayed in a graphic organizer. For example, a map or time line might help a reader better understand the geography and events involved in Sherman's March. Encourage students to consider whether graphics or visuals would be appropriate for their own topics.

introduced to mitigate [soften] the asperities [hardships] of war. Houses are pillaged and burned, churches are defaced, towns are ransacked, clothing of women and infants is stripped from their persons, jewelry and mementoes of the dead are stolen . . . means of subsistence [survival] are wantonly [cruelly] wasted to produce beggary, . . . the last morsel of food has been taken from families." (qtd. in Clinton 111)

Doubtless fear and hatred of the advancing army gave rise to many rumors, and some accounts may have been exaggerated. However, credible testimony from Southern eyewitnesses concurs with the description above. Eliza Andrews' "The War-Time Journal of a Georgia Girl, 1864–1865," describes the destruction left by Sherman's army:

> There was hardly a fence left standing. . . . The fields were trampled down and the road was lined with carcasses of horses, hogs, and cattle that the invaders, unable either to consume or to carry away with them, had wantonly shot down to starve out the people. . . . The dwellings that were standing all showed signs of pillage, and . . . here and there, lone chimney-stacks, "Sherman's Sentinels," told of homes laid in ashes. (19)

Understandably, Southern historians were anxious to keep the memory of Sherman's March alive. <u>Story of the Confederate States</u>, written in 1895, asserts, "Sherman's army . . . [took] everything that was valuable . . . and sometimes set fire to the house itself. Rings were taken from the fingers of ladies, and old men were hung up to make them tell where their treasures were concealed" (Derry 386). The bitterness of Southerners has not been assuaged by the passage of time. In <u>A Ruined Land: The End of the Civil War</u>, published in 1999, Golay describes Sherman's men as thieves and arsonists (36). Such accounts keep the bitterness alive.

Was Sherman's March a brilliant military tactic, a march for freedom, an act of psychological warfare, or a war crime? It seems likely that all these perspectives are at least partially true. Beyond a doubt, the march heightened the will and the morale of the North, demoralized the South, and hastened the end of the war. Some Southerners exaggerated the destructiveness of Sherman's troops, while the U.S. government had reason to downplay the troops' excesses. Ironically, Sherman himself may have had the most balanced view. He knew the march was cruel, but felt that victory was worth the cost. Perhaps Sherman's March is one of those historical events that defies a final, definitive judgment.

Author named in text

Point 3: Continued bitterness

Summary

CONCLUSION
Restatement of thesis

Summary of main points

Thought-provoking idea

(continued)

(continued)

Works Cited

Andrews, Eliza Frances. "The War-Time Journal of a Georgia Girl, 1864–1865: Electronic Edition." Documenting the American South, or The Southern Experience in 19th-century America. 1997. U of North Carolina at Chapel Hill Libs. 14 May 2001 <http://docsouth.unc.edu/andrews/andrews.html>.

Brother Against Brother: Time-Life Books History of the Civil War. New York: Prentice, 1990.

Clinton, Catherine. Tara Revisited: Women, War, and the Plantation Legend. New York: Abbeville, 1995.

Derry, Joseph T. Story of the Confederate States. New York: Arno, 1979.

Golay, Michael. A Ruined Land: The End of the Civil War. New York: Wiley, 1999.

Holzer, Harold. Witness to War: The Civil War: 1861–1865. New York: Berkley, 1996.

Inglehart, David. Fateful Lightening: A Narrative History of the Civil War. CD-ROM. Troubadour Interactive. 1998.

Janda, Lance. "Shutting the Gates of Mercy: The American Origins of Total War, 1860–1880." The Journal of Military History. 59.1: 7–26.

Miles, Jim. To the Sea: A History and Tour Guide of Sherman's March. Nashville: Rutledge Hill, 1989.

Nevin, David, and the Editors of Time-Life Books. The Civil War: Sherman's March: Atlanta to the Sea. Alexandria: Time-Life Books, Inc., 1986.

"Sherman and the March to the Sea." Civil War Journal II. Prod. Greg Goldman. Videocassette. A&E Home Video, 1994.

Sherman, William Tecumseh. Memoirs of General W. T. Sherman. New York: Lib. of America, 1951.

---. "Special Field Orders Issued by Gen. Sherman, Nov. 9, 1864." GeorgiaInfo. Carl Vinson Institute of Government, U of Georgia. 14 May 2001 <http://www.cviog.uga.edu/Projects/gainfo/order2.htm>.

TIP Research papers and their *Works Cited* lists are normally double-spaced. Due to limited space, they are represented single-spaced here.

INTERNET
More Writer's Models
Keyword: LE5 11-4

PRACTICE & APPLY 2

Guided and Independent Practice

Ask students to keep their outlines on their desks as they write. Suggest that they check off each part of the outline as they complete it. This practice will help them see their progress and also indicate to you whether they are moving along or stalled in the process.

PRACTICE & APPLY 2 As you write the first draft of your historical research paper, refer to the framework and the Writer's Model, including the *Works Cited* list.

Revising

Evaluate and Revise Content, Organization, and Style

Twice Is Nice To assess your writing effectively, read through your paper at least twice. The first time, evaluate and revise content and organization. Then, in your second reading, revise for style.

PEER REVIEW
Exchange your research paper with a classmate, who may have suggestions for improving the clarity of your summaries and paraphrases.

▶ **First Reading: Content and Organization** The following chart can help you determine whether you have clearly communicated your research. If you need help answering the questions in the first column, use the tips in the middle column. Then, revise your paper by making the changes suggested in the last column.

Rubric: Reporting Historical Research

Evaluation Questions	▶ Tips	▶ Revision Techniques
❶ Does the introduction draw readers into the research, give an overview of the research, and state the thesis?	▶ **Underline** the sentence that draws readers into the research; **bracket** the overview of research; **circle** the thesis statement.	▶ **Add** a quotation or interesting detail to the opening sentence. **Add** overview information, or **elaborate** on existing information. **Add** a thesis statement.
❷ Do several main ideas develop the thesis? Do facts and details support the main ideas?	▶ In the margin, **check** each main idea that develops the thesis. In the text, **double-check** at least one piece of supporting evidence for each idea. If there are not at least three main ideas and support for each, revise.	▶ **Add** main ideas to develop your thesis; consult your outline and note cards for ideas you may have missed. **Delete** ideas that do not support the thesis. **Elaborate** on each idea with material drawn from your research.
❸ Does the paper include summaries and paraphrases in addition to direct quotations?	▶ **Circle** all direct quotations. If direct quotations comprise more than 1/3 of the paper, revise.	▶ **Replace** some direct quotations with paraphrases or summaries.
❹ Are sources cited when necessary? Are the citations in the correct MLA format?	▶ **Place stars** by direct quotations and by facts that are not common knowledge.	▶ **Add** documentation for quoted, summarized, or paraphrased material. **Revise** incorrect citations.
❺ Does the conclusion restate the thesis and summarize the paper's main points? Does the writer close with a concluding thought or a thought-provoking idea?	▶ **Bracket** the restatement of the thesis. **Highlight** the summary of main ideas. **Circle** the thought-provoking ending.	▶ **Add** a sentence that returns the reader to the thesis of the paper. **Add** a summary of main ideas. **Add** a concluding thought or a thought-provoking idea.

Rubric: Reporting Historical Research

Advise students to use the **Rubric** chart on this page as a think sheet by having students answer the questions in their notebooks. Explain to students that using think sheets to summarize their notes allows students to place their thoughts, observations, and questions on paper, which, in turn, helps improve the content and organization of their reports.

Elaboration

Point out to students that even interesting facts can be dull reading if presented one after another. Suggest that students strive to balance their facts and statistics with description. Direct students' attention to the first paragraph of **A Writer's Model** and the descriptions of the various viewpoints on Sherman's March. Encourage students to use this example as a model when developing descriptive detail in their own reports.

Responding to the Revision Process

Answers

1. Without the citation, the writer would have been guilty of plagiarism.

2. It varies the sentence beginning by adding an adverb clause.

Independent Practice

As students revise their papers, point out to them that when including many facts and details it is sometimes easy to forget basic things such as writing in complete, clear sentences. Students should make sure the structures of their sentences are as well organized and as easy to follow as the structures of their papers.

Second Reading: Style Your style, how you express your ideas, is important in a long and complex research paper. If every sentence begins the same way, such as with the subject and verb of a main clause, your paper may bore readers. You can make your paper more interesting by **varying sentence beginnings.** For example, you can begin some sentences with adverb clauses. Adverb clauses answer the questions *How? When? Where? Why?* and *To what extent?* Use the following style guidelines to evaluate and refine your sentence beginnings.

Style Guidelines

Evaluation Question	▶ Tip	▶ Revision Technique
● Do many of the paper's sentences begin the same way?	▶ **Underline** the first five words of each sentence. If most subjects and verbs are underlined, revise.	▶ **Rearrange** and **combine** sentences to place adverb clauses at the beginning. Rephrase when necessary.

ANALYZING THE REVISION PROCESS

Study these revisions, and answer the questions that follow.

On November 12, 1864, Sherman set out with an army of

62,000 men on a 250-mile march from Atlanta to Savannah

(Inglehart). His army destroyed a strip of land 60 miles wide

add/add — and inflicted $100 million in damages. *(Holzer 172) While the annals of the* Sherman's march across *American Civil War are filled with controversial actions,*

delete — Georgia remains one of the most debated ~~action of the Civil War.~~

Responding to the Revision Process

1. Why is the information that the writer added to the second sentence necessary?

2. Why did the writer decide to change the last sentence?

SKILLS FOCUS

Writing Skills
Revise for content and style.

PRACTICE & APPLY 3 Using the guidelines in the charts on these two pages, revise the content, organization, and style of your research paper. If possible, collaborate with a peer throughout the revision process.

Publishing

Proofread and Publish Your Paper

Take Care of Business So that your readers will fully appreciate your historical research report, proofread it carefully. The last thing you want is for your readers to dismiss your work completely because they run into basic errors in grammar, usage, and mechanics. Therefore, take care to find and correct such errors. Having a peer help you proofread your paper is a good idea, too. You might be so familiar with your paper that you read over the errors.

Everything You Wanted to Know About . . . Doing a research paper requires a lot of hard work. Now that you've done that hard work, don't let your accomplishment go unnoticed. Find a larger audience for your paper. Here are some ways you might share your historical research paper with others.

- Save your historical research paper as a writing sample to submit for a college or job application.

- If the topic would be of interest to students in lower grades, send your paper to a teacher who teaches a related subject to those students. Consider scanning pictures of people and places involved in the event into your document to enhance its appeal to a younger audience.

- Surf the Web to discover sites related to your historical research topic, and submit your paper for possible online publication. As you prepare your work for a wider audience, look for places where you might incorporate **visuals** and **graphics** such as maps, charts, tables, or graphs to make your information more accessible.

Reflect on Your Paper

Take Stock Writing thoughtful responses to the following questions will help you develop as a thinker, a writer, and a researcher.

- How would you describe the extent of your knowledge of your topic before you researched it?

- How did your research experience affect your understanding of your topic? How did it affect your understanding of the study of history?

- If you had to list four fundamental principles of research for a student younger than you, what would they be?

 **PRACTICE & APPLY** First, proofread your paper, paying particular attention to the placement and punctuation of your citations. Then, publish your paper for a wider reading audience. Finally, reflect on your paper by answering the reflection questions above.

 TIP Proofreading will help ensure that your paper follows the **conventions** of standard American English and the documenting format required by your teacher. For example, pay particular attention to the placement and punctuation of parenthetical citations.

 COMPUTER TIP

If you have access to a computer and advanced publishing software, consider using those tools to design and format graphics and visuals to enhance the content of your research paper. For more on **graphics** and **visuals,** see Designing Your Writing in the Writer's Handbook.

SKILLS FOCUS

Writing Skills
Proofread, especially for punctuation and parenthetical citations. Use graphics and visuals to enhance a report.

Proofread and Publish Your Essay

If students decide to publish their essays on an online site, you need to be aware that Internet resources are sometimes public forums, and their content can be unpredictable.

Integrating with Grammar, Usage, and Mechanics

If students make mistakes with clear references or with using verbs correctly as they are proofreading, you may want to review section 3 in the Language Handbook.

PRACTICE & APPLY 4

Guided and Independent Practice

You may ask students to give their reports interesting and informative titles as part of the publishing process. Rather than *A Research Paper on Charlie Parker,* have students search for a title that hints at their theses and sparks curiosity, such as *Beautiful Surprises from an Alto Sax: Charlie Parker's Place in Jazz History.* Explain to students that sometimes a title appears on a separate page.

Presenting Historical Research

Speaking Assignment
Adapt a historical investigation report, and present it orally before an audience.

Professional historians routinely publish books and articles on the results of their research. They also present their research in oral presentations to their peers at conferences and meetings of historical organizations. To make these oral presentations interesting, historians use verbal and nonverbal techniques.

Adapt Your Report

Maintain Your Focus Your **purpose** in giving an oral report of historical research is to present your findings in a clear, concise, and interesting way. Your oral report could be shorter or longer than your written report, depending upon the time limit set by your teacher. Decide whether you need to shorten or lengthen your written report, and then use the following guidelines to adapt it.

- If your listening audience is different from your reading audience, consider revising the **introduction** by providing additional background information. Then, state your **thesis** so that it clearly communicates conclusions about the topic.

- If you have to cut your paper because of time limitations, be sure to maintain a balance of **primary** and **secondary sources** that represent relevant **perspectives** on the topic and show that you have analyzed several historical records. If you need to add information to your presentation, make sure you consider the **validity** and **reliability** of the new sources.

- Use a combination of rhetorical strategies to present your analysis of historical records. Use **exposition** to explain similarities and differences in the historical records and **persuasion** to convince readers of the validity of your conclusions. Look for places where you can effectively use **narration** and **description** because these rhetorical strategies make audiences feel as if they are listening to an exciting story rather than a dull report on research results.

- Since your audience will not have access to your *Works Cited* list, name the author and source of all quotations, statistics, important facts, and conclusions and judgments that are not your own.

- Check the **conclusion** in your paper to see if your summary of main ideas and restatement of the thesis are obvious to a listening audience. If you used long, complex sentences in the paper, simplify them so that listeners can understand you.

SKILLS FOCUS

Listening and Speaking Skills
Deliver an oral research report.

Present Your Report

The Natural Sound Speakers who read a speech often sound stiff and dull. Extemporaneous speakers, on the other hand, usually have note cards or an outline to glance at as the need arises. They also rehearse their presentations until they feel confident that they know their material and that they sound natural and spontaneous.

Prepare to deliver your presentation extemporaneously by writing on note cards your thesis, the main supporting ideas, and brief reminders of details you want to include. Arrange your note cards in the same pattern you used for your paper. Then, review your presentation to see if the order is clear for a listening audience. If the order seems confusing, experiment with new arrangements until you find one that is easy to follow.

Do a Dress Rehearsal To learn your text and master your performance, rehearse your oral report until you feel comfortable presenting it. You might want to videotape your presentation, practice in front of a mirror, or present your report to an audience of friends or family. Refer to the following table to improve your use of **verbal and nonverbal techniques.**

> **TIP** To ensure the best possible communication with your audience, use **standard American English.** Also be sure that your vocabulary is appropriate for your audience. For example, avoid terms that are likely to be unfamiliar to your audience. If your report requires the use of technical language, use the terms correctly and define them.

VERBAL TECHNIQUES	NONVERBAL TECHNIQUES
• **Tone:** maintain a formal tone to help your audience focus on the information	• **Eye contact:** involve your audience by making eye contact with your listeners
• **Volume:** speak loudly enough for everyone to hear you; emphasize important words by speaking slightly louder and with more force	• **Facial expression:** allow your face to express your feelings and attitude
• **Pause:** pause for a moment after an important point to allow your audience to catch up with you	• **Gestures:** use natural gestures as you speak; feel free to move around, but don't pace or fidget
• **Rate:** speak slowly enough to allow your audience to follow you, but not so slowly that they become bored	• **Posture:** use good posture to convey a sense of confidence

PRACTICE & APPLY 5 Use the instruction in this workshop to adapt, rehearse, and present orally your historical investigation report. Ask your classmates for feedback on the quality of your presentation.

SKILLS FOCUS

Listening and Speaking Skills Use effective verbal and nonverbal techniques.

Listening and Speaking Workshop: Presenting Historical Research **549**

■ *One-Stop Planner* CD-ROM with ExamView Test Generator

Internet
■ go.hrw.com (Keyword: LE5 11-4)
■ *Elements of Literature Online*

Present Your Report

Suggest that students create gestures or stylized movements as they memorize their speeches or key points of the speech. Repeating the same gesture at the same point in the speech will reinforce learning and help students to remember the speech's content.

DIFFERENTIATING INSTRUCTION

Learners Having Difficulty

As students practice delivering their oral reports, encourage them to use the following questions to help them evaluate their or peers' presentations for effectiveness.

- Did the introduction grab the audience's attention?
- Was the speech tailored to the audience's knowledge and interests?
- Were the purpose and the main ideas obvious to listeners?
- Did the conclusion summarize the main ideas and provide a sense of completion?
- Did the speaker seem relaxed and confident?
- Did the speaker make eye contact?
- Were facial expressions, gestures, and movements natural and used appropriately?

PRACTICE & APPLY 5

Guided and Independent Practice

Have each student freewrite for five minutes about the changes they intend to make in their written reports in order to present the research orally. You may circulate among students to check for understanding. Then, have students complete **Practice and Apply 5** for independent practice.

Collection 4: Skills Review

Comparing Literature

SKILLS FOCUS, pp. 550–553

Grade-Level Skills

- **Literary Skills**
Compare and contrast major literary works from different historical periods.

INTRODUCING THE SKILLS REVIEW

Use this review to assess students' ability to contrast literary works from different periods.

DIRECT TEACHING

A **Reading Skills**

? **Comparing and contrasting.** How are the men in the column different from the other soldiers and the support people on the road? [The soldiers in the column are unified, energetic, and highly motivated; the others are disorganized and "trying to dribble down" the road.]

B **Literary Focus**

? **Imagery.** What does Crane mean when he speaks of "the heart of the din"? [the part of the battle-field where the noise is loudest, where the fiercest fighting is taking place]

Collection 4: Skills Review
Comparing Literature

 **Test Practice**   The following two pieces of literature were written almost a hundred years apart. Both deal with the horrors of war.

Stephen Crane (1871–1900) was born after the Civil War, but his best-known work is *The Red Badge of Courage,* a short novel that supposedly takes place at the battle of Chancellorsville in Virginia. This classic work of fiction is told through the eyes of young Henry Fleming, a Union soldier.

The poet Yusef Komunyakaa (1947–   ) won the Pulitzer Prize in 1994 for his poetry collection *Neon Vernacular.* Much of Komunyakaa's work, including "Camouflaging the Chimera," is based on his experiences in the Vietnam War, where he served as an information specialist.

DIRECTIONS: Read the following novel excerpt and poem. Then, read each multiple-choice question that follows, and write the letter of the best response.

This excerpt from The Red Badge of Courage *describes a column of soldiers headed into battle. The "youth" is Henry Fleming, Crane's protagonist in the novel.*

from The Red Badge of Courage

Stephen Crane

A Presently the calm head of a forward-going column of infantry[1] appeared in the road. It came swiftly on. Avoiding the obstructions gave it the sinuous movement of a serpent. The men at the head butted mules with their musket stocks. They prodded teamsters[2] indifferent to all howls. The men forced their way through parts of the dense mass by strength. The blunt head of the column pushed. The raving teamsters swore many strange oaths.

B The commands to make way had the ring of a great importance in them. The men were going forward to the heart of the din. They were

SKILLS FOCUS

Pages 550–553 cover
Literary Skills
Compare and contrast works from different literary periods.

---

1. **infantry** *n.:* foot soldiers.
2. **teamsters** *n. pl.:* drivers of teams of horses used for hauling.

READING MINI-LESSON

Reviewing Word-Attack Skills
Activity. Display the following sets of words. Have students identify the two words in each set in which the given letters stand for the same sounds. Encourage students to check a dictionary if they are unsure of a pronunciation. Answers are underlined.

1. se <u>release</u> <u>decrease</u> appease
2. ch achieve <u>archive</u> <u>anchorage</u>
3. gn vignette <u>insignia</u> <u>dignify</u>
4. ch <u>chrysalis</u> <u>chrome</u> churlish
5. se abstruse <u>confuse</u> <u>diffuse</u>
6. gn <u>ignorant</u> <u>ignition</u> benign
7. se carouse <u>grouse</u> <u>blouse</u>
8. ch <u>leech</u> <u>larch</u> lichen
9. gn <u>gnostic</u> <u>agnostic</u> cognitive
10. ch <u>bachelor</u> <u>brooch</u> brachial

Activity. In some words, the letters se are pronounced /s/ or /z/, depending on the part of speech. Have students compose sentences for each of the following words to demonstrate the two pronunciations.

to confront the eager rush of the enemy. They felt the pride of their onward movement when the remainder of the army seemed trying to dribble down this road. They tumbled teams about with a fine feeling that it was no matter so long as their column got to the front in time. This importance made their faces grave and stern. And the backs of the officers were very rigid. **C**

As the youth looked at them the black weight of his woe returned to him. He felt that he was regarding a procession of chosen beings. The separation was as great to him as if they had marched with weapons of flame and banners of sunlight. He could never be like them. He could have wept in his longings. **D**

He searched about in his mind for an adequate malediction[3] for the indefinite cause, the thing upon which men turn the words of final blame. It—whatever it was—was responsible for him, he said. There lay the fault.

The haste of the column to reach the battle seemed to the forlorn young man to be something much finer than stout fighting. Heroes, he thought, could find excuses in that long seething lane. They could retire with perfect self-respect and make excuses to the stars.

He wondered what those men had eaten that they could be in such haste to force their way to grim chances of death. As he watched his envy grew until he thought that he wished to change lives with one of them. He would have liked to have used a tremendous force, he said, throw off himself and become a better. Swift pictures of himself, apart, yet in himself, came to him—a blue desperate figure leading lurid charges with one knee forward and a broken blade high—a blue, determined figure standing before a crimson and steel assault, getting calmly killed on a high place before the eyes of all. He thought of the magnificent pathos[4] of his dead body. **E** **F**

These thoughts uplifted him. He felt the quiver of war desire. In his ears, he heard the ring of victory. He knew the frenzy of a rapid successful charge. The music of the trampling feet, the sharp voices, the clanking arms of the column near him made him soar on the red wings of war. For a few moments he was sublime.[5]

---

3. **malediction** *n.:* curse.
4. **pathos** *n.:* the quality in something experienced or observed, which arouses a sense of sorrow or pity.
5. **sublime** *adj.:* noble; majestic.

C **Literary Focus**

? **Imagery.** Why do you think Crane mentions the rigid backs of the officers? [Possible response: The officers' rigid backs suggest that they are resolute and unyielding.]

D **Reading Skills**

? **Comparing and contrasting.** What images does Crane use to contrast the youth's attitude with that of the soldiers? [Possible response: Crane uses images of darkness and light. The boy feels the "black weight of his woe." The soldiers in the column seem to carry "weapons of flame" and "banners of sunlight."]

E **Reading Skills**

? **Comparing and contrasting.** How does the youth's emotional state differ from that of the other soldiers in the infantry column? [Possible response: The soldiers in the column are confident, determined, and eager to reach the front. The youth lacks their confidence and sense of purpose and longs to share in their certainty.]

F **Literary Focus**

? **Irony.** Why is the youth's image of himself in battle ironic? [Soldiers typically hope to survive battle, but the youth takes pleasure in imagining himself being "calmly killed."]

---

1. house [We built a shed behind the house. Marie decided to house her fish in a fishbowl.]
2. abuse [She tried not to abuse her privileges. They decided to report the abuse.]
3. refuse [I think he will refuse to go. Refuse was piling up in the yard.]
4. misuse [Fran would always misuse semicolons. This sentence demonstrates the misuse of the word *fulsome*.]

Activity. Have students analyze the following words by detaching the prefix and dividing the remainder of the word into syllables. Remind students that each syllable must contain a vowel sound.

1. preoccupation [pre + oc-cu-pa-tion]
2. nonvernacular [non + ver-nac-u-lar]
3. uncorroborated [un + cor-rob-o-rat-ed]
4. semielliptical [semi + el-lip-ti-cal]
5. reaffirmation [re + af-fir-ma-tion]
6. preponderant [pre + pon-der-ant]

DIRECT TEACHING

A Reading Skills

❓ Interpreting the title. In what ways did the American military forces in Vietnam resemble a chimera? [Possible responses: Helicopters and armored vehicles may have seemed like fire-breathing monsters; the military apparatus was terrifying, like a lion or a serpent; the effectiveness of the army proved illusory, like a chimera.]

B Literary Focus

❓ Imagery. What senses do the images in the first ten lines appeal to? [Possible responses: sight (the faces painted with mud, the grass hanging from the tiger suits); touch (hugging bamboo, leaning against the breeze).]

C Literary Focus

❓ Comparing literature from different periods. How do the battle preparations of the soldiers in this poem compare with those of the soldiers in the previous excerpt? [Possible response: These soldiers prepare for a surprise attack by blending into their surroundings and waiting quietly. The column of soldiers in the Crane excerpt stand out in their bright blue uniforms and rush headlong into the fight.]

D Reading Skills

❓ Drawing conclusions. What is the world that "revolved under each man's eyelid"? [Possible response: It is the world within; the soldiers have blended in with their surroundings and have now turned inward to focus on their private thoughts, hopes, and fears.]

ⒶCamouflaging the Chimera°

Yusef Komunyakaa

We tied branches to our helmets.
We painted our faces & rifles
with mud from a riverbank,

5 blades of grass hung from the pockets
of our tiger suits.° We wove
ourselves into the terrain,
content to be a hummingbird's target.

We hugged bamboo & leaned
against a breeze off the river,
10 slow-dragging with ghosts

from Saigon to Bangkok,
with women left in doorways
reaching in from America.
We aimed at dark-hearted songbirds.

15 In our way station of shadows
rock apes° tried to blow our cover,
throwing stones at the sunset.
Chameleons

crawled our spines, changing from day
to night: green to gold,
20 gold to black. But we waited
till the moon touched metal,

till something almost broke
inside us. VC° struggled
with the hillside, like black silk°

25 wrestling iron through grass.
We weren't there. The river ran
through our bones. Small animals took
refuge
against our bodies; we held our breath,

ready to spring the L-shaped
30 ambush, as a world revolved
under each man's eyelid.

---

23. VC: The Viet Cong were Communist forces that opposed the U.S. and South Vietnamese governments during the Vietnam War.
24. black silk: The Viet Cong wore black silk to camouflage themselves at night.

° **Chimera** (kī·mir′ə): a monster in Greek mythology. The word today also refers to a fanciful creation of the imagination.
5. tiger suits: camouflage uniforms with black and green stripes.
16. rock apes: apes or tailless monkeys known to throw rocks at humans, often scaring soldiers in Vietnam into thinking they were being attacked by the enemy.

Using Academic Language

Review of Literary Terms
Have students show their grasp of skills from the collection that illustrate the meanings of these terms.

Realism (p. 391); **Comparing Points of View** (p. 396); **Metaphors** (p. 398); **External Conflicts** (p. 406); **Internal Conflicts** (p. 406); **Situational Irony** (p. 434); **Verbal Irony** (p. 442); **Tall Tale** (p. 459); **Hyperbole** (p. 459); **Understatement** (p. 459); **Satire** (p. 468); **Writer's Purpose** (p. 468); **Naturalism** (p. 480); **Imagery** (p. 499).

Collection 4: Skills Review

1. Which of the following statements is *not* true, based on *The Red Badge of Courage* excerpt?
   - A The soldiers are proud to go to battle.
   - B The youth feels alienated from the soldiers leading the march.
   - C The soldiers are delaying their charge into battle.
   - D The youth imagines his own heroic death.

2. Which statement *best* represents the **situational irony** in the Crane excerpt?
   - F Although the youth is fearless, he does not look forward to the battle.
   - G The youth feels pride when looking at the enemy rather than when looking at his fellow soldiers.
   - H The youth feels ecstatic when he fantasizes about his death.
   - J Although he does not want to be a hero, the youth fights bravely.

3. Which of the animals mentioned in the Komunyakaa poem *best* **symbolizes** the soldiers?
   - A Hummingbirds
   - B Songbirds
   - C Rock apes
   - D Chameleons

4. The words that *best* describe the **tone** of Komunyakaa's poem are —
   - F judgmental and condemning
   - G adoring and extravagant
   - H tense and apprehensive
   - J bitter and sarcastic

5. Which statement accurately describes a contrast between the two selections?
   - A Crane's piece is bitter, whereas Komunyakaa's poem is uplifting.
   - B Crane's piece is written from one man's viewpoint, whereas Komunyakaa's poem uses the collective voice of a group of soldiers.
   - C Crane's piece focuses on events the narrator remembers from the past, whereas Komunyakaa's poem takes place in the present.
   - D Crane's piece emphasizes the loud sounds of the battle, whereas Komunyakaa's poem focuses on the smells of war.

6. Which of the following statements expresses a shared **theme** of these two selections?
   - F Peace can be obtained only through bloodshed.
   - G War requires ordinary people to perform extraordinary tasks.
   - H Soldiers are incapable of true heroism.
   - J Nature is ultimately ruined by war.

Essay Question

In a brief essay, compare and contrast these two pieces of literature. Pay particular attention to the impression of war created by the imagery in each work. How does each writer use **descriptive details** and **sensory images** to enhance the realistic nature of his work? How does imagery contribute to the **tone** of each work?

Answers and Model Rationales

1. **C** Students can eliminate A; Crane emphasizes how proud the soldiers are. B and D are also incorrect; the youth does feel alienated from the others and does imagine his own heroic death.

2. **H** The youth's feelings are ironic because we would not expect him to feel this way about his own death. It is clear that the youth is not fearless (F). The excerpt does not reveal his feelings about the enemy (G). The excerpt does not show the youth in battle (J).

3. **D** Like chameleons changing color to match their surroundings, the soldiers have camouflaged themselves for attack.

4. **H** The poet describes the tension the soldiers feel while waiting to ambush the enemy. The poem passes no judgment on the soldiers' actions (F). The poem expresses no bitterness or sarcasm (J). The tone of the poem is neutral, not adoring or extravagant (G).

5. **B** Crane's piece is told from the viewpoint of one man. The poem is told from the standpoint of the entire group.

6. **G** The ordinary soldiers in each piece are engaged in extraordinary actions.

Test-Taking Tips

For information on answering multiple-choice questions, refer students to **Test Smarts**.

Assessment

- *Holt Assessment: Literature, Reading, and Vocabulary*

Essay Question

Stephen Crane relies mainly on visual and auditory images to depict a tumultuous scene on the road leading to battle. We see the column moving like a sinuous serpent, men butting mules with muskets, and teams tumbling in all directions. We hear the loud commands of the soldiers and the oaths of those being pushed out of their way. Yusef Komunyakaa uses images that appeal mainly to sight and touch to depict a silent, hidden army lying in ambush. We see the colors of day changing from green to gold to black. We feel the small animals against the soldiers' bodies, the touch of bamboo and river grasses, and the river breeze. The images in Crane's piece create an agitated tone. The imagery of the hidden army in Komunyakaa's poem creates a tense mood.

Vocabulary Skills

Synonyms

Modeling. Model the thought process of a good reader answering item 1. "Peyton promised his allegiance to the Confederacy. When people pledge allegiance, they are promising to be loyal citizens. People don't promise their hatred or bitterness, so A and C can't be correct. I have never heard of anyone pledging their income, so D is unlikely. B, *loyalty,* is the best answer."

Answers and Model Rationales

1. **B** See rationale above.
2. **H** A candid description would show the war sincerely.
3. **A** While in hiding, Jacobs looked for comfort—not clarity, knowledge, or power.
4. **H** This sentence suggests that *wit* and *humor* are antonyms of *solemnity*. The best answer is therefore *seriousness.*
5. **B** People are often advised to avoid dangers, so it is likely that *dangerous* is a synonym for *perilous.*
6. **J** Aunt Georgiana loved music, so J and G are possible choices. Joyful music generally doesn't make people cry (G).
7. **B** Since Mary Chesnut was a southerner, Atlanta's capture would be bad news. B is the best choice.
8. **J** The best synonym for *inevitable* is *unavoidable.*
9. **D** It seems absurd that someone with everything to live for would kill himself. Therefore, D is correct.
10. **F** Reuniting a nation was a difficult task.

Test Practice

Synonyms

DIRECTIONS: Choose the best synonym for the underlined word in each sentence.

1. Peyton Farquhar promised his allegiance to the Confederacy.
   A hatred
   B loyalty
   C bitterness
   D income

2. Stephen Crane's writing offers a candid description of the harsh reality of war.
   F false
   G crafty
   H sincere
   J critical

3. Harriet Jacobs found solace in reading the Scriptures.
   A comfort
   B clarity
   C knowledge
   D power

4. Mark Twain is known for his wit and humor, rather than for his solemnity.
   F harshness
   G anger
   H seriousness
   J informality

5. Against the advice of others, the man faced the perilous cold on his own.
   A unbearable
   B dangerous
   C freezing
   D unending

6. Aunt Georgiana was moved to tears by the bewitching music.
   F repulsive
   G joyful
   H evil
   J captivating

7. Mary Chesnut wrote the lamentable news of Atlanta's capture in her diary.
   A wonderful
   B distressing
   C unexpected
   D refreshing

8. Frederick Douglass believed the battle with Mr. Covey was inevitable.
   F unlikely
   G unjust
   H questionable
   J unavoidable

9. Richard Cory's death seemed preposterous considering all he had to live for.
   A fitting
   B questionable
   C miraculous
   D absurd

10. Abraham Lincoln had the arduous task of reuniting a divided nation.
    F difficult
    G important
    H honorable
    J remarkable

SKILLS FOCUS

Vocabulary Skills
Analyze synonyms.

Vocabulary Review

Use this activity to determine whether students have retained the collection Vocabulary. Ask students to complete each of the analogies below with a Vocabulary word from the box.

intangible	pivotal	comply
deference	protruding	

1. RENDER : MAKE :: _____ : obey [comply]
2. CONCRETE : OBJECT :: _____ : thought [intangible]
3. SCORN : SCOUNDREL :: _____ : statesman [deference]
4. TANGENTIAL : SECONDARY :: _____ : primary [pivotal]
5. RECESSED : EYE SOCKETS :: _____ : nose [protruding]

Collection 4: Skills Review
Writing Skills

Test Practice

DIRECTIONS: The following paragraph is from a draft of a student's historical research paper. Read the questions below it, and choose the best answer to each question.

Before the battle of Gettysburg, Major General J. E. B. Stuart—with General Robert E. Lee's permission—attempted to take his cavalry unit completely around the Union army of the Potomoc. Because the Union army was far more spread out than he had supposed, Stuart lost touch with Lee for ten days. General Lee was, therefore, unaware that the Union army had moved north of the Potomoc River and thus believed he had positioned the Confederate army correctly. Lee was certain Stuart would have informed him if the Union army had changed its position. When Lee found out otherwise, he hastily moved his army into positions around Gettysburg. From there he was forced to fight before he was ready—just one of the reasons the Confederates lost the battle of Gettysburg.

1. Which of the following research questions does the information in the paragraph best answer?
   A Who was the Confederate army's leader?
   B Why did the Confederate army lose the battle at Gettysburg?
   C Where did Major General Stuart fight during the Civil War?
   D How did the Civil War affect Southerners and Northerners?

2. To support the main idea, which sentence could the writer add?
   F Stuart was supposed to inform Lee of the Union army's location.
   G Stuart was one of the most flamboyant of Lee's subordinates.
   H The battle of Gettysburg was an important battle of the war.
   J The battle site in Pennsylvania is now a national park.

3. To find more information, which primary source could the writer consult?
   A an encyclopedia article on the battle
   B a letter written by General Stuart
   C a journal article analyzing the battle
   D a biography of General Robert E. Lee

4. If the writer wanted to include a visual in his paper, which would be best?
   F a timeline showing the major battles of the Civil War
   G a table listing the number of soldiers in each unit of the Union army
   H a picture of the Confederate and Union soldiers' uniforms
   J a map illustrating the movements of Stuart's cavalry

5. To present this information in an oral presentation, the speaker should
   A use only secondary sources because they will be more reliable
   B delete all references to sources
   C give only one perspective
   D weave parenthetical citation information into the speech

SKILLS FOCUS

Writing Skills
Write a historical research report.

Collection 4 Skills Review   **555**

RESOURCES: WRITING

Assessment
- *One-Stop Planner* CD-ROM with ExamView Test Generator
- *Holt Assessment: Writing, Listening, and Speaking*

Internet
- *Holt Online Assessment*
- *Holt Online Essay Scoring*

Collection 4: Skills Review
Writing Skills

APPLICATION

People Posters

Have students choose famous mathematicians or scientists from the past. Then, ask them to use their research skills to prepare biographical posters. In the center of the poster, students should draw or paste a picture of the person. Around the picture, students then write ten short factual statements about the person's life. Finally, students should write the name of their subject at the top of their posters and a significant quotation by or about the subject at the bottom. Remind students to document their sources.

EXTENSION

Short Story

Have students use their research to produce a work of historical fiction for homework. Point out to students that though they will not provide citations in their short stories, their details should be as historically accurate as possible. Tell students having difficulty thinking of a premise for a story to consider the question, *What if the historical event had turned out differently?* Students' stories may be an investigation of the resulting effects, and may point out as well as any amount of research the importance of the event occurring the way it did.

Homework

Grade-Level Skills

■ **Literary Skills**
Evaluate the philosophical, political, religious, ethical, and social influences of a historical period.

Preview

Think About . . .

Before students read "The Moderns," have them preview the art that appears in the essay. Ask them to write down a few words that come to mind as they examine each picture. After students read the essay, have them look at the words they wrote. Do they see the pictures differently now that they know about the historical context in which the paintings were created?

DIRECT TEACHING

Ⓐ Literary Connections
World War I in British Literature
Little American literature of note deals directly with the war. In contrast, an entire generation of British writers gained immortality by turning their combat experiences into prose and poetry. Siegfried Sassoon, Robert Graves, Rupert Brooke, and Wilfred Owen came of age in the trenches and wrote vividly of the horrors of combat.

Ⓑ Content-Area Connections
Humanities: The Armory Show
In 1913, the Armory Show (held in New York's old 69th Regiment Armory) introduced Americans to modern movements. The work of artists like Paul Cezanne, Edvard Munch, Henri Matisse, and Marcel Duchamp made it clear that European artists had advanced far beyond their American counterparts.

The Moderns 1914–1939
by John Leggett *and* John Malcolm Brinnin

PREVIEW

Think About . . .

Life during the early part of the twentieth century was marked by tremendous change—political, social, psychological, and spiritual. Each decade seemed to bring new upheaval, and each upheaval required a new adjustment in attitude. These changes were reflected in a new period in American literature, called modernism.

As you read about this period, look for answers to these questions:

● What is the American dream?
● What happened to the American dream in the early twentieth century?
● In what ways did modernism challenge tradition—especially in what people valued in art and literature?

Ⓐ **W**orld War I, the so-called Great War, was one of the events that changed the American voice in fiction. The country appeared to have lost its innocence. Idealism had turned to cynicism for many Americans, who began to question the authority and tradition that was thought to be our bedrock. American writers, like their European counterparts, were also being profoundly affected by Ⓑ the **modernist** movement. This movement in literature, painting, music, and the other arts was swept along by disillusionment with traditions that seemed to have become spiritually empty. Modernism called for bold experimentation and wholesale rejection of traditional themes and styles.

The American Dream: Pursuit of a Promise

Before we look at the upheavals that marked the first part of the twentieth century, we should review some of the uniquely American beliefs that had for centuries played a major role in the formation of the "American mind." There are three central assumptions, explained below, that we have come to call the **American dream.**

■ America as a New Eden

First, there is admiration for America as a new Eden: a land of beauty, bounty, and unlimited promise. Both the promise and the disappointment of this idea are reflected in one of the greatest American novels, *The Great Gatsby* (1925), by F. Scott Fitzgerald (page 621). This work appeared at a time when great wealth and the pursuit of pleasure had become ends in themselves for many people.

SKILLS FOCUS

Collection introduction (pages 562–569) covers

Literary Skills
Evaluate the philosophical, political, religious, ethical, and social issues of a historical period.

DIFFERENTIATING INSTRUCTION

Learners Having Difficulty
To help students understand the main ideas in this essay, have them create a simple outline by writing down the subheadings in the text and boxed features. Instruct them to jot down one or two important ideas under each heading as they read.

Invite learners having difficulty to read the introductory historical essay in interactive format in *The Holt Reader* and to use the sidenotes as aids to understanding the selection.

English-Language Learners
For lessons designed for English-language learners and special education students, see *Holt Reading Solutions*.

The Voice of the City of New York Interpreted: The Brooklyn Bridge (The Bridge) (1920–1922) by Joseph Stella. Oil and tempera on canvas (88¼″ × 54″).

VIEWING THE ART

Joseph Stella (1877–1946), an Italian immigrant, was fascinated by the architecture and technology of modern America. One of his favorite subjects was the Brooklyn Bridge, which he painted a number of times. Stella called it a "shrine containing all the efforts of the new civilization of America." The bridge, linking Manhattan with Brooklyn, was completed in 1883; at the time it was the longest suspension bridge in the world. Stella's painting alters the appearance of the bridge and its surroundings, but is clearly based on the actual view from the bridge's pedestrian walkway.

Activity. Ask students to discuss how Stella's depiction of the bridge underscores his comment that the bridge might be called a "shrine." [The bridge has pointed arches, suggesting the architecture of a Gothic cathedral; Stella's panel resembles a medieval altarpiece.]

Primary and Secondary Sources

The Soldier's View
All Quiet on the Western Front (1929), probably the finest of all World War I novels, was written by a former German soldier, Erich Maria Remarque. The novel went through nineteen printings in its first eight months of publication in the United States. Its preface reads, "This book is to be neither an accusation nor a confession, and least of all an adventure, for death is not an adventure to those who stand face to face with it. It will try simply to tell of a generation of men who, even though they may have escaped its shells, were destroyed by the war."

The Historian's View
Paul Fussell wrote in 1976 that World War I began "in what was, compared with ours, a static world, where the values appeared stable and where the meanings of abstractions seemed permanent and reliable. Everyone knew what Glory was, and what Honor meant. It was not until eleven years after the war that [Ernest] Hemingway could declare in *A Farewell to Arms* that 'abstract words such as glory, honor, courage, or hallow were obscene beside the concrete names of villages, the numbers of roads, the names of rivers, the numbers of regiments and the dates.' In the summer of 1914 no one would have understood what on earth he was talking about."

A **Reading Skills**

? **Making predictions.** Have students read the boxed feature titled "Tenets of the American Dream." Given what you have already read, how do you predict World War I will affect those tenets? [Possible responses: Americans will cease to believe in the American dream as they find themselves caught in circumstances beyond their control; despite their self-reliance and ingenuity, they will find their opportunities limited and their lives worsening.]

A CLOSER LOOK

The most popular forms of entertainment during the 1930s were radio and films, which offered an escape from the harsh realities of life during the Depression.

B **Reading Informational Text**

? **Finding the main idea.** Why were these forms of entertainment so popular? [Both offered a relatively cheap way to escape from the realities of life in Depression-era America, and they also provided hard news.]

C **Content-Area Connections**

Humanities: The Ratings Race
Welles's radio scare was to some extent deliberate. The first "news bulletin" interrupting the story was timed to occur ten or twelve minutes into the program, when Edgar Bergen's popular radio show would be taking a break for music. Many listeners naturally changed stations to hear what else was playing, and having missed the beginning of *War of the Worlds,* thought the program was announcing an actual invasion.

Tenets of the American Dream

A
- America is a new Eden, a promised land of beauty, unlimited resources, and endless opportunities.
- The American birthright is one of ever-expanding opportunity. Progress is a good thing, and we can optimistically expect life to keep getting better and better.
- The independent, self-reliant individual will triumph. Everything is possible for the person who places trust in his or her own powers and potential.

The title character, Gatsby, is a self-made man whose wealth has mysterious and clearly illegal origins. Gatsby tries to woo both society and the woman he loves with lavish expenditures. His extravagant gestures are in pursuit of a dream. Unfortunately Gatsby's capacity for dreaming is far greater than any opportunity offered by the Roaring Twenties, and he meets a grotesquely violent end. But Gatsby's greatness is bound up with his tragedy: He believes in an America that has virtually disappeared under the degradations of modern life.

It is left to Nick Carraway, the narrator, to reflect at the end of the novel on the original promise of the American dream:

> 66 Gradually I became aware of the old island here that flowered once for Dutch sailors' eyes—a fresh, green breast of the new world. Its vanished trees, the trees that had made way for Gatsby's house, had once pandered in whispers to the last and greatest of all human dreams; for a transitory enchanted moment man must have held his breath in the presence of this continent, compelled into an aesthetic contemplation he neither understood nor desired, face to face for the last time in history with something commensurate to his capacity for wonder. 99

—F. Scott Fitzgerald, from *The Great Gatsby*

A CLOSER LOOK: SOCIAL INFLUENCES

Popular Entertainment

B **Radio.** Perhaps the most popular form of entertainment during the 1930s was the radio. By 1933, two thirds of American households owned at least one radio. People also relied on radios for news, as was demonstrated by a famous Halloween broadcast of 1938. Six million listeners tuned in to Orson Welles's radio play *Invasion from Mars*—a series of convincing but fictional news bulletins about a Martian invasion near New York City, based on H. G. Wells's science fiction novel *War of the Worlds.* Believing that the broadcast was reporting a real invasion, hundreds of people clogged eastern highways in an attempt to escape the alien invaders.

C

Movies. To get Americans' minds off the hardships of the Depression, Hollywood produced slapstick comedies by Laurel and Hardy and the Marx Brothers and romantic musicals with Fred Astaire. The cost of going to a movie was relatively inexpensive, and each week millions of Americans flocked to watch cartoons, newsreels, and feature films at elaborate movie palaces with romantic names like the Bijou, the Roxy, and the Ritz. To top off the decade, audiences in 1939 thronged to see Clark Gable and Vivien Leigh in the long-awaited blockbuster *Gone with the Wind.*

INFORMATIONAL TEXT

CONTENT-AREA CONNECTIONS

Film: *King of the Hill*
Whole-class activity. You may want to show students Steven Soderbergh's *King of the Hill* (1993), a film set during the Great Depression. The film shows some of the more harrowing aspects of the times through the eyes of a young boy. For instance, characters who cannot pay their rent are locked out of their apartments and end up in Hoovervilles.

Music: Jazz and Blues
Small-group activity. Have students form groups of three to research three great African American jazz and blues singers of the 1930s: Bessie Smith, Billie Holiday, and Ella Fitzgerald. Instruct students to listen to recordings of the artist they have chosen, paying particular attention to the lyrics and tone of the songs. How do they reflect the modern age?

■ A Belief in Progress

The second element in the American dream is optimism, justified by the ever-expanding opportunity and abundance that many people had come to expect. Americans had come to believe in progress—that life will keep getting better and that we are always moving toward an era of greater prosperity, justice, and joy.

■ Triumph of the Individual

The final element in the American dream is the importance and ultimate triumph of the individual—the independent, self-reliant person. This ideal of the self-reliant individual was championed by Ralph Waldo Emerson (page 179), who probably deserves most of the credit for defining the essence of the American dream, including its roots in the promise of the "new Eden" and its faith that "things are getting better all the time." Trust the universe and trust yourself, Emerson wrote. "If the single man plant himself indomitable on his instincts, and there abide, the huge world will come round to him."

A Crack in the World: Breakdown of Beliefs and Traditions

The devastation of World War I and the economic crash a decade later severely damaged these inherited ideas of an Edenic land, an optimism in the future, and a faith in individualism. Postwar writers became skeptical of the New England Puritan tradition and the gentility that had been central to the literary ideal. In fact, the center of American literary life finally started to shift away from New England, which had been the native region of America's most brilliant writers during the nineteenth century. Many modernist writers were born in the South, the Midwest, or the West.

In the postwar period two new intellectual theories or movements, **Marxism** and **psychoanalysis,** combined to influence previous beliefs and values.

Marxism and the Challenge to Free Enterprise

In Russia during World War I, a Marxist revolution had toppled and even murdered an anointed ruler, the czar. The socialistic beliefs of Karl Marx (1818–1883) that had powered the Russian Revolution in 1917 conflicted with the American system of capitalism and free enterprise, and Marxists threatened to export their revolution everywhere. Some Americans, however, believed that certain elements of Marxism would provide much-needed rights to workers. After visiting Russia, the American writer and social reformer Lincoln Steffens reported, "I have seen the future and it works."

Elements of Modernism

- Emphasis on bold experimentation in style and form, reflecting the fragmentation of society

- Rejection of traditional themes, subjects, and forms

- Sense of disillusionment and loss of faith in the American dream

- Rejection of sentimentality and artificiality

- Rejection of the ideal of a hero as infallible in favor of a hero who is flawed and disillusioned but shows "grace under pressure"

- Interest in the inner workings of the human mind, sometimes expressed through new narrative techniques, such as stream of consciousness

- Revolt against the spiritual debasement of the modern world

(D)

(E)

(D) Literary Connections
Elements of Modernism

(?) Have students review the boxed feature. Then, ask them, "Which items describe what modernism stands for as a movement?"
[Modernism espouses bold experimentation in style and form, a flawed hero or "antihero," and an interest in psychology.]

(E) Content-Area Connections
History: Marx and the Bolshevik Revolution

Karl Marx argued that the economic structure of a society shapes every aspect of life in that society. He believed that the capitalist system could not be reformed from within and had to be destroyed to make way for a classless society, in which all property would be owned communally and everyone would receive equal benefits and rewards. His ideas greatly influenced Vladimir Ilyich Lenin, who in 1903 became the head of the Bolshevik faction of the Social Democratic Party in Russia. In 1917, the Bolsheviks took control of the revolution that had deposed the czar and established a government based theoretically on Marxist ideals.

Village Speakeasy, Closed for Violation (c. 1934) by Ben Shahn.
Tempera on masonite ($16^3/_8'' \times 47^7/_8''$).

Museum of the City of New York. Permanent Deposit of the Public Art Project through the Whitney Museum.
© Estate of Ben Shahn/Licensed by VAGA, New York.

Ⓐ *The liberty of the individual is no gift of civilization. It was greatest before there was any civilization.*

—Sigmund Freud
from *Civilization and Its Discontents* (1930)

Freud and the Unconscious Mind

In Vienna there was another ground-shaking movement. Sigmund Freud (1856–1939), the founder of psychoanalysis, had opened the workings of the unconscious mind to scrutiny and called for a new understanding of human sexuality and the role it plays in our unconscious thoughts. Throughout America there was a growing interest in this new field of psychology and a resulting anxiety about the amount of freedom an individual really had. If our actions were influenced by our subconscious and if we had no control over our subconscious, there seemed to be little room left for free will.

One literary result of this interest in the psyche was the narrative technique called **stream of consciousness.** This writing style abandoned chronology and attempted to imitate the moment-by-Ⓑ moment flow of a character's perceptions and memories. The Irish writer James Joyce (1882–1941) radically changed the very concept of the novel by using stream of consciousness in *Ulysses* (1922), his monumental "odyssey" set in Dublin. Soon afterward the American writers Katherine Anne Porter (page 695) and William Faulkner (page 643) used the stream-of-consciousness technique in their works.

At Home and Abroad: The Jazz Age

Ⓒ In 1919, the Constitution was amended to prohibit the manufacture and sale of alcohol, which was singled out as a central social evil. But far from shoring up traditional values, Prohibition ushered in an age characterized by the bootlegger, the speak-easy, the cocktail, the short-skirted flapper, the new rhythms of jazz, and the dangerous but lucrative profession of the gangster. Recording the Roaring Twenties and making the era a vivid chapter in our history, F. Scott Fitzgerald gave it its name: the Jazz Age.

During the Jazz Age, women too played a prominent role. In 1920, women won the right to vote, and they began to create a presence in artistic, intellectual, and social circles. As energetic as the Roaring Twenties were in America, the pursuit of pleasure abroad was even more attractive to some than was its enjoyment at home. F. Scott Fitzgerald was among the many American writers and artists who abandoned their own shores after the war for the expatriate life in France. After World War I, living was not only cheap in Paris and on the sunny French Riviera but also somehow better; it was more exotic, filled with more grace and luxury, and there was no need to go down a cellar stairway to get a drink. This wave of expatriates (Americans living abroad) was another signal that something had gone wrong with the American dream—with the idea that America was Eden, with our belief in progress, and especially with the conviction that America was a land of heroes.

Grace Under Pressure: The New American Hero

The most influential of all the post–World War I writers was Ernest Hemingway (page 608). Hemingway is perhaps most famous for his literary style, which affected the style of American prose fiction for several generations. Like the Puritans, who strove for a plain style centuries earlier, Hemingway reduced the flamboyance of literary language to the bare bones of the truth it must express.

Hemingway also introduced a new kind of hero to American fiction, a character type that many readers embraced as a protagonist and a role model. This Hemingway hero is a man of action, a warrior, and a tough competitor; he has a code of honor, courage, and endurance. He shows, in Hemingway's own words, "grace under pressure." But the most important trait of this Hemingway hero is his thorough disillusionment, a quality that reflected the author's own outlook—that at the mysterious center of creation lay nothing at all.

Hemingway found his own answer to this crisis of faith in a belief in the self and in such qualities as decency, bravery, competence, and skillfulness. He clung to this conviction in spite of what he saw as the absolutely unbeatable odds waged against us all. A further part of the Hemingway code was the importance of recognizing and snatching up the rare, good, rich moments that life offers before those moments elude us.

FAST FACTS

Political Highlights

- In 1917, the United States enters World War I on the side of the Allied nations.

- Women win the right to vote when the Nineteenth Amendment is passed in 1920.

- The stock market crash of 1929 ushers in the Great Depression.

Philosophical Views

- Marxism, which embraced socialism as the desired social structure, takes hold in Russia and finds some support in the United States.

- The science of psychoanalysis encourages exploration of the human subconscious and the meaning of dreams.

Social Influences

- Speak-easies and jazz clubs spring up during Prohibition. The underground social scene becomes popular.

- During the 1920s, many young women flout tradition and become more independent in thought, dress, and attitude.

D Literary Connections
Zelda Fitzgerald

F. Scott Fitzgerald (1896–1940) married Zelda Sayre in 1920. For many, the couple epitomized the Jazz Age: wealthy, beautiful, talented, extravagant, and pleasure seeking. Fitzgerald's novel *Tender Is the Night* (1934) is based on their marriage.

E Content-Area Connections

History: A War of Attrition
On the western front, World War I was largely a war of attrition. Both sides suffered extremely heavy casualties while achieving few of their objectives.

F Exploring the Culture
THE AMERICAN HERO

Hemingway's heroes—tough, solitary, self-reliant, independent—are modern versions of a type that first captured the imagination of the reading public in the frontier tales of James Fenimore Cooper. American film was strongly influenced by this type of hero: The actors Gary Cooper, Humphrey Bogart, and John Wayne had long and successful careers playing Hemingway-type heroes.

Critic's Commentary: Wilson on Hemingway

In 1939, the critic Edmund Wilson wrote, "[Hemingway's] whole work is a criticism of society: he has responded to every pressure of the moral atmosphere of the time, as it is felt at the roots of human relations, with a sensitivity almost unrivaled. Even his preoccupation with licking the gang in the next block and being known as the best basketball player in high school has its meaning in the present epoch. After all, whatever is done in the world, political as well as athletic, depends on personal courage and strength. . . . Hemingway has expressed with genius the terrors of the modern man at the danger of losing control of his world, and he has also, within his scope, provided his own kind of antidote. This antidote, paradoxically, is almost entirely moral. Despite Hemingway's preoccupation with physical contests, his heroes are almost always defeated physically, nervously, practically: their victories are moral ones."

VIEWING THE ART

Pablo Picasso (1881–1973) played a major role in the development of modern art. Together with Georges Braque (1882–1963), Picasso developed cubism, one of the most radical movements the world of art has ever seen. Departing from the tradition of illusionist art, in which perspective is used to indicate depth, Picasso freely acknowledged the flatness of his canvases, creating an ambiguous sense of space. In the 1930s, he began using a bright, colorful palette and curving, rhythmic lines to define shapes.

Activity. Ask students to identify the ways Picasso unifies the shapes in his painting. [Possible response: He uses repeated colors and shapes to unify the painting's forms.]

Ⓐ Literary Connections
H. D.

Another important imagist poet was H. D. (p. 293), born Hilda Doolittle in Pennsylvania in 1886. Confused by her off-and-on romance with Ezra Pound and unsure of her future, H. D. drifted to London, where she published her first volume of poems, *Sea Garden* (1916). Critics hailed it as "the most perfect exemplar of Imagism."

Ⓑ Exploring the Culture
THE HARLEM RENAISSANCE

In the words of David Levering Lewis, "The Harlem Renaissance was . . . institutionally encouraged and directed by leaders of the national civil rights establishment for the paramount purpose of improving race relations in a time of extreme national backlash, caused in large part by economic gains won by Afro-Americans during the Great War." As a result, many black artists felt they had a dual mission: expressing their own artistic vision while calling for social justice.

Still Life on a Table (1931) by Pablo Picasso.

Modern Voices in Poetry: A Dazzling Period of Experimentation

By the second decade of the century, the last traces of British influence on American poetry were washed away, and American poets entered into their most dazzling period of experimentation. Many poets began to explore the artistic life of Europe, especially Paris. With other writers, artists, and composers from all over the world, they absorbed the lessons of modernist painters like Henri Matisse and Pablo Picasso, who were exploring new ways to see and represent reality. In the same way, poets sought to create poems that invited new ways of seeing and thinking. Ezra Pound (page 574) and T. S. Eliot (page 581) used the suggestive techniques of **symbolism** to fashion a new, modernist poetry (see page 571). Pound also spearheaded a related poetic movement called **imagism.** Exemplified by brilliant poets like E. E. Cummings (page 601), the imagist and symbolist styles would prevail in poetry until the mid–twentieth century.

Voices of American Character

Meanwhile other American poets rejected modernist trends. While their colleagues found inspiration in Paris, these poets stayed at home, ignoring or defying the revolution of modernism. These poets preferred to say what they had to say in plain American speech. Their individual accents reveal the regional diversity of American life and character.

Of these poets the greatest was unquestionably Robert Frost (page 716). Frost's independence was grounded in his ability to handle ordinary New England speech and in his surprising skill at taking the most conventional poetic forms and giving them a twist all his own. In an era when "good" was being equated by many artists with "new," the only new thing about Robert Frost was old: individual poetic genius. Using this gift to impose his own personality on the iambic line in verse, Frost created a poetic voice that was unique and impossible to imitate.

The Harlem Renaissance: Voices of the African American Experience

In the early 1920s, a group of black poets focused directly on the unique contributions of African American culture to America. Their poetry based its rhythms on spirituals and jazz, its lyrics on songs known as the blues, and its diction on the street talk of the ghettos.

Foremost among the African American lyric poets were James Weldon Johnson, Claude McKay (page 784), Langston Hughes

568 Collection 5   The Moderns: 1914–1939

CONTENT-AREA CONNECTIONS

Humanities: Prose Writers of the Harlem Renaissance

Prominent prose writers of the Harlem Renaissance include Jessie Redmon Fauset, Nella Larsen, Arna Bontemps, Jean Toomer, and Zora Neale Hurston (p. 762). Fauset wrote four novels, in which she addressed stereotypes of blacks and issues of race, class, and gender. Larsen wrote two acclaimed novels, *Quicksand* (1928) and *Passing* (1929), in which she explored the social restrictions that prevented women, especially black women, from defining their own identities and living fulfilling lives. Bontemps wrote poetry, history, and fiction as well as memoirs and critical essays about his time and its literary figures. In his novel *Cane*, Toomer wrote about the southern black culture he believed was disappearing with industrialization and the migration of African Americans to the North.

(page 749), and Countee Cullen (page 744). These poets brought literary distinction to the broad movement of artists known as the **Harlem Renaissance** (page 742). The geographical center of the movement was Harlem, the neighborhood of New York City north of 110th Street in Manhattan. Its spiritual center, though, was a place in the consciousness of African Americans—a people too long ignored, patronized, or otherwise shuffled to the margins of American art. When African American poetry, hand in hand with the music echoing from New Orleans, Memphis, and Chicago, became part of the Jazz Age, it was a catalyst for a new appreciation of the role of black talent in American culture.

The American Dream Revised

In some respects the modernist era is the richest period of American writing since the flowering of New England in the first half of the nineteenth century. The writers of this era—some of the best that America has produced—experimented boldly with forms and subject matter. But they were also still trying to find the answers to basic human questions: Who are we? Where are we going? What values should guide us on the search for our human identity?

REVIEW

Talk About . . .

Turn back to the Think About questions at the start of this introduction to the modern period (page 562), and discuss your views.

Write About . . .

Contrasting Literary Periods

The American dream, then and now. In 1929, Gertrude Stein, a leading modernist literary figure among the American expatriates in Paris, declared, "Everything is the same and everything is different." Apply her remark to the American dream of the early twentieth century, and then apply it to today—and tomorrow. Note the ways in which the American dream remains the same and ways in which it has changed.

War and economics, then and now. A major war and a major economic disaster marked the first decades of the twentieth century. How do you think historians of the future will describe the past twenty years? What forces—political and economic—contributed to the way people lived, what they hoped for and feared, and what they wrote about? Write your responses, and then share them with a partner.

The Moderns: 1914–1939 **569**

Check Test: True-False

Monitoring students' progress. Guide the class in answering these questions.

1. World War I is often seen as the beginning of America's loss of innocence. [T]

2. Interest in psychoanalysis led to a general anxiety about the influence of the unconscious on people's actions. [T]

3. Poets from New England maintained their dominant position in American literature after World War I. [F]

4. American writers were reluctant to leave the country and live in Europe after World War I. [F]

5. Stream of consciousness and other experimental techniques gained popularity. [T]

Review

Talk About . . .

• **Modeling.** You might model answering the first bulleted question on p. 562 by saying, "The three subheadings of the section 'The American Dream: Pursuit of a Promise' are 'America as a New Eden,' 'A Belief in Progress,' and 'Triumph of the Individual.' These headings suggest that the American dream is a vision of the United States as a land of bounty and limitless progress where the self-reliant individual will always triumph."

• In the early twentieth century, the idea of the American dream was rejected by an America traumatized by World War I and the Great Depression.

• Modernism challenged tradition by offering new ways to see and represent reality in art and literature. Traditional themes, subjects, and forms were viewed as outdated.

Write About . . .

The American dream, then and now. To help students get started, have them review the boxed feature on the tenets of the American dream. Then, ask students to think about what they hope to achieve in their own lives and whether they feel that outside forces (economic, political, cultural) will allow them to fulfill those goals.

War and economics, then and now. To help students get started, remind them of the following events: the AIDS explosion in the 1980s, the fall of the Berlin Wall in 1989, the breakup of the Soviet Union in 1991, the events of September 11, 2001, and the ongoing Israeli-Palestinian conflict,

THE QUOTATION

Activity. Have students read Pound's challenge and then write a brief interpretation. What does Pound mean by "new" art? Why does he emphasize the "joyous" quality of artistic creation? [Possible response: Pound feels that art should reflect a spontaneous joy in creation. That spontaneity constantly demands new forms and artistic strategies.]

VIEWING THE ART

Pablo Picasso (1881–1973) was the most widely exhibited and discussed artist of the modern era. Famous for his frequent changes in style, he assimilated developments in the art around him and influenced other artists in turn. Born and educated in Spain, Picasso began working as an artist in Barcelona before moving permanently to Paris in 1904. Interested in both the art of his time and place and the visual traditions of non-Western cultures, Picasso shocked the public with the way in which he dispensed with traditional methods of depicting space.

In *Girl Before a Mirror,* Picasso depicts a woman's face as two semicircular shapes that can be interpreted as a moon or a sun.

Activity. Ask students to compare literary innovations in this subchapter's selections with Picasso's artistic innovations.

Make It New!

Pound
Eliot
Williams
Moore
Cummings

Make it new!
Art is a joyous thing.

—Ezra Pound

INTERNET
Collection Resources
Keyword: LE5 11-5

Girl Before a Mirror (detail) (1932) by Pablo Picasso.

Symbolism, Imagism, and Beyond

by John Malcolm Brinnin

Sometime in the early twentieth century, Americans awoke to a sense that their own national culture had come of age. This was true in poetry and in painting, in music and in dance, even in the new architecture of the skyscraper. Ironically American poets found their new inspiration in Paris rather than their homeland. Learning from the French symbolist poets, who dominated French literature from about 1875 to 1895, Americans were able to produce a new type of poetry through which the true American genius could speak.

Symbolism: The Search for a New Reality

Symbolism is a form of expression in which the world of appearances is violently rearranged by artists who seek a different and more truthful version of reality. The symbolist poets did not merely describe objects; they tried to portray the emotional effects that objects can suggest. But don't be misled by the term *symbolism*. It has nothing to do with the religious, national, or psychological symbols we are all familiar with. In fact, the symbolists were concerned with getting rid of such symbols, which they saw as having become dull and meaningless through overuse. The symbolists stressed instead the need for a trust in the nonrational. Imagination is more reliable than reason, the symbolists argued, and just as precise. With their emphasis on the mysterious and the intuitive, symbolists hoped to bring revelation—self-discovery—to the reader through poems that lead the imagination to discover truths.

Symbolism was a new manifestation of the Romanticism that had swept over Europe and the United States in the nineteenth century. The Romantics had stressed the importance of feeling and the independence of the individual, and they had made a great stand against the mechanization of human life. In the natural world the Romantics found messages that spoke to the soul and gave it strength.

The symbolists, however, could find neither solace nor spiritual renewal in nature. By the start of the twentieth century, nature had been subjected to so much scientific classification and interpretation that it had been stripped of much of its mystery. Artists now faced the onslaught of the modern world, which in spite of advances in science and technology suffered increased poverty, violence, and conflict. The symbolist poets saw this new world as spiritually corrupt, and they faced it with a distaste amounting to outrage. They knew they could not transform or erase the modern

DIRECT TEACHING

A Literary Connections
Charles Baudelaire
An important forerunner of both the symbolists and the imagists, the French poet Charles Baudelaire (1821–1867) sought reality in the sordid details of modern life. He was prosecuted and fined for obscenity and blasphemy for his influential collection of poems, *Les Fleurs du Mal* (*The Flowers of Evil*) (1857).

B Exploring the Culture
Symbols
❓ What are some of the religious, national, and psychological symbols people today are familiar with? [Possible responses: cross, Star of David, crescent; eagle, buffalo, rising sun; heart (love), red (anger or passion).] **Why did the symbolists avoid using such symbols?** [Possible response: The symbolists rejected these symbols as stale and hackneyed.]

C Reading Skills
❓ **Comparing and contrasting.**
What are the similarities between symbolism and Romanticism? What are the differences? [Possible response: Both movements tried to reveal the reality beneath physical appearances by emphasizing emotion and intuition over rational thought; both saw mass culture and industrialization as threats to individuality and spirituality. Where the Romantics saw nature as a source of spiritual fulfillment and a mirror of human feelings, however, the symbolists felt that science had robbed nature of its mystery.]

DIFFERENTIATING INSTRUCTION

Learners Having Difficulty
Ask students to fill in the following outline by identifying the main ideas and facts in this essay. Then, have them extend the outline to include the last section, "A New Poetic Order."

I. Symbolist movement
  A. Dates:
  B. Main idea:
  C. Differences from Romanticism:
  D. Relation to industrial society:
II. Imagism
  A. Dates:
  B. Important poets:
  C. Main idea:
  D. Source of inspiration:
  E. Definition of *poetic image*:

VIEWING THE ART

Joseph Stella (1877–1946) was one of the pioneers of modernist art in the United States. Born in Italy, he came through Ellis Island in 1896. In his early paintings, Stella focused on social themes, such as the miserable conditions of Pittsburgh's industrial workers. A visit to Europe in 1910–1912 and the New York Armory Show of 1913 exposed Stella to the art of the cubists, who deconstructed the real world into geometric shapes, and the futurists, who focused on the machine age and its effects.

Activity. Ask students to find sentences in the essay that show why *Night Fires* is an appropriate illustration. [Possible responses: "The symbolist poets did not merely describe objects"; "Artists now faced the onslaught"; "They tried to redefine what it meant to be human. . . ." (pp. 571–572)] **Ask students to contrast this painting with the painting by Thomas Cole that opens Collection 2, "American Romanticism."** [Make sure students note the change from unspoiled nature to smoking industry, from sun and water to flames and steel, from unbounded freedom to steel walls. Cole's painting focuses on the magnificence of nature; Stella's painting depicts an industrial world.]

Ⓐ Exploring the Historical Period
1912–1917

Remind students that in the United States, the years 1912–1917 were marked by great industrial and economic growth, peak immigration, and a world war.

Night Fires (c. 1919) by Joseph Stella. Pastel on paper (22 ½" × 29").
Milwaukee Art Museum, Gift of Friends of Art.

world, though, so their revolt was spiritual. They tried to redefine what it meant to be human in a time when individualism was succumbing to the power of mass culture.

Imagism: "The *Exact* Word"

The two Americans who first came into close contact with symbolism and introduced the techniques of the movement to the United States were Ezra Pound (page 574) and T. S. Eliot (page 581). With the help of several British poets, a group of Americans led by Pound founded a school perhaps better known and understood in the United States than symbolism itself. This was **imagism,** which flourished in the years 1912–1917.

Ⓐ Like the symbolists, imagists believed that poetry can be made purer by concentration on the precise, clear, unqualified image. Imagery alone, the imagists believed, could carry a poem's emotion and message. It could do this almost instantly, without all the elaborate metrics and stanza patterns that were part of poetry's traditional mode. The imagists took on the role of reformers. They would rid poetry of its prettiness, sentimentality, and artificiality,

572 Collection 5 The Moderns: 1914–1939

CONTENT-AREA CONNECTIONS

Art: Symbolist Painters
Small-group activity. Divide the class into small groups, and have each group research a symbolist artist. Possibilities include the French artists Odilon Redon, Paul Gauguin, Gustave Moreau, and Henri Rousseau; the Dutch artist Vincent Van Gogh; the Belgian artist James Ensor; the Norwegian artist Edvard Munch; and the American artist Albert Ryder. Ask students to bring in copies of paintings by the artists and explain to the class how the works relate to the symbolist poets.

concentrating instead on the raw power of the image to communicate feeling and thought.

The imagists issued a "manifesto," or public declaration, proposing "to use the language of common speech," as well as "the *exact* word, not merely the decorative word." In the same spirit they called for a poetry "hard and clear, never blurred or indefinite." Some of the imagists' inspiration was drawn from Eastern art forms, particularly Japanese haiku, a verse form that often juxtaposes two distinct images and invites the reader to experience the emotion created by the juxtaposition.

Pound defined an image as "that which presents an intellectual and emotional complex in an instant of time." Here is a famous imagist poem that illustrates this concept:

In a Station of the Metro

The apparition of these faces in the crowd;
Petals on a wet, black bough.

　　　　　　　　　　—Ezra Pound

A New Poetic Order

Today poems with imagistic technique are commonplace. But at the time the imagists published their manifesto on poetry's nature and function, their theory created a great stir. It insisted that the range of poetic subject matter might include the kitchen sink as well as the rising of the moon, the trash can as well as the Chinese porcelain vase. The strongest opposition to the imagists was caused by their proposal "to create new rhythms—as the expression of new moods. . . . We do believe that the individuality of a poet may often be better expressed in free verse than in conventional forms." To tradition-minded poets this **free verse**—poetry without regular rhyming and metrical patterns—was deplorable. It meant a loosening of poetic standards and an assault on the very craft of poetry. These poets did not yet realize that successful free verse was at least as difficult to create as verse written in traditional forms.

Although imagism was a short-lived movement, it gave rise to some of our greatest poets. Many in the forefront of imagism went beyond the movement's limitations and expanded its insights. Besides Pound, these included William Carlos Williams (page 591), Marianne Moore (page 597), and E. E. Cummings (page 601). Eventually, imagism came to stand for a whole new order of poetry in the United States. Most Americans became familiar with the movement mainly as the school of free verse. But the imagist program was not only a call for a new method of organizing lines and stanzas; it was also an invitation to a new way of seeing and experiencing the world.

Symbolism, Imagism, and Beyond　　573

B Literary Connections
Haiku
Haiku shares with imagism an emphasis on the use of precise images (traditionally ones from nature) to suggest emotion. Unlike imagist poetry, however, it is structured according to rigid rules: A haiku consists of seventeen syllables arranged in three unrhymed lines of five, seven, and five syllables each.

C Background
The *Exact* Word
Ezra Pound recalled the inspiration for this poem: "Three years ago in Paris I got out of a 'metro' train at La Concorde, and saw suddenly a beautiful face, and then another and another, and then a beautiful child's face, and then another beautiful woman, and I tried all that day to find words for what this had meant to me, and I could not find any words that seemed to me worthy, or as lovely as that sudden emotion." This poem, although short, took a long time to write. Pound's first version contained thirty lines; his second contained fifteen. Over a year after that subway ride he finally finished this two-line poem.

D Literary Connections
Free Verse: Pro and Con
Robert Frost, a poet who favored traditional verse forms, once compared writing free verse to playing tennis without a net. He was referring not to the tightly structured poems of Ezra Pound and William Carlos Williams but to poems by unskilled writers that sounded like chopped-up prose.

Advanced Learners
Enrichment. Amy Lowell, a relative of the poets James Russell Lowell (1819–1891) and Robert Lowell (1917–1977), was a leading imagist poet. When she replaced Ezra Pound as the de facto leader of the imagists, he nicknamed the group the "Amygists," in recognition of her outspoken, dominant personality.

A celebrated eccentric, Lowell kept many dogs and smoked large black cigars.
Activity. Encourage students to read several poems by Lowell and explain how they reflect the ideas of the imagists.

Grade-Level Skills

■ **Literary Skills**

Analyze the way poets use imagery.

Review Skills

■ **Literary Skills**

Analyze various literary devices, including, figurative language, imagery, allegory, and symbolism.

More About the Writer

Background. In a letter to Archibald MacLeish written in 1943, Ernest Hemingway discusses his reaction to Ezra Pound's activities in support of Benito Mussolini. In the letter, Hemingway states, "[Pound] has a long history of generosity and unselfish aid to other artists and he is one of the greatest living poets. It is impossible to believe that anyone could utter the vile, absolutely idiotic drivel he has broadcast. His friends who knew him and who watched the warping and twisting and decay of his mind and his judgement should defend him and explain him on that basis."

Ezra Pound
(1885–1972)

Boris De Rachewitz/New Directions Publishing.

Ezra Pound is remembered by many people as the man who was charged with treason during World War II and spent many years in a psychiatric hospital. This notoriety has tended to obscure Pound's impact on American poetry. But his influence is still apparent everywhere; the generations of poets who have come after Pound have kept alive a complex memory of a man whose career wavered between brilliance and episodic madness.

Pound was born in Hailey, Idaho, and grew up in Pennsylvania. He taught at a conservative religious college for a while, but his bohemian lifestyle was out of tune with his surroundings.

In search of greater personal freedom and contacts with European poets, Pound settled in London in 1908. There he became a self-appointed spokesperson for the new poetic movement known as imagism. He also became a self-exiled critic of American life and a torchbearer for any art that challenged the complacent middle class.

Pound—whose slogan was "Make it new!"—was a born teacher whose advice was sought by the most brilliant writers of the period. T. S. Eliot acknowledged Pound's valuable advice when he dedicated his great poem *The Waste Land* (1922) to him.

After World War I, Pound felt the need for even broader horizons than London offered him. He moved to Paris in 1921 and to Italy three years later, where he continued to write poetry and criticism. And now came a tragic turning point in Pound's life. His interest in economics and social theory led him to support Benito Mussolini, the Fascist dictator of Italy.

RESOURCES: READING

Planning
■ *One-Stop Planner* CD-ROM with ExamView Test Generator

Differentiating Instruction
■ *The Holt Reader*
■ *Holt Reading Solutions*
■ *Supporting Instruction in Spanish*
■ *Audio CD Library, Selections and Summaries in Spanish*

Grammar and Language
■ *Daily Language Activities*

Assessment
■ *Holt Assessment: Literature, Reading, and Vocabulary*
■ *One-Stop Planner* CD-ROM with ExamView Test Generator
■ *Holt Online Assessment*

When World War II broke out, Pound stayed in Italy and turned propagandist for Mussolini's policies. In his radio broadcasts from Italy, Pound denounced the struggle of the United States and its allies against Germany, Italy, and Japan. Many of these broadcasts were viciously anti-Semitic.

When the American army advanced northward up the Italian peninsula in 1945, Pound was taken prisoner. He was confined to a cage on an airstrip near Pisa and eventually returned to the United States to be tried for treason. Psychiatrists judged him mentally incompetent, however, and in 1946 the poet was committed to St. Elizabeth's, at the time designated a hospital for the criminally insane, in Washington, D.C.

Twelve years later he was released through the intercession of writers, including Archibald MacLeish and Robert Frost, who argued that his literary contributions outweighed his disastrous lack of judgment and his notorious bigotry. Pound returned to Italy, where he lived the rest of his life. During these last years of exile, a reporter once asked Pound where he was living. "In hell," Pound answered. "Which hell?" the reporter asked. "Here," said Pound, pressing his heart. "Here."

When he died, in Venice, Pound left behind a body of work extending from the delicate lyrics he wrote at the turn of the century to *The Cantos,* an enormous epic he did not complete until well over fifty years later. He also left a public record that still uncomfortably involves scholars and historians in "the case of Ezra Pound."

Before You Read

The River-Merchant's Wife: A Letter

Make the Connection

In this letter-poem, Pound assumes the voice of a Chinese river-merchant's wife as she thinks about her growing love for her husband. This poem is a tribute to Li Po (701–762), one of the greatest Chinese poets. Pound had to cross generations, cultures, continents, and genders to write the poem; its intimate tone creates a bridge for the reader. If you have ever been moved to write a letter to someone you loved and missed, you will identify at once with the feelings of this eighth-century Chinese speaker.

Literary Focus
Imagery

Pound's poem is not a word-for-word translation of Li Po's poem but an adaptation based on the **images** and feelings that Pound experienced when he read translations of the original. Pound's images are simple and concrete; they help the reader to see the speaker and her setting clearly and to imagine how she is feeling.

> **Imagery** is language that creates vivid sense impressions and suggests emotional states.
>
> *For more on Imagery, see the Handbook of Literary and Historical Terms.*

Literary Skills
Understand imagery.

Ezra Pound   575

PRETEACHING

Summary ⬌ *at grade level*

Through a series of flashbacks, the speaker evokes various stages of her life and her feelings toward her husband at those times: during their childhood; at their marriage, when she was fourteen; and now, when she is sixteen and he has gone away. The final images reveal how the beauty of the natural world aggravates the pain she feels over her husband's long absence. She closes her "letter" by asking him to tell her when he will be returning so that she can come out to meet him.

Selection Starter

Motivate. Invite a volunteer to read the title of the poem. Point out to students that the speaker who writes the "letter" in the poem is a young woman about their age. As students read, have them note ways in which her views on male-female relationships differ from the views of an average American teenager. How do these differences reflect the culture and historical period in which she lives?

Skills Starter

Build review skills. Explain to students that poets use imagery to evoke a picture or impression of a person, a thing, a place, or an experience. Point out that although most imagery appeals to the sense of sight, it may appeal to other senses as well.

Internet
- go.hrw.com (Keyword: LE5 11-5)
- *Elements of Literature Online*

Media
- *Audio CD Library*
- *Audio CD Library, Selections and Summaries in Spanish*

Ⓐ Literary Focus

❓ Imagery. What emotions and character traits do the images in these lines suggest? [Possible response: The images convey the self-sufficiency of both children, as well as the speaker's nostalgia for those days of innocence.]

Ⓑ Reading Skills

❓ Speculating. What do these lines suggest about the circumstances of the speaker's marriage and the way she felt about it for the first year? Cite specific details to support your answer. [The speaker's bashful silence before her husband and her reference to him as "My Lord" suggest that it was a formal, arranged marriage and that for the first year the speaker was uncertain of her feelings for her husband.]

Ⓒ Learners Having Difficulty

❓ Paraphrasing. How would you paraphrase this line? [Possible responses: Why should I look back on my old life now that I am happily married? Why should I seek happiness in faraway places when I am so content where I am?]

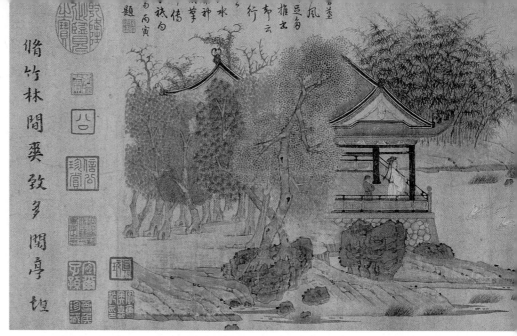

Wang Hsi-chih Watching Geese (detail) (c. 1235–before 1307) by Ch'ien Hsüan. Handscroll. Ink and color on paper (9¹⁄₈″ × 36¹⁄₂″).

The River-Merchant's Wife: A Letter

Ezra Pound

While my hair was still cut straight across my forehead
Played I about the front gate, pulling flowers.
Ⓐ You came by on bamboo stilts, playing horse,
You walked about my seat, playing with blue plums.
5 And we went on living in the village of Chokan:
Two small people, without dislike or suspicion.

At fourteen I married My Lord you.
Ⓑ I never laughed, being bashful.
Lowering my head, I looked at the wall.
10 Called to, a thousand times, I never looked back.

At fifteen I stopped scowling,
I desired my dust to be mingled with yours
Forever and forever and forever.
Ⓒ Why should I climb the lookout?

DIFFERENTIATING INSTRUCTION

Learners Having Difficulty
Invite learners having difficulty to read "The River-Merchant's Wife: A Letter" in interactive format in *The Holt Reader* and to use the side-notes as aids to understanding the selection. The interactive version provides additional instruction, practice, and assessment of the literary skill taught in the Student Edition. Monitor students' responses to the selection, and correct any misconceptions that arise.

English-Language Learners
Remind students that poets sometimes use unusual word order to emphasize a word or to create a rhythm. Point out two instances of unusual word order. [Possible responses: "Played I" in l. 2; "I married My Lord you" in l. 7.] Have students explain how these lines would be written in normal word order. ["I played"; "I married you, My Lord."]

Special Education Students
Read aloud the first six lines, and ask students to identify the "I" and the "you." Have students construct a two-column graphic organizer as they read the rest of the poem. Ask them to list details about the speaker, "I," in the first column and to list the same information for the absent "you" in the second column.

The Metropolitan Museum of Art, Gift of The Dillon Fund, 1973 (1973.120.6).
Photograph © 1981 The Metropolitan Museum of Art, New York.

VIEWING THE ART

Ch'ien Hsüan (c. 1235–before 1307) was an artist of the late Sung dynasty (960–1279) in China, a period noted for landscape painting. The founder of a circle of artists called the Eight Talents of Wu-hsing, Ch'ien excelled at painting birds, flowers, figures, and landscapes.

Activity. Discuss how the delicacy and understatement of the painting reflect Pound's poem. [Possible responses: The muted colors are like the poem's quiet language; the small figures gazing across the water suggest the speaker's longing.]

---

15   At sixteen you departed
      You went into far Ku-to-yen, by the river of swirling eddies,
      And you have been gone five months.
      The monkeys make sorrowful noise overhead.

      You dragged your feet when you went out.
20   By the gate now, the moss is grown, the different mosses,
      Too deep to clear them away!
      The leaves fall early this autumn, in wind.
      The paired butterflies are already yellow with August
      Over the grass in the West garden;
25   They hurt me. I grow older.
      If you are coming down through the narrows of the river Kiang,
      Please let me know beforehand.
      And I will come out to meet you
                  As far as Cho-fu-Sa.

                                    —*Li T'ai Po*

Ezra Pound   **577**

D Literary Focus

❷ Imagery. To which senses do the images "swirling eddies" and "sorrowful noise" appeal? Why do you think Pound includes these descriptions? [Possible response: "Swirling eddies" appeals to the senses of sight and touch. "Sorrowful noise" appeals to the sense of hearing. These images help the reader imagine the place where the man went and the loneliness that the woman feels.]

E Literary Focus

❷ Imagery. A series of images helps create a mood. What do these images reveal about the speaker's feelings? [Possible response: Images of time passing and of autumn suggest feelings of loss, longing, and sadness. The image of the paired butterflies reveals the speaker's sadness at being separated from her husband.]

DEVELOPING FLUENCY

Individual activity. Have students compose a return letter from the speaker's husband that parallels the form of her letter. In other words, instruct them to use images to convey his feelings about each stage of their relationship.

Summary ↔ *at grade level*

This imagist poem describes a woman walking through Kensington Gardens in London. The poet begins by comparing the woman to a length of silk. He contrasts her fragility and over-refinement with the vigor of a group of poor children, painting a picture of an aloof, emotionally repressed woman frightened of interacting with others.

DIRECT TEACHING

A **Literary Focus**

❓ **Imagery.** To what does the poet compare the woman? [a skein of silk blown against a wall] Why do you think the poet uses the word *skein*, which usually refers to a loose bundle of thread or yarn? [Possible responses: He liked the alliterative qualities of the words *skein* and *silk*; he uses *skein*, which can mean "tangle" or "coil," to suggest the state of the woman's emotions.]

B **Reading Skills**

❓ **Interpreting.** What does this verse show about the woman? [Possible response: The woman's boredom is a facade. She wants to interact with the speaker but fears that it would be unseemly.]

Before You Read

The Garden

Make the Connection

"*En robe de parade*" is a quotation from the nineteenth-century French poet Albert Samain. It means "dressed for show" or, in military terms, "in full regalia." In this poem a beautifully dressed woman is observed walking in a London park called Kensington Gardens. Many poor children are playing nearby. As you read, use Pound's images to picture the scene.

The Garden

Ezra Pound

Lillah McCarthy (c. 1920) by Ambrose McEvoy. Oil on canvas (39¾" × 30").
National Portrait Gallery, London.

En robe de parade.
—Samain

A Like a skein of loose silk blown against a wall
She walks by the railing of a path in Kensington Gardens,
And she is dying piecemeal
        of a sort of emotional anemia.

5   And round about there is a rabble
Of the filthy, sturdy, unkillable infants of the very poor.
They shall inherit the earth.

In her is the end of breeding.
Her boredom is exquisite and excessive.
10 She would like someone to speak to her,
B and is almost afraid that I
        will commit that indiscretion.

Youngsters in an East End slum, London.

Comparing and Contrasting Texts

Explain to students that looking for similarities and differences between poems written by the same person often yields insights into the poet and his or her view of life. Use these questions to help students compare and contrast "The River-Merchant's Wife: A Letter" and "The Garden."

• How would you compare and contrast the subjects of the poems? [Possible response: The woman in "The River-Merchant's Wife: A Letter" learns to love her husband and feels lonely and sad when he is gone. Although the woman in "The Garden" is also lonely, her sense of decorum prevents her from expressing her feelings and reaching out to others.]

• How do the themes of the two poems compare? [Possible response: Both poems deal with loneliness and people's need for human contact.]

Ezra Pound wrote the following "rules" for poets in an article in the March 1913 issue of Poetry *magazine. Many of these rules are useful to all writers.* **INFORMATIONAL TEXT**

A Few Don'ts by an Imagiste

It is better to present one Image in a lifetime than to produce voluminous works. . . .

Pay no attention to the criticism of men who have never themselves written a notable work. Consider the discrepancies between the actual writing of the Greek poets and dramatists, and the theories of the Greco-Roman grammarians, concocted to explain their meters.

Language

Use no superfluous word, no adjective, which does not reveal something.

Don't use such an expression as "dim lands of peace." It dulls the image. It mixes an abstraction with the concrete. It comes from the writer's not realizing that the natural object is always the *adequate* symbol.

Go in fear of abstractions. Don't retell in mediocre verse what has already been done in good prose. Don't think any intelligent person is going to be deceived when you try to shirk all the difficulties of the unspeakably difficult art of good prose by chopping your composition into line lengths. . . .

Don't imagine that the art of poetry is any simpler than the art of music, or that you can please the expert before you have spent at least as much effort on the art of verse as the average piano teacher spends on the art of music.

Be influenced by as many great artists as you can, but have the decency either to acknowledge the debt outright, or to try to conceal it. . . .

Rhythm and Rhyme

Let the neophyte know assonance and alliteration, rhyme immediate and delayed, simple and polyphonic, as a musician would expect to know harmony and counterpoint and all the minutiae of his craft. No time is too great to give to these matters or to any one of them, even if the artist seldom have need of them. . . .

Consider the way of the scientists rather than the way of an advertising agent for a new soap.

The scientist does not expect to be acclaimed as a great scientist until he has *discovered* something. He begins by learning what has been discovered already. He goes from that point onward. He does not bank on being a charming fellow personally. He does not expect his friends to applaud the results of his freshman classwork. Freshmen in poetry are unfortunately not confined to a definite and recognizable classroom. They are "all over the shop." Is it any wonder "the public is indifferent to poetry"?

Don't chop your stuff into separate *iambs.* Don't make each line stop dead at the end, and then begin every next line with a heave. Let the beginning of the next line catch the rise of the rhythm wave, unless you want a definite longish pause. . . .

If you are using a symmetrical form, don't put in what you want to say and then fill up the remaining vacuums with slush.

E. L. Pound

Ezra Pound **579**

Literary Criticism

Critic's Commentary: Free Verse
Pound also had a critical perspective on the writing of free verse: "[Free verse] has brought faults of its own. The actual language and phrasing is often as bad as that of our elders without even the excuse that the words are shoveled in to fill a metric pattern or to complete the noise of a rhyme-sound."

Critic's Commentary: Using the Concrete
Pound advises poets to "use no superfluous word, no adjective, which does not reveal something." E. B. White (1899–1985) gave similar advice in his addition to William Strunk, Jr.'s *The Elements of Style:* "Write with nouns and verbs, not with adjectives and adverbs. The adjective hasn't been built that can pull a weak or inaccurate noun out of a tight place."

INDEPENDENT PRACTICE

Response and Analysis

The River-Merchant's Wife: A Letter

Thinking Critically

1. (1) The girl and boy play together as children. (2) The girl marries the boy. (3) The wife stops scowling. (4) The husband departs on a long journey.

2. It reveals her change from shy wariness to deep commitment. She expresses her acceptance of and contentment with a life she initially resisted.

3. He drags his feet as he leaves.

4. The sight of the "paired butter-flies" deepens the girl's sense of loneliness and makes her more conscious of the passage of time.

5. The husband may have been called to fight in a war; he may have been delayed by unforeseen cir-cumstances. Perhaps he met with danger and was killed.

The Garden

Thinking Critically

1. The poet compares the woman to "a skein of loose silk blown against a wall."

2. Possible answer: *Anemia* refers here to listlessness or lack of vigor. Pound seems to suggest that emotional repression kills a person little by little.

3. In the second stanza, the poet introduces a noisy group of "sturdy, unkillable" children.

4. Possible answer: Those who will inherit the earth are poor, but not meek. In fact, they are resilient.

5. Possible answer: The speaker is suggesting that the woman comes from a family of high social stand-ing. The phrase could also mean that the woman's fragility and emotional reserve will prevent her from ever becoming close to a man and having a child.

The River-Merchant's Wife: A Letter

Thinking Critically

1. What events are referred to in the first four stanzas of "The River-Merchant's Wife"?

2. How is the third stanza a **turning point** in the poem? What do you think the river-merchant's wife means by line 14?

3. What **image** suggests that the river-merchant was reluctant to leave home?

4. What hurts the young wife in line 25, and why? In the same line, why does she say, after only five months, that she grows "older"?

5. Think of possible reasons why the river-merchant left. Do you think he will ever return? What may have delayed him?

The Garden

Thinking Critically

1. What **simile** in the first stanza of "The Garden" describes what the woman looks like as she walks in the park?

2. How would you explain "emotional anemia"? How might it cause the woman to die "piecemeal"?

3. What contrast to the woman is set up in the second stanza?

INTERNET
Projects and Activities
Keyword: LE5 11-5

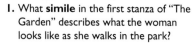

SKILLS FOCUS

Literary Skills
Analyze imagery.

Writing Skills
Write a poem describing an image.

4. Line 7, "They shall inherit the earth," is an allusion to the Bible (Matthew 5:5). There Jesus says, "Blessed are the meek, for they shall inherit the earth." What does the statement mean in this context?

5. *Breeding* can mean "producing offspring" or "good upbringing or good training." How would you explain the double meaning of the word in line 8?

6. In line 10, what does the speaker imagine the woman wants? What is she afraid of?

7. "The Garden" is a poem about two individuals, the woman and the speaker, but it is also about something broader. What is Pound's larger subject?

WRITING

Imagine It

Write a very brief **poem** making use of Pound's "A Few Don'ts by an Imagiste" (see the *Primary Source* on page 579). First, choose a topic you feel strongly about, perhaps a topic from one of these poems: love, parting, the contrast between rich and poor, the need for human contact. Then, think of a single concrete image that suggests the situation and your feelings about it. Describe the image as specifically as you can. Use Pound's "In a Station of the Metro" (page 573) as a model—Pound sets a mood by describing a single, strong image.

6. The speaker says that although the woman wants someone to speak to her, she fears that such an interaction would be improper.

7. Possible answers: Pound is condemning the restrictions imposed by society; Pound is criticizing the rigid conventions of tradi-tional poetry and art.

ASSESSING

Assessment

■ *Holt Assessment: Literature, Reading, and Vocabulary*

RETEACHING

For a lesson reteaching poetic devices, see **Reteaching**, p. 1117A.

T. S. Eliot
(1888–1965)

At the time when he was regarded as America's most eminent living poet, T. S. Eliot announced that he was a "classicist in literature, royalist in politics, and Anglo-Catholic in religion." In 1927, Eliot gave up his U.S. citizenship and became a subject of the king of England. The same year he was received into the Church of England. By a kind of poetic justice, this loss to America was later to be made up for: W. H. Auden (page 883), the leading British poet of his time, became a naturalized American citizen in 1946. But residence in an adopted country does not necessarily change the philosophy or the style of a poet. Eliot continued to speak in a voice first heard in the Puritan pulpits of Massachusetts. Auden retained a British sense of language unaffected by the inroads of American speech.

Thomas Stearns Eliot's family was rooted in New England, though he was born in St. Louis, Missouri, where his grandfather had been a founder and chancellor of Washington University. Eliot's childhood awareness of his native city would show itself in his poetry, but only after he had moved far away from St. Louis. He graduated from Harvard and went on to do postgraduate work at the Sorbonne in Paris.

Just before the outbreak of World War I, Eliot took up residence in London, the city that would become his home for the rest of his life. There he worked for a time in a bank, suffered a nervous breakdown, married an emotionally troubled Englishwoman, and finally took up the business of literature. He became active as a publisher in the outstanding firm of Faber and Faber and, on his own, edited *The Criterion*, a literary magazine. As a critic he was responsible for reviving interest in many neglected poets, notably the seventeenth-century English poet John Donne.

Complex Poetry for a Complex World

Long before he decided to live abroad permanently, Eliot had developed a taste for classical literature. He was as familiar with European and Eastern writings as he was with the masterpieces of English. But the most crucial influence on his early work came from the late-nineteenth-century French poets who, as a group, came to be known as the symbolists. (For more on the symbolists, see page 571.) When he was nineteen, Eliot came upon a book by the British critic Arthur Symons titled *The Symbolist Movement in Literature*. "I myself owe Mr. Symons a great debt," wrote Eliot. "But for having read his book, I should not . . . have heard of Laforgue and Rimbaud; I should probably not have begun to read Verlaine; and but for reading Verlaine, I should not have heard of Corbière. So the Symons book is one of those which have affected the course of my life."

Background. I. A. Richards, a leading literary critic of his time, knew Eliot when the poet worked for Lloyd's Bank in London. Richards recalls meeting a senior banker who asked him what he thought of Eliot's poetry. When Richards praised it, the banker was pleased; he had debated whether banking and poetry mixed. He added that if Eliot continued doing well at the bank, he might be promoted—and might even become a branch manager someday. Richards loved to tease Eliot by repeating the banker's prediction.

The poets Eliot mentions were men of distinctly different talents. Yet they all believed in poetry as an art of suggestion rather than statement. They saw poetry as an art of re-creating states of mind and feeling, as opposed to reporting or confessing them. These beliefs became the basis of Eliot's own poetic methods. When people complained that this poetic method of suggestion was complex and difficult to understand, Eliot retorted that poetry had to be complex to express the complexities of modern life. More or less ignoring the still undervalued contribution of Walt Whitman, Eliot and other American poets also believed that, divorced from British antecedents, they would once and for all bring the rhythms of their native speech into the mainstream of world literature. Eliot and these other poets are often referred to as modernists.

Words for a Wasteland

Eliot had an austere view of poetic creativity; he disagreed with those who regarded a poem as a means of self-expression, as a source of comfort, or as a kind of spiritual pep talk. Practicing what he preached, Eliot startled his contemporaries with "The Love Song of J. Alfred Prufrock" in 1915 and "Portrait of a Lady" in 1917. Then, in 1922, with the editorial advice and encouragement of Ezra Pound, Eliot published *The Waste Land,* a long work considered the most significant poem of the early twentieth century. The poem describes a civilization that is spiritually empty and paralyzed by indecision.

Assembled in the manner of a painter's collage or a moviemaker's montage, *The Waste Land* proved that it is possible to write an epic poem of classical scope in the space of 434 lines. Critics pored over the poem's complex structure and its dense network of allusions to world literature, Eastern religions, and anthropology. A few years after *The Waste Land* appeared, Eliot published a series of notes identifying many of his key references. (He was dismayed to find that some of his more ardent admirers were more interested in the notes than in the poem itself.)

In 1925, Eliot published a kind of lyrical postscript to *The Waste Land* called "The Hollow Men," which predicted in its somber conclusion that the world would end not with a bang but with a whimper. In "The Hollow Men," Eliot repeats and expands some of the themes of his longer poem and arrives at that point of despair beyond which lie but two alternatives: renewal or annihilation.

A Submission to Peace

For critics surveying Eliot's career, it has become commonplace to say that, after the spiritual dead end of "The Hollow Men," Eliot chose hope over despair and faith over the world-weary cynicism that marked his early years. But there is much evidence in his later poems to indicate that, for Eliot, hope and faith were not conscious choices. Instead, they were the consequences of a submission, even a surrender, to that "peace which passeth understanding," referred to in the last line of *The Waste Land.*

Eliot spent the remainder of his poetic career in an extended meditation on the limits of individual will and the limitless power of faith in the presence of grace.

Cited for his work as a pioneer of modern poetry, Eliot was awarded the Nobel Prize in literature in 1948. In the decades that followed, he came frequently to the United States to lecture and to read his poems, sometimes to audiences so large that he had to appear in football stadiums. Some of those who fought to buy tickets on the fifty-yard line were probably unaware of the irony in all of this: that a man once regarded as the most difficult and obscure poet of his era had achieved the drawing power of a rock star.

Ezra Pound (who called Eliot "Possum") wrote a few final words on the death of his old friend, ending with this passage:

"Am I to write 'about' the poet Thomas Stearns Eliot? Or my friend 'the Possum'? Let him rest in peace, I can only repeat, but with the urgency of fifty years ago: READ HIM."

Before You Read

The Love Song of J. Alfred Prufrock

Make the Connection

In the PBS television series *The Power of Myth,* the noted scholar of myths Joseph Campbell says, "The hero is today running up against a hard world that is in no way responsive to his spiritual need." Modern society has become a "stagnation of inauthentic lives and living . . . that evokes nothing of our spiritual life, our potentialities, or even our physical courage." According to Campbell, the times we live in are hostile to heroism. Heroes are people of action, but the drudgery of modern life has made many people observers rather than participants in life's adventures. See if you agree that the protagonist of this poem is a person of profound self-absorption and passivity. Does he fit the profile of antihero, the disillusioned and ineffectual protagonist we find in much modern and contemporary literature?

Literary Focus
Dramatic Monologue

This poem is written as a **dramatic monologue**—a poem in which a character speaks directly to one or more listeners. The words are being spoken by a man named Prufrock.

In a dramatic monologue we must learn everything about the setting, the situation, the other characters, and the personality of the speaker through what the speaker tells us. Sometimes Prufrock's line of reasoning is interrupted by an unexpected thought. You will often have to supply the missing connections in the speaker's stream of thoughts and associations.

> A **dramatic monologue** is a poem in which a character speaks directly to one or more listeners.
>
> *For more on Dramatic Monologue, see the Handbook of Literary and Historical Terms.*

Reading Skills
Identifying Main Ideas

Read the poem through twice. The first time, aim for a general sense of Prufrock's thoughts. As you read the poem again, write down examples of how his thoughts reflect the following ideas about his own time (the poem was published in 1915, during World War I) and perhaps about our time as well: (1) people are spiritually empty, and (2) contemporary life is unromantic and unheroic.

go.hrw.com

INTERNET
More About
T. S. Eliot
Keyword: LE5 11-5

SKILLS FOCUS

Literary Skills
Understand dramatic monologue.

Reading Skills
Identify main ideas.

T. S. Eliot **583**

Summary ⬆ *above grade level*

A question trembles on the lips of J. Alfred Prufrock, but he cannot bring himself to ask it. He recalls wandering through deserted streets. He worries about his appearance, knowing he is well dressed but painfully aware of his weak, thin arms and legs and his bald spot. He longs for the courage to assert himself and yearns for romantic love. But his fear of being ridiculed or misunderstood makes genuine communication with others impossible. In the end he recognizes that his shyness, lack of confidence, and fear of failure will always keep him from realizing his dreams.

Skills Starter

Build review skills. Discuss poets' and playwrights' use of dramatic monologue to reveal characters' innermost thoughts and feelings. The monologue often gives the audience previously unknown information. In a play the character delivering the monologue usually speaks while other characters onstage listen. In a poem it is up to the reader to imagine the audience.

A Literary Focus

❓ Dramatic monologue.
Dramatic monologues often have complex or multiple settings. What do you know about the setting so far? [It is evening; the mention of half-deserted streets indicates a town or city.]

Responses to Margin Questions

Line 3. It is compared to an anesthetized patient lying on an operating table.
Line 7. He wants to take his companion on a tour of run-down streets, hotels, and restaurants—the kinds of places he apparently frequents. He may be speaking to an acquaintance, the reader, or another side of himself.

THE LOVE SONG

OF J. ALFRED PRUFROCK

T. S. Eliot

T. S. Eliot (1930) by Powys Evans.

*S'io credessi che mia risposta fosse
a persona che mai tornasse al mondo,
questa fiamma staria senza più scosse.
Ma per ciò che giammai di questo fondo
non tornò vivo alcun, s'i'odo il vero,
senza tema d'infamia ti rispondo.*

Let us go then, you and I,
When the evening is spread out against the sky
Like a patient etherized upon a table;
Let us go, through certain half-deserted streets,
5   The muttering retreats
Of restless nights in one-night cheap hotels
And sawdust restaurants with oyster-shells:
Streets that follow like a tedious argument
Of insidious intent
10   To lead you to an overwhelming question . . .
Oh, do not ask, "What is it?"
Let us go and make our visit.

In the room the women come and go
Talking of Michelangelo.°

Epigraph. This quotation is from Dante's epic poem *The Divine Comedy* (1321). The speaker is Guido da Montefeltro, a man sent to Hell for dispensing evil advice. He speaks from a flame that quivers when he talks: "If I thought my answer were to one who ever could return to the world, this flame should shake no more; but since none ever did return alive from this depth, if what I hear be true, without fear of infamy I answer this" (*Inferno,* Canto 27, lines 61–66). Think of Prufrock as speaking from his own personal hell.

❓ 3. *What is the evening compared to?*

❓ 7. *Where does the speaker want to take his companion? Whom could he be talking to?*

14. Michelangelo: Michelangelo Buonarroti (1475–1564), a great artist of the Italian Renaissance.

Learners Having Difficulty
Modeling. To help students read this poem, model the skill of identifying main ideas and supporting details. Say, "One main idea seems to be that Prufrock feels empty inside. The first stanza is set in the evening on 'half-deserted streets'—a detail that supports this main idea."

Invite learners having difficulty to read

"The Love Song of J. Alfred Prufrock" in interactive format in *The Holt Reader* and to use the sidenotes as aids to understanding the selection.

English-Language Learners
For lessons designed for English-language learners and special education students, see *Holt Reading Solutions.*

Advanced Learners
Enrichment. There are many parallels between Dante's *Inferno* and "Prufrock." Like Dante, Prufrock wanders through a nightmarish landscape, though in his case it is constructed of his own fears. Have students read the section of the *Inferno* from which the epigraph is taken; ask them to note connections between Dante's and Eliot's poems.

15 The yellow fog that rubs its back upon the window-panes,
    The yellow smoke that rubs its muzzle on the window-panes,
    Licked its tongue into the corners of the evening,
    Lingered upon the pools that stand in drains,
    Let fall upon its back the soot that falls from chimneys,
20 Slipped by the terrace, made a sudden leap,
    And seeing that it was a soft October night,
    Curled once about the house, and fell asleep.

    And indeed there will be time
    For the yellow smoke that slides along the street
25 Rubbing its back upon the window-panes;
    There will be time, there will be time
    To prepare a face to meet the faces that you meet;
    There will be time to murder and create,
    And time for all the works and days of hands
30 That lift and drop a question on your plate;
    Time for you and time for me,
    And time yet for a hundred indecisions,
    And for a hundred visions and revisions,
    Before the taking of a toast and tea.

35 In the room the women come and go
    Talking of Michelangelo.

    And indeed there will be time
    To wonder, "Do I dare?" and, "Do I dare?"
    Time to turn back and descend the stair,
40 With a bald spot in the middle of my hair—
    (They will say: "How his hair is growing thin!")
    My morning coat, my collar mounting firmly to the chin,
    My necktie rich and modest, but asserted by a simple pin—
    (They will say: "But how his arms and legs are thin!")
45 Do I dare
    Disturb the universe?
    In a minute there is time
    For decisions and revisions which a minute will reverse.

    For I have known them all already, known them all—
50 Have known the evenings, mornings, afternoons,
    I have measured out my life with coffee spoons;
    I know the voices dying with a dying fall°
    Beneath the music from a farther room.
        So how should I presume?

B

? **22.** What details of this setting are you given?

C

? **27.** How would you paraphrase this line?

? **34.** What words are repeated in this stanza for poetic effect?

D

? **38.** What could he want to dare to do?

? **41.** Who are "they"?

? **42.** A morning coat is formal daytime dress for men. What does Prufrock look like? Is he young, middle-aged, or elderly?

? **51.** Has a life that is measured in coffee spoons been exciting or heroic?

52. dying fall: in music, notes that fade away.

T. S. Eliot **585**

DIRECT TEACHING

B Literary Focus

❷ Figures of speech: Metaphor. What is the fog compared to in this famous extended metaphor? [a cat] Why does Prufrock explore this metaphor at such length? [Possible responses: It suggests confusion and indecision; it hints at Prufrock's feelings of anxiety and uneasiness, which accompany him silently like a cat.]

C Literary Focus

❷ Repetition. What effect does the repetition of "there will be time" and "time" have? [It suggests both eternity and hesitation.]

D Reading Skills

❷ Finding the main idea. What are the main things you know about Prufrock so far? [Possible responses: He is insecure; he worries about what others think of him; he is timid and indecisive.]

Responses to Margin Questions

Line 22. The setting is a dirty, dreary street on a foggy evening.

Line 27. Possible response: to put on a mask or assume an attitude that will enable you to face other people.

Line 34. The words and phrases "There will be time," "time," "for a hundred," and "and" are repeated.

Line 38. Possible responses: He wishes he dared to speak honestly to others; he wishes he had the courage to talk to a particular person at the gathering.

Line 41. They are people whom Prufrock meets socially, especially women.

Line 42. He is dressed formally; he is balding and has thin arms and legs. He seems to be middle-aged.

Line 51. No, the image of the coffee spoons suggests the life of a cautious, fearful person.

CONTENT-AREA CONNECTIONS

Art: Collage

Small-group activity. Eliot's poem is intensely visual. Suggest that students keep a list of the images in the poem that help them visualize a scene. (The list might begin with the evening sky, the patient on the operating table, and the half-deserted streets.) After students read the poem, have them work in small groups to make a "Prufrock" collage.

Psychology: Self-Esteem

Paired activity. Discuss with students how people's opinions of themselves affect their actions. Ask students to describe Prufrock's opinion of himself and the way it has shaped his life. Then, have students work in pairs, writing a prose diary entry for Prufrock that shows how he feels about himself.

A Reading Skills

? Making judgments. Which poem strikes you as more purely imagist, "The Great Figure" or "The Red Wheelbarrow"? [Possible responses: "The Great Figure" is more purely imagist, because the speaker presents images entirely without comment; in contrast, by saying "so much depends" in the other poem, the poet adds a layer of meaning to the pure image. "The Red Wheelbarrow" is more purely imagist, because it describes objects in literal terms, whereas "The Great Figure" personifies the fire truck as "tense."]

VIEWING THE ART

The Figure 5 in Gold, by **Charles Demuth** (1883–1935), is his best-known work. The painting, which is based on Williams's poem, contains several direct references to Williams himself: the words *Bill* (at the top) and *Carlo*[s] (under the top bar of the largest 5) and the initials *W.C.W.* (bottom center).

Activity. Have students discuss how the raylike projections in the painting suggest a fire truck like the one in Williams's poem. [Possible response: The dark and light rays suggest speed and power or headlights cutting through the night.]

The Great Figure

William Carlos Williams

A
Among the rain
and lights
I saw the figure 5
in gold
5   on a red
fire truck
moving
tense
unheeded
10 to gong clangs
siren howls
and wheels rumbling
through the dark city.

The Figure 5 in Gold (1928) by Charles Henry Demuth. Oil on composition board (36″ × 29¾″).

The Metropolitan Museum of Art, Alfred Stieglitz Collection, 1949 (49.59.1). Photograph © 1986 The Metropolitan Museum of Art, New York.

DEVELOPING FLUENCY

Individual activity. Have students experiment with different ways of reading these poems aloud. For example, they might emphasize the adjectives *red, white,* and *glazed* in one reading of "The Red Wheelbarrow," and the prepositions *upon, with,* and *beside* in another reading.

When students read "The Great Figure" aloud, have them stress the end of each line and show through their reading why it makes sense to break the line there—for example, to emphasize the colors gold and red or the descriptive word *unheeded.* Then, have students recreate the sounds of the scene—especially the howling, clanging, and rumbling of the fire engine—in a second reading.

This Is Just to Say

William Carlos Williams

I have eaten
the plums
that were in
the icebox

B

5   and which
you were probably
saving
for breakfast

Forgive me
10   they were delicious
so sweet
and so cold

C

This Is Just to Say

INFORMATIONAL TEXT

When William Carlos Williams first began to write poems like this, hardly anybody took him seriously. His lines had no meter and no rhyme, no simile or metaphor, none of the familiar elements of poetry at all except for imagery and a kind of rhythm that was entirely personal. He did not even use punctuation! But gradually readers and critics of poetry began to see that even a little note left on the refrigerator door can be poetry and that the simplest expressions of everyday life have their own special phrasing and a kind of spontaneity that is apt to be missing from more formal attempts to make them sound "poetic."

Throwaway is a term that was often used in the 1960s for poetry written not to be published and preserved but, like facial tissue, to be used and then tossed away. Behind this idea was the belief that poetry ought to be considered not literature but an easy part of ordinary existence. Emily Dickinson had the same idea a hundred years earlier when she would enclose a poem with the gift of a pie she'd baked or with a jar of preserves she'd put up or when a birthday or a holiday called for the kind of sentiments we nowadays find mainly on greeting cards.

D

Most greeting-card verse is trite because the people who are hired to write it use the same old words and rhymes over and over again. But little messages of affection or gratitude don't *have* to be trite. Both Dickinson and Williams have shown us that when our feelings are expressed honestly, we are all poets.

William Carlos Williams   **595**

DIRECT TEACHING

B Literary Focus

? Imagery. The images in the previous poems are visual and (in "The Great Figure") auditory. To what senses do the images in this poem appeal? [Possible response: taste and touch.] **What words does the poet use to appeal to those senses?** [Possible responses: *plums; icebox; delicious; sweet; cold.*]

C Content-Area Connections

Art: Found Objects
The artists of Williams's time developed the concept of the *found object,* an ordinary item (a rock, a newspaper clipping, part of a machine) regarded as art. Found objects were often incorporated into artworks. Explain that this poem might itself have been a found object—an actual note of apology that Williams turned into poetry. Help students see the poem as an everyday object (like the wheelbarrow, chickens, and fire engine) that surprises the reader with its simple force and beauty.

Critical Comment

This feature discusses Williams's creation of "unpoetic" poetry and the reading public's gradual recognition that unrhymed, simple writings could be looked at as poems.

D Reading Informational Text

? Author's argument. Why does the writer mention Emily Dickinson's poetry? [to show that the idea of poetry as a simple expression of everyday life is not a new one]

DEVELOPING FLUENCY

Individual activity. Have students read "This Is Just to Say" aloud, showing the reaction of the person reading the note—perhaps irritation that the plums are gone or amusement at discovering that the note of apology is a poem. Then, have them read the poem the way the writer composing the note might read it, starting out by apologizing and then savoring the memory of the plums.

FAMILY/COMMUNITY ACTIVITY

Invite students to find their own poetry in the everyday. Have them look in such sources as newspapers, television and radio broadcasts, product labels, recipes, family photo albums, and casual notes. Ask students to invite other family members to join them in this hunt for "found" poetry. Have each student make a scrapbook of poems from his or her household.

Response and Analysis

Thinking Critically

1. Possible answers: Williams might be pointing to the importance of juxtaposition or of noticing the everyday in art and poetry. He might be saying that poetry, like art, captures moments when we feel especially alive—and "so much depends" on that feeling.

2. Possible answers: Like the wheelbarrow, chickens, and rain in "The Red Wheelbarrow," the fire engine and the dish of plums are everyday objects. The poet enables the reader to see them all in a new light.

3. Possible answer: Diagonal lines create a sense of movement in the painting, as does the figure 5, which seems to speed toward (or away from) the viewer. In the poem the reader seems to hear the gongs, sirens, and rumbling wheels.

4. *tense*

5. Possible answer: The colors red and gold create a feeling of excitement and energy. Darker colors would give the poem an ominous tone; pastel colors would weaken the effect.

6. It appeals primarily to taste, with the words *delicious* and *sweet*. The word *coldness* appeals to the sense of touch.

7. Possible answer: The speaker may be addressing a husband or wife—someone who lives with the speaker and knows him or her well. The imagined person reading the note might be charmed and amused by the apology or angered by the writer's thoughtlessness and attempt to charm his or her way out of the consequences of a selfish act.

Response and Analysis

The Red Wheelbarrow
The Great Figure
This Is Just to Say

Thinking Critically

1. Think about what Williams has in mind when he says, "so much depends upon a red wheel barrow." What might he be saying about poetry or art? Do you agree with him?

2. In "The Red Wheelbarrow," Williams focuses on an ordinary workday object. Are the subjects of "The Great Figure" and "This Is Just to Say" equally ordinary? Explain.

3. The painter Charles Henry Demuth (1883–1935) was so struck by the dynamic **imagery** in "The Great Figure" that he painted *The Figure 5 in Gold* (see page 594). What movement do you *see* in the painting? What do you *hear* in the poem itself?

INTERNET
Projects and Activities
Keyword: LE5 11-5

SKILLS FOCUS

Literary Skills
Analyze imagery.

Writing Skills
Write an imagist poem.

4. What one word is used **metaphorically** to describe the fire truck as if it were a person?

5. How would the feeling of "The Great Figure" change if the colors were different? Try it and see.

6. Which one of the five senses does the **imagery** in "This Is Just to Say" primarily appeal to?

7. Whom do you think the speaker of "This Is Just to Say" is addressing? What response do you imagine he or she will receive, and why?

WRITING

As Is

Write a brief imagist **poem** describing some subject from your everyday life. Use sensory images to convey the sight, smell, sound, taste, and feel of what you are describing. Try to capture your subject exactly as it is, without using it as a symbol or giving it any significance beyond what it simply is. You might open with one of Williams's opening lines. (The first line of "This Is Just to Say" has been used in hundreds of other poems, many of them parodies or mockery of Williams's humble subjects and simple free verse.)

Assessment

■ *Holt Assessment: Literature, Reading, and Vocabulary*

For a lesson reteaching poetic devices, see **Reteaching**, p. 1117A.

Marianne Moore
(1887–1972)

Marianne Moore is remembered by many people as the woman who wrote a poem in 1955 celebrating the only World Series the Brooklyn Dodgers ever won. Moore spent almost half her life in Brooklyn, where she became one of the most famous supporters of the local baseball team.

She was born in Kirkwood, a suburb of St. Louis, Missouri. After graduating from Bryn Mawr College, outside Philadelphia, Moore worked as a teacher and a librarian and later served as editor of *The Dial,* a magazine that encouraged young writers. She spent a good part of her life caring for her brother and mother. When her mother died, Moore lost her best friend—and her toughest critic.

All the while, Moore was writing and publishing her poems in the prestigious journals of the time. By 1921, she was living in New York City and had just published her first collection of poetry, *Poems.* Among the literary celebrities in New York, she was easily identifiable by her antique capes and other nineteenth-century touches in costume.

Behind the costume, however, Moore was a serious poet of meticulous detail, clarity, and humor. Mixing with the literati did not mean that she endorsed their tolerance in matters of personal behavior or their embrace of anything in the arts that seemed new or bold or simply amusing.

In fact, the only thing modern about Moore was her poetry. Like a bird building an intricate nest, she carefully pieced together her poems by combining her own writing with quotations and excerpts from social-science and natural-history journals. It has been said of her that no one was ever more indebted to other writers for material and, at the same time, more original. Her poetry reflects some of the influence of the imagists, and it also makes constant use of the concrete in the tradition of William Carlos Williams. Williams himself assessed his colleague's achievement when he said, "The magic name, Marianne Moore . . . I don't think there is a better poet writing in America today or one who touches so deftly a great range of our thought."

Like the visual artists of the twentieth century, Moore was able to join apparently unrelated elements of what she observed and bring them into a picture with a single focus. In some of her poems, Moore works like a painter whose nervous strokes and jagged edges capture a hundred details in one moment stopped in time. What she says in one famous poem, "The Steeple-Jack," might apply to readers approaching her work for the first time: "It is a privilege to see so much confusion."

Marianne Moore **597**

SKILLS FOCUS, pp. 597–600

Grade-Level Skills

■ **Literary Skills**
Analyze ways poets use imagery to convey meaning.

More About the Writer

Background. Marianne Moore's first book, *Poems* (1921), was not published until she was in her thirties. Three decades later, she won the Pulitzer Prize for her *Collected Poems* (1951). Despite the twists and turns in her poems, Moore expressed a fondness for writing "in a patterned arrangement, with rhymes . . . to secure an effect of flowing continuity." She loved zoos, and many of her poems include references to animals, especially exotic ones. Once she was invited by the Ford Motor Company to suggest a name for their newest car. Moore came up with "Utopian Turtletop." Ford decided to go with "Edsel" instead, a name that became notorious because of the car's historic failure on the market.

RESOURCES: READING

Planning
■ *One-Stop Planner* CD-ROM with ExamView Test Generator

Differentiating Instruction
■ *Supporting Instruction in Spanish*
■ *Audio CD Library, Selections and Summaries in Spanish*

Assessment
■ *Holt Assessment: Literature, Reading, and Vocabulary*
■ *One-Stop Planner* CD-ROM with ExamView Test Generator
■ *Holt Online Assessment*

Internet
■ go.hrw.com (Keyword: LE5 11-5)
■ *Elements of Literature Online*

Media
■ *Audio CD Library*
■ *Audio CD Library, Selections and Summaries in Spanish*

PRETEACHING

Summary ↔ *at grade level*

The speaker meditates on the purpose of poetry and on the characteristics of good poems. She begins by claiming that she, like many people, dislikes poetry, calling it "fiddle," or nonsense. But she then acknowledges that poetry has value because it conveys genuine human experience.

Selection Starter

Motivate. Write the following comments about poetry on the chalkboard. Have students choose the one they like best and discuss the reasons for their preferences.

1. "A poem . . . begins as a lump in the throat, a sense of wrong, a homesickness, a lovesickness."
   —Robert Frost

2. "A poem is a meteor."
   —Wallace Stevens

3. "Prose—words in their best order; poetry—the best words in their best order."
   —Samuel Taylor Coleridge

4. "Poetry must be as new as foam and as old as the rock."
   —Ralph Waldo Emerson

DIRECT TEACHING

A Reading Skills

? Making judgments. Do you think the speaker dislikes poetry? [Possible response: No; she wants to grab readers' attention.]

B Literary Focus

? Imagery. Moore presents a series of concrete images while exploring the abstract question of what poetry should be. How do these images illustrate a crucial point in Moore's thinking about poetry? [Possible response: They illustrate the speaker's belief that poetry should be useful and intelligible to the audience.]

Poetry

Make the Connection
Quickwrite

Without knowing why, many people complain, "I hate poetry! I never understand it." In this poem, Moore directly and humorously explains the usefulness and characteristics of good poetry. Moore takes on the role of the critic, daring to set standards for poets and readers alike.

Before you read, jot down your thoughts about poetry. Be honest: What do you like about poetry? What don't you like?

Literary Focus
Imagery and Meaning

The imagists believed that imagery alone could carry a poem's meaning. Their use of imagery was not merely to decorate, not merely to use a lot of sensory images to describe something. Instead, they wanted to find the exact image to describe the poet's perception in simple language.

SKILLS FOCUS

Literary Skills
Understand how imagery conveys meaning.

Background

Since the days of the Latin poet Horace (65–8 B.C.), poets have tried to explain what poetry is. Some poets have written poems about poetry, hoping to *show* rather than tell what the art of poetry is. Marianne Moore's "Poetry" and Archibald MacLeish's "Ars Poetica" (see the **Connection** on page 599) are in this tradition of poets writing about poetry.

Poetry

Marianne Moore

A I, too, dislike it: there are things that are important beyond all this fiddle.°
Reading it, however, with a perfect contempt for it, one discovers in
it after all, a place for the genuine.
Hands that can grasp, eyes
5   that can dilate, hair that can rise
        if it must, these things are important not because a

high-sounding interpretation can be put upon them but because they are
useful. When they become so derivative° as to become unintelligible,
the same thing may be said for all of us, that we
10   do not admire what
B   we cannot understand: the bat
        holding on upside down or in quest of something to

---

1. **fiddle** *n.:* slang for "nonsense."
8. **derivative** *adj.:* based on the work of others; unoriginal.

598   Collection 5   The Moderns: 1914–1939

DIFFERENTIATING INSTRUCTION

Learners Having Difficulty
Point out to students that to make sense of this poem, they must pay attention to the punctuation and continue past the ends of lines, and even of stanzas. Read the poem aloud once. Then, go through it again, helping students identify subjects and verbs in the sentences.

Advanced Learners
Enrichment. According to the biographical material on p. 597, Moore was influenced by the imagists but also focused on the concrete, as did William Carlos Williams. Like Williams, Moore studied biology in college. Have students analyze this poem in the light of these observations.

eat, elephants pushing, a wild horse taking a roll, a tireless wolf under
     a tree, the immovable critic twitching his skin like a horse that feels a flea, the base-
15   ball fan, the statistician—
          nor is it valid
               to discriminate against "business documents and

school-books"; all these phenomena are important. One must make a distinction
     however: when dragged into prominence by half poets, the result is not poetry,
20   nor till the poets among us can be
          "literalists of
               the imagination"—above
                    insolence and triviality and can present

for inspection, "imaginary gardens with real toads in them," shall we have
25   it. In the meantime, if you demand on the one hand,
     the raw material of poetry in
          all its rawness and
               that which is on the other hand
                    genuine, then you are interested in poetry.

CONNECTION / POEM

Archibald MacLeish (1892–1982), an American poet and Moore's contemporary, reflects on the means and ends of poetry in the following poem. Ars poetica is Latin for "the art of poetry."

Ars Poetica

Archibald MacLeish

A poem should be palpable and mute
As a globed fruit,

Dumb
As old medallions to the thumb,

5   Silent as the sleeve-worn stone
Of casement ledges where the moss has
     grown—

A poem should be wordless
As the flight of birds.

                    •

10   A poem should be motionless in time
As the moon climbs,

Leaving, as the moon releases
Twig by twig the night-entangled trees,

Leaving, as the moon behind the winter
     leaves,
Memory by memory the mind—

15   A poem should be motionless in time
As the moon climbs.

                    •

A poem should be equal to:
Not true.

For all the history of grief
20   An empty doorway and a maple leaf.

For love
The leaning grasses and two lights above
     the sea—

A poem should not mean
But be.

Marianne Moore   **599**

Comparing and Contrasting Texts

Ask the class to compare MacLeish's statement that a poem should be "palpable and mute" with Moore's call for "imaginary gardens with real toads in them." Have the class think of other images from the two poems that can be compared, and make cluster diagrams for the images on the chalkboard. Ask students whether the poems differ in their descriptions of what poetry is and what it does for the reader. Which theory do they prefer?

DIRECT TEACHING

C Content-Area Connections

Literature: Allusion to Tolstoy
Moore alludes to a comment in the diary of Leo Tolstoy, in which he writes that "poetry is everything with the exception of business documents and schoolbooks."

Connection

Summary *at grade level*

> The speaker maintains that a poem should be composed of images "equal to" the emotions and experiences found in life, and concludes by stating, "A poem should not mean / But be."

D Literary Focus

❓ Theme. What is the poet suggesting in these two lines? [Possible response: He is suggesting that a poem should be concrete and should not explain itself.]

E Literary Focus

❓ Paradox. A paradox is a statement that seems self-contradictory but actually reveals a truth. How is it possible for a poem to be "wordless"? [Possible response: A poem should be experienced not as an interesting selection of words but as a vivid emotion or perception.]

F Literary Focus

❓ Imagery. How might these two images be "equal to," or stand for, love? [Possible responses: The grasses' leaning position suggests people's need for companionship and their fulfillment of one another's needs; the two lights above the sea suggest companionship amid vast emptiness.]

Marianne Moore   599

Response and Analysis

Thinking Critically

1. Possible answer: She addresses readers who dislike poetry. Her tone is understanding and congenial. As she develops her ideas, her tone becomes increasingly serious and earnest.

2. Possible answer: She likes poems that surprise readers by evoking strong emotions and dealing with subjects they care about.

3. Possible answer: She dislikes poetry that is based on the ideas of others rather than on direct experience and that is therefore inaccessible to most people.

4. It should have imagination.

5. Possible answer: Moore means that images in poetry must be concretely described and rooted in experience.

6. MacLeish says that poetry should be "palpable and mute / As a globed fruit"; "Dumb / As old medallions"; "Silent as the sleeve-worn stone / Of casement ledges"; "wordless / As the flight of birds"; "motionless in time / As the moon climbs"; and "Leaving, as the moon releases . . . trees."

7. Possible answer: MacLeish means that although the poem is composed of words, the reader should think not of the words but of the images and experiences they evoke. The last lines suggest that rather than talking about an experience, a poem should actually re-create the experience for the reader.

8. Possible answer: The empty doorway suggests separation or absence. The single maple leaf suggests autumn, a time when natural things are dying.

Extending and Evaluating

9. Be sure that students have included paraphrases and quotations from the poems in their answers.

Response and Analysis

Thinking Critically

1. This poem suggests that someone has just made a remark to Moore. Whom do you think Moore is addressing in this poem? What **tone** does she take toward her audience?

2. According to lines 4–7, what kind of poetry does Moore like?

3. What kind of poetry, according to lines 8–11, does Moore dislike?

4. According to lines 20–25, what elements does Moore think "useful" poetry should have?

5. Moore says in lines 21–22 that poets must be "literalists of the imagination." What do you think she means? How is this idea related to her **image** of "imaginary gardens with real toads in them" (line 24)?

6. MacLeish's poem (see the **Connection** on page 599) also defines poetry, using a series of **similes**. List all the things MacLeish says poetry should be.

7. Some of MacLeish's **similes** are puzzling because they seem to be self-contradictory. For example, how can a poem, which is made of words, be "word-less"? How does MacLeish explain all his similes in the last two lines?

8. How do the two **images** in line 20 of MacLeish's poem suggest grief?

Extending and Evaluating

9. Did Moore and MacLeish give you any new ideas about what poetry should be? (Review your Quickwrite notes before you answer.) Cite details from each poem to illustrate your evaluation (which may be positive or negative). ✏️

go.hrw.com

INTERNET
Projects and Activities
Keyword: LE5 11-5

SKILLS FOCUS

Literary Skills
Analyze the way imagery conveys meaning.

Writing Skills
Write a poem with concrete images.

Listening and Speaking Skills
Deliver an oral interpretation of a poem.

WRITING

Poetry Is . . .

The most famous line in Moore's poem is the one that says that poetry should show us "imaginary gardens with real toads in them." Write your own **poem** about poetry. Use concrete images to illustrate what a poem is or can do. You may want to begin with the words "Poetry is . . ."

LISTENING AND SPEAKING

"Poetry" Reading

With a partner, take turns reading "Poetry" aloud. Pay attention to line and stanza breaks and to the placement of end punctuation. Note also the alternation of long and short lines. Decide where you would read quickly and where you would slow down for emphasis. Record or perform two or three readings for your class, and discuss with your audience the effects of the different readings.

Marianne Moore, a long-time Dodgers fan, tries out a boy's new baseball bat in New York City.

ASSESSING

Assessment

■ *Holt Assessment: Literature, Reading, and Vocabulary*

RETEACHING

For a lesson reteaching poetic devices, see **Reteaching,** p. 1117A.

E. E. Cummings
(1894–1962)

Self-Portrait by E. E. Cummings.

Edward Estlin (E. E.) Cummings was born in Cambridge, Massachusetts, the son of a Unitarian minister. After a childhood spent within walking distance of Harvard, he attended the university at a time when French symbolism and free verse were major new influences on American poetry. Like other poets, Cummings found guidelines in the imagist manifesto that allowed him to experiment and to break old rules.

If there is such a thing as rugged individualism in poetry, Cummings may be its prime example. All by himself he altered conventional English syntax and made typography and the division of words part of the shape and meaning of a poem. And—in the age of celebration of the common person—he went against the grain by championing the virtues of elitism. "So far as I am concerned," he wrote, "poetry and every other art was and is and forever will be strictly and distinctly a question of individuality. . . . Poetry is being, not doing. If you wish to follow, even at a distance, the poet's calling . . . you've got to come out of the measurable doing universe into the immeasurable house of being. . . . Nobody else can be alive for you; nor can you be alive for anybody else."

Graduating from college in the midst of World War I, Cummings became part of the conflict well before American soldiers appeared on European battlefields in 1917. He volunteered for an ambulance corps privately financed by Americans and staffed by young men. Crossing to Bordeaux on a French troop ship threatened by German U-boats, Cummings had hardly begun his duties when a French censor, intercepting one of his typographically odd letters, imprisoned him on suspicion of espionage. Released within three months, Cummings drew on the experience to produce his first important book of prose, *The Enormous Room* (1922).

After World War I, Cummings returned to France. He was one of the American literary expatriates who found in Paris the freedom and inspiration they felt were denied them by the restrictive Puritan climate of their own country. During this period, Cummings refined the eccentric shifts of syntax and typography that would become his trademark. In 1923, he published his first collection of verse, *Tulips and Chimneys*, which was followed by & (1925), *XLI Poems* (1925), and *is 5* (1926). His poetry is often marked by jubilant lyricism as he celebrates love, nature's beauty, and an almost Transcendentalist affirmation of the individual. He reserved his mischievous wit for the satire of the "unman," by which he meant the unthinking, unfeeling temperament of urban "humans."

Back in the United States, Cummings split his time between an apartment in Greenwich Village in New York City and a house in Silver Lake, New Hampshire. He died still believing that "when skies are hanged and oceans drowned, / the single secret will still be man."

SKILLS FOCUS, pp. 601–604

Grade-Level Skills

■ **Literary Skills**
Analyze ways poets use imagery, figures of speech, and sounds.

■ **Reading Skills**
Analyze syntax.

More About the Writer

Background. Cummings wrote his name *e. e. cummings* and had his name legally changed to be represented that way. Many critics thought the poet's unconventional use of typography to be arbitrary (as students may). In fact, Cummings's typographical quirks were not arbitrary but deliberately chosen, and they were extremely important to the poet.

PRETEACHING

Summary  *at grade level*

In "what if a much of a which of a wind" the speaker insists that in spite of every kind of earthly destruction, "the single secret will still be man." In "somewhere i have never travelled,gladly beyond," the speaker uses synesthesia (images that appeal to one sense but are expressed in terms of another), paradoxes, and similes to describe the effect his beloved has on him.

DIRECT TEACHING

Ⓐ Literary Focus

❓ **Style.** How would you describe the style of the poem's first line? What expectations does it set up for the poem as a whole? [Possible responses: The style is unconventional and hard to understand at first. The sounds of the words *much* and *which* create a sense of agitation, which is reinforced by the word *wind*. The first line creates the expectation that the poem will be challenging and that it will depend more on the sound of words than on their literal sense.]

Ⓑ Literary Focus

❓ **Style.** Cummings is noted for using verbs, adjectives, and adverbs as nouns. What examples can you find? [Possible responses: *much* (l. 1); *seem* (l. 5); *keen* (l. 9); *ago* (l. 12); *blind* (l. 13); *forever* (l. 19); *soon, never, twice* (l. 21); *isn't, was* (l. 22).]

Ⓒ Literary Focus

❓ **Paradox.** How do you explain the paradox in the third stanza, in which the universe is reduced to nothing, but "we" (humanity) live on? [Possible response: The meaning of human existence goes beyond the physical and does not depend on the presence of living people.]

Before You Read

what if a much of a which of a wind
somewhere i have never travelled,gladly beyond

Make the Connection

Have you ever been at a loss for words, unable to find the right way to express a deep feeling? Poets, too, search for ways of using language that will come close to conveying their complex feelings and thoughts. In a sense, therefore, a poem can be thought of as an attempt to put on paper what cannot quite be expressed in words. Think about what Cummings might be trying to say as you read the following poems.

Reading Skills
Untangling Syntax

In all languages, words are arranged in certain ways in order to make utterances that are easily understood. The way words are arranged in a sentence is called **syntax.** Writers, particularly poets, in their search for fresh ways to express experience, sometimes experiment with syntax. Cummings is known for his unconventional syntax and usage (his punctuation is unorthodox, he uses parts of speech interchangeably, his spacing is such that sometimes words bump into one another). Reading his poems can be challenging. You may have to begin your reading process by doing something very basic: Look for where Cummings begins and ends his sentences. Then, look for the subject and predicate of each sentence. Once you have done this, half of your work will have been done.

SKILLS FOCUS

Reading Skills Understand syntax.

what if a much of a which of a wind

E. E. Cummings

Ⓐ what if a much of a which of a wind
gives the truth to summer's lie;
bloodies with dizzying leaves the sun
and yanks immortal stars awry?°
5 Blow king to beggar and queen to seem
(blow friend to fiend:blow space to time)
Ⓑ —when skies are hanged and oceans drowned,
the single secret will still be man

what if a keen of a lean wind flays°
10 screaming hills with sleet and snow:
strangles valleys by ropes of thing
and stifles forests in white ago?
Blow hope to terror;blow seeing to blind
(blow pity to envy and soul to mind)
15 —whose hearts are mountains,roots are trees,

it's they shall cry hello to the spring
what if a dawn of a doom of a dream
bites this universe in two,
Ⓒ peels forever out of his grave
20 and sprinkles nowhere with me and you?
Blow soon to never and never to twice
(blow life to isn't:blow death to was)
—all nothing's only our hugest home;
the most who die,the more we live

---

4. **awry** (ə·rī′) *adv.*: out of place.
9. **flays** *v.*: here, whips; lashes.

DIFFERENTIATING INSTRUCTION

Learners Having Difficulty
Point out to students that in the first six lines of each stanza, Cummings sets up a scene of destruction and upheaval. Ask them to identify some of the images of turmoil and destruction. Then, ask them what message of hope is offered by the last two lines of each stanza.

English-Language Learners
Explain that Cummings is playing with language and that the sentences are not strictly logical. Advise them to enjoy the flow of the words and to try to get the gist of each poem rather than follow the syntax of each sentence.

Advanced Learners
Enrichment. Ask students to pay special attention to the way Cummings plays with language, particularly word usage and syntax, in both poems. For example, he uses the

"Miracles are to come"

INFORMATIONAL TEXT

The poems to come are for you and for me and are not for mostpeople
—it's no use trying to pretend that mostpeople and ourselves are alike. Mostpeople have less in common with ourselves than the squarerootofminusone. You and I are human beings;mostpeople are snobs. . . .

you and I are not snobs. We can never be born enough. We are human beings;for whom birth is a supremely welcome mystery,the mystery of growing:the mystery which happens only and whenever we are faithful to ourselves. You and I wear the dangerous looseness of doom and find it becoming. Life, for eternal us,is now;and now is much too busy being a little more than everything to seem anything,catastrophic included. . . .

Miracles are to come. With you I leave a remembrance of miracles:they are by somebody who can love and who shall be continually reborn,a human being;somebody who said to those near him,when his fingers would not hold a brush "tie it into my hand"—

—from *New Poems*

somewhere i have never travelled,gladly beyond

E. E. Cummings

somewhere i have never travelled,gladly beyond
any experience,your eyes have their silence:
in your most frail gesture are things which enclose me,
or which i cannot touch because they are too near

5   your slightest look easily will unclose me
though i have closed myself as fingers,
you open always petal by petal myself as Spring opens
(touching skilfully,mysteriously)her first rose

or if your wish be to close me,i and
10   my life will shut very beautifully,suddenly,
as when the heart of this flower imagines
the snow carefully everywhere descending;

nothing which we are to perceive in this world equals
the power of your intense fragility:whose texture
15   compels me with the colour of its countries,
rendering death and forever with each breathing

(i do not know what it is about you that closes
and opens;only something in me understands
the voice of your eyes is deeper than all roses)
20   nobody,not even the rain,has such small hands

The Kiss (Der Kuss) (1907–1908) by
Gustav Klimt.
Oesterreichische Galerie, Vienna, Austria. Courtesy
Erich Lessing/Art Resource, NY.

E. E. Cummings   **603**

Comparing and Contrasting Texts

adverb *ago* as a noun in "stifles forests in white ago." Discuss the images this phrase evokes, and ask students what they think it means. Then, have them work in pairs, with each student writing three or four sentences playing with language the way Cummings does. Have them exchange papers and interpret their partners' unconventional sentences.

In the Primary Source on p. 603, Cummings makes several statements about poetry and his audience while revealing his attitude toward life itself. Have students write a brief essay discussing whether these statements relate to the message of "what if a much of a which of a wind" or "somewhere i have never travelled,gladly beyond." Ask them to support their opinions with specific lines.

Response and Analysis

what if a much . . .

Thinking Critically

1. *Possible questions*—What if the earth is devastated by a massive hurricane or blizzard? What if a cataclysm destroys the universe? *Possible answers*—The mystery of human existence and consciousness will endure. Human beings will welcome the return of spring. The human spirit will survive.

2. He seems to be referring to hurricanes and blizzards of cataclysmic destructiveness, and to the annihilation of the universe.

3. Possible answer: Cummings is celebrating life by implying that the human spirit will endure.

4. The rhyme scheme is (roughly) *abcbddac*. Examples of internal rhyme include *will/still* and *keen/lean*.

5. Possible answer: The speaker's tone is hopeful, and suggests an instinctive faith.

somewhere i have never . . .

Thinking Critically

1. He uses similes to compare his love to spring and snow and to describe love opening him up and closing him down like a flower.

2. Possible answer: "Your delicacy is more powerful than anything else in the world. With each breath, you make me feel both death and eternal life."

3. in the line "the voice of your eyes is deeper than all roses"

4. In l. 3, "in your most frail gesture are things which enclose me" may mean that the lover's slightest gesture has the power to hold the speaker captive. In l. 14, "The power of your intense fragility" may refer to the spell exerted by the lover's delicacy.

Response and Analysis

what if a much . . .

Thinking Critically

1. Cummings opens each stanza with a question. What are the questions? What are the answers?

2. What are the three kinds of mass destruction that Cummings refers to in the first six lines of each stanza?

3. What do you think Cummings means by the last two lines? Is he celebrating life or death? Explain your response.

4. Identify the **rhyme scheme** of the poem. Where do you hear **internal rhyme**?

5. What **tone** do you hear in Cummings's poem—is the speaker cynical, despairing, solemn, hopeful, triumphant, or something else besides?

somewhere i have never . . .

Thinking Critically

1. In the first three stanzas, what **figures of speech** does Cummings use to talk about how he feels about his love and how she affects him?

2. The poem rises in intensity in the fourth stanza. **Paraphrase** this stanza, making clear what you think the speaker means by "death and forever."

3. In line 2, the phrase "your eyes have their silence" is an example of **synesthesia** (sin'əs·thē'zhə)—the juxtaposition of one sensory image with another that appeals to a different sense. Where in the last stanza does Cummings use synesthesia again?

4. A **paradox** is a statement that appears contradictory but actually reveals a kind of truth. Find two paradoxes in the poem, and explain what they mean.

SKILLS FOCUS

Reading Skills
Analyze syntax.

Writing Skills
Write a response to a poem. Write a descriptive paragraph.

5. In what way could the rain be said to have small hands? What is the speaker suggesting about his love by using this beautiful and mysterious **metaphor**?

Extending and Evaluating

6. Find examples in the poems of Cummings's unconventional **syntax**, or word order, and of words used in unusual ways. Do you think his linguistic inventions add to or detract from the effectiveness of the poems? Explain your evaluations.

WRITING

"for you and for me . . ."

In the comment called "Miracles are to come" (see the *Primary Source* on page 603), Cummings talks to you, the readers of his poems. Respond to Cummings in the form of a **letter** or **poem**.

Images in Prose

Imagery is not limited to poetry. Prose writers also use imagery to make a setting or a person or an event vivid to the reader. Think back on the imagist poems you have read. Does one of them suggest a topic for a **descriptive paragraph**—in prose? You might find a topic just by thinking about the topics of these poems: a journey, a garden, a farmyard, a fire truck, plums in the refrigerator, wind, a person you love. Find a topic, and describe it in a prose paragraph. Descriptive paragraphs can be organized spatially: Where are the items located in space (front, back, side, and so on)? You can also organize a descriptive paragraph by order of importance: What is the first important thing you see, what is the second? Give your paragraph a good title.

▶ **For help with this assignment, use "Writing a Descriptive Essay," pages 605–606.**

---

5. Possible answers: The sensation of raindrops striking the skin is like the touch of small hands. The speaker is commenting on the delicacy of the lover's touch.

Extending and Evaluating

6. Examples will vary. Cummings's unusual syntax and usage make the poems difficult, but some students may find them imaginative.

ASSESSING

Assessment

■ *Holt Assessment: Literature, Reading, and Vocabulary*

RETEACHING

For a lesson reteaching irony, tone, and author's style, see **Reteaching**, p. 1117A.

Writing a Descriptive Essay

The poets featured in this chapter were able to create vivid, unforgettable descriptions in just a few well-crafted lines. Like writing memorable poetry, describing a subject in an essay also requires the careful choice of details that add up to an overall impression. In this Mini-Workshop you'll write a **descriptive essay** that paints a vivid picture, helping your readers share an experience of a person, place, or thing that has been important to you.

Choose a Subject A compelling essay doesn't have to describe a famous person or place. An everyday subject can be fresh, interesting, and dramatic when you choose precise details and vivid, descriptive words. Choose a subject that meets the following criteria.

- **The subject is very familiar to you.** In other words, don't try to describe the Hoover Dam if you only rode over it in a car once. Instead, describe the small stream that flows through the woods near your school.

- **The subject holds some meaning for you.** No matter how many details you might come up with for a subject, if you don't care about it, your readers won't either.

- **The subject has some complexity.** Be sure you can say something fresh in your essay, either by choosing an unusual subject for your description or by choosing a subject with facets your readers might not have considered.

- **The subject is narrow.** Pick a subject that you can examine closely in a 1,500-word essay. If you choose a large subject—a city, for example—you may not be able to describe it adequately. Instead, choose a small part of a large subject and describe this part in detail, such as one block, building, or park within a city.

Note Details Observe your subject at length, and jot down notes about the following kinds of details.

- **concrete sensory details**—sights, sounds, smells, and textures

- **action details**—movements, gestures, or other specific actions related to the subject

- **details about changes,** including images that depend on specific circumstances (such as the time of day) and shifting vantage points of the subject (such as its appearance when viewed from a different angle)

  As you take notes, use **fresh, natural language** to describe the details you observe. For example, rather than saying, "The spider's web is

Writing Assignment
Write a descriptive essay about a person, place, or thing that is important to you.

SKILLS FOCUS

Writing Skills
Write a descriptive essay. Use sensory details.

PRETEACHING

Motivate. Have students recall lines of poetry that have stuck in their memories, and ask students what makes the lines so memorable. Ask students where else lively, precise imagery can be found. [music lyrics, travel brochures, eyewitness accounts]

DIRECT TEACHING

Choose a Subject
Suggest to students that choosing subjects that surprise them in some way will help them write descriptive essays that bring their subjects to life in a fresh manner for their readers. Writers who discover new things about their subject as they write will better capture their readers' attention with creative descriptions.

DIFFERENTIATING INSTRUCTION

Learners Having Difficulty
Students' difficulty in turning their descriptions into compelling essays might come from a lack of action, or "story," on which to base their descriptions. Encourage students to focus on a set of actions or a movement toward a certain goal in their descriptions. For example, a description as seemingly devoid of action as a description of one's backyard could be made more interesting for the reader if the narrator is struggling to rake up a sea of fallen leaves.

COLLECTION 5 RESOURCES: WRITING

Planning
- *One-Stop Planner* CD-ROM with ExamView Test Generator

Differentiating Instruction
- *Workshop Resources: Writing, Listening, and Speaking*
- *Family Involvement Activities in English and Spanish*
- *Supporting Instruction in Spanish*

Writing and Language
- *Workshop Resources: Writing, Listening, and Speaking*
- *Daily Language Activities*
- *Language Handbook Worksheets*

Assessment
- *Holt Assessment: Writing, Listening, and Speaking*

- *One-Stop Planner* CD-ROM with ExamView Test Generator
- *Holt Online Assessment*
- *Holt Online Essay Scoring*

Internet
- go.hrw.com (Keyword: LE5 11-5)
- *Elements of Literature Online*

Make an Impression

Students may have trouble choosing a single controlling impression about their subjects. Ask students to freewrite for five minutes on their emotional reactions to their subjects. Then, have students review their notes and throw out any elements that do not fit a general impression. Point out to students that they are left with a collection of reactions that need some shaping force. Ask students, "Is there one emotion that is stronger than any other? Can many of the emotions be organized under a broader, more general impression?" For example, if students felt fear, dizziness, happiness, an appreciation for beauty, and awe when looking at the Grand Canyon, they could probably organize their emotions under the controlling impression of awe.

Guided and Independent Practice

Guide students to think about what their audience will find most interesting about their descriptions by having students answer the following questions:

- What is unusual about your subject?
- How will your description surprise readers?
- What language can you use to bring out these elements of interest and surprise?

Students can then complete **Practice and Apply** independently.

---

difficult to see unless the sun hits it just right," you might say, "The spider's web is an invisible snare until a sunbeam catches the delicate fibers, making them gleam." The language you use to describe your details will set the **tone,** or attitude, for your essay.

Make an Impression Bringing your unique view of your subject to life is your **purpose** for writing your descriptive essay. To achieve this purpose, consider your **controlling impression**—the overall idea or feeling you want readers to get about your subject. Perhaps the most important thing about a beautiful downtown park is that it was a barren, dusty field before students helped with a landscaping project. A writer's controlling impression of this subject is the field's transformation for the better. The details and background information that the writer provides develop that impression.

As the **speaker** in your essay, it's your job to help readers, or your **audience,** see what *you* think makes the subject special. Even if several classmates describe the same subject, only your essay will share this unique perspective. Identify the controlling impression you want to create and choose the details for your essay, or the **form** your ideas will take. Then, write a statement of your controlling impression that prepares your audience for your ideas.

Select and Elaborate on Details To focus readers on a controlling impression of your subject, winnow the details down to the essentials. To decide which details to keep, answer these questions.

- Which details will help readers visualize the subject as you see it? Give readers the most important details so that they can imagine it through your eyes.

- Which details let readers know your feelings about your subject? Choose details that create the controlling impression you want—that your subject is forbidding or welcoming, pleasant or disgusting.

Delete any details that don't contribute to your controlling impression, and elaborate on those that do, clearly connecting each contributing detail to the statement of your controlling impression.

Organize Your Ideas Decide on the most effective arrangement of the details you will include. Most descriptions are arranged in **spatial order,** moving from left to right, top to bottom, front to back, or some other progression. However, because your description explains the subject's importance to you, you might instead arrange details in **order of importance,** moving from the least important detail to the most important detail or vice versa.

DO THIS →

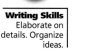

SKILLS FOCUS

Writing Skills
Elaborate on details. Organize ideas.

PRACTICE & APPLY Follow the preceding instructions to plan and write a descriptive essay about a person, place, or thing that is important to you. Then, share your finished description with your classmates.

Advanced Learners

Enrichment. Challenge students to use a combination of ways to organize their essays. They could use chronological order to set the scene for their descriptions, spatial order to give their readers an overview of the subject, and order of importance to focus the readers' attention on the details and to leave readers with a lasting final impression.

Modern American Fiction

Hemingway

Fitzgerald

Faulkner

A writer's problem does not change. He himself changes, but his problem remains the same. It is always how to write truly and, having found what is true, to project it in such a way that it becomes a part of the experience of the person who reads it.

—Ernest Hemingway

INTERNET

Collection Resources

Keyword: LE5 11-5

Americana (detail) (1931) by Charles Sheeler.
Oil on canvas (48″ × 36″).

The Metropolitan Museum of Art, Edith and Milton Lowenthal Collection, Bequest of Edith Abrahamson Lowenthal, 1991 (1992.24.8). Photograph © 2000–2002 The Metropolitan Museum of Art, New York.

607

VIEWING THE ART

Painter and photographer **Charles Sheeler** (1883–1965) was a versatile artist who attempted to establish a type of modernism that was uniquely American. He developed a style known as precisionism, characterized by flat planes and precise forms. Sheeler represented both the forms of modern machines and cities as well as preindustrial furniture. Sheeler admired the vernacular forms of Shaker furniture, and prized their simplicity. In *Americana,* he used an overhead angle from which he drew his home, which he had furnished with the simple American furnishings he admired.

Activity. Does this room seem lived in? Why or why not? [There are no people in the scene, but this is a space that is designed for living, with its furniture and backgammon game.]

THE QUOTATION

Ask a volunteer to read aloud the quotation by Ernest Hemingway. Ask students, "What does it mean to write truly?" [Possible responses: Writing truly means writing honestly. It means discovering the stories in your own experiences and writing frankly about them.] Then, ask students, "When does writing become a part of the experience of the person who reads it?" [Possible responses: Writing becomes a part of the experience of the person who reads it when the reader identifies with the characters, themes, or setting of a story; when the writer reveals some universal truth; or when the reader feels changed by what he or she has read.] Next, invite volunteers to share when they have felt particularly moved by a piece of writing. Have them discuss what made the writing memorable.

Grade-Level Skills

■ **Literary Skills**

Analyze the protagonist as an antihero.

■ **Reading Skills**

Read for details about a character.

Review Skills

■ **Literary Skills**

Analyze the way a work of literature relates to the themes and issues of its historical period. (Historical approach)

More About the Writer

Background. The heroes in Hemingway's short stories are often wounded both physically and psychologically. They carry with them the memory of violence. Facing a hypocritical world, they seek to find some code by which to live. When Hemingway was recuperating from his knee injury, he wrote his family from a Milan hospital: "Wounds don't matter. I wouldn't mind being wounded again so much because I know just what it is like . . . and it does give you an awfully satisfactory feeling to be wounded." During his lifetime, Hemingway was repeatedly injured—in car crashes, airplane crashes, shooting accidents, and fires. Like many of the heroes in his novels, he too was a wounded man.

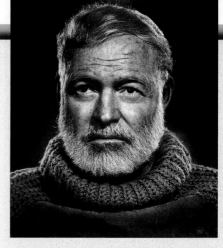

Ernest Hemingway
(1899–1961)

Few American authors have offered as powerful a definition of the twentieth-century hero as Ernest Hemingway has. Hemingway's fiction presents a strict code of contemporary heroism. His vision centers on disillusionment with the conventions of an optimistic, patriotic society and a belief that the essence of life is violence, from which there is no refuge. As Hemingway saw it, the only victory that can be won from life lies in a graceful stoicism, a willingness to accept gratefully life's few moments of pleasure.

Although this ideal of rugged machismo may now seem superficial, it powerfully affected generations of American readers. Moreover, Hemingway launched a new style of writing so forceful in its simplicity that it became a measure of excellence around the world.

Hemingway's life, like F. Scott Fitzgerald's, bore a notable resemblance to the lives of his fictional characters. He was born in the Chicago suburb of Oak Park on July 21, 1899. His father, a doctor, initiated him early into a love for the Michigan woods and the hunting and fishing that could be found there. Growing up, Hemingway boxed and played football devotedly, but he also wrote poetry, short stories, and a column for the school newspaper. Graduating from high school in 1917, just as the United States entered World War I, he yearned to enlist, but he was rejected by the army because of a boxing injury to his eye. He landed a job as a reporter for *The Kansas City Star.* Hemingway reached the war a year later as an ambulance driver for the Red Cross in Italy, but after six weeks he was wounded in the knee, seriously enough to require a dozen operations. This wound was a central episode in both Hemingway's real life and his creative one. During his long convalescence in an Italian hospital, he fell in love with a nurse who became the model for the heroine of his novel *A Farewell to Arms.*

After the armistice in 1918, Hemingway returned to Michigan. His experience of coming to terms with the war is reflected in his story "Big Two-Hearted River." In the story, Nick Adams, a war veteran, camps and fishes alone in the woods, escaping from the world in order to heal himself from both a physical and a psychological shattering.

An American in Paris

In 1921, newly married and with a commission as a roving reporter for *The Toronto Star,* Hemingway set off for Paris. It was the era of the American expatriates, when writers and painters crowded the cafes of the Left Bank of the Seine. Here Hemingway worked at the craft of fiction and met other important writers, among them F. Scott Fitzgerald, James Joyce, and Ezra Pound. But most important, he met the American writer Gertrude Stein (1874–1946). She read all his work and advised him to prune his descriptions and to "concentrate." Hemingway took her advice and spoke fervently of writing "the truest sentence that you know" and of arriving through straight presentation of unvarnished fact at a "true, simple declarative sentence."

Hemingway's first book, *Three Stories and Ten Poems* (1923), along with *The Torrents of Spring* (1926), a parody of his friend Sherwood Anderson's work, drew scant notice. Then, late in 1926, he published *The Sun Also Rises*, a novel based on his life in Paris but transplanted to Pamplona, the Spanish town famous for its annual running of the bulls through the streets. The novel brought Hemingway widespread critical attention. Gertrude Stein's remark, "You are all a lost generation," was the novel's epigraph, and the book did reveal the postwar epoch to itself. Many readers of Hemingway's age embraced it as a portrait of their shattered lives.

Hemingway, around thirty years old and married for the second time, went on to write an even more powerful and successful novel, *A Farewell to Arms* (1929). This is the beautifully told story of Frederic Henry, a wounded ambulance driver. Disillusioned with the war, he falls in love with Catherine Barkley, an English nurse, and flees with her to Switzerland, where she dies in childbirth. Frederic's farewell to the dying Catherine is one of the great love scenes in fiction.

Author and Adventurer

After the major success of *A Farewell to Arms,* Hemingway established himself as a worldwide adventurer, as though a heroic style was as important to his life as to his fiction.

During the early 1930s, Hemingway brought out two nonfiction books that revealed his fascination with bullfighting and big-game hunting—*Death in the Afternoon* (1932) and *Green Hills of Africa* (1935). In 1940, just as the literary world was writing Hemingway off as a has-been novelist, he presented another triumph, *For Whom the Bell Tolls.*

The outbreak of World War II drew Hemingway back into uniform. Although officially a correspondent, he gathered around himself a small army of adventurers. During one battle, Hemingway's band was sixty miles in front of the Americans' advancing line. When the Allies at last reached Paris in 1944, they found that Hemingway had already "liberated" the bar at the Ritz Hotel.

By 1952, Hemingway's celebrated literary accomplishments and his continuous pursuit of excitement and danger had made him as famous as any film star. In spite of his flamboyant exploits, he produced yet another widely acclaimed novel in that year, *The Old Man and the Sea,* which won the 1953 Pulitzer Prize. It tells of an old Cuban fisherman who hooks a giant marlin far out at sea and battles the fish for two days and nights. Although he finally succeeds in subduing the great fish and lashing it to the side of his boat, sharks tear at the carcass until the man is left with only the marlin's skeleton. The tale has been interpreted as Hemingway's metaphor for life: a vision of the hero weighed down by the years but still able to use his skill to taunt fate and so win a kind of victory from it.

In 1954, Hemingway won the Nobel Prize in literature. He now divided his time between his house in Ketchum, Idaho, and his restless travels all over the world: to Cuba, China, Venice, Spain, and Africa. His health deteriorated, and periods of elation alternated with episodes of severe depression. After a visit to the Mayo Clinic for treatment, he returned to Idaho. On the morning of July 2, 1961, he rose early, and with two charges of a double-barreled shotgun, he killed himself.

"He put life back on the page," wrote the critic Alfred Kazin, "made us see, feel, and taste the gift of life. . . . To read Hemingway was always to feel more alive."

For Independent Reading

Try these famous novels by Hemingway:

- *A Farewell to Arms*
- *For Whom the Bell Tolls*
- *The Old Man and the Sea*

More About the Writer

Background. Hemingway's faith in what he called "the truest sentence" helped produce his distinctive style: "Sometimes when I was starting a new story and I could not get it going, I would sit in front of the fire and squeeze the peel of the little oranges into the edge of the flame and watch the sputter of the blue that they made. I would stand and look out over the roofs of Paris and think, 'Do not worry. You have always written before and you will write now. All you have to do is write one true sentence. Write the truest sentence that you know.' So finally I would write one true sentence, and then go on from there. It was easy then because there was always one true sentence that I knew or had seen or had heard someone say."

For Independent Reading

- *A Farewell to Arms* blends masterful description, sculptured dialogue, and powerful action, especially in the scenes of the disastrous retreat from Caporetto. It is a gripping story about the consequences of love in wartime.
- *For Whom the Bell Tolls* is set during the Spanish civil war of the 1930s. This story also explores the meaning of heroism and the necessity of self-sacrifice.
- *The Old Man and the Sea,* one of Hemingway's most popular novels, is a story about endurance, courage, and the human struggle against nature.

CONTENT-AREA CONNECTIONS

History: Hemingway on War

Hemingway never forgot his combat experience. In 1935, as he watched Hitler prepare to launch World War II, he wrote, "They wrote in the old days that it is sweet and fitting to die for one's country. But in modern war there is nothing sweet or fitting in your dying. You will die like a dog for no good reason. . . . In a modern war there is no victory. The Allies won the war but the regiments that marched in triumph were not the men who fought the war. The men who fought the war were dead. More than seven million of them were dead and it is the murder of over seven million more that [Hitler and Mussolini] look forward hysterically to today."

Summary ⟷ *at grade level*

It is the summer of 1919 in a small Oklahoma town. Hemingway's protagonist, Harold Krebs, has just come home from World War I. He finds that he is too late for a hero's welcome and that he cannot speak honestly about his war experiences. He makes little effort to readjust to life with his parents and sisters and soon drifts into a passive routine of sleeping late, reading, and playing pool. He notices several pretty young women in town, but he can't make the effort to get to know them. The story's climax takes place when his worried mother confronts him about his future, and he decides to leave home for good.

Selection Starter

Build background. In order to understand Krebs's state of mind, students should know that the soldiers in France spent their days and nights in mud-filled trenches reeking of urine, poisonous gas, wet sandbags, and decomposing bodies. They fought rain, cold, lice, and rats, as well as diseases such as trench mouth, gangrene, and dysentery. The worst horror, however, was the constant threat of death from the enemy trenches. At any moment, a shell could be lobbed across no-man's land, the barren stretch between the two trenches.

Before You Read

Soldier's Home

Make the Connection

World War I was greeted as the "war to end all wars," and songs like "Over There" celebrated the heroism of hundreds of thousands of American soldiers who were shipped off to fight in the trenches of Europe. But advances in weaponry made the Great War (a name it held until World War II) devastating, both physically and psychologically. Returning soldiers sometimes couldn't readjust to life back home, which seemed to offer little they could relate to or believe in. As you can imagine, some became disillusioned, cynical, isolated, and overwhelmed by hopelessness. They became the most lost of Gertrude Stein's lost generation.

Literary Focus
Protagonist: The Antihero

In literature the **protagonist** is the main actor in the plot, the one who initiates the story's action. The protagonist need not be a hero. In fact, the antihero is a type of protagonist who appears in much modern literature. The **antihero** contrasts with the hero archetype, or model, which appears over and over again in the traditional literature of many cultures. The traditional hero responds to challenges with courage and self-sacrifice. The modern antihero gives in to disillusionment, hopelessness, and inaction.

INTERNET

Vocabulary
Practice
•
Cross-Curricular
Connection
•
More About
Ernest Hemingway

Keyword: LE5 11-5

SKILLS FOCUS

Literary Skills
Understand the protagonist and the antihero archetype.

Reading Skills
Identify details about a character.

> The **protagonist** is the central character of a work of literature. Heroes are protagonists, but not all protagonists are heroes. Some may be antiheroes.
>
> *For more on Protagonist, see the Handbook of Literary and Historical Terms.*

Reading Skills
Reading for Details

As you read the story, try to piece together a **character profile** of the returned soldier Harold Krebs. Take notes on Krebs's feelings, attitudes, and views on the war, his return home, his family, other people, his hometown, and his future.

Background

Soldiers who returned home from World War I were often described as shellshocked —suffering from a mental and emotional condition of confusion, exhaustion, anxiety, and depression. In the past the condition— now termed *post-traumatic stress disorder*— was not well understood, and friends and relatives often found themselves at a loss. They could not understand why some soldiers seemed unable to plunge back into civilian life.

Vocabulary Development

hysteria (hi·ster′ē·ə) *n.:* uncontrolled excitement.

atrocity (ə·träs′ə·tē) *n.* used as *adj.:* horrible; brutal.

apocryphal (ə·päk′rə·fəl) *adj.:* of questionable authority; false.

alliances (ə·lī′əns·iz) *n. pl.:* close associations entered into for mutual benefit.

intrigue (in′trēg′) *n.:* scheming; plotting.

Previewing Vocabulary

Have students read the Vocabulary words and definitions on p. 610. Then, have them work in pairs. The first student says a word, and the second student has to find one synonym and one antonym for it. Have partners alternate roles until they have worked through all the words. Then, have each pair complete the following matching item exercise.

1. hysteria [c]
2. atrocity [a]
3. apocryphal [b]
4. intrigue [d]
5. alliances [e]

a. savage
b. false
c. frenzied excitement
d. plotting
e. partnerships

(Pages 611–613) Photographs of Ernest Hemingway in Italy and France during World War I (1918).

Soldier's Home Ⓐ

Ernest Hemingway

Krebs went to the war from a Methodist college in Kansas. There is a picture which shows him among his fraternity brothers, all of them wearing exactly the same height and style collar. He enlisted in the Marines in 1917 and did not return to the United States until the second division returned from the Rhine[1] in the summer of 1919.

There is a picture which shows him on the Rhine with two German girls and another corporal. Krebs and the corporal look too big for their uniforms. The German girls are not beautiful. The Rhine does not show in the picture.

By the time Krebs returned to his home town in Oklahoma the greeting of heroes was over.

He came back much too late. The men from the town who had been drafted had all been welcomed elaborately on their return. There had been a great deal of hysteria. Now the reaction had set in. People seemed to think it was rather ridiculous for Krebs to be getting back so late, years after the war was over.

At first Krebs, who had been at Belleau Wood, Soissons, the Champagne, St. Mihiel and in the Argonne[2] did not want to talk about the war at all. Later he felt the need to talk but no one

---

1. **Rhine:** river that flows through Germany toward the North Sea.

2. **Belleau** (be·lō′) **Wood . . . Argonne** (är′gän′): sites of World War I battles that demonstrated the Allies' superior strength against the Germans.

Vocabulary
hysteria (hi·ster′ē·ə) *n.:* uncontrolled excitement.

DIRECT TEACHING

Ⓐ Reading Skills

❓ Interpreting. What different meanings does the title suggest? [Possible responses: It could mean "soldier is home from the war," "the home of the soldier," or "rest home for old soldiers."] Have students continue to ask themselves about the meaning of the title as they read.

Ⓑ Reading Skills

❓ Reading for details. What do the details in this sentence imply about Krebs's war experience? [Possible response: The war was not a romantic adventure.]

Ⓒ Reading Skills

Making inferences. Point out the word *years*. Ask students if they know when the war ended. [The war ended in November 1918, but Krebs did not return until the summer of 1919.] Ask students what this discrepancy in the town's treatment of soldiers allows them to infer about the town's mood. [Possible response: People feel they have done their duty to the veterans. They now want to forget about the war.]

DIFFERENTIATING INSTRUCTION

English-Language Learners
Make sure students understand the military terms in the opening paragraphs. Ask a volunteer to explain the difference between *enlisting* and *being drafted*. Be sure students know that the Marines are a part of the U.S. armed forces and that a division is a large unit of soldiers with its own command.

A Literary Focus

? Protagonists: The antihero.
In Hemingway's work, lies often have a corrupting influence on the protagonist and can poison every aspect of an experience. How do lies cause—or at least contribute to—a change in Krebs's attitude toward his war experiences? [Lying about the war makes it even more distasteful. Eventually he prefers to not talk about it at all rather than lie about it.]

B Literary Focus

? Protagonists: The antihero.
What "one thing" might have made Krebs feel "cool and clear"? [He might have killed other men in war.] What is the "something else" that he might have done? How does he feel now about his choice? [Possible response: He might have run or refused to fight. At the time, he was proud of his choice; now he is not so sure.]

C Reading Skills

? Reading for details. What do these details tell you about Krebs's relationship with his sisters and his parents? [Possible responses: He cannot communicate with them. His mother loves him, but she doesn't really want to hear details of the war. His father is detached, and his sisters have an idealized, unrealistic view of him.]

---

wanted to hear about it. His town had heard too many atrocity stories to be thrilled by actualities. Krebs found that to be listened to at all he had to lie, and after he had done this twice he, too, had a reaction against the war and against talking about it. A distaste for everything that had happened to him in the war set in because of the lies he had told. All of the times that had been able to make him feel cool and clear inside himself when he thought of them; the times so long back when he had done the one thing, the only thing for a man to do, easily and naturally, when he might have done something else, now lost their cool, valuable quality and then were lost themselves.

His lies were quite unimportant lies and consisted in attributing to himself things other men had seen, done or heard of, and stating as facts certain apocryphal incidents familiar to all soldiers. Even his lies were not sensational at the pool room. His acquaintances, who had heard detailed accounts of German women found chained to machine guns in the Argonne forest and who could not comprehend, or were barred by their patriotism from interest in, any German machine gunners who were not chained, were not thrilled by his stories.

Krebs acquired the nausea in regard to experience that is the result of untruth or exaggeration, and when he occasionally met another man who had really been a soldier and they talked a few minutes in the dressing room at a dance he fell into the easy pose of the old soldier among other soldiers: that he had been badly, sickeningly frightened all the time. In this way he lost everything.

During this time, it was late summer, he was sleeping late in bed, getting up to walk down town to the library to get a book, eating lunch at home, reading on the front porch until he became bored and then walking down through the town to spend the hottest hours of the day in the cool dark of the pool room. He loved to play pool.

In the evening he practised on his clarinet, strolled down town, read and went to bed. He was still a hero to his two young sisters. His

mother would have given him breakfast in bed if he had wanted it. She often came in when he was in bed and asked him to tell her about the war, but her attention always wandered. His father was non-committal.

Before Krebs went away to the war he had never been allowed to drive the family motor car. His father was in the real estate business and always wanted the car to be at his command when he required it to take clients out into the country to show them a piece of farm property. The car always stood outside the First National Bank building where his father had an office on

Vocabulary
atrocity (ə·träs′ə·tē) *n.* used as *adj.*: horrible; brutal.
apocryphal (ə·päk′rə·fəl) *adj.*: of questionable authority; false.

CONTENT-AREA CONNECTIONS

History: World War I
Help students understand why World War I was considered such a tragedy that it would "end all wars." Military commanders sent boys armed with bayonets into the face of automatic machine-gun fire, poisonous gas, and armored tanks. As a result of this colossal mismatch between old-fashioned military tactics and modern technology, casualties were greater than in any previous war. Russia lost 1,700,000 men; France, 1,358,000; and Great Britain close to 1 million. In many cases, soldiers were literally blown to bits by grenades or they choked to death after being exposed to chemical weapons.

Small-group activity. Interested students might compare casualty statistics from World War I with statistics from other wars and report their findings to the class.

stockings and flat shoes. He liked their bobbed hair and the way they walked.

When he was in town their appeal to him was not very strong. He did not like them when he saw them in the Greek's ice cream parlor. He did not want them themselves really. They were too complicated. There was something else. Vaguely he wanted a girl but he did not want to have to work to get her. He would have liked to have a girl but he did not want to have to spend a long time getting her. He did not want to get into the intrigue and the politics. He did not want to have to do any courting. He did not want to tell any more lies. It wasn't worth it.

He did not want any consequences. He did not want any consequences ever again. He wanted to live along without consequences. Besides he did not really need a girl. The army had taught him that. It was all right to pose as though you had to have a girl. Nearly everybody did that. But it wasn't true. You did not need a girl. That was the funny thing. First a fellow boasted how girls mean nothing to him, that he never thought of them, that they could not touch him. Then a fellow boasted that he could not get along without girls, that he had to have them all the time, that he could not go to sleep without them.

That was all a lie. It was all a lie both ways. You did not need a girl unless you thought about them. He learned that in the army. Then sooner or later you always got one. When you were really ripe for a girl you always got one. You did not have to think about it. Sooner or later it would come. He had learned that in the army.

Now he would have liked a girl if she had come to him and not wanted to talk. But here at home it was all too complicated. He knew he could never get through it all again. It was not worth the trouble. That was the thing about French girls and German girls. There was not all this talking. You couldn't talk much and you did not need to talk. It was simple and you were

the second floor. Now, after the war, it was still the same car.

Nothing was changed in the town except that the young girls had grown up. But they lived in such a complicated world of already defined alliances and shifting feuds that Krebs did not feel the energy or the courage to break into it. He liked to look at them, though. There were so many good-looking young girls. Most of them had their hair cut short. When he went away only little girls wore their hair like that or girls that were fast. They all wore sweaters and shirt waists with round Dutch collars. It was a pattern. He liked to look at them from the front porch as they walked on the other side of the street. He liked to watch them walking under the shade of the trees. He liked the round Dutch collars above their sweaters. He liked their silk

---

Vocabulary

alliances (ə·li′əns·iz) *n. pl.:* close associations entered into for mutual benefit.
intrigue (in′trēg′) *n.:* scheming; plotting.

Ernest Hemingway   **613**

Ernest Hemingway   **613**

Music: George M. Cohan
The colorful life of songwriter and performer George M. Cohan (1878–1942)—composer of "Over There" and "I'm a Yankee Doodle Dandy"—has been the subject of a 1942 movie, a Broadway musical, and many books. Cohan became associated with patriotic music in childhood, partly because his father recorded his birthday as July 4 (it was July 3).

Whole-class activity. Have students listen to "Over There" and contrast Krebs's experiences and postwar feelings with the impression of war conveyed in this rousing, positive song. What could the song suggest about the way people at home wanted to think about the war? What does the song suggest about the feelings of Americans before World War I?

? **Reading for details.** What does this exchange with his mother reveal about Krebs's relationship with his parents? [Possible response: His mother hopes that taking the car out will give Krebs an increased sense of responsibility and may help him to focus on the future. Krebs's questioning of his mother suggests that he believes his father views him as irresponsible. He doubts the honesty and good intentions of even his parents.]

A CLOSER LOOK

This feature describes the flapper fashions, wild excesses, new freedoms, and cultural crazes that dominated the Roaring Twenties.

B **Reading Informational Text**

Evaluating the social influences. Ask students to consider whether Krebs's behavior may be, in part, a reaction to the frivolity and materialism of the postwar era. [Possible response: Because the behavior and look of the women has changed since Krebs was at war, he may feel more isolated from the girls he once knew.]

---

friends. He thought about France and then he began to think about Germany. On the whole he had liked Germany better. He did not want to leave Germany. He did not want to come home. Still, he had come home. He sat on the front porch.

He liked the girls that were walking along the other side of the street. He liked the look of them much better than the French girls or the German girls. But the world they were in was not the world he was in. He would like to have one of them. But it was not worth it. They were such a nice pattern. He liked the pattern. It was exciting. But he would not go through all the talking. He did not want one badly enough. He liked to look at them all, though. It was not worth it. Not now when things were getting good again.

He sat there on the porch reading a book on the war. It was a history and he was reading about all the engagements he had been in. It was the most interesting reading he had ever

done. He wished there were more maps. He looked forward with a good feeling to reading all the really good histories when they would come out with good detail maps. Now he was really learning about the war. He had been a good soldier. That made a difference.

One morning after he had been home about a month his mother came into his bedroom and sat on the bed. She smoothed her apron.

"I had a talk with your father last night, Harold," she said, "and he is willing for you to take the car out in the evenings."

"Yeah?" said Krebs, who was not fully awake. "Take the car out? Yeah?"

"Yes. Your father has felt for some time that you should be able to take the car out in the evenings whenever you wished but we only talked it over last night."

"I'll bet you made him," Krebs said.

"No. It was your father's suggestion that we talk the matter over."

A CLOSER LOOK: SOCIAL INFLUENCES

The Decade That Roared

INFORMATIONAL TEXT

Harold Krebs finds his hometown much the same as he left it before the war, except for new styles in women's hair and clothing. He especially notices girls' short, bobbed hair—a style that had marked a girl as fast only a few years earlier, when he shipped out to the trenches of France.

The flap over flappers. Krebs was right on target. As the slick, sophisticated ads of the era show, nothing symbolized the decade after World War I so well as the flapper—a liberated young woman who cropped her hair into a cap-like shape, wore half the amount of clothing of her Victorian-era counterpart, and boldly wore rouge and lipstick. The flapper abandoned the confines of the corset and opted instead for loose, long-waisted dresses that ended at or above the knee. She showed off her legs in the new silk or rayon stockings that were affordable at every income level. And she kicked, shim-

mied, and swayed in a wild, new dance called the Charleston.

An era of excess. Tired of war and disillusioned with political and social causes, city dwellers and even small-town residents yearned for fun and excitement in the Roaring Twenties. Millions of Americans purchased automobiles and took to the road on touring vacations. Consumerism grew by leaps and bounds, fueled by abundant advertising and easy credit plans. Popular entertainment filled people's leisure time: Commercial radio and the movies changed American life by forming a national mass culture. People devoured the sensational stories of the day—vivid reports of scandals, crimes, freak disasters, and sports exploits. Young and old alike reveled in learning details of the private lives of movie stars like Rudolph Valentino, writers like Edna St. Vincent Millay (page 127), sports figures like Babe Ruth and the American Indian athlete Jim Thorpe, and celebrities like the pilot Charles Lindbergh.

SKILLS REVIEW

Analyzing cause and effect. Review cause and effect with students. They should remember that a cause answers the question "Why did something happen?" and that an effect answers the question "What happened?" A single cause can have any number of effects, and an effect may have multiple causes.

Activity. Have students read through the story and list main events and their causes. For example, one important effect of Krebs's delayed return home is that he does not receive a big welcome. Be sure students speculate on the deeper causes of Krebs's behavior. What could his family do to change his state of mind? After students have read the story, have them predict the effect of Krebs's decision to leave home. Have them consider the reactions of Mr. Krebs, Mrs. Krebs, and Helen.

"Yeah. I'll bet you made him," Krebs sat up in bed.

"Will you come down to breakfast, Harold?" his mother said.

"As soon as I get my clothes on," Krebs said.

His mother went out of the room and he could hear her frying something downstairs while he washed, shaved and dressed to go down into the dining-room for breakfast. While he was eating breakfast his sister brought in the mail.

"Well, Hare," she said. "You old sleepy-head. What do you ever get up for?"

Krebs looked at her. He liked her. She was his best sister.

"Have you got the paper?" he asked.

She handed him *The Kansas City Star* and he shucked off its brown wrapper and opened it to the sporting page. He folded *The Star* open and propped it against the water pitcher with his cereal dish to steady it, so he could read while he ate.

"Harold," his mother stood in the kitchen doorway, "Harold, please don't muss up the paper. Your father can't read his *Star* if it's been mussed."

"I won't muss it," Krebs said.

His sister sat down at the table and watched him while he read.

"We're playing indoor over at school this afternoon," she said. "I'm going to pitch."

"Good," said Krebs. "How's the old wing?"[3]

"I can pitch better than lots of the boys. I tell them all you taught me. The other girls aren't much good."

"Yeah?" said Krebs.

"I tell them all you're my beau.[4] Aren't you my beau, Hare?"

"You bet."

---

3. **wing** *n.*: arm.
4. **beau** (bō) *n.*: boyfriend.

Charleston endurance contest (1926).

Crazes spread throughout the country—manias for the Chinese game of mahjong, six-day bicycle races, dance marathons, and even flagpole sitting. Jazz, one of the great African American contributions to popular culture, provided the exciting soundtrack to the era.

The young rebels. Women and men alike, more aware of modernist thought and the psychoanalytic theories of Sigmund Freud, called for new social freedoms. Young people rebelled against the tight moral codes and even the good manners of the prewar years. They scoffed at the prohibition on alcohol by inventing the private cocktail party. With the new availability of motorcars, people roared off to dances in places where no one knew them, where they could feel free of their inhibitions. Couples danced together closer than ever before, tangoing and fox-trotting cheek to cheek to the sound of the saxophone.

The twenties' emphasis on youth and openness is recognizably modern. At the time many Americans were shocked and outraged by what they saw as the deterioration of culture and values. The 1920s were a rowdy, roisterous time—a decade that roared.

Ernest Hemingway **615**

A Literary Focus

❓ **Protagonists: The antihero.** What does this conversation reveal about Harold's mood? [Possible responses: His short answers reveal that Harold does not want to talk or that he is not paying attention to his sister.] What is antiheroic about Harold's reply "Maybe"? [Possible response: It embodies his lack of commitment.]

B Reading Skills

❓ **Reading for details.** What does this exchange reveal about Krebs's relationship with his mother? [Possible responses: She does not really want to know what his problems are, but wants him to think about the future. She places her faith in traditional religion, which makes Krebs feel alienated from her.]

C Literary Focus

❓ **Protagonists: The antihero.** What does the reference to the Civil War add to the character profile of Krebs? [Possible response: It shows that Krebs is not the first in his family to experience the horrors of war; it shows the Krebs's experience is universal to those who have fought in war.]

D Literary Focus

❓ **Protagonists: The antihero.** Why is the mention of Charley Simmons important to the profile of Harold's character? [Possible response: Simmons is important because he serves as a contrast or foil for Harold—Simmons has a job, has a fiancée, and is "settling down." Although readers are not told anything about his private life, Simmons represents a normalcy that Krebs cannot relate to.]

A "Couldn't your brother really be your beau just because he's your brother?"

"I don't know."

"Sure you know. Couldn't you be my beau, Hare, if I was old enough and if you wanted to?"

"Sure. You're my girl now."

"Am I really your girl?"

"Sure."

"Do you love me?"

"Uh, huh."

"Will you love me always?"

"Sure."

"Will you come over and watch me play indoor?"

"Maybe."

"Aw, Hare, you don't love me. If you loved me, you'd want to come over and watch me play indoor."

Krebs's mother came into the dining-room from the kitchen. She carried a plate with two fried eggs and some crisp bacon on it and a plate of buckwheat cakes.

"You run along, Helen," she said. "I want to talk to Harold."

She put the eggs and bacon down in front of him and brought in a jug of maple syrup for the buckwheat cakes. Then she sat down across the table from Krebs.

B "I wish you'd put down the paper a minute, Harold," she said.

Krebs took down the paper and folded it.

"Have you decided what you are going to do yet, Harold?" his mother said, taking off her glasses.

"No," said Krebs.

"Don't you think it's about time?" His mother did not say this in a mean way. She seemed worried.

"I hadn't thought about it," Krebs said.

"God has some work for every one to do," his mother said. "There can be no idle hands in His Kingdom."

"I'm not in His Kingdom," Krebs said.

"We are all of us in His Kingdom."

Krebs felt embarrassed and resentful as always.

"I've worried about you so much, Harold," his mother went on. "I know the temptations you must have been exposed to. I know how weak men are. I know what your own dear grandfather, my own father, told us about the Civil War and I have prayed for you. I pray for you all day long, Harold."

C Krebs looked at the bacon fat hardening on his plate.

"Your father is worried, too," his mother went on. "He thinks you have lost your ambition, that you haven't got a definite aim in life. Charley Simmons, who is just your age, has a good job and is going to be married. The boys are all settling down; they're all determined to get somewhere; you can see that boys like Charley Simmons are on their way to being really a credit to the community."

D Krebs said nothing.

"Don't look that way, Harold," his mother said. "You know we love you and I want to tell you for your own good how matters stand. Your father does not want to hamper your freedom. He thinks you should be allowed to drive the car. If you want to take some of the nice girls out riding with you, we are only too pleased. We want you to enjoy yourself. But you are going to have to settle down to work, Harold. Your father doesn't care what you start in at. All work is honorable as he says. But you've got to make a start at something. He asked me to speak to you this morning and then you can stop in and see him at his office."

"Is that all?" Krebs said.

"Yes. Don't you love your mother, dear boy?"

"No," Krebs said.

His mother looked at him across the table. Her eyes were shiny. She started crying.

"I don't love anybody," Krebs said.

It wasn't any good. He couldn't tell her, he couldn't make her see it. It was silly to have said it. He had only hurt her. He went over and took hold of her arm. She was crying with her head in her hands.

"I didn't mean it," he said. "I was just angry at something. I didn't mean I didn't love you."

His mother went on crying. Krebs put his arm on her shoulder.

"Can't you believe me, mother?"

READING MINI-LESSON

Developing Word-Attack Skills

Write the selection word *corporal* on the chalkboard. Point out that the written word *corporal* has three syllables, but it can be pronounced as if there were just two—/kôr′prəl/. Explain that *corporal* is an example of a word with an elided syllable. Instead of pronouncing all three syllables, people might leave out the second vowel sound and slur the second and third syllables together.

Write these words from the selection on the chalkboard. Have volunteers read the words aloud and decide if any syllables are elided in their pronunciations of the words. Elided syllables are underlined.

history

naturally

interesting

evening

Help students make the generalization that

East Wind over Weehawken (1934) by Edward Hopper. Oil on canvas (34″ × 50¼″).

His mother shook her head.

"Please, please, mother. Please believe me."

"All right," his mother said chokily. She looked up at him. "I believe you, Harold."

Krebs kissed her hair. She put her face up to him.

"I'm your mother," she said. "I held you next to my heart when you were a tiny baby."

Krebs felt sick and vaguely nauseated.

"I know, Mummy," he said. "I'll try and be a good boy for you."

"Would you kneel and pray with me, Harold?" his mother asked.

They knelt down beside the dining-room table and Krebs's mother prayed.

"Now, you pray, Harold," she said.

"I can't," Krebs said.

"Try, Harold."

"I can't."

"Do you want me to pray for you?"

"Yes."

So his mother prayed for him and then they stood up and Krebs kissed his mother and went out of the house. He had tried so to keep his life from being complicated. Still, none of it had touched him. He had felt sorry for his mother and she had made him lie. He would go to Kansas City and get a job and she would feel all right about it. There would be one more scene maybe before he got away. He would not go down to his father's office. He would miss that one. He wanted his life to go smoothly. It had just gotten going that way. Well, that was all over now, anyway. He would go over to the schoolyard and watch Helen play indoor baseball. ■

E

Ernest Hemingway   617

Ernest Hemingway   617

the vowel sounds in unaccented second syllables might be omitted in pronunciation and the consonant sounds incorporated into the next syllable.

Activity. Display these word pairs. Have volunteers compare the pronunciations of the two words and tell which word is more likely to have an elided syllable. Answers are underlined.

1. <u>desperate</u>   disparate
2. <u>general</u>   generate
3. <u>elaborately</u>   elaboration
4. diffident   <u>different</u>
5. <u>mystery</u>   mystical
6. familial   <u>family</u>

DIRECT TEACHING

VIEWING THE ART

Edward Hopper (1882–1967) was the quintessential American realist painter of the twentieth century. His images of solitary watchers in lonely Victorian houses, empty theaters, and hotel rooms symbolize modern alienation for many people. Weehawken, pictured here, is a town in the Palisades of New Jersey; it's just across the Hudson River from New York City.

Activity. Compare this painting to what you know about Krebs's hometown. Do you think this is what it looks like? Why or why not? [Possible responses: Yes, the homes seem very comfortable and old-fashioned, and many have front porches. The absence of people suggests Krebs's alienation.]

E **Reading Skills**

❓ **Reading for details.** How does the title of the story take on special meaning at the end of this sentence? [Possible response: To Harold, his home has become merely a house. The associations of warmth and safety in the title are now gone and replaced by an impersonal word that, like Krebs himself, houses no emotion.]

GUIDED PRACTICE

Monitoring students' progress. Guide the class in answering these questions.

True-False

1. Krebs returns from the war in the summer of 1919. [T]
2. Krebs does not enjoy reading about the engagements he had been in. [F]
3. Krebs's father gives him permission to drive the car. [T]
4. Krebs takes part in community life. [F]

Ernest Hemingway   617

Primary Source

Hemingway offers observations on the craft of writing and the loneliness of literary life. He says a good writer must not worry about his popularity or public stature but "face eternity" each day. He describes the difficulty of innovating in the shadow of the great writers of the past, and he says that writers should write, not speak.

DIRECT TEACHING

A Reading Informational Text

❓ Building background knowledge. Hemingway refers to "great writers who did not receive the prize." Since the Nobel Prize was instituted in 1901, writers who were never considered include some of the giants of world literature, including Leo Tolstoy, Anton Chekhov, Mark Twain, Joseph Conrad, Ezra Pound, Marcel Proust, James Joyce, D. H. Lawrence, Robert Frost, and Jorge Luis Borges. Why would a writer be denied the Nobel Prize? [Possible response: A writer might be denied because of a lack of adequate translations, controversial political beliefs, and personal preferences of the Nobel Prize committee.]

B Reading Informational Text

❓ Recognizing philosophical assumptions. What philosophical belief does Hemingway reveal when he says that each day a writer "must face eternity"? [Possible response: He believes that the opportunities for writing are endless, but writing well is also endlessly challenging.]

C Reading Informational Text

❓ Protagonists: The antihero. How is Hemingway like the antihero of one of his stories? [Possible responses: He is alone; he dislikes organizations. He succeeds only sometimes and must live with failure.]

Nobel Prize Acceptance Speech, 1954

Having no facility for speech making and no command of oratory nor any domination of rhetoric, I wish to thank the administrators of the generosity of Alfred Nobel for this prize.

A   No writer who knows the great writers who did not receive the prize can accept it other than with humility. There is no need to list these writers. Everyone here may make his own list according to his knowledge and his conscience.

It would be impossible for me to ask the ambassador of my country to read a speech in which a writer said all of the things which are in his heart. Things may not be immediately discernible in what a man writes, and in this sometimes he is fortunate; but eventually they are quite clear and by these and the degree of alchemy[1] that he possesses he will endure or be forgotten.

Writing, at its best, is a lonely life. Organizations for writers palliate[2] the writer's loneliness, but I doubt if they improve his writing. He grows in public stature as he sheds his loneliness, and often his work deteriorates.
B For he does his work alone, and if he is a good enough writer he must face eternity, or the lack of it, each day.

For a true writer each book should be a new beginning where he tries again for something that is beyond attainment. He should always try for something that has never been

Ernest Hemingway (left) receiving the medal for the Nobel Prize in literature (1954).

done or that others have tried and failed. Then sometimes, with great luck, he will succeed.
C How simple the writing of literature would be if it were only necessary to write in another way what has been well written. It is because we have had such great writers in the past that a writer is driven far out past where he can go, out to where no one can help him.

I have spoken too long for a writer. A writer should write what he has to say and not speak it. Again I thank you.

1. **alchemy** *n.:* magical power to transform the ordinary into the extraordinary. Alchemy was a branch of medieval science, one aim of which was to change common metals such as lead into gold.
2. **palliate** (pal′ē·āt′) *v.:* ease; lessen.

Comparing and Contrasting Texts

In order to compare Hemingway's battlelike vision of a writer's life with his vision of a soldier's experience, have students replace the word *writer* with the word *soldier* throughout the Nobel Prize speech. Then, have them identify statements or attitudes in the speech with which Harold Krebs would agree. Krebs, for example, would probably agree with the following statements:

- A soldier cannot express "all of the things which are in his heart."
- A soldier's life is "lonely."
- A soldier must "face eternity" every day.
- A soldier needs "great luck" in order to survive, let alone succeed.
- A soldier often feels "driven far out past where he can go."

Response and Analysis

Reading Check

1. Describe the way Krebs spends his days.
2. What is Krebs's reaction to reading a history of the battles he fought in?
3. What makes Krebs decide to leave home?

Thinking Critically

4. By the time Krebs returned, his hometown had quit "the greeting of heroes" and "the reaction had set in." What is this reaction? How does it affect Krebs?
5. What does Krebs mean by wanting "to live along without consequences"? Why might he feel that way?
6. What does Krebs's statement "You did not need a girl unless you thought about them" reveal about how he adapted to the hardships of war? How might such an adjustment affect his life at home?
7. Describe the **conflicts** revealed in the conversation between Mrs. Krebs and Harold at the end of the story. What losses on Harold's part does the talk reveal?
8. How would you state the **theme** of "Soldier's Home"—what does the story reveal to you about the way war can affect a young soldier?
9. How is Krebs an example of an **antihero**? How does he compare with the young **protagonists** of today's books and movies?
10. Ernest Hemingway himself was viewed as a member of the lost generation, scarred by the horrors of World War I. What details in his Nobel Prize acceptance speech (see the **Primary Source** on page 618) reflect the attitudes of a modern antihero?

WRITING

Krebs in Analysis

Write a **character profile** of Krebs, using the notes you took as you read the story. Be sure to support your analysis of Krebs with details from the story.

The Tip of the Iceberg

Ernest Hemingway once remarked of his writing style, "I always try to write on the principle of the iceberg. There is seven-eighths of it underwater for every part that shows." In a brief **essay,** explain what you think he means, and use examples from "Soldier's Home" to explain the "iceberg principle." Be sure to answer the question: What parts of "Soldier's Home" are underwater?

The Decade That . . .

On pages 614–615 is a description of the Roaring Twenties. Using this essay as a model, write a **description** of a recent decade that you know fairly well. Be sure to describe the following aspects of life in your decade: fashions; gender issues; popular entertainment; social and philosophical attitudes; and crazes, or fads.

INTERNET

Projects and Activities

Keyword: LE5 11-5

SKILLS FOCUS

Literary Skills
Analyze the protagonist and the antihero archetype.

Reading Skills
Identify details about a character.

Writing Skills
Write a character profile. Write an essay explaining an author's comment. Write a description of a historical period.

Vocabulary Skills
Demonstrate word knowledge.

Vocabulary Development

What If?

In a small group, discuss the possible outcomes of these scenarios:

1. What if hysteria spread through a crowd of fans at a rock concert?
2. What if an atrocity charge against the military were covered up?
3. What if an employer discovered that the work history on a résumé was apocryphal?
4. What if the United States were to pull out of all of its military alliances?
5. How could an ambitious person use intrigue to get ahead?

Ernest Hemingway   **619**

Response and Analysis

Thinking Critically

4. The reaction is a desire to forget the war. Krebs lies to hold the interest of people, but his lies become distasteful to him.
5. Having seen the terrible consequences of war, Krebs simply wants to live without incident, intimacy, or responsibility.
6. Krebs's strategy of adapting to hardships by not thinking about them (learned during the war) now isolates him from his family.
7. Mrs. Krebs wants Harold to settle down but Harold wants to put off making adult decisions. Harold has lost his faith, his ability to love, and his desire to participate fully in life.
8. Possible theme: War disillusions young people, alienating them from the very values they fought to protect.
9. Possible answer: Krebs is an antihero because he is disillusioned, passive, and defeated by life. He may remind students of Holden Caulfield in *The Catcher in the Rye.*
10. Hemingway's views of the writer reflect the attitudes of the lost generation in the emphasis on separation from the community.

Vocabulary Development

Sample Answer

1. The crowd may become angry and violent; people may rush the concert area, trampling others in their way.

Reading Check

1. He sleeps late, walks to the library, eats lunch, reads, plays pool, practices the clarinet, and takes walks.
2. He is proud of having been a good soldier; reading about the battles makes him feel that he accomplished something.
3. He decides to leave after the painful talk with his mother in which he tells her that he does not love her and that he cannot pray. He does not want to live with his parents and bring them grief.

Grammar Link

Practice

1. *Subject*—Most. *Verb*—are.
2. *Subject*—Harold Krebs. *Verb*—returns.
3. *Subjects*—father, mother. *Verb*—tries.
4. *Subject*—crowd. *Verb*—has.

ASSESSING

Assessment

- *Holt Assessment: Literature, Reading, and Vocabulary*

Grammar Link

Avoiding Subject-Verb Agreement Problems: Making Things Match

One rule of grammar is that the subject and the verb in a sentence have to agree in number. Here are some situations in which it's not easy to tell whether the subject is singular or plural:

The subject has more than one part. If two or more subjects are joined by *and,* the verb is usually plural. If two singular subjects are joined by *or* or *nor,* the verb is singular. If both are plural, the verb is plural. But, if one subject is singular and the other is plural, the verb agrees with the physically closer subject.

PLURAL	Harold's <u>father</u> *and* <u>mother</u> **are** worried.
SINGULAR	His <u>father</u> *or* his <u>mother</u> **needs** to talk to him.
PLURAL	Neither Harold *nor* his <u>parents</u> **want** to talk about the war.
SINGULAR	Neither his <u>parents</u> *nor* his <u>sister</u> **understands** him.

The subject is indefinite. Pronouns that refer to unspecified people or things are called **indefinite pronouns.** Most such pronouns are singular (*anybody, anyone, each, either, everybody, everyone, everything, neither, no one, somebody, someone*); some are plural (*both, many, several*); and a few can be either singular or plural, depending on how they're used (*all, any, more, most, none, some*).

SOMETIMES SINGULAR	All work **is** honorable, according to Harold's <u>father</u>.
SOMETIMES PLURAL	All the other soldiers **return** to a hero's <u>welcome</u>.

The subject is a group. Nouns that name a group (like *audience, class, crowd, couple*) are called **collective nouns.** If the group refers to a unit, use a singular verb. If the group refers to its members as individuals, use a plural.

SINGULAR	Harold's <u>family</u> **is** not helping him with his trauma.
PLURAL	His family **are** the last people he would go to for help.

SKILLS FOCUS

Grammar Skills
Revise errors in subject-verb agreement.

Apply to Your Writing

Re-read a current writing assignment, and correct any sentences with subject-verb-agreement problems.

▶ **For more help, see Agreement of Subject and Verb, 2a–i, in the Language Handbook.**

PRACTICE

In each sentence, circle the subject, and choose the correct verb from the underlined pair.

1. Most of the heroes in Hemingway's fiction (is/are) wounded—physically, psychologically, or both.

2. Harold Krebs, who is the hero of one of Hemingway's stories, (returns/return) from World War I to his hometown in Oklahoma.

3. Neither his father nor his mother really (tries/try) to talk with Harold about his experiences during the war.

4. The crowd that he spends time with (has/have) heard many sensational war stories.

Note: *None* takes a singular verb if it refers to an amount (*none of it*) and a plural verb if it refers to individuals (*none of them*).

None of the water **is** left.

None of the dancers **are** here.

DIFFERENTIATING INSTRUCTION

Learners Having Difficulty

Write the following sentences on the chalkboard. Have students choose the correct verb form in each sentence. Have students explain why they made their choices—why the subjects and verbs agree.

1. Krebs's division return/returns to America from the Rhine. [returns; collective noun]

2. Neither Harold's family nor his friends share/shares his disillusion. [share; closer subject]

3. All the townsfolk seem/seems alien to him. [seem; collective noun]

4. Among all the girls in the town, none want/wants to date him. [wants; singular indefinite pronoun]

5. Because of his painful past, neither his present nor his future look/looks bright. [looks; singular compound subjects joined by *nor*]

F. Scott Fitzgerald
(1896–1940)

If ever there was a writer whose life and fiction were one, it was F. Scott Fitzgerald. Fitzgerald—handsome, charming, and uncommonly gifted—was not only part of the crazy, wonderful, irresponsible era of the 1920s; he helped to name it the Jazz Age. He made a literary legend of it and, with his wife Zelda, lived it out in all of its excesses. He also almost certainly died of it.

Early Failures—And a Smash Hit

Fitzgerald was born in 1896 in St. Paul, Minnesota, the son of a father with claims to an aristocratic Maryland family. Scott was named for an ancestor, Francis Scott Key, the composer of "The Star-Spangled Banner." His mother was the daughter of a rich Irish immigrant. The young Scott was a spoiled boy, a failure at schoolwork and—to his own great disappointment—at sports. But he was a success at daydreaming and, while still in his teens, at writing stories and plays.

At Princeton University, which he entered in 1913, he wrote one of the Triangle Club musical shows, contributed to a literary magazine, and befriended the writers Edmund Wilson and John Peale Bishop. When the United States entered World War I, in 1917, Fitzgerald left college for officers' training school, yearning for heroic adventure on the battlefields of France. He was never sent overseas, but in camp he began a novel, *The Romantic Egoist,* which was twice turned down by the publishing company Scribner's.

While he was stationed at Camp Sheridan in Alabama, romance of a different sort overtook him. He fell deeply in love with Zelda Sayre, a high-spirited and gorgeous woman whose escapades had scandalized her hometown of Montgomery. Like Scott, Zelda hungered for new experiences. She was sure of her appeal and felt it was bound to bring her a full measure of luxury and gaiety. Although Scott courted her persistently, he had not nearly enough money to offer her the kind of marriage she wanted, and at first she turned him down.

Now out of the army, Fitzgerald took a low-paying job he hated; he sent his novel, rewritten and retitled *This Side of Paradise,* off to Scribner's for the third time. In 1919, the company agreed to publish it.

"I was an empty bucket," he said of the experience, "so mentally blunted by the summer's writing that I'd taken a job repairing car roofs at the Northern Pacific shops. Then the postman rang, and that day I quit work and ran along the streets, stopping automobiles to tell friends and acquaintances about it—my novel *This Side of Paradise* was accepted for publication. That week the postman rang and rang, and I paid off my terrible small debts, bought a suit, and woke up every morning with a world of ineffable toploftiness and promise."

When it was published, in 1920, *This Side of Paradise* was a sensation. The old, prewar world with its Victorian code of behavior had been dumped in favor of a great, gaudy spree of new freedoms. Girls bobbed their hair and shortened their skirts while boys filled their flasks with bootleg gin. To the wail of

SKILLS FOCUS, pp. 621–642

Grade-Level Skills

- **Reading Skills**
Draw inferences about characters.

Review Skills

- **Literary Skills**
Analyze influences on characters (such as motivation) and the way those influences affect the plot.

More About the Writer

Background. Fitzgerald rarely addressed his ideas or gave advice about his writing. However, his fiction offers some insights into his thoughts. In *The Last Tycoon,* he writes that "Writers aren't people exactly. Or if they're any good, they're a whole lot of people trying so hard to be one person." In "The Crack-Up," Fitzgerald complains, "When the first-rate author wants an exquisite heroine or a lovely morning, he finds that all the superlatives have been worn shoddy by his inferiors. It should be a rule that bad writers must start with plain heroines and ordinary mornings, and, if they are able, work up to something better."

RESOURCES: READING

Planning
- *One-Stop Planner* CD-ROM with ExamView Test Generator

Differentiating Instruction
- *Holt Adapted Reader*
- *Supporting Instruction in Spanish*
- *Audio CD Library, Selections and Summaries in Spanish*

Vocabulary
- *Vocabulary Development*

Grammar and Language
- *Daily Language Activities*

Assessment
- *Holt Assessment: Literature, Reading, and Vocabulary*
- *One-Stop Planner* CD-ROM with ExamView Test Generator

- *Holt Online Assessment*

Internet
- go.hrw.com (Keyword: LE5 11-5)
- *Elements of Literature Online*

Media
- *Audio CD Library*
- *Audio CD Library, Selections and Summaries in Spanish*
- *Fine Art Transparencies*

For Independent Reading

Most students will find the length and style of *The Great Gatsby* manageable. They may also identify with the narrator, Nick Carraway, who provides a straightforward and often sympathetic glimpse into the mysterious world of his wealthy neighbor, Jay Gatsby. The drama Carraway observes—that of Gatsby's unrequited love and ultimate demise—will also captivate the imaginations of young readers.

---

saxophones, couples danced the Charleston across the nation's dance floors. In Fitzgerald's novel the Jazz Age had found its definition.

Taking Aim at the American Dream

Zelda married Scott in April of that year. The newlyweds moved to New York and became the center of a round of parties while Scott turned out scores of stories. In the first years of the decade, he published two collections of stories and a second novel. After a stay in France, the Fitzgeralds returned to St. Paul, where their only child, a daughter named Frances, was born.

Scott announced to Maxwell Perkins, his editor at Scribner's, that he was going to write "something new—something extraordinary and beautiful and simple and intricately patterned." He fulfilled that ambition in *The Great Gatsby,* his nearly flawless masterpiece, which was published in 1925. It tells the story of James Gatz, a poor boy from the Middle West who dreams of success and elegance and finds their incarnation in a Louisville girl named Daisy Fay. When Gatz returns from the war, he learns that she has become Daisy Buchanan, married to a rich Chicagoan and leading a careless, sumptuous life on Long Island. The hero, now a successful bootlegger known as Jay Gatsby, hopes to win Daisy from what he believes is a loveless, unhappy marriage. The story ends with Gatsby's death, but we can see that his dreams and his feelings are admirable. The Buchanans, on the other hand, are insulated from life's possibilities by their wealth and self-indulgence.

The central triumph of *The Great Gatsby* is its revelation of the rich in all their seductive luxury and heedlessness, accompanied by an implicit condemnation of their way of life. In a remarkably concise work, Fitzgerald probed deeply the ambiguities of the American dream.

An Epitaph for the Jazz Age

The Great Gatsby won some critical praise, but it was a financial disappointment. Fitzgerald had to work even harder to keep up with the high cost of his and Zelda's international lifestyle. He turned out more potboiling short stories and went to Hollywood to write movie scripts. In 1930, the tenth year of their marriage, Zelda suffered a mental breakdown and spent the rest of her life in and out of asylums. Hers was a search for both sanity and identity. She aspired to be a dancer and a writer and in 1932 produced her own novel, *Save Me the Waltz.* This was her thinly disguised account of her troubled marriage.

Scott's novel *Tender Is the Night,* published in 1934, was his rebuttal of Zelda's novel. Its hero, Dick Diver, is the protector and healer of the mad heroine, Nicole. However, the stock market crash of 1929 had put an end to Fitzgerald's era, and readers had lost interest in the problems of expatriates like Dick Diver. Still, the book displays Fitzgerald's hard-won experience of life, the commitment to early dreams, the self-destructiveness of charm, and a whole generation's craving for endless youth and irresponsibility. In its despair, *Tender Is the Night* is an epitaph for the Jazz Age.

It was Fitzgerald's epitaph as well. After its publication he struggled with mounting debts, failing health, drinking, and depression. When he could, he continued to do serious work. Through his love affair with Sheilah Graham, a British journalist, he grew interested in the work of the Hollywood producer Irving Thalberg and began to write a novel about him. He was at work on this novel, *The Last Tycoon,* in 1940 when he died of heart failure. *The Last Tycoon* was compiled and edited by his friend Edmund Wilson and was published to wide critical praise after Fitzgerald's death.

For Independent Reading

Fitzgerald's American classic, *The Great Gatsby,* is available in many editions.

Literary Criticism

Critic's Commentary: Dexter Green and Jay Gatsby

Fitzgerald published "Winter Dreams" in 1922, three years before his masterpiece, *The Great Gatsby.* Critic Rose Adrienne Gallo points out that Fitzgerald saw "Winter Dreams" as "a sort of first draft of the *Gatsby* idea." While the two works share the same theme—"the pursuit of romantic illusions at the bitter price of inevitable disenchantment"—they are different in significant ways. Although Dexter and Gatsby both acquire great fortunes and fall in love with beautiful but shallow women, Dexter is accepted into the Joneses' social class because he acquires education along with wealth. More significantly, Dexter loses hope of ever winning Judy and becomes engaged to Irene Scheerer, a girl who has both sensitivity and intellect. Gatsby, in contrast, never untangles his dream from the allure of Daisy's beauty. His downfall comes in part from his inability to see Daisy's innate selfishness.

Before You Read

Winter Dreams

Make the Connection

Have you ever met someone and thought, "That's the person I want to marry"? If you have had this thought—or if you ever do someday—you might find yourself facing the same kinds of problems that Dexter Green faces. In fiction as well as in life, what individuals hope and long for is not always what they get.

Literary Focus
Motivation

Motivation refers to the reasons why characters behave as they do. Motivation can come from internal sources (ambition, insecurity, shyness) or from external factors (poverty, an ambitious parent, the crash of the stock market). In one-dimensional literature, motivation comes from a single cause. But in more sophisticated fiction, as in the complexity of life itself, motivation may come from many sources and is sometimes hard to pin down. In many stories, characters aren't even aware of their own motivation.

> **Motivation** refers to the reasons for a character's behavior.
>
> *For more on Motivation, see the Handbook of Literary and Historical Terms.*

Reading Skills
Drawing Inferences About Characters

When you make an **inference,** you make an educated guess based on facts presented in the text and on your own life experience. As you read this story, jot down the inferences you make to answer these questions about the characters: How are Dexter's two ambitions—achieving material success and win-

ning Judy's hand—tied together? What picture of Judy's character do you put together from what she says and does in the story? Why can't Dexter fully escape from Judy's magnetic charms?

Background

This story is one of several that Fitzgerald wrote about the dreams and illusions that marked the Jazz Age. "Winter Dreams" was written in 1922, when Fitzgerald's stories were commanding top prices from *The Saturday Evening Post* and other popular magazines. The story opens around 1911, when fourteen-year-old Dexter is caddying for wealthy golfers, and it spans eighteen years of Dexter's life.

Vocabulary Development

elation (ē·lā'shən) *n.*: celebration.

perturbation (pʉr'tər·bā'shən) *n.*: feeling of alarm or agitation.

malicious (mə·lish'əs) *adj.*: intentionally hurtful.

reserve (ri·zʉrv') *n.*: self-restraint.

petulance (pech'ə·ləns) *n.*: irritability; impatience.

mirth (mʉrth) *n.*: joyfulness.

divergence (dī·vʉr'jəns) *n.*: variance; difference.

turbulence (tʉr'byə·ləns) *n.*: wild disorder.

ludicrous (loo'di·krəs) *adj.*: laughable; absurd.

plaintive (plān'tiv) *adj.*: expressing sadness.

INTERNET

Vocabulary Practice
•
More About F. Scott Fitzgerald

Keyword: LE5 11-5

SKILLS FOCUS

Literary Skills
Understand motivation.

Reading Skills
Make inferences about characters.

F. Scott Fitzgerald   623

PRETEACHING

Summary *at grade level*

Fourteen-year-old Dexter Green abruptly quits his caddying job when told that he must caddy for eleven-year-old Judy Jones, a rich, impatient girl who fascinates him. Judy becomes part of Dexter's "winter dreams" of achieving wealth and glamour. After graduating from college in the East, Dexter returns to Minnesota and makes his fortune in the laundry business. While playing golf, Dexter again encounters Judy Jones, now grown up and gorgeous, and falls in love. Judy, however, toys with Dexter; he is merely one of the many men who worship her. After a year and a half, Dexter gives up on Judy and proposes to Irene Scheerer. A week before the announcement, Judy proposes to Dexter. Dexter accepts, but their engagement lasts only a month. Dexter joins the army to fight in World War I. Seven years later, Dexter learns that Judy, bereft of spirit and beauty, is married to a man who treats her badly. Dexter weeps as he realizes that his dream is irretrievably lost.

Selection Starter

Build background. Many of the settings and events of "Winter Dreams" mirror those in Fitzgerald's own life. According to his daughter, "He was like a surgeon performing an operation upon himself, hurting terribly but watching the process with a fascinated detachment."

Previewing Vocabulary

Have students read the definitions of the Vocabulary words listed on p. 623. Then, have students work in pairs. The first student gives his or her partner antonyms for a Vocabulary word, and the partner has to name the word. Have partners switch roles after they have used all the words and play another round. Then, have them complete the following matching item activity.

1. malicious [e]
2. petulance [i]
3. mirth [h]
4. turbulence [a]
5. ludicrous [g]
6. elation [b]
7. reserve [j]

8. plaintive [c]
9. divergence [f]
10. perturbation [d]

a. wild disorder
b. celebration
c. expressing sadness
d. feeling of alarm
e. intentionally hurtful
f. variance; difference
g. laughable; absurd

h. joyfulness
i. irritability; impatience
j. self-restraint

Building background knowledge. Explain that Judy's "nurse" is what we today would call a nanny, a companion hired to take care of a child.

B Reading Skills

? Making inferences about characters. What does the phrase "white linen nurse" suggest about Judy's attitude toward her caretaker? [It suggests that she views her nurse as an object.]

C Content-Area Connections

Culture: Bloomers
Bloomers were full, loose pants gathered at the knees, formerly worn by women for athletics. They were named after nineteenth-century American social reformer Amelia Bloomer.

D Reading Skills

? Making inferences about characters. Why do you think Dexter is so captivated by Judy Jones? [Possible response: Judy is radiant, charming, and uniquely self-confident and daring for her age.]

E Reading Skills

? Making judgments. Is it appropriate for Judy to call Dexter "Boy"? Why? [Possible responses: No, as a responsible caddy, Dexter has shown he is more mature than his years. Also, Judy is herself a child, three years younger than Dexter. On the other hand, Dexter is a boy—and not a wealthy one, as the demeaning term reminds him.]

---

wanted to quit? You promised that next week you'd go over to the State tournament with me."

"I decided I was too old."

Dexter handed in his "A Class" badge, collected what money was due him from the caddy-master, and walked home to Black Bear Village.

"The best—caddy I ever saw," shouted Mr. Mortimer Jones over a drink that afternoon. "Never lost a ball! Willing! Intelligent! Quiet! Honest! Grateful!"

The little girl who had done this was eleven—beautifully ugly as little girls are apt to be who are destined after a few years to be inexpressibly lovely and bring no end of misery to a great number of men. The spark, however, was perceptible. There was a general ungodliness in the way her lips twisted down at the corners when she smiled, and in the—Heaven help us!—in the almost passionate quality of her eyes. Vitality is born early in such women. It was utterly in evidence now, shining through her thin frame in a sort of glow.

She had come eagerly out on to the course at nine o'clock with a white linen nurse and five small new golf clubs in a white canvas bag which the nurse was carrying. When Dexter first saw her she was standing by the caddy house, rather ill at ease and trying to conceal the fact by engaging her nurse in an obviously unnatural conversation graced by startling and irrelevant grimaces from herself.

"Well, it's certainly a nice day, Hilda," Dexter heard her say. She drew down the corners of her mouth, smiled, and glanced furtively around, her eyes in transit falling for an instant on Dexter.

Then to the nurse:

"Well, I guess there aren't very many people out here this morning, are there?"

The smile again—radiant, blatantly artificial—convincing.

> *There was a general ungodliness in the way her lips twisted down at the corners when she smiled, and in the—Heaven help us!—in the almost passionate quality of her eyes.*

"I don't know what we're supposed to do now," said the nurse, looking nowhere in particular.

"Oh, that's all right. I'll fix it up."

Dexter stood perfectly still, his mouth slightly ajar. He knew that if he moved forward a step his stare would be in her line of vision—if he moved backward he would lose his full view of her face. For a moment he had not realized how young she was. Now he remembered having seen her several times the year before—in bloomers.[5]

Suddenly, involuntarily, he laughed, a short abrupt laugh—then, startled by himself, he turned and began to walk quickly away.

"Boy!"

Dexter stopped.

"Boy—"

Beyond question he was addressed. Not only that, but he was treated to that absurd smile, that preposterous smile—the memory of which at least a dozen men were to carry into middle age.

"Boy, do you know where the golf teacher is?"

"He's giving a lesson."

"Well, do you know where the caddy-master is?"

"He isn't here yet this morning."

"Oh." For a moment this baffled her. She stood alternately on her right and left foot.

"We'd like to get a caddy," said the nurse. "Mrs. Mortimer Jones sent us out to play golf, and we don't know how without we get a caddy."

Here she was stopped by an ominous glance from Miss Jones, followed immediately by the smile.

"There aren't any caddies here except me," said Dexter to the nurse, "and I got to stay here in charge until the caddy-master gets here."

---

5. **bloomers** *n. pl.*: baggy pants gathered at the knee, formerly worn by females for athletic activities.

CONTENT-AREA CONNECTIONS

Culture: Popular Sports
In the 1920s, sports like golf and tennis, which had been the pastimes of the wealthy, grew more democratic, a trend that has continued to the present.
Individual activity. Ask students to chart the popularity of sports from the 1920s to the present. Encourage them to name at least one sport that has remained popular [baseball, college football], one that was popular in the 1920s but has declined [polo, horse racing], one that existed in the 1920s but is more popular today [soccer], and one sport that did not exist in the 1920s [skateboarding].

"Oh."

Miss Jones and her retinue[6] now withdrew, and at a proper distance from Dexter became involved in a heated conversation, which was concluded by Miss Jones taking one of the clubs and hitting it on the ground with violence. For further emphasis she raised it again and was about to bring it down smartly upon the nurse's bosom, when the nurse seized the club and twisted it from her hands.

"You damn little mean old *thing!*" cried Miss Jones wildly.

Another argument ensued. Realizing that the elements of the comedy were implied in the scene, Dexter several times began to laugh, but each time restrained the laugh before it reached audibility. He could not resist the monstrous conviction that the little girl was justified in beating the nurse.

The situation was resolved by the fortuitous[7] appearance of the caddy-master, who was appealed to immediately by the nurse.

"Miss Jones is to have a little caddy, and this one says he can't go."

"Mr. McKenna said I was to wait here till you came," said Dexter quickly.

"Well, he's here now." Miss Jones smiled cheerfully at the caddy-master. Then she dropped her bag and set off at a haughty mince[8] toward the first tee.

"Well?" the caddy-master turned to Dexter. "What you standing there like a dummy for? Go pick up the young lady's clubs."

"I don't think I'll go out today," said Dexter.

"You don't—"

"I think I'll quit."

The enormity of his decision frightened him. He was a favorite caddy, and the thirty dollars a month he earned through the summer were not to be made elsewhere around the lake. But he had received a strong emotional shock, and his perturbation required a violent and immediate outlet.

---

6. **retinue** (ret'n·o͞o)*n.:* group of followers or servants attending a person of rank.
7. **fortuitous** (fôr·to͞o'ə·təs) *adj.:* fortunate.
8. **mince** *v.* used as *n.:* prim, affected walk.

It is not so simple as that, either. As so frequently would be the case in the future, Dexter was unconsciously dictated to by his winter dreams.

II

Now, of course, the quality and the seasonability of these winter dreams varied, but the stuff of them remained. They persuaded Dexter several years later to pass up a business course at the State university—his father, prospering now, would have paid his way—for the precarious[9] advantage of attending an older and more famous university in the East, where he was bothered by his scanty funds. But do not get the impression, because his winter dreams happened to be concerned at first with musings on the rich, that there was anything merely snobbish in the boy. He wanted not association with glittering things and glittering people—he wanted the glittering things themselves. Often he reached out for the best without knowing why he wanted it—and sometimes he ran up against the mysterious denials and prohibitions in which life indulges. It is with one of those denials and not with his career as a whole that this story deals.

He made money. It was rather amazing. After college he went to the city from which Black Bear Lake draws its wealthy patrons. When he was only twenty-three and had been there not quite two years, there were already people who liked to say: "Now *there's* a boy—" All about him rich men's sons were peddling bonds precariously, or investing patrimonies[10] precariously, or plodding through the two dozen volumes of the "George Washington Commercial Course," but Dexter borrowed a thousand dollars on his college degree and his confident mouth, and bought a partnership in a laundry.

---

9. **precarious** (pri·ker'ē·əs) *adj.:* uncertain.
10. **patrimonies** (pa'trə·mō'nēz) *n. pl.:* inheritances.

Vocabulary

perturbation (pʉr'tər·bā'shən) *n.:* feeling of alarm or agitation.

F Literary Focus

? Irony. How is Fitzgerald being ironic here? What does the irony suggest about Judy's character? [A *retinue* includes several servants—more than you would expect to attend a young girl. The irony suggests that Judy considers royal treatment her due.]

G Reading Skills

? Making inferences about characters. Why does Dexter quit his job? [Possible response: He does not want to be humiliated by caddying for a girl younger than he is.]

H Learners Having Difficulty

? Identifying pronoun antecedents. What is the antecedent of the pronoun *they*? Why is it important to link pronouns and their antecedents? [*They* refers to the noun *dreams*. Dexter's dreams influence him to choose the eastern school over the state university. Linking pronouns to their antecedents helps readers clarify a writer's train of thought and understand longer passages.]

I Literary Focus

? Motivation. What does this passage suggest about Dexter's motivation for seeking "the glittering things"? [Possible response: It suggests that Dexter is seeking an ideal life for his own satisfaction, not merely to impress other people.]

J Literary Focus

? Theme. What theme does this passage suggest Fitzgerald will address in this story? [Possible responses: Some things may be denied to us through no fault of our own; despite human efforts, destiny controls our fate.]

A Literary Focus

Philosophical and social influences of the period. In some ways, Dexter's life is a Horatio Alger story. Alger (1832–1899) wrote more than one hundred books for boys, many of them about newsboys or shoeshine boys who earned success and achieved the American dream through hard work, pluck, and virtue. Have students evaluate whether Dexter is a good model of this ideal.

B Reading Skills

❓ Making inferences about characters. What does Judy's behavior suggest about her character? [She is selfish and rude. Students are likely to think she is self-absorbed.]

A It was a small laundry when he went into it but Dexter made a specialty of learning how the English washed fine woolen golf stockings without shrinking them, and within a year he was catering to the trade that wore knickerbockers.[11] Men were insisting that their Shetland hose and sweaters go to his laundry just as they had insisted on a caddy who could find golf balls. A little later he was doing their wives' lingerie as well—and running five branches in different parts of the city. Before he was twenty-seven he owned the largest string of laundries in his section of the country. It was then that he sold out and went to New York. But the part of his story that concerns us goes back to the days when he was making his first big success.

When he was twenty-three Mr. Hart—one of the gray-haired men who like to say "Now there's a boy"—gave him a guest card to the Sherry Island Golf Club for a weekend. So he signed his name one day on the register, and that afternoon played golf in a foursome with Mr. Hart and Mr. Sandwood and Mr. T. A. Hedrick. He did not consider it necessary to remark that he had once carried Mr. Hart's bag over this same links, and that he knew every trap and gully with his eyes shut—but he found himself glancing at the four caddies who trailed them, trying to catch a gleam or gesture that would remind him of himself, that would lessen the gap which lay between his present and his past.

It was a curious day, slashed abruptly with fleeting, familiar impressions. One minute he had the sense of being a trespasser—in the next he was impressed by the tremendous superiority he felt toward Mr. T. A. Hedrick, who was a bore and not even a good golfer any more.

Then, because of a ball Mr. Hart lost near the fifteenth green, an enormous thing happened. While they were searching the stiff grasses of the rough there was a clear call of "Fore!"[12] from behind a hill in their rear. And as they all turned abruptly from their search a bright new ball sliced abruptly over the hill and caught Mr. T. A. Hedrick in the abdomen.

"By Gad!" cried Mr. T. A. Hedrick, "they ought to put some of these crazy women off the course. It's getting to be outrageous."

A head and a voice came up together over the hill:

"Do you mind if we go through?"

"You hit me in the stomach!" declared Mr. Hedrick wildly.

"Did I?" The girl approached the group of men. "I'm sorry. I yelled 'Fore!'"

Her glance fell casually on each of the men—then scanned the fairway for her ball.

"Did I bounce into the rough?"

It was impossible to determine whether this question was ingenuous[13] or malicious. In a moment, however, she left no doubt, for as her partner came up over the hill she called cheerfully:

B "Here I am! I'd have gone on the green except that I hit something."

As she took her stance for a short mashie[14] shot, Dexter looked at her closely. She wore a blue gingham dress, rimmed at throat and shoulders with a white edging that accentuated her tan. The quality of exaggeration, of thinness, which had made her passionate eyes and downturning mouth absurd at eleven, was gone now. She was arrestingly beautiful. The color in her cheeks was centered like the color in a picture—it was not a "high" color, but a sort of fluctuating and feverish warmth, so shaded that it seemed at any moment it would recede and disappear. This color and the mobility of her mouth gave a continual impression of flux, of intense life, of passionate vitality—balanced only partially by the sad luxury of her eyes.

---

11. **knickerbockers** *n. pl.*: short, loose pants gathered at the knees, formerly worn by golfers.
12. **fore** *interj.*: warning cry that a golfer gives before hitting a ball down the fairway.

13. **ingenuous** (in·jen′yo͞o·əs) *adj.*: innocent; without guile.
14. **mashie** *n.*: number five iron (golf club).

Vocabulary
malicious (mə·lish′əs) *adj.*: intentionally hurtful.

Literary Criticism

Critic's Commentary: Fitzgerald's Follies

In an article titled "Fitzgerald Before *The Great Gatsby*," critic Paul Rosenfeld says: "The utmost that can be charged against F. Scott Fitzgerald is that too oftentimes his good material eludes him. . . . Salty and insipid, exaggeratedly poetical and bitterly parodistic, his writing pours exuberantly out of him. Flat paragraphs are redeemed by brilliant metaphors, and conventional descriptions by witty, penetrating turns. Ideas of diamond are somewhat indiscriminately mixed with ideas of rhinestone and ideas of window glass; yet purest rays serene are present in variable abundance." Invite students to debate Rosenfeld's comments, and, if possible, to find examples of the qualities he assigns to Fitzgerald's writing.

She swung her mashie impatiently and without interest, pitching the ball into a sand-pit on the other side of the green. With a quick, insincere smile and a careless "Thank you!" she went on after it.

"That Judy Jones!" remarked Mr. Hedrick on the next tee, as they waited—some moments—for her to play on ahead. "All she needs is to be turned up and spanked for six months and then to be married off to an old-fashioned cavalry captain."

"My God, she's good-looking!" said Mr. Sandwood, who was just over thirty.

"Good-looking!" cried Mr. Hedrick contemptuously, "she always looks as if she wanted to be kissed! Turning those big cow-eyes on every calf in town!"

It was doubtful if Mr. Hedrick intended a reference to the maternal instinct.

"She'd play pretty good golf if she'd try," said Mr. Sandwood.

"She has no form," said Mr. Hedrick solemnly.

"She has a nice figure," said Mr. Sandwood.

"Better thank the Lord she doesn't drive a swifter ball," said Mr. Hart, winking at Dexter.

Later in the afternoon the sun went down with a riotous swirl of gold and varying blues and scarlets, and left the dry, rustling night of Western summer. Dexter watched from the veranda of the Golf Club, watched the even overlap of the waters in the little wind, silver molasses under the harvest moon. Then the moon held a finger to her lips and the lake became a clear pool, pale and quiet. Dexter put on his bathing suit and swam out to the farthest raft, where he stretched dripping on the wet canvas of the springboard.

There was a fish jumping and a star shining and the lights around the lake were gleaming. Over on a dark peninsula a piano was playing

> *The color in her cheeks was centered like the color in a picture—it was not a "high" color, but a sort of fluctuating and feverish warmth, so shaded that it seemed at any moment it would recede and disappear.*

the songs of last summer and of summers before that—songs from "Chin-Chin" and "The Count of Luxemburg" and "The Chocolate Soldier"—and because the sound of a piano over a stretch of water had always seemed beautiful to Dexter he lay perfectly quiet and listened.

The tune the piano was playing at that moment had been gay and new five years before when Dexter was a sophomore at college. They had played it at a prom once when he could not afford the luxury of proms, and he had stood outside the gymnasium and listened. The sound of the tune precipitated in him a sort of ecstasy and it was with that ecstasy he viewed what happened to him now. It was a mood of intense appreciation, a sense that, for once, he was magnificently attuned to life and that everything about him was radiating a brightness and a glamour he might never know again.

A low, pale oblong[15] detached itself suddenly from the darkness of the Island, spitting forth the reverberate[16] sound of a racing motorboat. Two white streamers of cleft water rolled themselves out behind it and almost immediately the boat was beside him, drowning out the hot tinkle of the piano in the drone of its spray. Dexter raising himself on his arms was aware of a figure standing at the wheel, of two dark eyes regarding him over the lengthening space of water—then the boat had gone by and was sweeping in an immense and purposeless circle of spray round and round in the middle of the lake. With equal eccentricity one of the circles flattened out and headed back toward the raft.

"Who's that?" she called, shutting off her motor. She was so near now that Dexter could

---

15. **oblong** *n.:* rectangular figure longer than it is broad.
16. **reverberate** *adj.:* reflected; echoed.

C Reading Skills

? Analyzing. How do the men feel about Judy? Why doesn't Dexter add his opinion to the conversation? [Possible responses: While Mr. Sandwood finds Judy attractive, Mr. Hedrick seems immune to her charms. This suggests that Judy's appeal is not universal. Dexter remains silent because he does not want to reveal how attracted he is to Judy.]

D Advanced Learners

? Analyzing style. How does the style of this passage reflect Dexter's feelings for Judy? [Possible responses: The rich imagery suggests the beauty and depth of Dexter's feelings. Dexter is attuned to the beauty of nature—personified as a woman—in the same way he is attuned to Judy's beauty.]

E Literary Focus

? Imagery. How does Fitzgerald use sound imagery to build up to the meeting between Dexter and Judy? [He introduces the piano tune coming across the water and then the drone of a motorboat.]

CONTENT-AREA CONNECTIONS

Music: Jazz
Developed by African Americans, jazz music flourished during the 1920s. With roots in West African folk music, jazz is characterized by improvisation, repeated chord progressions, subtle modulations of pitch, and tonal effects such as growls and wails. Near the end of the decade, George Gershwin composed two significant works that blended jazz with European classical music: *Rhapsody in Blue*

(1924) and *An American in Paris* (1928).
Whole-class activity. As students read the story, play an excerpt from *Rhapsody in Blue* or *An American in Paris*. Ask students to discuss how the freedom and improvisation of jazz reflect the lifestyle of the characters in "Winter Dreams." Have students comment on what they think today's musical styles reveal about contemporary Americans.

? **Motivation.** Why does Judy leave the man waiting at her house? [Possible responses: She is motivated by revulsion at his fawning, an urge to taunt him, or a desire to save him pain since she knows that she is not what he thinks she is.]

B **Reading Skills**

? **Drawing inferences about characters.** What inferences can you draw about Judy's character based on the way she swims? [Possible response: You can infer that she is not only beautiful, but also methodical, strong, and repetitive—sometimes painfully so, as the word *stabbing* suggests.]

C **Reading Skills**

? **Analyzing.** In what way is Dexter not really moving in a new direction? [Possible response: He has been intrigued by Judy, and for many years has sought the glamour she represents.]

---

see her bathing suit, which consisted apparently of pink rompers.[17]

The nose of the boat bumped the raft, and as the latter tilted rakishly, he was precipitated[18] toward her. With different degrees of interest they recognized each other.

"Aren't you one of those men we played through this afternoon?" she demanded.

He was.

(A) "Well, do you know how to drive a motorboat? Because if you do I wish you'd drive this one so I can ride on the surfboard behind. My name is Judy Jones"—she favored him with an absurd smirk—rather, what tried to be a smirk, for, twist her mouth as she might, it was not grotesque, it was merely beautiful—"and I live in a house over there on the Island, and in that house there is a man waiting for me. When he drove up at the door I drove out of the dock because he says I'm his ideal."

There was a fish jumping and a star shining and the lights around the lake were gleaming. Dexter sat beside Judy Jones and she explained how her boat was driven. Then she was in the water, swimming to the floating surfboard with a sinuous[19] crawl. Watching her was without effort to the eye, watching a branch waving or **(B)** a seagull flying. Her arms, burned to butternut, moved sinuously among the dull platinum ripples, elbow appearing first, casting the forearm back with a cadence of falling water, then reaching out and down, stabbing a path ahead.

They moved out into the lake; turning, Dexter saw that she was kneeling on the low rear of the now uptilted surfboard.

"Go faster," she called, "fast as it'll go."

---

17. **rompers** *n. pl.:* one-piece outfit with loose pants gathered at the knee.
18. **precipitated** *v.:* thrown headlong.
19. **sinuous** *adj.:* curving back and forth; snakelike.

> *"My name is Judy Jones"—she favored him with an absurd smirk—rather, what tried to be a smirk, for, twist her mouth as she might, it was not grotesque, it was merely beautiful . . .*

Obediently he jammed the lever forward and the white spray mounted at the bow. When he looked around again the girl was standing up on the rushing board, her arms spread wide, her eyes lifted toward the moon.

"It's awful cold," she shouted. "What's your name?"

He told her.

"Well, why don't you come to dinner tomorrow night?"

(C) His heart turned over like the flywheel[20] of the boat, and, for the second time, her casual whim gave a new direction to his life.

III

Next evening while he waited for her to come downstairs, Dexter peopled the soft deep summer room and the sunporch that opened from it with the men who had already loved Judy Jones. He knew the sort of men they were—the men who when he first went to college had entered from the great prep schools with graceful clothes and the deep tan of healthy summers. He had seen that, in one sense, he was better than these men. He was newer and stronger. Yet in acknowledging to himself that he wished his children to be like them he was admitting that he was but the rough, strong stuff from which they eternally sprang.

When the time had come for him to wear good clothes, he had known who were the best tailors in America, and the best tailors in America had made him the suit he wore this evening. He had acquired that particular <u>reserve</u> peculiar

---

20. **flywheel** *n.:* wheel that regulates the speed of a machine.

Vocabulary
reserve (ri·zurv′) *n.:* self-restraint.

DIFFERENTIATING INSTRUCTION

Advanced Learners
Enrichment. Encourage students to experiment with style by writing imitations of several sentences by Fitzgerald. Here are two sentences from the story, followed by models of imitative writing.

1. "Dexter stood perfectly still, his mouth slightly ajar." *The new truck idled softly, its power momentarily caged.*

2. "Perhaps from so much youthful love, so many youthful lovers, she had come, in self-defense, to nourish herself wholly from within." *Doubtless in response to so many homework assignments, so little free time, they had asked, in desperation, that the date of the test be postponed.*

After explaining the process, let students imitate five sentences on their own.

to his university, that set it off from other universities. He recognized the value to him of such a mannerism and he had adopted it; he knew that to be careless in dress and manner required more confidence than to be careful. But carelessness was for his children. His mother's name had been Krimslich. She was a Bohemian of the peasant class and she had talked broken English to the end of her days. Her son must keep to the set patterns.

At a little after seven Judy Jones came downstairs. She wore a blue silk afternoon dress, and he was disappointed at first that she had not put on something more elaborate. This feeling was accentuated when, after a brief greeting, she went to the door of a butler's pantry and pushing it open called: "You can serve dinner, Martha." He had rather expected that a butler would announce dinner, that there would be a cocktail. Then he put these thoughts behind him as they sat down side by side on a lounge and looked at each other.

"Father and mother won't be here," she said thoughtfully.

He remembered the last time he had seen her father, and he was glad the parents were not to be here tonight—they might wonder who he was. He had been born in Keeble, a Minnesota village fifty miles farther north, and he always gave Keeble as his home instead of Black Bear Village. Country towns were well enough to come from if they weren't inconveniently in sight and used as footstools by fashionable lakes.

They talked of his university, which she had visited frequently during the past two years, and of the nearby city which supplied Sherry Island with its patrons, and whither Dexter would return next day to his prospering laundries.

During dinner she slipped into a moody depression which gave Dexter a feeling of uneasiness. Whatever <u>petulance</u> she uttered in her throaty voice worried him. Whatever she smiled at—at him, at a chicken liver, at nothing—it disturbed him that her smile could have no root in <u>mirth</u>, or even in amusement. When the scarlet corners of her lips curved down, it was less a smile than an invitation to a kiss.

Then, after dinner, she led him out on the dark sunporch and deliberately changed the atmosphere.

"Do you mind if I weep a little?" she said.

"I'm afraid I'm boring you," he responded quickly.

"You're not. I like you. But I've just had a terrible afternoon. There was a man I cared about, and this afternoon he told me out of a clear sky that he was poor as a church mouse. He'd never even hinted it before. Does this sound horribly mundane?"[21]

"Perhaps he was afraid to tell you."

"Suppose he was," she answered. "He didn't start right. You see, if I'd thought of him as poor—well, I've been mad about loads of poor men, and fully intended to marry them all. But in this case, I hadn't thought of him that way, and my interest in him wasn't strong enough to survive the shock. As if a girl calmly informed her fiancé that she was a widow. He might not object to widows, but—"

"Let's start right," she interrupted herself suddenly. "Who are you, anyhow?"

For a moment Dexter hesitated. Then:

"I'm nobody," he announced. "My career is largely a matter of futures."

"Are you poor?"

"No," he said frankly, "I'm probably making more money than any man my age in the Northwest. I know that's an obnoxious remark, but you advised me to start right."

There was a pause. Then she smiled and the corners of her mouth drooped and an almost imperceptible sway brought her closer to him, looking up into his eyes. A lump rose in Dexter's throat, and he waited breathless for the experiment, facing the unpredictable compound that would form mysteriously from the elements of their lips. Then he saw—she communicated her excitement to him, lavishly, deeply, with kisses

---

21. **mundane** *adj.:* ordinary; everyday.

Vocabulary
petulance (pech'ə·ləns) *n.:* irritability; impatience.
mirth (murth) *n.:* joyfulness.

F. Scott Fitzgerald **631**

D Literary Focus

❓ Repetition. What word does Fitzgerald repeat for emphasis? How does this repetition hint at the story's theme? [He repeats the word *care* in *careless, careful,* and *carelessness.* The repetition suggests the need for Dexter to be careful in love as well as dress—especially when the object of his love is quite careless.]

E Learners Having Difficulty

Building background knowledge. Explain that Krimslich is an eastern European name and that Dexter's mother speaks "broken," or imperfect, English because she is an immigrant.

F Literary Focus

❓ Motivation. Why does Dexter lie about his hometown? [Admitting to living in middle-class Black Bear Village would emphasize the social distance between himself and the wealthy lake residents.]

G Literary Focus

❓ Social and ethical influences of the period. What does Dexter mean when he says that his career is "a matter of futures"? [Possible response: He doesn't work in a family business or have family money, but he does have a promising future that he is creating for himself.]

READING SKILLS REVIEW

Remind students that, depending on the context, a work of fiction may be read for a number of different purposes, such as for enjoyment or to find out information. A single reader may have more than one purpose for reading a work.

Activity. Discuss with students what their purposes might be for reading "Winter Dreams" in the contexts listed here. For each, have students state which aspects of the story they might pay more attention to.

1. Context: *Metropolitan Magazine, 1922*
   [Purpose—to enjoy a love story; you might pay attention to plot and characters.]

2. Context: a course in American studies
   [Purpose—to understand the Jazz Age; you might pay attention to details of social life.]

3. Context: a course in composition
   [Purpose—to find out how to write; you might pay attention to plot, characterization, and style.]

4. Context: a reading group
   [Purpose—to enjoy a story and share interpretations with friends; you might pay attention to themes and motifs.]

❓ **Drawing inferences about characters.** What does the kiss symbolize for Dexter? [Possible responses: the fulfillment of his winter dreams; the deepening of his desire for Judy.]

B **Content-Area Connections**

Literature: *The Great Gatsby*
This kiss prefigures the crucial kiss in *The Great Gatsby:* "[Gatsby knew] that when he kissed [Daisy], and forever wed his unutterable visions to her perishable breath, his mind would never romp again like the mind of God. So he waited, listening for a moment longer to the tuning-fork that had been struck upon a star. Then he kissed her. At his lips' touch she blossomed for him like a flower and the incarnation was complete."

C **Literary Focus**

❓ **Motivation.** Fitzgerald says that Judy goes directly after whatever she wants, but what exactly *does* she want? [Possible responses: love; respect; power; romance.]

D **Reading Skills**

❓ **Drawing inferences about characters.** There are elements of Judy's character that Dexter does not like, yet he doesn't want to change her. How do you explain his feelings? [Possible responses: It is Judy's very inconsistency that appeals to Dexter. He admires the way she lives in the moment, without regard for what others may think. Her beauty and vitality are so important to him that her faults don't matter.]

E **Reading Skills**

❓ **Evaluating.** Does Judy's character seem realistic to you? [Possible responses: No; she seems overly two-dimensional and stereotypical. Yes; some people are indeed that capricious, fickle, and insensitive.]

A that were not a promise but a fulfillment. They aroused in him not hunger demanding renewal but surfeit[22] that would demand more surfeit . . . kisses that were like charity, creating want by holding back nothing at all.

B It did not take him many hours to decide that he had wanted Judy Jones ever since he was a proud, desirous little boy.

IV

It began like that—and continued, with varying shades of intensity, on such a note right up to the dénouement.[23] Dexter surrendered a part of himself to the most direct and unprincipled personality with which he had ever come in **C** contact. Whatever Judy wanted, she went after with the full pressure of her charm. There was no <u>divergence</u> of method, no jockeying for position or premeditation of effects—there was a very little mental side to any of her affairs. She simply made men conscious to the highest degree of her physical loveliness. Dexter had no **D** desire to change her. Her deficiencies were knit up with a passionate energy that transcended and justified them.

When, as Judy's head lay against his shoulder that first night, she whispered, "I don't know what's the matter with me. Last night I thought I was in love with a man and tonight I think I'm in love with you—" —it seemed to him a beautiful and romantic thing to say. It was the exquisite excitability that for the moment he controlled and owned. But a week later he was **E** compelled to view this same quality in a different light. She took him in her roadster to a picnic supper, and after supper she disappeared, likewise in her roadster, with another man. Dexter became enormously upset and was scarcely able to be decently civil to the other people present. When she assured him that she had not kissed the other man, he knew she was lying—yet he was glad that she had taken the trouble to lie to him.

---

22. **surfeit** *n.:* discomfort resulting from excess or overindulgence.
23. **dénouement** (dā′nōō•män′) *n.:* final outcome.

He was, as he found before the summer ended, one of a varying dozen who circulated about her. Each of them had at one time been favored above all others—about half of them still basked in the solace of occasional sentimental revivals. Whenever one showed signs of dropping out through long neglect, she granted

Vocabulary
divergence (dĭ•vur′jəns) *n.:* variance; difference.

Point of view. Point of view is the vantage point from which the writer tells a story. In the first-person point of view, the narrator explains the events through his or her own eyes. In the third-person-omniscient point of view, the narrator looks through the eyes of all the characters and is all-knowing. In the third-person-limited point of view, the narrator sees the story through the eyes of only one character and reports only what he or she experiences.

Activity. All of the story's action is seen through Dexter's eyes; all the feeling, through his emotions. Even the passages told from an omniscient point of view seem to reflect Dexter's mature vantage point as he looks nostalgically back at his youth. Have students discuss how the story shifts between limited and omniscient points of view and whether they suggest that "Winter Dreams" is a cautionary tale or a moral lesson.

him a brief honeyed hour, which encouraged him to tag along for a year or so longer. Judy made these forays[24] upon the helpless and defeated without malice, indeed half unconscious that there was anything mischievous in what she did.

When a new man came to town every one dropped out—dates were automatically cancelled.

The helpless part of trying to do anything about it was that she did it all herself. She was not a girl who could be "won" in the kinetic[25] sense—she was proof against[26] cleverness, she was proof against charm; if any of these assailed her too strongly she would immediately resolve the affair to a physical basis, and under the magic of her physical splendor the strong as well as the brilliant played her game and not their own. She was entertained only by the gratification of her desires and by the direct exercise of her own charm. Perhaps from so much youthful love, so many youthful lovers, she had come, in self-defense, to nourish herself wholly from within.

Succeeding Dexter's first exhilaration came restlessness and dissatisfaction. The helpless ecstasy of losing himself in her was opiate rather than tonic.[27] It was fortunate for his work during the winter that those moments of ecstasy came infrequently. Early in their acquaintance it had seemed for a while that there was a deep and spontaneous mutual attraction—that first August, for example—three days of long evenings on her dusky veranda, of strange wan kisses through the late afternoon, in shadowy alcoves or behind the protecting trellises of the garden arbors, of mornings when she was fresh as a dream and almost shy at meeting him in the clarity of the rising day. There was all the ecstasy of an engagement about it, sharpened by his realization that there was no engagement. It was during those three days that, for the first

---

24. **forays** (fôr′āz) *n. pl.:* raids.
25. **kinetic** (ki·net′ik) *adj.:* coming about through action or energy.
26. **proof against:** able to withstand.
27. **opiate . . . tonic:** calming rather than stimulating.

time, he had asked her to marry him. She said "maybe some day," she said "kiss me," she said "I'd like to marry you," she said "I love you" —she said—nothing. **H**

The three days were interrupted by the arrival of a New York man who visited at her house for half September. To Dexter's agony, rumor engaged them. The man was the son of the president of a great trust company. But at the end of a month it was reported that Judy was yawning. At a dance one night she sat all evening in a motorboat with a local beau, while the New Yorker searched the club for her frantically. She told the local beau that she was bored with her visitor, and two days later he left. She was seen with him at the station, and it was reported that he looked very mournful indeed.

On this note the summer ended. Dexter was twenty-four, and he found himself increasingly in a position to do as he wished. He joined two clubs in the city and lived at one of them. Though he was by no means an integral part of the stag-lines[28] at these clubs, he managed to be on hand at dances where Judy Jones was likely to appear. He could have gone out socially as

---

28. **stag-lines** *n. pl.:* lines of unaccompanied men at a dance, waiting for available dance partners.

F **Literary Focus**

? Point of view. From what point of view is this description of Judy written? [third-person-omniscient point of view] How does the description help express the story's theme? [Possible response: It emphasizes Judy's inaccessibility and suggests that "winter dreams" do not by their very nature come true.]

G **Literary Focus**

? Motivation. Why do Dexter and all the other young men put up with Judy's careless behavior? [Possible responses: Dexter and the other suitors endure her behavior because they find her irresistible; each hopes that she will finally reject the others and choose him; for Dexter, she may also represent upward social mobility.]

H **Reading Skills**

? Speculating. What does the narrator mean when he says that Judy says "nothing"? [Possible responses: She avoids answering his questions; her answers are so glib and changeable that they cannot be taken seriously.]

Culture: Twenties Technology
The 1920s was an age in which machines entered the home and began to affect daily life. In addition to the automobile and airplane, the 1920s saw the increased use of the radio, vacuum cleaner, and washing machine. **Small-group activity.** Have groups of students select one machine that was invented or refined during the 1920s and report on its cultural impact.

Culture: The Automobile
With the ever-increasing production of cars, people conquered distances in the 1920s that would hardly have seemed possible just a few years earlier. The typical middle-class family now owned an automobile; in 1929, there were more than 23 million cars on the road. As a result, the tempo of life increased. Some people saw automobiles as contributing to the decline of morals, since it provided opportunities for young men and women to socialize away from a chaperone's watchful eye.

? **Drawing inferences about characters.** Have Dexter's dreams changed? Explain why or why not. [Possible response: No, they have not. Even though Dexter has achieved material success and is no longer awed by the local upper class, the actual fulfillment of his dreams still lies with Judy.]

B Literary Focus

? **Motivation.** What moves Dexter to become engaged to Irene? [Possible responses: He is trying to forget Judy; he is trying to make Judy jealous; he knows that Irene will be a suitable wife.]

C Vocabulary Development

Synonyms and antonyms. Explain that *slight* as an adjective means "small" and that as a noun it means "a snub or mild insult." Have students think of an antonym for the noun *slight*. [Possible responses: praise; compliment.]

D Reading Skills

? **Evaluating.** Is Judy a worthy object of Dexter's idealism? [Possible responses: Yes, because she is beautiful, aloof, and self-contained; no, because she is arrogant, unreliable, and selfish.]

E Content-Area Connections

Culture: Dance Floor Etiquette Ask a volunteer to explain the custom in which a man who wants to dance with a woman taps the shoulder of her dancing partner to "cut in."

---

much as he liked—he was an eligible young man, now, and popular with downtown fathers. His confessed devotion to Judy Jones had rather solidified his position. But he had no social aspirations and rather despised the dancing men who were always on tap for the Thursday or Saturday parties and who filled in at dinners with the younger married set. Already he was playing with the idea of going East to New York. He wanted to take Judy Jones with him. No disillusion as to the world in which she had grown up could cure his illusion as to her desirability.

Remember that—for only in the light of it can what he did for her be understood.

Eighteen months after he first met Judy Jones he became engaged to another girl. Her name was Irene Scheerer, and her father was one of the men who had always believed in Dexter. Irene was light-haired and sweet and honorable, and a little stout, and she had two suitors whom she pleasantly relinquished when Dexter formally asked her to marry him.

Summer, fall, winter, spring, another summer, another fall—so much he had given of his active life to the incorrigible[29] lips of Judy Jones. She had treated him with interest, with encouragement, with malice, with indifference, with contempt. She had inflicted on him the innumerable little slights and indignities possible in such a case—as if in revenge for having ever cared for him at all. She had beckoned him and yawned at him and beckoned him again and he had responded often with bitterness and narrowed eyes. She had brought him ecstatic happiness and intolerable agony of spirit. She had caused him untold inconvenience and not a little trouble. She had insulted him, and she had ridden over him, and she had played his interest in her against his interest in his work—for fun.

She had done everything to him except to criticize him—this she had not done—it seemed to him only because it might have sullied[30] the utter indifference she manifested and sincerely felt toward him.

When autumn had come and gone again it occurred to him that he could not have Judy Jones. He had to beat this into his mind but he convinced himself at last. He lay awake at night for a while and argued it over. He told himself the trouble and the pain she had caused him, he enumerated her glaring deficiencies as a wife. Then he said to himself that he loved her, and after a while he fell asleep. For a week, lest he imagined her husky voice over the telephone or her eyes opposite him at lunch, he worked hard and late, and at night he went to his office and plotted out his years.

> When autumn had come and gone again it occurred to him that he could not have Judy Jones.

At the end of a week he went to a dance and cut in on her once. For almost the first time since they had met he did not ask her to sit out with him or tell her that she was lovely. It hurt him that she did not miss these things—that was all. He was not jealous when he saw that there was a new man tonight. He had been hardened against jealousy long before.

He stayed late at the dance. He sat for an hour with Irene Scheerer and talked about books and about music. He knew very little about either. But he was beginning to be master of his own time now, and he had a rather priggish[31] notion that he—the young and already fabulously successful Dexter Green—should know more about such things.

That was in October, when he was twenty-five. In January, Dexter and Irene became engaged. It was to be announced in June, and they were to be married three months later.

The Minnesota winter prolonged itself interminably, and it was almost May when the winds

---

29. **incorrigible** *adj.*: incapable of correction or reform.

30. **sullied** *v.*: tainted; soiled.
31. **priggish** *adj.*: annoyingly precise and proper.

came soft and the snow ran down into Black Bear Lake at last. For the first time in over a year Dexter was enjoying a certain tranquility of spirit. Judy Jones had been in Florida, and afterward in Hot Springs, and somewhere she had been engaged, and somewhere she had broken it off. At first, when Dexter had definitely given her up, it had made him sad that people still linked them together and asked for news of her, but when he began to be placed at dinner next to Irene Scheerer people didn't ask him about her any more—they told him about her. He ceased to be an authority on her.

May at last. Dexter walked the streets at night when the darkness was damp as rain, wondering that so soon, with so little done, so much of ecstasy had gone from him. May one year back had been marked by Judy's poignant, unforgivable, yet forgiven turbulence—it had been one of those rare times when he fancied she had grown to care for him. That old penny's worth of happiness he had spent for this bushel of content. He knew that Irene would be no more than a curtain spread behind him, a hand moving among gleaming teacups, a voice calling to children . . . fire and loveliness were gone, the magic of nights and the wonder of the varying hours and seasons . . . slender lips, downturning, dropping to his lips and bearing him up into a heaven of eyes. . . . The thing was deep in him. He was too strong and alive for it to die lightly.

In the middle of May when the weather balanced for a few days on the thin bridge that led to deep summer he turned in one night at Irene's house. Their engagement was to be announced in a week now—no one would be surprised at it. And tonight they would sit together on the lounge at the University Club and look on for an hour at the dancers. It gave him a sense of solidity to go with her—she was so sturdily popular, so intensely "great."

He mounted the steps of the brownstone house and stepped inside.

"Irene," he called.

Mrs. Scheerer came out of the living room to meet him.

"Dexter," she said, "Irene's gone upstairs with a splitting headache. She wanted to go with you but I made her go to bed."

"Nothing serious, I—"

"Oh, no. She's going to play golf with you in the morning. You can spare her for just one night, can't you, Dexter?"

Her smile was kind. She and Dexter liked each other. In the living room he talked for a moment before he said good-night.

Returning to the University Club, where he had rooms, he stood in the doorway for a moment and watched the dancers. He leaned against the doorpost, nodded at a man or two—yawned.

"Hello, darling."

The familiar voice at his elbow startled him. Judy Jones had left a man and crossed the room to him—Judy Jones, a slender enameled doll in cloth of gold: gold in a band at her head, gold in two slipper points at her dress's hem. The fragile glow of her face seemed to blossom as she smiled at him. A breeze of warmth and light blew through the room. His hands in the pockets of his dinner jacket tightened spasmodically. He was filled with a sudden excitement.

"When did you get back?" he asked casually.

"Come here and I'll tell you about it."

She turned and he followed her. She had been away—he could have wept at the wonder of her return. She had passed through enchanted streets, doing things that were like provocative music. All mysterious happenings, all fresh and quickening hopes, had gone away with her, come back with her now.

She turned in the doorway.

"Have you a car here? If you haven't, I have."

"I have a coupé."

In then, with a rustle of golden cloth. He slammed the door. Into so many cars she had stepped—like this—like that—her back against the leather, so—her elbow resting on the door—waiting. She would have been soiled long since

Vocabulary
turbulence (tur′byə·ləns) *n.:* wild disorder.

F. Scott Fitzgerald **635**

F **Reading Skills**

❓ **Drawing inferences about characters.** What causes the fluctuations in Dexter's mood in this scene? What do you think will be the result of his feelings? [Possible responses: Dexter's mood swings are caused by his relationship with Judy, which is mirrored in the changing seasons. Dexter is trying to get over Judy, but the fact that his "tranquility of spirit" is a result of her absence suggests that she still holds sway over him.]

G **Reading Skills**

❓ **Making judgments.** Did Dexter make the right decision? Why? [Possible responses: Yes, because clinging to Judy would only bring him misery; no, because he doesn't love Irene.]

H **Literary Focus**

❓ **Symbol.** Why is Judy pictured in gold? [Possible responses: The color symbolizes Dexter's dreams—the wealth he longed for, achieved, and found wanting. It also symbolizes Judy and the elusive glamour she represents.]

I **Learners Having Difficulty**

❓ **Breaking down difficult text.** What is the narrator saying about Judy's character in the description of her entering "so many cars"? [Possible response: She has ridden in so many men's cars that it could have ruined her reputation, except that she always remained in control and never let any of her suitors touch her emotionally.]

CONTENT-AREA CONNECTIONS

Culture: Flappers
Review the term *flapper*, which describes young women of the 1920s who broke down conventions by cutting their hair short, wearing form-fitting dresses, and dancing the Charleston. Judy's aggressive allure and coy, flirtatious manner make her an ideal flapper, although she lacks a flapper's zaniness and seems calculating instead.

Whole-class activity. Ask the class to name and discuss other unconventional types of people that have dominated later decades. [Possible responses: the Jitterbugger of the 1940s; the beatnik of the 1950s; the hippie of the 1960s; the disco dancer of the 1970s; and the punk, grunge, and hip-hop fans of more recent years.]

A Literary Focus

❓ Motivation. Why does Dexter agree to go for a ride with Judy if, as he says, he has "put her behind him"? [Possible response: Dexter may go for the ride because he is not being truthful with himself—because he is still very much in love with Judy.]

B Reading Skills

❓ Drawing inferences about characters. What are Judy and Dexter saying between the lines? [Judy is asking whether Dexter still loves her; Dexter is saying that he does, but he is ambiguous about whether as a friend or a lover.]

C Reading Skills

❓ Drawing inferences about characters. Why does Dexter wonder if Judy knows about Irene? [Possible response: Dexter wonders if Judy's actions are motivated by jealousy of Irene.]

D Literary Focus

Diction. Note the reappearance of the word *careless*. Fitzgerald also uses it to describe Tom and Daisy's actions in *The Great Gatsby*: "I saw that what he had done was, to him, entirely justified. It was all very careless and confused. They were careless people, Tom and Daisy—they smashed up things and creatures and then retreated back into their money or their vast carelessness . . . and let other people clean up the mess they had made."

had there been anything to soil her—except herself—but this was her own self outpouring.

With an effort he forced himself to start the car and back into the street. This was nothing, he must remember. She had done this before, and he had put her behind him, as he would have crossed a bad account from his books.

He drove slowly downtown and, affecting abstraction, traversed the deserted streets of the business section, peopled here and there where a movie was giving out its crowd or where consumptive[32] or pugilistic[33] youth lounged in front of pool halls. The clink of glasses and the slap of hands on the bars issued from saloons, cloisters of glazed glass and dirty yellow light.

She was watching him closely and the silence was embarrassing, yet in this crisis he could find no casual word with which to profane[34] the hour. At a convenient turning he began to zigzag back toward the University Club.

"Have you missed me?" she asked suddenly.

"Everybody missed you."

---

32. **consumptive** *adj.:* destructive; wasteful.
33. **pugilistic** (pyo͞o′jə•lis′tik) *adj.:* eager to fight.
34. **profane** *v.:* curse.

He wondered if she knew of Irene Scheerer. She had been back only a day—her absence had been almost contemporaneous with his engagement.

"What a remark!" Judy laughed sadly—without sadness. She looked at him searchingly. He became absorbed in the dashboard.

"You're handsomer than you used to be," she said thoughtfully. "Dexter, you have the most rememberable eyes."

He could have laughed at this, but he did not laugh. It was the sort of thing that was said to sophomores. Yet it stabbed at him.

"I'm awfully tired of everything, darling." She called every one darling, endowing the endearment with careless, individual comraderie. "I wish you'd marry me."

The directness of this confused him. He should have told her now that he was going to marry another girl, but he could not tell her. He could as easily have sworn that he had never loved her.

"I think we'd get along," she continued, on the same note, "unless probably you've forgotten me and fallen in love with another girl."

Her confidence was obviously enormous. She had said, in effect, that she found such a thing impossible to believe, that if it were true he had merely committed a childish indiscretion—and probably to show off. She would forgive him, because it was not a matter of any moment but rather something to be brushed aside lightly.

"Of course you could never love anybody but me," she continued. "I like the way you love me. Oh, Dexter, have you forgotten last year?"

"No, I haven't forgotten."

"Neither have I!"

E Was she sincerely moved—or was she carried along by the wave of her own acting?

"I wish we could be like that again," she said, and he forced himself to answer:

"I don't think we can."

"I suppose not. . . . I hear you're giving Irene Scheerer a violent rush."

There was not the faintest emphasis on the name, yet Dexter was suddenly ashamed.

"Oh, take me home," cried Judy suddenly; "I don't want to go back to that idiotic dance—with those children."

Then, as he turned up the street that led to the residence district, Judy began to cry quietly to herself. He had never seen her cry before.

The dark street lightened, the dwellings of the rich loomed up around them, he stopped his coupé in front of the great white bulk of the Mortimer Joneses house, somnolent,[35] gorgeous, drenched with the splendor of the damp moonlight. Its solidity startled him. The strong walls, the steel of the girders, the breadth and beam and pomp of it were there only to bring out the contrast with the young beauty beside him. It was sturdy to accentuate her slightness—as if to show what a breeze could be generated by a butterfly's wing.

He sat perfectly quiet, his nerves in wild clamor, afraid that if he moved he would find her irresistibly in his arms. Two tears had rolled down her wet face and trembled on her upper lip.

"I'm more beautiful than anybody else," she said brokenly, "why can't I be happy?" Her moist eyes tore at his stability—her mouth turned slowly downward with an exquisite sadness: "I'd

---
35. **somnolent** *adj.:* sleepy.

like to marry you if you'll have me, Dexter. I suppose you think I'm not worth having, but I'll be so beautiful for you, Dexter."

A million phrases of anger, pride, passion, hatred, tenderness fought on his lips. Then a perfect wave of emotion washed over him, carrying off with it a sediment of wisdom, of convention,[36] of doubt, of honor. This was his girl who was speaking, his own, his beautiful, his pride.

F "Won't you come in?" He heard her draw in her breath sharply.

Waiting.

G "All right," his voice was trembling, "I'll come in."

V

It was strange that neither when it was over nor a long time afterward did he regret that night. Looking at it from the perspective of ten years, the fact that Judy's flare for him endured just one month seemed of little importance. Nor did it matter that by his yielding he subjected himself to a deeper agony in the end and gave serious hurt to Irene Sheerer and to Irene's parents, who had befriended him. There was nothing sufficiently pictorial about Irene's grief to stamp itself on his mind.

Dexter was at bottom hard-minded. The attitude of the city on his action was of no importance to him, not because he was going to leave the city, but because any outside attitude on the situation seemed superficial. He was completely indifferent to popular opinion. Nor, when he had seen that it was no use, that he did not possess in himself the power to move fundamentally or to hold Judy Jones, did he bear any malice toward her. He loved her, and he would love her until the day he was too old for loving—but he could not have her. So he tasted the deep pain that is reserved only for the strong, just as he had tasted for a little while the deep happiness. **H**

---
36. **convention** *n.:* accepted practices of social behavior.

DIRECT TEACHING

E **Literary Focus**

? **Motivation.** Why does Judy make a renewed play for Dexter? [Possible responses: She is jealous of Irene; she wants to test her power over Dexter; she really loves Dexter.]

F **Literary Focus**

? **Irony.** What is ironic about the fact that Dexter thinks of Judy as "his own"? [She is not "his own" and never has been; she continues to be capricious and elusive.]

G **Literary Focus**

? **Motivation.** Why does Dexter accept Judy's invitation? [Possible responses: He is too much in love with her to refuse; he believes this is the sole chance he has to get and keep Judy; he can't pass up a chance to fulfill his fantasy.]

H **Reading Skills**

? **Analyzing.** Does the narrator sympathize with Dexter or think that he is a fool for falling for Judy? [Possible responses: The narrator sympathizes with Dexter, as shown by the way he stresses Dexter's solidity, virtue, and strength. The narrator understands Dexter's dreams but also considers him foolish.] **Is Dexter "hard-minded" and "strong"? Why or why not?** [Possible responses: No; even if he has those traits, he is passive with Judy and accepts the superficial values of his society. Yes; he pursues his goals with determination.]

CONTENT-AREA CONNECTIONS

Art: Portrait of Judy
Individual activity. Dexter worships Judy and all that she represents to him. Have students create a portrait of Judy as she is described in the story. The portrait can be in any medium but must capture what Judy symbolizes to Dexter.

Creative Writing: Diary Entries
Individual activity. Have students write five diary entries for Judy Jones for the days when

- she goes for a golf lesson with her nurse
- she meets Dexter on the lake
- she leaves Dexter stranded at the picnic
- she returns from Florida
- she has been married for five years

Print and distribute the diaries. Then, use them as a springboard for a class discussion of Judy.

A Reading Skills

? Drawing inferences about characters. Biographer Matthew J. Bruccoli writes: "Fitzgerald developed a new American figure: the determined girl-woman. Not the cartoon flapper, but the warm, courageous, attractive, and chastely independent young woman competing at life and love for the highest stakes—her future." **Does Judy fit this description?** [Possible responses: Yes, Judy is courageous, attractive, and fiercely independent. No, Judy is not a warm person; she competes at life and love in order to make herself feel special, not to assure herself a happy future.]

B Literary Focus

? Irony. **What is ironic about Devlin's comment?** [Possible response: It is ironic because Dexter sees himself as a trespasser in the world of the rich, while Devlin sees him as a natural part of that world.]

C Literary Focus

? Motivation. **Why does Dexter want to take a train to Detroit?** [Possible responses: He wants to save Judy from her husband; he wants to assess the situation for himself; he still has a fantasy of being with Judy.]

A Even the ultimate falsity of the grounds upon which Judy terminated the engagement, that she did not want to "take him away" from Irene—Judy, who had wanted nothing else—did not revolt him. He was beyond any revulsion or any amusement.

He went East in February with the intention of selling out his laundries and settling in New York—but the war came to America in March and changed his plans. He returned to the West, handed over the management of the business to his partner, and went into the first officers' training camp in late April. He was one of those young thousands who greeted the war with a certain amount of relief, welcoming the liberation from webs of tangled emotion.

VI

This story is not his biography, remember, although things creep into it which have nothing to do with those dreams he had when he was young. We are almost done with them and with him now. There is only one more incident to be related here, and it happens seven years farther on.

It took place in New York, where he had done well—so well that there were no barriers too high for him. He was thirty-two years old, and, except for one flying trip immediately after the war, he had not been West in seven years. A man named Devlin from Detroit came into his office to see him in a business way, and then and there this incident occurred, and closed out, so to speak, this particular side of his life.

B "So you're from the Middle West," said the man Devlin with careless curiosity. "That's funny—I thought men like you were probably born and raised on Wall Street. You know—wife of one of my best friends in Detroit came from your city. I was an usher at the wedding."

Dexter waited with no apprehension of what was coming.

"Judy Simms," said Devlin with no particular interest; "Judy Jones she was once."

"Yes, I knew her." A dull impatience spread over him. He had heard, of course, that she was married—perhaps deliberately he had heard no more.

"Awfully nice girl," brooded Devlin meaninglessly, "I'm sort of sorry for her."

"Why?" Something in Dexter was alert, receptive, at once.

"Oh, Lud Simms has gone to pieces in a way. I don't mean he ill-uses her, but he drinks and runs around—"

"Doesn't she run around?"

"No. Stays at home with her kids."

"Oh."

"She's a little too old for him," said Devlin.

"Too old!" cried Dexter. "Why, man, she's only twenty-seven."

C He was possessed with a wild notion of rushing out into the streets and taking a train to Detroit. He rose to his feet spasmodically.

"I guess you're busy," Devlin apologized quickly. "I didn't realize—"

SKILLS REVIEW

Recognizing the theme. The pairing of the words *dreams* and *winter* in the story's title suggests that the dreams in question are fated to die—that they are nothing but faint consolations in the chilly landscape of reality. But do they die? Does Dexter wake up from his dreams, or does he only tell himself that he does? More broadly, Fitzgerald makes one wonder, "Can—or should—all dreams be attained?"

Activity. Have students make a comparison-contrast chart showing aspects of Dexter's dream and of his reality. Instruct students to include on their charts actions, images, events, and quotations from the story.

"No, I'm not busy," said Dexter, steadying his voice. "I'm not busy at all. Not busy at all. Did you say she was—twenty-seven? No, I said she was twenty-seven."

"Yes, you did," agreed Devlin dryly.

"Go on, then. Go on."

"What do you mean?"

"About Judy Jones."

Devlin looked at him helplessly.

"Well, that's—I told you all there is to it. He treats her like the devil. Oh, they're not going to get divorced or anything. When he's particularly outrageous she forgives him. In fact, I'm inclined to think she loves him. She was a pretty girl when she first came to Detroit."

A pretty girl! The phrase struck Dexter as ludicrous.

"Isn't she—a pretty girl, anymore?"

"Oh, she's all right."

"Look here," said Dexter, sitting down suddenly, "I don't understand. You say she was a 'pretty girl' and now you say she's 'all right.' I don't understand what you mean—Judy Jones wasn't a pretty girl, at all. She was a great beauty. Why, I knew her, I knew her. She was—"

Devlin laughed pleasantly.

"I'm not trying to start a row," he said. "I think Judy's a nice girl and I like her. I can't understand how a man like Lud Simms could fall madly in love with her, but he did." Then he added: "Most of the women like her."

Dexter looked closely at Devlin, thinking wildly that there must be a reason for this, some insensitivity in the man or some private malice.

"Lots of women fade just like *that*," Devlin snapped his fingers. "You must have seen it happen. Perhaps I've forgotten how pretty she was at her wedding. I've seen her so much since then, you see. She has nice eyes."

A sort of dullness settled down upon Dexter. For the first time in his life he felt like getting very drunk. He knew that he was laughing loudly at something Devlin had said, but he did not know what it was or why it was funny. When, in a few minutes, Devlin went, he lay down on his lounge and looked out the window at the New York skyline into which the sun was sinking in dull lovely shades of pink and gold.

He had thought that having nothing else to lose he was invulnerable at last—but he knew that he had just lost something more, as surely as if he had married Judy Jones and seen her fade away before his eyes.

> The dream was gone. Something had been taken from him.

The dream was gone. Something had been taken from him. In a sort of panic he pushed the palms of his hands into his eyes and tried to bring up a picture of the waters lapping on Sherry Island and the moonlit veranda, and gingham on the golf links and the dry sun and the gold color of her neck's soft down. And her mouth damp to his kisses and her eyes plaintive with melancholy and her freshness like new fine linen in the morning. Why, these things were no longer in the world! They had existed and they existed no longer.

For the first time in years the tears were streaming down his face. But they were for himself now. He did not care about mouth and eyes and moving hands. He wanted to care, and he could not care. For he had gone away and he could never go back anymore. The gates were closed, the sun was gone down, and there was no beauty but the gray beauty of steel that withstands all time. Even the grief he could have borne was left behind in the country of illusion, of youth, of the richness of life, where his winter dreams had flourished.

"Long ago," he said, "long ago, there was something in me, but now that thing is gone. Now that thing is gone, that thing is gone. I cannot cry. I cannot care. That thing will come back no more." ∎

Vocabulary
ludicrous (lōō′di·krəs) *adj.*: laughable; absurd.
plaintive (plān′tiv) *adj.*: expressing sadness.

Check Test: True-False

Monitoring students' progress. Guide the class in answering these questions.

1. Dexter first sees Judy at the lake. [F]
2. Dexter becomes wealthy from laundries. [T]
3. When Dexter gets engaged to Irene, Judy does not care. [F]
4. Dexter's courtship of Judy ends when he rejects her. [F]
5. When Dexter hears of Judy again, she is married with children. [T]

D Reading Skills

Drawing inferences about characters. How has Judy changed? [Possible response: Her character is completely transformed, as well as her looks. Instead of being desired by men, she is now liked by women.] What brought about these changes in Judy? Are they believable? [Possible responses: The changes could be the result of a disappointing marriage, childbearing, or aging. Yes; people can change dramatically. No; such radical change is improbable.]

E Literary Focus

Symbol. What does the sunset represent? [Possible responses: The sunset symbolizes the death of Dexter's dream. The pink represents Judy's beauty; the gold, her glamour.]

F Reading Skills

Analyzing. In the conclusion of *The Great Gatsby*, Nick Carraway describes the dream that motivated Gatsby: "Gatsby believed in the . . . future that year by year recedes before us. It eluded us then, but that's no matter—tomorrow we'll run faster, stretch out our arms farther. . . ." Would Dexter agree with Gatsby? Why or why not? [Possible response: Dexter would not agree, because he feels that he has lost his dream.]

G Reading Skills

Analyzing theme. Think about Dexter's romantic dream as a symbol for the American dream. What possible themes for the story can you infer from Dexter's words? [Possible responses: The American dream can never be fulfilled; the American dream will only lead to disappointment and loss.]

Vocabulary Development
Possible Answers

- *perturbation.* Sentence—The noise created such a <u>perturbation</u> that Jesse couldn't sleep. *Synonym*—The shocking news added to our <u>agitation</u>.

- *malicious.* Sentence—The wrestler made a <u>malicious</u> attempt to hurt his opponent. *Antonym*—The <u>benevolent</u> acts were intended to ease the plight of the homeless.

- *reserve.* Sentence—I demonstrated <u>reserve</u> by managing to keep my strong opinions to myself. *Antonym*—Larry's <u>rashness</u> showed that he couldn't always control his impulses.

- *petulance.* Sentence—The child's <u>petulance</u> spread throughout the room, and soon we were all irritable. *Synonym*—Her <u>patience</u> made us think she could endure even the most boring meetings.

- *mirth.* Sentence—The <u>mirth</u> the family demonstrated at dinner lifted our spirits. *Antonym*—Those who attended the funeral were overcome by <u>sadness</u>.

- *divergence.* Sentence—The jazz composition was a <u>divergence</u> from the hip-hop artist's repertoire. *Synonym*—Beatrice's strict routine was void of any <u>variance</u>.

- *turbulence.* Sentence—The stock market crash initiated a period of <u>turbulence</u> on Wall Street. *Antonym*—The <u>tranquility</u> of the countryside was a relief after living in the big city.

- *ludicrous.* Sentence—The clown's <u>ludicrous</u> costume made the audience laugh. *Synonym*—The meager amount of time we had to finish our assignment was <u>laughable</u>.

- *plaintive.* Sentence—The dog made <u>plaintive</u> sounds when its owner left for work. *Synonym*—The <u>melancholy</u> tone of Glenn's voice revealed his sadness.

WRITING
Fitzgerald's Fairy Tale?

In a book review of Fitzgerald's stories, the novelist and critic Jay McInerney wrote the following comment:

> The young (poor) boy's quest for the hand of the beautiful, rich princess is undoubtedly Fitzgerald's best plot, the fairy-tale skeleton of his jazz age tales. One supposes that magazine editors preferred the stories in which the quest is successful, but in the better ones, like "Winter Dreams" (1922) and "The Sensible Thing" (1924), the success is qualified or the quest ends in failure.

In a brief **essay**, analyze the ways in which "Winter Dreams" is like and unlike a fairy tale. Consider the story's **plot, characterization, tone,** and **theme.**

F. Scott and Zelda Fitzgerald (1921).

Vocabulary Development
Synonym and Antonym Mapping

elation	mirth
perturbation	divergence
malicious	turbulence
reserve	ludicrous
petulance	plaintive

Synonyms are words with the same or similar meanings. **Antonyms** are words with more or less opposite meanings. Make either a synonym or an antonym word map like the following one for each of the Vocabulary words (the first one has been done for you). You will have to think of either a synonym or an antonym for each word and then write sentences illustrating your understanding of the word. Feel free to consult a dictionary or a thesaurus.

Word	Sentence
elation	Dexter's feelings of <u>elation</u> were directly linked to how much attention Judy paid to him.
Antonym dejection	Dexter's <u>dejection</u> could be explained by the loss of his ideal.

ASSESSING

Assessment

- *Holt Assessment: Literature, Reading, and Vocabulary*

Be

A Ro

Make t

Faulkner,
tale, knew
and its po
in "A Rose
castes, the
ness with
of life, and
joy in it.

The fac
sensationa
in scandal
checkouts
of outrage
ture, thou
the event
one eccer
some imp
her comm
past, its p
its fierce i
all that is

Literar
Setting

Setting is
a story tal
customs a
including,
stereotyp
an offensiv
Miss Emily
It comes a
some of t
this langua
that Faulk
cally as po
of the rur
twentieth

William Faulkner
(1897–1962)

Yoknapatawpha County, Mississippi, is surely the hardest of American literary place-names to pronounce. Still, it is wise to learn how (yäk′nə·pə·tô′fə), for it is famous as the imagined world of William Faulkner, the scene of his most celebrated novels and stories. Imaginary Yoknapatawpha is similar in many ways to the actual impoverished farm-land, with its red-clay hills, that rings Oxford, Mississippi, home of the state's main university. It was there that William's father, Murry Falkner (William added the *u* to the family name), ran a livery stable and later became the university's business manager. William Faulkner lived and wrote there throughout most of his life.

The South Provides a Theme

Faulkner was a mediocre student and quit high school in the tenth grade, but he read widely and wrote poetry. At the outbreak of World War I, the U.S. Army rejected him because he failed to meet its height and weight requirements. However, he enlisted in the Royal Air Force of Canada and trained for flight duty, only to see the war end before he was commissioned. Returning to Oxford after the war, he took some courses at the university and did poorly in English. With neither profession nor skill and a marked distaste for regular employment, he seemed a moody and puzzling young man to his neighbors.

Faulkner took several short-lived jobs,

among them that of postmaster for the university. Resigning from that job, he wrote, "I will be damned if I propose to be at the beck and call of every itinerant scoundrel who has two cents to invest in a postage stamp."

In 1924, Faulkner left Oxford for New Orleans, where he met Sherwood Anderson, who had attracted much attention with the publication of *Winesburg, Ohio* (1919), his study of small-town life. Impressed and encouraged by Anderson, Faulkner tried his hand at fiction. In five months he completed a first novel, *Soldier's Pay,* a self-conscious story about the lost generation. Thereafter, Faulkner wrote with a tireless energy.

Within the next three years, Faulkner found his great theme: the American South as a microcosm for the universal themes of time, the passions of the human heart, and the destruction of the wilderness. Faulkner saw the South as a nation unto itself, with a strong sense of its noble past and an array of myths by which it clung to its pride, despite the humiliating defeat of the Civil War and the enforced acceptance of the distasteful values of an industrial North. Faulkner started to explore these themes in *Sartoris* (the first story set in mythical Yoknapatawpha) and *The Sound and the Fury,* two novels published within months of each other in 1929. *The Sound and the Fury* was a milestone in American literature, owing to Faulkner's bold manipulation of point of view and its stream-of-consciousness narrative technique.

In the decade that followed, Faulkner produced a succession of dazzling books: *As I Lay Dying* (1930), *Sanctuary* (1931), *Light in August* (1932), *Absalom, Absalom!* (1936)—considered by many readers to be his finest work— *The Unvanquished* (1938), and *The Hamlet* (1940). These works reveal Faulkner as equally skillful in the tragic or comic mode. He portrayed the South accurately, perceptively, and with a poignant ambivalence—on the one hand affectionate, on the other critical. He once said of the South, "Well, I love it and I hate it."

William Faulkner **643**

Grade-Level Skills
■ **Reading Skills**
Make inferences about character.

Review Skills
■ **Literary Skills**
Analyze the importance of the setting to the mood, tone, and meaning of the text.

More About the Writer
Background. Looking back over his career at the age of fifty-six, Faulkner wrote: "And now, at last, I have some perspective on all I have done. I mean, the work apart from me, the work which I did, apart from what I am. . . . And now I realize for the first time what an amazing gift I had: uneducated in every formal sense, without even very literate, let alone literary, companions, yet to have made the things I made. I don't know where it came from. I don't know why God or gods, or whoever it was, selected me to be the vessel. Believe me, this is not humility, false modesty; it is simply amazement."

(

Previ

To reinfo
use the \
plete the

1. The
   [tran

2. Her
   [arch

3. Beca
   he b

RESOURCES: READING

Planning
■ *One-Stop Planner* CD-ROM with ExamView Test Generator

Differentiating Instruction
■ *The Holt Reader*
■ *Holt Adapted Reader*
■ *Holt Reading Solutions*
■ *Supporting Instruction in Spanish*
■ *Audio CD Library, Selections and*

Summaries in Spanish
Vocabulary
■ *Vocabulary Development*

Grammar and Language
■ *Daily Language Activities*

Assessment
■ *Holt Assessment: Literature, Reading, and Vocabulary*
■ *One-Stop Planner* CD-ROM with

ExamView Test Generator
■ *Holt Online Assessment*

Internet
■ go.hrw.com (Keyword: LE5 11-5)
■ *Elements of Literature Online*

Media
■ *Audio CD Library*
■ *Audio CD Library, Selections and Summaries in Spanish*

Vocabulary Development

Practice

1. Possible answers:
   - *—anthropo—*: philanthropy
   - *—mono—*: monarch
   - *—physic—*: physical
   - *—flu—*: fluent
   - *—cept—*: intercept
   - *—duc—, —duct—*: educate
   - *—grad—, —gress—*: graduate
   - *—sed—, —sid—, —sess—*: preside

2. *astronomy.* Meaning of Word—the scientific study of the universe beyond the earth. *Family Word*—disaster.

   monograph. Meaning of Word—a scholarly paper or treatise. *Family Word*—photograph.

   psychiatry. Meaning of Word—the medical study of mental illness. *Family Word*—psychological.

   illuminate. Meaning of Word—to brighten with light; to clarify. *Family Word*—lucid.

   telescope. Meaning of Word—device for observing distant objects. *Family Word*—microscope.

   television. Meaning of Word—apparatus used for transmitting and receiving images of moving and stationary objects. *Family Word*—visual.

ASSESSING

Assessment

- *Holt Assessment: Literature, Reading, and Vocabulary*

RETEACHING

For a lesson reteaching theme and meaning, see **Reteaching,** p. 1117A.

Greek

Word	Root	Meaning of Root	Meaning of Word	Family Words
anthropoid	—anthropo—	human being	resembling a human	anthropology, anthropocentric
monotonous	—mono—	one	one tone; lacking variety	monad, monolith
physician	—physic—	of nature	doctor of medicine	physics, physiology

Latin

Word	Root	Meaning of Root	Meaning of Word	Family Words
influenced	—flu—	flow	affected	fluid, confluence
perceptible	—cept—	take hold	grasped by the senses	concept, precept
produced	—duc—, —duct—	lead; draw	brought forth	reduce, induction
progression	—grad—, —gress—	step; degree	advancement by steps	gradation, regression
subsided	—sed—, —sid—, —sess—	settle; sit	settled; became less active	sediment, sedate

PRACTICE

1. For each root listed in the charts, find one additional word in the same word family. You may use a dictionary for help.

2. Make a chart like the ones above for the following mathematical and scientific terms. Find the root and the meaning of the root given in parentheses for each word. Use a dictionary to find the meaning of the word. Then, find at least one family word. (You will note that several words also have common prefixes.)

   astronomy (—aster—, —astro—, "star")
   monograph (—graph—, "write; draw; record")
   psychiatry (—psych—, "mind; soul; spirit")
   illuminate (—luc—, —lumin—, "light")
   telescope (—scop—, "see")
   television (—vis—, —vid—, "see; look")

crystalloid

humanoid

android

—oid, suffix meaning "like"

Family Tree

Analyzing Literature

As you've seen from the works in this section, modern short stories pack a lot of ideas into just a few pages. Short story writers don't say *everything* they want to communicate. They also depend on their readers to figure out some ideas. To delve into a writer's meaning, you must **analyze** a story, breaking it down into its parts and examining how those parts work together to produce an overall effect. In this workshop you will write an essay that does just that.

Choose a Story You may choose to analyze a short story you already know and like. If you prefer to choose something new, look through anthologies or this textbook to find a complex, interesting story. Check with your teacher to make sure your choice is appropriate.

Analyze the Story Analyzing a literary work is like taking apart an engine to see how it works. First, read the story to become familiar with the plot and to understand the story's significant ideas. Then, use the questions in the left-hand column of the chart below to analyze specific elements of the story. The sample answers are for an analysis of Ernest Hemingway's story "Soldier's Home" (page 611).

Writing Assignment
Write a literary analysis of a short story.

ANALYZING A LITERARY WORK

Analysis Questions	Sample Answers
What happens in the **plot?** How is the main conflict resolved?	A young soldier returns from war and finds himself alienated from his family. The soldier ends up living a lie.
What changes take place within the main **character?**	At the beginning of the story, the soldier wants to talk about his experiences, but he soon learns to lie or avoid discussing them at all.
What mood does the **setting** convey? Does the setting affect the plot?	The setting is an ordinary small town. The ordinariness of the town contrasts with the soldier's experiences in war and creates a mood of understated anxiety.
What **universal themes** are addressed in the story?	The story addresses the theme of alienation.
Does the story contain any **symbols** (objects or characters that have meanings of their own but also stand for something else)?	The girls that the soldier watches symbolize the normal life he cannot have.
Are there any **ambiguities** (things that can be understood in more than one way), **nuances** (fine shades of meaning), or **complexities** (interrelated ideas) in the text?	Hemingway never tells exactly what happened to the soldier during the war—he allows the reader to infer this information from the effects the experiences have had on the character.

(continued)

Mini-Workshop: Analyzing Literature   665

PRETEACHING

Motivate. Ask students to name short stories they have enjoyed reading. Have students discuss the specific literary elements they liked in the stories, and lead students to give reasons why those elements worked so well. For example, if they enjoyed the scary atmosphere and tone of a short story by Edgar Allan Poe, have students recall images, details, and, if possible, diction that contributed to the effect. Point out to students that analyzing something means providing specific evidence for one's conclusions.

DIRECT TEACHING

Analyze the Story
Direct students to create charts similar to the one on this page to help them analyze the stories they choose. Tell students that, even though they will not address every literary element in their analyses, writing notes on each element can help them choose the most significant elements, draw connections among those elements, and develop details for their analyses.

DIFFERENTIATING INSTRUCTION

Advanced Learners
Enrichment. Challenge students to analyze a story on the reading list for the next grade level, or to analyze a well-known story by a famous author they have never before read.

COLLECTION 5 RESOURCES: WRITING

Planning
- *One-Stop Planner* CD-ROM with ExamView Test Generator

Differentiating Instruction
- *Workshop Resources: Writing, Listening, and Speaking*
- *Family Involvement Activities in English and Spanish*
- *Supporting Instruction in Spanish*

Writing and Language
- *Workshop Resources: Writing, Listening, and Speaking*
- *Daily Language Activities*
- *Language Handbook Worksheets*

Assessment
- *Holt Assessment: Writing, Listening, and Speaking*

- *One-Stop Planner* CD-ROM with ExamView Test Generator
- *Holt Online Assessment*
- *Holt Online Essay Scoring*

Internet
- go.hrw.com (Keyword: LE5 11-5)
- *Elements of Literature Online*

Grade-Level Skills

■ **Literary Skills**

Analyze archetypes drawn from myth and tradition.

Review Skills

■ **Literary Skills**

Analyze influences on characters (such as internal and external conflict) and the way those influences affect the plot.

More About the Writer

Background. The stories in *The Red Pony* are among John Steinbeck's earliest works of fiction. The Tiflin ranch in the stories is based on the ranch that Steinbeck's grandparents owned.

Another early novel, *Tortilla Flat* (1935) is named for a shabby district overlooking Monterey on the California coast, where Steinbeck lived as a young man. The locale is inhabited by a colorful gang whose exploits are reminiscent of Steinbeck's own literary heroes—the knights of King Arthur.

Although his later novels, especially *East of Eden* (1952) and *The Winter of Our Discontent* (1961), did not achieve the critical success of his earlier work, Steinbeck enjoyed both financial success and great popularity among the reading public.

For Independent Reading

Mention to students that *Of Mice and Men* (1937) is a story about the bond of friendship and the hopes of simple men. It has a remarkable ending.

John Steinbeck
(1902–1968)

Most writers would probably agree that fiction that delivers a political message may be effective propaganda but it is unlikely to be art. John Steinbeck would *not* have agreed with this precept, and he is a notable exception to it.

During the 1930s, the Great Depression cost millions of people their jobs and shook their faith in the American dream. But big business and the corporate farm seemed untouched by hard times; they were angrily perceived by many as impersonal and indifferent to human hardship.

Many novelists of the time were moved by this sense of injustice and turned their pens to a byproduct of the Depression known as the protest novel. Among these writers, John Steinbeck was the most widely praised.

Steinbeck was born in California's Salinas Valley in 1902, the son of a county treasurer and a schoolteacher. Although he graduated from high school and spent some time at Stanford University, he took more pride in the many jobs he held as a young man than in his formal education. He worked as a mason's assistant, fruit picker, apprentice painter, laboratory assistant, caretaker, surveyor, and journalist. He also wrote seventeen novels, in addition to stories, plays, and screenplays.

Steinbeck's first major success came in 1937 with *Of Mice and Men,* a short, bestselling novel that Steinbeck himself adapted for the Broadway theater. It is a tale of two itinerant farmhands: George and the powerful but simple-minded Lennie. Steinbeck took a pathetic situation and transformed it into an affirmative acceptance of life's brutal conflicts, along with life's possibilities for fellowship and courage.

He followed this success by living and working with some Oklahoma farmers—known as Okies—over the next two years. The result was his strongest and most enduring novel, *The Grapes of Wrath* (1939). This novel tells of the Joad family and their forced migration from the Dust Bowl of Oklahoma to California, the region that promised work at decent wages and a chance to buy land. Once in California, however, the Joads find only the exploitation and poverty of labor camps. Gradually they learn what *Okies* really means—people who never even had a chance.

The Grapes of Wrath is an angry book that speaks out on behalf of the migrant workers. Steinbeck sharply criticizes a system that bankrupted thousands of farmers and turned them from their own land, making them into paid help for the big growers. When the novel appeared, it was both praised and condemned, and it became the most widely read of all the novels of the 1930s.

The Grapes of Wrath won a Pulitzer Prize in 1940. After this major success, however, Steinbeck's eminence waned. In 1962, Steinbeck was awarded the Nobel Prize in literature and published *Travels with Charley,* a nostalgic account of his odyssey across America with his aged poodle, Charley. But Steinbeck's reputation is grounded on those earlier novels that portray California as the land of American promise.

For Independent Reading

These works by Steinbeck are recommended:

- *Of Mice and Men* (novel)
- *The Grapes of Wrath* (novel)
- *Travels with Charley* (nonfiction)

RESOURCES: READING

Planning
- *One-Stop Planner* CD-ROM with ExamView Test Generator

Differentiating Instruction
- *Supporting Instruction in Spanish*
- *Audio CD Library, Selections and Summaries in Spanish*

Vocabulary
- *Vocabulary Development*

Grammar and Language
- *Daily Language Activities*

Assessment
- *Holt Assessment: Literature, Reading, and Vocabulary*
- *One-Stop Planner* CD-ROM with ExamView Test Generator

- *Holt Online Assessment*

Internet
- go.hrw.com (Keyword: LE5 11-5)
- *Elements of Literature Online*

Media
- *Audio CD Library*
- *Audio CD Library, Selections and Summaries in Spanish*

The Leader of the People

Make the Connection
Quickwrite

It seems that in every generation there are older people who say, "It was different in my day." These people feel nostalgic about their past, remembering it as a golden age when everything was somehow better, happier, more heroic. In fact, some people end up living mainly in memories of a past that no longer exists and may never have been as they remember it.

Do you believe that the time of heroes is long past? Who are today's heroes, or are there none worthy of the label? What opportunities do you see for heroism today? Quickwrite your thoughts.

Literary Focus
Conflict

"The Leader of the People" shows three generations of a family in conflict because of differences in age, gender, personal histories, and the roles they play on the family ranch. Some conflicts in the story are **external conflicts:** They occur between two or more people. Others are **internal conflicts:** Those occur inside a person's mind. To understand one of the conflicts in the story, take a close look at the recurring dream of a more heroic American past.

> **Conflict** is a struggle between opposing forces or characters in a story.
>
> Conflict can be **internal** (a character struggles with conscience, for example) or **external** (a character struggles against a force of nature, another character, or a whole society).
>
> *For more on Conflict, see the Handbook of Literary and Historical Terms.*

Background

In "The Leader of the People," John Steinbeck explores the conflict between dream and reality at the heart of so much American fiction. This story appears as the fourth and final part of Steinbeck's novel *The Red Pony* (1945). Each part of this novel was published as a complete story. The stories, all connected by their characters and settings, are "The Gift," "The Great Mountains," "The Promise," and "The Leader of the People."

Vocabulary Development

arrogant (ar′ə·gənt) *adj.*: proud and overly confident.

immune (i·myo͞on′) *adj.*: protected.

cleft (kleft) *n.*: opening or crack in something.

contemptuously (kən·temp′cho͞o·əs·lē) *adv.*: scornfully.

judiciously (jo͞o·dish′əs·lē) *adv.*: wisely, like a judge.

rancor (raŋ′kər) *n.*: anger.

convened (kən·vēnd′) *v.*: assembled.

listlessly (list′lis·lē) *adv.*: wearily; without energy or interest in anything.

retract (ri·trakt′) *v.*: take back; draw back.

disconsolately (dis·kän′sə·lit·lē) *adv.*: unhappily.

INTERNET

Vocabulary Practice
•
Cross-Curricular Connection
•
More About John Steinbeck

Keyword: LE5 11–5

SKILLS FOCUS

Literary Skills
Understand internal and external conflict.

John Steinbeck **669**

PRETEACHING

Summary ⟷ *at grade level*

When Jody Tiflin's grandfather visits the family, Jody eagerly anticipates hearing the old man retell his stories of leading a wagon train west to California. Jody's father Carl is impatient with Grandfather's stories but grudgingly allows him to tell them at dinner. However, the next morning, Grandfather overhears Carl complaining about the tedious stories. Carl apologizes, but Grandfather realizes that the heroism he hoped to evoke with his stories has died, along with the dream of "westering"—a hunger for the frontier. Seeing his grandfather's despair, Jody tries to comfort him with a lemonade.

Selection Starter

Build background. In "The Gift," the first story of four in *The Red Pony,* set on the Tiflin ranch, Jody is thrilled to receive a red pony for his tenth birthday. Although Jody and the ranch-hand Billy Buck take good care of the pony, it dies. In "The Great Mountains," an old Mexican stranger named Gitano returns to his birthplace—the Tiflin ranch—to die. Although Jody and his mother want Gitano to stay, Mr. Tiflin forces him to leave the next day. In the third story, "The Promise," Jody works all summer to get another colt. When the colt is being born, Billy Buck realizes he must kill the mare to save the colt.

Previewing Vocabulary

Ask students to read the definitions of the Vocabulary words listed in the Vocabulary Development box on p. 669. Then, have them choose the Vocabulary word that best completes each analogy below.

1. EMOTION : HARDENED :: disease : [immune]

2. ACTIVE : EXCITEDLY :: passive : [listlessly]

3. QUICKLY : RAPIDLY :: unhappily : [disconsolately]

4. ENERGETICALLY : LETHARGICALLY :: admiringly : [contemptuously]

5. MARRIAGE : LOVE :: revenge : [rancor]

6. OUTSIDE : PROJECT :: inside : [retract]

7. HUMBLE : MODEST :: proud : [arrogant]

8. STUDENTS : ASSEMBLED :: jury : [convened]

9. HOLE : OPENING :: cave : [cleft]

10. DUNCE : FOOLISHLY :: sage : [judiciously]

VIEWING THE ART

Phil Paradise (1905–1997) was a California painter, sculptor, illustrator, graphic artist, and teacher. During the 1940s, he also served as a film art director for Paramount Studios. He is known for western subjects. San Luis Obispo lies 112 miles south of Salinas, California.

Activity. Ask students to comment on how the shapes, colors, and action of the painting help them to determine the time of day. [Possible responses: Contrasts of light and dark suggest early evening; the men in the center seem to be transferring the day's last load of hay into a loft.] **Ask students to describe the painting's mood.** [Possible response: The mood is peaceful and idyllic.]

670 Collection 5 The Moderns: 1914–1939

DIFFERENTIATING INSTRUCTION

Learners Having Difficulty
Activity. Since there is a great deal of dialogue in this story, you may wish to assign roles (narrator included). Have a few students read parts of the story aloud while others listen and jot down plot summaries after each page. Direct listeners to include at least five comments on the story's events, a question about the action, or a personal reaction to the action. Rotate roles so that everyone gets a chance to read and to create a plot summary.

Advanced Learners
Enrichment. Invite students to read the other three stories in *The Red Pony* to find out how they relate to "The Leader of the People." Students should consider plot, theme, setting, characters, and tone in their analysis. Invite students to share their findings with the class.

The Leader of the People

John Steinbeck

On Saturday afternoon Billy Buck, the ranch-hand, raked together the last of the old year's haystack and pitched small forkfuls over the wire fence to a few mildly interested cattle. High in the air small clouds like puffs of cannon smoke were driven eastward by the March wind. The wind could be heard whishing in the brush on the ridge crests, but no breath of it penetrated down into the ranch-cup.

The little boy, Jody, emerged from the house eating a thick piece of buttered bread. He saw Billy working on the last of the haystack. Jody tramped down scuffing his shoes in a way he had been told was destructive to good shoe-leather. A flock of white pigeons flew out of the black cypress tree as Jody passed, and circled the tree and landed again. A half-grown tortoise-shell[1] cat leaped from the bunkhouse porch, galloped on stiff legs across the road, whirled and galloped back again. Jody picked up a stone to help the game along, but he was too late, for the cat was under the porch before the stone could be discharged. He threw the stone into the cypress tree and started the white pigeons on another whirling flight.

Arriving at the used-up haystack, the boy leaned against the barbed wire fence. "Will that be all of it, do you think?" he asked.

The middle-aged ranch-hand stopped his careful raking and stuck his fork[2] into the ground. He took off his black hat and smoothed down his hair. "Nothing left of it that isn't soggy from ground moisture," he said. He replaced his hat and rubbed his dry leathery hands together.

"Ought to be plenty mice," Jody suggested.

---

1. **tortoise-shell** *n.* used as *adj.:* having a pattern of brown and yellow markings, as commonly seen on the shell of a tortoise.
2. **fork** *n.:* pitchfork.

Ranch Near San Luis Obispo, Evening Light (c. 1935) by Phil Paradise. Oil on canvas (28″ × 34″).

The Buck Collection, Laguna Hills, California.

John Steinbeck   671

A Literary Focus

❓ Conflict. Why does Steinbeck use such elevated language—"the time of disaster had come"—to describe Jody's plans to kill the mice? [Possible response: Steinbeck exaggerates the conflict with the mice to introduce the themes of doom, disaster, and survival. Explain that this conflict will lead into the major conflicts in the story: the loss of heroic opportunities, the past versus the present, Grandfather versus Carl Tiflin, and Jody versus his father.]

B Literary Focus

❓ Conflict. How does this conversation suggest that there is a conflict between Jody and his father? [Possible response: "Ominously" and "You know how he is" hint at a problem between Jody and his father.]

C Literary Focus

❓ Characterization. What clues to the character of Carl Tiflin does the narrator provide here? [Possible responses: The dog's fear of him suggests that Tiflin has a dominant and perhaps unpredictable personality. Tiflin's silhouette against the sky suggests that Tiflin is independent and authoritative.]

D English-Language Learners

❓ Idioms. Based on the context, what do you think the name Big-Britches means? Is it something you would like to be called? Why or why not? [Possible responses: Literally, it means someone who is too big for his or her pants. Figuratively, it mocks people whose ambition outstrips their experience and ability. Most students would not like to be called this.]

"Lousy with them," said Billy. "Just crawling with mice."

"Well, maybe, when you get all through, I could call the dogs and hunt the mice."

"Sure, I guess you could," said Billy Buck. He lifted a forkful of the damp ground-hay and threw it into the air. Instantly three mice leaped out and burrowed frantically under the hay again.

A Jody sighed with satisfaction. Those plump, sleek, arrogant mice were doomed. For eight months they had lived and multiplied in the haystack. They had been immune from cats, from traps, from poison and from Jody. They had grown smug in their security, overbearing and fat. Now the time of disaster had come; they would not survive another day.

Billy looked up at the top of the hills that surrounded the ranch. "Maybe you better ask your father before you do it," he suggested.

"Well, where is he? I'll ask him now."

"He rode up to the ridge ranch after dinner. He'll be back pretty soon."

Jody slumped against the fence post. "I don't think he'd care."

B As Billy went back to his work he said ominously, "You'd better ask him anyway. You know how he is."

Jody did know. His father, Carl Tiflin, insisted upon giving permission for anything that was done on the ranch, whether it was important or not. Jody sagged farther against the post until he was sitting on the ground. He looked up at the little puffs of wind-driven cloud. "Is it like to rain, Billy?"

"It might. The wind's good for it, but not strong enough."

"Well, I hope it don't rain until after I kill those damn mice." He looked over his shoulder to see whether Billy had noticed the mature profanity. Billy worked on without comment.

Jody turned back and looked at the side-hill where the road from the outside world came down. The hill was washed with lean March sunshine. Silver thistles, blue lupins[3] and a few

---

3. **lupins** (loo′pinz) *n. pl.*: flowering plants of the bean family; more often spelled *lupines*.

---

poppies bloomed among the sage bushes. Halfway up the hill Jody could see Doubletree Mutt, the black dog, digging in a squirrel hole. He paddled for a while and then paused to kick bursts of dirt out between his hind legs, and he dug with an earnestness which belied the knowledge he must have had that no dog had ever caught a squirrel by digging in a hole.

C Suddenly, while Jody watched, the black dog stiffened, and backed out of the hole and looked up the hill toward the cleft in the ridge where the road came through. Jody looked up too. For a moment Carl Tiflin on horseback stood out against the pale sky and then he moved down the road toward the house. He carried something white in his hand.

The boy started to his feet. "He's got a letter," Jody cried. He trotted away toward the ranch house, for the letter would probably be read aloud and he wanted to be there. He reached the house before his father did, and ran in. He heard Carl dismount from his creaking saddle and slap the horse on the side to send it to the barn where Billy would unsaddle it and turn it out.

Jody ran into the kitchen. "We got a letter!" he cried.

His mother looked up from a pan of beans. "Who has?"

"Father has. I saw it in his hand."

Carl strode into the kitchen then, and Jody's mother asked, "Who's the letter from, Carl?"

He frowned quickly. "How did you know there was a letter?"

She nodded her head in the boy's direction. "Big-Britches Jody told me."

D Jody was embarrassed.

His father looked down at him contemptuously. "He *is* getting to be a Big-Britches," Carl

---

Vocabulary

arrogant (ar′ə·gənt) *adj.*: proud and overly confident.
immune (i·myoon′) *adj.*: protected.
cleft (kleft) *n.*: opening or crack in something.
contemptuously (kən·temp′choo·əs·lē) *adv.*: scornfully.

DEVELOPING FLUENCY

Paired activity. Pair students to read the story out loud to each other. At the end of each page, partners should independently write a prediction about what will happen next. Have partners trade papers and jot down their reactions to the other's predictions. Encourage students to point out and read sections of the text that support their predictions. As students read, have them check and revise the predictions they made for previous pages.

said. "He's minding everybody's business but his own. Got his big nose into everything."

Mrs. Tiflin relented a little. "Well, he hasn't enough to keep him busy. Who's the letter from?"

Carl still frowned on Jody. "I'll keep him busy if he isn't careful." He held out a sealed letter. "I guess it's from your father."

Mrs. Tiflin took a hairpin from her head and slit open the flap. Her lips pursed <u>judiciously</u>. Jody saw her eyes snap back and forth over the lines. "He says," she translated, "he says he's going to drive out Saturday to stay for a little while. Why, this is Saturday. The letter must have been delayed." She looked at the postmark. "This was mailed day before yesterday. It should have been here yesterday." She looked up questioningly at her husband, and then her face darkened angrily. "Now what have you got that look on you for? He doesn't come often."

Carl turned his eyes away from her anger. He could be stern with her most of the time, but when occasionally her temper arose, he could not combat it.

"What's the matter with you?" she demanded again.

In his explanation there was a tone of apology Jody himself might have used. "It's just that he talks," Carl said lamely. "Just talks."

"Well, what of it? You talk yourself."

"Sure I do. But your father only talks about one thing."

"Indians!" Jody broke in excitedly. "Indians and crossing the plains!"

Carl turned fiercely on him. "You get out, Mr. Big-Britches! Go on, now! Get out!"

Jody went miserably out the back door and closed the screen with elaborate quietness. Under the kitchen window his shamed, downcast eyes fell upon a curiously shaped stone, a stone of such fascination that he squatted down and picked it up and turned it over in his hands.

The voices came clearly to him through the open kitchen window. "Jody's damn well right," he heard his father say. "Just Indians and crossing the plains. I've heard that story about how the horses got driven off about a thousand times. He just goes on and on, and he never changes a word in the things he tells."

When Mrs. Tiflin answered her tone was so changed that Jody, outside the window, looked up from his study of the stone. Her voice had become soft and explanatory. Jody knew how her face would have changed to match the tone. She said quietly, "Look at it this way, Carl. That was the big thing in my father's life. He led a wagon train clear across the plains to the coast, and when it was finished, his life was done. It was a big thing to do, but it didn't last long enough. Look!" she continued, "it's as though he was born to do that, and after he finished it, there wasn't anything more for him to do but think about it and talk about it. If there'd been any farther west to go, he'd have gone. He's told me so himself. But at last there was the ocean. He lives right by the ocean where he had to stop."

She had caught Carl, caught him and entangled him in her soft tone.

"I've seen him," he agreed quietly. "He goes down and stares off west over the ocean." His voice sharpened a little. "And then he goes up to the Horseshoe Club in Pacific Grove, and he tells people how the Indians drove off the horses."

She tried to catch him again. "Well, it's everything to him. You might be patient with him and pretend to listen."

Carl turned impatiently away. "Well, if it gets too bad, I can always go down to the bunkhouse and sit with Billy," he said irritably. He walked through the house and slammed the front door after him.

Jody ran to his chores. He dumped the grain to the chickens without chasing any of them. He gathered the eggs from the nests. He trotted into the house with the wood and interlaced it so carefully in the wood-box that two armloads seemed to fill it to overflowing.

His mother had finished the beans by now.

Vocabulary

judiciously (jōō·dish′əs·lē) *adv.*: wisely, like a judge.

John Steinbeck **673**

E **Literary Focus**

❓ **Conflict.** What is the conflict in this scene? Who do you think has the upper hand? Why? [Possible responses: Mr. Tiflin doesn't want Grandfather to visit, but Mrs. Tiflin does. She seems more dominant now since Mr. Tiflin, normally stern and inflexible, backs away from his wife's anger.]

F **Literary Focus**

❓ **Conflict.** Why does Carl yell at Jody? What does this action indicate about Jody's position in the family? [Possible responses: Carl misdirects his anger for his wife and her father onto Jody. This suggests that Jody is not respected because he is still a child.]

G **Reading Skills**

❓ **Drawing inferences.** What does Steinbeck mean when he says that Jody's mother "had caught Carl, caught him and entangled him in her soft tone"? [Possible responses: Her soft, gentle manner defuses Carl's anger; her gentle tone exposes how harsh and unfair he is being.]

H **English-Language Learners**

Building background knowledge. Explain that a *bunkhouse* is a separate structure where the ranch workers sleep.

CONTENT-AREA CONNECTIONS

History: Westward Ho!
Individual activity. Ask students to research the westward movement in the mid-nineteenth century and read about the difficulties experienced by pioneers who made the overland trek. Have students narrow their topic to a specific destination—perhaps California or another western region that students have connections to. Students may present their research either as a report to the rest of the class or as a research paper. Tell them to include illustrations, photographs, and maps.

? **Imagery.** How does Steinbeck evoke the ranch setting? [Possible responses: He creates vivid images that appeal to the senses. For example, tearing off the sage and rubbing it appeals to touch and smell; the dogs' yapping appeals to hearing.]

B English-Language Learners

Multiple-meaning words. Explain that in this context *flirted* means "moved in a rapid and jerky manner." Have students identify another common meaning for *flirted*. [played at being in love; considered an idea]

C Literary Focus

? **Characterization.** What does this description reveal about Grandfather's character? [Possible responses: His giant shadow, flickering darkly behind him, symbolizes his reputation. This image suggests that his greatest achievements are in the past; also his "granite dignity" and purposefulness may make him unable or unwilling to adapt to change.]

She stirred up the fire and brushed off the stove-top with a turkey wing. Jody peered cautiously at her to see whether any rancor toward him remained. "Is he coming today?" Jody asked.

"That's what his letter said."

"Maybe I better walk up the road to meet him."

Mrs. Tiflin clanged the stove-lid shut. "That would be nice," she said. "He'd probably like to be met."

"I guess I'll just do it then."

Outside, Jody whistled shrilly to the dogs. "Come on up the hill," he commanded. The two dogs waved their tails and ran ahead. Along the roadside the sage had tender new tips. Jody tore off some pieces and rubbed them on his hands until the air was filled with the sharp wild smell. With a rush the dogs leaped from the road and yapped into the brush after a rabbit. That was the last Jody saw of them, for when they failed to catch the rabbit, they went back home.

Jody plodded on up the hill toward the ridge top. When he reached the little cleft where the road came through, the afternoon wind struck him and blew up his hair and ruffled his shirt. He looked down on the little hills and ridges below and then out at the huge green Salinas Valley. He could see the white town of Salinas far out in the flat and the flash of its windows under the waning sun. Directly below him, in an oak tree, a crow congress had convened. The tree was black with crows all cawing at once.

Then Jody's eyes followed the wagon road down from the ridge where he stood, and lost it behind a hill, and picked it up again on the other side. On that distant stretch he saw a cart slowly pulled by a bay[4] horse. It disappeared behind the hill. Jody sat down on the ground and watched the place where the cart would reappear again. The wind sang on the hilltops and the puff-ball clouds hurried eastward.

Then the cart came into sight and stopped. A man dressed in black dismounted from the seat and walked to the horse's head. Although it was

---

4. **bay** *adj.:* reddish brown.

---

so far away, Jody knew he had unhooked the check-rein, for the horse's head dropped forward. The horse moved on, and the man walked slowly up the hill beside it. Jody gave a glad cry and ran down the road toward them. The squirrels bumped along off the road, and a roadrunner flirted its tail and raced over the edge of the hill and sailed out like a glider.

Jody tried to leap into the middle of his shadow at every step. A stone rolled under his foot and he went down. Around a little bend he raced, and there, a short distance ahead, were his grandfather and the cart. The boy dropped from his unseemly[5] running and approached at a dignified walk.

The horse plodded stumble-footedly up the hill and the old man walked beside it. In the lowering sun their giant shadows flickered darkly behind them. The grandfather was dressed in a black broadcloth suit and he wore kid congress gaiters[6] and a black tie on a short, hard collar. He carried his black slouch hat in his hand. His white beard was cropped close and his white eyebrows overhung his eyes like mustaches. The blue eyes were sternly merry. About the whole face and figure there was a granite dignity, so that every motion seemed an impossible thing. Once at rest, it seemed the old man would be stone, would never move again. His steps were slow and certain. Once made, no step could ever be retraced; once headed in a direction, the path would never bend nor the pace increase nor slow.

When Jody appeared around the bend, Grandfather waved his hat slowly in welcome, and he called, "Why, Jody! Come down to meet me, have you?"

Jody sidled[7] near and turned and matched

---

5. **unseemly** *adj.:* improper.
6. **kid congress gaiters:** high leather (kid) boots with elastic inserts in each side.
7. **sidled** (sīd'ld) *v.:* approached sideways.

Vocabulary

rancor (raŋ'kər) *n.:* anger.
convened (kən·vēnd') *v.:* assembled.

Primary Source

In an introduction to a critical study of his short novels, John Steinbeck recalled, "*The Red Pony* was written a long time ago, when there was desolation in my family. The first death had occurred. And the family, which every child believes to be immortal, was shattered. Perhaps this is the first adulthood of any man or woman. The first tortured question 'Why?' and then acceptance, and then the child becomes a man. *The Red Pony* was an attempt, an experiment if you wish, to set down this loss and acceptance and growth."

his step to the old man's step and stiffened his body and dragged his heels a little. "Yes, sir," he said. "We got your letter only today."

"Should have been here yesterday," said Grandfather. "It certainly should. How are all the folks?"

"They're fine, sir." He hesitated and then suggested shyly, "Would you like to come on a mouse hunt tomorrow, sir?"

"Mouse hunt, Jody?" Grandfather chuckled. "Have the people of this generation come down to hunting mice? They aren't very strong, the new people, but I hardly thought mice would be game for them."

"No, sir. It's just play. The haystack's gone. I'm going to drive out the mice to the dogs. And you can watch, or even beat the hay a little."

The stern, merry eyes turned down on him. "I see. You don't eat them, then. You haven't come to that yet."

Jody explained, "The dogs eat them, sir. It wouldn't be much like hunting Indians, I guess."

"No, not much—but then later, when the troops were hunting Indians and shooting children and burning teepees, it wasn't much different from your mouse hunt."

They topped the rise and started down into the ranch cup, and they lost the sun from their shoulders. "You've grown," Grandfather said. "Nearly an inch, I should say."

"More," Jody boasted. "Where they mark me on the door, I'm up more than an inch since Thanksgiving even."

Grandfather's rich throaty voice said, "Maybe you're getting too much water and turning to pith and stalk. Wait until you head out, and then we'll see."[8]

Jody looked quickly into the old man's face to see whether his feelings should be hurt, but there was no will to injure, no punishing nor putting-in-your-place light in the keen blue eyes. "We might kill a pig," Jody suggested.

"Oh, no! I couldn't let you do that. You're just humoring me. It isn't the time and you know it."

"You know Riley, the big boar, sir?"

"Yes. I remember Riley well."

"Well, Riley ate a hole into that same haystack, and it fell down on him and smothered him."

"Pigs do that when they can," said Grandfather.

"Riley was a nice pig, for a boar, sir. I rode him sometimes, and he didn't mind."

A door slammed at the house below them, and they saw Jody's mother standing on the porch waving her apron in welcome. And they saw Carl Tiflin walking up from the barn to be at the house for the arrival.

The sun had disappeared from the hills by now. The blue smoke from the house chimney hung in flat layers in the purpling ranch-cup. The puff-ball clouds, dropped by the falling wind, hung listlessly in the sky.

Billy Buck came out of the bunkhouse and

---

8. **Maybe . . . we'll see:** Like an overwatered plant, Jody may grow tall but not be very productive. Not until he "heads out" will anyone know what he is capable of.

Vocabulary

listlessly (list'lis·lē) *adv.:* wearily; without energy or interest in anything.

D **Literary Focus**

❷ Conflict. What does Grandfather's reaction suggest about his relationship to the people of this new generation? [Possible response: His laughter at the idea of a mouse hunt suggests that Grandfather has little respect for the next generation; he seems to believe that the present generation lacks strength and courage.]

E **Content-Area Connections**

History: Pioneers

In 1841, the first pioneers traveled in covered wagons across the plains. By 1843, more than one thousand people had risked their lives trekking across America. Within three decades, more than 350,000 settlers had moved to the Pacific territories of Oregon and California. Grandfather's comparison of hunting Indians and hunting mice is ambiguous—he may be gloating over or condemning actions that pioneers and their government took against the Native Americans over their land.

CONTENT-AREA CONNECTIONS

Health: Disease Prevention

Jody is excited about killing the mice for the thrill of the hunt, but mice and rats do pose a serious health risk. In addition to damaging food in storehouses, rodents transmit diseases, such as rabies and typhus. They also attack animals, poultry, and occasionally humans.

Small-group activity. Have students find out about the risks and costs of rodent infestations in modern cities and on farms. What methods are the most successful for controlling these pests?

VIEWING THE ART

Helen Lundeberg (1908–1999) captures the sense of a "heroic time" in *Pioneers of the West,* an idealized portrait of pioneer families.

Activity. Ask students how the artist's emphasis on large, stylized human shapes and golden tones, rather than a realistically detailed wagon train, connects with Jody's thoughts on p. 679—his dreams of "a race of giants," "phantoms" crossing westward. [Possible responses: The lack of fine detail, the golden shades, and the stylized human figures make the pioneers seem proud, noble, and almost godlike.]

A **Reading Skills**

? **Speculating.** Why do you think Billy and Grandfather feel this mutual admiration? [Possible responses: Both seem to be independent men who have worked with animals, lived alone, and retained a youthful sense of adventure.]

Pioneers of the West (1934) by Helen Lundeberg. Oil on canvas (40″ × 50¼″).
National Museum of American Art, Washington D.C./Courtesy Art Resource, New York.

A flung a wash basin of soapy water on the ground. He had been shaving in mid-week, for Billy held Grandfather in reverence, and Grandfather said that Billy was one of the few men of the new generation who had not gone soft. Although Billy was in middle age, Grandfather considered him a boy. Now Billy was hurrying toward the house too.

When Jody and Grandfather arrived, the three were waiting for them in front of the yard gate.

Carl said, "Hello, sir. We've been looking for you."

Mrs. Tiflin kissed Grandfather on the side of his beard, and stood still while his big hand patted her shoulder. Billy shook hands solemnly, grinning under his straw mustache. "I'll put up your horse," said Billy, and he led the rig away.

Grandfather watched him go, and then, turning back to the group, he said as he had said a hundred times before, "There's a good boy. I knew his father, old Mule-tail Buck. I never

676 Collection 5 The Moderns: 1914–1939

CONTENT-AREA CONNECTIONS

Music: Aaron Copland
The American composer Aaron Copland (1900–1990) wrote the score for the film version of *The Red Pony.* Copland's suite has six parts, including "Grandfather's Story," which goes with "The Leader of the People."
Mixed-ability group activity. Have students listen to Copland's music as they read "The Leader of the People" and then discuss how it captures the tone and spirit of the tale.

Film: Westerns
Invite students to watch one of the classic western movies mentioned on pp. 678–679.
Individual activity. Have students write a critique of the movie, examining how it presents the archetype of the western hero and glorifies the myth of the Old West. Students can compare the film to a contemporary heroic action movie to see if the same techniques are used to create the same effect.

knew why they called him Mule-tail except he packed mules."

Mrs. Tiflin turned and led the way into the house. "How long are you going to stay, Father? Your letter didn't say."

"Well, I don't know. I thought I'd stay about two weeks. But I never stay as long as I think I'm going to."

In a short while they were sitting at the white oilcloth table eating their supper. The lamp with the tin reflector hung over the table. Outside the dining-room windows the big moths battered softly against the glass.

Grandfather cut his steak into tiny pieces and chewed slowly. "I'm hungry," he said. "Driving out here got my appetite up. It's like when we were crossing. We all got so hungry every night we could hardly wait to let the meat get done. I could eat about five pounds of buffalo meat every night."

"It's moving around does it," said Billy. "My father was a government packer. I helped him when I was a kid. Just the two of us could about clean up a deer's ham."

"I knew your father, Billy," said Grandfather. "A fine man he was. They called him Mule-tail Buck. I don't know why except he packed mules."

"That was it," Billy agreed. "He packed mules."

Grandfather put down his knife and fork and looked around the table. "I remember one time we ran out of meat—" His voice dropped to a curious low sing-song, dropped into a tonal groove the story had worn for itself. "There was no buffalo, no antelope, not even rabbits. The hunters couldn't even shoot a coyote. That was the time for the leader to be on the watch. I was the leader, and I kept my eyes open. Know why? Well, just the minute the people began to get hungry they'd start slaughtering the team oxen. Do you believe that? I've heard of parties that just ate up their draft cattle. Started from the middle and worked toward the ends. Finally they'd eat the lead pair, and then the wheelers. The leader of a party had to keep them from doing that."

In some manner a big moth got into the room and circled the hanging kerosene lamp. Billy got up and tried to clap it between his hands. Carl struck with a cupped palm and caught the moth and broke it. He walked to the window and dropped it out.

"As I was saying," Grandfather began again, but Carl interrupted him. "You'd better eat some more meat. All the rest of us are ready for our pudding."

Jody saw a flash of anger in his mother's eyes. Grandfather picked up his knife and fork. "I'm pretty hungry, all right," he said. "I'll tell you about that later."

When supper was over, when the family and Billy Buck sat in front of the fireplace in the other room, Jody anxiously watched Grandfather. He saw the signs he knew. The bearded head leaned forward; the eyes lost their sternness and looked wonderingly into the fire; the big lean fingers laced themselves on the black knees. "I wonder," he began, "I just wonder whether I ever told you how those thieving Piutes[9] drove off thirty-five of our horses."

"I think you did," Carl interrupted. "Wasn't it just before you went up into the Tahoe country?"

Grandfather turned quickly toward his son-in-law. "That's right. I guess I must have told you that story."

"Lots of times," Carl said cruelly, and he avoided his wife's eyes. But he felt the angry eyes on him, and he said, " 'Course I'd like to hear it again."

Grandfather looked back at the fire. His fingers unlaced and laced again. Jody knew how he felt, how his insides were collapsed and empty. Hadn't Jody been called a Big-Britches that very afternoon? He arose to heroism and opened himself to the term Big-Britches again. "Tell about Indians," he said softly.

Grandfather's eyes grew stern again. "Boys

---

9. **Piutes** (pī′yōōts′): usually spelled *Paiutes*. The Paiutes are an American Indian people who originally lived in Utah, Arizona, Nevada, and California.

John Steinbeck   677

DIRECT TEACHING

B Literary Focus

❓ Conflict. What conflict is hinted at in Grandfather's comment about the length of his stay? [Possible response: Grandfather may tend to shorten his stay because of conflicts with his son-in-law.]

C Literary Focus

❓ Author's purpose. Why does Steinbeck have Grandfather tell his tales in such detail? [Possible response: The tales help characterize Grandfather as someone who lives in his memories and feels out of place in the present.]

D Content-Area Connections

History: Native Americans
The Paiutes are two different Native American groups. The Southern Paiutes at one time lived in Utah, Arizona, Nevada, and southeastern California. The Northern Paiutes lived in California, Nevada, and Oregon. After 1840, because the rush of settlers and prospectors had destroyed their meager food supplies, the Northern Paiutes armed themselves and fought the settlers until 1874, when the federal government seized the last of their lands. In 2000, between 10,000 and 13,000 persons identified themselves as of Paiute ancestry.

E Literary Focus

❓ Conflict. Why is Carl cruel toward Grandfather? [Possible responses: He is cruel by nature; he is bored by the old man's stories; he is envious of the old man's heroism.]

F Reading Skills

❓ Drawing inferences. What internal conflict is Jody experiencing? [Possible response: He wants to make Grandfather feel better but is afraid to anger his father.]

Literary Criticism

Critic's Commentary: The Faculty of Pity

Critic Joseph Henry Jackson writes, "There is at least one notable characteristic of Steinbeck's writing on which otherwise conflicting critics agree: he is a man in whom the faculty of pity is strong and close to the surface. Steinbeck is always aware of mankind's weaknesses, frustrations, failures, grotesqueries. But he is also always the artist, by Conrad's noble definition, the man who 'speaks to our capacity for delight and wonder; to the sense of mystery surrounding our lives; to our sense of pity, and beauty, and pain.' " Have students suggest ways in which Steinbeck shows pity for the characters in "The Leader of the People."

This piece outlines the role Hollywood films had in the development of the American public's idealized vision of the legendary West. However, life in the historical West was more complicated and less romantic than that portrayed in classic western films.

DIRECT TEACHING

A Content-Area Connections

Film: Law and Order
The Man Who Shot Liberty Valance (1962) stars James Stewart, John Wayne, and Vera Miles. The story concerns a greenhorn lawyer (Stewart) who tries to bring order to the West with help from the more experienced westerner, played by John Wayne.

B Literary Focus

? Characterization. Why does Grandfather suddenly appear uninterested in his own stories? [Possible responses: Grandfather is affected by the audience's lack of response to his stories. He is depressed; he feels that his present life is so limited that he has nothing else to contribute.]

C Content-Area Connections

Film: The Lone Hero
High Noon (1952) is a legendary western drama that concerns a crisis of conscience for a town marshal (Gary Cooper) who, on the day of his wedding and retirement, learns that a gang of vengeful outlaws is after him. The marshal feels it is his duty to face the gang—but no one is willing to help him. Directed by Fred Zinnemann, *High Noon* is a masterpiece of economy, pacing, and suspense, and it has influenced filmmakers around the world.

---

always want to hear about Indians. It was a job for men, but boys want to hear about it. Well, let's see. Did I ever tell you how I wanted each wagon to carry a long iron plate?"

Everyone but Jody remained silent. Jody said, "No. You didn't."

"Well, when the Indians attacked, we always put the wagons in a circle and fought from between the wheels. I thought that if every wagon carried a long plate with rifle holes, the men could stand the plates on the outside of the wheels when the wagons were in the circle and they would be protected. It would save lives and that would make up for the extra weight of the iron. But of course the party wouldn't do it. No party had done it before and they couldn't see why they should go to the expense. They lived to regret it, too."

Jody looked at his mother, and knew from her expression that she was not listening at all. Carl picked at a callus on his thumb and Billy Buck watched a spider crawling up the wall.

Grandfather's tone dropped into its narrative groove again. Jody knew in advance exactly what words would fall. The story droned on, speeded up for the attack, grew sad over the wounds, struck a dirge[10] at the burials on the great plains. Jody sat quietly watching Grandfather. The stern blue eyes were detached. He looked as though he were not very interested in the story himself.

When it was finished, when the pause had been politely respected as the frontier of the story, Billy Buck stood up and stretched and hitched his trousers. "I guess I'll turn in," he said. Then he faced Grandfather. "I've got an old powder horn and a cap and ball pistol down to the bunkhouse. Did I ever show them to you?"

Grandfather nodded slowly. "Yes, I think you did, Billy. Reminds me of a pistol I had when I was leading the people across." Billy stood po-

---

10. **dirge** (dʉrj) *n.:* sad song that accompanies a funeral or expresses grief.

A CLOSER LOOK: SOCIAL INFLUENCES

The West: Its Mythmakers and Archetypes

INFORMATIONAL TEXT

A *"This is the West, sir. When the legend becomes fact, print the legend."*

—*from* "The Man Who Shot Liberty Valance" *by* Dorothy Johnson

When Jody lies in bed thinking of "the impossible world of Indians and buffaloes" that he has heard about from his grandfather's tales, he muses that "a race of giants had lived then, fearless men, men of a staunchness unknown in this day." Jody's idealized vision of the West is a vision firmly entrenched in the popular imagination. Hollywood filmmakers played a major role in creating this larger-than-life vision. Starting with silent films such as *The Great Train Robbery* (1903), western movies have presented a world of heroes, evildoers, epic cattle drives, and heart-stopping action, all against a backdrop of spectacular scenery.

The archetypal hero. Dominating the action in western films is the western hero: self-reliant, solitary, often shadowed by a mysterious or tragic past, and ever ready to take matters into his hands. He is fearless, possessed of awesome skills, at home with nature and animals (especially his horse), in command of people as well as things. He usually is awkward with women. He routinely punishes evildoers and rescues the good (usually women). Above all, he displays integrity and honor. This character of the heroic, solitary man who emerges from a mysterious past to save a threatened people is an **archetype**—a model for countless heroes, ranging from the ancient superhero Beowulf to the latest *Star Wars* hero.

C Western screen heroes have been played by such stars as Gary Cooper (most notably in *High Noon*, 1952); Alan Ladd, who was perhaps

litely until the little story was done, and then he said, "Good night," and went out of the house.

Carl Tiflin tried to turn the conversation then. "How's the country between here and Monterey? I've heard it's pretty dry."

"It is dry," said Grandfather. "There's not a drop of water in the Laguna Seca. But it's a long pull from '87. The whole country was powder then, and in '61 I believe all the coyotes starved to death. We had fifteen inches of rain this year."

"Yes, but it all came too early. We could do with some now." Carl's eye fell on Jody. "Hadn't you better be getting to bed?"

Jody stood up obediently. "Can I kill the mice in the old haystack, sir?"

"Mice? Oh! Sure, kill them all off. Billy said there isn't any good hay left."

Jody exchanged a secret and satisfying look with Grandfather. "I'll kill every one tomorrow," he promised.

Jody lay in his bed and thought of the impossible world of Indians and buffaloes, a world that had ceased to be forever. He wished he could have been living in the heroic time, but he knew he was not of heroic timber.[11] No one living now, save possibly Billy Buck, was worthy to do the things that had been done. A race of giants had lived then, fearless men, men of a staunchness unknown in this day. Jody thought of the wide plains and of the wagons moving across like centipedes. He thought of Grandfather on a huge white horse, marshaling[12] the people. Across his mind marched the great phantoms, and they marched off the earth and they were gone.

He came back to the ranch for a moment, then. He heard the dull rushing sound that space and silence make. He heard one of the dogs, out in the doghouse, scratching a flea and bumping his elbow against the floor with every

---

11. **timber** *n.:* character.
12. **marshaling** *v.* used as *adj.:* leading; guiding.

Clint Eastwood.

the most archetypal western hero in *Shane* (1953); and John Wayne, the actor who became *the* rugged western hero in many Americans' minds in films like *She Wore a Yellow Ribbon* (1949) and *True Grit* (1969). Clint Eastwood has become John Wayne's successor as the archetype of the lone western hero.

Revising the myth. But historians tell us that the West—and the western hero—was a far cry from movie depictions. The myth tells of a land where rugged individualists lived in harmony with nature, where men settled scores with shootouts on the town's main street. But in the historical West, eastern investors and federal government programs played major roles in land development. Certain farming practices created environmental catastrophes, and the some-times terrifying loneliness and hardships of the prairie tore apart families and drove some homesteaders mad. (Also, cattle rustlers, burglars, and other criminals were often shot unceremoniously in the back, not in well-orchestrated shootouts.)

If we know the truth about the West, why do most of us still prefer the legend? Perhaps because the myth shows us the people we wish we were and the world we wish we lived in. The world of the mythic West is a simpler, much more romantic one than ours, one in which there's no question about distinguishing right from wrong. Indeed, filmmakers, writers, and other mythmakers of the American West have always found an audience that eagerly embraces the transformation of reality into legend.

John Steinbeck **679**

D **Literary Focus**

❷ **Characterization.** What trait of Grandfather's is shown here again when he refers to earlier drought years while discussing the weather? [Possible response: His comment shows he is living in the past—a golden age when everything, even droughts, was more impressive and powerful.]

E **Reading Informational Text**

❷ **Finding the main idea.** In the paragraph beginning "Revising the myth," the article acknowledges that filmmakers are now more informed and have made films that refute the myths of pioneer life. Why, according to the article, do "most of us" prefer the myths? [We have a need for the simpler romantic view of our past.]

F **Reading Skills**

❷ **Interpreting figures of speech.** What does this simple simile suggest about Jody's vision of "westering"? [Possible response: Jody's vision of the wagons as centipedes, like elements of nature themselves, and the image of Grandfather on the huge horse elevate "westering" to even more heroic heights. It is an ironic counterpoint to Carl's disregard for Grandfather and illustrates Jody's youth and innocence.]

A **Literary Focus**

Characterization. Although in Grandfather's eyes the mouse hunt indicates the triviality and inferiority of the next generation, it is an epic undertaking for Jody. Yet Jody is able to play his heroic game precisely because Grandfather's generation endured the hardships of "westering" and frontier settlement.

B **Literary Focus**

❷ **Irony.** How are Jody's actions ironic in light of Grandfather's past? [Possible response: Jody's adventure is postponed for a meal, an ironic juxta-position with Grandfather's pressing on even when he is hungry.]

C **Reading Skills**

❷ **Drawing inferences.** Why has Billy's statement "staggered" Jody? [Possible responses: It has never occurred to Jody that people can't always control their own destiny. He might also be thinking of his grandfather, who has participated in a grand event but has lost his power and purpose.]

D **Literary Focus**

❷ **Conflict.** In what tone of voice do you think Carl makes this remark? How does this reveal the conflict between the two men? [Possible response: Carl is probably using a sarcastic tone to show that he resents his father-in-law.]

E **Reading Skills**

❷ **Recognizing author's style.** What mechanical, grammatical, and vocabulary choices does Steinbeck make to convey emotion here? [Possible responses: dashes for pauses; action verbs ("jerked"); and diction ("sir") to indicate forced deference.]

---

stroke. Then the wind arose again and the black cypress groaned and Jody went to sleep.

He was up half an hour before the triangle sounded for breakfast. His mother was rattling the stove to make the flames roar when Jody went through the kitchen. "You're up early," she said. "Where are you going?"

A "Out to get a good stick. We're going to kill the mice today."

"Who is 'we'?"

"Why, Grandfather and I."

"So you've got him in it. You always like to have someone in with you in case there's blame to share."

"I'll be right back," said Jody. "I just want to have a good stick ready for after breakfast."

He closed the screen door after him and went out into the cool blue morning. The birds were noisy in the dawn and the ranch cats came down from the hill like blunt snakes. They had been hunting gophers in the dark, and although the four cats were full of gopher meat, they sat in a semi-circle at the back door and mewed piteously for milk. Doubletree Mutt and Smasher moved sniffing along the edge of the brush, performing the duty with rigid cere-mony, but when Jody whistled, their heads jerked up and their tails waved. They plunged down to him, wriggling their skins and yawn-ing. Jody patted their heads seriously, and moved on to the weathered scrap pile. He se-lected an old broom handle and a short piece of inch-square scrap wood. From his pocket he took a shoelace and tied the ends of the sticks

B loosely together to make a flail.[13] He whistled his new weapon through the air and struck the ground experimentally, while the dogs leaped aside and whined with apprehension.

Jody turned and started down past the house toward the old haystack ground to look over

---

13. **flail** *n.*: farm tool for hand-threshing grain. A flail is made of a short stick fastened with a leather strap to a longer handle. The user lets the short stick swing freely from the handle to knock the heads from the grain stalks.

the field of slaughter, but Billy Buck, sitting patiently on the back steps, called to him, "You better come back. It's only a couple of minutes till breakfast."

Jody changed his course and moved toward the house. He leaned his flail against the steps. "That's to drive the mice out," he said. "I'll bet they're fat. I'll bet they don't know what's going to happen to them today."

"No, nor you either," Billy remarked philo-sophically, "nor me, nor anyone."

C Jody was staggered by this thought. He knew it was true. His imagination twitched away from the mouse hunt. Then his mother came out on the back porch and struck the triangle, and all thoughts fell in a heap.

Grandfather hadn't appeared at the table when they sat down. Billy nodded at his empty chair. "He's all right? He isn't sick?"

"He takes a long time to dress," said Mrs. Tiflin. "He combs his whiskers and rubs up his shoes and brushes his clothes."

D Carl scattered sugar on his mush. "A man that's led a wagon train across the plains has got to be pretty careful how he dresses."

Mrs. Tiflin turned on him. "Don't do that, Carl! Please don't!" There was more of threat than of request in her tone. And the threat irritated Carl.

"Well, how many times do I have to listen to the story of the iron plates, and the thirty-five horses? That time's done. Why can't he forget it, now it's done?" He grew angrier while he talked, and his voice rose. "Why does he have to tell them over and over? He came across the plains. All right! Now it's finished. Nobody wants to hear about it over and over."

The door into the kitchen closed softly. The four at the table sat frozen. Carl laid his mush spoon on the table and touched his chin with his fingers.

Then the kitchen door opened and Grand-father walked in. His mouth smiled tightly and his eyes were squinted. "Good morning," he said, and he sat down and looked at his mush dish.

E Carl could not leave it there. "Did—did you hear what I said?"

Grandfather jerked a little nod.

Analyzing prefixes and suffixes. Remind students that they can figure out many words by recognizing common prefixes. Read each of the following words from the story, and have students identify its base word and its affix(es). Then, have students discuss the meanings:

1. entangled [tangle; *en*–]

2. overbearing [bearing; *over*–]

3. profanity [profane; *–ity*]

4. interlaced [lace; *inter*–]

5. dismounted [mount; *dis*–]

6. tonal [tone; *–al*]

7. heroism [hero; *–ism*]

8. staunchness [staunch; *–ness*]

9. piteous [pity; *–ous*]

10. unsaddle [saddle; *un*–]

"I don't know what got into me, sir. I didn't mean it. I was just being funny."

Jody glanced in shame at his mother, and he saw that she was looking at Carl, and that she wasn't breathing. It was an awful thing that he was doing. He was tearing himself to pieces to talk like that. It was a terrible thing to him to retract a word, but to retract it in shame was infinitely worse.

Grandfather looked sidewise. "I'm trying to get right side up," he said gently. "I'm not being mad. I don't mind what you said, but it might be true, and I would mind that."

"It isn't true," said Carl. "I'm not feeling well this morning. I'm sorry I said it."

"Don't be sorry, Carl. An old man doesn't see things sometimes. Maybe you're right. The crossing is finished. Maybe it should be forgotten, now it's done."

Carl got up from the table. "I've had enough to eat. I'm going to work. Take your time, Billy!" He walked quickly out of the dining-room. Billy gulped the rest of his food and followed soon after. But Jody could not leave his chair.

"Won't you tell any more stories?" Jody asked.

"Why, sure I'll tell them, but only when—I'm sure people want to hear them."

"I like to hear them, sir."

"Oh! Of course you do, but you're a little boy. It was a job for men, but only little boys like to hear about it."

Jody got up from his place. "I'll wait outside for you, sir. I've got a good stick for those mice."

He waited by the gate until the old man came out on the porch. "Let's go down and kill the mice now," Jody called.

"I think I'll just sit in the sun, Jody. You go kill the mice."

"You can use my stick if you like."

"No, I'll just sit here a while."

Jody turned disconsolately away, and walked down toward the old haystack. He tried to whip up his enthusiasm with thoughts of the fat juicy mice. He beat the ground with his flail. The dogs coaxed and whined about him, but he could not go. Back at the house he could see Grandfather sitting on the porch, looking small and thin and black.

Jody gave up and went to sit on the steps at the old man's feet.

"Back already? Did you kill the mice?"

"No, sir. I'll kill them some other day."

The morning flies buzzed close to the ground and the ants dashed about in front of the steps. The heavy smell of sage slipped down the hill. The porch boards grew warm in the sunshine.

Jody hardly knew when Grandfather started to talk. "I shouldn't stay here, feeling the way I do." He examined his strong old hands. "I feel as though the crossing wasn't worth doing." His eyes moved up the side-hill and stopped on a motionless hawk perched on a dead limb. "I tell those old stories, but they're not what I want to tell. I only know how I want people to feel when I tell them.

"It wasn't Indians that were important, nor adventures, nor even getting out here. It was a whole bunch of people made into one big crawling beast. And I was the head. It was westering and westering. Every man wanted something for himself, but the big beast that was all of them wanted only westering. I was the leader, but if I hadn't been there, someone else would have been the head. The thing had to have a head.

"Under the little bushes the shadows were black at white noonday. When we saw the mountains at last, we cried—all of us. But it wasn't getting here that mattered, it was movement and westering.

"We carried life out here and set it down the way those ants carry eggs. And I was the leader. The westering was as big as God, and the slow steps that made the movement piled up and piled up until the continent was crossed.

"Then we came down to the sea, and it was done." He stopped and wiped his eyes until the rims were red. "That's what I should be telling instead of stories."

When Jody spoke, Grandfather started and looked down at him. "Maybe I could lead the people some day," Jody said.

Vocabulary

retract (ri·trakt′) v.: take back; draw back.
disconsolately (dis·kän′sə·lit·lē) adv.: unhappily.

John Steinbeck 681

DIRECT TEACHING

F Literary Focus

? Conflict. Although the external conflict between Carl and Grandfather has been avoided, what internal conflicts remain? [Possible responses: Carl is caught between stubborn pride and the need to apologize; Grandfather is caught between clinging to his self-respect and acknowledging that he lingers in the past.]

G Reading Skills

? Drawing inferences. Why doesn't Jody kill the mice? [Possible responses: The fun has gone out of the game without his grandfather to help; he wants to cheer up his grandfather.]

FAMILY/COMMUNITY ACTIVITY

Invite students to make an audiotape or videotape of an interview with one of their grandparents or an older relative, neighbor, or friend whom they view as heroic. The following items are some sample questions the students can prepare before the interview:

• How do you define heroism?

• What do you think is the most important contribution that you have made to society?

What made this act significant to you?

• Do you feel that society today still values these types of contributions? Why or why not?

• What people do you feel are having a powerful positive impact on society today? Explain.

Remind students to check their equipment and to write a note thanking the person interviewed for sharing his or her time. Have students summarize their interviews for the whole class. Be sure that students have gotten permission from their interview subjects before sharing the results of their interviews.

A Literary Focus

? Conflict. What causes Jody's mother to stop being critical? [Possible response: She recognizes that Jody has a mature motive for wanting to get his grandfather lemonade.]

Monitoring students' progress. Guide the class in answering these questions.

True-False

1. Jody wants to kill the mice under the haystack. [T]
2. Carl enjoys Grandfather's stories. [F]
3. As a young man, Grandfather was the leader of a wagon train. [T]
4. At the end of the story, Jody wants to make Grandfather iced tea. [F]

Response and Analysis

Reading Check

1. Jody enjoys his visit.
2. He dreads hearing the stories.
3. leading a wagon train
4. He directed the wagon train.

Thinking Critically

5. It represented the desire to push to the limits of human possibility.
6. Possible answer: Grandfather's visit causes conflict between Mr. and Mrs. Tiflin. Carl's boredom with Grandfather's stories creates a generational conflict. Carl's determination to control his son creates another generational conflict. Jody's internal conflict revolves around wanting to help

---

The old man smiled. "There's no place to go. There's the ocean to stop you. There's a line of old men along the shore hating the ocean because it stopped them."

"In boats I might, sir."

"No place to go, Jody. Every place is taken. But that's not the worst—no, not the worst. Westering has died out of the people. Westering isn't a hunger any more. It's all done. Your father is right. It is finished." He laced his fingers on his knee and looked at them.

Jody felt very sad. "If you'd like a glass of lemonade I could make it for you."

Grandfather was about to refuse, and then he saw Jody's face. "That would be nice," he said. "Yes, it would be nice to drink a lemonade."

Jody ran into the kitchen where his mother was wiping the last of the breakfast dishes. "Can I have a lemon to make a lemonade for Grandfather?"

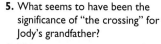

His mother mimicked—"And another lemon to make a lemonade for you."

"No, ma'am. I don't want one."

"Jody! You're sick!" Then she stopped suddenly. "Take a lemon out of the cooler," she said softly. "Here, I'll reach the squeezer down to you." ■

Response and Analysis

SKILLS FOCUS

Literary Skills
Analyze internal and external conflict and archetypes.

Writing Skills
Write an essay comparing and contrasting a story and a poem. Write an essay comparing and contrasting the themes from a novel and a story.

Vocabulary Skills
Clarify word meanings.

Reading Check

1. How does Jody feel about his grandfather's visit?
2. Why does Jody's father dread the visit?
3. What are Grandfather's stories about?
4. In what way was Grandfather "the leader of the people"?

Thinking Critically

5. What seems to have been the significance of "the crossing" for Jody's grandfather?
6. This story centers on several **conflicts**—some external, between members of the family, and some internal, existing in a character's mind. Describe the conflicts in the story, and explain how each conflict is resolved by the story's conclusion. (Are all the conflicts resolved?) Do you think the story is more about the stresses of family life than it is about the changing attitudes of each new generation? Explain your responses.
7. Re-read *A Closer Look* (pages 678–679). How does Jody's grandfather in his prime resemble the **archetypal**

character of the western hero? (Do you think Grandfather's view of the past reflects more myth than reality or vice versa?)
8. There is another **archetype** in this story, one that is also found in many other stories through the ages and in actual life as well. The archetype is not a character but an attitude: It involves a conviction that there was a time and place in the past that was more perfect, more heroic than the present. Some people call this a yearning for a golden age. (A Greek myth tells us that the first people lived in a golden age, a time of perfect happiness.) How is this archetypal longing for a past golden age expressed in Steinbeck's story? Where do you hear or see this longing for a more perfect past expressed in actual life? Think of stories, TV shows, films, and even commercials.
9. The story is full of **ironies,** or surprising departures from what is expected. How does Steinbeck use the mouse hunt ironically, to contrast the modern age with the heroic past?

---

his grandfather without alienating his father. Most students will conclude that some conflicts will continue. Students may be divided on the question of family stresses versus changing attitudes.

7. Like the western hero, Jody's grandfather was self-reliant and in command of himself and people in his care. Grandfather's view probably combines myth and reality.

8. Jody's grandfather contrasts the people and events of the present generation unfavorably with the past. Students may cite contemporary films, TV shows, or commercials which portray the past in an idealized way.

9. The mouse hunt is an ironic contrast with the struggle between the wagon train pioneers and the American Indians. It suggests that the present generation is weak.

10. Think about the **theme** of the story. What does the story reveal about the relationship between dreams and reality and the loss of the heroic ideal?

11. Look back at your Quickwrite notes. Do you believe, as Jody's grandfather does, that there are no longer any worlds for young people to conquer? If not, where do you see opportunities for Jody and other young people to prove themselves as heroes? 🖉

12. In your opinion, is Jody right to want to listen to Grandfather's stories over and over again, or is Carl right in wanting to forget the past and concentrate on the future? Are there, perhaps, ways in which both characters are right? Give reasons to support your views.

WRITING

Comparing Literature

In an **essay,** compare and contrast Steinbeck's story with Whitman's poem "I understand the large hearts of heroes" (page 316). Focus on three of these topics for your points of comparison:

- main theme in each text
- what each text says about heroism
- what each text says about America
- tone of each text (positive, negative, cynical, sad, uplifting)
- view of life in each text
- how each text's historical context affects its theme and tone

Be sure to use passages from each text to support your points.

Variations on a Theme

Review the major **theme** of Steinbeck's story as you see it. You may want to focus on the contrast between dream and reality, on the loss of heroism, on the conflicts between generations, on disillusionment, or on the limitations of the American dream. Then, choose a novel from your own reading that deals with a similar theme. Write an **essay** comparing and contrasting the ways in which the novel and the story develop the theme. In your essay, focus on what the characters in the story and in the novel discover as they work out their conflicts.

▶ Use "Analyzing a Novel," pages 774–781, for help with this assignment.

Vocabulary Development
What's the Difference?

To show that you understand the meaning of each Vocabulary word, answer the following questions. Use a dictionary for help.

1. How is *arrogant* different from *ignorant?*
2. How is *immune* different from *immure?*
3. How is *cleft* different from *cliff?*
4. How is *contemptuously* different from *contemporaneously?*
5. How is *judiciously* different from *judgmentally?*
6. How is *rancor* different from *rigor?*
7. How is *convened* different from *convinced?*
8. How is *listlessly* different from *liberally?*
9. How is *retract* different from *repeat?*
10. How is *disconsolately* different from *discontinuously?*

John Steinbeck **683**

---

10. Possible answer: The story explores the clash between our spiritual hunger for heroism and the mundane realities of life. It demonstrates the power of a dream, the importance of reality checks, and the importance of creating new goals and ideals.

11. Possible answers: Space and the oceans are examples of worlds to conquer. Heroes today may fight terrorism or other injustices.

12. Possible answers: Jody is right; the stories are his heritage. Carl is right; Grandfather's obsession keeps him from living in the present.

Vocabulary Development

1. *Arrogant* means "proud or overly confident," and *ignorant* means "lacking knowledge."

2. *Immune* means "protected," and *immure* means "to enclose."

3. A *cleft* is an opening or crack, and a *cliff* is a steep face of a rock.

4. *Contemptuously* means "scornfully," and *contemporaneously* means "at the same time."

5. *Judiciously* means "wisely," and *judgmentally* means "in a judging way."

6. *Rancor* means "anger," and *rigor* means "severity" or "difficulty."

7. *Convened* means "assembled," and *convinced* means "persuaded."

8. *Listlessly* means "without energy," and *liberally* means "in a liberal or free way."

9. *Retract* means "to take back," and *repeat* means "to do again."

10. *Disconsolately* means "unhappily," and *discontinuously* means "in a way that is not continuous, or steady."

ASSESSING

Assessment

Holt Assessment: Literature, Reading, and Vocabulary

RETEACHING

For a lesson reteaching archetypes, see **Reteaching,** p. 1117A.

Summary at grade level

In this stream-of-consciousness narrative, a nearly eighty-year-old grandmother, Ellen Weatherall, lies dying. Passing in and out of consciousness, she interacts with her doctor and her daughter Cornelia and thinks back on her long life. Although many of her memories are pleasant, she also recalls being jilted by a man named George on their wedding day. Weatherall tells herself that she was "given back everything he took away and more" by the man she ultimately married and by her children, but this memory actually reflects a deep inner hurt. As death nears, a priest gives Granny her last rites and Porter evokes a "tiny point in the center of her brain" surrounded by blackness as a metaphor for Granny's life. Out of this blackness, Granny seeks a sign from God, the divine bridegroom, but at the story's climax, no sign appears. In her last thought, Granny decides that she will never forgive this final "jilting," and she herself blows out the light of her life.

Skills Starter

Motivate. Ask students to recall times when they have reflected on their own lives. Do their thoughts follow a completely logical pattern, or does one memory tend to lead to another unrelated one?

Before You Read

The Jilting of Granny Weatherall

Make the Connection

Most people, even those in middle or old age, look forward to what life has in store for them. They ask, "What's the weather going to be tomorrow? Where shall we go on vacation next year?" Some older persons, however, start to look backward more than forward. Events from long ago seem more vivid than events from yesterday or the recent past. That is surely true of Ellen Weatherall, the nearly eighty-year-old narrator of this story. Granny Weatherall has little interest in the future, of which she knows she has very little. But the past! Now *there's* something to think about, and she does.

The point of this story is what Granny Weatherall recalls most vividly of all. It happened sixty years ago, Granny tells us, and the memory still hurts.

Literary Focus
Stream of Consciousness

Although Porter uses some dialogue in this story, she mostly uses the modernist narrative technique called **stream of consciousness**. This technique gives readers the impression that they are listening in on the main character's thoughts and memories as they flow randomly through that person's mind. In this story the thoughts and memories of Granny Weatherall come and go in no special order. They shift back and forth, from what is happening in her present to what happened in her life long ago.

Since the thoughts that stream freely through the mind are often irrational and contradictory, stream-of-consciousness narratives often contain many **ambiguities**, or meanings that are unclear or open to more than one interpretation.

INTERNET

Vocabulary
Practice

Keyword: LE5 11–5

SKILLS FOCUS

Literary Skills
Understand stream of consciousness and ambiguity.

Reading Skills
Read closely for clues to meaning.

Stream of consciousness is a style of writing that conveys the inner—and sometimes chaotic—workings of a character's mind.

For more on Stream of Consciousness, see the Handbook of Literary and Historical Terms.

Reading Skills
Reading Closely

Like a good detective, you will have to sift clues carefully as you share Granny's stream of consciousness. Here are some suggestions: Pay careful attention to tenses of verbs, since they help distinguish past from present. Also, pay attention to quotation marks. They enclose words actually spoken aloud as opposed to unspoken thoughts. Finally, be patient. If the identity of a character is not immediately clear, keep reading until you have enough clues to figure out who he or she is.

Vocabulary Development

tactful (takt′fəl) *adj.*: skilled in saying the right thing.

clammy (klam′ē) *adj.*: cold and damp.

plague (plāg) *v.*: annoy.

vanity (van′ə·tē) *n.*: excessive pride.

jilted (jilt′id) *v.*: rejected (as a lover).

disputed (di·spyo͞ot′id) *v.*: contested.

nimbus (nim′bəs) *n.*: aura; halo.

dwindled (dwin′dəld) *v.*: diminished.

Previewing Vocabulary

Have students read the Vocabulary words listed on p. 696. Then, have them write imaginative sentences using one new Vocabulary word in each sentence. When they finish writing their sentences, ask students to match each word in the left column with its synonym in the right column.

1. disputed [e]
2. plague [g]
3. tactful [c]
4. vanity [a]
5. dwindled [h]
6. jilted [f]
7. clammy [b]
8. nimbus [d]

a. pride
b. damp
c. polite
d. halo
e. argued
f. rejected
g. annoy
h. shrank

DIFFERENTIATING INSTRUCTION

Learners Having Difficulty
Modeling. To help students read "The Jilting of Granny Weatherall," model the reading skill of reading closely. Say, "Suppose you read that Granny Weatherall brushes off the doctor's warning. Knowing this, you can conclude that Granny is not willing to admit how ill she is." Encourage students, as they read, to ask themselves, "How in or out of touch is Granny with what is happening in real time around her?"

could collect in twenty-four hours! The box in the attic with all those letters tied up, well, she'd have to go through that tomorrow. All those letters—George's letters and John's letters and her letters to them both—lying around for the children to find afterward made her uneasy. Yes, that would be tomorrow's business. No use to let them know how silly she had been once.

D

While she was rummaging around she found death in her mind and it felt clammy and unfamiliar. She had spent so much time preparing for death there was no need for bringing it up again. Let it take care of itself now. When she was sixty she had felt very old, finished, and went around making farewell trips to see her children and grandchildren, with a secret in her mind: This is the very last of your mother, children! Then she made her will and came down with a long fever. That was all just a notion like a lot of other things, but it was lucky too, for she had once for all got over the idea of dying for a long time. Now she couldn't be worried. She hoped she had better sense now. Her father had lived to be one hundred and two years old and had drunk a noggin[2] of strong hot toddy[3] on his last birthday. He told the reporters it was his daily habit, and he owed his long life to that. He had made quite a scandal and was very pleased about it. She believed she'd just plague Cornelia a little.

E

"Cornelia! Cornelia!" No footsteps, but a sudden hand on her cheek. "Bless you, where have you been?"

"Here, Mother."

"Well, Cornelia, I want a noggin of hot toddy."

"Are you cold, darling?"

"I'm chilly, Cornelia. Lying in bed stops the circulation. I must have told you that a thousand times."

Well, she could just hear Cornelia telling her husband that Mother was getting a little childish and they'd have to humor her. The thing that most annoyed her was that Cornelia thought she was deaf, dumb, and blind. Little

2. **noggin** *n*.: mug.
3. **hot toddy:** drink made of liquor mixed with hot water, sugar, and spices.

hasty glances ar
her and over he
let her have her
she sitting there
cage. Sometime
mind to pack u
house where no
minute that she
till your own ch
back!

In her day sh
had got more w
for Lydia to be
when one of the
Jimmy still drop
"Now, Mammy
want to know w
Cornelia could
without asking.
had been so swe
wished the old
children young
It had been a ha
her. When she t
cooked, and all
sewed, and all ti
the children sho
out of her, and
Sometimes she
point to them a
did I? But that v
tomorrow. She
but now all the
father, and he w
saw him now. It
something wro
possibly recogn
dred acres once
and clamping th
help. That chan
looking for a yo
Spanish comb i
Digging postho

Vocabulary
clammy (klăm′ē)
plague (plāg) *v*.: ar

New England Woman (1895) by Cecilia Beaux. Oil on canvas (43″ × 24¼″). The Pennsylvania Academy of the Fine Arts, Philadelphia. Joseph E. Temple Fund.

The Jilting of Granny Weatherall

Katherine Anne Porter

697

A Reading Skills

Reading closely. What is happening to Granny at this point? [She is so ill that her sight and other bodily sensations are affected. In her distorted perceptions, her bones feel loose within her, and Doctor Harry seems to be floating.]

B Literary Focus

Character. What does this paragraph reveal about Granny's feelings regarding Cornelia? [Possible responses: She resents Cornelia for treating her as an incompetent being. She feels insulted by Cornelia talking about her behind her back and by what she sees as Cornelia's affected solicitousness.]

C Literary Focus

Stream of consciousness. Trace the associations that lead Granny from one thought to the next in this paragraph. ["Tomorrow" reminds her of tidying the house, which reminds her of the box of letters she wants to sort through.]

A Reading Skills

Interpreting dialogue. What do you think the neighbor's statement means? [Possible response: To remain on friendly terms, neighbors should create clear boundaries so they won't encroach on each other's territory.] How does the neighbor's statement relate to the poem's title? [Possible responses: Working together to repair a wall can improve relations between neighbors; mending a wall can mend a relationship.]

B English-Language Learners

Interpreting idioms. Help students distinguish between the idiomatic expressions *walling in* ("enclosing") and *walling out* ("keeping out" or "excluding") by physically demonstrating each action.

C Literary Focus

Ambiguity. How does the speaker's behavior contradict the opinion he voices about walls between neighbors? [Possible responses: He helps mend the wall even though he doesn't think it is necessary or helpful; he enjoys building the wall with his neighbor even though he has doubts that walls contribute to good neighborly relations.]

D Literary Focus

Simile. Why does the speaker compare his neighbor to "an old-stone savage"? [Possible response: He is suggesting that his neighbor's values are like those of a primitive cave man: reactionary, ignorant, and suspicious.]

E Literary Focus

Ambiguity. How does the final line affect the reader's search for the poem's overall meaning? [Possible response: The neighbor has the last word, leaving the reader to wonder if the poet agrees with him or with the speaker.]

We have to use a spell to make them balance:
"Stay where you are until our backs are turned!"
20 We wear our fingers rough with handling them.
Oh, just another kind of outdoor game,
One on a side. It comes to little more:
There where it is we do not need the wall:
He is all pine and I am apple orchard.
25 My apple trees will never get across
And eat the cones under his pines, I tell him.
He only says, "Good fences make good neighbors."
Spring is the mischief in me, and I wonder
If I could put a notion in his head:
30 "*Why* do they make good neighbors? Isn't it
Where there are cows? But here there are no cows.
Before I built a wall I'd ask to know
What I was walling in or walling out,
And to whom I was like to give offense.
35 Something there is that doesn't love a wall,
That wants it down." I could say "Elves" to him,
But it's not elves exactly, and I'd rather
He said it for himself. I see him there,
Bringing a stone grasped firmly by the top
40 In each hand, like an old-stone savage armed.
He moves in darkness as it seems to me,
Not of woods only and the shade of trees.
He will not go behind his father's saying,
And he likes having thought of it so well
45 He says again, "Good fences make good neighbors."

DIFFERENTIATING INSTRUCTION

Advanced Learners

Enrichment. Share this quotation from Frost: "Poetry provides the one permissible way of saying one thing and meaning another. People say, 'Why don't you say what you mean?' We never do that, do we, being all of us too much poets." Ask students to discuss how this comment sheds light on the ambiguity of "Mending Wall." [Possible response: It implies that the poem's ambiguity is deliberate, the result of Frost's poetic intent to say "one thing" and mean "another."]

This poem was written by a teacher in Lakeside, California.

Mending Test

(Apologies to Robert Frost)
Penelope Bryant Turk

Something there is that doesn't love a test,
That sends the frozen mind-set under it
And spills the grade objectives in the room,
And makes gaps students often fall between. **F**

5 No one has seen them made or heard them made
But at spring testing time we find them here.
I let my classes know within my room
And on a day we meet to take the test
And set the norms between us once again.

10 We wear our minds quite rough with handling them.
Oh, just another kind of indoor game,
One on a side. It comes to little more.
There where it is, we do not need the test.
The teachers can assess their goals, I tell him,

15 The district's high inquisitor, once more.
He only says, "Good tests will make good students."
Spring is the mischief in me, and I wonder
If I could put a notion in his head.
"Why do they make good students?" I inquire.

20 "Before I gave a test, I'd ask to know
What I was testing in or testing out.
And to whom I was like to do some good.
Something there is that doesn't love a test,
That wants it done." I could say this to him

25 But it's not politic, and then I'd rather
He said it for himself. I see him there
Bringing a test grasped firmly in each hand,
With pencils like an old-time pedant° armed.
He moves in darkness as it seems to me, **G**

30 Not of woods only and the shade of trees.
He will not go behind the state's command,
And he likes having thought of it so well,
He says again, "Good tests will make good students."

---

28. pedant (ped**'**nt) *n.:* fussy, narrow-minded teacher.

In a 1995 opinion written for the Supreme Court, Justice Antonin Scalia justified a "high wall" separating the levels of government by quoting the neighbor in Frost's poem. The New York Times *published an editorial reminding Justice Scalia that Frost did not think good fences made good neighbors. Here is one letter about the controversy:*

To the Editor:
Robert Frost's "Mending Wall" has been subjected to many conflicting interpretations, but your April 22 editorial gives the correct one. The "pro-wall" speaker was Frost's French Canadian neighbor, Napoleon Guay. In the opening lines,

Something there is that doesn't love a wall,
That sends the frozen-ground-swell under it

the "something," a natural force that breaks down the wall and indicates the poet's point of view, is frost. Frost liked to pun on his name, calling his satire "frostbite." **H**

 When this poem was translated into Russian and printed in the newspapers for Frost's official visit to the Soviet Union in 1962, many writers and intellectuals saw a negative reference to the Berlin Wall put up by East Germany in 1961. So the Soviet translators jump-started the poem with line two. **I**

     —Jeffrey Meyers
     April 22, 1995

Connection

Summary ⬌ *at grade level*

The poem "Mending Test" is a parody of Frost's poem "Mending Wall." The speaker, a teacher, expresses doubts to the district supervisor about the value of tests in the promotion of learning.

 The letter to *The New York Times* from Jeffrey Meyers (a biographer of Frost) continues the debate over Frost's ambiguity in "Mending Wall."

DIRECT TEACHING

F Reading Skills

❓ Making inferences. What are the "gaps" students often fall between? [Possible responses: Students may learn to pass the test but fail to learn anything of lasting value. Other students may know the material but not test well and be unfairly penalized.]

G Reading Skills

❓ Comparing and contrasting. What is the darkness to which the speaker refers? Is it different from the darkness in "Mending Wall"? [Possible response: In both poems the darkness is a lack of imagination, curiosity, and daring, along with a stubborn clinging to conventional ideas.]

H Reading Skills

❓ Interpreting puns. If the "something" that doesn't love a wall is winter "frost," what does the pun on the poet's name suggest about Frost's view of walls? [It implies that he would like to get rid of them.]

I Content-Area Connections

History: Cold War Wall
Remind students that the Berlin Wall was erected to keep East Germans "walled in" Communist East Germany and West Germans "walled out." The Berlin Wall was torn down in 1989.

Comparing and Contrasting Texts

A parody and its source. "Mending Test" implies that tests, like walls, can separate people from what is really important. In "Mending Wall," the separation is between people. In "Mending Test," it is between people (students) and knowledge or the joy of learning.
Whole-class activity. Ask students to hold a class discussion on the theme of separation versus inclusion in Frost's poem and its parody. Have them consider ambiguity, tone, humor, and author purpose in both poems. Students might also discuss the purpose and effect of Penelope Turk's subtitle, "Apologies to Robert Frost." Finally, encourage students to bring up real-life situations when it might be better to break down walls, rules, or traditions in order to achieve a greater good.

Response and Analysis

Thinking Critically

1. The speaker observes that the wall is routinely broken down by natural forces. Hunters may break down walls.

2. The speaker and his neighbor meet at their boundary wall and work together to rebuild it. Possible answer: Rebuilding is a game or symbolic exercise, because the wall will fall down again and its effectiveness as a boundary is merely symbolic.

3. The speaker wants to know what is being kept in or enclosed and what is being kept out or excluded.

4. Possible answer: The speaker wishes to suggest that there are mysterious or unseen forces at work in the world, but he is unsure how to express this idea to his neighbor in a way that he could understand or accept.

5. from his father

6. Possible answer: The two characters could represent the progressive and conservative poles in any contemporary cultural or political debate.

7. Possible answers: It means the darkness of ignorance. By comparing his neighbor to a pre-historic "savage," the speaker is suggesting that the man's thinking is unenlightened and backward.

8. Possible answers: barriers to human communication and understanding; social and economic barriers.

9. Possible answer: The speaker makes an effort to bridge the gap between himself and his neighbor in the hope that some mutual understanding might develop.

10. Possible answer: The first-person point of view suggests Frost's identification with the speaker, who makes careful observations and raises questions about the wall.

Response and Analysis

Thinking Critically

1. What makes the speaker say that "something" doesn't love a wall? Besides this "something," who else sometimes knocks down walls?

2. Describe what is happening in lines 13–16. According to the speaker, why is rebuilding the wall merely a game (lines 23–26)?

3. What questions does the speaker think should be settled before building a wall, according to lines 32–34?

4. Why would the speaker say "Elves" (line 36)?

5. From whom did the neighbor get his saying: "Good fences make good neighbors"?

6. Frost creates two characters in this poem, and we come to know them by what they say and do and think. What persons or points of view in contemporary life do Frost's characters reflect?

7. What do you think the word *darkness* means in line 41? What could the **simi-le** in line 40 have to do with darkness?

8. What might the wall in the poem **symbolize**?

9. How do you explain the fact that the man who doesn't see the need for a wall is the one who, every spring, is the first to call upon his neighbor and so make sure the wall is rebuilt? Might he want something more from his neighbor than merely a hand with repair work? Explain your response.

10. This poem is **ambiguous**—it presents opposing views about the wall. Do you think Frost favors the view of the speaker or of the neighbor? Which details from the poem lead you to this interpretation?

11. What historical walls or boundaries have separated neighbors? (Be sure to check your Quickwrite notes.) 🖉

SKILLS FOCUS

Literary Skills
Analyze ambiguity.

730 Collection 5 The Moderns: 1914–1939

Extending and Evaluating

12. Do you believe that "Good fences make good neighbors"? Do you think the generalization could apply in some situations but not all? Give your reasons. (See the **Connection** on page 729 for Justice Antonin Scalia's position on walls.)

13. The poem "Mending Test" (see the **Connection** on page 729) is a **parody** (a work that makes fun of another work) of Frost's poem. Do you think Penelope Turk makes a serious point about test-taking, or is her poem just a clever imitation of Frost's form and style? Explain the reasons for your evaluation.

Women walking next to the Berlin Wall (1985).

---

11. Possible answers: the Berlin Wall; the Great Wall of China; the Mason-Dixon line; the Iron Curtain.

Extending and Evaluating

12. Possible answers: Yes, walls promote privacy, define boundaries, and protect rights. No, walls encourage separateness, isolation, and suspicion. Walls are helpful in some situations and harmful in others.

13. Possible answers: Turk's poem makes a serious point by detailing how testing harms students and teachers. No, the humor resulting from the parody dilutes any seriousness.

ASSESSING

Assessment

■ *Holt Assessment: Literature, Reading, and Vocabulary*

Before You Read

The Death of the Hired Man

Make the Connection
Quickwrite

One of Frost's most famous lines is from this poem: "Home is the place where, when you have to go there, / They have to take you in." The poem also offers another definition of home: "Something you somehow haven't to deserve." To some people, home is a definite place; to others, it is a state of mind, a sense of connectedness and belonging. Quickwrite your definition of home.

Literary Focus
A Narrative Poem

A **narrative poem** is a poem that tells a story—a series of related events. Most of this narrative poem consists of **dialogue** written in **blank verse** (see page 738). The poem's main character, Silas the hired man, does not speak for himself, yet his presence dominates the poem. By the last line we have heard enough about Silas's background, habits, and attitudes to feel we know him. In gradually learning about him, we also come to know the husband and wife whose dialogue tells the poem's story.

A **narrative poem** is a poem that tells a story—a series of related events with a beginning, a middle, and an end. A narrative poem also features characters and, frequently, dialogue.

For more on Narrative Poem, see the Handbook of Literary and Historical Terms.

Reading Skills
Drawing Inferences About Characters

Read this poem as if it were a short story. As you read, make notes about the feelings you sense between Warren and Mary. Think too about the feelings each of them has toward Silas. Note your own responses to each of these characters. Do your feelings change as you read on through the poem?

INTERNET

More About
Robert Frost

Keyword: LE5 11-5

SKILLS
FOCUS

Literary Skills
Understand the characteristics of a narrative poem.

Reading Skills
Make inferences about characters.

PRETEACHING

Summary ⬌ *at grade level*

Mary and Warren discuss Silas, who once worked for them and has now returned. For practical reasons, Warren does not want to take Silas back, but Mary senses that Silas has come "home" to die and believes they must take him in. After a dialogue, they decide to let the man stay. When Warren goes to tell Silas, he finds him dead.

Selection Starter

Build background. Like short stories, narrative poems have characters who appear in a specific setting and take action in response to a conflict. As students read, help them identify the conflict Warren and Mary face.

DIRECT TEACHING

A **Reading Skills**

? **Drawing inferences about characters.** What can you infer about Warren from Mary's warning to him to "Be kind"? [Possible responses: He can be tactless or harsh; there is some problem between him and Silas.]

The Death of the Hired Man

Robert Frost

Mary sat musing on the lamp-flame at the table,
Waiting for Warren. When she heard his step,
She ran on tiptoe down the darkened passage
To meet him in the doorway with the news
5   And put him on his guard. "Silas is back."
She pushed him outward with her through the door **A**
And shut it after her. "Be kind," she said.

Robert Frost 731

RESOURCES: READING

Planning
- *One-Stop Planner* CD-ROM with ExamView Test Generator

Differentiating Instruction
- *Holt Reading Solutions*
- *The Holt Reader*
- *Supporting Instruction in Spanish*
- *Audio CD Library, Selections and Summaries in Spanish*

Grammar and Language
- *Daily Language Activities*

Assessment
- *Holt Assessment: Literature, Reading, and Vocabulary*
- *One-Stop Planner* CD-ROM with ExamView Test Generator
- *Holt Online Assessment*

Internet
- go.hrw.com (Keyword: LE5 11-5)
- *Elements of Literature Online*

Media
- *Audio CD Library*
- *Audio CD Library, Selections and Summaries in Spanish*

A Literary Focus

? **Sound effects.** Have a volunteer read the first four lines of Warren's speech aloud (omitting "he said"). What do you notice about the meter? [When the lines are spoken naturally, they are not strictly iambic.] Why is this irregularity appropriate? [Possible response: Human beings don't actually speak in strict meter.]

B Reading Skills

? **Drawing inferences about characters.** What does this statement reveal about Silas? [Possible responses: He is too proud to beg; he does not want the humiliation of being financially dependent on others.]

C Literary Focus

Narrative poetry. Explain to students that in this passage Warren is relating an earlier conversation he had with Silas. The single quotation marks indicate when each character starts and stops speaking. Suggest to students that they may have to read the lines more than once to figure out who is speaking and who is replying.

D Learners Having Difficulty

Paraphrasing. Have students restate in their own words Warren's grievance against Silas. [Possible response: Silas deserted Warren during the busy season because he got a better job offer; then, he came back in the slow season looking for work when Warren no longer needed him.]

E Reading Skills

? **Drawing inferences about characters.** What does this exchange reveal about Mary's and Warren's characters? [Mary is kinder and more compassionate than Warren; Warren is more impatient and blunt than Mary.]

She took the market things from Warren's arms
And set them on the porch, then drew him down
10   To sit beside her on the wooden steps.

A   "When was I ever anything but kind to him?
But I'll not have the fellow back," he said.
"I told him so last haying, didn't I?
If he left then, I said, that ended it.
15   What good is he? Who else will harbor° him   15. **harbor** v.: provide safe shelter
At his age for the little he can do?   for.
What help he is there's no depending on.
Off he goes always when I need him most.
He thinks he ought to earn a little pay,
20   Enough at least to buy tobacco with,
B   So he won't have to beg and be beholden.°   21. **beholden** adj.: indebted.
'All right,' I say, 'I can't afford to pay
C   Any fixed wages, though I wish I could.'
'Someone else can.' 'Then someone else will have to.'
25   I shouldn't mind his bettering himself
If that was what it was. You can be certain,
D   When he begins like that, there's someone at him
Trying to coax him off with pocket money—
In haying time, when any help is scarce.
30   In winter he comes back to us. I'm done."

E   "Sh! not so loud: He'll hear you," Mary said.

"I want him to: He'll have to soon or late."

"He's worn out. He's asleep beside the stove.
When I came up from Rowe's I found him here,
35   Huddled against the barn door fast asleep,
A miserable sight, and frightening, too—
You needn't smile—I didn't recognize him—
I wasn't looking for him—and he's changed.
Wait till you see."

                        "Where did you say he'd been?"

40   "He didn't say. I dragged him to the house,
And gave him tea and tried to make him smoke.
I tried to make him talk about his travels.
Nothing would do: He just kept nodding off."

        "What did he say? Did he say anything?"

"But little."

                "Anything? Mary, confess
45   He said he'd come to ditch° the meadow for me."   46. **ditch** v.: dig drainage channels
                                                                               in.
"Warren!"

DIFFERENTIATING INSTRUCTION

Learners Having Difficulty

Activity. Students may find this long and reflective poem easier to follow if they work together to present it as reader's theater. Have a pair of students block out the dialogue in the poem and create a script. Another student can function as a casting director, auditioning and selecting students for the roles of narrator, Warren, Mary, and Silas. Tell the scriptwriters that they are free to do some rewriting and editing of the poem in order to make it work as a dramatic reading, but they must be able to justify their changes. For instance, they may decide to have Silas speak directly (which he does not do in the poem), but if they do so, they must create dialogue that is in tune with Silas's character as presented in the poem.

Invite learners having difficulty to read "The Death of the Hired Man" in interactive format in *The Holt Reader* and to use the sidenotes as aids to understanding the selection.

"But did he? I just want to know."

"Of course he did. What would you have him say?
Surely you wouldn't grudge the poor old man
50   Some humble way to save his self-respect.
He added, if you really care to know,
He meant to clear the upper pasture, too.
That sounds like something you have heard before?
Warren, I wish you could have heard the way
55   He jumbled everything. I stopped to look
Two or three times—he made me feel so queer°—
To see if he was talking in his sleep.
He ran on° Harold Wilson—you remember—
The boy you had in haying four years since.
60   He's finished school, and teaching in his college.
Silas declares you'll have to get him back.
He says they two will make a team for work:
Between them they will lay this farm as smooth!
The way he mixed that in with other things.
65   He thinks young Wilson a likely lad, though daft
On education—you know how they fought
All through July under the blazing sun,
Silas up on the cart to build the load,
Harold along beside to pitch it on."

70   "Yes, I took care to keep well out of earshot."

"Well, those days trouble Silas like a dream.
You wouldn't think they would. How some things linger!
Harold's young college-boy's assurance piqued° him.
After so many years he still keeps finding
75   Good arguments he sees he might have used.
I sympathize. I know just how it feels
To think of the right thing to say too late.
Harold's associated in his mind with Latin.
He asked me what I thought of Harold's saying
80   He studied Latin, like the violin,
Because he liked it—that an argument!
He said he couldn't make the boy believe
He could find water with a hazel prong°—
Which showed how much good school had ever done him.
85   He wanted to go over that. But most of all
He thinks if he could have another chance
To teach him how to build a load of hay—"

"I know, that's Silas' one accomplishment.
He bundles every forkful in its place,
90   And tags and numbers it for future reference,
So he can find and easily dislodge it

56. queer *adj.*: uncomfortable; ill at ease.

58. ran on: kept talking in a rambling way about.

73. piqued *v.*: provoked.

83. hazel prong: forked branch used to find water underground.

Robert Frost   **733**

F Reading Skills

? Drawing inferences about characters. Is Warren justified in being suspicious of or angry with Silas? [Possible response: Yes, Silas had not been a dependable worker; he left Warren shorthanded in the middle of the busy season and returned in winter, when no one else would hire him. Warren does not want to be taken advantage of again.]

G Reading Skills

? Interpreting characters' feelings. Why does Mary feel uncomfortable? [Possible response: Silas rambles and doesn't seem fully conscious.]

H Reading Skills

? Drawing inferences about characters. Why do you think Silas doesn't get along with Harold Wilson? [Possible responses: Silas envies Harold, who has a future. As Mary says in ll. 100–101, Silas is an old man who has little to be proud of in his past and no hope for a better future. Harold represents everything Silas could never be.]

I Literary Focus

? Indirect characterization. What does Silas's comment about Harold reveal about Silas? [Possible responses: Silas has had little formal education but has learned skills through experience. Silas is insecure and wants Harold to respect him.]

English-Language Learners
Activity. To give students practice speaking conversational English, have them pair up with an English-proficient partner and role-play the following scenarios:
(1) Silas and Harold talk while they work together on the farm, and (2) Warren informs Silas's brother of Silas's death. Encourage students to look in the poem for clues about how the characters talk, what they want, and how they feel about one another. Partners should rehearse their dialogues before presenting them to the group.

Advanced Learners
Enrichment. Ask students to work in a small group to create dialogue and stage directions for the scene in which Silas returns to the farm. Tell them they can think of themselves as writing the script for the opening scene of a one-act play, based on "The Death of the Hired Man." Have students write the dialogue between Silas and Mary in prose or blank verse.

A **Reading Skills**

❓ Drawing inferences about characters. What does this stanza suggest about Silas? What does it suggest about Warren? [Silas has a legitimate skill to offer. Warren is both observant and fair.]

B **Literary Focus**

❓ Imagery. What does Frost suggest about Mary here? [Possible response: The image of playing the harp suggests that she exerts a soothing influence on those around her.]

C **Reading Skills**

❓ Drawing inferences about characters. What do Warren's and Mary's different definitions of "home" suggest about their feelings toward Silas? [Possible responses: Warren believes that Silas is imposing on their generosity. Mary believes that Silas trusts their kindness and has no other home.]

D **Learners Having Difficulty**

By this point in the poem, students may have lost track of which character is speaking which lines. Suggest that they mark *M* for Mary and *W* for Warren on small adhesive notes and put these next to each character's lines on the page. This will help them follow the dialogue and keep track of the poem's final complications.

A
In the unloading. Silas does that well.
He takes it out in bunches like big birds' nests.
You never see him standing on the hay
95   He's trying to lift, straining to lift himself."

"He thinks if he could teach him that, he'd be
Some good perhaps to someone in the world.
He hates to see a boy the fool of books.
Poor Silas, so concerned for other folk,
100   And nothing to look backward to with pride,
And nothing to look forward to with hope,
So now and never any different."

Part of a moon was falling down the west,
Dragging the whole sky with it to the hills.
105   Its light poured softly in her lap. She saw it
And spread her apron to it. She put out her hand
B   Among the harplike morning-glory strings,
Taut with the dew from garden bed to eaves,
As if she played unheard some tenderness
110   That wrought° on him beside her in the night.
"Warren," she said, "he has come home to die:
You needn't be afraid he'll leave you this time."

"Home," he mocked gently.

                      "Yes, what else but home?
It all depends on what you mean by home.
115   Of course he's nothing to us, any more
Than was the hound that came a stranger to us
Out of the woods, worn out upon the trail."

"Home is the place where, when you have to go there,
They have to take you in."
C
                      "I should have called it
120   Something you somehow haven't to deserve."

Warren leaned out and took a step or two,
Picked up a little stick, and brought it back
And broke it in his hand and tossed it by.
"Silas has better claim on us you think
125   Than on his brother? Thirteen little miles
As the road winds would bring him to his door.
Silas has walked that far no doubt today.
Why doesn't he go there? His brother's rich,
A somebody—director in the bank."

D
"He never told us that."

130   "We know it, though."

110. **wrought** *v.:* worked.

Analyzing plot and conflict. Remind students that conflicts are the struggles at the heart of any narrative. They can occur between characters; between one character and nature or society; between feelings or wishes within a character; or between forces or conditions, such as good and evil or innocence and experience. Explain that conflicts are usually worked out through the plot of a narrative. The exposition introduces the problem; complications, which develop as characters try to deal with the conflict, lead to the point of greatest intensity, the climax. The resolution brings an end to the conflict, but it is not always satisfactory to all characters.

Activity. Have the students chart the various conflicts between the characters in "The Death of the Hired Man." Be sure they identify the conflicts and complications and how they are resolved. [Possible responses: *Characters*—Silas, Mary, and Warren. *Conflict*—Warren does not trust Silas. *Complication*—Warren must decide whether to take Silas in. *Resolution*—Mary convinces Warren, but Silas dies.]

"I think his brother ought to help, of course.
I'll see to that if there is need. He ought of right
To take him in, and might be willing to—
He may be better than appearances.
135   But have some pity on Silas. Do you think
If he had any pride in claiming kin
Or anything he looked for from his brother,
He'd keep so still about him all this time?"

"I wonder what's between them."

                                        "I can tell you.
140   Silas is what he is—we wouldn't mind him—
But just the kind that kinsfolk can't abide.
He never did a thing so very bad.
He don't know why he isn't quite as good
As anybody. Worthless though he is,
145   He won't be made ashamed to please his brother."

"*I* can't think Si ever hurt anyone."

"No, but he hurt my heart the way he lay
And rolled his old head on that sharp-edged chair-back.
He wouldn't let me put him on the lounge.
150   You must go in and see what you can do.
I made the bed up for him there tonight.
You'll be surprised at him—how much he's broken.
His working days are done; I'm sure of it."

"I'd not be in a hurry to say that."

155   "I haven't been. Go, look, see for yourself.
But, Warren, please remember how it is:
He's come to help you ditch the meadow.
He has a plan. You mustn't laugh at him.
He may not speak of it, and then he may.
160   I'll sit and see if that small sailing cloud
Will hit or miss the moon."

                                        It hit the moon.
Then there were three there, making a dim row,
The moon, the little silver cloud, and she.

Warren returned—too soon, it seemed to her—
165   Slipped to her side, caught up her hand and waited.

"Warren?" she questioned.
                                        "Dead," was all he answered.

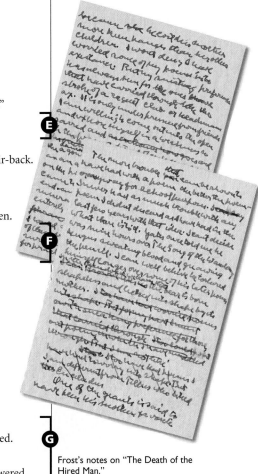

Frost's notes on "The Death of the Hired Man."

E **Reading Skills**

❓ **Drawing inferences about characters.** Warren calls Silas by a nickname here. What does this suggest about Warren's mood? [Possible response: His conversation with Mary has softened his attitude.]

F **Reading Skills**

❓ **Analyzing cause and effect.** Warren's attitude has completely changed. He now tries to reassure Mary that Silas is in good health. What has caused this change? [Possible responses: Mary's compassion has awakened Warren's softer side; he pities Silas's loneliness and separation from his family; he respects Silas's pride; he feels sorry that Silas is old and sick.]

G **Reading Skills**

❓ **Drawing inferences about characters.** What contrasting traits does Warren show at the end of the poem? [Possible response: He shows tenderness and sensitivity when he takes hold of Mary's hand to tell her the news of Silas's death, yet he also demonstrates his characteristic bluntness and practicality in the way he tells her.]

FAMILY/COMMUNITY ACTIVITY

Have students write letters to family members or to members of the community in which they tell the story of Silas's return to the farm as if it were something that happened to them or their neighbors. Tell students that the purpose of their letters is to share their feelings about home and community and discuss ways to provide for relatives and neighbors who can no longer support themselves.

Primary Source

In this excerpt from a 1917 interview with a *New York Times* reporter, Frost explains his preference for blank verse over free verse. He sees modernist poets as achieving some striking, immediate effects but not creating anything of lasting beauty.

DIRECT TEACHING

A Content-Area Connections

Literature: Free Verse
Students may be surprised by Frost's vigorous rejection of free verse. Explain to them that his views reflect his personal preference for metered poetry and they are not generally held by today's poets. Be sure students also understand that all versification is the conscious art of expressing ideas in some sort of poetic frame or structure. Poets can use a variety of techniques to create that structure, including rhythm, rhyme, compression, repetition, word choice, and sound effects, as well as meter. For this reason, there is really no such thing as "free verse" in the sense of verse without any structure or form. In other words, poetry must be more than prose arranged on the page to look like a poem.

"I must have the pulse beat of rhythm . . ."

These comments are from an interview in The New York Times *in 1917. Here Frost has been talking about American poetry.*

We're still a bit afraid. America, for instance, was afraid to accept Walt Whitman when he first sang the songs of democracy. His influence on American poetry began to be felt only after the French had hailed him as a great writer, a literary revolutionist. Our own poet had to be imported from France before we were sure of his strength.

Today almost every man who writes poetry confesses his debt to Whitman. Many have gone very much further than Whitman would have traveled with them. They are the people who believe in wide straddling.

I, myself, as I said before, don't like it for myself. I do not write free verse; I write blank verse. I must have the pulse beat of rhythm, I like to hear it beating under the things I write.

That doesn't mean I do not like to read a bit of free verse occasionally. I do. It some-times succeeds in painting a picture that is very clear and startling. It's good as something created momentarily for its sudden startling effect; it hasn't the qualities, however, of something lastingly beautiful.

And sometimes my objection to it is that it's a pose. It's not honest. When a man sets out consciously to tear up forms and rhythms and measures, then he is not interested in giving you poetry. He just wants to perform; he wants to show you his tricks. He will get an effect; nobody will deny that, but it is not a harmonious effect.

Sometimes it strikes me that the free-verse people got their idea from incorrect proof sheets. I have had stuff come from the printers with lines half left out or positions changed about. I read the poems as they stood, distorted and half finished, and I confess I get a rather pleasant sensation from them. They make a sort of nightmarish half-sense. . . .

Robert Frost

Robert Frost at John F. Kennedy's inauguration, January 20, 1961.

Comparing and Contrasting Texts

Whitman versus Frost. Have groups of students look back over Walt Whitman's poems in Chapter 3 and discuss the differences between the verse forms of Whitman and Frost. They may also want to consider whether Whitman's free-verse poems are less beautiful and harmonious than Frost's metered verse.

Response and Analysis

Thinking Critically

1. All stories are built around conflict. Sum up the basic problem facing Warren, Mary, and Silas as it unfolds in the dialogue between Mary and Warren. Some might say that Mary sees the hired man's situation in an emotional sense and Warren views it in a business sense. Do you agree? Explain.

2. Based on their dialogue, what **inferences** can you make about the relationship between Warren and Mary and about the way in which each relates to Silas?

3. Identify the details in lines 103–110 that create a vivid image of the **setting** of this narrative poem. What does this passage tell you about Mary's **character**?

4. Do any of the main characters change in the course of the narrative? Quote passages to support your answer.

5. Does the conclusion of this narrative poem strike you as inevitable, or unavoidable? Why or why not? What would your feelings have been if Warren, instead of answering "Dead" to Mary's question, had answered "Asleep" or "Sharpening his scythe"?

6. Find the two definitions of *home* offered in the poem. A critic has said that one definition is based on law and duty, and the other on mercy. Identify each. Do you agree with the critic's observation? Which definition is closer to yours? Be sure to refer to your Quickwrite notes. ✏️

7. State in your own words the poem's **theme,** or what it reveals to you about our lives. How could its theme apply to social issues faced in both rural and urban areas today?

Extending and Evaluating

8. In the *Primary Source* on page 736, Frost says he aimed to give the speech of each character in his poetry a distinct sound, just as people's voices sound different in real life. Does he successfully differentiate Warren's and Mary's dialogue? Give reasons for your opinion.

WRITING

Frost Bites

The critic Louise Bogan pointed out the "tensions, dark conflicts, and passionate involvements" that appear in Frost's poetry and "pervade certain poems with almost nightmare intensity." In a brief **essay,** explore examples of the "dark conflicts" in the Frost poems you have read here. What attitudes does Frost share with the Dark Romantics (page 148)?

Accident or Design?

In a brief essay, **compare and contrast** Frost's "Design" with Emily Dickinson's "Apparently with no surprise" (page 344). Before you write, gather your data in a chart like the one below:

	Dickinson	Frost
Message		
Symbols		
Rhyme and rhythm		
Imagery		

INTERNET
Projects and Activities
Keyword: LE5 11-5

SKILLS FOCUS

Literary Skills
Analyze a narrative poem and blank verse.

Reading Skills
Make inferences about characters.

Writing Skills
Write an essay analyzing a poem. Write an essay comparing and contrasting two poems.

Listening and Speaking Skills
Perform an oral interpretation of a poem.

Robert Frost **737**

Literary Criticism

Critic's Commentary: Tennis Without a Net

In defense of Frost's attack on the aesthetics of free verse, the British poet Robert Graves tells us: "Frost has always respected meter. When, during the *Vers Libre* (Free Verse) period of the Nineteen Twenties and Thirties, his poems were disdained as old-fashioned, he remarked disdainfully that writing free verse was like playing tennis without a net. . . . That you can't achieve much in poetry, without, so to speak, a taut net and straight whitewashed lines is shown by the difficulty of memorizing free verse; it does not fix itself firmly enough in the imagination." Ask students whether they agree with Frost and Graves or whether they do find free verse poetic.

In *The Veteran in a New Field,* **Winslow Homer** (1836–1910) simultaneously conveys a realistic moment in the working life of a farmer, gives an impression of peace, and makes a biblical allusion to war and reconciliation (Isaiah 2:4, "swords into plowshares").

Activity. Ask students how Homer's and Frost's work are similar in style. [Possible response: Both portray the dignity of ordinary country people.]

INDEPENDENT PRACTICE

Literary Focus

Possible Answers

• Listening only to ll. 1–10, we note strict iambic pentameter in ll. 4 and 6–10. Lines 2, 3, and 5 are in loose iambic pentameter, with one instance each of an irregular stress or an extra unstressed syllable at the end of the line. Line 1 is looser, yet has thirteen syllables and an irregular rhythm.

• No, the occasional looseness of the rhythm suits the earthy subject matter and diction.

• Students' rewrites will vary. Remind students to emphasize cadence, parallelism, and repetition of words, phrases, and imagery.

• Some students may prefer the strength and straightforwardness of free verse, while others may prefer the discipline that regular rhyme and rhythm impose on poetry.

ASSESSING

Assessment

■ *Holt Assessment: Literature, Reading, and Vocabulary*

RETEACHING

For a lesson reteaching poetic devices, see **Reteaching,** p. 1117A.

The Veteran in a New Field (detail) (1865) by Winslow Homer. Oil on canvas.

The Metropolitan Museum of Art.
Bequest of Miss Adelaide Milton de Groot, 1967 (67.187.131).
Photograph © 1995, The Metropolitan Museum of Art, New York.

LISTENING AND SPEAKING

Dynamic Dialogue

With a partner, prepare an oral reading of "The Death of the Hired Man." Begin by thoroughly discussing the characters of Warren and Mary. Be sure you know what each character wants. How can their different personalities be conveyed by varying the speed, volume, and tone of their speech? Practice these variations along with appropriate gestures and movements. When you are satisfied with your interpretation, perform it for your class or group.

Literary Focus
Blank Verse

"The poet goes in like a rope skipper to make the most of his opportunities," Frost wrote in an essay called "The Constant Symbol." "If he trips himself he stops the rope. He is of our stock and has been brought up by ear to choice of two meters, strict iambic and loose iambic (not to count varieties of the latter)." Like most of Frost's poems, "The Death of the Hired Man" is written in **blank verse,** which is unrhymed iambic pentameter. It is called *blank verse* because the lines do not have end rhymes. Iambic pentameter means that there are five iambs to each line; an iamb is an unaccented syllable followed by an accented syllable:

da DUM (˘ ´)

• Scan the first ten lines, and recite them aloud to hear the meter. (For help scanning a poem, see page 171.)

• Look over the poem, and find examples of strict iambic and loose iambic meter.

• Do you think Frost ever "trips" himself in this poem?

• Take ten lines from this poem, and rewrite them in the free verse style of Walt Whitman (for more on free verse, see page 313). Where will you break the lines? What rearrangement of words will have to be made to break the iambic meter?

• Look at Frost's comments on free verse in the **Primary Source** on page 736. What is *your* opinion of Frost's ideas?

Writing a Biographical Narrative

"There's more there than meets the eye" is an expression you could apply to Granny Weatherall and Walter Mitty, two of the interesting characters you encountered in the preceding literature section. Like fictional characters, real people also have stories—stories that writers like you can tell. In this workshop you'll tell another person's story by writing a **biographical narrative,** a true story based on an incident in the life of someone you know.

Choose a Subject As you consider a subject for your biographical narrative—a person to write about—choose someone you already know well or someone you can interview if you need extra information. Make sure you have specific knowledge of at least one incident that reveals that person's character. If necessary, interview your subject to learn more details about the incident.

Add Details To make the **characterization** of your subject vivid and to bring the incident you're describing to life, use narrative and descriptive details.

- **Narrative details** tell what happened; they are the sequence of events that make up the incident. Narrative details also provide information about the specific actions, movements, gestures, and feelings of the people involved in the incident.

- **Descriptive details** give information about the subject's **appearance** and personality. Descriptive details also explain the setting or **specific places** where the incident occurs.

Take notes on the narrative and descriptive details you want to include in your paper. Then, add **concrete sensory details**—details that appeal to the senses of touch, taste, smell, sight, and hearing—to create specific **images** in the reader's mind of each part of the incident.

Use Stylistic Devices One technique you can use to portray your subject as a unique, fully developed individual is **interior monologue,** in which your subject "thinks out loud." Interior monologue allows the reader to experience your subject's thoughts directly. Use interior monologue for thoughts that the subject has told you about, such as the one below.

> Benny carefully picked the sparrow up from the ground. "Come on, little bird," he thought, "you're going to be fine."

Writing Assignment
Write a biographical narrative about an incident that shows another person's character.

SKILLS FOCUS

Writing Skills
Write a biographical narrative. Include narrative and descriptive details.

Mini-Workshop: Writing a Biographical Narrative **739**

COLLECTION 5 RESOURCES: WRITING

Planning
- *One-Stop Planner* CD-ROM with ExamView Test Generator

Differentiating Instruction
- *Workshop Resources: Writing, Listening, and Speaking*
- *Family Involvement Activities in English and Spanish*
- *Supporting Instruction in Spanish*

Writing and Language
- *Workshop Resources: Writing, Listening, and Speaking*
- *Daily Language Activities*
- *Language Handbook Worksheets*

Assessment
- *Holt Assessment: Writing, Listening, and Speaking*

(continued on p. 740)

PRETEACHING

Motivate. Have students think of a person who has made a positive impression on them in some way. Ask students to share with the class the trait or traits this person has that contributes to this impression. Then, ask students to think about a specific instance when they observed these traits in action. Explain to students that they will write about such an instance in this workshop.

DIRECT TEACHING

Writing a Biographical Narrative

Explain to students that a biographical narrative is much more similar to a narrative—a story—than to a biography—a history of a person's life. A biographical narrative should not chronicle an entire life or even a large part of one. Instead, it should tell the specific story or stories that best reveal an aspect of the subject's character.

RETEACHING

Add Details

To help students organize their impressions and feelings toward a subject, encourage them to create graphic organizers such as word clusters or cause-and-effect diagrams. Word clusters can help students brainstorm descriptive details and label emotional responses they have when they think about their subjects. Cause-and-effect diagrams can help a student see the results of the impact the subject has had on the student.

English-Language Learners

A large part of a student's success in writing a biographical narrative depends on a student's descriptive abilities: He or she must be able to create specific images. You might teach a mini-lesson on the correct use of adjectives in English. Review the placement of adjectives as well as the fact that in English, adjectives do not have inflected forms.

Advanced Learners

Enrichment. Ask students to review the selections in other Writing Workshops of their text and find clear examples of authors' use of pace. Ask students to describe the pace and explain specifically how the author achieved it. For example, did the author use short sentences, repetition, single-syllable words, or words with multiple syllables to create a particular pace? Analyzing other models should help students plan their own stories.

PRACTICE & APPLY

Guided and Independent Practice

You might guide students in devising criteria to help them determine which incidents they will write about in their biographical narratives. Discuss with students what makes one incident more suitable than another, and help students turn this information into criteria. After students have chosen their subjects and determined what incidents to narrate, they will be ready to complete **Practice and Apply** independently.

TIP The words you choose and the way you arrange those words in sentences make up the **style** of your paper. Sometimes those words and sentences can be used to convey **irony**, a contrast between what is expected and what is real, as in the towering and gruff appearance of a caring and gentle person.

| DO THIS →

Establish a Point of View You'll generally write from your own **point of view** to show readers how you see your subject. Occasionally, however, it may be helpful to include someone else's point of view. Changing from one point of view to another and back again is called **shifting perspectives.** As you write, make sure any transitions between perspectives are clear to readers. Notice how the student shifts perspectives in the example below to show a different view of her subject.

> Because of Benny's enormous build and somber nature, my friend Janis thought of him as a stereotypical athlete who cared only about himself and lifting weights. She was surprised to learn that Benny helped rescue a sparrow that had fallen from its nest.

Organize and Pace Your Narrative Once you've gathered all the details for your biographical narrative, plan its organization and pace. In general, your biography should be in **chronological order.** Within this framework, however, you may need to use other organizational strategies. For instance, you might use **spatial order** to describe your subject's appearance or the setting of an important event.

The **pace** of your biographical narrative—the rate at which you relate events—should vary to accommodate spatial (place) changes, temporal (time) changes, and dramatic mood changes. Look at the following chart to see how the student writer plans to accommodate spatial, temporal, and mood changes.

> **Spatial changes:** I'll describe our walk in the woods in detail to slow the pace and give readers time to absorb the setting.
>
> **Temporal changes:** Because Benny and I attended a wildlife camp, I'll include a flashback to explain why I knew what to do with the sparrow.
>
> **Mood changes:** I'll add details about Benny's difficulty in climbing the tree to increase the pace gradually and show our growing anticipation at replacing the baby bird in its nest.

Explain the Meaning The events and details you include in your narrative will show your subject's character. Save any direct statement about the person's character until the last paragraph, after your readers have had a chance to draw conclusions about the subject for themselves.

SKILLS FOCUS

Writing Skills
Organize the narrative.

PRACTICE & APPLY
Using the information on these two pages, plan and write a biographical narrative. Then, share your biographical narrative with your classmates.

COLLECTION 5 RESOURCES: WRITING

- *One-Stop Planner* CD-ROM with ExamView Test Generator
- *Holt Online Assessment*
- *Holt Online Essay Scoring*

Internet
- go.hrw.com (Keyword: LE5 11-5)
- *Elements of Literature Online*

The Harlem Renaissance

Cullen

Hughes

Hurston

I, too, sing America.

—Langston Hughes

INTERNET

Collection Resources

Keyword: LE5 11–5

The Migration of the Negro (1940–1941), No. 1, by Jacob Lawrence. Tempera on masonite (12″ × 18″).

The Phillips Collection, Washington, D.C. Acquired 1942, Courtesy of the Jacob and Gwendolyn Lawrence Foundation.

741

THE QUOTATION

The quotation from Langston Hughes alludes to Walt Whitman's famous poem "I Hear America Singing" (see p. 311). Although Whitman includes all men and women in his vision of America, not all nineteenth-century Americans thought and felt as he did. In the twentieth century, Hughes felt the impulse to add his voice to the national song. What do people feel when they experience exclusion—such as being banned from group activities or being forbidden membership in an organization? [Possible responses: loneliness; shame; depression; anger.] What does the expression "I, too" suggest about Hughes's attitude? [Possible response: He has a voice and wishes to be heard. He expects to be recognized as a contributor to the national experience.]

VIEWING THE ART

Jacob Lawrence (1917–2000) carefully researched the history behind his sixty-panel Migration series. He was the first artist to recognize the magnitude of what was the biggest internal migration in American history—the movement of as many as one million African Americans from the rural South to the industrial North in the early decades of the twentieth century.

Activity. What details suggest the goals of migrating African Americans? [The signs over the gates suggest that the migrants sought opportunities in large cities.] Note the impression of urgency in the image of the mobs surging onto the trains.

A Exploring the Culture
HARLEM RENAISSANCE

The word *renaissance,* meaning "rebirth or revival," usually refers to the Renaissance that flourished in Europe between 1300 and 1600—an era characterized by its spirit of innovation, curiosity, and adventure in fields ranging from architecture to science to fine art. The European Renaissance was considered a rebirth of the Golden Age of classical culture in ancient Greece and Rome. The upsurge in African American cultural expression that took place in Harlem, New York, in the 1920s occurred with such force and had so much influence that it became known as the Harlem Renaissance.

B Exploring the Historical Period
MARCUS GARVEY

Marcus Garvey (1887–1940) was a Jamaican-born American who exhorted African Americans to view Africa as their primary homeland and urged them to emigrate there.

C Content-Area Connections

Music: Jazz

Jazz, a truly original American art form, evolved from African American folk music. Its roots lie in African rhythms, European harmonies, American gospel sounds, and the work songs that flourished among plantation workers during and after slavery. These last two forms, along with "sorrow songs," influenced the rise of the blues, which in turn contributed to jazz. Ragtime and Dixieland, both arising in New Orleans in the 1890s, were the earliest jazz styles. Jazz spread to Chicago, Kansas City, and other cities after 1917 and developed rapidly into an improvisational music that was played by big bands and small groups alike. Jazz remains popular around the world today.

A The Harlem Renaissance

In the early 1920s, African American artists, writers, musicians, and performers were part of a great cultural movement known as the Harlem Renaissance. The huge migration to the north after World War I brought African Americans of all ages and walks of life to the thriving New York City neighborhood called Harlem. Doctors, singers, students, musicians, shopkeepers, painters, and writers congregated, forming a vibrant mecca of cultural affirmation and inspiration.

As Langston Hughes wrote, "It was the period when the Negro was in vogue." Marcus Garvey's "Back to Africa" movement was in full swing. The blues were vibrantly alive; jazz was just beginning. An all-black show, *Shuffle Along,* opened on Broadway in 1921, with music composed by Eubie Blake and lyrics by Noble Sissle. *Shuffle Along* introduced audiences to three performers soon to become famous: Josephine Baker, Paul Robeson, and Florence Mills. Meanwhile, mainstream America was developing a new respect for African art and culture, thanks in part to its reflection in the work of the modernist artists Pablo Picasso and Georges Braque.

Against this backdrop, Harlem Renaissance artists insisted that the African American be accepted as "a collaborator and participant in American civilization," in the words of the educator and critic Alain Locke. Writers such as Jean Toomer and Zora Neale Hurston (page 762) wrote about the African American experience. Artists such as Aaron Douglas and William H. Johnson painted it. The photographer James Van Der Zee recorded it with his camera. The trumpeter Louis Armstrong and the pianist Fletcher Henderson set it to music, and the vocalists Bessie Smith and Ma Rainey sang it.

Bessie Smith.

CONTENT-AREA CONNECTIONS

Music: Bessie Smith

Bessie Smith (1894?–1937) was born in Chattanooga, Tennessee, and began her music career around 1910. In New York during the 1920s, she made the bold, powerful recordings that earned her the nickname "Empress of the Blues."

Whole-class activity. Encourage students to listen to recordings of authentic blues singers of the past, such as Blind Lemon Jefferson, as well as recordings of contemporary blues masters, such as B. B. King. Have students compare the old and new styles, and discuss with them how the form and attitude of the blues have remained basically unchanged through the years.

Harlem newspapers and journals, such as *Crisis* and *Opportunity*, published the work of both new and established African American writers. To promote and support intellectually gifted young people, the journals sponsored literary contests that encouraged creative writing and rewarded it with cash prizes and social introductions to the top writers of the time.

In autobiographies, poetry, short stories, novels, and folklore, African American writers affirmed the role of black talent in American culture and focused on different aspects of black life in Harlem, the South, Europe, the Caribbean, and even Russia. They addressed issues of race, class, religion, and gender. Some writers focused entirely on black characters, while others addressed relationships among people of different races. Some writers attacked racism; others addressed issues within black communities. A byproduct of African American writing was the affirmation that black dialects were as legitimate as standard English.

Unfortunately, by the early 1930s, the Great Depression had depleted many of the funds that had provided financial support to individual African American writers, institutions, and publications. Nevertheless, Harlem and African American culture were forever changed. The foundation was laid for Ralph Ellison, James Baldwin, Gwendolyn Brooks, Alice Walker, Toni Morrison, Maya Angelou, Terry McMillan, Rita Dove, and thousands of other African American writers, painters, composers, and singers to make their feelings and experiences part of American artistic expression: "I, too, sing America."

Louis Armstrong.

The Harlem Renaissance   **743**

DIRECT TEACHING

D **Exploring the Historical Period**
LOUIS ARMSTRONG

Louis Armstrong (1901–1971) was born in New Orleans and raised in extreme poverty. At age eleven, he was sent to reform school (for firing a gun in the air on New Year's Eve). It was there that he learned to play the cornet. He gained prominence in the 1920s as a member of King Oliver's band and then as leader of his own Hot Five and Hot Seven bands. His brilliant trumpet and cornet playing brought the role of the Dixieland soloist to greater prominence. He also pioneered the improvisational singing style known as scat, in which sound syllables replace words.

SKILLS REVIEW

Asking questions. Encourage students to browse the HRW Web site, where they can conduct an Internet search on the Harlem Renaissance.

Activity. Using the site, groups of students should generate three relevant, interesting questions about the Harlem Renaissance. They might focus on jazz; blues; an African American writer, artist, or musician; or the social scene in Harlem in the 1920s. Have groups choose one question, research further via the Internet or other electronic sources, and present a brief written report. Have students supplement their reports with an illustration, a poster, a graph, a time line, an audiotape, or a videotape.

Grade-Level Skills

■ **Literary Skills**
Analyze the way poets use metaphor.

More About the Writer

Background. Countee Cullen once said that "good poetry is a lofty thought beautifully expressed," a thing that "should not be too intellectual" but should "deal more . . . with the emotions." While Cullen aimed to transcend the issue of race, his poems never abandoned the predicaments faced by African Americans.

VIEWING THE ART

Winold Reiss (1886–1953), a German artist who lived in New York City during the 1920s and 1930s, is known for his striking portraits of Native Americans and African Americans.

Activity. Why might Reiss have added color only to Cullen's face and tie? [Possible response: Reiss wished to emphasize these features as expressive of Cullen's personality.] What character traits does the portrait suggest? [thoughtfulness, seriousness, dignity]

Countee Cullen
(1903–1946)

Countee Porter Cullen (c. 1925) by Winold Reiss.
Pastel on artist board (30^{1}/$_{16}$" × 21^{1}/$_{2}$").

Countee Cullen grew up in New York City as the adopted son of Rev. and Mrs. Frederick Cullen. He was a brilliant student, and during high school he was already writing accomplished poems in traditional forms. He graduated Phi Beta Kappa from New York University in 1925. While in college, Cullen won the Witter Bynner Poetry Prize; that same year, *Color,* his first volume of poetry, was published. This collection won a gold medal from the Harmon Foundation and established the young poet's reputation.

After earning his master's degree from Harvard in 1926, Cullen worked as an assistant editor of the important African American magazine *Opportunity.* His poems were published in such influential periodicals as *Harper's, Poetry,* and *Crisis.* In 1927, he published *Copper Sun,* a collection of poems, and *Caroling Dusk,* an anthology of poetry by African Americans. *Caroling Dusk* was a significant contribution to the Harlem Renaissance, but the introduction Cullen wrote for the book was controversial. He called for black poets to write traditional verse and to avoid the restrictions of solely racial themes.

At the peak of his career, Cullen married the daughter of the famous black writer W.E.B. Du Bois and published a third collection of poems, *The Ballad of the Brown Girl.* In 1929, he published a fourth volume, *The Black Christ.* Although he continued to write prose until the end of his life, this was his last collection of poetry. During the Great Depression of the 1930s, unable to make a living solely from writing, he began teaching in Harlem public schools, a job that he held until his early death.

Cullen's verse was heavily influenced by the poetry of the English Romantics, especially John Keats. He thought of himself primarily as a lyric poet in the Romantic tradition, not as a black poet writing about social and racial themes. Nevertheless, Cullen found himself repeatedly drawn to such themes: "Somehow or other I find my poetry of itself treating of the Negro, of his joys and his sorrows—mostly of the latter—and of the heights and depths of emotion which I feel as a Negro."

RESOURCES: READING

Planning
■ *One-Stop Planner* CD-ROM with ExamView Test Generator

Differentiating Instruction
■ *Supporting Instruction in Spanish*
■ *Audio CD Library, Selections and Summaries in Spanish*

Assessment
■ *Holt Assessment: Literature, Reading, and Vocabulary*
■ *One-Stop Planner* CD-ROM with ExamView Test Generator
■ *Holt Online Assessment*

Internet
■ go.hrw.com (Keyword: LE5 11-5)

■ *Elements of Literature Online*
Media
■ *Audio CD Library*
■ *Audio CD Library, Selections and Summaries in Spanish*
■ *Fine Art Transparencies*

Before You Read

Tableau

Make the Connection

The history of race relations in the United States is long and tragic, the cause of much pain and misunderstanding. Knowledge of the great public confrontations such as the Civil War and the civil rights movement can illuminate that history, but in the end, it may be the personal experiences of individual blacks and whites that provide us with the deepest understanding of our past and of our possible future. As you read the following two poems by Cullen, think about the impact of the encounters on the individuals involved—and on the society in which they lived.

A *tableau* is "a scene or an action stopped cold," like a still picture in a reel of film.

Literary Focus
Metaphor

A **metaphor** is a **figure of speech,** an imaginative comparison between two unlike things. Some metaphors are stated directly, using a linking verb: *That boy is a streak of lightning.* Often they are more indirect. This poem uses four metaphors to reveal the way the poet feels about the sight of two boys crossing a street. Watch for the metaphors that end the first and last stanzas.

SKILLS FOCUS

Literary Skills
Understand metaphor.

> A **metaphor** is a figure of speech that makes a comparison between two unlike things without the use of a specific word of comparison.
>
> *For more on Metaphor, see the Handbook of Literary and Historical Terms.*

Tableau

(For Donald Duff)

Countee Cullen

Locked arm in arm they cross the way,
    The black boy and the white,
The golden splendor of the day,
    The sable pride of night.

5   From lowered blinds the dark folk stare,
    And here the fair folk talk,
Indignant that these two should dare
    In unison to walk.

Oblivious to look and word
10   They pass, and see no wonder
That lightning brilliant as a sword
    Should blaze the path of thunder.

Countee Cullen   **745**

VIEWING THE ART

Raphael Soyer (1899–1987) came to New York City from Russia in 1913. He became famous for his sensitive portraits of urban life in America.

Activity. Ask students how Soyer's scene both resembles and differs from that shown in Cullen's poem "Incident." [Both depict whites and blacks riding public transportation together, but while Cullen focuses on two boys interacting, Soyer focuses on the discomfort of a mother and child.] Ask students to interpret the body language of the black mother, the child, and the white passenger in the painting. [Possible response: The black mother stares straight ahead, as if she is tense and wary of some imminent trouble. The child edges away from the white woman. The white woman seems to be keeping to herself, not hostile but unwilling to appear too friendly.]

CONTENT-AREA CONNECTIONS

Literature: Further Reading
Other experiences of young African Americans are recounted by Zora Neale Hurston (see p. 763), Richard Wright (see p. 968), James Baldwin (see p. 1015), and Alice Walker (see p. 1007). Students might also read selections by Ralph Ellison and Malcolm X.

History: Civil Rights
Both of Cullen's poems were written when

American society was largely segregated. The civil rights movement that began in the 1950s aimed to end segregation and racial discrimination. Have students report on one of the following events:

• Montgomery bus boycott

• "I Have a Dream" speech by Martin Luther King, Jr.

• Civil Rights Act of 1964

• registration of African American voters

Art: Illustrating Cullen
Both "Tableau" and "Incident" present one powerful image or picture and then comment on it. Have students draw or paint the scene described in one of Cullen's poems. Students' work should convey the scene's emotional impact. Encourage them to use any style they find effective.

Before You Read

Incident

Make the Connection
Quickwrite ✏️

The power of a word to taunt, to criticize, to dehumanize can't be underestimated. You might be shaken by the offensive word in this poem—imagine how it would affect a child.

Before you read "Incident," quickwrite your response to the poem's title. Does it suggest something serious, or something relatively minor? How would you react if the title were "Catastrophe"?

Incident

Countee Cullen

Once, riding in old Baltimore,
    Heart-filled, head-filled with glee,
I saw a Baltimorean
    Keep looking straight at me.

5 Now I was eight and very small,
    And he was no whit bigger,
And so I smiled, but he poked out
    His tongue, and called me "Nigger."

I saw the whole of Baltimore
10   From May until December;
Of all the things that happened there
    That's all that I remember.

Passengers (1953) by Raphael Soyer. Oil on canvas.
© Estate of Raphael Soyer, Forum Gallery, New York. Image
courtesy of Sotheby's.

Countee Cullen   **747**

Response and Analysis

Tableau

Thinking Critically

1. The two boys, locked arm in arm, are walking across a street.

2. The observers are indignant because the friendship violates the enforced separation of the races, which is founded on prejudice. The boys pay no attention at all.

3. *Black boy*—"the sable pride of night." *White boy*—"the golden splendor of the day."

4. Possible answers: Both lightning and thunder are compared to the boys' jolting act of friendship. The thunder may be the rumbling of social change.

5. Many students will express admiration for the boys.

6. Possible answer: You must know that racial prejudice was prevalent.

Incident

Thinking Critically

1. The people are two boys, one black and one white, riding public transportation. When the black boy smiles, the white boy calls him "Nigger."

2. Possible answers: Parental influence, meanness, and ignorance might prompt an insult. A child's prejudice may be more disturbing because it is learned at home or less disturbing because the child may learn to reevaluate his bias.

3. Possible answer: An incident is an extraordinary event. Cullen chose the title to suggest how critical and traumatic the event was.

4. By telling us that this remains his only memory from that long stay in Baltimore, the speaker dramatizes its profound impact.

Extending and Evaluating

5. Possible answer: The poems capture the persistence of racial prejudice. Neither the details nor the messages are outdated.

Response and Analysis

Tableau

Thinking Critically

1. What exactly are the two boys in the tableau doing?

2. Why are "the dark folk" and "the fair folk" indignant? How do the boys respond?

3. What **metaphor** in the first stanza describes the black boy? the white boy?

4. Two more **metaphors** are used in the third stanza. Who or what is "lightning brilliant as a sword"? Who or what is "the path of thunder"?

5. How do the metaphors make you feel about the boys?

6. What do you have to know about the social context of the poem in order to understand why such a commonplace thing as a friendship between two boys could evoke such a dramatic response?

Incident

Thinking Critically

go.hrw.com

INTERNET

Projects and Activities

Keyword: LE5 11-5

1. Who are the two people in this poem, and what exactly happens between them?

2. What do you think leads the "Baltimorean" to act as he does? Are his actions more disturbing or less disturbing because he is a child? Explain your responses.

3. What does the word *incident* suggest to you? Why do you think Cullen chose this as his title? Be sure to refer to your Quickwrite notes. 🖉

4. The speaker never directly states his emotional response to the experience. How does the last stanza indirectly make clear the impact the encounter had on him?

SKILLS FOCUS

Literary Skills
Analyze metaphor.

Writing Skills
Write an essay analyzing two poems.

Extending and Evaluating

5. Do you think that the content and messages of "Tableau" and "Incident" are relevant only to the time in which Cullen wrote? Or are the incidents described in these poems still occurring today? Explain.

WRITING

Analyzing Literature

When you analyze a piece of literature, you take it apart to see how its elements work together to create meaning. In an **essay**, analyze these two poems, "Incident" and "Tableau." Before you start to write, gather your details in a chart like the following one:

	Tableau	Incident
Message		
Tone		
Images or figures of speech		
Use of rhyme		
Use of meter		

Analyze each poem separately, first "Tableau" and then "Incident." At the end of your analysis, include a comment that describes your response to each poem. Which element of the poem has the strongest impact on your response?

▶ **Use "Analyzing Literature," pages 665–666, for help with this assignment.**

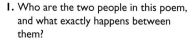

ASSESSING

Assessment

■ *Holt Assessment: Literature, Reading, and Vocabulary*

RETEACHING

For a lesson reteaching poetic devices, see **Reteaching, p. 1117A.**

Langston Hughes

(1902–1967)

One evening toward the end of 1925, the poet Vachel Lindsay was eating dinner in the Wardman Park Hotel in Washington, D.C. The busboy, a twenty-three-year-old African American, left three poems near Lindsay's plate. Lindsay was so impressed by the poems that he presented them in his reading that night, telling the audience that he had discovered a true poet—a young black man who was working as a busboy in the hotel restaurant. Over the next few days, articles about the "busboy poet" appeared in newspapers up and down the East Coast.

The busboy, Langston Hughes, was no beginning writer. In fact, when he shyly approached Lindsay, Hughes's first book of poetry, *The Weary Blues,* was about to be published by a prestigious New York company, and individual poems had appeared in numerous places. Lindsay warned the young poet about literary "lionizers" who might exploit him for their own purpose: "Hide and write and study and think. I know what factions do. Beware of them. I know what lionizers do. Beware of them." In response to Lindsay, Hughes wrote back: "If anything is important, it is my poetry, not me. I do not want folks to know me, but if they know and like some of my poems I am glad. Perhaps the mission of an artist is to interpret beauty to the people—the beauty within themselves. That is what I want to do, if I consciously want to do anything with poetry."

Before this encounter, Hughes had attended Columbia University and worked his way to Africa and back as a crew member on an ocean freighter. Ambitious and energetic, Hughes had learned early to rely on himself. He spoke German and Spanish; he had lived in Mexico, France, and Italy. In the years that followed his "overnight" celebrity, he earned his degree at

Lincoln University, wrote fifteen volumes of poetry, six novels, three books of short stories, eleven plays, and a variety of nonfiction works.

Born in Joplin, Missouri, Hughes spent most of his childhood in Lawrence, Kansas, with his grandmother. When he was thirteen, she died, and he moved to Lincoln, Illinois, and then to Cleveland, Ohio, to live with his mother and stepfather.

Hughes began writing poems in the eighth grade, and he began publishing his work as a high school student in his school literary magazine. He read voraciously and greatly admired the work of Edgar Lee Masters, Vachel Lindsay, Amy Lowell, Carl Sandburg, and Walt Whitman.

Portrait of Langston Hughes by Winold Reiss.

The most important influences on Hughes's poetry were Walt Whitman and Carl Sandburg. Both poets broke from traditional poetic forms and used free verse to express the humanity of all people regardless of their age, gender, race, and class. Encouraged by the examples of Whitman and Sandburg, Hughes celebrated the experiences of African Americans, often using jazz rhythms and the repetitive structure of the blues in his poems. Toward the end of his life, he wrote poems specifically for jazz accompaniment. He was also responsible for the founding of several black theater companies, and he wrote and translated a number of dramatic works. His work, he said, was an attempt to "explain and illuminate the Negro condition in America." It succeeded in doing that with both vigor and compassion.

Langston Hughes   **749**

SKILLS FOCUS, pp. 749–761

Grade-Level Skills

■ **Literary Skills**
Analyze the way an author's style achieves specific rhetorical or aesthetic purposes.

■ **Literary Skills**
Analyze the way poets use rhythm, mood, and repetition.

Review Skills

■ **Literary Skills**
Evaluate the aesthetic qualities of style, including the effect of diction, figurative language, tone, and mood.

More About the Writer

Background. In his autobiography, Langston Hughes wrote about his early work: "I had been . . . a writer who wrote mostly because, when I felt bad, writing kept me from feeling worse; it put my inner emotions into exterior form, and gave me an outlet for words that never came in conversation."

RESOURCES: READING

Planning
■ *One-Stop Planner* CD-ROM with ExamView Test Generator

Differentiating Instruction
■ *Holt Reading Solutions*
■ *The Holt Reader*
■ *Supporting Instruction in Spanish*
■ *Audio CD Library, Selections and Summaries in Spanish*

Grammar and Language
■ *Daily Language Activities*

Assessment
■ *Holt Assessment: Literature, Reading, and Vocabulary*
■ *One-Stop Planner* CD-ROM with ExamView Test Generator
■ *Holt Online Assessment*

Internet
■ go.hrw.com (Keyword: LE5 11-5)
■ *Elements of Literature Online*

Media
■ *Audio CD Library*
■ *Audio CD Library, Selections and Summaries in Spanish*

Summary *at grade level*

> The speaker re-creates the sounds and emotions he experiences while listening to an African American piano player singing the blues in a Harlem cafe. The speaker suggests that even after the musician has gone to bed, the blues will keep playing in the player's mind.

Skills Starter

Build review skills. Remind students that poets use sound to achieve a wide variety of specific effects. Sounds in poetry can imitate the natural world, human voices, animal sounds, or musical instruments.

DIRECT TEACHING

A Literary Focus

? Rhythm. How would you describe the rhythm of this poem? [Possible responses: bluesy; syncopated; slowly rocking.] What techniques does Hughes use to create this rhythm? [Possible responses: alternating accented and unaccented syllables ("the tune o' those Weary Blues"); alternating long and short lines (ll. 2–3); repetition ("He did a lazy sway"); alliteration ("droning" / "drowsy"); assonance ("lazy sway"); onomatopoeia ("drowsy," "thump").]

Make the Connection
Quickwrite 🖉

Among the great contributions from American culture to the world is the music created by African Americans: orchestral, blues, ragtime, soul, rap, and new musical expressions that are being developed every day.

The music known as the blues started to attract attention at the turn of the twentieth century. Eventually the blues became widely popular in the United States and abroad, making stars of such singers as Bessie Smith and Ethel Waters. In this poem, Hughes describes his experience of listening to "a sad raggy tune" and captures some of its rhythms in words.

Jot down your associations with the word *blues* and the music it describes. What feelings or words are associated with blues music? Is there any blues influence on the music you like?

Literary Focus
Rhythm

Rhythm in poetry is the rise and fall of the voice, produced by alternating stressed and unstressed syllables. Langston Hughes uses several kinds of rhythms in "The Weary Blues." As he says in the first line, he uses the "syncopated tune" of a piano. He also uses the rhythm of everyday speech, the soulful rhythm of the blues, and even the formal meter of traditional poetry. His poems are true originals.

> **Rhythm** is the alternation of stressed and unstressed syllables in a line of prose or poetry.
>
> *For more on Rhythm, see the Handbook of Literary and Historical Terms.*

go.hrw.com

INTERNET

Cross-Curricular Connection
•
More About Langston Hughes

Keyword: LE5 11–5

SKILLS FOCUS

Literary Skills
Understand rhythm.

Background

On a March night in 1922, Langston Hughes sat in a small Harlem cabaret and wrote "The Weary Blues." In this poem, Hughes incorporated the many elements of his life—the music of Southern black speech, the lyrics of the first blues he ever heard, and conventional poetic forms he learned in school. While the body of the poem took shape quickly, it took the poet two years to get the ending right: "I could not achieve an ending I liked, although I worked and worked on it." When he at last completed the poem, "The Weary Blues" marked the beginning of his literary career.

Solo Sax by Phoebe Beasley.

DIFFERENTIATING INSTRUCTION

Learners Having Difficulty
After students have read the poem, ask them to identify their favorite lines in the poem. To help students sense the musical quality of the poem, have them read their favorite lines aloud in several different ways, emphasizing different words, changing speeds, or suggesting different emotions.

Advanced Learners
Like many other first-rate poems, "The Weary Blues" is carefully and subtly crafted to seem simple. Encourage students to find details and touches that mark the hand of a master poet. Examples include shifting the stress to syncopate the line in which the word *syncopation* appears (l. 1); the slow, flexible beat that resembles the bass line of a blues piano; and the startling simile in the last line.

The Block (1971) by Romare Bearden.

The Weary Blues

Langston Hughes

Droning a drowsy syncopated tune,°
Rocking back and forth to a mellow croon,
   I heard a Negro play.
Down on Lenox Avenue° the other night
5 By the pale dull pallor of an old gas light
   He did a lazy sway . . .
   He did a lazy sway . . .
To the tune o' those Weary Blues.
With his ebony hands on each ivory key
10 He made that poor piano moan with melody.
   O Blues!
Swaying to and fro on his rickety stool
He played that sad raggy tune like a musical fool.
   Sweet Blues!
15 Coming from a black man's soul.
   O Blues!
In a deep song voice with a melancholy tone
I heard that Negro sing, that old piano moan—
   "Ain't got nobody in all this world,
20   Ain't got nobody but ma salf.
   I's gwine to quit ma frownin'
   And put ma troubles on the shelf."
Thump, thump, thump, went his foot on the floor.
He played a few chords then he sang some more—
25   "I got the Weary Blues
   And I can't be satisfied.
   Got the Weary Blues
   And can't be satisfied—
   I ain't happy no mo'
30   And I wish that I had died."
And far into the night he crooned that tune.
The stars went out and so did the moon.
The singer stopped playing and went to bed
While the Weary Blues echoed through his head.
35 He slept like a rock or a man that's dead.

A

1. **syncopated tune:** melody in which accents
are placed on normally unaccented beats.

4. **Lenox Avenue:** street in Harlem.

B

C

D

E

Lazy Sway by Phoebe Beasley.

Langston Hughes   **751**

DIRECT TEACHING

B English-Language Learners

Interpreting colloquialisms. Ask volunteers to explain the connotations of *rickety* [unsteady], *raggy* [in a ragtime rhythm; tattered like a rag], and *fool* [used affectionately here for a person completely devoted to something]. **Discuss the connotations these words share and what impression they leave of the musician.** [Possible response: They all link him with poverty, uncertainty, and fatigue.]

C Literary Focus

❓ Rhythm and structure.
Where in the poem do song lyrics appear? [ll. 19–22, 25–30] How does the poet differentiate the song from the other lines? [Short, basically iambic lines of the song create the slow, walking rhythm of the blues.]

D Literary Focus

❓ Style. What does the language of the song lyrics reveal about the singer? [Possible response: The song's refrain emphasizes his unhappiness. His burdens might be loneliness, discrimination, and heartache.]

E Reading Skills

❓ Evaluating. Hughes did not arrive at the right ending to this poem for two years. Do you think his final version is effective? Why or why not? [Most students will praise the stark drama of the ending.]

CONTENT-AREA CONNECTIONS

Music: Blues
Composer and bandmaster W. C. Handy (1873–1958) helped make the blues successful as popular music. His famous "St. Louis Blues" has been recorded by hundreds of performers.

Whole-class activity. Have students listen to a recording of "St. Louis Blues" or another blues recording and then re-read Hughes's poem with a focus on its rhythm and musical sound effects.

DEVELOPING FLUENCY

Individual or small-group activity. Have students read this poem aloud, or have them read aloud the lyrics to blues songs. Individuals or small groups can perform the lyrics without the accompanying music, using only the words to convey the blues rhythm.

VIEWING THE ART

Romare Bearden (1914–1988) was a prominent African American painter, collagist, and illustrator. He trained in New York in the 1930s and in Paris after World War II army service. The young Bearden criticized other black visual artists for failing to develop a technique as original as jazz or the spiritual, but later he became an advocate for African American artists. The title *Out Chorus* refers to the final chorus of a jazz piece.

Activity. Ask students how the painting relates to the text. [The group may be playing the blues.] Have students identify the instruments in the picture. [bass, percussion, guitar, saxophones, trumpet, piano]

Out Chorus by Romare Bearden. Silkscreen (12⅜″ × 16½″).

New Britain Museum of Art, New Britain, Connecticut. Friends Purchase Fund. Photo by E. Irving Blomstrann.
© Romare Bearden Foundation/Licensed by VAGA, New York, New York.

CONTENT-AREA CONNECTIONS

Music: Form and Word Choice
While blues songs often feature informal language, they usually follow a tight formal structure, much like a sonnet or a haiku. In the blues stanza, the second line repeats the first or varies it slightly, and the third line elaborates or resolves the problem posed in the first two. An instrumental part then echoes the voice. In Hughes's poem, the speaker's descriptions take the instrumental part.

Birth of the Blues

When asked about the origins of the blues, a veteran New Orleans fiddler once said: "The blues? Ain't no first blues! The blues always been." The first form of blues, country blues, developed in several parts of the United States, most notably the Mississippi Delta, around 1900. Country blues tunes were typically sung by men—usually share-croppers. The subject was often the relationship between men and women. As the contemporary blues singer B. B. King once said, the blues is about a man losing his woman.

From the start, blues music was improvisational—it changed with every singer and performance. Parts of lyrics were freely borrowed from other songs or based on folk songs or figures of speech. Lines might be repeated two or three times, with different accents and emphases, then answered or completed by a rhyming line:

> Black cat on my doorstep, black cat on my window sill. (repeat)
> If some black cat don't cross me, some other black cat will.
>
> —Ma Rainey

The blues catch on. The earliest blues singers, among them Charley Patton, Robert Johnson, and Blind Lemon Jefferson, played at country stores, at Friday- and Saturday-night dances, at cafes, and at picnics. The first popular blues recordings, made in the 1920s, featured female singers such as Ma Rainey and Bessie Smith backed by a piano or a jazz band.

When rural Southern African Americans migrated after World War I to cities like Chicago, New York, Detroit, St. Louis, and Memphis, the blues sound evolved further. Musicians sang about their experiences in the city, adding the electric guitar, amplified harmonica, bass, and drums to blues ensembles. Musicians such as Sunnyland Slim, T-Bone Walker, and Memphis Minnie pioneered the urban blues sound in the 1930s and 1940s; the next generation included the blues greats Muddy Waters, Howlin' Wolf, and B. B. King. Since then, blues music has influenced virtually every genre of music, including folk, country and western, and—most profoundly—rock. Elvis Presley, Bob Dylan, the Rolling Stones, Eric Clapton, and Bonnie Raitt have all borrowed freely from the blues tradition. Today, blues music is still being played and created by such artists as Buddy Guy, Otis Rush, Koko Taylor, Keb' Mo', and Robert Cray. They are carrying on a musical tradition that was invented at a particular time and place—the American South in the early 1900s—to express the African American experience. The genius of the blues is that it has honored its origins even as it expresses universal hopes, fears, and sorrows.

A CLOSER LOOK

Originating as an improvisational lament, the blues developed into an art form that significantly influenced the country and rock music of today.

DIRECT TEACHING

A **Reading Informational Text**

❓ **Recognizing organizational structure.** What is the basic structure of this essay? [chronological] What elements provide clues to its structure? [headings; the succession of dates]

B **Content-Area Connections**

Literature: Blues Brother
Harlem Renaissance scholar Edward E. Waldron writes, "Many writers/poets have attempted for years to incorporate the essence of the blues into works outside the reference of music—i.e., into stories and poetry. One of the most successful in this endeavor was Langston Hughes. . . . In his blues poetry Langston Hughes captures the mood, the feel, and the spirit of the blues; his poems have the rhythm and the impact of the musical form they incorporate. Indeed, the blues poems of Langston Hughes are blues as well as poetry." Ask students to look for prose fiction that incorporates "the essence of the blues."

C **Reading Informational Text**

❓ **Finding the main idea.**
Which sentence or expression in the essay best conveys its main idea? [Possible response: the final sentence.] **Express the main idea of the essay in your own words.** [Possible response: An American form invented to express sorrow and loss, the blues is still a vibrant musical style that has influenced many styles of popular music.]

PRETEACHING

Summary ⟷ *at grade level*

The speaker employs irony, figurative language, and free verse to evoke the economic and emotional distress of African Americans "on the edge of hell" in Depression-era Harlem.

Selection Starter

Build background. Review basic historical information about the United States during the Great Depression, such as the year it began (1929), the devastatingly high unemployment rate, and the general mood of pessimism, especially when compared with the Roaring Twenties.

DIRECT TEACHING

A Literary Focus

❷ Mood. What images does the single word *hell* conjure up? [Possible responses: endless suffering; death.] What mood does the poem immediately establish? [deprivation and despair]

B Literary Focus

❷ Mood. How do ll. 3–6 contribute to the mood? [They add details that make the emotion palpable.] What is the effect of the repetition of *old*? [*Old* recalls slavery and its effects that still remain.]

C Learners Having Difficulty

❷ Finding details. Why does the speaker mention such small details? [These details illustrate the people's everyday life. The rise in food prices, for example, may mean making do with less.]

Harlem

Make the Connection

Quickwrite ✏️

INTERNET

More About Langston Hughes

Keyword: LE5 11–5

SKILLS FOCUS

Literary Skills
Understand mood.

The Harlem Renaissance writers responded to the oppression and feelings of powerlessness that pervaded the lives of their Harlem neighbors. Hughes himself wrote several poems called "Harlem." This one is set during the Great Depression of the 1930s, a time when even a one-cent increase in the price of bread could be disastrous, a time also when being black usually meant being poor with little opportunity to earn more.

How does it feel to be a victim of discrimination? Jot down some notes.

Literary Focus

Mood

In literature, **mood** refers to the feelings aroused by words and by sounds. A poem, for example, might make a reader feel sad or amused or thoughtful. Poems can create more than one feeling, but often they have one dominant mood. (Often, in talking about a work of literature, the words *mood* and *atmosphere* are used interchangeably.) As you read "Harlem," look for words and images that create a particular mood.

> **Mood** is the overall feeling created in a piece of writing.
>
> *For more on Mood, see the Handbook of Literary and Historical Terms.*

Harlem

Langston Hughes

A Here on the edge of hell
Stands Harlem—
B Remembering the old lies,
The old kicks in the back,
5 The old "Be patient"
They told us before.

Sure, we remember.
Now when the man at the corner store
Says sugar's gone up another two cents,
10 And bread one,
C And there's a new tax on cigarettes—
We remember the job we never had,

Never could get,
And can't have now
15 Because we're colored.

So we stand here
On the edge of hell
In Harlem
D And look out on the world
20 And wonder
What we're gonna do
In the face of what
We remember.

DIFFERENTIATING INSTRUCTION

Learners Having Difficulty

Ask students to imagine an anthology of music that summarizes their experience as teenagers in the twenty-first century. Have them list the selections of music that they would include in such an anthology, and for each selection, have them provide a one-sentence statement of what the music says about being a contemporary teenager.

Invite learners having difficulty to read "Harlem" in interactive format in *The Holt Reader* and to use the sidenotes as aids to understanding the selection.

English-Language Learners

For lessons designed for English-language learners and special education students, see *Holt Reading Solutions*.

Harlem Street Scene (1975) by Jacob Lawrence. Serigraph (27″ × 24″).

Langston Hughes   **755**

VIEWING THE ART

Jacob Lawrence (1917–2000) usually painted in tempera, but *Harlem Street Scene* is a serigraph, or silk-screen print. The process involves printing flat colors through a piece of silk or fine cloth. A stencil is cut for the areas to be printed in one specific color, another stencil is cut for each additional color, and the print is made one color at a time.

Activity. Have students contrast the mood of Lawrence's print with the mood of Hughes's poem "Harlem." [Possible response: The poem presents disturbing aspects of Harlem life; the painting seems more cheerful, perhaps because of the musician, the children at play, and the hint of a smile on the face of the man with the cane.]

D Literary Focus

? **Mood.** How does the mood shift in the last stanza? [Possible response: The mood of oppression shifts to a mood of possible action. The residents of Harlem look "out on the world," wondering what they will "do."]

DEVELOPING FLUENCY

Individual or small-group activity. Have students read the poem aloud, identifying which words in the poem should receive emphasis. They might, for example, want to emphasize the repeated expression "we remember." Also, remind students that the ends of lines do not require full stops; encourage them to read each sentence as a continuous thought.

Comparing and Contrasting Texts

Cullen and Hughes. Have students compare "Harlem" with Cullen's poems "Tableau" and "Incident." Ask students to compare and contrast the different ways in which each poem speaks out against racial oppression.

VIEWING THE ART

Harlem was not the only center for the renaissance of African American culture in the 1920s. Another cultural center was the South Side of Chicago, where jazz was cultivated and where artists like **Archibald John Motley, Jr.** (1891–1981) painted the high-energy scenes of the area's night-clubs. Yet another center was Paris. Attracted by its reputation for racial tolerance, many African American artists, writers, and musicians went to Paris to live and work. Motley was in Paris when he painted this scene of the Jockey Club, a nightclub frequented by African Americans. Note the diversity of social types and the skin tones of the figures painted by Motley.

Activity. What about this club suggests its American theme? [its English name, as well as the stylized cowboy and Native American painted around its door]

Primary Source

In this excerpt from his memoir *The Big Sea,* Hughes describes the ironies, contradictions and pleasures of the years when African American culture in Harlem became fashionable among the white elite of New York.

Ⓐ Reading Informational Text

Repetition as organizing principle. Alert students to Hughes's use of "It was a period when" here and several more times in this paragraph. Lead a discussion on when repetition holds prose together as opposed to when it distracts readers.

Jockey Club (1929) by Archibald John Motley, Jr. Oil on canvas.

Heyday in Harlem

Langston Hughes describes the vigor and excitement of Harlem in the 1920s and 1930s.

White people began to come to Harlem in droves. For several years they packed the expensive Cotton Club on Lenox Avenue. But I was never there, because the Cotton Club was a Jim Crow club[1] for gangsters and monied whites. They were not cordial to Negro patronage, unless you were a celebrity like Bojangles.[2] So Harlem Negroes

did not like the Cotton Club and never appreciated its Jim Crow policy in the very heart of their dark community....

Ⓐ It was a period when, at almost every Harlem upper-crust dance or party, one would be introduced to various distinguished white celebrities there as guests. It was a period when almost any Harlem Negro of any social importance at all would be likely to say casually: "As I was remarking the other day to Heywood—," meaning Heywood Broun.[3] Or: "As I said to George—," referring to George

INFORMATIONAL TEXT

---

1. **Jim Crow club:** segregated nightclub.
2. **Bojangles:** Bill "Bojangles" Robinson (1879–1949), star of black musical comedies and vaudeville.

3. **Heywood Broun** (1888–1939): American journalist during the 1920s and 1930s.

Taking notes. Remind students that note-taking involves writing down the important points of a text, usually in words and phrases instead of complete sentences. Effective note takers recognize main ideas and supporting details and then record them in their own words. They may also construct graphic organizers as part of their notes.
Activity. Have students form three groups to take notes on the lives of Countee Cullen,

Langston Hughes, and Zora Neale Hurston, using the author biographies and other material in the textbook. In each group, students should take notes individually, then read their notes aloud and discuss why they chose to include specific pieces of information.
Activity. Have each group design and fill in two graphic organizers using their notes. Possible types of graphic organizers include a chart showing the writer's works with their

Gershwin.[4] It was a period when local and visiting royalty were not at all uncommon in Harlem. And when the parties of A'Lelia Walker, the Negro heiress, were filled with guests whose names would turn any Nordic[5] social climber green with envy.... It was a period when every season there was at least one hit play on Broadway acted by a Negro cast. And when books by Negro authors were being published with much greater frequency and much more publicity than ever before or since in history. It was a period when white writers wrote about Negroes more successfully (commercially speaking) than Negroes did about themselves. It was the period (God help us!) when Ethel Barrymore[6] appeared in blackface in *Scarlet Sister Mary*! It was the period when the Negro was in vogue....

Then it was that house-rent parties began to flourish—and not always to raise the rent either. But, as often as not, to have a get-together of one's own, where you could do the black-bottom[7] with no stranger behind you trying to do it, too. Nontheatrical, non-intellectual Harlem was an unwilling victim of its own vogue. It didn't like to be stared at by white folks. But perhaps the downtowners never knew this—for the cabaret owners, the entertainers, and the speakeasy[8] proprietors treated them fine—as long as they paid.

The Saturday night rent parties that I attended were often more amusing than any night club, in small apartments where God knows who lived—because the guests seldom did—but where the piano would often be augmented by a guitar, or an odd cornet, or somebody with a pair of drums walking in off the street. And where awful bootleg whiskey and good fried fish or steaming chitterling[9] were sold at very low prices. And the dancing and singing and impromptu entertaining went on until dawn came in at the windows.

These parties, often termed whist[10] parties or dances, were usually announced by brightly colored cards stuck in the grille of apartment house elevators. Some of the cards were highly entertaining in themselves:

Some wear pajamas, some wear pants, what does it matter
just so you can dance, at

A Social Whist Party

GIVEN BY

MR. & MRS. BROWN

AT 258 W. 115TH STREET, APT. 9

SATURDAY EVE., SEPT. 14, 1929

The music is sweet and everything good to eat!

Almost every Saturday night when I was in Harlem I went to a house-rent party. I wrote lots of poems about house-rent parties, and ate thereat many a fried fish and pig's foot—with liquid refreshments on the side. I met ladies' maids and truck drivers, laundry workers and shoeshine boys, seamstresses and porters. I can still hear their laughter in my ears, hear the soft slow music, and feel the floor shaking as the dancers danced.

from "When the Negro Was in Vogue"

---

4. **George Gershwin** (1898–1937): great American composer of both popular and serious music.
5. **Nordic:** white.
6. **Ethel Barrymore** (1879–1959): American stage and movie actress.
7. **black-bottom** *n.:* popular dance of the late 1920s.
8. **speakeasy** *n.:* club where alcoholic drinks were sold illegally during Prohibition.

9. **chitterling** (chit′lin) *n.:* food made from small intestines of pigs, deep-fried in hot oil.
10. **whist** *n.:* card game.

Langston Hughes **757**

DIRECT TEACHING

B Content-Area Connections

History: 1930s Harlem

According to historian David Levering Lewis, the leading lights of the Harlem Renaissance took part in "a moveable feast to which the anointed were invited" in Harlem apartments, where guests might include British poet Sir Osbert Sitwell, the crown prince of Sweden, singer-actor Paul Robeson, novelist Sinclair Lewis, journalist H. L. Mencken, and composer George Gershwin.

Conditions for average Harlem residents were not nearly so glamorous, however, and as the Depression deepened, they typically faced much worse living conditions than whites. Median family income in Harlem was cut almost in half. Harlemites lived with a tuberculosis rate five times that of white Manhattanites, and rates of pneumonia and typhoid were double those of the rest of the borough. African American rates of infant mortality and maternal death were also double those of whites. Apartment rent for Harlem residents took double the percentage of family income that it did for whites.

This was the backdrop against which house-rent parties, also called rent parties, became customary both as a boost to the party giver's income and as psychological relief from economic and social stress.

READING SKILLS REVIEW

subjects and themes, a cluster diagram showing a character profile of the writer, an outline indicating the central themes of the writer's life and work, or a time line of the writer's life and career. Ask each group to present its organizers to the class.

Tracing etymologies. Point out that most English words are derived from older English words and words from other languages. Idioms, colloquialisms, slang terms, and regional or ethnic vocabulary often have especially interesting derivations. Have students trace the etymologies of the selection words and phrases at right. Besides standard dictionaries, students may wish to use specialized resources, such as *The Dictionary of American Regional English*.

1. Jim Crow
2. Negro
3. upper-crust
4. cabaret
5. speak-easy

6. guitar
7. cornet
8. bootleg
9. chitterling
10. whist

Langston Hughes **757**

Response and Analysis

The Weary Blues

Thinking Critically

1. Possible answer: In a crowded cafe, dark and smoky, a black musician sways at the piano as he plays and sings the blues. The exhausted and depressed blues singer goes home and sleeps in order to forget his pain.

2. In the first verse the singer sings that despite his isolation, he will nevertheless put aside his troubles. In the second verse, however, the singer despairs and says that nothing can free him from his troubles.

3. The singer sleeps "like a rock" or like "a man that's dead." Possible answer: The singer has given up hope; sleep is the only place he finds relief; his spirit is dead.

4. Possible answer: The mood is melancholy, world-weary, even despairing. Contributing words include *droning, poor, sad, melancholy,* and *moan.*

5. The repetition of words and phrases and the syncopation of longer lines when combined with shorter lines contribute to the rhythmic effect.

6. Examples of alliteration include "droning a drowsy" (l. 1), "Pale dull pallor of an old gas light" (l. 5), and "poor piano moan with melody" (l. 10). Line 23— "Thump, thump, thump"—is onomatopoeic.

Harlem

Thinking Critically

1. Possible answer: The mood of the poem is one of suffering, gloom, oppression, and unjust punishment. The people are on the edge of despair.

2. The poem suggests that many remember the lies they were told, physical abuse, poverty, and employment discrimination.

Response and Analysis

The Weary Blues

Thinking Critically

1. What **scene** do you see as you read this poem?

2. How does the message of the blues singer's first verse contrast with that of the second verse?

3. What **similes** in the poem's last line describe how the singer sleeps? What do you think the last five words suggest?

4. Think of how the blues singer, the listener, and you feel as you hear the blues song. How would you describe the overall **mood** of the poem? What words help to create this mood? (Be sure to check your Quickwrite notes.)

5. Describe how the poem's structure suggests the **rhythms** of blues music.

6. Hughes also uses alliteration and onomatopoeia to create his music. **Alliteration** is the repetition of similar consonant sounds in words that are close together. **Onomatopoeia** is the use of words that actually *sound* like what they name (*swish, slap,* and *pop* are examples). Read aloud examples of **alliteration** and **onomatopoeia** that add to the musical effect of "The Weary Blues."

**go.
hrw
.com**

INTERNET
Projects and
Activities
Keyword: LE5 11-5

**SKILLS
FOCUS**

Literary Skills
Analyze rhythm
and mood.

Writing Skills
Write a historical
research report.

**Listening and
Speaking Skills**
Perform an oral
interpretation of
a poem.

Harlem

Thinking Critically

1. What **mood** does the speaker immediately create with this description of the poem's **setting**: "Here on the edge of hell / Stands Harlem—"?

2. Name the specific hardships and injustices that the people of Harlem remember, according to the speaker.

3. What is the effect of the **repetition** of the word *remember*?

4. How do you interpret the poem's final stanza? Is it an expression of powerlessness, of opposition, or of something else? Be sure you can defend your interpretation.

5. Did any adjectives in your Quickwrite describe the feelings expressed in this poem? If not, what adjective would you use to describe the overall **mood** of the poem?

WRITING

An Investigation into the Harlem Renaissance

Find out more about some of the writers and artists of the Harlem Renaissance. You may want to read more of Hughes's poetry or research some of the musicians mentioned in his essay "Heyday in Harlem." (See the *Primary Source* on page 756.) Alternatively, you could investigate the works of other writers of that time, such as Claude McKay or Paul Laurence Dunbar. You might investigate one of the great Harlem Renaissance artists, such as Aaron Douglas or William H. Johnson. Write a brief **research report** on some topic related to the Harlem Renaissance. Share your findings with the rest of the class.

▶ Use "Reporting Historical Research," pages 528–547, for help with this assignment.

LISTENING AND SPEAKING

From the Soul

Paying careful attention to punctuation and line breaks, read "The Weary Blues" and "Harlem" aloud to express each poem's unique **rhythm** and **mood.** Let another group of students evaluate your performance.

3. Possible answer: The repetition emphasizes the anger, frustration, and bitterness they feel.

4. Possible answer: The final stanza is an expression of powerlessness, because knowing the brutality and injustice of the past, they have little hope for the future. The final stanza indicates a stubborn resolve to do something, *anything,* to redress past wrongs.

5. Possible answer: Adjectives might include *angry, bitter,* and *frustrated.* The mood might be described as hot with repressed rage, simmering with righteous indignation, or tense with the expectation of some action.

RETEACHING

For a lesson reteaching poetic devices, see **Reteaching,** p. 1117A.

Before You Read

The Negro Speaks of Rivers

Make the Connection

Imagery is the use of language to create pictures. Images can appeal not only to our sense of sight but also to our senses of hearing, smell, taste, and touch. Some images appear again and again in art. There seems to be no end to the capacity of these images to stir our imaginations and move our emotions. In this poem by Langston Hughes and in the poem that follows by the contemporary writer Lucille Clifton, the recurring image is that of a river. What do you think of when you see or imagine a mighty river?

Literary Focus
Repetition

Poets create rhythm and musical effects by using **repetition**—of sounds, words, phrases, or even entire lines. A repeated line in a poem or song is called a **refrain**. Repetition not only affects the sound of a poem; it also emphasizes important ideas and builds up certain feelings and expectations.

> **Repetition** is the recurrence of certain sounds, words, phrases, or lines in a poem to achieve rhythmic or emotional effects. A repeated line is called a **refrain.**
>
> *For more on Refrain, see the Handbook of Literary and Historical Terms.*

INTERNET
More About Langston Hughes
Keyword: LE5 11–5

SKILLS FOCUS

Literary Skills
Understand repetition.

PRETEACHING

Summary ⬄ *at grade level*

In one of Hughes's most famous poems, the speaker describes his deep-seated knowledge of the spirit of the world's great rivers.

Selection Starter

Motivate. In *The Big Sea*, Hughes describes the genesis of the poem: "All day on the train I had been thinking of my father. Now it was just sunset and we crossed the Mississippi . . . and I began to think what that river, the old Mississippi, had meant to Negroes in the past. . . . Then I began to think of other rivers in our past—the Congo, and the Niger, and the Nile in Africa—and the thought came to me: 'I've known rivers,' and I put it down on the back of an envelope I had in my pocket, and within the space of ten or fifteen minutes, . . . I had written this poem."

The Negro Speaks of Rivers

Langston Hughes

I've known rivers:
I've known rivers ancient as the world and older than the flow
    of human blood in human veins.

My soul has grown   deep like rivers.

   I bathed in the Euphrates when dawns were young.
5 I built my hut near the Congo and it lulled me to sleep.
   I looked upon the Nile and raised the pyramids above it.
   I heard the singing of the Mississippi when Abe Lincoln went
       down to New Orleans, and I've seen its muddy bosom turn
       all golden in the sunset.

I've known rivers:
Ancient, dusky rivers.

10 My soul has grown   deep like rivers.

Langston Hughes   **759**

DIRECT TEACHING

A **Reading Skills**
❓ **Recognizing rhetorical devices.** How does the poet indicate that this line is important? [The line stands alone.]

B **Literary Focus**
❓ **Repetition.** How does the repetition in these lines help to identify the "I"? [It conveys the idea that the "I" is actually a multitude of speakers.]

C **Literary Focus**
❓ **Imagery.** What might the change in the river's color suggest? [Possible response: Beauty may be born out of darkness and adversity.]

D **Literary Focus**
❓ **Repetition.** What do you think the speaker means by the repeated expression "grown deep"? [Possible response: He has achieved wisdom.]

DIFFERENTIATING INSTRUCTION

Learners Having Difficulty

Help students recognize exaggeration as an element in comedy. Say, "Suppose you read that a character complains that he'd rather face a swarm of killer bees than attend a party. The exaggerated comparison is not only funny, it also tells us something about the character." Encourage students as they read to find when exaggeration is being used to create humor and to develop characters.

VIEWING THE ART

In addition to creating numerous paintings, prints, and collages, **Phoebe Beasley** serves on the board of the Museum of African American Art and has helped to direct the Los Angeles County Arts Commission. According to Maya Angelou, "Phoebe Beasley's eye has never failed her, has never lied to her, and her art generously gives us beauty, information and always the truth." *The Negro Speaks of Rivers,* directly inspired by Langston Hughes, colorfully captures both the sense of history and timelessness embodied in Hughes's poem.

Activity. Ask students why Beasley might have included pyramids in her painting. [Hughes specifically mentions pyramids in his poem.]

Connection

Summary ⬌ *at grade level*

The poem describes the flow of rivers as blood in the body of the earth.

A **Reading Skills**

? **Recognizing rhetorical devices.** What effect does the poet achieve by flowing the first line directly from the title? [The device suggests the river's continuous flow.]

B **Literary Focus**

Figurative language. Explain the metaphor and the simile. [The water is the circulation of the body of the earth—metaphor personifying the planet. The water is like the blood of gods—simile revealing the divine life force in nature.]

C **Reading Skills**

Interpreting. Explain why the person is "mistaken." [Possible response: The experience is timeless and universal.]

The Negro Speaks of Rivers by Phoebe Beasley.

760 Collection 5 The Moderns: 1914–1939

DIFFERENTIATING INSTRUCTION

Learners Having Difficulty
Ask students to use a map or a historical atlas to find the exact locations of the Euphrates, the Congo, the Nile, and the Mississippi. Point out to students the wide geographical range that Hughes suggests.

English-Language Learners
Point out that *bosom* is a deliberately old-fashioned, poetic term for the source of inmost thoughts and feelings.

Advanced Learners
Ask students to research and report on the civilizations that flourished around each of the rivers mentioned in the poem. What major contributions did each group of people make to the progress of the human race?

the mississippi river empties into the gulf

Lucille Clifton

and the gulf enters the sea and so forth,
none of them emptying anything,
all of them carrying yesterday
forever on their white tipped backs,
5   all of them dragging forward tomorrow.
it is the great circulation
of the earth's body, like the blood
of the gods, this river in which the past
is always flowing. every water
10   is the same water coming round.
everyday someone is standing on the edge
of this river, staring into time,
whispering mistakenly:
only here. only now.

Response and Analysis

Thinking Critically

1. What specific rivers does the speaker name?

2. Like Whitman (see page 307), this speaker speaks for a multitude. Who or what does the poet imagine is the "I" in this poem? (The title provides one clue.)

3. What special connections may African Americans have with each of these rivers? (Note the verbs that follow the word "I" at the beginning of each line in the third stanza.)

4. In the last line, what comparison does the speaker make?

5. What instances of **repetition** occur in the poem? What line acts as a **refrain**? What is the emotional effect of this repetition?

6. After you read Hughes's poem aloud, think about the **tone** you hear. Which word best describes that tone: sad? bitter? thoughtful? joyful? Give details from the poem to support your response.

7. In the *Connection* on this page, Lucille Clifton also writes about a river. What river is she describing? What does the river remind this speaker of, according to lines 6–10? How do both Clifton's speaker and Hughes's speaker identify rivers with human life?

SKILLS FOCUS

Literary Skills
Analyze repetition.

Langston Hughes   **761**

ASSESSING

Assessment

- *Holt Assessment: Literature, Reading, and Vocabulary*

RETEACHING

For lessons reteaching poetic devices, see **Reteaching,** p. 1117A.

Response and Analysis

Thinking Critically

1. The speaker names the Euphrates, the Congo, the Nile, and the Mississippi.

2. "I" represents the persona of the poet and all African Americans of the past, present, and future.

3. The Euphrates River flowed through Mesopotamia, the site of one of the earliest recorded civilizations. The Congo River was a focal point of central African culture and an important inroad for the European colonization of central Africa. The Nile River was the site of the ancient Egyptian civilization and its dominating dynasties. The Mississippi was important in the lives of many African American slaves.

4. The speaker compares the depth of his soul to the depth of rivers.

5. Repeated expressions include "I've known rivers" and the words *I* and *ancient*. The refrain is "My soul has grown deep like rivers." The repetition creates a meditative effect, as if the speaker is communing with the rivers he invokes.

6. Possible answers: The tone is deeply thoughtful or meditative. The speaker steps back into his own experience ("I've known") and into the experience of an entire group of people when he recalls historical events along the banks of these rivers.

7. Clifton describes the Mississippi, which reminds her of blood circulating through a body. Hughes's speaker identifies rivers with human life through the civilizations that flourished near them and through the comparison of his soul's depth to the rivers' depth. Clifton's speaker identifies the river with human life by explicitly comparing it to blood flowing through a body.

VIEWING THE ART

The photograph shown in various details on pp. 764–765, 767, and 768 was taken at Hurston's school in Quincy, Florida.

Activity. Invite students to survey the poems in the Harlem Renaissance section (pp. 741–772) and select a line or phrase to use as a caption for this photo. [Possible response: The flags might suggest Langston Hughes's line "I, too, sing America."]

More About the Writer

Background. According to Hurston, the folk tradition she was born into was so familiar that it fit her "like a tight chemise," which she could not see because she was wearing it. "It was only when I was off in college," she added, "away from my native surroundings, that I could see myself like somebody else and stand off and look at my garment. Then I had to have the spyglass of Anthropology to look through at that."

from Dust Tracks on a Road

DIFFERENTIATING INSTRUCTION

Learners Having Difficulty
Some students may be challenged by Hurston's distinctive blend of erudite diction and regional slang. Remind students to modify their reading strategies if their understanding breaks down. For example, they might re-read challenging passages more slowly or ask themselves questions about the text to help with understanding.

Invite learners having difficulty to read *Dust Tracks on a Road* in interactive format in *The Holt Reader* and to use the sidenotes as aids to understanding the selection.

English-Language Learners
Tell students that Hurston's style gains color from the creative use of idiom and metaphor. Encourage students to decipher idiomatic and metaphoric expressions such as "go a piece of the way" [travel partway], "carried the point" [convinced them], "If the village was singing a chorus, I must have missed the tune" [the village did not interest me], "as a squelcher" [to deter mischief], and "I'm going to catch it" [I will be punished].

Zora Neale Hurston

My grandmother worried about my forward ways a great deal.

I used to take a seat on top of the gatepost and watch the world go by. One way to Orlando ran past my house, so the carriages and cars would pass before me. The movement made me glad to see it. Often the white travelers would hail me, but more often I hailed them, and asked, "Don't you want me to go a piece of the way with you?"

They always did. I know now that I must have caused a great deal of amusement among them, but my self-assurance must have carried the point, for I was always invited to come along. I'd ride up the road for perhaps a half-mile, then walk back. I did not do this with the permission of my parents, nor with their foreknowledge. When they found out about it later, I usually got a whipping. My grandmother worried about my forward ways a great deal. She had known slavery and to her my brazenness was unthinkable.

"Git down offa dat gatepost! You li'l sow, you! Git down! Setting up dere looking dem white

Vocabulary

hail v.: greet.
brazenness (brā′zən·nis) n.: boldness.

Dunbar High School, Quincy, Florida (pages 763–765, 767, 768).
Florida State Archives.

Zora Neale Hurston **765**

Building background knowledge. If necessary, clarify *lynch*, which means "murder by mob action." Explain that even after slavery ended, mobs of whites sometimes murdered blacks.

B Content-Area Connections

History: Segregated Schools Hurston grew up when racial segregation of schools and other public facilities was legal in the South. Her childhood predated much of the great migration of African Americans from the South to the North. Thus, whites who came from the North were curious about Hurston's all-black school.

C Literary Focus

❓ Autobiography. How do idiomatic expressions like "cut one caper" contribute to this autobiography? [Possible responses: They let the reader "hear" Hurston's lively speech mannerisms; they make the writing personal and unique.]

D Literary Focus

❓ Autobiography. What do subjective details in this passage reveal about the young Hurston's previous experience of white people? [Her preoccupation with the visitors' hands and hair suggests that she has seen few whites and thus finds them strange and exotic.]

---

folks right in de face! They's gowine[1] to lynch you, yet. And don't stand in dat doorway gazing out at 'em neither. Youse too brazen to live long."

Nevertheless, I kept right on gazing at them, and "going a piece of the way" whenever I could make it. The village seemed dull to me most of the time. If the village was singing a chorus, I must have missed the tune.

Perhaps a year before the old man[2] died, I came to know two other white people for myself. They were women.

It came about this way. The whites who came down from the North were often brought by their friends to visit the village school. A Negro school was something strange to them, and while they were always sympathetic and kind, curiosity must have been present, also. They came and went, came and went. Always, the room was hurriedly put in order, and we were threatened with a prompt and bloody death if we cut one caper while the visitors were present. We always sang a spiritual, led by Mr. Calhoun himself. Mrs. Calhoun always stood in the back, with a palmetto switch[3] in her hand as a squelcher. We were all little angels for the duration, because we'd better be. She would cut her eyes[4] and give us a glare that meant trouble, then turn her face toward the visitors and beam as much as to say it was a great privilege and pleasure to teach lovely children like us. They couldn't see that palmetto hickory in her hand behind all those benches, but we knew where our angelic behavior was coming from.

Usually, the visitors gave warning a day ahead and we would be cautioned to put on shoes, comb our heads, and see to ears and fingernails. There was a close inspection of every one of us before we marched in that morning. Knotty heads, dirty ears, and fingernails got hauled out

---

1. **gowine:** dialect for "going."
2. **old man:** white farmer who knew Hurston's family, took her fishing, and gave her advice.
3. **palmetto switch:** whip made from the stem of a large, fanlike leaf of a kind of palm tree. Teachers sometimes used these switches to discipline students.
4. **cut her eyes:** slang for "look scornfully."

---

of line, strapped, and sent home to lick the calf[5] over again.

This particular afternoon, the two young ladies just popped in. Mr. Calhoun was flustered, but he put on the best show he could. He dismissed the class that he was teaching up at the front of the room, then called the fifth grade in reading. That was my class.

So we took our readers and went up front. We stood up in the usual line, and opened to the lesson. It was the story of Pluto and Persephone.[6] It was new and hard to the class in general, and Mr. Calhoun was very uncomfortable as the readers stumbled along, spelling out words with their lips, and in mumbling undertones before they exposed them experimentally to the teacher's ears.

Then it came to me. I was fifth or sixth down the line. The story was not new to me, because I had read my reader through from lid to lid, the first week that Papa had bought it for me.

That is how it was that my eyes were not in the book, working out the paragraph which I knew would be mine by counting the children ahead of me. I was observing our visitors, who held a book between them, following the lesson. They had shiny hair, mostly brownish. One had a looping gold chain around her neck. The other one was dressed all over in black and white with a pretty finger ring on her left hand. But the thing that held my eyes were their fingers. They were long and thin, and very white, except up near the tips. There they were baby pink. I had never seen such hands. It was a fascinating discovery for me. I wondered how they felt. I would have given those hands more attention, but the child before me was almost

---

5. **lick the calf:** slang for "wash up."
6. **Pluto and Persephone** (pər·sefʹə·nē): In classical mythology, Pluto, or Hades, is the god who rules the underworld; Persephone, also known as Proserpina, is his wife, queen of the underworld. In this version of the origin of the seasons, Hurston uses the names of Roman and Greek gods interchangeably.

Vocabulary
caper (kāʹpər) *n.*: foolish prank.

SKILLS REVIEW

Analyzing idioms. Point out that Hurston skillfully uses idioms (expressions that mean more than the literal definitions of their parts) to give her autobiography the flavor of her personality and her environment. For example, *lick the calf* is a regional Southern idiom, meaning "wash oneself." Tell students to note idioms in this selection and to infer their meanings by using footnotes and context clues.

Activity. Ask students to translate the following idioms.

1. "if we cut one caper" (p. 766) [if we played any pranks]
2. "just popped in" (p. 766) [arrived with no warning]
3. "I got on my mark" (p. 767) [I got ready]
4. "left me cold" (p. 769) [did not interest me]

through. My turn next, so I got on my mark, bringing my eyes back to the book and made sure of my place. Some of the stories I had reread several times, and this Greco-Roman myth was one of my favorites. I was exalted by it, and that is the way I read my paragraph.

"Yes, Jupiter[7] had seen her (Persephone). He had seen the maiden picking flowers in the field. He had seen the chariot of the dark monarch pause by the maiden's side. He had seen him when he seized Persephone. He had seen the black horses leap down Mount Aetna's[8] fiery throat. Persephone was now in Pluto's dark realm and he had made her his wife."

The two women looked at each other and then back to me. Mr. Calhoun broke out with a proud smile beneath his bristly moustache, and instead of the next child taking up where I had ended, he nodded to me to go on. So I read the story to the end, where flying Mercury, the messenger of the Gods, brought Persephone back to the sunlit earth and restored her to the arms of Dame Ceres, her mother, that the world might have springtime and summer flowers, autumn and harvest. But because she had bitten the pomegranate while in Pluto's kingdom, she must return to him for three months of each year, and be his queen. Then the world had winter, until she returned to earth.

The class was dismissed and the visitors smiled us away and went into a low-voiced conversation with Mr. Calhoun for a few minutes. They glanced my way once or twice and I began to worry. Not only was I barefooted, but my feet and legs were dusty. My hair was more uncombed than usual, and my nails were not shiny

7. **Jupiter:** in Roman mythology, king of the gods.
8. **Mount Aetna's:** Mount Aetna (also spelled *Etna*) is a volcanic mountain in eastern Sicily.

clean. Oh, I'm going to catch it now. Those ladies saw me, too. Mr. Calhoun is promising to 'tend to me. So I thought.

Then Mr. Calhoun called me. I went up thinking how awful it was to get a whipping before company. Furthermore, I heard a snicker run over the room. Hennie Clark and Stell Brazzle did it out loud, so I would be sure to hear them. The smart aleck was going to get it. I slipped one hand behind me and switched my dress tail at them, indicating scorn.

"Come here, Zora Neale," Mr. Calhoun cooed as I reached the desk. He put his hand on my shoulder and gave me little pats. The ladies smiled and held out those flower-looking fingers toward me. I seized the opportunity for a good look.

"Shake hands with the ladies, Zora Neale," Mr. Calhoun prompted and they took my hand one after the other and smiled. They asked me if I loved school, and I lied that I did. There was *some* truth in it, because I liked geography and reading, and I liked to play at recess time. Whoever it was invented writing and arithmetic got no thanks from me. Neither did I like the arrangement where the teacher could sit up there with a palmetto stem and lick me whenever he saw fit. I hated things I couldn't do anything about. But I knew better than to bring that up right there, so I said yes, I *loved* school.

"I can tell you do," Brown Taffeta gleamed. She patted my head, and was lucky enough not to get sandspurs in her hand. Children who roll and tumble in the grass in Florida are apt to get sandspurs in their hair. They shook hands with me again and I went back to my seat.

Vocabulary
exalted (eg·zôlt′id) *v.:* lifted up.
realm (relm) *n.:* kingdom.

> The ladies smiled and held out those flower-looking fingers toward me.

DIRECT TEACHING

E **Literary Focus**

❷ **Autobiography.** To which aspects of the young Hurston's character do you think this myth appeals? [Possible responses: The dramatic setting and action may appeal to Hurston's imagination and taste for adventure; the parallelism and rolling cadences may appeal to her love of language.]

F **Literary Focus**

❷ **Autobiography.** What tone do you notice in Hurston's narrative of this incident? [subtle humor or irony] Why do you think Hurston adopts this tone? [Possible response: As an adult writing the autobiography, she knows what she did not know as a child: that she was to be rewarded, not punished.]

G **Literary Focus**

❷ **Autobiography.** What do you think these details reveal about the young Hurston's character? [Possible responses: She is strategic and perceptive, understanding that this is not the time for total honesty; she has strong opinions; she values control over her own life.]

H **Advanced Learners**

❷ **Enrichment.** Metonymy is a figure of speech in which a part represents the whole. What is the effect of equating this visitor with her "brown taffeta"? [Possible responses: It underscores her comparative affluence (her dress is made of fine fabric). It also creates a slightly irreverent tone.]

Response and Analysis

Reading Check

1. Her memories of the days of slavery make her worry that whites will harm Zora.

2. The visitors are two young white women from Minnesota.

3. They send a box of books and used clothes.

4. Her favorites include *Norse Tales, Greek and Roman Myths,* Kipling's Jungle Books, books by Hans Christian Andersen and Robert Louis Stevenson, an Episcopal hymnal, and the Old Testament.

Thinking Critically

5. Possible answers: They are curious to see an all-black school. They want to do a good deed.

6. Their difference fascinates her; she scrutinizes them. She feels that they are judging her; she worries about her grooming and tells them what she surmises they want to hear.

7. They think that she is gifted; they give her presents that encourage her to continue her education.

8. Her introduction to literature is most lasting. Some students may doubt that anything could have stopped her from becoming a writer. Others may conclude that these early rewards were critical to her career.

9. She is lively and adventurous (she likes the biblical David and stories by Robert Louis Stevenson), self-assured (she identifies with Odin and Hercules), imaginative (she enjoys Andersen's tales and Kipling's talking snakes), attuned to language (she hears music in hymns with no written notes), down-to-earth and fun-loving (she scorns didactic stories).

10. Her responses to literature, eye for detail, ear for language, and perceptiveness about other people suggest a future as a writer.

Response and Analysis

Reading Check

1. Why is Hurston's grandmother afraid of her granddaughter's boldness?

2. Who visits Zora's school?

3. What do the visitors send from Minnesota?

4. What are the narrator's favorite books?

Thinking Critically

5. Why do you think the two visitors come to Zora's school?

6. What does Zora feel about the two visitors? How do you know?

7. What do the visitors think of Zora? How do you know?

8. What do you think is the most lasting effect of Zora's encounter with the visitors? Do you think her life might have taken a different direction if this meeting had not taken place? Explain.

9. How would you describe the **character** of the narrator? Cite examples from the text that support your analysis, especially the passages in which Hurston talks about her favorite books.

10. What details from this **autobiography** shed light on why Zora became a writer when she grew up?

11. Hurston's unmistakable voice comes through very clearly in this autobiography. What **tone** do you hear in her story of the white visitors?

Literary Criticism

12. **Philosophical approach.** Some of Hurston's contemporaries criticized her for not emphasizing in her writing the oppression of African Americans by the white community. Using references from this excerpt, explain whether or not you think this is a valid criticism. Would the quality of Hurston's work have been improved by comments on those political and social issues? Explain your response.

go.hrw.com

INTERNET
Projects and Activities
Keyword: LE5 11-5

SKILLS FOCUS

Literary Skills
Analyze an autobiography. Analyze the political and social influences of a historical period.

Writing Skills
Write an essay analyzing a title.

Vocabulary Skills
Create semantic maps.

WRITING

Judging a Book by Its Cover

The title of an autobiography can reveal a great deal about how the writer views his or her own life. Write an **essay** in which you give your reactions to Hurston's title, *Dust Tracks on a Road.* Use what you learned about Hurston from the biography on page 762 and from this autobiographical excerpt to speculate about why she chose this title. What does it reveal about Hurston's life experiences and her responses to them?

Vocabulary Development

Mapping an Unfamiliar Word

hail	avarice
brazenness	tread
caper	profoundly
exalted	resolved
realm	conceive

One way to own a word is to think of examples of how it is used. Take the word *caper,* for example. Filling out a word map like the one that follows will help you know the word better. Study this map for *caper,* and then make word maps of your own for the other Vocabulary words. If you prefer, use the base form of each word (*brazen,* not *brazenness; profound,* not *profoundly*).

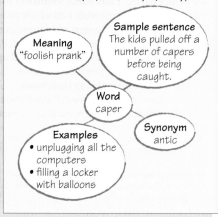

Meaning
"foolish prank"

Sample sentence
The kids pulled off a number of capers before being caught.

Word
caper

Synonym
antic

Examples
• unplugging all the computers
• filling a locker with balloons

11. Possible answer: Her tone in this anecdote is lively, forthright, irreverent, and at times ironic.

Literary Criticism

12. Possible answer: Direct comments on political and social issues would weaken this excerpt, since Hurston's goal here is to re-create a time when she did not know the sting of oppression.

Vocabulary Development

Sample Answer

Word—resolved. *Meaning*—"came to a decision." *Sample sentence*—The band resolved to play weekly. *Synonym*—decided. *Examples*—making up your mind to study more; deciding to save money.

Check students' maps of the remaining words for appropriate definitions, sentences, synonyms, and examples.

Grammar Link

Avoiding Misplaced and Dangling Modifiers: Saying What You Mean

A single-word modifier. A **modifier** is a word, a phrase, or a clause that makes the meaning of another word more specific. (The two kinds of modifiers are **adjectives** and **adverbs**.) A **misplaced modifier** is one that accidentally attaches itself to the wrong word in a sentence, usually because it's too far away from the right word. Although your readers *might* understand what you're trying to say, you're expecting them to do a lot of extra work to figure out your meaning.

Single-word modifiers, such as *only, always, often, almost, even,* and *nearly,* should go directly in front of or after the words or phrases they're intended to describe. Sometimes the meaning of the sentence changes depending on where you place this type of word.

MISPLACED	Zora Neale only rode part of the way with the travelers she hailed.
CLEAR	Zora Neale rode only part of the way with the travelers she hailed.

Phrases and clauses. Modifying phrases and clauses should also go as close as possible to the words they modify. Otherwise, the sentence can be confusing or even ridiculous. Sometimes the best way to fix a misplaced phrase or clause is to move it closer to the right word; other sentences require more tinkering to solve the problem.

MISPLACED	Zora Neale Hurston was the daughter of a minister and a teacher who published her first story in 1921. [It was Zora Neale, not her mother, who published the story.]
CLEAR	The daughter of a minister and a teacher, Zora Neale Hurston published her first story in 1921.

Dangling modifiers. While a misplaced modifier attaches itself to the wrong word, a **dangling modifier** doesn't logically modify *any* word in the sentence. The most common example is called a **dangling participle.** An introductory **participial phrase** (a word group beginning with an *–ing* or an *–ed* verb form) should modify the noun or the pronoun that comes directly after it. If that word doesn't make sense as the "doer" of the action described in the participial phrase, then the phrase is dangling. You can fix the problem by (1) naming the doer immediately after the participial phrase, (2) turning the phrase into a clause that names the doer as its subject, or (3) rewriting the whole sentence.

DANGLING	Sitting on the gatepost, the carriages and cars passed by Zora Neale's house. [It was Zora Neale who was sitting on the gatepost, not the carriages and cars.]

Grammar Skills
Avoid misplaced and dangling modifiers.

Zora Neale Hurston **771**

Grammar Link

Practice

Possible Answers

1. When Mr. Calhoun called Zora Neale up to his desk, she was afraid she would be punished.

2. Only Zora Neale received a box of clothes and books from the two white women who visited her class.

3. Zora Neale loved the books that she received from the two women.

4. After scrubbing Zora Neale and warning her about her behavior, her mother sent her to the hotel.

5. Zora Neale resolved to be like Hercules and ignored the other Greek gods and goddesses.

ASSESSING

Assessment

- *Holt Assessment: Literature, Reading, and Vocabulary*

RETEACHING

For a lesson reteaching the philosophical approach to literature, see **Reteaching**, p. 1117A.

CLEAR	Sitting on the gatepost, Zora Neale watched the carriages and cars pass by her house.
CLEAR	While Zora Neale was sitting on the gatepost, the carriages and cars passed by her house.

PRACTICE

In the following sentences, correct any misplaced or dangling modifiers. You may need to add or change words or rewrite sentences.

1. Afraid she would be punished, Mr. Calhoun called Zora Neale up to his desk.

2. Zora Neale only received a box of clothes and books from the two white women who visited her class.

3. Zora Neale loved the books from the two women that she received.

4. Scrubbed and warned about her behavior, Zora Neale's mother sent her to the hotel.

5. Resolving to be like Hercules, the other Greek gods and goddesses were ignored by Zora Neale.

Apply to Your Writing

Re-read a current writing assignment or one that you've already completed. Correct any misplaced or dangling modifiers.

▶ **For more help, see Placement of Modifiers, 5f–5g, in the Language Handbook.**

Zora Neale Hurston.

DIFFERENTIATING INSTRUCTION

Learners Having Difficulty

Write the following sentences on the chalkboard. Have students rewrite each to correct the misplaced or dangling modifiers. Possible answers are shown.

1. The schoolchildren fidgeted before the bell rang often. [The schoolchildren often fidgeted before the bell rang.]

2. Mr. Calhoun was the terror of the children who carried a palmetto switch. [Mr. Calhoun, who carried a palmetto switch, was the terror of the children.]

3. Dropping in unannounced, one visitor's dress caught Zora's attention. [One visitor, who dropped in unannounced, wore a dress that caught Zora's attention.]

4. Proud of the children's singing, a smile creased Mr. Calhoun's face. [Mr. Calhoun was proud of the children's singing, and a smile creased his face.]

5. Filled with shiny pennies, Zora gasped when she opened the cylinder. [Zora gasped when she opened the cylinder, which was filled with shiny pennies.]

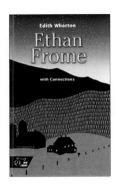

FICTION

Strange Twists of Fate

Winters in Starkville, Massachusetts, are harsh and lonely, and no one feels this loneliness more than Ethan Frome, who is stuck in his broken-down farmhouse with a sick and unpleasant wife. When his wife's attractive cousin, Mattie, comes to stay with the Fromes, Ethan feels a sense of hope and renewal that he hasn't felt in years, and he's overjoyed to learn that Mattie feels the same way. *Ethan Frome,* by Edith Wharton, is a classic story of an ill-fated romance that ends with a shocking twist.

This title is available in the HRW Library.

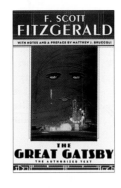

FICTION

Lifestyles of the Rich and Famous

He's rich, he's handsome, he throws great parties—so why does Jay Gatsby stand outside his opulent Long Island mansion, gazing longingly at a light across the water? The narrator, Nick Carraway, tries to unlock the puzzle in *The Great Gatsby,* F. Scott Fitzgerald's novel of American dreams and disappointments during the Jazz Age.

This title is available in the HRW Library.

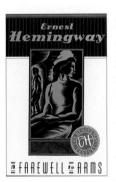

FICTION

Wounds of War

Ernest Hemingway is famous for his realistic, almost journalistic accounts of the triumphs and tragedies of warfare. In *A Farewell to Arms,* he sets a tragic romance against the backdrop of World War I Italy. In *For Whom the Bell Tolls,* the backdrop changes to the Spanish civil war.

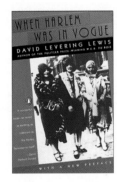

NONFICTION

Take the "A" Train

From about 1919 to 1932, New York City experienced a blossoming of African American culture known as the Harlem Renaissance (see page 742). Langston Hughes, Zora Neale Hurston, and James Weldon Johnson are just three of the many creative talents featured in *When Harlem Was in Vogue,* a highly readable social history by David Levering Lewis.

Read On   **773**

DIFFERENTIATING INSTRUCTION

Estimated Word Counts and Reading Levels of Read On Books:

Fiction			Nonfiction		
The Great Gatsby	⬌	57,400	*When Harlem Was in Vogue*	⬆	115,500
A Farewell to Arms	⬌	39,900			
For Whom the Bell Tolls	⬌	196,900			
Ethan Frome	⬇	57,400			

KEY: ⬆ *above grade level*   ⬌ *at grade level*   ⬇ *below grade level*

Read On

For Independent Reading

If students enjoyed the themes and topics explored in this collection, you might recommend the following titles for independent reading.

Assessment Options

The following projects can help you evaluate and assess your students' outside reading.

- **Present a play.** After students have read *The Great Gatsby,* ask them to select a pivotal scene to use as the basis for a reader's theater presentation. Have students script, cast, and rehearse their scenes. Have students perform them for the class and videotape the presentations.

- **Make a collage.** As students read either Hemingway novel, ask them to pay particular attention to the images of battle and its aftermath. Then, have students make a collage based on these images and write a statement explaining it. Display the collages in the classroom.

- **Draw a character.** After students have read *Ethan Frome,* ask them to select the character who interests them the most and to draw or paint their image of the character. (If drawing or painting is not practical, students might print an image from the Internet or cut out a magazine illustration.) Have students present their work to the class.

- **Create a summary chart.** As students read *When Harlem Was in Vogue,* ask them to make notes for a summary chart. The chart should include the names of writers and other important figures of the Harlem Renaissance, their works, and major social and historical events.

Skills Starter

Motivate. Ask students to name a novel they have read that made a strong impression on them. Have students rate the novels they select, using a descriptive scale such as *awful, so-so,* and *terrific.* Point out that this informal reaction is one type of response to a novel; students will be learning a similar but more formal type of response, called a literary analysis, in this workshop.

Read and Analyze

You may want to provide a list of classic and contemporary works that are on students' reading level and that would make good subjects for analysis. If students choose a novel from a source other than your list or the school library, have them check with you before reading. Students who may have trouble reading a novel-length work could read and analyze a short story instead. Encourage students wishing to read works by authors of varying ethnic backgrounds to consider distinguished authors such as Julia Alvarez, Sandra Cisneros, Ralph Ellison, Toni Morrison, Amy Tan, Toshiko Uchida, or Richard Wright.

Integrating with Grammar, Usage, and Mechanics

As students start their literary analyses, they may have trouble with capitalization and punctuation. You may want to review sections 11 and 12 in the Language Handbook.

Analyzing a Novel

Writing Assignment
Write a literary analysis that focuses on a literary element of a novel.

The works of Harlem Renaissance writers can be appreciated more deeply when you look below the surface to analyze their messages and techniques. Similarly, literary analysis adds depth to your understanding of a great novel. To develop your unique viewpoint about a novel, analyze the themes and techniques the author uses. By writing a **literary analysis,** you can help others discover deeper layers of meaning in a novel and add to their appreciation of it.

Prewriting

Read and Analyze

Once Is Not Enough First, choose an appropriate novel—one that is complex enough for you to analyze in a 1,500-word essay—and read it for enjoyment and general understanding. (If you need help choosing a novel to analyze, ask your teacher or librarian for suggestions.) Then, review your novel, and make notes about the significant ideas presented in it. To develop a **comprehensive understanding** of the author's ideas, consider the literary elements of your novel by answering the analysis questions in the right-hand column of the chart below.

QUESTIONS FOR LITERARY ANALYSIS	
Literary Element	**Analysis Questions**
Characters	How do the important characters in the novel think, talk, and act? In what ways do their actions or attitudes change over the course of the novel?
Setting	What is the time and place of the novel? How does the setting affect the mood or the development of the plot?
Plot	What is the central conflict, or problem, of the story? How does the outcome of the story relate to the theme?
Point of View	Is the story told by a first-person or a third-person narrator? What does the narrator think about the characters and events in the story?
Theme	What universal truths does the novel express about human nature, experiences, problems, or relationships? What details reflect this theme?
Symbolism	Do any objects or elements show up repeatedly? Does any person, place, or thing seem to represent an abstract idea? If so, what?

(continued)

Stylistic Devices

Imagery	What feelings do sensory descriptions of people, places, events, and ideas suggest? What effects are created through the use of imagery?
Diction	Is the author's word choice straightforward, or is the language connotative (having meaning beyond a simple definition)? What is the novel's tone? How does the word choice affect the tone of the story?
Figurative Language	Does the author use similes and metaphors? If so, what effects do these comparisons create?

TIP As you analyze these elements in your novel, consider **unique aspects of the text,** such as an author's unusual use of point of view, language, or plot structure. For example, you might focus on how J. D. Salinger's use of a first-person narrator with a distinct attitude and way of speaking affects a reader's impression of *The Catcher in the Rye.*

Write a Thesis Statement

Zoom In To plan your essay, focus on analyzing a single element over the entire course of the novel. Look at your notes to decide which element seems most important or interesting. Identify a few major points that make that element so strong—for example, the most surprising plot events or the characters whose lives point out the theme. Then, write a sentence that presents your perspective about the novel—a conclusion based on the major points about your chosen element. This sentence, your working **thesis statement,** will serve as a guide. If necessary, you can revise this statement later. Here is how one student expressed a viewpoint in a working thesis statement.

Through the empty lives of three <u>characters</u> from this novel— <u>George Wilson</u>, <u>Jay Gatsby</u>, and <u>Daisy Buchanan</u>—<u>Fitzgerald</u> <u>shows that chasing hollow dreams leads only to misery.</u>

Literary element
Major points
Conclusion about the novel

Gather Evidence

Get the Facts Find and make notes of evidence to support your working thesis statement. Your most important support will be **literary evidence**—detailed references to the text of the novel. Literary evidence includes quotations, paraphrases, and summaries of specific details and passages in the text. Although most of your evidence will come from the **primary source,** the novel itself, you might also find evidence in **secondary sources**—reference materials such as encyclopedias, periodicals, biographies of authors, or literary criticism. Such sources can bolster your major points and provide background information your readers may need to understand the context of the novel.

SKILLS FOCUS

Writing Skills
Write an analysis of a novel. Analyze literary elements and the author's style. Write a thesis statement.

Speaking
- *One-Stop Planner* CD-ROM with ExamView Test Generator
- *Holt Online Assessment*
- *Holt Online Essay Scoring*

Internet
- go.hrw.com (Keyword: LE5 11-5)
- *Elements of Literature Online*

Advanced Learners

Enrichment. Challenge students to use two or three different secondary sources in their analyses. If students are writing about a recently published work, they can cite book reviews and author interviews for their secondary sources; if students are writing about a classic work, they should have no trouble locating critical studies. You may want to review with students the method of citation you want them to use in their papers.

PRACTICE & APPLY 1

Guided and Independent Practice

Guide students in constructing a critical response to the novel they read by asking them to review their personal responses to the work and to ask why they felt that way. Students can use these suggestions to help them develop a thesis:

• Review your notes on your novel. On which elements have you written the most information? Which elements stood out in your reading?

• Make a generalization about the role the elements play in the novel. Narrow the focus of this generalization until you can develop an insight about the work you can support with evidence from the novel.

Spell It Out Explain how each piece of evidence supports your thesis and develops your major points. To do this, elaborate on the importance of each idea and its connection to your thesis. As part of your elaboration, explain how the author uses ambiguities, nuances, and complexities, and how those devices relate to your thesis.

● **ambiguities:** language or situations that can be interpreted in more than one way or have more than one meaning

● **nuances:** fine shades of meaning, especially any changes in the way the author expresses a recurring idea

● **complexities:** details in the novel that at first seem self-contradictory, requiring some thought to understand thoroughly

One student gathered evidence for her thesis using the notes below.

> **Thesis:** Through the empty lives of three characters from <u>The Great Gatsby</u>, Fitzgerald shows that chasing hollow dreams leads only to misery.
>
> **Major point:** Jay Gatsby's shallow pursuit of wealth and Daisy
>
> **Evidence:** Daisy says to Gatsby: "Oh, you want too much!" (133)
>
> **Elaboration:** Gatsby's desire to have it all—money, class, power, and Daisy, no matter the cost—has corrupted his spirit.

TIP Document quotations from the novel by enclosing the words in quotation marks and including the page number, as shown to the right. When you use material from secondary sources to support your thesis, identify the author and title in your essay to avoid **plagiarism**—using other authors' words or ideas without giving proper credit. Also, be sure to copy the quotation exactly as it appears in the original source.

| DO THIS ⟶

SKILLS FOCUS

Writing Skills Organize your ideas.

Arrange Your Ideas

Map the Course How you organize your ideas will depend on your thesis. For example, if you were examining how a character changes over time, you would use **chronological order.** Then again, if you were examining the importance of individual characters to a novel's theme, you could discuss them in **order of importance.** Once you've picked an order, map or outline your ideas. Here is one student's plan in order of importance.

> Show how Wilson chases empty dreams as first support. Use his attempt to buy a car and his weak marriage as examples. ⟶ Use Gatsby's shallow life as second support. Use as examples the wealth he gained illegally and his attempt to get Daisy back. ⟶ Use Daisy as the most important support of thesis. Use the examples of her marriage and her love for Gatsby to show the hollowness of her life.

PRACTICE & APPLY 1 Read and analyze an appropriate novel. Develop a thesis that states a conclusion about the novel, gather evidence, and organize your ideas.

Writing

Analyzing a Novel

A Writer's Framework

Introduction	Body	Conclusion
• Present background information that provides a context for your analysis.	• Organize major points in a logical order.	• Restate your thesis and summarize your major points.
• Give the novel's author and title.	• Include literary evidence from the text or secondary sources.	• End your analysis with a memorable statement—an idea your readers can ponder.
• Include a clear thesis statement.	• Elaborate on how evidence supports major points.	

A Writer's Model

Hollow Dreams—Empty Lives

After World War I, America seemed to promise unlimited financial and social opportunities for anyone willing to work hard—an American Dream. For some, however, striving for and realizing that dream corrupted them, as they acquired wealth only to pursue pleasure. Even though the characters in F. Scott Fitzgerald's <u>The Great Gatsby</u> appear to relish the freedom of the 1920s, their lives demonstrate the emptiness that results when wealth and pleasure become ends in themselves. Specifically, the empty lives of three characters from this novel—George Wilson, Jay Gatsby, and Daisy Buchanan—show that chasing hollow dreams results only in misery.

One character who chases an empty dream is George Wilson, the owner of a garage. Wilson has gone into business with the hope of becoming rich, but he has not been successful. Wilson thinks that if Tom Buchanan, Daisy's wealthy husband, will sell him a fancy car, he can then turn a profit by reselling it. When Tom and the narrator Nick Carraway meet Wilson at his garage, Nick says that there is a "damp gleam of hope" in Wilson's eyes (25). Wilson complains that the sale is going slowly, and Tom replies, "[I]f you feel that way about it, maybe I'd better sell it somewhere else after all"(25). Wilson instantly backs down. This exchange suggests that Wilson has no chance of either making a profit off Tom's car or realizing his dream of wealth. His hope for economic security is doomed to failure.

(continued)

INTRODUCTION
Background information

Author and title

Thesis statement

BODY
Major point #1

Evidence

Elaboration

DIRECT TEACHING

A Writer's Framework
Point out to students that **A Writer's Model** begins with a description of the time period in which the work appears. Tell students that the historical era of a novel can provide a context for students' analyses. The context could also include the important ideas in the work and the parallels students can draw between the novel and their own lives. Encourage students to be creative—but also very clear—when providing a context for their analyses. Remind them that the context provides the first impression of their work and that they want that impression to be favorable.

DIFFERENTIATING INSTRUCTION

Learners Having Difficulty
Students having trouble incorporating quotations in their own work may benefit from locating the sources of the quotations used in **A Writer's Model.** Provide small groups of students with a marked-up copy of *The Great Gatsby* so they can discuss the variety of ways in which the writer included quotations from Fitzgerald's novel. Students can use these instances as models for their own citations.

Major point #2
Background information
Evidence

Elaboration

Another character who holds tightly to an illusion is the title character, Jay Gatsby. Before the war, Gatsby and Daisy fell deeply in love. However, Daisy's family prevented her from marrying Gatsby because, as a young soldier, he was penniless. As a result, he spent his years after the war becoming very rich, but he did so by engaging in illegal activities. Having made his fortune, he moves near Daisy and puts on lavish parties in the hope that Daisy might leave her husband for him. Unfortunately, his newfound wealth does not earn him respect or acceptance into a higher social class. Rumors about his tainted past circulate, even as the partygoers devour the extravagant food and drink he provides. Gatsby is an outsider, and even when Daisy comes back to him, their love is tainted by money. In a final conversation, Daisy cries out to Gatsby: "Oh, you want too much!" (133) She is right: Gatsby's desire to have it all—money, class, power, and Daisy, no matter the cost—has corrupted his spirit.

Major point #3
Evidence

Elaboration

Unlike Gatsby, Daisy Buchanan seems perfectly at ease in her wealthy social circle. Money, rather than love, has determined her choice of husbands. Despite her love for Gatsby, she married Tom Buchanan, who gave her "a string of pearls valued at three hundred and fifty thousand dollars" for a wedding gift (77). Betraying Gatsby's love for Buchanan's money, Daisy is herself betrayed by her husband for another woman. Daisy returns to Gatsby, but she is still unable to free herself from the constraints of her wealthy society, particularly from her husband, who sneers at Gatsby's background and newfound wealth. The dream of happiness—the love she and Gatsby once shared—is doomed, because she believes that money is more important.

CONCLUSION
Restatement of thesis and major points

Memorable statement

Throughout the novel, F. Scott Fitzgerald portrays a society that has corrupted the true meaning of the American Dream through Wilson, Gatsby, and Daisy's hollow pursuit of wealth. If the characters in The Great Gatsby come from various classes of American society, then a major theme of The Great Gatsby is that no one in 1920s America was safe from vacant dreams and their negative results.

INTERNET
More Writer's Models
Keyword: LE5 11–5

TIP When you incorporate a quotation into a sentence, use capitalization appropriate to the sentence, even if the capitalization is different in the source. To indicate that you have made such a change, put brackets around the letter that has been changed, as shown in the second paragraph of the Writer's Model.

PRACTICE & APPLY 2 Write the first draft of your literary analysis of a novel, using the framework on page 777 and the Writer's Model above as guides.

TECHNOLOGY TIP

Use a search engine to find Web sites concerning *The Great Gatsby* on the Internet. Show students locations that include reviews and commentary on the novel. Students can visit the sites and note examples of literary evidence for points the authors make. Discuss with students how different perspectives can lead to many different analyses of a single work.

You need to be aware that Internet resources sometimes serve as public forums and that their content can be unpredictable.

CRITICAL THINKING

After students have read **A Writer's Model,** have them evaluate it for its balance of quotations, summaries, arguments, evidence, and elaboration. Lead students with these questions:

• Is **A Writer's Model** well balanced? Why or why not?

• What changes would you propose to improve **A Writer's Model**?

Have students give reasons for their suggestions.

PRACTICE & APPLY 2

Guided and Independent Practice

Guide students by offering them these questions to help them evaluate the literary evidence they plan to use in their analyses:

• Does the quotation, paraphrase, or summary go beyond the thesis statement or merely repeat it?

• Is the literary evidence relevant to the main idea in the thesis?

The evidence students choose to include should be both supportive and relevant. Have students then complete **Practice and Apply 2** as independent practice.

Revising

Evaluate and Revise Your Analysis

Do a Double Take Your analysis isn't complete until you've revised it carefully. Read through your draft at least twice. Use the first-reading guidelines below to look critically at content and organization. Then, use the style guidelines on page 780 to evaluate and revise the style of your analysis.

▶ **First Reading: Content and Organization** Using the chart below, evaluate and revise the content and organization of your literary analysis.

PEER REVIEW

Before you revise, trade papers with a peer and ask for input on where you need to integrate literary evidence more smoothly in your paper.

Rubric: Analyzing a Novel

Evaluation Questions	▶ Tips	▶ Revision Techniques
❶ Does the introduction include background information to give the analysis context? Does it include the author's name and the novel's title?	▶ **Circle** the information that provides context for the analysis. **Underline** the name of the author and the title of the novel.	▶ **Add** information that provides context, such as details about the author's life or the novel's historical setting. **Add** the name of the author or the novel's title.
❷ Does a clear thesis statement present a conclusion about the novel based on a literary element?	▶ **Bracket** the element identified in the thesis and the writer's conclusion about the novel.	▶ **Add** a conclusion about the novel or a clearer statement of the literary element on which the analysis focuses.
❸ Does each body paragraph develop a major point that supports the thesis?	▶ **Label** the major point of each body paragraph in the margin next to the paragraph.	▶ **Replace** sentences or paragraphs that don't support the thesis.
❹ Does evidence support each major point?	▶ **Draw a jagged line** under each piece of evidence. If a paragraph includes little evidence or evidence that doesn't clearly support its point, revise.	▶ **Add** quotations, paraphrases, or summaries from the novel or other sources. **Elaborate** on how the evidence supports the paragraph's point.
❺ Are the paper's major points organized effectively?	▶ **Number** ideas in sequence for chronological order. For order of importance, **underline** the most important point.	▶ **Reorder** a chronological essay in correct time order. For order of importance, **reorder** to place the most important point first or last.
❻ Does the conclusion restate the thesis and sum up the major points? Does it close the essay with a memorable statement?	▶ **Circle** the sentences that restate the essay's thesis and sum up major points. **Double underline** a memorable concluding statement.	▶ **Add** a sentence or two restating the thesis and summarizing major points. **Elaborate** with a memorable statement.

DIRECT TEACHING

Rubric: Analyzing a Novel

Advise students to use the **Rubric** chart on this page as a think sheet by answering the questions in their notebooks. Explain to students that using think sheets to summarize their notes allows them to place their thoughts, observations, and questions on paper—which in turn helps improve the content and organization of their essays.

RETEACHING

Elaboration

If students struggle with elaborating on evidence, point out that the use of allusion may be an effective technique. Clarifying or elaborating by referring to another work, another section of the same work, or another character or symbol is often very helpful.

Second Reading: Style To improve the style of your literary analysis, look at how you **introduce quotations.** To weave quotations smoothly into your sentences, introduce them with a brief clause. Look at these examples:

Original: A "damp gleam of hope" is what the narrator, Nick, says the character Wilson has in his eyes (25).

Revision: Nick says that there is a "damp gleam of hope" in Wilson's eyes (25).

Use the guidelines below to evaluate your style.

Style Guidelines

Evaluation Question	▶ Tip	▶ Revision Technique
● Are quotations woven into the structure of the sentence? Does each quotation have an introduction?	▶ **Draw a box** around each sentence that includes a quotation. **Underline** the introduction of each quotation.	▶ **Reword** sentences that are confusing by using a brief clause before quotations to introduce them.

ANALYZING THE REVISION PROCESS
Study these revisions, and answer the questions that follow.

reword

Wilson complains that the sale is going slowly, *, and Tom replies,* "[I]f you feel

that way about it, maybe I'd better sell it somewhere else after

elaborate

all" ~~is what Tom says~~ (25). Wilson instantly backs down. His

hope for economic security is doomed to failure.

This exchange suggests that Wilson has no chance of either making a profit off Tom's car or realizing his dream of wealth.

Responding to the Revision Process
1. How does the revision of the first two sentences make the paragraph easier to follow?
2. Why did the writer add a sentence? How does the new sentence explain the literary evidence?

PRACTICE & APPLY 3 Use the guidelines on pages 779 and 780 to evaluate and revise your essay's content, organization, and style. Consider peer comments as well.

SKILLS FOCUS
Writing Skills
Revise for content and style.

GUIDED PRACTICE

Responding to the Revision Process

Answers

1. The revision provides a smooth transition into the quotation.

2. The addition provides a reflection on the literary evidence that supports the writer's thesis. Without the addition, it might not be clear to the reader how the evidence supports the thesis.

PRACTICE & APPLY 3

Independent Practice
To help students focus their revision efforts, provide these questions:

• Which is your strongest point? Is any point unclear?

• Have you provided enough literary evidence? Why do you think so?

• Are the quotations adequately woven into the flow of your composition? If not, how can their use be improved?

DIFFERENTIATING INSTRUCTION

English-Language Learners
In many languages, the conventions relating to the punctuation of quotations are different from those in English. Offer students a quick review of how to include quoted material in a composition, and provide ongoing support as needed.

Publishing

Proofread and Publish Your Analysis

To Err Is Human All writers make mistakes. A good writer catches and corrects mistakes before the work is published. Carefully check your draft—individually and collaboratively—for grammar, usage, spelling, and punctuation errors before you submit the final copy.

Get the Word Out Your analysis presents your unique perspective on a literary work. Don't limit the audience for that perspective to just your classmates and teacher. Here are some ways you might share your literary analysis with a wider audience.

- Collaborate with other students on a booklet of related analyses. You might collect analyses that discuss various works by the same author or works by authors from the same era, or you could group essays that analyze the same literary element in different works or that examine similar themes. Bind your booklet, and add it to a class or library display of student work.

- Create a bulletin board for your class. Arrange your literary analysis next to a photo of the novel's author. Add other supplementary material related to the novel or its author to catch a reader's eye.

- Find a Web site about the author of the novel you analyzed. Send an e-mail message to ask the producers of the site if they will publish your analysis there.

Reflect on Your Literary Analysis

Get Some Perspective Now that your literary analysis is complete, take time to reflect on your writing. Writing responses to the following questions will help you identify and build on what you learned in this workshop.

- How did you choose the focus of your analysis? What other elements of the novel or major points might you have analyzed instead?

- How has writing the analysis deepened your understanding of the literary work?

- What important revisions did you make to your draft? How did they improve it?

- What will you do differently if you write another literary analysis?

PRACTICE & APPLY 4 Proofread your revised analysis to correct any errors in grammar, usage, or mechanics. Then, publish your analysis using one of the suggestions above. Finally, answer the questions above, and attach your responses to your analysis.

TIP Proofread carefully for English-language **conventions.** One convention writers of literary analyses use is the literary present tense. Because the events in a novel are constantly unfolding for new readers, use the present tense to refer to events that occur in the novel you analyze. For more on the **literary present tense,** see Tenses and Their Uses, 3b, in the Language Handbook.

SKILLS FOCUS

Writing Skills
Proofread, especially for use of the literary present tense.

Writing Workshop: Analyzing a Novel **781**

Proofread and Publish Your Analysis

If students choose to publish their essays on the Internet, you need to be aware that the World Wide Web sometimes functions as a public forum and that its content may be unpredictable.

PRACTICE & APPLY 4

Guided and Independent Practice

Challenge students to consider these alternative ways in which to publish their essays:

- Students could enter their work in a contest run by the school, local library, or student periodical.

- Volunteers could conduct research to identify periodicals interested in receiving student submissions.

Then, have students complete **Practice and Apply 4** as independent practice.

782 Collection 5 The Moderns: 1914–1939

PRETEACHING

Motivate. Ask students if, while they were brainstorming for ways to publish their literary analysis, they thought of sharing it with an audience by presenting it orally. Encourage volunteers to suggest changes they would have to make to their literary analyses in order to present them orally.

DIRECT TEACHING

Adapt Your Analysis

To help students prepare to give extemporaneous speeches, offer these tips:

- Outline your presentation on note cards, but do not memorize it.

- Practice until you are able to deliver your presentation with only quick periodic glances at your notes.

- Mark your note cards in a way that reminds you to use verbal and nonverbal techniques, such as pauses and eye contact.

- Write your note cards clearly enough to avoid having to decipher your own writing in front of an audience.

RETEACHING

Give Orders

If students have trouble organizing a presentation their audience will easily be able to follow, review additional transitional expressions that indicate order of importance and chronological order. Have volunteers use each of the transitions in context. Suggest to students that they begin each of their note cards with one of the expressions, in order to make sure the organization of their ideas is clear to them. By rehearsing, students can determine how many of the transitional expressions are needed to make the organization of their ideas clear to an audience.

Presenting a Literary Analysis

Speaking Assignment
Adapt your written literary analysis into an oral response to literature, and deliver it your class.

Writing an essay isn't the only way for you to share your analysis of a novel. You can also tell a group of listeners your ideas in an **oral response to literature.** You'll use slightly different ideas and techniques in your oral presentation, though. This workshop will help you adapt your written ideas and present them to a listening audience.

Adapt Your Analysis

Think Out Loud You crafted your written literary analysis for an audience of classmates and teachers. Even if you have the same audience for your presentation, you'll need to adjust your analysis to fit their needs as listeners rather than readers. Use the following tips.

Keep It Short If you have a time limit, make sure you can deliver your presentation within it. Even without a time limit, focus on a limited number of points and evidence to hold your listeners' interest.

Plan Content Your **thesis statement** will show your comprehensive understanding of the significant ideas in the work. Adapt your written thesis statement by shortening or simplifying it to make it easier for listeners to understand, and summarize your points up front to prepare listeners for the ideas you will present.

Focus your speech on the most important points about the element you analyzed in your essay. Remember that these points can include descriptions and explanations of other literary elements, including **universal themes,** point of view, symbolism, **stylistic devices** such as **imagery** and the author's choice of **language,** and other **unique aspects** of the text.

Support your thesis and each major point you discuss with evidence in the form of accurate and detailed references to the text or to other works. Identify the title and author of any secondary source you quote. Elaborate on the evidence by showing how it relates to the assertion your thesis makes about the work. If appropriate, explain any significant **ambiguities, nuances,** or **complexities** in the work to help you develop your major points or your elaboration.

Use Rhetorical Techniques To make your presentation easier for listeners to understand and remember, try using the following techniques.

- **rhetorical questions,** or questions with debatable answers asked for effect—for example, the student analyzing *The Great Gatsby* might begin by asking, "Which is more important, love or money?"

- **parallel structure,** or using the same grammatical form for similar ideas—for example, "While *Gatsby has loved* only Daisy, *Daisy has loved* Tom and his money as well as Gatsby."

SKILLS FOCUS

Listening and Speaking Skills
Present an oral response to a literary work. Use effective rhetorical techniques.

COLLECTION 5 RESOURCES: LISTENING & SPEAKING

Planning
- *One-Stop Planner* CD-ROM with ExamView Test Generator

Differentiating Instruction
- *Workshop Resources: Writing, Listening, and Speaking*
- *Family Involvement Activities in English and Spanish*

- *Supporting Instruction in Spanish*

Listening and Speaking
- *Workshop Resources: Writing, Listening, and Speaking*
- *Daily Language Activities*
- *Language Handbook Worksheets*

Give Orders Like your written literary analysis, your presentation will follow **chronological order** or **order of importance.** Plan to give listeners clues that indicate the order you will use, such as *first, then,* and *finally* for chronological order or *for one thing, further,* and *most important* for order of importance. Make brief notes on note cards to remind you of what you want to say, and number the cards in order. The note card below is for an oral presentation based on the Writer's Model that begins on page 777.

5 ——— Card number

Gatsby's spirit corrupted by desire for money, class, ——— Summary
power, and, most important, Daisy

Daisy to Gatsby: "Oh, you want too much!" ——— Direct quotation

Rehearse and Present Your Analysis

Take Command In order to make a successful presentation, you must master the material you will present and fine-tune the details of your speech. To do this, try these rehearsal strategies.

- Videotape or audiotape your presentation and play it back, noting two specific ways you might improve it. Practice and record again, focusing on two more ways to improve. Repeat the process as needed.

- Practice your presentation in front of a mirror. First, concentrate on nonverbal elements, such as facial expressions and gestures. When you feel comfortable with the nonverbal elements, work on the verbal elements, such as volume and enunciation.

- Give your presentation to a group of friends or family, and ask for feedback. Practice, and then give your presentation again to another group of listeners, repeating the process until you feel confident.

Once you are comfortable and confident with both your material and the performance details of your delivery, present your analysis to your classmates.

PRACTICE & APPLY 5 — Adapt the literary analysis you wrote for the Writing Workshop to plan an oral presentation. Then, rehearse and deliver your oral response to literature to your classmates.

Reference Note

For more on **delivery techniques,** see page 369.

TIP When quoting dialogue from the novel, consider using movements, gestures, or speaking styles suited to the character you are quoting. Research appropriate dialect for the characters, if necessary, and look up any words you don't know how to pronounce.

SKILLS FOCUS

Listening and Speaking Skills Rehearse and present your literary analysis.

Listening and Speaking Workshop: Presenting a Literary Analysis **783**

SKILLS FOCUS, pp. 784–787

Grade-Level Skills

■ **Literary Skills**
Compare major literary forms of different historical periods.

INTRODUCING THE SKILLS REVIEW

Use this review to assess students' ability to contrast works from different periods.

DIRECT TEACHING

Ⓐ Literary Focus

❷ Comparing literature. To what does "bread of bitterness" and "tiger's tooth" refer? [American racism] What conflicting feelings are expressed toward America? [Possible response: love and defiance.]

Ⓑ Literary Focus

❷ Comparing literature. What does the speaker foresee? [decline, oblivion]

Test Practice

The two poems that follow are concerned with the state of America in the twentieth century. The first was written in the 1920s by Claude McKay, who was born in 1890 in Jamaica and later became one of the leading writers of the Harlem Renaissance. The other poem was written more than fifty years later by the activist poet Allen Ginsberg, who was born in 1926 and who for many years made his home on the teeming Lower East Side of New York City.

DIRECTIONS: Read the following poems. Then, read each multiple-choice question that follows, and write the letter of the best response.

America

Claude McKay

Ⓐ   Although she feeds me bread of bitterness,°
     And sinks into my throat her tiger's tooth,
     Stealing my breath of life, I will confess
     I love this cultured hell that tests my youth!
5   Her vigor flows like tides into my blood,
     Giving me strength erect against her hate.
     Her bigness sweeps my being like a flood.
     Yet as a rebel fronts° a king in state,
     I stand within her walls with not a shred
10   Of terror, malice, not a word of jeer.
Ⓑ   Darkly I gaze into the days ahead,
     And see her might and granite wonders there,
     Beneath the touch of Time's unerring hand,
     Like priceless treasures sinking in the sand.

---

1. **bread of bitterness:** allusion to Psalm 80:5, "Thou feedest them with the bread of tears; and givest them tears to drink in great measure."
8. **fronts** *v.:* confronts.

SKILLS FOCUS

Pages 784–787 cover **Reading Skills** Compare and contrast works from different literary periods.

READING MINI-LESSON

Reviewing Word-Attack Skills
Activity. Display these words. Have students count the syllables in their pronunciation of each word. Answers may vary.

1. practically [3 or 4]   2. temperament [3 or 4]

3. preference [2 or 3]   4. privilege [2 or 3]

5. inseparable [4 or 5]   6. elementary [4 or 5]

Activity. Display these pairs of words and their meanings in parentheses, and have students underline the accented syllable in each one. Answers are underlined.

1. <u>in</u>cense (make very angry)
   in<u>cense</u> (substance burned for fragrance)

2. <u>pres</u>ent (in attendance)
   pre<u>sent</u> (offer for viewing)

3. com<u>pound</u> (put together)
   <u>com</u>pound (fenced area)

4. <u>con</u>tent (substance)
   con<u>tent</u> (satisfied)

DIRECT TEACHING

C **Literary Focus**

? **Comparing literature.** What changes would "washing" bring to the world? [Possible response: It would clean up pollution, remove the scars of wars, and right political wrongs.]

Homework

Homage Kenneth Koch

Allen Ginsberg

If I were doing my Laundry I'd wash my dirty Iran
I'd throw in my United States, and pour on the Ivory Soap, scrub
    up Africa, put all the birds and elephants back in
    the jungle,
I'd wash the Amazon river and clean the oily Carib & Gulf of
    Mexico,
Rub that smog off the North Pole, wipe up all the pipelines in
    Alaska,
Rub a dub dub for Rocky Flats and Los Alamos, Flush that
5   sparkly Cesium out of Love Canal
Rinse down the Acid Rain over the Parthenon & Sphinx,
    Drain the Sludge out of the Mediterranean basin &
    make it azure again,
Put some blueing back into the sky over the Rhine, bleach the
    little Clouds so snow return white as snow,
Cleanse the Hudson Thames & Neckar, Drain the Suds out
    of Lake Erie
Then I'd throw big Asia in one giant Load & wash out the
    blood & Agent Orange,
Dump the whole mess of Russia and China in the wringer,
    squeeze out the tattletail Gray of U.S. Central American
10   police state,
& put the planet in the drier & let it sit 20 minutes or an Aeon
    till it came out clean.

April 26, 1980

Activity. Display these words. Have students identify the two words in each set in which the boldface letter stands for the same sound. Answers are underlined.

1. t**y**pical   t**y**pify   t**y**pographic
2. fa**c**tory   fa**c**tual   manufa**c**ture
3. **g**esture   **g**esticulate   **g**estation
4. h**y**perbole   h**y**pnotic   h**y**steria
5. gra**d**ual   gra**d**ation   gra**d**uate
6. pe**t**ulant   pe**t**unia   pos**t**ulate
7. p**y**thon   pap**y**rus   p**y**gmy
8. mo**d**ular   mo**d**ulate   mo**d**icum

TestPractice

Answers and Model Rationales

1. **B** Lines 3–4 read in part, ". . . I will confess / I love this cultured hell. . . ."

2. **F** Lines 1–4 include no references to suggest a nurse (H) or a nightmare (J). While l. 1 suggests a mother (G), ll. 2–3 describe a tiger (F).

3. **B** McKay, an African American, wrote the poem in the 1920s, when racism (B) was legal and ubiquitous. Line 7 suggests that he found America's size (A) invigorating, not hateful. He is not referring to prejudice against poets (C), or hatred of the poor (D).

4. **F** The speaker suggests sorrow (F), not admiration (H). Line 10 directly states that the speaker feels no terror (G) or malice (J).

5. **A** Although references to a king and a rebel (B) and a tiger (C) are mentioned in the poem, they are descriptive images, not expressions of a central conflict. America's fate (D) is mentioned only in the poem's last lines.

6. **G** There is neither reference to time destroying America (F) nor the speaker's moving to Europe (H). The speaker does not sound powerless (J).

7. **C** There is no reference to violence (A) or great leadership (B). The speaker does not say that America will no longer exist (D), but that her glory will not last (C).

8. **J** The poem includes no references to pornography (G), to Washington, D.C. scandals (H), or to poverty (F).

9. **C** In ll. 11–12, the speaker says "put the planet in the drier & let it sit 20 minutes or an Aeon."

---

1. In the first four lines of McKay's poem, what does he confess about his feelings for America?
   A He dislikes her.
   B He loves her.
   C He does not understand her.
   D He wishes to leave her.

2. In the first four lines, what does McKay **personify** America as?
   F A tiger
   G A mother
   H A nurse
   J A nightmare

3. Consider McKay's background and the time he wrote this poem. How would you explain what he means by "her hate" in line 6?
   A He refers to America's size.
   B He refers to racism.
   C He refers to prejudice against poets.
   D He refers to hatred of the poor.

4. Which words *best* describe the **tone** of lines 11–14 of "America"?
   F Defiant and sad
   G Terrified and mocking
   H Admiring and triumphant
   J Bitter and angry

5. The central **conflict** in "America" takes place between —
   A the speaker's contradictory feelings
   B the king and the rebel
   C the tiger and the poet
   D America and her tragic fate

6. In lines 8–10 of "America," the speaker does not revolt against America because —
   F time will destroy America
   G he loves his country
   H he moves to Europe
   J he feels powerless

7. In "America," what does the speaker see as the future of the country?
   A America will be overcome by violence.
   B America will lead the world.
   C America's glory will not endure.
   D America will no longer exist.

8. In the laundry **metaphor** that runs throughout "Homework," what does the speaker want cleaned up?
   F Urban decay and rural poverty
   G Pornographic books and films
   H Scandals in Washington, D.C.
   J Political and environmental problems

9. In Ginsberg's poem, how long does the speaker say he'll wait for the wash to come "out clean"?
   A Until the end of time
   B A minute or two
   C Twenty minutes or an aeon
   D Half an hour

Using Academic Language

Review of Literary Terms
After they review the meanings of the terms listed below, have students cite passages from the collection that illustrate their meanings.
Modernism (pp. 562, 565); **Stream of Consciousness** (pp. 566, 696); **Symbolism** (p. 571); **Imagism** (p. 572); **Free Verse** (p. 573); **Imagery** (pp. 575, 592, 759); **Dramatic Monologue** (p. 583); **Syntax** (p. 602); **Protagonist, Antihero** (p. 610);

Motivation (p. 623); **Setting** (p. 645); **Conflict** (p. 669); **Theme** (p. 685); **Parody** (p. 707); **Sonnet** (p. 718); **Allusion** (p. 721); **Ambiguity** (p. 727); **Narrative Poem** (p. 731); **Blank Verse** (p. 738); **Metaphor** (p. 745); **Rhythm** (p. 750); **Mood** (p. 754); **Repetition** (p. 759); **Autobiography** (p. 763).

10. Which word *best* describes Ginsberg's **tone**?

    F Tragic

    G Threatening

    H Playful

    J Bitter

11. Which statement would the speaker of "Homework" most likely agree with?

    A America's problems are easy to solve.

    B The speaker has a responsibility to help America.

    C America's problems are unsolvable.

    D America is not a good place to live.

12. Which statement is true of *both* "America" and "Homework"?

    F The speakers of both poems describe their love of America.

    G Both poets refer to America as a female.

    H Both poets have a negative outlook for America's future.

    J Both poets use metaphors to describe their feelings.

13. With which of the following statements about the United States do you think McKay and Ginsberg would agree?

    A America and the world are not perfect and need reform.

    B We should not let the natural world become polluted.

    C Individuals are powerless in society today.

    D This is the best of all possible worlds.

14. What do McKay and Ginsberg have in common with other twentieth-century American writers, such as Hemingway and Fitzgerald?

    F They prefer lyrical, romantic language.

    G They have a critical attitude toward modern life.

    H They all have amusing tones.

    J They think that American society is perfect.

Essay Question

Speaking from different eras and different experiences, Claude McKay and Allen Ginsberg present personal visions of the modern world. Write an essay in which you first summarize each poet's main message. Then, compare the views of these poets with the reality of the world as you see it today.

10. **H** The poem's light and playful tone (H) precludes bitterness (J) or threats (G). Though many of the world's problems are tragic (F), Ginsberg's tone is not.

11. **B** The speaker's light tone suggests that he does not view America's problems as unsolvable (C). However, the poem's long list of problems suggests that the speaker does not think the problems will be easy to solve (A). Nothing in the poem suggests that America is not a good place to live (D).

12. **J** While McKay clearly mentions his love of America, Ginsberg alludes to a love for the planet as a whole (F). McKay personifies America as female, but Ginsberg does not mention gender (G). McKay alludes to America losing its grandeur, but Ginsberg seems hopeful about its future. However, both poets use metaphors.

13. **A** Both McKay and Ginsberg highlight problems and the need for reform (A), the opposite of D. Neither poet focuses on personal powerlessness (C). Ginsberg refers to pollution (B), a key issue of the 1970s and '80s, but McKay, writing in the 1920s, does not.

14. **G** Twentieth-century writers generally do not prefer romantic language (F) or consider American society perfect (J). A few—including Ginsberg but not McKay—adopt amusing tones (H).

Test-Taking Tips

For information on answering multiple-choice items, refer students to **Test Smarts**.

ASSESSING

Assessment

■ *Holt Assessment: Literature, Reading, and Vocabulary*

Essay Question

McKay focuses on America and the African American experience. He emphasizes the personal strength that the modern "cultured hell" demands, and he calls up a vision of America's obliterated grandeur. To some students, this poem may seem like a bleak warning; to others, a vow to work for change. Some might note improvements in civil rights; for others, changes are still needed.

Ginsberg's focus is more global. The speaker wistfully imagines cleansing the world of its problems. Though the tone is light, the problems are not. For some students, this contrast may reinforce the impossibility of the task. Others may find Ginsberg more optimistic. Some may say that today's technological advances bring the fantasy closer to reality; others may say recent problems push it further away.

Collection 5: Skills Review

Vocabulary Skills

Analogies

Modeling. Model the thought process of a good reader getting the answer to item 1 by saying: "*Ludicrous* and *absurd* are synonyms. In A, B, and C, the word pairs are antonyms. *Peaceful* and *undisturbed* are synonyms, so D is the best choice."

Answers and Model Rationales

1. **D** See rationale above.
2. **J** A criminal is not respectable (F), a professor is not ignorant (G), and a painter isn't necessarily trustworthy (H).
3. **A** *Hail* and *greet* are synonyms, as are *avoid* and *dodge* (A). The word pairs in B, C, and D are all antonyms.
4. **H** In F, the relationship is attribute to person. In G and J, the word pairs are synonyms.
5. **B** Word pairs in A, C, and D show no relationship of quality to setting.
6. **H** The word pairs in G and J are synonyms; the words in F show cause-effect relationship.
7. **D** Word pairs in A, B, and C are antonyms.
8. **G** In J, the words are merely synonyms; *Fancy* does not mean "very elaborate." The word pairs in F and H are antonyms.
9. **B** A judge must not be biased (A); a bully need not be a braggart (D). The words in C are synonyms.
10. **F** The word pairs in G, H, and J show no causal relationship.

Test Practice

Analogies

DIRECTIONS: For each of the following items, choose the lettered pair of words that expresses a relationship that is most similar to the relationship between the capitalized pair of words.

1. LUDICROUS : ABSURD ::
   - **A** pure : filthy
   - **B** quick : unmoving
   - **C** ill : healthy
   - **D** peaceful : undisturbed

2. PAUPER : POOR ::
   - **F** criminal : respectable
   - **G** professor : ignorant
   - **H** painter : trustworthy
   - **J** comedian : funny

3. HAIL : GREET ::
   - **A** avoid : dodge
   - **B** deny : give
   - **C** destroy : restore
   - **D** find : lose

4. ARCHAIC : MODERN ::
   - **F** immature : novice
   - **G** shy : timid
   - **H** violent : peaceful
   - **J** wild : untamed

5. BEDLAM : WAR ::
   - **A** order : beach
   - **B** quiet : library
   - **C** comfort : court
   - **D** distress : supermarket

6. CONVENED : DISPERSED ::
   - **F** retreated : repelled
   - **G** welcomed : accepted
   - **H** froze : melted
   - **J** imagined : created

7. DISTRAUGHT : TROUBLED ::
   - **A** giddy : bored
   - **B** injured : well
   - **C** excited : lethargic
   - **D** confused : bewildered

8. DIMINUTIVE : SMALL ::
   - **F** complicated : easy
   - **G** gorgeous : good-looking
   - **H** dull : brilliant
   - **J** fancy : elaborate

9. CRAVEN : COWARD ::
   - **A** biased : judge
   - **B** stingy : miser
   - **C** frightening : scary
   - **D** braggart : bully

10. PANDEMONIUM : RIOT ::
    - **F** illness : virus
    - **G** sorrow : excitement
    - **H** environment : pollution
    - **J** verdict : guilty

SKILLS FOCUS

Vocabulary Skills
Analyze word analogies.

Vocabulary Review

Use this activity to assess whether students have retained the collection Vocabulary.
Activity. Ask students to complete each analogy below with a Vocabulary word from the box.

> reverberated virulent punctures
> plague brazenness

1. SOUR : SWEET :: _____ : harmless [virulent]
2. _____ : ANNOY :: adore : love [PLAGUE]
3. NEEDLE : _____ :: knife : cuts [PUNCTURES]
4. LIGHT : REFLECTED :: sound : _____ [reverberated]
5. _____ : TIMIDITY :: joy : sorrow [BRAZENNESS]

Test Practice

DIRECTIONS: Read the following paragraph from a literary analysis. Mark on your own paper the best answer to each question.

(1) In the novel *Passing*, the two main characters are masked. (2) The novel proved Nella Larsen one of the most influential writers of the Harlem Renaissance. (3) Although the characters in *Passing,* Clare and Irene, come from African American families, both are able to "pass" as white women. (4) Early in the novel, Irene describes Clare's face as an "ivory mask" which she uses to break away "from all that was familiar and friendly to take [her] chance in another environment" (24). (5) Irene also passes, and at the end of the novel "her face ha[s] become a mask" that she uses to hide her emotions (99). (6) While masking themselves allows Clare and Irene entrance into other social spheres, they soon learn the greater consequences of not being true to themselves.

1. Which sentence could replace sentence 1 to express a clearer perspective?
   A *Passing* uses the metaphor of a mask to show how characters hide their true identities.
   B *Passing* contrasts Clare and Irene's lifestyles and families.
   C *Passing* explains how and why light-skinned African Americans entered white society.
   D *Passing,* a Harlem Renaissance novel, explores issues of race.

2. Which sentence would explain the quotations in sentence 4?
   F Passing causes Clare to lose family, friends, and heritage.
   G Irene passes because she enjoys fooling others.
   H Through passing, Clare experiences white society.
   J Clare doesn't miss the friends and family she leaves behind.

3. To further support his viewpoint, the student could
   A summarize his major points
   B include more detailed and accurate references to the text
   C analyze in this paragraph other elements of the novel
   D ignore ambiguities and complexities within the text

4. Which sentence should be moved to another paragraph to improve organization?
   F 2   H 5
   G 4   J 6

5. To present this analysis orally, the student should
   A make the thesis statement longer and more complex
   B read the entire analysis aloud from note cards
   C rehearse one time only
   D focus on the strongest main points and evidence

SKILLS FOCUS

Writing Skills
Write an analysis of a novel.

RESOURCES: WRITING

Assessment
- *Holt Assessment: Writing, Listening, and Speaking*
- *One-Stop Planner* CD-ROM with ExamView Test Generator

Internet
- *Holt Online Assessment*
- *Holt Online Essay Scoring*

Writing Skills
Answers
1. A
2. H
3. B
4. F
5. D

APPLICATION

Short Story
For homework, have students use their familiarity with literary elements to write their own short stories. Tell students that though they should be concerned with establishing a vivid setting and introducing the reader to realistic characters, their main focus should be on telling an interesting and unusual story that will entertain their readers. Students may want to meet in small groups to discuss plot ideas. Ask volunteers to share their stories by reading them aloud to the class.

Homework

EXTENSION

Ad Analysis
Ask students to choose a print or TV advertisement and to analyze the commercial as they would analyze a literary work. Lead them with these questions:
- What is the theme of the advertisement?
- What do the characters do?
- How important is the setting?

Finally, students should evaluate the effectiveness of the persuasive message and consider how literary analysis can help them make better decisions as consumers. Ask students to share their results in the form of posters you can display around the classroom.

Collection 6
Contemporary Literature: 1939 to Present

About Collection 6

In Collection 6, students will master the following skills:

- **Literary Skills:** Evaluate traditions in American literature; analyze implied metaphor, subjective and objective reporting, persuasion, satire, magic realism, dialogue in nonfiction, personal essay, allusion, poetic devices, figurative language, and archetypes; analyze and compare political points of view on a topic; compare and contrast works from different literary periods.
- **Reading Skills:** Analyze an author's credibility, a writer's message, historical context; make inferences about characters; identify main ideas and supporting details; evaluate an author's argument.
- **Vocabulary Skills:** Understand connotations of synonyms and etymologies of words used in political science and history; use context clues; recognize synonyms; analyze word analogies.
- **Media Skills:** Develop, write, and revise a multimedia presentation.
- **Listening and Speaking Skills:** Present and evaluate an oral recitation of literature.

Minimum Course of Study

Most skills can be taught with a minimum number of selections and features. In the chart to the right, lessons highlighted in green constitute the minimum course of study that provides coverage of the skills taught in Collection 6.

Selection ▪ Feature	Literary Skills
Contemporary Literature: 1939 to Present *by* John Leggett, Susan Allen Toth, John Malcolm Brinnin, *and* Thomas Hernacki	• Evaluate genres and traditions in American literature
Introducing Political Points of View: World War II	
Main Readings: • The Death of the Ball Turret Gunner *by* Randall Jarrell ↔ *at grade level*	• Analyze implied metaphor
• *from* Night *by* Elie Wiesel ↔ *at grade level* • A Noiseless Flash *from* Hiroshima *by* John Hersey ↔ *at grade level*	• Analyze subjective and objective report
• "The Arrogance and Cruelty of Power" *from* Speech at the Nuremberg Trials, November 21, 1945 *by* Robert H. Jackson ↑ *above grade level*	• Analyze persuasion and argument
Connected Readings: • *from* The Diary of a Young Girl *by* Anne Frank ↔ *at grade level* • "The Biggest Battle of All History" *by* John Whitehead *from* The Greatest Generation Speaks *by* Tom Brokaw ↔ *at grade level* • *from* April in Germany *by* Margaret Bourke-White ↓ *below grade level*	

Resource Manager

(see pp. 790I–790P)

Lesson and workshop resources are referenced in the Resource Manager on the pages that follow. These resources can be used to reinforce the skills taught in Collection 6, remediate students who are having difficulty, and provide supporting activities for English-language learners.

Reading Skills	Vocabulary Skills	Writing ▪ Grammar and Language ▪ Listening and Speaking Skills
• Analyze credibility		• Write a multimedia report • Write a historical research report
• Analyze a writer's message • Read closely for details	• Understand connotations of synonyms • Demonstrate word knowledge • Understand denotations and connotations • Understand etymologies of words used in political science and history	• Write an essay comparing and connecting texts • Write an essay analyzing suspense • Write an essay extending a statement from the text

(continued)

Scope and Sequence

Selection ▪ Feature	Literary Skills	Reading Skills
CONTEMPORARY FICTION		
Speaking of Courage *by Tim O' Brien* ↔ *at grade level*	• Analyze external and internal conflict • Analyze historical context	• Use context clues
Game *by Donald Barthelme* ↔ *at grade level*	• Analyze theme and title • Understand satire	
Everything Stuck to Him *by Raymond Carver* ↔ *at grade level*	• Analyze a writer's style	• Analyze questions about characters
Daughter of Invention *by Julia Alvarez* ↔ *at grade level*	• Analyze external and internal conflict	• Make inferences about characters
Literature of the Americas: Colombia The Handsomest Drowned Man in the World *by Gabriel García Márquez* ↔ *at grade level*	• Analyze use of magic realism	
Rules of the Game *from* The Joy Luck Club *by Amy Tan* ↔ *at grade level*	• Analyze motivation	
When Mr. Pirzada Came to Dine *by Jhumpa Lahiri* ↔ *at grade level*	• Analyze theme and conflict	
The Book of the Dead *by Edwidge Danticat* ↔ *at grade level*	• Analyze irony, including verbal, situational, and dramatic irony	
Writing Mini-Workshop *Writing an Autobiographical Narrative*		
CONTEMPORARY NONFICTION		
from Black Boy *by Richard Wright* ↔ *at grade level*	• Analyze dialogue in nonfiction	
The Girl Who Wouldn't Talk *from* The Woman Warrior *by Maxine Hong Kingston* ↔ *at grade level*	• Analyze characterization	• Make inferences about characters

Vocabulary Skills	Writing ▪ Grammar and Language ▪ Listening and Speaking Skills
• Write an essay comparing and contrasting two characters	• Write an essay explaining the use of contrast in a story
• Recognize synonyms	• Write an essay analyzing two literary characters
• Use words in context	• Write an essay explaining a statement in a text • Write an interior monologue • Use verb tenses correctly
• Demonstrate word knowledge	• Write an essay analyzing conflict in a story
• Demonstrate word knowledge	• Write an expository essay • Write an essay analyzing the use of magic realism in a story
• Demonstrate word knowledge	• Write an essay describing two literary characters in another context • Write an autobiographical narrative • Use transitional expressions to connect ideas
• Create semantic maps • Understand and use analogies	• Write a historical research report • Write an essay comparing two stories
• Demonstrate word knowledge	• Write an essay analyzing theme in a story
	• Write an autobiographical narrative
• Understand synonyms	• Write an essay analyzing a character • Use parallel structure
• Complete word analogies	• Write a character analysis

Scope and Sequence

Selection ▪ Feature	Literary Skills	Reading Skills
from The Way to Rainy Mountain *by* N. Scott Momaday ↑ *above grade level*	• Analyze setting	• Identify main ideas and supporting details
from In Search of Our Mothers' Gardens *by* Alice Walker ↔ *at grade level*	• Analyze a personal, or informal, essay	• Analyze the main idea
Autobiographical Notes *by* James Baldwin ↔ *at grade level*	• Analyze tone	• Evaluate an author's arguments
Straw into Gold *by* Sandra Cisneros ↔ *at grade level*	• Analyze allusion	• Analyze a writer's background
Writing Mini-Workshop *Analyzing Nonfiction*		
CONTEMPORARY POETRY		
Night Journey *by* Theodore Roethke ↔ *at grade level*	• Analyze rhyme and rhythm	
The Beautiful Changes *by* Richard Wilbur ↔ *at grade level*	• Analyze ambiguity	
The Fish	• Analyze symbols	
One Art *by* Elizabeth Bishop ↔ *at grade level*	• Analyze a villanelle	
Mirror Mushrooms *by* Sylvia Plath ↔ *at grade level*	• Analyze a poem's speaker • Analyze tone	
The Bells Young *by* Anne Sexton ↔ *at grade level*	• Analyze imagery	

Vocabulary Skills	Writing ▪ Grammar and Language ▪ Listening and Speaking Skills
• Demonstrate word knowledge	• Write a description of a setting
• Create word histories	• Write a personal essay • Write a summary evaluating the personal essay
• Demonstrate word knowledge	• Write an essay containing an assertion
• Demonstrate word knowledge	• Write an essay exploring the impact of a writer's background on her work
	• Write an essay analyzing nonfiction
	• Write an essay comparing two poems • Perform an oral recitation of a poem
	• Write an essay evaluating a writer's comment • Write three lines of a poem
	• Write a narration of a poem • Write a villanelle
	• Write a poem in the voice of an object • Write an essay comparing tone in different texts
	• Write a poem or a paragraph containing visual images • Perform an oral recitation of a poem

Selection ▪ Feature	Planning	Differentiating Instruction ▪ Lesson Plans with ELL Strategies and Practice	Reading ▪ Vocabulary
Contemporary Literature: 1939 to Present *by* John Leggett, Susan Allen Toth, John Malcolm Brinnin, *and* Thomas Hernacki		• Holt Adapted Reader	• Holt Adapted Reader
Introducing Political Points of View: World War II **Main Readings:** • The Death of the Ball Turret Gunner *by* Randall Jarrell • *from* Night *by* Elie Wiesel • A Noiseless Flash *from* Hiroshima *by* John Hersey • "The Arrogance and Cruelty of Power" from Speech at the Nuremberg Trials, November 21, 1945 *by* Robert H. Jackson **Connected Readings:** • *from* The Diary of a Young Girl *by* Anne Frank • "The Biggest Battle of All History" *by* John Whitehead *from* The Greatest Generation Speaks *by* Tom Brokaw • *from* April in Germany *by* Margaret Bourke-White	• One-Stop Planner with ExamView Test Generator	• The Holt Reader • Holt Reading Solutions: Lesson Plans • Supporting Instruction in Spanish • Audio CD Library, discs 20, 21 NOTE: Allselections appear on • Audio CD Library, Selections and Summaries in Spanish	• The Holt Reader • Holt Reading Solutions • Vocabulary Development, pp. 45, 46, 47
CONTEMPORARY FICTION			
Speaking of Courage *by* Tim O'Brien	• One-Stop Planner with ExamView Test Generator	• The Holt Reader • Supporting Instruction in Spanish • Audio CD Library, disc 22	• The Holt Reader • Vocabulary Development, p. 48
Game *by* Donald Barthelme	• One-Stop Planner with ExamView Test Generator • PowerNotes: Satire and Irony	• The Holt Reader • Supporting Instruction in Spanish • Audio CD Library, disc 22	• The Holt Reader • Vocabulary Development, p. 49

The Holt Reader

The Holt Reader is a consumable paperback book which can be used alone or to accompany *Elements of Literature*. It offers guided support throughout the reading process and encourages students to become active readers by circling, underlining, questioning, and jotting down responses as they read. *The Holt Reader* works well for homework, students who have missed class, additional instructional time, reteaching, and remediation.

Holt Reading Solutions (HRS)

Holt Reading Solutions pulls together reading resources in the *Elements of Literature* program to create a powerful tool for intervention and whole-class instruction. *HRS* includes diagnostic assessment tools, lesson plans for English-language learners and special education students, adaptations of selected reading selections, vocabulary and comprehension worksheets, information on phonics and decoding, and additional instruction and practice in remedial reading skills.

Writing ▪ Grammar and Language ▪ Listening and Speaking	Assessment
• Daily Language Activities	• Holt Assessment: Literature, Reading, and Vocabulary • Holt Online Assessment • One-Stop Planner with ExamView Test Generator
	• Holt Assessment: Literature, Reading, and Vocabulary • Holt Online Assessment • One-Stop Planner with ExamView Test Generator
	• Holt Assessment: Literature, Reading, and Vocabulary • Holt Online Assessment • One-Stop Planner with ExamView Test Generator

Technology

INTERNET

- go.hrw.com
- Holt Online Assessment
- Holt Online Essay Scoring
- Elements of Literature Online

MEDIA

 • One-Stop Planner with ExamView Test Generator

 • PowerNotes

 • Audio CD Library, discs 20–27

 • Audio CD Library, Selections and Summaries in Spanish

 • Visual Connections Videocassette Program, Segment 10

 • Fine Art Transparencies, 16, 17

 Transparency   Video

 CD-ROM Audio CD

One-Stop Planner with ExamView Test Generator

The *One-Stop Planner* CD-ROM contains electronic versions of print-based teaching resources, clips from the video program, and valuable assessment tools. The *One-Stop Planner* resources are presented in easy-to-follow, point-and-click menu formats. To preview resources or print out worksheets and tests, you simply make a selection and click.

 One-Stop Planner CD-ROM

Selection ▪ Feature	Planning	Differentiating Instruction ▪ Lesson Plans with ELL Strategies and Practice	Reading ▪ Vocabulary
The Memory of Elena *by* Carolyn Forché	• One-Stop Planner with ExamView Test Generator	• The Holt Reader • Supporting Instruction in Spanish • Audio CD Library, disc 27	• The Holt Reader
Literature of the Americas: El Salvador Ars Poetica *by* Claribel Alegría	• One-Stop Planner with ExamView Test Generator	• The Holt Reader • Supporting Instruction in Spanish • Audio CD Library, disc 27	• The Holt Reader
The Latin Deli: An Ars Poetica *by* Judith Ortiz Cofer	• One-Stop Planner with ExamView Test Generator	• The Holt Reader • Holt Reading Solutions: Lesson Plans • Supporting Instruction in Spanish • Audio CD Library, disc 27	• The Holt Reader • Holt Reading Solutions
Testimonial *by* Rita Dove	• One-Stop Planner with ExamView Test Generator	• The Holt Reader • Supporting Instruction in Spanish • Audio CD Library, disc 27	• The Holt Reader
Coastal *by* Mark Doty	• One-Stop Planner with ExamView Test Generator	• The Holt Reader • Supporting Instruction in Spanish • Audio CD Library, disc 27	• The Holt Reader
Visions and Interpretations *by* Li-Young Lee	• One-Stop Planner with ExamView Test Generator	• The Holt Reader • Supporting Instruction in Spanish • Audio CD Library, disc 27	• The Holt Reader
Medusa *by* Agha Shahid Ali	• One-Stop Planner with ExamView Test Generator	• The Holt Reader • Supporting Instruction in Spanish • Audio CD Library, disc 27	• The Holt Reader
Man Listening to Disc *by* Billy Collins	• One-Stop Planner with ExamView Test Generator	• The Holt Reader • Supporting Instruction in Spanish • Audio CD Library, disc 27	• The Holt Reader
Media Workshop: *Analyzing and Using Media*	• One-Stop Planner with ExamView Test Generator	• Workshop Resources: Writing, Listening, and Speaking • Supporting Instruction in Spanish	
Listening and Speaking Workshop: *Reciting Literature*	• One-Stop Planner with ExamView Test Generator	• Workshop Resources: Writing, Listening, and Speaking • Supporting Instruction in Spanish	
Skills Review: *Literary Skills* *Vocabulary Skills* *Writing Skills*			

Writing ▪ Grammar and Language ▪ Listening and Speaking	Assessment
	• Holt Assessment: Literature, Reading, and Vocabulary • Holt Online Assessment • One-Stop Planner with ExamView Test Generator
	• Holt Assessment: Literature, Reading, and Vocabulary • Holt Online Assessment • One-Stop Planner with ExamView Test Generator
	• Holt Assessment: Literature, Reading, and Vocabulary • Holt Online Assessment • One-Stop Planner with ExamView Test Generator
	• Holt Assessment: Literature, Reading, and Vocabulary • Holt Online Assessment • One-Stop Planner with ExamView Test Generator
	• Holt Assessment: Literature, Reading, and Vocabulary • Holt Online Assessment • One-Stop Planner with ExamView Test Generator
	• Holt Assessment: Literature, Reading, and Vocabulary • Holt Online Assessment • One-Stop Planner with ExamView Test Generator
	• Holt Assessment: Literature, Reading, and Vocabulary • Holt Online Assessment • One-Stop Planner with ExamView Test Generator
	• Holt Assessment: Literature, Reading, and Vocabulary • Holt Online Assessment • One-Stop Planner with ExamView Test Generator
• Daily Language Activities • Workshop Resources: Writing, Listening, and Speaking	• Holt Assessment: Writing, Listening, and Speaking • Holt Online Assessment • One-Stop Planner with ExamView Test Generator
• Workshop Resources: Writing, Listening, and Speaking	• Holt Assessment: Writing, Listening, and Speaking • Holt Online Assessment • One-Stop Planner with ExamView Test Generator
	• Holt Assessment: Writing, Listening, and Speaking • One-Stop Planner with ExamView Test Generator

Technology

INTERNET

- go.hrw.com
- Holt Online Assessment
- Holt Online Essay Scoring
- Elements of Literature Online

MEDIA

 • One-Stop Planner with ExamView Test Generator

 • PowerNotes

• Audio CD Library, discs 20–27

• Audio CD Library, Selections and Summaries in Spanish

• Visual Connections Videocassette Program, Segment 10

• Fine Art Transparencies, 16, 17

Transparency   Video

CD-ROM   Audio CD

Collection 6

INTRODUCING THE COLLECTION

Collection 6 begins with an opportunity for students to analyze political points of view of a selection of works about World War II. The rest of the collection is divided into studies of contemporary literature by genre: beginning with the fiction of such new voices as Jhumpa Lahiri and Amy Tan. In the nonfiction subcollection, students will read works by James Baldwin and Richard Wright and master the skills of analyzing an author's argument. In the collection of contemporary poetry, students will find a wide range of poets from Anne Sexton and Sylvia Plath to Agha Shahid Ali and Billy Collins. Collection 6 ends with a media workshop on analyzing and using media.

VIEWING THE ART

Much of the tension in the art of the twentieth century has arisen from the struggle between figuration and abstraction—the portrayal of recognizable forms versus the non-representational arrangement of paint on a canvas. **Richard Diebenkorn** (1922–1993), one of the best-known artists to emerge from California, explored this issue in compelling ways. Beginning as an abstract expressionist, Diebenkorn shifted to painting figurative works in the 1950s—but retained some of the compositional developments of his earlier style. Then, beginning in 1967, Diebenkorn made another major stylistic transition. He departed from his figurative style in a series of paintings known as the Ocean Park series in reference to the Santa Monica neighborhood in which he lived. These paintings use networks of lines, shape, and color to negotiate and define spaces linked to the landscape of the American West.

Activity. What sort of landscape does this remind you of? [Possible response: It is reminiscent of land seen from above, as from an airplane.]

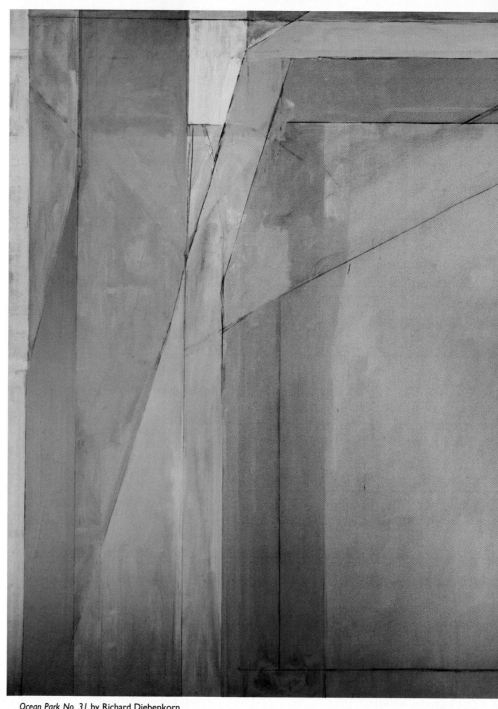

Ocean Park No. 31 by Richard Diebenkorn.

COLLECTION 6 RESOURCES: READING

Planning
- *One-Stop Planner* CD-ROM with ExamView Test Generator

Differentiating Instruction
- *The Holt Reader*
- *Holt Adapted Reader*
- *Holt Reading Solutions*
- *Family Involvement Activities in English and Spanish*

- *Supporting Instruction in Spanish*
- *Audio CD Library, Selections and Summaries in Spanish*

Vocabulary
- *Vocabulary Development*

Grammar and Language
- *Language Handbook Worksheets*
- *Daily Language Activities*

Collection 6

Contemporary Literature 1939 to Present

You can't say it that way any more.

—John Ashbery

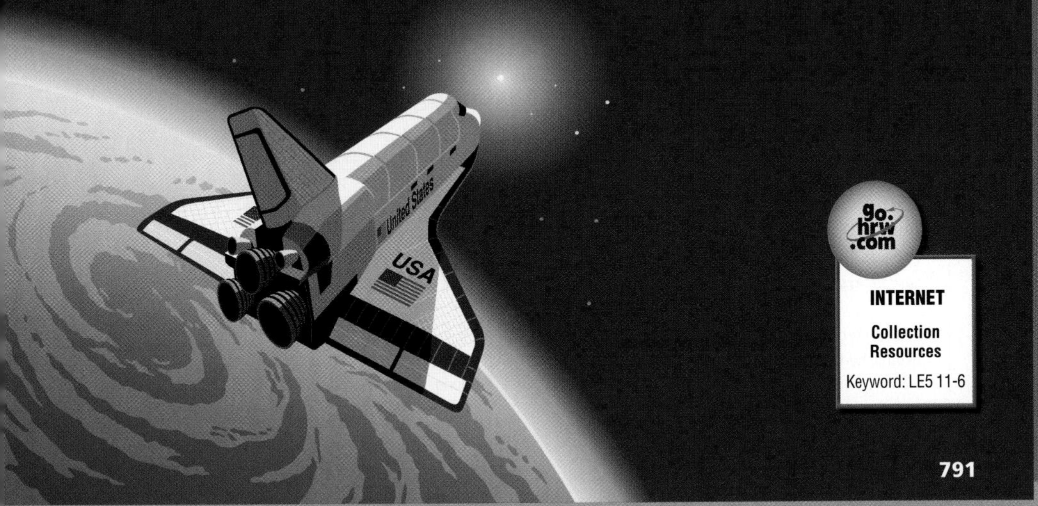

go.hrw.com

INTERNET

Collection Resources

Keyword: LE5 11-6

THE QUOTATION

The miracles and horrors made possible by twentieth-century technological advances, particularly since World War II, made Americans feel especially cut off from the past. Ask students what Ashbery might mean by "any more" and whether they agree with him that a new consciousness calls for a new way of communicating. [Possible response: "Any more" could refer to the present time, in which people live with phenomena like the threat of nuclear war, rapid mass communication, and space travel. This new reality has altered people's sense of space and time, and it cannot be adequately described by earlier modes of communication.]

Assessment

- *Holt Assessment: Literature, Reading, and Vocabulary*
- *One-Stop Planner* CD-ROM with ExamView Test Generator
- *Holt Online Assessment*

Internet

- go.hrw.com (Keyword: LE5 11-6)
- *Elements of Literature Online*

Media

- *Audio CD Library*
- *Audio CD Library, Selections and Summaries in Spanish*
- *Fine Art Transparencies*
- *Visual Connections Videocassette Program*

Time Line

■ 1959
Lorraine Hansberry

Lorraine Hansberry died from cancer in 1965, at the age of thirty-four, just six years after winning the New York Drama Critics Circle Award for her first completed play, *A Raisin in the Sun.* Two other Hansberry plays, *The Sign in Sidney Brustein's Window* and *Les Blancs,* were published, and most of her other writings later appeared in the book *To Be Young, Gifted, and Black.* Students might also wish to read *Young, Black, and Determined: A Biography of Lorraine Hansberry* written by Pat McKissack in 1998.

■ 1963
Dr. Martin Luther King, Jr.

Dr. Martin Luther King, Jr.'s "I Have a Dream" speech reached an audience of more than 200,000 people gathered in Washington, D.C., in a passionate demonstration for civil rights and racial justice, and millions more watching on television. Standing on the steps of the Lincoln Memorial, King proclaimed the need for change through nonviolent political action and peaceful demonstration. He said, "I have a dream that one day this nation will rise up and live out the true meaning of its creed: 'We hold these truths to be self-evident; that all men are created equal.'" King's efforts helped bring about the passage of the Civil Rights Act of 1964 and the Voting Rights Act of 1965, two landmark pieces of legislation designed to guarantee all Americans equal access to the political process, regardless of color or creed. King was awarded the Nobel Peace Prize in 1964.

Contemporary Literature
1939 to Present

LITERARY EVENTS

1940

1940 Richard Wright publishes his brutal novel *Native Son*

1945 Tennessee Williams's memory play *The Glass Menagerie* opens on Broadway

Tennessee Williams.

1946 William Carlos Williams publishes the first part of his long poem *Paterson*

1948 William Faulkner publishes *Intruder in the Dust,* about the growing moral awareness of a white boy in the South

1949 Arthur Miller's tragedy *Death of a Salesman* opens

1950

1951 J. D. Salinger publishes his novel *The Catcher in the Rye*

1952 Ralph Ellison publishes his novel *Invisible Man*

1959 Lorraine Hansberry's play *A Raisin in the Sun* opens

1960 Harper Lee publishes her novel *To Kill a Mockingbird*

1962 John Steinbeck wins the Nobel Prize in literature

1965 *The Autobiography of Malcolm X* is published

1966 Truman Capote publishes his "nonfiction novel," *In Cold Blood*

1967 Colombian writer Gabriel García Márquez publishes *One Hundred Years of Solitude*

POLITICAL AND SOCIAL EVENTS

1940

1941 U.S. enters World War II after Japan attacks Pearl Harbor, Hawaii

1944 Allies begin final drive against German forces on D-day, June 6

May 1945 Germany surrenders

1945 United States explodes atomic bombs over Hiroshima (August 6) and Nagasaki (August 9); Japan surrenders (August 14)

1945 United Nations is established

1950 Senator Joseph McCarthy charges that 205 Communists have infiltrated the State Department

1953 Korean War ends with division of the country into North Korea and South Korea

1954 U.S. Supreme Court rules that segregation in public schools is unconstitutional

1957 Soviet Union launches first artificial satellite, *Sputnik I,* beginning the "space race" with the United States

1960

1961 U.S. invasion of Bay of Pigs, in Cuba, fails

1963 Martin Luther King, Jr., delivers "I Have a Dream" speech during the March on Washington

1963 President John F. Kennedy is assassinated

1964 An estimated 73 million viewers tune in to *The Ed Sullivan Show* to watch the North American debut of the Beatles

1965 U.S. involvement in the Vietnam War escalates

1969 Two U.S. astronauts become the first human beings to walk on the moon

Edwin "Buzz" Aldrin, Jr. (July 20, 1969).

Using the Time Line

Activity. Divide students into small groups, and instruct each group to choose one of the following categories: U.S. politics, geopolitics, economics, sociocultural trends, scientific developments, or artistic achievements. Have each group identify the events from the political and social portion of the Time Line that fall into their particular category. (Accept some overlap among categories as long as the students can justify their classifications.) Have the groups share their classifications with the class. Then, ask each group to select two events and collaborate on writing a paragraph that answers the following question for each event: How would the world be different today if this event had never happened? Have groups share their paragraphs and discuss them in class.

Time Line

1980		**2000**	
1970 Maya Angelou publishes her autobiography *I Know Why the Caged Bird Sings*	**1981** John Updike publishes his third "Rabbit" novel, *Rabbit Is Rich*	**1990** Tim O'Brien publishes *The Things They Carried*	**2000** Jhumpa Lahiri wins the Pulitzer Prize for her short story collection *Interpreter of Maladies*
1975 E. L. Doctorow publishes *Ragtime,* a novel mixing fictional and real characters	**1982** Alice Walker publishes her novel *The Color Purple*	**1991** Sandra Cisneros publishes a story collection called *Woman Hollering Creek*	**2001** Billy Collins is named U.S. poet laureate
1976 Alex Haley publishes *Roots,* a fictional history of his family, beginning with its African origins	**1983** Raymond Carver publishes *Cathedral,* a collection of short stories	**1993** Toni Morrison wins the Nobel Prize in literature	
	1989 Amy Tan publishes *The Joy Luck Club*		

American soldiers in Vietnam.

1980		**2000**	
1973 Peace treaty provides for a cease-fire in Vietnam and withdrawal of U.S. forces	**1985** Era of great change in the Soviet Union begins as Mikhail Gorbachev rises to power	**1990** West Germany and East Germany unite	**2001** Terrorist attacks at the World Trade Center in New York, at the Pentagon in Washington, D.C., and in a plane crash in Pennsylvania kill thousands
1974 Watergate scandal forces Richard M. Nixon to resign as president of the United States	**1986** U.S. space shuttle *Challenger* explodes soon after liftoff	**1990–1991** Iraq invades Kuwait but is forced to retreat by the U.S.-led Operation Desert Storm	
1979 Iranian militants seize the U.S. embassy in Tehran and take fifty-two American hostages, beginning a 444-day "hostage crisis"	**1987** U.S. and Soviet Union sign a treaty reducing medium-range nuclear weapons	**1991** Soviet Union is dissolved	
	1989 Berlin Wall is knocked down	**1995** Bomb explosion kills 168 at the Murrah Federal Building in Oklahoma City, Oklahoma	
1979 Soviet Union invades Afghanistan	**1989** Pro-democracy demonstrations are crushed in Tiananmen Square, Beijing	**2001** American veteran Timothy McVeigh is executed for the bombing of the federal building in Oklahoma City	

Contemporary Literature: 1939 to Present   **793**

Activity. To involve students with the Time Line, ask the following questions:

- What events in the 1960s and '70s involved the United States in long-term foreign entanglements? [the Vietnam War and the Iranian hostage crisis]

- Who are the authors of *In Cold Blood* and *Ragtime,* and what do these two works have in common? [Truman Capote wrote *In Cold Blood* and E.L. Doctorow wrote *Ragtime.* Both mix fiction and nonfiction.]

- Which American wars are noted on this Time Line, and when did the U.S. involvement in each end? [World War II, 1945; the Korean War, 1953; the Vietnam War, 1973; Operation Desert Storm (the Gulf War), 1991]

■ **1979–1981**
Iranian Hostage Crisis

In 1979, the Ayatollah Ruhollah Khomeini led Islamic fundamentalists in ousting the shah of Iran from power. The shah had created many enemies in Iran because of his secular, pro-Western policies and his government's abuse of human rights. While the shah's thirty-eight years in power were hardly democratic, his regime was characterized by technological advances and an expansion of women's rights. Largely reversing the shah's changes, the Ayatollah Khomeini declared Iran an Islamic state, with laws based on Islamic teachings. When the shah fled to the United States, militants seized the U.S. embassy in Tehran and took a large group of U.S. citizens hostage, refusing to release them until the shah was returned for trial. The United States refused, and the hostage crisis ensued. The shah died of cancer six months before the hostages were finally returned in January 1981, on the day of President Ronald Reagan's inauguration.

■ **1991**
Dissolution of the Soviet Union

In August 1991, Soviet President Mikhail Gorbachev survived an attempted coup by his country's Communist hardliners. Days after he reassumed power, Gorbachev dramatically swept away much of the institutional clout of the Communist Party in the Soviet Union, enacting measures that made the nation's government separate from the Party apparatus. Gorbachev did not abolish Communism, but he weakened it considerably. The tide of change moved swiftly, and Gorbachev himself was unable to stay ahead of it. By December 1991, various Soviet republics created the Commonwealth of Independent States in part of the former Soviet Union. On December 25, Gorbachev resigned as president of the Soviet Union, which by then no longer existed. He was soon replaced by Boris Yeltsin as the nation's political leader.

Political and Social Milestones

■ 1939–1945
World War II

On Sunday morning, December 7, 1941, Japanese warplanes attacked the United States naval base at Pearl Harbor in Hawaii. Until that attack, the United States had remained technically neutral in World War II, although the nation had provided financial support to the forces fighting against Germany, Italy, and Japan. The United States had also frozen Japanese assets and maintained an embargo against selling essential war goods, such as petroleum, to Japan. These actions prompted the Japanese government to regard the United States as a hostile power. Before the attack on Pearl Harbor, the war had been seen by many Americans as a foreign problem. This attitude melted in the outrage over Japan's attack, which killed 2,395 Americans and destroyed or damaged 21 ships and 323 aircraft.

■ 1945–1991
The Cold War

The most tense moment of the cold war was during the Cuban Missile Crisis in October 1962. Three years before, Cuban revolutionary Fidel Castro had established a Communist government allied with the Soviet bloc. The Soviet premier Nikita Khrushchev had promised to protect Cuba against its superpower neighbor, and U.S.-Cuban hostility deepened in 1961 after the Kennedy administration's ill-fated attack on Cuba at the Bay of Pigs. In August 1962, U.S. reconnaissance flights revealed that the Soviet Union was building missile sites in Cuba. President Kennedy called on the Soviet Union to dismantle the bases. He declared a naval quarantine around Cuba to prevent the delivery of "offensive weapons." No Soviet ships tried to enter the quarantine zone, and eventually Khruschev ordered that the missile bases be dismantled.

World War II, 1939–1945

The second great war of the twentieth century officially began in 1939, when Britain and France declared war on Germany after Hitler's armies invaded Poland. The United States was drawn into the conflict in 1941, when Japan bombed the U.S. naval base at Pearl Harbor, in Hawaii. By the time the war ended, in 1945 (after the United States dropped atomic bombs that wasted two Japanese cities), the conflict had become global.

Hiroshima, Japan, after the atomic bombing (1945).

The Cold War, 1945–1991

The United States emerged from World War II an economic and political powerhouse, but U.S. dominance did not go unchallenged for long. Soon after the war ended, the Soviet Union seized control of most of Eastern Europe and installed one-party Communist governments behind what Winston Churchill called an "iron curtain."

With the Soviet Union's development of nuclear weapons in the 1950s and 1960s, the ideological conflict between the United States and the Soviet Union hardened into a long and expensive arms race. Smaller countries, such as Korea and Vietnam, became bloody battlegrounds on which the great powers played out their rivalries in a standoff dubbed the cold war.

In the late 1980s, the Soviet Union began to unravel. In 1991, under the combined weight of Western pressure and internal failures, it collapsed. A new Russian republic with democratic aspirations (and plenty of domestic problems) took its place. Suddenly all over Eastern Europe the iron curtain lifted.

Milestones 1939 to Present

The Digital Revolution and Economic Prosperity

In the second half of the twentieth century, life for the average American may well have been most profoundly changed by the introduction of computer technology into daily life. In the 1950s and 1960s, business and government were revolutionized by giant mainframe computers, which made quick electronic storage and retrieval of vast amounts of data possible for the first time. Then, in the 1980s and 1990s, desktop computers began to appear in offices, schools, and homes. Yet more changes came in the late 1990s, when Internet communication and wireless telephone technology promised to keep Americans constantly connected. All of these innovations fueled a surge in the stock market in the 1990s, which, like all giddy upturns, ended with a thud in the spring of 2000. The greatest period of economic prosperity was sputtering out when, on September 11, 2001, foreign terrorists carried out the worst attack on native soil in our history.

President Reagan, a bust of Lenin behind him, speaks at Moscow State University (1988).

■ The Digital Revolution and Economic Prosperity

On September 11, 2001, hijackers took control of four commercial airliners in the United States, crashing two of them into the twin towers of the World Trade Center in New York City and one into the Pentagon in Washington, D.C. The fourth plane crashed in Pennsylvania, the hijackers' plans probably thwarted by the resistance of the passengers. The attack, which killed nearly three thousand civilians and wiped out a section of the New York City skyline, was a damaging blow to the country's flagging economy.

Grade-Level Skills

■ **Literary Skills**
Evaluate the philosophical, political, religious, ethical, and social influences of the historical period.

Preview

Think About . . .

Ask students to list the headings they find, both major and secondary. (For example, "Contemporary Fiction: Diversity and Vitality" on p. 802 is a major heading, followed by a secondary heading, "Perspectives in Postmodern Fiction.") Then, have students write a question about each major section of the essay.

DIRECT TEACHING

A **Background**

The Atomic Bomb

When the atomic bomb was detonated over Hiroshima, nearly every building within a half-mile radius of ground zero (directly below the detonation) was demolished. Twelve-inch-thick brick walls a mile away were cracked and homes two miles away were severely damaged. About 92,000 people died in the blast, and many more died later as a result of burns and radioactive fallout.

Contemporary Literature
1939 to Present

by John Leggett, Susan Allen Toth, John Malcolm Brinnin, *and* Thomas Hernacki

P R E V I E W

Think About . . .

During the second half of the twentieth century, the United States emerged victorious from two wars, one hot and one cold. In the final decades of the century, however, when the United States was the undisputed military and economic leader of the world, American culture seemed unwilling to identify exclusively with any one group or class. America's emphasis on cultural and ethnic inclusion is reflected in the postmodern literature of the period.

As you read this introduction to the contemporary period, look for answers to these questions:

● How did rapid developments in technology after World War II affect everyday life?

● What does *postmodern* mean?

● How did political and economic development shape people's lives in the second half of the twentieth century?

A On August 6, 1945, at 8:15 A.M., an atomic bomb was dropped on the Japanese city of Hiroshima from the U.S. airplane *Enola Gay.* Within seconds the center of Hiroshima had disappeared. The bomb in effect ended World War II, and its mushroom cloud has cast a shadow over every generation since.

Although many Americans disapproved of the use of the atomic bomb to end World War II, most agreed with the purpose of the war itself. They were fighting against tyranny, against regimes that would destroy the American way of life. Only twenty years later, however, the United States became deeply involved in another overseas war—this time in Vietnam—that would sharply divide the nation. In the 1960s, demonstrations against the government, both peaceful and violent, became commonplace.

To some writers the madness of the war-torn world was an inescapable condition of modern life, and the only appropriate response was hard-edged laughter at life's tragic ironies. The term *gallows humor*—ironic humor arising from an acknowledgment of

SKILLS FOCUS

Collection introduction (pages 796–809) covers
Literary Skills
Evaluate genres and traditions in American literature.

DIFFERENTIATING INSTRUCTION

Learners Having Difficulty
Have students survey the essay before they read it, noting the major divisions and special features. Explain that the section "A Closer Look: Social Influences" is related to the essay but is not part of the essay itself, as are the other boxed features, which are primarily quotations. Then, as they read, encourage students to write a one- or two-sentence summary for each of the essay's major sections.

English-Language Learners
Have students create a glossary of words relating to contemporary literature and culture. Encourage them to use an unabridged or college dictionary to define the terms. When they have finished, ask them to review their glossaries with a partner to make sure that they have correctly spelled and defined the words and know how to pronounce them.

Advanced Learners
Enrichment. Have students research and report on one contemporary literary technique or cultural movement. Students might consider magic realism, feminist criticism, cultural literacy, semiotics, or new historicism. Skimming an encyclopedia of contemporary culture will increase students' awareness of movements or techniques to research.

The Whitney Museum of American Art, New York.

War Series: Victory (1947) by Jacob Lawrence. Egg tempera on board (20″ × 16″).

Contemporary Literature: 1939 to Present   **797**

DIRECT TEACHING

VIEWING THE ART

Jacob Lawrence (1917–2000) established himself as one of the country's leading African American artists with his 1941 *Migration* series, but his career was temporarily interrupted by World War II. Drafted into the Coast Guard, he served on the first integrated ship in the Navy, where his captain allowed him time to pursue his art. After the war, Lawrence received a Guggenheim fellowship and used it to develop his war series. Many African Americans served during the Second World War in segregated units; as a result of their heroism, immediately after the war racial policies were reconsidered and the armed forces were gradually integrated. This integration formed an important prelude to the integration of American society at large.

CONTENT-AREA CONNECTIONS

History: The Atomic Bomb

Explain that the first atomic bomb was developed by a team of American and European scientists working for the U.S. government during World War II. The project was called the Manhattan Project. The government was motivated by its belief that the Nazis were also working on such a weapon. However, the war in Europe ended in April 1945, before either side developed a workable bomb. The fact that the atomic bomb was used against Japanese civilians, rather than against Hitler's Nazis, upset a number of the scientists whose opposition to Hitler had been their prime justification for developing such a terrible weapon.

A Exploring the Historical Period
WATERGATE'S AFTERMATH

President Richard M. Nixon, a Republican, resigned from office on August 9, 1974, after the House Judiciary Committee voted to recommend three articles of impeachment against him. These articles were based on evidence from the Watergate scandal, which began with the arrest and conviction of several of Nixon's 1972 campaign employees—for an attempted burglary at the Democratic Party's national headquarters in the Watergate office–apartment house complex in Washington, D.C. Nixon was charged with obstructing justice, abusing presidential powers, and disobeying subpoenas.

B Exploring the Historical Period
THE CONTINUING NUCLEAR THREAT

Nuclear capability is no longer limited to two superpowers. Now, other nations, such as India and Pakistan, have tested nuclear weapons, greatly complicating international relations.

C Reading Skills

❓ **Making judgments.** According to John Updike, what is the role of the artist in society? Do you agree? [Possible responses: The artist's creation provides an alternative vision to an unsettled world; the artist helps society see positive meaning in the uncertainty and chaos of historical change. Students may agree with Updike, or they may feel that artists, more than other people, tend to delight in change and upheaval for their own sake.]

A CLOSER LOOK

This feature describes how Americans adapted to living under the shadow of nuclear war in the 1950s and '60s, particularly by constructing bomb shelters.

Toppled statue of the Soviet dictator Joseph Stalin, Russia (1991).

> At all times, an old world is collapsing and a new world arising; we have better eyes for the collapse than the rise, for the old one is the world we know. The artist, in focusing on his creation, finds, and offers, relief from the tension and sadness of being burdened not just with consciousness but with historical consciousness.
>
> —John Updike, from *Hugging the Shore*

the absurd or grotesque—was often used to describe the work of writers who flourished after World War II. In the works of writers like Tim O'Brien (page 865), madness and war are inextricably mixed, not because madness is a result of war but because war is the result of madness.

The 1970s saw the winding down of the Vietnam War, but another focus of disillusionment filled the news: the Watergate scandal, which in 1974 forced the only resignation of a U.S. president, Richard M. Nixon.

Then came the 1980s, which many Americans now regard as the time of the "me generation," when individual enjoyment and material success seemed to overshadow other concerns. As the 1980s ended, so did the cold war, the struggle between the United States and the Soviet Union that had dominated international politics since shortly after the end of World War II. The Soviet Union collapsed as its republics and satellite nations declared independence. The end of the cold war reduced but did not end the threat of nuclear violence.

A CLOSER LOOK: SOCIAL INFLUENCES

Atomic Anxiety

INFORMATIONAL TEXT

Things are probably going to look different when you get outside.

—from *How to Survive an Atomic Bomb* (1950)

Americans testing a bomb-shelter escape hatch (1952), Bronxville, New York.

CONTENT-AREA CONNECTIONS

Science: Nuclear Power in Daily Life
Individual activity. Have interested students research and report on the ways in which nuclear power is being used to improve people's lives. Students might consider such topics as the use of nuclear energy to provide electricity and the use of nuclear technology in medicine.

Science: NASA in Space
Individual activity. Encourage students to visit the Web site of the National Aeronautics and Space Administration (NASA) to learn more about its extraordinary accomplishments since the 1969 moon landing. They might explore topics such as other moon landings, the investigations of the surface of Mars, the Hubble Telescope, the space shuttle program, communications satellites, and deep-space probes.

Nuclear explosion in the Nevada desert (1955).

In many ways the nuclear bomb is the dramatic symbol of the last half of the twentieth century. Its infamous mushroom cloud represents the triumph of science and technology, the purpose of which was, ironically enough, to benefit humankind, to make life richer and easier for all.

Peace Today by Rube Goldberg.
The Granger Collection, New York.

At the end of World War II, Americans confronted two new, unsettling facts of life: the atomic bomb and the cold war with the Soviet Union. U.S. scientists published chilling calculations of what would happen if atomic (and, later, hydrogen) bombs were dropped on American cities. Meanwhile, a vivid image of a malignant Soviet leadership, with its collective finger poised over the red button that would launch a nuclear attack, was created in the American psyche—an image memorably evoked in the 1963 film *Dr. Strangelove or: How I Learned to Stop Worrying and Love the Bomb.* Politicians warned that war would come, in the words of New York's governor Thomas E. Dewey, "whenever the fourteen evil men in Moscow decide to have it break out." It was high time, experts of various stripes agreed, to devise a new national civil-defense plan.

The possible options in response to nuclear attack were succinctly described by one U.S. government official as "dig, die, or get out." The second option aside, getting out meant leaving big cities, which presumably would be targets of

Soviet bombs. Some policymakers urged that major cities be relocated under mountain ranges or in thirty-foot strips alongside highways. Government officials ultimately rejected these and other relocation schemes. Even the less ambitious idea of evacuating cities drove planners to despair as they pondered maps of New York City and Los Angeles.

What was left but to dig? The notion of burrowing underground took root partly because it allowed every citizen a personal response to nuclear war: Build a bomb shelter. Companies selling shelters proliferated in the 1950s, and marketing creativity soared. Using fictitious "protection factor" ratings, shelter ads promised blastproof rooms; one ad featured a decontamination room for latecomers. Bomb shelters generated so much enthusiasm that by the end of 1960, industrious Americans had constructed about one million of them.

The fears that inspired those bunkers are now, sadly, entirely understandable to twenty-first-century Americans facing new threats to their security.

A Exploring the Culture
FACT VS. FICTION IN THE NEWS MEDIA

The contemporary tendency to blur the lines between fact and fiction may actually affect interpretation of the news and politics, with serious legal and ethical ramifications. To capture viewers' attention, prime-time television news programs often use techniques borrowed from filmmakers. For example:

- Newsmagazine shows may dramatize or re-create an event so that the audience can visualize something that was not actually captured on film.
- Rumor, speculation, and sensational details may be emphasized to grab the attention of channel surfers.
- Background music may be used to enhance the drama of a news story or interview.

In journalism, accurate information has traditionally been more important than entertainment. However, the advent of a new, hybrid form of journalism, "infotainment," presents a challenge to serious journalists.

B Exploring the Culture
REALITY TV

The blurring of fact and fiction occurs not only in literature but also on television. At the turn of this century, a new type of programming called reality TV emerged, using cameras to record the words and actions of everyday people placed in different situations. Although the shows claim to record events as they occur, the very presence of camera operators and film editors blurs the line between factual reality and fictional entertainment.

Nonfiction is the place where much of the best writing of the day is being done. Yet many writers and teachers of writing continue to feel vaguely guilty if they prefer it to fiction—nonfiction is the slightly disreputable younger brother in the royal house of literature. No such guilt is necessary. While the keepers of the temple weren't looking, nonfiction crept in and occupied the throne.

—William Zinsser

Contemporary Nonfiction: Breaking the Barriers

Until fairly recently *nonfiction* meant whatever was *not* fiction—suggesting that nonfiction was not a literary form and not art. Nonfiction writers were lumped together with journalists, who in turn were defined as nonliterary folk whose work was quickly written, read, and discarded. Critics tended to concentrate on the search for the elusive Great American Novel, which was thought to be more important than anything a nonfiction writer could produce.

Since the 1970s, however, nonfiction has come into its own. Featured reviews now discuss the art (not just the factual content) of books on computers, architecture, travel, history, film, and other subjects. Lists of bestsellers, which have always included self-help books, cookbooks, and exercise manuals, now regularly feature memoirs, biographies, and histories as well.

■ Does It Have to Be Accurate?

Critics, however, are still uncertain about the terminology we should apply to nonfiction. For instance, when discussing fiction, we can talk about point of view, character, plot, theme, and setting; in discussing more complex fiction, we can analyze irony, metaphors, symbols, and levels of meaning. These traditional literary terms don't always apply to nonfiction, however.

Peter Matthiessen.

A More troubling is the problem of accuracy. Truth or accuracy is often a test applied to nonfiction, with frequently unsatisfactory results. For example, a class read Peter Matthiessen's *The Snow Leopard* (1978), a travel memoir about wildlife in the Himalayas and the writer's search for the meaning of life. The class praised the book for its penetrating observations, philosophical depth, and narrative technique. Students were then asked whether they would like it just as much if they learned that it was fiction, that Matthiessen had done extensive research in a library but had never gone to the Himalayas at all. (This, of course, is *not* the case.) No, many students said; they would not like the book as **B** well. It would no longer be true. Wasn't truth what distinguished nonfiction from fiction?

Summarizing. Remind students that stopping to summarize a portion of a long essay is an effective reading and studying strategy. The task of summarizing is made easier when an essay is divided into sections with descriptive headings.

Activity. Have students write a two- or three-sentence summary of the major sections of this essay. Then, have students exchange summaries with a partner, noting areas of similarities and differences.

Activity. Have students find and read a review of a contemporary book, either fiction or nonfiction, and then summarize the review. Each summary should be one paragraph long, contain a clear statement of the review's main idea, and give several supporting ideas.

■ The New Journalism

This question was often raised in the 1960s, when the new journalism (also called literary journalism) began to appear. Truman Capote, Tom Wolfe, Joan Didion, Norman Mailer, and others attracted attention by describing contemporary culture and actual events in strongly individual voices. They used many of the devices of fiction, including complex characterization, plot, suspense, setting, symbolism, and irony.

A new journalist did not feel obliged to keep his or her opinion and presence out of the writing; in fact, presence and participation were often crucial. Joan Didion bought a dress for a defendant in a trial she was covering as a journalist. Truman Capote befriended the murderers he was writing about in *In Cold Blood,* which he called a nonfiction novel—a perfect example of the overlapping of genres. Readers wanted to know just what the writer was thinking or feeling about the subject, and so the tone of a book became nearly as important as its facts.

If facts alone do not distinguish nonfiction from fiction, what does? No one is sure. What readers *are* sure about is their interest in nonfiction that uses the traditional attractions of accomplished fiction: characters to care about, suspense, and compelling use of language. Many readers, eager for literature that will illuminate their lives, enrich their knowledge, and entertain them, have become as willing to turn to nonfiction as to fiction.

Contemporary Poetry: Varied and Intensely Personal

In recent years more Americans have been writing poetry than ever before. It is a special challenge to determine which poets and movements will last.

■ The Decline of Modernism

There are a number of clear, significant differences between American poetry written before World War II and poetry written in the decades since. The twenty years between the two world wars marked the flowering and near monopoly of modernist poetry. That was the kind of poetry defined by and large by the theories and practices of T. S. Eliot, Ezra Pound, and, somewhat later, W. H. Auden.

In 1917, Eliot had called for an impersonal, objective poetry that was not concerned with the subjective emotions of the poet. The poem, said Eliot, should be impersonal, allusive (it should make references, or allusions, to other works), and intellectually challenging.

C

Joan Didion visiting the closed Alcatraz Prison (1967).

C Literary Connections

T. S. Eliot

Poet T. S. Eliot was born in St. Louis, Missouri, but moved to London and eventually became a British subject.

In *The Waste Land* (1922), Eliot contrasts what he perceives to be the spiritual bankruptcy of modern Europe with the values that unified life in the past. He uses myths and allusions to world literature and cultures to embody those values. Eliot won the Nobel Prize in literature in 1948.

Outlining. Remind students that outlining is an effective study strategy for recognizing and clarifying the relationships among ideas and facts in a text.

Activity. Have students read each section of this introduction, paying special attention to the headings and subheadings. Then, have them identify one or two main ideas for each section and write them in outline format, leaving spaces for supporting material. Finally, have students identify at least three supporting details for each of the main ideas and add them in appropriate outline format.

A **Literary Connections**

Projective Verse

During the 1950s, some poets found a track other than modernism, called "projective verse." Led by Charles Olson, Robert Duncan, and Robert Creeley, the Black Mountain Poets (named for the college where they taught) produced poems strongly influenced by Ezra Pound and William Carlos Williams. Projective verse favored "open form," which meant treating each poem as an individual organic entity creating its own form as it proceeded. Open-form poems avoided regular meter and rhyme, as well as other traditional forms. Open-form poets aimed to imitate the spontaneity and complexity of reality itself. Other open-form poets included Denise Levertov, Paul Blackburn, Ed Dorn, and Louis Zukofsky.

> *One judges an age, just as one judges a poet, by its best poems.*
>
> —Randall Jarrell

Modernist writers followed Pound's insistence that the image was all-important and that any unnecessary words should be omitted; but in doing this, they often eliminated material that could have made their poetry more understandable to more people.

A By the early 1950s, there was a growing sense that modernism was somehow played out, that it was no longer appropriate for the times. The era itself may have had something to do with the shift away from modernism. A generation had returned from war to a country where conformity and material success were the main values. The Soviet Union and the atomic bomb worried Americans in the late 1940s and early 1950s, but acquiring a house and a car and making money were generally of more immediate importance. "These are the tranquilized *Fifties,*" Robert Lowell wrote in a poem toward the end of that decade, as he ironically described the conformity he saw around him:

> I hog a whole house on Boston's
> "hardly passionate Marlborough Street,"
> where even the man
> scavenging filth in the back alley trash cans,
> has two children, a beach wagon, a helpmate,
> and is a "young Republican."
>
> —Robert Lowell,
>   from "Memories of West Street and Lepke"

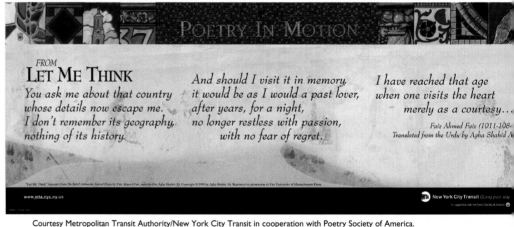

FROM
LET ME THINK
You ask me about that country
whose details now escape me.
I don't remember its geography,
nothing of its history.

And should I visit it in memory,
it would be as I would a past lover,
after years, for a night,
no longer restless with passion,
with no fear of regret.

I have reached that age
when one visits the heart
    merely as a courtesy...

Faiz Ahmed Faiz (1911-108-)
Translated from the Urdu by Agha Shahid A

Courtesy Metropolitan Transit Authority/New York City Transit in cooperation with Poetry Society of America.

English-Language Learners

The shift from the modernism of T. S. Eliot and W. H. Auden to contemporary poetry is marked by contemporary poets' attempts to capture the idioms and patterns of everyday speech.

Activity. Have students choose a favorite modernist American poem to read out loud, explaining what makes the poem a modernist work and why they like it. Then, have students use the library or Internet to locate and listen to a recording of a contemporary poem of their choice, looking at the differences in word choice, cadence, phrasing, and syntax between the modernist and contemporary poems.

■ The Beat Poets

In 1956, a long poem called *Howl* was published by Allen Ginsberg, a writer who could by no stretch of the imagination be described as dull. A cry of outrage against the conformity of the 1950s, *Howl* was far removed from the safe confines of modernism. *Howl* begins, "I saw the best minds of my generation destroyed by madness, starving hysterical naked," and it continues at the same intense pitch for hundreds of lines.

Beatnik poet reading to the accompaniment of a musician in New York's Greenwich Village (1959).

Together with *On the Road* (1957), Jack Kerouac's novel celebrating the bohemian life, *Howl* quickly became a kind of bible for the young nonconformists who made up what became known as the beat generation. Beat poetry and the beat lifestyle—marked by poetry readings, jazz performances, and the appearance of late-night coffeehouses in San Francisco and New York's Greenwich Village—had an immediate impact on American popular culture.

Howl provided the first clear alternative to poetry that seemed to be written for analysis in the classroom. *Howl* addressed the concerns of contemporary life. Many of Ginsberg's concerns—the injustices of modern life, the importance of the imagination—would become the principal themes of the next decade's poetry.

■ Poetry and Personal Experience

In 1959, Robert Lowell published *Life Studies,* one of the most important and influential volumes of verse to appear since World War II. These poems are about personal experiences that modernist poets had avoided dealing with directly: emotional distress, alcoholism, illness, and depression. In *Life Studies,* Lowell clearly and decisively broke with Eliot's theory that poetry should be impersonal. In doing so, he helped to reunite, for himself and for other writers, "the man who suffers and the mind which creates."

Shortly after *Life Studies* appeared, a critic described Lowell's poems as "confessional." The label stuck, and the **confessional school** of poets, mostly friends or students of Lowell's, was officially born. Those poets—including Sylvia Plath, Anne Sexton, and John Berryman—wrote frank, sometimes brutal poems about their private lives.

FAST FACTS

Political Highlights

- World War II ends in 1945.
- The Soviet Union becomes a nuclear power in 1949, touching off a dangerous arms race with the United States.
- Mikhail Gorbachev presides over the dissolution of the Soviet Union in 1991, ending the cold war.

Philosophical Views

- In the 1950s, America creates a culture marked by conformity and vigorous anti-Communism.
- In the 1980s, postmodernism takes root in philosophy, linguistics, and literature.
- Proponents of multiculturalism challenge traditional views of what writers should write and what students should read.

Social Influences

- The counterculture movement of the late 1960s rejects conformity in politics and art in favor of dissent and experimentation.
- The communications revolution of the 1990s promises new levels of prosperity.

DIRECT TEACHING

B Background
The Beats

The beat movement of the 1950s maintained a critical stance toward mainstream American culture. Also known as beatniks, the beats praised individuality while speaking out against social injustice and middle-class conformity.

C Content-Area Connections
Humanities: Bohemians

The word *bohemian*—meaning "an unconventional and nonconforming person, often an artist"—originated from the fact that the nomadic Gypsies, or Romany, passed through Bohemia (a region of Czechoslovakia) to reach western Europe. The term's popular use grew in 1896, when Italian composer Giacomo Puccini unveiled his opera *La Bohème,* a popular portrayal of a group of struggling artists in Paris's Latin Quarter.

D Literary Connections
The Confessional School

The Confessional poets listed here all won the Pulitzer Prize in poetry, an annual award given for a distinguished book of verse by an American author. The prize was awarded to John Berryman (1965, *77 Dream Songs*); Anne Sexton (1967, *Live or Die*); and, posthumously, Sylvia Plath (1982, *The Collected Poems*).

E Exploring the Historical Period
FAST FACTS

? What did the proponents of multiculturalism in the late twentieth century have in common with the counterculture movement of the late 1960s? [Possible response: Both movements criticized traditional American cultural values in favor of new ones that implicitly or explicitly favored greater diversity and social justice.]

Secondary Source

The Beats and Rock Music

Stephen Holden, a writer for *The New York Times,* wrote that the influence of beat writers Allen Ginsberg, Jack Kerouac, and William Burroughs radiated far beyond academia. According to Holden, the beats not only loosened the "straitjacket constricting American literature," but they also had a "profound impact on rock culture." He argues that the "rough-hewn rock poetry" of Bob Dylan, Lou Reed, and Patti Smith reflected the beat aesthetic.

Small-group activity. Have students choose one of the above rock artists, study his or her lyrics, and then find parallels between the lyrics and the incantations, prophesies, and rantings of the beats.

A Background

Poetry "Slams"

Poetry "slams" have become popular in many American cities. They often occur in environments that encourage self-expression, such as urban coffeehouses. The Nuyorican Poets Café on the Lower East Side of New York City was founded in the 1970s by a group of Puerto Rican American writers, including Miguel Piñero and Miguel Algarin. There, the slam format is often "open mike"—that is, anyone can take the floor and read. A reader at a poetry slam generally renders a poem in a deeply moved, impassioned voice, "slamming" the poetry with a force and boldness intended to stir up audiences. Poetry slams can also take the form of contests, in which the audiences decide the winners.

Poetry reading at Nuyorican Poets Café in New York City (1995).

■ History of the Human Heart

Today American poetry is characterized by diversity. The extraordinary variety in style and attitude has attracted large new audiences. Poetry performances have sprung up throughout America, with live poetry slams at such places as the Nuyorican Poets Café in New York City. Technology has made available thousands of readings on audiotape and videotape, and television broadcasts and numerous Web sites are devoted to poetry.

Much contemporary poetry reflects a democratic quality, often influenced by the works of Walt Whitman and William Carlos Williams. Poetry lives in the people, contemporary poets seem to say, and any walk of life, any experience, any style of expression can result in authentic poetry. Contemporary poets often write in the language of common speech, and they do not hesitate to surprise or even shock with their language, their attitudes, and the details of their private lives. Poetry today is anything but impersonal.

Will today's poetry reach audiences a hundred years from now? The answer by the poet laureate Billy Collins suggests that it will: "It's the only history of the human heart we have," he says.

808   Collection 6   Contemporary Literature: 1939 to Present

READING SKILLS REVIEW

Making generalizations. A *generalization* is a type of inference in which readers combine information in a text with information that they already know to make a judgment that extends beyond the text. Remind students that when they include generalizations in an essay about a work of literature, they should support each generalization with evidence from the text and examples from their own experience.

Activity. Have students identify one generalization in this essay. Do students agree with it? Have students explain whether they think the generalization is supported sufficiently in the text.

Activity. Have students make one generalization about the literature of their own time. Each generalization should be adequately supported with facts, examples, or reasons.

Where the Present Meets the Past on the Way to the Future

The literature that captures a wide audience often does so by offering a fresh voice and a new attitude, for those are the powerful needs of each new generation. Yet much of contemporary American literature deals with the same themes that concerned our greatest writers of the nineteenth century: Poe, Hawthorne, Whitman, Dickinson, Melville, Emerson, and Thoreau. The characters created by the novelist John Updike, for example, seek spiritual revelations in ordinary life. "The invariable mark of wisdom," Emerson wrote, "is to find the miraculous in the common." It is more difficult, however, to find transcendent spiritual values in the cheap clutter of modern life than it was in the woods around Emerson's Concord. Still, Updike's characters continue the search. "I find myself . . . circling back to man's religious nature," Updike has written of his own work, "and the real loss to man and art alike when that nature has nowhere to plug itself in." Those words could serve to describe the work of a great number of contemporary writers whose intellectual roots can be traced to the Transcendentalists of the nineteenth century and perhaps even further back, to those hardy, practical Puritans who braved the two-month voyage across the Atlantic in small wooden ships.

> *Everything is connected in the end.*
> —Don DeLillo, from *Underworld*

REVIEW

Talk About . . .

Turn back to the Think About questions at the start of this essay (page 796), and discuss your views.

Write About . . .

Contrasting Literary Periods

Today versus the past. On page 803, Václav Havel says that he thinks we are in an age of transition, that something is on the way out and something new is being born. In a paragraph, explain your response to Havel's comment. From what you know of the past, tell what you think is on the way out. From what you know of the present, tell what you think might be on the way in. Try to focus on the old and the new in terms of things like books, dance, music, values, dress.

DIRECT TEACHING

B Literary Connections
American Memoirists
The search for values in the contemporary period may be illuminated by the current outpouring of memoirs. Here are some notable American memoirs from the contemporary period:

- *The Woman Warrior: Memoirs of a Girlhood Among Ghosts,* by Maxine Hong Kingston (1976)
- *Growing Up,* by Russell Baker (1982)
- *Having Our Say: The Delany Sisters' First 100 Years,* by Sarah and A. Elizabeth Delany with Amy Hill Hearth (1993)
- *Always Running: LA Vida Loca, Gang Days in L.A.,* by Luis J. Rodriguez (1994)
- *Something to Declare,* by Julia Alvarez (1998)

Review

Talk About . . .

- **Modeling.** Model your thought process in responding to the second question on p. 796 by saying, "First, I will review the text about postmodern literature. Then, I will generalize this information to cover other artistic areas such as art and music. Obviously, one characteristic is cultural diversity. I know that the self-conscious borrowing of sounds from other cultures to create a whole new sound is typical of musical artists. I can infer that this is one characteristic of postmodernism."

Write About . . .

Today vs. the past. To help students get started, ask them to brainstorm by listing styles and trends that seem past their prime, as well as those that seem to be on the cutting edge. Remind students to focus on popular culture (dance, music, and clothing); art and literature; and values and morals.

Check Test: Short Answer
Monitoring students' progress. Guide the class in answering the following short-answer questions.

1. What are two tenets of T. S. Eliot's modernist theory of poetry? [impersonality and allusive language]

2. What are two characteristics of postmodern literature? [multiple meanings/ multiple words; nontraditional forms; self-consciousness; cultural diversity; blending of fiction and nonfiction; borrowing or manipulating ideas from the past]

3. What is the New Journalism? [an approach to writing nonfiction that employs many of fiction's techniques]

4. What school of poets was influenced by Robert Lowell's *Life Studies*? [the Confessional school]

THE QUOTATION

Before he was elected president, Dwight D. Eisenhower was the supreme commander of the Allied forces in Europe during World War II. His career as a soldier began when, as a young man seeking a college education, he applied to the Military Academy at West Point, New York. Eisenhower was disappointed not to participate in combat during World War I, but his work consistently impressed his superiors, and by the time the United States entered World War II, he was selected to lead several European invasions. Soon after heading the Allied forces' D-day invasion, Eisenhower was promoted to the U.S. Army's highest rank—general of the army. Ask students to discuss Eisenhower's statement. How does knowing Eisenhower's background (that of a long and successful military career) affect how you interpret his words? [Possible response: Eisenhower witnessed the tragedy of war firsthand. His experiences must have taught him a great deal about the misery and destruction of war.]

VIEWING THE ART

This digital montage uses an image of a mushroom cloud superimposed over text that describes the effects of a detonated atomic bomb. A third layer of black lines, derived from a diagram of subatomic particles, implies the potential peaceful uses for atomic research.

Activity. What political statement do you think is made by this image? [Possible response: The artist's use of both text and image to convey the destructive power of the atomic bomb suggests that the negative use of atomic research has overshadowed its potential positive uses.]

**Political
Points of View:
World
War II**

Jarrell
Wiesel
Hersey
Jackson
Frank
Whitehead
Bourke-White

I hate war as only a
soldier who has lived it
can, only as one who has
seen its brutality, its
futility, its stupidity.
—Gen. Dwight D. Eisenhower

Introducing **Political Points** *of* **View**

World War II

The seven selections listed above are included in this Political Points of View feature on World War II. In the top corner of the pages in this feature, you'll find three stars. Smaller versions of the stars appear next to the questions on pages 815, 827, 828, 843, and 852 that focus on World War II. At the end of the feature (page 862), you'll compare the various points of view expressed in these selections—points of view about war, about responsibility, about the effects of evil, about the impulse toward good.

Examining the Issue: World War II

The twentieth century might become known as the Century of War. Only twenty-one years after the end of the so-called Great War, the world was plunged into another horror. World War II began on a September morning in 1939 when an enormous German army invaded Poland.

On December 7, 1941, Japanese forces bombed America's Pacific fleet as it lay at anchor in Pearl Harbor in the Hawaiian Islands. The next day the United States declared war on Japan. By December 11, the United States was also at war in Europe.

The war in Europe ended with the fall of Berlin and the surrender of Germany on May 8, 1945. The Japanese emperor surrendered on August 14, 1945, but only after the Japanese cities of Hiroshima and Nagasaki were devastated by atomic bombs.

(Opposite) *Nuclear Holocaust* by J. B. Weekes.
Digital composite.

SKILLS FOCUS

Pages 811–863
cover
Literary Skills
Analyze
political points
of view on a
topic.

**Reading
Skills**
Evaluate
credibility.

Contemporary Literature: 1939 to Present   **811**

Political Points of View

SKILLS FOCUS, pp. 811–863

Grade-Level Skills

■ **Literary Skills**
Analyze political points of view of a selection of literary works on a topic.

■ **Reading Skills**
Evaluate credibility.

Review Skills

■ **Reading Skills**
Analyze and elaborate on ideas presented in primary and secondary sources.

Political Issue: World War II

The readings in this section present events of the Second World War from the points of view of an Air Force crew member, a concentration camp inmate, the civilian victims of the Hiroshima bombing, a judge at the Nuremberg trials, a young Jewish girl in hiding, a Navy officer at the D-day invasion, and a reporter visiting a recently liberated concentration camp.

Selection Starter

Build background. World War I, which was known in Great Britain as the Great War for Civilization, began in Europe in August 1914 and continued until 1918. It ranks second to World War II as the most costly and bloody war in history. The United States tried to remain neutral in the early years of the war, but the sinking of unarmed passenger ships and other acts by Germany led the United States to enter the war in 1917 on the side of the Allies.

Many historians have noted that World War I set the stage for World War II. The Versailles Peace Treaty, which forced Germany to disarm, give up territory, and pay reparations, caused widespread suffering and resentment. In addition, World War I and its aftermath led to the worst economic depression in history, aiding the rise of dictatorships in Germany and Italy.

Selection Starter

Build background. After World War II began in Europe in 1939, Americans debated whether to participate in the fighting or not. Isolationists wanted to stay out of the fighting at all costs, while interventionists urged that the United States fight on behalf of the Allies. Eventually, the U.S. government prepared for war by expanding its armed services and building new defense plants.

About 360 Japanese planes attacked the naval base at Pearl Harbor on December 7, 1941, sinking or damaging 21 ships and destroying or damaging 323 U.S. planes. Although the attack crippled the Pacific fleet, it united American opinion and forced the United States to declare war on Japan. When Germany and Italy declared war on the United States on December 11, the U.S. Congress responded in kind.

On July 26, 1945, the United States, Great Britain, and China issued an ultimatum calling for Japan's unconditional surrender. When Japan ignored the ultimatum, the first atomic bomb was dropped by the United States on Hiroshima on August 6, killing more than 70,000 people. Three days later, a second atomic bomb was dropped on Nagasaki, killing at least 40,000. On September 2, the Japanese signed a surrender agreement, ending World War II.

U.S. warships on fire in Pearl Harbor after a surprise Japanese attack (December 7, 1941).

The exact number of casualties of World War II is not known. It is estimated that Russia alone lost about eighteen million people in the war. When Gen. Dwight D. Eisenhower and the U.S. military entered Germany after its surrender, they found the concentration camps abandoned by the Nazis. Millions of Jews and members of other persecuted groups had perished in those camps.

Reading Skills
Evaluating Credibility

When you read about historical events, it is important to evaluate the credibility of your sources. There are two types of sources. **Primary sources** are firsthand, original accounts, such as interviews, autobiographies, letters, diaries, memoirs, and newsreels. Primary sources provide reliable eyewitness information. **Secondary sources** are materials like newspaper articles, biographies, history books, and encyclopedia articles. The credibility of secondary sources depends on their authorship and on the dates they were written. In other words, you want reliable and up-to-date secondary sources.

Prisoners in the concentration camp at Dachau, Germany, cheering their liberators, the U.S. Army (May 1945).

Randall Jarrell
(1914–1965)

One of the most careful and learned readers of contemporary poetry, Randall Jarrell was, at the same time, both an abrasive critic and a generous promoter of the art of poetry.

Born in Nashville, Tennessee, Jarrell was brought up in California. His childhood experiences included close observation of the gaudy remnants of the old Hollywood, a personal acquaintance with the MGM lion, and an appreciation of the difference between fantasy and fact—between life and myths about life—that would provide him with themes for poetry for years to come.

After graduating from Vanderbilt University in his native city, Jarrell began a career that led to positions in the English departments of many colleges and universities from Texas to New York. In 1942, he joined the Army Air Corps and served for a time as a pilot and then, for a longer time, as celestial navigation trainer of pilots assigned to fly the famous B-29 bombers of World War II. Out of this experience came two notable books of poetry, *Little Friend, Little Friend* (1945) and *Losses* (1948). Many critics say these books rank among the best American contributions to the literature of World War II.

A man of extraordinary wit, Jarrell gave full play to his gifts in his often caustic and devastating critical articles and essays, particularly in the collection *A Sad Heart at the Supermarket* (1962). In poetry, however, his faculty for contemptuous criticism is kept under wraps: His wit shows itself only in mellow good humor ("I feel like the first men who read Wordsworth. / It's so simple I can't under-

stand it") and in a resigned toleration of the more absurd aspects of American life.

Jarrell died when struck by a car while walking on a North Carolina highway in 1965. His tragic death raised a question: Was it actually a suicide? But of the loss to American letters and to the poets who had counted upon him to explain, judge, and celebrate their art there was no question at all.

Internet
- go.hrw.com (Keyword: LE5 11-6)
- *Elements of Literature Online*
Media
- *Audio CD Library*
- *Audio CD Library, Selections and Summaries in Spanish*

PRETEACHING

Summary *at grade level*

> The speaker tells the story of his own life and death in World War II, as if the poem were an epitaph on a gravestone.

DIRECT TEACHING

A Literary Focus

? Imagery. What do you associate with the image of "my mother's sleep"? [Possible responses: time before birth; the safety of the womb; comfort; innocence.]

B Literary Focus

? Implied metaphor. What implied comparison does the speaker make when he says he is in the "belly" of the State? [Possible response: He is comparing the ball turret of the bomber to the womb. It is an ironic comparison, since rather than warmth and safety, in the womb of the State the speaker finds freezing cold, "black flak and the nightmare fighters," and gruesome death.]

C Political Issue

? World War II. Do you think the last line has a meaning beyond shock value? Why or why not? [Possible response: By suggesting that the speaker is not an individual but just so much blood and protoplasm, the line evokes a revulsion in the reader against the war.]

Before You Read

The Death of the Ball Turret Gunner

Political Points *of* View

Quickwrite 🖉

These five lines, written in 1945, make up the most famous poem to come out of World War II. Before you read, write your thoughts on these questions: What attitude toward war do you expect to find in a poem written in 1945? What attitude toward war do you find in most literature and films about war produced today?

Literary Focus
Implied Metaphor

Some metaphors are directly stated. Emily Dickinson uses a direct metaphor when she says, "Hope is the thing with feathers." Other metaphors are implied; that is, they are not directly stated. We recognize an **implied metaphor** from the language the writer uses. If Dickinson had written, "Hope nests in my soul and warms me with its feathers," she would have used an implied metaphor. The words *nest* and *feathers* provide clues that the poet is comparing hope to a bird. What metaphor is implied in this poem by Jarrell?

> An **implied metaphor** is a comparison between two unlike things that is implied, or suggested, but not directly stated.
>
> *For more on Metaphor, see the Handbook of Literary and Historical Terms.*

SKILLS FOCUS

Literary Skills
Analyze political points of view on a topic. Understand implied metaphor.

The Death of the Ball Turret Gunner

Randall Jarrell

From my mother's sleep I fell into the State,
And I hunched in its belly till my wet fur froze.
Six miles from earth, loosed from its dream of life,
I woke to black flak and the nightmare fighters.
When I died they washed me out of the turret with a hose.

A Czech fighter pilot in England (1940).

DIFFERENTIATING INSTRUCTION

Learners Having Difficulty
Invite learners having difficulty to read "The Death of the Ball Turret Gunner" in interactive format in *The Holt Reader* and to use the sidenotes as aids to understanding the selection. The interactive version provides additional instruction, practice, and assessment of the literature standard taught in the Student Edition. Monitor students' responses to the selection, and correct any misconceptions that arise.

▶ Resources Reminder

For lessons designed for English-language learners and special education students, see *Holt Reading Solutions*.

The Ball Turret

A ball turret was a plexi-glass sphere set into the belly of a B-17 or B-24, and inhabited by two .50 caliber machine guns and one man, a short, small man. When this gunner tracked with his machine guns a fighter attacking his bomber from below, he revolved with the turret; hunched upside down in his little sphere, he looked like the fetus in the womb. The fighters which attacked him were armed with cannon firing explosive shells. The hose was a steam hose.

—Randall Jarrell

Response and Analysis

Thinking Critically

1. Who is speaking in this poem?

2. What is the temperature like in the ball turret?

3. What happens to the speaker?

4. How do you know that the speaker didn't enter the army on the basis of a rational decision?

5. "Belly" in line 2 of the poem can be read on two levels. What is the literal meaning? What is the **metaphoric** meaning?

6. What is the speaker's "wet fur"? Why do you think he compares himself to an animal?

7. Explain the **implied metaphor** in the poem. (In other words, what is the ball turret gunner compared to?) What specific words develop the metaphor?

8. What details in Jarrell's explanation of the ball turret (see the **Primary Source** above) add levels of meaning to his poem?

9. How would you describe the emotional effect of Randall's metaphor?

10. What is this poem really about? What statement about war is made in only five lines? Explain your views, and provide details from the text to support them.

Extending and Evaluating

11. Review your Quickwrite notes. How well did you predict Jarrell's attitude toward war? Did you find his attitude old-fashioned or surprisingly contemporary? Explain. ✏️

SKILLS FOCUS

Literary Skills
Analyze political points of view on a topic. Analyze implied metaphor.

Randall Jarrell 815

Thinking Critically

1. the dead ball turret gunner

2. The temperature is cold enough to freeze the fur on the gunner's jacket.

3. He is killed by enemy fighter planes.

4. "I fell into the State" suggests an unplanned entry into the service.

5. On a literal level, the gunner is in the airplane's ball turret; on a metaphorical level, the gunner is in the "belly" of the State, caught up in a huge military effort.

6. Possible answers: The wet fur could be his fleece-lined flight suit, sweat-soaked from fear. Fear has reduced the gunner to an animal frozen in the sight of the enemy.

7. Possible answers: The gunner is compared to an inborn fetus ("my mother's sleep"; "hunched in its belly"); the gunner is compared to a helpless animal devoured by a beast-like military ("fell into the State"; "hunched in its belly till my wet fur froze").

D Primary Source

Here, Randall Jarrell provides some technical background information that helps explain the imagery of the poem and the harsh reality of the event he describes.

Response and Analysis

8. Important details include the size of the gunner (small), his position ("hunched . . . like the fetus in the womb"), and the enemy fire (cannons).

9. The contrast that Jarrell implies between the warmth and security of a fetus's existence in the womb and the short, horror-filled life of the ball turret gunner is saddening. The reader feels indignation that the State did not protect the speaker as a mother should protect her child.

10. Possible answer: The poem suggests that the ball turret gunner, perhaps like many World War II fighting men, was no more than a child who had never learned the meaning of his life before dying.

Extending and Evaluating

11. Students may be surprised by Jarrell's antiwar stance.

Assessment

■ *Holt Assessment: Literature, Reading, and Vocabulary*

For a lesson reteaching poetic devices, see **Reteaching,** p. 1117A.

SKILLS FOCUS,
pp. 816–828

Grade-Level Skills

■ **Literary Skills**
Analyze political points of view on a topic.

■ **Reading Skills**
Analyze a writer's message.

More About the Writer

Background. Well after his liberation from the concentration camp, Wiesel learned that his two older sisters, Hilda and Batya, had also managed to survive the Nazis. After the war, Wiesel relocated to France, living first in Normandy and later in Paris, where he attended the Sorbonne from 1948 to 1951. As a writer, French became Wiesel's preferred language. *Night,* his best-known work, was originally published in French as *La Nuit* in 1958. It was written as a memorial to his parents and youngest sister. In 1960, Wiesel published a sequel, *Dawn,* which deals with a concentration camp survivor struggling to help establish Israel in 1948. A third novel with the French title *Le Jour* (*Day*) was published in English as *The Accident.* It deals with the moral crisis faced by a Holocaust survivor involved in a near-fatal car crash. The three novels were later published together as the *Night Trilogy.*

Elie Wiesel
(1928–   )

In March of 1944, when Elie Wiesel (el′ē vē·zel′) was fifteen, his life changed forever. At the time, Wiesel was living in the little town where he was born—Sighet, a remote village in the Carpathian Mountains of Hungary (now Romania). Raised in the Jewish mystical tradition of Hasidism, Wiesel had spent his childhood years immersed in the heritage of his extended family and in intense religious study. But in March 1944, the German army invaded Hungary. Soon Wiesel, his family, and some fifteen thousand other Jews from his region were rounded up and deported to extermination camps in Nazi-occupied Poland.

What Wiesel experienced in the camps was an unremitting horror. He saw his mother and youngest sister sent to die in a gas chamber, he saw his father succumb to dysentery and senseless violence, and he saw great numbers of fellow prisoners, many of them children, tortured and murdered by the Nazis.

After Wiesel was liberated from Buchenwald concentration camp in April 1945, he could not bring himself to write of the Holocaust for a decade, for fear "that words might betray it." Yet he also remembered the promise he had made to himself: "If, by some miracle, I survive, I will devote my life to testifying on behalf of all those whose shadows will be bound to mine forever." The result of this promise was *Night,* Wiesel's devastating memoir of his experiences under the Nazi terror, originally published in Yiddish as *Un di velt hot geshvign* (*And the World Kept Silent*) in 1956. In the same year he came to the United States to cover the United Nations as a reporter. He became a U.S. citizen in 1963 and is now a professor at Boston University.

For over four decades, Wiesel has continued to be a powerful advocate for human dignity—as a novelist, dramatist, journalist, religious scholar, and international activist. Seeking to maintain global awareness of the Nazi atrocities and to prevent similar crimes against humanity, he has spoken out against human-rights abuses in Cambodia, the former Soviet Union, Bosnia and Herzegovina, and South Africa under the apartheid regime. Such work earned Wiesel a Nobel Peace Prize in 1986. In his acceptance speech he reflected on his past and his purpose in life.

"This is what I say to the young Jewish boy wondering what I have done with his years. It is in his name that I speak to you and that I express to you my deepest gratitude. No one is as capable of gratitude as one who has emerged from the Kingdom of Night. We know that every moment is a moment of grace, every hour an offering; not to share them would mean to betray them. Our lives no longer belong to us alone; they belong to all those who need us desperately."

816 | Collection 6 | Contemporary Literature: 1939 to Present

RESOURCES: READING

Planning
■ *One-Stop Planner* CD-ROM with ExamView Test Generator

Differentiating Instruction
■ *Supporting Instruction in Spanish*
■ *Audio CD Library, Selections and Summaries in Spanish*

Vocabulary
■ *Vocabulary Development*

Grammar and Language
■ *Daily Language Activities*

Assessment
■ *Holt Assessment: Literature, Reading, and Vocabulary*
■ *One-Stop Planner* CD-ROM with ExamView Test Generator
■ *Holt Online Assessment*

Internet
■ go.hrw.com (Keyword: LE5 11-6)
■ *Elements of Literature Online*

Media
■ *Audio CD Library*
■ *Audio CD Library, Selections and Summaries in Spanish*

816 | Collection 6 | Contemporary Literature: 1939 to Present

Before You Read

from **Night**

Political Points *of* View

Wiesel's memoir takes us inside the Nazi concentration camps of World War II. Part of Wiesel's power as a writer is his ability to make us feel enormous empathy and deep fear. When a writer fulfills his responsibility as a witness, what is your responsibility as a reader?

Reading Skills
Analyzing a Writer's Message

Wiesel's *Night* is a **memoir,** which means it is a true account of a personal experience. Wiesel is a moralist, yet he does not directly state any message to us in this part of his memoir. Instead, he allows the horror of the experience and the responses of different people to their suffering to speak for themselves. As you read, think about what Wiesel's writing reveals about the power of faith, the power of evil, the power of art. What implicit philosophical beliefs underlie Wiesel's message?

Background

World War II forced people to face not only battlefield atrocities but also the grim reality that an industrialized, civilized society was capable of profound evil. The Nazis of Germany deliberately tortured, starved, and murdered millions who posed no military threat. In the Holocaust, or Shoah, the Nazis and their collaborators made a systematic attempt to implement a "Final Solution" that would destroy all the Jews of Europe. By the end of the war in 1945, the Nazis had killed more than six million Jews. They had also killed five million other civilians whom they deemed undesirable—Romany (Gypsies), homosexuals, and "non-Aryans"—as well as political opponents and resistance fighters.

On the following pages you will find three excerpts from Wiesel's memoir about his personal experience of the Holocaust. The events described in the first excerpt occurred on a train headed for Auschwitz (oush'vits'), the most notorious Nazi concentration camp. Wiesel, who was fifteen at the time, and his family had been forced into a railroad car with eighty other Hungarian Jews.

Vocabulary Development

abyss (ə·bis') *n.:* bottomless gulf or void.

pestilential (pes'tə·len'shəl) *adj.:* dangerous and harmful, like a deadly infection.

abominable (ə·bäm'ə·nə·bəl) *adj.:* nasty and disgusting.

encumbrance (en·kum'brəns) *n.:* hindrance; burden.

semblance (sem'bləns) *n.:* appearance; likeness.

conscientiously (kän'shē·en'shəs·lē) *adv.:* carefully; painstakingly; thoroughly.

apathy (ap'ə·thē) *n.:* indifference; lack of emotion.

INTERNET

Vocabulary Practice

Keyword: LE5 11-6

SKILLS FOCUS

Literary Skills
Analyze political points of view on a topic.

Reading Skills
Understand a writer's message.

Elie Wiesel   **817**

Previewing Vocabulary

Have students complete each of the following sentences with the correct Vocabulary word from p. 817.

1. Filled with _____, Cody didn't care where we went or what we did. [apathy]

2. Millions died from the _____ virus. [pestilential]

3. Weighed down by the heavy _____, we made slow progress. [encumbrance]

4. The mountain climber kept her eyes averted from the _____ between the canyon walls. [abyss]

5. May tried to assume a _____ of contentment, but I could see she was unhappy. [semblance]

6. Working _____ all year, Mia graduated with a straight-A average. [conscientiously]

7. The _____ odor of rotting garbage filled the air. [abominable]

PRETEACHING

Summary *at grade level*

In the first excerpt from his memoir, Wiesel describes the forced transport of his family and other Jews to Poland. Packed in a cattle car without water, food, or sanitation, they are forced to travel for days, as claustrophobia and terror rise. Madame Schächter, separated from husband and older sons, loses control and screams for hours. Her cries so unnerve the other prisoners that they gag and beat her.

The second excerpt describes the death-selection process at Buna. Wiesel makes it through the selection, but his father, unsure he has passed the selection, insists Wiesel accept a spoon and knife as a tragic "inheritance." Wiesel spends a day in terror of losing this last surviving member of his family. While his father narrowly escapes death, others are not so lucky. Wiesel describes the death sentence of a man named Akiba Drumer, and mourns how quickly he is forgotten by the others in the camp.

The third excerpt describes a grisly death march from Buna to Gleiwitz. The Nazi guards shoot prisoners who slow their pace, and Rabbi Eliahou becomes terrified when he can't find his son. With horror, Wiesel remembers that he has seen Eliahou's son—pushing to the front to escape responsibility for his elderly father. The next night, the prisoners arrive at the overcrowded barracks of Gleiwitz and are pushed inside into a sea of dead and dying human bodies. Struggling for air, Wiesel hears Juliek, a violin player he has met earlier, playing a Beethoven concerto for this audience of dying prisoners. In the morning, Wiesel finds Juliek dead beside his crushed violin.

from Night

Elie Wiesel

translated by **Stella Rodway**

Identity card and yellow star for a Jew living in Amsterdam in 1943.

A The train stopped at Kaschau,[1] a little town on the Czechoslovak frontier. We realized then that we were not going to stay in Hungary. Our eyes were opened, but too late.

The door of the car slid open. A German officer, accompanied by a Hungarian lieutenant-interpreter, came up and introduced himself.

"From this moment, you come under the authority of the German army. Those of you who still have gold, silver, or watches in your possession must give them up now. Anyone who is later found to have kept anything will be shot on the spot. Secondly, anyone who feels ill may go to the hospital car. That's all."

The Hungarian lieutenant went among us with a basket and collected the last possessions from those who no longer wished to taste the bitterness of terror.

"There are eighty of you in this wagon," added the German officer. "If anyone is missing, you'll all be shot, like dogs. . . ."

They disappeared. The doors were closed. We were caught in a trap, right up to our necks. The doors were nailed up; the way back was finally cut off. The world was a cattle wagon hermetically sealed.[2]

We had a woman with us named Madame Schächter.[3] She was about fifty; her ten-year-old son was with her, crouched in a corner. Her husband and two eldest sons had been deported with the first transport by mistake. The separation had completely broken her.

I knew her well. A quiet woman with tense,

burning eyes, she had often been to our house. Her husband, who was a pious man, spent his days and nights in study, and it was she who worked to support the family.

B Madame Schächter had gone out of her mind. On the first day of the journey she had already begun to moan and to keep asking why she had been separated from her family. As time went on, her cries grew hysterical.

On the third night, while we slept, some of us sitting one against the other and some standing, a piercing cry split the silence:

"Fire! I can see a fire! I can see a fire!"

There was a moment's panic. Who was it who had cried out? It was Madame Schächter. Standing in the middle of the wagon, in the pale light from the windows, she looked like a withered tree in a cornfield. She pointed her arm toward the window, screaming:

"Look! Look at it! Fire! A terrible fire! Mercy! *Oh, that fire!*"

Some of the men pressed up against the bars. There was nothing there; only the darkness.

The shock of this terrible awakening stayed with us for a long time. We still trembled from it. With every groan of the wheels on the rail, we felt that an abyss was about to open beneath our bodies. Powerless to still our own anguish, we **C** tried to console ourselves:

"She's mad, poor soul. . . ."

Someone had put a damp cloth on her brow, to calm her, but still her screams went on:

"Fire! Fire!"

---

1. **Kaschau** (kä′shou′); also called Košice (kô′shē·tse).
2. **hermetically** (hər·met′ik·lē) **sealed:** airtight.
3. **Schächter** (shekh′tər).

Vocabulary
abyss (ə·bis′) *n.:* bottomless gulf or void.

Arriving at Auschwitz from Hungary (spring 1944).
© All rights reserved. Yad Vashem Film and Photo Archive, Jerusalem.

Her little boy was crying, hanging onto her skirt, trying to take hold of her hands. "It's all right, Mummy! There's nothing there. . . . Sit down. . . ." This shook me even more than his mother's screams had done.

Some women tried to calm her. "You'll find your husband and your sons again . . . in a few days. . . ."

She continued to scream, breathless, her voice broken by sobs. "Jews, listen to me! I can see a fire! There are huge flames! It is a furnace!"

It was as though she were possessed by an evil spirit which spoke from the depths of her being.

We tried to explain it away, more to calm ourselves and to recover our own breath than to comfort her. "She must be very thirsty, poor thing! That's why she keeps talking about a fire devouring her."

But it was in vain. Our terror was about to burst the sides of the train. Our nerves were at breaking point. Our flesh was creeping. It was as though madness were taking possession of us all. We could stand it no longer. Some of the young men forced her to sit down, tied her up, and put a gag in her mouth.

Silence again. The little boy sat down by his mother, crying. I had begun to breathe normally again. We could hear the wheels churning out

that monotonous rhythm of a train traveling through the night. We could begin to doze, to rest, to dream. . . .

An hour or two went by like this. Then another scream took our breath away. The woman had broken loose from her bonds and was crying out more loudly than ever:

"Look at the fire! Flames, flames everywhere. . . ."

Once more the young men tied her up and gagged her. They even struck her. People encouraged them:

"Make her be quiet! She's mad! Shut her up! She's not the only one. She can keep her mouth shut. . . ."

They struck her several times on the head—blows that might have killed her. Her little boy clung to her; he did not cry out; he did not say a word. He was not even weeping now.

An endless night. Toward dawn, Madame Schächter calmed down. Crouched in her corner, her bewildered gaze scouring[4] the emptiness, she could no longer see us.

She stayed like that all through the day, dumb, absent, isolated among us. As soon as night fell, she began to scream: "There's a fire over there!" She would point at a spot in space, always the same one. They were tired of hitting her. The heat, the thirst, the pestilential stench, the suffocating lack of air—these were as nothing compared with these screams which tore us to shreds. A few days more and we should all have started to scream too.

But we had reached a station. Those who were next to the windows told us its name:

"Auschwitz."

No one had ever heard that name.

The train did not start up again. The afternoon passed slowly. Then the wagon doors slid

---

4. **scouring** v. used as adj.: roaming about; searching.

Vocabulary

pestilential (pes'tə·len'shəl) adj.: dangerous and harmful, like a deadly infection.

Elie Wiesel   819

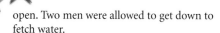

A Political Issue

World War II: Nazi ideology.
How does the calm, and perhaps even polite, tone that the officer takes with the terrified prisoners make actions and ideology seem all the more horrifying? [Possible response: The officer's calm and businesslike manner demonstrates how anti-Semitic ideology allowed the Nazis to thoroughly dehumanize their victims; they send Jews to their deaths calmly, without expressions of anger or guilt.]

B Literary Focus

Atmosphere. What atmosphere do the few stark details in this passage evoke? [Possible response: The flames shooting into the darkness and the abominable odor everywhere present an image of hell.]

C Literary Focus

Irony. What ironies appear at the end of this excerpt? [Possible response: The "delusions" of Madame Schächter turn out to be dreadfully accurate.]

D Political Issue

World War II: Auschwitz-Birkenau. The Auschwitz-Birkenau camp was the largest of the Nazi concentration camps, and it is estimated that about 1.5 million Jews were murdered there, mostly in gas chambers. As the inmates entered this factory of death, they were greeted by a huge sign in German that read, "Work makes free" (*Arbeit macht frei*)—intended to convince the new arrivals that only a labor camp awaited them. In reality, the majority were killed within twenty-four hours of their arrival.

---

open. Two men were allowed to get down to fetch water.

When they came back, they told us that, in exchange for a gold watch, they had discovered that this was the last stop. We would be getting out here. There was a labor camp. Conditions were good. Families would not be split up. Only the young people would go to work in the factories. The old men and invalids would be kept occupied in the fields.

The barometer of confidence soared. Here was a sudden release from the terrors of the previous nights. We gave thanks to God.

Madame Schächter stayed in her corner, wilted, dumb, indifferent to the general confidence. Her little boy stroked her hand.

As dusk fell, darkness gathered inside the wagon. We started to eat our last provisions. At ten in the evening, everyone was looking for a convenient position in which to sleep for a while, and soon we were all asleep. Suddenly:

"The fire! The furnace! Look, over there! . . ."

Waking with a start, we rushed to the window. Yet again we had believed her, even if only for a moment. But there was nothing outside save the darkness of night. With shame in our souls, we went back to our places, gnawed by fear, in spite of ourselves. As she continued to scream, they began to hit her again, and it was with the greatest difficulty that they silenced her.

The man in charge of our wagon called a German officer who was walking about on the platform, and asked him if Madame Schächter could be taken to the hospital car.

"You must be patient," the German replied. "She'll be taken there soon."

Toward eleven o'clock, the train began to move. We pressed against the windows. The convoy was moving slowly. A quarter of an hour later, it slowed down again. Through the windows we could see barbed wire; we realized that this must be the camp.

We had forgotten the existence of Madame Schächter. Suddenly, we heard terrible screams:

"Jews, look! Look through the window! Flames! Look!"

And as the train stopped, we saw this time that flames were gushing out of a tall chimney into the black sky.

Madame Schächter was silent herself. Once more she had become dumb, indifferent, absent, and had gone back to her corner.

We looked at the flames in the darkness. There was an abominable odor floating in the air. Suddenly, our doors opened. Some odd-looking characters, dressed in striped shirts and black trousers, leapt into the wagon. They held electric torches[5] and truncheons.[6] They began to strike out to right and left, shouting:

"Everybody get out! Everyone out of the wagon! Quickly!"

We jumped out. I threw a last glance toward Madame Schächter. Her little boy was holding her hand.

In front of us flames. In the air that smell of burning flesh. It must have been about midnight. We had arrived—at Birkenau,[7] reception center for Auschwitz. . . .

The following section of Night *takes place in Buna* (bōō'nə), *another camp in Poland, where Wiesel and his father were sent from Auschwitz. It documents the horrifying process of selection, in which the Nazis separated those prisoners judged fit to perform slave labor from those who were to be killed immediately. It was after such a selection that Wiesel's mother and sister were murdered in the Auschwitz gas chamber.*

The head of our block had never been outside concentration camps since 1933. He had already been through all the slaughterhouses, all the

---

5. **electric torches:** flashlights.
6. **truncheons** (trun'chənz) *n. pl.:* short, thick clubs.
7. **Birkenau** (bir'kə·nou).

Vocabulary
abominable (ə·bäm'ə·nə·bəl) *adj.:* nasty and disgusting.

CONTENT-AREA CONNECTIONS

Art: The Holocaust
Whole-class activity. Ask students to locate and prepare for the class a display of one of the following:

• Reproductions of art or photographs housed in the Holocaust Memorial Museum.

• Selections from Art Spiegelman's two-part Pulitzer Prize–winning novel, *Maus,* which uses a cartoon format to tell the story of his parents' experience in a concentration camp.

Cinema: The Holocaust
Individual activity. Ask students to watch and write a review of Steven Spielberg's Academy Award–winning movie, *Schindler's List,* which recounts how a German businessman gradually becomes involved in a risky venture to save the lives of hundreds of Jews. Ask students to evaluate the movie's effectiveness in communicating the moral dilemmas faced by gentile civilians like Schindler.

factories of death. At about nine o'clock, he took up his position in our midst:

"Achtung!"[8]

There was instant silence.

"Listen carefully to what I am going to say." (For the first time, I heard his voice quiver.) "In a few moments the selection will begin. You must get completely undressed. Then one by one you go before the SS[9] doctors. I hope you will all succeed in getting through. But you must help your own chances. Before you go into the next room, move about in some way so that you give yourselves a little color. Don't walk slowly, run! Run as if the devil were after you! Don't look at the SS. Run, straight in front of you!"

He broke off for a moment, then added:

"And, the essential thing, don't be afraid!"

Here was a piece of advice we should have liked very much to be able to follow.

I got undressed, leaving my clothes on the bed. There was no danger of anyone stealing them this evening.

Tibi and Yossi, who had changed their unit at the same time as I had, came up to me and said:

"Let's keep together. We shall be stronger."

Yossi was murmuring something between his teeth. He must have been praying. I had never realized that Yossi was a believer. I had even always thought the reverse. Tibi was silent, very pale. All the prisoners in the block stood naked between the beds. This must be how one stands at the last judgment.

E

"They're coming!"

There were three SS officers standing round the notorious Dr. Mengele,[10] who had received

F

---

8. **achtung** (äkh′tʊʊŋ): German for "attention."
9. **SS:** Abbreviation for *Schutzstaffel* (shoots′shtə′fəl), German for "protection squad," the elite Nazi guards who oversaw the operation of the concentration camps.
10. **Dr. Mengele:** Josef Mengele (yō′zef′men′ə·lə) (1911–1979) was a Nazi doctor and SS officer infamous for torturing camp prisoners, often children, sometimes in pseudoscientific experiments.

---

us at Birkenau. The head of the block, with an attempt at a smile, asked us:

"Ready?"

Yes, we were ready. So were the SS doctors. Dr. Mengele was holding a list in his hand: our numbers.[11] He made a sign to the head of the block: "We can begin!" As if this were a game!

The first to go by were the "officials" of the block: *Stubenaelteste*,[12] Kapos,[13] foremen, all in perfect physical condition of course! Then came the ordinary prisoners' turn. Dr. Mengele took stock of them from head to foot. Every now and then, he wrote a number down. One single thought filled my mind: not to let my number be taken; not to show my left arm.

There were only Tibi and Yossi in front of me. They passed. I had time to notice that Mengele had not written their numbers down. Someone pushed me. It was my turn. I ran without looking back. My head was spinning: You're too thin, you're weak, you're too thin, you're good for the furnace. . . . The race seemed interminable. I thought I had been running for years. . . . You're too thin, You're too weak. . . . At last I had arrived exhausted. When I regained my breath, I questioned Yossi and Tibi:

"Was I written down?"

"No," said Yossi. He added, smiling: "In any case, he couldn't have written you down, you were running too fast. . . ."

I began to laugh. I was glad. I would have liked to kiss him. At that moment, what did the others matter! I hadn't been written down.

Those whose numbers had been noted stood apart, abandoned by the whole world. Some were weeping in silence. . . .

G

---

11. **our numbers:** Concentration camp prisoners were identified by a number, which was usually tattooed on the left arm shortly after arrival.
12. *Stubenaelteste* (shtoob′ən·el′tɔst·ə): German for "barracks leaders" or "room leaders."
13. **Kapos** (kä′pōz): prisoners appointed by the Nazis to head work gangs, often in exchange for better treatment.

DIRECT TEACHING

E **Literary Focus**

❓ **Analyzing author's beliefs.** What does the description of Yossi and Tibi reveal about Wiesel's religious beliefs? [Possible responses: The fear of imminent death can cause one to reveal hidden or buried religious beliefs; at the end of life we stand naked and afraid of the unknown.]

F **Content-Area Connections**

History: Josef Mengele Mengele personally selected nearly 500,000 prisoners to be gassed at Auschwitz-Birkenau. He was infamous for his so-called scientific experiments on prisoners. Such experiments often involved torture and mutilation, including the excision of genital organs, harmful injections directly into the veins or heart, and extreme starvation.

G **Reading Skills**

❓ **Analyzing a writer's message.** How does Wiesel use this passage to show that he internalized, in spite of himself, some of the camp's structure and ideology? [Possible responses: Young Wiesel finds himself valuing strength and survival alone, accepting that the thin and the weak are "good for the furnace." He feels a momentary indifference for those who have been selected.]

Primary Source

Wiesel on *Night*

Regarding the writing style of Night, Elie Wiesel made these comments in his 1995 memoir, *All Rivers Run to the Sea*: "All my subsequent works are written in the same deliberately spare style as *Night*. It is the style of the chroniclers of the ghettos, where everything had to be said swiftly, in one breath. You never knew when the enemy might kick in the door, sweeping us away into nothingness. Every phrase was a testament. There was no time or reason for anything superfluous. Words must not be imprisoned or harnessed, not even in the silence of the page. And yet, it must be held tightly. If the violin is to sing, its strings must be stretched so tight as to risk breaking; slack, they are merely threads."

DIRECT TEACHING

A Learners Having Difficulty

? Noting details. Why does the cell block head read out the numbers "in a soft voice"? [because he knows that the people whose numbers have been selected are almost certain to be killed]

B English-Language Learners

? Appositive phrases. Remind students that an appositive phrase consists of a noun or pronoun and its modifiers—and is placed beside (usually after) another noun or pronoun to identify or explain it. How do the two appositive phrases that follow "from the block" evoke the setting and atmosphere? [The appositives make it clear that the cell barracks are indelibly associated with death and torment for Wiesel.]

C Reading Skills

Making predictions. Have students pause here to predict what will happen to the narrator's father. After students have read the next page, have them check the accuracy of their predictions.

D Reading Skills

? Analyzing a writer's message. What does the father's gift to the son reveal about their relationship? [Possible response: The heartrending gift of the knife and spoon affirms that Wiesel and his father have managed to retain love and loyalty despite their situation.]

Several days had elapsed. We no longer thought about the selection. We went to work as usual, loading heavy stones into railway wagons. Rations had become more meager: This was the only change.

We had risen before dawn, as on every day. We had received the black coffee, the ration of bread. We were about to set out for the yard as usual. The head of the block arrived, running.

"Silence for a moment. I have a list of numbers here. I'm going to read them to you. Those whose numbers I call won't be going to work this morning; they'll stay behind in the camp."

And, in a soft voice, he read out about ten numbers. We had understood. These were numbers chosen at the selection. Dr. Mengele had not forgotten.

The head of the block went toward his room. Ten prisoners surrounded him, hanging onto his clothes:

"Save us! You promised . . . ! We want to go to the yard. We're strong enough to work. We're good workers. We can . . . we will. . . ."

He tried to calm them, to reassure them about their fate, to explain to them that the fact that they were staying behind in the camp did not mean much, had no tragic significance.

"After all, I stay here myself every day," he added.

It was a somewhat feeble argument. He realized it, and without another word went and shut himself up in his room.

The bell had just rung.

"Form up!"

It scarcely mattered now that the work was hard. The essential thing was to be as far away as possible from the block, from the crucible of death, from the center of hell.

I saw my father running toward me. I became frightened all of a sudden.

"What's the matter?"

Out of breath, he could hardly open his mouth.

"Me, too . . . me, too . . . ! They told me to stay behind in the camp."

They had written down his number without his being aware of it.

"What will happen?" I asked in anguish.

But it was he who tried to reassure me.

"It isn't certain yet. There's still a chance of escape. They're going to do another selection today . . . a decisive selection."

I was silent.

He felt that his time was short. He spoke quickly. He would have liked to say so many things. His speech grew confused; his voice choked. He knew that I would have to go in a few moments. He would have to stay behind alone, so very alone.

"Look, take this knife," he said to me. "I don't need it any longer. It might be useful to you. And take this spoon as well. Don't sell them. Quickly! Go on. Take what I'm giving you!"

The inheritance.

"Don't talk like that, Father." (I felt that I would break into sobs.) "I don't want you to say that. Keep the spoon and knife. You need them as much as I do. We shall see each other again this evening, after work."

He looked at me with his tired eyes, veiled with despair. He went on:

"I'm asking this of you. . . . Take them. Do as I ask, my son. We have no time. . . . Do as your father asks."

Our Kapo yelled that we should start.

The unit set out toward the camp gate. Left, right! I bit my lips. My father had stayed by the block, leaning against the wall. Then he began to run, to catch up with us. Perhaps he had forgotten something he wanted to say to me. . . . But we were marching too quickly. . . . Left, right!

We were already at the gate. They counted us, to the din of military music. We were outside.

The whole day, I wandered about as if sleepwalking. Now and then Tibi and Yossi would throw me a brotherly word. The Kapo, too, tried to reassure me. He had given me easier work today. I felt sick at heart. How well they were

Literary Criticism

Wiesel's Universality

Have students consider these comments by critics, all of which touch on the universality of Wiesel's message. In a class discussion, examine each opinion and debate its validity.

• Wiesel "touches universal chords" because "in writing about the Jewish condition, he thereby writes about the human condition. For the human condition is not generalized existence; it is a huge, crazy-quilt sum of particularized existences all woven together."

—Robert McAfee Brown,
The Christian Century

• "Wiesel has taken the Jew as his metaphor—and his reality—in order to unite a moral and aesthetic vision in terms of all men."

—Daniel Stern,
The Washington Post Book World

treating me! Like an orphan! I thought: Even now, my father is still helping me.

I did not know myself what I wanted—for the day to pass quickly or not. I was afraid of finding myself alone that night. How good it would be to die here!

At last we began the return journey. How I longed for orders to run!

The military march. The gate. The camp.

I ran to Block 36.

Were there still miracles on this earth? He was alive. He had escaped the second selection. He had been able to prove that he was still useful. . . . I gave him back his knife and spoon.

Akiba Drumer left us, a victim of the selection. Lately, he had wandered among us, his eyes glazed, telling everyone of his weakness: "I can't go on. . . . It's all over. . . ." It was impossible to raise his morale. He didn't listen to what we told him. He could only repeat that all was over for him, that he could no longer keep up the struggle, that he had no strength left, nor faith. Suddenly his eyes would become blank, nothing but two open wounds, two pits of terror.

He was not the only one to lose his faith during those selection days. I knew a rabbi from a little town in Poland, a bent old man, whose lips were always trembling. He used to pray all the time, in the block, in the yard, in the ranks. He would recite whole pages of the Talmud from memory, argue with himself, ask himself questions and answer himself. And one day he said to me: "It's the end. God is no longer with us."

And, as though he had repented of having spoken such words, so clipped, so cold, he added in his faint voice:

"I know. One has no right to say things like that. I know. Man is too small, too humble and inconsiderable to seek to understand the mysterious ways of God. But what can I do? I'm not a sage, one of the elect, nor a saint. I'm just an ordinary creature of flesh and blood. I've got eyes, too, and I can see what they're doing here. Where is the divine Mercy? Where is God? How

Slave laborers in the barracks of Buchenwald concentration camp (April 16, 1945). Elie Wiesel is the man whose face can be seen on the far right of the center bunk.

can I believe, how could anyone believe, in this merciful God?"

Poor Akiba Drumer, if he could have gone on believing in God, if he could have seen a proof of God in this Calvary,[14] he would not have been taken by the selection. But as soon as he felt the first cracks forming in his faith, he had lost his reason for struggling and had begun to die.

When the selection came, he was condemned in advance, offering his own neck to the executioner. All he asked of us was:

"In three days I shall no longer be here. . . . Say the Kaddish[15] for me."

We promised him. In three days' time, when we saw the smoke rising from the chimney, we

---

14. **Calvary:** Wiesel compares Drumer's tragedy to the crucifixion of Jesus, which took place at the site near Jerusalem called Golgotha, or Calvary.
15. **Kaddish** (käd′ish): Jewish prayer in praise of God, one form of which is recited to mourn a death.

Elie Wiesel   **823**

- "Wiesel is one of the few writers who . . . has succeeded in revealing in the Jewish tragedy those features by which it has become again and again a paradigm of the human condition."
  —Manes Sperber,
  The New York Times Book Review

- "Wiesel is a messenger to mankind. . . . His message is one of peace, atonement and human dignity."
  —Egil Aarvik, Chairman of the Nobel Prize committee

❓ Irony. Why is the ending of this excerpt ironic? [The prisoners' promise that they would say the Kaddish enabled Drumer to go peacefully to his death. However, the prisoners forget their promise in just three days.]

B **Reading Skills**

❓ Making inferences. Why might a rabbi's words of comfort provoke rebellion? [Possible response: The extreme inhumanity and apocalyptic horror of the Holocaust made it hard for anyone to claim that it was in any way a result of "God's will"—and a rabbi who advanced such traditional theology might deeply hurt and offend his congregation.]

C **Reading Skills**

❓ Drawing conclusions. Why is Wiesel glad that Rabbi Eliahou continues searching for his "beloved son"? [Possible responses: He hopes Rabbi Eliahou will not discover his son's betrayal.]

D **Reading Skills**

❓ Analyzing a writer's message. What does it mean to pray to a God in whom one no longer believes? Has Wiesel lost his faith, and if so, what has he retained? [Possible response: Wiesel clings to the rituals he has grown up with and which define him as a Jew, but he seems to have lost his faith in a God who intervenes in the world, for such a God could not have allowed the Holocaust to happen.]

---

would think of him. Ten of us would gather together and hold a special service. All his friends would say the Kaddish.

Then he went off toward the hospital, his step steadier, not looking back. An ambulance was waiting to take him to Birkenau.

A These were terrible days. We received more blows than food; we were crushed with work. And three days after he had gone, we forgot to say the Kaddish. . . .

The next section of Night *occurs toward the end of Wiesel's eleven months in the concentration camps. It opens during a brutal march toward a new camp, Gleiwitz (glī′vits). The Nazi guards have forced the prisoners to run for miles in the snow without adequate rest or clothing. As a result, hundreds will die before they reach the dangerously overcrowded barracks.*

The door of the shed opened. An old man appeared, his moustache covered with frost, his lips blue with cold. It was Rabbi Eliahou,[16] the rabbi of a small Polish community. He was a very good man, well loved by everyone in the camp, even by the Kapos and the heads of the blocks. Despite the trials and privations, his face still shone with his inner purity. He was the only rabbi who was always addressed as "Rabbi" at Buna. He was like one of the old prophets, always in the midst of his people to comfort them. And, strangely, his words of comfort never provoked rebellion; they really brought peace.

He came into the shed and his eyes, brighter than ever, seemed to be looking for someone:

"Perhaps someone has seen my son somewhere?"

He had lost his son in the crowd. He had looked in vain among the dying. Then he had scratched up the snow to find his corpse. Without result.

For three years they had stuck together. Al-

---
16. Eliahou (el·ē·ä′hoō′).

ways near each other, for suffering, for blows, for the ration of bread, for prayer. Three years, from camp to camp, from selection to selection. And now—when the end seemed near—fate had separated them. Finding himself near me, Rabbi Eliahou whispered:

"It happened on the road. We lost sight of one another during the journey. I had stayed a little to the rear of the column. I hadn't any strength left for running. And my son didn't notice. That's all I know. Where has he disappeared? Where can I find him? Perhaps you've seen him somewhere?"

"No, Rabbi Eliahou, I haven't seen him."

He left then as he had come: like a windswept shadow.

He had already passed through the door when I suddenly remembered seeing his son running by my side. I had forgotten that, and I didn't tell Rabbi Eliahou!

Then I remembered something else: his son had seen him losing ground, limping, staggering back to the rear of the column. He had seen him. And he had continued to run on in front, letting the distance between them grow greater.

A terrible thought loomed up in my mind: He had wanted to get rid of his father! He had felt that his father was growing weak, he had believed that the end was near and had sought this separation in order to get rid of the burden, to free himself from an encumbrance which could lessen his own chances of survival.

C I had done well to forget that. And I was glad that Rabbi Eliahou should continue to look for his beloved son.

D And, in spite of myself, a prayer rose in my heart, to that God in whom I no longer believed.

My God, Lord of the Universe, give me strength never to do what Rabbi Eliahou's son has done.

Shouts rose outside in the yard, where dark-

Vocabulary

encumbrance (en·kum′brəns) *n.*: hindrance; burden.

SKILLS REVIEW

Analyzing style. Remind students that style is the distinctive way in which an author uses language. Explain that Wiesel struggled for years to find a style of writing appropriate for an account of his Holocaust experiences. He finally decided to adopt a spare, declarative style because the short sentences and fragments created a breathless, somewhat fractured tone that was appropriate for the camps. (See Primary Source on p. 821.)

Activity. Ask students why Wiesel relates events in such a simple, literal fashion rather than using figurative language or presenting his own emotions and reactions. [Possible responses: Figurative language is unnecessary because the immense terror, guilt, and dismay in these scenes are obvious; using figurative language or speaking directly of his own emotions might somehow trivialize the experience or do a disservice to his fellow victims.]

ness had fallen. The SS ordered the ranks to form up.

The march began again. The dead stayed in the yard under the snow, like faithful guards assassinated, without burial. No one had said the prayer for the dead over them. Sons abandoned their fathers' remains without a tear.

On the way it snowed, snowed, snowed endlessly. We were marching more slowly. The guards themselves seemed tired. My wounded foot no longer hurt me. It must have been completely frozen. The foot was lost to me. It had detached itself from my body like the wheel of a car. Too bad. I should have to resign myself; I could live with only one leg. The main thing was not to think about it. Above all, not at this moment. Leave thoughts for later.

Our march had lost all semblance of discipline. We went as we wanted, as we could. We heard no more shots. Our guards must have been tired.

But death scarcely needed any help from them. The cold was conscientiously doing its work. At every step someone fell and suffered no more.

E

From time to time, SS officers on motorcycles would go down the length of the column to try and shake us out of our growing apathy:

"Keep going! We are getting there!"

"Courage! Only a few more hours!"

"We're reaching Gleiwitz."

These words of encouragement, even though they came from the mouths of our assassins, did us a great deal of good. No one wanted to give up now, just before the end, so near to the goal. Our eyes searched the horizon for the barbed wire of Gleiwitz. Our only desire was to reach it as quickly as possible.

The night had now set in. The snow had ceased to fall. We walked for several more hours before arriving.

We did not notice the camp until we were just in front of the gate.

Some Kapos rapidly installed us in the barracks. We pushed and jostled one another as if

this were the supreme refuge, the gateway to life. We walked over pain-racked bodies. We trod on wounded faces. No cries. A few groans. My father and I were ourselves thrown to the ground by this rolling tide. Beneath our feet someone let out a rattling cry:

"You're crushing me . . . mercy!"

A voice that was not unknown to me.

"You're crushing me . . . mercy! mercy!"

The same faint voice, the same rattle, heard somewhere before. That voice had spoken to me one day. Where? When? Years ago? No, it could only have been at the camp.

"Mercy!"

I felt that I was crushing him. I was stopping his breath. I wanted to get up. I struggled to disengage myself, so that he could breathe. But I was crushed myself beneath the weight of other bodies. I could hardly breathe. I dug my nails into unknown faces. I was biting all round me, in order to get air. No one cried out.

F

Suddenly I remembered. Juliek![17] The boy from Warsaw who played the violin in the band at Buna. . . .

"Juliek, is it you?"

"Eliezer[18] . . . the twenty-five strokes of the whip. Yes . . . I remember."

He was silent. A long moment elapsed.

"Juliek! Can you hear me, Juliek?"

"Yes . . . ," he said, in a feeble voice. "What do you want?"

He was not dead.

"How do you feel, Juliek?" I asked, less to know the answer than to hear that he could speak, that he was alive.

"All right, Eliezer. . . . I'm getting on all

---

17. **Juliek** (yoo'lē·ek).
18. **Eliezer** (ā·lē·ā'zər).

Vocabulary

semblance (sem'bləns) *n.:* appearance; likeness.

conscientiously (kän'shē·en'shəs·lē) *adv.:* carefully; painstakingly; thoroughly.

apathy (ap'ə·thē) *n.:* indifference; lack of emotion.

Elie Wiesel   **825**

E **Literary Focus**

? **Personification.** Identify the use of personification in this passage, and describe how it affects the atmosphere. [Possible response: Wiesel personifies the cold, which, like the SS officers, carries out the work of killing with a careful and ruthless efficiency. The personification adds to the atmosphere of detached despair: Even nature has turned against the Jews.]

F **Reading Skills**

? **Analyzing a writer's message.** What is the effect of Wiesel's simple observation that "No one cried out"? [Possible response: It is devastating in its simplicity. "No one cried out" encapsulates the dehumanization, brutality, and utter despair of the prisoners.] In what way is the writing of *Night* an attempt to redress the suffering of the prisoners? [Possible responses: Wiesel's book cries out for those prisoners who could not; it is a way to tell the world about their suffering.]

CONTENT-AREA CONNECTIONS

History: The Holocaust

Individual activity. Have students research and report on different aspects of the Holocaust. Some students might report on the eyewitness accounts of other survivors, such as Simon Wiesenthal or Primo Levi. Other students can research a particular exhibit at the Holocaust Memorial Museum in Washington, D.C., such as the Tower of Life

display. Or students can report on specific concentration camps, such as Buchenwald or Auschwitz.

VIEWING THE ART

Ben Shahn (1898–1969) was an artist whose painting addressed social issues and often reflected a sense of bitter irony. As a boy, Shahn immigrated with his family to the United States from Lithuania. As a young man, he worked as a lithographer's apprentice in order to earn enough to study at a series of New York art schools; he completed his art education with trips to Europe in 1927 and 1929. Shahn made his name as a painter of social conscience with his 1931–1932 series on the politically explosive Sacco-Vanzetti case of the 1920s. During the late 1930s and the 1940s, he designed several murals for the Federal Art Project and a series of dramatic posters for the Office of War Information. Shahn often sets stylized figures against a landscape, as he does in *Concentration Camp*.

Activity. Have students select lines from Wiesel's memoir that could be used as alternate titles for the painting. [Possible responses: "We were caught in a trap"; "'Let's keep together. We shall be stronger.'"]

A **Literary Focus**

❓ **Symbol.** In such a place, what might the violin represent for Juliek? [Possible responses: The violin might symbolize civilization, beauty, joy, and hope for a return to a normal life; it might symbolize Juliek's own individuality.]

B **Literary Focus**

❓ **Atmosphere.** What feelings does this passage arouse in you? [Possible responses: horror; revulsion; terror.] Which words and phrases contribute to that effect? [Possible responses: *suffocation; invisible assassin; tore; decaying; dying.*]

Concentration Camp (1944) by Ben Shahn. Tempera (24″ × 24″).
© Estate of Ben Shahn/Licensed by VAGA, New York. Courtesy Sotheby's New York.

right . . . hardly any air . . . worn out. My feet are swollen. It's good to rest, but my violin . . ."

A I thought he had gone out of his mind. What use was the violin here?

"What, your violin?"

He gasped.

"I'm afraid . . . I'm afraid . . . that they'll break my violin. . . . I've brought it with me."

I could not answer him. Someone was lying full length on top of me, covering my face. I was unable to breathe, through either mouth or nose. Sweat beaded my brow, ran down my spine. This was the end—the end of the road. A silent death, suffocation. No way of crying out, of calling for help.

B I tried to get rid of my invisible assassin. My whole will to live was centered in my nails. I scratched. I battled for a mouthful of air. I tore at decaying flesh which did not respond. I could not free myself from this mass weighing down my chest. Was it a dead man I was struggling against? Who knows?

I shall never know. All I can say is that I won. I succeeded in digging a hole through this wall of dying people, a little hole through which I could drink in a small quantity of air.

"Father, how are you?" I asked, as soon as I could utter a word.

I knew he could not be far from me.

"Well!" answered a distant voice, which

FAMILY/COMMUNITY ACTIVITY

Tell students that after his experiences in the camps, Elie Wiesel vowed never to be silent in the face of human suffering. Point out that Wiesel kept his promise, eventually winning the Nobel Peace Prize for his efforts. Invite students to create a "Speaking Out Against Suffering" bulletin-board display. Ask each student to work with his or her family to choose one person who has spoken out against conditions that cause suffering. Students can choose members of their own community or people who have worked in other states or countries. After choosing a person, have students prepare a brief summary of the person's work for the bulletin board.

seemed to come from another world. I tried to sleep.

He tried to sleep. Was he right or wrong? Could one sleep here? Was it not dangerous to allow your vigilance to fail, even for a moment, when at any minute death could pounce upon you?

I was thinking of this when I heard the sound of a violin. The sound of a violin, in this dark shed, where the dead were heaped on the living. What madman could be playing the violin here, at the brink of his own grave? Or was it really an hallucination?

It must have been Juliek.

He played a fragment from Beethoven's concerto. I had never heard sounds so pure. In such a silence.

How had he managed to free himself? To draw his body from under mine without my being aware of it?

It was pitch-dark. I could hear only the violin, and it was as though Juliek's soul were the bow. He was playing his life. The whole of his life was gliding on the strings—his lost hopes, his charred past, his extinguished future. He played as he would never play again.

I shall never forget Juliek. How could I forget that concert, given to an audience of dying and dead men! To this day, whenever I hear Beethoven played my eyes close and out of the dark rises the sad, pale face of my Polish friend, as he said farewell on his violin to an audience of dying men.

I do not know for how long he played. I was overcome by sleep. When I awoke, in the daylight, I could see Juliek, opposite me, slumped over, dead. Near him lay his violin, smashed, trampled, a strange overwhelming little corpse. ■

Response and Analysis

Reading Check

1. What does Madame Schächter see on the journey? How do her cries affect her son? her fellow prisoners?

2. When the prisoners arrive at Auschwitz, what do they see that proves Madame Schächter's visions were tragically accurate?

3. In the second excerpt, what does the head of Wiesel's block advise the prisoners to do before the selection process? Why?

4. What is Akiba Drumer's last request?

5. In the third excerpt, what does Juliek play at Gleiwitz? Who is his audience?

Thinking Critically

6. In the first excerpt, what do you think causes Madame Schächter's terrible visions?

7. In the second excerpt, how has Akiba Drumer "begun to die" when he starts to lose his faith in God? What do you think kept Wiesel from giving up?

8. In the third excerpt, why is it **ironic** that Rabbi Eliahou will "continue to look for his beloved son"? Why is Wiesel glad that he will keep looking?

9. At the end of the third excerpt, why do you think Wiesel uses the **metaphor** of "a strange overwhelming little corpse" to describe Juliek's violin? What might the violin **symbolize** for Wiesel?

10. What **message** is Wiesel communicating to us in telling these stories of terrible human suffering? Think of what these stories say about the power of faith, the power of evil, and the power of art.

Literary Skills
Analyze political points of view on a topic.

Reading Skills
Analyze a writer's message.

Writing Skills
Write an essay comparing and connecting texts.

Vocabulary Skills
Understand connotations of synonyms.

Elie Wiesel **827**

Reading Check

1. Madame Schächter sees a flaming furnace. Her cries terrify the others.

2. The prisoners see the flames and smoke of the Auschwitz crematory and smell the odor of burning flesh.

3. He advises them to jump around to bring color into their bodies and to run by the

SS doctors, who will mark them for death if they look weak or unhealthy.

4. He asks that his friends recite the Kaddish for him after his corpse has been sent to Buna crematory, but they forget.

5. Juliek plays a fragment of a Beethoven concerto on his violin for the dead and dying prisoners, who are being crushed in the barracks.

Response and Analysis

Thinking Critically

6. She has "gone out of her mind." She also may have a premonition of her terrible fate.

7. Possible answer: Drumer loses his sense of purpose when he questions his faith. Wiesel clings to his love for his father and his prayers to a god in whom he "no longer believed."

8. We know that the rabbi's son has abandoned him to increase his own chances of survival. Wiesel is glad that the rabbi isn't forced to understand what the camps have done to his son, and can live with his memories of their strong bond.

9. He may describe it as a corpse because its owner has been crushed to death. The crushed violin may also symbolize the state of civilization.

10. Wiesel seems to suggest that the power of evil, represented by the Nazis, can overwhelm an individual's faith in a righteous and caring God. At the same time, he shows through the writing of *Night* that life can be affirmed through art.

Vocabulary Development

malignant (mə·lig′nənt) *adj.*: destructive; evil.

vengeance (ven′jəns) *n.*: revenge; punishment in return for a wrongdoing.

vindicate (vin′də·kāt′) *v.*: prove correct; justify.

magnitude (mag′nə·tōōd′) *n.*: importance; greatness of scope.

reproached (ri·prōcht′) *v.*: blamed; disgraced.

precariously (pri·ker′ē·əs·lē) *adv.*: in a shaky or unstable way.

arrogance (ar′ə·gəns) *n.*: overbearing pride; self-importance.

invincible (in·vin′sə·bəl) *adj.*: unconquerable.

prostrate (präs′trāt′) *adj.*: helpless; overcome.

dissident (dis′ə·dənt) *adj.*: disagreeing; differing in belief or opinion.

(Photographs, pages 846–849)
Among the Nazis on trial at Nuremberg were top leaders Hermann Goering (far left), the designated successor to Adolf Hitler, and Rudolf Hess (seated next to Goering), Hitler's deputy. The Nazis wearing headphones are listening to a German translation of the proceedings.

Previewing Vocabulary

Have students look up synonyms and antonyms for the Vocabulary words on p. 846. Then, ask the following questions.

1. If someone <u>reproached</u> you, would you have done something good or bad? [bad]

2. Would a politician with a <u>dissident</u> opinion be likely to agree or disagree with the government in power? [disagree]

3. Would you expect an <u>invincible</u> army to win or lose a battle? [win]

4. If you lived <u>precariously</u>, would you be secure or insecure? [insecure]

5. If a court were to <u>vindicate</u> you, would you be happy or unhappy? [happy]

6. Would a <u>prostrate</u> nation be easy or hard to conquer? [easy]

7. Would people usually encourage or oppose a <u>malignant</u> force? [oppose]

8. Does a man filled with <u>arrogance</u> have a high or low opinion of <u>himself</u>? [high]

9. Is choosing a movie or choosing a college a decision of greater <u>magnitude</u>? [choosing a college]

10. Are criminals or their <u>victims</u> more likely to want <u>vengeance</u>? [victims]

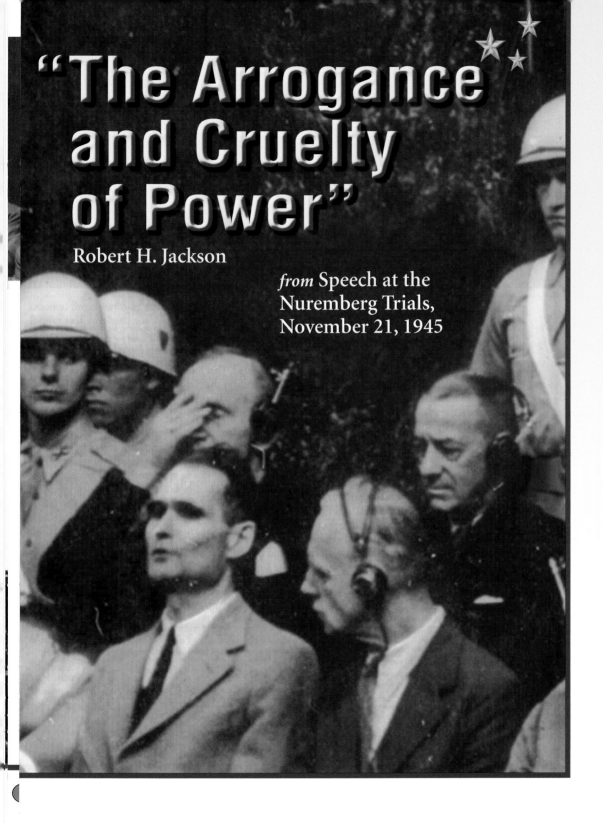

"The Arrogance and Cruelty of Power"

Robert H. Jackson

from Speech at the Nuremberg Trials, November 21, 1945

Connected Reading

Summary ⬌ at grade level

In this letter, John Whitehead, an American boat officer, recalls a quiet moment during the D-day invasion. After successfully ferrying two loads of troops and supplies from his ship to the beachhead, Whitehead takes a moment to survey the invasion scene. The landing, which earlier in the day seemed so chaotic that Whitehead feared it would fail, is beginning to take shape. Whitehead realizes that the invasion may well succeed, and his small part in the overall effort fills him with great pride.

Selection Starter

Build background. Tell students that the D-day invasion, known officially as Operation Overlord, involved 3 million troops, about 4,000 large ships, approximately 2,500 smaller landing craft, and more than 11,000 aircraft. The invaders waded ashore across a 50-mile front, and Allied engineers used prefabricated harbors and docks to unload supplies.

Political Points *of* View

Before You Read

The television journalist Tom Brokaw (1940–   ) walked the beaches of Normandy in northern France on the fortieth and fiftieth anniversaries of D-day—the June 6, 1944, Allied invasion of Nazi-occupied France that signaled the beginning of the final stage of World War II in Europe. As Brokaw walked, he began to realize how much he owed the generation who had fought World War II. It was his parents' generation, people shaped by the Great Depression of the 1930s and the war years of the 1940s—a generation little known or understood by people coming of age in the 1980s and 1990s, an era of prosperity. He decided to thank that generation for its legacy of "duty and honor, sacrifice and accomplishment" by telling its stories in a book he called *The Greatest Generation* (1998).

Response proved so enthusiastic that Brokaw compiled a second book. *The Greatest Generation Speaks* (1999) contains letters and reflections by men and women who directly experienced World War II. The excerpt you are about to read comes from a letter written by John Whitehead, who served in the U.S. Navy as a supply officer on the U.S.S. *Thomas Jefferson*. World War II "was a long war," Whitehead said earlier in his letter, but one that was "universally accepted by all of us who participated as a 'just war.' . . . It was a war that had to be won and we would willingly stay the course."

For the D-day mission on June 6, 1944, Whitehead was assigned to be a boat officer. The following excerpt begins after Whitehead and his crew had landed two thousand soldiers on the beaches of Normandy, France, for the planned attack.

U.S. infantrymen wading ashore during D-day landing.

Allied forces at the beach in Normandy.

Primary Source

Winston Churchill's Oratory

In October 1940, the British prime minister Winston Churchill broadcast a speech to Nazi-occupied France that ended with this promise: "Good night, then: sleep to gather strength for the morning. For the morning will come. Brightly will it shine on the brave and the true, kindly upon all who suffer for the cause, glorious upon the tombs of the heroes. Thus, will shine the dawn."

Whole-class activity. Have students discuss the purpose of Churchill's words. What might he have been referring to when he spoke of "the morning"? [the liberation of Nazi-occupied France] How did historical events fulfill Churchill's promise to France? [The Allies won the war.]

LETTER

"The Biggest Battle of All History"

A

John Whitehead

from **The Greatest Generation Speaks**
by **Tom Brokaw**

There was one moment of D-day which, rather strangely, remains more vivid in my mind than anything else. It was a quiet moment, a moment of peace and introspection after a very long day of noise and fear, of chaos and seasickness, of little acts of courage, and of death.

It was about 3:00 and we had made our second landing of the day and would soon be starting again the two-hour trip back to the *T.J.*[1] The beach was now secure. My five little boats had all made it in without serious problems and we were actually a little ahead of schedule. The ship's crew had only had two casualties from the landing. The Army lieutenant from my boat was now busy trying to get ashore a large machine gun and, for the first time since 2:00 A.M., I had a free moment.

I clambered off the boat—we were stuck on a little shoal in about two feet of water—and walked a few yards up the beach. I took a few deep breaths and looked around me. The dead and wounded had been moved up to the first dune and were being cared for. Equipment— guns and food and ammunition—was being unloaded, along with more troops. As far as I could see, in both directions, LCVPs[2] were landing, unloading, and withdrawing, and I realized that what I could see was less than 5 percent of the landing beaches. It wasn't orderly, but it wasn't chaos either. I got the sense that it was going to work, that what had looked like such a disaster only a few hours earlier was beginning to look like it had a chance.

B

I felt thankful, of course, that I seemed to have survived the worst part. I took a few deep breaths and felt suddenly elated, proud to be having even a tiny part in what was maybe the biggest battle of all history. At that moment, soaked to the skin, seasick, dead tired, cold, still scared, I would not have wanted to be anywhere else.

C

---

1. **T.J.:** Whitehead's abbreviation for the U.S.S. *Thomas Jefferson*.
2. **LCVPs:** plural form of the acronym for "landing craft, vehicle, personnel," small U.S. Navy boats designed to carry personnel from ship to shore.

John Whitehead   **859**

DIRECT TEACHING

A Political Issue

? World War II. According to John Whitehead, World War II was "universally accepted by all of us who participated as a 'just war.'" Why would this attitude help the Allied forces on D-day? [Possible responses: Working for a just cause would give the soldiers added confidence and determination; people are more willing to fight and die for a cause in which they truly believe.]

B Literary Focus

? Tone. How would you describe the tone of Whitehead's letter? [Possible response: Whitehead begins with an objective, somewhat philosophical tone and ends with an optimistic and idealistic tone.]

C Political Issue

? World War II. Why do you think Whitehead decides he would rather be on the beachhead at Normandy than anywhere else? [Possible responses: He realizes that taking part in this historic event is a unique opportunity; for the first time, he senses that the invasion will succeed.]

Secondary Source

D-Day Casualty Statistics

To put the D-day invasion and the fighting that followed in perspective, you might want to share these comments and statistics from two World War II historians: "For those who walk the silent cemeteries of Normandy, the cost of victory may seem steep indeed. The fighting between 6 June and 29 August cost the Twenty-First Army Group (consisting of British, Canadian, and Polish troops) 83,045 casualties.

American ground troops suffered a further 125,847 casualties. In addition, the RAF and USAAF each lost over 8,000 men. . . . Altogether, Allied losses were approximately 225,000. On the other side, the Germans suffered over 200,000 casualties. with an additional 200,000 captured. By any standard, the summer campaign of 1944 was a bloodbath. . . . "

Summary ↔ *at grade level*

On Independence Day, Paul Berlin, a Vietnam veteran, drives repeatedly around a small lake in his hometown and imagines the conversation he longs to have with his father. The conversation concerns an incident that haunts Paul from his service in Vietnam, where he believes he had an opportunity to win a Silver Star for valor. In that incident, Paul had failed to probe a Viet Cong tunnel after a fellow soldier had been killed there. In the imaginary conversation, his father reassures him of his bravery. Preoccupied with the soldier's death and his own sense of failure, Paul stops for a meal at a drive-in, and, as the day ends, watches the holiday fireworks display.

Selection Starter

Build background. The Vietnam War lasted from the late 1950s to 1975. During this conflict, communist North Vietnam attempted to gain control of non-communist South Vietnam. The early stages of the war were fought mainly between the South Vietnamese army and communist-trained rebels (known as the Viet Cong) in South Vietnam. By 1964–1965, both the United States and North Vietnam had become directly involved. The United States began withdrawing its 500,000 troops in 1969, but continued bombing. The last troops did not leave until March 1973. In 1975, South Vietnam surrendered. Almost 60,000 Americans died in this much-protested war; Vietnamese deaths numbered between 3 and perhaps more than 5 million.

Before You Read

Speaking of Courage

Make the Connection
Quickwrite 🖉

What is courage? Can it be measured by awards and medals? In this story, Paul Berlin looks back, wishing he had *really* been courageous in war—especially during one particular incident. He finds himself unable to discuss with his father what happened. Why might it be difficult for a young soldier to speak with a parent about a war experience? Write down reasons why such conversations might be strained.

Literary Focus
Conflict

A **conflict** is a struggle between opposing forces or characters. An **external conflict** can involve two people, or a person and a natural or artificial force. An **internal conflict** involves opposing forces within a person's mind. "Speaking of Courage" focuses mainly on an internal conflict within the mind of Paul Berlin.

INTERNET
Vocabulary Practice
Keyword: LE5 11-6

> **Conflict** is a struggle between opposing forces or characters.
>
> *For more on Conflict, see the Handbook of Literary and Historical Terms.*

Reading Skills
Identifying Historical Context

The setting of a story includes not only its time and place but also its historical context—the social and political environment unique to that time and place. Atmosphere, characterization, and the central conflicts of a story often flow directly from historical context, as they do in "Speaking

SKILLS FOCUS

Literary Skills
Understand external and internal conflict.

Reading Skills
Identify historical context.

of Courage." As you read, take notes on contrasts between the attitudes and values of small-town Iowa, Paul Berlin's home, and the realities of jungle warfare in Vietnam, which Paul has just experienced.

Background

Before O'Brien completed his war novel, *Going After Cacciato,* he published earlier versions of some sections as short stories. This story, which appears in a different form in the novel, was named one of the O. Henry Prize Stories of 1978.

The novel describes the war as experienced by a young soldier named Paul Berlin. In "Speaking of Courage," Paul has recently returned home from battle duty in Vietnam. Like many other veterans of that war, Paul is vaguely dissatisfied and confused about the meaning of his experiences.

Vocabulary Development

affluent (af′lōō·ənt) *n.*: well-to-do people.

tepid (tep′id) *adj.*: lukewarm.

mesmerizing (mez′mər·īz′iŋ) *v.* used as *adj.*: hypnotic.

drone *n.*: steady hum.

recede (ri·sēd′) *v.*: become more distant and indistinct.

valor (val′ər) *n.*: great courage.

municipal (myōō·nis′ə·pəl) *adj.*: belonging to a city or town.

profundity (prō·fun′də·tē) *n.*: intellectual depth.

tactile (tak′təl) *adj.*: able to be perceived by touch.

Previewing Vocabulary

Have students work in groups to read the Vocabulary words listed on p. 866. To reinforce understanding, have students match each of the following words with its definition.

1. valor [f]
2. tepid [b]
3. affluent [a]
4. recede [e]
5. profundity [h]
6. municipal [g]
7. mesmerizing [c]
8. tactile [i]
9. drone [d]

a. wealthy people
b. lukewarm
c. hypnotic
d. constant hum
e. fade
f. bravery
g. of a city
h. depth of thought
i. can be touched

SPEAKING OF COURAGE

Tim O'Brien

His father would not talk. His father had been in another war, so he knew the truth already, and there was no one left to talk with.

867

A Reading Skills

Identifying historical context.
Remind students that "the war" refers to the Vietnam War. Although the war technically ended in 1975, the last of the U.S. troops departed Vietnam in 1973.

B Reading Skills

? Making inferences. What can you infer about Paul Berlin from the first two sentences? [Possible responses: He has been in a war and has returned home; he is alone; he seems aimless and troubled.]

C Literary Focus

? Conflict. What conflict is revealed in the narrator's repeated comment that everything is the same? [Possible response: The repetition suggests ironically that everything is not the same—that the narrator has changed and is now experiencing a conflict with his community.]

D Reading Skills

Identifying historical context.
Explain that Paul's father probably participated in World War II.

E Reading Skills

? Making inferences. What is "the truth" that Paul's father knows? [Possible response: Paul's father knows that war is a shameful, humiliating horror that cannot be expressed in words.]

F Literary Focus

? Imagery. How does this image reflect Paul's internal state? [Possible response: Like the man with his motorboat, Paul finds himself "stalled," confused, and frustrated.]

(A) (B) The war was over, and there was no place in particular to go. Paul Berlin followed the tar road in its seven-mile loop around the lake, then he started all over again, driving slowly, feeling safe inside his father's big Chevy, now and again looking out onto the lake to watch the boats and waterskiers and scenery. It was Sunday and it was summer, and things seemed pretty much the same. The lake was the same. (C) The houses were the same, all low-slung and split level and modern, porches and picture windows facing the water. The lots were spacious. On the lake-side of the road, the houses were handsome and set deep in, well-kept and painted, with docks jutting out into the lake, and boats moored and covered with canvas, and gardens, and sometimes even gardeners, and stone patios with barbecue spits and grills, and wooden shingles saying who lived where. On the other side of the road, to his left, the houses were also handsome, though less expensive and on a smaller scale and with no docks or boats or wooden shingles. The road was a sort of boundary between the affluent and the almost affluent, and to live on the lake-side of the road was one of the few natural privileges in a town of the prairie—the difference between watching the sun set over cornfields or over the lake.

It was a good-sized lake. In high school he'd driven round and round and round with his friends and pretty girls, talking about urgent matters, worrying eagerly about the existence of God and theories of causation,[1] or wondering whether Sally Hankins, who lived on the lake-side of the road, would want to pull into the shelter of Sunset Park. Then, there had not been a war. But there had always been the lake. It had been dug out by the southernmost advance of the Wisconsin glacier. Fed by neither springs nor streams, it was a tepid, algaed lake that depended on fickle prairie rains for replenishment. Still, it was the town's only lake, the only one in twenty-six miles, and at night the moon made a white swath across its waters, and on sunny days it was nice to look at, and that evening it would dazzle with the reflections of fireworks, and it was the center of things from the very start, always there to be driven around, still mesmerizing and quieting and a good audience for silence, a seven-mile flat circumference that could be traveled by slow car in twenty-five minutes. It was not such a good lake for swimming. After college, he'd caught an ear infection that had almost kept him out of the war. And the lake had drowned Max Arnold, keeping him out of the war entirely. Max had been one who liked to talk about the existence of God. "No, I'm not saying *that*," he would say carefully against the drone of the engine. "I'm saying it is possible as an idea, even necessary as an idea, a final cause in the whole structure of causation." Now he knew, perhaps. Before the war, they'd driven around the lake as friends, but now Max was dead and most of the others were living in Des Moines or Sioux City, or going to school somewhere, or holding down jobs. None of the girls was left. Sally Hankins was married. His father would not talk. (D) His father had been in another war, so he knew the truth already, and he (E) would not talk about it, and there was no one left to talk with.

He turned on the radio. The car's big engine fired machinery that blew cold air all over him. Clockwise, like an electron spinning forever around its nucleus, the big Chevy circled the lake, and he had little to do but sit in the air-conditioning, both hands on the wheel, letting the car carry him in orbit. It was a lazy Sunday. The town was small. Out on the lake, a man's motorboat had stalled, and the fellow was bent (F) over the silver motor with a wrench and a frown, and beyond him there were waterskiers and smooth July waters and two mud hens.

Vocabulary

affluent (af'lōō·ənt) n.: well-to-do people.
tepid (tep'id) adj.: lukewarm.
mesmerizing (mez'mər·īz'in) v. used as adj.: hypnotic.
drone n.: steady hum.

---

1. **theories of causation:** philosophical theories holding that events are connected through cause-and-effect relationships.

DIFFERENTIATING INSTRUCTION

Learners Having Difficulty
Modeling. To help students read "Speaking of Courage," model the reading skill of identifying historical context. Say, "From the first line of the story, I know that its action takes place after the ending of a war—the Vietnam War. I also know that the narrator lacks purpose and direction. These two facts seem to be linked. That is, the story's historical context—the postwar period—is directly influencing the character of Paul Berlin. I can guess that the historical context will have an impact on the story's plot, too."

English-Language Learners
Help students choose a word or phrase that is repeated in the story. Then, have them make a cluster diagram to record associated ideas and images. For example, students can write "no place in particular to go" in a cen-

The road curved west. The sun was low in front of him, and he figured it was close to five o'clock. Twenty after, he guessed. The war had taught him to figure time. Even without the sun, waking from sleep, he could usually place it within fifteen minutes either way. He wished his father were there beside him, so he could say, "Well, looks about five-twenty," and his father would look at his watch and say, "Hey! How'd you do that?" "One of those things you learn in the war," he would say. "I know exactly what you mean," his father would then say, and the ice would be broken, and then they would be able to talk about it as they circled the lake.

He drove past Slater Park and across the causeway and past Sunset Park. The radio announcer sounded tired. He said it was five-thirty. The temperature in Des Moines was eighty-one degrees, and "All you on the road, drive carefully now, you hear, on this fine Fourth of July." Along the road, kicking stones in front of them, two young boys were hiking with knapsacks and toy rifles and canteens. He honked going by, but neither boy looked up. Already he'd passed them six times, forty-two miles, nearly three hours. He watched the boys <u>recede</u> in his rearview mirror. They turned purply colored, like clotted blood, before finally disappearing.

"How many medals did you win?" his father might have asked.

"Seven," he would have said, "though none of them were for valor."

"That's all <u>right</u>," his father would have answered, knowing full well that many brave men did not win medals for their bravery, and that others won medals for doing nothing. "What are the medals you won?"

And he would have listed them, as a kind of starting place for talking about the war: the Combat Infantryman's Badge, the Air Medal, the Bronze Star (without a V-device for valor),

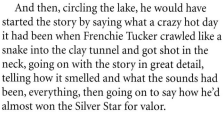

"Though none of them were for valor."

the Army Commendation Medal, the Vietnam Campaign Medal, the Good Conduct Medal, and the Purple Heart, though it wasn't much of a wound, and there was no scar, and it didn't hurt and never had. While none of them was for valor, the decorations still looked good on the uniform in his closet, and if anyone were to ask, he would have explained what each signified, and eventually he would have talked about the medals he did not win, and why he did not win them, and how afraid he had been.

"Well," his father might have said, "that's an impressive list of medals, all right."

"But none were for valor."

"I understand."

And that would have been the time for telling his father that he'd almost won the Silver Star, or maybe even the Medal of Honor.

"I almost won the Silver Star," he would have said.

"How's that?"

"Oh, it's just a war story."

"What's wrong with war stories?" his father would have said.

"Nothing, except I guess nobody wants to hear them."

"Tell me," his father would have said.

And then, circling the lake, he would have started the story by saying what a crazy hot day it had been when Frenchie Tucker crawled like a snake into the clay tunnel and got shot in the neck, going on with the story in great detail, telling how it smelled and what the sounds had been, everything, then going on to say how he'd almost won the Silver Star for valor.

"Well," his father would have said, "that's not a very pretty story."

"I wasn't very brave."

"You have seven medals."

Vocabulary
recede (ri·sēd′) v.: become more distant and indistinct.
valor (val′ər) n.: great courage.

G **Literary Focus**

? **Conflict.** Point out that external and internal conflicts are often closely linked. What are Paul Berlin's conflicts, and how are they linked? [For Paul, the external conflict of the war has created an internal conflict about courage and self-worth.]

H **Reading Skills**

? **Evaluating ethical influences.** What does this imaginary exchange reveal about Paul's views of "right" and "wrong" behavior? [Possible response: "Right" behavior is courage, and "wrong" behavior is cowardice.]

tral circle and then, in surrounding circles, write repetitions or elaborations of the idea.

Advanced Learners
Enrichment. Have each student write a letter from Paul to his father that expresses everything he wants to say. To begin, students can review the story and take notes on Paul's imaginary conversations with his father. Then, students can brainstorm a list of emotions Paul might feel toward his father. Students should use their notes to write their letters. Invite volunteers to read their letters aloud.

Ⓐ Literary Focus

❓ Conflict. What does Paul's repeated imagined conversation indicate about his inner conflict? [Possible response: The fact that he cannot think of anything else hints at his great need for resolution of the conflict.]

Vietnam Veterans Memorial (detail), Washington, D.C.

"True, true," he would have said, "but I might have had eight," but even so, seven medals was pretty good, hinting at courage with their bright colors and heavy metals. "But I wasn't brave," he would have admitted.

"You weren't a coward, either," his father would have said.

"I might have been a hero."

"But you weren't a coward," his father would have insisted.

"No," Paul Berlin would have said, holding the wheel slightly right of center to produce the constant clockwise motion, "no, I wasn't a coward, and I wasn't brave, but I had the chance." He would have explained, if anyone were there to listen, that his most precious medal, except for the one he did not win, was the Combat Infantryman's Badge. While not strictly speaking a genuine medal—more an insignia of soldierdom—the CIB meant that he had seen the war as a real soldier, on the ground. It meant he'd had the opportunity to be brave, it meant that. It meant, too, that he'd . . . seen Frenchie Tucker crawl into the tunnel so that just his feet were left showing, and heard the sound when he got shot in the neck. With its crossed rifles and silver and blue colors, the CIB was really not such a bad decoration, not as good as the Silver Star or Medal of Honor, but still evidence that he'd once been there with the chance to be very brave. "I wasn't brave," he would have said, "but I might have been."

The road descended into the outskirts of town, turning northwest past the junior college and tennis courts, then past the city park where tables were spread with sheets of colored plastic as picnickers listened to the high school band, then past the municipal docks where a fat woman stood in pedal-pushers and white socks, fishing for bullheads.[2] There were no other fish in the lake, excepting some perch and a few

---

2. **bullheads** *n. pl.*: type of freshwater catfish with hornlike growths near its mouth.

Vocabulary
municipal (myo͞o·nis′ə·pəl) *adj.*: belonging to a city or town.

Comparing and Contrasting Texts

Comparing experiences of war. "Speaking of Courage" and "Game" (p. 878) both focus on the mental states of men affected by military experiences. You might ask the following questions after students read both stories:

• Who has been damaged more by war—Paul Berlin or Barthelme's narrator?

• Which story is more sympathetic toward its protagonist? Explain.

• Which story's setting has a stronger effect on you? Why?

• Which story is more optimistic about the future? How can you tell?

• Which story do you prefer? Why?

worthless carp. It was a bad lake for swimming and fishing both.

He was in no great hurry. There was no place in particular to go. The day was very hot, but inside the Chevy the air was cold and oily and secure, and he liked the sound of the big engine and the radio and the air-conditioning. Through the windows, as though seen through one-way glass, the town shined like a stop-motion photograph, or a memory. The town could not talk, and it would not listen, and it was really a very small town anyway. "How'd you like to hear about the time I almost won the Silver Star for valor?" he might have said. The Chevy seemed to know its way around the lake.

It was late afternoon. Along an unused railway spur, four men were erecting steel launchers for the evening fireworks. They were dressed alike in khaki trousers, work shirts, visored caps and black boots. They were sweating. Two of them were unloading crates of explosives from a city truck, stacking the crates near the steel launchers. They were talking. One of them was laughing. "How'd you like to hear about it?" he might have murmured, but the men did not look up. Later they would blow color into the sky. The lake would be like a mirror, and the picnickers would sigh. The colors would open wide. "Well, it was this crazy hot day," he would have said to anyone who asked, "and Frenchie Tucker took off his helmet and pack and crawled into the tunnel with a forty-five and a knife, and the whole platoon stood in a circle around the mouth of the tunnel to watch him go down. 'Don't get blowed away,' said Stink Harris, but Frenchie was already inside and he didn't hear. You could see his feet wiggling, and you could smell the dirt and clay, and then, when he got shot through the neck, you could smell the gunpowder and you could see Frenchie's feet jerk, and that was the day I could have won the Silver Star for valor."

The Chevy rolled smoothly across the old railroad spur. To his right, there was only the open lake. To his left, the lawns were scorched dry like October corn. Hopelessly, round and round, a rotating sprinkler scattered water into Doctor Mason's vegetable garden. In August it would get worse. The lake would turn green, thick with bacteria and decay, and the golf course would dry up, and dragonflies would crack open for lack of good water. The summer seemed permanent.

The big Chevy curled past the A&W[3] and Centennial Beach, and he started his seventh revolution around the lake.

He followed the road past the handsome low-slung houses. Back to Slater Park, across the causeway, around to Sunset Park, as though riding on tracks.

Out on the lake, the man with the stalled motorboat was still fiddling with the engine.

The two boys were still trudging on their hike. They did not look up when he honked.

The pair of mud hens floated like wooden decoys. The waterskiers looked tan and happy, and the spray behind them looked clean.

It was all distant and pretty.

Facing the sun again, he figured it was nearly six o'clock. Not much later the tired announcer in Des Moines confirmed it, his voice seeming to rock itself into a Sunday afternoon snooze.

Too bad, he thought. If Max were there, he would say something meaningful about the announcer's fatigue, and relate it to the sun low and red now over the lake, and the war, and courage. Too bad that all the girls had gone away. And his father, who already knew the difficulties of being brave, and who preferred silence.

Circling the lake, with time to talk, he would have told the truth. He would not have faked it. Starting with the admission that he had not been truly brave, he would have next said he hadn't been a coward, either. "I almost won the Silver Star for valor," he would have said, and, even so, he'd learned many important things in the war. Like telling time without a watch. He had learned to step lightly. He knew, just by the sound, the difference between friendly and enemy mortars,[4] and with time to talk and with an audience, he could explain the difference in

---

3. **A&W:** chain of drive-in fast-food restaurants.
4. **mortars** *n. pl.:* cannons used to fire explosive shells.

DIRECT TEACHING

A **Reading Skills**

Identifying historical context. Students may not understand why "nobody believed it was really a war at all." Explain that the Vietnam War was unpopular. Some Americans felt that the U.S. presence in South Vietnam only supported a corrupt government.

B **Learners Having Difficulty**

? Paraphrasing. In your own words, what happens in this passage? [Possible response: Paul crawls into the tunnel where Frenchie was shot, smells Frenchie's blood, and passes out. He is dragged out of the tunnel by his comrades.]

C **Advanced Learners**

? Enrichment. What is the truth that Paul desperately wants to communicate, and why is it "not profound"? [He wants to work through the simple, but overwhelming truth of his day-by-day experiences in Vietnam. By "not profound," he means that he cannot portray them as part of a righteous cause, ideological quest, or philosophical journey.]

---

great detail. He could tell people that the enemy fired 82-millimeter mortar rounds, while we fired 81's, and that this was a real advantage to the enemy since they could steal our rounds and shoot them from their own weapons. He knew many lies. Simple, unprofound things. He knew it is a lie that only stupid men are brave. He knew that a man can die of fright, literally, because it had happened just that way to Billy Boy Watkins after his foot had been blown off. Billy Boy had been scared to death. Dead of a heart attack caused by fright, according to Doc Peret, who would know. He knew, too, that it is a lie, the old saying that you never hear the shot that gets you, because Frenchie Tucker was shot in the neck, and after they dragged him out of the tunnel he lay there and told everyone his great discovery; he'd heard it coming the whole way, he said excitedly; and then he raised his thumb and bled through his mouth, grinning at the great discovery. So the old saying was surely a lie, or else Frenchie Tucker was lying himself, which under the circumstances was hard to believe. He knew a lot of things. They were not new or profound, but they were true. He knew that he might have won a Silver Star, like Frenchie, if he'd been able to finish what Frenchie started in the foul tunnel. He knew many war stories, a thousand details, smells and the confusion of the senses, but nobody was there to listen, and nobody knew a damn about the war because nobody believed it was really a war at all. It was not a war for war stories, or talk of valor, and nobody asked questions about the details, such as how afraid you can be, or what the particular sounds were, or whether it hurts to be shot, or what you think about and hear and see on ambush, or whether you can really tell in a firefight which way to shoot, which you can't, or how you become brave enough to win the Silver Star, or how it smells of sulfur against your cheek after firing eighteen fast rounds, or how you crawl on hands and knees without knowing direction, and how, after crawling into the red-mouthed tunnel, you close your eyes like a mole and follow the tunnel walls and smell Frenchie's fresh blood and know a bullet cannot miss in there, and how there is nowhere to go but forward or backward, eyes closed, and how you can't go forward, and lose all sense, and are dragged out by the heels, losing the Silver Star. All the details, without profundity, simple and age old, but nobody wants to hear war stories because they are age old and not new and not profound, and because everyone knows already that it hadn't been a war like other wars. If Max or his father were ever to ask, or anybody, he would say, "Well, first off, it was a war the same as any war," which would not sound profound at all, but which would be the truth. Then he would explain what he meant in great detail, explaining that, right or wrong or win or lose, at root it had been a real war, regardless of corruption in high places or politics or sociology or the existence of God. His father knew it already, though. Which was why he didn't ask. And Max could not ask. It was a small town, but it wasn't the town's fault, either.

He passed the sprawling ranch-style homes. He lit a cigarette. He had learned to smoke in the war. He opened the window a crack but kept the air-conditioner going full, and again he circled the lake. His thoughts were the same. Out on the lake, the man was frantically yanking the cord to his stalled outboard motor. Along the causeway, the two boys marched on. The pair of mud hens sought sludge at the bottom of the lake, heads under water and tails bobbing.

Six-thirty, he thought. The lake had divided into two halves. One half still glistened. The other was caught in shadow. Soon it would be dark. The crew of workers would shoot the sky full of color, for the war was over, and the town would celebrate independence. He passed Sunset Park once again, and more houses, and the junior college and tennis courts, and the picnickers and the high school band, and the municipal docks where the fat woman patiently waited for fish.

Vocabulary

profundity (prō·fun′də·tē) *n.:* intellectual depth.

CONTENT-AREA CONNECTIONS

Geography: Vietnam

Individual activity. Have students research photographs and sketches of the Vietnamese countryside, including the mountains, hills, and jungles that made combat so difficult for Americans. Students can use these images to help them contrast the appearance of Vietnam with that of Paul's hometown in Iowa.

Music: George Crumb's *Black Angels*

One of the most powerful pieces of music to emerge from the Vietnam War is George Crumb's *Black Angels: Thirteen Images from the Dark Land* (1970). This eerie string quartet evokes the terrifying environment of the war and presents a "journey" through the conflict in three stages: "Departure," "Absence," "Return." Try to locate the gripping recording by the Kronos Quartet.

Already, though it wasn't quite dusk, the A&W was awash in neon lights.

He maneuvered his father's Chevy into one of the parking slots, let the engine idle, and waited. The place was doing a good holiday business. Mostly kids in their fathers' cars, a few farmers in for the day, a few faces he thought he remembered, but no names. He sat still. With the sound of the engine and air-conditioning and radio, he could not hear the kids laughing, or the cars coming and going and burning rubber. But it didn't matter, it seemed proper, and he sat patiently and watched while mosquitoes and June bugs swarmed off the lake to attack the orange-colored lighting. A slim, hipless, deft young blonde delivered trays of food, passing him by as if the big Chevy were invisible, but he waited. The tired announcer in Des Moines gave the time, seven o'clock. He could trace the fall of dusk in the orange lights which grew brighter and sharper. It was a bad war for medals. But the Silver Star would have been nice. Nice to have been brave. The tactile, certain substance of the Silver Star, and how he could have rubbed his fingers over it, remembering the tunnel and the smell of clay in his nose, going forward and not backward in simple bravery. He waited patiently. The mosquitoes were electrocuting themselves against a Pest-Rid machine. The slim young carhop ignored him, chatting with four boys in a Firebird, her legs in nylons even in mid-summer.

He honked once, a little embarrassed, but she did not turn. The four boys were laughing. He could not hear them, or the joke, but he could see their bright eyes and the way their heads moved. She patted the cheek of the driver.

He honked again, twice. He could not hear the sound. The girl did not hear, either.

He honked again, this time leaning on the horn. His ears buzzed. The air-conditioning shot cold air into his lap. The girl turned slowly,

"I almost won the Silver Star."

as though hearing something very distant, not at all sure. She said something to the boys, and they laughed, then she moved reluctantly toward him. EAT MAMA BURGERS said the orange and brown button on her chest. "How'd you like to hear about the war," he whispered, feeling vengeful. "The time I almost won the Silver Star."

She stood at the window, straight up so he could not see her face, only the button that said, EAT MAMA BURGERS. "Papa Burger, root beer, and french fries," he said, but the girl did not move or answer. She rapped on the window.

"Papa Burger, root beer, and french fries," he said, rolling it down.

She leaned down. She shook her head dumbly. Her eyes were as lovely and fuzzy as cotton candy.

"Papa Burger, root beer, and french fries," he said slowly, pronouncing the words separately and distinctly for her.

She stared at him with her strange eyes. "You blind?" she chirped suddenly. She gestured toward an intercom attached to a steel post. "You blind or something?"

"Papa Burger, root beer, and french fries."

"Push the button," she said, "and place your order." Then, first punching the button for him, she returned to her friends in the Firebird.

"Order," commanded a tinny voice.

"Papa Burger, root beer, and french fries."

"Roger-dodger," the voice said. "Repeat: one Papa, one beer, one fries. Stand by. That's it?"

"Roger," said Paul Berlin.

"Out," said the voice, and the intercom squeaked and went dead.

"Out," said Paul Berlin.

When the slim carhop brought him his tray,

Vocabulary

tactile (tak′təl) *adj.:* able to be perceived by touch.

Tim O'Brien   873

D Literary Focus

? Symbol. What does Paul's father's car symbolize, here and throughout the story? [Possible responses: insulation; alienation; aimlessness; Paul's need to control his own destination.]

E Literary Focus

? Conflict. How does Paul's external conflict with the carhop mirror one of his internal conflicts? [Possible response: Paul cannot "connect" with the carhop. This mirrors Paul's inability to connect the meaning of his wartime experiences with his present life.]

GUIDED PRACTICE

Monitoring students' progress. Guide the class in answering the following questions.

True-False

1. Paul is amazed at how much everything has changed in his hometown. [F]
2. Paul receives seven medals, but none of them are for valor. [T]
3. Paul believes he could have won the Silver Star the day Frenchie Tucker died. [T]
4. In Vietnam, Paul learned that a man can die from fright. [T]
5. Paul is glad he was not awarded the Silver Star. [F]

SKILLS REVIEW

Analyzing theme. Ask students to try to express the story's theme in one or two sentences. Then, discuss with students what the story reveals about the "wages" of war. For example, does the country owe Paul a "debt"? How will that debt be paid? Has Paul been "paid" in a currency that he does not want or that he does not deserve?

A Literary Focus

? Theme. What does the man's inability to fix his boat suggest about the theme? [Possible response: It points to the devastation and dysfunction that war can cause in a person's life.]

INDEPENDENT PRACTICE

Response and Analysis

Reading Check

1. The story takes place on a Sunday, July 4, in Paul's home-town near Des Moines, Iowa, and in Paul's memory of a tunnel in Vietnam in which a comrade is killed by enemy fire.

2. Paul wishes his father would talk to him about the war.

3. Possible answers: He learned how to tell time without a watch, to step lightly, and to differentiate between sounds of friendly and enemy fire.

4. People don't want to hear about the war because nobody believes it was a war like other wars.

5. Paul wishes he had won a medal for valor. He wants to tell his father how he almost won the Silver Star and how he feels about the war and about himself.

Thinking Critically

6. From his own experience, Paul's father knows that war is filled with harsh moments. He may be resisting hearing about the pain his child endured at war.

7. Paul's revolutions about the lake and repeated estimates of the hour symbolize inertia and suggest that he is locked in a loop.

8. The Fourth of July celebrates national pride and freedom. No one acknowledges Paul's work to safeguard this ideal.

---

he ate quickly, without looking up, then punched the intercom button.

"Order," said the tinny voice.

"I'm done."

"That's it?"

"Yes, all done."

"Roger-dodger, over n' out," said the voice.

"Out."

On his ninth revolution around the lake he passed the hiking boys for the last time. The man with the stalled motorboat was paddling toward shore. The mud hens were gone. The fat woman was reeling in her line. The sun had left a smudge of watercolor on the horizon, and the bandshell[5] was empty, and Doctor Mason's sprinkler went round and round.

On his tenth revolution, he switched off the

---

5. **bandshell** *n.*: open-air stage with a rear sounding board shaped like the shell of a scallop.

---

air-conditioning, cranked open a window, and rested his elbow comfortably on the sill, driving with one hand. He could trace the contours of the tunnel. He could talk about the scrambling sense of being lost, though he could not describe it even in his thoughts. He could talk about the terror, but he could not describe it or even feel it anymore. He could talk about emerging to see sunlight, but he could not feel the warmth, or see the faces of the men who looked away, or talk about his shame. There was no one to talk to, and nothing to say.

On his eleventh revolution, the sky went crazy with color.

He pulled into Sunset Park and stopped in the shadow of a picnic shelter. After a time, he got out and walked down to the beach and stood with his arms folded and watched the fireworks. For a small town, it was a pretty good show. ■

Response and Analysis

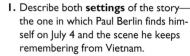
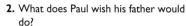

SKILLS FOCUS

Literary Skills
Analyze external and internal conflict.

Reading Skills
Analyze historical context.

Writing Skills
Write an essay comparing and contrasting two characters. Write an essay explaining the use of contrast in a story.

Vocabulary Skills
Use context clues.

Reading Check

1. Describe both **settings** of the story— the one in which Paul Berlin finds himself on July 4 and the scene he keeps remembering from Vietnam.

2. What does Paul wish his father would do?

3. List the things Paul has learned as a result of the war.

4. According to Paul, why don't people want to hear about the war?

5. What does Paul wish he had done in Vietnam? What does he want to tell his father?

Thinking Critically

6. Explain why it is so difficult for Paul and his father to talk. What do you think Paul means when he says that his father "knew the truth already"? (Be sure to check your Quickwrite notes.) ✏

7. Discuss the **symbolic** meaning of the repeated circular actions in the story and the repeated references to time.

8. Considering the historical context of the story, what is **symbolic** about the date on which these events take place? 🚢

9. Given Paul's experiences, what is **ironic** about the military language used over the intercom at the A&W drive-in?

10. Find the passages in which Paul mentions conversations about God. What purpose do you think these passages serve?

11. What is Paul's **internal conflict**? Has it been resolved by the end of the story? Explain.

12. Is Paul being too hard on himself? Do you think he is a courageous person? Explain your responses to Paul's character.

---

9. Nobody wants to hear Paul's stories, yet people use the words of war casually.

10. The first reference to God juxtaposes ephemeral conversations about God with the inescapable reality of war and death; the second, the debatable nature of God's existence with the certainty of war.

11. Paul is conflicted about whether he showed courage or cowardice in war. This conflict remains unresolved.

12. Most will agree that Paul is too hard on himself and that he is courageous.

13. How could a greater awareness of historical context—specifically, knowledge of the Vietnam War and American attitudes toward the war—help explain why Paul has a hard time finding anyone who is willing to talk about the war?

WRITING

Comparing Stories

In a brief **essay,** compare and contrast the situation and character of Paul Berlin with those of Harold Krebs in Ernest Hemingway's "Soldier's Home" (page 611). What can you infer about the similarities and differences in the experiences of soldiers returning from World War I and those returning from Vietnam?

War and Peace

"Speaking of Courage" deals indirectly with the horror of warfare by contrasting war with small-town life. In a brief **essay,** explain how the story uses contrast to present a picture of war versus peace.

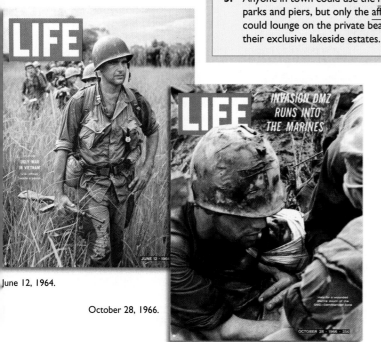

June 12, 1964.

October 28, 1966.

Vocabulary Development
Using Context Clues

Define each underlined word, and identify the **context clues** that give hints to its meaning. Then, go back to "Speaking of Courage," and see if O'Brien provides context clues for each word.

1. The veteran had earned a Purple Heart for his bravery, but dreams of greater <u>valor</u> continued to haunt him, even as the war itself continued to <u>recede</u> into the past.

2. Though the car salesman's pitch lacked <u>profundity</u>, his charming, rapid-fire delivery proved <u>mesmerizing</u> to the man who kept staring at the new car.

3. The coffee proved to be <u>tepid</u>, not hot, when the woman gave it a quick <u>tactile</u> test by dipping her finger into it.

4. We were alerted to the power outage by the sudden silencing of the usual <u>drone</u> of lights, fans, and household appliances.

5. Anyone in town could use the <u>municipal</u> parks and piers, but only the <u>affluent</u> could lounge on the private beaches of their exclusive lakeside estates.

Grade-Level Skills

■ **Literary Skills**

Analyze the way the theme and title of a selection represent a comment on life.

■ **Literary Skills**

Analyze characteristics of satires.

More About the Writer

Background. Donald Barthelme began writing in high school, but did not fully establish his writing style until after he moved to New York in 1962. He was influenced by the French Symbolists and borrowed words and phrases from a variety of sources, including songs and advertisements. His first novel, *Snow White,* was replete with stylistic and structural innovations, and Barthelme continued to delight readers with his experimentation until his death from cancer in 1989.

Donald Barthelme
(1931–1989)

© Nancy Crampton.

Donald Barthelme (bär′thəl·mē) was an experimenter in fiction and a true member of the avant-garde. Sometimes known as a postmodernist, he is widely regarded as one of the ablest and most versatile American stylists—witty, adventurous, and profound.

In broad terms, Barthelme believed that while literature of the past functioned to revitalize the imagination, storytelling had largely lost the power to inspire, persuade, or even entertain us. He felt that our language had gone bankrupt. Since words no longer effectively communicated feelings, he said, they had lost the power to move us. Contemporary language, Barthelme asserted, is thick with sludge and stuffing. Its use of clichés and its wordiness obscure truth rather than reveal it. As Snow White, the title character of Barthelme's 1967 novel, says, "Oh I wish there were some words in the world that were not the words I always hear!"

Barthelme saw the problems with language as a reflection of a society so dehumanized, so lacking in quality, that it could no longer sustain the kinds of myths that once gave us our identity. Thus, he felt, the whole point of storytelling was lost.

In his fiction, Barthelme set out to create a banal world that fails to make distinctions of quality in people, things, and ideas. Then, since he felt it was no longer possible to write about real life or the real world, he took writing itself for his subject—the art of making art out of language. His interest lay in the form and sound of language, and he tended to play with words, to make art out of fragments, much as some contemporary sculptors fashion works out of everyday objects and some pop artists transform cartoons into art.

Barthelme's plots are also unconventional. They are episodic, a clutter of styles, absurdities, and slapstick. "Fragments are the only forms I trust," says one of his narrators. His characters are types rather than fully developed individuals.

In Barthelme's hands, myth may turn into realism and realism into absurdity; readers can lose their way as they try to identify with the proceedings and wonder about the writer's point. Barthelme explained to the puzzled: "Art is not difficult because it wishes to be difficult, rather because it wishes to be art. However much the writer might long to be, in his work, simple, honest, straightforward, these virtues are no longer available to him. He discovers that in being simple, honest, straightforward, nothing much happens. . . . We are looking for the as yet unspeakable, the as yet unspoken."

Barthelme was born in Philadelphia, the son of an avant-garde architect, and was raised and educated in Texas. After serving with the U.S. Army, he worked as a reporter for the *Houston Post,* as a museum director, as the editor of an art and literature review, as a professor of English at the City University of New York, and as a teacher of creative writing at the University of Houston. He was a regular contributor to *The New Yorker* magazine. Collections of his stories include *Come Back, Dr. Caligari* (1964), *Unspeakable Practices, Unnatural Acts* (1968), in which "Game" appears, *Sixty Stories* (1981), and *Overnight to Many Distant Cities* (1983).

Before You Read

Game

Make the Connection

How we view the world determines in large measure how we live our lives and how we react to the people with whom we live. The following story offers a disturbing view of our times. "Game" won't give you a clear picture of your world, but it may start you thinking.

Literary Focus
Theme and Title

Think about the word *game*. How many meanings can you identify? What does *game* mean to a child? to an athlete? to a hunter? Does the word suggest something serious or something frivolous? As you read Barthelme's story, jot down each new meaning of *game* that seems to apply. Then, think about how Barthelme's title reveals a theme of the story.

> **Theme** is the insight into human life that is communicated by a work as a whole. The **title** of a story often suggests or supports the theme.
>
> *For more on Theme, see the Handbook of Literary and Historical Terms.*

Vocabulary Development

sated (sāt′id) *v.*: satisfied.

simultaneously (sī′məl·tā′nē·əs·lē) *adv.*: at the same time.

ruse (rōōz) *n.*: trick; deception.

scrupulously (skrōōp′yə·ləs·lē) *adv.*: painstakingly; with great care.

precedence (pres′ə·dəns) *n.*: priority because of superiority in rank.

exemplary (eg·zem′plə·rē) *adj.*: serving as a model; worth imitating.

acrimoniously (ak′ri·mō′nē·əs·lē) *adv.*: bitterly; harshly.

stolidly (stäl′id·lē) *adv.*: in a way that shows little emotion; impassively.

go.
hrw
.com

INTERNET
Vocabulary
Practice
Keyword: LE5 11–6

SKILLS
FOCUS

Literary Skills
Understand
theme and title.

Donald Barthelme   877

PRETEACHING

Summary ⬌ *at grade level*

The first-person narrator and his co-worker Shotwell are responsible for a nuclear weapon they may be ordered to launch. If ordered, they must simultaneously turn their control keys to launch the weapon. The men have been locked underground for 133 days and don't know why they haven't been relieved of duty. Each is supposed to shoot the other if he acts strangely. But as the story opens, both men have slipped into childish behavior such as writing on the walls and playing jacks. As we travel deeper into the psyche of the narrator, we learn he suspects that Shotwell wants him to help launch the missile. He indicates that he may do it, but only if Shotwell lets him play with his jacks.

Selection Starter

Build background. Point out that "Game" was published in the late 1960s, during the height of the nuclear arms race and only a few years after the Cuban missile crisis, which occurred when the United States learned that the Soviet Union had built nuclear missile bases in Cuba, just ninety miles off the southern coast of Florida. Although the conflict was ultimately resolved diplomatically, most experts agree that it brought the United States and the Soviet Union perilously close to nuclear war.

Skills Starter

Motivate. Remind students that a **theme** is an insight or message expressed by a work of literature. Remind them, too, that a theme is usually stated in a complete sentence, while a topic can be stated in one or two words. Write the topic *game* on the board. Then, write the sample theme *Games help people forget the stresses of "real life."* Have students give other sample themes related to games. After students read the selection, help them discuss the irony in Barthelme's story and title.

Previewing Vocabulary

Have students complete the following sentences with the correct Vocabulary word from p. 877.

1. The team ——— endured the coach's criticism. [stolidly]

2. If the disguise is realistic, the ——— will definitely work. [ruse]

3. Mark always checks his work ——— before handing it in. [scrupulously]

4. The phone and doorbell rang ———. [simultaneously]

5. After the accident, they argued ———. [acrimoniously]

6. We hope to imitate his ——— behavior. [exemplary]

7. Safety always takes ———. [precedence]

8. He ate until he was ———. [sated]

Donald Barthelme   877

DIFFERENTIATING INSTRUCTION

Learners Having Difficulty
Students may have difficulty identifying the conflicts between the narrator and Shotwell. Have students keep notes in a two-column chart as they read. In one column, students should list details about the narrator and in the other column, students should describe Shotwell. Have students identify the two characters' similarities and differences.

English-Language Learners
Students may have difficulty identifying the narrator's tone in this story. Help them to recognize that at different times he speaks like a spoiled child; a sensitive, suffering man; a mental patient; and a military man. Point out that Barthelme deliberately creates an ambiguity that keeps readers off balance.

Advanced Learners
Enrichment. Encourage students to read another of Barthelme's strange, unsettling stories and to compare it with "Game." You might put the focus on such typical Barthelme topics and devices as ambiguity, paranoia, humor, wordplay, and the unreliable narrator. Students might also discuss ways in which all of Barthelme's stories are "games."

If I behave strangely Shotwell is supposed to shoot me.

Game

Donald Barthelme

Shotwell keeps the jacks and the rubber ball in his attaché case and will not allow me to play with them. He plays with them, alone, sitting on the floor near the console[1] hour after hour, chanting "onesies, twosies, threesies, foursies" in a precise, well-modulated voice, not so loud as to be annoying, not so soft as to allow me to forget. I point out to Shotwell that two can derive more enjoyment from playing jacks than one, but he is not interested. I have asked repeatedly to be allowed to play by myself, but he simply shakes his head. "Why?" I ask. "They're mine," he says. And when he has finished, when he has <u>sated</u> himself, back they go into the attaché case.

It is unfair but there is nothing I can do about it. I am aching to get my hands on them.

Shotwell and I watch the console. Shotwell and I live under the ground and watch the console. If certain events take place upon the console, we are to insert our keys in the appropriate locks and turn our keys. Shotwell has a key and I have a key. If we turn our keys <u>simultaneously</u> the bird flies, certain switches are activated and the bird flies. But the bird never flies. In one hundred thirty-three days the bird has not flown. Meanwhile Shotwell and I watch each other. We each wear a .45 and if Shotwell behaves strangely I am supposed to shoot him. If I behave strangely Shotwell is supposed to shoot me. We watch the console and think about shooting each other and think about the bird. Shotwell's behavior with the jacks is strange. Is it strange? I do not know. Perhaps he is merely

_____

1. **console** (kän′sōl′) *n.:* desklike control panel.

Vocabulary
sated (sāt′id) *v.:* satisfied.
simultaneously (sī′məl·tā′nē·əs·lē) *adv.:* at the same time.

Donald Barthelme   **879**

? Making inferences. What does the repetition suggest about the speaker? [Possible responses: The obsessive repetition of key words may indicate that he is nervous, paranoid, or even losing his mind.]

B Literary Focus

? Theme. Responsibility—both personal and national—is at the root of one of the story's themes. Point out that the passive voice ("an error had been made") and an impersonal euphemism ("Owing to an oversight") leave the responsibility for the narrator's situation ambiguous. What do such expressions suggest about the government? [Possible responses: It is distant; it is bureaucratic.]

C Literary Focus

? Satire. Incongruity, a common satiric device, is evident here. What is so shocking about these characters' attitudes? [Possible responses: They seem unaware of their responsibility; they are losing their minds.]

---

selfish . . . perhaps his character is flawed, perhaps his childhood was twisted. I do not know.

Each of us wears a .45 and each of us is supposed to shoot the other if the other is behaving strangely. How strangely is strangely? I do not know. In addition to the .45 I have a .38 which Shotwell does not know about concealed in my attaché case, and Shotwell has a .25 caliber Beretta which I do not know about strapped to his right calf. Sometimes instead of watching the console I pointedly watch Shotwell's .45, but this is simply a ruse, simply a maneuver, in reality I am watching his hand when it dangles in the vicinity of his right calf. If he decides I am behaving strangely he will shoot me not with the .45 but with the Beretta. Similarly, Shotwell pretends to watch my .45 but he is really watching my hand resting idly atop my attaché case, my hand resting idly atop my attaché case, my hand. My hand resting idly atop my attaché case.

In the beginning I took care to behave normally. So did Shotwell. Our behavior was painfully normal. Norms of politeness, consideration, speech, and personal habits were scrupulously observed. But then it became apparent that an error had been made, that our relief was not going to arrive. Owing to an oversight. Owing to an oversight we have been here for one hundred thirty-three days. When it became clear that an error had been made, that we were not to be relieved, the norms were relaxed. Definitions of normality were redrawn in the agreement of January 1, called by us, The Agreement. Uniform regulations were relaxed, and mealtimes are no longer rigorously scheduled. We eat when we are hungry and sleep when we are tired. Considerations of rank and precedence were temporarily put aside, a handsome concession on the part of Shotwell, who is a captain, whereas I am only a first lieutenant. One of us watches the console at all times rather than two of us watching the console at all times, except when we are both on our feet. One of us watches the console at all times and if the bird flies then that one wakes the other and we turn our keys in the locks simultaneously and the

bird flies. Our system involves a delay of perhaps twelve seconds but I do not care because I am not well, and Shotwell does not care because he is not himself. After the agreement was signed Shotwell produced the jacks and the rubber ball from his attaché case, and I began to write a series of descriptions of forms occurring in nature, such as a shell, a leaf, a stone, an animal. On the walls.

Shotwell plays jacks and I write descriptions of natural forms on the walls.

Shotwell is enrolled in a USAFI[2] course which leads to a master's degree in business administration from the University of Wisconsin (although we are not in Wisconsin, we are in Utah, Montana or Idaho). When we went down it was in either Utah, Montana or Idaho, I don't remember. We have been here for one hundred thirty-three days owing to an oversight. The pale green reinforced concrete walls sweat and the air conditioning zips on and off erratically and Shotwell reads *Introduction to Marketing* by Lassiter and Munk, making notes with a blue ballpoint pen. Shotwell is not himself but I do not know it, he presents a calm aspect and reads *Introduction to Marketing* and makes his exemplary notes with a blue ballpoint pen, meanwhile controlling the .38 in my attaché case with one-third of his attention. I am not well.

We have been here one hundred thirty-three days owing to an oversight. Although now we are not sure what is oversight, what is plan. Perhaps the plan is for us to stay here permanently, or if not permanently at least for a year, for

---

2. **USAFI:** United States Armed Forces Information, an organization that supervises courses taken by service members.

Vocabulary

ruse (ro͞oz) *n.*: trick; deception.

scrupulously (skro͞op′yə·ləs·lē) *adv.*: painstakingly; with great care.

precedence (pres′ə·dəns) *n.*: priority because of superiority in rank.

exemplary (eg·zem′plə·rē) *adj.*: serving as a model; worth imitating.

Making predictions. Remind students that they must support predictions with solid textual evidence and back them up with their own experience. Predicting what a character will do is a way of participating actively in the drama and suspense of fiction.

Activity. Point out the narrator's obsession with Shotwell's jacks. When students have read about half the story, ask them to predict

whether the narrator will have a turn with the jacks.

Activity. Have students predict what might happen after the story's ending. Ask them to provide a quotation from the story and a personal observation for support. Most importantly, will the missile be fired? If so, why? How? What will the result be?

Developing Word-Attack Skills
Use the term *attaché case* to introduce two letter-sound correspondences in words from French: *ch* for /sh/ and *é* for /ā/. Write the English word *attach* on the chalkboard, and read it aloud, stressing the final sound, /ch/. Then, write the word *attaché,* and read it aloud. Contrast

three hundred sixty-five days. Or if not for a year for some number of days known to them and not known to us, such as two hundred days. Or perhaps they are observing our behavior in some way, sensors[3] of some kind, perhaps our behavior determines the number of days. It may be that they are pleased with us, with our behavior, not in every detail but in sum. Perhaps the whole thing is very successful, perhaps the whole thing is an experiment and the experiment is very successful. I do not know. But I suspect that the only way they can persuade sun-loving creatures into their pale green sweating reinforced concrete rooms under the ground is to say that the system is twelve hours on, twelve hours off. And then lock us below for some number of days known to them and not known to us. We eat well although the frozen enchiladas are damp when defrosted and the frozen devil's food cake is sour and untasty. We sleep uneasily and acrimoniously. I hear Shotwell shouting in his sleep, objecting, denouncing, cursing sometimes, weeping sometimes, in his sleep. When Shotwell sleeps I try to pick the lock on his attaché case, so as to get at the jacks. Thus far I have been unsuccessful. Nor has Shotwell been successful in picking the locks on my attaché case so as to get at the .38. I have seen the marks on the shiny surface. I laughed, in the latrine, pale green walls sweating and the air conditioning whispering, in the latrine.

I write descriptions of natural forms on the walls, scratching them on the tile surface with a diamond. The diamond is a two and one-half carat solitaire I had in my attaché case when we went down. It was for Lucy. The south wall of the room containing the console is already

3. **sensors** (sen′sərz) *n. pl.:* detecting devices.

covered. I have described a shell, a leaf, a stone, animals, a baseball bat. I am aware that the baseball bat is not a natural form. Yet I described it. "The baseball bat," I said, "is typically made of wood. It is typically one meter in length or a little longer, fat at one end, tapering to afford a comfortable grip at the other. The end with the handhold typically offers a slight rim, or lip, at the nether[4] extremity, to prevent slippage." My description of the baseball bat ran to 4500 words, all scratched with a diamond on the south wall. Does Shotwell read what I have written? I do not know. I am aware that Shotwell regards my writing-behavior as a little strange. Yet it is no stranger than his jacks-behavior, or the day he appeared in black bathing trunks with the .25 caliber Beretta strapped to his right calf and stood over the console, trying to span with his two arms outstretched the distance between the locks. He could not do it, I had already tried, standing over the console with my two arms outstretched, the distance is too great. I was moved to comment but did not comment, comment would have provoked counter-comment,

4. **nether** (ne*th*′ər) *adj.:* lower.

Vocabulary
acrimoniously (ak′ri·mō′nē·əs·lē) *adv.:* bitterly; harshly.

Donald Barthelme   **881**

D Literary Focus

? Theme. What ironic messages about the idea of control do you find here? [Possible responses: The narrator and Shotwell are losing control of themselves, even though they control a weapon of mass destruction. The two men, fighting for control over each other, may be in a controlled-behavior experiment. A government that controls nuclear weapons cannot control the irrationality of two men.]

E Vocabulary Development

? Word meaning and synonyms. Interpreting the word *strange* is essential for both the characters and the reader. Point out that *strange* comes from the Latin word *extraneus*, meaning "on the outside." How does the meaning of the word *strange* change in the context of the narrator's and Shotwell's insularity and paranoia? [Possible response: *Strange* becomes relative to whatever the two men "inside" agree is acceptable behavior—that is, behavior that will not induce one to shoot the other.] What synonyms for *strange* would work in this story? [Possible responses: violent, incoherent, insane, threatening.] How do these synonyms compare to more typical synonyms for the word *strange*? [They are more extreme than typical synonyms such as *weird, odd,* and *unusual*.]

F Reading Skills

? Making inferences. Why does Shotwell try to reach both locks at once? [Possible responses: He wants to figure out if he can launch the missile himself. He may be exercising a morbid curiosity or trying to torment the narrator; he may believe that if "the bird flies," they will be released from their captivity.]

---

the sound of *ch* in the two words. Show more examples of *ch* for /sh/ and é for /ā/.

champagne   éclair   chandelier

Activity. Write these sentences on the chalkboard, and have students read aloud the underlined words.

1. A message appeared in <u>chartreuse</u> chalk.
2. It was written with elegance and <u>élan</u>.
3. It told where to find choice <u>chanterelles</u>.
4. We found a <u>cache</u> of them under a birch.
5. We gave them to the chief <u>chef</u>.
6. He will <u>sauté</u> them to sate our hunger.
7. We all agree they make a tasty <u>entrée</u>.

A Literary Focus

❓ Theme. Who are "they"? [Possible responses: scientists; military leaders; government officials.] **With whom are "they" being ironically compared?** [Possible response: "They" are being compared with God, who can be thought of as having planned the universe, set up the rules of the "game," and left us with the job of figuring out the ultimate purpose.] **What might this comparison suggest about the story's theme?** [Possible response: Ironically, when people "play God," the outcome may be destruction and dehumanization.]

B Reading Skills

❓ Interpreting. What do you think each man "has in mind"? [Possible response: launching the missile.]

C Reading Skills

❓ Interpreting. What does the end of the story suggest? [Possible response: The ending suggests that the men will take the game to its logical conclusion and launch the missile.]

Monitoring students' progress. Guide the class in answering the following questions.

True-False

1. Each man has a hidden weapon. [T]
2. Each man has tried to reach both locks at once. [T]
3. The narrator writes poetry on the walls. [F]
4. The men are ordered to launch the missile. [F]
5. The men know where the missile is aimed. [F]

A comment would have led God knows where. They had in their infinite patience, in their infinite foresight, in their infinite wisdom already imagined a man standing over the console with his two arms outstretched, trying to span with his two arms outstretched the distance between the locks.

Shotwell is not himself. He has made certain overtures. The burden of his message is not clear. It has something to do with the keys, with the locks. Shotwell is a strange person. He appears to be less affected by our situation than I. He goes about his business stolidly, watching the console, studying *Introduction to Marketing*, bouncing his rubber ball on the floor in a steady, rhythmical, conscientious manner. He appears to be less affected by our situation than I am. He is stolid. He says nothing. But he has made certain overtures, certain overtures have been made. I am not sure that I understand them. They have something to do with the keys, with the locks. Shotwell has something in mind. Stolidly he shucks the shiny silver paper from the frozen enchiladas, stolidly he stuffs them into the electric oven. But he has something in mind. **B** But there must be a quid pro quo.[5] I insist on a quid pro quo. I have something in mind.

I am not well. I do not know our target. They do not tell us for which city the bird is targeted. I do not know. That is planning. That is not my responsibility. My responsibility is to watch the console and when certain events take place upon the console, turn my key in the lock. Shotwell bounces the rubber ball on the floor in a steady, stolid, rhythmical manner. I am aching

---

5. **quid pro quo:** Latin for "something for something." The phrase is used here to mean an even exchange.

---

to get my hands on the ball, on the jacks. We have been here one hundred thirty-three days owing to an oversight. I write on the walls. Shotwell chants "onesies, twosies, threesies, foursies" in a precise, well-modulated voice. Now he cups the jacks and the rubber ball in his hands and rattles them suggestively. I do not know for which city the bird is targeted. Shotwell is not himself.

Sometimes I cannot sleep. Sometimes Shotwell cannot sleep. Sometimes when Shotwell cradles me in his arms and rocks me to sleep, singing Brahms' "Guten Abend, gute Nacht,"[6] or I cradle Shotwell in my arms and rock him to sleep, singing, I understand what it is Shotwell wishes me to do. At such moments we are very close. But only if he will give me the **C** jacks. That is fair. There is something he wants me to do with my key, while he does something with his key. But only if he will give me my turn. That is fair. I am not well. ■

---

6. **Guten Abend, gute Nacht** (go͞ot'n ä'bənt go͞ot'ə näkht): German for "good evening, good night." This line is from the musical composition popularly known as "Brahms's Lullaby" by Johannes Brahms (1833–1897).

Vocabulary

stolidly (stäl'id·lē) *adv.:* in a way that shows little emotion; impassively.

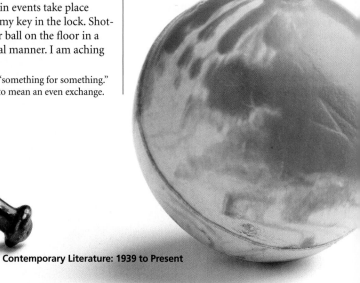

DEVELOPING FLUENCY

Paired activity. Have students read the story aloud with a partner. Encourage partners to comment on the ways the speaker's paranoia and obsessiveness come through in the patterns of his speech. Students can take notes on specific examples and share them with the class after they have read the story.

The Unknown Citizen

W. H. Auden

Social Programs (detail) by Robert Graham. Sculpture at the Franklin D. Roosevelt Memorial in Washington, D.C.

To JS/07/M/378
This Marble Monument Is Erected by the State

He was found by the Bureau of Statistics to be
One against whom there was no official complaint,
And all the reports on his conduct agree
That, in the modern sense of an old-fashioned word,
    he was a saint,
5 For in everything he did he served the Greater Community.
Except for the War till the day he retired
He worked in a factory and never got fired,
But satisfied his employers, Fudge Motors Inc.
Yet he wasn't a scab or odd in his views,
10 For his Union reports that he paid his dues,
(Our report on his Union shows it was sound)
And our Social Psychology workers found
That he was popular with his mates and liked a drink.
The Press are convinced that he bought a paper every day
15 And that his reactions to advertisements were normal in every way.
Policies taken out in his name prove that he was fully insured,
And his Health-card shows he was once in hospital but left it cured.
Both Producers Research and High-Grade Living declare
He was fully sensible to the advantages of the Installment Plan
20 And had everything necessary to the Modern Man,
A gramophone, a radio, a car, and a frigidaire.
Our researchers into Public Opinion are content
That he held the proper opinions for the time of year;
When there was peace, he was for peace; when there was war, he went.
25 He was married and added five children to the population,
Which our Eugenist says was the right number for a parent of his generation,
And our teachers report that he never interfered with their education.
Was he free? Was he happy? The question is absurd:
Had anything been wrong, we should certainly have heard.

D

E

Donald Barthelme   **883**

Connection

Summary ⬆ *above grade level*

In this poem, Auden describes a citizen of the modern world. He played by the rules, paid his dues, and held appropriate opinions. The poem concludes with the ironic observation that the man's life must have been happy.

DIRECT TEACHING

D Literary Focus

❷ Rhyme. How does rhyme affect the mood or feel of this poem? [Possible response: The sing-song rhyme scheme creates a generic, impersonal mood.] **How is this mood ironic?** [Possible response: The poem is about a person.]

E Literary Focus

❷ Irony. What does the final couplet add to the poem? [Possible responses: It underscores society's belief that conformity will lead to a good, happy life. It adds irony.]

Comparing and Contrasting Texts

"Game" and "The Unknown Citizen" both address the issue of authority in the modern world. Ask students the following questions about the two texts. Each response should be supported with evidence from the text.

• How is authority represented in each text—as a personal or an impersonal force?

• What attitude toward authority does each author seem to hold?

• To what extent have "The Unknown Citizen" and the men in "Game" been dehumanized? In each case, who or what is responsible?

Summary *at grade level*

The story begins with a frame story, told from a third-person limited point of view, in which a father and daughter meet in Milan, and she asks to hear about her childhood. In the inner story, the father recalls the early years of his marriage, using a third-person perspective, as if describing an anonymous "boy" and "girl." The conflict of the inner story begins with the young father's plan to go on a hunting trip, leaving his wife alone with their sick baby girl. They argue, the wife insisting that her husband choose his family or his trip. Although the husband begins to leave, he returns, makes up with his wife, and accidentally spills his breakfast, which comically sticks to his long underwear. The frame story suggests that this happiness was transient. The story's title becomes ironic as it becomes clear that in the long run, the man refused to let marriage, family, and his other emotional obligations "stick" to him at all.

Selection Starter

Motivate. Ask students if they like to hear stories about their own childhood. Discuss with them how hearing these stories from a parent's point of view makes these stories so special.

Skills Starter

Build review skills. Remind students that a writer's style depends on many variables, such as diction, tone, mood, use of figurative language and imagery, and even sentence length and complexity. If necessary, review with students the definitions of some of these terms before they begin reading.

Before You Read

Everything Stuck to Him

Make the Connection

If we think in simple terms about human feelings, reducing them to clear-cut patterns, we may trick ourselves into believing that feelings themselves are simple. Great fiction, no matter how simple on the surface, enables us to discover the depths of feelings. We respond to such fiction because we recognize in it the give-and-take of real experience, the gains and the losses, and the complex interactions of people who defy stereotyping.

Literary Focus
Style

One of the most striking elements of Raymond Carver's writing is his **style,** the unique way in which he uses language. Carver's prose has a chiseled quality, as if he has chipped away every unnecessary word. His style includes some oddities, however. He uses no quotation marks around dialogue, and he often doesn't give his characters names. These are not mere tricks, however. Each element of Carver's style has a purpose.

go.
hrw
.com

INTERNET

Vocabulary Practice

Keyword: LE5 11-6

> **Style** is the unique way in which a writer uses language.
>
> *For more on Style, see the Handbook of Literary and Historical Terms.*

SKILLS FOCUS

Literary Skills
Understand a writer's style.

Reading Skills
Identify questions about characters.

L (1986) by Mike and Doug Starn. Toned silver print on polyester, tape, wood (48″ × 48″).

Image courtesy Leo Castelli Photo Archives. © 2003 Mike and Doug Starn/Artists Rights Society (ARS), New York.

Reading Skills
Learning Through Questioning

As you read "Everything Stuck to Him," make a list of questions that occur to you about the characters. You might ask about their feelings, for instance, or what they are *not* saying to each other.

Vocabulary Development

coincide (kō′in·sīd′) *v.*: occur at the same time.

striking *adj.*: impressive; attractive.

fitfully *adv.*: irregularly; in stops and starts.

888   Collection 6   Contemporary Literature: 1939 to Present

---

Previewing Vocabulary

Members of small groups should take turns reading aloud one Vocabulary word and its definition from p. 888. Have groups discuss the meanings until all members are familiar with the words. Then, ask groups to brainstorm preliminary ideas for short stories; the ideas should use the words *coincide, striking,* and *fitfully*. For example: "This story is about a character of *striking* appearance who *fitfully* makes a decision that *coincides* with a specific event." The groups do not need to develop the plot. Have each group share its idea with the class.

Everything Stuck to Him

Raymond Carver

They were kids themselves, but they were crazy in love.

She's in Milan[1] for Christmas and wants to know what it was like when she was a kid. Tell me, she says. Tell me what it was like when I was a kid. She sips Strega,[2] waits, eyes him closely.

She is a cool, slim, attractive girl, a survivor from top to bottom.

That was a long time ago. That was twenty years ago, he says.

You can remember, she says. Go on.

What do you want to hear? he says. What else can I tell you? I could tell you about something that happened when you were a baby. It involves you, he says. But only in a minor way.

Tell me, she says. But first fix us another so you won't have to stop in the middle.

He comes back from the kitchen with drinks, settles into his chair, begins.

They were kids themselves, but they were crazy in love, this eighteen-year-old boy and this seventeen-year-old girl when they married. Not all that long afterwards they had a daughter.

The baby came along in late November during a cold spell that just happened to coincide with the peak of the waterfowl season. The boy loved to hunt, you see. That's part of it.

The boy and girl, husband and wife, father and mother, they lived in a little apartment under a dentist's office. Each night they cleaned the dentist's place upstairs in exchange for rent and utilities. In summer they were expected to maintain the lawn and the flowers. In winter the boy shoveled snow and spread rock salt on the walks. Are you still with me? Are you getting the picture?

I am, she says.

That's good, he says. So one day the dentist finds out they were using his letterhead for their personal correspondence. But that's another story.

He gets up from his chair and looks out the window. He sees the tile rooftops and the snow that is falling steadily on them.

Tell the story, she says.

The two kids were very much in love. On top of this they had great ambitions. They were always talking about the things they were going to do and the places they were going to go.

Now the boy and girl slept in the bedroom, and the baby slept in the living room. Let's say the baby was about three months old and had only just begun to sleep through the night.

---

1. **Milan** (mi·lan′): city in northwestern Italy.
2. **Strega:** sweet Italian liqueur.

Vocabulary

coincide (kō′in·sīd′) v.: occur at the same time.

DIRECT TEACHING

A Reading Skills

? Learning through questioning. What question might you ask about the girl, based on this sentence? [Possible responses: What has she survived? How old is she?]

B Reading Skills

? Learning through questioning. What is the connection between the frame story and the inner story? Who are "he" and "she" in Milan, and who are the boy, girl, and baby daughter? [In the frame story, the man tells his daughter the inner story as an incident from her childhood. "He" and "she" in the frame story are father and daughter. In the inner story, "he" is the frame-story father, "she" is his wife, and the baby is the daughter—the "she" in the frame story.]

C English-Language Learners

Compound words. Have students find the two smaller words in *waterfowl*. Explain that waterfowl, such as ducks and geese, are swimming game birds that live near lakes and ponds.

D Reading Skills

? Speculating. Why do you think the father asks the daughter these questions? [Possible response: He may feel that his daughter has an insufficient sense of her parents' marriage, and he wishes to convey their hard work, their hope, or some other quality.]

E Literary Focus

? Style. So far, what specifics have you noticed in Carver's style? [Possible responses: ordinary language; no quotation marks; unnamed characters.]

DIFFERENTIATING INSTRUCTION

Learners Having Difficulty
Modeling. To help students read "Everything Stuck to Him," model how to learn by asking questions. Say, "I read at the beginning that the man's story involves his daughter only in a minor way. To learn more about the story, I can ask myself, 'What does he mean by "in a minor way"?' I conclude that the story may be more about him than about his daughter. I'll keep reading to find out if this is so." Encourage students to ask themselves questions as they read.

English-Language Learners
Help students separate the frame and the inner story by pointing out the sentences "He comes back from the kitchen with drinks, settles into his chair, begins" and "He gets up from his chair and refills their glasses," which begin and end the inner story.

On this one Saturday night after finishing his work upstairs, the boy stayed in the dentist's office and called an old hunting friend of his father's.

Carl, he said when the man picked up the receiver, believe it or not, I'm a father.

Congratulations, Carl said. How is the wife?

She's fine, Carl. Everybody's fine.

That's good, Carl said, I'm glad to hear it. But if you called about going hunting, I'll tell you something. The geese are flying to beat the band. I don't think I've ever seen so many. Got five today. Going back in the morning, so come along if you want to.

I want to, the boy said.

The boy hung up the telephone and went downstairs to tell the girl. She watched while he laid out his things. Hunting coat, shell bag, boots, socks, hunting cap, long underwear, pump gun.

What time will you be back? the girl said.

Probably around noon, the boy said. But maybe as late as six o'clock. Would that be too late?

It's fine, she said. The baby and I will get along fine. You go and have some fun. When you get back, we'll dress the baby up and go visit Sally.

The boy said, Sounds like a good idea.

Sally was the girl's sister. She was striking. I don't know if you've seen pictures of her. The boy was a little in love with Sally, just as he was a little in love with Betsy, who was another sister the girl had. The boy used to say to the girl, If we weren't married, I could go for Sally.

What about Betsy? the girl used to say. I hate to admit it, but I truly feel she's better looking than Sally and me. What about Betsy?

Betsy too, the boy used to say.

After dinner he turned up the furnace and helped her bathe the baby. He marveled again at the infant who had half his features and half the girl's. He powdered the tiny body. He powdered between fingers and toes.

He emptied the bath into the sink and went upstairs to check the air. It was overcast and cold. The grass, what there was of it, looked like canvas, stiff and gray under the street light.

Snow lay in piles beside the walk. A car went by. He heard sand under the tires. He let himself imagine what it might be like tomorrow, geese beating the air over his head, shotgun plunging against his shoulder.

Then he locked the door and went downstairs.

In bed they tried to read. But both of them fell asleep, she first, letting the magazine sink to the quilt.

It was the baby's cries that woke him up.

The light was on out there, and the girl was standing next to the crib rocking the baby in her arms. She put the baby down, turned out the light, and came back to the bed.

He heard the baby cry. This time the girl stayed where she was. The baby cried fitfully and stopped. The boy listened, then dozed. But the baby's cries woke him again. The living-room light was burning. He sat up and turned on the lamp.

I don't know what's wrong, the girl said, walking back and forth with the baby. I've changed her and fed her, but she keeps on crying. I'm so tired I'm afraid I might drop her.

You come back to bed, the boy said. I'll hold her for a while.

He got up and took the baby, and the girl went to lie down again.

Just rock her for a few minutes, the girl said from the bedroom. Maybe she'll go back to sleep.

The boy sat on the sofa and held the baby. He jiggled it in his lap until he got its eyes to close, his own eyes closing right along. He rose carefully and put the baby back in the crib.

It was a quarter to four, which gave him forty-five minutes. He crawled into bed and dropped off. But a few minutes later the baby

Vocabulary

striking *adj.:* impressive; attractive.
fitfully *adv.:* irregularly; in stops and starts.

was crying again, and this time they both got up.

The boy did a terrible thing. He swore.

For God's sake, what's the matter with you? the girl said to the boy. Maybe she's sick or something. Maybe we shouldn't have given her the bath.

The boy picked up the baby. The baby kicked its feet and smiled.

Look, the boy said, I really don't think there's anything wrong with her.

How do you know that? the girl said. Here, let me have her. I know I ought to give her something, but I don't know what it's supposed to be.

The girl put the baby down again. The boy and the girl looked at the baby, and the baby began to cry.

The girl took the baby. Baby, baby, the girl said with tears in her eyes.

Probably it's something on her stomach, the boy said.

The girl didn't answer. She went on rocking the baby, paying no attention to the boy.

The boy waited. He went to the kitchen and put on water for coffee. He drew his woolen underwear on over his shorts and T-shirt, buttoned up, then got into his clothes.

What are you doing? the girl said.

Going hunting, the boy said.

I don't think you should, she said. I don't want to be left alone with her like this.

Carl's planning on me going, the boy said. We've planned it.

I don't care about what you and Carl

Couple in Open Doorway (1977) by George Segal. Painted plaster, wood, and metal (96″ × 69″ × 52″).

Image courtesy Sidney Janis Gallery, New York. © The George and Helen Segal Foundation/Licensed by VAGA, New York.

Raymond Carver   891

VIEWING THE ART

George Segal (1924–2000) gained recognition in the late 1950s for his life-size sculptures. Made using white plaster, chicken wire, burlap, and molds taken from living models, these sculptures are placed in lonely "environments" defined by a few common objects, such as chairs, tables, and beds. Segal cast in plaster of Paris directly from human forms, producing mummylike molds that look as though they might still contain bodies. Segal's figures usually have a rough finish, with individual features not clearly defined. They seldom appear to communicate with each other, and they often appear disaffected.

Activity. Have students compare Carver's and Segal's styles as well as their implied commentaries on contemporary American life. [Students might note that they both create sparse representations with little ornament; both focus on couples, and on people who seem trapped in static postures.]

© English-Language Learners

? Interpreting idioms. How does the context of this conversation help you determine what the boy means by the idiom "it's something on her stomach"? [She has eaten something that has created stomach cramps or nausea.]

CONTENT-AREA CONNECTIONS

Art: Abstraction

Individual activity. Have students illustrate the concept of romantic love in an abstract fashion—with colors, shapes, forms, objects, and symbols, but not with images of people or scenes. Invite students to choose a visual medium they feel comfortable with, such as drawing, painting, photography, or collage. Have them write a caption explaining what their work of art says about love. Display their work in the classroom.

SKILLS REVIEW

Analyzing stylistic devices. Discuss with students what they think the selection would be like if it were made into a television drama. Discuss how a director might use elements such as sets and music to enhance Carver's spare style.

Activity.

• Divide students into pairs, and have them act out a scene from the story.

Ask them to demonstrate Carver's style through their actions, mannerisms, choice of words, and tone of voice.

• Invite each group, remaining in character, to discuss the family's history and their feelings about one another.

• Have students (out of character) discuss the insights they gained from this dramatization.

Raymond Carver   891

? **Style.** Discuss that this scene represents a climactic point in the story. Point out that some writers emphasize such scenes with dramatic descriptions and excitement. How would you describe Carver's style here? [Possible response: spare—with short sentences, everyday verbs, no adjectives or other description.]

B Reading Skills

? **Learning through questioning.** Is this just a slapstick moment, or does it have deeper implications, and if so, what? [Possible response: The incident helps the couple laugh off their dispute. It may also hint that the boy is not comfortable with his decision not to go, and that he is "stuck" in something (a family) that he will ultimately want to escape.]

C Reading Skills

? **Learning through questioning.** What questions and answers can you suggest about the period between the inner story and the frame story? [Possible question: "What happened to the boy and girl in the inner story?" Possible response: "The boy left, the marriage broke up, and the wife took custody of their daughter; the wife died."]

D Reading Skills

? **Learning through questioning.** What else might be included in "everything else"? [Possible responses: conflicts in the marriage; the adult daughter's bitterness or sense of loss.] What was "the cold, and where he'd go in it"? [Possible response: the tempting but loveless world outside family, commitment, and intimacy.]

planned, she said. And I don't care about Carl, either. I don't even know Carl.

You've met Carl before. You know him, the boy said. What do you mean you don't know him?

That's not the point and you know it, the girl said.

What is the point? the boy said. The point is we planned it.

The girl said, I'm your wife. This is your baby. She's sick or something. Look at her. Why else is she crying?

I know you're my wife, the boy said.

The girl began to cry. She put the baby back in the crib. But the baby started up again. The girl dried her eyes on the sleeve of her night-gown and picked the baby up.

The boy laced up his boots. He put on his shirt, his sweater, his coat. The kettle whistled on the stove in the kitchen.

You're going to have to choose, the girl said. Carl or us. I mean it.

A What do you mean? the boy said.

You heard what I said, the girl said. If you want a family, you're going to have to choose.

They stared at each other. Then the boy took up his hunting gear and went outside. He started the car. He went around to the car windows and, making a job of it, scraped away the ice.

He turned off the motor and sat awhile. And then he got out and went back inside.

The living-room light was on. The girl was asleep on the bed. The baby was asleep beside her.

The boy took off his boots. Then he took off everything else. In his socks and his long under-wear, he sat on the sofa and read the Sunday paper.

The girl and the baby slept on. After a while, the boy went to the kitchen and started frying bacon.

The girl came out in her robe and put her arms around the boy.

Hey, the boy said.

I'm sorry, the girl said.

It's all right, the boy said.

I didn't mean to snap like that.

It was my fault, he said.

You sit down, the girl said. How does a waffle sound with bacon?

Sounds great, the boy said.

She took the bacon out of the pan and made waffle batter. He sat at the table and watched her move around the kitchen. — STOP > 12

B She put a plate in front of him with bacon, a waffle. He spread butter and poured syrup. But when he started to cut, he turned the plate into his lap.

I don't believe it, he said, jumping up from the table.

If you could see yourself, the girl said.

The boy looked down at himself, at every-thing stuck to his underwear.

I was starved, he said, shaking his head.

You were starved, she said, laughing.

He peeled off the woolen underwear and threw it at the bathroom door. Then he opened his arms and the girl moved into them.

We won't fight anymore, she said.

The boy said, We won't.

He gets up from his chair and refills their glasses.

That's it, he says. End of story. I admit it's not much of a story.

I was interested, she says.

He shrugs and carries his drink over to the window. It's dark now but still snowing.

C Things change, he says. I don't know how they do. But they do without your realizing it or wanting them to.

Yes, that's true, only—But she does not finish what she started.

She drops the subject. In the window's reflec-tion he sees her study her nails. Then she raises her head. Speaking brightly, she asks if he is going to show her the city, after all.

He says, Put your boots on and let's go.

But he stays by the window, remembering.

D They had laughed. They had leaned on each other and laughed until the tears had come, while everything else—the cold, and where he'd go in it—was outside, for a while anyway. ∎

Check Test: True-False

Monitoring students' progress. Guide the class in answering these questions.

1. The opening conversation takes place between a man and his daughter. [T]

2. The husband wants to go bowling with a friend. [F]

3. The husband decides to stay with his wife and child. [T]

4. The couple agree never to argue again. [T]

This is an excerpt from an article on Raymond Carver.

A Still, Small Voice

Jay McInerney

The recurring image I associate with Raymond Carver is one of people leaning toward him, working very hard at the act of listening. He mumbled. T. S. Eliot once described Ezra Pound, qua mentor, as "a man trying to convey to a very deaf person the fact that the house is on fire." Raymond Carver had precisely the opposite manner. The smoke could be filling the room, flames streaking across the carpet, before Carver would ask, "Is it, uh, getting a little hot in here, maybe?" And you would be sitting in your chair, bent achingly forward at the waist, saying, "Beg pardon, Ray?" Never insisting, rarely asserting, he was an unlikely teacher. I once sat in and listened while Carver was interviewed for two and a half hours. The writer conducting the interview moved the tape recorder closer and closer and finally asked if Carver would put it in his lap. A few days later the interviewer called up, near despair: Ray's voice on the tapes was nearly inaudible. The word "soft-spoken" hardly begins to do justice to his speech; this condition was aggravated whenever he was pressed into the regions of generality or prescription. . . .

One aspect of what Carver seemed to say to us—even to someone who had never been inside a lumber mill or a trailer park—was that literature could be fashioned out of strict observation of real life, whenever and however it was lived, even if it was lived with a bottle of Heinz ketchup on the table and the television set droning. This was news at a time when academic metafiction was the regnant° mode. His example reinvigorated realism as well as the short-story form. . . .

Having fallen under Carver's spell on reading his first collection, *Will You Please Be Quiet, Please?,* a book I would have bought on the basis of the title alone, I was lucky enough to meet him a few years later and

---
°**regnant** *adj.*: ruling.

eventually to become his student at Syracuse University in the early 80s. . . .

My first semester, Ray somehow forgot to enter my grade for workshop. I pointed this out to him, and we went together to the English office to rectify the situation. "You did some real good work," he said, informing me that I would get an A. I was very pleased with myself, but perhaps a little less so when Ray opened the grade book and wrote an A next to my name underneath a solid column of identical grades. Everybody did good work, apparently. In workshop he approached every story with respect—treating each as if it were a living entity, a little sick, possibly, or lame, but something that could be nursed and trained to health.

Though Ray was always encouraging, he could be rigorous if he knew criticism was welcome. Fortunate students had their stories subjected to the same process he employed on his own numerous drafts. Manuscripts came back thoroughly ventilated with Carver deletions, substitutions, question marks and chicken-scratch queries. I took one story back to him

---

Connection

Summary ⬌ *at grade level*

> Novelist Jay McInerney discusses Carver's influence on students. To illustrate Carver's attention to editing, McInerney describes a debate in which Carver tries to persuade him to use *ground* instead of *earth*.

DIRECT TEACHING

E Content-Area Connections

Literature: Metafiction
Explain that **metafiction** is fiction that deals with the writing of fiction or its conventions. For example, a metafiction story might explicitly state that the story is coming to a close because the conflict has been resolved.

F Reading Skills

❷ Speculating. Why do you think McInerney includes the story about Carver's grading? [Possible response: It shows that Carver wanted his students to focus on their writing rather than on grades.]

READING MINI-LESSON

Developing Word-Attack Skills
Tell students that recognizing prefixes can help them figure out a word's meaning and pronunciation. Write the selection word *coincide* on the board. Explain that if they didn't recognize the prefix *co-* in the word, they might read it as /koyn sīd/ instead of /kō in sīd/.

Help students explore the importance of recognizing the prefixes in these words:

cooperate   preempt
unclear   extramural

Activity. Display these words and have volunteers identify the prefix in each one. Prefixes are underlined.

1. preeminent
2. restage
3. underline
4. trilinear
5. coinsure
6. semiannual
7. readdress
8. anticlimax
9. unidentified
10. preexisting

A **Reading Skills**

? **Comparing and contrasting.**
How does this view of Carver contrast with the description at the beginning of the article? [Possible response: At the beginning Carver is described as very quiet, but when helping writers with their work he speaks with conviction.]

B **Reading Informational Text**

? **Assessing the author's argument.** How, if at all, does McInerney prove that Carver was a good teacher? [Possible responses: Students may say that the story about the grade proves it. Others may need to hear more to decide.]

seven times; he must have spent fifteen or twenty hours on it. He was a meticulous, obsessive line editor. One on one, in his office, he almost **A** became a tough guy, his voice gradually swelling with conviction.

Once we spent some ten or fifteen minutes debating my use of the word *earth*. Carver felt it had to be *ground,* and he felt it was worth the trouble of talking it through. That one exchange was invaluable; I think of it constantly when I'm working. Carver himself used the same example later in an essay he wrote that year, in discussing the influence of his mentor, John Gardner. "Ground is ground, he'd say, it means ground, dirt, that kind of stuff. But if you say *earth,* that's something else, that word has other ramifications." . . .

B For someone who claimed he didn't love to teach, he made a great deal of difference to a great many students. He certainly changed my life irrevocably and I have heard others say the same thing.

I'm still leaning forward with my head cocked to one side, straining to hear his voice.
—from *The New York Times*
August 6, 1989

Raymond Carver giving a lecture at Syracuse University (early 1980s).
Ohio State University Libraries.

894 Collection 6 Contemporary Literature: 1939 to Present

Comparing and Contrasting Texts

Comparing author and character.
Discuss with students how in "Everything Stuck to Him," the character in the frame story and the younger version of that character in the inner story do not verbally express feelings. Next, remind students that McInerney describes Raymond Carver as "soft-spoken."

Whole-class activity. Have students discuss how much of "Everything Stuck to Him" may be autobiographical. Instruct them to base their ideas on the excerpts from "A Still, Small Voice" and on the biography on p. 887.

Response and Analysis

Reading Check

1. This story has a frame story and an inner story. A **frame story** is just that: a "frame" for an inner story. What is the **setting,** and who are the **characters** in the frame story (the introductory narrative within which a character proceeds to tell the inner story)?

2. In the inner story (the one told by one of the characters), what is the **setting,** and who are the **characters**? Which characters appear in both stories?

3. What happened during the night when the baby kept crying?

4. What promise did the couple make on Sunday morning?

Thinking Critically

5. What is the main **conflict** between the husband and wife in the inner story?

6. What thoughts and emotions do you think the boy experienced as he "sat awhile" in the car?

7. After telling the inner story, the man says that "things change." What do you think has changed since the time of the inner story? What has the man learned?

8. Near the end of the frame story, the woman replies, "Yes, that's true, only—" She does not finish. What do you think she intended to say, and why did she stop?

9. The **title** of the story refers to an incident in the inner story. Explain how the title also refers to something much more important to the man.

10. What is the **theme** of the story—what does the story reveal about the human condition? How does the theme relate to the story's title?

11. One aspect of Carver's **style** in this story is the omission of names for his main characters. Why do you think he did this? Why do you think he uses the terms *boy* and *girl* instead of *man* and *woman* or *father* and *mother*?

Literary Criticism

12. In the **Connection** on page 893, Jay McInerney says, "One aspect of what Carver seemed to say to us . . . was that literature could be fashioned out of strict observation of real life, whenever and however it was lived. . . ." Do you agree with this statement? Use details from this story and from other stories or novels you have read to support your response.

WRITING

Major or Minor?

Early on, the man says that the inner story involves the woman, "but only in a minor way." Do you agree with this comment, or was the man using **understatement,** a manner of speaking that downplays the importance of something? In a brief **essay,** explain how important the woman's role is in the inner story. Defend your interpretation with evidence from the story.

Writing an Interior Monologue

Write an **interior monologue** that reveals the unspoken thoughts and feelings of one of the characters in "Everything Stuck to Him." Write your monologue from the first-person point of view, using the pronoun "I." Choose one of the following scenes: (1) the girl sitting up alone with the baby, (2) the boy sitting alone in the car, or (3) the woman looking at her fingernails after hearing the story.

SKILLS FOCUS

Literary Skills
Analyze a writer's style.

Reading Skills
Analyze questions about the characters.

Writing Skills
Write an essay explaining a statement in a text. Write an interior monologue.

Vocabulary Skills
Use words in context.

Vocabulary Development
Using Words in Context

Write a short paragraph that uses all three of the Vocabulary words and provides clues to their meaning: *coincide, striking, fitfully.*

Response and Analysis

7. Possible answers: He and his wife grew apart. He learns that people's lives are always changing.

8. Possible answers: "We are responsible for our actions"; "you and mother could have tried harder to stay together." She doesn't want to create conflict.

9. Possible answers: Family needs "stuck" to him only temporarily; the pain that comes from his choices still "stick" to him.

10. Possible answer: To be intimate, people must reveal hopes, fears, and dreams to each other. If they don't, they will not "stick" to one another. The boy doesn't express (and may not understand) his feelings.

11. Possible answer: He wants to emphasize the characters' actions and the details of the setting. The words *boy* and *girl* denote youth and immaturity.

Literary Criticism

12. Possible answers: Some students may agree that profound experiences are often based on everyday details of people's lives and that literature develops from feelings generated by these experiences. Others may say that Carver's use of details tie him to reality and prevent him from exploring more abstract ideas in his stories.

Vocabulary Development

Students' paragraphs should include all the Vocabulary words and provide clear context clues.

Reading Check

1. The setting is Milan, Italy, at Christmas. The characters are a father and his grown daughter.

2. The setting is an American apartment under a dentist's office in November, twenty years before. The characters are a husband, a wife, and their child. The husband is the father in the frame story and the baby is the daughter.

3. The husband and wife took turns rocking the baby; they argued.

4. They promise not to fight anymore.

Thinking Critically

5. Possible answer: They have conflicting ideas about family life.

6. Possible answers: guilt; the need to be responsible; the need to escape.

Grammar Link

Practice

1. Carver's first collection of stories was nominated for a National Book Award in 1976, and he went on to publish four more collections of stories and five volumes of poetry before he died in 1988.

2. In "Everything Stuck to Him," the frame story suggests that the father is no longer married to the mother in the inner story.

3. In the inner story the girl is furious that her husband wants to go fishing when their baby is sick.

4. OK

Assessment

- *Holt Assessment: Literature, Reading, and Vocabulary*

For a lesson reteaching irony, tone, and author's style, see **Reteaching, p. 1117A.**

Grammar Link

Avoiding Shifts in Verb Tense: Keeping Things Consistent

In "Everything Stuck to Him," Raymond Carver tells two stories: an outer frame story about a father and his twenty-year-old daughter and an inner story that takes place when the father was much younger. One of the ways Carver signals the switch between the two stories is by shifting verb tenses—using the present tense for the frame story and the past tense for the inner story.

PRESENT	He gets up from the chair and looks out the window.
PAST	The two kids were very much in love.

The **tense** of a verb indicates the time of the action or state of being that is expressed by the verb. Sometimes you have to shift tenses within a passage or even a single sentence. For example, when you're describing events that took place at different times, you may need to use different tenses to show the correct sequence in time. In the following example the writer needs to shift from the present tense to the past tense.

NECESSARY SHIFT	The father tells his adult daughter a story about an incident that happened when she was a baby.

Problems occur when a writer shifts verb tenses arbitrarily. Unless you have a good reason for switching tenses, you should stick to one consistent tense.

INCONSISTENT	At first the boy decides to go hunting, but then he changed his mind.
CONSISTENT	At first the boy decides to go hunting, but then he changes his mind.

Use the present tense when you're writing about what happens in a work of literature. This is called the *literary present.*

PRESENT	In "Everything Stuck to Him," the young father accidentally spills his breakfast onto his lap.

Apply to Your Writing

Re-read a current writing assignment or one that you've already competed. Underline every verb, and then check each one to make sure that you've used the correct tense.

▶ **For more help, see Tenses and Their Uses, 3b–3c, in the Language Handbook.**

Grammar Skills
Use verb tenses correctly.

Rewrite the following sentences, and correct any unnecessary shifts in verb tenses or incorrect use of tenses. If you think the verb tenses are correct, write *OK.* (There may be more than one error in a sentence.)

1. Carver's first collection of stories was nominated for a National Book Award in 1976, and he goes on to publish four more collections of stories and five volumes of poetry before he died in 1988.

2. In "Everything Stuck to Him," the frame story suggested that the father was no longer married to the mother in the inner story.

3. In the inner story the girl is furious that her husband wanted to go hunting when their baby was sick.

4. Carver revised many of his earlier, minimalist stories; for example, "A Small, Good Thing" is a fleshed-out version of "The Bath."

DIFFERENTIATING INSTRUCTION

Learners Having Difficulty

Explain that when students write about the action of a story, they should use the present tense regardless of the tense in the story itself. Write the following sentences on the chalkboard. Have students rewrite the sentences in the present tense.

1. The boy picked up his hunting gear and went outside. [The boy picks up his hunting gear and goes outside.]

2. When he came back into the house, he saw the girl asleep on the bed with the baby. [When he comes back into the house, he sees the girl asleep on the bed with the baby.]

3. The boy went to the kitchen and started to fry some bacon. [The boy goes to the kitchen and starts to fry some bacon.]

4. When her father finished telling the story, the daughter started to say something to him. [When her father finishes telling the story, the daughter starts to say something to him.]

Julia Alvarez
(1950–   )

"**A**ll my childhood I had dressed like an American, eaten American foods, and befriended American children. I had gone to an American school and spent most of the day speaking and reading English. At night, my prayers were full of blond hair and blue eyes and snow. . . . All my childhood I had longed for this moment of arrival. And here I was, an American girl, coming home at last."

With these words, Julia (pronounced hŏō′lē·ä) Alvarez describes stepping back into America. Although born in New York City, Alvarez spent her early childhood in the Dominican Republic. In 1960, just before her father was to be arrested for his involvement in a secret plot to overthrow the dictator Rafael Trujillo Molina, Alvarez and her family were tipped off by an American agent and escaped to the United States.

Paradoxically, her homecoming was filled with all the difficulties of adjusting to a brand-new life. Learning contemporary American English was only part of the adjustment. Alvarez also had to learn to compromise in order to resolve conflicts between American customs and her parents' more traditional views. This theme is at the heart of her fiction—particularly her short stories and her best-known work, the novel *How the Garcia Girls Lost Their Accents* (1991).

Before concentrating on writing fiction, Alvarez taught courses in poetry for twelve years in schools in Kentucky, California, Vermont, Illinois, and Washington, D.C. Her first collection of poems, appropriately titled *Homecoming,* was published in 1984. Alvarez has also won the American Academy of Poetry Prize, but it is as a novelist that she has received the most notice.

How the Garcia Girls Lost Their Accents is a novel of fifteen interlocking stories with engaging and memorable characters. The Garcia family, with its four daughters, struggles to overcome a variety of cultural and generational conflicts, and comparisons with Alvarez's own family make it clear that the novel is highly autobiographical. Her 1994 novel, *In the Time of the Butterflies,* is a fictionalized account of the lives and deaths of three sisters, Patria, Minerva, and María Teresa Mirabal, the wives of political prisoners in the Dominican Republic. The women, who had been visiting their husbands, were murdered in 1960 by thugs connected to the Trujillo regime. Alvarez's 1997 novel *¡Yo!* is populated by some of the *Garcia Girls* characters.

It is clear that Alvarez has forged, out of memory and imagination, a novelist's sensibility. As one critic said about *Garcia Girls,* Alvarez has "beautifully captured the threshold experience of the new immigrant, where the past is not yet a memory and the future remains an anxious dream."

For Independent Reading

For more about the characters in the following story, read
- *How the Garcia Girls Lost Their Accents* (novel)

SKILLS FOCUS, pp. 897–910

Grade-Level Skills
■ **Reading Skills**
Make inferences about characters.

Review Skills
■ **Literary Skills**
Analyze influences on characters (including internal and external conflict) and the way those influences affect the plot.

More About the Writer

Background. At the age of thirteen, Alvarez was sent to boarding school along with her older sister because her parents were "afraid of public schools." For the next twenty-five years, she was on the move, never staying long in any one place. Then, in 1988, she took a job teaching at Middlebury College in Vermont. There she met her husband, an opthalmologist. She is now Writer-in-Residence at the college.

For Independent Reading

How the Garcia Girls Lost Their Accents was named a notable book by the American Library Association in 1992.

Summary ⬌ at grade level

The story, told from the first-person point of view, focuses on the narrator's immigrant family from the Dominican Republic. The story reveals interrelated conflicts that arise out of the family's Dominican heritage: the pressure to assimilate into U.S. culture, and the creative ambitions of both the narrator and her mother. The story opens with the narrator's recollections of her mother's nightly "inventing" of time- and labor-saving gadgets and of how the rest of the family scoffed at them. When the narrator is chosen to deliver a speech at school, she puts off preparing the speech for weeks. Finally, some lines by Whitman inspire her to write a passionate and personal speech. Although her mother approves, her father is infuriated by the speech, which he sees as dangerously disrespectful of authority. In the story's climax, he tears up the manuscript. The narrator's mother intervenes and helps her daughter construct a new speech saying all the "right" things. The next day, the narrator's revised speech is a success. That night the narrator's contrite father brings home an electric typewriter, which the narrator will use to become a writer, following her mother's creative tradition.

Selection Starter

Build background. The Dominican Republic is located on the eastern part of the island of Hispaniola in the West Indies (the western part is Haiti). It achieved its independence from Haiti in 1844. The population is approximately 8.5 million, and the capital is Santo Domingo. New York City has a sizable Dominican population.

Before You Read

Daughter of Invention

Make the Connection

From the biblical parable of the prodigal son to a short story written this morning, literature will probably always tell stories of children and parents struggling to understand one another. "Experience is the greatest teacher, so trust us," says the older generation. "We want to live our own lives, not yours," say the children. What are some other phrases, sayings, or typical pieces of advice that parents use when they talk to their children?

Literary Focus
Conflict

Stories run on **conflict,** and this story is no exception. It takes its strength and much of its fun from the clash between the anxious values of Latin American parents and the liberated values of their New York–raised daughter. Each major character experiences both **external conflict** (clashes with other people, a government, or society in general) and **internal conflict** (problems that exist within his or her own mind).

External conflict is a clash of opposing forces, which can exist between two people, between a person and a force of nature, or between a person and society.
Internal conflict is a clash between opposing forces that exist within a person's mind.

For more on Conflict, see the Handbook of Literary and Historical Terms.

go.
hrw
.com

INTERNET

Vocabulary
Practice
•
Cross-
Curricular
Connection
•
More About
Julia Alvarez

Keyword: LE5 11–6

**SKILLS
FOCUS**

Literary Skills
Understand
external and
internal conflict.

Reading Skills
Make inferences
about
characters.

Reading Skills
Making Inferences About Characters

"Daughter of Invention" is one of the fifteen interwoven stories in *How the Garcia Girls Lost Their Accents.* It is fascinating to watch how the characters in this story adapt so differently to the liberty the family enjoys in its new country. As a skilled reader, you will want to go beneath the surface events of the story and try to understand why these characters respond to new social customs in such different ways. In other words, you'll make **inferences,** or educated guesses, about the psychology of the characters, based on clues provided in the story and on your own experience with people.

Vocabulary Development

disembodied (dis′im·bäd′ēd) v. used as adj.: separated from the body.

labyrinth (lab′ə·rinth′) n.: place full of complex passageways; maze.

communal (kə·myōon′əl) adj.: belonging to an entire group (in this case, Mami's daughters).

eulogy (yōo′lə·jē) n.: public speech of praise.

noncommittal (nän′kə·mit′′l) adj.: neutral; giving no clear indication of feeling or attitude.

florid (flôr′id) adj.: showy.

ultimatum (ul′tə·māt′əm) n.: last offer; final proposition.

vengeful (venj′fəl) adj.: intent on revenge.

reconcile (rek′ən·sīl′) v.: make peace.

Previewing Vocabulary

Have students review the Vocabulary words on p. 898. Then, have students complete each of the following analogies with the correct Vocabulary word.

1. ANCIENT : CONTEMPORARY : : INDIVIDUAL : [COMMUNAL]

2. CAUTIOUS : DARING : : SUBDUED : [FLORID]

3. BASEMENT : CELLAR : : MAZE : [LABYRINTH]

4. EARLY : PROPOSAL : : FINAL : [ULTIMATUM]

5. TRAGIC : COMIC : : PHYSICAL : [DISEMBODIED]

6. POEM : HAIKU : : SPEECH : [EULOGY]

7. PATIENTS : HEAL : : ENEMIES : [RECONCILE]

8. SUPERIOR : AVERAGE : : ENTHUSIASTIC : [NONCOMMITTAL]

9. JUBILANT : DEPRESSED : : FORGIVING : [VENGEFUL]

Daughter of Invention

Julia Alvarez

She always invented at night, after settling her house down.

A Reading Skills

❓ Making inferences about characters. What inferences can you make about the mother from this paragraph? [She has a traditional view of female roles, yet she longs to create something of lasting value.]

B English-Language Learners

❓ Interpreting idioms. What sayings does the mother mangle? ["You'll be sorry" mixed with "Better safe than sorry"; "green" ("inexperienced") with "Wet behind the ears"; "When in Rome, do as the Romans do" with "Do unto others as you would have them do unto you."]

C Literary Focus

❓ Conflict. What internal conflict does Mami face? [She loves her daughters and is hurt by the hostility they face, but she feels she must "teach" them to get along because she cannot control how others treat them.]

D English-Language Learners

Interpreting idioms. Explain that Mami's expression "It takes two to tangle" is from "It takes two to tango," meaning that both people usually contribute to a conflict.

She wanted to invent something, my mother. There was a period after we arrived in this country, until five or so years later, when my mother was inventing. They were never pressing, global needs she was addressing with her pencil and pad. She would have said that was for men to do, rockets and engines that ran on gasoline and turned the wheels of the world. She was just fussing with little house things, don't mind her.

She always invented at night, after settling her house down. On his side of the bed my father would be conked out for an hour already, his Spanish newspaper draped over his chest, his glasses, propped up on his bedside table, looking out eerily at the darkened room like a disembodied guard. But in her lighted corner, like some devoted scholar burning the midnight oil, my mother was inventing, sheets pulled to her lap, pillows propped up behind her, her reading glasses riding the bridge of her nose like a schoolmarm's. On her lap lay one of those innumerable pads of paper my father always brought home from his office, compliments of some pharmaceutical company, advertising tranquilizers or antibiotics or skin cream; in her other hand, my mother held a pencil that looked like a pen with a little cylinder of lead inside. She would work on a sketch of something familiar, but drawn at such close range so she could attach a special nozzle or handier handle, the thing looked peculiar. Once, I mistook the spiral of a corkscrew for a nautilus shell, but it could just as well have been a galaxy forming.

It was the only time all day we'd catch her sitting down, for she herself was living proof of the *perpetuum mobile*[1] machine so many inventors had sought over the ages. My sisters and I would seek her out now when she seemed to have a moment to talk to us: We were having

trouble at school or we wanted her to persuade my father to give us permission to go into the city or to a shopping mall or a movie—in broad daylight! My mother would wave us out of her room. "The problem with you girls . . ." I can tell you right now what the problem always boiled down to: We wanted to become Americans and my father—and my mother, at first—would have none of it.

"You girls are going to drive me crazy!" She always threatened if we kept nagging. "When I end up in Bellevue,[2] you'll be safely sorry!"

She spoke in English when she argued with us, even though, in a matter of months, her daughters were the fluent ones. Her English was much better than my father's, but it was still a mishmash of mixed-up idioms and sayings that showed she was "green behind the ears," as she called it.

If my sisters and I tried to get her to talk in Spanish, she'd snap, "When in Rome, do unto the Romans . . ."

I had become the spokesman for my sisters, and I would stand my ground in that bedroom. "We're not going to that school anymore, Mami!"

"You have to." Her eyes would widen with worry. "In this country, it is against the law not to go to school. You want us to get thrown out?"

"You want us to get killed? Those kids were throwing stones today!"

"Sticks and stones don't break bones . . ." she chanted. I could tell, though, by the look on her face, it was as if one of those stones the kids had aimed at us had hit her. But she always pretended we were at fault. "What did you do to provoke them? It takes two to tangle, you know."

> We wanted to become Americans and my father—and my mother, at first—would have none of it.

---

2. **Bellevue:** large New York City hospital known for its psychiatric department.

Vocabulary
disembodied (dis′im·bäd′ēd) v. used as *adj.*: separated from the body.

---

1. *perpetuum mobile* (per·pe′tōō·əm mō′bi·lā): Latin for "perpetual motion."

DIFFERENTIATING INSTRUCTION

Learners Having Difficulty
Modeling. To help students read the story, model the skill of making inferences. Say, "I read that the mother invents only at night, after she finishes her family duties. From this, I infer that she puts her family first. As you read, ask yourself, 'Where else do we see what the mother considers important?'"

English-Language Learners
Mami struggles with idioms, sometimes mixing two different sayings. Ask students to watch for other mixed-up sayings in the story, including, "Sticks and stones don't break bones" and "He didn't put all his pokers on a back burner."

"Thanks, thanks a lot, Mom!" I'd storm out of that room and into mine. I never called her *Mom* except when I wanted her to feel how much she had failed us in this country. She was a good enough Mami, fussing and scolding and giving advice, but a terrible girlfriend parent, a real failure of a Mom.

Back she'd go to her pencil and pad, scribbling and tsking and tearing off paper, finally giving up, and taking up her *New York Times*. Some nights, though, she'd get a good idea, and she'd rush into my room, a flushed look on her face, her tablet of paper in her hand, a cursory knock on the door she'd just thrown open: "Do I have something to show you, Cukita!"

This was my time to myself, after I'd finished my homework, while my sisters were still downstairs watching TV in the basement. Hunched over my small desk, the overhead light turned off, my lamp shining poignantly on my paper, the rest of the room in warm, soft, uncreated darkness, I wrote my secret poems in my new language.

"You're going to ruin your eyes!" My mother would storm into my room, turning on the overly bright overhead light, scaring off whatever shy passion I had just begun coaxing out of a <u>labyrinth</u> of feelings with the blue thread of my writing.

"Oh Mami!" I'd cry out, my eyes blinking up at her. "I'm writing."

"Ay, Cukita." That was her <u>communal</u> pet name for whoever was in her favor. "Cukita, when I make a million, I'll buy you your very own typewriter." (I'd been nagging my mother for one just like the one father had bought her to do his order forms at home.) "Gravy on the turkey" was what she called it when someone was buttering her up. She'd butter and pour. "I'll hire you your very own typist."

Down she'd plop on my bed and hold out her pad to me. "Take a guess, Cukita?" I'd study her rough sketch a moment: soap sprayed from the nozzle head of a shower when you turned the knob a certain way? Coffee with creamer already mixed in? Time-released water capsules for your plants when you were away? A key chain with a timer that would go off when your parking meter was about to expire? (The ticking would help you find your keys easily if you mislaid them.) The famous one, famous only in hindsight, was the stick person dragging a square by a rope—a suitcase with wheels? "Oh, of course," we'd humor her. "What every household needs: a shower like a car wash, keys ticking like a bomb, luggage on a leash!" By now, as you can see, it'd become something of a family joke, our Thomas Edison Mami, our Benjamin Franklin Mom.

Her face would fall. "Come on now! Use your head." One more wrong guess, and she'd tell me, pressing with her pencil point the different highlights of this incredible new wonder. "Remember that time we took the car to Bear Mountain, and we re-ah-lized that we had forgotten to pack an opener with our pick-a-nick?" (We kept correcting her, but she insisted this is how it should be said.) "When we were ready to eat we didn't have any way to open the refreshments cans?" (This before fliptop lids, which she claimed had crossed her mind.) "You know what this is now?" A shake of my head. "Is a car bumper, but see this part is a removable can opener. So simple and yet so necessary, no?"

"Yeah, Mami. You should patent it." I'd shrug. She'd tear off the scratch paper and fold it, carefully, corner to corner, as if she were going to save it. But then, she'd toss it in the wastebasket on her way out of the room and give a little laugh like a disclaimer.[3] "It's half of one or two dozen of another . . ."

I suppose none of her daughters was very encouraging. We resented her spending time on those dumb inventions. Here, we were trying to fit in America among Americans; we needed

---

3. **disclaimer** *n.*: refusal to accept responsibility; denial.

Vocabulary

labyrinth (lab′ə·rinth′) *n.*: place full of intricate passageways; maze.
communal (kə·myōon′əl) *adj.*: belonging to an entire group (in this case, Mami's daughters).

E Reading Skills

❷ Evaluating social influences. What does the narrator say is the difference between a Mami and a Mom? What might account for this difference? [A Mami is a traditional mother who corrects and guides her children, but a Mom is more of a friend who offers support. Mami's approach to parenting has been shaped by the social norms of her homeland.]

F English-Language Learners

❷ Interpreting idioms. To "butter up" someone is to say nice things to put that person in a good mood. Why does Mami butter up the narrator? [Mami wants the narrator to like her invention.]

G Reading Skills

❷ Making inferences about characters. What does Mami's reaction to the narrator's lack of enthusiasm tell you about Mami? [Possible responses: She is perceptive, sensing that her daughter is not giving her an honest opinion; she doesn't have as much self-confidence as she seems to.]

CONTENT-AREA CONNECTIONS

Math: Drafting

Independent activity. Ask students to come up with an idea for an invention that might solve a common household problem. They may modify an ordinary object, as Mami often does, or create an object. Have them present their ideas to the class, using scale drawings or other visual aids.

VIEWING THE ART

In *Madre e hija,* **Oscar Pardo** uses predominantly dark tones with expressive application, producing a feeling of bittersweet love between mother and daughter.

Activity. Point out to students, or ask a volunteer to explain, that *Madre e hija* is Spanish for "mother and daughter." Then, have students discuss what the placement of the two figures might suggest about their attitude toward one another. [Possible response: They are not facing each other, perhaps indicating that they are not communicating.] Why might this painting have been chosen to illustrate the story? [Possible response: The girl is looking at her mother, who is not looking at her. Maybe the daughter in the story needs more attention from her mother.]

help figuring out who we were, why these Irish kids whose grandparents were micks two generations ago, why they were calling us spics. Why had we come to the country in the first place? Important, crucial, final things, you see, and here was our own mother, who didn't have a second to help us puzzle any of this out, inventing gadgets to make life easier for American moms. Why, it seemed as if she were arming our own enemy against us!

One time, she did have a moment of triumph. Every night, she liked to read *The New York Times* in bed before turning off her light, to see what the Americans were up to. One night, she let out a yelp to wake up my father beside her, bolt upright, reaching for his glasses which, in his haste, he knocked across the room. *"Que pasa? Que pasa?"*[4] What is wrong? There was terror in his voice, fear she'd seen in his eyes in the Dominican Republic before we left. We were being watched there; he was being followed; he and mother had often exchanged those looks. They could not talk, of course, though they must have whispered to each other in fear at night in the dark bed. Now in America, he was safe, a success even; his Centro Medico in Brooklyn was thronged with the sick and the homesick. But in dreams, he went back to those awful days and long nights, and my mother's screams confirmed his secret fear: We had not gotten away after all; they had come for us at last.

"Ay, Papi, I'm sorry. Go back to sleep, Cukito. It's nothing, nothing really." My mother held up the *Times* for him to squint at the small print, back page headline, one hand tapping all over the top of the bedside table for his glasses, the other rubbing his eyes to wakefulness.

---

4. *Que pasa?* (kä pä′sä): Spanish for "What's going on?"

(Opposite) *Madre e hija* (1995) by Oscar Pardo. Pastel on paper (19″ × 12½″). Courtesy of the artist.

"Remember, remember how I showed you that suitcase with little wheels so we would not have to carry those heavy bags when we traveled? Someone stole my idea and made a million!" She shook the paper in his face. She shook the paper in all our faces that night. "See! See! This man was no *bobo!*[5] He didn't put all his pokers on a back burner. I kept telling you, one of these days my ship would pass me by in the night!" She wagged her finger at my sisters and my father and me, laughing all the while, one of those eerie laughs crazy people in movies laugh. We had congregated in her room to hear the good news she'd been yelling down the stairs, and now we eyed her and each other. I suppose we were all thinking the same thing: Wouldn't it be weird and sad if Mami did end up in Bellevue as she'd always threatened she might?

"Ya, ya! Enough!" She waved us out of her room at last. "There is no use trying to drink spilt milk, that's for sure."

It was the suitcase rollers that stopped my mother's hand; she had weather vaned a minor brainstorm. She would have to start taking herself seriously. That blocked the free play of her ingenuity. Besides, she had also begun working at my father's office, and at night, she was too tired and busy filling in columns with how much money they had made that day to be fooling with gadgets!

She did take up her pencil and pad one last time to help me out. In ninth grade, I was chosen by my English teacher, Sister Mary Joseph, to deliver the teacher's day address at the school assembly. Back in the Dominican Republic, I was a terrible student. No one could ever get me to sit down to a book. But in New York, I needed to settle somewhere, and the natives were unfriendly, the country inhospitable, so I took root in the language. By high school, the nuns were reading my stories and compositions

---

5. *bobo:* Spanish for "fool."

> They could not talk, of course, though they must have whispered to each other in fear at night in the dark bed.

Julia Alvarez   903

Julia Alvarez   903

DIRECT TEACHING

A Literary Focus

❓ Conflict. What conflict does this paragraph tell us exists between the mother and her daughters? [The mother has a need to create, which takes time that her daughters feel she should spend helping them in their new life.]

B Reading Skills

❓ Evaluating political influences. Who might have been watching and following Papi in the Dominican Republic? How did this experience affect him? [Possible responses: Government agents or the police were watching Papi, whom they suspected of having anti-government opinions. The experience left him fearful that they might still be pursuing him.]

C English-Language Learners

❓ Interpreting figurative language. Explain that a weather vane is a device with four arms, one for each of the four main points of the compass, that swings to show the direction the wind is coming from. The author here forms a verb *weather vaned* from the noun to create an image of what Mami had done: She had pointed her attention in the direction from which a brainstorm, or good new idea, was coming.

D Learners Having Difficulty

❓ Interpreting. What effect does the fact that one of her ideas made a lot of money (even though it was for someone else) have on Mami? [The notion that her ideas could actually be worth a great deal of money inhibits her from brainstorming freely.]

CONTENT-AREA CONNECTIONS

Psychology: Peer Counseling

Small-group activity. Ask groups of four to six students to think about the issues that Mami's daughters face as immigrants. What advice would they give the girls? Students should answer based on their own experiences in new situations as well as on what they have learned from the story. Then, at this point or later in the story, ask each group to write the script of a conversation in which two or more of the characters calmly and rationally resolve a conflict. Some members of the group can then act out the conversation for the rest of the class.

A Literary Focus

❓ **Conflict.** What internal conflict is the narrator experiencing here? [She wants to give the speech because she is proud of her creativity, but she is afraid her classmates will make fun of her accent.]

B Reading Skills

❓ **Expressing an opinion.** How useful to the narrator do you think her father's advice is? [Possible responses: It is not very useful, as the narrator's problem is not delivery but content; the purpose of her speech is quite different from the one he recites to her; and she has a hard time understanding his formal Spanish.]

C Reading Skills

❓ **Making inferences about characters.** What does the narrator's response to Whitman's poetry tell you about her? [Possible responses: She is open to people with different ideas; she appreciates people who reveal their true selves.]

out loud to my classmates as examples of imagination at work.

This time my imagination jammed. At first I didn't want and then I couldn't seem to write that speech. I suppose I should have thought of it as a "great honor," as my father called it. But I was mortified. I still had a pronounced lilt to my accent, and I did not like to speak in public, subjecting myself to my classmates' ridicule. Recently, they had begun to warm toward my sisters and me, and it took no great figuring to see that to deliver a eulogy for a convent full of crazy, old overweight nuns was no way to endear myself to the members of my class.

But I didn't know how to get out of it. Week after week, I'd sit down, hoping to polish off some quick, noncommittal little speech. I couldn't get anything down.

The weekend before our Monday morning assembly I went into a panic. My mother would just have to call in and say I was in the hospital, in a coma. I was in the Dominican Republic. Yeah, that was it! Recently, my father had been talking about going back home to live.

My mother tried to calm me down. "Just remember how Mister Lincoln couldn't think of anything to say at the Gettysburg, but then, Bang! 'Four score and once upon a time ago,'" she began reciting. Her version of history was half invention and half truths and whatever else she needed to prove a point. "Something is going to come if you just relax. You'll see, like the Americans say, 'Necessity is the daughter of invention.' I'll help you."

All weekend, she kept coming into my room with help. "Please, Mami, just leave me alone, please," I pleaded with her. But I'd get rid of the goose only to have to contend with the gander. My father kept poking his head in the door just to see if I had "fulfilled my obligations," a phrase he'd used when we were a little younger, and he'd check to see whether we had gone to the bathroom before a car trip. Several times that

weekend around the supper table, he'd recite his valedictorian speech from when he graduated from high school. He'd give me pointers on delivery, on the great orators and their tricks. (Humbleness and praise and falling silent with great emotion were his favorites.)

My mother sat across the table, the only one who seemed to be listening to him. My sisters and I were forgetting a lot of our Spanish, and my father's formal, florid diction was even harder to understand. But my mother smiled softly to herself, and turned the Lazy Susan at the center of the table around and around as if it were the prime mover,[6] the first gear of attention.

That Sunday evening, I was reading some poetry to get myself inspired: Whitman in an old book with an engraved cover my father had picked up in a thrift shop next to his office a few weeks back. "I celebrate myself and sing myself . . ." "He most honors my style who learns under it to destroy the teacher." The poet's words shocked and thrilled me. I had gotten used to the nuns, a literature of appropriate sentiments, poems with a message, expurgated texts. But here was a flesh and blood man, belching and laughing and sweating in poems. "Who touches this book touches a man."

That night, at last, I started to write, recklessly, three, five pages, looking up once only to see my father passing by the hall on tiptoe. When I was done, I read over my words, and my eyes filled. I finally sounded like myself in English!

When I was done, I read over my words, and my eyes filled. I finally sounded like myself in English!

---

6. **prime mover:** in philosophy, the self-moved being that is the source of all motion; in machinery, the source of power, such as a windmill or an engine.

Vocabulary

eulogy (yōō′lə·jē) *n.:* public speech of praise.
noncommittal (nän′kə·mit″l) *adj.:* neutral; giving no clear indication of feeling or attitude.
florid (flôr′id) *adj.:* showy.

SKILLS REVIEW

Analyzing cause and effect. Remind students that a cause makes something happen; that "something" is the effect. Sometimes an author may show an effect without explicitly stating its cause. In those cases, readers must infer the probable cause in order to understand the story more fully. Point out that cause-and-effect relationships may be self-perpetuating: One situation or event causes another, which causes the first one to happen again.

Activity. Have students draw a diagram showing one of the cause-and-effect relationships set into motion by the narrator's family's moving to the United States.

As soon as I had finished that first draft, I called my mother to my room. She listened attentively, as she had to my father's speech, and in the end, her eyes were glistening too. Her face was soft and warm and proud. "That is a beautiful, beautiful speech, Cukita. I want for your father to hear it before he goes to sleep. Then I will type it for you, all right?"

Down the hall we went, the two of us, faces flushed with accomplishment. Into the master bedroom where my father was propped up on his pillows, still awake, reading the Dominican papers, already days old. He had become interested in his country's fate again. The dictatorship had been toppled. The interim government was going to hold the first free elections in thirty years. There was still some question in his mind whether or not we might want to move back. History was in the making, freedom and hope were in the air again! But my mother had gotten used to the life here. She did not want to go back to the old country where she was only a wife and a mother (and a failed one at that, since she had never had the required son). She did not come straight out and disagree with my father's plans. Instead, she fussed with him about reading the papers in bed, soiling those sheets with those poorly printed, foreign tabloids. "*The Times* is not that bad!" she'd claim if my father tried to humor her by saying they shared the same dirty habit.

The minute my father saw my mother and me, filing in, he put his paper down, and his face brightened as if at long last his wife had delivered a son, and that was the news we were bringing him. His teeth were already grinning from the glass of water next to his bedside lamp, so he lisped when he said, "Eh-speech, eh-speech!"

"It is so beautiful, Papi," my mother previewed him, turning the sound off on his TV. She sat down at the foot of the bed. I stood before both of them, blocking their view of the soldiers in helicopters landing amid silenced gun reports and explosions. A few weeks ago it had been the shores of the Dominican Republic. Now it was the jungles of Southeast Asia they

were saving. My mother gave me the nod to begin reading.

I didn't need much encouragement. I put my nose to the fire, as my mother would have said, and read from start to finish without looking up. When I was done, I was a little embarrassed at my pride in my own words. I pretended to quibble with a phrase or two I was sure I'd be talked out of changing. I looked questioningly to my mother. Her face was radiant. She turned to share her pride with my father.

But the expression on his face shocked us both. His toothless mouth had collapsed into a dark zero. His eyes glared at me, then shifted to my mother, accusingly. In barely audible Spanish, as if secret microphones or informers were all about, he whispered, "You will permit her to read *that*?"

My mother's eyebrows shot up, her mouth fell open. In the old country, any whisper of a challenge to authority could bring the secret police in their black V.W.'s. But this was America. People could say what they thought. "What is wrong with her speech?" my mother questioned him.

"What ees wrrrong with her eh-speech?" My father wagged his head at her. His anger was always more frightening in his broken English. As if he had mutilated the language in his fury— and now there was nothing to stand between us and his raw, dumb anger. "What is wrong? I will tell you what is wrong. It shows no gratitude. It is boastful. 'I celebrate myself'? 'The best student learns to destroy the teacher'?" He mocked my plagiarized words. "That is insubordinate. It is improper. It is disrespecting of her teachers—" In his anger he had forgotten his fear of lurking spies: Each wrong he voiced was a decibel higher than the last outrage. Finally, he was yelling at me, "As your father, I forbid you to say that eh-speech!"

My mother leapt to her feet, a sign always that she was about to make a speech or deliver an ultimatum. She was a small woman, and she

---

Vocabulary

ultimatum (ul′tə·māt′əm) *n*.: last offer; final proposition.

D **Advanced Learners**

? **Characterization.** What basic personality differences between the narrator's mother and father are revealed by these details? [Possible responses: Her father is more conservative, craving a return to traditional ways, while her mother is more interested in and open to change.]

E **Reading Skills**

? **Making predictions.** How do you predict the narrator's father will react to her speech? Why do you think so? [Possible responses: He will be pleased because it was he who brought home the Whitman book that inspired her speech; he will be shocked by her references to Whitman's ideas.]

F **Reading Skills**

? **Making inferences about characters.** What do Papi's expression and tone of voice suggest about his reaction to the speech? [Possible responses: They suggest an effort to control himself; they suggest shock, nearly to the point of speechlessness.]

G **Literary Focus**

? **Conflict.** What inner conflict of Papi's is evident here? [He escaped a repressive regime but has internalized its authoritarian attitudes.]

A Reading Skills

❓ Interpreting metaphors. The story has occasional lyrical passages such as this metaphor. What does it suggest about the parents' relationship? [Mami loves Papi in spite of the anguish he causes her.]

B Literary Focus

❓ Conflict. According to Mami, what keeps the "war" between her and Papi going? [his inability to accept that he is safe and free in the United States]

A CLOSER LOOK

This essay explains the patent system, describes unusual inventions, and relates the stories of some popular patented devices.

C Reading Informational Text

❓ Understanding author's purpose. What is the author's main purpose? [to give an engaging overview of the function and activities of the Patent Office]

D Reading Informational Text

❓ Understanding structure. What is the point of this list? [to show that many ideas on record at the Patent Office are amusing]

---

spoke all her pronouncements standing up, either for more protection or as a carry-over from her girlhood in convent schools where one asked for, and literally took, the floor in order to speak. She stood by my side, shoulder to shoulder; we looked down at my father. "That is no tone of voice, Eduardo—" she began.

By now, my father was truly furious. I suppose it was bad enough I was rebelling, but here was my mother joining forces with me. Soon he would be surrounded by a house full of independent American women. He too leapt from his bed, throwing off his covers. The Spanish newspapers flew across the room. He snatched my speech out of my hands, held it before my panicked eyes, a <u>vengeful</u>, mad look in his own, and then once, twice, three, four, countless times, he tore my prize into shreds.

"Are you crazy?" My mother lunged at him. "Have you gone mad? That is her speech for tomorrow you have torn up!"

"Have *you* gone mad?" He shook her away. "You were going to let her read that . . . that insult to her teachers?"

"Insult to her teachers!" My mother's face had crumpled up like a piece of paper. On it was written a love note to my father. Ever since they had come to this country, their life together was a constant war. "This is America, Papi, America!" she reminded him now. "You are not in a savage country any more!"

I was on my knees, weeping wildly, collecting all the little pieces of my speech, hoping that I could put it back together before the assembly tomorrow morning. But not even a sibyl[7]

---

7. **sibyl** (sib'əl) *n.:* in ancient Greece and Rome, a woman who foretold the future.

Vocabulary
vengeful (venj'fəl) *adj.:* intent on revenge.

A CLOSER LOOK: SOCIAL INFLUENCES

Patently American Inventions

INFORMATIONAL TEXT

Have an invention of your own you'd like to protect? Consider patenting it. A U.S. patent gives you the right to exclude all others from making, using, or selling your invention within the United States for a limited number of years. To start, put your idea in writing, illustrate your device or process, and sign and date the document (use indelible ink). But before you reach for pad and pen, you might want to learn a little more about patents and inventions.

Patents are granted by the U.S. Patent and Trademark Office, in Arlington, Virginia. The Patent Office is flooded with over 150,000 applications a year, each of which takes about two years to process. If you can convince the patent officer that your invention is (1) new, (2) useful, and (3) original, a patent is yours. But be warned: You'll need deep pockets, since patent fees typically exceed $1,000.

Patented inventions we haven't seen in stores. Anyone wanting an afternoon's—or a lifetime's—entertainment could do worse than browse through the five million patents on record at the Patent Office. Ideas on record include these:

- eye protectors for chickens
- a device combining a plow and a gun
- a locket for storing used chewing gum
- a wake-up device consisting of suspended wood blocks that fall on the sleeper's face
- a device to create or maintain dimples
- balloons powered by large birds
- farms that rest on giant saucers floating in the sea

Did you know . . . ? The narrator's mother in "Daughter of Invention" is one in a long list of female American inventors. Since 1793, U.S. patents have been granted to women for inventions ranging from the brown paper bag, the modern coffeepot, and the disposable diaper to

---

CONTENT-AREA CONNECTIONS

History: Dominican Republic
Individual and whole-class activity. Ask some students to research events in the Dominican Republic, just before and after the time in which "Daughter of Invention" is set (the early 1960s). Ask others to find out about recent events in the country. Discuss as a class the information students collect.

Humanities: Spanish
Small-group activity. Ask students who speak or have studied Spanish to come up with a list of proverbs and folk sayings in Spanish and to provide translations for students who do not understand the language.

could have made sense of all those scattered pieces of paper. All hope was lost. "He broke it, he broke it," I moaned as I picked up a handful of pieces.

Probably, if I had thought a moment about it, I would not have done what I did next. I would have realized my father had lost brothers and comrades to the dictator Trujillo.[8] For the rest of his life, he would be haunted by blood in the streets and late night disappearances. Even after he had been in the states for years, he jumped if a black Volkswagen passed him on the street. He feared anyone in uniform: the meter maid giving out parking tickets, a museum guard

___

8. **Trujillo** (trōō·hē'yō): Rafael Leonidas Trujillo Molina, general who took over as president of the Dominican Republic and ruled oppressively from 1930 to 1938 and from 1942 until 1961, when he was assassinated.

approaching to tell him not to touch his favorite Goya at the Metropolitan.[9]

I took a handful of the scraps I had gathered, stood up, and hurled them in his face. "Chapita!" I said in a low, ugly whisper. "You're just another Chapita!"

It took my father only a moment to register the hated nickname of our dictator, and he was after me. Down the halls we raced, but I was quicker than he and made it to my room just in time to lock the door as my father threw his weight against it. He called down curses on my head, ordered me on his authority as my father to open that door this very instant! He throttled that doorknob, but all to no avail. My mother's love of gadgets saved my hide that night. She

___

9. **Goya...Metropolitan:** painting by the Spanish artist Francisco José de Goya y Lucientes at the Metropolitan Museum of Art in New York City.

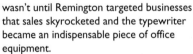
Julia Alvarez   **907**

FAMILY/COMMUNITY ACTIVITY

Encourage students to interview relatives to find out when, why, and from where members of the family originally came to the United States. Interested students can then meet in small groups to discuss similarities and differences among their findings and to share their responses to the family stories they have gathered.

VIEWING THE ART

Alejandro Xul Solar
(1888–1963) was an unconventional and imaginative Argentinian painter. Xul Solar used bold colors and fantastic forms to reveal human spirituality and heightened awareness.

Activity. Ask students what they see in the work. [Possible responses: a human; a robot; candles; buildings.] What emotion does the central figure suggest? [Possible responses: independence; assertiveness; anger; jubilation.] Which character in the story does the figure suggest? [Possible responses: the father or the narrator, because the figure stands alone raising its arms, perhaps in protest; the daughter as seen by the father—that is, as boastful.]

Ⓐ Literary Focus

❓ Conflict. What conflict is resolved here? [The narrator's desire for more time with her mother is fulfilled when Mami helps with a new speech.]

GUIDED PRACTICE

Monitoring students' progress. Guide the class in answering these comprehension questions.

Short Answer

1. Where did the family emigrate from? [They came from the Dominican Republic.]

2. Where does the narrator's father work? [He works at a medical center.]

3. Where do the narrator and her sisters go to school? [They attend a Catholic school.]

4. What equipment does the mother use to design her inventions? [paper and pencil]

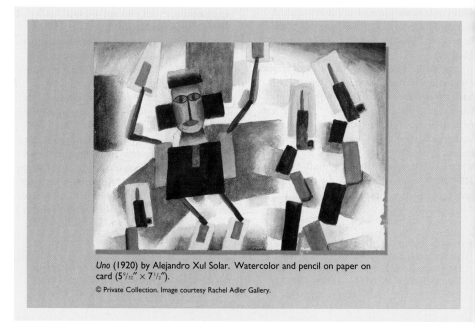

Uno (1920) by Alejandro Xul Solar. Watercolor and pencil on paper on card (5⁹/₃₂″ × 7¹/₂″).
© Private Collection. Image courtesy Rachel Adler Gallery.

had hired a locksmith to install good locks on all the bedroom doors after our house had been broken into while we were away the previous summer. In case burglars broke in again, and we were in the house, they'd have a second round of locks to contend with before they got to us.

"Eduardo," she tried to calm him down. "Don't you ruin my new locks."

He finally did calm down, his anger spent. I heard their footsteps retreating down the hall. I heard their door close, the clicking of their lock. Then, muffled voices, my mother's peaking in anger, in persuasion, my father's deep murmurs of explanation and of self-defense. At last, the house fell silent, before I heard, far off, the gun blasts and explosions, the serious, self-important voices of newscasters reporting their TV war.

A little while later, there was a quiet knock at my door, followed by a tentative attempt at the doorknob. "Cukita?" my mother whispered. "Open up, Cukita."

"Go away," I wailed, but we both knew I was glad she was there, and I needed only a mo-

ment's protest to save face before opening that door.

What we ended up doing that night was putting together a speech at the last moment. Two brief pages of stale compliments and the polite commonplaces on teachers, wrought by necessity without much invention by mother for daughter late into the night in the basement on the pad of paper and with the same pencil she had once used for her own inventions, for I was too upset to compose the speech myself. After it was drafted, she typed it up while I stood by, correcting her misnomers and mis-sayings.

She was so very proud of herself when I came home the next day with the success story of the assembly. The nuns had been flattered, the audience had stood up and given "our devoted teachers a standing ovation," what my mother had suggested they do at the end of my speech.

She clapped her hands together as I re-created the moment for her. "I stole that from your father's speech, remember? Remember how he put that in at the end?" She quoted him in

Spanish, then translated for me into English.

That night, I watched him from the upstairs hall window where I'd retreated the minute I heard his car pull up in front of our house. Slowly, my father came up the driveway, a grim expression on his face as he grappled with a large, heavy cardboard box. At the front door, he set the package down carefully and patted all his pockets for his house keys—precisely why my mother had invented her ticking key chain. I heard the snapping open of the locks downstairs. Heard as he struggled to maneuver the box through the narrow doorway. Then, he called my name several times. But I would not answer him.

"My daughter, your father, he love you very much," he explained from the bottom of the stairs. "He just want to protect you." Finally, my mother came up and pleaded with me to go down and reconcile with him. "Your father did not mean to harm. You must pardon him. Always it is better to let bygones be forgotten, no?"

I guess she was right. Downstairs, I found him setting up a brand new electric typewriter on the kitchen table. It was even better than the one I'd been begging to get like my mother's. My father had outdone himself with all the extra features: a plastic carrying case with my initials, in decals, below the handle, a brace to lift the paper upright while I typed, an erase cartridge, an automatic margin tab, a plastic hood like a toaster cover to keep the dust away. Not even my mother, I think, could have invented such a machine!

But her inventing days were over just as mine were starting up with my schoolwide success. That's why I've always thought of that speech my mother wrote for me as her last invention rather than the suitcase rollers everyone else in the family remembers. It was as if she had passed on to me her pencil and pad and said, "Okay, Cukita, here's the buck. You give it a shot." ∎

Vocabulary

reconcile (rek′ən·sīl′) v.: make peace

Response and Analysis

Reading Check

1. Which of the mother's ideas for an invention is a huge success for somebody else?

2. Why did the daughters resent the time their mother spent on inventions?

3. The narrator's mother uses many English-language **aphorisms** (af′ə·riz′əmz)—brief, wise sayings—but she gets them slightly wrong. Give the correct version of two or three of her sayings.

4. How does the daughter insult her father after he destroys her speech?

5. How do the father and daughter become reconciled?

Thinking Critically

6. The narrator wants to use Whitman's words, "He most honors my style who learns under it to destroy the teacher" (page 904). How does her father interpret the words? What do you think Whitman really meant?

7. The narrator says that her mother was "a good enough Mami" but "a terrible girlfriend parent, a real failure of a Mom" (page 901). What does the narrator mean? What do you think of her conflicting feelings for her mother? Are these typical American responses, or are they found in many cultures? Explain.

8. What **conflicts** does the father face in the story? How does the narrator deal with these conflicts?

SKILLS FOCUS

Literary Skills
Analyze external and internal conflict.

Reading Skills
Make inferences about characters.

Writing Skills
Write an essay analyzing conflict in a story.

Vocabulary Skills
Demonstrate word knowledge.

Julia Alvarez **909**

---

9. Possible answers: Papi is resistant to change; he yearns to return to his homeland, where people's roles are more defined. The narrator is open to change but is unsure of herself. Mami embraces change; she is ambitious and, for the most part, confident.

10. Possible answer: The title plays on the saying "Necessity is the mother of invention." This relates to the story's theme by suggesting not only Mami's inventions but also Mami's setting aside her inventing in order to meet her daughters' needs. In the process, Mami passes along her creativity to the narrator. The title is clever and apt.

11. Possible answer: Yes, it is realistic; the experience of living in fear may inflict lasting emotional distress. Students may cite their own or their friends' experiences or those of other immigrants from countries that have undergone political turmoil.

Vocabulary Development
Possible Answers

1. I'd be terrified.

2. I would find my way out of the maze.

3. We'd argue that a group meeting hall should be for everyone.

4. People would be shocked to hear insults in a speech that is supposed to praise someone.

5. I would insist that he or she decide.

6. I would try to write more simply and clearly in the future.

7. I would think carefully before making a decision.

8. The attacker might get hurt.

9. I would regret not being able to make peace.

9. What inferences can you make about the **characters** based on the ways they have adapted (or failed to adapt) to their new country?

10. A good **title** has what is sometimes called resonance (rez′ə·nəns). That means that the title resounds or echoes with meanings. Think of how and why Alvarez's title works. In what ways does it relate to the story's **theme**? How do you feel about her choice of title?

11. In this story the father's experience with authority in his home country influences his behavior in the United States. Do you think this is a realistic portrayal of a person who has come to America from a country with an oppressive government? How does it compare with the experiences of immigrants you know or have heard about? Explain your responses.

WRITING
Analyzing Conflicts

"Daughter of Invention" builds upon a variety of **external** and **internal conflicts.** Make a four-column chart like the one below to organize your thoughts about the conflicts in the story. In the first column, list all the types of conflicts you can identify, such as social, interpersonal, cultural, and political conflicts. In the second column, tell who is involved in each conflict: for example, mother-daughter, father-daughter, husband-wife. In the third column, describe how the conflict is—or is not—resolved in the story. In the fourth column, evaluate each conflict's power to hold your interest and to evoke reactions. Finally, use your chart as the basis of an **essay** analyzing the conflicts in "Daughter of Invention."

Type of Conflict	Who Is Involved	Resolution	Evaluation
Social			
Interpersonal			
Cultural			
Political			

Vocabulary Development
What If?

In a small group, discuss the possible outcomes of these scenarios.

1. What if a disembodied hand gripped your shoulder?

2. What if you found yourself in a labyrinth?

3. What if a communal meeting hall was off-limits to teenagers?

4. What if a eulogy said negative things about its subject?

5. What if your date suddenly became noncommittal about going to the prom?

6. What if a teacher said you wrote florid prose?

7. What if you were given a tough ultimatum?

8. What if a vengeful victim confronted her attacker?

9. What if you could not reconcile with an old friend?

ASSESSING

■ *Holt Assessment: Literature, Reading, and Vocabulary*

Literature of the Americas
Colombia

Gabriel García Márquez
(1928–   )

Gabriel García Márquez (gä′brē·el′ gär·sē′ä mär′kes) was born in Aracataca, Colombia, the town that became the model for the fictional village of Macondo in his popular novel *One Hundred Years of Solitude* (1967). He spent his early years with his maternal grandparents, whom he regards as "wonderful beings." According to García Márquez, "They had an enormous house, full of ghosts. They were people of great imagination and superstitions. In every corner there were dead people and memories, and after six o'clock in the [evening] the house was untraversable. It was a world prodigious with terror. There were conversations in code."

After attending universities in Bogotá and Cartagena, García Márquez worked as a journalist in Colombia and in Rome, Paris, Barcelona, Caracas, and New York. Newspaper work helped García Márquez (like Ernest Hemingway) develop a style of writing fiction. Even after ending his newspaper career in 1965, García Márquez considered himself to be at heart a journalist, which is one reason for the factual or realistic basis for his fiction. It also accounts for his occasional nonfiction books, such as *News of a Kidnapping* (1997). Because of serious political differences with the Colombian government, he lives in Mexico City.

García Márquez has achieved international renown mainly for his fiction, which includes, besides *One Hundred Years of Solitude*, *The Autumn of the Patriarch* (1976), *Love in the Time of Cholera* (1988), *Strange Pilgrims* (1993), and *Of Love and Other Demons* (1995).

García Márquez's novels have often been compared with those of William Faulkner, who created a mythical county in Mississippi as the background for bizarre and sometimes hilarious events that reflect exaggerated historical reality. Faulkner's influence can also be seen in García Márquez's use of long, rhythmic sentences and shifting points of view. However, it is the rich storytelling traditions and the unique imaginative fantasies of Latin America that García Márquez has found most valuable. Awarded the Nobel Prize for literature in 1982, García Márquez deplored, in his acceptance speech, the way many Latin American writers ignore their own heritage and accept the hand-me-downs of European history and culture.

Gabriel García Márquez signing autographs in the streets of Cartagena.

SKILLS FOCUS, pp. 911–918

Grade-Level Skills

- **Literary Skills**
Analyze characteristics of magic realism.

- **Literary Skills**
Analyze recognized works of world literature.

- **Literary Skills**
Analyze archetypes drawn from myth and tradition.

More About the Writer

Background. Like several other great fiction writers from Henry Fielding to Franz Kafka, Gabriel García Márquez was educated as a lawyer. He entered the law school of the National University of Colombia in 1947 and transferred to Cartagena after one year. While continuing his law studies, he began a career in journalism, and it was in newspapers that his first short stories were published.

Skills Starter

Build prerequisite skills. Before students read the selection, review some of the characteristics of the archetypal hero: extraordinary physical prowess, courage, cunning, and goodness; a mysterious origin; a life of dangerous encounters with evil; a death that occasions great mourning, unites a community, and inspires hopes for the hero's return.

RESOURCES: READING

Planning
- *One-Stop Planner* CD-ROM with ExamView Test Generator

Differentiating Instruction
- *Holt Reading Solutions*
- *The Holt Reader*
- *Supporting Instruction in Spanish*
- *Audio CD Library, Selections and Summaries in Spanish*

Vocabulary
- *Vocabulary Development*

Grammar and Language
- *Language Handbook Worksheets*
- *Daily Language Activities*

Assessment
- *Holt Assessment: Literature, Reading, and Vocabulary*
- *One-Stop Planner* CD-ROM with

ExamView Test Generator
- *Holt Online Assessment*

Internet
- go.hrw.com (Keyword: LE5 11-6)
- *Elements of Literature Online*

Media
- *Audio CD Library*
- *Audio CD Library, Selections and Summaries in Spanish*

Summary ↔ at grade level

This magic realist story begins with the discovery of the body of a drowned man. In itself, this is not an extraordinary event in a village by the sea, but as the people begin to examine the body, trying to figure out who the man was and how he lived and died, they make some extraordinary discoveries. As the women clean the corpse, they are struck by its great size, strength, and beauty, and they begin to imagine the dead man as having had superhuman qualities. The oldest woman among them, however, looks at the man's face and declares that he is surely "someone called Esteban"—a far more ordinary figure whose great size could have led to his mistreatment by others when he was alive. Now, the women begin to feel pity and affection for the drowned man and convince their husbands to give him a lavish funeral. The villagers return the body to the sea without an anchor in case the man (who has now attained mythical status) wishes to return. As the villagers resume their lives, the memory of the drowned man gives them a new sense of their own importance and the will to transform their barren village into a flowering oasis.

Selection Starter

Build background. Tell students that "The Handsomest Drowned Man in the World" was originally collected in García Márquez's 1972 book of short stories, called *Leaf Storm and Other Stories*. In addition to the title story and "The Handsomest Drowned Man in the World," the volume includes another remarkable magic realist tale, called "A Very Old Man with Enormous Wings," which, like this one, García Márquez labeled a children's story.

Before You Read

The Handsomest Drowned Man in the World

Make the Connection

Archetypes sound complicated but they are only very basic patterns that you probably first encountered in stories from childhood. **Archetype** (är′kə·tīp′) means "an original pattern or a basic pattern." Archetypes have recurred in writing throughout the centuries; they can be plots, characters, events, or just things. An example of an archetype is the superhuman hero. The comic-strip hero Superman is an example of that archetype, still alive and well today. Another example of an archetype is a metamorphosis, a marvelous transformation from one form to another. You have read about metamorphoses in myths and fairy tales: In a version of the Cinderella story, for example, a pumpkin is magically transformed into a fabulous carriage. What other superheroes can you name? What metamorphoses can you remember from the stories you have read?

Literary Focus
Magic Realism

Magic realism is a literary style that combines incredible events with realistic details and relates them all in a matter-of-fact tone. The style was invented in Latin America around the middle of the twentieth century and has since gained worldwide popularity. Magic realism blurs the lines that usually separate what seems real from what seems imagined or fantastic. Its incorporation of magic, myth, imagination, and religious elements into literature aims to expand rigid notions of what constitutes reality. You can find echoes of magic realism in works by such noted American authors as Donald Barthelme (page 876), Thomas Pynchon, and Kurt Vonnegut, as well as in the novels of Günter Grass of Germany and John Fowles of England.

go.
hrw
.com

INTERNET
Vocabulary Practice
Keyword: LE5 11-6

SKILLS FOCUS

Literary Skills
Understand characteristics of magic realism.

Magic realism is a literary style that combines incredible events with realistic details and relates them all in a matter-of-fact tone.

For more on Magic Realism, see the Handbook of Literary and Historical Terms.

Vocabulary Development

bountiful (bɔun′tə·fəl) *adj.*: generous.

haggard (hag′ərd) *adj.*: gaunt; worn out.

virile (vir′əl) *adj.*: manly; masculine.

destitute (des′tə·tōōt′) *adj.*: poverty-stricken.

frivolity (fri·väl′ə·tē) *n.*: silliness.

mortified (môrt′ə·fīd′) *v.* used as *adj.*: humiliated; deeply embarrassed.

© DC Comics.

Previewing Vocabulary

Remind students that **connotations** are the feelings associated with a word, which go beyond the word's dictionary meaning. Often, connotations show shades of meaning or degrees of intensity. Have students work with a partner to determine which word in each pair has a stronger connotation. Possible answers are underlined.

1. virile   <u>heroic</u>
2. frivolity   <u>absurdity</u>
3. destitute   poor
4. <u>bountiful</u>   abundant
5. <u>haggard</u>   tired
6. <u>mortified</u>   humiliated

The Handsomest Drowned Man in the World

Gabriel García Márquez

translated by **Gregory Rabassa**

A Tale for Children

The first children who saw the dark and slinky bulge approaching through the sea let themselves think it was an enemy ship. Then they saw it had no flags or masts and they thought it was a whale. But when it was washed up on the beach, they removed the clumps of seaweed, the jellyfish tentacles, and the remains of fish and flotsam, and only then did they see that it was a drowned man.

They had been playing with him all afternoon, burying him in the sand and digging him up again, when someone chanced to see them and spread the alarm in the village. The men who carried him to the nearest house noticed that he weighed more than any dead man they had ever known, almost as much as a horse, and they said to each other that maybe he'd been floating too long and the water had got into his bones. When they laid him on the floor they said he'd been taller than all other men because there was barely enough room for him in the house, but they thought that maybe the ability to keep on growing after death was part of the nature of certain drowned men. He had the smell of the sea about him and only his shape gave one to suppose that it was the corpse of a human being, because the skin was covered with a crust of mud and scales.

They did not even have to clean off his face to know that the dead man was a stranger. The village was made up of only twenty-odd wooden houses that had stone courtyards with no flowers and which were spread about on the end of a desertlike cape. There was so little land that mothers always went about with the fear that the wind would carry off their children and the few dead that the years had caused among them had to be thrown off the cliffs. But the sea

Art on pages 911, 913, 914, and 918 by Sergio Bustamente/Photos by Clint Clemens.

Ⓐ Reading Skills

❓ Analyzing archetypes. What archetypal heroic terms does the author use to describe the dead man? [Like the Greek hero Odysseus, he crosses "faraway oceans," makes his way through "labyrinths," and projects a certain pride and self-sufficiency.] What is ironic about his heroic attributes? [Possible response: He is a posthumous hero.]

Ⓑ Literary Focus

❓ Magic realism. Here the women endow the man with godlike traits. What details suggest a myth? [calling fish from the sea; causing springs to burst forth; growing flowers on barren cliffs]

was calm and <u>bountiful</u> and all the men fit into seven boats. So when they found the drowned man they simply had to look at one another to see that they were all there.

That night they did not go out to work at sea. While the men went to find out if anyone was missing in neighboring villages, the women stayed behind to care for the drowned man. They took the mud off with grass swabs, they removed the underwater stones entangled in his hair, and they scraped the crust off with tools used for scaling fish. As they were doing that they noticed that the vegetation on him came from faraway oceans and deep water and that his clothes were in tatters, as if he had sailed through labyrinths of coral. They noticed too that he bore his death with pride, for he did not have the lonely look of other drowned men who came out of the sea or that <u>haggard</u>, needy look of men who drowned in rivers. But only when they finished cleaning him off did they become aware of the kind of man he was and it left them breathless. Not only was he the tallest, strongest, most <u>virile</u>, and best-built man they had ever seen, but even though they were looking at him there was no room for him in their imagination.

They could not find a bed in the village large enough to lay him on nor was there a table solid enough to use for his wake. The tallest men's holiday pants would not fit him, not the fattest ones' Sunday shirts, nor the shoes of the one with the biggest feet. Fascinated by his huge size and his beauty, the women then decided to make him some pants from a large piece of sail and a shirt from some bridal brabant linen[1] so that he could continue through his death with dignity. As they sewed, sitting in a circle and gazing at the corpse between stitches, it seemed to them that the wind had never been so steady nor the sea so restless as on that night and they supposed that the change had something to do with the dead man. They thought that if that magnificent man had lived in the village, his house would have had the widest doors, the highest ceiling, and the strongest floor, his bedstead would have been made from a midship frame held together by iron bolts, and his wife would have been the happiest woman. They thought that he would have had so much authority that he could have drawn fish out of the sea simply by calling their names and that he would have put so much work into his land that springs would have burst forth from among the rocks so that he would have been able to plant flowers on the cliffs. They secretly compared him to their own men, thinking that for all their lives theirs were incapable of doing what he could do in one night, and they ended up dismissing them deep in their hearts as the weakest, meanest, and most useless creatures on earth. They were wandering through that maze of fantasy when the oldest woman, who as the oldest had looked upon the drowned man with more compassion than passion, sighed:

---

1. **brabant** (brə·bant′) **linen:** linen from Brabant, a province of Belgium known for its fine lace and cloth.

Vocabulary
bountiful (boun′tə·fəl) *adj.:* generous.
haggard (hag′ərd) *adj.:* gaunt; worn out.
virile (vir′əl) *adj.:* manly; masculine.

DIFFERENTIATING INSTRUCTION

Advanced Learners
Enrichment. Students may research the history of magic realism and read other Latin American writers, including Jorge Luis Borges, Julio Cortázar, Alejo Carpenter, Carlos Fuentes, José Donoso, and Mario Vargas Llosa.

CONTENT-AREA CONNECTIONS

Science: Flora and Fauna
Paired activity. Invite partners to use geographical atlases and other sources to research the flora and fauna of coastal Colombia. Encourage students to start with life forms mentioned in the story and then to widen their search to include plants and other animals from the region. They can present their findings orally and display photographs and maps.

"He has the face of someone called Esteban."[2] It was true. Most of them had only to take another look at him to see that he could not have any other name. The more stubborn among them, who were the youngest, still lived for a few hours with the illusion that when they put his clothes on and he lay among the flowers in patent leather shoes his name might be Lautaro.[3] But it was a vain illusion. There had not been enough canvas, the poorly cut and worse sewn pants were too tight, and the hidden strength of his heart popped the buttons on his shirt. After midnight the whistling of the wind died down and the sea fell into its Wednesday drowsiness.[4] The silence put an end to any last doubts: he was Esteban. The women who had dressed him, who had combed his hair, had cut his nails and shaved him were unable to hold back a shudder of pity when they had to resign themselves to his being dragged along the ground. It was then that they understood how unhappy he must have been with that huge body since it bothered him even after death. They could see him in life, condemned to going through doors sideways, cracking his head on crossbeams, remaining on his feet during visits, not knowing what to do with his soft, pink, sea lion hands while the lady of the house looked for her most resistant chair and begged him, frightened to death, sit here, Esteban, please, and he, leaning against the wall, smiling, don't bother, ma'am, I'm fine where I am, his heels raw and his back roasted from having done the

same thing so many times whenever he paid a visit, don't bother, ma'am, I'm fine where I am, just to avoid the embarrassment of breaking up the chair, and never knowing perhaps that the ones who said don't go, Esteban, at least wait till the coffee's ready, were the ones who later on would whisper the big boob finally left, how nice, the handsome fool has gone. That was what the women were thinking beside the body a little before dawn. Later, when they covered his face with a handkerchief so that the light would not bother him, he looked so forever dead, so defenseless, so much like their men that the first furrows of tears opened in their hearts. It was one of the younger ones who began the weeping. The others, coming to, went from sighs to wails, and the more they sobbed the more they felt like weeping, because the drowned man was becoming all the more Esteban for them, and so they wept so much, for he was the most destitute, most peaceful, and most obliging man on earth, poor Esteban. So when the men returned with the news that the drowned man was not from the neighboring villages either, the women felt an opening of jubilation in the midst of their tears.

"Praise the Lord," they sighed, "he's ours!"

The men thought the fuss was only woman-ish frivolity. Fatigued because of the difficult nighttime inquiries, all they wanted was to get rid of the bother of the newcomer once and for all before the sun grew strong on that arid, windless day. They improvised a litter with the remains of foremasts and gaffs,[5] tying it to-gether with rigging so that it would bear the weight of the body until they reached the cliffs. They wanted to tie the anchor from a cargo ship to him so that he would sink easily into the deepest waves, where fish are blind and divers die of nostalgia, and bad currents would not bring him back to shore, as had happened with

---

2. **Esteban** (es·te′bän): Spanish equivalent of "Stephen." In Christian tradition, Stephen was the first martyr. He was stoned to death because of his beliefs.

3. **Lautaro** (lou·tä′rô): leader of the Araucanian Indian people who resisted the Spanish conquistadors en-tering their land, in what is now Chile, during the sixteenth century. Lautaro is now seen as a Chilean national hero.

4. **Wednesday drowsiness** (and later **Wednesday meat** and **Wednesday dead body**): *Wednesday* is a collo-quial expression for "tiresome." In many fishing villages, fishers returned from the sea on Thursday, so by Wednesday, people began running out of food and were generally weary and bored.

5. **gaffs** *n. pl.:* poles used on a boat to support a sail.

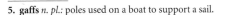

Vocabulary
destitute (des′tə·tōōt′) *adj.:* poverty-stricken.
frivolity (fri·väl′ə·tē) *n.:* silliness.

Gabriel García Márquez   915

C Reading Skills

? Interpreting details. How does the observation that the drowned man looks like an Esteban (and not a Lautaro) change his sta-tus among the women? [Possible responses: With the simple name Esteban, as opposed to the heroic name Lautaro, the man is recast as a sad, humble, awkward, and even tragic giant. In Christianity, Stephen (Esteban) was a martyr who suffered for being who he was.] Now, what do the women imagine his life was like? [Possible response: Just as Stephen's extreme faith led to his death, the women imagine that the drowned man's extreme size led to the scorn of village women who feigned politeness.]

D English-Language Learners

Interpreting slang. Point out to students that *the big boob* means "the big fool" or "the big oaf."

E Reading Skills

? Comparing and contrasting. How do the men's reactions differ from the women's? [Possible response: The women create a past for the man (first as a hero, then as an awkward loner) and imagine how he felt. The men see the body as a nuisance and consider how to remove it.]

F Literary Focus

? Magic realism "[W]here . . . divers die of nostalgia" is classic magic-realist imagery. How is the description fantastic, and how is it realistic? [Possible response: It's fan-tastic because divers do not literally die of nostalgia. It's realistic; if they venture too far, divers may endanger their lives and, in so doing, long for home.]

Mixed-ability group activity. To help stu-dents follow and appreciate the shifting points of view in the narrative, they can prepare and present a choral reading of the story. They will need to go back over the narrative to decide how many readers they want to use to tell the story, which characters the readers will represent, and which portions of the text

each character will read. For example, they may want to use individual readers for the narrator, the old woman, and the drowned man and small groups of readers to represent the village men and women. Emphasize the importance of preparing a script and rehears-ing as a group.

other bodies. But the more they hurried, the more the women thought of ways to waste time. They walked about like startled hens, pecking with the sea charms[6] on their breasts, some interfering on one side to put a scapular[7] of the good wind on the drowned man, some on the other side to put a wrist compass on him, and after a great deal of *get away from there, woman, stay out of the way, look, you almost made me fall on top of the dead man,* the men began to feel mistrust in their livers and started grumbling about why so many main-altar decorations for a stranger, because no matter how many nails and holy-water jars he had on him, the sharks would chew him all the same, but the women kept piling on their junk relics, running back and forth, stumbling, while they released in sighs what they did not in tears, so that the men finally exploded with *since when has there ever been such a fuss over a drifting corpse, a drowned nobody, a piece of cold Wednesday meat.* One of the women, mortified by so much lack of care, then removed the handkerchief from the dead man's face and the men were left breathless too.

He was Esteban. It was not necessary to repeat it for them to recognize him. If they had been told Sir Walter Raleigh, even they might have been impressed with his gringo accent, the macaw[8] on his shoulder, his cannibal-killing blunderbuss,[9] but there could be only one Esteban in the world and there he was, stretched out like a sperm whale, shoeless, wearing the pants of an undersized child, and with those stony nails that had to be cut with a knife. They only had to take the handkerchief off his face to see that he was ashamed, that it was not his fault that he was so big or so heavy or so handsome, and if he had known that this was going to hap-

pen, he would have looked for a more discreet place to drown in, seriously, I even would have tied the anchor off a galleon around my neck and staggered off a cliff like someone who doesn't like things in order not to be upsetting people now with this Wednesday dead body, as you people say, in order not to be bothering anyone with this filthy piece of cold meat that doesn't have anything to do with me. There was so much truth in his manner that even the most mistrustful men, the ones who felt the bitterness of endless nights at sea fearing that their women would tire of dreaming about them and begin to dream of drowned men, even they and others who were harder still shuddered in the marrow of their bones at Esteban's sincerity.

That was how they came to hold the most splendid funeral they could conceive of for an abandoned drowned man. Some women who had gone to get flowers in the neighboring villages returned with other women who could not believe what they had been told, and those women went back for more flowers when they saw the dead man, and they brought more and more until there were so many flowers and so many people that it was hard to walk about. At the final moment it pained them to return him to the waters as an orphan and they chose a father and mother from among the best people, and aunts and uncles and cousins, so that through him all the inhabitants of the village became kinsmen. Some sailors who heard the weeping from a distance went off course and people heard of one who had himself tied to the mainmast, remembering ancient fables about sirens.[10] While they fought for the privilege of

---

6. **sea charms:** magic charms worn to protect the wearer from dangers at sea.
7. **scapular** (skap′yə·lər) *n.:* pair of small cloth squares showing images of saints, joined by string and worn under clothing by some Roman Catholics as a symbol of religious devotion.
8. **macaw** *n.:* large, brightly colored parrot.
9. **blunderbuss** *n.:* now-outdated gun with a short, flaring muzzle.

---

10. **sirens** *n. pl.:* In Greek mythology, the sirens are sea maidens whose seductive singing lures men to wreck their boats on coastal rocks. Odysseus, hero of Homer's *Odyssey,* fills his crew's ears with wax so that they can pass the sirens safely. Odysseus, however, has his crew tie him to the ship's mast so that he can listen to the sirens' songs without plunging into the sea.

Vocabulary
mortified (môrt′ə·fīd′) *v.* used as *adj.:* humiliated; deeply embarrassed.

carrying him on their shoulders along the steep escarpment by the cliffs, men and women became aware for the first time of the desolation of their streets, the dryness of their courtyards, the narrowness of their dreams as they faced the splendor and beauty of their drowned man. They let him go without an anchor so that he could come back if he wished and whenever he wished, and they all held their breath for the fraction of centuries the body took to fall into the abyss. They did not need to look at one another to realize that they were no longer all present, that they would never be. But they also knew that everything would be different from then on, that their houses would have wider doors, higher ceilings, and stronger floors so that Esteban's memory could go everywhere without bumping into beams and so that no one in the future would dare whisper the big boob finally died, too bad, the handsome fool has finally died, because they were going to

E

paint their house fronts gay colors to make Esteban's memory eternal and they were going to break their backs digging for springs among the stones and planting flowers on the cliffs so that in future years at dawn the passengers on great liners would awaken, suffocated by the smell of gardens on the high seas, and the captain would have to come down from the bridge in his dress uniform, with his astrolabe,[11] his polestar, and his row of war medals and, pointing to the promontory of roses on the horizon, he would say in fourteen languages, look there, where the wind is so peaceful now that it's gone to sleep beneath the beds, over there, where the sun's so bright that the sunflowers don't know which way to turn, yes, over there, that's Esteban's village. ∎

---

11. **astrolabe** (as′trō·lāb′) *n.:* instrument used to find a star's altitude and to help navigators determine their position at sea.

Response and Analysis

Reading Check

1. How is the drowned man discovered?
2. What is unusual about the drowned man? How do the villagers explain these characteristics?
3. What name do the villagers give the drowned man? Why?
4. What do the villagers do with the body of the drowned man?
5. How does the drowned man transform the people and their village?

Thinking Critically

6. Where is the story set? What details about the setting are examples of **magic realism**?
7. A strong **theme** of this story concerns the human need for dreams and heroes. What does this story say about our need for heroes, about how heroes are

created, and about how heroes can transform societies? Use details from the text to support your statement of theme.

8. In Homer's *Odyssey*, the hero, Odysseus, who has been away from home for twenty years, is washed up from the sea onto the shores of his own kingdom. What echoes of this myth can you find in this story?

9. Where do you find these **archetypes** in the story: the superhuman hero; metamorphoses; a hope for a hero who will transform our everyday lives?

10. **Satire** is the kind of writing that is critical of some aspect of society. Satire often uses humor and exaggeration to make its points. Do you find any hints in this story that García Márquez is making fun of some aspects of human nature? Explain your responses.

SKILLS FOCUS

Literary Skills
Analyze the use of magic realism.

Writing Skills
Write an expository essay. Write an essay analyzing the use of magic realism in a story.

Vocabulary Skills
Demonstrate word knowledge.

Gabriel García Márquez   **917**

Reading Check

1. Children see his corpse wash up on the beach.
2. He is unusually large. They think he is waterlogged or somehow grew while dead.
3. They call him Esteban when they realize he has the face of an ordinary, sincere person.
4. They clean and clothe his body and carry it, covered with flowers, to the edge of the cliff, where they drop it into the sea.

5. The memory of him inspires the people to turn their arid village into a flowering garden.

Thinking Critically

6. The story is set in a very narrow, desert-like strip of land that juts out into the sea. Magic-realist details include the village's unusually small size, remoteness, and uniform appearance.

DIRECT TEACHING

E **Literary Focus**

? **Style.** Márquez often runs many sentences into a particularly long one. What is the effect of this device on the reader? [Possible responses: It creates a sense of the narrative gathering steam; it emphasizes the interconnectedness of phenomena.]

INDEPENDENT PRACTICE

7. Possible answer: When the women finally see the man as someone more ordinary, they honor not only the man but also themselves by transcending their own limitations and transforming their lives.

8. Like Odysseus, the drowned man is strong and handsome and apparently traveled great distances.

9. *Superhuman hero*—"he could have drawn fish out of the seas simply by calling their names"; *Metamorphoses*—"everything would be different from then on"; *Transforming hero*—"They thought that if that magnificent man had lived in the village, his house would have had the widest doors."

10. Possible answer: García Márquez is making fun of the human need to look for a superhuman or magic solution to everyday problems and limitations. The fact that the women in the story would find a dead man covered in scales an object of desire gently mocks the blind need that often drives people to choose unworthy heroes.

Literary Criticism

11. Possible answers: Most students will agree that García Márquez effectively and humorously combines realistic elements with the kind of magical effects associated with myths, legends, etc. Examples of the latter include the men's conjecture that the drowned man's body continued to grow after death, the presumption that the dead Esteban might return from the sea, the drowned man's association with water and its life-giving qualities, and the wasteland transformed into a garden. The author's joke is that the people do not really need anyone other than their best selves for salvation.

Vocabulary Development

1. True
2. False
3. True
4. True
5. True

ASSESSING

Assessment

■ *Holt Assessment: Literature, Reading, and Vocabulary*

RETEACHING

For a lesson reteaching archetypes, see **Reteaching**, p. 1117A.

Literary Criticism

11. The literary critic David Young says this about magic realism:

> One way to understand magic realism is as a kind of pleasant joke on realism. . . . [Magic realism] manages to combine the truthful and verifiable aspects of realism with the magical effects we associate with myth, folk tale, tall story, and that being in all of us—our childhood self, perhaps—who loves the spell that narrative casts even when it is perfectly implausible.

Which passages of García Márquez's story remind you of myth, legend, folk tale, or tall tale? How well does the story as a whole exemplify Young's definition of magic realism?

WRITING

Do We Need Heroes?

Answer that question in a brief **essay.** In your answer, refer to García Márquez's story and to one other story in this book that also focuses on the topic of heroism. Note how heroism can transform the world (or, if it is absent, how that absence can affect it). In addition to "The Handsomest Drowned Man in the World," you could refer to "Miniver Cheevy" (page 524); "Soldier's Home" (page 611); "The Leader of the People" (page 671); "The Secret Life of Walter Mitty" (page 708); or "Speaking of Courage" (page 867). In your essay, explain why you think we need heroes.

Analyzing Magic Realism

In a brief **essay**, analyze García Márquez's use of **magic realism** in this story. Before you write, review the story to locate some particularly realistic details. Then, locate some of the story's fantastic elements. You might organize your details on a chart like the one below. At the end of your essay, state your general response to the use of magic realism. Do you like this blending of fantasy and reality? Or do you prefer either pure fantasy or pure realism?

Fantastic Events	Realistic Details

Vocabulary Development
True or False?

Each sentence that follows makes a statement about García Márquez's story. Show your understanding of the underlined words by labeling each sentence true or false. Be able to explain the reason for your choice.

1. The villagers made their living fishing the <u>bountiful</u> sea.
2. The drowned man looked sickly and <u>haggard</u>.
3. Esteban appeared <u>destitute</u>, yet handsome and exceptionally <u>virile</u>.
4. The women were annoyed with the <u>frivolity</u> of the men's businesslike attitudes toward the body.
5. The women imagined that, in life, Esteban often felt <u>mortified</u> about his great size.

FAMILY/COMMUNITY ACTIVITY

García Márquez subtitled his story "A Tale for Children," and the story does contain many elements that would appeal to children, such as a mysterious creature emerging from the sea, a man of gigantic proportions, allusions to magic transformations, and a splendid funeral ritual. Most children, however, would not be able to follow García Márquez's text. Suggest that students rewrite the story for a child in their family or community, retaining some of García Márquez's magical elements, but revising the plot, language, and theme to appeal to a child's mind. Have students read their revised stories to the children for whom they were written and observe which elements the children find most appealing.

Amy Tan
(1952–)

Amy Tan had not planned to become a fiction writer. In fact, for years she worked as a freelance writer for high-technology companies, a career in which flights of imagination are not permitted. To ease the pressures of her job, she decided to take jazz piano lessons—and she began writing fiction. The result was the release of a dazzling new storyteller.

Tan's parents had fled Communist China and had come to the United States shortly before she was born in Oakland, California. Her mother, a nurse, was originally from Shanghai; her father, an engineer and a Baptist minister, came from Beijing.

After her father and young brother both died of brain tumors when Amy Tan was just fifteen, her mother took her away from the "diseased" house to Switzerland, where she finished high school. Her mother expected her talented daughter to become a neurosurgeon, as well as a pianist, in her spare time. When they returned to the United States, Tan enrolled as a pre-med student at Linfield College, a Baptist school in Oregon, which had been selected by her mother. But she defied her mother by leaving Linfield to join her boyfriend at San Jose State University, where she changed her major from pre-med to English. Tan's mother took this defiance as a sort of death between them, and mother and daughter did not speak for six months.

Tan was well aware of her mother's narrative gift, a gift that may have prompted her own desire to write. However, Tan was thirty-three before she wrote her first story, "Endgame" (retitled "Rules of the Game"). This story and others were collected in 1989 into a bestselling volume, *The Joy Luck Club* (also made into a popular movie). The collection interweaves stories about four Chinese American young women with stories of their mothers, born in China, who are members of a mah-jongg club in San Francisco.

In Tan's 1991 novel, *The Kitchen God's Wife,* a mother tells her grown daughter about life in China during World War II—and the daughter begins to see both her mother and herself with new eyes. A third novel, *The Hundred Secret Senses* (1995), explores another familial relationship—one between two sisters whose lives are transformed during a visit to a small village in China.

Tan's mother died in 1999, and the final days of her life helped shape Tan's fourth best-seller, *The Bonesetter's Daughter* (2001). The novel, moving between San Francisco of today and a Chinese village of the past, tells the story of a mother and daughter who find themselves through their dreams and their histories. Her mother, Tan said, will continue to serve as her muse. "She is a voice. A voice that can do all kinds of things. . . . She'll insist that she has a role in the next book. She's not done with me yet."

SKILLS FOCUS, pp. 919–931

Review Skills

■ **Literary Skills**
Analyze influences on characters (including internal and external conflict and motivation) and the way those influences affect the plot.

More About the Writer

Background. A woman of many interests, Amy Tan is part of a rock band made up mostly of writers, including Stephen King, Dave Barry, Barbara Kingsolver, and Matt Groening. Calling themselves the Rock Bottom Remainders, they made their debut at the 1992 American Booksellers Association convention.

Of her writing, Tan has said: "Writing is a bit like sculpting. You just have to start by cutting away until you have something and can feel what you're molding. Then you refine and polish it."

RESOURCES: READING

Planning
■ *One-Stop Planner* CD-ROM with ExamView Test Generator

Differentiating Instruction
■ *Holt Reading Solutions*
■ *The Holt Reader*
■ *Supporting Instruction in Spanish*
■ *Audio CD Library, Selections and Summaries in Spanish*

Vocabulary
■ *Vocabulary Development*

Grammar and Language
■ *Language Handbook Worksheets*
■ *Daily Language Activities*

Assessment
■ *Holt Assessment: Literature, Reading, and Vocabulary*
■ *One-Stop Planner* CD-ROM with

ExamView Test Generator
■ *Holt Online Assessment*

Internet
■ go.hrw.com (Keyword: LE5 11-6)
■ *Elements of Literature Online*

Media
■ *Audio CD Library*
■ *Audio CD Library, Selections and Summaries in Spanish*

A Learners Having Difficulty

❓ Paraphrasing. How would you paraphrase what the mother says after she scans the rules book? [Possible response: Immigrants are expected to know the rules. No one gives them a helping hand, so they must figure out things for themselves.]

B Reading Skills

❓ Making generalizations. How might these comments about chess strategy apply to life as well? [Possible responses: To be successful in life, a person needs to plan and be willing to anticipate challenges.]

C Literature Focus

❓ Comparing works from different cultures. How does the intergenerational relationship between Waverly and Lau Po compare with the other intergenerational relationships in this story and in Julia Alvarez's "Daughter of Invention"? [Possible responses: Both stories describe the strains between parents and children. The relationship between Lau Po and Waverly seems free of emotional conflict, so the two players enjoy one another's company as well as the game of chess.]

---

with a pawn in his hand. "Pawn. P-A-W-N. Pawn. Read it yourself."

My mother patted the flour off her hands. "Let me see book," she said quietly. She scanned the pages quickly, not reading the foreign English symbols, seeming to search deliberately for nothing in particular.

A "This American rules," she concluded at last. "Every time people come out from foreign country, must know rules. You not know, judge say, Too bad, go back. They not telling you why so you can use their way go forward. They say, Don't know why, you find out yourself. But they knowing all the time. Better you take it, find out why yourself." She tossed her head back with a satisfied smile.

I found out about all the whys later. I read the rules and looked up all the big words in a dictionary. I borrowed books from the Chinatown library. I studied each chess piece, trying to absorb the power each contained.

I learned about opening moves and why it's important to control the center early on; the shortest distance between two points is straight down the middle. I learned about the middle game and why tactics between two adversaries are like clashing ideas; the one who plays better has the clearest plans for both attacking and getting out of traps. I learned why it is essential in the endgame to have foresight, a mathematical understanding of all possible moves, and patience; all weaknesses and advantages become evident to a strong adversary and are obscured to a tiring opponent. I discovered that for the whole game one must gather invisible strengths and see the endgame before the game begins.

I also found out why I should never reveal "why" to others. A little knowledge withheld is a great advantage one should store for future use. That is the power of chess. It is a game of secrets in which one must show and never tell.

I loved the secrets I found within the sixty-four black and white squares. I carefully drew a handmade chessboard and pinned it to the wall next to my bed, where at night I would stare for hours at imaginary battles. Soon I no longer lost any games or Life Savers, but I lost my adver-

saries. Winston and Vincent decided they were more interested in roaming the streets after school in their Hopalong Cassidy[2] cowboy hats.

On a cold spring afternoon, while walking home from school, I detoured through the playground at the end of our alley. I saw a group of old men, two seated across a folding table playing a game of chess, others smoking pipes, eating peanuts, and watching. I ran home and grabbed Vincent's chess set, which was bound in a cardboard box with rubber bands. I also carefully selected two prized rolls of Life Savers. I came back to the park and approached a man who was observing the game.

"Want to play?" I asked him. His face widened with surprise and he grinned as he looked at the box under my arm.

C "Little sister, been a long time since I play with dolls," he said, smiling benevolently. I quickly put the box down next to him on the bench and displayed my retort.

Lau Po, as he allowed me to call him, turned out to be a much better player than my brothers. I lost many games and many Life Savers. But over the weeks, with each diminishing roll of candies, I added new secrets. Lau Po gave me the names. The Double Attack from the East and West Shores. Throwing Stones on the

---

2. **Hopalong Cassidy:** cowboy hero of movies and television from the 1930s through the early 1950s.

Vocabulary
obscured (əb·skyoord′) v.: concealed; hidden.
retort (ri·tôrt′) n.: quick, sharp answer.

(Opposite) Scene from the movie *The Joy Luck Club*.
© Buena Vista Distribution, Inc.

CONTENT-AREA CONNECTIONS

Art: The Theme of Competition
Paired activity. Games and competition have been a common subject of art across cultures for centuries. Have pairs of students do independent research to locate drawings, paintings, sculpture, or other works of art that depict competition or games. Ask them to bring in copies of the works they find and share them with the class. They should give some information on the artist, the medium, and the style of each work. Have the rest of the class compare and contrast the various works and discuss what attitude or feeling about games or competition each expresses.

Amy Tan **925**

FAMILY/COMMUNITY ACTIVITY

Invite a teacher or advanced student of Chinese languages to introduce the class to basic words and phrases. Ask the speaker to explain the basic syntax of spoken Chinese. Does Mrs. Jong's English speech patterns bear any resemblance to the syntax of her native language? Ask the speaker also to list the different dialects of Chinese (and which one the narrator's mother is likely to have spoken).

A Literary Focus

❓ Motivation. What motivates Waverly to say the opposite of what she really feels? [She is using a stratagem (sometimes called reverse psychology) to get her mother to allow her to be in the tournament.]

B Literature Focus

❓ Comparing works from different cultures. Point out to students that in Chinese culture, jade symbolizes good fortune. The red tablets symbolize the southern point of the compass and pay homage to Earth. Then, mention to students the scapulars that the women in the García Márquez story (p. 913) put on the drowned man. What connects the women in that story and Mrs. Jong in this one? [Possible response: They both have faith in objects that they can give, with love, to another.]

C Literary Focus

Style. Point out to students that Tan occasionally inserts lyrical passages, like this one, that show, in interior monologue, the imagination of her main character.

D Reading Skills

❓ Drawing conclusions. What might the wind represent to the narrator? [Possible responses: quiet strength; strategy.] How does the wind's advice echo the narrator's earlier comments about chess? [Possible responses: She keeps her opponent guessing; she avoids her opponent's traps and effectively distracts him.]

Drowning Man. The Sudden Meeting of the Clan. The Surprise from the Sleeping Guard. The Humble Servant Who Kills the King. Sand in the Eyes of Advancing Forces. A Double Killing Without Blood.

There were also the fine points of chess etiquette. Keep captured men in neat rows, as well-tended prisoners. Never announce "Check" with vanity, lest someone with an unseen sword slit your throat. Never hurl pieces into the sandbox after you have lost a game, because then you must find them again, by yourself, after apologizing to all around you. By the end of the summer, Lau Po had taught me all he knew, and I had become a better chess player.

A small weekend crowd of Chinese people and tourists would gather as I played and defeated my opponents one by one. My mother would join the crowds during these outdoor exhibition games. She sat proudly on the bench, telling my admirers with proper Chinese humility, "Is luck."

A man who watched me play in the park suggested that my mother allow me to play in local chess tournaments. My mother smiled graciously, an answer that meant nothing. I desperately wanted to go, but I bit back my tongue. I knew she would not let me play among strangers. So as we walked home I said in a small voice that I didn't want to play in the local tournament. They would have American rules. If I lost, I would bring shame on my family.

"Is shame you fall down nobody push you," said my mother.

During my first tournament, my mother sat with me in the front row as I waited for my turn. I frequently bounced my legs to unstick them from the cold metal seat of the folding chair. When my name was called, I leapt up. My mother unwrapped something in her lap. It was her *chang,* a small tablet of red jade which held the sun's fire. "Is luck," she whispered, and tucked it into my dress pocket. I turned to my opponent, a fifteen-year-old boy from Oakland. He looked at me, wrinkling his nose.

As I began to play, the boy disappeared, the color ran out of the room, and I saw only my white pieces and his black ones waiting on the other side. A light wind began blowing past my ears. It whispered secrets only I could hear.

"Blow from the South," it murmured. "The wind leaves no trail." I saw a clear path, the traps to avoid. The crowd rustled. "Shhh! Shhh!" said the corners of the room. The wind blew stronger. "Throw sand from the East to distract him." The knight came forward ready for the sacrifice. The wind hissed, louder and louder. "Blow, blow, blow. He cannot see. He is blind now. Make him lean away from the wind so he is easier to knock down."

"Check," I said, as the wind roared with laughter. The wind died down to little puffs, my own breath.

My mother placed my first trophy next to a new plastic chess set that the neighborhood Tao society had given to me. As she wiped each piece with a soft cloth, she said, "Next time win more, lose less."

"Ma, it's not how many pieces you lose," I said. "Sometimes you need to lose pieces to get ahead."

"Better to lose less, see if you really need."

At the next tournament, I won again, but it was my mother who wore the triumphant grin.

"Lost eight piece this time. Last time was eleven. What I tell you? Better off lose less!" I was annoyed, but I couldn't say anything.

I attended more tournaments, each one farther away from home. I won all games, in all divisions. The Chinese bakery downstairs from our flat displayed my growing collection of trophies in its window, amidst the dust-covered cakes that were never picked up. The day after

---

Generating and evaluating questions. Remind students that they can improve their comprehension of a story by generating questions and responding to them as they read. Make sure they understand that readers make sense of what they read not only by studying the text but also by drawing on what they already know from their own life experience and from other stories.

Activity. Have students make a list of general questions regarding the essential elements of any short story, such as title, characters, motivation, conflict, resolution, and author's purpose. Then, have students answer the edited questions as they read the story, and share their answers when everyone has finished reading. Urge them also to discuss how they arrived at their answers.

I won an important regional tournament, the window encased a fresh sheet cake with whipped-cream frosting and red script saying, "Congratulations, Waverly Jong, Chinatown Chess Champion." Soon after that, a flower shop, headstone engraver, and funeral parlor offered to sponsor me in national tournaments. That's when my mother decided I no longer had to do the dishes. Winston and Vincent had to do my chores.

"Why does she get to play and we do all the work," complained Vincent.

"Is new American rules," said my mother. "Meimei play, squeeze all her brains out for win chess. You play, worth squeeze towel."

By my ninth birthday, I was a national chess champion. I was still some 429 points away from grand-master status,[3] but I was touted as the Great American Hope, a child prodigy and a girl to boot. They ran a photo of me in *Life* magazine next to a quote in which Bobby Fischer[4] said, "There will never be a woman grand master." "Your move, Bobby," said the caption.

The day they took the magazine picture I wore neatly plaited braids clipped with plastic barrettes trimmed with rhinestones. I was playing in a large high school auditorium that echoed with phlegmy coughs and the squeaky rubber knobs of chair legs sliding across freshly waxed wooden floors. Seated across from me was an American man, about the same age as Lau Po, maybe fifty. I remember that his sweaty brow seemed to weep at my every move. He wore a dark, malodorous suit. One of his pockets was stuffed with a great white kerchief on which he wiped his palm before sweeping his hand over the chosen chess piece with great flourish.

In my crisp pink-and-white dress with scratchy lace at the neck, one of two my mother had sewn for these special occasions, I would clasp my hands under my chin, the delicate points of my elbows poised lightly on the table in the manner my mother had shown me for posing for the press. I would swing my patent leather shoes back and forth like an impatient child riding on a school bus. Then I would pause, suck in my lips, twirl my chosen piece in midair as if undecided, and then firmly plant it in its new threatening place, with a triumphant smile thrown back at my opponent for good measure.

I no longer played in the alley of Waverly Place. I never visited the playground where the pigeons and old men gathered. I went to school, then directly home to learn new chess secrets, cleverly concealed advantages, more escape routes.

But I found it difficult to concentrate at home. My mother had a habit of standing over me while I plotted out my games. I think she thought of herself as my protective ally. Her lips would be sealed tight, and after each move I made, a soft "Hmmmmph" would escape from her nose.

"Ma, I can't practice when you stand there like that," I said one day. She retreated to the kitchen and made loud noises with the pots and pans. When the crashing stopped, I could see out of the corner of my eye that she was standing in the doorway. "Hmmmph!" Only this one came out of her tight throat.

My parents made many concessions to allow

---

3. **grand-master status:** top rank in international chess competition.
4. **Bobby Fischer** (1943–   ): American chess master, the youngest player in the world to attain the rank of grand master, in 1958.

Vocabulary
touted (tout′id) *v.:* highly praised.
prodigy (präd′ə·jē) *n.:* extremely gifted person.
malodorous (mal·ō′dər·əs) *adj.:* bad-smelling.
concessions (kən·sesh′ənz) *n. pl.:* acts of giving in.

Amy Tan   **927**

READING MINI-LESSON

Developing Word-Attack Skills
Remind students that prefixes and combining forms can change or add meaning. Suffixes change the word's part of speech. Sometimes affixes can also help with the pronunciation of a word, as shown by the selection word *malodorous,* which is made up of the combining form *mal–* ("bad"), the base word *odor,* and the adjective-forming suffix *–ous.*

Analyzing *malodorous* helps a reader understand what it means—"bad-smelling"— and helps with its pronunciation /mal ōd ər əs/.
Activity. Have students read and analyze these words by dividing them into their component parts.

1. overrefinement   [over re fine ment]
2. omnidirectional   [omni direct ion al]

3. postmodernism   [post modern ism]
4. nonconformist   [non con form ist]
5. multimillionaire   [multi million aire]
6. neorealism   [neo real ism]
7. interchangeable   [inter change able]
8. disfigurement   [dis figure ment]

A Literary Focus

❓ Motivation. What does this passage suggest about the different attitudes of the narrator and her mother toward the daughter's mastery of chess? [Possible response: While the narrator enjoys the challenge of winning at chess for its own sake, the mother enjoys the daughter's success for the attention and admiration it brings to her.]

B Reading Skills

❓ Making inferences. What does this comment reveal about the mother's feelings? [Possible responses: The comment shows that she was hurt by the way the narrator spoke to her earlier; she thinks the narrator is not concerned about her feelings.]

Monitoring students' progress. Guide the class in answering the true-false statements that follow.

True-False

1. The narrator receives a brand new chess set at the Christmas party. [F]
2. The narrator first plays chess with her brothers. [T]
3. Other players are intimidated by the narrator's appearance. [F]
4. The narrator's brothers have to do her chores. [T]

---

me to practice. One time I complained that the bedroom I shared was so noisy that I couldn't think. Thereafter, my brothers slept in a bed in the living room facing the street. I said I couldn't finish my rice; my head didn't work right when my stomach was too full. I left the table with half-finished bowls and nobody complained. But there was one duty I couldn't avoid. I had to accompany my mother on Saturday market days when I had no tournament to play. My mother would proudly walk with me, visiting many shops, buying very little. "This my daughter Wave-ly Jong," she said to whoever looked her way.

One day, after we left a shop I said under my breath, "I wish you wouldn't do that, telling everybody I'm your daughter." My mother stopped walking. Crowds of people with heavy bags pushed past us on the sidewalk, bumping into first one shoulder, then another.

"Aiii-ya. So shame be with mother?" She grasped my hand even tighter as she glared at me.

I looked down. "It's not that, it's just so obvious. It's just so embarrassing."

"Embarrass you be my daughter?" Her voice was cracking with anger.

"That's not what I meant. That's not what I said."

"What you say?"

I knew it was a mistake to say anything more, but I heard my voice speaking. "Why do you have to use me to show off? If you want to show off, then why don't you learn to play chess?"

My mother's eyes turned into dangerous black slits. She had no words for me, just sharp silence.

I felt the wind rushing around my hot ears. I jerked my hand out of my mother's tight grasp and spun around, knocking into an old woman. Her bag of groceries spilled to the ground.

"Aii-ya! Stupid girl!" my mother and the woman cried. Oranges and tin cans careened down the sidewalk. As my mother stooped to help the old woman pick up the escaping food, I took off.

I raced down the street, dashing between

people, not looking back as my mother screamed shrilly, "Meimei! Meimei!" I fled down an alley, past dark, curtained shops and merchants washing the grime off their windows. I sped into the sunlight, into a large street crowded with tourists examining trinkets and souvenirs. I ducked into another dark alley, down another street, up another alley. I ran until it hurt and I realized I had nowhere to go, that I was not running from anything. The alleys contained no escape routes.

My breath came out like angry smoke. It was cold. I sat down on an upturned plastic pail next to a stack of empty boxes, cupping my chin with my hands, thinking hard. I imagined my mother, first walking briskly down one street or another looking for me, then giving up and returning home to await my arrival. After two hours, I stood up on creaking legs and slowly walked home.

The alley was quiet and I could see the yellow lights shining from our flat like two tiger's eyes in the night. I climbed the sixteen steps to the door, advancing quietly up each so as not to make any warning sounds. I turned the knob; the door was locked. I heard a chair moving, quick steps, the locks turning—click! click! click!—and then the door opened.

"About time you got home," said Vincent. "Boy, are you in trouble."

He slid back to the dinner table. On a platter were the remains of a large fish, its fleshy head still connected to bones swimming upstream in vain escape. Standing there waiting for my punishment, I heard my mother speak in a dry voice.

"We not concerning this girl. This girl not have concerning for us."

Nobody looked at me. Bone chopsticks clinked against the inside of bowls being emptied into hungry mouths.

I walked into my room, closed the door, and lay down on my bed. The room was dark, the

---

Vocabulary

careened (kə·rēnd′) v.: lurched sideways.

Comparing and Contrasting Texts

Comparing plots. Ask students to compare and contrast the main conflicts in this story with those in "Daughter of Invention" by Julia Alvarez (p. 899). Ask students to conclude their analyses with a consideration of this question: Which aspects of intergenerational conflicts seem relevant to all cultures and which seem specific to particular cultures?

ceiling filled with shadows from the dinnertime lights of neighboring flats.

In my head, I saw a chessboard with sixty-four black and white squares. Opposite me was my opponent, two angry black slits. She wore a triumphant smile. "Strongest wind cannot be seen," she said.

Her black men advanced across the plane, slowly marching to each <u>successive</u> level as a single unit. My white pieces <u>screamed</u> as they scurried and fell off the board one by one. As her men drew closer to my edge, I felt myself grow-

ing light. I rose up into the air and flew out the window. Higher and higher, above the alley, over the tops of tiled roofs, where I was gathered up by the wind and pushed up toward the night sky until everything below me disappeared and I was alone.

I closed my eyes and pondered my next move. ■

Vocabulary
successive (sək·ses′iv) *adj.*: consecutive.

Response and Analysis

Reading Check

1. Describe where Waverly lives.
2. How do the Jongs acquire their first chess set?
3. How does Waverly persuade her brothers to let her play chess too?
4. What are some ways in which Waverly's mother shows she is ambitious for her daughter and proud of her accomplishments?
5. As a result of Waverly's success at chess, what **conflicts** arise between her and her mother?

Thinking Critically

6. What does Waverly's mother mean on page 923 when she says about the used chess set, "She not want it. We not want it"? How does the boys' reaction show cultural and generational **conflicts** between the mother and her children?
7. Review your Quickwrite notes. How do the rules of chess relate to the relationship between Waverly and her mother? ✏
8. What do you see as Mrs. Jong's **motivation** for showing off her daughter? Why does Waverly resent her mother's actions?

9. Toward the end of the story, Waverly's imaginary opponent says, "Strongest wind cannot be seen." Where else in the story is that statement used? What do you think it means?
10. What do you think Waverly's fantasy at the end of the story means? What do you predict as her "next move"?
11. Find passages in the story where rules of various sorts are talked about. What multiple meanings might the **title** have?

Literary Criticism

12. In a review of *The Joy Luck Club*, the critic Susan Dooley wrote the following comment:

> These women from China find trying to talk to their daughters like trying to plug a foreign appliance into an American outlet. The current won't work. Impulses collide and nothing flows through the wires except anger and exasperation.

How does this comment apply to "The Rules of the Game"? Use specific examples from the story to support your conclusions.

SKILLS FOCUS

Literary Skills
Analyze motivation.

Writing Skills
Write an essay describing two literary characters in another context. Write an autobiographical narrative.

Vocabulary Skills
Demonstrate word knowledge.

Amy Tan   929

DIRECT TEACHING

C Literary Focus
Imagery. Note how Tan uses the imagery of a chessboard to represent the conflict between mother and daughter.

INDEPENDENT PRACTICE

Response and Analysis

8. Possible answer: The mother is very proud of Waverly and wants to share the attention. Waverly is resentful because she feels her mother is using her to make herself feel more important.
9. The mother uses it in the second paragraph. It refers to the importance of hiding strategies or feelings from an opponent.
10. Possible answer: Her fantasy may reflect her desire to escape her mother. Her next overt move may be to say she is sorry while quietly distancing herself from her mother.
11. Possible answers: Santa Claus's rules about being a good girl; the rules of chess; the American rules and procedures; the rules of chess etiquette. The title could refer to chess, family relationships, or life.

Literary Criticism

12. Possible answers: The narrator and her mother frequently misunderstand one another. For example, Waverly tells her mother, "I wish you wouldn't do that, telling everybody I'm your daughter." The mother thinks Waverly is ashamed of her, but she is really protesting her mother's appropriation of her accomplishments.

Reading Check

1. The narrator lives in an apartment above a bakery in San Francisco's Chinatown.
2. Vincent receives it at a Christmas party.
3. She bribes them with candy.
4. She displays the trophies, excuses Waverly from chores, and makes her new clothes.
5. She is embarrassed by the pride her mother takes in the victories. The mother is hurt by the daughter's rejection.

Thinking Critically

6. She does not want anything that someone else does not value. The boys are not so proud; they just want to play chess.
7. Waverly must learn to live within the restrictions of her mother's rules.

Vocabulary Development

Possible Answers

1. Hair color is an <u>ancestral</u> trait.

2. A spider web is an <u>intricate</u> maze.

3. The clouds <u>obscured</u> the moon.

4. The student asked, "What strategy did you use?" The master's <u>retort</u> was this: "Clearly, one that was invisible to you."

5. May has been <u>touted</u> for her brains and beauty.

6. He was a musical <u>prodigy</u>, composing symphonies at age five.

7. The stench from the <u>malodorous</u> dumpster was like that of rotting meat.

8. Besides *compromises*, another word for *concessions* is *businesses*.

9. The car <u>careened</u> into the bushes.

10. The numbers *2, 3, 4, 5,* and *6* are <u>successive</u>.

WRITING

Visitors from Other Stories

In a brief **essay,** tell what you think would happen if Mrs. Jong and Mrs. Garcia (the narrator's mother from "Daughter of Invention" by Julia Alvarez, page 899) were to enter each other's story. If Mrs. Jong could be brought into Alvarez's story, whose side would she take—that of Mrs. Garcia or that of the narrator's father? If Mrs. Garcia from "Daughter of Invention" could be introduced to Mrs. Jong, what advice would she give Mrs. Jong? Write one paragraph about each mother. Be sure to explain *why* you think each character would behave the way she does.

Rules of Your Game

Have you ever had an experience like Waverly has had in this story? Think back to a time when you learned about the rules of life. What happened? Whose rules did you break? In a few paragraphs, write a **narrative** about this incident.

▶ Use **"Writing an Autobiographical Narrative," pages 964–965, for help with this assignment.**

Grammar Link

SKILLS FOCUS

Grammar Skills
Use transitional expressions to connect ideas.

Using Transitional Expressions: Making Things Coherent

Transitional expressions are words or phrases that provide a smooth flow from one idea to the next, making your writing more coherent and logical. Transitional expressions help the reader follow your train of thought and see connections within sentences or between sentences or paragraphs. Transitional expressions often show **chronological** or **spatial** relationships. They may also show connections based on **comparison and contrast, cause and effect,** or **exemplification-restatement.** In the following passages from Amy Tan's "Rules of the Game," notice the transitional words that connect the sentences:

"I knew she would not let me play among strangers. <u>So</u> as we walked home I said in a small voice that I didn't want to play in the local tournament." [**So** indicates a cause-and-effect relationship.]

Vocabulary Development

Own It

1. Give an example of an <u>ancestral</u> trait.

2. Describe an <u>intricate</u> object.

3. Explain how something might be <u>obscured</u>.

4. Write a few lines of dialogue, with an example of a <u>retort</u>.

5. Describe something you have been <u>touted</u> for.

6. Use the word *prodigy* in a sentence.

7. Write a brief description of a <u>malodorous</u> person.

8. Look in the dictionary to find another meaning for the word *concessions*.

9. Describe an incident with the word *careened*.

10. List five numbers in <u>successive</u> order.

"One time I complained that the bedroom I shared was so noisy that I couldn't think. Thereafter, my brothers slept in a bed in the living room facing the street." [**Thereafter** indicates a chronological relationship.]

In the first example the transitional word *so* explains why Waverly says what she does to her mother—her motivation. In the second example the word *thereafter* tells the order in which these two linked events occurred—and by implication, that the change in sleeping arrangements occurred as a result of Waverly's complaint.

Transitional words and phrases are like the string that holds together a beaded necklace, keeping it from scattering into separate pieces. Whenever your writing sounds choppy or disjointed, consider adding a transitional word or phrase that clarifies the connection between your ideas.

Transitional Words and Phrases			
Chronological	then	first	meanwhile
	finally	before	eventually
	soon	at last	after
	next	later	afterward
Spatial	above	across	next to
	below	inside	over
	near	outside	under
	there	here	around
Comparison	also	like	likewise
	similarly	too	moreover
Contrast	yet	still	nevertheless
	however	although	in spite of
	unlike	in contrast	on the other hand
Cause and Effect	because	so that	consequently
	since	therefore	as a result
	thus	since	for this reason
Exemplification-Restatement	specifically	for example	for instance
	that is	in fact	in other words

Apply to Your Writing

Re-read a current writing assignment or one that you've already completed. Are there any passages that seem choppy or confusing because your ideas don't flow smoothly together? See if you can clarify the coherence of your writing by adding a transitional expression.

▶ **For more help, see Combining Sentences for Variety, 10a–d, in the Language Handbook.**

PRACTICE

In the following passages, add transitional expressions to create a smoother flow and to strengthen the connection between ideas. You may choose to combine sentences or keep them separate.

1. In Amy Tan's story "Rules of the Game," Waverly's brother Vincent gets a chess set at a church Christmas party. Their mother tells him to throw it away.

2. Waverly learns to play chess better than her brothers. They lose interest in playing with her.

3. Waverly becomes a chess champion. Her mother is proud of her. Waverly is uncomfortable with her mother's way of showing her pride.

4. Waverly sees her conflict with her mother in terms of chess. She runs away from her mother after their fight. She says that the alley contains "no escape routes," a term she previously used to describe "chess secrets."

Grammar Link

Practice

Possible Answers

1. In Amy Tan's story "Rules of the Game," Waverly's brother Vincent gets a chess set at a church Christmas party; afterward their mother tells him to throw it away.

2. Waverly learns to play chess better than her brothers. As a result, they lose interest in playing with her.

3. Waverly becomes a chess champion. Although her mother is proud of her, Waverly is uncomfortable with her mother's way of showing her pride.

4. Waverly sees her conflict with her mother in terms of chess. For instance, when she runs away from her mother after their fight, she says that the alley contains "no escape routes," a term she previously used to describe "chess secrets."

ASSESSING

Assessment

■ *Holt Assessment: Literature, Reading, and Vocabulary*

DIFFERENTIATING INSTRUCTION

Learners Having Difficulty

Write the following sentences on the chalkboard. Have students choose the correct transitional expression in each sentence.

1. The children of immigrants often feel torn in two directions after/because their loyalties are divided between the culture of their parents and that of their new home. [because]

2. Immigrant parents want their children to succeed in their new country; nevertheless/consequently, they are sorry to see them give up the old ways and traditions. [nevertheless]

3. First-generation immigrant children sometimes feel ashamed of their foreign-born parents. On the other hand/For example, they sometimes refuse to bring their American friends home to meet their families. [For example]

4. When the children of immigrants are young and struggling, they often do not want to hear about life in the old country. Therefore/Later, they may wish they had paid more attention to their parents' precious memories. [Later]

A Literary Focus

? Theme. What does Lilia learn by watching her parents during the war? [Possible response: By seeing how they set aside personal comfort to help Mr. Pirzada, she learns the concept of putting others' needs above one's own desires.]

B Reading Skills

? Evaluating a resolution. Throughout this story, the whereabouts and safety of Mr. Pirzada's family were always in question; now, the suspense is over. Were Mr. Pirzada's worries justified? Why or why not? [Possible responses: No, the family was safe the whole time. Yes, it was the *not* knowing that made Mr. Pirzada's fears real and the story suspenseful.]

C Literary Focus

? Theme. Why do you think that it is only now that Lilia realizes she misses Mr. Pirzada? [Possible responses: Until the card arrives, Mr. Pirzada's absence seems not quite real; Lilia can imagine that he is nearby and just too busy to visit.]

GUIDED PRACTICE

Monitoring students' progress. Guide the class in answering these comprehension questions.

True-False

1. Mr. Pirzada has left East Pakistan to study in New England. [T]

2. Lilia learns about East Pakistan in school. [F]

3. Lilia prays for Mr. Pirzada's family. [T]

4. The last time that Lilia sees Mr. Pirzada is on Halloween. [F]

5. When her family receives a card from Mr. Pirzada, Lilia realizes that she misses him deeply. [T]

the most part, a remote mystery with haphazard clues. What I remember during those twelve days of the war was that my father no longer asked me to watch the news with them, and that Mr. Pirzada stopped bringing me candy, and that my mother refused to serve anything other than boiled eggs with rice for dinner. I remember some nights helping my mother spread a sheet and blankets on the couch so that Mr. Pirzada could sleep there, and high-pitched voices hollering in the middle of the night when my parents called our relatives in Calcutta to learn more details about the situation. Most of all I remember the three of them operating during that time as if they were a single person, sharing a single meal, a single body, a single silence, and a single fear.

In January, Mr. Pirzada flew back to his three-story home in Dacca, to discover what was left of it. We did not see much of him in those final weeks of the year; he was busy finishing his manuscript, and we went to Philadelphia to spend Christmas with friends of my parents. Just as I have no memory of his first visit, I have no memory of his last. My father drove him to the airport one afternoon while I was at school. For a long time we did not hear from him. Our evenings went on as usual, with dinners in front of the news. The only difference was that Mr. Pirzada and his extra watch were not there to accompany us. According to reports Dacca was repairing itself slowly, with a newly formed parliamentary government. The new leader, Sheikh Mujib Rahman,[15] recently re-

Dacca residents celebrating the homecoming of Sheikh Mujib Rahman (1972).

leased from prison, asked countries for building materials to replace more than one million houses that had been destroyed in the war. Countless refugees returned from India, greeted, we learned, by unemployment and the threat of famine. Every now and then I studied the map above my father's desk and pictured Mr. Pirzada on that small patch of yellow, perspiring heavily, I imagined, in one of his suits, searching for his family. Of course, the map was outdated by then.

Finally, several months later, we received a card from Mr. Pirzada commemorating the Muslim New Year, along with a short letter. He was reunited, he wrote, with his wife and children. All were well, having survived the events of the past year at an estate belonging to his wife's grandparents in the mountains of Shillong. His seven daughters were a bit taller, he wrote, but otherwise they were the same, and he still could not keep their names in order. At the end of the letter he thanked us for our hospitality, adding that although he now understood the meaning of the words "thank you," they still were not adequate to express his gratitude. To celebrate the good news, my mother prepared a special dinner that evening, and when we sat down to eat at the coffee table, we toasted our water glasses, but I did not feel like celebrating. Though I had not seen him for months, it was only then that I felt Mr. Pirzada's absence. It was only then, raising my water glass in his name, that I knew what it meant to miss someone who was so many miles and hours away, just as he had missed his wife and daughters for so many months. He had no reason to return to us, and my parents predicted, correctly, that we would never see him again. Since January, each night before bed, I had continued to eat, for the sake of Mr. Pirzada's family, a piece of candy I had saved from Halloween. That night there was no need to. Eventually, I threw them away. ■

---

15. **Sheikh Mujib Rahman** (1920–1975): Bengali leader who demanded independence for East Pakistan. He became the first prime minister of Bangladesh in 1972 and its president in 1975.

FAMILY/COMMUNITY ACTIVITY

Lilia's parents met Mr. Pirzada by looking for familiar surnames in the directory of a local university. Today, as well, some high schools and many colleges and universities host students and teachers visiting from other countries. Have students work together to contact such visitors at a local school. (You may want to call schools ahead of time to determine the best way to make contacts.) Students can invite their contacts to visit the class and share information about their homeland and some of their experiences since coming to the United States.

WR

Look

Write
of the
might
tion c
of Ind
Befor
sure i
your
your
recor
and ir
differe
carefu
biblio;
the C

▶ U:
pages
assigi

Com

Comr
univei
equall
frustr
exper
Came
narra
(page
writte
will fi
you w
one t

Narr

Conf

Disc

CONNECTION / NEWSPAPER ARTICLE

INFORMATIONAL TEXT

The Ravaged People of East Pakistan

Alvin S. Toffler

East Pakistani refugees taking shelter near Calcutta, India (1971).

A planetary catastrophe is taking place in Asia, a human disaster so massive that it could bathe the future in blood, not just for Asians, but for those of us in the West as well. Yet the response of the global community has been minimal at best. In the United States, the official response has been worse than minimal and morally numb.

I have just returned from Calcutta and the border of East Pakistan, where I conducted interviews with refugees avalanching into India as a result of the West Pakistanis' genocidal attack on them. Since March 25, West Pakistani troops have bombed, burned, looted, and murdered the citizens of East Pakistan in what can only be a calculated campaign to decimate them or to drive them out of their villages and over the border into India.

Part of the time I traveled with a Canadian parliamentary delegation. We saw babies' skin stretched tight, bones protruding, weeping women who told us they would rather die today in India than return to East Pakistan after the tragedies they had witnessed, the total wretchedness of refugee camps, and the unbelievable magnitude of this forced human migration—6.7 million refugees pouring into India within a matter of four months.

I saw Indian villages deluged by masses of destitute refugees, every available inch crammed with bodies seeking shelter from the blistering sun and the torrential rain. I saw refugees still streaming along the roads unable to find even a resting place. I saw miserable Indian villagers sharing their meager food with the latest frightened and hungry arrivals. I saw thousands of men, women, and babies lined up, waiting patiently under the sun for hours to get their rations. These pitiful few ounces of rice, wheat, and dhal provide a level of nutrition so low that it will inevitably create protein breakdown, liver illness, and a variety of other diseases in addition to the cholera, pneumonia, and bronchitis that are already rampant. I saw Indian relief officials struggling heroically, and with immense personal sympathy, to cope with the human tidal wave—and to do so on a budget of one rupee a day—about 13 cents per human.

It is now clear that famine will further devastate East Pakistan this fall, and that millions more will seek refuge in an India already staggering under the burden.

—from *The New York Times*
August 5, 1971

Jhumpa Lahiri 947

Comparing and Contrasting Texts

10. P
a
t
e

Analyzing theme or meaning. After students have read the short story and the newspaper article, have them work in small groups to compare and contrast the selections. First, students should discuss similarities and differences in the tone, style, and purpose of each piece. Then, ask them to focus on comparing the theme or meaning of each text.

Have students record their discussions, and report their conclusions to the class. Then, have the class discuss the question, "Which text presents its theme or meaning more effectively?" Students should use specific examples from the texts to support their responses.

Connection
Summary ⬌ at grade level

In this article from the August 5, 1971, edition of *The New York Times*, reporter Alvin S. Toffler describes the Pakistani refugees he witnessed on a recent trip to Calcutta, India, and the border of East Pakistan. After a brief explanation of the West Pakistani attacks on East Pakistan, Toffler focuses on the plight of the starving refugees and on the Indian villagers and relief officials struggling to help them.

DIRECT TEACHING

D Reading Informational Text

❓ Analyzing author's assumptions. What does Toffler believe the role of the global community is in this situation? How do you know? [The global community has a responsibility to recognize and respond to the events in East Pakistan. He states that the response from the world has been "minimal at best," and the United States's response has been "worse than minimal and morally numb."]

E Reading Informational Text

❓ Author's argument. What primary type of appeal does Toffler use? What are some examples of this appeal? Do you find his appeal effective? [Possible responses: Toffler appeals to readers' emotions by describing starving infants and crying women. He uses words such as "wretchedness," "destitute," "miserable," "heroically," and "sympathy" to describe the refugees and the Indian villagers and relief officials; he talks about the "meager" and "pitiful" food rations and diseases that are "rampant." Most students will find this appeal based on personal experience effective.]

A **Literary Focus**

? **Analyzing author's style.** This story takes place in the present tense and has a first-person narrator. What is the effect of these elements of style? [Possible response: Present tense makes the story more immediate and, along with first-person narration, immediately pulls readers into the story.]

B **Reading Skills**

? **Making inferences.** What can you infer about the father's time in prison? [Possible response: He was mistreated—tortured or beaten.]

C **Literary Focus**

? **Irony.** *Dimanche* is the French word for "Sunday," considered by Christians as the Lord's Day. In what way is the name of the prison ironic? [Possible response: From what the narrator has told us, it does not sound as if the prisoners were treated in a way consistent with Christian principles.]

D **Reading Skills**

? **Making inferences.** From the narrator's description of her sculpture, how do you think she views her father? [Possible response: She sees her father as vulnerable.] Even though the narrator doesn't reveal her answer to the officer's question, in what way is the description of the sculpture an answer? [Possible response: The narrator's thoughts indicate that she loves her father and can't imagine any reason he would run away from her.]

E **Content-Area Connections**

Art: Minimalism
Tell students that minimalism is an art movement that began in the 1960s. Art done in this style is characterized by simplistic designs, structures, and forms.

My father is gone. I am slouched in a cast-aluminum chair across from two men, one the manager of the hotel where we're staying and the other a policeman. They are waiting for me to explain what has become of him, my father.

The manager—"Mr. Flavio Salinas," the plaque on his office door reads—has the most striking pair of chartreuse[1] eyes I have ever seen on a man with an island-Spanish lilt to his voice.

The officer is a baby-faced, short white Floridian with a pot belly.

"Where are you and your daddy from, Ms. Bienaimé?" he asks.

I answer "Haiti," even though I was born and raised in East Flatbush, Brooklyn, and have never visited my parents' birthplace. I do this because it is one more thing I have longed to have in common with my parents.

The officer plows forward. "You down here in Lakeland from Haiti?"

"We live in New York. We were on our way to Tampa."

I find Manager Salinas's office gaudy. The walls are covered with orange-and-green wallpaper, briefly interrupted by a giant gold-leaf-bordered print of a Victorian cottage that somehow resembles the building we're in. Patting his light-green tie, he whispers reassuringly, "Officer Bo and I will do the best we can to help you find your father."

We start out with a brief description: "Sixty-four, five feet eight inches, two hundred and twenty pounds, moon-faced, with thinning salt-and-pepper hair. Velvet-brown eyes—"

"Velvet-brown?" says Officer Bo.

"Deep brown—same color as his complexion."

My father has had partial frontal dentures for ten years, since he fell off his and my mother's bed when his prison nightmares began. I mention that, too. Just the dentures, not the nightmares. I also bring up the claw-shaped marks that run from his left ear down along his cheek to the corner of his mouth—the only visible reminder of the year he spent at Fort Dimanche,

the Port-au-Prince prison ironically named after the Lord's Day.

"Does your daddy have any kind of mental illness, senility?" asks Officer Bo.

"No."

"Do you have any pictures of your daddy?"

I feel like less of a daughter because I'm not carrying a photograph in my wallet. I had hoped to take some pictures of him on our trip. At one of the rest stops I bought a disposable camera and pointed it at my father. No, no, he had protested, covering his face with both hands like a little boy protecting his cheeks from a slap. He did not want any more pictures taken of him for the rest of his life. He was feeling too ugly.

"That's too bad," says Officer Bo. "Does he speak English, your daddy? He can ask for directions, et cetera?"

"Yes."

"Is there anything that might make your father run away from you—particularly here in Lakeland?" Manager Salinas interjects. "Did you two have a fight?"

I had never tried to tell my father's story in words before now, but my first sculpture of him was the reason for our trip: a two-foot-high mahogany figure of my father, naked, crouching on the floor, his back arched like the curve of a crescent moon, his downcast eyes fixed on his short stubby fingers and the wide palms of his hands. It was hardly revolutionary, minimalist at best, but it was my favorite of all my attempted representations of him. It was the way I had imagined him in prison.

The last time I had seen my father? The previous night, before falling asleep. When we pulled into the pebbled driveway, densely lined with palm and banana trees, it was almost midnight. All the restaurants in the area were closed. There was nothing to do but shower and go to bed.

Vocabulary

gaudy (gô′dē) *adj.:* showy but lacking in good taste.

---

1. **chartreuse** (shär·trōōz′) *adj.:* pale yellowish green.

DIFFERENTIATING INSTRUCTION

Learners Having Difficulty
Help students make their way through the opening scene with the narrator, the police officer, and the hotel manager by telling them that quotation marks signal what the narrator says aloud. The parts of her response not in quotation marks are her unspoken thoughts. Have students use a two-column chart with the headings "What She Said" and "What She

Thought" to note what they learn about the narrator and her father.

English-Language Learners
Point out that when the narrator uses the past tense, she is telling what happened either in the distant ("I was born and raised . . .") or recent past ("We were on our way . . .").

"It is like a paradise here," my father said when he saw the room. It had the same orange-and-green wallpaper as Salinas's office, and the plush green carpet matched the walls. "Look, Annie," he said, "it is like grass under our feet." He was always searching for a glimpse of paradise, my father.

He picked the bed closest to the bathroom, removed the top of his gray jogging suit, and unpacked his toiletries. Soon after, I heard him humming, as he always did, in the shower.

After he got into bed, I took a bath, pulled my hair back in a ponytail, and checked on the sculpture—just felt it a little bit through the bubble padding and carton wrapping to make sure it wasn't broken. Then I slipped under the covers, closed my eyes, and tried to sleep.

I pictured the client to whom I was delivering the sculpture: Gabrielle Fonteneau, a young woman about my age, an actress on a nationally syndicated television series. My friend Jonas, the principal at the East Flatbush elementary school where I teach drawing to fifth-graders, had shown her a picture of my *Father* sculpture, and, the way Jonas told it, Gabrielle Fonteneau had fallen in love with it and wished to offer it as a gift to her father on his birthday.

Since this was my first big sale, I wanted to make sure that the piece got there safely. Besides, I needed a weekend away, and both my mother and I figured that my father, who watched a lot of television, both in his barbershop and at home, would enjoy meeting Gabrielle, too. But when I woke up the next morning, my father was gone.

I showered, put on my driving jeans and a T-shirt, and waited. I watched a half hour of mid-morning local news, smoked three mentholated cigarettes even though we were in a nonsmoking room, and waited some more. By noon, four hours had gone by. And it was only then that I noticed that the car was still there but the sculpture was gone.

I decided to start looking for my father: in the east garden, the west garden, the dining room, the exercise room, and in the few guest rooms cracked open while the maid changed the sheets; in the little convenience store at the Amoco gas station nearby; even in the Salvation Army thrift shop that from a distance seemed to blend into the interstate. All that waiting and looking actually took six hours, and I felt guilty for having held back so long before going to the front desk to ask, "Have you seen my father?"

I feel Officer Bo's fingers gently stroking my wrist. Up close he smells like fried eggs and gasoline, like breakfast at the Amoco. "I'll put the word out with the other boys," he says. "Salinas here will be in his office. Why don't you go back to your room in case he shows up there?"

I return to the room and lie in the unmade bed, jumping up when I hear the click from the electronic key in the door. It's only the housekeeper. I turn down the late-afternoon cleaning and call my mother at the beauty salon where she perms, presses, and braids hair, next door to my father's barbershop. But she isn't there. So I call my parents' house and leave the hotel number on their machine. "Please call me as soon as you can, Manman. It's about Papi."

Once, when I was twelve, I overheard my mother telling a young woman who was about to get married how she and my father had first met on the sidewalk in front of Fort Dimanche the evening that my father was released from jail. (At a dance, my father had fought with a soldier out of uniform who had him arrested and thrown in prison for a year.) That night, my mother was returning home from a sewing class when he stumbled out of the prison gates and collapsed into her arms, his face still bleeding from his last beating. They married and left for New York a year later. "We were like two seeds planted in a rock," my mother had told the young woman, "but somehow when our daughter, Annie, came, we took root."

My mother soon calls me back, her voice staccato[2] with worry.

---

2. **staccato** (stə·kät′ō) *adj.:* made up of abrupt, distinct sounds.

Edwidge Danticat **955**

Edwidge Danticat **955**

Summary ⟷ *at grade level*

In this selection from his auto-biography, Wright uses a neutral, objective tone to detail the extreme hardships of his forma-tive years in Memphis. After his father abandons the family, Richard, his mother, and his brother suffer from malnutrition and crushing poverty. His mother urges her sons to be self-reliant, but they are all filled with a vague dread of the future. In order to buy groceries without being robbed on the way, Richard learns (at his mother's insistence) to beat the local bullies with a stick. Later, he is brought to his parents' alimony trial, where he watches his father con a judge into believing that he, despite his comfort-able lifestyle, can't support the family. Wright's mother is unable to provide for her sons on her income as a cook, and she places them in an orphanage, where con-ditions are harsh and bleak. After Wright tries unsuccessfully to flee, he accompanies his mother to beg his father again for money. How-ever, he is so disgusted by the condescension of his father and the strange woman with him that he refuses the nickel they offer him. Twenty-five years later, Wright sees his father again, now a sharecropper in Mississippi. This time, Wright forgives and pities him, realizing there is an unbridge-able gap between them.

Skills Starter

Motivate. Initiate a discussion on hunger for food—how it feels physi-cally, how it feels psychologically. Proceed to listing types of hunger that people suffer from beyond the hunger for food. Explain that part of the following selection appears in many anthologies under the title "Hunger." Ask students to keep var-ious kinds of hunger in mind as they read the selection.

Before You Read

from Black Boy

Make the Connection

What does it mean to grow up and to par-ticipate in the world as mature and respon-sible adults? What elements of childhood do we carry with us forever? The discoveries we make as children, awakening to what the world is like, can be harsh or sweet, shock-ing or gradual, depending on the specific circumstances of our lives. Through our in-dividual experiences, we are each deeply affected by our childhood awakenings.

Literary Focus
Dialogue and Nonfiction

We often associate **dialogue,** the directly quoted words of people speaking to one another, with drama and fiction. Nowadays dialogue also plays an important part in nonfiction, particularly in autobiography and journalism. Dialogue in nonfiction, however, can become controversial. Reporters, for instance, have been challenged in court to prove that the words they put in quotation marks were the actual words spoken by the people they interviewed.

In Wright's autobiography, most of the scenes are dramatized by means of dialogue. Wright's use of dialogue gives his autobiog-raphy the feel of a novel, even though he is writing about actual events. The passage you are about to read provides a good example of how nonfiction writers often use the ele-ments of fiction to make their texts come alive. As a critical reader you have to decide if the extensive use of dialogue, which the writer could not possibly have recalled accu-rately, affects the veracity, or truthfulness, of his text. Does Wright use the dialogue to reveal the essence of the characters he is presenting to us? Could he have brought his mother and father to life without the use of dialogue?

INTERNET

Vocabulary Practice
•
More About Richard Wright
Keyword: LE5 11–6

SKILLS FOCUS

Literary Skills
Understand dialogue in nonfiction.

Dialogue is the directly quoted words of two or more people in conversation.

For more on Dialogue, see the Hand-book of Literary and Historical Terms.

Vocabulary Development

enthralled (en·thrôld′) *v.:* fascinated.

clamor (klam′ər) *n.:* loud noise; loud demand or complaint.

dispirited (di·spir′it·id) *adj.:* discouraged.

frenzy (fren′zē) *n.:* frantic behavior; wildness.

ardently (är′dənt·lē) *adv.:* intensely; eagerly.

copiously (kō′pē·əs·lē) *adv.:* abundantly.

futile (fyoot′'l) *adj.:* useless; pointless.

eluded (ē·lood′id) *v.:* escaped detection or notice.

withering (with′ər·iŋ) *v.* used as *adj.:* drying up; weakening.

968 Collection 6 Contemporary Literature: 1939 to Present

Previewing Vocabulary

Several of the Vocabulary words can be acted out or pantomimed by students. After dividing students into groups, have them take turns acting out a word of their choice for their group while the others in the group try to guess the word. One or two clues may be given; after two clues, the actor should reveal the word. Then have the class work on the following activity for each word.

1. Locate the sentence in which Wright first uses the word.
2. Write a new sentence that uses the word. Use the same structure as Wright's sen-tence, but change most of the other words.
3. Have volunteers read their sentences aloud to the class.

from

Black Boy

Richard Wright

Where was I going? I did not know. The farther I walked the more frantic I became. **A**

One day my mother told me that we were going to Memphis on a boat, the *Kate Adams,* and my eagerness thereafter made the days seem endless. Each night I went to bed hoping that the next morning would be the day of departure.

"How big is the boat?" I asked my mother.

"As big as a mountain," she said.

"Has it got a whistle?"

"Yes."

"Does the whistle blow?"

"Yes."

"When?"

"When the captain wants it to blow."

"Why do they call it the *Kate Adams*?"

"Because that's the boat's name."

"What color is the boat?"

"White."

"How long will we be on the boat?"

"All day and all night."

"Will we sleep on the boat?"

"Yes, when we get sleepy, we'll sleep. Now, hush." **B**

For days I had dreamed about a huge white boat floating on a vast body of water, but when my mother took me down to the levee on the day of leaving, I saw a tiny, dirty boat that was not at all like the boat I had imagined. I was disappointed and when time came to go on board I cried and my mother thought that I did not want to go with her to Memphis, and I could not tell her what the trouble was. Solace came when I wandered about the boat and gazed at Negroes throwing dice, drinking whiskey,

969

A Reading Skills

? Making inferences. Knowing that she never before told her son to fight, what can you infer about Richard's mother? [Possible response: She wants him to have a sense of decency, but she knows he must learn how to survive.]

B English-Language Learners

Clarifying idioms. Make sure students know that *I let the stick fly* means Richard swung (not threw) it; *egging on* means "prodding into action"; and *tore out* means "ran."

C Reading Skills

? Analyzing an author's assumptions and beliefs. What belief might this episode have instilled in Richard? [Possible responses: You have to stand up for yourself; the only effective way to respond to violence is with violence.]

D Literary Focus

? Tone. How would you describe the tone with which Wright introduces this scene? Explain. [Possible response: The tone is disapproving. Wright speaks of his mother's faith as a dominating force, and he calls the preacher a "guise" in his representation of God.]

E Reading Skills

? Finding the main idea. What do you see as the main idea of this passage? [Possible response: The passage emphasizes Richard's frustration with a world that provides few breaks for him.] What details in the passage support that idea? [Possible responses: the smiling but gluttonous preacher; Richard's inability to eat his soup]

---

she said. "Go to the store and buy those groceries. If those boys bother you, then fight."

I was baffled. My mother was telling me to fight, a thing that she had never done before.

"But I'm scared," I said.

"Don't you come into this house until you've gotten those groceries," she said.

"They'll beat me; they'll beat me," I said.

"Then stay in the streets; don't come back here!"

I ran up the steps and tried to force my way past her into the house. A stinging slap came on my jaw. I stood on the sidewalk, crying.

"Please, let me wait until tomorrow," I begged.

"No," she said. "Go now! If you come back into this house without those groceries, I'll whip you!"

She slammed the door and I heard the key turn in the lock. I shook with fright. I was alone upon the dark, hostile streets and gangs were after me. I had the choice of being beaten at home or away from home. I clutched the stick, crying, trying to reason. If I were beaten at home, there was absolutely nothing that I could do about it; but if I were beaten in the streets, I had a chance to fight and defend myself. I walked slowly down the sidewalk, coming closer to the gang of boys, holding the stick tightly. I was so full of fear that I could scarcely breathe. I was almost upon them now.

"There he is again!" the cry went up.

They surrounded me quickly and began to grab for my hand.

"I'll kill you!" I threatened.

They closed in. In blind fear I let the stick fly, feeling it crack against a boy's skull. I swung again, lamming another skull, then another. Realizing that they would retaliate if I let up for but a second, I fought to lay them low, to knock them cold, to kill them so that they could not strike back at me. I flayed with tears in my eyes, teeth clenched, stark fear making me throw every ounce of my strength behind each blow. I hit again and again, dropping the money and the grocery list. The boys scattered, yelling, nursing their heads, staring at me in utter disbe-

lief. They had never seen such frenzy. I stood panting, egging them on, taunting them to come on and fight. When they refused, I ran after them and they tore out for their homes, screaming. The parents of the boys rushed into the streets and threatened me, and for the first time in my life I shouted at grownups, telling them that I would give them the same if they bothered me. I finally found my grocery list and the money and went to the store. On my way back I kept my stick poised for instant use, but there was not a single boy in sight. That night I won the right to the streets of Memphis. . . .

After my father's desertion, my mother's ardently religious disposition dominated the household and I was often taken to Sunday school where I met God's representative in the guise of a tall, black preacher. One Sunday my mother invited the tall, black preacher to a dinner of fried chicken. I was happy, not because the preacher was coming but because of the chicken. One or two neighbors also were invited. But no sooner had the preacher arrived than I began to resent him, for I learned at once that he, like my father, was used to having his own way. The hour for dinner came and I was wedged at the table between talking and laughing adults. In the center of the table was a huge platter of golden-brown fried chicken. I compared the bowl of soup that sat before me with the crispy chicken and decided in favor of the chicken. The others began to eat their soup, but I could not touch mine.

"Eat your soup," my mother said.

"I don't want any," I said.

"You won't get anything else until you've eaten your soup," she said.

The preacher had finished his soup and had asked that the platter of chicken be passed to him. It galled me. He smiled, cocked his head this way and that, picking out choice pieces. I

Vocabulary

frenzy (fren′zē) *n.*: frantic behavior; wildness.
ardently (är′dənt·lē) *adv.*: intensely; eagerly.

FAMILY/COMMUNITY ACTIVITY

Although Wright had a difficult childhood that left him frustrated and bitter, he eventually found success as a writer. Ask students to discuss with classmates and family members (for whom they should summarize this selection) the personal strengths Wright developed as a child that enabled him to succeed in spite of the difficulties that he faced. Students then can work individually or collaboratively to develop lists of skills that they think people need in order to succeed today. You may wish to specify different contexts—for example, success in school, success in personal relationships, economic success, social success, ethical success, and success in your particular community.

forced a spoonful of soup down my throat and looked to see if my speed matched that of the preacher. It did not. There were already bare chicken bones on his plate, and he was reaching for more. I tried eating my soup faster, but it was no use; the other people were now serving themselves chicken and the platter was more than half empty. I gave up and sat staring in despair at the vanishing pieces of fried chicken.

"Eat your soup or you won't get anything," my mother warned.

I looked at her appealingly and could not answer. As piece after piece of chicken was eaten, I was unable to eat my soup at all. I grew hot with anger. The preacher was laughing and joking and the grownups were hanging on his words. My growing hate of the preacher finally became more important than God or religion and I could no longer contain myself. I leaped up from the table, knowing that I should be ashamed of what I was doing, but unable to stop, and screamed, running blindly from the room.

"That preacher's going to eat *all* the chicken!" I bawled.

The preacher tossed back his head and roared with laughter, but my mother was angry and told me that I was to have no dinner because of my bad manners.

When I awakened one morning my mother told me that we were going to see a judge who would make my father support me and my brother. An hour later all three of us were sitting in a huge crowded room. I was overwhelmed by the many faces and the voices which I could not understand. High above me was a white face which my mother told me was the face of the judge. Across the huge room sat my father, smiling confidently, looking at us. My mother warned me not to be fooled by my father's friendly manner; she told me that the judge might ask me questions, and if he did I must tell him the truth. I agreed, yet I hoped that the judge would not ask me anything.

For some reason the entire thing struck me as being useless; I felt that if my father were going

That night I won the right to the streets of Memphis . . .

973

DIRECT TEACHING

F **Literary Focus**

? **Dialogue.** How did you respond to this line of dialogue and its aftermath? [Some students may laugh, but many will feel sorry for Richard.] **What impression of Richard does it give you?** [Possible responses: He is a bright but frustrated child who doesn't yet know how to get what he wants. When he tries to speak up for himself, he is punished.]

G **Correcting Misconceptions**

The "gap." Make sure that students understand that a gap in text, as illustrated here, indicates an important shift in scene—the close of one episode and the beginning of another. Explain that the decision to use or not to use gaps is up to the writer and the editor; for example, Wright and his editor did not include a gap on page 979, even though the events described are separated by a quarter of a century.

Comparing and Contrasting Texts

Comparing characters' responses to a shared circumstance. Much of this selection explores Richard's response to poverty. Invite students to compare Richard's attitude on the subject with that of the following people and characters: Benjamin Franklin, who arrives in Philadelphia with practically no money (page 66); Henry David Thoreau, who decides to live in the woods (page 191); Frederick Douglass, who confronts Mr. Covey (page 398); Mrs. Sommers, Kate Chopin's character, who considers what to do with an unexpected sum of money (page 503); Phoenix Jackson, Eudora Welty's character, who interacts with various people in Natchez (page 685).

VIEWING THE ART

Hughie Lee-Smith (1915–2000) was born in Eustis, Florida, to parents who supported his passion for art. As a young child, he moved to Cleveland, where he studied at Karamu House, a community center known for its arts program. Later, he taught for nearly two decades at the Art Students League in New York City, where students select the faculty. He chose to paint the urban ghetto, and his paintings address the contradictions of loneliness and community, poverty and wealth. Many show young people in scenes of isolation or alienation, with urban decay around them. Although primarily realistic, the paintings convey a mystery, an almost surreal quality, that disturbs some viewers. His figures often have their backs to the viewer, yet they also seem alert and poised for action; and they are treated with sympathy but not sentimentality. *Boy with Tire* is one of Lee-Smith's most famous works. Critics have called it "allegorical" for the symbolic implications of the boy, tire, buildings, and shadows.

Activity. Ask students to discuss what elements of the painting are realistic, what elements seem stylized or abstract, and how the painting makes them feel. [Possible response: The details of the scene are generally realistic; however, the desolation of the landscape seems stylized and adds a sense of alienation and isolation.]

Boy with Tire (1952) by Hughie Lee-Smith. Oil on prestwood panel (60.3 cm × 82.6 cm).

The Detroit Institute of Arts, Gift of Dr. S. B. Milton, Dr. James A. Owen, Dr. B. F. Seabrooks, and Dr. A. E. Thomas, Jr. Photograph ©1988 The Detroit Institute of Arts © Hughie Lee-Smith/Licensed by VAGA, New York.

974 Collection 6 Contemporary Literature: 1939 to Present

Literary Criticism

Critic's Commentary: The Wright Stuff
In his review of *Black Boy,* Orville Prescott wrote: "Mr. Wright in this explosive autobiography does not suggest any constructive means for improving the lot of the Negro in this country. . . . [H]e can only display suffering and cruelty with harsh dramatic power, he can only arouse anger and sympathy. If enough such books are written, if enough millions of people read them, maybe, some day, in the fullness of time, there will be a greater understanding and a more true democracy." You might have students discuss what Prescott meant by "a greater understanding" and whether "enough such books" have been written or "enough millions of people" have read them.

to feed me, then he would have done so regardless of what a judge said to him. And I did not want my father to feed me; I was hungry, but my thoughts of food did not now center about him. I waited, growing restless, hungry. My mother gave me a dry sandwich and I munched and stared, longing to go home. Finally I heard my mother's name called; she rose and began weeping so copiously that she could not talk for a few moments; at last she managed to say that her husband had deserted her and two children, that her children were hungry, that they stayed hungry, that she worked, that she was trying to raise them alone. Then my father was called; he came forward jauntily, smiling. He tried to kiss my mother, but she turned away from him. I only heard one sentence of what he said.

"I'm doing all I can, Your Honor," he mumbled, grinning.

It had been painful to sit and watch my mother crying and my father laughing and I was glad when we were outside in the sunny streets. Back at home my mother wept again and talked complainingly about the unfairness of the judge who had accepted my father's word. After the court scene, I tried to forget my father; I did not hate him; I simply did not want to think of him. Often when we were hungry my mother would beg me to go to my father's job and ask him for a dollar, a dime, a nickel . . . But I would never consent to go. I did not want to see him.

My mother fell ill and the problem of food became an acute, daily agony. Hunger was with us always. Sometimes the neighbors would feed us or a dollar bill would come in the mail from my grandmother. It was winter and I would buy a dime's worth of coal each morning from the corner coalyard and lug it home in paper bags. For a time I remained out of school to wait upon my mother, then Granny came to visit us and I returned to school.

At night there were long, halting discussions about our going to live with Granny, but

Vocabulary
copiously (kō′pē·əs·lē) *adv.:* abundantly.

A Reading Skills

❓ **Analyzing an author's assumptions and beliefs.** Why does the young Richard no longer want his father to feed him? [Possible responses: He is too disillusioned to hope for help from the man; he is too proud to ask for help from someone who deserted him; he is so hungry that he no longer cares.]

B Literary Focus

❓ **Dialogue.** Why do you think that the judge rules in the father's favor? [Possible responses: The judge is a fool; the judge takes a man's word over a woman's; the judge's prejudices about African Americans blind him to the reality of the case.]

CONTENT-AREA CONNECTIONS

Culture: On the Move

In some cultures, frequent change of residence is an accepted part of life; for example, nomadic groups of Native Americans, Eskimos, and Bushmen traditionally moved to follow the game that they hunted. In other cultures, moves are rare; a nineteenth-century English farmer, for example, might have lived in the same spot all his life. In our own time, many Americans have grown used to moving as a result of job changes, and refugees often are forced to move because of political or economic turmoil.

Small-group activity. Ask groups of students to discuss the possible effects of frequent moving on young people and to share their comments with the class.

A Advanced Learners

Enrichment. Point out that as a boy, Wright preferred the simplicity of action to the complexities of words but that as an adult Wright lived by words. Invite students to discuss how such a change might occur. [Possible responses: Education and adult experience can help one appreciate the power of words; Wright was inherently a verbally gifted person but did not discover his gift until later in his life.]

B Learners Having Difficulty

Finding sequence of events. Have students list in chronological order the events that lead to sending Richard and his brother to live in an orphanage. [His mother loses her child-support case in court; his mother falls ill, increasing the difficulties; the idea of living with the grandmother comes up and is rejected; there is no longer enough money to pay the rent; the mother searches for and finds an orphanage.]

C Vocabulary Development

❓ Denotation and connotation. Look at the adjectives (*silent, hostile, vindictive, complaining*) and nouns (*nervousness, intrigue*) that Wright uses in this passage. What feelings do you think he intends to stir in the reader by using such words? [Possible response: He wants readers to share his own remembered distaste for the orphanage and worry about what might happen to him there.]

D Reading Skills

❓ Comparing and contrasting. How is this description of hunger's effects similar to and different from the description on p. 970, which begins, "Hunger stole upon me so slowly . . ."? [Possible response: Both describe the physical effects of hunger, but here the hunger is at a more advanced stage.]

---

nothing came of it. Perhaps there was not enough money for railroad fare. Angered by having been hauled into court, my father now spurned us completely. I heard long, angrily whispered conversations between my mother and grandmother to the effect that "that woman ought to be killed for breaking up a home."

What irked me was the ceaseless talk and no action. If someone had suggested that my father be killed, I would perhaps have become interested; if someone had suggested that his name never be mentioned, I would no doubt have agreed; if someone had suggested that we move to another city, I would have been glad. But there was only endless talk that led nowhere and I began to keep away from home as much as possible, preferring the simplicity of the streets to the worried, futile talk at home.

Finally we could no longer pay the rent for our dingy flat; the few dollars that Granny had left us before she went home were gone. Half sick and in despair, my mother made the rounds of the charitable institutions, seeking help. She found an orphan home that agreed to assume the guidance of me and my brother provided my mother worked and made small payments. My mother hated to be separated from us, but she had no choice.

The orphan home was a two-story frame building set amid trees in a wide, green field. My mother ushered me and my brother one morning into the building and into the presence of a tall, gaunt, mulatto woman who called herself Miss Simon. At once she took a fancy to me and I was frightened speechless; I was afraid of her the moment I saw her and my fear lasted during my entire stay in the home.

The house was crowded with children and there was always a storm of noise. The daily routine was blurred to me and I never quite grasped it. The most abiding feeling I had each day was hunger and fear. The meals were skimpy and there were only two of them. Just before we went to bed each night we were given a slice of bread smeared with molasses. The children were silent, hostile, vindictive, continuously complaining of hunger. There was an overall atmosphere of nervousness and intrigue, of children telling tales upon others, of children being deprived of food to punish them.

The home did not have the money to check the growth of the wide stretches of grass by having it mown, so it had to be pulled by hand. Each morning after we had eaten a breakfast that seemed like no breakfast at all, an older child would lead a herd of us to the vast lawn and we would get to our knees and wrench the grass loose from the dirt with our fingers. At intervals Miss Simon would make a tour of inspection, examining the pile of pulled grass beside each child, scolding or praising according to the size of the pile. Many mornings I was too weak from hunger to pull the grass; I would grow dizzy and my mind would become blank and I would find myself, after an interval of unconsciousness, upon my hands and knees, my head whirling, my eyes staring in bleak astonishment at the green grass, wondering where I was, feeling that I was emerging from a dream . . .

During the first days my mother came each night to visit me and my brother, then her visits stopped. I began to wonder if she, too, like my father, had disappeared into the unknown. I was rapidly learning to distrust everything and everybody. When my mother did come, I asked her why had she remained away so long and she told me that Miss Simon had forbidden her to visit us, that Miss Simon had said that she was spoiling us with too much attention. I begged my mother to take me away; she wept and told me to wait, that soon she would take us to Arkansas. She left and my heart sank.

Miss Simon tried to win my confidence; she asked me if I would like to be adopted by her if my mother consented and I said no. She would take me into her apartment and talk to me, but her words had no effect. Dread and mistrust had already become a daily part of my being and my memory grew sharp, my senses more

---

Vocabulary
futile (fyo͞ot′l) *adj.*: useless; pointless.

READING MINI-LESSON

Developing Word-Attack Skills
Remind students that when the spelling pattern *i*-consonant-*e* occurs in one-syllable words the vowel sound is long *i*. Write on the chalkboard words they suggest to this letter-sound correspondence.

Using the following selection words, explain that when *i*-consonant-*e* occurs at the end of a multisyllable word, the vowel sound is not always long *i*.

hostile final vowel sound is /ə/ or /ī/
massive final vowel sound is /i/
routine final vowel sound is /ē/
deprive final vowel sound is /ī/

Help students conclude that when *i*-consonant-*e* occurs at the end of a multisyllabic word, the vowel sound can be long or short *i*, long *e*, or the unaccented schwa (ə) sound.

Individual activity. Have students group the words by final vowel sound: /ī/, /i/, /ē/, or /ə/.

impressionable; I began to be aware of myself as a distinct personality striving against others. I held myself in, afraid to act or speak until I was sure of my surroundings, feeling most of the time that I was suspended over a void. My imagination soared; I dreamed of running away. Each morning I vowed that I would leave the next morning, but the next morning always found me afraid.

One day Miss Simon told me that thereafter I was to help her in the office. I ate lunch with her and, strangely, when I sat facing her at the table, my hunger vanished. The woman killed something in me. Next she called me to her desk where she sat addressing envelopes.

"Step up close to the desk," she said. "Don't be afraid."

I went and stood at her elbow. There was a wart on her chin and I stared at it.

"Now, take a blotter from over there and blot each envelope after I'm through writing on it," she instructed me, pointing to a blotter that stood about a foot from my hand.

I stared and did not move or answer.

"Take the blotter," she said.

I wanted to reach for the blotter and succeeded only in twitching my arm.

"Here," she said sharply, reaching for the blotter and shoving it into my fingers.

She wrote in ink on an envelope and pushed it toward me. Holding the blotter in my hand, I stared at the envelope and could not move.

"Blot it," she said.

I could not lift my hand. I knew what she had said; I knew what she wanted me to do; and I had heard her correctly. I wanted to look at her and say something, tell her why I could not move; but my eyes were fixed upon the floor. I could not summon enough courage while she sat there looking at me to reach over the yawning space of twelve inches and blot the wet ink on the envelope.

"Blot it!" she spoke sharply.

Still I could not move or answer.

"Look at me!"

I could not lift my eyes. She reached her hand to my face and I twisted away.

"What's wrong with you?" she demanded.

I began to cry and she drove me from the room. I decided that as soon as night came I would run away. The dinner bell rang and I did not go to the table, but hid in a corner of the hallway. When I heard the dishes rattling at the table, I opened the door and ran down the walk to the street. Dusk was falling. Doubt made me stop. Ought I go back? No; hunger was back there, and fear. I went on, coming to concrete sidewalks. People passed me. Where was I going? I did not know. The farther I walked the more frantic I became. In a confused and vague way I knew that I was doing more running *away* from than running *toward* something. I stopped. The streets seemed dangerous. The buildings were massive and dark. The moon shone and the trees loomed frighteningly. No, I could not go on. I would go back. But I had walked so far and had turned too many corners and had not kept track of the direction. Which way led back to the orphan home? I did not know. I was lost.

I stood in the middle of the sidewalk and cried. A "white" policeman came to me and I wondered if he was going to beat me. He asked me what was the matter and I told him that I was trying to find my mother. His "white" face created a new fear in me. I was remembering the tale of the "white" man who had beaten the "black" boy. A crowd gathered and I was urged to tell where I lived. Curiously, I was too full of fear to cry now. I wanted to tell the "white" face that I had run off from an orphan home and that Miss Simon ran it, but I was afraid. Finally I was taken to the police station where I was fed. I felt better. I sat in a big chair where I was surrounded by "white" policemen, but they seemed to ignore me. Through the window I could see that night had completely fallen and that lights now gleamed in the streets. I grew sleepy and dozed. My shoulder was shaken gently and I opened my eyes and looked into a "white" face of another policeman who was sitting beside me. He asked me questions in a quiet, confidential tone, and quite before I knew it he was not "white" any more. I told him that I had run

Richard Wright   977

E

F

G

DIRECT TEACHING

E Literary Focus

? Dialogue. What are Miss Simon's emotions as she keeps telling Wright to blot the envelope? [Possible responses: increasing anger; incomprehension; irritation; frustration.] What are Richard's emotions? [Possible responses: terror; numbness; confusion.]

F Reading Skills

? Making inferences. Why does Wright enclose the word *white* in quotation marks in this paragraph? [Possible response: to emphasize the absurdity of racial classification.]

G Reading Skills

? Tracing recurring themes. What crucial act by the police wins Wright's trust? [The police feed him.]

magazine /ē/	discipline /i/	peregrine /i/
determine /i/	subjective /i/	predestine /i/
futile /ə/	asinine /ī/	tactile /ə/
infantile /ī/	sterile /ə/	projectile /ə/
collective /i/	medicine /ə/	crystalline /i/
gabardine /ē/	divine /ī/	collide /ī/
franchise /ī/	fertile /ə/	missile /ə/
bibliophile /ī/	executive /i/	saline /ē/

VIEWING THE ART

John Wilson (1922–) is a socially conscious painter, print-maker, sculptor, illustrator, and teacher. In the 1940s, Wilson's teacher at the School of the Museum of Fine Arts, Boston, encouraged him to use social art as a means of fighting racism. *My Brother* is an intimate portrait that reveals a deep bond of sympathy between the artist and the sub-ject. The finely rendered portrait stands out against a sketchy urban landscape.

Activity. Ask students to discuss what personal qualities the artist is trying to convey and why this portrait seems appropriate (or not appropriate) to the word por-trait of the young Richard Wright.

Ⓐ **Learners Having Difficulty**

Summarizing. Help students continue with their time line project and summarize the events that have taken place since Wright entered the orphanage. [Possible response: The children are made to pull grass by hand; they are inadequately fed; Wright is repelled by Miss Simon; Wright runs away from the orphan-age and is picked up and given a meal by the police; he is returned to the orphanage, where Miss Simon beats him.]

My Brother (1942) by John Wilson. Oil on panel (12″ × 10⁵⁄₈″).

Smith College Museum of Art, Northampton, Massachusetts.

away from an orphan home and that Miss Simon ran it.

Ⓐ It was but a matter of minutes before I was walking alongside a policeman, heading toward the home. The policeman led me to the front gate and I saw Miss Simon waiting for me on the steps. She identified me and I was left in her charge. I begged her not to beat me, but she yanked me upstairs into an empty room and lashed me thoroughly. Sobbing, I slunk off to bed, resolved to run away again. But I was watched closely after that.

My mother was informed upon her next visit that I had tried to run away and she was terribly upset.

"Why did you do it?" she asked.

"I don't want to stay here," I told her.

"But you must," she said. "How can I work if I'm to worry about you? You must remember that you have no father. I'm doing all I can."

"I don't want to stay here," I repeated.

"Then, if I take you to your father . . ."

"I don't want to stay with him either," I said.

"But I want you to ask him for enough money for us to go to my sister's in Arkansas," she said.

Again I was faced with choices I did not like, but I finally agreed. After all, my hate for my fa-ther was not so great and urgent as my hate for the orphan home. My mother held to her idea

978 Collection 6 Contemporary Literature: 1939 to Present

Economics: Comparative Costs
Paired activity. Have pairs of students research what five cents could buy in 1917 in order to determine what Wright was refusing when he did not take his father's nickel (p. 979). Have them use a time line to chart the change in what that sum could buy over the years. In addition, have pairs of students research the cost of three bus tickets (one adult and two children) from Memphis,

Tennessee, to Little Rock, Arkansas (p. 978). Ask students to calculate the price of the tick-ets in 1917 and then guess how much money Wright's mother wanted from his father.

Social Studies: Orphanages
In the late nineteenth and early twentieth centuries, it was not uncommon for poverty-stricken parents to seek placement of their children outside the family as a matter of survival.

Small-group activity. Have students research the orphanage as an institution in the United States in the 1910s and 1920s. Students should consider the administration of orphanages, the living conditions in orphanages, the population of children, and the rate of adoption. Have students report their findings to the class and relate them to the selection.

and one night a week or so later I found myself standing in a room in a frame house. My father and a strange woman were sitting before a bright fire that blazed in a grate. My mother and I were standing about six feet away, as though we were afraid to approach them any closer.

"It's not for me," my mother was saying. "It's for your children that I'm asking you for money."

"I ain't got nothing," my father said, laughing.

"Come here, boy," the strange woman called to me.

I looked at her and did not move.

"Give him a nickel," the woman said. "He's cute."

"Come here, Richard," my father said, stretching out his hand.

I backed away, shaking my head, keeping my eyes on the fire.

"He is a cute child," the strange woman said.

"You ought to be ashamed," my mother said to the strange woman. "You're starving my children."

"Now, don't you-all fight," my father said, laughing.

"I'll take that poker and hit you!" I blurted at my father.

He looked at my mother and laughed louder.

"You told him to say that," he said.

"Don't say such things, Richard," my mother said.

"You ought to be dead," I said to the strange woman.

The woman laughed and threw her arms about my father's neck. I grew ashamed and wanted to leave.

"How can you starve your children?" my mother asked.

"Let Richard stay with me," my father said.

"Do you want to stay with your father, Richard?" my mother asked.

"No," I said.

"You'll get plenty to eat," he said.

"I'm hungry now," I told him. "But I won't stay with you."

"Aw, give the boy a nickel," the woman said.

My father ran his hand into his pocket and pulled out a nickel.

"Here, Richard," he said.

"Don't take it," my mother said.

"Don't teach him to be a fool," my father said. "Here, Richard, take it."

I looked at my mother, at the strange woman, at my father, then into the fire. I wanted to take the nickel, but I did not want to take it from my father.

"You ought to be ashamed," my mother said, weeping. "Giving your son a nickel when he's hungry. If there's a God, He'll pay you back."

"That's all I got," my father said, laughing again and returning the nickel to his pocket.

We left. I had the feeling that I had had to do with something unclean. Many times in the years after that the image of my father and the strange woman, their faces lit by the dancing flames, would surge up in my imagination so vivid and strong that I felt I could reach out and touch it; I would stare at it, feeling that it possessed some vital meaning which always <u>eluded</u> me.

A quarter of a century was to elapse between the time when I saw my father sitting with the strange woman and the time when I was to see him again, standing alone upon the red clay of a Mississippi plantation, a sharecropper,° clad in ragged overalls, holding a muddy hoe in his gnarled, veined hands—a quarter of a century during which my mind and consciousness had become so greatly and violently altered that when I tried to talk to him I realized that, though ties of blood made us kin, though I could see a shadow of my face in his face, though there was an echo of my voice in his voice, we were forever strangers, speaking a different language, living on vastly distant planes

---

°**sharecropper** n.: farmer who works a piece of land for its owner and gets a small portion of the crop in return.

Vocabulary
eluded (ē·lōōd′id) v.: escaped detection or notice.

Richard Wright   **979**

B Literary Focus

? Setting. What does this setting suggest about whether Wright's father was lying in court? [Possible response: Wright's father and his girlfriend live in a frame house (rather than a crumbling tenement) and can afford wood for a fire. These details indicate that he was lying in court.]

C Literary Focus

? Dialogue. What do the comments by Wright's father, the father's girlfriend, and Wright's mother suggest about each of these people? [Possible responses: The father tries to control the awkward situation by treating it as a joke; his girlfriend seems generous, but she does not acknowledge the seriousness of the confrontation; the mother's anger over the other woman's role is stronger than any discomfort that she may be feeling.]

D Literary Focus

? Dialogue. What does young Wright reveal about himself by responding to his father's invitation and then by falling silent? [Possible responses: He proves that he his hunger cannot sway him now; he shows himself to be of stronger character than his father. His silence underscores his determination not to be swayed from his decision.]

E Reading Skills

? Synthesizing. How has Wright's father changed? [Possible response: He has become aged and destitute, no longer an imposing, frightening figure.] How has Wright himself changed? [Possible response: He has become an educated, sophisticated, modern writer and urban resident.]

SKILLS REVIEW

Relating a work of literature to its historical period. After students have read this excerpt from *Black Boy,* share or review the comments in "More About the Writer" (p. 967). Discuss these questions.

1. What episodes in this narrative show Wright exploring what Ellison notes are potential problems that come when races "strive for mutual understanding"? [Possible response: the episode in which Wright's father talks a white judge into not forcing him to pay child support; the episode in which young Wright sees white policemen in a new, more kindly way.]

2. *Black Boy* came out in 1945. How does that fact help you understand why Clarke said that Wright "came like a sledgehammer"? [Possible response: Wright exposed black America to a white audience years before the civil rights movement.]

A Reading Skills

? Interpreting. What is Wright's final assessment of his father? [Possible response: His father was a black peasant who had gone to the city and failed. He endured without regrets—but without hopes.]

GUIDED PRACTICE

Monitoring students' progress. Guide the class in answering these comprehension questions.

Short Answer

1. In what city do most of the events in this excerpt take place? [Memphis, Tennessee]

2. What did Wright have to do before his mother would let him back into the house? [He had to buy groceries.]

3. Why did Wright's father not have to support his family financially? [He convinced a judge that he already was doing his best.]

4. Why did Wright's mother put him and his brother into an orphanage? [She could not make enough money to support them.]

5. How did Wright react when his father offered him a nickel? [He refused it.]

INDEPENDENT PRACTICE

Response and Analysis

Reading Check

1. The neighborhood was bleak and living quarters were cramped.

2. A gang of boys knocked him down and stole his grocery money.

3. He was offhand, condescending. He used humor to take charge of each situation.

4. At first, he felt detachment; later, he felt resentment.

---

of reality. That day a quarter of a century later when I visited him on the plantation—he was standing against the sky, smiling toothlessly, his hair whitened, his body bent, his eyes glazed with dim recollection, his fearsome aspect of twenty-five years ago gone forever from him—I was overwhelmed to realize that he could never understand me or the scalding experiences that had swept me beyond his life and into an area of living that he could never know. I stood before him, poised, my mind aching as it embraced the simple nakedness of his life, feeling how completely his soul was imprisoned by the slow flow of the seasons, by wind and rain and sun, how fastened were his memories to a crude and raw past, how chained were his actions and emotions to the direct, animalistic impulses of his withering body . . .

From the white landowners above him there had not been handed to him a chance to learn the meaning of loyalty, of sentiment, of tradition. Joy was as unknown to him as was despair.

As a creature of the earth, he endured, hearty, whole, seemingly indestructible, with no regrets and no hope. He asked easy, drawling questions about me, his other son, his wife, and he laughed, amused, when I informed him of their destinies. I forgave him and pitied him as my eyes looked past him to the unpainted wooden shack. From far beyond the horizons that bound this bleak plantation there had come to me through my living the knowledge that my father was a black peasant who had gone to the city seeking life, but who had failed in the city; a black peasant whose life had been hopelessly snarled in the city, and who had at last fled the city—that same city which had lifted me in its burning arms and borne me toward alien and undreamed-of shores of knowing. ■

Vocabulary
withering (wi*th*ʹər·iŋ) v. used as *adj.:* drying up; weakening.

Response and Analysis

Literary Skills
Analyze dialogue in nonfiction.

Writing Skills
Write an essay analyzing a character.

Vocabulary Skills
Understand synonyms.

Reading Check

1. What was life like for Richard and his family when they arrived in Memphis?

2. What happened when Richard went to buy groceries?

3. How did Richard's father behave in the courtroom scene and when Richard and his mother went to see him at home?

4. How did Richard feel about his father during most of his childhood?

Thinking Critically

5. What **details** does Wright use to make the reader feel the physical and emotional hunger he experienced as a boy?

6. When Richard's mother sent him back to face the boys who robbed him, what lesson was she trying to teach him? What else could she have done?

7. Why couldn't Richard eat his soup while the preacher was devouring the chicken? What does this incident reveal about the boy's **character**?

8. Wright uses vivid **dialogue** to dramatize scenes of great emotional conflict between Richard and people he was forced to depend on. Find and read two of these scenes aloud, and then discuss what they reveal about Richard's emotions.

9. On page 977, Wright describes his feelings about the white policeman who took him to the police station. At first Wright was scared but then he remarks, ". . . before I knew it he was not 'white' any more." What does his initial fear of the policeman and then this later comment reveal about Wright's beliefs about white people at the time?

Thinking Critically

Possible Answers

5. The main detail is Wright's association of the emotional image of his father with his physical hunger.

6. She was trying to teach him to stand up for himself. She could have confronted the boys or called the police.

7. Richard resented the preacher's buoyant spirits and huge appetite. Richard is stubborn—also somewhat self-destructive.

8. Richard clashed with his mother about hunger and facing up to the bullies; both clashes suggest fear. He responded with silence to attempts at conversation from Miss Simon and his father; his silence suggests rebellion.

9. His fear was of whites as a group. When an individual treated him with respect, Wright lost his fear.

10. Remembering his father and the strange woman, "their faces lit by the dancing flames," Wright says this **image** "possessed some vital meaning which always eluded me" (page 979). What do you think he means?

11. When Wright saw his father again after twenty-five years, what did he realize about his father? How was the city's effect on his father different from its effect on Wright himself?

Extending and Evaluating

12. Review Wright's use of **dialogue** in this portion of his autobiography. Does the use of dialogue Wright could not possibly have accurately recalled detract from the power or authority of his story? Discuss your responses in class.

WRITING

"The Simple Nakedness of His Life . . ."

In a short **essay,** analyze the **character** of Wright's father as Wright presents him. Consider the father when he lived in Memphis and, twenty-five years later, when he lived as a sharecropper in rural Mississippi. Had the father changed a great deal over the years? Had Wright himself changed? What assessment did Wright make of his father at the end? Do you think his evaluation fits the facts of his father's life? Before you write, collect details for your analysis in a chart like the following one:

	Details from Text
Father's words and actions in Memphis	
Father's words and actions 25 years later	
General assessment of father	

▶ Use "Analyzing Literature," pages 665–666, for more help with this assignment.

House in rural Tennessee (1945).

Vocabulary Development
Synonym Maps

enthralled	frenzy	futile
clamor	ardently	eluded
dispirited	copiously	withering

Use a dictionary or a thesaurus to find a synonym for each Vocabulary word. Then, go back to the text, and replace each Vocabulary word with the synonym you have found. For each word, decide whether the synonym works as well, or not as well, in the context of the sentence. See the following example:

```
clamor
```
```
Synonym
noise
```
```
Sentence
Whenever I begged for food now my
mother would pour me a cup of tea
which would still the noise in my
stomach for a moment or two.
```
```
Judgment
Noise could also work, but clamor
suggests a person complaining
loudly and is more powerful.
```

Richard Wright **981**

Vocabulary Development

- *enthralled. Synonym*—fascinated. *Judgment*—*Enthralled* better suggests the power that the machines had over Wright's attention.
- *dispirited. Synonym*—discouraged. *Judgment*—*Dispirited* is stronger than *discouraged.*
- *frenzy. Synonym*—wildness. *Judgment*—*Frenzy* seems more intense than *wildness.*
- *ardently. Synonym*—intensely. *Judgment*—*Ardently* suggests that something is done "with heart."
- *copiously. Synonym*—abundantly. *Judgment*—*Copiously* fits better with *weeping* than *abundantly* does.
- *futile. Synonym*—pointless. *Judgment*—*Futile* seems stronger than *pointless.*
- *eluded. Synonym*—escaped. *Judgment*—*Eluded* has connotations of mysteriousness.
- *withering. Synonym*—weakening. *Judgment*—*Withering* suggests a greater loss of strength.

10. He means that the image had symbolic significance for him, but he never figured out just what it meant.

11. He realized that, despite blood, they were strangers, and his father never would understand him. City life strengthened Wright; his father, however, wherever he resided, lived by "direct, animalistic impulses."

Evaluation

12. Yes, knowing that he could not have quoted accurately makes us suspect everything that he says. No, the narrative would be powerful even if it were completely fictional; the account is so true to life that there's no point in questioning its authority.

Grammar Link

Using Parallel Structure: Keeping Things in Balance

You create **parallel structure** when you state equal, or parallel, ideas in the same grammatical form. In this sentence from *Black Boy,* notice how Richard Wright uses parallelism. All the underlined phrases start with the preposition *of* and end with a noun.

PARALLEL   "From the white landowners above him there had not been handed to him a chance to learn the meaning of loyalty, of sentiment, of tradition."

If Wright had written the following sentence, he would have created a grammatical error. The underlined words are not in parallel grammatical form.

NOT PARALLEL   From the white landowners above him there had not been handed to him a chance to learn the meaning of loyalty, sentiment, of having tradition.

The key to parallel structure is balance: You must pair a noun with a noun, a verb with a verb, a prepositional phrase with a prepositional phrase, a clause with the same kind of clause. In the following sentence the underlined elements are *not* parallel in structure:

NOT PARALLEL   To read *Black Boy* will teach people more about the African American experience than listening to rap music. [*To read* is an infinitive paired with *listening,* a gerund.]

To read is an infinitive, but *listening* is a gerund. You can correct the error and make the verbs parallel by using the same grammatical form for both verbs.

PARALLEL   Reading *Black Boy* will teach people more about the African American experience than listening to rap music. [gerund paired with gerund]

NATIVE SON A Play
By PAUL GREEN and RICHARD WRIGHT

A MERCURY PRODUCTION
Produced by Orson Welles and John Houseman

This powerful play is based on the phenomenally successful novel, Native Son, by Richard Wright, of which Clifton Fadiman said in The New Yorker: "Powerful...overwhelming...It does for the Negro what Theodore Dreiser's American Tragedy did for the bewildered, inarticulate American white."

HARPER & BROTHERS ~ ESTABLISHED 1817

Drafts of Wright's writings.
(Above and right) Yale Collection of American Literature, Beinecke Rare Book and Manuscript Library.

DIFFERENTIATING INSTRUCTION

Learners Having Difficulty
Have students identify the faulty parallelism (underlined) in each of the following sentences adapted from *Black Boy.* Then, work with students as a group to suggest possible corrections (there may be more than one possible correction for some sentences).

1. Now I began to wake up at night to find hunger standing at my bedside, <u>and it stared</u> at me gauntly. [staring]

2. We must learn as soon as possible to take care of ourselves, <u>dress ourselves,</u> and to prepare our own food. [to dress]

3. She sat down at once, wrote another note, gave me more money, <u>and she sent</u> me out to the grocery again. [and sent]

4. At last she managed to say that her husband had deserted her and her two children, that her children were hungry, that they stayed hungry, <u>and she worked and was trying</u> to raise them alone. [that she worked, and that she was trying]

Following are some situations in which you'll want to check your sentences for parallel structure:

- Linking ideas by using **coordinating conjunctions** (such as *and, but, or, nor,* and *yet*)

  Wright's mother tells the judge <u>that her husband has deserted his family</u> **and** <u>that their children are hungry.</u> [noun clause paired with noun clause]

- Connecting several ideas in a series

  The boys were <u>yelling, nursing</u> their heads, and <u>staring</u> at Wright in disbelief. [three verbs in the present progressive]

- Linking ideas by using **correlative conjunctions** (pairs of words such as *either . . . or, neither . . . nor,* and *both . . . and*)

  Wright **not only** <u>threatens</u> to hit his father with a poker **but also** <u>tells</u> his companion that she ought to be dead. [verb paired with verb]

Apply to Your Writing

Re-read a current writing assignment or one that you've already completed. Correct any examples of faulty parallelism, paying particular attention to the situations discussed above.

▶ **For more help, see Using Parallel Structure, 9c, in the Language Handbook.**

PRACTICE

In the following sentences, correct any examples of faulty parallelism:

1. Richard Wright is most famous for the novel *Native Son* and for having written the autobiography *Black Boy.*

2. In this excerpt from *Black Boy,* Wright decides that it would be worse to get beaten at home than if he got beat up on the streets.

3. Wright's father is neither generous nor does he show remorse.

4. When Wright visits his father twenty-five years later, he feels forgiveness, pity, and that he understands the old man.

Grammar Link

Practice

Possible Answers

1. Richard Wright is most famous for the novel *Native Son* and the autobiography *Black Boy.*

2. In this excerpt from *Black Boy,* Wright decides that it would be worse to get beaten at home than to get beaten on the streets.

3. Wright's father shows neither generosity nor remorse.

4. When Wright visits his father twenty-five years later, he feels forgiveness, pity, and understanding for the old man.

ASSESSING

Assessment

- *Holt Assessment: Literature, Reading, and Vocabulary*

Grade-Level Skills

■ **Reading Skills**
Draw inferences about character.

Review Skills

■ **Literary Skills**
Analyze the methods writers use to reveal character.

More About the Writer
Background. Kingston's parents married in China. Her father emigrated to New York City and worked in a laundry for fifteen years, during which time he sent his wife money to study for certifications in medicine and midwifery in China. She established a practice in China but gave it up when her husband sent for her to come to the United States. Here she worked as a laundress and a field hand. Kingston may have found in her parents a model for some of the Chinese immigrants in her writing.

Maxine Hong Kingston
(1940–   )

Maxine Hong Kingston burst onto the literary scene in 1976 with an extraordinary and innovative book—*The Woman Warrior: Memoirs of a Girlhood Among Ghosts.* Kingston, who was born in California of Chinese immigrant parents, uses a mixture of autobiography, myth, poetic meditation, and fiction to convey her memories and feelings about growing up in a strange world (the United States) populated by what she and her family thought of as white-skinned "ghosts."

The book received immediate acclaim. William McPherson of *The Washington Post* wrote: "*The Woman Warrior* is a strange, sometimes savagely terrifying and, in the literal sense, wonderful story about growing up caught between two highly sophisticated and utterly alien cultures, both vivid, often menacing, and equally mysterious." Paul Gray said in *Time:* "Exiles and refugees tell sad stories of the life they left behind. Even sadder, sometimes, is the muteness of their children. They are likely to find the old ways and old language excess baggage, especially if their adopted homeland is the United States, where the race is to the swift and the adaptable. Thus a heritage of centuries can die in a generation of embarrassed silence. *The Woman Warrior* gives that silence a voice."

When *The Woman Warrior* won the National Book Critics Circle Award for general nonfiction in 1976, Kingston gained national attention. The suddenness of her appearance as an important literary figure was startling.

Where had Kingston been until the age of thirty-six? Named for an American woman in the gambling house where her father worked for a time, Maxine Hong grew up in the Chinatown of Stockton, California. She earned a B.A. from the University of California at Berkeley in 1962 and married the actor Earll Kingston. After their son was born, the Kingstons lived in Hawaii for a time, where Maxine taught English at the high school and college levels, before returning to California.

In 1980, Kingston published a companion piece to *The Woman Warrior,* a kind of ancestral history called *China Men.* The critic Susan Currier has described this book as "a sort of vindication of all the Chinese who helped build America but who were rewarded with abuse and neglect." In 1988, Kingston published an extravagant novel called *Tripmaster Monkey: His Fake Book,* blending Chinese history and myth and vivid storytelling in the adventures of a young Chinese American named Wittman Ah Sing. The noted novelist Anne Tyler called *Tripmaster Monkey* "a novel of satisfying complexity and bite and verve." In the 1990s, Kingston taught creative writing at the University of California at Berkeley and worked on a book of nonfiction.

Despite the attention given to her books, Kingston has remained relatively private. She seldom gives interviews or appears at public readings. In her two memoirs she does not answer all of the personal questions raised by her writing. In the selection that follows, even a careful reader will not be able to decide what is truth, what is fiction, and what is simply left unsaid. This ambiguity gives Kingston's work much of its haunting quality.

RESOURCES: READING

Planning
■ *One-Stop Planner* CD-ROM with ExamView Test Generator

Differentiating Instruction
■ *Supporting Instruction in Spanish*
■ *Audio CD Library, Selections and Summaries in Spanish*

Vocabulary
■ *Vocabulary Development*

Grammar and Language
■ *Daily Language Activities*

Assessment
■ *Holt Assessment: Literature, Reading, and Vocabulary*
■ *One-Stop Planner* CD-ROM with ExamView Test Generator
■ *Holt Online Assessment*

Internet
■ go.hrw.com (Keyword: LE5 11-6)
■ *Elements of Literature Online*

Media
■ *Audio CD Library*
■ *Audio CD Library, Selections and Summaries in Spanish*

The Girl Who Wouldn't Talk

Make the Connection

It happens just about every day to all of us. For one reason or another, we don't tell others what we really think or feel about something important. Out of self-doubt, politeness, fear, or even because we are trying to keep the truth from ourselves, we are silent. Sometimes we act out what we don't say in ways that hurt ourselves and others, but at other times we find positive ways that express our feelings in writing, painting, music, or some other art form.

Literary Focus
Characterization

Just like fiction writers, nonfiction writers use all the devices of **characterization** to bring the people in their texts to life. It is the expert use of these fictional devices that sometimes makes us feel as if we are reading fiction—when what we are reading is supposed to be factually true.

Maxine Hong Kingston reveals the personalities of her narrator and of the other characters in her **memoir** (mem'wär') by describing how they look, dress, act, and speak (including *if* they speak). She also shows us how her characters affect other people and what other people think of them. Since Kingston writes in the first person, we are also given access to the private thoughts and feelings of the narrator.

> **Characterization** is the process by which a writer reveals the personality of a character.
>
> *For more on Character, see the Handbook of Literary and Historical Terms.*

Reading Skills
Drawing Inferences About Characters

As you read, take notes on how the writer characterizes the narrator and the silent girl. Look for clues that reveal how the narrator views her white American classmates and how she feels about them. Then, stop near the top of page 992, and write down what you think the silent girl is *not* saying—that is, what are her unexpressed thoughts and feelings? You might also jot down what you think the narrator is not saying.

Background

The Chinese American family in this excerpt from *The Woman Warrior* lives in Stockton, California. Just before the episode starts, the narrator describes Chinese voices, which she says are louder than American voices. Describing her own voice, the narrator says, "You could hear splinters in my voice, bones rubbing jagged against one another. I was loud, though. I was glad I didn't whisper."

The "ghosts" mentioned by the narrator are white Americans, who seemed so strange to this Chinese family.

Vocabulary Development

loitered (loit'ərd) v.: spent time; hung around.

nape n.: back of the neck.

habitually (hə·bich'oo·ə·lē) adv.: usually; by habit.

sarcastic (sär·kas'tik) adj.: scornful; mocking.

temples (tem'pəlz) n. pl.: sides of the forehead, just above and in front of the ears.

INTERNET

Vocabulary
Practice
•
Cross-Curricular
Connection

Keyword: LE5 11-6

SKILLS FOCUS

Literary Skills
Understand
characterization.

Reading Skills
Make inferences
about characters.

Maxine Hong Kingston   985

PRETEACHING

Summary   *at grade level*

This thematic exploration of assimilation and cultural difference begins with the Chinese American narrator's description of her attempts to create an, "American-feminine speaking personality" to compensate for her "strong and bossy" Chinese voice. She then recalls a Chinese American classmate who refuses to speak unless reading aloud (and whispering even then). The narrator, as a child, finds some similarities between herself and the "quiet girl" and has a largely irrational hatred for the girl—perhaps because they do share some attributes. One day in sixth grade, the narrator and the quiet girl are alone in the lavatory. The narrator tries to force the girl to speak— threatening her, hurting her, and even bribing her. When the girl cries but will not speak, the narrator ends up crying in frustration. After this encounter, the narrator is kept at home for eighteen months by a "mysterious illness." When she returns to school, she discovers that the girl has not changed. She remains immune to social pressures, and is sheltered even into adulthood by her family.

Selection Starter

Build background. Point out that in the passages surrounding this excerpt, Kingston elaborates on the differences in communication between Chinese immigrants and native-born Americans. According to the narrator's father, American speech and music were too soft for the Chinese to enjoy hearing, while Americans found Chinese speech too loud and its sharply varying tones too unfamiliar. The desire of Chinese children to fit in was one reason for their adoption of a quiet persona; another was their need to keep family secrets. Fear of immigration authorities helped motivate such secrecy, because some immigrants had arrived as stowaways or with improper papers.

Maxine Hong Kingston   **985**

Previewing Vocabulary

Challenge pairs of students to compose sentences using the Vocabulary words as follows:

1. Compose a sentence using both nouns.
2. Compose a sentence using one of the nouns and one of the other words.
3. Compose a sentence using two of the words that are not nouns.

A **Reading Skills**

❷ Drawing inferences about characters. What can you infer about the quiet girl, based on what the narrator says she heard when walking past the girl's house? [Possible responses: The girl can talk and assert herself at home where she is comfortable; she is very frightened at school.]

A CLOSER LOOK

This feature discusses some of the ways in which Chinese Americans seek to preserve their heritage and sense of community.

B **Reading Informational Text**

❷ Verifying statements. How could you further document what the writer is saying about Chinese names? [Possible responses: by interviewing Chinese Americans; by researching books or Internet resources about Chinese culture]

---

know his father's name. We laughed and were relieved that our parents had had the foresight to tell us some names we could give the teachers. "If you're not stupid," I said to the quiet girl, "what's your name?" She shook her head, and some hair caught in the tears; wet black hair stuck to the side of the pink and white face. I reached up (she was taller than I) and took a strand of hair. I pulled it. "Well, then, let's honk your hair," I said. "Honk. Honk." Then I pulled the other side—"ho-o-n-nk"—a long pull; "ho-o-n-n-nk"—a longer pull. I could see her little white ears, like white cutworms curled underneath the hair. "Talk!" I yelled into each cutworm.

A I looked right at her. "I know you talk," I said. "I've heard you." Her eyebrows flew up. Something in those black eyes was startled, and I pursued it. "I was walking past your house when you didn't know I was there. I heard you yell in English and in Chinese. You weren't just talking.

You were shouting. I heard you shout. You were saying, 'Where are you?' Say that again. Go ahead, just the way you did at home." I yanked harder on the hair, but steadily, not jerking. I did not want to pull it out. "Go ahead. Say, 'Where are you?' Say it loud enough for your sister to come. Call her. Make her come help you. Call her name. I'll stop if she comes. So call. Go ahead."

She shook her head, her mouth curved down, crying. I could see her tiny white teeth, baby teeth. I wanted to grow big strong yellow teeth. "You do have a tongue," I said. "So use it." I pulled the hair at her temples, pulled the tears out of her eyes. "Say, 'Ow,'" I said. "Just 'Ow.' Say, 'Let go.' Go ahead. Say it. I'll honk you again

---

Vocabulary

temples (tem′pəlz) *n. pl.:* sides of the forehead, just above and in front of the ears.

A CLOSER LOOK: CULTURAL INFLUENCES

The Chinese American Family

In her story, Maxine Hong Kingston mentions that the girl who wouldn't talk was supported and protected by her family. This isn't surprising, given the importance of family relationships in Chinese culture. As the Chinese American writer Leslie Li notes, solitude is not a coveted state among most Chinese people. "They love their family and friends and want them around, along with the *renao* they bring, the heat and noise of human relationships."

B **Family ties.** In Chinese culture, one's name does not so much signify individual identity as relationship to others, such as daughter, son, aunt, uncle, and so on. In Chinese tradition the family name is given first—for example, "Chan Jackie," not the Americanized "Jackie Chan"—and family members are often introduced not by their names but by their family relationships. Children may address family members not

by name but as Aunt, Second Older Brother, Grandfather, and so on. In Kingston's story a boy is laughed at in class because he doesn't know his father's name; at home, he says, his father is called only "father of me." In the story "Rules of the Game" by the Chinese American writer

> **INFORMATIONAL TEXT**

Literary Criticism

Critic's Commentary: Finding a Voice
Scholar Amy Ling writes: "A major theme in Kingston's *The Woman Warrior* is the importance of articulateness. Finding one's voice and telling one's stories represents power, just as having one's stories buried is powerlessness." Have students discuss how this comment relates to "The Girl Who Wouldn't Talk."

if you don't say, 'Let me alone.' Say, 'Leave me alone,' and I'll let you go. I will. I'll let go if you say it. You can stop this anytime you want to, you know. All you have to do is tell me to stop. Just say, 'Stop.' You're just asking for it, aren't you? You're just asking for another honk. Well then, I'll have to give you another honk. Say, 'Stop.' " But she didn't. I had to pull again and again.

Sounds did come out of her mouth, sobs, chokes, noises that were almost words. Snot ran out of her nose. She tried to wipe it on her hands, but there was too much of it. She used her sleeve. "You're disgusting," I told her. "Look at you, snot streaming down your nose, and you won't say a word to stop it. You're such a nothing." I moved behind her and pulled the hair growing out of her weak neck. I let go. I stood silent for a long time. Then I screamed, "Talk!" I would scare the words out of her. If she had had

little bound feet, the toes twisted under the balls, I would have jumped up and landed on them—crunch!—stomped on them with my iron shoes. She cried hard, sobbing aloud. "Cry, 'Mama,' " I said. "Come on. Cry, 'Mama.' Say, 'Stop it.' "

I put my finger on her pointed chin. "I don't like you. I don't like the weak little toots you make on your flute. Wheeze. Wheeze. I don't like the way you don't swing at the ball. I don't like the way you're the last one chosen. I don't like the way you can't make a fist for tetherball. Why don't you make a fist? Come on. Get tough. Come on. Throw fists." I pushed at her long hands; they swung limply at her sides. Her fingers were so long, I thought maybe they had an extra joint. They couldn't possibly make fists like other people's. "Make a fist," I said. "Come on. Just fold those fingers up; fingers on the inside, thumbs on the outside. Say some-

Amy Tan (page 921), the character Waverly is called "Waverly" for the benefit of outsiders, but at home she is "Meimei" (Little Sister).

Bridging two worlds. Ultimately many Chinese Americans choose to integrate the cultures of both China and the United States in their family life. They embrace some traditional beliefs of their immigrant parents or grandparents, but they also take part in mainstream American traditions. They may celebrate both Chinese and American holidays, for example, or enjoy traditional Chinese foods one day, grilled steak the next. They may use American names with outsiders but their Chinese middle names at home. In addition to attending regular public or private school all day, some Chinese American children spend three or four hours at Chinese school (often held on Saturdays), where their parents expect them to learn Chinese language, literature, history, and philosophy.

Maxine Hong Kingston   991

C Reading Skills

❓ Drawing inferences about characters. Why might the quiet girl be so unresponsive? What more are we learning about the narrator? [Possible responses: She fears the narrator; she has resolved never to talk at school except for reading aloud; she views her silence as a form of strength. The narrator is blaming the quiet girl for being a victim.]

D Reading Informational Text

❓ Evaluating credibility. Does the writer effectively support the statement that many Chinese Americans participate in "mainstream American traditions"? Explain. [Most students will consider the support effective; the writer gives four examples.]

E Content-Area Connections

Culture: Bound Feet
The narrator is referring to the ancient Chinese custom of binding the feet of girls to keep their feet small enough to fit into shoes that were three inches long. This was intended to identify women with high social status. The practice, which crippled generations of upper-class Chinese women, was the object of protests and was finally outlawed in 1911, after the end of the Manchu Dynasty.

A Literary Focus

❓ Character interaction and plot. The plot builds in suspense because the narrator continues to torment the girl despite her hunger and her own fear of staying so late in the building. Why does this struggle mean so much to her? [Possible response: The narrator feels she must dominate the quiet girl, bend the girl to her will, perhaps to prove that her own decision to assimilate rather than to fade away in silence is the better path.]

B Literary Focus

❓ Characterization. How does the ongoing verbal assault help to characterize the narrator and the quiet girl? [Possible response: By not responding, the girl reinforces the narrator's view that she is weak and fearful. By continuing to terrorize the girl, the narrator displays her cruelty—and her own issues of self-identity.]

C Vocabulary Development

Multiple meanings of words. Point out that one meaning of *dumb* is "mute, not speaking, or unable to speak"—a definition that fits the quiet girl's behavior. The more common meaning, however, is "unintelligent"—a definition that probably does not fit her but that the narrator uses to try to shame the girl into speaking.

D Literary Focus

❓ Cultural influences on plot. How does the narrator use cultural pressure to try to manipulate the girl? [Possible response: She says that a silent girl will not find a husband. Marriage was a goal of many American girls in the 1950s, so her claim is meant to apply pressure.]

---

thing. Honk me back. You're so tall, and you let me pick on you.

"Would you like a hanky? I can't get you one with embroidery on it or crocheting along the edges, but I'll get you some toilet paper if you tell me to. Go ahead. Ask me. I'll get it for you if you ask." She did not stop crying. "Why don't you scream, 'Help'?" I suggested. "Say, 'Help.' Go ahead." She cried on. "O.K. O.K. Don't talk. Just scream, and I'll let you go. Won't that feel good? Go ahead. Like this." I screamed not too loudly.

A My voice hit the tile and rang it as if I had thrown a rock at it. The stalls opened wider and the toilets wider and darker. Shadows leaned at angles I had not seen before. It was very late. Maybe a janitor had locked me in with this girl for the night. Her black eyes blinked and stared, blinked and stared. I felt dizzy from hunger. We had been in this lavatory together forever. My mother would call the police again if I didn't bring my sister home

B soon. "I'll let you go if you say just one word," I said. "You can even say 'a' or 'the,' and I'll let you go. Come on. Please." She didn't shake her head anymore, only cried steadily, so much water coming out of her. I could see the two duct holes where the tears welled out. Quarts of tears but no words. I grabbed her by the shoulder. I could feel bones. The light was coming in queerly through the frosted glass with the chicken wire embedded in it. Her crying was like an animal's—a seal's—and it echoed around the basement. "Do you want to stay here all night?" I asked. "Your mother is wondering what happened to her baby. You wouldn't want to have her mad at you. You'd better say something." I shook her shoulder. I pulled her hair again. I squeezed her face. "Come on! Talk! Talk! Talk!" She didn't seem to feel it anymore when I pulled her hair. "There's nobody here but you

and me. This isn't a classroom or a playground or a crowd. I'm just one person. You can talk in front of one person. Don't make me pull harder and harder until you talk." But her hair seemed to stretch; she did not say a word. "I'm going to pull harder. Don't make me pull anymore, or your hair will come out and you're going to be bald. Do you want to be bald? You don't want to be bald, do you?"

Far away, coming from the edge of town, I heard whistles blow. The cannery was changing shifts, letting out the afternoon people, and still we were here at school. It was a sad sound—work done. The air was lonelier after the sound died.

"Why won't you talk?" I started to cry. What if I couldn't stop, and everyone would want to know what happened? "Now look what you've done," I scolded.

"You're going to pay for this. I want to know why. And you're going to tell me why. You don't see I'm trying to help you out, do you? Do you want **C** to be like this, dumb (do you know what dumb means?), your whole life? Don't you ever want to be a cheerleader? Or a pom-pom girl? What are you going to do for a living? Yeah, you're going to have to work because you can't be a housewife. Somebody has to marry you before you can be a housewife. And you, you are a plant. Do you know that? That's all you are if you don't talk. If you don't talk, you **D** can't have a personality. You'll have no personality and no hair. You've got to let people know you have a personality and a brain. You think somebody is going to take care of you all your stupid life? You think you'll always have your big sister? You think somebody's going to marry you, is that it? Well, you're not the type that gets dates, let alone gets married. Nobody's going to notice you. And you have to talk for interviews,

> "I'll let you go if you say just one word," I said. "You can even say 'a' or 'the,' and I'll let you go. Come on. Please."

speak right up in front of the boss. Don't you know that? You're so dumb. Why do I waste my time on you?" Sniffling and snorting, I couldn't stop crying and talking at the same time. I kept wiping my nose on my arm, my sweater lost somewhere (probably not worn because my mother said to wear a sweater). It seemed as if I had spent my life in that basement, doing the worst thing I had yet done to another person. "I'm doing this for your own good," I said. "Don't you dare tell anyone I've been bad to you. Talk. Please talk."

I was getting dizzy from the air I was gulping. Her sobs and my sobs were bouncing wildly off the tile, sometimes together, sometimes alternating. "I don't understand why you won't say just one word," I cried, clenching my teeth. My knees were shaking, and I hung on to her hair to stand up. Another time I'd stayed too late, I had had to walk around two Negro kids who were bonking each other's head on the concrete. I went back later to see if the concrete had cracks in it. "Look. I'll give you something if you talk. I'll give you my pencil box. I'll buy you some candy. O.K.? What do you want? Tell me. Just say it, and I'll give it to you. Just say, 'yes,' or, 'O.K.,' or, 'Baby Ruth.'" But she didn't want anything.

I had stopped pinching her cheek because I did not like the feel of her skin. I would go crazy if it came away in my hands. "I skinned her," I would have to confess.

Suddenly I heard footsteps hurrying through the basement, and her sister ran into the lavatory calling her name. "Oh, there you are," I said. "We've been waiting for you. I was only trying to teach her to talk. She wouldn't cooperate, though." Her sister went into one of the stalls and got handfuls of toilet paper and wiped her off. Then we found my sister, and we walked home together. "Your family really ought to force her to speak," I advised all the way home. "You mustn't pamper her."

The world is sometimes just, and I spent the next eighteen months sick in bed with a mysterious illness. There was no pain and no symptoms, though the middle line in my left palm broke in two. Instead of starting junior high school, I lived like the Victorian recluses° I read about. I had a rented hospital bed in the living room, where I watched soap operas on TV, and my family cranked me up and down. I saw no one but my family, who took good care of me. I could have no visitors, no other relatives, no villagers. My bed was against the west window, and I watched the seasons change the peach tree. I had a bell to ring for help. I used a bedpan. It was the best year and a half of my life. Nothing happened.

But one day my mother, the doctor, said, "You're ready to get up today. It's time to get up and go to school." I walked about outside to get my legs working, leaning on a staff I cut from the peach tree. The sky and trees, the sun were immense—no longer framed by a window, no longer grayed with a fly screen. I sat down on the sidewalk in amazement—the night, the stars. But at school I had to figure out again how to talk. I met again the poor girl I had tormented. She had not changed. She wore the same clothes, hair cut, and manner as when we were in elementary school, no make-up on the pink and white face, while the other Asian girls were starting to tape their eyelids. She continued to be able to read aloud. But there was hardly any reading aloud anymore, less and less as we got into high school.

I was wrong about nobody taking care of her. Her sister became a clerk-typist and stayed unmarried. They lived with their mother and father. She did not have to leave the house except to go to the movies. She was supported. She was protected by her family, as they would normally have done in China if they could have afforded it, not sent off to school with strangers, ghosts, boys. ∎

° **Victorian recluses:** characters in Victorian novels who, because of some illness or incapacity, lived shut away from the world.

Response and Analysis

Reading Check

1. She regards the girl as weak. The others consider her unfriendly.

2. The narrator abuses her physically and verbally. The girl seems alarmed but endures the torments with tears and sobs and still refuses to speak.

3. The narrator falls ill and spends a year and a half in bed.

Thinking Critically

Possible Answers

4. The narrator seems angry at her own family, at American society, at herself, and at the conflict between assimilation and tradition. Her internal conflict consists of wondering if she will be accepted by American society.

5. The narrator does not say if the classmates agreed that "normal Chinese women's voices are loud and bossy," if they ever accepted the boy they ridiculed, or how they reacted to the narrator's illness. In short, she says little about her white classmates.

6. The images make the quiet girl seem weak to the narrator, and that response makes the reader view the narrator as mean.

7. The girl may view her silence as a badge of honor; she may wish that she could respond more effectively.

8. She may have hated school and the stress of growing up between cultures. She needed this time alone before she could appreciate the world again. Perhaps she came to accept how similar she was to the silent girl.

9. The fact that "solitude is not a coveted state among most Chinese people" helps readers grasp the power in the narrator's taunt that the quiet girl

---

Response and Analysis

Reading Check

1. What reasons does the narrator give for hating the silent girl? What do the other students think of the silent one?

2. How does the narrator try to make the silent girl talk? How does the girl respond?

3. What happens to the narrator to make her say that "the world is sometimes just"?

Thinking Critically

4. The narrator's intense anger seems directed solely at the silent girl, but why is she so angry with her? Perhaps she is angry for other reasons and not admitting her feelings. Is she affected by an **internal conflict**—a struggle occurring in her own mind? Explain your response, using details from the text.

5. The author **characterizes** the narrator by showing us what she says, does, thinks, and feels, but we can also make inferences about her character based on what she does *not* express. What, for example, do you think the narrator does *not* say about her white American classmates? (Check your reading notes.)

6. **Imagery** is the use of language to evoke a picture of a person, a place, or a thing. Find the images that Kingston uses to help us imagine the silent girl's skin, her fingers, her ears, and her crying. What do these images reveal about the narrator's feelings toward the silent girl? What can you infer about the narrator from her description of the girl?

7. The silent girl is obviously able to speak. Why do you think she does not speak? (Review the notes you made while reading.) What do you imagine she is thinking and feeling—but not saying?

8. What inference can you draw from the fact that the narrator says that her time in bed "was the best year and a half of my life"? What discoveries about herself or about the silent girl might she have made during that time?

9. Review *A Closer Look* on pages 990–991 about the Chinese American family. Do any details in this feature connect with details in Kingston's memoir? How do you think the story would have differed if the narrator had been a member of a different culture?

Extending and Evaluating

10. A character's **motivation** is what causes him or her to act the way he or she does. Motivation can come from needs, fears, and desires. What do you think is the motivation behind the narrator's wanting to make the silent girl speak? Do her feelings and actions strike you as believable? Give reasons for your evaluation based on your own experiences.

SKILLS FOCUS

Literary Skills
Analyze characterization.

Reading Skills
Make inferences about characters.

Writing Skills
Write a character analysis.

Vocabulary Skills
Complete word analogies.

---

never would find a husband; the reference to the importance of Chinese school sheds light on the narrator's discomfort over staying so long after school. Students may suggest that if the narrator had not been Chinese, she might have ignored the quiet girl, or taunted her in a different way.

Extending and Evaluating

10. To the narrator, the quiet girl represents an image of submissiveness brought on by fear of what white Americans think of Chinese Americans. The narrator's compulsion to make the girl speak may reflect the narrator's rejection of such an image. Students may suggest that the feeling is believable.

Vocabulary Development

1. sarcastic
2. loitered
3. habitually
4. temples
5. nape

ASSESSING

Assessment

■ *Holt Assessment: Literature, Reading, and Vocabulary*

WRITING

Tortured Character

Write a brief **character analysis** of the narrator. (Be sure to review your reading notes.) Focus on how this character is revealed through her words, actions, appearance, private thoughts, and influence on others. Before you write, gather details from the text in a cluster diagram like the one below:

Conclude your analysis by discussing your own assessment of the narrator with a classmate.

Vocabulary Development

Analogies

loitered   sarcastic
nape   temples
habitually

In an **analogy** the words in one pair relate to each other in the same way as the words relate in a second pair. Fill in each blank below with the Vocabulary word that best completes the analogy:

1. *Scarlet* is to *color* as _____ is to *tone.*
2. *Swell* is to *shrink* as _____ is to *rushed.*
3. *Rarely* is to *seldom* as _____ is to *usually.*
4. *Nostrils* are to *nose* as _____ are to *forehead.*
5. *Sole* is to *foot* as _____ is to *neck.*

Grade-Level Skills

■ **Reading Skills**

Identify main ideas and supporting details.

Review Skills

■ **Literary Skills**

Analyze the importance of the setting to the mood, tone, and meaning of the text.

More About the Writer

Background. When N. Scott Momaday was a youngster, his family lived at various times on the Navajo reservation, two Apache reservations, and at the Pueblo of Jemez. Thus, Momaday had "a Pan-Indian experience before [he] knew what that term meant."

Momaday once said: "I can take credit for setting down those Kiowa stories in English, in *The Way to Rainy Mountain,* but I didn't invent them. The imagination that informs those stories is really not mine, though it exists, I think, in my blood. It's an ancestral imagination."

N. Scott Momaday
(1934–   )

Among American voices, one that has made itself heard at long last is that of the Native American. Previously American Indians were presented in literature and the other arts as the crudest of stereotypes, either as noble, primitive warriors or as fearsome, ignorant savages. One has only to look at westerns—movies from the 1940s and 1950s—to see how blatant the stereotypes were. Even American history textbooks seldom questioned the popular view that the white settlers' gradual "winning" of the West was a virtuous struggle against the unwarranted resistance of American Indians. Few Americans gave much thought either to the moral basis on which the United States expanded or to the history of the American Indians.

When the civil rights movement of the 1950s and 1960s brought discrimination against African Americans to the forefront of public discussion, other minority groups began to demand a fairer social and political standing for themselves. Native Americans spoke loudly and clearly of loss, injustice, and prejudice.

Navarre Scott Momaday was born in Lawton, Oklahoma, of Kiowa ancestry on his father's side, and some Cherokee on his mother's. After receiving an undergraduate degree from the University of New Mexico, Momaday studied creative writing at Stanford University, where he earned a doctorate.

But Momaday broke loose from the standard academic mold with three works grounded in his knowledge of American Indian life: a Pulitzer Prize–winning novel, *House Made of Dawn* (1968), and two memoirs, *The Way to Rainy Mountain* (1969) and *The Names* (1976).

The Way to Rainy Mountain is part legend, part history, and part poetry, with striking illustrations by Momaday's father, Alfred Momaday. Following the introduction, Momaday describes Kiowa history in a form that is associative and imagistic; it works on

the reader's imagination in subtle ways that do not depend on a straightforward narrative. On one page he sets down a Kiowa myth or legend; on the facing page he places a short excerpt from a traditional history and then a personal memory of his own. In the mind of the reader, the inner truth blends with the outer; emotion mixes with fact.

The Kiowas' journey to Rainy Mountain begins in the hidden mists of time, when a tribe of unknown origin descends from the headwaters of the Yellowstone River eastward to the Black Hills (in present-day South Dakota) and south to the Wichita Mountains. It ends in a cemetery where many of Momaday's Kiowa relatives are buried. Momaday says that "the journey is an evocation of three things in particular: a landscape that is incomparable, a time that is gone forever, and the human spirit, which endures."

The incomparable landscape is the Great Plains, wind-swept and lonely, in turn brilliant with summer sun and buried in winter snows. Momaday's love of the land where he grew up suffuses everything he writes. He reminds us of both the spiritual richness and the rigors of living close to the land, under a wide, open sky, in harmony with the changing seasons. In his work, Momaday has looked at his own particular landscape from so many angles that his pictures often shimmer like prisms.

996　Collection 6　Contemporary Literature: 1939 to Present

Before You Read

from The Way to Rainy Mountain

Make the Connection

Why do we honor the generations that preceded us? Perhaps it's because we realize that not only did they build civilizations and give us life—but also that they *knew* something. We search in thousands of ways for the secrets of what they must have known. We search in history, archaeology, anthropology, art, linguistics, architecture, music, mythology, literature. In many ways, what we are doing as we search for the past is searching for knowledge of ourselves.

Literary Focus

Setting

Like a storyteller, Momaday is a master at describing **setting,** the time and location in which events occur or in which characters are placed. The following excerpt from Momaday's memoir contains descriptions of several settings. In some cases, Momaday's description is made up of just one or two well-chosen images. Note how these settings are used to create mood, or atmosphere.

> **Setting** is the time and location in which events occur or in which characters are placed.
>
> *For more on Setting, see the Handbook of Literary and Historical Terms.*

Reading Skills

Identifying Main Ideas and Supporting Details

As you read (or as you re-read), take notes on Momaday's **main ideas** and their **supporting details.** Use the following format for your notes:

Main idea:
Supporting detail:
Supporting detail:

Background

This excerpt from *The Way to Rainy Mountain* is not a straightforward narrative. Momaday uses frequent **flashbacks** to earlier times, and he often omits transitional passages. The text is like a poem in which the narrator traces, in his imagination, the heroic and ultimately tragic history of his people, the Kiowas.

Vocabulary Development

infirm (in·fʉrm′) *adj.*: physically weak.

preeminently (prē·em′ə·nənt·lē) *adv.*: above all else.

luxuriant (lug·zhoor′ē·ənt) *adj.*: rich; abundant.

tenuous (ten′yōō·əs) *adj.*: slight; insubstantial; not firm.

wariness (wer′ē·nis) *n.*: carefulness; caution.

disperse (di·spʉrs′) *v.*: scatter.

opaque (ō·pāk′) *adj.*: not transparent; not letting light pass through.

vital (vīt′'l) *adj.*: filled with life.

enmities (en′mə·tēz) *n. pl.*: hatreds.

indulge (in·dulj′) *v.*: satisfy; please; humor.

go.hrw.com

INTERNET
Vocabulary Practice
Keyword: LE5 11–6

SKILLS FOCUS

Literary Skills
Understand setting.

Reading Skills
Identify main ideas and supporting details.

N. Scott Momaday   **997**

VIEWING THE ART

Although the word *powwow* originally referred to a spiritual healer, a new meaning for the term has recently developed. It was only in the late nineteenth century that Native Americans began to hold powwows, or meetings, to celebrate their heritage. This photograph was taken at a powwow in 1946, a time when the popular view of Native Americans was rife with stereotypes.

Activity. Ask students to discuss what mood this photograph conveys. What might this woman be reflecting on as she listens to the sound of the powwow going on in the background? [Possible responses: The mood is reflective, peaceful, sad. She might be old enough to be remembering great moments of Kiowa history.]

Kosahn, a blind Kiowa woman, at Carnegie, Oklahoma, powwow (1946). Photo by Pierre Tartoue.

Tartoue Negative Collection, 20912.14.150. Archives and Manuscripts Division of the Oklahoma Historical Society.

from

THE WAY TO RAINY MOUNTAIN

N. Scott Momaday

998 Collection 6 Contemporary Literature: 1939 to Present

DIFFERENTIATING INSTRUCTION

Learners Having Difficulty
Modeling. Model the skill of identifying the main idea and supporting details. Say, "I read at the beginning this main idea: The weather at Rainy Mountain is 'the hardest weather in the world.' I look for which details in the paragraph support this main idea. I find 'the grass turns brittle and brown.' " Ask students where other main ideas and supporting details appear together.

English-Language Learners
Students will benefit from a discussion of topographical terms used in the selection. Give them a list of the following words, and discuss the definitions with them:

knoll, prairie, groves, range, plains, canyon, high country, highland meadow, creek. Photographs or drawings of the types of landscapes found along the route of the Kiowa migration also may be helpful.

A single knoll rises out of the plain in Oklahoma north and west of the Wichita Range. For my people, the Kiowas, it is an old landmark, and they gave it the name Rainy Mountain. The hardest weather in the world is there. Winter brings blizzards, hot tornadic winds arise in the spring, and in summer the prairie is an anvil's edge. The grass turns brittle and brown, and it cracks beneath your feet. There are green belts along the rivers and creeks, linear groves of hickory and pecan, willow and witch hazel. At a distance in July or August the steaming foliage seems almost to writhe in fire. Great green and yellow grasshoppers are everywhere in the tall grass, popping up like corn to sting the flesh, and tortoises crawl about on the red earth, going nowhere in the plenty of time. Loneliness is an aspect of the land. All things in the plain are isolate; there is no confusion of objects in the eye, but *one* hill or *one* tree or *one* man. To look upon that landscape in the early morning, with the sun at your back, is to lose the sense of proportion. Your imagination comes to life, and this, you think, is where Creation was begun. ❶

Devils Tower, Wyoming.

❶
❓ Why is Rainy Mountain so important to the writer?

I returned to Rainy Mountain in July. My grandmother had died in the spring, and I wanted to be at her grave. She had lived to be very old and at last infirm. Her only living daughter was with her when she died, and I was told that in death her face was that of a child.

I like to think of her as a child. When she was born, the Kiowas were living that last great moment of their history. For more than a hundred years they had controlled the open range from the Smoky Hill River to the Red, from the headwaters of the Canadian to the fork of the Arkansas and Cimarron. In alliance with the Comanches, they had ruled the whole of the southern Plains. War was their sacred business, and they were among the finest horsemen the world has ever known. But warfare for the Kiowas was preeminently a matter of disposition rather than of survival, and they never understood the grim, unrelenting advance of the U.S. Cavalry. When at last, divided and ill-provisioned, they were driven onto the Staked Plains in the cold rains of autumn, they fell into panic. In Palo Duro Canyon they abandoned their crucial stores to pillage[1] and had nothing then but their lives. In order to save themselves, they surrendered to the soldiers at Fort Sill and were imprisoned in the old stone corral that now stands as a military museum. My grandmother was spared the humiliation of those high gray walls by eight or ten years, but she must have known from birth the affliction of defeat, the dark brooding of old warriors. ❷

❷
❓ Why did the Kiowas surrender to the U.S. Cavalry?

Her name was Aho, and she belonged to the last culture to evolve in North America. Her forebears came down from the high country in western Montana nearly three centuries ago. They were a mountain people, a mysterious tribe of hunters whose language has never been positively classified in any major group. In the late seventeenth century they began a long migration to the south and east. It was a journey toward the dawn, and it led to a golden age. Along the way the Kiowas were befriended by the Crows, who gave them the culture and religion of the Plains. They acquired horses, and their ancient nomadic spirit was suddenly free

1. **pillage** *n.*: loot; that which is stolen.

Vocabulary
infirm (in·fʉrm′) *adj.*: physically weak.
preeminently (prē·em′ə·nənt·lē) *adv.*: above all else.

N. Scott Momaday   **999**

DIRECT TEACHING

Ⓐ Literary Focus
❓ **Setting.** What word would you use to describe the setting the author portrays in this paragraph? [Possible responses: rugged, harsh, desolate, lonely]

Ⓑ Reading Skills
❓ **Speculating.** In the past, why had warfare for the Kiowas not been a matter of survival? [Possible response: In the past, the Kiowas and their opponents had similar weapons and operated with an understanding and respect of each other's rules of warfare; there was enough land and food for all.]

Ⓒ Learners Having Difficulty
❓ **Summarizing.** Where did the journey of the Kiowas originate and end? In what ways did this journey change them, according to the author? [Possible response: The journey, which started in Montana and ended in the southern Plains, gave the Kiowa people a new culture, which included a new religion and a sense of pride.]

Responses to Boxed Questions
1. It is an old Kiowa landmark. He is Kiowa.
2. The cavalry divided the Kiowa forces, and they had few provisions. The Kiowa surrendered to save themselves.

Advanced Learners
Enrichment. Review or teach the definition of *elegy*. Read a few excerpts from a famous elegy, such as Bryant's "Thanatopsis" (p. 166) or Tennyson's *In Memoriam*. Point out that while most elegies are written in verse, the mournful, pensive tone that is common to them may also be captured in prose. When they have finished reading the selection, ask students to write a paragraph explaining why they think it is or is not an elegy.

A Reading Skills

? Interpreting. What does the author mean when he says that the Kiowas were "bent and blind"? [Possible response: He means that forested mountains limited the Kiowas' vision of themselves and their future.]

B Literary Focus

? Setting. What mood does this description evoke? What words contribute to the mood? [Possible responses: a mood of contentment, expansiveness; words that contribute to the mood include: *luxuriant, unfolds, wonder, immense, billowing.*]

C English-Language Learners

? Interpreting cultural concepts. What words might describe the "character" of a god? [Possible responses: powerful, omnipotent, brilliant.] Discuss how the sun on the plains might be more "godlike" than the sun on the mountains.

D Content-Area Connections

Geography: Devils Tower Devils Tower is a shaft of now-hardened molten rock looming above the Belle Fourche River in Wyoming.

Responses to Boxed Questions

3. They acquired a sense of destiny and pride.

4. He wanted to visit his grandmother's grave.

5. They began to worship the sun when they came to the plains.

---

of the ground. They acquired Tai-me, the sacred Sun Dance doll, from that moment the object and symbol of their worship, and so shared in the divinity of the sun. Not least, they acquired the sense of destiny, therefore courage and pride. When they entered upon the southern Plains they had been transformed. No longer were they slaves to the simple necessity of survival; they were a lordly and dangerous society of fighters and thieves, hunters and priests of the sun. According to their origin myth, they entered the world through a hollow log. From one point of view, their migration was the fruit of an old prophecy, for indeed they emerged from a sunless world. ❸

> ❸ **?** How did the Kiowas become transformed as a result of their long migration south and east?

Although my grandmother lived out her long life in the shadow of Rainy Mountain, the immense landscape of the continental interior lay like memory in her blood. She could tell of the Crows, whom she had never seen, and of the Black Hills, where she had never been. I wanted to see in reality what she had seen more perfectly in the mind's eye, and traveled fifteen hundred miles to begin my pilgrimage. ❹

> ❹ **?** Why did the narrator decide to return to Rainy Mountain?

Yellowstone, it seemed to me, was the top of the world, a region of deep lakes and dark timber, canyons and waterfalls. But, beautiful as it is, one might have the sense of confinement there. The skyline in all directions is close at hand, the high wall of the woods and deep cleavages of shade. There is a perfect freedom in the mountains, but it belongs to the eagle and the elk, the badger and the bear. The Kiowas reckoned their stature by the distance they could see, and they were bent and blind in the wilderness. ❹

Descending eastward, the highland meadows are a stairway to the plain. In July the inland slope of the Rockies is luxuriant with flax and buckwheat, stonecrop and larkspur. The earth unfolds and the limit of the land recedes. Clus-

ters of trees, and animals grazing far in the distance, cause the vision to reach away and wonder to build upon the mind. The sun follows a longer course in the day, and the sky is immense beyond all comparison. The great billowing clouds that sail upon it are shadows that move upon the grain like water, dividing light. Farther down, in the land of the Crows and Blackfeet, the plain is yellow. Sweet clover takes hold of the hills and bends upon itself to cover and seal the soil. There the Kiowas paused on their way; they had come to the place where they must change their lives. The sun is at home on the plains. Precisely there does it have the certain character of a god. When the Kiowas came to the land of the Crows, they could see the dark lees[2] of the hills at dawn across the Bighorn River, the profusion of light on the grain shelves, the oldest deity ranging after the solstices.[3] Not yet would they veer southward to the caldron of the land that lay below; they must wean their blood from the northern winter and hold the mountains a while longer in their view. They bore Tai-me in procession to the east. ❺

> ❺ **?** What does this paragraph tell you about the Kiowas' religious beliefs?

A dark mist lay over the Black Hills, and the land was like iron. At the top of a ridge I caught sight of Devils Tower upthrust against the gray sky as if in the birth of time the core of the earth had broken through its crust and the motion of the world was begun. There are things in nature that engender[4] an awful quiet in the heart of man; Devils Tower is one of them. Two centuries ago, because they could not do otherwise, the Kiowas made a legend at the base of the rock. My grandmother said:

---

2. **lees** *n. pl.:* shelters.
3. **solstices** *n. pl.:* The solstices are the points where the sun is farthest north and farthest south of the celestial equator, creating the longest day (June 21) and the shortest day (December 21) of sunlight in the Northern Hemisphere.
4. **engender** *v.:* cause; produce.

Vocabulary
luxuriant (lug·zhoor′ē·ənt) *adj.:* rich; abundant.

CONTENT-AREA CONNECTIONS

Literature: Legends
Individual activity. Discuss the legend (or myth) of the seven sisters, the brother/bear, and the Big Dipper. Ask students to create a legend explaining a natural phenomenon. They should try to write a legend that might help a certain group of people give meaning to something in their world that is otherwise inexplicable. Point out that many legends involve metamorphosis, and encourage students to include such transformations in their legends.

Eight children were there at play, seven sisters and their brother. Suddenly the boy was struck dumb; he trembled and began to run upon his hands and feet. His fingers became claws, and his body was covered with fur. Directly there was a bear where the boy had been. The sisters were terrified; they ran, and the bear after them. They came to the stump of a great tree, and the tree spoke to them. It bade them climb upon it, and as they did so it began to rise into the air. The bear came to kill them, but they were just beyond its reach. It reared against the tree and scored the bark all around with its claws. The seven sisters were borne into the sky, and they became the stars of the Big Dipper.

From that moment, and so long as the legend lives, the Kiowas have kinsmen in the night sky. Whatever they were in the mountains, they could be no more. However tenuous their well-being, however much they had suffered and would suffer again, they had found a way out of the wilderness. **G**

My grandmother had a reverence for the sun, a holy regard that now is all but gone out of mankind. There was a <u>wariness</u> in her, and an

? **6** What does it mean that the Kiowas "have kinsmen in the night sky"?

ancient awe. She was a Christian in her later years, but she had come a long way about, and she never forgot her birthright. As a child she had been to the Sun Dances; she had taken part in those annual rites, and by them she had learned the restoration of her people in the presence of Tai-me. She was about seven when the last Kiowa Sun Dance was held in 1887 on the Washita River above Rainy Mountain Creek. The buffalo were gone. **F** In order to consummate[5] the ancient sacrifice—to impale the head of a buffalo bull upon the medicine tree—a delegation of old men journeyed into Texas, there to beg and barter for an animal from the Goodnight herd. She was ten when the Kiowas came together for the last time as a living Sun Dance culture. They could find no buffalo; they had to hang an old hide from the sacred tree. Before the dance could begin, a company of soldiers rode out from Fort Sill under orders to disperse the tribe. Forbidden without cause the <u>essential</u> act of their faith, having seen the wild herds slaughtered and left to rot upon the ground, the Kiowas backed away forever from the medicine tree. That was July 20, 1890, at the great bend of the Washita. My grandmother was there. Without bitterness, and for as long as she lived, she bore a vision of deicide.[6] **?** **H**

? **7** In what sense had his grandmother witnessed deicide, the murder of a god?

Now that I can have her only in memory, I see my grandmother in the several postures that

---

5. **consummate** *v.:* finish; make complete.
6. **deicide** (dē'ə·sīd') *n.:* murder of a god.

Vocabulary
tenuous (ten'yōō·əs) *adj.:* slight; insubstantial; not firm.
wariness (wer'ē·nis) *n.:* carefulness; caution.
disperse (di·spurs') *v.:* scatter.

N. Scott Momaday   **1001**

READING SKILLS REVIEW

Analyzing text structures for comparison/contrast. Momaday uses comparison and contrast to show changes for the Kiowa and his family. But rather than stating them directly, he expects readers to make connections between passages.

Activity.

1. On pp. 999 and 1000, Momaday describes homes of the Kiowas. Have students make a chart that shows the similarities and differences among their home in what is now Montana, their home in what is Wyoming and South Dakota, and their home in what is Oklahoma.

2. Have students locate passages in which Momaday contrasts his grandmother's house when she was alive with the house after her death (pp. 1002–1003).

3. Discuss the contrast in the Kiowas' life before and after the arrival of whites.

DIRECT TEACHING

E **Reading Skills**

? **Synthesizing.** Why might the legend be important to Kiowas? [Possible response: Kiowas judged themselves by how far they could see; "kinsmen" in the heavens looking down at Earth raised Kiowa stature.]

F **Content-Area Connections**
Geography: Buffalo
To the Kiowa, the buffalo provided both material and spiritual essentials. By 1885, however, the buffalo were gone. Students may want to do research to learn how the Kiowa used the various parts of the buffalo and why the buffalo disappeared.

G **Reading Skills**

? **Identifying cause and effect.** Why was the Sun Dance so important to the Kiowas? Why did the government send soldiers to stop it? [Possible responses: The Sun Dance unified the Kiowas and reaffirmed their pride as a people. Perhaps the government feared the power of religion.]

H **Reading Skills**

? **Identifying main idea and supporting details.** Supporting details may come *before* a stated main idea. What details lead up to and support the idea that killing off the buffalo was deicide? [White settlers had herded and killed off the buffalo, which were integral to the Kiowas' worship of their deity; the soldiers forcibly prevented the Kiowas from worshipping.]

Responses to Boxed Questions

6. According to legend, seven Kiowa girls were transformed into the stars that form the Big Dipper.

7. When the Kiowa could no longer perform the Sun Dance, they lost an essential part of their culture.

N. Scott Momaday   **1001**

Grade-Level Skills

■ **Literary Skills**
Analyze characteristics of subgenres of nonfiction, including personal essays.

■ **Reading Skills**
Analyze the main idea.

More About the Writer

Background. During an interview Alice Walker was once asked why she wrote. She responded, "I'm really paying homage to people I love, the people who are thought to be dumb and backward but who were the ones who first taught me to see beauty."

Alice Walker

(1944–   )

In her poetry, essays, and novels, Alice Walker has celebrated the endurance, the strength, and the creativity of African American women like her mother—unsung women who carried immense familial and social burdens even as they struggled against low status and a complete lack of recognition.

Walker was born in Eatonton, Georgia, and grew up on a succession of farms in the area. Her father was a sharecropper, and her mother labored side-by-side with him in the fields, cared for their eight children, and still never failed, wherever they were living, to cultivate a large and beautiful flower garden. Her mother's hard work and determination to enrich her own life have served as an inspiration to Walker throughout her career.

A childhood accident that blinded Walker in one eye made her feel for a time disfigured and outcast. Seeking solace, she turned to writing poetry and reading, and also to closely observing people around her. Walker later attended Spelman College in Atlanta for two and a half years, before transferring to Sarah Lawrence College, near New York City. There she studied with the noted poet Muriel Rukeyser before graduating in 1965.

During her college years, Walker was active in the civil rights movement in Georgia and Mississippi, and she traveled in Africa. Many of the poems in her first published collection, *Once: Poems* (1968), were inspired by these activities. The poems were written in a burst of creativity while Walker was at Sarah Lawrence. As quickly as she completed a poem, she would rush over to Muriel Rukeyser's classroom (a converted gardener's cottage in the center of the campus) and shove it under the door, then go back to her own room and write some more. This immense outpouring of creative energy continued night and day for the short period it lasted, but Walker didn't

even care what Rukeyser did with the poems —the point was the creative surge of expression, not the end goal of publication. But the result was that Rukeyser gave the poems to her agent, and *Once: Poems* was published a few years later.

After graduating from college, Walker began a career of teaching and writing. She was among the first to teach university courses on the work of African American women writers, and she has since brought an understanding of their work to a wider audience. Walker edited an important collection of the writings of Zora Neale Hurston (page 762) called *I Love Myself When I Am Laughing . . .* (1979). In addition to poetry, short stories, and essays, Walker has written a number of well-received novels, including the Pulitzer Prize–winning *The Color Purple* (1982).

According to the critic Donna Haisty Winchell, Walker "comes across in her writing from the 1980s and 1990s as a woman at peace with herself and with the universe. Some of the anger of her youth remains, but it is more tempered and more focused." This mellowing is evident in her 1983 collection of essays, *In Search of Our Mothers' Gardens.* In 1996, Walker published *The Same River Twice,* a memoir about the filming of her novel *The Color Purple.*

Before You Read

from In Search of Our Mothers' Gardens

Make the Connection

The selection that follows is the second part of an essay about the creative spirit of African American women. In this section of her personal essay, Walker attempts to answer some questions she raises earlier: What did it mean for black women of previous generations to be artists? How were black women able to be creative despite limited opportunity and freedom? Walker explores these questions by examining her mother's own life.

Literary Focus
Personal Essay

There are two types of essays, formal essays, such as Thomas Paine's *The Crisis* (see page 87), and informal essays, sometimes called personal essays. A **personal essay** is a short prose work of nonfiction that explores a topic in a personal way. Some of the best personal essays show how the individual experience of the writer connects with larger, more universal concerns. Such essays typically tap deeply into the emotional life of a writer.

> A **personal**, or **informal, essay** is a short prose work of nonfiction that takes a personal look at some topic.
>
> For more on the Essay, see the Handbook of Literary and Historical Terms.

Reading Skills
Identifying the Main Idea: Outlining

Personal essays are often discursive, even rambling—that is, they are not as tightly organized as more formal essays. For that reason, it may be harder to recognize the main idea in a personal essay. When you read Walker's essay for the first time, note each time she introduces a new topic. When you have finished your first reading, go back over the text, and expand your notes into an outline. First, write each main idea you find in her essay on a separate line. Then in an indented list under each main idea, provide details, examples, or anecdotes from the text that support and illustrate each main idea. Review your notes to see if you can find one general, overriding idea that covers *all* these separate ideas. Note also any key passages that seem to point to or support your statement of a main idea. Be sure to consider the significance of the essay's unusual title.

Vocabulary Development

vibrant (vī′brənt) *adj.*: full of energy.

medium (mē′dē·əm) *n.*: material for an artist.

profusely (prō·fyōōs′lē) *adv.*: in great quantities.

conception (kən·sep′shən) *n.*: mental formation of ideas.

ingenious (in·jēn′yəs) *adj.*: clever.

go.
hrw
.com

INTERNET
Vocabulary Practice
•
More About Alice Walker
Keyword: LE5 11-6

SKILLS FOCUS

Literary Skills
Understand a personal, or informal, essay.

Reading Skills
Identify the main idea by outlining.

Alice Walker   1007

PRETEACHING

Summary ⟷ *at grade level*

In this excerpt, Walker details the life of her mother—marriage at seventeen, eight children, unceasing work—and wonders when this woman could "feed the creative spirit." Looking for the answer, Walker recalls a quilt created by an "anonymous black woman." Its beauty demonstrates to Walker that the genius of generations of African American women came through in practical projects passed on to their daughters. Her mother's creative spark, for example, manifested itself in storytelling and in ambitious gardens.

Selection Starter

Build background. You may want to outline for students the first part of Walker's essay, which is not printed here. Walker describes the harsh lives of black women in the South, wonders how the creativity of these women was kept alive in an inhospitable climate, recalls Virginia Woolf's dictum that a writing woman must have a room of her own and money to support herself, and wonders about Phillis Wheatley (p. 60), whose life she describes in detail. Walker then suggests that in looking for the source of black women's creativity, she found the answer to be very close to her.

Skills Starter

Motivate. Invite students to describe the work of a creative writer or visual artist who has inspired them. For example, pictures taken by a photojournalist may have inspired them to write a poem or to analyze a timely topic with friends. Then, have them discuss how the work expresses the writer's or visual artist's philosophical beliefs.

Previewing Vocabulary

Call on students to read aloud the definitions of the Vocabulary words at the bottom of the selection pages. Then, have volunteers use each Vocabulary word in a sentence. To reinforce their understanding of the words, have students complete the following exercise by choosing the Vocabulary word that fits best in each sentence.

1. While he enjoyed working in watercolors, oil was his favorite _____. [medium]

2. The budding inventor came up with a(n) _____ solution to the problem. [ingenious]

3. Weeds sprouted _____ in the untended garden. [profusely]

4. Pictures in _____ colors covered the walls of the room. [vibrant]

5. The witness's _____ of what led to the crash differed from the driver's. [conception]

Grade-Level Skills

■ **Literary Skills**

Analyze the way an author's tone and style achieve specific rhetorical or aesthetic purposes.

■ **Reading Skills**

Make reasonable assertions about an author's argument by using elements of the text to defend interpretations.

More About the Writer

Background. After his 1942 graduation from De Witt Clinton High School, James Baldwin held a number of jobs to support himself while writing book reviews for national publications like *The New Leader* and *The Nation*. He was befriended by Richard Wright (p. 967), who helped him obtain a writing fellowship.

James Baldwin
(1924–1987)

James Baldwin felt compelled to write at length about being an African American "because it was the gate I had to unlock before I could hope to write about anything else." His essays flow from his conviction that a writer's duty is "to examine attitudes, to go beneath the surface, to tap the source."

One of the most controversial and stirring writers of the twentieth century, James Baldwin was born and raised in New York City's Harlem, where his stepfather was the minister of a small evangelical church. As a young man, Baldwin read voraciously and served as a junior minister for a few years at the Fireside Pentecostal Assembly. At the age of twenty-four, he used funds from a fellowship to move to Europe. While living in Paris, he completed his first—and some say best—novel, *Go Tell It on the Mountain* (1953). *Notes of a Native Son,* a collection of autobiographical essays published in 1955, established Baldwin as an American writer of the first rank. The critic Irving Howe said Baldwin was among "the two or three greatest essayists this country has ever produced."

Although he lived much of his life in France, Baldwin never relinquished his U.S. citizenship, and in later years he traveled back to his homeland so often that he considered himself a transatlantic commuter. While abroad, he wrote in a variety of forms, including novels, plays, essays, poetry, and book reviews. Two of Baldwin's plays, *The Amen Corner* (1955) and *Blues for Mister Charlie* (1964), were produced on Broadway.

In the 1950s, the decade that witnessed the early growth of the American civil rights movement, Baldwin's audacious, searing scrutiny of racial injustice played a major role in forcing leaders, black and white, to come to terms with one of the nation's most anguishing problems—the treatment of African Americans. He saw himself as a "disturber of the peace," and some chided him for his unrelenting criticism. For instance, Benjamin DeMott wrote in the *Saturday Review,* "To function as a voice of outrage month after month for a decade and more strains heart and mind, and rhetoric as well; the consequence is a writing style ever on the edge of being winded by too many summonses to intensity."

In the early sixties, Baldwin's reputation grew with the publication of additional essays, *Nobody Knows My Name: More Notes of a Native Son* (1961) and *The Fire Next Time* (1963), a groundbreaking book on race relations that had wide influence. He later published several novels, participated in TV documentaries, and remained a prominent, humane advocate of racial justice in American life.

At the time of his death in France, Baldwin was working on a biography of the Reverend Martin Luther King, Jr. Soon after Baldwin died, two noted African American writers praised his lifework. Orde Coombs wrote, "Because he existed we felt that the racial miasma that swirled around us would not consume us, and it is not too much to say that this man saved our lives." Juan Williams of *The Washington Post* said, "America and the literary world are far richer for [Baldwin's] witness. The proof of a shared humanity across the divides of race, class, and more is the testament that the preacher's son, James Arthur Baldwin, has left us."

RESOURCES: READING

Planning
■ *One-Stop Planner* CD-ROM with ExamView Test Generator

Differentiating Instruction
■ *Supporting Instruction in Spanish*
■ *Audio CD Library, Selections and Summaries in Spanish*

Vocabulary
■ *Vocabulary Development*

Grammar and Language
■ *Daily Language Activities*

Assessment
■ *Holt Assessment: Literature, Reading, and Vocabulary*
■ *One-Stop Planner* CD-ROM with ExamView Test Generator
■ *Holt Online Assessment*

Internet
■ go.hrw.com (Keyword: LE5 11-6)
■ *Elements of Literature Online*

Media
■ *Audio CD Library*
■ *Audio CD Library, Selections and Summaries in Spanish*

Before You Read

Autobiographical Notes

Make the Connection

The ancient Greek philosopher Socrates believed that only an examined life is worth living. What exactly does it mean to live an examined life? At the least it means stepping back from the whirl of daily activities and gaining some perspective on who you are, where you have been, and where you are heading. It means creating new angles of vision, asking questions, proposing answers. It means making self-assessment a part of self-creation. As you will see, James Baldwin certainly took Socrates's words to heart. The autobiographical notes that follow first appeared as a preface to Baldwin's acclaimed *Notes of a Native Son*.

Literary Focus

Tone

Since Baldwin is writing his autobiography, his main subject is himself and his life experience. Therefore, when we speak of his **tone,** we mean his attitude toward himself and the world in which he lived. We sense that attitude by the words he chooses and by the style or manner in which he arranges those words. Tone can often by summed up in a single adjective, such as *ironic* or *lighthearted;* the way in which that tone is achieved must be examined by detailed analysis.

> The **tone** of a literary work is the attitude the writer takes toward the subject and the audience.
>
> *For more on Tone, see the Handbook of Literary and Historical Terms.*

Reading Skills

Evaluating an Author's Arguments

In this essay, Baldwin assesses his life experience. He tells us what conclusions he has drawn about a number of important subjects, such as the racial divide in American society and the dilemma of the African American writer. Often, he explicitly states his beliefs and gives reasons for his assertions. As you read, jot down statements that reveal Baldwin's beliefs and the reasons he gives for making those assertions. After you read, think about your own responses to Baldwin's text. What assertions will *you* make about Baldwin's beliefs?

Vocabulary Development

bleak *adj.:* cheerless.

censored (sen′sərd) *v.:* cut or changed to remove material deemed objectionable.

assess (ə·ses′) *v.:* evaluate; judge the value of.

conundrum (kə·nun′drəm) *n.:* riddle.

coherent (kō·hir′ənt) *adj.:* clear, logical, and consistent.

crucial (krōō′shəl) *adj.:* critical; decisive.

interloper (in′tər·lō′pər) *n.:* intruder; meddler.

appropriate (ə·prō′prē·āt′) *v.:* take over.

explicit (eks·plis′it) *adj.:* clear; definite.

pulverized (pul′vər·īzd′) *v.:* crushed; destroyed.

SKILLS
FOCUS

Literary Skills
Understand tone.

Reading Skills
Understand an author's arguments.

James Baldwin **1015**

PRETEACHING

Summary *at grade level*

"Autobiographical Notes" offers a compelling portrait of Baldwin's development as a writer and thinker. His tone is sometimes lightly ironic, other times more direct. He relies on wit, understatement, and literary allusions to express some serious and moving insights about writing, personal integrity, and the paradoxes of African American identity. Baldwin begins with a self-deprecating and satirical account of his childhood as "the usual bleak fantasy," illustrating the heavy responsibilities he bore in caring for his younger siblings under difficult circumstances. He describes his early ambitions as a writer and reader. For much of the selection, he reflects on what he sees as the difficult position of the African American writer. Writers who happen to be African American must not only first achieve some kind of clarity regarding the "Negro problem" in America but also establish a stance toward Western culture in general, a culture in which they are "interlopers." He closes with a witty and engaging discussion of his own personal principles: his likes and dislikes, his ambivalent but fierce love for America, his faith in his own "moral center," and his duties as a writer.

Selection Starter

Motivate. Have students discuss their ambitions for the future. Ask, "How would you like to be remembered, and what contribution to the world would you like to make?"

Previewing Vocabulary

To reinforce students' understanding of the Vocabulary words, have them read the definitions given on this page. Then, have students match each of the words listed on the left with its synonym or definition on the right.

1. censored [f]
2. conundrum [i]
3. crucial [d]
4. assess [e]
5. pulverized [b]
6. interloper [h]
7. appropriate [a]
8. bleak [c]
9. explicit [g]
10. coherent [j]

a. take over
b. smashed to pieces
c. miserable
d. vitally important
e. make a judgment about
f. cut or changed
g. clearly stated
h. intruder
i. puzzle
j. well thought out

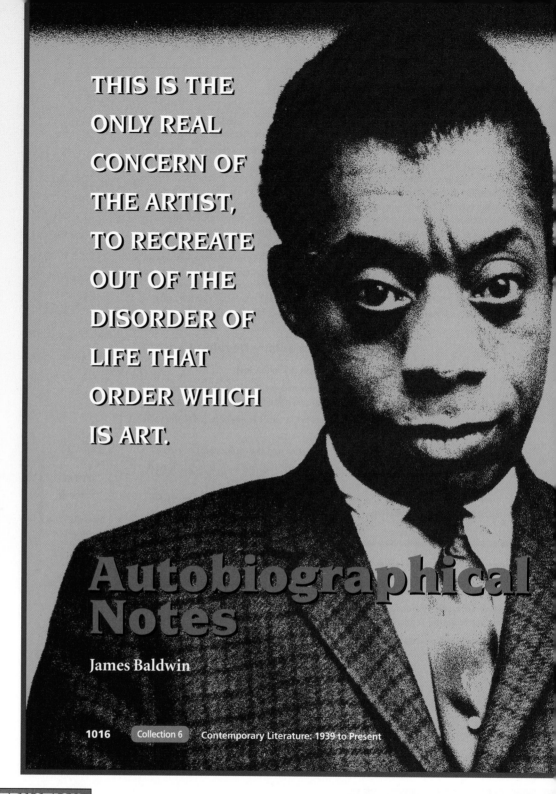

THIS IS THE ONLY REAL CONCERN OF THE ARTIST, TO RECREATE OUT OF THE DISORDER OF LIFE THAT ORDER WHICH IS ART.

Autobiographical Notes

James Baldwin

DIFFERENTIATING INSTRUCTION

Learners Having Difficulty
Modeling. Model how you evaluate an author's argument. Say, "I see that after 'On the other hand,' Baldwin argues that an uncaring audience makes a writer work harder. He doesn't offer examples to prove his point, but his logic makes sense." Ask students to read the rest of the essay and to ask, "How well does Baldwin develop his arguments?"

English-Language Learners
Explain that Baldwin uses a style that deliberately mixes high-level prose with informal terms ("goings-on") and sentence fragments ("Did another book . . . Harlem."). Help students with other examples as they come up.

Advanced Learners
Enrichment. Ask students to identify a subject or an avocation that gives them a sense of accomplishment. How would they describe what they went through to reach their level of skill? Ask students to write self-interviews to be titled "The Created Self."

I was born in Harlem thirty-one years ago. I began plotting novels at about the time I learned to read. The story of my childhood is the usual bleak fantasy, and we can dismiss it with the restrained observation that I certainly would not consider living it again. In those days my mother was given to the exasperating[1] and mysterious habit of having babies. As they were born, I took them over with one hand and held a book with the other. The children probably suffered, though they have since been kind enough to deny it, and in this way I read *Uncle Tom's Cabin* and *A Tale of Two Cities* over and over and over again; in this way, in fact, I read just about everything I could get my hands on—except the Bible, probably because it was the only book I was encouraged to read. I must also confess that I wrote—a great deal—and my first professional triumph, in any case, the first effort of mine to be seen in print, occurred at the age of twelve or thereabouts, when a short story I had written about the Spanish revolution won some sort of a prize in an extremely short-lived church newspaper. I remember the story was censored by the lady editor, though I don't remember why, and I was outraged.

Also wrote plays, and songs, for one of which I received a letter of congratulations from Mayor La Guardia,[2] and poetry, about which the less said, the better. My mother was delighted by all these goings-on, but my father wasn't; he wanted me to be a preacher. When I was fourteen I became a preacher, and when I was seventeen I stopped. Very shortly thereafter I left home. For God knows how long I struggled with the world of commerce and industry—I guess they would say they struggled with *me*—and when I was about twenty-one I had enough done of a novel to get a Saxton Fellowship. When I was twenty-two the fellowship was over, the novel turned out to be unsalable, and I started waiting on tables in a Village[3] restaurant and writing book reviews—mostly, as it turned out, about the Negro problem, concerning which the color of my skin made me automatically an expert. Did another book, in company with photographer Theodore Pelatowski, about the store-front churches in Harlem. This book met exactly the same fate as my first—fellowship, but no sale. (It was a Rosenwald Fellowship.) By the time I was twenty-four I had decided to stop reviewing books about the Negro problem—which, by this time, was only slightly less horrible in print than it was in life—and I packed my bags and went to France, where I finished, God knows how, *Go Tell It on the Mountain.*

Any writer, I suppose, feels that the world into which he was born is nothing less than a conspiracy against the cultivation of his talent—which attitude certainly has a great deal to support it. On the other hand, it is only because the world looks on his talent with such a frightening indifference that the artist is compelled to make his talent important. So that any writer, looking back over even so short a span of time as I am here forced to assess, finds that the things which hurt him and the things which helped him cannot be divorced from each other; he could be helped in a certain way only because he was hurt in a certain way; and his help is simply to be enabled to move from one conundrum to the next—one is tempted to say that he moves from one disaster to the next. When one begins looking for influences one finds them by the

---

1. **exasperating** *adj.*: irritating; very annoying.
2. **Mayor La Guardia:** Fiorello La Guardia, mayor of New York City from 1934 to 1945.
3. **Village:** Greenwich Village, a section of Manhattan noted as a center for writers and other artists.

Vocabulary

bleak *adj.*: cheerless.
censored (sen′sərd) *v.*: cut or changed to remove material deemed objectionable.
assess (ə·ses′) *v.*: evaluate; judge the value of.
conundrum (kə·nun′drəm) *n.*: riddle.

James Baldwin **1017**

Advanced Learners

Enrichment. Students will probably agree that literary nonfiction, sometimes called creative nonfiction, has entertainment value. Ask them to consider if it also has educational value. For example, ask them how memoir excerpts and essays might be appropriately placed in a history text. [Possible answers: Literary nonfiction could present different perspectives on an issue or help explain the motivation of people involved in an event.]

RETEACHING

State and Support Your Thesis

To help students generate effective thesis statements, you may have them work through the following activity. Give students several minutes to write their preliminary thesis statements. Next, pair students to evaluate each other's thesis. Have students focus on identifying literary elements and clearly stated main ideas in each other's thesis statement. Make a thesaurus available, and ask students to offer suggestions to each other for replacing overused or vague words, such as *good*. Invite several students to read their preliminary thesis statements to the class. After each one is read, ask the class what literary elements will be discussed and what the writer's main idea is.

PRACTICE & APPLY

Guided and Independent Practice

Encourage students to write down every example of a literary element they notice initially in their chosen piece of nonfiction. Later, they can discard some elements or intentionally search for additional examples of other elements to include in their analyses. Have them complete **Practice and Apply** independently.

TIP Keep in mind that not every work will necessarily include all of the stylistic devices listed below. Writers often use one or two devices more than the others, or use several of them sparingly to achieve their intended effect.

STYLISTIC DEVICES AND EXAMPLES

Device	Example
Irony—a contrast or discrepancy between expectation and reality	The writer's mother, although "hindered and intruded upon" (1012), made art a daily part of her life.
Diction—choice of words; can be neutral and objective, or emotionally charged	Strong verbs, such as "battled" and "labored" (1009), reflect the strength of the writer's mother.
Imagery—language that appeals to the senses; can evoke emotions	The vivid images of the Smithsonian quilt, the mother's garden, and the determined woman described in the poem make the reader feel a sense of awe.
Sound effects—such as the **repetition** of vowel or consonant sounds (**assonance, alliteration**), sound patterns (**rhythm**), or words and phrases	Repeating "She" as the subject of four consecutive sentences strongly reinforces the mother's endless tasks (1009). Highlighting her creative spirit are the phrases "so brilliant," "so original," and "so magnificent" (1011).
Other stylistic devices include **allusions, figurative language, parallelism,** and **sentence structure.**	The writer's mother is metaphorically described as "Creator." Her garden is the universe she made.

SKILLS FOCUS

Writing Skills
Write an essay analyzing nonfiction. Choose a nonfiction work. Consider purpose, audience, and form. Survey the work. State and support your thesis. Organize your essay.

State and Support Your Thesis Choose the literary elements that contribute most to making the work effective and appealing. Then, write a **thesis statement** that identifies the elements and expresses your main idea about them. Next, support your thesis statement with **precise and relevant examples.** Use direct quotations, paraphrases, and summaries of the text to support the ideas in your analysis. Provide at least two examples for each element you select. Document your direct quotations with parenthetical citations.

Organize Your Essay Finally, make sure the organization of your essay is clear and logical by using the following two common organizational patterns for analyses.

- **Chronological order** traces the writer's use of one literary element from its first appearance in the work until its last.

- **Order of importance** arranges discussion of more than one element from most important to least important, or vice versa.

PRACTICE & APPLY Using the guidelines in this workshop, plan and write an essay that analyzes how a writer uses literary elements in a nonfiction work. Then, share your analysis with your classmates.

COLLECTION 6 RESOURCES: WRITING

(continued from p. 1031)

Assessment

- *Holt Assessment: Writing, Listening, and Speaking*
- *One-Stop Planner* CD-ROM with ExamView Test Generator
- *Holt Online Assessment*
- *Holt Online Essay Scoring*

Internet

- go.hrw.com (Keyword: LE5 11-6)
- *Elements of Literature Online*

Contemporary Poetry

Roethke	Forché
Wilbur	Cofer
Bishop	Dove
Plath	Doty
Sexton	Lee
Brooks	Ali
Walcott	Collins

If we are looking for something which is new and something which is vital, we must look first into the chaos within ourselves. That will help us in the directions that we need to go—that's why our poetry is so essential, so vital.

—Audre Lorde

Untitled (detail) (1952) by Kenneth Noland.
Oil on plywood (21³/₈″ × 13¹/₈″).
Smithsonian American Art Museum, Washington, D.C./Art Resource, NY.
© Kenneth Noland. Licensed by VAGA, New York.

1033

THE QUOTATION

Audre Lorde (1934–1992) grew up in New York City, where as a child she recited poems to express her feelings. Eventually, she began writing her own. Her first poem was published in *Seventeen* magazine when Lorde was still in high school. During the politically charged 1970s, Lorde distinguished herself as a teacher, a poet, and an activist, working to advance the causes of women, African Americans, and gays and lesbians. A decade before her death in 1992, Lorde published her first prose collection, *The Cancer Journals,* about confronting breast cancer.

What might Lorde mean by "the chaos within ourselves"? How might this chaos give us "directions"? [Possible responses: She may be referring to our secret inner lives—where we struggle with hopes as well as fears. Sorting through the chaos inspires personal growth.]

VIEWING THE ART

Created in 1952, before **Kenneth Noland** (1924–   ) had arrived at his signature style, this abstract expressionist painting uses lines and patterns reminiscent of so-called primitive art. Many American painters of the 1940s and 1950s were inspired by art and mythology from other cultures. Noland later developed a style of painting featuring large color-saturated shapes.

Activity. What image does this painting suggest? [It looks like a face—its lines imply eyes, a nose, and other facial features.]

Grade-Level Skills

■ **Literary Skills**
Analyze the way poets use sounds, including rhyme and rhythm.

More About the Writer

Background. Roethke struggled all his life with self-doubt. Even as an adult, he felt he could do nothing to win his father's approval. In high school he craved acceptance by his peers, who thought his love of reading unmanly. When he began to write poetry in college, he did so in secret.

For Independent Reading

■ "The Bat" provides young readers and writers with an excellent model for descriptive poetry.

■ "My Papa's Waltz" and "Elegy for Jane" show the range of the poet's exquisitely tuned emotions.

Theodore Roethke
(1908–1963)

"**E**verything that lives is holy: I call upon these holy forms of life." These words of Theodore Roethke's, which sound like the words of a religious ceremony, are at the core of his intense vision. For Roethke (ret′kē) the function of poetry is to represent in words the sanctified forms and experiences of life.

A native of Saginaw, Michigan, Roethke grew up in a family that had an enormous influence on his poetry. His father owned the largest greenhouse complex in the state, and Roethke's childhood was spent close to nature, nurturing cuttings and small plants and walking in the vast acres of woodlands owned by his family. This childhood world provided the foundation for much of his poetry, which often looks at the smallest aspects of nature—worms, snails, tiny seedlings—through the eyes of a child. "I have a genuine love of nature," he wrote when he was a sophomore in college. "When I get alone under an open sky where man isn't too evident—then I'm tremendously exalted and a thousand vivid ideas and sweet visions flood my consciousness."

Roethke studied law and worked in public relations for some time after graduating from college, but his desire to become a writer finally led him to graduate school. He began a teaching career at Lafayette College in Easton, Pennsylvania (where he also coached the tennis team); taught at Pennsylvania State University; and, from 1947 until his death, taught at the University of Washington.

A passionate and dedicated teacher, Roethke brought the same energy to the classroom that he brought to poetry. In teaching he sought the same rewards he searched for in his writing: transcendence and illumination.

The search for illumination and ecstasy was a fundamental concern for Roethke in life as well as in poetry. This search brought with it a psychological imbalance that he tried to face openly and employ honestly in his verse. "My heart keeps open house," he wrote in an early poem.

Between 1947 and 1958, Roethke published four volumes of poetry and received a number of honors, including a Pulitzer Prize, a National Book Award, and a Bollingen Prize. A poet of both pain and joy, the dark and the light, Roethke tried to find in both extremes the same transcendent moment, "a consciousness beyond the mundane," as he once put it, "a purity, a final innocence."

For Independent Reading

Try these poems by Roethke:
• "The Bat"
• "My Papa's Waltz"
• "Elegy for Jane"

1034 Collection 6 Contemporary Literature: 1939 to Present

Railroad Sunset (1929) by Edward Hopper. Oil on canvas (28¼″ × 47¾″; 71.8 cm × 121.3 cm).

Before You Read

Night Journey

Make the Connection

A cross-country train ride is a real journey. From coast to coast, a train ride takes about three days. Today we can fly across the country in about five hours. What once had to be a journey can now be merely a trip. What would we experience during a train ride that we would miss while we were thousands of feet up in a plane?

Pullman berth in line 3 refers to a car with sleeping arrangements. The Pullman car was named after its inventor, G. M. Pullman.

Literary Focus
Rhyme and Rhythm

Rhyme is the repetition of vowel sounds in accented syllables and in all succeeding syllables (*wonder/thunder*). Rhymes can be **internal** (appearing within lines), or they can be **end rhymes** (coming at the ends of

lines). Not all poets use rhyme; some poets use it so subtly that unless you listen closely, you may miss the rhyme altogether.

Rhythm is the alternation of stressed and unstressed syllables in oral and written language. Rhythm occurs in all uses of language, but it is most obvious in poetry.

> **Rhyme** is the repetition of vowel sounds in accented syllables and in all succeeding syllables.
>
> **Rhythm** is the alternation of stressed and unstressed syllables in oral and written language.
>
> *For more on Rhyme and Rhythm, see the Handbook of Literary and Historical Terms.*

SKILLS
FOCUS

Literary Skills
Understand rhyme and rhythm.

Theodore Roethke **1035**

Theodore Roethke **1035**

DIRECT TEACHING

VIEWING THE ART

> **Edward Hopper** (1882–1967) was a leading realist painter of the twentieth century.
>
> **Activity.** Ask students to compare the atmosphere of the painting with that of Theodore Roethke's "Night Journey." [Possible response: Both convey exaltation in nature seen from the road, but the painting suggests a contemplative, static atmosphere, while the poem suggests an exciting night.]

PRETEACHING

Summary *at grade level*

> The speaker stares into the night from his berth on a train. He describes a view of bridges, trees, and mountains. He merges with the train as he strains "at a curve," his muscles moving with the steel. The train rushes on; the speaker is exhilarated.

Skills Starter

Build review skills. Give students photocopies of a poem with regular rhyme and rhythm. Review how to identify rhyme schemes—both internal and end rhymes. Have students identify the rhythm by having them assign a different letter to each line's end sounds (perhaps, *abab*) and marking syllables as unstressed (˘) or stressed (´). Before students read "Night Journey," explain that Roethke uses irregular rhyme and rhythm. Have them consider how the poem's irregularity is appropriate for its subject.

A Literary Focus

Ambiguity. Make sure students identify the two ways of reading the title, as discussed in Skills Starter on p. 1039.

B Learners Having Difficulty

❓ Breaking down difficult text. Who is "One," and what is One doing? [One is anyone who is wading (that is, walking) through a meadow of wildflowers in autumn.]

C Reading Skills

❓ Analyzing. How can a chameleon and a praying mantis change a forest? [Possible response: Their camouflaged harmony with their environment creates a subtly deeper range of natural color.]

D Literary Focus

❓ Ambiguity. How is the manner in which the roses are held ambiguous? [The person holding the roses does so in a way that suggests paradoxically, that they cannot be "held," or possessed, at all.]

Ⓐ The Beautiful Changes

Richard Wilbur

Ⓑ One wading a Fall meadow finds on all sides
The Queen Anne's Lace lying like lilies
On water; it glides
So from the walker, it turns
5 Dry grass to a lake, as the slightest shade of you
Valleys my mind in fabulous blue Lucernes.

The beautiful changes as a forest is changed
By a chameleon's tuning his skin to it;
Ⓒ As a mantis, arranged
10 On a green leaf, grows
Into it, makes the leaf leafier, and proves
Any greenness is deeper than anyone knows.

Ⓓ Your hands hold roses always in a way that says
They are not only yours; the beautiful changes
15 In such kind ways,
Wishing ever to sunder
Things and things' selves for a second finding, to lose
For a moment all that it touches back to wonder.

Learners Having Difficulty
Learners having difficulty might work with advanced learners to rewrite the poem as prose. After they have completed their rewrites, have students respond individually to the process and the product in their journals. Have students state whether the rewriting contributed to, or detracted from, the poem's meaning, and explain why.

Invite learners having difficulty to read "The Beautiful Changes" in interactive format in *The Holt Reader* and to use the side-notes as aids to understanding the selection.

English-Language Learners
Have students find the definitions of *mantis* in a dictionary. Point out that in l. 6, the word *valleys* is acting as a verb.

Ask students what this verb might mean, especially in conjunction with the words *blue Lucernes* at the end of the line.

Response and Analysis

Thinking Critically

1. According to the speaker, how does Queen Anne's lace change a meadow of dry grass?

2. Who could be "you" in line 5?

3. How does "you" affect the speaker?

4. How does a chameleon change a forest? How does a mantis change a green leaf?

5. What is "you" doing in the last stanza?

6. To understand what the speaker says about the beautiful changes, paraphrase the last stanza. (The verb *sunder* in line 16 means "separate; break apart.")

7. In your own words, explain the **ambiguity** of the title. Does the poem as a whole support just one meaning or all meanings?

8. Is this a love poem? If so, whom or what does the speaker love? Pick out the lines that support your answer.

WRITING

"Glorious Energy"

In an interview, Wilbur made this statement:

> To put it simply, I feel that the universe is full of glorious energy, that the energy tends to take pattern and shape, and that the ultimate character of things is comely and good.

SKILLS FOCUS

In a brief **essay**, discuss how "The Beautiful Changes" supports Wilbur's statement. Do you agree with him? Why or why not?

The Beautiful Changes

Write three lines of a **poem** in which you tell how *you* think the beautiful changes. You could structure your verse with these words: "The beautiful changes as . . . is changed into . . ."

Literary Skills
Analyze ambiguity.

Writing Skills
Write an essay evaluating a writer's comment. Write three lines of a poem.

Richard Wilbur **1041**

INDEPENDENT PRACTICE

Response and Analysis

Thinking Critically

1. It causes a meadow of dry grass to resemble a lake.

2. Possible answers: a loved one or the reader or both

3. Like the Queen Anne's Lace, "you" inspires an expanse of beautiful images and heightened perceptions.

4. Both creatures change their environment by enhancing it and expanding it—by giving it more range, depth, and vitality.

5. "You" is holding roses.

6. Possible answers: The beautiful both inspires and renews our perception, which lets us rediscover the world with fresh meaning and wonder. The way your hands hold roses show us that when the beautiful touches something, that something radiates wonder again.

7. Possible answer: Beautiful things and people change, as does our perception of them. Changes in nature and in human perception are beautiful. The poem supports both meanings.

8. Possible answers: References to "you" (ll. 5, 13–14) suggest a specific beloved person. References to "the beautiful" (ll. 7, 14) indicate a general love of beauty.

ASSESSING

Assessment

- *Holt Assessment: Literature, Reading, and Vocabulary*

Response and Analysis

Mirror

Critical Thinking

1. The speaker is the mirror.

2. Possible answers: The speaker claims to possess the capacity to see and reflect reality without illusions. The speaker claims to have an omniscient perspective—yet it only sees surface reality.

3. Possible answer: Candlelight and moonlight soften the woman's appearance, while the mirror gives an "honest" reflection.

4. Possible answers: The monstrous image suggests distortions of identity and self-worth, brought on by a fear of aging. The image may call up associations with sharks and the leviathan, called a "great fish" in the Bible.

5. Possible answers: The real subject is vanity, or the way people use physical appearance to confirm who they are; the poem is about how people can be self-critical.

Mushrooms

Critical Thinking

1. The speakers are mushrooms.

2. They describe the growth of fungi in dark, damp environments. Possible answer: She uses images that are tactile and powerful— taking hold "on the loam," "fists," acquiring air, hammering, ramming, and shoving.

3. The speakers allude to the expression in ll. 31–32. Possible answer: The speakers are not meek. They exhibit aggressive behavior.

4. Possible answer: The poem is about the bland, persistent, and disturbing urge to dominate that may exist in some people and perhaps in nature itself.

5. Possible answer: cold, calculating, and confident tones.

Response and Analysis

Mirror

Thinking Critically

1. Identify the **speaker** of the poem— who is the "I"?

2. What qualities does the speaker claim to possess? What does the speaker imply by saying it is "the eye of a little god" (line 5)?

3. Why would the speaker refer to the candles and the moon as "liars" (line 12)?

4. The last line of "Mirror" contains the striking **image** of "a terrible fish." How would you explain this last image? What associations and emotional overtones does the image of a terrible fish have for you?

5. What would you say is the real subject of this poem? (It is not really about a mirror.) What *is* it about?

Mushrooms

Thinking Critically

1. Who are the speakers of this poem?

2. What natural process do the speakers describe? How does the poet use **personification**—a figure of speech in which an object or an animal is given human characteristics—to help you visualize what is happening in the poem?

SKILLS FOCUS

Literary Skills
Analyze a poem's speaker. Analyze tone.

Writing Skills
Write a poem in the voice of an object. Write an essay comparing tone in different texts.

3. "Blessed are the meek, for they shall inherit the earth" is a well-known expression from Matthew 5:5 in the Bible. Where do the speakers of the poem allude to this saying? Are the speakers truly meek? Explain your responses to this stanza.

4. What kind of people do you think the mushrooms **symbolize**? Explain.

5. You have read two poems by Plath. What **tones** do you hear in these poems? (Are the tones similar?)

WRITING

Mirror Poem

Write your own **poem** in which you give a mirror a voice. Let your mirror speak as "I." Make clear to the reader what kind of mirror is speaking (wall mirror, hand mirror, car mirror, and so on). What does *your* mirror think about the people and events it reflects?

Comparing Texts

In a brief **essay,** compare Plath's attitude toward nature in "Mushrooms" with the attitude toward nature revealed in another text, such as Emerson's *Nature* (page 182), Thoreau's *Walden* (page 192), Dickinson's "Apparently with no surprise" (page 344), or Bishop's "The Fish" (page 1044). Focus on these points for your comparison of the writers' ideas:

- attitude toward nature
- view of the universe as benign, hostile, or indifferent
- tone in each text

ASSESSING

Assessment

■ *Holt Assessment: Literature, Reading, and Vocabulary*

RETEACHING

For a lesson reteaching poetic devices, see **Reteaching,** p. 1117A.

Anne Sexton
(1928–1974)

From the very beginning of her literary career, Anne Sexton was recognized as a spirit in turmoil. The writer James Dickey put it this way: "Anne Sexton's poems so obviously come out of deep, painful sections of the author's life that one's literary opinions scarcely seem to matter; one feels tempted to drop them furtively into the nearest ashcan, rather than be caught with them in the presence of so much naked suffering."

Sexton's poetry was an eruption of her stormy emotional life into art. The titles of her most gripping volumes indicate a preoccupation with bouts of anxiety and mental illness and with the need to confront ultimate questions: *To Bedlam and Part Way Back* (1960), *Live or Die* (1966), *The Death Notebooks* (1974), and *The Awful Rowing Toward God* (1975).

Anne Gray Harvey was born in Newton, Massachusetts, and attended the public schools in nearby Wellesley. In 1947, she enrolled in the Garland School, a finishing school for women, and in 1948 married Alfred Sexton. Anne Sexton worked for a time as a fashion model, gave birth to two daughters, and then, at age twenty-eight, began writing poetry.

Sexton studied with Robert Lowell in his graduate writing seminar at Boston University and developed friendships with other important poets, including Sylvia Plath (page 1049), Maxine Kumin, and George Starbuck. One of the strongest influences on her was the work of her friend W. D. Snodgrass, whose volume of poetry, *Heart's Needle* (1959), traced the emotional consequences of a difficult midlife divorce.

Sexton traveled to Europe and Africa, taught at Boston University, gave readings, and earned numerous prizes for her poetry, including a Pulitzer Prize for *Live or Die*. In 1968, she formed a rock-music group called Anne Sexton and Her Kind: Sexton read her poems to the accompaniment of guitar, flute, saxophone, drums, bass, and keyboards.

Sexton's poetry was intended to be, as she said, "a shock to the senses." In her second book, *All My Pretty Ones* (1962), she quoted Franz Kafka: "The books we need are the kind that act upon us like a misfortune, that make us suffer like the death of someone we love more than ourselves. . . . [A] book should serve as the ax for the frozen sea within us." Her books were personal axes, but they also opened up a wider vision of contemporary women. Many of her poems portray women in moments of crisis.

The general public as well as other poets responded enthusiastically to Sexton's poems. Artistic success did not strengthen her fragile personality, though. As her close friend Robert Lowell remembered: "At a time when poetry readings were expected to be boring, no one ever fell asleep at Anne's. I see her as having the large, transparent, breakable, and increasingly ragged wings of a dragonfly—her poor, shy, driven life, the blind terror behind her bravado, her deadly increasing pace . . . her bravery while she lasted."

For Independent Reading

These poems by Sexton are comic and ironic takeoffs of popular fairy tales:

- "Snow White and the Seven Dwarfs"
- "Rumpelstiltskin"
- "Rapunzel"
- "Cinderella"

SKILLS FOCUS, pp. 1055–1059

Grade-Level Skills

■ **Literary Skills**
Analyze ways poets use imagery, figures of speech, and sounds.

More About the Writer

Background. Anne Sexton began writing poetry at the suggestion of the doctor who was treating her for mental illness. Poet and critic Alicia Ostriker later wrote about this period in Sexton's life. "When she began taking classes in poetry and meeting poets, Sexton discovered another group who spoke 'language.' [Sexton said] 'I found I belonged to the poets, that I was *real* there.'" Ostriker goes on to describe the "language" that attracted Sexton: "[It] is intimacy, authenticity, love in a loveless world; it is what the inner self uses to communicate with other inner selves."

For Independent Reading

Suggest that students work in small groups to read aloud Sexton's sardonic versions of traditional fairy tales. Have them discuss how Sexton's retellings highlight women's issues. What lines reveal Sexton's intention to create "a shock to the senses"?

Summary ⟷ *at grade level*

In "The Bells," Sexton illustrates the relationship between a father and child through a memory of a trip to the circus. The speaker mentions her father's patient explanations of the circus, his kindness, and their love for one another. The "sound where it began," the speaker tells us, is the sound of the bells for the "flying man," whose identity seems to merge with that of her father. She closes the poem by rejoicing in the time when "all the trembling bells" of her father belonged to her.

In "Young," the speaker describes herself as a "lonely kid," lying on the grass outside her parents' big house on a summer night. She is looking at her parents' windows, asking the stars questions, and believing that God watches over all.

Skills Starter

Build review skills. Invite students to share Quickwrite notes that describe childhood memories based on sensory experiences. Explain that imagery is simply a description that helps the reader experience such sensations more directly. For example, a poet might describe a "sunny kitchen filled with the tickle of freshly baked cinnamon rolls" rather than saying "the kitchen was pleasant."

VIEWING THE ART

Marc Chagall (1887–1985) was fascinated by the theatricality of circuses, and produced several paintings and series of prints based on the circus.

Activity. Ask students to comment on Chagall's view of the circus. How does his vision coincide with Sexton's? [Possible responses: Both seem to be inspired by colorful memories of the circus; Sexton's musical and paradelike imagery of rings and flying men is echoed in Chagall's painting.]

Before You Read

The Bells
Young

Make the Connection
Quickwrite ✏

Some events, major or minor at the time, stick in our minds many years later. A parade, a kiss, a summer night, a song—it could be anything that brings back the past for us and reminds us of our younger selves. Jot down an experience from the past that makes you feel joy. What images or sounds prompt your memory of the experience?

Literary Focus
Imagery

Imagery is the use of language to evoke a picture or a concrete sensation of a person, a place, a thing, or an experience. Most images appeal to our sense of sight. An image can, however, also appeal to our senses of taste, smell, hearing, and touch. In poetry, imagery is used to help us participate in an experience and evoke emotional responses. Imagery is so important in poetry that we can even make distinctions among poets based purely on the images they use.

> **Imagery** is the use of language to evoke a picture or a concrete sensation of a person, a place, a thing, or an experience.
>
> *For more on Imagery, see the Handbook of Literary and Historical Terms.*

Literary Skills
Understand imagery.

1056

DIFFERENTIATING INSTRUCTION

Learners Having Difficulty
In both poems, Sexton describes a moment in childhood and the feelings attached to those moments. While "The Bells" is fairly straightforward, struggling readers may need help with "Young." Read the poem aloud, and ask them to imagine the speaker's life at that point. Does she seem content, sad, angry? What outlook do the last four lines suggest?

Invite learners having difficulty to read "The Bells" in interactive format in *The Holt Reader* and to use the sidenotes as aids to understanding the selection.

English-Language Learners
The "three rings of danger" may not mean anything to students unfamiliar with large circuses. Explain that large circuses often have three circles with three different acts going on

THE BELLS

Anne Sexton

Today the circus poster
is scabbing off the concrete wall
and the children have forgotten
if they knew at all.
5 Father, do you remember?
Only the sound remains,
the distant thump of the good elephants,
the voice of the ancient lions
and how the bells
10 trembled for the flying man.
I, laughing,
lifted to your high shoulder
or small at the rough legs of strangers,
was not afraid.
15 You held my hand
and were instant to explain
the three rings of danger.
Oh see the naughty clown
and the wild parade
20 while love love
love grew rings around me.
This was the sound where it began;
our breath pounding up to see
the flying man breast out
25 across the boarded sky
and climb the air.
I remember the color of music
and how forever
all the trembling bells of you
30 were mine.

Circus (Le Cirque) by Marc Chagall.

Anne Sexton   **1057**

Anne Sexton   **1057**

DIRECT TEACHING

A **Literary Focus**

❓ Speaker. To whom is the speaker speaking? How does knowing this help you identify the speaker? [She is speaking to her father. This helps identify the speaker as the father's son or daughter recalling a childhood memory.]

B **Literary Focus**

❓ Imagery. Sexton uses sounds to help the reader feel the speaker's feelings. What sounds does she describe? [thump of elephants; voice of lions; trembling bells] What feelings do these sounds convey? [fear; anxiety]

C **Literary Focus**

❓ Imagery. How does Sexton use this imagery to create the feeling of a child in a crowd of adults? [The "rough legs of strangers" helps us sense the child's size and feel the people in the crowd brushing by.]

D **Literary Focus**

❓ Repetition. Why does the speaker describe "the three rings of danger" and then say, "love love / love grew rings around me"? [Possible response: Sexton wants to contrast the confusion of the three-ring circus with the love encompassing the speaker when she is with her father.]

E **Reading Skills**

❓ Interpreting. Why does Sexton have the speaker say "all the trembling bells of you" to describe her father? [Possible responses: to convey the joy he brought her; to suggest she conflated the flying man and her father] What kind of bell sounds do you hear in this line? [Possible responses: echoing chimes; cascading bells; sounds causing a shiver of thrill or joy]

---

at the same time (as opposed to smaller, one-ring circuses). Ask why the speaker might call them "rings of danger." You may wish to introduce the simile "like a three-ring circus," used to suggest a chaotic scene.

Advanced Learners
Enrichment. Ask students to compare and contrast the speakers' views of the father in the poems. Could the speaker in each poem

be the same person at different ages? If so, what seems to have changed by the time of the scene recorded in the second poem?

? **Imagery.** What effect do these images of the natural world have on the tone of the poem? [Possible responses: They suggest that the speaker is enveloped by a benevolent natural universe; because they suggest that the speaker is at peace but also isolated from others, they contribute to a bittersweet tone.]

B **Literary Focus**

? **Metaphor.** To what does the speaker compare her parents' windows? [a funnel of yellow heat; a half-shut eye]

C **Reading Skills**

? **Making inferences.** Does the speaker still believe this? Explain. [Possible response: No, the sing-song–like end suggests the belief is childlike; she may no longer believe in a God who pays attention to her personal concerns.]

VIEWING THE ART

Arthur G. Dove (1880–1946) was one of the first American abstract artists. By 1910, his works reflected his belief that elements such as line, shape, color, and balance can capture a reality beneath the exterior of things. Though nonrepresentational, his paintings suggest forms of nature. *Me and the Moon,* for example, suggests a moon embraced by Earth.

Activity. Ask students to discuss how the colors and shapes match the mood of "Young." [Possible responses: The darkness might call up the loneliness of the speaker; the bright moon could suggest the peaceful tone of most of the poem.]

Anne Sexton said that "Young" should be "said in one breath" and that the poem is composed of a single sentence in order to capture a single moment in time.

Young

Anne Sexton

A thousand doors ago
when I was a lonely kid
in a big house with four
garages and it was summer
5 as long as I could remember,
I lay on the lawn at night,
clover wrinkling under me,
the wise stars bedding over me,
my mother's window a funnel
10 of yellow heat running out,
my father's window, half shut,
an eye where sleepers pass,

and the boards of the house
were smooth and white as wax
15 and probably a million leaves
sailed on their strange stalks
as the crickets ticked together
and I, in my brand new body,
which was not a woman's yet,
20 told the stars my questions
and thought God could really see
the heat and the painted light,
elbows, knees, dreams, goodnight.

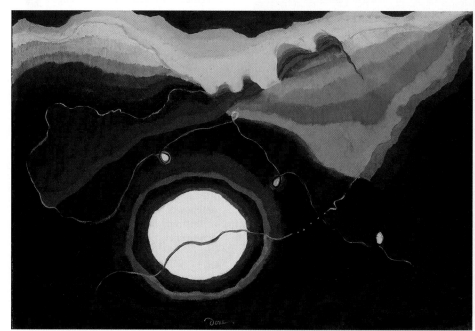

Me and the Moon (1937) by Arthur G. Dove.
Wax emulsion on canvas (18″ × 26″).

Response and Analysis

The Bells

Thinking Critically

1. What prompts the speaker to remember the scene from her past?

2. In line 5, whom do we learn the speaker is talking to?

3. According to line 6, what "remains"?

4. How does the speaker feel about her father? What lines give you the answer?

5. Rings are mentioned twice in the poem. What are the "rings of danger"? What are the other rings?

6. Describing a perception of one sense in terms of another sense is called **synesthesia** (sin'əs·thē'zhə). What senses does Sexton mix in line 27?

7. One **theme** of the poem is conveyed with childlike simplicity in lines 28–30. How would you paraphrase these lines—that is, how would you state their message in your own words?

Young

Thinking Critically

1. "Young" overflows with visual **imagery**. Make a list of all the images that this poem helps you see. What image helps you *hear* a sound?

2. Sexton reminds us that this poem is one long sentence. A sentence always contains a doer and an action. What did the speaker do "a thousand doors ago" when she was a lonely kid? What did she tell the stars? What did she think God could really see?

3. Why might the speaker say that her youth took place "a thousand doors ago"?

4. What **metaphors** does the poet use to describe the windows of her house? How could these metaphors reflect the speaker's different feelings for her mother and her father?

5. Describe the **tone** of the poem—the attitude the speaker conveys toward that summer night long ago.

WRITING

Respond to a Critic

Sexton believed that a book "should serve as the ax for the frozen sea within us" (see page 1055). In a brief **essay,** write a response to that statement. Address these questions in your essay:

- How would you explain this quotation in your own words?

- How could these two poems break a reader's "frozen sea"?

Writing a Description

Write a **poem** or a **paragraph** in which you use visual images to re-create an experience from your childhood that made you feel joy. You might try to model your poem after Sexton's and write just one long sentence. Be sure to refer to your Quickwrite notes. 🖉

LISTENING AND SPEAKING

Oral Performance

Perform "Young" aloud, as Sexton recommends. Where must you pause slightly for breath? Where is it a good idea to pause slightly for emphasis? How could you use your voice to make the poem sound as if a young girl were speaking?

Response and Analysis

Young

Critical Thinking

1. Possible answers: Visual images include the house with four garages; wrinkling clover; stars above; a funnel of yellow heat; a half-shut window like an eye; the white, smooth boards; a million leaves. The crickets ticking together helps the reader hear a sound.

2. She lay on grass at night. She told the stars her questions. She felt God saw everything about her.

3. It suggests she has gone through many "doors," or stages.

4. Her mother's window is a funnel sending out heat and light. Her father's is a half-shut eye. Possible answer: The metaphors may suggest that the speaker feels her mother is open to her, but her father is more closed off.

5. Possible answers: The tone could be described as bittersweet, peaceful, or nostalgic.

ASSESSING

Assessment

■ *Holt Assessment: Literature, Reading, and Vocabulary*

RETEACHING

For a lesson reteaching poetic devices, see **Reteaching,** p. 1117A.

The Bells

Critical Thinking

1. She sees an old circus poster.

2. She is talking to her father.

3. Only the sound of the circus remains.

4. She feels secure with him. This feeling comes out in ll. 11–14. She also feels love.

5. The "rings of danger" are the rings of the circus—one of the realities in front of the child. The other rings are those of "love love love," which she feels protect her.

6. She mixes sight and sound.

7. Possible answers: A loving parent gives a child a sense of security that the child thinks will last forever. The intensity of the experience of the circus and the love of her father are linked forever in the speaker's memory.

Grade-Level Skills

■ **Literary Skills**

Analyze the way an author's style achieves specific rhetorical or aesthetic purposes.

Review Skills

■ **Literary Skills**

Identify the literary devices that define a writer's style.

More About the Writer

Background. Collins says that he writes rapidly, often doing a first draft in one sitting. "I have a feeling of momentum when I'm writing, . . . the poem for me is like a ride and I'm the first one to take the ride. . . . And so I'm the first one to arrive. . . . And I couldn't just write eight lines of a poem and then come back to it a few days later. I have to complete this ride and discover the destination of the poem." Then during revision, he works on "getting the rhythm right and getting the cadence. . . ."

For Independent Reading

You might point out to students that "Sunday Morning with the Sensational Nightingales" is also a poem about music.

Billy Collins
(1941–   )

When Billy Collins was named poet laureate of the United States in 2001, he said, "It came completely out of the blue, like a soft wrecking ball from outer space." This contradictory image of a soft wrecking ball is characteristic of Collins's poetry—surprising, playful, almost casual, but with a hint of danger.

Born in New York City, Billy Collins has been a professor of English at the City University of New York for more than thirty years—as he modestly puts it, a "lifter of chalk in the Bronx." During his career he has won many poetry awards, including fellowships from the National Endowment for the Arts and the Guggenheim Foundation. He has also won wide popularity—some have called him the most popular poet in America—largely because his poems are anything but dry, heavy, or academic. Collins tries to be reader friendly:

> I have one reader in mind, someone who is in the room with me, and who I'm talking to, and I want to make sure I don't talk too fast, or too glibly. Usually I try to create a hospitable tone at the beginning of a poem. Stepping from the title to the first lines is like stepping into a canoe. A lot of things can go wrong.

Billy Collins's collections include *The Apple That Astonished Paris* (1988); *Questions About Angels* (1991), which was selected for the National Poetry Series; *The Art of Drowning* (1995); and *Sailing Alone Around the Room* (2001). He conducts poetry workshops during the summer and has recorded many of his poems. Collins's poems may at first seem deceptively low-key, but they usually convey a subtle message. As his fellow poet Edward

Hirsch says: "Billy Collins is an American original, a metaphysical poet with a funny bone and a sly questioning intelligence. . . . His poems —witty, playful, and beautifully turned—bump up against the deepest human mysteries."

For Independent Reading

For more by Billy Collins, read these poems from *The Art of Drowning*:

• "Center"

• "Sunday Morning with the Sensational Nightingales"

RESOURCES: READING

Planning

■ *One-Stop Planner* CD-ROM with ExamView Test Generator

Differentiating Instruction

■ *Supporting Instruction in Spanish*

■ *Audio CD Library, Selections and Summaries in Spanish*

Assessment

■ *Holt Assessment: Literature, Reading, and Vocabulary*

■ *One-Stop Planner* CD-ROM with ExamView Test Generator

■ *Holt Online Assessment*

Internet

■ go.hrw.com (Keyword: LE5 11-6)

■ *Elements of Literature Online*

Media

■ *Audio CD Library*

■ *Audio CD Library, Selections and Summaries in Spanish*

Before You Read

Man Listening to Disc

Make the Connection

Here's what Billy Collins has to say about the poem you're about to read, "Man Listening to Disc":

> I am usually not one of those people who walks around town with earphones on his head. I prefer to listen to the unpredictable noises of the city—people talking to themselves, a metal grate being thrown open, the sound of a messenger-bike with no brakes bearing down on me. But this day, I was wired to a metallic-blue Discman I had tucked in my coat pocket. The music sounded so intimate and immediate as I walked up one street and down another, I could not help feeling that I was in the physical company of the musicians.

So put on the headphones, turn up the volume, and take a stroll with Billy Collins.

Literary Focus

Style

When we talk about **style** in literature, we refer to the way a writer uses language. Style can be ornate, slangy, plain, informal, elegant, personal, complex, and so on. People in many professions—athletes and politicians, for example—are sometimes criticized for having more style than substance. In literature and the arts, however, style and substance are deeply intertwined. In fact, the best writers make style part of the substance of their works. The Puritan plain style reflected an entire community's faith in the saving power of simplicity. Whitman's free verse embodied his wide-ranging democratic energy. Hemingway's muscular, sculptured prose conveyed his belief in the value of strength and grace in both literature and life.

In twenty-first-century American literature many different styles coexist. They range from formal and objective to informal and immediate.

> **Style** is the distinctive way in which a writer uses language.
>
> *For more on Style, see the Handbook of Literary and Historical Terms.*

Background

As he bops down the street, Collins is listening to a classic jazz CD, *Thelonious Monk/ Sonny Rollins*. The disc features Thelonious Monk on piano, Sonny Rollins on tenor saxophone, Tommy Potter on bass, and Arthur Taylor on drums, along with several other musicians. Their vibrant version of the popular romantic song "The Way You Look Tonight," by Jerome Kern and Dorothy Fields, was recorded in 1954.

Thelonious Monk (1960).

SKILLS FOCUS

Literary Skills
Understand style.

Billy Collins   **1097**

PRETEACHING

Summary   *at grade level*

As the speaker walks down a street in New York City listening to jazz by Sonny Rollins and others, he imagines that he and the musicians are in each other's company. He starts mixing into his casual language the formal—some might say pretentious—style of an emcee introducing the musicians to an audience. He prides himself on his familiarity with the musicians and announces, perhaps with some tongue in cheek, that his place in the universe is much more important than anyone else's.

Skills Starter

Motivate. To initiate a discussion of writing styles, have students discuss clothing styles. What label do they put to each style? Discuss what elements make up style in the context of clothing. Then, remind students that vocabulary and sentence structure are two of the tools writers use to create a distinctive style of writing. Have them contrast the styles of American writers they have read—such as Mark Twain and Richard Wright.

DIFFERENTIATING INSTRUCTION

Learners Having Difficulty

The breezy style with which the poem starts changes at l. 10, where the poet introduces more formal vocabulary. Help students use context to determine the meanings of *profusion* (l. 10), *suffused* (l. 12), *surpassed* (l. 15), *gratitude* (l. 15), and *esteemed* (l. 19).

English-Language Learners

Elicit from students experiences they have had in selecting the correct register of English to use in various situations. Have they been informal when they should have been formal or vice versa?

Advanced Learners

Enrichment. Collins says that as a young poet, before finding his own voice, he wrote in the style of Lawrence Ferlinghetti and Richard Brautigan, among others. Have students read poems by these authors and contrast their style with the style Collins uses in this poem.

? **Style.** The title of the poem is a straightforward description of the subject of the poem. It also sounds somewhat like the title of a work of a painting. What style do you expect in the poem itself? [Possible responses: plain, clear, direct.]

B Literary Focus

? **Style.** Where does the style start migrating from plain to formal? [Some students may cite l. 4, where the poet uses a technical term, *calipers;* most students will point to l. 10, where the first of several more difficult words appears, or ll. 12 and 15, where the passive voice takes over.]

C Literary Focus

? **Style.** Where does the speaker, still sounding and acting formal, fall back on informal language? [In l. 22, the speaker reports that he bows deeply—a rather formal move—but in l. 24, he uses the colloquialism *whatever,* which means "anything else of the sort."]

D Reading Skills

? **Summarizing.** Having introduced the musicians, the speaker moves on to a new topic. What is he feeling, and whom is he talking to? [Possible response: He thinks of himself at the center the universe and advises anyone else to, in effect, get out of his (and the band's) way.]

A Man Listening to Disc

Billy Collins

This is not bad—
ambling along 44th Street
with Sonny Rollins for company,
his music flowing through the soft calipers
5   of these earphones,

as if he were right beside me
on this clear day in March,
the pavement sparkling with sunlight,
pigeons fluttering off the curb,
10   nodding over a profusion of bread crumbs.

B In fact, I would say
my delight at being suffused
with phrases from his saxophone—
some like honey, some like vinegar—
15   is surpassed only by my gratitude

to Tommy Potter for taking the time
to join us on this breezy afternoon
with his most unwieldy bass
and to the esteemed Arthur Taylor
20   who is somehow managing to navigate

C this crowd with his cumbersome drums.
And I bow deeply to Thelonious Monk
for figuring out a way
to motorize—or whatever—his huge piano
25   so he could be with us today.

D The music is loud yet so confidential
I cannot help feeling even more
like the center of the universe
than usual as I walk along to a rapid
30   little version of "The Way You Look Tonight,"

and all I can say to my fellow pedestrians,
to the woman in the white sweater,
the man in the tan raincoat and the heavy glasses,
who mistake themselves for the center of the universe—
35   all I can say is watch your step

because the five of us, instruments
and all,
are about to angle over
to the south side of the street
and then, in our own tightly knit way,
40   turn the corner at Sixth Avenue.

And if any of you are curious
about where this aggregation,
this whole battery-powered crew,
is headed, let us just say
45   that the real center of the universe,

the only true point of view,
is full of the hope that he,
the hub of the cosmos
with his hair blown sideways,
will eventually make it all the way
50   downtown.

(Opposite) *Summer Madness* (1993) by Michael Escoffery. Mixed media.

Private collection. © Michael Escoffery/Art Resource, New York. © Copyright ARS, New York.

CONTENT-AREA CONNECTIONS

Music: Jazz
Jazz emerged as a distinctive form in the late nineteenth century, but its roots go back both to rhythms that originated in Africa and to the musical structures of western Europe. Jazz borrowed from the traditions of spirituals, work songs, field hollers, and, later, from blues and popular music. A distinguishing characteristic is improvisation. For jazz musicians, a known work is the starting point around which improvisations are built.

Whole-class activity. Play a recording of "The Way You Look Tonight" as originally composed by Jerome Kern and Dorothy Fields. Fred Astaire sang the song in the 1936 film *Swing Time.* Frank Sinatra also made a popular recording. Then, play the jazz version of the song by Thelonnious Monk and Sonny Rollins. Ask students to discuss the differences.

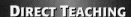
VIEWING THE ART

While this illustration by **Michael Escoffery** represents a single band, the anonymity of the musicians suggests that the artist's interests lie elsewhere. Indeed, his goal seems to be to comment upon the enormous influence of African Americans on American music, in the form of jazz, blues, and rock & roll.

Activity: The electric guitarist is in the center of the composition; the other musicians, who play instruments more associated with jazz seem to swirl about him. What does the centrality of the electric guitar player suggest about the importance of African Americans to American culture? [Possible response: Music largely developed by African Americans has become central to American life.]

Literary Criticism

Critic's Commentary: Differing Opinions of Billy Collins

Collins may have been named poet laureate of the United States, but that title didn't assure him universal critical acclaim. Dwight Garner, an editor at the *New York Times Book Review,* says, "Collins writes like a man with a pile of those poetry refrigerator magnet sets who happened to get pretty handy with them." Still, Collins has probably inspired more admiration than disdain. Poet Miller Williams has this to say: "There is a lobby of obscurantists in this country, who believe that a poem is not to be experienced but solved. People who subscribe to this are contemptuous of anyone whose poetry can be followed. Anyone can be hard to understand. . . . What is rare and difficult is the ability to be clear and mysterious at the same time." For Williams, this pairing is Collins's talent. Have students discuss which of these two views is closer to their own.

Response and Analysis

Critical Thinking

1. The poem is set on 44th Street in New York City on a clear, breezy day in March.

2. The speaker imagines that a group of musicians playing "The Way You Look Tonight" is accompanying him as he walks down the street.

3. Possible answers: The music makes him feel delighted (l. 12), grateful (l. 15), and important ("like the center of the universe," l. 28).

4. He is listening to the music through headphones, played loudly but only he can hear it.

5. He wants to say, "Watch your step. You are not the real center of the universe."

6. Possible answer: The "hub of the cosmos" who hopes he'll make it downtown may be the speaker.

7. Possible answers: Students will find in "Man Listening to Disc" examples of vocabulary and syntax to support each of the adjectives.

8. Possible answers: Yes, the poem left me disoriented because I wasn't always sure who was speaking and where this poem was going. No, the poem simply describes a cheerful little interlude in the speaker's life.

ASSESSING

Assessment

■ *Holt Assessment: Literature, Reading, and Vocabulary*

RETEACHING

For a lesson reteaching irony, tone, and author's style, see **Reteaching**, p. 1117A.

Response and Analysis

Thinking Critically

1. Where is the poem set?

2. What does the speaker imagine is happening in lines 1–25?

3. How does the music make the speaker feel? Find lines of the poem that describe his feelings.

4. What makes the music "loud yet so confidential" (line 26)?

5. What does the speaker want to say to the other pedestrians?

6. In the last verse, who is the "hub of the cosmos" who hopes he'll make it downtown?

7. Which of these words best describes Collins's **style**? More than one descriptive word can be correct.
   - formal
   - informal
   - complex
   - elegant
   - personal
   - humorous

SKILLS FOCUS

Literary Skills
Analyze style.

Writing Skills
Write an essay evaluating a poem. Write an essay or a poem about a song.

8. Collins says, "Poetry is my cheap form of transportation. By the end of the poem, the reader should be in a different place from where he started. I would like him to be slightly disoriented at the end, like I drove him outside of town at night and dropped him off in a cornfield." Did "Man Listening to Disc" work on you the way Collins hoped it would? Explain your response to the poem.

WRITING

Ars Poetica

Some critics wonder if Collins's work belongs on the shelf with the work of the best living American poets. To think about that question, review two famous poems on pages 598 and 599 that talk about the art of poetry. Then, select one of these poems, and relate what it says to Collins's poem. In a brief **essay**, tell whether Collins's poem qualifies as a genuine poem, based on what Moore or MacLeish says a poem should be. Use at least two specifics from Moore's or MacLeish's poem to apply to Collins's.

"Listening to . . . "

Choose a song or a CD that might be *your* own private soundtrack. Write an **essay** or a **poem** about the experience of listening to the music most meaningful to you. Be sure to explain *why* the music moves you. Feel free to experiment with a style that matches your thoughts and feelings.

DIFFERENTIATING INSTRUCTION

Learners Having Difficulty

Have students answer question 7 as a group. First, model for them choosing appropriate words to describe the style, by saying, "I ask myself, 'Is the style of this poem formal?' When I look at the first line, it sounds like someone talking. That isn't formal language."

Have students discuss each word in the list, looking for examples of vocabulary and structure in the poem that support or undercut the word as an accurate description of Collins's style.

Many works of contemporary literature use realistic language and graphic descriptions. Be sure to check with your teacher and a parent or guardian before reading any of the following books.

FICTION

Objects of War
A Bible used as a pillow, a pebble kept under the tongue, a can of peaches—these objects may puzzle us, but they mean the world to the young soldiers depicted in Tim O'Brien's *The Things They Carried.* This work of interconnected short stories straddles the line between reality and imagination, relating the stories of soldiers both on and off the battlefield.

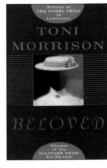

FICTION

Both Sides of the Story
Toni Morrison (page 1020) writes of the debilitating effects of the oppression of African Americans on victim and perpetrator alike; she also explores the other side of the coin: the richness of the African American community and its traditions. Her novel *Beloved* tells the story of a mother's desperate attempt to save her children from slavery.

NONFICTION

Irrational Acts
Into the Wild and *Into Thin Air,* both by the journalist Jon Krakauer, are examples of nonfiction writing at its best. *Into the Wild* is the tragic story of a young man who set off to experience the wilderness. His adventure ended in an abandoned school bus in Denali National Park in Alaska. *Into Thin Air* is Krakauer's account of his guided ascent of Mount Everest.

POETRY

A Nation of Poets
More people are writing poetry than ever before, and happily, the audience for poetry is also growing. *Unsettling America: An Anthology of Contemporary Multicultural Poetry,* edited by Maria M. Gillan and Jennifer Gillan, contains thematically grouped poems by American poets of many cultures. To explore the more recent work of poets such as Charles Olson, Denise Levertov, and Jimmy Santiago Baca, see *Postmodern American Poetry,* edited by Paul Hoover.

Read On 1101

Read On

For Independent Reading
If students enjoyed the themes and topics explored in this collection, you might recommend the following titles for independent reading.

Assessment Options
The following projects can help you evaluate and assess your students' outside reading.

- **Design a book jacket.** Have students design and create an alternative jacket for a book they have read. The cover should include an illustration; the book's title, author or editor, and publisher; and an original critical comment to encourage reader interest.

- **Make a map.** Ask students to create a map based on *The Things They Carried* or one of John Krakauer's books. They can use symbols to designate important locations.

- **Adapt a film.** Have students work in pairs to rewrite, as a movie script, important scenes from *Beloved.* Remind students that scripts focus more on dialogue and action than on descriptions. Suggest that students practice reading their scripts aloud before performing them for the class.

- **Read poetry.** Have a group of students who have read *Unsettling America* or *Postmodern American Poetry* prepare a reading for the class. Students should prepare two poems to read. Suggest that they work as a group to rehearse the readings and to prepare the order of the program.

DIFFERENTIATING INSTRUCTION

Estimated Word Counts and Reading Levels of Read On Books:

Fiction			Nonfiction			Poetry		
The Things They Carried	↔	61,000	Into Thin Air	↓	114,400	Unsettling America: An Anthology of Contemporary Multicultural Poetry	↔	75,500
Beloved	↑	115,900				Postmodern American Poetry	↔	151,400

KEY: ↑ *above grade level* ↔ *at grade level* ↓ *below grade level*

Independent Practice: Identifying implicit beliefs. As homework, ask students to read Halimah Abdullah's "Honoring African Heritage" (p. 62) and identify statements where Abdullah's beliefs and opinions are implicitly expressed. Have students list these on a chart like the one below. Then, ask them to work with a partner to infer beliefs and values that are implicit in the statements they identified. Have students list these implicit beliefs in the second column of their charts and then share their charts with the class. (Possible responses appear in brackets.) As a class, have students evaluate the implicit beliefs partners identified and speculate on any biographical details that may have contributed to the beliefs of the reporter and of the people quoted in the article. (All appear to be African Americans with a strong interest in their African ancestry.)

Statements	Implicit Beliefs
["The ocean view represented a symbolic connection to their African ancestors' voyages here."]	[Symbolic connections are important and can change attitudes and lives.]
[" 'We're paying tribute to both those who died during that African holocaust and the survivors.' "]	[Tributes to the dead are meaningful to the living.]
[" 'It's important for us to do these things to regain a sense of pride.' "]	[Honoring ancestors instills pride in descendants.]
[" 'We need to think about what they must have gone through.' "]	[Reflecting on the sufferings of one's ancestors builds a sense of ethnic solidarity and identity.]

Critiquing Public Documents

Objective: Critique the validity, appeal, and truthfulness of arguments in public documents.

Direct Teaching: Share the following ideas with students.

Because many of the most famous public documents in American history, such as the Declaration of Independence and Lincoln's Gettysburg Address, are so familiar and express values so widely accepted, it is easy to forget that they are statements of opinion. When they were written, these political statements and speeches were intended not only to announce and explain policy but also to persuade Americans to support the writers' position or point of view. Likewise, when we read or listen to political statements or speeches today, it is important to remember that their purpose too is to persuade. The best way to approach a persuasive document is to decide exactly what the writer wants us to do or to believe. Then we can examine how the writer tries to persuade us to share his or her point of view. We can expect writers to make appeals to our intellect and emotions, and both of these methods of persuasion can be either effective or ineffective. Their success depends on the soundness of the reasoning and the power of the emotional appeal. Also, effective persuaders often try to anticipate and address what they know to be the doubts and concerns of their audience and to counter the objections their opponents are likely to raise. For example, a writer trying to persuade readers to support a ban on commercial timbering on public lands might call for job-retraining programs for displaced workers in the timber industry in order to counter those who would raise the prospect of unemployment as an objection to the ban.

Guided Practice: Critiquing public documents. Discuss with students the difference between logical and emotional appeals. Review examples of faulty reasoning, such as false generalization in which something that is *sometimes* true in individual cases is presented as *always* true for an entire class or group. Remind them that emotional appeals are usually signaled by loaded or heightened language, which is designed to stir the audience to anger, fear, or pity or to elicit identification with one group and rejection of another.

Have students look back at Patrick Henry's "Speech to the Virginia Convention" (p. 79). Remind them that the speech was given the year before the Declaration of Independence was written and the Revolutionary War began. Explain that although Colonial leaders were distressed over the treatment of the Colonies by Great Britain and by the build-up of British military forces on American soil, they did not agree on how to respond to these problems. Begin a discussion by asking students what Patrick Henry is trying to persuade his listeners to do about their problems with Britain. [He wants the colonists to take up arms against the British immediately.] Then, have students think about some of the questions that Patrick Henry's call to arms might have raised in his audience. [Possible responses: How could a Colonial army be raised and financed? Could the colonists win? Were there any less drastic solutions to the problems with Britain? Did the colonists really want to sever all political, economic, and cultural ties with Britain?] List on the chalkboard the questions the students cite, and ask them to look again at the speech to see if Henry anticipates and addresses them.

After students have read the speech, draw on the chalkboard a chart like the one on p. 1117I. Read aloud each excerpt in the first column, and discuss with students whether the passage appeals to logic, emotion, or both. Then, ask what, if any, audience concern or objection the excerpt addresses or counters. (Possible responses appear in brackets.) Work with students to be as specific as possible in identifying Henry's persuasive techniques.

When you have filled the web with all the evidence students have gathered from the poem, ask students to reflect on what they have discovered. Encourage them to discuss what comment on life Edwin Arlington Robinson is making through the speaker in his poem. Tell them that there is more than one way to express Robinson's theme, and then write several student's theme statements on the chalkboard. Ask the class to evaluate each one, referencing the poem and their own experience. [Possible theme statements: The lives of the rich are not necessarily happier because they are wealthy and admired; appearances can be deceiving; the inner lives of others are mysterious and unknowable; envy based on appearances is often misplaced.]

Independent Practice: Analyzing themes. Have students read Kate Chopin's short story "A Pair of Silk Stockings" (p. 503) or another short story from their textbook. Then, have them work with a partner to gather evidence from the story that will help them discover the comment on life that the writer is making. Urge them to organize their evidence on a web like the one below. (Possible responses appear in brackets.) Ask partners to use their webs to write a short paragraph, stating the writer's theme as they see it and explaining the process they used to arrive at their conclusion. Have them exchange their essays with partners who analyzed the same story, and encourage them to compare and contrast their various theme statements. [Possible theme statements: Flights from routine deprivations bring at least temporary pleasure and relief; even the most selfless people need to indulge themselves occasionally; temporary escapes don't make returning to reality any easier.]

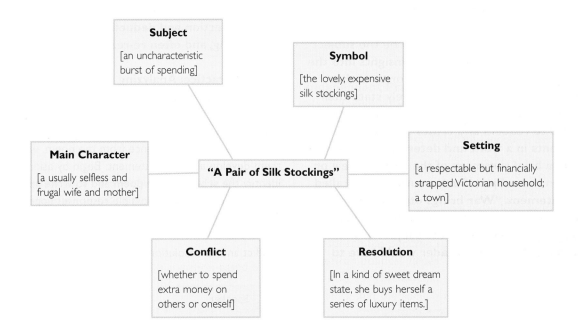

Subject
[an uncharacteristic burst of spending]

Symbol
[the lovely, expensive silk stockings]

Main Character
[a usually selfless and frugal wife and mother]

"A Pair of Silk Stockings"

Setting
[a respectable but financially strapped Victorian household; a town]

Conflict
[whether to spend extra money on others or oneself]

Resolution
[In a kind of sweet dream state, she buys herself a series of luxury items.]

Irony, Tone, and Author's Style

Objective: Analyze the way an author's style achieves specific rhetorical or aesthetic purposes.

Direct Teaching: Share the following information with students.

Style is the distinctive manner in which writers present their ideas. Diction, the choice of words, is one of the ways that a writer creates a style. For example, a writer can choose an informal, everyday word, such as *work,* or a more formal, less commonplace one, such as *toil.* Writers can also choose between words that are plain or fancy, modern or old-fashioned, specific or general—to name just a few of the many choices open to them. Writers can also choose words based on their connotations— that is, on the emotions, images, and ideas associated with the words. On p. 186 of the excerpt from "Self-Reliance," for instance, Ralph Waldo Emerson chooses the highly evocative word *hobgoblin,* with its connotations of mischief and otherworldly power, instead of less imaginative options, like *stumbling block* or *obsession.* It's a bold choice, and it affects the tone of the entire passage, reinforcing Emerson's assertion of the value of individuality. The use of figurative language, such as similes and metaphors, is another way of using words that affects a writer's overall style.

Regardless of the words they choose, writers must form sentences. Sentence structure, then, is another important component of style. The unique rhythm—the pattern of repeated sounds—of a passage is created by the way its words, phrases, and clauses are strung together. Sequences of short, simple sentences, for example, create one effect while strings of long, complex sentences create another.

As you read, pay careful attention to the writer's choice of words and to the rhythm created by the sentence structure. Look to see if the words and sentences create an overall *tone,* or attitude toward the subject. Ask yourself questions like these:

- Are most of the words simple or elaborate, formal or slangy, restrained or charged?

- **What attitude toward the subject do the words and sentence structure convey?**

- **Does the writer use figurative language—original and imaginative comparisons that give the work a personal stamp? The responses to these questions will help you evaluate the impact of the author's style on the tone and message of the work.**

Guided Practice: Analyzing style and tone. Read aloud the first sentence from Ralph Waldo Emerson's essay "Self-Reliance" (p. 184). Begin an analysis of Emerson's style in this passage by asking students to put Emerson's message in their own words. [Possible response: Individuals should not compare themselves with others but should accept themselves as they are, directing their efforts to making the most of what they have been given.] Next, ask, "How would you describe Emerson's attitude toward his subject? Is he lighthearted? discouraged? critical? serious?" [serious] Discuss Emerson's word choices. Point out words like *conviction, imitation, portion, universe,* and *bestowed.* Ask students to describe the diction. Give them simple synonyms (such as *belief, copying, lot, world,* and *given*) if they are having trouble seeing that the diction is elevated and formal. Call their attention to the metaphor "no kernel of nourishing corn can come to him but through his toil bestowed on that plot of ground which is given to him to till." Have students analyze what are being compared, and discuss with them the effect of the metaphor. [Possible responses: Growing corn on one's own land is compared to nurturing one's inborn talents. The metaphor gives a familiar, concrete form to a less familiar, abstract idea.] Then, ask students to look at the sentence structure. Point out that the passage is one long sentence, with a repeating pattern of clauses beginning with the word *that.* Read the passage aloud again, and ask the class to listen to the sound of the language. Point out the smooth, flowing rhythm of the clauses and suggest to them that the sound creates a feeling of clarity, harmony, and conviction. Explain that the style seems to underscore Emerson's self-assured beliefs and that his flowing prose inspires assurance in the reader as well.

Independent Practice: Comparing authors' styles. As homework, ask students to read Sor Juana Inés de la Cruz's sonnet "World, in hounding me . . ." (p. 32). Explain that there will be a class discussion comparing and contrasting the poet's style with that of Emerson in the excerpt from "Self Reliance." Encourage students to begin by summarizing the message of the sonnet. Next, have them examine the diction, the use of figurative and connotative language, and the sentence structure of the poem. Ask them to consider how each element contributes to the overall tone. Then, have them compare and contrast these with the conclusions about Emerson's style that the class reached in the Guided Practice. Students may want to make a simple, two-column comparison and contrast chart to organize their ideas. Class discussion should cover the many similarities in the message and style of the two writers. [Possible responses: Both are assertive, committed believers in their own personal values. One prizes individuality; the other, the life of the mind. The diction of both is serious, elevated, and somewhat aphoristic. Sor Juana personifies time as a victor, use rhetorical questions, and hints at paradoxes. The tone of both writers is serious, intellectual, and assertive, although Sor Juana's choice of the sonnet form may suggest more of a desire for self-expression and less of a need to persuade than Emerson displays.]

Poetic Devices

Objective: Analyze ways poets use imagery, figures of speech, and sounds.

Direct Teaching: Share the following thoughts with students.

Skilled poets are able to excite readers with new sensations, ideas, and feelings or to make the familiar become fresh and alive. What is amazing is that poets achieve these effects with words alone, by making use of a variety of poetic devices. These devices include imagery, figures of speech, and various sound effects. Imagery is the use of words to make vivid sense impressions on readers' imaginations. Imagery makes it possible for readers to see, hear, smell, and feel what the writer wants them to experience. Figurative language links objects or experiences that seem at first to have no similarity but turn out to be connected in some unexpected and revealing way. Sound effects—like alliteration, assonance, and rhyme—are what give poetry its musical quality. Imagery, figures of speech, and sound effects all work together to stir readers' emotions and imaginations at a level deeper than ordinary prose can achieve.

Guided Practice: Identifying poetic devices. Review with students the definitions of *simile, metaphor, personification, alliteration, assonance,* and *rhyme* in the Handbook of Literary and Historical Terms (p. 1169). Go over with students any provided examples, and ask them to offer additional examples from their favorite poems. Remind students that poems are meant to be read aloud and listened to carefully and that more than one reading is usually needed to get their full meaning. Then, have student volunteers read aloud Walt Whitman's "A Sight in Camp in the Daybreak Gray and Dim" (p. 321). As the students are reading the poem, draw on the chalkboard a chart like the one below. Tell students that the middle column of the chart includes examples of poetic devices. Have students take turns identifying the device(s) used in each passage. Be sure to tell them that many passages display more than one of the devices you have been discussing. Write their responses in the third column of the chart. (Possible responses appear in brackets.)

Passage from Poem	Poetic Device	Emotional Effect
"A sight in camp in the daybreak gray and dim,"	[imagery; alliteration]	[creates a sense of immediacy, mystery, and foreboding; pulls reader into the scene]
"Who are you elderly man so gaunt and grim, with well-gray'd hair . . . "	[alliteration; imagery; assonance]	[stirs feelings of compassion, fear, and foreboding]
"Young man I think I know you—I think this face is the face of the Christ himself."	[metaphor]	[stirs feelings of universal compassion and human solidarity as well as spiritual or religious feelings in some]

Independent Practice: Analyzing emotional effects. Add a fourth column to the chart as shown above. For each example, have student pairs discuss how the poetic devices make them feel or help them imagine an experience in the poem. (Possible responses appear in brackets.) When partners have finished their discussions, have them regroup as a class and compare and contrast their responses.

For further practice, ask students to read "The Raven" by Edgar Allan Poe (p. 273). For homework, have them find and analyze examples of the poetic devices they have been studying, using a three-column chart like the one in the Guided Practice. When they have completed their charts, ask them to write a short essay on the emotional effects that Poe creates by means of his poetic devices.

Archetypes

Objective: Analyze archetypes drawn from myth and tradition.

Direct Teaching: Share the following information with students.

The English word *archetype* comes from a Greek word meaning "original," which in turn came from the Greek root for "stamp" or "model." A literary archetype, then, is a pattern or model that forms the basis for many different, but related, versions of a character, plot, setting, image, or theme. Since myths, religious texts, and folk tales are the earliest forms of literature, they are the source for many of the archetypal patterns on which so much later literature is based. For example, the larger-than-life hero of the Greek myths is an archetypal character, and his or her quest to overcome evil or regain a lost paradise is an archetypal plot. This same character
and plot structure recur in the literature of many cultures, times, and places. The details change, but the core remains the same, suggesting that human beings everywhere share the same concerns and use their imaginations in similar ways.

Guided Practice: **Identifying archetypes.** On the chalkboard, draw a web like the one below. Help students think of examples of the five kinds of archetypes indicated on the web, and write their examples on the chalkboard. (Possible responses appear in brackets.) It may help students to know that archetypes are still being used in movies, such as Westerns or science-fiction films, and in other forms of popular media, such as television shows, music videos, and even in advertisements.

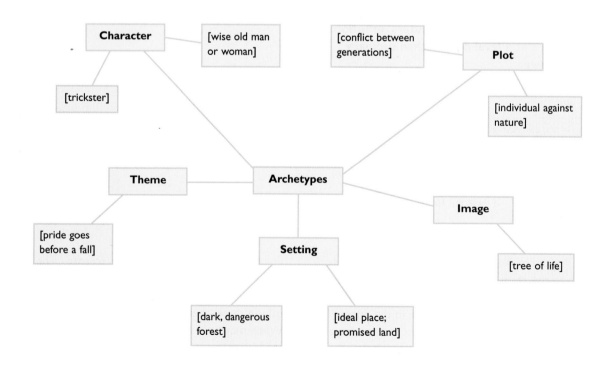

Read aloud Edgar Allan Poe's poem "Eldorado"(p. 280), and ask students to read the excerpt from *The Way to Rainy Mountain* by N. Scott Momaday (p. 997) or "The Leader of the People" by John Steinbeck (p. 669). Have students identify common archetypes in these texts or in others with which they are familiar. [Possible responses: a search for an ideal place or better land; a questing hero, or in Momaday's case, a questing people; failure to find or hold on to the ideal.] Then, lead students in a discussion of why these patterns keep reappearing in texts from different authors, times, and cultures. Ask if they think people today are still searching for an ideal place and how they deal with their disappointment when they don't find it. Help students understand that archetypes recur because human beings everywhere face similar problems, devise similar solutions, and have similar feelings in the face of adversity.

Independent Practice: Analyzing archetypes. Have students read Nathaniel Hawthorne's story "Dr. Heidegger's Experiment" (p. 227) or Jack London's "To Build a Fire" (p. 480). Next, ask them to work with a partner who has read the same story, collaborating to identify archetypes in the work. [Possible responses: *Hawthorne*—the search for eternal youth; the "mad scientist"; the magic mirror; failure to learn from experience. *London*—man humbled by nature; the overconfident rookie; the animal companion; the saving power of fire.] Have students find a contemporary story, television program, or movie that makes use of the same archetype(s) as one of these stories by Hawthorne or London and prepare to discuss how the contemporary version compares. Encourage them to use a chart or a Venn diagram to organize their analysis of the works' similarities and differences. Students can refer to their charts or diagrams in a class discussion about how writers have used archetypes over the ages. You might conclude by asking students the following questions:

- Why do you think archetypes often turn up in advertisements?

- What television ads, for example, present an image of eternal youth or an ideal place which will solve all problems and bring lasting happiness?

Philosophical Approach to Literature

> **Objective:** Analyze the philosophical arguments in literary works and their impact on the quality of each work.

Direct Teaching: Share the following information with students.

The ideas that form the foundation of a writer's work come from many sources. Writers draw from their own knowledge, experiences, and interests. Their writing also reflects what they understand and believe about the world and the people in it. This pattern of beliefs and values can be thought of as their philosophy of life. Often a writer's philosophy coincides with a particular religious, scientific, or literary body of thought (such as Jack London's interest in the literary theory of naturalism), or it may be a very personal set of beliefs that doesn't conform to any one philosophical system. Writers' philosophies affect how they write about such subjects as the nature of good and evil, the role of nature in human life, the possibility of happiness, and the meaning of death. Careful readers will look to see if writers have successfully integrated their philosophical beliefs into their work and will evaluate whether characters and other details ring true or function merely as mouthpieces for the writers' philosophical positions.

Guided Practice: Analyzing philosophical positions. Tell students that the role of nature is the subject of many works of literature, both in poetry and prose, and that underlying every one of these works is a philosophical belief about the relationship between the human and the natural worlds. Read aloud Emily Dickinson's poem "Apparently with no surprise" (p. 344). On the chalkboard, draw a diagram like the one below, and guide students in formulating a statement that identifies the belief about nature expressed in the poem. As students volunteer statements, ask them to provide details from the poem that support their conclusions, and write these at the bottom of the diagram. (Possible responses appear in brackets.) Keep the discussion going until all agree on a single statement of the speaker's philosophy on the subject of nature.

Next, ask students if they think Emily Dickinson, through her speaker in the poem, made a good case for her philosophical position. Explain to students that they do not have to accept a belief in order to judge whether a writer has made a convincing case for it; rather, they need only evaluate the strength of the evidence—in this case, the vividness of Dickinson's imagery.

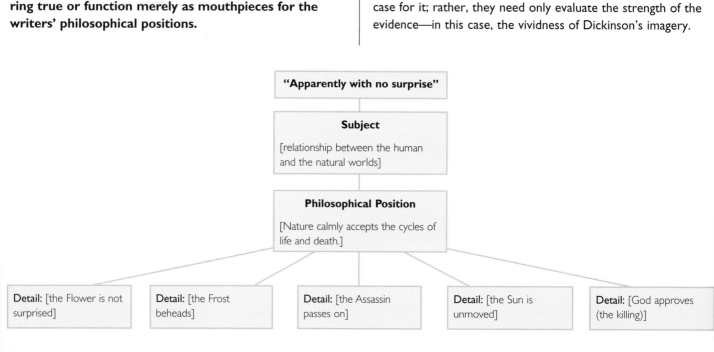

"Apparently with no surprise"

Subject

[relationship between the human and the natural worlds]

Philosophical Position

[Nature calmly accepts the cycles of life and death.]

Detail: [the Flower is not surprised]

Detail: [the Frost beheads]

Detail: [the Assassin passes on]

Detail: [the Sun is unmoved]

Detail: [God approves (the killing)]

Independent Practice: Evaluating philosophical positions in literature. Ask students to read Jack London's story "To Build a Fire" (p. 480). Then, have pairs compare and contrast London's view of the relationship between nature and human beings with that of Emily Dickinson as expressed in "Apparently with no surprise." Help students get started by asking them if they think the narrator of London's story would agree with the statement of Dickinson's philosophical position developed in the Guided Practice. [Most students will see the similarity between the two authors' view that nature is supremely indifferent to those it kills, but some may see London's philosophy as less benign and more deterministic than Dickinson's view of an approving God who watches over all.] Next, have partners note details from "To Build a Fire" that support their conclusions about London's philosophical position. [Possible responses: the detached narrator echoes nature's detachment; the main character is so unimportant in the scheme of things that he isn't given a name; the cold, gray images of nature link it with pain and death.] Finally, work as a class in considering the input of various pairs to refine evaluation of the two works. Ask, "Which writer do you think illustrates his or her philosophical position more effectively, and why?" In the case of the story, remind students to consider whether the fate of London's main character seems believable or merely a contrivance to prove London's philosophical point.

As you progress through each stage in the writing process, make sure you do the following.

- **Keep your ideas coherent and focused.** Present a tightly reasoned argument that will help you achieve your specific purpose. Every idea should focus on the point you make in your thesis statement.

- **Share your own perspective.** Give readers a piece of your mind by clearly communicating your viewpoint on the topic. Leave no doubt about who is the speaker in your writing, whether that person is you as a writer or a character you create to narrate a fictional piece.

- **Keep your audience in mind.** Use your understanding of your specific audience's backgrounds and interests to make your writing speak directly to them. If you have the option, choose a form that will be familiar or appealing to your readers—for example, a song, poem, memoir, editorial, screenplay, pamphlet, or letter.

- **Plan to publish.** Develop every piece as if it might be submitted for publication. When you proofread, work with a classmate who can help you find errors and inconsistencies. Use the following questions to guide you. The numbers in parentheses indicate the sections in which instruction on each topic begins in the Language Handbook.

QUESTIONS FOR PROOFREADING

1. Is every sentence complete, not a fragment or run-on? (9d, e)

2. Are punctuation marks used correctly? (12a–r, 13a–n, 14a–n)

3. Do sentences and proper nouns and adjectives begin with a capital letter? (11a, c)

4. Does each verb agree in number with its subject? (2a) Are verb forms and tenses used correctly? (3a–c)

5. Are subject and object forms of personal pronouns used correctly? (4a–d) Does every pronoun agree with a clear antecedent in number and gender? (4j)

To mark corrections, use the following symbols.

SYMBOLS FOR REVISING AND PROOFREADING

Symbol	Example	Meaning of Symbol
≡	Spence college	Capitalize a lowercase letter.
/	our Best friend	Lowercase a capital letter.
∧	on *the* fourth of July	Insert a missing word, letter, or punctuation mark.
	the capital of *Ohio* ~~Iowa~~	Replace a word.
ℓ	hoped ~~for~~ to go	Delete a word, letter, or punctuation mark.

Paragraphs

The Parts of a Paragraph

Paragraphs come in all sorts of shapes and sizes. They can be as short as one sentence or as long as many pages; they can seamlessly connect several items or develop a single idea.

In works of nonfiction, including essays that you write for school, paragraphs usually develop one main idea. These main-idea paragraphs are often made up of a **topic sentence, supporting sentences,** and a **clincher sentence,** as explained in the chart below.

PARTS OF PARAGRAPHS	
Topic Sentence	• states the main idea, or central focus, of the paragraph • is often the first or second sentence of a paragraph • can be placed at or near the end of a paragraph to create surprise or to summarize ideas
Supporting Sentences	• support or prove the main idea in the topic sentence • use the following kinds of details: *sensory details*—images of sight, sound, taste, smell, and texture *facts*—statements that can be proved true *examples*—specific instances or illustrations of a general idea; examples must be relevant to the main idea and precise rather than general *anecdotes*—brief biographical or autobiographical stories used to illustrate a main idea *analogies*—comparisons between ideas familiar to readers and unfamiliar concepts being explained
Clincher Sentence	• is a final sentence that emphasizes or summarizes the main idea • can help readers grasp the main idea of a longer paragraph

TIP Many paragraphs—even those that develop a main idea—do not use a clincher sentence. Use clinchers sparingly in your writing to avoid boring readers by restating an obvious main idea.

TIP Not all paragraphs have or need topic sentences. In fiction, paragraphs rarely include topic sentences. Paragraphs in nonfiction works that relate a sequence of events or steps frequently do not contain topic sentences. In much of the writing you do for school, however, you'll find topic sentences useful. They provide a focus for readers, and they keep you from straying off the topic as you develop the rest of your paragraph.

Putting the Parts Together Look carefully at the parts of the following paragraph. Notice that the topic sentence at the beginning expresses the main idea.

Topic Sentence

Supporting Sentences

Clincher Sentence

> In the past forty years, however, anthropologists have done some very thorough digging into the life of the North American Indians and have discovered a bewildering variety of cultures and societies beyond anything the schoolbooks have taught. There were Indian societies that dwelt in permanent settlements, and others that wandered; some were wholly democratic, and others had very rigid class systems based on property. Some were ruled by gods carried around on litters; some had judicial systems; to some the only known punishment was torture. Some lived in caves, others in tepees of bison skins, others in cabins. There were tribes ruled by warriors or by women, by sacred elders or by councils. . . .There were tribes who worshiped the bison or a matriarch or the maize they lived by. There were tribes that had never heard of war, and there were tribes debauched by centuries of fighting. In short, there was a great diversity of Indian nations, speaking over five hundred languages.
>
> Alistair Cooke, *Alistair Cooke's America*

Qualities of Paragraphs

You wouldn't build a house without thinking about how the boards, bricks, and shingles fit together. Paragraphs need to be just as carefully constructed. A well-written paragraph has **unity** and **coherence.**

Unity Unity simply means that a paragraph "hangs together." In other words, all the supporting sentences work together to develop a focused main idea. A paragraph should have unity whether the main idea is directly stated or merely suggested. Unity is achieved when all sentences relate to a stated or implied main idea or when all sentences relate to a sequence of events. In paragraphs that relate a series of actions or events, you can achieve unity by providing all the steps in the sequence, with no digressions.

Coherence In a coherent paragraph, the relationship between ideas is clear—the paragraph flows smoothly. You can go a long way toward making paragraphs coherent by paying attention to two things:

• the structure, or **order,** you use to arrange your ideas

• the **connections** you make between ideas

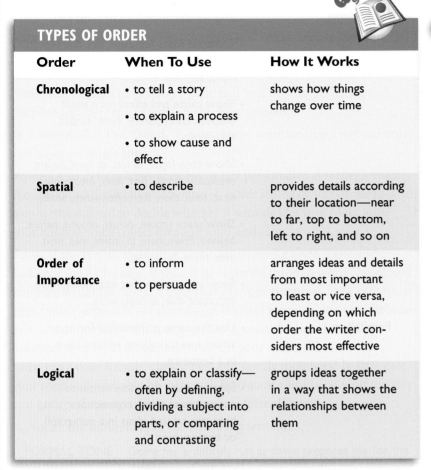

TYPES OF ORDER

Order	When To Use	How It Works
Chronological	• to tell a story • to explain a process • to show cause and effect	shows how things change over time
Spatial	• to describe	provides details according to their location—near to far, top to bottom, left to right, and so on
Order of Importance	• to inform • to persuade	arranges ideas and details from most important to least or vice versa, depending on which order the writer considers most effective
Logical	• to explain or classify— often by defining, dividing a subject into parts, or comparing and contrasting	groups ideas together in a way that shows the relationships between them

TIP At times, you may need to use multiple orders. In explaining an effect, for example, you may trace it **chronologically** from its cause. If one effect has four simultaneous causes, you would place these causes in **logical order** or **order of importance.** To avoid confusing your readers, use multiple orders in a sustained way and only when necessary.

In addition to presenting details in an order that makes sense, a paragraph that has coherence also shows how these details are connected. You can show connections by using **direct references** (or repetition of ideas), **transitional expressions,** and **parallelism.**

CONNECTING IDEAS

Connecting Strategy	How To Use It
Direct References, or Repetition of Ideas	• Refer to a noun or pronoun used earlier in the paragraph. • Repeat a word used earlier. • Use a word or phrase that means the same thing as one used earlier.

TIP Direct references and transitional expressions can also build coherence in longer compositions, leading readers from one sentence, paragraph, or idea to another. Try not to overuse these connecting strategies in your writing, though, as doing so can result in writing that sounds artificial and stilted.

(continued)

example, if most of your sentences start with a subject, occasionally move a phrase from later in the sentence to the beginning.

A Rhetorical Point To make your writing more effective, use the **rhetorical devices** of parallelism, repetition, and analogy.

Parallelism Use the same grammatical forms to connect related ideas within a sentence. Also, consider linking two ideas that appear in different sentences by using the same sentence structure. Use this latter technique sparingly to create an "echo" in readers' minds that will help them see the connections between important points.

Repetition Repeating words or phrases can cement important ideas in readers' minds and make your writing more coherent. Significant words, when repeated, can also create an emotional response, as in Martin Luther King, Jr.'s famous "I Have a Dream" speech.

Analogy An analogy is an extended comparison between two things. You can use an analogy to explain something unfamiliar to readers in terms they will understand, or you can enhance your tone through an analogy, such as this one: "The island emerged from the ocean in the same way that movie monsters suddenly appear from the darkness."

A Descriptive Model As you read the following passage, notice its voice and tone, word choice, sentence variety, and rhetorical devices.

A Writer's Model

Analogy
Precise language

Voice and tone

Repetition

Tone

The day I went to Alcatraz was as bleak as the island prison's past. It was cold and windy, and the waters of the bay were gunmetal gray. Along with the other tourists, my family and I crowded onto the ferry to the island, and the boat set out. Alcatraz loomed out of the waters of the bay, its peak crowned with concrete prison buildings and an old lighthouse. Gray, gray, everything looked gray. Later I would notice that wildflowers grew all over the island. At that moment, though, there was no color to be seen.

PRACTICE & APPLY Revise the following paragraph to improve its style.

I went to the Muir Woods last Saturday with my friend. We saw a big cross section of a redwood tree that showed that the tree was very old. We walked in the forest all day. The trees were tall. There were lots of other people walking in the forest. Afterward we went to the gift shop. I bought a bracelet made of redwood. It reminds me of the forest.

Designing Your Writing

A poorly designed document won't communicate even strong information effectively. In a well-designed document, the design supports the content, making it easy for readers to navigate through ideas and using visuals to share information that is difficult to communicate in words. You can create effective design and visuals by hand, or you can use advanced publishing software and graphics programs to design pages and to integrate databases, graphics, and spreadsheets into your documents.

Page Design

User-Friendly As a reader, you know that some document designs make text look inviting and others make you want to turn the page. As a writer, design your documents to be as appealing and easy to read as possible. Use these design elements to improve readability:

Columns and Blocks **Columns** arrange text in separate sections printed side by side. A **block** is a rectangle of text shorter than a page separated from other text by white space. The text in advertisements is usually set in blocks so that it may be read quickly. Text in reference books and newspapers usually appears in columns.

Bullets A **bullet** (•) is a symbol used to separate information into lists like the one on the next page. Bullets attract attention and help readers remember the information included in the lists.

Headings and Subheadings A **heading** at the beginning of a section of text, such as a chapter, gives a general idea of what that section will be about. A **subheading** indicates a new idea within the section. Several subheadings often appear under one heading. Headings and subheadings are usually set in larger type or in a different style than the rest of the text.

Pull-quotes Many magazine articles catch your attention with pull-quotes. A **pull-quote** is a significant sentence from the text that is printed in a large font and set in a box.

White Space **White space** is any area on a page where there is little or no text, visuals, or graphics. Usually, white space is limited to the margins and the spaces between words, lines, columns, and blocks. Advertisements usually have more white space than do books or articles.

Captions **Captions** are lines of text that explain the meaning or importance of photographs or illustrations and connect them to the main text. Captions may appear in italics or in smaller type than the main text.

Contrast Contrast refers to the balance of light and dark areas on a page. Dark areas are those that contain blocks of text or graphics. Light areas have little type. A page with high contrast, or roughly balanced light and dark areas, is easier to read than a page with low contrast, such as one that is filled with text and images.

Emphasis Emphasis is how a page designer indicates which information on a page is important. For example, the front page of a newspaper uses photographs and large headlines to place emphasis on a particular story. Because readers' eyes are drawn naturally to color, large print, and graphics, these elements are often used to create emphasis.

Type

Just My Type The kind of type you choose affects the readability of your documents. You can use type to provide emphasis and interest by varying the case and the font of your letters.

Case You can vary case in your documents in the following ways.

- **Uppercase letters** Words in all uppercase, or capital, letters attract readers' attention and may be used in headings or titles. Text in all capital letters can be difficult to read. Therefore, use it sparingly.

- **Initial letter** An initial letter is a large first letter used to draw readers into an essay. You can draw your initial letter by hand, or you can enlarge a letter using a word-processing program.

- **Small caps** Small caps are uppercase letters reduced in size. They appear in abbreviations of time, such as 9:00 A.M. and A.D. 1500. Small caps may be combined with capitals for an artistic effect.

Font A **font** is one complete set of characters (such as letters, numbers, and punctuation marks) of a given size and design. All fonts belong to one of the three categories shown in the chart below.

CATEGORIES OF FONTS		
Category	**Explanation**	**Uses**
decorative, or **script**	elaborately designed characters that convey a distinct mood or feeling	Decorative fonts are difficult to read and should be used in small amounts for an artistic effect.
serif	characters with small strokes (serifs) attached at each end	Because the strokes on serif characters help guide the reader's eyes from letter to letter, serif type is often used for large bodies of text.
sans serif	characters formed of straight lines, with no serifs (*sans serif* means "without strokes")	Sans serif fonts are easy to read and are used for headings, subheadings, callouts, and captions.

1150 Resource Center   **Writer's Handbook**

- **Font size** The size of the type in a document is called the font size or point size. Many newspapers use type measured at 12 points, with larger type for headings and smaller type for captions.

- **Font style** Most text is set in *roman* ("not slanted") style. *Italic,* or slanted, style has special uses, as for captions or book titles. Underscored or boldface type can be used for emphasis.

Visuals

Get Visual Some ideas can be communicated more effectively visually than as part of the text. For instance, a line graph showing how your club's membership has grown over the last four years would be more effective than simply writing about the information. If available, use technology, such as computer software and graphics programs, to create visuals and to integrate databases, graphics, and spreadsheets into documents. Whether you create them with software or by hand, the following types of visuals can help you effectively share ideas.

Graphs A **bar graph** can compare quantities at a glance or indicate the parts of a whole. A **line graph** such as the example below can compare trends or show how two or more variables interact. Both kinds of graphs can show trends or changes over time.

TIP You can copy databases or spreadsheets and paste them into word-processed documents. For example, imagine that you are writing a letter to your school administration asking for more money for the prom. Your letter will be more effective if you include in the letter a spreadsheet showing the budget and estimated expenses for the prom.

EXAMPLE

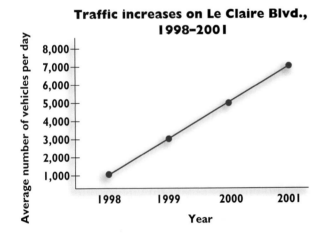

Traffic increases on Le Claire Blvd., 1998–2001

Tables use rows and columns to provide detailed information arranged in an accessible, organized way. A **spreadsheet** is a special kind of table created on a computer. The cells of a spreadsheet are associated with mathematical equations. Spreadsheets are especially useful for budgets or schedules in which the numbers are variables in an equation. In the spreadsheet on the next page, the last row totals the figures in each column.

EXAMPLE

Club Account Balances by Month				
Month	September	October	November	December
deposit (dues)	150.00	150.00	165.00	165.00
deposit (other)	75.00	38.00	17.75	119.00
total	225.00	188.00	182.75	284.00

Pictures You may scan a drawing or photograph into your document on the computer or paste it in manually. Place a picture as close as possible to the reference in the text, and use a caption.

Charts Charts show relationships among ideas or data. Two types of charts you are likely to use are flowcharts and pie charts. A **flowchart** uses geometric shapes linked by arrows to show the sequence of events in a process. A **pie chart** is a circle that is divided into wedges. Each wedge represents a certain percentage of the total, and a legend tells what concept each wedge color represents.

EXAMPLE

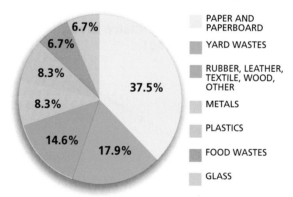

What Creates Solid Wastes?
(Percentage of solid waste)

- PAPER AND PAPERBOARD
- YARD WASTES
- RUBBER, LEATHER, TEXTILE, WOOD, OTHER
- METALS
- PLASTICS
- FOOD WASTES
- GLASS

Time Lines Time lines identify the events dealing with a particular subject that have taken place over a given period of time. (See page 2 for an example of a time line.)

PRACTICE & APPLY Use the instructions in this section to choose and create the visual you think would most effectively communicate the following information.

Last year, the total production cost for the Eureka High yearbook was $2,000. Paper cost $400, printing cost $1,000, and binding cost $600. This year, production costs have gone up. Paper will cost $500, printing will cost $1,250, and binding will cost $725, for a total of $2,475.

Test Smarts

by **Flo Ota De Lange** *and* **Sheri Henderson**

Strategies for Taking Multiple-Choice Tests

You have now reached your junior year and are almost at the end of your high school career. To graduate, however, you still need to pass a lot of tests. You'll have plenty of quizzes, midterm exams, and finals to get through. You'll take the state's standardized tests, and if you plan to go on to college, you'll need to tackle the *Scholastic Assessment Test (SAT)* or the *American College Testing Program (ACT)*.

The following pages can help you prepare for all your standardized tests. They are designed to help you meet three goals:

- to become familiar with the different types of questions you will be asked
- to learn some strategies for approaching the questions
- to discover the kinds of questions that give you trouble

Once you have met those goals, you will want to practice answering the kinds of questions that give you trouble until you feel comfortable with them. Here are some basic strategies that will help you approach your multiple-choice tests with confidence:

Stay Calm

You have studied the material, and you know your stuff, but you're still nervous. That's OK. A little nervousness helps you focus, but so does a calm body. **Take a few deep breaths** before you begin.

Track Your Time

First, take a few minutes to estimate how much time you have for each question. Then, set checkpoints for yourself—how many questions should be completed at a quarter of the time, half the time, and so on. That way you can **pace yourself** as you work through the test. If you're behind, you can speed up. If you're ahead, you can—and should—slow down.

Master the Directions

Read the directions carefully to be sure you know exactly what to do and how to do it. If you are supposed to fill in a bubble, fill it in cleanly and carefully. Be careful to match each question's number to the number on the answer sheet.

Study the Questions

Read each question once, twice, three times—until you are absolutely certain you know what the question is asking you. Watch out for words like *not* and *except:* They tell you to look for choices that are false, different, or opposite.

Anticipate Answers

Once you are sure you understand the question, **anticipate the answer** before you read the choices. If the answer you guessed is there, it is probably correct. To be sure, though, check out each choice. If you understand the question but don't know the answer, eliminate any choices you think are wrong. Then, make an educated—not a wild—guess. Take care to **avoid distracters,** choices that are true but don't fit the question.

Don't Give Up

If you are having a hard time with a test, take a deep breath, and **keep on going.** On most tests the questions do not get more difficult as you go, and an easier question is probably coming up soon. The last question on a test is worth just as many points as the first, so give your all—all the way to the end.

Types of Test Questions

You will feel more confident if you are familiar with the kinds of questions given on a test. Following are examples of and tips for taking the different types of questions on many standardized tests.

Thus, you are looking for a word that means "good." **E is your best choice.**

But let's imagine for a moment that the choices are all unfamiliar words. (What? You say they *are* unfamiliar words?) You can still think them through. **Use what you know to eliminate incorrect choices.** For instance, you know that a nebula is a hazy cloud of dust and gas in space, so choice **A** (*nebulous*—like a nebula) probably means "hazy" too.

Choice **B** (*noxious*) may be an unfamiliar word, but you can guess it's related to *obnoxious*, which means "totally unpleasant." **C** (*partial*) gives its meaning away in its root word: *part*. However, you may have heard someone say he or she is partial to chocolate, as in liking it. That *could* be a match, but it's a stretch. Keep looking for a better choice.

D (*intractable*) has a familiar prefix (*in–*, meaning "not") and suffix (*able*). Not able to *tract*. Hmmm. A word that means "not able to do something" isn't going to fit the blank.

So what's left? Bingo! You might even have connected the ancient tradition of augury (telling the future) with the modern word *auspicious* in **E.**

Two Blanks to Fill In

Some sentence-completion questions contain two blanks. The trick is to find the choice that fits both blanks correctly—in the order given. **As a shortcut, determine the choices that fit *one* blank, whichever blank seems easier to you.** Cross out all the choices that don't fit. **Then, consider *only* the remaining choices when filling in the other blank.**

9. Comprehending that a million is a truly _____ quantity to visualize, the professor _____ to the class that one million dollar bills stacked atop one another would reach more than four hundred feet high and weigh one ton.

   A knotty, pontificated

   B prodigious, explained

   C immense, refused

   D cuboid, lampooned

   E scant, illuminated

Answer: Before you look at the choices, make sense of the sentence. You know from the sentence that the first blank will reflect a *large* quantity, because the second half describes its considerable height and weight. Now, look at the choices. **You can immediately eliminate any first-blank choices that do not reflect the sentence's meaning.** Eliminate **A** (*knotty*) and **D** (*cuboid*) as irrelevant. Eliminate **E** (*scant*) because it's an antonym for the word you want. That leaves **B** (*prodigious*) and **C** (*immense*). Even if you don't know the definitions of those words, consider them. **Now, go on to the second blank, checking only the choices that fit the first blank**—in this case **B** and **C.** The second blank describes what the professor did. Of the two choices left, **B** (*explained to the class*) fits well, but **C** (*refused to the class*) makes no sense. **Thus, the best answer is B.**

ANALOGY QUESTIONS require that you figure out the relationship between one pair of words and then select another pair with the same relationship. Analogies use many kinds of relationships, among them, **classification, degree, cause and effect, part and whole, object and performer, performer and action, characteristic, synonym, antonym,** and **use.** For more about analogies, see pages 163, 714, and 950.

The more comprehensive your vocabulary, the better off you will be when you face an analogy question. If you are stumped, try breaking an unfamiliar word into its prefix, suffix, and root. In some tests the analogy questions get harder as you go, but don't give up. Everyone's vocabulary is different, and a word that seems difficult to others may be easy for you. Let's try one out:

10. CHEAPSKATE : STINGINESS ::

   A donor : generosity

   B grouch : cheerfulness

   C bully : merriment

   D beggar : excess

   E flatterer : truthfulness

Begin by turning the first pair of words (the stem words) into a sentence that defines their relationship. Your sentence should begin with the first word in the pair and end with the second word; you fill in the middle. A sentence for item 10 might be *A characteristic of a cheapskate is stinginess.* Now, try out each choice in that sentence: A characteristic of a donor is generosity? A characteristic of a grouch is cheerfulness? A characteristic of a bully is merriment? A characteristic of a beggar is excess? A characteristic of a flatterer is truthfulness?

Answer: **A is the best answer** because it preserves the same relationship in both word pairs, which in this case is a person and a characteristic. Both a cheapskate and a donor are kinds of people. Both stinginess and generosity are characteristics of people, and each is, indeed, a characteristic of its paired type of person. All other choices—**B, C, D,** and **E**—mismatch people and characteristics. Oh, there's just one more thing about the words in item 10. On the *SAT* the words would be much more difficult, like this:

11. MISER : PARSIMONY ::

   A philanthropist : largesse

   B curmudgeon : felicity

   C lout : joviality

   D mendicant : surfeit

   E sycophant : verity

Answer: **The correct answer is still A.** In item 11, every word is a synonym of the corresponding word in item 10.

You may have already noticed that words in vocabulary questions are anything but commonplace. What's a student to do in the face of such *egregious, inordinate,* and *maliciously pedantic* word choices? Study them. Study them. Study them. The best way, though, to learn vocabulary words is to read. Read many different kinds of materials. Don't just skim over words you don't know: Look them up. Then, think about the meaning they add to the passage you are reading. If you follow those suggestions, you'll increase your vocabulary *exponentially,* and questions on vocabulary tests will be much less *formidable.*

Here are two more analogy questions—the kind with easy words:

12. LYRICS : SONG ::

   A table : lamp

   B dialogue : script

   C poetry : prose

   D trial : judgment

   E plow : tractor

Answer: To define the relationship in the stem words, you might make up this sentence: *Lyrics are part of a song.* (The relationship is that of part and whole.) Then, try out that same sentence with all of the choices. You can eliminate **A, C,** and **E** because they don't make sense in your sentence. **B** makes sense: The dialogue *is* part of a script. **D** would have made sense if the words were in reverse order (a judgment is part of a trial)—but they're not. **So B is the correct answer.**

13. PAINTER : CANVAS ::

   A experiment : science

   B concentration : distraction

   C athlete : spine

   D dentist : molars

   E cathedral : architect

Answer: **The answer is D.** The relationship in this analogy is that of a performer (the doer) and object: *A painter works on a canvas.* You can quickly eliminate **B** (the words are antonyms) and **C** (*spine* doesn't fit; if the choice were *race,* that might work). **A** doesn't make sense in your sentence, and **E** gives the words in the wrong order. The only choice that fits is **D:** A dentist works on molars.

Multiple-Choice Writing Questions

Multiple-choice writing questions are designed to test your knowledge of standard written English. Some questions ask you to spot errors in a sentence's grammar or punctuation. Some ask you to spot the best written form of a sentence. Some ask when a paragraph is (or isn't) properly developed. You will need to know the rules of punctuation and grammar. Here are some question formats you might encounter:

IDENTIFYING-SENTENCE-ERROR QUESTIONS

ask you to look at underlined sections of a sentence and choose the section that includes an error. You are *not* expected to correct the error.

14. When Daniel P. Mannix, a sword
swallower, <u>being</u> accused of using retract-
       A

ing swords to fool his <u>audience, Mannix</u>
                 B

swallowed a neon <u>tube and then turned</u>
               C

it on, bringing new meaning to the old
adage <u>"Light of my life."</u> <u>No error.</u>
   D   E

Answer: **The correct answer is A.** Replace the participle *being* with the verb *was*. Remember, however, that that kind of question asks you only to *find* the error, *not* to correct it. By the way, don't try Daniel's trick at home.

IMPROVING-SENTENCES QUESTIONS

ask you to correct an underlined section by choosing the best version offered. It is helpful to find the error before you look at the choices. Then, anticipate how it could best be corrected. The answers to questions like these are often confusing to read because they are long and very poorly written (remember that all but one of them are wrong). Take some time with such questions.

Directions: Read the sentence below. Then, choose the answer that best improves the underlined portion of the sentence. Remember: The answers do not replace the whole sentence; they replace only the underlined part.

15. <u>The water strider is a type of insect, it walks on water</u> with padlike feet that skate over the water's surface tension.

   A The water strider is a type of insect, which it is able to walk on water

   B To walk on water, a type of insect called the water strider walks on water

   C The water strider, a type of insect, walks on water

   D Walking on water, the water strider, a type of insect, walks on water

   E The water strider, which has the ability to walk on water, is a type of insect that walks on water

Answer: **C is the best answer.** It corrects the run-on in the original sentence by creating an appositive, *a type of insect.* Choice **A** is grammatically incorrect because the word *it* follows *which*. Choices **B** and **D** are grammatically correct, but they're unnecessarily repetitious. The introductory infinitive phrase in **B** (*To walk on water*) and the introductory participial phrase in **D** (*Walking on water*) create sentences that awkwardly repeat *walks on water* later in the sentence. **E** is grammatically correct and would be a good choice except for the repetition of *walk/walks on water*. Notice that the correct answer, **C,** wastes no words—it's streamlined, clear, and direct.

IMPROVING-THE-PARAGRAPH QUESTIONS

present a paragraph followed by questions. You may be asked to pick a choice that combines or rewrites portions of sentences. You may be asked to decide which sentences could be added or removed from the paragraph. You may be asked which sentence could be used to strengthen the argument of the writer or to pick a thesis statement for the paragraph.

Directions: Read the paragraph below. Then, find the best answer to the following questions.

(1) A professional baseball pitcher's fast ball crosses the plate in about .4 seconds from the time it is thrown. (2) You could literally blink and miss it. (3) And a swing that is 7/1,000th of a second too early or too late will foul out. (4) The best spot on the bat to hit a ball is really small. (5) It is only about as big as a tube of lipstick. (6) If the batter doesn't hit that spot, the ball doesn't go all that far, and the vibration up the bat stings like crazy. (7) A professional baseball player swings the bat at about 70 mph with a force of about three horse-power. (8) When everything lines up just right, that swing at 70 mph meets the ball with about four tons of pressure, which flattens it for a split second to about half its diameter and then sets it flying at 110 mph over the fence.

16. Which of the following statements represents the best way to combine sentences 4 and 5?

   A The best spot on the bat to hit a ball is really small, it is only about as big as a tube of lipstick.

   B The best spot on the bat to hit a ball is really small, only about as big as a tube of lipstick.

   C The best spot on the bat to hit a ball is really small like a tube of lipstick is really small.

   D The best spot on the bat to hit a ball is only about as big as a tube of lipstick.

   E The best spot on the bat to hit a ball is only a tube of lipstick.

Answer: You are looking for the sentence that contains all of the important information with the *least* amount of repetition. **A** is a run-on sentence, so that clearly won't work. **C** is awkwardly repetitious, and **E** is just plain silly. **B** is a good possibility, but **D** says it in fewer words. **Your best answer is D,** which cuts the repetitious *really small* since you have preserved *only about as big.*

17. You want to add the following sentences to the paragraph on the left. Where is the best place to put them?

   So you think baseball is easy to play? Think again.

   A Before sentence 1

   B After sentence 8

   C Between sentences 2 and 3

   D Between sentences 5 and 6

   E Between sentences 7 and 8

Answer: If you try out the two sentences in the places mentioned, you'll quickly discover that **C, D,** and **E** are wrong. The two sentences interrupt the thought—the logic—of the paragraph and ruin the paragraph's coherence. Both **A** (at the beginning) and **B** (at the end) seem possible, but the sentence *Think again* suggests that information will follow that will contradict your notion that baseball is easy to play. **Therefore, A is the best answer.**

Strategies for Taking Writing Tests

Writing a Response to Literature

On a test you may be asked to respond in writing to a poem. To do so effectively, you must not only understand the poem on the surface but also draw conclusions that lead you to understand the poem's deeper meaning. Follow the steps below. The sample responses provided are based on the prompt to the right.

Prompt

In an essay, explain the meaning of the following poem by Emily Dickinson. Support your ideas with examples from the poem and from your own knowledge.

Tell all the Truth but tell it slant—
Success in Circuit lies
Too bright for our infirm Delight
The Truth's superb surprise
As Lightning to the Children eased
With Explanation kind
The Truth must dazzle gradually
Or every man be blind —

THINKING IT THROUGH ∘ **Writing a Response to Literature**

STEP 1 **First, read the prompt carefully; then, read the selection.** Decide what tasks the prompt calls for, and read the selection for understanding.

This poem talks about telling the whole truth, but not telling it all right away.

STEP 2 **Draw a conclusion about the deeper meaning of the piece.** Base your conclusion on your own knowledge and on details that seem important in the selection.

I think the poet is saying that the really important truths in life can't be understood unless you learn them indirectly or gradually. She's talking about important, life-and-death things, because Truth with a capital "T" (which appears 3 times) doesn't mean something small, like admitting you forgot your homework.

STEP 3 **Gather support for your thesis.** Choose strong details and examples, and elaborate on those details and examples using your own knowledge and experience.

Capitalized words: Truth (3 times), Circuit, Delight, Lightning, Explanation, Children
Repetition: Truth, images of bright lights (Too bright, Lightning, dazzle)
The Truth is the bright light.

STEP 4 **Develop a thesis statement for your essay.** Your thesis statement will sum up your main points and state your conclusion about the piece.

Dickinson's poem suggests that the only way to help someone understand an important truth in life is to reveal it gradually or indirectly.

STEP 5 **Write your essay.** Make clear how examples you use from the text relate to your thesis. As you draft your essay, maintain a serious, objective tone. Proofread your finished draft, and correct any errors in grammar, usage, and mechanics.

Writing a Response to Expository Text

You read **expository** text, such as instructions for a task, a chapter in a textbook, or a magazine article, to gain information. Such text is usually clearly organized to help you learn from it. When you write a response to expository text, you must demonstrate what you have learned and show that you understand how that information is organized. Use the steps below. ("The Most Remarkable Woman of This Age" begins on page 418.)

("The Most Remarkable Woman of This Age" begins on page 418.)

Prompt

The article "The Most Remarkable Woman of This Age" was first published during the Civil War. What do you think the author hoped to achieve by writing the article? In an essay, note details from the article that support the purpose you identify.

THINKING IT THROUGH   Writing a Response to Expository Text

STEP 1 **First, read the prompt carefully. Then, read the text.** Decide what tasks the prompt calls for, and get an overview of the selection.

I need to read the article looking for clues about the author's purpose, keeping in mind that the article was published during the Civil War.

STEP 2 **Decide on your general answer, and identify your main supporting points.** Skim the selection to identify the main points you will make to support your answer to the prompt.

Even though it isn't a persuasive piece, I think the author wants people to admire Harriet Tubman and support her cause. The article discusses her difficult life, her efforts toward helping people to freedom, and her personal outlook.

STEP 3 **Develop a thesis statement for your essay.** Your thesis statement will sum up your main points and draw a conclusion about your topic.

Although it isn't stated directly, the author probably supports the abolition of slavery based on the ideas in the article and on what I know about the Civil War. My thesis will be: This article was written to win support for Harriet Tubman's efforts and for the larger cause of abolishing slavery in the United States.

STEP 4 **Gather support for your thesis.** Choose details and examples that will provide strong support, and elaborate on those details and examples by drawing on your own knowledge and experience.

Details such as Tubman's head injury, the sedated infant, and Tubman's statement about the lengths necessary to avoid betrayal point out the evils of slavery and the difficulty involved in finding freedom. The final paragraph shows that the writer feels that God supports Harriet Tubman's cause.

STEP 5 **Write your essay.** Begin with an attention-getter, such as a question or a surprising statement. Organize ideas clearly and logically, using transitions to show readers the links among those ideas. Then, find and correct any errors in English-language conventions in your draft.

Test Smarts   1163

Writing a Biographical Narrative

An effective **biographical narrative** relates an event in someone's life so vividly that readers feel that they, too, have experienced it. It also presents a conclusion about the person involved in the event, helping readers learn something more about him or her. To write a biographical narrative in response to a test prompt, follow the steps below.

Prompt

Heroic deeds come in many forms, from acts that make front-page news to those that affect only one person. Think of something you consider heroic that someone you know has done, and write a narrative describing the event.

THINKING IT THROUGH

Writing a Biographical Narrative

STEP 1 Carefully read the prompt, and choose a subject.

I have to describe a heroic act by someone I know. I'll tell about the time when my brother saved a dog that was caught in a storm sewer during a thunderstorm.

STEP 2 Identify the parts of the event you will relate. Jot down in sequence the smaller events that make up your chosen event.

1. We were excited, listening to the thunder and watching the radar on TV, when we heard a faint howling.
2. We went out with a flashlight and found the dog a few yards back from where the storm sewer opens to the creek behind our house.
3. My brother waded into the knee-deep water that was pouring out of the storm sewer and carried the dog out.
4. We took care of it and let it sleep in the garage, then found its owner the next day.

STEP 3 Identify important details about the people, events, and setting. Details should be relevant and specific to bring the incident to life.

Important details include the flashes of lightning, the way the water roaring out of the storm sewer sounded and looked, the determined look on my brother's face, and the sound and appearance of the bedraggled dog.

STEP 4 Draw a conclusion based on the details. Decide why the incident is significant; this conclusion will be the basis for your narrative's thesis.

Despite his discomfort and the possible dangers of wading into deep, fast-moving water, my brother was a hero to a helpless animal that night.

STEP 5 Write a draft of your biographical narrative. Include an introduction to provide context for readers. Make sure you consistently relate the event from your own point of view, not from your subject's, and check that every detail you include helps support your thesis or bring the event to life. Finally, correct any errors in grammar, usage, and mechanics.

Writing an Expository Composition

When you write an **expository composition,** you provide information to an audience of curious readers. To help readers understand your ideas, answer questions they might have about your topic and clear up any potential misunderstandings or biases about the topic. Use the steps below to write an effective expository composition for a test. The sample responses provided are based on the prompt to the right.

Prompt

There is a wide variety of after-school activities in which you might participate. Choose two of your favorite activities, and write an essay in which you explain how they are similar and different—not only in *what* you do, but in *why* you participate and what you get out of them.

THINKING IT THROUGH | Writing an Expository Composition

STEP 1 Carefully read the prompt, and choose a topic you know well.

I need to explain the similarities and differences between two after-school activities I participate in, including what I get out of participating. I'll compare and contrast my two favorite activities—drama club and track.

STEP 2 Divide the topic into parts. Note the main categories of information you will provide about your topic.

Similarities: In both I challenge myself, try new things, and represent the school.
Differences: Track is more physical, while drama is more mental. Also, in track I usually race alone, while in drama I work as part of a cast.

STEP 3 Brainstorm details about each part of the topic. Details should answer the *5W-How?* questions (Who? What? Where? When? Why? How?).

People already know the obvious details about these activities, so I'll focus on the kinds of challenges and on details about mental preparation and teamwork. For example, my comparison can note how much time I spend practicing alone for both activities. My contrast can explain the importance of other cast members' actions to my performance in drama, as well as how my track performance is independent of how my teammates do.

STEP 4 Synthesize your ideas to plan a thesis. Draft a thesis sentence explaining the point made by all of your information about your topic.

While track and drama seem on the surface to be very different activities, they also share similarities in how they affect me personally.

STEP 5 Write a draft of your expository composition. To provide clear, useful information for readers, avoid simply stringing together obvious ideas about your topic. Instead, include striking or unusual ideas and explain them thoroughly for readers. Organize all of your ideas in an easy-to-follow way. Finally, proofread to correct any errors in grammar, usage, and mechanics.

their skilled use of dialect are Mark Twain, Eudora Welty, William Faulkner, and Langston Hughes.

See page 459.
See also *Vernacular*.

DIALOGUE **The directly quoted words of people speaking to one another.** Writers use dialogue to advance the plot and develop characters.

See pages 731, 968.
See also *Dialect, Diction, Tone*.

DICTION **A speaker's or writer's choice of words.** Diction can be formal, informal, colloquial, full of slang, poetic, ornate, plain, abstract, concrete, and so on. Diction depends on the writer's subject, purpose, and audience. Some words, for example, are suited to informal conversations but are inappropriate in a formal speech. Diction has a powerful effect on the **tone** of a piece of writing.

See also *Tone*.

DRAMATIC MONOLOGUE **A poem in which a character speaks to one or more listeners whose responses are not known.** The reactions of the listener must be inferred by the reader. From the speaker's words the reader learns about the setting, the situation, the identity of the other characters, and the personality of the speaker. The outstanding dramatic monologue in American literature is T. S. Eliot's "The Love Song of J. Alfred Prufrock" (Collection 5).

See page 583.

ELEGY **A poem of mourning, usually about someone who has died.** Most elegies are written to mark a particular person's death, but some extend their subject to reflect on life, death, and the fleeting nature of beauty. William Cullen Bryant's poem "Thanatopsis" (Collection 2) is an elegy. The excerpt from N. Scott Momaday's *The Way to Rainy Mountain* (Collection 6) is partly elegiac in that it mourns the death of a particular person and, by extension, the passing of an entire way of life.

See page 1004.

ENJAMBMENT **The running on of sense from the end of one line of verse into the next, without a punctuated pause.** Poets often use enjambment to add rhythmic diversity. Enjambment is contrasted with an end-stopped line (a line that is a grammatical unit and ends with punctuation). Enjambed lines allow the poet to create a pause in the middle of a sentence. This mental and physical "breath" creates an unexpected moment for the reader.

EPIC **A long narrative poem, written in heightened language, which recounts the deeds of a heroic character who embodies the values of a particular society.** Epics in English include *Beowulf* (c. 700) and John Milton's *Paradise Lost* (1667). Some critics of Walt Whitman's *Leaves of Grass* see his collection as an American epic in which the hero is the questing poet.

EPITHET **A descriptive word or phrase that is frequently used to characterize a person or a thing.** The epithet "the father of our country" is often used to characterize George Washington. New York City's popular epithet, "the Big Apple," is frequently used by advertisers. Epics such as Homer's *Odyssey* and *Illiad* frequently use **stock epithets** over and over again to describe certain characters or places: "patient Penelope," "wily Odysseus," and "earthshaker" for Poseidon.

ESSAY **A short piece of nonfiction prose in which the writer discusses some aspect of a subject.** The word *essay* come from French *essai*, meaning "to try," a derivation that suggests that the essay form is not an exhaustive treatment of a subject. Essays are sometimes classified as **formal** or **informal** (or personal). The essay form was especially popular in the twentieth century, particularly among American writers. Some famous American essayists of the past include Thomas Paine (Collection 1), Ralph Waldo Emerson (Collection 2), and Henry David Thoreau (Collection 2). More recent essayists include E. B. White, Alice Walker (Collection 6), James Baldwin (Collection 6), Annie Dillard, and Joan Didion.

See page 1007.

EXPOSITION **One of the four major forms of discourse, in which something is explained or set forth.** Exposition is most commonly used in nonfiction. The word *exposition* also refers to that part of a plot in which the reader is given important background information on the characters, their setting, and their problems. Such exposition is usually provided at the opening of a story or play. See the opening paragraph of Nathaniel Hawthorne's "The Minister's Black Veil" (Collection 2) for an example. The other three major forms of discourse are **description, narration,** and **persuasion.**

See also *Plot.*

FABLE **A very short story told in prose or poetry that teaches a practical lesson about how to succeed in life.** In many fables the characters are animals that behave like people. The most ancient fabulist is the Greek Aesop; the most famous American fabulist is James Thurber (Collection 5), who wrote *Fables for Our Time* and *Further Fables for Our Time.*

FARCE **A type of comedy in which ridiculous and often stereotyped characters are involved in silly far-fetched situations.** The humor in a farce is often physical and slapstick, with characters being hit in the face with pies or running into closed doors. American cinema has produced many farces, including those starring Laurel and Hardy, Abbott and Costello, and the Marx Brothers.

FIGURE OF SPEECH **A word or phrase that describes one thing in terms of something else and that is not meant to be taken literally.** Figures of speech almost always involve a comparison of two things that are basically very dissimilar. Hundreds of figures of speech have been identified by scholars; the most common ones are **simile, metaphor, personification,** and **symbol.** Figures of speech, also called, more generally, **figurative language,** are basic to everyday speech. Statements like "She is a tower of strength" and "He is a pain in the neck" are figures of speech.

See pages 45, 184, 191.
See also *Conceit, Metaphor, Personification, Simile, Symbol.*

FIRESIDE POETS **A group of nineteenth-century poets from Boston including Henry Wadsworth Longfellow, John Greenleaf Whittier, Oliver Wendell Holmes, and James Russell Lowell.** Their poems were often read by the fireside as family entertainment and memorized and recited by students in classrooms. They were also known as the Schoolroom Poets.

See page 146.

FLASHBACK **A scene that interrupts the normal chronological sequence of events in a story to depict something that happened at an earlier time.** Although the word was coined to describe a technique used by moviemakers, the technique itself is at least as old as ancient Greek literature. Much of Homer's epic poem the *Odyssey* is a flashback. Willa Cather uses frequent flashbacks to reveal the past of Georgiana in "A Wagner Matinée" (Collection 4).

See page 997.

FOIL **A character who acts as a contrast to another character.** In Maxine Hong Kingston's "The Girl Who Wouldn't Talk" (Collection 6), the quiet girl who takes refuge in her Chinese family is a foil for the narrator who is aggressively trying to fit into American society.

FOOT **A metrical unit of poetry.** A foot always contains at least one stressed syllable and, usually, one or more unstressed syllables. An **iamb** is a common foot in English poetry: It consists of an unstressed syllable followed by a stressed syllable (ˇ ´).

See also *Anapest, Blank Verse, Dactyl, Iamb, Iambic Pentameter, Meter, Spondee, Trochee.*

FORESHADOWING **The use of hints and clues to suggest what will happen later in a plot.** A writer might use foreshadowing to create suspense or to prefigure later events. In "To Build a Fire" (Collection 4), for example, Jack London places hints throughout the text that foreshadow the story's conclusion.

FRAME STORY **A literary device in which a story is enclosed in another story, a tale within a tale.** The best-known example of a frame story is the Persian collection *The Thousand and One Nights* (also known as *Arabian Nights*). Raymond Carver uses the frame device in "Everything Stuck to Him" (Collection 6). His story begins and ends with a frame in which an unnamed man tells a woman a story. The story that the man tells is the main body of Carver's tale.

FREE ENTERPRISE **The practice of allowing private businesses to operate competitively for profit with little government regulation.** Free enterprise was threatened by Marxist beliefs. Several novelists of the 1920s and 1930s satirized the free-enterprise system and the gross materialism of American business of the time. Sinclair Lewis's *Babbitt* (1922) is a major example.

See page 565.

Handbook of Literary and Historical Terms **1175**

FREE VERSE Poetry that does not conform to regular meter or rhyme scheme. Poets who write in free verse try to reproduce the natural rhythms of spoken language. Free verse uses the traditional poetic elements of **imagery, figures of speech, repetition, internal rhyme, alliteration, assonance,** and **onomatopoeia.** The first American practitioner of free verse was Walt Whitman (Collection 3). Some of Whitman's heirs are William Carlos Williams (Collection 6), Carl Sandburg (Collection 6), and Allen Ginsberg (Collection 5).

See pages 313, 573.
See also *Cadence, Meter, Rhythm.*

HAIKU A short, unrhymed poem developed in Japan in the fifteenth century. A haiku consists of three unrhymed lines and a total of seventeen syllables. The first and third lines of a traditional haiku have five syllables each, and the middle line has seven syllables. Haiku often convey feelings through a descriptive snapshot of a natural object or scene. Imagists like Ezra Pound were influenced by the haiku form.

HARLEM RENAISSANCE A cultural movement of the early 1920s led by African American artists, writers, musicians, and performers, located in Harlem. After World War I, vast numbers of African Americans migrated north and settled in the New York City neighborhood called Harlem. Important contributors to the Harlem Renaissance were the writers Langston Hughes and Countee Cullen, the artists Jacob Lawrence and Aaron Douglas, and the performers Paul Robeson and Josephine Baker.

See pages 568, 741.

HYPERBOLE (hī·pur′bə·lē) A figure of speech that uses an incredible exaggeration, or overstatement, for effect. In "The Celebrated Jumping Frog of Calaveras County" (Collection 4), Mark Twain uses hyperbole for comic effect. In his poetry, Walt Whitman often uses overstatement to create a larger-than-life persona, or speaker, as in the line below.

> I sound my barbaric yawp over the roofs of the world.
>
> —Walt Whitman,
> from *Song of Myself,* 54

See page 459.
See also *Understatement.*

IAMB A metrical foot in poetry that has an unstressed syllable followed by a stressed syllable, as in the word *protect.* The iamb (ˇ ′) is a common foot in poetry written in English.

See pages 171, 173.
See also *Anapest, Blank Verse, Dactyl, Foot, Iambic Pentameter, Meter, Spondee, Trochee.*

IAMBIC PENTAMETER A line of poetry that contains five iambic feet. The iambic pentameter line is most common in English and American poetry. Shakespeare and John Milton, among others, used iambic pentameter in their major works. So did such American poets as William Cullen Bryant, Ralph Waldo Emerson, Robert Frost, and Wallace Stevens. Here, for example is the opening line of a poem by Emerson:

> In May, when sea-winds pierced our solitudes
>
> —Ralph Waldo Emerson, from "The Rhodora"

See page 173.
See also *Blank Verse, Foot, Iamb, Meter, Scanning.*

IDIOM An expression particular to a certain language that means something different from the literal definitions of its parts. "Falling in love" is an American idiom, as is "I lost my head."

See also *Figure of Speech.*

IMAGERY The use of language to evoke a picture or a concrete sensation of a person, a thing, a place, or an experience. Although most images appeal to the sense of sight, they may appeal to the sense of taste, smell, hearing, and touch as well.

See pages 181, 499, 575, 592, 598, 1056, 1070.

IMAGISM A twentieth-century movement in European and American poetry that advocated the creation of hard, clear images, concisely expressed in everyday speech. The leading Imagist poets in America were Ezra Pound, Amy Lowell, H. D. [Hilda Doolittle], and William Carlos Williams.

See pages 568, 572.

IMPRESSIONISM A nineteenth-century movement in literature and art that advocated recording one's personal impressions of the world, rather than attempting a strict representation of reality. Some famous American impressionists in art are Mary Cassatt, Maurice Prendergast, and William Merritt Chase. In fiction, Stephen Crane pioneered a kind of literary impressionism in which he portrayed not objective reality but one character's impressions of reality. Crane's impressionistic technique is best seen in his novel *The Red Badge of Courage*.

INCONGRUITY (in'kän·groo'i·tē) **The deliberate joining of opposites or of elements that are not appropriate to each other.** T. S. Eliot's famous opening simile in "The Love Song of J. Alfred Prufrock" (Collection 5) joins two incongruous elements: a sunset and a patient knocked out by ether on an operating table. Incongruity can also be used for humor: We laugh at the sight of an elephant dressed in a pink tutu because the two elements are incongruous. Writers also use incongruity for dramatic effect. In Donald Barthelme's "Game" (Collection 6), the childish actions of the characters are in sharp contrast with the devastation they can cause by turning a key.

INTERIOR MONOLOGUE **A narrative technique that records a character's internal flow of thoughts, memories, and associations.** Parts of James Joyce's *Ulysses* and William Faulkner's *The Sound and the Fury* are written as interior monologues.

> See also *Stream of Consciousness*.

INTERNAL RHYME **Rhyme that occurs within a line of poetry or within consecutive lines.** The first line of the following couplet includes an internal rhyme.

> And so, all the night-**tide,** I lie down by the **side**
> Of my darling—my darling—my life and my
> bride. . . .
>
> —Edgar Allan Poe, from "Annabel Lee"

> See also *Rhyme*.

INVERSION **The reversal of the normal word order in a sentence or phrase.** An English sentence is normally built on subject-verb-complement, in that order. An inverted sentence reverses one or more of those elements. In poetry written many years ago, writers often inverted word order as a matter of course, in order to have words conform to the meter, or to create rhymes. The poetry of Anne Bradstreet

contains many inversions, as in the first line of the poem on the burning of her house:

> In silent night when rest I took

In prose, inversion is often used for emphasis, as when Patrick Henry, in his fiery speech to the Virginia Convention (Collection 1), thundered "Suffer not yourselves to be betrayed with a kiss" (instead of "Do not suffer [allow] yourselves," and so on).

> See pages 28, 166.

IRONY **In general, a discrepancy between appearances and reality.** There are three main types of irony:

1. **Verbal irony** occurs when someone says one thing but really means something else. The first line of Stephen Crane's poem "War Is Kind" is an example of verbal irony: "Do not weep, maiden, for war is kind." The speaker really believes that war is *not* kind and warrants weeping.

2. **Situational irony** takes place when there is a discrepancy between what is expected to happen, or what would be appropriate to happen, and what really does happen. A famous use of situational irony is in Stephen Crane's "A Mystery of Heroism" (Collection 4), in which a soldier risks his life to get water that is then spilled.

3. **Dramatic irony** is so called because it is often used on stage. In this kind of irony a character in the play or story thinks one thing is true, but the audience or reader knows better. In Edwin Arlington Robinson's "Miniver Cheevy" (Collection 4), Miniver thinks he is too refined for his time, but to the reader he seems foolish and somewhat pathetic.

> See pages 347, 434, 442, 952.

LYRIC POEM **A poem that does not tell a story but expresses the personal feelings or thoughts of a speaker.** The many lyric poems in this textbook include "Thanatopsis" by William Cullen Bryant (Collection 2) and the optimistic "what of a much of a which of a wind" by E. E. Cummings (Collection 5).

MAGIC REALISM **A genre developed in Latin America that juxtaposes the everyday with the marvelous or magical.** Myths, folk tales, religious beliefs, and tall tales are the raw material for many magic realist writers. Gabriel García Márquez's work, particularly his novel *One Hundred Years of Solitude* (1967), established him as a master of the genre. Other prominent Latin American magic realists include Jorge Luis Borges, Julio Cortázar, and Isabel Allende. Among American writers, Donald Barthelme (Collection 6) and Thomas Pynchon have been influenced by magic realism.

See page 912.

MARXISM **The political and economic philosophy developed by Karl Marx and his followers in the mid-nineteenth century.** In contrast to capitalists, Marxists believe greater economic unity can be reached by a classless society.

See page 565.

MEMOIR **A type of autobiography that often focuses on a specific time period or historical event.** Elie Wiesel's *Night* (Collection 6) is a memoir about the author's harrowing experience in a concentration camp.

See page 817.
See also *Autobiography*.

METAPHOR **A figure of speech that makes a comparison between two unlike things without the use of such specific words of comparison as *like*, *as*, *than*, or *resembles*. There are several kinds of metaphor:**

1. A **directly stated metaphor** states the comparison explicitly: "Fame is a bee" (Emily Dickinson).
2. An **implied metaphor** does not state explicitly the two terms of the comparison: "I like to see it lap the Miles" (Emily Dickinson) contains an implied metaphor in which the verb *lap* implies a comparison between "it," which is a train, and some animal that "laps" up water.
3. An **extended metaphor** is a metaphor that is extended or developed over a number of lines or with several examples. Dickinson's poem beginning "Fame is a bee" is an extended metaphor: the comparison of fame to a bee is extended for four lines:

> Fame is a bee.
> It has a song—
> It has a sting—
> Ah, too, it has a wing.

4. A **dead metaphor** is a metaphor that has been used so often that the comparison is no longer vivid: "The head of the house," "the seat of government," and a "knotty problem" are all dead metaphors.
5. A **mixed metaphor** is a metaphor that fails to make a logical comparison because its mixed terms are visually or imaginatively incompatible. If you say, "The president is a lame duck who is running out of gas," you've lost control of your metaphor and have produced a statement that is ridiculous (ducks do not run out of gas).

See pages 191, 398, 744, 814.
See also *Conceit, Figure of Speech, Simile*.

METER **A pattern of stressed and unstressed syllables in poetry.** The meter of a poem is commonly indicated by using the symbol (ˈ) for stressed syllables and the symbol (˘) for unstressed syllables. This is called **scanning** the poem.

Meter is described as **iambic, trochaic, dactylic,** or **anapestic.** These scanned lines from "Richard Cory" (Collection 4) are iambic. They are built on iambs—unstressed syllables followed by stressed syllables.

> ˘ ˈ ˘ ˈ ˘ ˈ ˘ ˈ ˘ ˈ
> And he was always quietly arrayed
> ˘ ˈ ˘ ˈ ˘ ˈ ˘ ˈ ˘ ˈ
> And he was always human when he talked

See page 171.
See also *Anapest, Cadence, Dactyl, Foot, Free Verse, Iamb, Iambic Pentameter, Rhythm, Scanning, Spondee, Trochee.*

METONYMY (mə·tän′ə·mē) **A figure of speech in which a person, place, or thing is referred to by something closely associated with it.** Referring to a king or queen as "the crown" is an example of metonymy, as is calling a car "wheels."

See also *Synecdoche*.

MODERNISM **A term for the bold new experimental styles and forms that swept the arts during the first third of the twentieth century.** Modernism called for changes in subject matter, in fictional styles, in poetic forms, and in attitudes. T. S. Eliot and Ezra Pound are associated with the modernist movement in poetry. Their aim was to rid poetry of its nineteenth-century prettiness and sentimentality.

See page 562.
See also *Imagism, Symbolism.*

MOOD **The overall emotion created by a work of literature.** Mood can usually be described with one or two adjectives such as *bittersweet, playful,* or *scary.* All the elements of literature, including sound effects, rhythm, and word choice, contribute to a work's mood. The mood of Horacio Quiroga's "The Feathered Pillow" (Collection 5) is cold and menacing.

See pages 151, 754.
See also *Atmosphere, Setting.*

MOTIVATION **The reasons for a character's behavior.** In order for us to understand why characters act the way they do, their motivation has to be believable, at least in terms of the story. At times a writer directly reveals motivation; in subtler fiction we must use details from the story to infer motivation.

See pages 503, 623, 920, 994.
See also *Character.*

MYTH **An anonymous traditional story that is basically religious in nature and that usually serves to explain a belief, ritual, or mysterious natural phenomenon.** Most myths have grown out of religious rituals, and almost all of them involve the exploits of gods and humans. Works of magic realism often draw on myths or mythlike tales.

See pages 24, 25.

NARRATIVE **The form of discourse that tells about a series of events.** Narration is used in all kinds of literature: fiction, nonfiction, and poetry. Usually a narrative is told in **chronological order**—in the order in which events occurred. The other three major forms of discourse are **description, exposition,** and **persuasion.**

NARRATIVE POEM **A poem that tells a story—a series of related events with a beginning, a middle, and an end.** A narrative poem also features characters and, frequently, dialogue. Henry Wadsworth Longfellow is famous for his long narrative poems based on figures from myth and from European and American history. *The Song of Hiawatha* and *Evangeline* are major examples of his narrative poems.

See page 731.

NARRATOR **In fiction the one who tells the story.** Narrators differ in their degree of participation in the story: (1) **Omniscient narrators** are all-knowing and outside the action; they can take us into minds and hearts of all the characters and behind all the events unfolding in the story; (2) **first-person narrators** are either witnesses to or participants in the story; (3) **third-person-limited narrators** are omniscient narrators too, but they zoom in on one character and allow us to experience the story through this one character's perceptions.

See also *Point of View.*

NATURALISM **A nineteenth-century literary movement that was an extension of realism and that claimed to portray life exactly as if it were being examined through a scientist's microscope.** The naturalists relied heavily on the new fields of psychology and sociology. They tended to dissect human behavior with complete objectivity, the way a scientist would dissect a specimen in the laboratory. The naturalists were also influenced by Darwinian theories of the survival of the fittest. Naturalists believed that human behavior is determined by heredity and environment; they felt that people have no recourse to supernatural forces and that human beings, like animals, are subject to laws of nature beyond their control. The outstanding naturalists among American writers are Theodore Dreiser, Jack London, and Frank Norris. Some people consider John Steinbeck's *The Grapes of Wrath* a naturalistic novel, in which characters are the pawns of economic conditions.

See pages 394, 480.
See also *Realism.*

OCTAVE **An eight-line poem, or the first eight lines of a Petrarchan, or Italian, sonnet.** In a Petrarchan sonnet the octave states the subject of the sonnet or poses a problem or question.

See also *Sestet, Sonnet.*

ODE **A lyric poem, usually long, on a serious subject and written in dignified language.** In ancient Greece and Rome, odes were written to be read in public at ceremonial occasions. In modern literature, odes tend to be more private, informal, and reflective.

ONOMATOPOEIA (än′ō·mat′ō·pē′ə) **The use of a word whose sound imitates or suggests its meaning.** The word *buzz* is onomatopoeic; it imitates the sound it names.

OXYMORON (äk′si·môr′än′) **A figure of speech that combines opposite or contradictory terms in a brief phrase.** *Sweet sorrow, deafening silence,* and *living death* are common oxymorons. (Some jokesters claim that phrases such as *jumbo shrimp, congressional leadership,* and *limited nuclear war* are also oxymorons.)

PARABLE A relatively short story that teaches a moral, or lesson, about how to lead a good life. The most famous parables are those told by Jesus in the Bible.

See pages 206, 249.

PARADOX A statement that appears self-contradictory but reveals a kind of truth. Many writers like to use paradox because it allows them to express the complexity of life by showing how opposing ideas can be both contradictory and true. Emily Dickinson often used paradoxes, as in "I taste a liquor never brewed" and "Much Madness is divinest Sense" (Collection 3).

See pages 210, 350.

PARALLEL STRUCTURE The repetition of words or phrases that have similar grammatical structures (also called *parallelism*). Lincoln, in his Gettysburg Address (Collection 4), uses several memorable parallel structures, as when he refers to "government of the people, by the people, for the people."

See pages 96, 313.

PARODY A work that makes fun of another work by imitating some aspect of the writer's style. Parodies often achieve their effects by humorously exaggerating certain features in the original work.

See page 707.

PASTORAL A type of poem that depicts country life in idyllic, idealized terms. The term *pastoral* comes from the Latin word for "shepherd" (the word survives today in our word *pastor*). Originally, in the Latin verse of ancient Rome, pastorals were about the loves of shepherds and nymphs and the simple idealized pleasures of country life. (Any work of literature that treats rural life as it really is would not be pastoral.) Today the term has a looser meaning, referring to any poem that portrays an idyllic rural setting or expresses nostalgia for an age or place of lost innocence. England has a long pastoral tradition; America has almost no pastoral tradition at all. The term *pastoral* is often used, misleadingly, to refer to poets who write about rural life. Robert Frost, for example, has been called a pastoral poet. No poet's work could be further from the idealized pastoral tradition. Frost is a deeply ironic, even dark poet.

PERSONIFICATION A figure of speech in which an object or animal is given human feelings, thoughts, or attitudes. Personification is a type of metaphor in which two dissimilar things are compared. In "Apparently with no surprise" (Collection 3), Emily Dickinson personifies the frost as a heedless killer and a flower as a playful child.

See pages 341, 1054.
See also *Anthropomorphism,*
Figure of Speech.

PERSUASION One of the four forms of discourse, which uses reason and emotional appeals to convince a reader to think or act in a certain way. Persuasive techniques are used in the Declaration of Independence (Collection 1), in Patrick Henry's "Give me liberty, or give me death" speech (Collection 1), and in Thomas Paine's *The Crisis, No. 1* (Collection 1). Persuasion is almost exclusively used in nonfiction, particularly in essays and speeches. The other three major forms of discourse are **description, exposition,** and **narration.**

See pages 79, 86, 208, 845.
See also *Argument.*

PLAIN STYLE A way of writing that stresses simplicity and clarity of expression. The plain style was favored by most Puritan writers, who avoided unnecessary ornamentation in all aspects of their lives, including church ritual and even the style of church structures. Simple sentences, everyday words from common speech, and clear and direct statements characterize the plain style. This style can be seen in Anne Bradstreet's works. One of the chief exponents of the plain style in recent American literature was Ernest Hemingway.

See page 28.
See also *Style.*

PLOT **The series of related events in a story or play, sometimes called the story line.** Most short story plots contain the following elements: **exposition,** which tells us who the characters are and introduces their conflict; **complications,** which arise as the characters take steps to resolve their conflicts; the **climax,** that exciting or suspenseful moment when the outcome of the conflict is imminent; and a **resolution** or **denouement,** when the story's problems are all resolved and the story ends.

The plots of dramas and novels are more complex because of their length. A schematic representation of a typical dramatic plot is shown below. It is based on a pyramid developed by the nineteenth-century German critic Gustav Freitag. The **rising action** refers to all the actions that take place before the **turning point** (sometimes called the **crisis**). The turning point is the point at which the hero experiences a decisive reversal of fortune: In a comedy, things begin to work out well at that turning point; in a tragedy they get worse and worse. (In Shakespeare's plays the turning point takes place in the third act. In *Romeo and Juliet,* for example, after he kills Tybalt in the third act, Romeo's fate is sealed and he experiences one disaster after another.) All the action after the turning point is called **falling action** because it leads to the final resolution (happy or unhappy) of the conflict. The major **climax** in most plays and novels takes place just before the ending; in Shakespeare's plays the final climax takes place in the fifth, or last, act. (In *Romeo and Juliet* the major climax takes place in the last act when the two young people kill themselves.)

Dramatic Plot

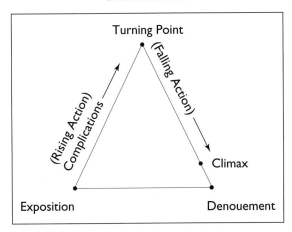

See page 162.

See also *Climax, Denouement, Exposition, Resolution.*

POINT OF VIEW **The vantage point from which the writer tells a story.** In broad terms, there are four main points of view: **first person, third person limited, omniscient,** and **objective.**

1. In the **first-person point of view,** one of the characters in the story tells the story, using first-person pronouns such as *I* and *we.* With this point of view, we can know only what the narrator knows. Mark Twain's novel *Adventures of Huckleberry Finn* is told from the first-person point of view, by the novel's main character, a boy named Huck Finn. One of the great pleasures of that novel, in fact, is that its point of view allows us to hear Huck's very distinct voice and dialect. It also allows us to see the complex adult world through the eyes of a young boy who is often victimized by that world.

2. In the **third-person-limited point of view,** an unknown narrator (usually thought of as the author) tells the story, but this narrator zooms in to focus on the thoughts and feelings of only one character. (This point of view gets its name because the narrator refers to all the characters as *he, she,* and *they;* this narrator does not refer to himself or herself with the first-person pronoun *I.*) Like the first-person point of view, however, this point of view also limits us to the perceptions of one character, but in this case the narrator can tell us many things that the character is unaware of. For example, Eudora Welty tells "A Worn Path" (Collection 5) from the third-person-limited point of view, which zooms in on her protagonist, an old woman named Phoenix Jackson. At one point, Welty's narrator tells us that Phoenix was "like an old woman begging a dignified forgiveness."

3. In the **omniscient point of view,** an omniscient, or all-knowing, narrator tells the story, also using the third-person pronouns. However, this narrator, instead of focusing on one character only, often tells us everything about many characters: their motives, weaknesses, hopes, childhoods, and sometimes even their futures. This narrator can also comment directly on the characters' actions. Nathaniel Hawthorne's "The Minister's Black Veil" (Collection 2) is told from the omniscient point of view.

4. In the **objective point of view,** a narrator who is totally impersonal and objective tells the story, with no comment on any characters or events. The objective point of view is like the point of view of a movie camera; it is totally impersonal, and what we know is only what the camera might see. This narrator never gives any direct revelation of the characters' thoughts

or motives. Ernest Hemingway uses this objective point of view, which is why his stories often seem so puzzling to readers. "What happened?" we ask. The *reader* must infer what happens in Hemingway's stories, just as in real life we have to infer the motives, thoughts, and feelings of people we meet.

See page 423.

POSTMODERNISM A term for the dominant trend in the arts since 1945 characterized by experiments with nontraditional forms and the acceptance of multiple meanings. The lines between real and imaginary worlds are often blurred in post-modern texts, as is the boundary between fiction and nonfiction. Other characteristics of postmodern texts are cultural diversity and an often playful self-consciousness, which is an acknowledgment that literature is not a mirror that accurately reflects the world, but a created world unto itself. Some well-known postmodern writers are Donald Barthelme, Toni Morrison, and Philip Roth.

See page 802.

PROTAGONIST The central character in a story, the one who initiates or drives the action. The protagonist might or might not be the story's hero; some protagonists are actually the villains in the story.

See page 610.
See also *Antagonist.*

PROVERB A short, pithy statement that expresses a common truth or experience. Many of Benjamin Franklin's sayings, such as "Fish and visitors smell in three days," have become proverbs in American culture.

See also *Aphorism.*

PSYCHOANALYSIS A method of examining the unconscious mind, developed primarily by the Austrian physician Sigmund Freud (1865–1939). Psychoanalysis is based on the assumption that many mental and emotional disorders are the result of the conscious mind repressing factors that persist in the unconscious and can cause conflicts. Modern writers often use the techniques of psychoanalysis. In "The Secret Life of Walter Mitty" (Collection 5), James Thurber uses the psychoanalytic technique of free association to give us a picture of a man with (comically) repressed desires.

See page 566.

PUN A play on words based on the multiple meanings of a single word or on words that sound alike but mean different things. An example of the first type of pun is a singer explaining her claim that she was locked out of an audition because she couldn't find the right key. The second kind of pun can be found in the opening lines of Shakespeare's *Julius Caesar,* where a man who repairs shoes claims to be a mender of men's souls (soles). Puns are often used for humor, but some puns are a serious element in poetry.

QUATRAIN A poem consisting of four lines, or four lines of a poem that can be considered as a unit. The typical ballad stanza, for example, is a quatrain.

RATIONALISM The belief that human beings can arrive at truth by using reason, rather than by relying on the authority of the past, on religious faith, or on intuition. The Declaration of Independence (Collection 1) is a document based on rationalist principles.

See page 14.

REALISM A style of writing, developed in the nineteenth century, that attempts to depict life accurately, as it really is, without idealizing or romanticizing it. Instead of writing about the long ago or far away, the realists concentrated on contemporary life and on middle- and lower-class lives in particular. Among the outstanding realistic novelists in America are Stephen Crane, Willa Cather, and John Steinbeck. European playwrights who wrote realistic dramas, including Henrik Ibsen, August Strindberg, and Anton Chekhov, discarded artificial plots in favor of themes centering on contemporary society. They also rejected extravagant language in favor of simple, every-day diction.

See pages 389, 393.
See also *Naturalism, Romanticism.*

REFRAIN A word, phrase, line, or group of lines that is repeated, for effect, several times in a poem. Refrains are often used in ballads and other narrative poems. "Nevermore" is a refrain in Poe's "The Raven" (Collection 2).

See page 759.

REGIONALISM Literature that emphasizes a specific geographic setting and that reproduces the speech, behavior, and attitudes of the people

who live in that region. Among the great regional writers of the twentieth century are Sinclair Lewis (Midwest); John Steinbeck (California); and William Faulkner, Flannery O'Connor, and Eudora Welty (South).

See page 391.

REPETITION A unifying property of repeated words, sounds, syllables, and other elements that appear in a work. Repetition occurs in most poetry and in some prose. Repetition is used to create rhythm, to reinforce a message, and to enhance a mood or emotional affect. **Rhyme, refrain, assonance, dissonance,** and other literary devices are all based on the repetition of certain sounds.

See pages 759, 1066.
See also *Assonance, Consonance, Dissonance, Refrain, Rhyme.*

RESOLUTION The conclusion of a story, when all or most of the conflicts have been settled. The resolution is also often called the *denouement.*

See also *Denouement, Plot.*

RHETORICAL QUESTION A question that is asked for effect and that does not actually require an answer. In his speech to the Virginia Convention (Collection 1), Patrick Henry asks several rhetorical questions. Such questions presume the audience agrees with the speaker on the answers.

RHYME The repetition of vowel sounds in accented syllables and all succeeding syllables. *Listen* and *glisten* rhyme, as do *chime* and *sublime.* When words within the same line of poetry have repeated sounds, we have an example of **internal rhyme. End rhyme** refers to rhyming words at the end of lines.

The pattern of rhymes in a poem is called a **rhyme scheme.** Rhyme scheme is commonly indicated with letters of the alphabet, each rhyming sound represented by a different letter of the alphabet. For example, the rhyme scheme of the following lines is *abab.*

Tell me not, in mournful numbers,	*a*
Life is but an empty dream!—	*b*
For the soul is dead that slumbers,	*a*
And things are not what they seem.	*b*

—Henry Wadsworth Longfellow,
from "A Psalm of Life"

Approximate rhymes (also called **off rhymes, half rhymes, imperfect rhymes,** or **slant rhymes**) are words that have some correspondence in sound but not an exact one. Examples of approximate rhymes are often found in Emily Dickinson's poems. *Flash* and *flesh* are approximate rhymes, as are *stream* and *storm,* and *early* and *barley.* Approximate rhyme has the effect of catching the reader off guard: Where you expect a perfect rhyme, you get only an approximation. The emotional effect is something like that of the sound of a sharp or flat note in music.

See pages 1035, 1061.
See also *Internal Rhyme, Rhythm, Slant Rhyme.*

RHYTHM The alternation of stressed and unstressed syllables in language. Rhythm occurs naturally in all forms of spoken and written English. The most obvious kind of rhythm is produced by **meter,** the regular pattern of stressed and unstressed syllables found in some poetry. Writers can also create less structured rhythms by using rhyme, repetition, pauses, and variations in line length and by balancing long and short words or phrases.

See pages 750, 1035.
See also *Cadence, Free Verse, Meter, Rhyme.*

ROMANCE In general, a story in which an idealized hero or heroine undertakes a quest and is successful. In a romance, beauty, innocence, and goodness usually prevail over evil. Romances are traditionally set in the distant past and use a great deal of fantasy. The laws of nature are often suspended in a romance, so that the hero often has supernatural powers, as we see in the adventures of King Arthur and his knights. Stories set in the American West are in the romance mode, except that the supernatural elements are eliminated (though the sheriff-hero usually has a nearly magical skill with his gun). Today we also use the word *romance* to refer to a kind of popular escapist love story, which often takes place in an exotic setting. A popular contemporary romance in the traditional sense is the bestselling trilogy by J.R.R. Tolkien, *The Lord of the Rings.*

ROMANTICISM A revolt against rationalism that affected literature and the other arts, beginning in the late eighteenth century and remaining strong throughout most of the nineteenth century. Romanticism is marked by these characteristics: (1) a conviction that intuition, imagination, and emotion are superior to reason; (2) a conviction that poetry is superior to science; (3) a belief that contemplation of the natural world is a means of discovering the truth that lies behind mere reality; (4) a distrust of industry and city life and an idealization of rural life and of the wilderness; (5) an interest in the more "natural" past and in the supernatural. Romanticism affected so many creative people that it was bound to take many different forms; the result is that it is difficult to define the word in a way that includes everyone who might be called a Romantic. In the nineteenth century, for example, Romantics were outspoken in their love of nature and contempt for technology. In the twentieth century, however, as nature was taken over by real-estate developers and highways, some writers took a romantic view of machines, buildings, and other products of technology.

See pages 140, 143, 144.
See also *Realism.*

ROMANTIC NOVEL **A novel with a happy ending that presents readers with characters engaged in adventures filled with courageous acts, daring chases, and exciting escapes.** James Fenimore Cooper is known for novels such as *The Last of the Mohicans* (1826) and *The Deerslayer* (1841), which are filled with romantic adventures.

See page 389.

SATIRE **A type of writing that ridicules the shortcomings of people or institutions in an attempt to bring about a change.** Satire can cover a wide range of tones, from gentle spoofing to savage mockery. In "The Secret Life of Walter Mitty" (Collection 5), for example, James Thurber pokes fun at the domesticated American male's tendency to escape into heroic fantasies. In Donald Barthelme's "Game" (Collection 6), the satire is harsh, as it points out the absurdity and illogic of nuclear war games. Satire is always intensely moral in its purpose. Mark Twain, in his essay "The Lowest Animal" (Collection 4), satirizes the moral infirmity of the entire human race by ironically comparing the behavior of humans with that of the animals and finding the latter to be morally superior.

See pages 162, 468, 886.

SCANNING **The analysis of a poem to determine its meter.** When you scan a poem, you describe the pattern of stressed and unstressed syllables in each line. Stresses or accents are indicated by the symbol (ˊ) and unstressed syllables by the symbol (ˇ).

> ˇ ˊ ˇ ˊ ˇ ˊ ˇ ˊ ˇ ˊ
> To him who in the love of Nature holds
> ˇ ˊ ˇ ˇ ˊ ˇ ˊˇ ˊ ˇ ˊ
> Communion with her visible forms, she speaks
> ˇ ˊ ˇ ˊ ˇ ˊ ˇ ˇ ˊ
> A various language: for his gayer hours
> ˇ ˊ ˇ ˊ ˇ ˊ ˇ ˇ ˇ ˊ
> She has a voice of gladness, and a smile.
>
> —William Cullen Bryant, from "Thanatopsis"

See also *Anapest, Blank Verse, Dactyl, Foot, Iamb, Iambic Pentameter, Meter, Spondee, Trochee.*

SESTET **Six lines of poetry, especially the last six lines of a Petrarchan, or Italian, sonnet.** In the Petrarchan sonnet the sestet offers a comment on the subject or problem presented in the first eight lines, or the octave, of the poem.

See pages 173, 178.
See also *Octave, Sonnet.*

SETTING **The time and location in which a story takes place.** Setting can have several functions in fiction:
1. Setting is often used to create **conflict.** In the purest and often simplest form of a story, a character is in conflict with some element of a setting. The narrator in Jack London's "To Build a Fire" (Collection 4), for example, is in conflict with extreme cold (the cold wins).
2. Often the setting helps to create **atmosphere** or **mood.** Edgar Allan Poe's setting of a dungeon in "The Pit and the Pendulum" (Collection 2) creates a mood of horror.
3. Setting can also create and delineate **character.** In William Faulkner's "A Rose for Emily" (Collection 5), Miss Emily Grierson's old-fashioned house with its musty rooms reflects her refusal to live in the present.

See pages 513, 645, 997.

SHORT STORY **A brief work of prose fiction.** A short story has a simpler plot than a novel and is not long enough to be published as a volume of its own. Short stories usually focus on a few characters and one major event. Edgar Allan Poe has often been called one of the originators and masters of the modern short story. Some of the great American short story writers include Nathaniel Hawthorne, Flannery O'Connor, Eudora Welty, and Raymond Carver.

SIMILE A figure of speech that makes an explicit comparison between two unlike things, using a word such as *like, as, than,* or *resembles.*

> Helen, thy beauty is to me
> Like those Nicéan barks of yore
>
> —Edgar Allan Poe, from "To Helen"

See also *Figure of Speech, Metaphor.*

SLANT RHYME A rhyming sound that is not exact. *Follow/fellow* and *mystery/mastery* are examples of slant or approximate rhyme. Emily Dickinson frequently uses the subtleties of slant rhyme.

See pages 337, 341.
See also *Rhyme.*

SOLILOQUY A long speech made by a character in a play while no other characters are onstage. A soliloquy is different from a monologue in that the speaker appears to be thinking aloud, not addressing a listener.

SONNET A fourteen-line poem, usually written in iambic pentameter, that has one of two basic structures. The **Petrarchan sonnet,** also called the **Italian sonnet,** is named after the fourteenth-century Italian poet Petrarch. Its first eight lines, called the **octave,** ask a question or pose a problem. These lines have a rhyme scheme of *abba, abba.* The last six lines, called the **sestet,** respond to the question or problem. These lines have a rhyme scheme of *cde, cde.*

The form used to such perfection by William Shakespeare is known as the **English, Elizabethan,** or **Shakespearean sonnet.** It has three four-line units, or **quatrains,** and it concludes with a **couplet.** The most common rhyme scheme for the Shakespearean sonnet is *abab, cdcd, efef, gg.*

Longfellow wrote many sonnets, such as "The Cross of Snow" (Collection 2), as did Edna St. Vincent Millay, Robert Frost, and E. E. Cummings.

See pages 32, 173, 178, 718.
See also *Octave, Sestet.*

SOUND EFFECTS The use of sounds to create specific literary effects. Writers use devices such as **rhythm, rhyme, meter, alliteration, ono-matopoeia, assonance, consonance,** and **repetition** to make the sounds of a work convey and enhance its meaning.

See pages 273, 279, 1082.

SPEAKER The voice that addresses the reader in a poem. The speaker may be the poet or a persona, a character whose voice and concerns do not necessarily reflect those of the poet. The speaker of T. S. Eliot's "The Love Song of J. Alfred Prufrock" (Collection 5) is one of the most famous personas in literature. The speaker in Sylvia Plath's poem "Mirror" (Collection 6) is the personified mirror itself.

See page 1050.

SPEECH A formal address delivered to an audience, or the printed version of the same address. Speeches are most commonly delivered by politicians, political activists, and other types of public figures. "The Arrogance and Cruelty of Power" from the Nuremberg Trials (Collection 6), delivered by Robert H. Jackson, is an example of a speech given to open a trial.

SPONDEE A metrical foot consisting of two syllables, both of which are stressed. The words *true-blue* and *nineteen* are made of spondees. When Walt Whitman writes "Beat! beat! drums," he uses spondees. Spondaic feet are rarely used extensively because of their *thump-thump* sound. However, poets sometimes use spondees to provide a brief change from an iambic or trochaic beat or to provide emphasis.

See also *Anapest, Dactyl, Foot, Iamb, Iambic Pentameter, Meter, Trochee.*

STANZA A group of consecutive lines that forms a structural unit in a poem. Stanzas come in varying numbers of lines, though four is the most common. On the page, stanzas are separated by spaces. Stanza patterns are determined by the number of lines, the kind of feet in each line, and metrical and rhyme schemes, if any.

STEREOTYPE A fixed idea or conception of a character or a group of people that does not allow for any individuality and is often based on religious, social, or racial prejudices. Some common stereotypes are the unsophisticated farmer, the socially inept honor student, the dumb athlete, and the lazy teenager. Stereotypes, also called **stock characters,** are often deliberately used in comedies and in melodramas, where they receive instant recognition from the audience and make fully fleshed characterization unnecessary. In Thurber's "The Secret Life of Walter Mitty" (Collection 5), Walter and Mrs. Mitty are stock characters—the henpecked husband and the domineering wife.

See also *Character.*

STREAM OF CONSCIOUSNESS **A style of writing that portrays the inner (and often chaotic) workings of a character's mind.** The stream-of-consciousness technique usually consists of a recording of the random flow of ideas, memories, associations, images, and emotions, as they arise spontaneously in a character's mind. This flow of the contents of a character's mind is called an **interior monologue.** William Faulkner, in his novel *The Sound and the Fury,* uses a stream-of-consciousness technique. Two other great writers that successfully use a stream-of-consciousness technique are the Irish writer James Joyce and the English writer Virginia Woolf.

See pages 566, 696.

STYLE **The distinctive way in which a writer uses language.** Style can be plain, ornate, metaphorical, spare, descriptive, and so on. Style is determined by such factors as sentence length and complexity, syntax, use of figurative language and imagery, and diction.

See pages 86, 523, 888, 1097.
See also *Plain Style, Stream of Consciousness, Tone.*

SUBJECTIVE AND OBJECTIVE WRITING **Subjectivity, in terms of writing, suggests that the writer's primary purpose is to express personal experiences, feelings, and ideas. Objectivity suggests that the writer's purpose is to report facts, avoiding personal judgments and feelings.** Subjective writing is typified by autobiographies and memoirs. Objective writing is used mostly in news reporting and other types of journalism. This is not to say that all writing must be one or the other. In fact, most writing will have elements of subjective and objective writing.

See page 830.

SURREALISM **A movement in art and literature that started in Europe during the 1920s. Surrealists wanted to replace conventional realism with the full expression of the unconscious mind, which they considered to be more real than the "real" world of appearances.** Surrealists, influenced by the psychoanalytic theories of Sigmund Freud, tried not to censor the images that came from their dreams or to impose logical connections on these images. This resulted in surprising combinations of "inner" and "outer" reality—a "suprareality." Surrealism affected writers as diverse as T. S. Eliot and Donald Barthelme. Two famous surrealist artists are the Spaniard Salvador Dali (1904–1989) and the Belgian René Magritte (1898–1967).

SUSPENSE **A feeling of uncertainty and curiosity about what will happen next in a story.** A key element in fiction and drama, suspense is one of the hooks a writer uses to keep the audience interested.

SYMBOL **A person, a place, a thing, or an event that has meaning in itself and that also stands for something more than itself.** We can distinguish between **public** and **personal** symbols. The dove, for example, is a public symbol of peace—that is, it is widely accepted the world over as such a symbol. The bald eagle is a public symbol that stands for the United States; a picture of a skull and crossbones is a public symbol of death; two snakes coiled around a staff is a widely accepted symbol of the medical profession.

Most symbols used in literature are personal symbols; even though a symbol may be widely used, a writer will usually adapt it in some imaginative, personal way so that it can suggest not just one, but a myriad of meanings. One of the most commonly used symbols in literature, for example, is the journey, which can stand for a search for truth, for redemption from evil, or for discovery of the self and freedom.

The writers known as the Dark Romantics—Poe, Hawthorne, and Melville—used symbolism heavily in their works. One of American literature's most famous symbols is Melville's white whale, Moby-Dick, used to symbolize the inexpressible nature of evil.

See pages 238, 255, 321, 1043.
See also *Figure of Speech.*

SYMBOLISM A literary movement that originated in late-nineteenth-century France, in which writers rearranged the world of appearances in order to reveal a more truthful version of reality. The symbolists believed that direct statements of feeling were inadequate. Instead, they called for new and striking imaginative images to evoke complexities of meaning and mood. The French symbolists were influenced by the poetry and critical writings of the American writer Edgar Allan Poe. The poetry of Ezra Pound, T. S. Eliot, and Wallace Stevens is in the symbolist tradition.

See pages 568, 571.

SYNECDOCHE (si·nek′də·kē) **A figure of speech in which a part represents the whole.** The capital city of a nation, for example, is often spoken of as though it were the government: *Washington and Moscow are both claiming popular support for their positions.* In "The Love Song of J. Alfred Prufrock" (Collection 5), T. S. Eliot writes "And I have known the arms already. . . ." *Arms* stands for all the women he has known.

See also *Metonymy.*

SYNESTHESIA (sin′əs·thē′zhə) **The juxtaposition of one sensory image with another image that appeals to an unrelated sense.** In synesthesia an image of sound might be conveyed in terms of an image of taste as in "sweet laughter," or an image that appeals to the sense of touch might be combined with an image that appeals to the sense of sight, as in the example from Emily Dickinson: "golden touch."

TALL TALE An outrageously exaggerated, humorous story that is obviously unbelievable. Tall tales are part of folk literature of many countries, including the United States. Perhaps the most famous tall tale in American literature is Mark Twain's "The Celebrated Jumping Frog of Calaveras County" (Collection 4).

See page 467.

THEME The insight about human life that is revealed in literary work. Themes are rarely stated directly in literature. Most often, a reader has to infer the theme of a work after considerable thought. Theme is different from **subject.** A story's subject might be stated as "growing up," "love," "heroism," or "fear." The theme is the statement the writer wants to make about that subject: "For most young people, growing up is a process that involves the pain of achieving self-knowledge." Theme must be stated in at least one sentence; most themes are complex enough to require several sentences, or even an essay.

See pages 166, 685, 877, 933, 1089.

TONE The attitude a writer takes toward the subject of a work, the characters in it, or the audience. In speaking we use voice inflections and even body language to show how we feel about what we are saying. Writers manipulate language in an attempt to achieve the same effect. For example, John Hersey takes an objective tone in telling about the nuclear explosion in *Hiroshima* (see "A Noiseless Flash," Collection 6). In contrast, the tone in Patrick Henry's speech to the Virginia Convention (Collection 1) is subjective, even impassioned. Tone is dependent on **diction** and **style,** and we cannot say we have understood any work of literature until we have sensed the writer's tone. Tone can usually be described in a single word: objective, solemn, playful, ironic, sarcastic, critical, reverent, irreverent, philosophical, cynical, and so on.

See pages 344, 1015, 1052, 1086.
See also *Diction, Style.*

TRAGEDY In general, a story in which a heroic character either dies or comes to some other unhappy end. In most tragedies the main character is in an enviable, even exalted, position when the story begins (in classical tragedies and in Shakespeare's plays, the tragic hero is of noble origin, often a king or queen, prince or princess). The character's downfall generally occurs because of some combination of fate, an error in judgment, or a personality failure known as a **tragic flaw** (Creon's stubbornness in *Antigone* or Hamlet's indecision, for example). The tragic character has usually gained wisdom at the end of the story, in spite of suffering defeat or even death. Our feeling on reading or viewing a tragedy is usually exaltation—despite the unhappy ending—because we have witnessed the best that human beings are capable of.

See also *Comedy.*

TRANSCENDENTALISM **A nineteenth-century movement in the Romantic tradition, which held that every individual can reach ultimate truths through spiritual intuition, which transcends reason and sensory experience.** The Transcendental movement was centered in Concord, Massachusetts, home of its leading exponents, Ralph Waldo Emerson and Henry David Thoreau. The basic tenets of the Transcendentalists were (1) a belief that God is present in every aspect of nature, including every human being; (2) the conviction that everyone is capable of apprehending God through the use of intuition; (3) the belief that all of nature is symbolic of the spirit. A corollary of these beliefs was an optimistic view of the world as good and evil as nonexistent.

See pages 146, 147.

TROCHEE **A metrical foot made up of an accented syllable followed by an unaccented syllable, as in the word _taxi_.** A trochee, the opposite of an iamb, is sometimes used to vary iambic rhythm.

See also _Anapest, Dactyl, Foot, Iamb, Iambic Pentameter, Meter, Spondee._

UNDERSTATEMENT **A statement that says less than what is meant.** Understatement, paradoxically, can make us recognize the truth of something by saying that just the opposite is true. If you are sitting down to enjoy a ten-course meal and say, "Ah! A little snack before bedtime," you are using an understatement to emphasize the tremendous amount of food you are about to eat. Understatement is often used to make an ironic point; it can also be used for humor.

See page 459.
See also _Hyperbole._

VERNACULAR **The language spoken by the people who live in a particular locality.** Regionalist writers try to capture the vernacular of their area.

See page 459.
See also _Dialect._

VILLANELLE **A nineteen-line poem consisting of five tercets (three-line stanzas) with the rhyme scheme _aba_ and with a final quatrain (four-line stanza) of _abaa_.** Two well-known villanelles in the English language are Dylan Thomas's "Do Not Go Gentle into That Good Night" and Elizabeth Bishop's "One Art" (Collection 6).

See page 1046.

NOTE Whenever possible, revise the sentence to avoid this awkward construction.

EXAMPLE
The **director was** not eager to rehearse the scene again, and neither **were** the **performers.**

2e. The verb agrees with its subject even when the verb precedes the subject, such as in sentences beginning with *here, there,* or *where.*

EXAMPLES
Here **is** [*or* here's] a **copy** of the Declaration of Independence.
Here **are** [*not* here's] two **copies** of the Declaration of Independence.

2f. A *collective noun* (such as *class, herd,* or *jury*) is singular in form but names a group of persons or things. A collective noun takes a singular verb when the noun refers to the group as a unit and takes a plural verb when the noun refers to the parts or members of the group.

SINGULAR The **cast** of *A Raisin in the Sun* **is made** up entirely of juniors. [The cast as a unit is made up of juniors.]

PLURAL After the play, the **cast are joining** their families for a celebration. [The members of the cast are joining their families.]

2g. An expression of an amount (a length of time, a statistic, or a fraction, for example) is singular when the amount is thought of as a unit or when it refers to a singular word. An amount is plural when it is thought of as many parts or when it refers to a plural word.

SINGULAR **Twenty years was** a long time for Rip Van Winkle to sleep. [one unit]

PLURAL **Fifty percent** of the students **have** already **read** *Walden.* [The percentage refers to *students.*]

Expressions of measurement (length, weight, capacity, area) are usually singular.

EXAMPLES
Seventy-five degrees below zero was the air temperature in "To Build a Fire."
Four and a half miles was how far the man walked in an hour.

2h. The title of a creative work (such as a book, song, film, or painting) or the

name of an organization, a country, or a city (even if the name is plural in form) takes a singular verb.

EXAMPLES
"Birches" **was written** by Robert Frost.
The **United States calls** its flag Old Glory.

2i. A verb agrees with its subject, not with its predicate nominative.

SINGULAR One **symptom** of flu **is** sore muscles
PLURAL Sore **muscles are** one symptom of flu.

AGREEMENT OF PRONOUN AND ANTECEDENT

A pronoun usually refers to a noun or another pronoun. The word to which a pronoun refers is called its *antecedent.*

2j. A pronoun agrees with its antecedent in number and gender. Singular pronouns refer to singular antecedents. Plural pronouns refer to plural antecedents. A few singular pronouns indicate gender (neuter, feminine, masculine).

EXAMPLES
Marianne Moore published **her** first book of poems in 1921. [singular, feminine]
Peyton Farquhar thinks **he** has escaped. [singular, masculine]
Benjamin Franklin wrote, "**Three** may keep a secret if two of **them** are dead." [plural]

2k. Indefinite pronouns may be singular, plural, or either.

(1) Singular pronouns are used to refer to the indefinite pronouns *anybody, anyone, anything, each, either, everybody, everyone, everything, neither, nobody, no one, nothing, one, somebody, someone,* and *something.* The gender of any of these pronouns is often determined by a word in a phrase following the pronoun.

EXAMPLES
Each of the **girls** has already memorized **her** part.
One of the **boys** gave **his** interpretation of "Nothing Gold Can Stay."

If the antecedent may be either masculine or feminine, use both the masculine and feminine pronouns to refer to it.

EXAMPLE
Anyone who is qualified for the job may submit **his** or **her** application.

NOTE Whenever possible, revise the sentence to avoid this awkward construction.

EXAMPLE

Anyone who is qualified for the job may submit an application.

(2) Plural pronouns are used to refer to the indefinite pronouns *both, few, many,* and *several.*

EXAMPLE

Both of the finalists played **their** best.

(3) Singular or plural pronouns may be used to refer to the indefinite pronouns *all, any, most, none,* and *some.* These indefinite pronouns are singular when they refer to singular words and are plural when they refer to plural words.

SINGULAR   **All** of our **planning** achieved **its** purpose.

PLURAL   **All** of your **suggestions** had **their** good points.

2l. A plural pronoun is used to refer to two or more singular antecedents joined by *and.*

EXAMPLE

Jerry and Francesca read the sonnets **they** wrote about Olaudah Equiano.

2m. A singular pronoun is used to refer to two or more singular antecedents joined by *or* or *nor.*

EXAMPLE

Neither **Cindy nor Carla** thinks **she** is ready to write the final draft.

2n. When a singular and a plural antecedent are joined by *or* or *nor,* the pronoun agrees with the nearer antecedent.

EXAMPLE

Either **Jerry or** the **twins** will bring **their** stereo.

 Revising Misleading Sentences

Sentences with antecedents joined by *or* or *nor* can be misleading when the antecedents are of different genders or numbers. Revise the sentences to avoid such constructions.

MISLEADING   Either Christopher or Tiffany will give her report on Transcendentalism. [The sentence suggests that Christopher may give Tiffany's report.]

REVISED   Either **Christopher** will give **his** report on Transcendentalism, or **Tiffany** will give **hers.**

2o. A collective noun (such as *audience, family,* or *team*) takes a singular pronoun when the noun refers to the group as a unit and takes a plural pronoun when the noun refers to the parts or members of the group.

SINGULAR   The **debate club** elected **its** new officers.

PLURAL   The **debate club** will practice **their** speeches in this week's workshop.

2p. The title of a creative work (such as a book, song, film, or painting) or the name of an organization, a country, or a city (even if it is plural in form) takes a singular pronoun.

EXAMPLES

The teacher read **"Mushrooms"** and then asked me to interpret **it.**

Anderson Outfitters advertises **itself** as "the first step in getting away from it all."

3 USING VERBS

REGULAR AND IRREGULAR VERBS

Every verb has four basic forms called the *principal parts:* the *base form,* the *present participle,* the *past,* and the *past participle.* A verb is classified as *regular* or *irregular* depending on the way it forms the past and past participle.

3a. A *regular verb* forms the past and past participle by adding *–d* or *–ed* to the base form. An *irregular verb* forms the past and the past participle in some other way.

The following examples include *is* and *have* in parentheses to show that helping verbs are used with the present participle and past participle forms.

Language Handbook 1193

Language Handbook

Resources ─────

Grammar and Language

• *Language Handbook Worksheets,* pp. 15–26

COMMON REGULAR AND IRREGULAR VERBS

BASE FORM	PRESENT PARTICIPLE	PAST	PAST PARTICIPLE
REGULAR			
ask	(is) asking	asked	(have) asked
attack	(is) attacking	attacked	(have) attacked
drown	(is) drowning	drowned	(have) drowned
plan	(is) planning	planned	(have) planned
try	(is) trying	tried	(have) tried
use	(is) using	used	(have) used
IRREGULAR			
be	(is) being	was, were	(have) been
begin	(is) beginning	began	(have) begun
catch	(is) catching	caught	(have) caught
drink	(is) drinking	drank	(have) drunk
drive	(is) driving	drove	(have) driven
go	(is) going	went	(have) gone
lend	(is) lending	lent	(have) lent
shake	(is) shaking	shook	(have) shaken
swim	(is) swimming	swam	(have) swum
tear	(is) tearing	tore	(have) torn
throw	(is) throwing	threw	(have) thrown

Before adding the suffix *–ing* or *–ed* to form the present participle or the past or past participle of a verb, double the final consonant if the base form satisfies both of these conditions:
(1) It has only one syllable or has the accent on the last syllable.
(2) It ends in a single consonant preceded by a single vowel.

EXAMPLES
grin + -ing = grin**ning**
refer + -ed = refer**red**

See 14m for exceptions.

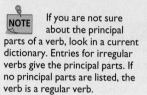 If you are not sure about the principal parts of a verb, look in a current dictionary. Entries for irregular verbs give the principal parts. If no principal parts are listed, the verb is a regular verb.

TENSES AND THEIR USES

3b. The *tense* of a verb indicates the time of the action or the state of being expressed by the verb.

(1) The *present tense* is used mainly to express an action or a state of being that is occurring now.

EXAMPLE
We **understand** now.

The present tense is also used

- to show a customary or habitual action or state of being
- to convey a general truth—something that is always true
- to make a historical event seem current (such use is called the *historical present*)
- to summarize the plot or subject matter of a literary work or to refer to an author's relationship to his or her work (such use is called the *literary present*)
- to express future time

EXAMPLES
For breakfast I **eat** cereal and **drink** orange juice. [customary action]

The earth **revolves** once around the sun each year. [general truth]
Several of the *Mayflower* passengers **die** before the ship **reaches** Plymouth. [historical present]
Moby-Dick **tells** the story of a man who **pursues** a white whale. [literary present]
The workshop **begins** tomorrow. [future time]

(2) The *past tense* is used to express an action or a state of being that occurred in the past but did not continue into the present.

EXAMPLES
Pepe **grabbed** his rifle and **crawled** into the brush.

(3) The *future tense* (*will* or *shall* + base form) is used to express an action or a state of being that will occur.

EXAMPLES
Elisa **will play** the part of Beneatha Younger.
I **will** [*or* shall] **serve** as her understudy.

(4) The *present perfect tense* (*have* or *has* + past participle) is used mainly to express an action or a state of being that occurred at some indefinite time in the past.

EXAMPLE
Have you **read** any stories by Sandra Cisneros?

The present perfect tense is also used to express an action or a state of being that began in the past and continues into the present.

EXAMPLE
My sister **has been** a Girl Scout for two years.

(5) The ***past perfect tense*** (*had* + past participle) is used to express an action or a state of being that was completed in the past before another action or state of being occurred.

EXAMPLE
Miss Emily returned the tax notice that she **had received.**

NOTE Use the past perfect tense in "if" clauses that express the earlier of two past actions.

EXAMPLE
If he **had taken** [*not* would have taken *or* took] more time, he would have won.

(6) The ***future perfect tense*** (*will have* or *shall have* + past participle) is used to express an action or a state of being that will be completed in the future before some other future occurrence.

EXAMPLE
By the time Rip Van Winkle returns to his village, the Revolutionary War **will have occurred.**

3c. Avoid unnecessary shifts in tense.

INCONSISTENT	Shiftlet marries Lucynell and then abandoned her.
CONSISTENT	Shiftlet **marries** Lucynell and then **abandons** her.
CONSISTENT	Shiftlet **married** Lucynell and then **abandoned** her.

When describing events that occur at different times, use verbs in different tenses to show the order of events.

EXAMPLE
She now **works** for *The New York Times,* but she **worked** for *The Wall Street Journal* last year.

ACTIVE VOICE AND PASSIVE VOICE

3d. *Voice* is the form a verb takes to indicate whether the subject of the verb performs or receives the action.

A verb is in the ***active voice*** when its subject performs the action.

ACTIVE VOICE	Julia Alvarez **wrote** "Daughter of Invention."

A verb is in the ***passive voice*** when its subject receives the action. A passive voice verb is always a verb phrase that includes a form of *be* and the past participle of an action verb.

PASSIVE VOICE	"Daughter of Invention" **was written** by Julia Alvarez.

3e. Use the passive voice sparingly.

In general, the passive voice is less direct and less forceful than the active voice. In some cases, the passive voice may sound awkward.

AWKWARD PASSIVE	A memorable speech was delivered by William Faulkner when the Nobel Prize was accepted by him in 1950.
ACTIVE	William Faulkner delivered a memorable speech when he accepted the Nobel Prize in 1950.

The passive voice is useful

1. when you do not know the performer of the action
2. when you do not want to reveal the performer of the action
3. when you want to emphasize the receiver of the action

EXAMPLES
Hemingway **was** severely **wounded** during the war.
Many careless errors **were made** in some of the essays about Amy Tan.
Madeline Usher **had been buried** alive!

4 USING PRONOUNS

CASE

Case is the form that a noun or a pronoun takes to indicate its use in a sentence. In English, there are three cases: *nominative, objective,* and *possessive.*

The form of a noun is the same for both the nominative case and the objective case. A noun changes form only in the possessive case. Unlike nouns, most personal pronouns have one form for each case. The form a pronoun takes depends on its function in a sentence.

Resources
Grammar and Language
- *Language Handbook Worksheets,* pp. 27–38

Language Handbook 1195

The Direct Object and the Indirect Object

8i. A *direct object* is a noun, a pronoun, or a word group that functions as a noun and tells *who* or *what* receives the action of a transitive verb.

EXAMPLES

Kerry called **me** at noon. [called whom? me]

Captain Ahab sacrifices his **ship** and almost **all** of his crew. [sacrifices what? ship and all—compound direct object]

8j. An *indirect object* is a word or word group that comes between a transitive verb and a direct object. An indirect object, which may be a noun, a pronoun, or a word group that functions as a noun, tells *to whom* or *to what* or *for whom* or *for what* the action of the verb is done.

EXAMPLES

Emily Dickinson sent **Thomas Wentworth Higginson** four poems. [sent to whom? Thomas Wentworth Higginson]

Ms. Cruz showed **José** and **me** pictures of her trip to Walden Pond. [showed to whom? José and me—compound indirect object]

 NOTE A sentence that has an indirect object must always have a direct object as well.

 For more information about verbs, see 3a–e.

The Objective Complement

8k. An *objective complement* is a word or word group that helps complete the meaning of a transitive verb by identifying or modifying the direct object. An objective complement, which may be a noun, a pronoun, an adjective, or a word group that functions as a noun or adjective, almost always follows the direct object.

EXAMPLES

Everyone considered her **dependable.** [The adjective *dependable* modifies the direct object *her.*]

Many literary historians call Poe **the master of the macabre.** [The word group *the master of the macabre* modifies the direct object *Poe.*]

The Subject Complement

8l. A *subject complement* is a word or word group that completes the meaning of a linking verb and identifies or modifies the subject. There are two kinds of subject complements: the *predicate nominative* and the *predicate adjective*.

(1) A **predicate nominative** is the word or group of words that follows a linking verb and refers to the same person or thing as the subject of the verb.

A predicate nominative may be a noun, a pronoun, or a word group that functions as a noun.

EXAMPLES

Of the three applicants, Carlos is the most competent **one.** [The pronoun *one* refers to the subject *Carlos.*]

The main characters are **Aunt Georgiana** and **Clark.** [The nouns *Aunt Georgiana* and *Clark* refer to the subject *characters.*]

(2) A **predicate adjective** is an adjective that follows a linking verb and modifies the subject of the verb.

EXAMPLES

Eben Flood felt very **lonely.** [The adjective *lonely* modifies the subject *Eben Flood.*]

Shiftlet is **sly** and **scheming.** [The adjectives *sly* and *scheming* modify the subject *Shiftlet.*]

SENTENCES CLASSIFIED ACCORDING TO STRUCTURE

8m. According to structure, sentences are classified as *simple, compound, complex,* and *compound-complex.*

(1) A **simple sentence** has one independent clause and no subordinate clauses.

EXAMPLE

Thornton Wilder's *Our Town* is one of my favorite plays.

(2) A **compound sentence** has two or more independent clauses but no subordinate clauses.

EXAMPLE

Jack London was a prolific writer; he wrote nearly fifty books in less than twenty years. [two independent clauses joined by a semicolon]

 NOTE Do not confuse a simple sentence that has a compound subject or a compound verb with a compound sentence.

(3) A **complex sentence** has one independent clause and at least one subordinate clause.

EXAMPLE
Before we read *The Great Gatsby,* let's talk about the Jazz Age. [The independent clause is *let's talk about the Jazz Age.* The subordinate clause is *before we read* The Great Gatsby.]

(4) A **compound-complex** sentence has two or more independent clauses and at least one subordinate clause.

EXAMPLE
The two eyewitnesses told the police officer what they saw, but their accounts of the accident were quite different. [The two independent clauses are *the two eyewitnesses told the police officer* and *their accounts of the accident were quite different.* The subordinate clause is *what they saw.*]

SENTENCES CLASSIFIED ACCORDING TO PURPOSE

8n. Sentences may be classified according to purpose.

(1) A **declarative sentence** makes a statement. It is followed by a period.

EXAMPLE
Swimming fast toward the ship was the white whale.

(2) An **interrogative sentence** asks a question. It is followed by a question mark.

EXAMPLE
Have you ever read *Blue Highways*?

(3) An **imperative sentence** makes a request or gives a command. It is usually followed by a period. A strong command, however, is followed by an exclamation point.

EXAMPLES
Please give me the dates for the class meetings.
Read Act I of *A Raisin in the Sun* by tomorrow.
Help me!

(4) An **exclamatory sentence** expresses strong feeling or shows excitement. It is followed by an exclamation point.

EXAMPLE
What a noble leader he was!

9 SENTENCE STYLE

WAYS TO ACHIEVE CLARITY

Coordinating Ideas

9a. To *coordinate* two or more ideas, or to give them equal emphasis, link them with a connecting word, an appropriate mark of punctuation, or both.

EXAMPLE
Edgar Allan Poe wrote "The Raven"; Edgar Lee Masters wrote *Spoon River Anthology.*

Subordinating Ideas

9b. To *subordinate* an idea, or to show that one idea is related to but less important than another, use an adverb clause or an adjective clause.

An **adverb clause** begins with a subordinating conjunction, which shows how the adverb clause relates to the main clause. Usually, the relationship is *time, cause or reason, purpose or result,* or *condition.*

EXAMPLES
Whenever I think of Boston, I think of the Lowells. [time]
Janet got a lead role in *Our Town* **because she is one of the best actors in our school.** [cause]
Let's finish now **so that we won't have to come back tomorrow.** [purpose]

An **adjective clause** usually begins with *who, whom, whose, which, that,* or *where.*

EXAMPLE
Tamisha is the one **whose essay won first prize.**

 For more about adjective clauses and adverb clauses, see 7d and f.

Using Parallel Structure

9c. Use the same grammatical form (*parallel structure*) to express ideas of equal weight.

Resources

Grammar and Language
• *Language Handbook Worksheets,* pp. 89–112

1. Use parallel structure when you link coordinate ideas.

EXAMPLE
The company guaranteed **that salaries would be increased and that working days would be shortened.** [noun clause paired with noun clause]

2. Use parallel structure when you compare or contrast ideas.

EXAMPLE
Thinking logically is as important as **calculating** accurately. [gerund compared with gerund]

3. Use parallel structure when you link ideas with correlative conjunctions (such as *both . . . and, either . . . or, neither . . . nor,* and *not only . . . but also*).

EXAMPLE
With *Ship of Fools,* Katherine Anne Porter proved she was talented not only **as a short-story writer** but also **as a novelist.** [Note that the correlative conjunctions come directly before the parallel terms.]

When you revise for parallel structure, you may need to repeat an article, a preposition, or a pronoun before each of the parallel terms.

UNCLEAR	Through Kate Chopin's stories, we can learn almost as much about the author as the social condition of women in her era.
CLEAR	Through Kate Chopin's stories, we can learn almost as much **about** the author as **about** the social condition of women in her era.

OBSTACLES TO CLARITY

Sentence Fragments

9d. Avoid using a *sentence fragment*— a word or word group that either does not contain a subject and a verb or does not express a complete thought.

Attach the fragment to the sentence that comes before or after it, or add words to or delete words from the fragment to make it a complete sentence.

FRAGMENT	Nina Otero was one of the first Mexican American women. To hold a major public post in New Mexico.
SENTENCE	Nina Otero was one of the first Mexican American women **to hold a major public post in New Mexico.**

 For more information about sentence fragments, see 8a.

Run-on Sentences

9e. Avoid using a *run-on sentence*—two or more complete thoughts that run together as if they were one complete thought.

There are two kinds of run-on sentences.

- A *fused sentence* has no punctuation at all between the complete thoughts.
- A *comma splice* has just a comma between the complete thoughts.

FUSED SENTENCE	Emerson praised Whitman's poetry most other poets sharply criticized it.
COMMA SPLICE	Emerson praised Whitman's poetry, most other poets sharply criticized it.

You may correct a run-on sentence in one of the following ways. Depending on the relationship you want to show between ideas, facts, and other information, one method will often prove to be more effective than another.

1. Make two sentences.

EXAMPLE
Emerson praised Whitman's poetry**.** **M**ost other poets sharply criticized it.

2. Use a comma and a coordinating conjunction.

EXAMPLE
Emerson praised Whitman's poetry**,** **but** most other poets sharply criticized it.

3. Change one of the independent clauses to a subordinate clause.

EXAMPLE
Emerson praised Whitman's poetry, **while most other poets sharply criticized it.**

4. Use a semicolon.

EXAMPLE
Emerson praised Whitman's poetry**;** most other poets sharply criticized it.

5. Use a semicolon and a conjunctive adverb followed by a comma.

EXAMPLE
Emerson praised Whitman's poetry**; however,** most other poets sharply criticized it.

Unnecessary Shifts in Sentences

9f. Avoid making unnecessary shifts in subject, in verb tense, and in voice.

AWKWARD	Athletes should be at the parking lot by 7:00 so that you can leave by 7:15. [shift in subject]
BETTER	**Athletes** should be at the parking lot by 7:00 so that **they** can leave by 7:15.
AWKWARD	She walked into the room, and she says, "The lights of the car outside are on." [shift in verb tense]
BETTER	She **walked** into the room, and she **said,** "The lights of the car outside are on."
AWKWARD	Russell Means starred as Chingachgook in *The Last of the Mohicans,* and an outstanding performance was delivered. [shift in voice]
BETTER	Russell Means **starred** as Chingachgook in *The Last of the Mohicans* and **delivered** an outstanding performance.

REVISING FOR VARIETY

9g. Use a variety of sentence beginnings.

The following examples show how a writer can revise sentences to avoid beginning with the subject every time.

SUBJECT FIRST	*Billy Budd* was published in 1924 and helped revive an interest in Melville's other works.
PARTICIPIAL PHRASE FIRST	**Published in 1924,** *Billy Budd* helped revive an interest in Melville's other works.
PREPOSITIONAL PHRASE FIRST	**In 1924,** *Billy Budd* was published and helped revive interest in Melville's other works.
ADVERB CLAUSE FIRST	**When** *Billy Budd* **was published in 1924,** it helped revive interest in Melville's other works.

Varying Sentence Structure

9h. Use a mix of simple, compound, complex, and compound-complex sentences in your writing.

The following paragraph shows a mix of sentence structures.

San Francisco is famous for its scenic views. [simple] Because the city sprawls over forty-two hills, driving through San Francisco is like riding a roller coaster. [complex] Atop one of San Francisco's hills is Chinatown; atop another is Coit Tower. [compound] The most popular place to visit is the San Francisco Bay area, where the Golden Gate Bridge and Fisherman's Wharf attract a steady stream of tourists. [complex]

 For information about the four types of sentence structure, see 8m.

Revising to Reduce Wordiness

9i. Avoid using unnecessary words in your writing.

The following guidelines suggest some ways to revise wordy sentences.

1. Take out a whole group of unnecessary words.

WORDY	After climbing down to the edge of the river, we boarded a small houseboat that was floating there on the surface of the water.
BETTER	After climbing down to the edge of the river, we boarded a small houseboat.

2. Replace pretentious words and expressions with straightforward ones.

WORDY	The young woman, who was at some indeterminate point in her teenage years, sported through her hair a streak of pink dye that could be considered extremely garish.
BETTER	The **teenager** sported a streak of **shocking-**pink dye in her hair.

3. Reduce a clause to a phrase.

WORDY	Emily Dickinson fell in love with Charles Wadsworth, who was a Presbyterian minister.
BETTER	Emily Dickinson fell in love with Charles Wadsworth, **a Presbyterian minister.**

4. Reduce a phrase or a clause to one word.

WORDY	One of the writers from the South was William Faulkner.
BETTER	One of the **Southern** writers was William Faulkner.

13b. Use italics (underlining) for words, letters, numerals, and symbols referred to as such and for foreign words that have not been adopted into English.

EXAMPLES

Should the use of *their* for *there* be considered a spelling error or a usage error?

The teacher couldn't tell whether I had written a script *S*, the number *5*, or an *&*.

All U.S. coins are now stamped with the inscription *e pluribus unum*.

QUOTATION MARKS

13c. Use quotation marks to enclose a *direct quotation*—a person's exact words.

EXAMPLE

Chief Joseph said, **"**The earth is the mother of all people, and all people should have equal rights upon it.**"**

Notice that a direct quotation begins with a capital letter. However, if the quotation is only part of a sentence, it does not begin with a capital letter.

EXAMPLE

Chief Joseph called the earth "the mother of all people."

(1) When the expression identifying the speaker divides a quoted sentence, the second part begins with a lowercase letter.

EXAMPLE

"I really have to leave now," said Gwen, "so that I will be on time." [Notice that each part of a divided quotation is enclosed in quotation marks.]

When the second part of a divided quotation is a new sentence, it begins with a capital letter.

EXAMPLE

"Teddy Roosevelt was the first U.S. President to express concern about the depletion of the nation's natural resources," explained Mr. Fuentes. "He established a conservation program that expanded the national park system."

(2) When used with quotation marks, other marks of punctuation are placed according to the following rules.

- Commas and periods are always placed inside the closing quotation marks.

EXAMPLES

"On the other hand**,"** he said, **"**your decision may be correct.**"**

- Semicolons and colons are always placed outside the closing quotation marks.

EXAMPLES

My neighbor said, **"**Sure, I'll buy a subscription**"**; it was lucky that I asked her on payday.

Edna St. Vincent Millay uses these devices in her poem **"**Spring**"**: alliteration, slant rhyme, and personification.

- Question marks and exclamation points are placed inside the closing quotation marks if the quotation itself is a question or an exclamation. Otherwise, they are placed outside.

EXAMPLES

Was it you who wrote the poem **"**Upon Turning Seventeen**"**?

"What a tortured soul Reverend Dimmesdale is!**"** said Mr. Klein.

(3) When quoting a passage that consists of more than one paragraph, put quotation marks at the beginning of each paragraph and at the end of only the last paragraph.

EXAMPLE

"As he neared the house, each detail of the scene became vivid to him. He was aware of some bricks of the vanished chimney lying on the sod. There was a door which hung by one hinge.

"Rifle bullets called forth by the insistent skirmishers came from the far-off bank of foliage. They mingled with the shells and the pieces of shells until the air was torn in all directions by hootings, yells, howls. The sky was full of fiends who directed all their wild rage at his head.**"**

—Stephen Crane, "A Mystery of Heroism"

(4) Use single quotation marks to enclose a quotation within a quotation.

EXAMPLES

The teacher requested, "Jorge, please explain what Emerson meant when he said, 'To be great is to be misunderstood.'"

"Have you read 'Rip Van Winkle'?" Jill asked.

(5) When writing *dialogue* (a conversation), begin a new paragraph every time the speaker changes, and enclose the speaker's words in quotation marks.

EXAMPLE

"How far is it to the Owl Creek bridge?**"** Farquhar asked.

"About thirty miles.**"**

"Is there no force on this side the creek?**"**

"Only a picket post half a mile out, on the railroad, and a single sentinel at this end of the bridge.**"**

—Ambrose Bierce, "An Occurrence at Owl Creek Bridge"

3d. Use quotation marks to enclose titles of short works, such as short stories, poems, essays, articles, songs, episodes of television series, and chapters and other parts of books.

TYPE OF NAME	EXAMPLES	
Short Stories	"The Magic Barrel"	"The Tell-Tale Heart"
Poems	"The Latin Deli"	"Thanatopsis"
Essays	"On the Mall"	"The Creative Process"
Articles	"Old Poetry and Modern Music"	
Songs	"On Top of Old Smoky"	
TV Episodes	"The Flight of the Condor"	
Chapters and Parts of Books	"The World Was New" "The Colonies' Struggle for Freedom"	

NOTE Neither italics nor quotation marks are used for titles of major religious works or titles of legal or historical documents.

EXAMPLES
Bible   Bill of Rights

☞ For a list of titles that are italicized rather than placed in quotation marks, see 13a.

ELLIPSIS POINTS

3e. Use three spaced periods called *ellipsis points* (. . .) to mark omissions from quoted material and pauses in a written passage.

ORIGINAL   The second half of the program consisted of four numbers from the *Ring,* and closed with Siegfried's funeral march. My aunt wept quietly, but almost continuously, as a shallow vessel overflows in a rainstorm. From time to time her dim eyes looked up at the lights which studded the ceiling, burning softly under their dull glass globes; doubtless they were stars in truth to her. I was still perplexed as to what measure of musical comprehension was left to her, she who had heard nothing but the singing of gospel hymns at Methodist services in the square frame schoolhouse on Section Thirteen for so many years. I was wholly unable to gauge how much of it had been dissolved in soapsuds, or worked into bread, or milked into the bottom of a pail.
—Willa Cather, "A Wagner Matinée"

(1) If the quoted material that comes before the ellipsis points is not a complete sentence, use three ellipsis points with a space before the first point.

EXAMPLE
The narrator notes, "The second half of the program . . . closed with Siegfried's funeral march."

(2) If the quoted material that comes before or after the ellipsis points is a complete sentence, use an end mark before the ellipsis points.

EXAMPLE
The narrator observes, "My aunt wept quietly. . . . "

(3) If one sentence or more is omitted, ellipsis points follow the end mark that precedes the omitted material.

EXAMPLE
Recalling the experience, the narrator says, "My aunt wept quietly, but almost continuously, as a shallow vessel overflows in a rainstorm. . . . I was still perplexed as to what measure of musical comprehension was left to her, she who had heard nothing but the singing of gospel hymns at Methodist services in the square frame schoolhouse on Section Thirteen for so many years."

(4) To show that a full line or more of poetry has been omitted, use an entire line of spaced periods.

ORIGINAL   If you were coming in the Fall,
I'd brush the Summer by
With half a smile, and half a spurn,
As Housewives do, a Fly.
—Emily Dickinson, "If you were coming in the Fall"

WITH OMISSION   If you were coming in the Fall,
I'd brush the Summer by
. . . .
As Housewives do, a Fly.

APOSTROPHES

13f. Use an apostrophe in forming the possessive of nouns and indefinite pronouns.

(1) To form the possessive of a singular noun, add an apostrophe and an *s*.

EXAMPLES
the minister's veil   Ross's opinion

NOTE When forming the possessive of a singular noun ending in an *s* sound, add only an apostrophe if the addition of *'s* will make the noun awkward to pronounce. Otherwise, add *'s*.

EXAMPLES
Douglass's autobiography   Texas' population

(2) To form the possessive of a plural noun ending in *s*, add only the apostrophe. If the plural noun does not end in *s*, add an apostrophe and an *s*.

EXAMPLES
the authors' styles   the Ushers' house
men's fashions   children's toys

(3) To form the possessive of an indefinite pronoun, add an apostrophe and an *s*.

EXAMPLES
each one's time   everybody's opinion

NOTE In such forms as *anyone else* and *somebody else*, the correct possessives are *anyone else's* and *somebody else's*.

(4) Form the possessive of only the last word in a compound word, in the name of an organization or business firm, or in a word group showing joint possession.

EXAMPLES
father-in-law's gloves   Roz and Denise's idea
Taylor, Sanders, and Weissman's law office

(5) Form the possessive of each noun in a word group showing individual possession of similar items.

EXAMPLE
Baldwin's and Ellison's writings

When a possessive pronoun is part of a word group showing joint possession, each noun in the word group is also possessive.

EXAMPLE
Walter Mitty's and **her** relationship

(6) When used in the possessive form, words that indicate time (such as *hour, week,* and *year*) and words that indicate amounts of money require apostrophes.

EXAMPLES
a week's vacation   five dollars' worth

13g. Use an apostrophe to show where letters, words, or numbers have been omitted in a contraction.

EXAMPLES
they had . . . **they'd**   Kerry is . . . **Kerry's**
let us . . . **let's**   of the clock . . . **o'clock**
where is . . . **where's**   1997 . . . **'97**

The word *not* can be shortened to *–n't* and added to a verb, usually without any change in the spelling of the verb.

EXAMPLES
is not . . . **isn't**   has not . . . **hasn't**

EXCEPTION
will not . . . **won't**

13h. Use an apostrophe and an *s* to form the plurals of all lowercase letters, some uppercase letters, numerals, and some words referred to as words.

EXAMPLES
There are two *r*'s and two *s*'s in *embarrassed*.
Soon after Tom and Lucynell said their *I do*'s, he abandoned her.

You may add only an *s* to form the plurals of such items—except lowercase letters—if the plural forms will not cause misreading.

EXAMPLES
Compact discs (**CDs**) were introduced in the **1980s**.
On her report card were three **A**'s and three **C**'s.

HYPHENS

13i. Use a hyphen to divide a word at the end of a line.

When dividing a word at the end of a line, remember the following rules:

(1) Do not divide a one-syllable word.

EXAMPLE
Peyton Farquhar was captured, and he was finally **hanged** from the bridge.

(2) Divide a word only between syllables.

EXAMPLE
Ernest Hemingway's *A Farewell to Arms* was **published** in 1929.

(3) Divide an already hyphenated word at the hyphen.

EXAMPLE
Stephen Crane died in Germany at the age of **twenty-eight**.

(4) Do not divide a word so that one letter stands alone.

EXAMPLE
One fine autumn day, Rip Van Winkle fell fast **asleep** in the mountains.

13j. Use a hyphen with compound numbers from twenty-one to ninety-nine and with fractions used as modifiers.

EXAMPLES
six hundred **twenty-five**
a **three-fourths** quorum [*but* three fourths of the audience]

DASHES

13k. Use dashes to set off abrupt breaks in thoughts.

EXAMPLE
The poor condition of this road—it really needs to be paved—makes this route unpopular.

13l. Use dashes to set off an appositive or a parenthetical expression that contains commas.

EXAMPLE
Several of the nineteenth-century American poets—Poe, Dickinson, and Whitman, for example—led remarkable lives.

PARENTHESES

13m. Use parentheses to enclose informative or explanatory material of minor importance.

EXAMPLES
Harriet Tubman (c. 1820–1913) is remembered for her work in the Underground Railroad.
On our vacation we visited Natchitoches (it's pronounced nak′ə·täsh′), Louisiana.
Thoreau lived at Walden Pond for two years. (See the map on page 350.)

BRACKETS

13n. Use brackets to enclose an explanation within quoted or parenthetical material.

EXAMPLE
I think that Hilda Doolittle (more commonly known as H. D. [1886–1961]) is best remembered for her Imagist poetry.

14 SPELLING

UNDERSTANDING WORD STRUCTURE

Many English words are made up of roots and affixes (prefixes and suffixes).

Roots

14a. The *root* of a word is the part that carries the word's core meaning.

ROOTS	MEANINGS	EXAMPLES
–bio–	life	biology, symbiotic
–duc–, –duct–	lead	educate, conductor
–mit–, –miss–	send	remit, emissary
–port–	carry, bear	transport, portable

NOTE To find the meaning of a root or an affix, look in a dictionary. Most dictionaries have individual entries for word parts.

Prefixes

14b. A *prefix* is one or more letters or syllables added to the beginning of a word or word part to create a new word.

PREFIXES	MEANINGS	EXAMPLES
a–	lacking, without	amorphous, apolitical
dia–	through, across, apart	diagonal, diameter, diagnose
inter–	between, among	intercede, international
mis–	badly, wrongly	misfire, misspell

Resources
Grammar and Language
• *Language Handbook Worksheets,* pp. 160–167

austere (ô·stir′) *adj.*: very plain.

autonomy (ô·tän′ə·mē) *n.*: independence; self-government.

avarice (av′ə·ris) *n.*: greed. —**avaricious** *adj.*

avert (ə·vʉrt′) *v.*: prevent; turn away.

B

bedlam (bed′ləm) *n.*: place or condition of great noise and confusion.

bewitch (bē·wich′) *v.*: entice; make someone or something irresistible. —**bewitching** *v.* used as *adj.*

bicker (bik′ər) *v.*: quarrel over something unimportant; squabble. —**bickering** *v.* used as *adj.*

blanch (blanch) *v.*: drain of color. —**blanched** *v.* used as *adj.*

bleak *adj.*: cheerless.

blithe (blīth) *adj.*: carefree.

bountiful (boun′tə·fəl) *adj.*: generous.

brazenness (brā′zən·nis) *n.*: boldness.

C

caliber (kal′ə·bər) *n.*: quality or ability.

candid (kan′did) *adj.*: unbiased; fair.

caper (kā′pər) *n.*: foolish prank.

careen (kə·rēn′) *v.*: lurch sideways.

celestial (sə·les′chəl) *adj.*: divine; perfect.

censor (sen′sər) *v.*: cut or change to remove material deemed objectionable.

circumvent (sʉr′kəm·vent′) *v.*: avoid by cleverness or deceit.

clammy (klam′ē) *adj.*: cold and damp.

clamor (klam′ər) *n.*: loud noise; loud demand or complaint.

cleft (kleft) *n.*: opening or crack in something.

coherent (kō·hir′ənt) *adj.*: clear, logical, and consistent.

coincide (kō′in·sīd′) *v.*: occur at the same time.

commodious (kə·mō′dē·əs) *adj.*: spacious.

communal (kə·myoon′əl) *adj.*: belonging to an entire group.

compel (kəm·pel′) *v.*: drive; force.

comply (kəm·plī′) *v.*: obey; agree to a request.

conceive (kən·sēv′) *v.*: think; imagine.

conception (kən·sep′shən) *n.*: mental formation of ideas.

concession (kən·sesh′ən) *n.*: act of giving in.

confiscation (kän′fis·kā′shən) *n.*: seizure of property by authority.

conflagration (kän′flə·grā′shən) *n.*: huge fire.

conjecture (kən·jek′chər) *v.*: guess; predict.

conscientious (kän′shē·en′shəs) *adj.*: careful; painstaking; thorough. —**conscientiously** *adv.*

consolation (kän′sə·lā′shən) *n.*: comfort.

consternation (kän′stər·nā′shən) *n.*: confusion resulting from fear or shock.

constitution (kän′stə·too′shən) *n.*: physical condition.

constrain (kən·strān′) *v.*: force.

contemptuous (kən·temp′choo·əs) *adj.*: scornful. —**contemptuously** *adv.*

contrivance (kən·trī′vəns) *n.*: scheme; plan.

conundrum (kə·nun′drəm) *n.*: riddle.

convene (kən·vēn′) *v.*: assemble.

conviction (kən·vik′shən) *n.*: fixed or strong belief.

convivial (kən·viv′ē·əl) *adj.*: jovial; sociable.

copious (kō′pē·əs) *adj.*: abundant. —**copiously** *adv.*

covet (kuv′it) *v.*: long for; want badly.

craven (krā′vən) *adj.*: very fearful; cowardly.

crucial (kroo′shəl) *adj.*: critical; decisive.

cunning (kun′iŋ) *adj.*: sly or crafty.

D

debris (də·brē′) *n.*: rubble; broken pieces.

deference (def′ər·əns) *n.*: respect.

deferential (def′ər·en′shəl) *adj.*: showing respect or courteous regard.

deluge (del′yooj) *n.*: rush; flood.

delusion (di·loo′zhən) *n.*: false belief or opinion.

deplore (dē·plôr′) *v.*: condemn as wrong; disapprove of.

derision (di·rizh′ən) *n.*: ridicule; contempt.

destitute (des′tə·toot′) *adj.*: poverty-stricken.

dilapidated (də·lap′ə·dāt′id) *adj.*: partially ruined; in need of repair.

diminutive (də·min′yoo·tiv) *adj.*: very small; tiny.

disconsolate (dis·kän′sə·lit) *adj.*: unhappy. —**disconsolately** *adv.*

disembody (dis′im·bäd′ē) *v.*: separate from the body. —**disembodied** *v.* used as *adj.*

disperse (di·spʉrs′) *v.*: scatter.

dispirited (di·spir′it·id) *adj.*: discouraged.

disposition (dis′pə·zish′ən) *n.*: nature; character.

dispute (di·spyoot′) *v.*: contest.

dissident (dis′ə·dənt) *adj.*: disagreeing; differing in belief or opinion.

distraction (di·strak′shən) *n.*: mental disturbance or distress.

distraught (di·strôt′) *adj.*: troubled.

distressed (di·strest′) *adj.*: suffering; troubled.

divergence (dī·vʉr′jəns) *n.*: variance; difference.

dominion (də·min′yən) *n.:* rule.

drone *n.:* steady hum.

dwindle (dwin′dəl) *v.:* diminish.

E

edible (ed′ə·bəl) *adj.:* capable of being eaten.

efface (ə·fās′) *v.:* erase; wipe out.

effectual (e·fek′choo·əl) *adj.:* productive; efficient.

effervescent (ef′ər·ves′ənt) *adj.:* bubbling up; foaming.

effete (e·fēt′) *adj.:* sterile; unproductive.

elation (ē·lā′shən) *n.:* celebration.

eloquence (el′ə·kwəns) *n.:* forceful, fluent, and graceful speech.

elude (ē·lood′) *v.:* escape detection or notice. —**eluding** *v.* used as *adj.*

encompass (en·kum′pəs) *v.:* surround; enclose. —**encompassed** *v.* used as *adj.*

encumbrance (en·kum′brəns) *n.:* burden; hindrance.

enmity (en′mə·tē) *n.:* hatred.

ensue (en·soo′) *v.:* result.

enthrall (en·thrôl′) *v.:* fascinate.

entreat (en·trēt′) *v.:* ask sincerely; beg.

eradicate (ē·rad′i·kāt′) *v.:* eliminate; wipe out; destroy.

eradication (ē·rad′i·kā′shən) *n.:* utter destruction; obliteration.

ethereal (ē·thir′ē·əl) *adj.:* not earthly; spiritual.

eulogy (yoo′lə·jē) *n.:* public speech of praise.

exalt (eg·zôlt′) *v.:* lift up.

excruciating (eks·kroo′shē·āt′iŋ) *adj.:* intensely painful.

exemplary (eg·zem′plə·rē) *adj.:* serving as a model; worth imitating.

expedient (ek·spē′dē·ənt) *n.:* convenience; means to an end.

expire (ek·spīr′) *v.:* die. —**expiring** *v.* used as *adj.*

explicit (eks·plis′it) *adj.:* clear; definite.

expunge (ek·spunj′) *v.:* erase; remove.

extremity (ek·strem′ə·tē) *n.:* limb of the body, especially a hand or foot. —**extremities** *n. pl.*

F

facilitate (fə·sil′ə·tāt′) *v.:* make easier.

fastidious (fa·stid′ē·əs) *adj.:* difficult to please; critical.

fervent (fur′vənt) *adj.:* having intense feeling. —**fervently** *adv.*

fitful *adj.:* irregular; in stops and starts. —**fitfully** *adv.*

florid (flôr′id) *adj.:* showy.

flourish (flur′ish) *v.:* thrive; prosper.

frenzy (fren′zē) *n.:* frantic behavior; wildness.

frivolity (fri·väl′ə·tē) *n.:* silliness.

furtive (fur′tiv) *adj.:* stealthy; hidden.

futile (fyoot′'l) *adj.:* useless; pointless.

G

garrulous (gar′ə·ləs) *adj.:* talking a great deal, especially about unimportant things.

gaudy (gô′dē) *adj.:* showy but lacking in good taste.

gesticulate (jes·tik′yoo·lāt′) *v.:* gesture, especially with the hands and arms. —**gesticulating** *v.* used as *adj.*

grotesque (grō·tesk′) *adj.:* strange; absurd.

gyration (jī·rā′shən) *n.:* circular movement; whirling.

H

habitual (hə·bich′oo·əl) *adj.:* usual; by habit. —**habitually** *adv.*

haggard (hag′ərd) *adj.:* gaunt; wasted or worn in appearance.

hail *v.:* greet.

hedonistic (hē′də·nis′tik) *adj.:* pleasure-loving; self-indulgent.

hysteria (hi·ster′ē·ə) *n.:* uncontrolled excitement.

I

idealist (ī·dē′əl·ist) *n.:* one who believes in noble though sometimes impractical goals; dreamer.

illumine (i·loo′mən) *v.:* light up.

immune (i·myoon′) *adj.:* protected.

impart (im·pärt′) *v.:* reveal.

impassive (im·pas′iv) *adj.:* controlled; not revealing any emotions.

impeccable (im·pek′ə·bəl) *adj.:* perfect; without error or defect. —**impeccably** *adv.*

imperative (im·per′ə·tiv) *adj.:* absolutely necessary; urgent.

---

at, āte, cär; ten, ēve; is, īce; gō, hôrn, look, tool; oil, out; up, fur; ə *for unstressed vowels, as* a *in* ago, u *in* focus; ′ *as in* Latin (lat′'n); chin; she; thin; *the*; zh *as in* azure (azh′ər); ŋ *as in* ring (riŋ)

imperceptible (im′pər·sep′tə·bəl) *adj.:* unnoticeable; so slight as not to be noticed; not clear or obvious to the senses or mind.

impervious (im·pʉr′vē·əs) *adj.:* resistant; incapable of being penetrated.

impetuous (im·pech′o͞o·əs) *adj.:* impulsive.

impious (im′pē·əs) *adj.:* irreverent.

impregnable (im·preg′nə·bəl) *adj.:* impossible to capture or enter by force.

improvident (im·präv′ə·dənt) *adj.:* careless; not providing for the future.

impulse (im′puls′) *n.:* sudden desire or urge.

impute (im·pyo͞ot′) *v.:* credit; assign.

incessant (in·ses′ənt) *adj.:* without stopping. —**incessantly** *adv.*

inconceivable (in′kən·sēv′ə·bəl) *adj.:* unimaginable; beyond understanding.

indolent (in′də·lənt) *adj.:* lazy.

induce (in·do͞os′) *v.:* persuade; force; cause.

indulge (in·dulj′) *v.:* satisfy; please; humor.

inert (in·ʉrt′) *adj.:* inactive; dull; motionless.

inevitable (in·ev′i·tə·bəl) *adj.:* not avoidable.

inexplicable (in·eks′pli·kə·bəl) *adj.:* unable to be explained.

inextricable (in·eks′tri·kə·bəl) *adj.:* unable to be freed or disentangled from.

infamous (in′fə·məs) *adj.:* having a bad reputation; disgraceful.

infirm (in·fʉrm′) *adj.:* physically weak.

ingenious (in·jēn′yəs) *adj.:* clever.

inherent (in·hir′ənt) *adj.:* inborn; built-in.

iniquity (i·nik′wi·tē) *n.:* wickedness.

inscrutable (in·skro͞ot′ə·bəl) *adj.:* mysterious.

insidious (in·sid′ē·əs) *adj.:* sly; sneaky.

insolent (in′sə·lənt) *adj.:* boldly disrespectful.

insuperable (in·so͞o′pər·ə·bəl) *adj.:* incapable of being overcome.

insurrection (in′sə·rek′shən) *n.:* rebellion; revolt.

intangible (in·tan′jə·bəl) *adj.:* difficult to define; vague.

integrate (in′tə·grāt′) *v.:* unify.

integrity (in·teg′rə·tē) *n.:* sound moral principles; honesty.

intent (in·tent′) *adj.:* purposeful.

interloper (in′tər·lō′pər) *n.:* intruder; meddler.

interminable (in·tʉr′mi·nə·bəl) *adj.:* endless; seeming to last forever.

interpose (in′tər·pōz′) *v.:* put forth in order to interfere.

intersperse (in′tər·spʉrs′) *v.:* place at intervals. —**interspersed** *v.* used as *adj.*

intimate (in′tə·māt′) *v.:* state indirectly; hint.

intricate (in′tri·kit) *adj.:* complicated; detailed.

intrigue (in′trēg′) *n.:* scheming; plotting.

intuitive (in·to͞o′i·tiv) *adj.:* without conscious reasoning. —**intuitively** *adv.*

invincible (in·vin′sə·bəl) *adj.:* unconquerable.

inviolate (in·vī′ə·lit) *adj.:* uncorrupted.

J

jilt (jilt) *v.:* reject (as a lover).

judicious (jo͞o·dish′əs) *adj.:* cautious; wise, like a judge. —**judiciously** *adv.*

L

laborious (lə·bôr′ē·əs) *adj.:* difficult; involving much hard work.

labyrinth (lab′ə·rinth′) *n.:* place full of complex passageways; maze.

lamentable (lə·men′tə·bəl) *adj.:* regrettable; distressing.

legacy (leg′ə·sē) *n.:* inheritance.

lethargy (leth′ər·jē) *n.:* abnormal drowsiness.

listless (list′lis) *adj.:* weary; without energy or interest in anything. —**listlessly** *adv.*

loiter (loit′ər) *v.:* spend time; hang around.

lucid (lo͞o′sid) *adj.:* clearheaded; not confused.

ludicrous (lo͞o′di·krəs) *adj.:* laughable; absurd.

luxuriant (lug·zhoor′ē·ənt) *adj.:* rich; abundant.

M

magnanimity (mag′nə·nim′ə·tē) *n.:* nobility of spirit.

magnitude (mag′nə·to͞od′) *n.:* importance; greatness of scope.

malice (mal′is) *n.:* deliberate ill will; desire to harm. —**malicious** *adj.*

malign (mə·līn′) *adj.:* harmful; evil.

malignant (mə·lig′nənt) *adj.:* destructive; evil.

malodorous (mal·ō′dər·əs) *adj.:* bad-smelling.

manifest (man′ə·fəst′) *adj.:* plain; clear.

martial (mär′shəl) *adj.:* warlike.

medium (mē′dē·əm) *n.:* material for an artist.

melancholy (mel′ən·käl′ē) *adj.:* sad; gloomy; sorrowful.

mesmerize (mez′mər·īz) *v.:* hypnotize. —**mesmerizing** *v.* used as *adj.*

mirth (mʉrth) *n.:* joyfulness.

mortify (môrt'ə·fī') *v.*: humiliate; deeply embarrass. —**mortified** *v.* used as *adj.*

municipal (myōō·nis'ə·pəl) *adj.*: belonging to a city or town.

myriad (mir'ē·əd) *adj.*: countless.

N

nape *n.*: back of the neck.

nimbus (nim'bəs) *n.*: aura; halo.

nomadic (nō·mad'ik) *adj.*: wandering.

noncommittal (nän'kə·mit''l) *adj.*: neutral; giving no clear indication of feeling or attitude.

nostalgia (nä·stal'jə) *n.*: longing.

notorious (nō·tôr'ē·əs) *adj.*: known widely and usually unfavorably.

O

oblique (ō·blēk') *adj.*: slanted. —**obliquely** *adv.*

obliterate (ə·blit'ər·āt) *v.*: erase or destroy.

obscure (əb·skyoor') *v.*: conceal; hide.

obscurity (əb·skyoor'ə·tē) *n.*: darkness.

occult (ə·kult') *adj.*: hidden.

ominous (äm'ə·nəs) *adj.*: threatening; menacing.

omnipotent (äm·nip'ə·tənt) *adj.*: all-powerful.

opaque (ō·pāk') *adj.*: not transparent; not letting light pass through.

oscillation (äs'ə·lā'shən) *n.*: regular back-and-forth movement.

ostentatious (äs'tən·tā'shəs) *adj.*: deliberately attracting notice.

P

pandemonium (pan'də·mō'nē·əm) *n.*: wild confusion.

parsimony (pär'sə·mō'nē) *n.*: stinginess.

pauper (pô'pər) *n.*: extremely poor person.

penitent (pen'i·tənt) *adj.*: sorry for doing wrong.

pensive (pen'siv) *adj.*: deeply thoughtful. —**pensively** *adv.*

perennial (pə·ren'ē·əl) *adj.*: persistent; constant.

perilous (per'ə·ləs) *adj.*: dangerous.

perseverance (pʉr'sə·vir'əns) *n.*: persistence.

persistent (pər·sist'ənt) *adj.*: continuing.

pertinent (pʉrt''n·ənt) *adj.*: to the point; applying to the situation.

perturbation (pʉr'tər·bā'shən) *n.*: feeling of alarm or agitation.

perverse (pər·vʉrs') *adj.*: odd; contrary.

pervert (pər·vʉrt') *v.*: misdirect; corrupt.

pestilential (pes'tə·len'shəl) *adj.*: dangerous and harmful, like a deadly infection.

petulance (pech'ə·ləns) *n.*: irritability; impatience.

pious (pī'əs) *adj.*: devoted to one's religion.

pivotal (piv'ət·'l) *adj.*: central; acting as a point around which other things turn.

placid (plas'id) *adj.*: peaceful; quiet.

plague (plāg) *v.*: annoy.

plaintive (plān'tiv) *adj.*: expressing sadness.

plausibility (plô'zə·bil'ə·tē) *n.*: believability.

plunder (plun'dər) *n.*: goods seized, especially during wartime.

poignant (poin'yənt) *adj.*: emotionally moving.

ponder (pän'dər) *v.*: think deeply.

ponderous (pän'dər·əs) *adj.*: very heavy.

portend (pôr·tend') *v.*: signify.

posterity (päs·ter'ə·tē) *n.*: generations to come.

potent (pōt''nt) *adj.*: powerful or effective.

precarious (pri·ker'ē·əs) *adj.*: uncertain; insecure; risky; unstable. —**precariously** *adv.*

precedence (pres'ə·dəns) *n.*: priority because of superiority in rank.

preeminent (prē·em'ə·nənt) *adj.*: above all else. —**preeminently** *adv.*

preposterous (prē·päs'tər·əs) *adj.*: ridiculous.

prestigious (pres·tij'əs) *adj.*: impressive; having distinction.

pretense (prē·tens') *n.*: false claim.

prevalent (prev'ə·lənt) *adj.*: widely existing; frequent.

prodigy (präd'ə·jē) *n.*: extremely gifted person.

profound (prō·found') *adj.*: deep. —**profoundly** *adv.*

profundity (prō·fun'də·tē) *n.*: intellectual depth.

profuse (prō·fyōōs') *adj.*: in great quantities. —**profusely** *adv.*

prostrate (präs'trāt') *adj.*: **1.** lying flat. **2.** helpless; overcome.

protrude (prō·trōōd') *v.*: stick out. —**protruding** *v.* used as *adj.*

---

at, āte, cär; ten, ēve; is, īce; gō, hôrn, look, tōōl; oil, out; up, fʉr; ə *for unstressed vowels, as* a *in* ago, u *in* focus; ' *as in* Latin (lat''n); chin; she; thin; *the*; zh *as in* azure (azh'ər); ŋ *as in* ring (riŋ)

provisional (prə·vizh′ə·nəl) *adj.*: temporary; serving for the time being.

provocation (präv′ə·kā′shən) *n.*: something that stirs up action or feeling.

provoke (prə·vōk′) *v.*: anger. —**provoked** *v.* used as *adj.*

proximity (präk·sim′ə·tē) *n.*: nearness.

prudence (prōō′dəns) *n.*: sound judgment.

pulverize (pul′vər·īz′) *v.*: crush; destroy.

puncture (puŋk′chər) *n.*: small hole.

R

rakish (rāk′ish) *adj.*: casual; stylish. —**rakishly** *adv.*

rancor (raŋ′kər) *n.*: anger.

ravage (rav′ij) *n.*: violent destruction.

realm (relm) *n.*: kingdom.

recede (ri·sēd′) *v.*: become more distant and indistinct.

recoil (ri·koil′) *v.*: shrink away; draw back.

reconcile (rek′ən·sīl′) *v.*: make peace.

rectitude (rek′tə·tōōd′) *n.*: correctness.

reiteration (rē·it′ə·rā′shən) *n.*: repetition.

relinquish (ri·liŋ′kwish) *v.*: give up.

remit (ri·mit′) *v.*: cancel; refrain from enforcing payment.

rend (rend) *v.*: violently rip apart. —**rending** *v.* used as *n.*

render (ren′dər) *v.*: make.

rendezvous (rän′dā·vōō′) *n.*: meeting. —**rendezvous** *n.* used as *adj.*

renounce (ri·nouns′) *v.*: give up.

reproach (ri·prōch′) *v.*: blame; disgrace.

reserve (ri·zurv′) *n.*: self-restraint.

resolute (rez′ə·lōōt′) *adj.*: determined; resolved; unwavering.

resolve (ri·zälv′) *v.*: make a decision; determine.

resonance (rez′ə·nəns) *n.*: capacity to intensify sound.

retort (ri·tôrt′) *n.*: quick, sharp answer.

retract (ri·trakt′) *v.*: take back; draw back.

retraction (ri·trak′shən) *n.*: withdrawal.

revel (rev′əl) *v.*: take pleasure.

reverberate (ri·vur′bə·rāt′) *v.*: resound; re-echo.

reverential (rev′ə·ren′shəl) *adj.*: deeply respectful.

rigorous (rig′ər·əs) *adj.*: precise; severe.

rotund (rō·tund′) *adj.*: round; plump.

ruse (rōōz) *n.*: trick; deception.

S

sagacious (sə·gā′shəs) *adj.*: wise; keenly perceptive.

sarcastic (sär·kas′tik) *adj.*: scornful; mocking.

sate (sāt) *v.*: satisfy.

savory (sā′vər·ē) *adj.*: appetizing; tasty.

scruple (skrōō′pəl) *v.*: hesitate because of feelings of guilt.

scrupulous (skrōōp′yə·ləs) *adj.*: painstaking; with great care. —**scrupulously** *adv.*

semblance (sem′bləns) *n.*: outward appearance; likeness.

sentinel (sent″n·əl) *n.*: guard; sentry.

simultaneous (sī′məl·tā′nē·əs) *adj.*: at the same time. —**simultaneously** *adv.*

singular (siŋ′gyə·lər) *adj.*: remarkable.

solace (säl′is) *v.*: comfort.

solemnity (sə·lem′nə·tē) *n.*: seriousness. —**solemn** *adj.*

sordid (sôr′did) *adj.*: dirty; cheap; shameful.

spurn (spurn) *v.*: reject.

stagnant (stag′nənt) *adj.*: not flowing or moving.

stolid (stäl′id) *adj.*: showing little emotion; impassive. —**stolidly** *adv.*

stolidity (stə·lid′ə·tē) *n.*: absence of emotional reactions.

striking *adj.*: impressive; attractive.

subsequent (sub′si·kwənt) *adj.*: following.

subside (səb·sīd′) *v.*: lessen.

subsist (səb·sist′) *v.*: stay alive. —**subsisting** *v.* used as *adj.*

successive (sək·ses′iv) *adj.*: consecutive.

superficial (sōō′pər·fish′əl) *adj.*: not profound; shallow.

superfluous (sə·pur′flōō·əs) *adj.*: more than is needed or wanted; useless.

supplication (sup′lə·kā′shən) *n.*: plea; prayer.

sustain (sə·stān′) *v.*: prolong. —**sustained** *v.* used as *adj.*

T

taboo (tə·bōō′) *n.*: social restriction.

tactful (takt′fəl) *adj.*: skilled in saying the right thing.

tactile (tak′təl) *adj.*: able to be perceived by touch.

tedious (tē′dē·əs) *adj.*: tiring; dreary.

temple (tem′pəl) *n.*: side of the forehead, just above and in front of the ear.

temporal (tem′pə·rəl) *adj.*: temporary.

tenuous (ten′yōō·əs) *adj.*: slight; insubstantial; not firm.

tepid (tep′id) *adj.*: lukewarm.

tout (tout) *v.*: praise highly.

tranquil (traŋ′kwəl) *adj.*: calm; quiet.

transcendent (tran·sen′dənt) *adj.*: excelling; surpassing.

transient (tran′shənt) *adj.*: temporary; passing quickly or soon.

transition (tran·zish′ən) *n.*: passage from one condition, form, or stage to another.

tread (tred) *n.*: step; walk.

trepidation (trep′ə·dā′shən) *n.*: anxious uncertainty.

tumultuous (tōō·mul′chōō·əs) *adj.*: violent; noisy and disorderly; greatly agitated or disturbed; stormy.

turbulence (tʉr′byə·ləns) *n.*: wild disorder.

tyranny (tir′ə·nē) *n.*: cruel use of power.

U

ultimatum (ul′tə·māt′əm) *n.*: last offer; final proposition.

undulation (un′jə·lā′shən) *n.*: wavelike motion.

unnerve (un·nʉrv′) *v.*: cause to lose one's courage.

V

valor (val′ər) *n.*: great courage.

vanity (van′ə·tē) *n.*: excessive pride.

venerable (ven′ər·ə·bəl) *adj.*: worthy of respect, usually by reason of age.

vengeance (ven′jəns) *n.*: revenge; punishment in return for a wrongdoing.

vengeful (venj′fəl) *adj.*: intent on revenge.

venture (ven′chər) *v.*: dare or risk going.

veracious (və·rā′shəs) *adj.*: honest; truthful.

veritable (ver′i·tə·bəl) *adj.*: genuine; true.

vibrant (vi′brənt) *adj.*: full of energy.

vigilant (vij′ə·lənt) *adj.*: watchful. —**vigilant** *adj.* used as *n.*

vindicate (vin′də·kāt′) *v.*: prove correct; justify. —**vindicated** *v.* used as *adj.*

virile (vir′əl) *adj.*: manly; masculine.

virulent (vir′yoo·lənt) *adj.*: full of hate; venomous.

vital (vīt′′l) *adj.*: filled with life.

vulnerability (vul′nər·ə·bil′ə·tē) *n.*: capability of being hurt.

W

wanton (wänt′′n) *adj.*: careless, often with deliberate ill will. —**wantonly** *adv.*

wariness (wer′ē·nis) *n.*: carefulness; caution.

wither (with′ər) *v.*: dry up; weaken. —**withering** *v.* used as *adj.*

---

at, āte, cär; ten, ēve; is, īce; gō, hôrn, look, tōōl; oil, out; up, fʉr; ə *for unstressed vowels, as* a *in* ago, u *in* focus; ′ *as in* Latin (lat′′n); chin; she; thin; *the*; zh *as in* azure (azh′ər); ŋ *as in* ring (riŋ)

deprimido.

disposition/disposición s. inclinación; carácter; tendencia.

dispute/disputa s. altercado; querella; contienda.

dissident/disidente adj. disconforme; contrario; discordante.

distraction/distracción s. 1. diversión; entretenimiento. 2. aturdimiento; confusión.

distraught/turbado adj. loco; enloquecido; trastornado.

distressed/afligido adj. desolado; angustiado.

divergence/divergencia s. discrepancia; variación.

dominion/dominio s. mando; autoridad.

drone/zumbido s. ronroneo; sonido; rumor.

dwindle/disminuir v. menguar; reducir.

E

edible/comestible adj. que se puede comer; alimenticio.

efface/borrar v. suprimir; anular.

effectual/eficaz adj. válido; eficiente; productivo.

effervescent/efervescente adj. espumoso; exaltado; agitado.

effete/agotado adj. exhausto; infructífero; poco fértil.

elation/júbilo s. gran alegría; regocijo; deleite.

eloquence/elocuencia adj. persuasión; palabra convincente y persuasiva.

elude/eludir v. evitar; esquivar; rodear.

encompass/abarcar v. englobar; abrazar; incorporar.

encumbrance/estorbo s. contrariedad; inconveniente; obstáculo.

enmity/enemistad s. hostilidad; odio; antipatía.

ensue/resultar v. producir; manifestar.

enthrall/cautivar v. fascinar; hechizar; encantar.

entreat/suplicar v. implorar; rogar; invocar.

eradicate/erradicar v. desarraigar plantas; extirpar una mala costumbre; eliminar; arrancar.

eradication/erradicación s. desarraigue; extirpación; eliminación; arranque.

ethereal/etéreo adj. celeste; que no es de la tierra; espiritual.—**ether/éter** s. esfera celeste

aparente que rodea a la Tierra.

eulogy/elogio s. encomio; aplauso; aclamación; discurso laudatorio público.

exalt/exaltar v. enaltecer; ensalzar; celebrar.

excrutiating/intolerable adj. insoportable; inaguantable; intensamente doloroso.

exemplary/ejemplar adj. intachable; excelente; que sirve de modelo; que merece copiarse.

expedient/conveniencia s. utilidad.

expire/expirar v. morir; fallecer; caducar.

explicit/explícito adj. claro; manifiesto; evidente.

expunge/borrar v. tachar; suprimir.

extremity/extremidad s. miembro del cuerpo, en particular los pies y las manos.

F

facilitate/facilitar v. proveer; allanar; posibilitar; simplificar.

fastidious/melindroso adj. delicado; quisquilloso; caprichoso.

fervent/ardiente adj. ferviente; vehemente; apasionado.

fitful/espasmódico adj. convulsivo; crispado.

florid/florido adj. adornado; estilo elocuente; labrado.

flourish/florecer v. brotar; prosperar.

frenzy/frenesí s. arrebato; delirio; agitación.

frivolity/frivolidad s. futilidad; trivialidad; superficialidad.

furtive/furtivo adj. 1. que actúa a escondidas. 2. que se hace en secreto.

futile/vano adj. inútil; frívolo; pueril.

G

garrulous/locuaz adj. parlanchín; indiscreto; que habla mucho de temas poco importantes.

gaudy/chillón adj. llamativo; vistoso; sobrecargado.

gesticulate/gesticular v. menear; moverse mucho especialmente con las manos y los brazos.

grotesque/grotesco adj. extraño; absurdo.

gyration/giro s. vuelta; rotación.

H

habitual/habitual *adj.* acostumbrado; inveterado; habituado.

haggard/ojeroso *adj.* pálido; exangüe; agotado; marchito.

hail/saludar *v.* llamar; aclamar.

hedonistic/hedonista *adj.* gozador; sensualista; indulgente consigo mismo.

hysteria/histeria *s.* nerviosismo; excitación fuera de control.

I

idealist/idealista *s.* persona guiada por sus ideales o sus principios de perfección.

illumine/iluminar *v.* alumbrar; encender; brillar.

immune/inmune *adj.* exento; libre; protegido.

impart/impartir *v.* revelar; inculcar; comunicar.

impassive/impasible *adj.* inalterable; inmutable.

impeccable/impecable *adj.* perfecto; correcto; sin error o defecto.

imperative/imperativo *adj.* absolutamente necesario; obligado; urgente.

imperceptible/imperceptible *adj.* gradual; paulatino, inapreciable.

impervious/insensible *adj.* indiferente; impasible; resistente; impenetrable.

impetuous/impetuoso *adj.* impulsivo; precipitado.

impious/impío *adj.* incrédulo; ateo; irreverente.

impregnable/invulnerable *adj.* inexpugnable; que no se puede capturar o penetrar.

improvident/gastador *adj.* derrochador; que no ahorra para el futuro.

impulse/impulso *s.* deseo repentino; estímulo.

impute/imputar *v.* hacer responsable; atribuir; asignar.

incessant/incesante *adj.* constante; continuo; perpetuo.

inconceivable/inconcebible *adj.* sorprendente; extraordinario; que no se puede comprender.

indolent/indolente *adj.* apático; perezoso.

induce/inducir *v.* persuadir; convencer; incitar.

indulge/mimar *v.* consentir; permitir.

inert/inerte *adj.* inactivo; inmóvil; quieto.

inevitable/inevitable *adj.* necesario; irremediable; fijo.

inextricable/inextricable *adj.* confuso; enredado; complicado.

infamous/infame *adj.* de mala fama; disoluto.

infirm/enfermizo *adj.* débil; enclenque; achacoso.

ingenous/ingenuo *adj.* cándido; inocente; sencillo; demasiado confiado.

inherent/inherente *adj.* congénito; innato; propio.

iniquity/iniquidad *s.* perversidad; maldad; perfidia.

inscrutable/inescrutable *adj.* insondable; recóndito; misterioso.

insidious/insidioso *adj.* pérfido; traidor; espía.

insolent/insolente *adj.* desvergonzado; fresco; ofensivo.

insuperable/insuperable *adj.* excelente; óptimo; impar; que no se puede mejorar.

insurrection/insurrección *s.* sedición; motín; revuelta.

intangible/intangible *adj.* impalpable; invisible; sutil.

integrate/integrar *v.* completar; suplir; añadir; reunir.

intent/atento *adj.* considerado; galante; dispuesto; vigilante.

interloper/intruso *s.* indiscreto; impostor; fisgón.

interminable/interminable *adj.* sin fin; imperecedero; eterno; perpetuo.

interpose/interponer *v.* intercalar; insertar; mezclar.

intersperse/esparcir *v.* entremezclar; diseminar.

intimate/insinuar *v.* sugerir; aludir; indicar.

intricate/intrincado *adj.* complicado; enredado; equívoco.

intrigue/intriga *s.* maquinación; complot; ardid.

intuitive/intuitivo *adj.* instintivo; automático; sin razonamiento consciente.

invincible/invencible *adj.* invulnerable; inmune.

inviolate/intacto *adj.* ileso, incorrupto.

L

laborious/laborioso *adj.* trabajoso; penoso; costoso.

labyrinth/laberinto *s.* lugar lleno de enredos; caos.

lamentable/lamentable *adj.* triste; deplorable; calamitoso.

legacy/legado *s.* herencia; cesión; dote.

lethargy/letargo *s.* sopor; modorra; somnolencia.

listless/decaído *adj.* indiferente; sin energía ni interés.

loiter/rezagarse *v.* vagar; deambular.

lucid/lúcido *adj.* consciente; claro; penetrante; fino.

ludicrous/absurdo *adj.* ridículo; irracional; incoherente.

luxuriant/exuberante *adj.* copioso; generoso; abundante.

M

magnanimity/magnanimidad *s.* generosidad; nobleza; altruismo.

magnitude/magnitud *s.* dimensión; importancia; alcance.

malice/malicia *s.* picardía; perfidia; deseo de hacer el mal.

malign/calumniar *v.* difamar; hablar mal de otro.

malignant/maligno *adj.* perverso; malo; destructivo.

malodorous/maloliente *adj.* fétido; hediondo; que hule mal.

manifest/manifiesto *adj.* evidente; notorio; ostensible.

martial/marcial *adj.* guerrero; bélico; valiente.

medium/medio *s.* instrumento; material para un artista.

melancholy/melancólico *adj.* triste; sombrío.

mesmerize/hipnotizar *v.* hechizar; magnetizar.

mirth/alegría *s.* regocijo; júbilo.

mortify/mortificar *v.* apesadumbrar; afligir; apenar.

municipal/municipal *adj.* comunal; administrativo; que pertenece a una comunidad.

myriad/miríada *s.* multitud; infinidad.

N

nape/nuca *s.* cogote; cerviz.

nimbus/nimbo *s.* aureola; corona; halo.

nomadic/nómada *adj.* errante; ambulante; vagabundo.

noncommittal/evasivo *adj.* ambiguo; impreciso.

nostalgia/nostalgia *s.* añoranza; recuerdo; melancolía.

notorious/célebre *adj.* famoso; popular; conocido; un criminal notorio.

O

oblique/oblicuo *adj.* inclinado; diagonal; torcido.

obliterate/obliterar *v.* impedir; eliminar; tachar.

obscure/oscurecer *v.* ocultar; disimular; esconder.

obscurity/oscuridad *s.* noche; tinieblas; sombra.

occult/oculto *adj.* recóndito; clandestino; escondido.

ominous/siniestro *adj.* inquietante; adverso.

omnipotent/omnipotente *adj.* todopoderoso; supremo; soberano.

opaque/opaco *adj.* oscuro; mate; turbio.

oscillation/oscilación *s.* vaivén; fluctuación; flujo.

ostentatious/ostentoso *adj.* aparatoso; teatral; grandioso.

P

pandemonium/caos *s.* gran confusión; anarquía; jaleo.

parsimony/parsimonia *s.* parquedad; frugalidad.

pauper/pobre *s.* persona indigente.

penitent/penitente *adj.* mortificado; arrepentido; contrito.

pensive/pensativo *adj.* meditabundo; ensimismado; absorto.

perennial/eterno *adj.* continuo; perenne.

perilous/peligroso *adj.* arriesgado; azaroso.

perseverance/perseverancia *s.* constancia; persistencia; firmeza.

persistent/persistente *adj.* continuo; constante.

pertinent/pertinente *adj.* oportuno; acertado; apto; una observación referente al tema.

perturbation/perturbación *s.* inquietud; nerviosismo.

perverse/perverso *adj.* perjudicial; contrario; nocivo.

pervert/pervertir *v.* trastornar; perturbar; depravar; corromper.

pestilential/pestilente *adj.* peligroso o dañino, como una infección mortal.

petulance/petulancia *s.* irritabilidad; impaciencia.

pious/piadoso *adj.* devoto; religioso; practicante; creyente.

pivotal/esencial *adj.* fundamental; que actúa como eje.

placid/plácido *adj.* apacible; tranquilo; sosegado.

plague/plaga *s.* calamidad; catástrofe; desastre.

plaintive/quejumbroso *adj.* lastimero; triste; apenado.

plausibility/plausibilidad *s.* veracidad; certeza; factible.

plunder/saqueo *s.* pillaje; botín.

poignant/conmovedor *adj.* patético; triste; melancólico; dolor agudo; mordaz.

ponder/considerar *v.* examinar; reflexionar; pensar.

ponderous/laborioso *adj.* pesado, que se mueve con lentitud.

portend/presagiar *v.* predecir; profetizar; pronosticar; augurar algo malo; vaticinar.

posterity/posteridad *s.* futuro; porvenir; futuras generaciones.

potent/potente *adj.* un argumento poderoso, un remedio eficaz; fuerte.

precarious/precario *adj.* inestable; inseguro.

precedence/precedencia *s.* primacía; prioridad debida al rango o a la edad.

preeminent/preeminente *adj.* relevante; de mayor importancia.

preposterous/absurdo *adj.* ridículo; extravagante.

prestigious/prestigioso *adj.* acreditado; famoso; popular; distinguido.

pretense/pretensión *s.* petición falsa.

prevalent/predominante *adj.* preponderante; frecuente.

prodigy/prodigio *s.* fenómeno; niño dotado de un talento extraordinario.

profound/profundo *adj.* hondo; penetrante; intenso.

profundity/profundidad *s.* fondo intelectual.

profuse/profuso *adj.* abundante; pródigo; copioso.

protrude/sobresalir *v.* resaltar; despuntar; predominar.

provisional/provisional *adj.* temporal; transitorio.

provocation/provocación *s.* desafío; reto; incitación.

provoke/provocar *v.* suscitar; irritar; excitar.

proximity/proximidad *s.* cercanía; vecindad; contacto.

prudence/prudencia *s.* sensatez; moderación; cautela.

pulverize/pulverizar *v.* machacar; destruir; demoler.

puncture/pinchazo *s.* punzada; perforación.

R

rakish/desenvuelto *adj.* resuelto; original.

rancor/rencor *s.* odio; resentimiento; aversión.

ravage/destrozar *v.* asolar; desfigurar; causar estragos; arrasar.

realm/reino *s.* terreno; esfera.

recede/retroceder *v.* retirarse; volverse atrás.

recoil/rechazar *v.* echarse atrás; sentir repugnancia por; tener horror.

reconcile/reconciliar *v.* interceder; mediar; arreglar; poner fin a una disputa.

rectitude/rectitud *s.* integridad; dignidad.

reiteration/reiteración *s.* repetición; confirmación; reincidencia.

relinquish/renunciar *v.* desistir; dimitir.

remit/remitir *v.* realizar un pago; enviar; expedir; facturar.

rend/rasgar *v.* rajar; hender; desgarrar.

render/rendir *v.* dar gracias a Dios; presentar; dar cuenta de; entregar.

rendez-vous/cita *s.* convocatoria; reunión.

renounce/renunciar *v.* desistir; dimitir; declinar.

reproach/reprender *v.* condenar; criticar; censurar.

reserve/reserva *s.* prudencia; discreción; reticencia.

resolute/resuelto *adj.* determinado; decidido; audaz; temerario.

resolve/resolución *s.* decisión; propósito; valor.

resonance/resonancia *s.* repercusión; eco; capacidad de intensificar un sonido.

retort/réplica *s.* argumento; objeción.

retract/retractar *v.* retirar; revocar; rescindir; anular.

retraction/retractación *s.* rescisión; anulación;

revocación.

revel/deleitarse *v.* gozar; divertirse; disfrutar.

reverberate/reverberar *v.* repercutir; resonar; retumbar.

reverential/reverencial *adj.* que actúa con un gran respeto.

rigorous/riguroso *adj.* duro; preciso; severo.

rotund/rotundo *adj.* redondo; corpulento; grueso.

ruse/ardid *s.* astucia; treta.

S

sagacious/sagaz *adj.* perspicaz; prudente; sensato.

sarcastic/sarcástico *adj.* punzante; que se burla de algo o de alguien; satírico.

sate/saciar *v.* hartar; satisfacer; colmar.

savory/sabroso *adj.* suculento; gustoso; apetitoso.

scruple/escrúpulo *s.* miramiento; recato; duda.

scrupulous/escrupuloso *adj.* cuidadoso; esmerado; aplicado.

semblance/semblante *s.* aspecto exterior; fisonomía; parecer.

sentinel/centinela *s.* guardián; vigilante.

simultaneous/simultáneo *adj.* sincrónico; paralelo; presente; que ocurre al mismo tiempo.

singular/singular *adj.* único; extraño; original.

solace/consuelo *s.* alivio; desahogo.

solemnity/solemnidad *s.* ceremonia; protocolo; seriedad.

sordid/sórdido *adj.* mezquino; indecoroso; vil.

spurn/despreciar *v.* rechazar; menospreciar; desfavorecer; desdeñar.

stagnant/estancado *adj.* estacionario; sin movimiento.

stolid/impasible *adj.* imperturbable; impávido.

stolidity/impasibilidad *s.* imperturbabilidad; equilibrio; serenidad.

striking/sorprendente *adj.* impresionante; admirable.

subsequent/subsiguiente *adj.* sucesivo.

subside/disminuir *v.* 1. hundirse una estructura o terreno. 2. dejarse caer.

subsist/subsistir *v.* perdurar; vivir; aguantar.

successive/sucesivo *adj.* continuo; repetido; cíclico.

superficial/superficial *adj.* frívolo; que solamente toca la superficie; somero.

superfluous/superfluo *adj.* prolijo; sobrante; redundante; más de lo necesario.

supplication/súplica *s.* ruego; demanda humilde; solicitud.

sustain/mantener *v.* sostener; conservar; alimentar; nutrir.

T

taboo/tabú *s.* prohibición; restricción social.

tactful/discreto *adj.* lleno de tacto; que sabe decir lo correcto.

tactile/táctil *adj.* palpable; tangible; que se percibe tocando.

tedious/tedioso *adj.* aburrido; pesado; fastidioso.

temple/sien *s.* lado de la frente, justo encima y en frente de los oídos.

temporal/temporal *adj.* transitorio; pasajero.

tenous/tenue *adj.* sutil; frágil; delicado.

tepid/tibio *adj.* templado; ni caliente ni frío.

tout/alabar *v.* ensalzar; vender algo.

tranquil/tranquilo *adj.* sereno; sosegado; apacible.

transcendent/trascendente *adj.* eminente; excelente; culminante.

transient/transitorio *adj.* temporal; provisorio; provisional.

transition/transición *s.* metamorfosis; evolución; etapa entre una condición a la otra.

tread/pisar *v.* andar; pasar; marcar.

trepidation/trepidación *s.* estremecimiento; conmoción; incertidumbre ansiosa; ansiedad.

tumultous/tumultuoso *adj.* disturbado; alborotado; turbulento; revuelto.

turbulence/turbulencia *s.* perturbación; revuelta; disturbio.

tyranny/tiranía *s.* opresión; despotismo; absolutismo; abuso de poder.

U

ultimatum/ultimátum *s.* exigencia; proposición final.

undulation/ondulación *s.* pulsación; onda.

unnerve/desconcertar *v.* turbar; desanimar; acobardar.

V

valor/valor *s.* valentía; coraje; audacia.

vanity/vanidad *s.* engreimiento; presunción; orgullo desmesurado.

venerable/venerable *adj.* respetable; honorable; noble; digno.

vengeance/venganza *s.* represalia; punición; castigo.

vengeful/vengativo *adj.* rencoroso; resentido; vengador.

venture/arriesgar *v.* emprender; aventurar; osar.

veracious/veraz *adj.* cierto; sincero; honesto.

veritable/verdadero *adj.* exacto; vigente; que es verdad.

vibrant/vibrante *adj.* excitante; apasionante; lleno de energía.

vigilant/vigilante *adj.* alerta; precavido; cuidadoso.

vindicate/vindicar *v.* justificar; rehabilitar.

virile/viril *adj.* varonil; masculino.

virulent/virulento *adj.* venenoso; mordaz; maligno.

vital/vital *adj.* enérgico; vigoroso; lleno de vida.

vulnerability/vulnerabilidad *s.* fragilidad; delicadeza.

W

wanton/desenfrenado *adj.* sin miramientos, ni precaución; negligente.

wariness/cautela *s.* precaución; recelo.

wither/marchitar *v.* debilitar; languidecer.

Liveright Publishing Company: From Introduction to *New Poems* (from *Collected Poems 1904–1962*) by E. E. Cummings, edited by George J. Firmage. Copyright 1938, © 1966, 1991 by the Trustees for the E. E. Cummings Trust. "what if a much of a which of a wind" and "#225: somewhere i have never travelled,gladly beyond" from *Complete Poems, 1904–1962* by E. E. Cummings, edited by George J. Firmage. Copyright 1931, 1944, © 1959, 1972, 1991 by the Trustees for the E. E. Cummings Trust; copyright © 1979 by George James Firmage.

Lotus Press: "Emily Dickinson" from *Songs for My Fathers* by Gary Smith. Copyright © 1984 by Gary Smith.

Jeffrey Meyers: "Foe of Walls," letter to the editor by Jeffrey Meyers from *The New York Times*, April 27, 1995. Copyright © 1995 by Jeffrey Meyers.

National Council of Teachers of English: "Mending Test" by Penelope Bryant Turk from *English Journal*, January 1993. Copyright © 1993 by the National Council of Teachers of English.

New Directions Publishing Corporation: "Helen" from *Collected Poems 1912–1944* by H. D. Doolittle. Copyright © 1982 by The Estate of Hilda Doolittle. From "Early Success" from *The Crack-up* by F. Scott Fitzgerald. Copyright © 1945 by New Directions Publishing Corporation. "A Pact," "In a Station of the Metro," "The Garden," and "The River Merchant's Wife: A Letter" from *Personae: The Collected Poems of Ezra Pound*. Copyright © 1926 by Ezra Pound. "The Great Figure," "The Red Wheelbarrow," and "This Is Just to Say" from *Collected Poems: 1909–1939*, vol. I, by William Carlos Williams. Copyright © 1938 by New Directions Publishing Corporation.

The New York Review of Books: From "Fitzgerald Revisited" by Jay McInerney from *The New York Review of Books*, August 15, 1991. Copyright © 1991 by NYREV, Inc.

The New York Times Company: From "Robert Frost Relieves His Mind" by Rose C. Feld (retitled "I must have the pulse beat of rhythm ...") from *The New York Times Book Review*, October 21, 1923. Copyright © 1923 by The New York Times Company. From "Mississippi Honors a 'Native Son' Who Fled" by Edwin McDowell from *The New York Times*, November 23, 1985. Copyright © 1985 by The New York Times Company. From "Raymond Carver: A Still, Small Voice" by Jay McInerney from *The New York Times*, August 16, 1989. Copyright © 1989 by The New York Times Company. Quote by Tim O'Brien from "A Storyteller for the War That Won't End" by D.J.R. Bruckner from *The New York Times*, April 3, 1990. Copyright © 1990 by The New York Times Company. From review of *How the Garcia Girls Lost Their Accent* by Julia Alvarez from *The New York Times Book Review*, October 6, 1991. Copyright © 1991 by The New York Times Company. From "The New Measure of Man" by Vaclav Havel from *The New York Times*, July 8, 1994. Copyright © 1994 by The New York Times Company. From "Honoring African Heritage" by Halimah Abdullah from *The New York Times*, June 22, 1997. Copyright © 1997 by The New York Times Company. "A Time of Gifts" by Stephen Jay Gould from *The New York Times*, September 26, 2001. Copyright © 2001 by The New York Times Company.

The New Yorker: From "James Thurber" from *E. B. White: Writings from "The New Yorker," 1927–1976*. Copyright © 1961, 1989 by E. B. White. Originally appeared in *The New Yorker*. Published by HarperCollins.

The Nobel Foundation: Acceptance speeches by William Faulkner and by Ernest Hemingway from *Nobel Lectures in Literature: 1901–1967*, edited by Horst Frenz. Copyright 1949 by The Nobel Foundation. From acceptance speech by Elie Wiesel. Copyright © 1986 by The Nobel Foundation.

W. W. Norton & Company, Inc.: "Medusa" from *A Nostalgist's Map of America* by Agha Shahid Ali. Copyright © 1991 by Agha Shahid Ali. "Testimonial" from *On the Bus with Rosa Parks* by Rita Dove. Copyright © 1999 by Rita Dove. "Emily Dickinson" from *PM/AM: New and Selected Poems* by Linda Pastan. Copyright © 1971 by Linda Pastan.

Tim O'Brien: Slightly adapted from "Speaking of Courage" by Tim O'Brien from *The Massachusetts Review*, Summer 1976. Copyright © 1979 by Tim O'Brien.

Teresa Palomo Acosta: "In the season of change" by Teresa Palomo Acosta. Copyright © 1994 by Teresa Palomo Acosta.

G. P. Putnam's Sons, a division of Penguin Putnam Inc.: From "Rules of the Game" from *The Joy Luck Club* by Amy Tan. Copyright © 1989 by Amy Tan.

Random House, Inc.: "The Unknown Citizen" from *W. H. Auden: The Collected Poems*. Copyright © 1976 by Edward Mendelson, William Meredith, and Monroe K. Spears, Executors of the Estate of W. H. Auden. "Man Listening to Disc" from *Sailing Alone Around the Room* by Billy Collins. Copyright © 2001 by Billy Collins. "A Rose for Emily" (and excerpts) from *Collected Stories of William Faulkner*. Copyright 1930 and renewed © 1958 by William Faulkner. From Appendix from *Hugging the Shore* by John Updike. Copyright © 1983 by John Updike. "Is Phoenix Jackson's Grandson Really Dead?" from *The Eye of the Story: Selected Essays* by Eudora Welty. Copyright © 1978 by Eudora Welty.

The Saturday Review: From "James Baldwin on the Sixties: Acts and Revelations" by Benjamin DeMott from *The Saturday Review*, May 27, 1972, pp. 63–64. Copyright © 1972 by General Media International, Inc.

Scribner, an imprint of Simon & Schuster Adult Publishing Group: "Soldier's Home" from *In Our Time* by Ernest Hemingway. Copyright 1925 by Charles Scribner's Sons; copyright renewed 1953 by Ernest Hemingway. "Poetry" (and excerpts) from *Collected Poems* by Marianne Moore. Copyright © 1935 by Marianne Moore; copyright renewed © 1963 by Marianne Moore and T. S. Eliot.

Simon & Schuster: From letter to Scottie Fitzgerald from *F. Scott Fitzgerald: A Life in Letters,* edited by Matthew J. Bruccoli. Copyright © 1994 by the Trustees under Agreement dated July 3, 1975. Created by Frances Scott Fitzgerald Smith.

Starr & Company: From *The Greatest Generation Speaks: Letters and Reflections* by Tom Brokaw. Copyright © 1999 by Tom Brokaw.

The Texas Folklore Society: Song lyrics from "Follow the Drinking Gourd" by H. B. Parks from *Follow de Drinkin' Gou'd, Publications of the Texas Folklore Society*, no. VII, edited by J. Frank Dobie. Copyright 1928 by the Texas Folklore Society.

Rosemary A. Thurber and The Barbara Hogenson Agency: From "A Biographical Sketch of James Thurber" from *Collecting Himself* by James Thurber. Copyright © 1989 by Rosemary A. Thurber. Originally published by HarperCollins Publishers. "The Secret Life of Walter Mitty" from *My World—and Welcome to It* by James Thurber. Copyright © 1942 and copyright renewed © 1971 by James Thurber. All rights reserved.

Time Inc.: From "Book of Changes" by Paul Gray from *Time*, December 6, 1976. Copyright © 1976 by Time Inc.

Alvin Toffler: From "The Ravaged People of East Pakistan" by Alvin Toffler from *The New York Times*, August 5, 1971. Copyright © 1971 by Alvin Toffler.

United States Holocaust Memorial Museum: Quote by Martin Niemöller from *Their Brothers' Keepers* by Philip Friedman. Copyright © by United States Holocaust Memorial Museum.

The University of New Mexico Press: From *The Way to Rainy Mountain* by N. Scott Momaday. Copyright © 1969 by The University of New Mexico Press. First published in *The Reporter*, January 26, 1967.

University of North Carolina Press: From *The Invasion of America* by Francis Jennings. Copyright © 1975 by the University of North Carolina Press.

University of Texas Press: "The Feather Pillow" from *The Decapitated Chicken and Other Stories* by Horacio Quiroga, translated by Margaret Sayers Peden. Copyright © 1976 by the University of Texas Press.

Picture C[redits]

The illustrations and/or phot[...] pages are picked up from page[...] for those works can be found e[...] on which they appear or in the[...]

Page x: © David Muench/CORBIS[...] Photofest; **3:** (top) © [...] Kirchoff/Wohlberg; (bottom [...] © Geoffrey Clemens/CORBIS; **4**[...] CORBIS; **5:** © Bettmann/CORBIS[...] (right): John Carter Brown Library[...] Rhode Island; **16–17:** Library [...] Westenberger; **24:** Jerry Jacka Pho[...] 10, Scottsdale, AZ/Jerry Jacka Pho[...] Generation Trading Company/Jer[...] CORBIS; **33:** Courtesy The S[...] Project/Dartmouth College; **37:** [...] **46:** Sinclair Hamilton Collection, G[...] Materials Division, Department [...] Collections, Princeton University [...] Marc and Evelyn Bernheim/Wood[...] Bettmann/CORBIS; **62:** AP/Wide [...] the Frankliniana Collection of the [...] Pennsylvania; **72:** B. Timmons/Th[...] North Wind Picture Archives; [...] Associates; **92:** Courtesy Nati[...] Management Program, and Guilfor[...] Park; **93:** Painting by [...] © Bettmann/CORBIS; **102:** Joe [...] © Smithsonian American Art Mu[...] **111:** © Bettmann/CORBIS; **113:** (t[...] *Leslie* by Catherine Maria Sedgwick[...] The State University of N[...] permission of Rutgers University F[...] tion from *Africans in America: Am[...] copyright © 1998 by WGGH Ed[...] exception of the fictional materia[...] material copyright © 1998 by C[...] permission of Harcourt, Inc.; (bot[...] *the Trail of the Wind* by John B[...] *Blackfoot Indian on Horseback,* [...] Bodmer. From *Travels in [...] Maximillian, Prince of Wied. Pu[...] Museum, Omaha, Nebraska). Rep[...] Straus and Giroux, LLC; (bottom [...] dery by Zelda Sperber; **134:** (top) [...] Patricio, New Mexico; (bottom) \[...] Oklahoma, © Carl Vinson In[...] University of Georgia; **135:** (to[...] CORBIS; (center right) © HRW[...] Sperber; **136:** National Archives; [...] of Matthew R. Isenburg, Oakland [...] Gold Rush; **137** (right): © Bettman [...] Inc.; **141:** Courtesy Schweitzer [...] Reprinted by permission of Warne[...] From *The Illustrated Edgar Allan Poe*[...]

Jenshel; **1097:** Herb Snitzer/TimePix; **1100:** © Getty Images; **1101:** (top left) from *The Things They Carried* (jacket cover) by Tim O'Brien, copyright. Used by permission of Broadway Books, a division of Random House, Inc.; (top right) *Beloved;* (bottom left)

Into Thin Air by Jon Krakauer, copyright © 1997 by Jon Krakauer. Used by permission of Villard Books, a division of Random House, Inc.; (bottom right) *Unsettling America: An Anthology of Contemporary Multicultural Poetry.*

Illustrations

Maps

Index of Skills

The boldface page numbers indicate an extensive treatment of the topic.

LITERARY SKILLS

Abstract language, **1078, 1169**
Allegory, **227, 1169**
Alliteration, 177, 279, 313, 723, 758, 1064, 1082, 1084, **1169**
Allusion, **36,** 43, 83, **721,** 723, **1024,** 1030, **1075,** 1076, **1169**
Ambiguity, 282, 696, 704, 720, **727,** 730, **1039,** 1041, 1084, **1169**
American Indian oratory, **455**
Analysis questions (Interpretations), 26, 30, 34, 43, 49, 63, 75, 83–84, 92, 104, 162, 169, 177, 178, 187, 206, 217, 237, 249, 269, 279, 282, 312, 318, 320, 327, 333, 341, 346, 352, 353, 404, 411, 431, 443, 444, 456, 467, 476, 495, 501, 511, 520, 526, 580, 589–590, 596, 600, 604, 619, 641, 645, 655, 662, 682–683, 694, 704, 713, 720, 723, 726, 730, 737, 748, 758, 761, 770, 815, 827, 843, 852, 874–875, 884–885, 895, 909–910, 917, 929, 948, 963, 980–981, 994, 1004, 1013, 1021, 1030, 1037, 1041, 1048, 1054, 1059, 1064, 1068, 1073, 1076, 1080, 1084, 1087, 1091, 1095, 1100
Analogy, 86, 92, **1169**
Anapest, **1170**
Anecdote, 86, 214, **1170**
Antagonist, **1170**
Anthropomorphism, **1170**
Antihero, **610,** 619
Aphorism, **73,** 909
Archetype, **21,** 26, **151,** 237, **280,** 282, **678–679,** 682, 685, **912,** 917, **1093, 1170**
Argument, 96, 845, **1170**
Assertion, 84, 1022
Assonance, 313, 1082, 1084, 1183
Atmosphere, **1171,** 1184
Autobiography, **51,** 63, **763,** 770, **1170**
Ballad, **1171**
Biography, **1171**
Blank verse, 724, 726, 731, **738, 1171**

Cadence, 96, 304, **313,** 318, **1171**
Caesura, **1171**
Catalog, **310,** 312, **1171**
Character, 162, 237, 249, 411, 511, 682, 694, 737, 770, 980, 985, **1171,** 1184
archetypal, 682
comic, **459,** 467
dynamic, **1172**
flat, **1172**
inferences about, **623, 645,** 731, 737, **898,** 910, 985, 994
round, **1172**
static, **1172**
stock, 713
Characterization, **985,** 994, **1171**
Chronological order, 423, 431, 1179
Cliché, **1172**
Climax, 235, 248, 641, 662, **1172**
Coda, 319
Comedy, **1172**
Comic devices, **459,** 467
Conceit, **1172**
Concrete language, **1078,** 1080, **1172**
Conflict, **406,** 619, 655, **669,** 682, **866,** 884, 895, **898,** 909, 929, 948, 994, **1172**
external, **406,** 411, **669,** 682, 866, **898**
internal, **406,** 411, **669,** 682, 866, 874, **898,** 948, 994
Connotation, 43, **523,** 526, **1172,** 1184
Consonance, **1173**
Couplet, **173,** 718, 720, **1173**
Dactyl, **1173**
Denouement, **1173**
Dialect, 459, **1173**
Dialogue, 731, **968,** 980, 981, **1174**
Diction, 720, **1174**
Dramatic irony, **952,** 963, **1177**
Dramatic monologue, **583, 1174**
Elegy, 1004, **1174**
Elizabethan (Shakespearean) sonnet, **173,** 178, 718, 1185
End rhyme, **1035,** 1064, 1183
English sonnet. See Elizabethan (Shakespearean) sonnet.
Enjambment, **1174**
Epic, **1174**
Epithet, **1174**

Essay, 1007, 1013, **1174**
Evaluation questions, 30, 34, 43, 49, 63, 75, 84, 92, 163, 169, 187, 188, 206, 217, 249, 269, 279, 282, 346, 411, 431, 467, 476, 495, 501, 511, 521, 526, 590, 600, 604, 694, 704, 726, 730, 737, 748, 815, 852, 885, 981, 994, 1005, 1021, 1048, 1073, 1091, 1095
Exact rhyme, **337**
Exaggeration, **442,** 468, 476
Exposition, **1174**
Extended metaphor, 30, 589, **1178**
External conflict, **406,** 411, **669,** 682, 866, **898, 1172**
Fable, **1175**
Fantasy, 886
Farce, **1175**
Figures of speech (figurative language), **45,** 49, **184,** 338, 590, 604, 745, 1030, 1048, 1066, **1175**
personification, 34, 169, 177, 341, 346, 352, 443, 526, 1048, 1054
simile, 49, 341, 459, 580, 589, 600, 720, 726, 730, 758, 1013, 1048, 1068
See also Metaphor.
Flashback, 520, 997, 1005, **1175**
Foil, 662, **1175**
Foot, **171, 1175**
Foreshadowing, 151, 495, 655, **1175**
Formal essay, 1007
Frame story, 467, 895, **1175**
Free verse, 304, **313,** 318, **1176**
Gothic tale, **658**
Haiku, **1176**
Hero, 144, 149, 318, 610, 917
antihero, **610,** 619
archetypal, **678–679**
Historical context, **503,** 511, **866**
Hyperbole, **459,** 886, **1176**
Iamb, **171,** 173, 726, **1176**
Iambic pentameter, 173, 178, **1176**
Idiom, 459, **1176**
Imagery, 177, 178, **181,** 187, 313, 338, 346, 443, **499,** 501, **575,** 580, **592,** 596, 981, 994, 1030, 1037, **1056,** 1059, **1070,** 1073, 1080, 1091, **1176**
Imagism, 568, **572–573,** 579, **1176**

Index of Art

Index of Authors and Titles